Oxford
Learner's Pocket
Dictionary

Fourth edition

T0346749

OXFORD
UNIVERSITY PRESS

OXFORD
UNIVERSITY PRESS

Great Clarendon Street, Oxford OX2 6DP

Oxford University Press is a department of the University of Oxford.
It furthers the University's objective of excellence in research, scholarship,
and education by publishing worldwide in

Oxford New York

Auckland Cape Town Dar es Salaam Hong Kong Karachi
Kuala Lumpur Madrid Melbourne Mexico City Nairobi
New Delhi Shanghai Taipei Toronto

With offices in

Argentina Austria Brazil Chile Czech Republic France Greece
Guatemala Hungary Italy Japan Poland Portugal Singapore
South Korea Switzerland Thailand Turkey Ukraine Vietnam

OXFORD and OXFORD ENGLISH are registered trade marks of
Oxford University Press in the UK and in certain other countries

© Oxford University Press 2008

Database right Oxford University Press (maker)

First published 1983
Second edition 1991
Third edition 2003
Fourth edition 2008

2027 2026 2025 2024
30 29 28 27 26 25 24

No unauthorized photocopying

ISBN: 978 0 19 439872 5

Text capture, processing and typesetting by Oxford University Press
Printed in China

ACKNOWLEDGEMENTS

Edited by: Victoria Bull

Contents

Guide to the dictionary

headword	**sandwich** /ˈsænwɪdʒ/ n [C] two slices of bread with meat, salad, etc between them: *a cheese ~*	pronunciation
meaning		example

---

differences between British and American spelling	**sceptre** (*US* **-er**) /ˈsɛptə(r)/ n [C] decorated rod carried by a king or queen as a symbol of power	
	■ **Secretary of 'State** n [C] **1** (*GB*) head of an important government department **2** (*US*) head of the department that deals with foreign affairs	differences in meaning between British and American English

---

words with the same spelling but different meanings, parts of speech and sometimes different pronunciation	O➡ **separate¹** /ˈsɛprət/ adj **1 ~ (from)** forming a unit by itself; not joined to sth else: *~ rooms* **2** different: *on three ~ occasions* ▶ **separately** adv	
	O➡ **separate²** /ˈsɛpəreɪt/ v **1** [I,T] (cause people or things to) move apart; divide into different parts or	

Oxford 3000™ keyword	O➡ **shake¹** /ʃeɪk/ v (pt **shook** /ʃʊk/ pp **~n** /ˈʃeɪkən/) **1** [I,T] (cause sb/sth to) move quickly from side to side or up and down **2** [I] **~ (with)** make short quick movements that you cannot control, eg because you are afraid **3** [I] (of sb's voice) sound unsteady, usu because you are afraid, etc **4** [T] shock or upset sb very much: *We were ~n by his death.* [**IDM**] **shake hands (with sb)** ∣ **shake sb's hand** take sb's hand and move it up and down as a greeting **shake your head** move your head from side to side to indicate 'no' or to show doubt, etc [**PV**] **shake sb/sth off** free yourself of sb/sth **shake sth up** make important changes in an organization, etc to make it more efficient ■ **'shake-up** n [C] major reorganization of a company, etc ▶ **shakily** /-ɪli/ adv ▶ **shaky** adj (**-ier, -iest**) **1** (of a person) shaking and	irregular verb forms
		preposition that usually follows the headword
idioms		
phrasal verbs		
derivatives		compound noun or adjective

	O➡ **shelf** /ʃelf/ n [C] (pl **shelves** /ʃelvz/) **1** flat piece of wood, etc attached to a wall, etc for things to stand on **2** (*geol*) piece of rock like a shelf on a cliff face or underwater	irregular plural
		subject area in which the word is used

---

help with spelling	**swig** /swɪg/ v (**-gg-**) [T] (*infml*) drink sth in large amounts	degree of formality

---

	swirl /swɜːl/ v [I,T] (cause air, water, etc to) move or flow with twists and turns ● **swirl** n [C] swirling movement or pattern	word with a similar meaning to the headword, but a different part of speech

Aa

A, a /eɪ/ n [C,U] (pl **A's, a's** /eɪz/) first letter of the English alphabet • **A abbr** amp(s) • **A level** n [C,U] (GB) exam in a particular subject at about the age of 18 and necessary for entrance to a university

0— **a** /ə/; strong form eɪ/ (also an /ən; strong form æn/) indefinite article (an is used before a vowel sound) **1** one: a book ∘ a million pounds **2** used of number, quantity, groups, etc: a lot of money **3** each: 70 miles an hour

aback /ə'bæk/ adv [IDM] be taken aback (by sb/sth) be shocked or surprised by sb/sth

abacus /'æbəkəs/ n [C] frame with small balls which slide on rods, used for counting

0— **abandon** /ə'bændən/ v [T] **1** leave sb/sth with no intention of returning **2** stop doing or having sth: ~ an idea **3** (lit) ~ yourself to feel an emotion so strongly that you can feel nothing else ▸ **abandonment** n [U]

abashed /ə'bæʃt/ adj embarrassed; ashamed

abate /ə'beɪt/ v [I] (fml) (esp of wind or pain) become less strong ▸ **abatement** n [U]

abattoir /'æbətwɑː(r)/ n [C] place where animals are killed for food

abbess /'æbes/ n [C] woman who is the head of a convent

abbey /'æbi/ n [C] building in which monks or nuns live

abbot /'æbət/ n [C] man who is the head of a monastery or an abbey

abbreviate /ə'briːvieɪt/ v [T] make a word, phrase, etc shorter ▸ **abbreviation** /ə,briːvi'eɪʃn/ n [C] short form of a word or phrase

abdicate /'æbdɪkeɪt/ v [I,T] give up a high position, responsibility, etc ▸ **abdication** /,æbdɪ'keɪʃn/ n [U,C]

abdomen /'æbdəmən/ n [C] part of the body containing the stomach ▸ **abdominal** /æb'dɒmɪnl/ adj

abduct /æb'dʌkt/ v [T] take sb away illegally, using force ▸ **abduction** /æb'dʌkʃn/ n [U,C]

aberration /,æbə'reɪʃn/ n [C,U] action or way of behaving that is not normal

abet /ə'bet/ v (-tt-) [IDM] aid and abet → AID

abhor /əb'hɔː(r)/ v (-rr-) [T] (fml) hate sth ▸ **abhorrence** /əb'hɒrəns/ n [U] ▸ **abhorrent** /-ənt/ adj

abide /ə'baɪd/ v [T] tolerate sb/sth **2** [I] ~ by keep or obey a law, promise, etc ▸ **abiding** adj (written) lasting for a long time and not changing

0— **ability** /ə'bɪləti/ n [C,U] (pl -ies) skill or power

abject /'æbdʒekt/ adj (fml) **1** terrible and without hope: ~ poverty **2** not having pride or respect for yourself ▸ **abjectly** adv

ablaze /ə'bleɪz/ adj (written) **1** burning; on fire **2** shining brightly

0— **able** /'eɪbl/ adj (~r, ~st) **1** ~ to having the power, means or opportunity to do sth: Are you ~ to come with us? **2** clever; skilled ▸ **ably** adv • **able-bodied** adj physically strong ▸ **ably** adv

abnormal /æb'nɔːml/ adj unusual in a way that is worrying, harmful, etc ▸ **abnormality** /,æbnɔː'mæləti/ n [C,U] (pl -ies) ▸ **abnormally** adv

aboard /ə'bɔːd/ adv, prep on or onto a ship, an aircraft, a train or a bus

abode /ə'bəʊd/ n [sing] (fml) house or home: people of no fixed ~ (= with no permanent home)

abolish /ə'bɒlɪʃ/ v [T] put an end to sth ▸ **abolition** /,æbə'lɪʃn/ n [U]

abominable /ə'bɒmɪnəbl/ adj extremely unpleasant and causing disgust ▸ **abominably** adv

Aboriginal /,æbə'rɪdʒənl/ (also **Aborigine** /,æbə'rɪdʒəni/) n [C] member of the race of people who were the original inhabitants of Australia ▸ **Aboriginal** adj

abort /ə'bɔːt/ v [I,T] **1** (cause sb to) end a pregnancy early in order to prevent a baby from developing **2** end sth before it is completed ▸ **abortion** /ə'bɔːʃn/ n [C,U] (instance of) aborting (1): have an ~ ▸ **abortive** adj not successful; failed

abound /ə'baʊnd/ v [I] ~ (in/with) have or exist in large numbers or quantities

0— **about** /ə'baʊt/ prep **1** on the subject of: a book ~ flowers **2** in many directions: walking ~ the town **3** concerned or occupied with: And while you're ~ it,... (= while you are doing that) [IDM] be about to do sth be going to do sth very soon **how/ what about...?** **1** used when making a suggestion: How ~ some more tea? **2** used when asking for information: What ~ the money – do we have enough? • **about adv 1** a little more or less than: It costs ~ £100. **2** in many different directions: The children were rushing ~. **3** here and there: papers lying ~ on the floor **4** able to be found in a place: There was no one ~. ▪ a**bout-turn** n [sing] complete change of position or opinion

0— **above** /ə'bʌv/ prep, adv **1** at or to a higher place or position than sb/ sth: the shelf ~ **2** more than sth; greater in number, level or age than sb/sth **3** of greater importance or of higher quality than sb/sth: I rate her ~ most players of her age. **4** earlier in

A B C D E F G H I J K L M N O P Q R S T U V W X Y Z

sth written or printed: *See ~, page 16.* **5** too good or too honest to do sth: *be ~ suspicion* [IDM] **above all** most important of all ● **above** *adj* mentioned or printed previously in a letter, book, etc: *Write to us at the ~ address.* ▶ **the above** *n* [sing, with sing or pl verb]: *Please notify us if the ~ is not correct.*

abrasion /əˈbreɪʒn/ *n* [C] injury where the skin has been scraped **2** [U] scraping or rubbing

abrasive /əˈbreɪsɪv/ *adj* **1** that scrapes or rubs sth away; rough **2** rude and harsh: *an ~ manner*

abreast /əˈbrest/ *adv* side by side [IDM] **keep abreast of sth** remain well informed about sth

abridge /əˈbrɪdʒ/ *v* [T] make a book, etc shorter ▶ **abridgement** *n* [C, U]

0– **abroad** /əˈbrɔːd/ *adv* in or to another country: *travel ~*

abrupt /əˈbrʌpt/ *adj* **1** sudden and unexpected: *an ~ stop* **2** (of behaviour) rude and unfriendly ▶ **abruptly** *adv* ▶ **abruptness** *n* [U]

abscess /ˈæbses/ *n* [C] painful swelling in the body, containing thick yellowish liquid (pus)

abscond /əbˈskɒnd/ *v* [I] (*fml*) **1** escape from a place that you are not allowed to leave without permission **2** leave secretly, esp with money that does not belong to you

abseil /ˈæbseɪl/ *v* [I] go down a steep hill or rock while attached to a rope, pushing against the slope with your feet

0– **absence** /ˈæbsəns/ *n* **1** [U,C] (occasion or period of) being away: *~ from school* **2** [U] fact of sb/sth not existing; lack: *the ~ of information*

0– **absent** /ˈæbsənt/ *adj* ~ **(from)** not present in a place ■ **absent-minded** *adj* with your mind on other things; forgetful

absentee /ˌæbsənˈtiː/ *n* [C] person who is not present

0– **absolute** /ˈæbsəluːt/ *adj* **1** complete; total: *~ trust* **2** not limited or restricted: *an ~ ruler* **3** not measured in relation to other things: *an ~ standard* ▶ **absolutely** *adv* **1** completely **2** /ˌæbsəˈluːtli/ (*infml*) used to emphasize that you agree with sb ■ **absolute maˈjority** *n* [C] (in an election) more than half of the total number of votes or winning candidates ■ **absolute ˈzero** *n* [U] the lowest temperature that is thought to be possible

absolve /əbˈzɒlv/ *v* [T] ~ **from/of** (*fml*) declare sb to be free from blame, a duty, etc

0– **absorb** /əbˈsɔːb/ *v* [T] **1** take in a liquid, heat, light, etc **2** hold sb's interest and attention: *~ed in her work* ▶ **absorbent** *adj* that absorbs

liquid easily ▶ **absorption** /əbˈsɔːpʃn/ *n* [U]

abstain /əbˈsteɪn/ *v* [I] **1** not vote; neither for nor against a proposal **2** ~ **(from)** keep yourself from drinking alcohol, eating meat, etc

abstemious /əbˈstiːmiəs/ *adj* not eating or drinking a lot; moderate

abstention /əbˈstenʃn/ *n* [C,U] instance of abstaining (1)

abstinence /ˈæbstɪnəns/ *n* [U] practice of abstaining (2), esp from alcoholic drink

abstract /ˈæbstrækt/ *adj* **1** existing as an idea, rather than having a physical or practical existence: *Beauty is ~.* **2** (of art) not showing objects in a realistic way **3** (of a noun) that refers to an abstract quality or state, eg *freedom* ● **abstract** *n* [C] short account of a book, etc; summary

absurd /əbˈsɜːd/ *adj* unreasonable; ridiculous ▶ **absurdity** *n* [U,C] (pl -ies) ▶ **absurdly** *adv*

abundance /əˈbʌndəns/ *n* [U,sing] quantity that is more than enough ▶ **abundant** /əˈbʌndənt/ *adj* ▶ **abundantly** *adv*

0– **abuse** /əˈbjuːz/ *v* [T] **1** make bad or wrong use of sth **2** treat sb in a cruel or violent way, esp sexually **3** say rude things to or about sb ● **abuse** /əˈbjuːs/ *n* **1** [U, sing] wrong or bad use of sth: *the ~ of power* **2** [U] unfair, cruel or violent treatment of sb: *child ~* **3** [U] rude or cruel words: *hurl ~ at sb* ▶ **abusive** *adj* using rude or cruel words

abysmal /əˈbɪzməl/ *adj* very bad: *an ~ failure* ▶ **abysmally** *adv*

abyss /əˈbɪs/ *n* [C] hole so deep that it seems to have no bottom

0– **academic** /ˌækəˈdemɪk/ *adj* **1** of (teaching or learning in) schools, colleges, etc **2** involving a lot of reading or studying rather than practical skills ● **academic** *n* [C] teacher at a university, college, etc ▶ **academically** /-kli/ *adv*

academy /əˈkædəmi/ *n* [C] (pl -ies) **1** school for special training: *a music ~* **2** society for people interested in the arts, etc

accede /əkˈsiːd/ *v* [I] ~ **(to)** (*fml*) agree to a request, suggestion, etc

accelerate /əkˈseləreɪt/ *v* [I,T] (cause sth to) move faster ▶ **acceleration** /əkˌseləˈreɪʃn/ *n* [U] ▶ **accelerator** /əkˈseləreɪtə(r)/ *n* [C] pedal in a car, etc that is pressed with the foot to increase the car's speed

0– **accent** /ˈæksent; -sənt/ *n* [C] **1** individual, local or national way of speaking **2** mark written over or under a letter, eg the symbol on the *e's* in *résumé* **3** special emphasis or force given to sth ▶ **accent** /ækˈsent/ *v* [T] put emphasis on sth

accentuate /əkˈsentʃueɪt/ *v* [T]

emphasize sth or make it more noticeable

0━ **accept** /ək'sept/ v **1** [I,T] agree to take sth offered; say yes to an invitation, etc: ~ *a present* **2** [T] agree to sth; recognize or believe sth: ~ *the truth* ▸ **acceptable** *adj* **1** agreed or approved of by most people in a society **2** that sb agrees is satisfactory or allowed ▸ **acceptance** n [U,C]

0━ **access** /'ækses/ n [U] **1** ~ **(to)** **1** way into a place **2** opportunity or right to use sth ● **access** v [T] open a computer file in order to get or add information ▸ **accessible** /ək'sesəbl/ *adj* easy to reach, use, etc

accession /æk'seʃn/ n [U] act of becoming a ruler of a country

accessory /ək'sesəri/ n [C] (pl **-ies**) **1** something extra that is useful but not essential: *car accessories* **2** (*law*) person who helps another in a crime

0━ **accident** /'æksɪdənt/ n [C] event that happens unexpectedly, esp causing injury or damage [IDM] **by accident** in a way that is not planned ▸ **accidental** /ˌæksɪ'dentl/ *adj* happening by chance ▸ **accidentally** /-təli/ *adv* ■ **accident and emergency** (*abbr* **A & E**) n = CASUALTY(2)

acclaim /ə'kleɪm/ v [T] (*fml*) praise or welcome sth/sb publicly ● **acclaim** n [U] (*fml*) enthusiastic welcome or approval

acclimatize (*also* **-ise**) /ə'klaɪmətaɪz/ v [I,T] ~ **(yourself) (to)** get used to a new climate or new conditions

accolade /'ækəleɪd/ n [C] (*fml*) praise or approval

accommodate /ə'kɒmədeɪt/ v [T] **1** provide sb with a place to live **2** do a favour to sb; oblige sb ▸ **accommodating** *adj* helpful

0━ **accommodation** /əˌkɒmə'deɪʃn/ n [U] room(s), esp for living in: *rented/temporary* ~

accompaniment /ə'kʌmpənimənt/ n [C,U] **1** music played to support a singer or another instrument **2** [C] something that you eat, drink or use together with sth else

accompanist /ə'kʌmpənist/ n [C] person who plays music to support a singer or another instrument

0━ **accompany** /ə'kʌmpəni/ v (pt, pp **-ied**) [T] **1** go somewhere with sb **2** happen or appear with sth else: *wind accompanied by rain* **3** play music to support a singer or another instrument

accomplice /ə'kʌmplɪs/ n [C] person who helps another do sth wrong

accomplish /ə'kʌmplɪʃ/ v [T] succeed in doing sth ▸ **accomplished** /-ɪʃt/ *adj* skilled ▸ **accomplishment** n [C] thing done or achieved after a lot of hard

work **2** [C,U] skill or special ability **3** [U] successful completing of sth

accord /ə'kɔːd/ n [IDM] **in accord (with sth/sb)** (*fml*) in agreement with sth/sb of your own accord without being asked or forced ● **accord** v [I] ~ **(with)** (*fml*) agree with or match sth

accordance /ə'kɔːdns/ n [IDM] **in accordance with sth** in agreement with sth

accordingly /ə'kɔːdɪŋli/ *adv* because of sth just mentioned; for that reason

0━ **according to** /ə'kɔːdɪŋ tə; *before vowels* tu/ *prep* **1** as stated by sb; as shown in sth: *A~ to the report, most people don't take enough exercise.* **2** following or agreeing with sth: *act* ~ *to your principles*

accordion /ə'kɔːdiən/ n [C] musical instrument with bellows and a keyboard

accost /ə'kɒst/ v [T] go up to and speak to sb, esp a stranger

0━ **account** /ə'kaʊnt/ n **1** [C] arrangement that sb has with a bank to keep money there: *open a bank* ~ **2** [usu pl] written record of money that is owed to a business and of money that has been paid by it: *the* ~*s department* **3** [C] written or spoken description of sth that has happened: *I gave the police a full* ~ *of the incident.* **4** [C] (*business*) regular customer: *to lose an important* ~ **5** [C] arrangement that sb has with a company that allows them to use the Internet, send emails, etc [IDM] **on account of sth** because of sth **on no account** not for any reason **take account of sth | take sth into account** consider particular facts, etc when making a decision about sth ● **account** v [PV] **account for sth 1** be an explanation of sth **2** give an explanation of sth: *How do you* ~ *for the play's success?* **3** be a particular amount or part of sth ▸ **accountable** *adj* responsible

accountant /ə'kaʊntənt/ n [C] person whose job is to keep or check financial accounts ▸ **accountancy** /-tənsi/ n [U] profession of an accountant

accredited /ə'kredɪtɪd/ *adj* officially recognized: *our* ~ *representative* ▸ **accreditation** /-'teɪʃn/ n [U] official approval given when sb/sth achieves a certain standard

accrue /ə'kruː/ v [I] (*fml*) come as an (esp financial) increase

accumulate /ə'kjuːmjəleɪt/ v [I,T] become or make sth greater in quantity over a period of time ▸ **accumulation** /-'leɪʃn/ n [U,C]

accurate

0— **accurate** /'ækjərət/ *adj* exact; correct ▸ **accuracy** /-rəsi/ *n* [U] ▸ **accurately** *adv*

accusation /,ækju'zeɪʃn/ *n* [C] statement accusing sb of having done sth wrong

0— **accuse** /ə'kjuːz/ *v* [T] ~ **(of)** say that sb has done wrong: ~ *sb of theft* ▸ **the accused** *n* [C] (pl **the accused**) person on trial for committing a crime ▸ **accuser** *n* [C]

accustom /ə'kʌstəm/ *v* [T] ~ **to** make yourself/sb get used to sth ▸ **accustomed** *adj* usual

ace /eɪs/ *n* [C] **1** playing card with a large single symbol on it **2** (*infml*) person who is extremely skilled: *an* ~ *footballer* **3** (in tennis) serve that is so good that your opponent cannot reach the ball

ache /eɪk/ *v* [I] **1** feel a continuous dull pain: *My head ~s.* **2** (*written*) want sth very much ● **ache** *n* [C] (often in compounds) continuous dull pain in a part of the body: *a tummy ~*

0— **achieve** /ə'tʃiːv/ *v* [T] gain or reach sth by effort; get sth done: ~ *your aim* ▸ **achievement** *n* [C,U]

Achilles heel /ə,kɪliːz 'hiːl/ *n* [sing] weak point or fault in sb's character, which can be attacked by other people ■ **Achilles 'tendon** *n* [C] tendon joining the muscles at the back of the leg to the heel

0— **acid** /'æsɪd/ *n* [U,C] (*chem*) substance that contains hydrogen and has a pH of less than seven ● **acid** *adj* **1** sour **2** (of remarks) very unkind ■ **acid 'rain** *n* [U] rain containing harmful chemicals that kills trees, crops, etc ■ **acid 'test** *n* [sing] way of deciding whether sth is successful or true

0— **acknowledge** /ək'nɒlɪdʒ/ *v* [T] **1** accept that sth is true **2** accept that sb/sth has a particular authority or status **3** tell sb that you have received sth (eg a letter) **4** show that you have noticed sb **5** publicly express thanks for help you have been given ▸ **acknowledgement** (also **acknowledgment**) *n* [U,C]

acne /'ækni/ *n* [U] spots on the face and neck

acorn /'eɪkɔːn/ *n* [C] fruit of the oak tree

acoustic /ə'kuːstɪk/ *adj* of sound ▸ **acoustics** *n* **1** [pl] qualities that make a room good or bad for hearing music or speeches in **2** [U] study of sound

acquaint /ə'kweɪnt/ *v* [T] ~ **with** make sb/yourself familiar with sth ▸ **acquaintance** *n* **1** [C] person that you know slightly **2** [U,C] ~ **(with)** (esp slight) knowledge of sb/sth [IDM] **make sb's acquaintance** (*fml*)

meet sb for the first time ▸ **acquainted** *adj* ~ **(with)** knowing sb personally

acquiesce /,ækwi'es/ *v* [I] ~ **(in)** (*fml*) accept sth without protest ▸ **acquiescence** *n* [U]

0— **acquire** /ə'kwaɪə(r)/ *v* [T] gain sth by your own ability, efforts, etc; obtain sth ▸ **acquisition** /,ækwɪ'zɪʃn/ *n* **1** [U] act of getting sth, esp knowledge, a skill, etc **2** [C] something that sb buys to add to what they already own ▸ **acquisitive** /ə'kwɪzətɪv/ *adj* (*fml, disapprov*) wanting very much to buy or get new possessions

acquit /ə'kwɪt/ *v* (**-tt-**) **1** [T] declare that sb is not guilty **2** ~ **yourself** behave in the way that is stated ▸ **acquittal** *n* [C,U]

acre /'eɪkə(r)/ *n* [C] measure of land; 4840 square yards (about 4050 square metres) ▸ **acreage** /'eɪkərɪdʒ/ *n* [U,C] area measured in acres

acrid /'ækrɪd/ *adj* (esp of smell or taste) sharp or bitter

acrimonious /,ækrɪ'məʊniəs/ *adj* (*fml*) (esp of quarrels) bitter ▸ **acrimony** /'ækrɪməni/ *n* [U]

acrobat /'ækrəbæt/ *n* [C] person who can do skilful physical acts, eg walking on a rope, esp at a circus ▸ **acrobatic** /-'bætɪk/ *adj* ▸ **acrobatics** *n* [pl]

acronym /'ækrənɪm/ *n* [C] word formed from the first letters of a name, eg *NATO*

0— **across** /ə'krɒs/ *adv, prep* **1** from one side to the other side: *swim ~ the lake* **2** on the other side of sth: *My house is just ~ the street.*

acrylic /ə'krɪlɪk/ *adj* made of a substance or fabric produced by chemical processes from a type of acid: ~ *fibres/paints*

0— **act¹** /ækt/ *v* **1** [I] do sth; behave: *We must ~ quickly.* **2** [I,T] perform a part in a play or film **3** ~ **as/like sth** perform a particular role or function ▸ **acting** *n* [U] skill or work of performing in plays, etc ● **acting** *adj* doing the work of another person for a short time: *the ~ing manager*

0— **act²** /ækt/ *n* [C] **1** particular thing that sb does: *an ~ of kindness* **2** law made by a government: *an A~ of Parliament* **3** way of behaving that is not sincere: *to put on an ~* **4** main division of a play **5** one of a series of short performances: *a circus ~* [IDM] **act of God** (*law*) event caused by natural forces beyond human control (eg a storm) **in the act (of doing sth)** while you are doing sth

0— **action** /'ækʃn/ *n* **1** [U] process of doing sth: *take ~ to stop the rise in crime* **2** [C] something sb does **3** [C] legal process to stop sb from doing sth, to make them pay for a mistake, etc: *bring a libel* ~ *against sb* **4** [U] fighting in war: *He was killed in* ~. **5** [U] events in a story, play, etc **6** [U] exciting events [IDM] **actions speak louder than words** what a person actually does means more than what they say they will do **into action** into operation **out of action** no longer working

activate /ˈæktɪveɪt/ v [T] start sth working

0‒ **active** /ˈæktɪv/ adj **1** doing things; busy or energetic **2** (gram) of the verb form used when the subject of a sentence does the action, as in 'She *drove* the car.' ▶ **the active** (*also* **active** voice) n [sing] active (2) form of a verb ▶ **actively** adv

0‒ **activist** /ˈæktɪvɪst/ n [C] person who works to achieve political and social change

0‒ **activity** /ækˈtɪvəti/ n (pl -**ies**) **1** [U] situation in which sth is happening or a lot of things are being done: *a lot of* ~ *in the street* **2** [C, usu pl] something you do for interest or pleasure: *leisure/social activities*

0‒ **actor** /ˈæktə(r)/ n [C] (fem **actress** /ˈæktrəs/) person who acts in plays, films, etc

0‒ **actual** /ˈæktʃuəl/ adj existing in fact; real ▶ **actually** adv **1** really; in fact: *what ~ly happened* **2** used for showing surprise: *He~ly expected me to pay!*

acumen /ˈækjəmən/ n [U] (fml) ability to understand and judge things clearly

acupuncture /ˈækjupʌŋktʃə(r)/ n [U] treatment of illness by sticking small needles into the body

acute /əˈkjuːt/ adj **1** very great; severe: *suffer* ~ *hardship* **2** very sensitive: *an* ~ *sense of hearing* ■ a**,cute 'accent** n [C] mark written over a letter, as over the *e*'s in *résumé* ■ a**,cute 'angle** n [C] angle of less than 90° ▶ **acutely** adv ▶ **acuteness** n [U]

AD /ˌeɪ ˈdiː/ abbr (in the Christian calendar) since the birth of Jesus Christ

0‒ **ad** /æd/ n [C] (infml) = ADVERTISEMENT

adamant /ˈædəmənt/ adj refusing to change your opinion

Adam's apple /ˌædəmz ˈæpl/ n [C] lump at the front of the throat

0‒ **adapt** /əˈdæpt/ v **1** [T] make sth suitable for a new use **2** [I,T] change your behaviour to deal with a new situation ▶ **adaptable** adj able to change ▶ **adaptation** /-ˈteɪʃn/ n [C,U] result or process of adapting: *an ~ation of the play for television* ▶ **adaptor** n [C] kind of electrical plug that allows several plugs to be connected to one socket

0‒ **add** /æd/ v [T] **1** put sth together with sth else: ~ *the flour to the milk* **2** put numbers together to get a total **3** say sth more [PV] **add up 1** (infml) seem reasonable; make sense *a TV* ~ **add up to sth** calculate the total of two or more numbers **add up to sth** result in sth; show sth

adder /ˈædə(r)/ n [C] small poisonous snake

addict /ˈædɪkt/ n [C] **1** person who cannot stop taking drugs, alcohol, etc **2** person strongly interested in sth: *a TV* ~ ▶ **addicted** /əˈdɪktɪd/ adj ~ **(to)** unable to stop taking or using sth ▶ **addiction** /əˈdɪkʃn/ n [U,C] ▶ **addictive** /əˈdɪktɪv/ adj

0‒ **addition** /əˈdɪʃn/ n **1** [U] process of adding numbers together to find their total **2** [C] thing that is added to sth else [IDM] **in addition (to sth/ sth)** as an extra person, thing, etc ▶ **additional** /-ʃənl/ adj extra ▶ **additionally** adv

additive /ˈædətɪv/ n [C] substance added to sth, esp food

0‒ **address** /əˈdres/ n [C] **1** details of where sb lives or works and where letters, etc can be sent: *What's your name and* ~? ◇ *an email* ~ **2** formal speech ● **address** v [T] **1** write a name and address on sth **2** give a speech to sb

adept /əˈdept/ adj ~ **(at/in)** skilled at (doing) sth

0‒ **adequate** /ˈædɪkwət/ adj enough; satisfactory ▶ **adequately** adv

adhere /ədˈhɪə(r)/ v [i] (fml) ~ **(to)** stick firmly to sth [PV] **adhere to sth** act according to a law, rule, etc; follow a set of beliefs ▶ **adherence** /-rəns/ n [U] ▶ **adherent** /ədˈhɪərənt/ n [C] supporter of a person, group, etc

adhesive /ədˈhiːsɪv/ adj able to stick to sth ▶ **adhesion** /ədˈhiːʒn/ n [U] ▶ **adhesive** n [C,U] substance, eg glue, that makes things stick together

ad hoc /ˌæd ˈhɒk/ adj, adv made or arranged for a particular purpose; not planned

adjacent /əˈdʒeɪsnt/ adj ~ **(to)** next to sth

adjective /ˈædʒɪktɪv/ n [C] (gram) word that describes a noun, eg *green* in *green grass* ▶ **adjectival** /ˌædʒekˈtaɪvl/ adj

adjoin /əˈdʒɔɪn/ v [I] (fml) be next to: ~*ing rooms*

adjourn /əˈdʒɜːn/ v [I,T] stop a meeting for a time, esp in a court of law ▶ **adjournment** n [C,U]

adjudicate /əˈdʒuːdɪkeɪt/ v [I,T] (fml) make an official decision or judgement on sth ▶ **adjudication** /-ˈkeɪʃn/ n [U] ▶ **adjudicator** n [C]

adjunct /ˈædʒʌŋkt/ n [C] **1** (gram) adverb or phrase that adds meaning to the verb, eg *yesterday* in *She left home yesterday.* **2** (fml) thing that is attached to sth larger or more important

0ᵐ **adjust** /əˈdʒʌst/ v **1** [T] change or correct sth to make it right **2** [I,T] ~ (**to**) get used to a new situation ▶ **adjustable** adj ▶ **adjustment** n [C,U]

ad lib /ˌæd ˈlɪb/ adj, adv spoken, performed, etc without preparation ● **ad lib** v (**-bb-**) [I] speak, perform, etc without preparation

administer /ədˈmɪnɪstə(r)/ v [T] **1** control or manage sth: ~ a hospital **2** (fml) give sth: ~ a drug ▶ **administration** /-ˈstreɪʃn/ n **1** [U] activities done in order to plan, organize and run a business, school, etc **2** [U] process of organizing the way that sth is done **3** (often Administration) [C] the government of a country, esp the US: *the Bush A~* ▶ **administrative** /ədˈmɪnɪstrətɪv/ adj ▶ **administrator** /ədˈmɪnɪstreɪtə(r)/ n [C]

admirable /ˈædmərəbl/ adj deserving admiration; excellent ▶ **admirably** adv

admiral /ˈædmərəl/ n [C] officer of very high rank in the navy

0ᵐ **admire** /ədˈmaɪə(r)/ v [T] have a good opinion of sb/sth; look at sb/sth with pleasure ▶ **admiration** /ˌædməˈreɪʃn/ n [U] feeling of respect, approval or pleasure ▶ **admirer** n [C] ▶ **admiring** adj

admissible /ədˈmɪsəbl/ adj **1** (law) that can be allowed: ~ evidence **2** (fml) acceptable

admission /ədˈmɪʃn/ n **1** [U] entering or being allowed to enter a building, school, etc **2** [U] money charged for being admitted to a public place **3** [C] statement that sth is true; confession

0ᵐ **admit** /ədˈmɪt/ v (**-tt-**) [T] **1** allow sb/sth to enter; let sb/sth in **2** agree that sth bad is true: *I ~ that I was wrong.* ▶ **admittance** n [U] right to enter ▶ **admittedly** adv used when you are accepting that sth is true

admonish /ədˈmɒnɪʃ/ v [T] (fml) tell sb firmly that they have done sth wrong

ad nauseam /ˌæd ˈnɔːziæm/ adv so often as to become annoying: *She played the CDs ~.*

ado /əˈduː/ n [U] trouble; delay: *without further ~*

adolescent /ˌædəˈlesnt/ adj, n [C] (of a) young person who is developing from a child into an adult ▶ **adolescence** /-ˈlesns/ n [U]

0ᵐ **adopt** /əˈdɒpt/ v [T] **1** take sb else's child into your family, making them legally your son or daughter **2** take and use a method, way of life, etc ▶ **adoption** /əˈdɒpʃn/ n [U,C] ▶ **adoptive** adj related by adoption

adore /əˈdɔː(r)/ v [T] **1** love sb very much **2** (infml) like sth very much ▶ **adorable** adj easy to love for: *an adorable child* ▶ **adoration** /ˌædəˈreɪʃn/ n [U]

adorn /əˈdɔːn/ v [T] decorate sth/sb ▶ **adornment** n [C,U]

adrenalin /əˈdrenəlɪn/ n [U] substance produced in the body by anger, fear, etc and which makes the heart beat faster

adrift /əˈdrɪft/ adj (of boats) floating freely; not fastened

adulation /ˌædjuˈleɪʃn/ n [U] (fml) too much praise or admiration

0ᵐ **adult** /ˈædʌlt; also əˈdʌlt/ n [C], adj (person or animal) grown to full size or strength ▶ **adulthood** n [U] state of being an adult

adulterate /əˈdʌltəreɪt/ v [T] make food or drink less pure by adding another substance

adultery /əˈdʌltəri/ n [U] sex between a married person and sb who is not their husband or wife ▶ **adulterer** n [C] person who commits adultery ▶ **adulterous** /-tərəs/ adj

0ᵐ **advance** /ədˈvɑːns/ n **1** [C,U] forward movement; progress **2** [C, usu sing] money paid for work before it has been done **3** (advances) [pl] attempts to start a sexual relationship with sb [IDM] **in advance (of sth)** before the time that is expected ● **advance** adj done or given before sth: *an ~ warning* ● **advance** v **1** [I] move forward **2** [I] give sb money before the time it would usu be paid ▶ **advanced** adj **1** having the most modern and recently developed ideas, etc: ~d technology **2** at a high or difficult level: ~d studies [IDM] **of advanced years** very old ▶ **advancement** n [U] act of advancing; progress or promotion

0ᵐ **advantage** /ədˈvɑːntɪdʒ/ n [C,U] **1** something useful that puts you in a better or more favourable position than other people **2** quality that makes sth better or more useful [IDM] **take advantage of sth/sb 1** make good use of sth (eg an opportunity) **2** make use of sb/sth in a way that is unfair or dishonest to get what you want ▶ **advantageous** /ˌædvənˈteɪdʒəs/ adj

advent /ˈædvent/ n (the advent) [sing] ~ the coming of an important event

0ᵐ **adventure** /ədˈventʃə(r)/ n **1** [C] exciting or dangerous journey or experience **2** [U] excitement; risk

▶ **adventurer** n [C] person who likes adventures ▶ **adventurous** adj **1** fond of adventures **2** exciting

adverb /'ædvɜːb/ n [C] (gram) word that adds information to a verb, adjective, phrase, or another adverb, eg *quickly* in *run quickly* ▶ **adverbial** /æd'vɜːbiəl/ adj, n [C]

adversary /'ædvəsəri/ n [C] (pl -ies) (fml) enemy; opponent

adverse /'ædvɜːs/ adj negative and unpleasant: ~ *weather conditions* ▶ **adversely** adv ▶ **adversity** /əd'vɜːsəti/ n [C,U], (pl -ies) trouble

0▬ **advert** /'ædvɜːt/ n [C] (infml) = ADVERTISEMENT

0▬ **advertise** /'ædvətaɪz/ v [T] make sth, esp sth for sale, known to people by notices in newspapers, on television, etc: ~ *a product, job or service* ▶ **advertisement** /əd'vɜːtɪsmənt/ n [C] notice in a newspaper, on television, etc, telling people about a product, job or service ▶ **advertiser** n [C] ▶ **advertising** n [U]

0▬ **advice** /əd'vaɪs/ n [U] opinion given to sb about what they should do

0▬ **advise** /əd'vaɪz/ v [T] **1** give advice to sb **2** ~ sb of sth (business) inform sb about sth: ~ *sb of a delivery date* ▶ **advisable** adj sensible or wise ▶ **adviser** (esp US **advisor**) n [C] ▶ **advisory** adj giving advice

advocate /'ædvəkət/ n [C] person who speaks in favour of sb (esp in a law court) or an idea ● **advocate** /'ædvəkeɪt/ v [T] support sth publicly

aerial /'eəriəl/ adj in, through or from the air: *an ~ photograph* ● **aerial** n [C] wire or rod that receives television or radio signals

aerobatics /,eərə'bætɪks/ n [pl] skilful and exciting movements performed by aircraft

aerobics /eə'rəʊbɪks/ n [U] physical exercise done to strengthen the heart and lungs

aerodynamics /,eərəʊdaɪ'næmɪks/ n [U] science which deals with the forces that act on objects moving through the air ▶ **aerodynamic** adj

aeronautics /,eərə'nɔːtɪks/ n [U] scientific study or practice of flying aircraft

aeroplane /'eərəpleɪn/ n [C] flying vehicle with wings and one or more engines

aerosol /'eərəsɒl/ n [C] small container from which a liquid is forced out as a fine spray

aerospace /'eərəʊspeɪs/ n [U] industry of building aircraft and equipment to be sent into space

aesthetic /iːs'θetɪk/ adj concerned with (the enjoyment of) beauty ▶ **aesthetically** /-klɪ/ adv ▶ **aesthetics** n [U] branch of philosophy dealing with beauty

afar /ə'fɑː(r)/ adv [IDM] **from afar** from a long distance away

affable /'æfəbl/ adj friendly and easy to talk to ▶ **affably** adv

0▬ **affair** /ə'feə(r)/ n **1** (affairs) [pl] important public or political events: ~*s of state* **2** [C, usu sing] event that people are talking about **3** [C] sexual relationship between two people, when one of them is married to sb else **4** (affairs) [pl] private business and financial matters **5** [sing] something that sb is responsible for: *How I spend my money is my ~.*

0▬ **affect** /ə'fekt/ v [T] have an influence on sb/sth: *The cold climate ~ed her health.* ▶ **affectation** /,æfek'teɪʃn/ n [C,U] behaviour or an action that is not natural or sincere ▶ **affected** adj not natural; artificial

0▬ **affection** /ə'fekʃn/ n [U] feeling of love; fondness ▶ **affectionate** /-ʃənət/ adj ▶ **affectionately** adv

affidavit /,æfə'deɪvɪt/ n [C] (law) sworn written statement used as evidence

affiliate /ə'fɪlieɪt/ v [I,T] (esp of an organization) join a larger organization ▶ **affiliation** /-'eɪʃn/ n [C,U]

affinity /ə'fɪnəti/ n [C,U] (pl -ies) **1** close relationship **2** strong liking: *She feels a strong ~ for him.*

affirm /ə'fɜːm/ v [T] (fml) state or declare that sth is true ▶ **affirmation** /,æfə'meɪʃn/ n [C,U] ▶ **affirmative** n [C], adj (word, reply, etc) meaning 'yes' or showing agreement: *I answered in the ~* (= I said yes).

affix /ə'fɪks/ v [T] (fml) stick or attach sth to sth else ● **affix** /'æfɪks/ n [C] (gram) prefix or suffix, such as *un-* or *-ly*

afflict /ə'flɪkt/ v [T] cause pain or trouble to sb/sth ▶ **affliction** /ə'flɪkʃn/ n [C,U] (fml) (cause of) suffering

affluent /'æfluənt/ adj rich; wealthy ▶ **affluence** /-ns/ n [U]

0▬ **afford** /ə'fɔːd/ v [T] **1** have enough money or time for sth **2** be able to do sth without risk to yourself: *We can't ~ to lose such experienced workers.*

affront /ə'frʌnt/ v [T] insult or offend sb ● **affront** n [C] insult

afield /ə'fiːld/ adv [IDM] **far/farther/further afield** far away from home

afloat /ə'fləʊt/ adj **1** floating on water **2** (of a business, etc) able to pay its debts

afoot /ə'fʊt/ adj being planned; happening

aforementioned /ə,fɔː'menʃənd/ (also **aforesaid** /ə'fɔːsed/) adj (fml) mentioned earlier

0▬ **afraid** /ə'freɪd/ adj ~ (of/to) frightened of sb/sth or that sth bad will happen: ~ *of spiders* ◇ *to go out in the dark* [IDM] **I'm afraid** (spoken) I'm sorry: *I'm ~ we'll arrive late.*

afresh /ə'freʃ/ *adv* (fml) again

0⎯ **after** /'ɑ:ftə(r)/ *prep* **1** later than sth: *leave ~ lunch* **2** following sth/sb: *Year ~ year he would visit her.* **3** because of sth: *A~ what he said, I never want to see him again.* **4** searching for sth or chasing sb: *The police are ~ him.* **5** in spite of sth: *A~ all I've done for you, you're leaving me!* **6** in the style of sb/sth; following the example of sb/sth: *We named the baby ~ my mother.* [IDM] **after all** in spite of what has been said or expected ■ **after** *adv, conj* later in time (than sth) ■ '**after-effect** *n* [usu pl] (esp unpleasant) effect that is experienced later ■ '**afterthought** *n* [C] idea that comes later

aftermath /'ɑ:ftəmæθ; -mɑ:θ/ *n* [C] result of a war or other bad event

0⎯ **afternoon** /,ɑ:ftə'nu:n/ *n* [U, C] part of the day from 12 midday until about 6 o'clock

0⎯ **afterwards** /'ɑ:ftəwədz/ (*US also* afterward) *adv* at a later time

0⎯ **again** /ə'gen; ə'geɪn/ *adv* **1** once more; another time: *try ~ later* ◇ *I've told you ~ and ~* (= many times) *not to do that.* **2** to or in the original place or condition: *I was glad to be home ~.* **3** in addition: *I'd like the same ~* (= the same amount or thing as before).

0⎯ **against** /ə'genst; ə'geɪnst/ *prep* **1** in contact with: *The ladder was leaning ~ the wall.* **2** opposing: *Are you for or ~ the death penalty?* ◇ *swim ~ the current* ◇ ~ *the law* **3** in contrast to: *The trees were black ~ the sky.* **4** in order to prevent sth from happening or causing harm: *an injection ~ measles*

0⎯ **age¹** /eɪdʒ/ *n* **1** [C, U] length of time sb has lived or sth has existed **2** [U] state of being old: *Wisdom comes with ~.* **3** [C] period of history: *the Elizabethan ~* (= the time of Queen Elizabeth I) **4** (ages) [pl] (infml) very long time: *I waited for ~s.* [IDM] **come of age** become an adult in law **under age** not legally old enough ■ '**age group** *n* [C] people of a similar age ▶ **ageism** /'eɪdʒɪzəm/ *n* [U] unfair treatment of people because they are considered too old ▶ **ageist** *adj* ■ '**age limit** *n* [C] oldest or youngest age at which you are allowed to do sth ■ '**age-old** *adj* having existed for a very long time

age² *v* (pres pt **ageing** or **aging** pp **aged** /eɪdʒd/) [I, T] (cause sb to) become old ▶ **ageing** (also **aging**) *n* [U] process of growing old ▶ **aged** /eɪdʒɪd/ *adj* very old ▶ **the aged** /eɪdʒɪd/ *n* [pl]

very old people ▶ **ageing** (also aging) *adj* becoming older

0⎯ **agency** /'eɪdʒənsi/ *n* [C] (pl -**ies**) business or organization that provides a particular service esp on behalf of other businesses or organizations: *a travel ~*

agenda /ə'dʒendə/ *n* [C] list of things to be discussed at a meeting

0⎯ **agent** /'eɪdʒənt/ *n* [C] **1** person who arranges business for other people: *an estate ~* **2** person who finds work for an actor, a musician, etc **3** person or thing that has an important effect on a situation

aggravate /'ægrəveɪt/ *v* [T] **1** make sth worse **2** (infml) annoy sb ▶ **aggravation** /,ægrə'veɪʃn/ *n* [C,U]

aggregate /'ægrɪgət/ *n* [C] total amount

aggression /ə'greʃn/ *n* [U] **1** angry feelings **2** violent attack or threats by one country against another ▶ **aggressor** /ə'gresə(r)/ *n* [C] person or country that attacks first

0⎯ **aggressive** /ə'gresɪv/ *adj* **1** having angry feelings **2** behaving in a very forceful and determined way in order to succeed: *an ~ salesman* ▶ **aggressively** *adv* ▶ **aggressiveness** *n* [U]

aggrieved /ə'gri:vd/ *adj* (written) feeling angry and bitter, esp because of unfair treatment

aghast /ə'gɑ:st/ *adj* filled with horror or shock

agile /'ædʒaɪl/ *adj* able to move quickly and easily ▶ **agility** /ə'dʒɪləti/ *n* [U]

aging → AGE²

agitate /'ædʒɪteɪt/ *v* **1** [T] make sb anxious or nervous **2** [I] ~ **for/against** argue publicly in favour of/against sth **3** [T] (tech) shake a liquid strongly ▶ **agitation** /,ædʒɪ'teɪʃn/ *n* [U] ▶ **agitator** *n* [C] person who tries to persuade people to take part in political protest

aglow /ə'gləʊ/ *adj* bright with colour or excitement

AGM /,eɪ dʒi: 'em/ *abbr* (esp GB) annual general meeting; meeting held once a year by a company, club, etc

agnostic /æg'nɒstɪk/ *n* [C], *adj* (person who is) not sure whether God exists or not

0⎯ **ago** /ə'gəʊ/ *adv* before now: *The train left five minutes ~.*

agog /ə'gɒg/ *adj* excited and very interested to find out sth

agonize (also -ise) /'ægənaɪz/ *v* [I] ~ (**over/about**) spend a long time thinking and worrying about sth ▶ **agonized** (also -ised) *adj*

agonizing (also -ising) *adj* causing great pain

agony /'ægəni/ *n* [U,C] (pl -**ies**) great pain ■ '**agony aunt** *n* [C] (GB) person who writes in a newspaper, etc giving advice in reply to people's letters about their personal problems

agoraphobia /ˌægərəˈfəʊbiə/ *n* [U] fear of being in public places where there are a lot of people
▶ **agoraphobic** *adj*

agrarian /əˈgreəriən/ *adj* of land, esp farmland

0━ **agree** /əˈgriː/ *v* **1** [I] ~ **(with)** have the same opinion as sb: *I ~ with you that money is the problem.* **2** [I] ~ **to** be willing to do sth; say yes to sth: *My boss ~d to let me go home early.* **3** [I,T] ~ **(on)** decide sth **4** [I,T] ~ **(with)** approve of or accept sth **5** [I] be the same as sth; match: *The two descriptions do not ~.* **6** [I] ~ **(with)** (gram) (of verbs, etc) have the same number, person, etc as another word in the same sentence [IDM] **be agreed** have the same opinion about sth [PV] **not agree with sb** (of food) make you feel ill
▶ **agreeable** *adj* **1** pleasant **2** willing ▶ **agreeably** *adv*
▶ **agreement** *n* **1** [C] arrangement, promise or contract made with sb **2** [U] state of sharing the same opinion

agriculture /ˈægrɪkʌltʃə(r)/ *n* [U] science or practice of farming
▶ **agricultural** /ˌægrɪˈkʌltʃərəl/ *adj*

agritourism /ˈægrɪtʊərɪzəm/ *n* [U] holidays in which tourists stay with local people who live in the countryside

agrochemical /ˌægrəʊˈkemɪkl/ *n* [C] any chemical used in farming

agronomist /əˈgrɒnəmɪst/ *n* [C] scientist who studies the relationship between crops and the environment ▶ **agronomy** *n* [U]

aground /əˈgraʊnd/ *adv, adj* (of ships) touching the ground in shallow water

0━ **ahead** /əˈhed/ *adv* further forward in space or time: *go/plan ~* ■ **a'head of** *prep* **1** further forward in space or time than **2** further advanced than: *be years ~ of your rivals*

AI /ˌeɪ ˈaɪ/ *abbr* **1** artificial insemination **2** artificial intelligence

0━ **aid** /eɪd/ *n* **1** [U] food, money, etc sent to a country in need **2** [U] help: *with the ~ of a friend* **3** [C] thing or person that helps: *visual ~s* [IDM] **what is... in aid of?** (GB, spoken) used to ask why sth is happening ● **aid** *v* [T] (fml) help sb/sth [IDM] **aid and abet** (law) help or encourage sb to do wrong

aide /eɪd/ *n* [C] assistant to sb with an important government job: *several presidential ~s*

Aids (also **AIDS**) /eɪdz/ *abbr* Acquired Immune Deficiency Syndrome; serious illness which destroys the body's ability to fight infection

ailing /ˈeɪlɪŋ/ *adj* (fml) ill and not improving ▶ **ailment** /ˈeɪlmənt/ *n* [C] illness, esp a slight one

0━ **aim** /eɪm/ *v* **1** [I] ~ **(at/for)** direct your efforts at sth; plan to achieve: *~ at increasing exports* **2** [I,T] ~ **(at)** point a weapon or object towards sth **3** [T] direct a comment, etc at sb ● **aim** *n* **1** [C] purpose; intention: *Her ~ is to be famous.* **2** [U] action of pointing a weapon at sb/sth
▶ **aimless** *adj* having no purpose
▶ **aimlessly** *adv*

ain't /eɪnt/ (used in non-standard spoken English) *short for* AM NOT, IS NOT, ARE NOT, HAS NOT, HAVE NOT

0━ **air¹** /eə(r)/ *n* **1** [U] mixture of gases that we breathe **2** [U] earth's atmosphere: *travel by ~* (= in an aircraft) **3** [C] impression or appearance: *an ~ of importance* **4** (airs) [pl] (disapprov) way of behaving that shows that sb thinks that they are more important, educated, etc than they really are: *I hate the way she puts on ~s.* [IDM] **in the air** felt by a number of people to exist or be happening **on/off (the) air** broadcasting/not broadcasting on television or the radio **up in the air** not yet decided ■ **'airbag** *n* [C] safety device in a car that fills with air if there is an accident, to protect the people in the car ■ **'airborne** *adj* **1** (of a plane or passengers) in the air **2** carried through the air ■ **'air conditioning** *n* [U] system of machines that supply a room or building with cool dry air
▶ **'air-conditioned** *adj* ■ **'aircraft** *n* [C] (pl **aircraft**) any vehicle that can fly and carry goods or passengers ■ **'aircraft carrier** *n* [C] large ship that carries aircraft which use it as a base to land on and take off from ■ **'airfield** *n* [C] area of open ground where aircraft can take off and land ■ **'air force** *n* [C] part of a country's military forces that is organized for fighting in the air ■ **'air hostess** *n* [C] woman whose job is to look after the passengers in an aircraft ■ **'airlift** *n* [C] transport of people or supplies by air ■ **'airlift** *v* [T] ■ **'airline** *n* [C] company that carries passengers or goods by plane ■ **'airliner** *n* [C] large passenger plane ■ **'airmail** *n* [U] system of sending letters, etc by air ■ **'air marshal** *n* [C] officer of very high rank in the British Air Force: *Air Marshal Richard Poole* ■ **'airplane** *n* [C] (US) = AEROPLANE ■ **'airport** *n* [C] place where aircraft land and take off, with buildings for passengers to wait in, etc ■ **'air raid** *n* [C] attack by aircraft ■ **'airship** *n* [C] large aircraft without wings, filled with a gas which is lighter than air, and driven by engines ■ **'airspace** *n*

air

[U] part of the earth's atmosphere above a country, considered to belong to that country ■ **airstrip** n [C] piece of land cleared for aircraft to take off and land ■ **air terminal** n [C] building at an airport that provides services for passengers travelling by plane ■ **airtight** adj not allowing air to get in or out ■ **air-to-air** adj (fired) from one aircraft to another while flying ■ **air traffic controller** n [C] person whose job is to give radio instructions to pilots about taking off and landing ■ **airway** n [C] passage from the nose and throat to the lungs ■ **airworthy** adj (of an aircraft) safe to fly

air² v [I,T] put clothes, etc in a warm place to dry completely **2** [T] let fresh air into a room **3** [T] express your opinions publicly ▶ **airing** n [sing]: *give the blankets a good ~ing* ■ **airing cupboard** n [C] warm cupboard for drying clean sheets, towels, etc

airless /'eələs/ adj not having enough fresh air

airy /'eəri/ adj (-ier, -iest) **1** with plenty of fresh air because there is a lot of space **2** not serious ▶ **airily** adv

aisle /aɪl/ n [C] passage between rows of seats in a theatre, church, plane, etc or between shelves in a supermarket

ajar /ə'dʒɑ:(r)/ adj (of a door) slightly open

akin /ə'kɪn/ adj ~ **to** (fml) similar to

à la carte /ˌɑː lɑː 'kɑːt/ adj (of a restaurant meal) ordered as separate items from the menu and not as a fixed price for the complete meal

alacrity /ə'lækrəti/ n [U] (fml) great willingness or eagerness

0─ alarm /ə'lɑːm/ n **1** [U] sudden feeling of fear, caused by danger **2** [C] (device that gives a) warning sound: *a fire ~ ◇ sound/raise the ~* ● **alarm** v [T] make sb anxious or afraid ■ **alarm clock** n [C] clock that can be set to make a noise at a particular time to wake you up ▶ **alarming** adj causing fear

alas /ə'læs/ exclam (old-fash or lit) used to show you are sad or sorry

albatross /'ælbətrɒs/ n [C] large white seabird

albeit /ˌɔːl'biːɪt/ conj (fml) although: *a useful, ~ brief, report*

albino /æl'biːnəʊ/ n [C] (pl ~s) person or animal with white skin and hair and pink eyes

album /'ælbəm/ n [C] **1** book in which a collection of photographs, stamps, etc can be kept **2** long-playing record

0─ alcohol /'ælkəhɒl/ n [U] (pure colourless liquid in) drinks such as beer, wine and whisky ● **alcoholic** /ˌælkə'hɒlɪk/ adj of or containing alcohol ● **alcoholic** n [C] person who drinks too much alcohol and cannot stop drinking, so it has become an illness ▶ **alcoholism** /'ælkəhɒlɪzəm/ n [U] (disease caused by) regular heavy drinking of alcohol

alcove /'ælkəʊv/ n [C] small area in a room formed by part of the wall being set back

ale /eɪl/ n [U,C] kind of strong beer

alert /ə'lɜːt/ adj fully awake and ready to act ● **alert** n **1** [sing, U] situation in which people are ready to deal with possible danger: *Be on the ~ for suspicious packages.* **2** [C] warning of danger ● **alert** v [T] ~ **to** warn sb of danger

algae /'ældʒiː; 'ælɡiː/ n [U] mass of very simple plants that are mainly found in water

algebra /'ældʒɪbrə/ n [U] branch of mathematics in which letters represent quantities

algorithm /'ælɡərɪðəm/ n [C] (computing) process or set of rules that must be followed when solving a particular problem

alias /'eɪliəs/ n [C] false name, used esp by a criminal ● **alias** adv also (falsely) called: *Joe Sykes, ~ John Smith*

alibi /'æləbaɪ/ n [C] evidence that proves that sb was somewhere else when a crime was committed

alien /'eɪliən/ n [C] **1** (law) person who is not a citizen of the country in which they live or work **2** creature from another world ● **alien** adj **1** strange and frightening **2** foreign

alienate /'eɪliəneɪt/ v [T] cause sb to become unfriendly ▶ **alienation** /ˌeɪliə'neɪʃn/ n [U]

alight¹ /ə'laɪt/ adj on fire ● **alight** v [I] (fml) **1** get off a bus, etc **2** (of a bird) come down from the air and settle

align /ə'laɪn/ v **1** [T] place sth in a straight line **2** ~ **yourself with** join or publicly support sb/sth ▶ **alignment** n [C,U]

alike /ə'laɪk/ adj like one another ▶ **alike** adv in the same way

alimentary canal /ˌælɪmentəri kə'næl/ n [C] passage in the body that carries food from the mouth to the anus

alimony /'ælɪməni/ n [U] money that sb has to pay regularly to a former wife or husband after they have been divorced

0─ alive /ə'laɪv/ adj **1** living **2** excited; lively **3** continuing to exist [IDM] **alive to sth** aware of sth **alive with sth** full of living things

alkali /'ælkəlaɪ/ n [C,U] (chem)

substance that forms a salt when combined with an acid

all /ɔːl/ det, pron **1** the whole of a thing or of a period of time: We've lost ~ (of) the money. ◇ I've been here ~ day. **2** every one of a group: A~ the people have come. ◇ They were ~ broken. **3** the only thing that; everything that: A~ I want is some peace! **4** any whatever: beyond ~ doubt [IDM] **all in all** when everything is considered (not) at all (not) in any way: I didn't enjoy it at ~. **in all** as a total not at all used as a polite reply when receiving thanks ▸ **all** adv **1** completely: dressed ~ in black **2** ~ too used to show that sth is more than you would like: I'm ~ too aware of the problems. **3** (in games) to each side: The scores was four ~. [IDM] **all along** (infml) all the time **all the better, harder, etc** so much better, harder, etc: We'll have to work ~ the harder with two people off sick. **all in** very tired **all over** everywhere **all the same** → SAME **all there** having a healthy mind; thinking clearly **be all for (doing) sth** believe strongly that sth should be done **be all the same to sb** not be important to sb: It's ~ the same to me when you go. **not all that good, well, etc** not very good, etc ■ **the ,all-'clear** n [sing] signal that the danger has ended ■ ,all-'in adj with everything included: an ~-in price ■ ,all-'out adj using all possible strength: an ~-out attack on the opposition ■ 'all out adv: The team is going ~ out to win. ■ ,all-'rounder n [C] person with a wide range of abilities

Allah /ˈælə/ n [sing] name of God among Muslims

allay /əˈleɪ/ v [T] (fml) make fears, doubts, etc less

allegation /ˌæləˈɡeɪʃn/ n [C] statement that is made without proof, accusing sb of doing wrong

allege /əˈledʒ/ v [T] (fml) state sth as a fact but without proof ▸ **alleged** adj ▸ **allegedly** adv

allegiance /əˈliːdʒəns/ n [U] support or loyalty to a ruler, belief, etc

allegory /ˈæləɡəri/ n [C] (pl -ies) story in which people are symbols of qualities such as truth or patience ▸ **allegorical** /ˌæləˈɡɒrɪkl/ adj

alleluia /ˌælɪˈluːjə/ n [C], exclam expression of praise to God

allergy /ˈælədʒi/ n [C] (pl -ies) medical condition that causes you to react badly or feel ill when you eat or touch a particular substance ▸ **allergic** /əˈlɜːdʒɪk/ adj

alleviate /əˈliːvieɪt/ v [T] make pain or suffering less ▸ **alleviation** /əˌliːviˈeɪʃn/ n [U]

alley /ˈæli/ n [C] narrow passage between or behind buildings

alliance /əˈlaɪəns/ n [C] relationship or agreement between countries, groups, etc to work together for the same purpose

allied /ˈælaɪd/ adj **1** (often Allied) of countries that unite to fight a war together: ~ forces/troops **2** /əˈlaɪd/ ~ (to/with sth) (written) connected to sth; similar

alligator /ˈælɪɡeɪtə(r)/ n [C] large reptile of the crocodile family that lives in rivers and lakes in America and China

alliteration /əˌlɪtəˈreɪʃn/ n [U] use of the same letter or sound at the beginning of words that are close together, as in 'He built a big boat.'

allocate /ˈæləkeɪt/ v [T] give sth officially for a particular purpose ▸ **allocation** /ˌæləˈkeɪʃn/ n [C, U]

allot /əˈlɒt/ v (-tt-) [T] give sth as a share ▸ **allotment** n [C] **1** (GB) small area of land rented for growing vegetables **2** amount of sth that is given or allowed to have; the process of giving sth to sb

allow /əˈlaʊ/ v [T] **1** give permission to sb to do sth; let sth be done: You're not ~ed to smoke in this room. **2** make sure you have enough of sth for a particular purpose [PV] **allow for sb/sth** include sb/sth when calculating sth: ~ for traffic delays ▸ **allowable** adj ▸ **allowance** n [C] money given to sb regularly [IDM] **make allowances (for sb)** allow sb to behave in a way that you would not usu accept, because of a problem or because of a special reason **make allowance(s) for sth** consider sth when making a decision

alloy /ˈælɔɪ/ n [C, U] mixture of metals

all 'right (also infml ,al'right) adj, adv **1** satisfactory; in a satisfactory manner **2** safe and well **3** that can be allowed: Is it all right to leave early? ▸ **all right** exclam showing that you agree to do what sb has asked

allude /əˈluːd/ v [PV] **allude to sb/sth** mention sb/sth indirectly ▸ **allusion** /əˈluːʒn/ n [C] indirect reference to sb/sth

alluring /əˈlʊərɪŋ/ adj attractive; charming

ally /ˈælaɪ/ n [C] (pl -ies) person or country that has agreed to support another ▸ **ally** /əˈlaɪ/ v (pt, pp -ied) [I, T] ~ (yourself) with sb/sth give your support to another group or country

almanac /ˈɔːlmənæk/ n [C] book published every year with information about the sun, moon, tides, etc

almighty /ɔːlˈmaɪti/ adj (infml) very great ▸ **the Almighty** n [sing] God

almond /ˈɑːmənd/ n [C] flat pale sweet nut of the almond tree

0━ almost /ˈɔːlməʊst/ *adv* very nearly: ~ *everywhere/impossible*

alms /ɑːmz/ *n* [pl] (*old-fash*) money, clothes, etc given to poor people

aloft /əˈlɒft/ *adv* (*fml*) high up in the air

0━ alone /əˈləʊn/ *adj, adv* **1** without other people: *living* ~ **2** only: *You can help me.* [IDM] **go it alone** do sth without help from anyone

0━ along /əˈlɒŋ/ *prep* **1** from one end to the other end of sth: *walk* ~ *the street* **2** close to or on: *a path* ~ *the river* ● **along** *adv* **1** forward; onward: *Come* ~! **2** with others: *Can I bring some friends* ~? [IDM] **along with sb/ sth** together with sb/sth
■ **a,long'side** *adv, prep* close to the side of sth

aloof /əˈluːf/ *adj* not friendly or interested in other people
▶ **aloofness** *n* [U]

0━ aloud /əˈlaʊd/ *adv* in a voice loud enough to be heard: *to read* ~

0━ alphabet /ˈælfəbet/ *n* [C] set of letters arranged in order, used when writing a language ▶ **alphabetical** /-ˈbetɪkl/ *adj* in the order of the alphabet ▶ **alphabetically** /-kli/ *adv*

0━ already /ɔːlˈredi/ *adv* **1** before now: *I've* ~ *told them what happened.* **2** earlier than expected: *You're not leaving us* ~, *are you?*

alright = ALL RIGHT (ALL)

Alsatian /ælˈseɪʃn/ *n* [C] large dog, often trained to help the police

0━ also /ˈɔːlsəʊ/ *adv* in addition; too

altar /ˈɔːltə(r)/ *n* [C] table used in a religious service

0━ alter /ˈɔːltə(r)/ *v* [I,T] (cause sb/ sth to) become different; change sb/ sth ▶ **alteration** /-ˈreɪʃn/ *n* [C, U]

0━ alternate /ɔːlˈtɜːnət/ *adj* **1** (of two things) happening or following one after the other: ~ *layers of fruit and cream* **2** every second: *on* ~ *days* (= eg on Monday, Wednesday and Friday) ▶ **alternately** *adv*
● **alternate** /ˈɔːltəneɪt/ *v* [I,T] ~ **(between/with)** (cause things or people to) follow one another in a repeated pattern: *The weather will* ~ *between sunshine and rain.*
■ **alternating 'current** *n* [U] electric current that regularly changes direction ▶ **alternation** /-ˈneɪʃn/ *n* [U,C]

0━ alternative /ɔːlˈtɜːnətɪv/ *adj* **1** that may be used or done instead: *an* ~ *means of transport* **2** not based on the usual methods or standards: ~ *medicine* ● **alternative** *n* [C] thing that you choose to do out of two or more possibilities ▶ **alternatively** *adv*

alternator /ˈɔːltəneɪtə(r)/ *n* [C] device, used esp in a car, that produces an alternating current

0━ although /ɔːlˈðəʊ/ *conj* though

altitude /ˈæltɪtjuːd/ *n* [C] height above sea level

alto /ˈæltəʊ/ *n* [C] (pl **~s**) **1** (*also* **contralto**) (music for a singer with the) highest adult male or lowest female voice **2** musical instrument with the second highest range of notes in its group

0━ altogether /ˌɔːltəˈgeðə(r)/ *adv* **1** completely: *It's not* ~ *surprising that I failed.* **2** including everything

altruism /ˈæltruɪzəm/ *n* [U] (*fml*) fact of caring about the needs of other people more than your own
▶ **altruistic** /ˌæltruˈɪstɪk/ *adj*

aluminium /ˌæljəˈmɪniəm/ (*US* **aluminum** /əˈluːmɪnəm/) *n* [U] light silver-grey metal used for making pans, etc

0━ always /ˈɔːlweɪz/ *adv* **1** at all times: *You should* ~ *wear a seat belt.* **2** for ever: *I'll* ~ *love her.*

Alzheimer's disease /ˈæltshaɪməz dɪziːz/ *n* [U] serious disease, esp affecting older people, that prevents the brain from functioning normally

0━ a.m. /ˌeɪ ˈem/ *abbr* between midnight and midday

am /æm; strong from æm/ → BE

amalgamate /əˈmælgəmeɪt/ *v* [I,T] (cause two or more things to) join together to form one
▶ **amalgamation** /-ˈmeɪʃn/ *n* [U,C]

amass /əˈmæs/ *v* [T] collect sth, esp in large quantities

amateur /ˈæmətə(r)/ *n* [C] person who does sth as a hobby, without receiving money for it ▶ **amateurish** *adj* without skill

0━ amaze /əˈmeɪz/ *v* [T] surprise sb greatly: ~*d at the news*
▶ **amazement** *n* [U] ▶ **amazing** *adj*

ambassador /æmˈbæsədə(r)/ *n* [C] official who represents his/her own country in a foreign country
▶ **ambassadorial** *adj*

amber /ˈæmbə(r)/ *n* [U] **1** hard yellowish-brown substance used for making jewels **2** yellowish-brown colour

ambidextrous /ˌæmbiˈdekstrəs/ *adj* able to use the right hand and left hand equally well

ambiguous /æmˈbɪgjuəs/ *adj* having more than one meaning ▶ **ambiguity** /ˌæmbɪˈgjuːəti/ *n* [U,C] (pl **-ies**)

0━ ambition /æmˈbɪʃn/ *n* **1** [U] strong desire to be successful **2** [C] something you want to do very much: *achieve your* ~ ▶ **ambitious** /æmˈbɪʃəs/ *adj*

ambivalent /æmˈbɪvələnt/ *adj* (*written*) having or showing both good and bad feelings about sth/sb ▶ **ambivalence** *n* [U, sing]

amble /ˈæmbl/ *v* [I] walk at a slow relaxed speed

ambulance /ˈæmbjələns/ n [C] vehicle for carrying sick people to hospital

ambush /ˈæmbʊʃ/ n [U, C] (waiting in a hidden position to make a) sudden attack ● **ambush** v [T] attack sb/sth from a hidden position

ameba (US) = AMOEBA

amen /ɑːˈmen; eɪˈmen/ exclam used at the end of a prayer, meaning 'may it be so'

amenable /əˈmiːnəbl/ adj willing to be guided by sb or to do sth

amend /əˈmend/ v [T] change sth slightly in order to correct it ▸ **amendment** n [C,U]

amends /əˈmendz/ n [pl] [IDM] **make amends (to sb) (for (doing) sth)** do sth for sb to show that you are sorry for sth wrong or unfair you have done

amenity /əˈmiːnəti/ n [C] (pl **-ies**) feature that makes a place pleasant or easy to live in

American /əˈmerɪkən/ n [C] person from America, esp the USA ▸ **American** adj ● A**merican football** (US **football**) n [U] American game of football, similar to rugby

amethyst /ˈæməθɪst/ n [C] purple semi-precious stone

amiable /ˈeɪmiəbl/ adj pleasant and friendly ▸ **amiably** adv

amicable /ˈæmɪkəbl/ adj friendly and peaceful ▸ **amicably** adv

amid /əˈmɪd/ (also **amidst** /əˈmɪdst/) prep (fml) in the middle of; among

amiss /əˈmɪs/ adj, adv wrong; not as it should be [IDM] **take sth amiss** be offended by sth

ammonia /əˈməʊniə/ n [U] gas with a strong smell, used in making explosives, fertilizers, etc

ammunition /ˌæmjuˈnɪʃn/ n [U] supply of bullets, bombs, etc, fired from weapons

amnesia /æmˈniːziə/ n [U] loss of memory

amnesty /ˈæmnəsti/ n [C] (pl **-ies**) general pardon, esp for political offences

amniocentesis /ˌæmniəʊsenˈtiːsɪs/ n [U, sing] medical test performed on a pregnant woman in order to find out if the baby has particular illnesses

amoeba (US also **ameba**) /əˈmiːbə/ n [C] (pl **~s** or **~ae** /-biː/) very small living creature consisting of only one cell

amok /əˈmɒk/ adv [IDM] **run amok** → RUN¹

among /əˈmʌŋ/ (also **amongst** /əˈmʌŋst/) prep **1** surrounded by: a house ~ the trees **2** in the number of; included in: ~ the best in the world **3** used when you are sharing sth

between people: divide the cake ~ the class

amorous /ˈæmərəs/ adj showing (esp sexual) love ▸ **amorously** adv

amount /əˈmaʊnt/ n [C] total or quantity: a large ~ of money ● **amount** v [PV] **amount to sth** add up to or be equal to sth

amp /æmp/ n [C] **1** (also **ampere** /ˈæmpeə(r)/) (abbr **A**) unit for measuring electric current **2** (infml) = AMPLIFIER

ampersand /ˈæmpəsænd/ n [C] the symbol (&) used to mean 'and'

amphetamine /æmˈfetəmiːn/ n [C,U] illegal drug that makes you feel excited and full of energy

amphibian /æmˈfɪbiən/ n [C] animal, e.g a frog, that can live both on land and in water ▸ **amphibious** adj

amphitheatre (US **-theater**) /ˈæmfiθɪətə(r)/ n [C] round building without a roof and with rows of seats rising round an open space

ample /ˈæmpl/ adj (more than) enough ▸ **amply** adv

amplify /ˈæmplɪfaɪ/ v (pt, pp **-ied**) [T] **1** increase sth in strength, esp sound **2** add details to sth ▸ **amplification** /ˌæmplɪfɪˈkeɪʃn/ n [U] ▸ **amplifier** n [C] (abbr **amp**) device that makes sounds or radio signals louder

amplitude /ˈæmplɪtjuːd/ n [U, C] (physics) greatest distance that a wave, esp a sound or radio wave, vibrates (= moves up and down)

amputate /ˈæmpjuteɪt/ v [I,T] cut off an arm or a leg ▸ **amputation** /ˌæmpjuˈteɪʃn/ n [U, C]

amulet /ˈæmjulət/ n [C] object worn to protect you from evil, etc

amuse /əˈmjuːz/ v [T] **1** make sb laugh or smile **2** make time pass pleasantly for sb ▸ **amusement** n **1** [C] something that makes time pass pleasantly **2** [U] state of being amused ▸ **amusing** adj causing you to laugh or smile

an → A

anachronism /əˈnækrənɪzəm/ n [C] person or thing thought to be out of date

anaemia /əˈniːmiə/ n [U] lack of red cells in the blood, causing a person to look pale ▸ **anaemic** adj

anaerobic /ˌæneəˈrəʊbɪk/ adj **1** not needing oxygen **2** (of physical exercise) not esp designed to improve the function of the heart and lungs

anaesthesia /ˌænəsˈθiːziə/ n [U] state of being unable to feel pain ▸ **anaesthetic** /ˌænəsˈθetɪk/ n [C] substance that stops you feeling pain ▸ **anaesthetist** /əˈniːsθətɪst/ n [C] person who is trained to give anaesthetics to patients

▶ **anaesthetize** (*also* -ise) /əˈniːsθətaɪz/ v [T] give sb an anaesthetic

anagram /ˈænəɡræm/ n [C] word made by changing the order of the letters of another word: '*Stare*' *is an* ~ *of* '*tears*'.

analgesic /ˌænəlˈdʒiːzɪk/ n [C] (*med*) substance that reduces pain

analogue /ˈænəlɒɡ/ adj (*tech*) **1** (of an electronic process) using a continuously changing range of physical quantities to measure or store data: *an* ~ *computer/signal* **2** (of a clock or watch) showing the time using hands on a dial and not with a display of numbers

analogy /əˈnælədʒi/ n (pl -**ies**) **1** comparison of one thing with another that has similar features: *draw an* ~ *between the heart and a pump* **2** [U] explaining one thing by comparing it to sth else
▶ **analogous** /əˈnæləɡəs/ adj similar

0━ **analyse** /ˈænəlaɪz/ v [T] examine or study sth, esp by separating sth into its parts

0━ **analysis** /əˈnæləsɪs/ n (pl -**yses** /-əsiːz/) **1** [U] study of sth by examining its parts **2** [C] result of such study ▶ **analyst** /ˈænəlɪst/ n [C] **1** person who makes (esp chemical) analyses: *a food/political*~ **2** = PSYCHOANALYST ▶ **analytical** /ˌænəˈlɪtɪkl/ (*also* **analytic** /-ˈlɪtɪk/) adj

analyze (*US*) = ANALYSE

anarchy /ˈænəki/ n [U] absence of government; disorder ▶ **anarchist** n [C] person who favours anarchy

anatomy /əˈnætəmi/ n [U,C] (pl -**ies**) (study of the) structure of human or animal bodies ▶ **anatomical** /ˌænəˈtɒmɪkl/ adj

ancestor /ˈænsestə(r)/ n [C] person in your family who lived a long time ago ▶ **ancestral** /ænˈsestrəl/ adj of or from your ancestors ▶ **ancestry** /-tri/ n [C] (pl -**ies**) line of ancestors

anchor /ˈæŋkə(r)/ n [C] heavy piece of metal lowered from a ship into the water in order to stop the ship from moving ● **anchor** v [I,T] lower a ship's anchor to stop it from moving ▶ **anchorage** /ˈæŋkərɪdʒ/ n [C,U] place where ships may anchor safely

anchovy /ˈæntʃəvi/ n [C,U] (pl -**ies**) small fish with a strong salty flavour

0━ **ancient** /ˈeɪnʃənt/ adj **1** belonging to times long ago: ~ *Greece* **2** very old: ~ *monuments*

ancillary /ænˈsɪləri/ adj giving support; additional

0━ **and** /ænd; ən; strong form ænd/ conj **1** also; in addition to: *bread* ~ *butter* **2** then; following this: *She*

came in ~ *sat down.* **3** as a result of this: *Work hard* ~ *you'll succeed.* **4** used between repeated words to show that sth is repeated or continuing: *for hours* ~ *hours* **5** (*infml*) used instead of *to* after certain verbs: *Try* ~ *come early.*

anecdote /ˈænɪkdəʊt/ n [C] short interesting story about a real person or event

anemia, anemic (*US*) = ANAEMIA, ANAEMIC

anemone /əˈneməni/ n [C] small plant with colourful flowers

anesthesia (*US*) = ANAESTHESIA

anew /əˈnjuː/ adv (*written*) again

angel /ˈeɪndʒl/ n [C] **1** messenger of God **2** beautiful or very kind person ▶ **angelic** /ænˈdʒelɪk/ adj

0━ **anger** /ˈæŋɡə(r)/ n [U] feeling that makes people want to quarrel or fight ● **anger** v [T] make sb angry

angina /ænˈdʒaɪnə/ n [U] very bad pain in the chest caused by a low supply of blood to the heart

0━ **angle** /ˈæŋɡl/ n [C] **1** space between two lines that meet **2** corner **3** point of view [IDM] **at an angle** not straight ● **angle** v **1** move or place sth so that it is not straight or not directly facing sb/sth **2** [T] present information, etc from a particular point of view **3** [I] catch fish with a line and hook [PV] **angle for sth** try to get a particular reaction from sb, without directly asking for what you want: ~ *for compliments* ▶ **angler** n [C] person who catches fish (= goes angling) as a hobby ▶ **angling** n [U]

anglicize (*also* -ise) /ˈæŋɡlɪsaɪz/ v [T] make sb/sth English in character

Anglo- /ˈæŋɡləʊ/ prefix English or British: *A~-American*

0━ **angry** /ˈæŋɡri/ adj (-**ier**, -**iest**) **1** filled with anger **2** (of a wound) red and infected ▶ **angrily** adv

angst /æŋst/ n [U] feeling of anxiety and worry about a situation

anguish /ˈæŋɡwɪʃ/ n [U] great mental or physical pain ▶ **anguished** adj

angular /ˈæŋɡjələ(r)/ adj **1** (of a person) thin and bony **2** having sharp corners

0━ **animal** /ˈænɪml/ n [C] **1** living creature that can feel and move **2** any such creature other than a human being **3** unpleasant wild person ● **animal** adj physical; basic ■ **animal ˈrights** n [pl] rights of animals to be treated well

animate /ˈænɪmeɪt/ v [T] give life and energy to sth ● **animate** /ˈænɪmət/ adj living ▶ **animated** /ˈænɪmeɪtɪd/ adj **1** lively **2** (of pictures, drawings, etc in a film) made to look as if they are moving: ~*d cartoons* ▶ **animation** /ˌænɪˈmeɪʃn/ n **1** (*also* energy and enthusiasm **2** [U] process of making animated cartoons **3** [C] animated film

animatronics /ˌænɪmə'trɒnɪks/ n [U] process of making and operating robots that look like real people or animals, used in films, etc

animosity /ˌænɪ'mɒsəti/ n [U, C] (pl **-ies**) strong hatred

0➡ **ankle** /'æŋkl/ n [C] joint connecting the foot with the leg

annals /'ænlz/ n [pl] historical records

annex /ə'neks/ v [T] take control of a country, etc, esp by force ► **annexation** /ˌænek'seɪʃn/ n [U, C]

annexe (esp US **annex**) /'æneks/ n [C] building added to a larger one

annihilate /ə'naɪəleɪt/ v [T] destroy sb/sth completely ► **annihilation** /-'leɪʃn/ n [U]

0➡ **anniversary** /ˌænɪ'vɜːsəri/ n [C] (pl **-ies**) day remembered for sth special which happened on that date in a previous year: a wedding ~

annotate /'ænəteɪt/ v [T] add notes to a book, etc ► **annotation** /ˌænə'teɪʃn/ n [C, U]

0➡ **announce** /ə'naʊns/ v [T] make sth known publicly ► **announcement** n [C] public statement ► **announcer** n [C] person who introduces programmes on radio or television

0➡ **annoy** /ə'nɔɪ/ v [T] make sb slightly angry; cause trouble to sb ► **annoyance** n [U, C]

0➡ **annual** /'ænjuəl/ adj **1** happening once every year **2** calculated for the year: ~ income ● **annual** n [C] **1** book published once a year, having the same title but different contents **2** plant that lives for one year ► **annually** adv

annuity /ə'njuːəti/ n [C] (pl **-ies**) fixed sum of money paid to sb every year

annul /ə'nʌl/ v (**-ll-**) [T] declare that sth is no longer legally valid ► **annulment** n [C, U]

anode /'ænəʊd/ n [C] place on a battery or other electrical device where the electric current enters

anoint /ə'nɔɪnt/ v [T] put oil or water on sb's head, esp as a religious ceremony

anomaly /ə'nɒməli/ n [C] (pl **-ies**) (fml) something different from what is normal ► **anomalous** /-ləs/ adj

anon. /ə'nɒn/ abbr anonymous

anonymous /ə'nɒnɪməs/ adj with a name that is not made known; without a name: The author wishes to remain ~. ◇ an ~ donor ► **anonymity** /ˌænə'nɪməti/ n [U]

anorak /'ænəræk/ n [C] waterproof jacket with a hood

anorexia /ˌænə'reksiə/ (also **anorexia nervosa** /nɜː'vəʊsə/) n [U] mental illness that causes fear of gaining weight and eating and leads to dangerous loss of weight ► **anorexic** /ˌænə'reksɪk/ adj

0➡ **another** /ə'nʌðə(r)/ adj, pron **1** an additional (one): have ~ cup of tea **2** a different (one): do that ~ time **3** a similar (one): ~ Einstein

0➡ **answer** /'ɑːnsə(r)/ n [C] **1** thing said or written in response to sb/sth; reply **2** solution: Do you know the ~ to question 8? ● **answer** n [I,T] give an answer to sb/sth: Think before you ~. ◇ ~ the phone (= lift the receiver and speak to the person calling) ◇ ~ the door (= open the door when sb has knocked at it) [PV] **answer (sb) back** reply rudely to sb **answer for sb/sth 1** accept responsibility for sth **2** speak in support of sb/sth ► **answerable** adj responsible: ~ for your actions

ant /ænt/ n [C] small insect that lives in organized groups

antagonism /æn'tægənɪzəm/ n [U] opposition; dislike ► **antagonist** /-nɪst/ n [C] opponent ► **antagonistic** /-'nɪstɪk/ adj

antagonize (also **-ise**) /æn'tægənaɪz/ v [T] do sth to make sb angry with you

Antarctic /æn'tɑːktɪk/ n [sing] (the Antarctic) very cold regions around the South Pole ► **Antarctic** adj ■ **the Antarctic Circle** n [sing] the line of latitude 66° 33′ South

antecedent /ˌæntɪ'siːdnt/ n **1** [C] (fml) thing or event that comes before another **2** (**antecedents**) [pl] ancestors

antediluvian /ˌæntɪdɪ'luːviən/ adj (fml) very out of date; old fashioned

antelope /'æntɪləʊp/ n [C] animal like a deer

antenatal /ˌæntɪ'neɪtl/ adj relating to the medical care given to pregnant women: an ~ clinic

antenna /æn'tenə/ n [C] **1** (pl **-e** /-niː/) insect's feeler (= one of two long thin parts on its head) **2** (pl **-s**, **-e**) (esp US) = AERIAL

anthem /'ænθəm/ n [C] piece of music sung in churches or written for a special occasion

anthology /æn'θɒlədʒi/ n [C] (pl **-ies**) collection of writings, esp poems

anthrax /'ænθræks/ n [U] serious disease that affects sheep and cows and sometimes people

anthropology /ˌænθrə'pɒlədʒi/ n [U] study of the human race ► **anthropologist** n [C]

0➡ **anti-** /'ænti/ prefix opposed to; against

antibiotic /ˌæntibaɪ'ɒtɪk/ n [C] (powerful substance, eg penicillin) that can destroy bacteria

antibody

antibody /'æntɪbɒdi/ n [C] (pl -ies) substance formed in the blood which destroys harmful bacteria

0— **anticipate** /æn'tɪsɪpeɪt/ v [T] **1** expect sth: We ~ trouble. **2** see what might happen in the future and take action ▶ **anticipation** /æn,tɪsɪ'peɪʃn/ n [U]

anticlimax /,ænti'klaɪmæks/ n [C] disappointing end to sth exciting

anticlockwise /,ænti'klɒkwaɪz/ adv, adj in the direction opposite to the movement of the hands of a clock

antics /'æntɪks/ n [pl] strange or amusing behaviour

anticyclone /,ænti'saɪkləʊn/ n [C] area of high pressure that produces calm weather conditions

antidepressant /,æntidɪ'presnt/ n [C] drug used to treat depression

antidote /'æntidəʊt/ n [C] substance that acts against the effects of a poison or disease

antifreeze /'æntifriːz/ n [U] substance added to water to stop it freezing, esp in car radiators

antihistamine /,ænti'hɪstəmiːn/ n [C,U] drug used to treat allergies

antiperspirant /,ænti'pɜːspərənt/ n [U,C] substance that prevents or reduces sweat

antiquated /'æntikweɪtɪd/ adj old-fashioned

antique /æn'tiːk/ adj, n **1** [C] old and valuable (object): ~ furniture **2** [C] old and valuable (object): ~ furniture

antiquity /æn'tɪkwəti/ n (pl -ies) **1** [U] ancient times **2** [C, usu pl] ancient building, painting, etc **3** [U] great age

antiretroviral /,ænti'retrəʊvaɪrəl/ adj of or connected with a class of drugs designed to stop viruses from damaging the body: A~ drugs are the only way to treat HIV.

antiseptic /,ænti'septɪk/ n [C], adj (substance) preventing disease by destroying bacteria

antisocial /,ænti'səʊʃl/ adj **1** not liking to meet other people; unfriendly **2** harmful to other people

antithesis /æn'tɪθəsɪs/ n (pl -ses /-siːz/) (fml) direct opposite

antler /'æntlə(r)/ n [C] horn of a deer

antonym /'æntənɪm/ n [C] word that is opposite in meaning to another

anus /'eɪnəs/ n [C] hole through which solid waste matter leaves the body

anvil /'ænvɪl/ n [C] heavy iron block on which metals are hammered into shape

0— **anxiety** /æŋ'zaɪəti/ n (pl -ies) **1** [U,C] concern and fear, esp about what might happen **2** [U] strong desire: ~ to please

0— **anxious** /'æŋkʃəs/ adj **1** feeling anxiety **2** causing anxiety: an ~ time **3** ~ for/to strongly wishing sth: He's ~ to meet you. ▶ **anxiously** adv

0— **any** /'eni/ adj, pron **1** some amount (of): Have you got ~ milk? ◇ No, I haven't got any. ◇ I haven't read ~ books by Tolstoy. **2** no matter which: Take ~ card you like. ● any adv at all: I can't run ~ faster.

0— **anybody** /'enibɒdi/ (also anyone /'eniwʌn/) pron **1** used instead of somebody in negative sentences and questions: Did ~ see you? **2** any person at all: A~ will tell you.

anyhow /'enihaʊ/ adv **1** = ANYWAY **2** carelessly: do the work ~

0— **anyone** = ANYBODY

anyplace /'enipleɪs/ (US) = ANYWHERE

0— **anything** /'eniθɪŋ/ pron **1** used instead of something in negative sentences and questions: Has ~ unusual happened? **2** any thing at all (whatever it is): I'm so hungry, I'll eat ~! [IDM] anything but definitely not

0— **anyway** /'eniweɪ/ adv **1** in spite of everything **2** used to change the subject of conversation

0— **anywhere** /'eniweə(r)/ adv used instead of somewhere in negative sentences and questions [IDM] get anywhere → GET

aorta /eɪ'ɔːtə/ n [C] main artery that carries blood from the heart to the rest of the body

0— **apart** /ə'pɑːt/ adv **1** separated by a distance, of space or time: The houses are 500 metres ~. **2** separate(ly): They're living ~. **3** into pieces: It fell ~. ● a part from prep **1** except for **2** as well as

apartheid /ə'pɑːthaɪt/ n [U] (in South Africa in the past) official government policy of keeping people of different races separate

0— **apartment** /ə'pɑːtmənt/ n [C] **1** (esp US) = FLAT² **2** set of rooms rented for a holiday

apathy /'æpəθi/ n [U] lack of interest or enthusiasm ▶ **apathetic** /,æpə'θetɪk/ adj

ape /eɪp/ n [C] large animal like a monkey, with no tail, eg a chimpanzee or gorilla ● ape v [T] copy sb's speech or behaviour

aperitif /ə,perə'tiːf/ n [C] alcoholic drink before a meal

aperture /'æpətʃə(r)/ n [C] (tech) narrow hole or opening, eg in a camera lens

apex /'eɪpeks/ n [C] (pl ~es) highest point: the ~ of a triangle

aphid /'eɪfɪd/ n [C] very small insect that is harmful to plants

apiece /ə'piːs/ adv each

aplomb /ə'plɒm/ n [U] confidence and success: do sth with great ~

apologetic /ə,pɒlə'dʒetɪk/ adj

B C D E F G H I J K L M N O P Q R S T U V W X Y Z

saying or feeling sorry for doing sth wrong ▸ **apologetically** /-kli/ *adv*

0-ᴡ **apologize** (*also* -ise) /əˈpɒlədʒaɪz/ *v* [I] say that you are sorry: *I must ~ for being late.*

apology /əˈpɒlədʒi/ *n* (pl -ies) statement saying that you are sorry for having done wrong, hurt sb's feelings, etc **IDM an apology for sth** very poor example of sth

apostle /əˈpɒsl/ *n* [C] **1** (Apostle) any of the twelve men sent out by Christ to spread his teaching **2** leader of a new faith or movement

apostrophe /əˈpɒstrəfi/ *n* [C] sign (') used to show that one or more letters have been left out, as in *I'm* for *I am*

0-ᴡ **appal** (*US also* appall) /əˈpɔːl/ *v* (-ll-) [T] fill sb with horror; shock sb deeply: *We were ~led at the news.* ▸ **appalling** *adj*

apparatus /ˌæpəˈreɪtəs/ *n* [U] set of tools or equipment used for a purpose: *laboratory ~*

0-ᴡ **apparent** /əˈpærənt/ *adj* **1** clearly seen: *for no ~ reason* **2** seen but not necessarily real: *an ~ lack of knowledge* ▸ **apparently** *adv*

apparition /ˌæpəˈrɪʃn/ *n* [C] ghost

0-ᴡ **appeal** /əˈpiːl/ *v* [I] **1** make a formal request to a higher court, etc for a new decision **2** ~ **to** attract or interest sb: *The design does not ~ to me.* **3** ~ (**for**) make a serious and urgent request: *~ for help/money* ● **appeal** *n* [C] **1** formal request to a court of law, etc **2** [U] quality that makes sb/sth attractive or interesting: *sex ~* **3** [C] urgent request ▸ **appealing** *adj* **1** attractive **2** wanting sb to show you pity

0-ᴡ **appear** /əˈpɪə(r)/ *v* [I] **1** give the impression of being; seem: *That explanation ~s (to be) reasonable.* **2** come into view; become visible: *A ship ~ed on the horizon.* **3** arrive **4** be published or broadcast: *Her latest book ~s in the spring.* **5** be present in a law court ▸ **appearance** *n* [C] act of arriving, esp unexpectedly **2** [C,U] way sb/sth looks to other people: *She was determined to keep up ~s (= hide the true situation and appear that everything is going well).* **IDM put in an appearance** go to a meeting, a party, etc, esp for a short time **to all appearances** so far as can be seen

appease /əˈpiːz/ *v* [T] (*fml*) make sb calm or stop sb being angry, esp by satisfying demands ▸ **appeasement** *n* [U]

append /əˈpend/ *v* [T] (*fml*) add or attach sth, esp in writing ▸ **appendage** /-dɪdʒ/ *n* [C] something added to or joined to sth larger

appendicitis /əˌpendəˈsaɪtɪs/ *n* [U] painful swelling of the appendix that can be very serious

appendix /əˈpendɪks/ *n* [C] **1** (pl **~es**) small organ attached to the large intestine **2** (pl **-dices** /-dɪsiːz/) section giving extra information at the end of a book

appetite /ˈæpɪtaɪt/ *n* [C, U] strong desire, esp for food

appetizer (*also* -iser) /ˈæpɪtaɪzə(r)/ *n* [C] small amount of food or drink that you have before a meal ▸ **appetizing** (*also* -ising) *adj* making you feel hungry

applaud /əˈplɔːd/ *v* **1** [I, T] show approval of sb/sth by clapping your hands **2** [T] express praise for sb/sth because you approve of them/it ▸ **applause** /əˈplɔːz/ *n* [U]

0-ᴡ **apple** /ˈæpl/ *n* [C] round fruit with shiny red or green skin and white flesh

applet /ˈæplət/ *n* [C] (*computing*) program which is run from within another program, eg from within a web browser

appliance /əˈplaɪəns/ *n* [C] device; machine: *electrical/household ~s*

applicable /əˈplɪkəbl; ˈæplɪkəbl/ *adj* ~ (**to**) that can be said to be true in the case of sb/sth

applicant /ˈæplɪkənt/ *n* [C] person who applies for a job, etc

0-ᴡ **application** /ˌæplɪˈkeɪʃn/ *n* **1** [C,U] request: *an ~ (form) for a job* **2** [U, C] act of putting sth to practical use: *the practical ~s of the invention* **3** [U] hard work; great effort **4** [C] (*computing*) program designed to do a particular job: *a database ~*

0-ᴡ **apply** /əˈplaɪ/ *v* (pt, pp -ied) **1** [I] ~ (**for**) ask officially for sth: *~ for a job/visa* **2** [I] ~ (**to**) concern or relate to sb/sth: *This rule does not ~ to you.* **3** [T] work at sth or study sth hard: *~ yourself/your mind to the problem* **4** [T] put sth into operation; use sth: *~ the brakes* **5** [T] rub or put sth onto a surface: *~ ointment to the cut* ▸ **applied** *adj* put to practical use: *applied science*

0-ᴡ **appoint** /əˈpɔɪnt/ *v* [T] **1** choose sb for a job **2** (*fml*) fix or decide sth: *the ~ed time* ▸ **appointment** *n* **1** [C] formal arrangement to meet sb, esp for a reason connected with their work: *make an ~* **2** [C] job to which sb is appointed **3** [C, U] act of appointing sb for a job

appraise /əˈpreɪz/ *v* [T] (*fml*) consider the value of sb/sth ▸ **appraisal** *n* [C, U] judgement of the value of sb/ sth: *staff ~s*

appreciable /əˈpriːʃəbl/ *adj* large enough to be noticed: *an ~ difference* ▸ **appreciably** *adv*

0-ᴡ **appreciate** /əˈpriːʃieɪt/ *v* **1** [T] recognize the good qualities of sb/

sth: *Her family doesn't ~ her.* **2** [T] be grateful for a skilled trade ▸ **apprentice** *I really ~ all your help.* **3** [T] understand sth completely: *I understand your problems, but I am not able to help.* **4** [I] (of land, etc) increase in value ▸ **appreciation** /əˌpriːʃiˈeɪʃn/ *n* [U,C] ▸ **appreciative** /əˈpriːʃətɪv/ *adj*

apprehend /ˌæprɪˈhend/ *v* [T] (*fml*) (of the police) arrest sb

apprehension /ˌæprɪˈhenʃn/ *n* [U,C] worry or fear ▸ **apprehensive** /ˌæprɪˈhensɪv/ *adj* worried

apprentice /əˈprentɪs/ *n* [C] person learning a skilled trade ▸ **apprentice** *v* [T] (*old-fash*) ~ (**to**) make sb an apprentice: *He is ~d to a plumber.* ▸ **apprenticeship** /əˈprentɪʃɪp/ *n* [C,U] (time of) being an apprentice

0━ **approach** /əˈprəʊtʃ/ *v* [I,T] come near(er) to sb/sth **2** [T] make a request or offer to sb: *~ the manager for a pay rise* **3** [T] begin to deal with a problem, task, etc ● **approach** *n* [C] **1** way of dealing with sb/sth **2** [usu sing] act of speaking to sb **3** road, way, etc ▸ **approachable** *adj* friendly and easy to talk to

0━ **appropriate** /əˈprəʊpriət/ *adj* suitable; correct ▸ **appropriately** *adv* ● **appropriate** /əˈprəʊprieɪt/ *v* [T] **1** take sth that does not belong to you for your own use **2** set sth aside for a particular purpose ▸ **appropriation** /əˌprəʊpriˈeɪʃn/ *n* [C,U]

0━ **approval** /əˈpruːvl/ *n* [U] feeling or showing that you think sb/sth is good or acceptable: *Your plans have my ~.* **[IDM] on approval** (of goods) to be returned without paying if not satisfactory

0━ **approve** /əˈpruːv/ *v* **1** [I] ~ (**of**) feel or show that sb/sth is good or acceptable **2** [T] agree to sth formally ▸ **approvingly** *adv*

0━ **approximate** /əˈprɒksɪmət/ *adj* almost correct or exact, but not completely so ▸ **approximately** *adv*: *~ly 100 students* ● **approximate** /əˈprɒksɪmeɪt/ *v* [I] ~ to come very near to sth ▸ **approximation** /əˌprɒksɪˈmeɪʃn/ *n* [C]

apricot /ˈeɪprɪkɒt/ *n* **1** [C] small orange-yellow fruit with a stone **2** [U] orange-yellow colour

0━ **April** /ˈeɪprəl/ *n* [U,C] fourth month of the year: *on the first* ◇ *on the first of A~* ◇ *(US) on A~ first* ◇ *She was born in A~.* ◇ *last A~*

apron /ˈeɪprən/ *n* [C] piece of clothing worn round the front part of your body to keep your clothes clean, eg when cooking

apt /æpt/ *adj* **1** suitable: *an ~ remark* **2** ~ **to** likely to do sth: *~ to be forgetful* **3** quick to learn ▸ **aptly** *adv* ▸ **aptness** *n* [U]

aptitude /ˈæptɪtjuːd/ *n* [C,U] natural ability or skill

aqualung /ˈækwəlʌŋ/ *n* [C] breathing unit for underwater swimming

aquamarine /ˌækwəməˈriːn/ *n* **1** [C] bluish-green semi-precious stone **2** [U] bluish-green colour

aquarium /əˈkweəriəm/ *n* [C] (building with) a large glass tank for keeping live fish

aquatic /əˈkwætɪk/ *adj* **1** (of animals or plants) living or growing in water **2** (of sports) taking place on or in water

aqueduct /ˈækwɪdʌkt/ *n* [C] bridge that carries water across a valley

Arabic /ˈærəbɪk/ *n* [U] *adj* (language) of the Arabs ● **Arabic numeral** *n* [C] symbol 0, 1, 2, 3, etc used for writing numbers in many countries

arable /ˈærəbl/ *adj* (of land) used or suitable for growing crops

arbitrage /ˈɑːbɪtrɑːʒ, -trɪdʒ/ *n* [U] (*business*) the practice of buying sth (eg shares or foreign money) in one place and selling it in another place where the price is higher ▸ **arbitrageur** /ˌɑːbɪtrɑːˈʒɜː(r)/ (*also* **arbitrager** /ˈɑːbɪtrɪdʒə(r)/) *n* [C]

arbitrary /ˈɑːbɪtrəri/ *adj* based on chance, not reason ▸ **arbitrarily** *adv*

arbitrate /ˈɑːbɪtreɪt/ *v* [I,T] ~ (**between**) settle a dispute, argument, etc between two groups ▸ **arbitration** /ˌɑːbɪˈtreɪʃn/ *n* [U] settlement of a dispute by sb chosen as a judge ▸ **arbitrator** *n* [C]

arc /ɑːk/ *n* [C] part of the curved line of a circle

arcade /ɑːˈkeɪd/ *n* [C] covered passage with shops

arch /ɑːtʃ/ *n* [C] curved structure, eg one that is part of the support of a bridge ● **arch** *v* [I,T] form an arch: *The cat ~ed its back.*

archaeology /ˌɑːkiˈɒlədʒi/ *n* [U] study of the remains of ancient buildings, etc ▸ **archaeological** /ˌɑːkiəˈlɒdʒɪkl/ *adj* ▸ **archaeologist** *n* [C]

archaic /ɑːˈkeɪɪk/ *adj* (esp of words) no longer in use; very old

archbishop /ˌɑːtʃˈbɪʃəp/ *n* [C] chief bishop

archer /ˈɑːtʃə(r)/ *n* [C] person who shoots with a bow and arrows ▸ **archery** *n* [U] skill or sport of shooting with a bow and arrows

archipelago /ˌɑːkɪˈpeləgəʊ/ *n* [C] (pl ~s or ~es) group of many small islands

architect /ˈɑːkɪtekt/ *n* [C] person who designs buildings ▸ **architecture** /ˈɑːkɪtektʃə(r)/ *n* [U] art of building; style of building ▸ **architectural** /ˌɑːkɪˈtektʃərəl/ *adj*

archives /ˈɑːkaɪvz/ *n* [pl] (collection of) historical records

Arctic /'ɑːktɪk/ adj **1** of the very cold region around the North Pole **2** (arctic) very cold ▸ **the Arctic** n [sing] the very cold region around the North Pole ■ **the Arctic Circle** n [sing] the line of latitude 66° 33′ North

ardent /'ɑːdnt/ adj (written) very enthusiastic ▸ **ardently** adv

arduous /'ɑːdjuəs; -dʒu-/ adj needing a lot of effort or energy: an ~ journey ▸ **arduously** adv

are /ə(r); strong form ɑː(r)/ → BE

0⇀ **area** /'eəriə/ n **1** [C] part of a place, town, etc, or a region of a country or the world: desert ~s **2** [C, U] extent or measurement of a surface **3** range of activity: different ~s of human experience

arena /ə'riːnə/ n **1** enclosed area used for sports, etc **2** area of activity: in the political ~

aren't /ɑːnt/ = ARE NOT

0⇀ **argue** /'ɑːgjuː/ v **1** [I] express disagreement; quarrel **2** [I] ~ **for/against** give reasons for/against sth **3** [T] (fml) discuss sth: The lawyers ~d the case. ▸ **arguable** /'ɑːgjuəbl/ adj not certain; questionable ▸ **arguably** adv

0⇀ **argument** /'ɑːgjumənt/ n **1** [C] disagreement **2** [C, U] discussion; reason for or against sth ▸ **argumentative** /ˌɑːgjuˈmentətɪv/ adj fond of arguing (1)

aria /'ɑːriə/ n [C] song for one voice in an opera, etc

arid /'ærɪd/ adj **1** (of land) very dry **2** dull; uninteresting

0⇀ **arise** /ə'raɪz/ v (pt **arose** /ə'rəʊz/ pp ~n /ə'rɪzn/) [I] (fml) come into existence: A difficulty may ~n.

aristocracy /ˌærɪˈstɒkrəsi/ n [C] (pl -ies) people born in the highest social class, who have special titles ▸ **aristocrat** /'ærɪstəkræt/ n [C] member of the aristocracy ▸ **aristocratic** /ˌærɪstəˈkrætɪk/ adj

arithmetic /ə'rɪθmətɪk/ n [U] branch of mathematics that deals with the adding, multiplying, etc of numbers ▸ **arithmetical** /ˌærɪθˈmetɪkl/ adj

ark /ɑːk/ n [C] (in the Bible) Noah's ship

0⇀ **arm** /ɑːm/ n **1** either of the two long parts of your body that connect your shoulder to your hand **2** part of clothing that covers this; sleeve **3** part of a chair where you rest your arms [IDM] **arm in arm** (of two people) with their arms linked ● **arm** v [I, T] supply sb or provide yourself with weapons [IDM] **armed to the teeth** having many weapons ■ **the armed forces** n [pl] a country's army, navy and air force ■ **'armchair** n [C] chair with supports for the arms ■ **armpit** n [C] hollow

part under the arm where it joins the shoulder

armada /ɑːˈmɑːdə/ n [C] large group of ships sailing together

armadillo /ˌɑːməˈdɪləʊ/ n [C] (pl ~s) American animal with a hard shell made of pieces of bone

armament /'ɑːməmənt/ n **1** [C, usu pl] weapons, esp large guns **2** [U] process of equipping military forces for war

armistice /'ɑːmɪstɪs/ n [C] agreement during a war to stop fighting for a time

armour (US -or) /'ɑːmə(r)/ n **1** protective metal covering for the body in battle **2** metal covering for tanks, ships, etc ▸ **armoured** (US -or-) adj ▸ **armoury** (US -or-) n [C] (pl -ies) place where weapons are kept

0⇀ **arms** /ɑːmz/ n [pl] weapons [IDM] **take up arms (against sb)** (fml) (prepare to) go to war **(be) up in arms (about/over sth)** (infml) (be) very angry about sth and ready to protest strongly about it ■ **the 'arms race** n [sing] competition among nations for military strength

0⇀ **army** /'ɑːmi/ n [C, with sing or pl verb] (pl -ies) **1** military forces of a country which fight on land: join the ~ **2** large group: an ~ of helpers

arnica /'ɑːnɪkə/ n [U] natural medicine used to treat bruises

aroma /ə'rəʊmə/ n [C] pleasant smell ▸ **aromatic** /ˌærəˈmætɪk/ adj

aromatherapy /əˌrəʊməˈθerəpi/ n [U] use of natural oils for controlling pain or for massage ▸ **aromatherapist** n [C]

arose pt of ARISE

0⇀ **around** /ə'raʊnd/ adv, prep **1** approximately: It's ~ six o'clock. **2** on all sides of sb/sth; surrounding sb/sth: He put his arms ~ her. **3** on, or from the other side of sb/sth: The bus came ~ the bend. **4** with a circular movement about sth: The earth moves ~ the sun. **5** in or to many places in an area: We walked all ~ the town. **6** to fit in with particular people, ideas, etc: I can't plan everything ~ your timetable! **7** present in a place; available: Is anyone ~?

arouse /ə'raʊz/ v **1** cause sth to appear or become active: ~ suspicion **2** excite sb sexually

arr. abbr **1** (in writing) arrive(s); arrival **2** (of music) arranged (by)

arraign /ə'reɪn/ v [T] (law) bring sb to court to formally accuse them of a crime ▸ **arraignment** n [C, U]

0⇀ **arrange** /ə'reɪndʒ/ v **1** [I, T] plan or organize sth in advance: We ~d to meet at one o'clock. ◇ I've ~d a loan with the bank. **2** [T] put sth in order;

make sth attractive: ~ *flowers* **3** [T] adapt a piece of music for a particular instrument ▶ **arrangement** n [C, usu pl] plan or preparation that you make so that sth can happen: *travel ~ments* **2** [C, usu pl] the way things are done or organized: *new security ~ments* **3** [C, U] agreement that you make with sb that you can both accept **4** [C] group of things that are organized or placed in a particular order: *a flower ~ment* **5** [C, U] (piece of) music that has been adapted for a particular instrument

array /əˈreɪ/ n [C] large impressive series of things

arrears /əˈrɪəz/ n [pl] money that is owing [IDM] **be in arrears** | **get/fall into arrears** be late in paying money that you owe

0━ **arrest** /əˈrest/ v [T] **1** seize sb by the authority of the law **2** (*fml*) stop a process **3** attract sb's attention ● **arrest** n [C] act of arresting [IDM] **under arrest** held prisoner by the police

0━ **arrival** /əˈraɪvl/ n **1** [U] act of arriving **2** [C] person or thing that arrives: *The new ~* (= baby) *is a girl.*

0━ **arrive** /əˈraɪv/ v [I] **1** reach a place: *~ home* **2** come: *The great day has ~d!* **3** (*infml*) become successful [PV] **arrive at sth** reach sth: *~ at a decision*

arrogant /ˈærəɡənt/ adj behaving in a proud and rude way ▶ **arrogance** /-ns/ n [U] ▶ **arrogantly** adv

0━ **arrow** /ˈærəʊ/ n [C] **1** pointed stick shot from a bow **2** sign (→) used for showing direction

arse /ɑːs/ n [C] (*GB*, ⚠, *sl*) **1** buttocks; bottom **2** stupid person ● **arse** v [PV] **arse about/around** (*GB*, ⚠, *sl*) behave in a silly way

arsenal /ˈɑːsənl/ n [C] **1** collection of weapons **2** place where weapons and explosives are stored or made

arsenic /ˈɑːsnɪk/ n [U] very strong poisonous substance

arson /ˈɑːsn/ n [U] crime of setting fire to property

0━ **art** /ɑːt/ n **1** [U] use of the imagination to express ideas or feelings, particularly in painting, drawing or sculpture **2** (*arts*) [pl] subjects of study, eg languages or history, that are in contrast to science **3** [C, U] skill in doing sth ■ **art gallery** (pl **-ies**) n [C] building where works of art are shown to the public

artefact (*esp US* **artifact**) /ˈɑːtɪfækt/ n [C] thing made by a human being

artery /ˈɑːtəri/ n [C] (pl **-ies**) **1** one of the tubes that carry blood from the heart to other parts of the body

2 main road, railway, etc ▶ **arterial** /ɑːˈtɪəriəl/ adj

artful /ˈɑːtfl/ adj clever at getting what you want, sometimes by not telling the truth ▶ **artfully** adv

arthritis /ɑːˈθraɪtɪs/ n [U] pain and swelling in a joint in the body ▶ **arthritic** /ɑːˈθrɪtɪk/ adj

artichoke /ˈɑːtɪtʃəʊk/ n [C] **1** (*also* **globe artichoke**) kind of plant with a lot of thick, green leaves, the bottom part of which can be eaten when cooked **2** = JERUSALEM ARTICHOKE

0━ **article** /ˈɑːtɪkl/ n [C] **1** piece of writing in a newspaper, etc **2** (*law*) separate part of an agreement or contract **3** separate thing: *~s of clothing* **4** (*gram*) word *a*, *an* or *the*

0━ **articulate** /ɑːˈtɪkjələt/ adj **1** (of a person) good at expressing ideas or feelings clearly in words **2** (of speech) clearly pronounced ▶ **articulately** adv ● **articulate** /ɑːˈtɪkjuleɪt/ v [I,T] express sth clearly ▶ **articulated** adj (of a lorry) having two parts connected by a joint which allows it to turn easily ▶ **articulation** /ɑːˌtɪkjuˈleɪʃn/ n [U]

artifact (*esp US*) = ARTEFACT

0━ **artificial** /ˌɑːtɪˈfɪʃl/ adj **1** not natural; made by human beings **2** false; not what it appears to be ■ **artificial intelligence** n [U] (*abbr* AI) (*computing*) area of study concerned with making computers copy intelligent human behaviour ■ **artificial respiration** n [U] process of helping a person who has stopped breathing begin to breathe again, usu by blowing into their mouth or nose ▶ **artificially** adv

artillery /ɑːˈtɪləri/ n [U] (branch of the army that uses) large heavy guns

artisan /ˌɑːtɪˈzæn/ n [C] (*fml*) person who does skilled work, making things with their hands

0━ **artist** /ˈɑːtɪst/ n [C] **1** person who creates works of art, esp paintings **2** = ARTISTE ▶ **artistic** /ɑːˈtɪstɪk/ adj **1** of art and artists **2** having or showing skill in art ▶ **artistically** /-kli/ adv ▶ **artistry** n [U] skill of an artist

artiste /ɑːˈtiːst/ n [C] professional singer, dancer, actor, etc

arty /ˈɑːti/ adj (*infml*) pretending to be artistic

arugula /æˈruːɡjulə/ n [U] (*US*) = ROCKET(3)

0━ **as** /əz/ strong form æz/ prep **1** appearing to be sb: *dressed as a policeman* **2** having the function or character of sb/sth: *a career as a teacher* ◇ *Treat me as a friend.* ● **as** adv (as...as) (used in comparisons) equally... as sb/sth: *as tall as his father* ◇ *Run as fast as you can!* ● **as** conj **1** during the time when: *I saw her as I was leaving.* **2** since;

because: *As you were out, I left a message.* **3** though: *Young as I am, I know what I want to be.* **4** in the way which: *Do as I say.* [IDM] **as for sb/sth** used to start talking about sb/sth ◇ **as from | as of** showing the time from which sth starts **as if/though** in a way that suggests sth **as it is** in reality **as it were** as it might be expressed **as much** so: *I thought as much.* **as per** according to: *Work as per instructions.* **as to sth | as regards sth** used when you are referring to sth

asbestos /æsˈbestəs/ *n* [U] soft grey material that does not burn

ascend /əˈsend/ *v* [I,T] (*fml*) go up sth [IDM] **ascend the throne** (*fml*) become king or queen
▶ **ascendancy** *n* [U] (*fml*) power; influence ▶ **ascendant** *n* [IDM] in the **ascendant** being or becoming more powerful or popular

ascent /əˈsent/ *n* [C] act of climbing or moving up; way up

ascertain /ˌæsəˈteɪn/ *v* [T] (*fml*) find out or make certain about sth

ASCII /ˈæski/ *n* [U] (*computing*) American Standard Code for Information Interchange; standard code used so that data can be moved between computers that use different programs

ascribe /əˈskraɪb/ *v* [T] ~ **to** consider sth to be caused by or to belong to sth/sb: *He ~d his failure to bad luck.*

aseptic /ˌeɪˈseptɪk/ *adj* free from harmful bacteria

asexual /ˌeɪˈsekʃuəl/ *adj* **1** without sex or sex organs **2** having no interest in sexual relations

ash /æʃ/ *n* **1** [U] grey or black powder left after sth has burnt: *cigarette ~* **2** (ashes) [pl] what is left after sth has been destroyed by burning **3** (ashes) [pl] remains of a dead human body after burning **4** (*also* 'ash tree*) [C] forest tree with grey bark **5** [U] hard pale wood of the ash tree ● 'ashtray *n* [C] small dish for tobacco ash

0‑ **ashamed** /əˈʃeɪmd/ *adj* feeling shame or embarrassment for sth you have done

ashore /əˈʃɔː(r)/ *adv* towards, onto or on land, having come from the water

0‑ **aside** /əˈsaɪd/ *adv* to one side; out of the way: *He laid the book ~.* ● **aside** *n* [C] remark that others are not supposed to hear

0‑ **ask** /ɑːsk/ *v* **1** [I,T] put a question to sb in order to get information: *I ~ed him where he lived.* ◇ *'What time is it?' she ~ed.* **2** [I,T] say to sb that you want them to do sth: *I ~ed them to close the window.* **3** [T] invite sb: *~ him to the party* [IDM] **ask for it/ trouble** (*infml*) behave in such a way that trouble is likely [PV] **ask after sb**

ask about sb's health **ask for sb/sth** say that you want to speak to sb or be given sth ■ **asking price** *n* [C] price that sb wants to sell sth for

askance /əˈskæns/ *adv* [IDM] **look askance (at sb/sth)** (*written*) look at sb/sth with suspicion or doubt

askew /əˈskjuː/ *adj, adv* not in a straight or level position

0‑ **asleep** /əˈsliːp/ *adj* **1** sleeping **2** (of an arm or leg) having no feeling

asp /æsp/ *n* [C] small poisonous snake of N Africa

asparagus /əˈspærəgəs/ *n* [U] plant whose green shoots are eaten as a vegetable

0‑ **aspect** /ˈæspekt/ *n* [C]
1 particular part or side of sth being considered **2** (*fml*) direction in which a building faces

aspersions /əˈspɜːʃnz/ *n* [pl] critical or unpleasant remarks or judgements: *cast ~ on sb's honesty*

asphalt /ˈæsfælt/ *n* [U] black sticky substance for making road surfaces ▶ **asphalt** *v* [T] cover sth, esp a road, with asphalt

asphyxiate /əsˈfɪksieɪt/ *v* [T] cause sb to become very ill or die by preventing them from breathing ▶ **asphyxiation** /əsˌfɪksiˈeɪʃn/ *n* [U]

aspirate /ˈæspərət/ *n* [C] sound of the letter 'h' ● **aspirate** /ˈæspəreɪt/ *v* [T] pronounce sth with an 'h' sound

aspire /əˈspaɪə(r)/ *v* [I] ~ **(to)** have a strong desire to achieve sth ▶ **aspiration** /ˌæspəˈreɪʃn/ *n* [C, U] strong desire

aspirin /ˈæsprɪn/ *n* [C, U] (*pl* **aspirin** *or* **~s**) drug used to reduce pain and fever

ass /æs/ *n* [C] **1** (*US*, ⚠, *sl*) = ARSE **2** (*GB*, *infml*) stupid person

assail /əˈseɪl/ *v* [T] (*fml*) attack sb violently, esp when this is a crime ▶ **assailant** /əˈseɪlənt/ *n* [C] (*fml*) person who attacks sb, esp physically

assassin /əˈsæsɪn/ *n* [C] person who murders sb important or famous ▶ **assassinate** /əˈsæsɪneɪt/ *v* [T] murder sb important or famous, esp for political reasons ▶ **assassination** /əˌsæsɪˈneɪʃn/ *n* [U, C]

assault /əˈsɔːlt/ *n* [C, U] sudden violent attack ● **assault** *v* [T] attack sb violently, esp when this is a crime ■ **assault course** *n* [C] area of land with many objects that are difficult to climb, jump over etc, used esp by soldiers, for training

assemble /əˈsembl/ *v* **1** [I, T] come together as a group; bring people or things together **2** [T] fit together the parts of sth

assembly /əˈsembli/ *n* (*pl* **-ies**) **1** [C] (Assembly) group of people who have been elected to meet and make decisions or laws for a region or country: *the UN General A~* **2** [C] group of people coming together for a purpose **3** [C,U] meeting of teachers and students in a school, usu at the start of the day **4** [U] process of fitting the parts of sth together ■ **assembly line** *n* [C] arrangement of machines and workers along which a product moves as it is put together in stages

assent /əˈsent/ *n* [U] *(fml)* agreement ● **assent** *v* [I] **~ (to)** *(fml)* agree to sth

assert /əˈsɜːt/ *v* [T] **1** state sth firmly **2** make others recognize your authority, by behaving firmly **3** **~ yourself** behave in a confident and forceful way ▸ **assertion** /əˈsɜːʃn/ *n* [U,C] ▸ **assertive** *adj* confident and forceful

assess /əˈses/ *v* [T] **1** judge the importance, worth, etc of sb/sth **2** calculate the value of sth ▸ **assessment** *n* [C,U] ▸ **assessor** *n* [C]

asset /ˈæset/ *n* [C] **1** valuable person or quality **2** [usu pl] thing owned, esp property, that can be sold to pay debts ■ **asset-stripping** *n* [U] *(business)* practice of buying a failing company at a low price and then selling all its assets (2) in order to make a profit

assign /əˈsaɪn/ *v* [T] **1** give sth as a share or task **2** provide sb for a task or position **3** fix sth as a time, place, etc; name sth ▸ **assignment** *n* [C] piece of work that sb is given to do; task **2** [U] act of giving sth to sb as a share or task

assimilate /əˈsɪməleɪt/ *v* **1** [T] take in or absorb food, information, ideas, etc **2** [I,T] (allow sb to) become part of another group or state ▸ **assimilation** /-ˈleɪʃn/ *n* [U].

0–▪ **assist** /əˈsɪst/ *v* [I,T] *(fml)* help sb to do sth ▸ **assistance** *n* [U] *(fml)* help ▸ **assistant** *n* [C] person who helps or supports sb, usu in their job

0–▪ **associate** /əˈsəʊʃieɪt/ *v* **1** **~ (with)** make a connection between people or things in your mind: *I always ~ the smell of baking with my childhood.* **2** [I] **~ with** spend time with sb: *I don't want to ~ with those people.* ● **associate** /əˈsəʊʃiət/ *n* [C] person you work with or do business with: *business ~s*

0–▪ **association** /əˌsəʊsiˈeɪʃn/ *n* **1** [C] official group of people joined together for a purpose **2** [C,U] connection or relationship between people or organizations **3** [C] connection in the mind [IDM] **in association with sb** together with sb ■ **As'sociation 'Football** *(GB, fml)* = FOOTBALL

assorted /əˈsɔːtɪd/ *adj* of different kinds; mixed ▸ **assortment** /əˈsɔːtmənt/ *n* [C] collection of different things or different types of the same thing

0–▪ **assume** /əˈsjuːm/ *v* [T] **1** believe sth to be true without proof **2** begin to use, take or have sth: *~ control* ◇ *~ a greater importance* **3** pretend to have a particular feeling or quality ▸ **assumption** /əˈsʌmpʃn/ *n* **1** something believed to be true without proof **2** act of assuming

assurance /əˈʃɔːrəns/ *n* **1** [U] belief in your own abilities **2** [C] promise: *give an ~* **3** [U] *(GB)* insurance: *life ~*

0–▪ **assure** /əˈʃʊə(r), -ʃɔː(r)/ *v* [T] **1** tell sb that sth is definitely true: *I ~ you that the money will be safe with me.* **2** **~ yourself (of sth)** make yourself certain of sth **3** *(GB)* insure against sth, esp against sb's death ▸ **assured** *adj* **1** confident **2** certain to happen

asterisk /ˈæstərɪsk/ *n* [C] star-shaped symbol (*)

asteroid /ˈæstərɔɪd/ *n* [C] any one of the small planets which go around the sun

asthma /ˈæsmə/ *n* [U] chest illness that causes difficulty in breathing ▸ **asthmatic** /æsˈmætɪk/ *adj*

astonish /əˈstɒnɪʃ/ *v* [T] surprise sb greatly ▸ **astonishing** *adj* very surprising ▸ **astonishment** *n* [U]

astound /əˈstaʊnd/ *v* [T] shock or surprise sb very much

astral /ˈæstrəl/ *adj* of the stars

astray /əˈstreɪ/ *adv* away from the right path

astride /əˈstraɪd/ *adj, prep* with one leg on each side (of)

astrology /əˈstrɒlədʒi/ *n* [U] study of the stars in the belief that they influence human affairs ▸ **astrologer** *n* [C] ▸ **astrological** /-ˈlɒdʒɪkl/ *adj*

astronaut /ˈæstrənɔːt/ *n* [C] person who travels in a spacecraft

astronomy /əˈstrɒnəmi/ *n* [U] scientific study of the stars, planets, etc ▸ **astronomer** *n* ▸ **astronomical** /ˌæstrəˈnɒmɪkl/ *adj* **1** of astronomy **2** *(infml)* (of an amount, a price, etc) very large

astute /əˈstjuːt/ *adj* clever at seeing quickly how to gain an advantage ▸ **astutely** *adv* ▸ **astuteness** *n* [U]

asylum /əˈsaɪləm/ *n* [U] *(also fml political a'sylum')* protection that a government gives to people who have left their own countries, usu because they were in danger for political reasons ■ **a'sylum seeker** *n* person who asks for asylum: *the rights of ~ seekers*

0–▪ **at** /ət; strong from æt/ *prep* **1** used to show where sb/sth is: *at the station* ◇ *She's at Yale* (= Yale University). **2** used to show when sth happens: *at two o'clock ◇ at the end of the week* **3** used to state the age at which sb does sth: *He got married at (the age of) 24.* **4** in the direction of or towards sb/sth: *look at her ◇ He pointed a gun at him.* **5** used to state the distance away from sth: *hold sth at arm's length* **6** used to show the situation sb/sth is in: *The country is now at war.* **7** used to show a rate, speed, etc: *driving at 70mph ◇ exports valued at £1 million* **8** used after an *adj* expressing ability: *good at music* **9** used after an *adj* to show the cause of sth: *shocked at the news*

ate *pt of* EAT

atheism /ˈeɪθiɪzəm/ *n* [U] belief that there is no God ▶ **atheist** *n* [C]

athlete /ˈæθliːt/ *n* [C] person trained for physical games ▶ **athletic** /æθˈletɪk/ *adj* **1** physically strong and fit **2** of athletics ▶ **athletics** *n* [U] sports that people compete in, esp running, jumping and throwing

atlas /ˈætləs/ *n* [C] book of maps

ATM /ˌeɪ tiː ˈem/ *n* [C] automated teller machine = CASH MACHINE

0━ **atmosphere** /ˈætməsfɪə(r)/ *n* [sing] **1** (the atmosphere) gases surrounding the earth **2** air in a room or enclosed space **3** general impression of a place: *a friendly ~* ▶ **atmospheric** /ˌætməsˈferɪk/ *adj* of the atmosphere

atoll /ˈætɒl/ *n* [C] island made of coral and shaped like a ring with a lake of sea water (lagoon) in the middle

0━ **atom** /ˈætəm/ *n* [C] smallest part of an element that can take part in chemical change ▶ **atomic** /əˈtɒmɪk/ *adj* of atoms ■ **atom bomb** (also a **tomic 'bomb**) *n* [C] bomb where explosive power comes from splitting atoms

atrocious /əˈtrəʊʃəs/ *adj* **1** very bad: *~ weather* **2** very cruel ▶ **atrociously** *adv*

atrocity /əˈtrɒsəti/ *n* [C, usu pl, U] (pl -**ies**) cruel violent act, esp in a war

0━ **attach** /əˈtætʃ/ *v* **1** [T] fasten or join sth to sth: *I ~ a copy of my report for your information.* **2** [T] join sth as a companion or member **3** [I, T] **~ to** (cause sth to) connect with sth: *~ importance to her speech* ▶ **attached** *adj* **1 ~ (to)** very fond of sb/sth **2 ~ to** forming part of an organization: *The research unit is ~ed to the university.* **3** joined to sth ▶ **attachment** *n* **1** [U] **~ (to)** strong feeling of affection for sb/sth **2** [C] thing that can be fixed onto a machine to make it do another job **3** [C] (*computing*) document that you send to sb using email

attaché /əˈtæʃeɪ/ *n* [C] person who works on the staff of an embassy ■ **at'taché case** *n* [C] small case for documents

0━ **attack** /əˈtæk/ *n* **1** [C, U] attempt to hurt or defeat sb/sth using force **2** [C, U] strong criticism in speech or writing **3** [C] short period when you suffer badly from a disease, etc ● **attack** *v* **1** [I, T] try to hurt or defeat sb/sth using force **2** [T] criticize sb/sth severely **3** [T] have a harmful effect on sth: *a disease that ~s the brain* **4** [T] deal with sth with a lot of energy and determination ▶ **attacker** *n* [C]

attain /əˈteɪn/ *v* [T] (*fml*) succeed in getting sth; achieve sth ▶ **attainable** *adj* ▶ **attainment** *n* **1** [C] skill or ability **2** [U] success in achieving sth

0━ **attempt** /əˈtempt/ *v* [T] try to do sth: *~ to escape* ● **attempt** *n* [C] effort to do sth [**IDM**] **an attempt on sb's life** an act of trying to kill sb

0━ **attend** /əˈtend/ *v* **1** [T] be present at an event: *~ a meeting* **2** [T] go regularly to a place: *~ school* **3** [I] **~ (to)** (*fml*) pay attention to sb/sth [**PV**] **attend to sb/sth** deal with sb/sth; take care of sb/sth ▶ **attendance** *n* **1** [U,C] act of being present at a place **2** [C,U] number of people present at an organized event ▶ **attendant** *n* [C] person whose job is to serve people in a public place

0━ **attention** /əˈtenʃn/ *n* [U] **1** careful thought: *pay~* **2** interest in sb/sth **3** special care or action: *in need of medical~* **4** position of a soldier standing upright and still ▶ **attentive** /əˈtentɪv/ *adj* giving attention to sb/sth ▶ **attentively** *adv*

attest /əˈtest/ *v* [I, T] **~ (to)** (*fml*) show or prove that sth is true

attic /ˈætɪk/ *n* [C] room in the roof of a house

0━ **attitude** /ˈætɪtjuːd/ *n* [C] **1** way of thinking or behaving **2** (*fml*) position of the body

attn (*esp US* **attn.**) *abbr* (*business*) (in writing) for the attention of: *Sales Dept, attn A Waters*

0━ **attorney** /əˈtɜːni/ *n* [C] (*US*) lawyer

0━ **attract** /əˈtrækt/ *v* [T] **1** get sb's attention or interest: *a display that ~s customers* **2** make sb/sth come somewhere: *The warm air ~s mosquitoes.* **3** cause people to have a particular reaction: *His remarks were bound to ~ criticism.* ▶ **attraction** /əˈtrækʃn/ *n* **1** [U, sing] feeling of liking sb, esp sexually **2** [C] interesting place to go or thing to do **3** [C] feature or quality that makes sth seem interesting ▶ **attractive** *adj* pleasing or interesting

0━ **attribute** /əˈtrɪbjuːt/ *v* [T] **~ to** say or believe that sth is caused by sb/sth:

attributive

He ~s his success to hard work.
● **attribute** /ˈætrɪbjuːt/ n [C] quality or feature of sth

attributive /əˈtrɪbjətɪv/ adj (gram) coming in front of a noun

aubergine /ˈəʊbəʒiːn/ n [C, U] large dark purple fruit, used as a vegetable

auburn /ˈɔːbən/ adj (esp of hair) reddish-brown

auction /ˈɔːkʃn/ n [C, U] public sale at which goods are sold to the person who offers the most money
● **auction** v [T] sell sth at an auction
▶ **auctioneer** /ˌɔːkʃəˈnɪə(r)/ n [C] person in charge of an auction

audacious /ɔːˈdeɪʃəs/ adj willing to take risks or do sth shocking
▶ **audaciously** adv ● **audacity** /ɔːˈdæsəti/ n [U] brave but rude or shocking behaviour

audible /ˈɔːdəbl/ adj able to be heard ▶ **audibly** adv

0━ **audience** /ˈɔːdiəns/ n [C] 1 group of people gathered together to hear or watch sb/sth 2 number of people who watch or listen to a broadcast programme 3 formal meeting with sb important

audio /ˈɔːdiəʊ/ adj of hearing or sound ▪ **audio-visual** adj using both sound and pictures

audit /ˈɔːdɪt/ n [C] official examination of business accounts
● **audit** v [T] examine accounts
▶ **auditor** n [C]

audition /ɔːˈdɪʃn/ n [C] short performance by an actor, singer, etc to test ability ● **audition** v [I, T] (ask sb to) give an audition

auditorium /ˌɔːdɪˈtɔːriəm/ (pl **auditoriums** or **auditoria** /-riə/) n [C] part of a building in which an audience sits

augment /ɔːɡˈment/ v [T] (fml) increase the amount, value, etc of sth

augur /ˈɔːɡə(r)/ v [IDM] **augur well/ill for sb/sth** (fml) be a good/bad sign for sb/sth in the future

0━ **August** /ˈɔːɡəst/ n [U, C] eighth month of the year (See examples of use at **April**.)

august /ɔːˈɡʌst/ adj (fml) impressive, making you feel respect

0━ **aunt** /ɑːnt/ n [C] 1 sister of your father or mother; wife of your uncle ▶ **auntie** (also **aunty**) n [C] (infml) aunt

au pair /ˌəʊ ˈpeə(r)/ n [C] young person who lives with a family in a foreign country in order to learn the language and take care of the children

aura /ˈɔːrə/ n [C] quality or feeling that seems to be produced by a person or place

aural /ˈɔːrəl/ adj of the ear or hearing

---

auspices /ˈɔːspɪsɪz/ n [pl] [IDM] **under the auspices of sb/sth** (fml) with the help or support of sb/sth

auspicious /ɔːˈspɪʃəs/ adj (fml) showing signs of future success; favourable ▶ **auspiciously** adv

austere /ɒˈstɪə(r), ɔːˈst-/ adj 1 without decoration; simple and plain 2 (used about a person) strict and serious 3 allowing nothing that gives pleasure; not comfortable
▶ **austerely** adv ● **austerity** /ɒˈsterəti, ɔːˈst-/ n [U, C] (pl -ies)

authentic /ɔːˈθentɪk/ adj known to be real or true ▶ **authentically** /-kli/ adv ● **authenticate** v [T] prove that sth is genuine, real or true
▶ **authentication** /-ˈkeɪʃn/ n [U]
● **authenticity** /-ˈtɪsəti/ n [U] quality of being genuine or true

0━ **author** /ˈɔːθə(r)/ n [C] 1 writer 2 person who creates or begins sth
▶ **authoring** n [U] (computing) creating computer programs without using programming language, for use in multimedia products ▶ **authorship** n [U] identity of the person who wrote sth

authoritative /ɔːˈθɒrətətɪv/ adj having or showing authority; that can be trusted ▶ **authoritatively** adv

0━ **authority** /ɔːˈθɒrəti/ n (pl -ies) 1 [U] power to give orders 2 [U] official permission to do sth 3 [C, usu pl] people or group with this power 4 [C] expert: He's an ~ on criminal law.

authorize (also -ise) /ˈɔːθəraɪz/ v [T] give official permission for sth
▶ **authorization** (also -isation) /ˌɔːθəraɪˈzeɪʃn/ n [U]

autobiography /ˌɔːtəbaɪˈɒɡrəfi/ n [C] (pl -ies) story of a person's life, written by that person
▶ **autobiographical** /ˌɔːtəˌbaɪəˈɡræfɪkl/ adj

autocrat /ˈɔːtəkræt/ n [C] 1 ruler who has complete power 2 person who expects to be obeyed
▶ **autocratic** /ˌɔːtəˈkrætɪk/ adj

autograph /ˈɔːtəɡrɑːf/ n [C] signature of sb famous
● **autograph** v [T] write your signature on sth

automate /ˈɔːtəmeɪt/ v [T] use machines and computers instead of people to do a job

0━ **automatic** /ˌɔːtəˈmætɪk/ adj 1 (of a machine) working by itself without human control 2 (of an action) done without thought
● **automatic** n [C] 1 gun that fires bullets continuously as long as the trigger is pressed 2 [C] car with a system of gears that operate without direct action from the driver
▶ **automatically** /-kli/ adv

automation /ˌɔːtəˈmeɪʃn/ n [U] use

of machines to do work previously done by people

automobile /ˈɔːtəməbiːl/ n [C] (US) = CAR

autonomous /ɔːˈtɒnəməs/ adj **1** (of a country, region, etc) able to govern itself **2** (of a person) able to do things without help from anyone else ▸ **autonomy** n [U] **1** freedom for a country, region, etc to govern itself independently **2** ability to act without being controlled by anyone else

autopsy /ˈɔːtɒpsi/ n [C] (pl **-ies**) medical examination of a body to find the cause of death

0-w **autumn** /ˈɔːtəm/ n [U, C] season of the year between summer and winter ▸ **autumnal** /ɔːˈtʌmnəl/ adj

auxiliary /ɔːɡˈzɪliəri/ adj (of workers) giving help or support to the main group of workers: ~ *nurses* ■ **auxiliary** n [C] (pl **-ies**) ■ **auxiliary verb** n [C] verb used with main verbs to show tense, etc and to form questions, eg *do* and *has* in: *Do you know where he has gone?*

0-w **avail** /əˈveɪl/ v (fml) ~ **yourself of** make use of sth ● **avail** n [IDM] **of little/no avail** of little or no use **to little/no avail** with little or no success

0-w **available** /əˈveɪləbl/ adj **1** that you can find or buy: *There are no tickets* ~. **2** (of a person) free to see or talk to people ▸ **availability** /-ˈbɪləti/ n [U]

avalanche /ˈævəlɑːnʃ/ n [C] mass of snow that falls down the side of a mountain

avarice /ˈævərɪs/ n [U] (fml) extreme desire for money ▸ **avaricious** /ˌævəˈrɪʃəs/ adj

avatar /ˈævətɑː(r)/ n **1** (in Hinduism and Buddhism) god appearing in a physical form **2** picture on a computer screen which represents a person, esp in a computer game or Internet chat room

avenge /əˈvendʒ/ v [T] hurt or punish sb for a wrong they have done to you: ~ *his father's murder*

avenue /ˈævənjuː/ n **1** (abbr **Ave.**) street in a town or city **2** (GB) road, esp one with trees on either side **3** choice or way of achieving sth: *explore several* ~s

0-w **average** /ˈævərɪdʒ/ n [C] result of adding several amounts together and dividing the total by the number of amounts **2** [U] usual level ● **average** adj: *the* ~ *age* ● **average** v **1** [I,T] find the average of sth **2** [T] be or do sth as an average: *Drivers* ~ *12 miles an hour.*

averse /əˈvɜːs/ adj ~ **to** (fml) opposed to sth: *not* ~ *to making money*

aversion /əˈvɜːʃn/ n [C,U] ~ (**to**) strong dislike of sb/sth

avert /əˈvɜːt/ v [T] **1** prevent sth unpleasant from happening **2** (fml) turn away your eyes, etc

avian /ˈeɪviən/ adj of or connected with birds ■ **avian flu** n [U] (fml) = BIRD FLU

aviary /ˈeɪviəri/ n [C] (pl **-ies**) large cage or building in which birds are kept

aviation /ˌeɪviˈeɪʃn/ n [U] science or practice of flying aircraft

avid /ˈævɪd/ adj very enthusiastic; keen ▸ **avidly** adv

avocado /ˌævəˈkɑːdəʊ/ n [C] (pl **-s**) pear-shaped green tropical fruit

0-w **avoid** /əˈvɔɪd/ v [T] **1** prevent sth bad from happening **2** keep away from sb/sth; try not to do sth ▸ **avoidable** adj that can be avoided ▸ **avoidance** n [U]

avow /əˈvaʊ/ v [T] (fml) declare sth openly

await /əˈweɪt/ v [T] (fml) wait for sb/sth

0-w **awake** /əˈweɪk/ adj not asleep ● **awake** v (pt **awoke** /əˈwəʊk/ pp **awoken** /əˈwəʊkən/) [I,T] (cause sb to) wake up

awaken /əˈweɪkən/ v **1** [I,T] (cause sb to) wake up **2** [T] cause sth to become active: ~ *sb's interest* [PV] **awaken (sb) to sth** (cause sb to) become aware of sth ▸ **awakening** n [sing] act of realizing sth

0-w **award** /əˈwɔːd/ v [T] make an official decision to give sth to sb: ~ *her first prize* ● **award** n [C] something awarded: *an* ~ *for bravery*

0-w **aware** /əˈweə(r)/ adj ~ (**of/that**) knowing or realizing sth: *I'm well* ~ *of the problem.* ▸ **awareness** n [U]

0-w **away** /əˈweɪ/ adv **1** at or at a distance from sth: *The sea is two miles* ~. **2** to a different place or in a different direction: *Go* ~? ◇ *Put your toys* ~. **3** not present: *He's* ~ *this week.* **4** continuously: *He was working* ~. **5** until disappearing completely: *The water boiled* ~. **6** (sport) at the ground of your opponents: *play the next match* ~ ■ **awayday** (also **a'way day**) n [C] day when a group of workers go to another place in order to discuss ideas or plans: *The* ~ *brought together all the department heads.*

awe /ɔː/ n [U] respect and fear ■ **'awe-inspiring** adj impressive; making you feel respect ▸ **awesome** /ˈɔːsəm/ adj **1** very impressive or difficult and making you feel frightening **2** (US, infml) very good, enjoyable, etc

0-w **awful** /ˈɔːfl/ adj **1** very bad or unpleasant: ~ *weather* **2** (spoken) used to emphasize that there is a large amount or too much of sth: *It*

cost an ~ lot of money. ▶ **awfully**
/'ɔːfli/ adv very: ~ly hot

awhile /ə'waɪl/ adv (fml) for a short time

0━ **awkward** /'ɔːkwəd/ adj
1 embarrassing: an ~ silence
2 difficult to deal with: an ~ customer
3 not convenient: arrive at an ~ time
4 difficult or dangerous because of its shape or design **5** not graceful; not comfortable: to sleep in an ~ position ▶ **awkwardly** adv
▶ **awkwardness** n [U]

awning /'ɔːnɪŋ/ n [C] sheet of cloth that stretches from above a door or window to keep off the rain or sun

awoke pt of AWAKE

awoken pp of AWAKE

axe (esp US ax) /æks/ n [C] tool for cutting wood [IDM] **have an axe to grind** have private reasons for doing sth ● **axe** v [T] greatly reduce jobs or services

axiom /'æksiəm/ n [C] statement accepted as true ▶ **axiomatic** /-'mætɪk/ adj true in such an obvious way that you do not need to prove it

axis /'æksɪs/ n [C] (pl **axes** /'æksiːz/)
1 imaginary line through the centre of a turning object: the earth's ~
2 (tech) fixed line against which the positions of points are measured, esp on a graph: horizontal ~

axle /'æksl/ n [C] rod on which a wheel turns

aye (also ay) /aɪ/ exclam (old-fash or used in dialects) yes ● **aye** n [C] (person who gives a) vote in favour of sth

azure /'æʒə(r); 'æʒjʊə(r)/ adj, n [U] (written) bright blue

Bb

B, b /biː/ n [C,U] (pl **B's, b's** /biːz/) the second letter of the English alphabet

b. abbr born

babble /'bæbl/ v [I] talk quickly in an excited way ▶ **babble** n [sing]

baboon /bə'buːn/ n [C] kind of large monkey

0━ **baby** /'beɪbi/ n [C] (pl **-ies**) **1** very young child or animal **2** (sl, esp US) word used affectionately to address your wife, husband or lover
▶ **babyish** adj or like a baby
■ **babysit** v (**-tt-** pt, pp **-sat**) [I] look after a child or children while the parents are out ■ **babysitter** n [C]

bachelor /'bætʃələ(r)/ n [C]
1 unmarried man **2** (Bachelor) holder of a first university degree: a B~ of Arts

0━ **back¹** /bæk/ n [C] part of a person's or an animal's body between the neck and the bottom

2 (usu sing) part or side of sth that is furthest from the front: sit in the ~ of the car ◇ Write your number on the ~ of the cheque. **3** [C] part of a chair that supports your upper body [IDM] **back to front** with the back where the front should be: You've got your jumper on ~ to front. **behind sb's back** without sb's knowledge **get sb's back up** (infml) annoy sb **get off sb's back** (infml) stop annoying sb **put your back into sth** work very hard at sth ● **back** adj **1** situated behind or at the back of sth: the ~ door **2** owed from a time in the past: ~ pay
■ **backache** n [U,C] continuous pain in the back ■ **back'bencher** n [C] (GB) member of Parliament who does not hold a senior position in the government or opposition
■ **backbone** n **1** [C] line of bones down the middle of the back
2 [sing] most important part of a system, an organization, etc that gives it support **3** [U] strength of character ■ **back-breaking** adj (of physical work) very hard and tiring
■ **background** n **1** [C] details of a person's family, education, etc
2 [sing, U] circumstances or past events which explain why sth is how it is; information about these
3 [C, usu sing] part of a scene behind the main objects, people, etc
4 [sing] position in which sb/sth can be seen/heard etc, but is not the centre of attention ■ **backhand** n [C] stroke in tennis, etc with the back of the hand forward ■ **back'handed** adj indirect or sarcastic: rather a ~handed compliment ■ **backless** adj (of a dress) not covering most of the back ■ **backlog** n [C] work still to be done ■ **back 'number** [C] issue of a newspaper, etc of an earlier date
■ **backpack** n [C] = RUCKSACK
● **backpack** v [I] travel on holiday carrying your equipment and clothes in a backpack: go ~ing
■ **backside** n [C] (infml) part of the body that you sit on ■ **backslash** n [C] mark (\) used in computer commands ■ **back'stage** adv behind the stage in a theatre
■ **backstroke** n [U] swimming stroke done on your back
■ **backwater** n [C] **1** part of a river away from the main part **2** place not affected by progress, new ideas, etc

0━ **back²** /bæk/ adv **1** towards or at the back; away from the front or centre: Stand ~, please. **2** in(to) an earlier position or condition: Put the book ~ on the shelf. **3** (of time) in the past: a few years ~ **4** in return: hit him ~ ◇ I'll phone you ~. [IDM] **back and forth** backwards and forwards
■ **backbiting** n [U] unkind talk about sb who is not present ■ **back'date** v [T] declare that sth is valid from an earlier date in the past ■ **back'fire** v [I] have the opposite effect to the

one intended, with bad or dangerous results ■ **backlash** n [sing] extreme, esp violent, reaction to an event

0─┳ **back**[3] /bæk/ v **1** [I,T] move (sth) backwards: ~ *a car into a space* **2** [I] ~ **onto** (of a building) face sth at the back: *The house* ~s *onto the park.* **3** [T] give help or support to sb/sth **4** [T] bet money on a horse, etc **5** [T] cover the back of sth [PV] **back down** withdraw a claim, etc made earlier; admit defeat **back out (of sth)** withdraw from an agreement **back sb/sth up 1** support or encourage sb **2** give evidence to prove sth **3** (*computing*) make a spare copy of a file, etc ▸ **backer** n [C] person who gives (esp financial) support ▸ **backing** n [U] **1** support or help **2** material that forms the back of sth ■ **backup** n [U,C] **1** extra help or support **2** (*computing*) spare copy of a file, etc that can be used if the original is lost or damaged

backgammon /ˈbækɡæmən/ n [U] game played with dice on a board marked with long thin triangles

0─┳ **backward** /ˈbækwəd/ *adj* **1** directed towards the back: *a* ~ *glance* **2** having made less than normal progress: *a* ~ *child* ▸ **backwards** (*esp US* **backward**) *adv* **1** towards a place or position that is behind **2** with the back or end first: *say the alphabet* ~s

bacon /ˈbeɪkən/ n [U] salted or smoked meat from the back or sides of a pig

0─┳ **bacteria** /bækˈtɪəriə/ n [pl] (sing **-ium** /-iəm/) very small living organisms, often the cause of disease ▸ **bacterial** /-riəl/ *adj*

0─┳ **bad** /bæd/ *adj* (**worse** /wɜːs/ **worst** /wɜːst/) **1** not good; unpleasant: *a* ~ *actor* **3** ~ **at** (of poor quality: *a* ~ *actor* **3** ~ **at** (of poor) not able to do sth well or easily: *be* ~ *at maths* **4** serious; severe: *a* ~ *mistake* ◊ *in a* ~ *mood* **5** (of food) not fresh or fit to eat; rotten: *The fish have gone* ~. **6** unhealthy; painful: *a* ~ *back* **7** (of a person) wicked; immoral **8** harmful: *Smoking is* ~ *for you.* **9** inappropriate: *a* ~ *time to phone* [IDM] **be in sb's bad books** → BOOK[1] **be bad luck** be unfortunate **go from bad to worse** (of a bad situation) get even worse **have a bad night** → NIGHT **not bad** (*spoken*) quite good **too bad** (*spoken*) unfortunate; regrettable: *It's too* ~ *she's ill.* ■ **bad debt** n [C] money owed that is unlikely to be paid back ▸ **baddy** n [C] (*pl* **-ies**) (*infml*) bad person in a film, etc ■ **bad language** n [U] rude or offensive words ▸ **badly** *adv* (**worse, worst**) **1** in a bad way; not good enough **2** seriously; severely: ~*ly wounded* **3** very much: *need some money* ~*ly*

[IDM] **badly off** poor; not having enough of sth ▸ **badness** n [U]

bade *pt* of BID(3)

badge /bædʒ/ n [C] something worn to show occupation, membership, rank, etc

badger /ˈbædʒə(r)/ n [C] small animal with black and white stripes on its head that lives in holes in the ground and is active at night ▸ **badger** v [T] put pressure on sb by repeatedly asking them questions

badminton /ˈbædmɪntən/ n [U] game similar to tennis, played by hitting a shuttlecock across a high net

0─┳ **bad-tempered** *adj* often angry; in an angry mood: *Giles often gets* ~ *when he's hungry.*

baffle /ˈbæfl/ v [T] confuse sb; be too difficult for sb to understand

0─┳ **bag** /bæɡ/ n **1** [C] flexible container with an opening at the top: *a paper/shopping* ~ **2** (*also* (**bags**)) [pl] (*GB, infml*) ~ **of** plenty of sth [IDM] **in the bag** (*infml*) certain to be won, achieved, etc ● **bag** v (**-gg-**) [T] **1** put sth into bags **2** catch or kill an animal (*GB, infml*) claim sth as yours

0─┳ **baggage** /ˈbæɡɪdʒ/ n [U] (*esp US*) = LUGGAGE

baggy /ˈbæɡi/ *adj* (**-ier, -iest**) (of clothing) hanging loosely: ~ *trousers*

bagpipes /ˈbæɡpaɪps/ n [pl] musical instrument with pipes and a bag to store air

bail /beɪl/ n **1** [U] money sb agrees to pay if an accused person fails to appear at their trial. When bail has been arranged, the accused person is allowed to go free until the trial: *He was released on* ~. **2** [C, usu pl] (in cricket) either of the two small pieces of wood over the stumps ● **bail** (*GB also* **bale**) v [PV] **bail out (of sth)** jump out of a plane that is going to crash **bail sb out 1** pay sb's bail for them **2** help sb out of (esp financial) difficulties **bail (sth) out** empty water from a boat using your hands or a container

bailiff /ˈbeɪlɪf/ n [C] **1** (GB) law officer who takes goods, etc from sb who owes money **2** (GB) person who manages land for sb else **3** (US) official who keeps order in a law court

bait /beɪt/ n [U] **1** food put on a hook or in a trap to catch fish or animals **2** thing used to tempt or attract sb ● **bait** v [T] **1** put bait on or in sth **2** deliberately try to make sb angry

0─┳ **bake** /beɪk/ v **1** [I,T] cook sth in an oven **2** [I,T] (cause sth to) become hard by heating **3** [I] (of a person or place) become very hot: *It's baking today!* ▸ **baker** n [C] person whose job is to bake and sell bread, etc ▶ **bakery** *n* [C] (pl -**ies**) place where bread is baked and/or sold ■ **baking powder** *n* [U] powder used for making cakes, etc rise and become light

0━ **balance**¹ /ˈbæləns/ *n* **1** [U, sing] condition when two opposites are equal or in correct proportions: *a ~ between work and play* **2** [U] ability to keep steady with an equal amount of weight on each side of the body: *keep/lose your ~* **3** [C, usu sing] amount of money in a bank account **4** [C, usu sing] amount owed after a part payment **5** [C] instrument used for weighing things [IDM] **in the balance** uncertain or undecided **on balance** having considered everything ■ **balance sheet** *n* [C] (*business*) record of money received and paid out

0━ **balance**² /ˈbæləns/ *v* [I, T] put your body or sth else into a position where it is steady and equal: *How long can you ~ on one leg?* **2** [T] compare two objects, plans, etc; give equal importance to two contrasting things **3** [T] (*business*) show that in an account the total money spent is equal to the total money received

balcony /ˈbælkəni/ *n* [C] (pl -**ies**) **1** platform built onto the outside of a building with a wall or rail around it **2** area of seats upstairs in a theatre

bald /bɔːld/ *adj* **1** having little or no hair on the head **2** without any extra explanation or detail: *a ~ statement* ▶ **balding** *adj* starting to lose the hair on your head ▶ **baldly** *adv* in a few words with nothing extra or unnecessary ▶ **baldness** *n* [U]

bale /beɪl/ *n* [C] large bundle of hay, cloth, etc tied tightly together ● **bale** *v* [T] **1** make sth into bales **2** (*GB*) = **BAIL**

balk (*esp US*) = **BAULK**

0━ **ball** /bɔːl/ *n* [C] **1** round object used in games **2** round mass: *a ~ of wool* **3** round part of the body: *the ~ of your foot* **4** (*usu pl*) (*infml*) testicle **5** large formal party with dancing [IDM] **get/start/keep the ball rolling** begin/continue an activity **have a ball** (*infml*) have a very good time **(be) on the ball** (*infml*) be alert and aware of new ideas, etc ■ **ball game** *n* [C] **1** any game played with a ball **2** (*US*) game of baseball [IDM] **a (whole) different/new ball game** (*infml*) a completely different kind of situation ■ **ballpoint** (*also* **ballpoint** 'pen) *n* [C] pen that uses a tiny ball at its point to roll ink onto the paper ■ **ballroom** *n* [C] large room used for dancing on formal occasions

ballad /ˈbæləd/ *n* [C] song or poem that tells a story

ballast /ˈbæləst/ *n* [U] heavy material placed in a ship or hot-air balloon to keep it steady

ballerina /ˌbæləˈriːnə/ *n* [C] female ballet dancer

ballet /ˈbæleɪ/ *n* **1** [U] style of dancing that tells a story with music but no talking or singing **2** [C] story performed by a group of ballet dancers **3** [C, with sing or pl verb] group of dancers who work and perform ballet together

ballistic /bəˈlɪstɪk/ *adj* connected with ballistics [IDM] **go ballistic** (*infml*) to become very angry ■ **ballistic missile** *n* [C] missile that is at first powered and guided but then falls freely

ballistics /bəˈlɪstɪks/ *n* [U] scientific study of the movement of objects shot or fired through the air

balloon /bəˈluːn/ *n* [C] **1** brightly coloured rubber bag filled with air **2** (*also* hot-'air balloon) large rounded bag filled with air or gas to make it rise in the air, with a basket to carry passengers ● **balloon** *v* [I] **1** suddenly swell out or get bigger **2** travel in a hot-air balloon as a sport: *go ~ing* ▶ **balloonist** *n* [C] person who flies in a balloon as a sport

ballot /ˈbælət/ *n* **1** [U, C] system of voting in secret; occasion on which such a vote is held **2** (*GB* 'ballot paper) [C] piece of paper on which sb marks who they are voting for **3** (the ballot) [sing] total number of votes in an election ● **ballot** *v* [T] ask sb to vote secretly about sth **2** [I] vote secretly about sth ■ 'ballot box *n* [C] box into which ballot papers are put

balm /bɑːm/ *n* [U, C] oil or cream that is used to make wounds less painful or skin softer ▶ **balmy** *adj* (-ier, -iest) (of the air, weather, etc) warm and pleasant

balsa /ˈbɔːlsə/ (*also* 'balsa wood) *n* [U] light wood of the tropical American balsa tree

balsamic vinegar /bɔːlˌsæmɪk ˈvɪnɪgə(r)/ *n* [U] dark sweet Italian vinegar

balti /ˈbɔːlti; ˈbʊlti/ *n* [C, U] type of meat or vegetable dish cooked in Pakistani style, usu served in a round metal pan

balustrade /ˌbæləˈstreɪd/ *n* [C] row of posts, joined together at the top, built along the edge of a balcony, bridge, etc

bamboo /ˌbæmˈbuː/ *n* [C, U] (pl ~s) tall plant of the grass family with hard hollow stems

0━ **ban** /bæn/ *v* (-nn-) forbid sth officially ● **ban** *n* [C] ~ (on) official rule that forbids sth

banal /bəˈnɑːl/ adj ordinary and uninteresting: ~ remarks

banana /bəˈnɑːnə/ n [C] long yellow tropical fruit

0—▪ band /bænd/ n [C] **1** group of musicians who play popular music **2** group of people: a ~ of robbers **3** thin flat strip of material for tying things together or putting round an object **4** range of numbers, amounts, etc within limits ▪ **band** v [I] ~ **together** unite in a group ▪ **Band-Aid**™ n (esp US) = PLASTER(3) ▪ **bandstand** n [C] covered platform outdoors, where musicians, esp a brass or military band, can play ▪ **bandwagon** n [IDM] **climb/jump on the bandwagon** (infml) join others in doing sth fashionable and successful

0—▪ bandage /ˈbændɪdʒ/ n [C] strip of cloth that is wrapped round a wound ▪ **bandage** v [T] wrap a bandage round sth

bandit /ˈbændɪt/ n [C] member of an armed group of thieves who attack travellers

bandwidth /ˈbændwɪdθ, -wɪtθ/ n [C,U] (computing) measurement of the amount of information that a particular computer network or Internet connection can send in a particular time. It is often measured in bits per second.

bandy /ˈbændi/ adj (-ier, -iest) (of the legs) curving outwards at the knees ▪ **bandy** v (pt, pp -ied) [IDM] **bandy words** (old-fash) quarrel [PV] **bandy sth about** mention a name, word, story, etc frequently

bang /bæŋ/ n [C] **1** sudden loud noise **2** violent blow to a part of the body: a ~ on the head ▪ **bang** v **1** [I,T] (cause sth to) make a loud noise: The door ~ed shut. **2** [T] hit a part of the body against sth: She ~ed her knee on the desk. [IDM] **be banging your head against a brick wall** → HEAD¹ ▪ **bang** adv (infml) exactly: ~ in the middle

banger /ˈbæŋə(r)/ n [C] (GB, infml) **1** sausage **2** noisy firework **3** noisy old car

bangle /ˈbæŋgl/ n [C] jewellery in the form of a large ring that is worn round the wrist

banish /ˈbænɪʃ/ v [T] ~ (**from**) **1** order sb to leave a place, esp as a punishment **2** (written) make sb/sth go away; get rid of sb/sth ▪ **banishment** n [U]

banister (also **bannister**) /ˈbænɪstə(r)/ n [C, usu pl] posts and rail at the side of a staircase

banjo /ˈbændʒəʊ/ n [C] (pl ~s) musical instrument with a round body, played by plucking the strings

0—▪ bank /bæŋk/ n [C] **1** place where money is kept safely **2** place for storing supplies: a blood ~ **3** land sloping up beside a river, etc

---

4 raised area of ground that slopes at the sides **5** mass of snow, clouds, etc **6** row or series of similar objects, esp machines: a ~ of switches ▪ **bank** v **1** [T] put money into a bank account **2** [I] (have an account with a particular bank) **3** [I] (of an aircraft) travel with one side higher than the other, while turning [PV] **bank on sb/ sth** rely on sb/sth ▶ **banker** n [C] owner, director or manager of a bank ▪ **bank 'holiday** n [C] (GB) official public holiday ▶ **banking** n [U] business activity of banks ▪ **banknote** n [C] piece of paper money

bankrupt /ˈbæŋkrʌpt/ adj **1** unable to pay your debts **2** completely lacking in anything good ▶ **bankrupt** n [C] (law) person who is declared bankrupt in a court of law ▶ **bankruptcy** /ˈbæŋkrʌptsi/ n [C,U] (pl -ies) state of being bankrupt

banner /ˈbænə(r)/ n [C] long strip of cloth with a message on it, carried by marchers

bannister = BANISTER

banns /bænz/ n [pl] public announcement in church of an intended marriage

banquet /ˈbæŋkwɪt/ n [C] large formal dinner

bantam /ˈbæntəm/ n [C] type of small chicken

banter /ˈbæntə(r)/ n [U] playful joking talk ▪ **banter** v [I] joke with sb

baptism /ˈbæptɪzəm/ n [C] ceremony of sprinkling water on sb or dipping sb in water, often giving them a name as well, as a sign of their membership of the Christian Church [IDM] **baptism of fire** difficult introduction to a new job or activity ▶ **baptize** (also **-ise**) /bæpˈtaɪz/ v [T] give sb baptism

0—▪ bar /bɑː(r)/ n **1** [C] room or counter where drinks and food are served **2** [C] piece of sth with straight sides: a ~ of chocolate **3** [C] long straight piece of wood or metal, esp across a door, window, etc: be behind ~s (= be in prison) **4** [C] narrow band of colour, light, etc **5** [C, usu sing] thing that stops sb from doing sth: Poor health is a ~ to success. **6** [C] (music) series of notes **7** (**the Bar**) [sing] (GB) the profession of barrister: He was called to the B~ (= became a qualified barrister). **8** (**the Bar**) [sing] (US) the profession of any kind of lawyer ▪ **'bar code** n [C] group of thick and thin parallel lines printed on goods for sale, containing information for a computer ▪ **barman** n [C] (pl -men) (fem **barmaid**) (US **bartender**) person who serves drinks at a bar

---

barb /bɑːb/ n [C] sharp curved point of an arrow or a hook ▸ **barbed** adj with short sharp points: ~ed wire

barbarian /bɑːˈbeəriən/ adj, n [C] uncivilized (person) ▸ **barbaric** /bɑːˈbærɪk/ adj cruel and violent and not as expected from civilized people ▸ **barbarity** /bɑːˈbærəti/ n [U,C] (pl -ies) great cruelty ▸ **barbarous** /ˈbɑːbərəs/ adj (written) cruel and shocking

barbecue /ˈbɑːbɪkjuː/ n [C] (abbr **BBQ**) **1** metal frame for cooking food outdoors **2** party at which food is cooked on a barbecue ● **barbecue** v [T] cook food on a barbecue

barber /ˈbɑːbə(r)/ n [C] person whose job is to cut men's hair

barbiturate /bɑːˈbɪtʃərət/ n [C] powerful drug that causes sleep

bare /beə(r)/ adj (~r, ~st) **1** without clothing or covering **2** empty: ~ cupboards **3** just enough; basic ● **bare** v [T] uncover sth; reveal sth ■ **bareback** adj, adv on a horse without a saddle ▸ **barefaced** adj shameless; very rude ▸ **barefoot** adj, adv without shoes or socks ▸ **barely** adv only just ▸ **bareness** n [U]

0̄ **bargain** /ˈbɑːgən/ n [C] **1** something sold cheaply **2** agreement between two or more people to do sth for each other [IDM] **into the bargain** also; as well ● **bargain** v [I] discuss prices, conditions, etc with sb in order to reach a satisfactory agreement [PV] **bargain for/on sth** expect and be prepared for sth to happen: I got more than I had ~ed for.

barge /bɑːdʒ/ n [C] flat-bottomed boat ● **barge** v (infml) [I] move awkwardly, pushing people out of the way or crashing into them [PV] **barge in (on sth)** interrupt rudely

barista /bəˈriːstə/ n [C] person who serves coffee in a bar or cafe

baritone /ˈbærɪtəʊn/ n [C] (man with a) singing voice between tenor and bass

bark /bɑːk/ n [U,C] **1** short loud sound made by a dog **2** outer covering of a tree ● **bark** v [I] (of dogs) make a short loud sound **2** [T] say sth in a loud unfriendly way

barley /ˈbɑːli/ n [U] (plant producing) grain used for food and for making beer and whisky

barmy /ˈbɑːmi/ adj (-ier, -iest) (GB, infml) slightly crazy

barn /bɑːn/ n [C] building for storing hay, etc on a farm

barnacle /ˈbɑːnəkl/ n [C] small shellfish that attaches itself to objects under water

barometer /bəˈrɒmɪtə(r)/ n [C] instrument for measuring air pressure to show changes in the weather: (fig) a ~ of public feeling

baron /ˈbærən/ n [C] **1** British nobleman of low rank **2** person who owns or controls a large part of a particular industry ▸ **baroness** n [C] **1** woman with the same rank as a baron **2** wife of a baron ▸ **baronet** /ˈbærənət/ n [C] nobleman with the lowest hereditary rank in Britain

baroque /bəˈrɒk/ adj used to describe European architecture, art and music of the 17th and early 18th centuries that have a grand and highly decorated style

barrack /ˈbærək/ v [I,T] shout loudly at sb to interrupt him/her

barracks /ˈbærəks/ n [C] (pl **barracks**) [with sing or pl verb] large building(s) for soldiers to live in

barrage /ˈbærɑːʒ/ n [C] **1** heavy continuous gunfire **2** large number of questions or comments that are directed at sb quickly and aggressively: a ~ of complaints **3** artificial barrier across a river

barrel /ˈbærəl/ n [C] **1** round container for liquids **2** contents of or the amount contained in a barrel **3** tube of a gun through which the bullet is fired ■ **barrel organ** n from which music is produced by turning a handle

barren /ˈbærən/ adj **1** (of soil or plants) not able to produce crops or fruit **2** not producing anything useful or successful

barricade /ˌbærɪˈkeɪd/ n [C] barrier of objects built to block a street, etc ● **barricade** v [T] block a street, etc

0̄ **barrier** /ˈbæriə(r)/ n [C] **1** something that prevents or controls movement or progress: the removal of trade ~s **2** thing that keeps people apart: the language ~

barring /ˈbɑːrɪŋ/ prep except for

barrister /ˈbærɪstə(r)/ n [C] lawyer in Britain who has the right to argue cases in higher courts

barrow /ˈbærəʊ/ n [C] **1** (GB) small cart, moved by hand, from which fruit and vegetables are sold in the street **2** = WHEELBARROW (WHEEL)

barter /ˈbɑːtə(r)/ v [I,T] exchange goods for other goods, without using money ▸ **barter** n [U]

0̄ **base** /beɪs/ n [C] **1** lowest part of sth, on which it stands **2** idea, fact, situation, etc from which sth is developed **3** main part to which other parts are added: a drink with a rum ~ **4** place from which the armed forces operate: *a naval ~* ● **base** v [T] **1 ~ on** develop sth using sth else as a starting point: *a story ~d on real life* **2** use a particular city, town, etc as the main place for a company's business, holiday, etc: *a company ~d in Cairo* ▶ **baseless** *adj* (*fml*) without cause or reason ● **base** *adj* (**-r, ~st**) (*fml*) immoral; dishonourable ● **base metal** *n* [C] metal that is not a precious metal such as gold

baseball /'beɪsbɔːl/ *n* [U] American game played with a bat and ball by two teams of nine players

basement /'beɪsmənt/ *n* [C] lowest floor of a building, below ground level

bases 1 *plural* of BASIS **2** *plural* of BASE

bash /bæʃ/ *v* [T] (*infml*) hit sb/sth very hard ● **bash** *n* [C] (*infml*) hard hit [IDM] **have a bash (at sth)** (*GB, spoken*) try to do sth

bashful /'bæʃfl/ *adj* shy ▶ **bashfully** *adv*

BASIC /'beɪsɪk/ *n* [U] simple language, using familiar English words, for writing computer programs

0━ **basic** /'beɪsɪk/ *adj* simplest or most important; fundamental: *the ~ facts* ▶ **basically** *adv* most importantly ▶ **basics** *n* [pl] basic parts or facts

basil /'bæzl/ *n* [U] sweet-smelling herb

basin /'beɪsn/ *n* [C] **1** = WASHBASIN (WASH¹) **2** round open bowl for liquids or food **3** area of land by a large river with streams running down into it: *the Amazon B~* **4** hollow place where water collects

0━ **basis** /'beɪsɪs/ *n* (pl **bases** /'beɪsiːz/) **1** [sing] reason why people take a particular action: *She was chosen for the job on the ~ of her qualifications.* **2** [sing] way in which sth is done: *a service run on a commercial ~* **3** [C, usu sing, U] most important part of sth from which it is developed; foundation: *arguments that have a firm ~*

bask /bɑːsk/ *v* [I] **~ (in)** sit or lie, esp in the sunshine, enjoying sth's warmth: (*fig*) *~ in sb's approval*

basket /'bɑːskɪt/ *n* [C] container made of woven strips of wood: *a shopping ~* ● **basketball** *n* [U] game in which two teams of five players try to throw a ball into a high net hanging from a ring

bass¹ /beɪs/ *n* **1** [U] lowest tone or part in music, for instruments or voices **2** [C] (man with) the lowest singing voice **3** = DOUBLE BASS (DOUBLE¹) ● **bass** *adj* low in tone

bass² /bæs/ *n* [C,U] (pl **bass**) kind of sea or freshwater fish, eaten as food

bassoon /bə'suːn/ *n* [C] wind

instrument made of wood, producing very low sounds

bastard /'bɑːstəd/ *n* [C] **1** (⚠, *sl*) used to insult sb, esp a man, who has been rude, unpleasant or cruel **2** (*sl*) word that some people use to refer to sb, esp a man, who they feel jealous of or sorry for

baste /beɪst/ *v* [T] pour fat over meat while cooking

bastion /'bæstiən/ *n* [C] **1** group of people or system that protects a way of life or belief that is threatened **2** place that military forces are defending

bat /bæt/ *n* [C] **1** piece of wood with a handle for hitting the ball in cricket, baseball, etc **2** animal like a mouse with wings that flies and feeds at night [IDM] **off your own bat** (*infml*) without being encouraged or helped by anyone else ● **bat** *v* (**-tt-**) [I] hit a ball with a bat (1) [IDM] **not bat an eyelid** (*infml*) show no sign of surprise ■ **batsman** *n* [C] (pl **-men**) (in cricket) player who is hitting the ball

batch /bætʃ/ *n* [C] **1** group of things or people **2** (*computing*) set of jobs processed together on a computer: *process a ~ job ◇ a ~ file/program*

0━ **bath** /bɑːθ/ *n* [C] (pl **~s** /bɑːðz/) **1** large container for water in which you sit to wash your body **2** water in a bath, ready to use: *a long soak in a hot ~* **3** act of washing your body while sitting in the bath ● **bath** *v* [T] (*US*) (*bathe*) give a bath to sb: *~ a baby* ■ **bathrobe** *n* [C] **1** loose piece of clothing worn before or after taking a bath **2** (*US*) = DRESSING GOWN ■ **bathroom** *n* [C] **1** room in which there is a bath, a washbasin and often a toilet **2** (*esp US*) = TOILET ■ **bathtub** *n* [C] (*esp US*) bath (1)

bathe /beɪð/ *v* **1** [T] wash sth with water, esp a part of the body: *B~ the wound.* **2** [I] (*old-fash*) swim in the sea, esp in the sea, etc ● **bathe** *n* [sing] (*GB*) swim in the sea, etc ▶ **bather** *n* [C] swimmer

baton /'bætɒn; -tɒ/ *n* [C] **1** short thin stick used by the conductor of an orchestra **2** (*esp GB*) police officer's short thick stick used as a weapon

battalion /bə'tæliən/ *n* [C] (*GB*) large group of soldiers that form part of a brigade

batten /'bætn/ *n* [C] long wooden board ● **batten** *v* [T] **~ down** fasten sth with battens

batter /'bætə(r)/ *v* [T] hit sb/sth hard and often ▶ **battered** *adj* out of shape because of old age, great use, etc ■ **battering ram** *n* [C] large heavy log formerly used for breaking down walls, etc ● **batter** *n* **1** [U] mixture of flour, eggs, milk, etc: *fish fried in ~* **2** [C] (*US*) (in baseball) player who is hitting the ball

0➔ **battery** /'bætri, -təri/ *n* (*pl* **-ies**) **1** [C] device for supplying electricity **2** [C] large number of things or people of the same type: *a ~ of cameras/reporters* **3** [C] number of big guns that are used together **4** [C] series of cages in which hens are kept: *~ hens/eggs* **5** [U] (*law*) crime of attacking sb physically

0➔ **battle** /'bætl/ *n* **1** [C,U] fight between armed forces **2** [C] competition, argument or struggle between people trying to win power or control: *a legal ~ for compensation* ● **battle** *v* [I] fight; struggle: *battling against poverty* ■ **'battlefield** *n* [C] place where a battle is fought ■ **'battleship** *n* [C] large warship with big guns and heavy armour

battlements /'bætlmənts/ *n* [pl] low wall around the top of a castle, with openings for shooting through

batty /'bæti/ *adj* (**-ier, -iest**) (*infml*) slightly crazy

bauble /'bɔːbl/ *n* [C] cheap showy ornament

baulk (*esp US* **balk**) /bɔːk/ *v* [I] *~ (at)* be very unwilling to try or do sth

bawdy /'bɔːdi/ *adj* (**-ier, -iest**) rude and amusing about sexual matters

bawl /bɔːl/ *v* [I,T] **1** shout loudly **2** cry loudly: *He was ~ing his eyes out.*

0➔ **bay** /beɪ/ *n* **1** area of the coast where the land curves widely inwards **2** area or division used for a particular purpose: *a loading ~* —**IDM** **hold/keep sb/sth at bay** prevent an enemy from coming near or a problem from having a bad effect ■ **'bay tree** *n* [C] tree whose dark green leaves are used in cooking ■ **,bay 'window** *n* [C] window, with glass on three sides, that projects from an outside wall ● **bay** *v* [I] (of large dogs) make a deep loud sound, esp when hunting

bayonet /'beɪənət/ *n* [C] long sharp blade fixed to the end of a rifle ▸ **bayonet** /'beɪənət; ˌbeɪə'net/ *v* [T] stab sb with a bayonet

bazaar /bə'zɑː(r)/ *n* [C] **1** (in some eastern countries) street or area where there are many small shops **2** (in Britain, the US, etc) sale of goods to raise money for charity

bazooka /bə'zuːkə/ *n* [C] long portable gun that rests on the shoulder and fires rockets esp against tanks

BBC /ˌbiː biː 'siː/ *abbr* British Broadcasting Corporation

BBQ *abbr* = BARBECUE

BC /ˌbiː 'siː/ *abbr* (in the year) before the birth of Jesus Christ

0➔ **be¹** /bi/ strong form biː/ *v* [NOTE] (I **am** (I'm), you **are** (you're), he/she/it **is** (he's/she's/it's), we **are** (we're), you **are** (you're), they **are** (they're) *Past tense*: I **was**, you **were**, he/she/it **was**, we **were**, you **were**, they **were** *Past participle*: **been**, *present participle*: **being**, *negative short forms*: **aren't, isn't, wasn't, weren't**) **1** *linking verb* (there is/are) exist; be present: *Is there a God?* **2** [I] be situated: *The lamp is on the table.* **3** *linking verb* used to give the date or age of sb/sth or to talk about time: *Today's Tuesday April 9th.* ◇ *She'll be 39 this month.* ◇ *It's two thirty.* **4** *linking verb* used when you are giving the name of people or things, describing them or giving more information about them: *This is Mrs Dawson.* ◇ *She's from Thailand.* ◇ *'How is your wife?' 'She's fine, thanks.'* **5** [I] (used only in the perfect tenses) go to a place; visit sb/sth: *I've never been to Japan.* ◇ *Has the doctor been yet?* **6** *linking verb* used to show possession: *The money's not yours, it's Mark's.* ◇ *The letter is for you.* **7** *linking verb* used to show equivalence in value, number, etc: *That will be £80.95.* ◇ *Two and two is four.*

0➔ **be²** /bi; strong form biː/ *aux v* (for full present and past tense forms → BE¹) **1** used with a *present participle* to form the continuous tense: *They are reading.* **2** used with a *past participle* to form the passive: *He was sacked.* **3** (be to do sth) used to show that sth must happen or that sth has been arranged: *You are to report to the police at 10 o'clock.*

0➔ **beach** /biːtʃ/ *n* [C] area covered by sand or small stones (shingle) beside the sea or a lake ● **beach** *v* [T] move a boat onto the shore from the water ■ **'beach ball** *n* [C] large light ball for games on the beach ■ **'beachhead** *n* [C] strong position on a beach established by an invading army ■ **'beachwear** *n* [U] clothes for sunbathing, swimming, etc

beacon /'biːkən/ *n* [C] light or fire used as a signal or warning

bead /biːd/ *n* [C] **1** small piece of glass, wood, etc with a hole through it, that can be put on a string with others of the same type and worn as jewellery, etc **2** drop of liquid: *~s of sweat*

beady /'biːdi/ *adj* (**-ier, -iest**) (of eyes) small and bright

0➔ **beak** /biːk/ *n* [C] hard pointed or curved outer part of a bird's mouth

beaker /'biːkə(r)/ *n* [C] **1** tall narrow cup for drinking from **2** glass container used in chemistry

beam /biːm/ *n* [C] **1** line of light, electric waves or particles: *~s of* sunlight ◇ a laser ~ **2** long piece of wood, metal, etc used to support weight, esp as part of the roof in a building **3** wooden bar that is used in gymnastics for people to move and balance on ● wide and happy smile ● beam v **1** [I] ~ (at) smile happily **2** [T] send out radio or television signals **3** [I] send out light and warmth

bean /biːn/ n [C] **1** seeds or seed containers (pods) of a climbing plant, eaten as vegetables: soya ~s **2** seed from a coffee plant or similar plant: coffee/cocoa ~s [IDM] **full of beans** (infml) having a lot of energy; lively

0~ bear¹ /beə(r)/ v (pt bore /bɔː(r)/ pp borne /bɔːn/) **1** [T] (used with can/could in negative sentences and questions) be able to accept and deal with sth unpleasant: I can't ~ the smell of fish. ◇ She couldn't ~ the pain any more. **2** (used in negative sentences) be fit for sth: The plan will not ~ close examination. **3** [T] (fml) take responsibility for sth: We'll ~ the cost of the improvements. **4** [T] (written) have a particular feeling, esp a negative feeling: I ~ them no resentment. **5** [T] support sb/sth: The ice is too thin to ~ your weight. **6** [T] (fml) show sth; carry sth so it can be seen: The letter bore her signature. **7** [T] (written) give birth to a child **8** [T] (fml) (of trees and plants) produce flowers or fruit **9** [I] go or turn in the direction mentioned: The road ~s left. [IDM] **bear the brunt of sth** suffer the main force of sth: ~ the brunt of an attack/sb's anger **bear sth in mind** → MIND¹ **bear witness to sth** show evidence of sth **bring sth to bear (on sb/sth)** (fml) use pressure, influence, etc to try to achieve sth or make sb do sth: Pressure was brought to ~ on him to finish the job. **can't bear sb/sth** dislike sb/sth very much [PV] **bear down on sb/sth** move quickly and threateningly towards sb/sth **bear sb/sth out** show that sb is right or that sth is true **bear up** be as cheerful as possible in difficult times **bear with sb** be patient with sb ▶ **bearable** adj that can be tolerated ●

bear² n [C] heavy wild animal with thick fur and sharp claws

0~ beard /bɪəd/ n [C,U] hair that grows on the chin and cheeks of a man's face ▶ **bearded** adj

bearer /'beərə(r)/ n [C] **1** person who carries sth, esp at a ceremony: coffin~ **2** person who brings a letter or message **3** (fml) person who has a cheque for payment

bearing /'beərɪŋ/ n **1** [U] ~ on relevance; connection: That has no ~ on the subject. **2** [sing] way of standing or behaving **3** [C] (tech)

direction shown on a compass [IDM] **get/find your bearings** become familiar with where you are **lose your bearings** → LOSE

beast /biːst/ n [C] **1** (old-fash or fml) large or dangerous animal **2** cruel person ▶ **beastly** adj (infml) unpleasant

0~ beat¹ /biːt/ v (pt beat pp ~en /'biːtn/) **1** [T] defeat sb; be better than sth: She ~ me at chess. **2** [I,T] hit sb/sth many times, usu very hard **3** [I,T] make a regular sound or movement: His heart ~ faster. **4** [T] mix sth thoroughly with a fork: ~ eggs **5** [T] change the shape of sth, esp metal, by hitting it [IDM] **beat about the bush** talk indirectly about sth **beat it** (sl) go away **beat a (hasty) retreat** go away or back quickly **beat time (to sth)** mark the rhythm of music by making regular movements **off the beaten track** far away from other people, houses, etc [PV] **beat down on sb/sth** (of the sun) shine with great heat **beat sb down** persuade a seller to reduce a price **beat sb up** hit and kick sb hard, many times: He was badly ~ en up. ▶ **beat** adj very tired: I'm dead ~. ▶ **beaten** adj shaped by beating ▶ **beater** n [C] tool for beating: a carpet ~er ◇ an egg ~er ▶ **beating** n [C] **1** punishment by hitting **2** very heavy defeat

0~ beat² /biːt/ n [C] **1** (sound of a) repeated stroke: the ~ of a drum **2** rhythm in music or poetry **3** route along which a police officer goes regularly

beautician /bjuː'tɪʃn/ n [C] person whose job is to give beauty treatments

0~ beautiful /'bjuːtɪfl/ adj very pretty or attractive; giving pleasure to the senses ▶ **beautifully** adv ▶ **beautify** /'bjuːtɪfaɪ/ v (pt, pp -ied) [T] make sth beautiful

0~ beauty /'bjuːti/ n (pl -ies) **1** [U] quality or state of being beautiful **2** [C] person or thing that is beautiful ■ **'beauty salon** (also **'beauty parlour**) [C] place where you can pay for treatment to your face, hair, nails, etc ■ **'beauty spot** n [C] (GB) place famous for its scenery

became pt of BECOME

0~ because /bɪ'kɒz/ conj for the reason that: I did it ~ they asked me. ● **because of** prep by reason of: He couldn't walk fast ~ of his bad leg.

beckon /'bekən/ v [I,T] call sb to come nearer by waving your hand or finger

become /bɪ'kʌm/ v (pt became /bɪ'keɪm/ pp become) (usu used with an adj) **1** linking verb begin to be sth: They soon became angry. ◇ He wants to ~ a doctor. **2** [T] (fml) look attractive on sb: Short hair ~s you. [IDM] what became, has become, will become of sb/sth? used to ask what has happened or will happen to sb/sth ▸ becoming adj (fml) attractive

bed¹ /bed/ n [C] **1** piece of furniture that you sleep on **2** bottom of the sea or a river **3** piece of ground for growing plants **4** layer of clay, rock, etc in the ground [IDM] go to bed with sb (infml) have sex with sb ■ bedclothes n [pl] sheets, blankets, etc on a bed ■ bedding n [U] bedclothes ■ bedpan n [C] container for use as a toilet by sb ill in bed ■ bedridden adj having to stay in bed all the time because of illness, old age, etc ■ bedroom n [C] room for sleeping in ■ bedside n [sing] area beside a bed ■ bedsit n [C] (also bedsitter) n [C] (GB) rented room for both living and sleeping in ■ bedspread n [C] decorative top cover for a bed ■ bedstead n [C] wooden or metal frame of a bed ■ bedtime n [U] time that sb normally goes to bed

bed² /bed/ v (-dd-) [T] place or fix sth firmly in sth: The bricks are ~ded in the concrete. [PV] bed down sleep in a place where you do not usu sleep

bedevil /bɪ'devl/ v (-ll-, US -l-) [T] (fml) cause a lot of problems for sb/sth

bedlam /'bedləm/ n [U] scene of noisy confusion

bedraggled /bɪ'dræɡld/ adj made wet, dirty or untidy by rain, mud, etc

bee /biː/ n [C] black and yellow stinging insect that makes honey [IDM] have a bee in your bonnet (about sth) think or talk about sth a lot and think that it is very important ■ beehive n [C] box for bees to live in ■ beeline n [C] [IDM] make a beeline for sth/sb (infml) go directly towards sth/sb

beech /biːtʃ/ n **1** [C] tree with smooth bark, shiny leaves and small nuts **2** [U] wood of this tree

beef /biːf/ n **1** [U] meat of a cow **2** [C] (infml) complaint ● beef v [I] (infml) complain about sth ■ beefsteak n [U] thick piece of beef ▸ beefy adj (-ier, -iest) (infml) big or fat

been /biːn; bɪn/ pp of BE

beer /bɪə(r)/ n [U,C] alcoholic drink made from malt and flavoured with hops ▸ beery adj smelling of or like beer

beet /biːt/ n [U,C] **1** plant with a fleshy root that is used as a vegetable, esp for feeding animals or for making sugar **2** (US) = BEETROOT ■ beetroot n [U,C] dark red fleshy root of beet, eaten as a vegetable

beetle /'biːtl/ n [C] insect, often large and black, with a hard case on its back, covering its wings

befall /bɪ'fɔːl/ v (pt befell /bɪ'fel/ pp ~en /bɪ'fɔːlən/) [I,T] (old-fash) happen to sb

befit /bɪ'fɪt/ v (-tt-) [T] (fml) be suitable for ▸ befitting adj suitable; proper

before /bɪ'fɔː(r)/ prep **1** earlier than sb/sth: the day ~ yesterday **2** in front of sb/sth; ahead of sb/sth: B comes ~ C in the alphabet. ● before conj **1** earlier than the time when: Do it ~ you forget. **2** until: It was some time ~ I realized the truth. ● before adv at an earlier time; already: I've seen that film ~.

beforehand /bɪ'fɔːhænd/ adv in advance; earlier

befriend /bɪ'frend/ v [T] make a friend of sb

beg /beɡ/ v [I,T] (-gg-) **1** ask sb for sth anxiously because you want or need it very much: He ~ged for forgiveness. **2** ~ (for) ask sb for money, food, etc, esp in the street [IDM] go begging (GB, spoken) (of things) be unwanted I beg to differ I disagree I beg your pardon **1** (fml) I am sorry **2** used to ask sb to repeat sth because you did not hear it

beggar /'beɡə(r)/ n [C] person who lives by asking people for money, food, etc

begin /bɪ'ɡɪn/ v (-nn- pt began /bɪ'ɡæn/ pp begun /bɪ'ɡʌn/) [I,T] start: ~ to read a new book ◇ The film ~s at ten. ◇~ to feel ill [IDM] to begin with at first; firstly ▸ beginner n [C] person who is just starting to learn sth ▸ beginning n [C,U] starting point

begrudge /bɪ'ɡrʌdʒ/ v [T] feel envy or resentment at sb/sth: I do not ~ them their success.

behalf /bɪ'hɑːf/ n [IDM] on behalf of sb | on sb's behalf as the representative of sb: I'm speaking on Ann's ~.

behave /bɪ'heɪv/ v **1** [I] act in a particular way: ~ well/badly **2** [T] ~ yourself act in the correct or appropriate way ▸ behaviour (US -ior) n [U] way of behaving

behead /bɪ'hed/ v [T] cut off sb's head

behind /bɪ'haɪnd/ prep **1** at, or to the back of sb/sth: Hide ~ the tree. **2** later or less good than sb/sth; making less progress than sb/sth:

He's ~ the rest of the class. **3** supporting or agreeing with sb/sth **4** responsible for causing or starting sth: What's ~ that happy smile, then? ● **behind adv 1** at or towards the back of sb/sth; further back: The others are a long way ~. **2** remaining after others have gone: stay ~ after school **3** ~ **(with/in)** late in paying money or completing work: be ~ with the rent ● **behind** n [C] (infml) person's bottom

beige /beɪʒ/ adj, n [U] (of a very light yellowish-brown colour

being¹ /ˈbiːɪŋ/ pres part BE

being² /ˈbiːɪŋ/ n **1** [U] existence: The society came into ~ in 2001. **2** [C] living creature: human ~s

belated /bɪˈleɪtɪd/ adj coming or happening late ► **belatedly** adv

belch /beltʃ/ v **1** [I] let air come up noisily from your stomach and out through your mouth **2** [T] send out a lot of smoke, etc ● **belch** n [C]

belfry /ˈbelfri/ n (pl -ies) tower for bells

0━ **belief** /bɪˈliːf/ n **1** ~ **(in)** feeling that sth/sb is real and true and can be trusted **2** [C] something accepted as true: religious ~s

0━ **believe** /bɪˈliːv/ v **1** [T] be sure of the truth of sth or that sb is telling the truth: I don't ~ you! **2** [T] think that sth is true or possible: I ~ they have moved house. **3** (in negative sentences) [T] used to show anger or surprise at sth **4** [I] have religious faith **[PV] believe in sb/sth 1** feel certain that sb/sth exists: I don't ~ in ghosts. **2** be sure of the value of sth: He ~s in getting plenty of exercise. ► **believable** adj that can be believed ► **believer** n [C] person who believes in the existence or truth of sth, esp a religious faith

belittle /bɪˈlɪtl/ v [T] make sb/sth seem unimportant: Don't ~ your achievements.

0━ **bell** /bel/ n [C] **1** metal object that makes a ringing sound when struck: church ~s **2** electrical device that makes a ringing sound when a button on it is pushed; the sound that it makes: Ring the ~ and see if they're in.

belligerent /bəˈlɪdʒərənt/ adj **1** unfriendly and aggressive **2** (fml) (of a country) fighting a war

bellow /ˈbeləʊ/ v [I,T] shout in a deep loud voice

bellows /ˈbeləʊz/ n [pl] device for blowing air into sth, eg a fire

belly /ˈbeli/ n [C] (pl -ies) part of the body below the chest, containing the stomach ■ **bellyache** n [C,U] (infml) stomach pain ■ **bellyache** v [I] (infml) complain constantly ■ **bellyful** /ˈbelifʊl/ n (infml) enough; too much: I've had a ~ful of your moaning.

35

benefactor

0━ **belong** /bɪˈlɒŋ/ v [I] **1** ~ to be owned by sb: These books ~ to me. **2** ~ to be a member of sth: ~ to a political party **3** have a right or usual place: The plates ~ in this cupboard. ► **belongings** n [pl] personal articles; possessions

beloved adj /bɪˈlʌvd; before a noun bɪˈlʌvɪd/ much loved: He was ~ by all who knew him. ◇ my ~ husband ► **beloved** /bɪˈlʌvɪd/ n dearly loved person

0━ **below** /bɪˈləʊ/ prep, adv at or to a lower place or level than sb/sth: We saw the sea ~ us. ◇ The temperature fell ~ freezing. ◇ For details, see ~.

0━ **belt** /belt/ n [C] **1** strip of material worn round the waist **2** circular piece of material that drives machinery or carries things along **3** area that has a particular feature or where a particular group of people live: the commuter ~ **[IDM] below the belt** (infml) unfair or cruel ● **belt** v **1** [T] (infml) hit sth very hard **2** [I] (infml) move very fast: ~ing along the road **3** [T] fasten sth with a belt: The dress was ~ed at the waist. **[PV] belt up** (spoken) used to tell sb rudely to be quiet

bemoan /bɪˈməʊn/ v [T] (fml) complain about sth

bench /bentʃ/ n **1** [C] long wooden or metal seat for two or more people **2** (the bench) [sing] (law) judge or place where a judge sits in a law court: address the ~ **3** [C, usu sing] (in British Parliament) seat where a particular group of politicians sit: the Opposition ~es ■ (the bench) [sing] (sport) seats where players sit when they are not playing in the game ■ **benchmark** n [C] standard that other things can be compared to

0━ **bend** /bend/ v (pt, pp bent /bent/) **1** [T] make sth that was straight into a curved shape: ~ the wire ◇ It hurts when I ~ my arm. **2** [I] be or become curved: The road ~s to the left here. **3** [I] move your body forwards and downwards: Slowly ~ from the waist and touch your toes. **[IDM] bend over backwards (to do sth)** make a great effort ● **bend** n **1** [C] curve or turn: a ~ in the road **2** (the bends) [pl] pain suffered by divers coming to the surface too quickly **[IDM] round the bend** (infml) crazy

0━ **beneath** /bɪˈniːθ/ prep, adv (fml) **1** below; under **2** not good enough for sb/sth: ~ contempt

benediction /ˌbenɪˈdɪkʃn/ n [C,U] religious blessing

benefactor /ˈbenɪfæktə(r)/ n [C] person who gives money or help to an organization such as a charity or school ► **benefactress**

/'benɪfæktrəs/ n [C] woman benefactor

beneficial /ˌbenɪˈfɪʃl/ adj having a good effect; useful

beneficiary /ˌbenɪˈfɪʃəri/ n (pl -ies) person who receives sth, esp money, from a will

0̶ benefit /'benɪfɪt/ n **1** [C] advantage; helpful or useful effect: have the ~ of a good education **2** [U,C] (GB) money given by the government to people who are ill, poor, unemployed, etc: sickness ~ **3** [C, usu pl] advantages that you get from a company in addition to the money you earn: a company car and other ~s [IDM] for sb's benefit in order to help sb **give sb the benefit of the doubt** accept that sb is right because there is no clear proof that they are not ● **benefit v 1** [T] be useful to sb **2** [i] be in a better position because of sth

benevolent /bəˈnevələnt/ adj kind and helpful ▸ **benevolence** /bəˈnevələns/ n [U]

benign /bɪˈnaɪn/ adj **1** (fml) (of a person) kind and gentle **2** (med) (of tumours growing in the body) not dangerous

bent¹ pt, pp of BEND

0̶ bent² /bent/ adj **1** not straight: with your knees ~ **2** (GB, infml) dishonest [IDM] be bent on (doing) sth be determined to do sth, esp sth bad ● **bent** n [C, usu sing] natural skill: have a ~ for languages

bequeath /bɪˈkwiːð/ v [T] leave property, etc to sb after your death ▸ **bequest** /bɪˈkwest/ n [C] (fml) something bequeathed to sb

berate /bɪˈreɪt/ v [T] (fml) speak angrily to sb

bereaved /bɪˈriːvd/ adj (fml) having lost a relative or friend by death ▸ **bereavement** /bɪˈriːvmənt/ n [U,C]

bereft /bɪˈreft/ adj ~ of (fml) completely without sth: ~ of all hope

beret /'bereɪ/ n [C] soft flat round hat

berry /'beri/ n [C] (pl -ies) small soft fruit with seeds: black~

berserk /bəˈzɜːk/ adj very angry: My father will go ~ when he finds out.

berth /bɜːθ/ n [C] **1** place for sleeping on a ship or train **2** place in a harbour where ships tie up ● **berth v** [I,T] tie up a ship

beseech /bɪˈsiːtʃ/ v (pt, pp besought /bɪˈsɔːt/ or ~ed) [T] (fml) ask sb for sth anxiously because you want or need it very much

beset /bɪˈset/ v (-tt- pt, pp beset) [T] (fml) (usu passive) trouble sb/sth constantly: ~ by problems

0̶ beside /bɪˈsaɪd/ prep next to or at the side of sb/sth: Sit ~ me. [IDM] **beside yourself (with sth)** unable to

control yourself because of the strength of emotion you are feeling

besides /bɪˈsaɪdz/ prep in addition to sb/sth; apart from sb/sth ● **besides** adv moreover; also

besiege /bɪˈsiːdʒ/ v [T] surround a place with armed forces: (fig) The actress was ~d by reporters.

bespoke /bɪˈspəʊk/ adj (of a product) made specially, according to the needs of the customer

0̶ best¹ /best/ adj superlative of GOOD¹ **1** of the most excellent type or quality: the ~ dinner I've ever tasted **2** most enjoyable; happiest: the ~ years of my life **3** most suitable or appropriate: It's ~ if you go now. ■ **best man** n [C] man who helps the bridegroom at a wedding ● **best** adv superlative of WELL² **1** most; to the greatest extent: Which one do you like ~? **2** in the most excellent way: I work ~ in the mornings. **3** in the most suitable or appropriate way [IDM] **as best you can** not perfectly, but as well as you are able ■ **best-seller** n [C] book, etc that sells in very large numbers

0̶ best² /best/ n [sing] **1** most excellent thing or person: We want the ~ for our children. **2** highest standard that sb/sth can reach: do your ~ **3** something that is as close as possible to what you need or want: That's the ~ I can do. [IDM] **all the best** (infml) used when saying goodbye to sb to give them your good wishes **at best** taking the most favourable view **at its/your best** in the best state or form **the best of both worlds** the benefits of two completely different situations that you can enjoy at the same time **make the best of sth** do as well as you can in a difficult situation

bestial /'bestɪəl/ adj cruel and disgusting ▸ **bestiality** /ˌbesti'æləti/ n [U]

bestow /bɪˈstəʊ/ v [T] (fml) give sth to sb: ~ an honour on her

0̶ bet /bet/ v (-tt- pt, pp bet) [I,T] **1** ~ (on) risk money on a race or event by trying to predict the result **2** (spoken) used to say you are almost sure sth will happen: I ~ they'll come late. ● **bet** n [C] **1** arrangement to risk money on a future event **2** money risked in this way ▸ **better** n [C] person who bets

betray /bɪˈtreɪ/ v [T] **1** give information about sb/sth to an enemy; make a secret known **2** hurt sb who trusts you by not being faithful to them **3** show sth unintentionally: His face ~ed his guilt. ▸ **betrayal** /bɪˈtreɪəl/ n [C,U] ▸ **betrayer** n [C]

betrothed /bɪˈtrəʊðd/ adj (fml) engaged to be married

0̶ better¹ /'betə(r)/ adj comparative of GOOD¹ **1** of a higher standard or less poor quality; not as bad as sth else: *He's in a much ~ mood.* **2** more able or skilled: *She's ~ at cooking than I am.* **3** more suitable or appropriate **4** less ill or unhappy: *He is slowly getting ~.* [IDM] one's **better half** (*hum*) one's wife or husband

0➤ **better²** /'betə(r)/ *adv* comparative of WELL² **1** in a more excellent or pleasant way; not as badly: *You play tennis ~ than I do.* **2** more; to a greater degree: *Wait till you get to know her ~.* **3** used to suggest that sth would be a suitable or appropriate thing to do: *Some things are ~ left unsaid.* [IDM] be **better off** in a better position, esp financially **had better (do sth)** should; ought to: *You'd ~ go soon.* **know better (than to do sth)** be sensible enough not to do sth

0➤ **better³** /'betə(r)/ *n* [sing,v] something that is better: *I expected ~ of him.* [IDM] **get the better of sb/sth** defeat sb/sth or gain an advantage

0➤ **better⁴** /'betə(r)/ *v* [T] **1** be better or do sth better than sb/sth else **2** ~ **yourself** improve your social position through education, etc

0➤ **between** /bɪ'twiːn/ *prep* **1** in or into the space or time that separates two points: *Q comes ~ P and R in the alphabet.* ◇ *Children must go to school ~ 5 and 16.* **2** from one place to another and back again: *We fly ~ Paris and Rome daily.* **3** used to show a connection or relationship: *the link ~ unemployment and crime* **4** shared by two or more people or things: *We drank a bottle of wine ~ us.* **5** by putting together the actions of two or more people: *B~ them, they collected £500.* ● **between** *adv* (usu **in between**) in the space or time that separates two points, objects, dates, etc: *The house was near a park but there was a road in ~.*

bevelled /'bevld/ (*US* beveled) *adj* having a sloping edge or surface: *a ~ mirror*

beverage /'bevərɪdʒ/ *n* [C] (*fml*) any kind of drink except water

bevy /'bevi/ *n* [sing] (*fml*) large group

beware /bɪ'weə(r)/ *v* [I,T] ~ (**of**) be careful about sb/sth dangerous or harmful: *B~ of the dog!*

bewilder /bɪ'wɪldə(r)/ *v* [T] confuse sb: *~ed by the noise and lights* ▶ **bewildering** *adj*

bewitch /bɪ'wɪtʃ/ *v* [T] **1** attract sb so much that they cannot think in a sensible way **2** put a magic spell on sb ▶ **bewitching** *adj*

0➤ **beyond** /bɪ'jɒnd/ *prep* **1** on or to the further side of sth: *The path continues ~ the village.* **2** further than the limits of: *What happened was ~ my control.* [IDM] **be beyond sb** (*infml*) be too difficult for sb to understand

● **beyond** *adv* on the other side; further on

bias /'baɪəs/ *n* [U,C] tendency to be unfair in your decisions by strongly favouring one side, person, etc ● **bias** *v* (**-s-, -ss-**) (*esp passive*) unfairly influence sb's opinions or decisions: *The jury was ~ed against her.*

bib /bɪb/ *n* [C] piece of cloth or plastic that you put under babies' chins while they eat

bible /'baɪbl/ *n* **1** (**the Bible**) [sing] holy book of the Jewish and Christian religions **2** [C] copy of the holy book **3** [C] authoritative book: *the gardener's ~* ▶ **biblical** /'bɪblɪkl/ *adj*

bibliography /ˌbɪbli'ɒɡrəfi/ *n* [C] (pl **-ies**) list of books and writings about one subject ▶ **bibliographer** /-'ɒɡrəfə(r)/ *n* [C]

bicentenary /ˌbaɪsen'tiːnəri/ *n* [C] (pl **-ies**) (*US* bicentennial) (celebration of) the 200th anniversary of an event

bicentennial /ˌbaɪsen'teniəl/ *n* [C] (*US*) = BICENTENARY ● **bicentennial** *adj*

biceps /'baɪseps/ *n* [C] (pl **biceps**) large muscle in the upper arm

bicker /'bɪkə(r)/ *v* [I] argue about unimportant things

0➤ **bicycle** /'baɪsɪkl/ *n* [C] (*also infml* **bike**) road vehicle with two wheels that you ride by pushing the pedals with your feet: *Let's go for a ~ ride.* ● **bicycle** *v* [I] (*old-fash*) ride a bicycle

0➤ **bid** /bɪd/ *v* (**-dd-** pt, pp **bid**, usu in sense 3: pt **bade** /bæd/ pp **-den** /'bɪdn/) **1** [I,T] offer to pay a particular price for sth, esp at an auction **2** [I] offer to do work or provide a service for a particular price, in competition with other companies **3** [T] (*fml*) say 'good morning', etc to sb ● **bid** *n* [C] **1** price offered to buy sth **2** offer to do work or provide a service for a particular price, in competition with other companies **3** attempt to do sth: *a desperate ~ to escape* ▶ **bidder** *n* [C] ▶ **bidding** *n* [U]

bide /baɪd/ *v* [IDM] **bide your time** wait for a good time to do sth

bidet /'biːdeɪ/ *n* [C] low bowl in the bathroom that you fill with water and sit on to wash your bottom

biennial /baɪ'eniəl/ *adj* happening every two years

bifocals /ˌbaɪ'fəʊklz/ *n* [pl] pair of glasses with lenses that are designed for both distant and near vision ▶ **bifocal** *adj*

0➤ **big** /bɪɡ/ *adj* (**~ger, ~gest**) **1** large in size, importance, etc: *~ feet* ◇ *a ~ match* **2** (*infml*) popular [IDM] **a big noise/shot** (*infml*) important

bigamy

person ■ ˌbig ˈgame n [U] large wild animals, hunted for sport ■ ˈbig-head n [C] (infml) person who is too proud ▶ ˈbig-headed adj (infml) ■ ˈbigwig n [C] (infml) important person

bigamy /'bɪgəmi/ n [U] crime of marrying a person when still legally married to sb else ▶ **bigamist** n [C] person guilty of bigamy ▶ **bigamous** adj

bigot /'bɪgət/ n [C] person who holds strong unreasonable opinions and will not change them ▶ **bigoted** adj intolerant and narrow-minded ▶ **bigotry** n [U]

0━ **bike** /baɪk/ n [C] (infml) short for BICYCLE

bikini /bɪ'ki:ni/ n [C] two-piece swimming costume worn by women

bilateral /ˌbaɪ'lætərəl/ adj between two sides: a ~ agreement

bile /baɪl/ n [U] liquid produced by the liver

bilge /bɪldʒ/ n 1 [C] (also bilges [pl]) almost flat part of the bottom of a boat or a ship 2 [U] dirty water that collects in a ship's bilge

bilingual /ˌbaɪ'lɪŋgwəl/ adj speaking or using two languages

bilious /'bɪliəs/ adj feeling sick

0━ **bill** /bɪl/ n [C] 1 statement of money owed for goods and services 2 proposed law to be discussed by parliament 3 (US) piece of paper money 4 printed notice 5 bird's beak [IDM] fill/fit the bill be suitable for a particular purpose ■ bill of exˈchange n [C] (pl ~s of exchange) (business) written order to pay a particular person a sum of money on a particular date ■ ˌbill of ˈlading n [C] (pl ~s of lading) (business) list giving details of the goods that a ship, etc is carrying ● **bill** v [T] 1 send a bill (1) to sb 2 announce sb/sth in a programme: He is ~ed to appear as Othello.

billet /'bɪlɪt/ n [C] private house in which soldiers are put to live temporarily ▶ **billet** v [T]

billiards /'bɪliədz/ n [U] game played on a table, using balls and long sticks

0━ **billion** /'bɪljən/ number one thousand million

billow /'bɪləʊ/ v [I] 1 (of a sail, skirt, etc) fill with air and swell out 2 (of smoke, cloud, etc) rise and move in a large mass ● **billow** n [C] (lit) moving mass of smoke, cloud, etc ▶ **billowy** adj

billy goat /'bɪli gəʊt/ n [C] male goat

0━ **bin** /bɪn/ n [C] large container for storing things in or for rubbish

binary /'baɪnəri/ adj of a system of numbers that uses only the digits 0 and 1

bind /baɪnd/ (pt, pp **bound** /baʊnd/) v 1 [T] tie or fasten sb/sth with a string or rope: ~ the prisoner's legs to the chair 2 [T] unite people, organizations, etc: bound by friendship 3 [T] fasten a book to a cover: a book bound in leather 4 [T] make sb obey a duty or promise: He bound her to secrecy. 5 [I,T] (cause sth to) stick together in a solid mass ● **bind** n [sing] (GB, infml) annoying situation that is difficult to avoid ▶ **binder** n [C] 1 hard cover that holds sheets of paper together 2 person or machine that binds books ▶ **binding** n [C] book cover

binge /bɪndʒ/ n [C] (infml) short time of doing too much of a particular activity, esp eating or drinking alcohol: ~ drinking is on the increase. ◇ go on a ~ ● **binge** v [I] ~ (on)

bingo /'bɪŋgəʊ/ n [U] gambling game using numbers

binoculars /bɪ'nɒkjələz/ n [pl] instrument with a lens for each eye, making distant objects seem nearer

biochemistry /ˌbaɪəʊ'kemɪstri/ n [U] study of the chemistry of living things ▶ **biochemist** n [C] scientist who studies biochemistry

biodata /'baɪəʊdeɪtə/ n [U] = CURRICULUM VITAE

biodegradable /ˌbaɪəʊdɪ'greɪdəbl/ adj that can be taken back into the earth naturally and so not harm the environment

biodiversity /ˌbaɪəʊdaɪ'vɜːsəti/ n [U] existence of many different kinds of animals and plants which make a balanced environment

biography /baɪ'ɒɡrəfi/ n [C] (pl -ies) story of a person's life, written by sb else ▶ **biographer** /baɪ'ɒɡrəfə(r)/ n [C] person who writes a biography ▶ **biographical** /ˌbaɪə'ɡræfɪkl/ adj

biohazard /'baɪəʊhæzəd/ n [C] risk to health or to the environment, from a biological source

0━ **biology** /baɪ'ɒlədʒi/ n [U] scientific study of living things ▶ **biological** /ˌbaɪə'lɒdʒɪkl/ adj ■ ˌbioˈlogical ˈweapon n [C] instrument of war that uses harmful bacteria ▶ **biologist** n [C] scientist who studies biology

biometric /ˌbaɪəʊ'metrɪk/ adj using measurements of human features in order to identify people: The major ~ methods include face, voice, fingerprint and iris (= the round, coloured part of the eye) recognition.

bipolar /ˌbaɪ'pəʊlə(r)/ (also ˌmanic-deˈpressive) adj suffering from bipolar disorder ■ ˌbiˌpolar disˈorder (also ˌmanic-deˈpression) n [U,C] mental illness causing sb to change suddenly from being very depressed to being very happy

birch /bɜːtʃ/ n [U,C] (hard wood of a)

kind of tree with smooth bark and thin branches

bird /bɜːd/ n [C] **1** creature with feathers and wings, usu able to fly **2** (GB, sl sometimes offens) young woman ■ 'bird flu (also 'avian flu, 'chicken flu) n [U] serious illness that can spread from birds to humans and that can cause death: Ten new cases of ~ flu were reported yesterday. ■ bird of 'prey n [C] bird that kills other animals for food

Biro™ /ˈbaɪrəʊ/ n (pl ~s) kind of ballpoint pen

birth /bɜːθ/ n **1** [C,U] (process of) being born **2** [U] family origin: Russian by ~ **3** [sing] beginning: the ~ of socialism [IDM] **give birth (to sb/sth)** produce a baby or young animal ■ 'birth control n [U] practice of preventing pregnancy ■ 'birthday n [C] anniversary of the day on which you were born ■ 'birthmark n [C] unusual mark on the skin from birth ■ 'birth rate n [C] number of births in one year to every thousand people

biscuit /ˈbɪskɪt/ n [C] (US cookie) small flat thin crisp cake

bisect /baɪˈsekt/ v [T] divide sth into two parts

bishop /ˈbɪʃəp/ n [C] **1** Christian clergyman of high rank **2** chess piece ■ bishopric /ˈbɪʃəprɪk/ n [C] office or district of a bishop

bison /ˈbaɪsn/ n [C] (pl bison) American buffalo; European wild ox

bistro /ˈbiːstrəʊ/ n [C] (pl ~s) small restaurant

bit¹ pt of BITE

bit² /bɪt/ n **1** (a bit) [sing] rather; a little: a ~ tired **2** (a bit) [sing] short time or distance: Move up a ~. **3** [C] ~ of small piece, amount or part of sth: useful ~s of information ◇ Which ~ of the film did you like best? **4** (a bit) [sing] (infml) a lot: He earns quite a ~. **5** [C] (computing) smallest unit of information **6** [C] metal bar that is put inside a horse's mouth so that the rider can control it **7** [C] part of a tool for drilling holes [IDM] **bit by bit** gradually ◇ **do your bit** (infml) do your share of a task **every bit as good, bad, etc (as sth)** just as good, etc ◇ **not a bit | not one (little) bit** not at all

bitch /bɪtʃ/ n **1** female dog **2** (sl, disapprov) unpleasant woman

bite /baɪt/ v (pt bit /bɪt/ pp bitten /ˈbɪtn/) **1** [I,T] cut into or through sth with your teeth **2** [I,T] (of an insect or snake) wound sb by making a small hole or mark in their skin **3** [I] (of fish) take the food from the hook of a fishing line **4** [I] have an unpleasant effect: The recession is beginning to ~. [IDM] **bite sb's head off** (infml) answer sb angrily ◇ **bite off more than you can chew** try to do too much ● **bite** n **1** [C] act of biting **2** [C] piece

cut off by biting **3** [sing] (infml) small amount of food: have a ~ to eat **4** [C] wound made by an animal or insect ● biting adj **1** sharp; painful: a biting wind ■ bite-sized (also 'bite-size) adj **1** small enough to put into the mouth and eat: Cut the meat into ~-sized pieces. **2** (infml) very short or short: The exams are taken in ~-sized chunks over two years.

bitmap /ˈbɪtmæp/ n [C] (computing) way in which an image is stored with a fixed number of bits (= units of information) ▶ bitmap v (-pp-) [T]

bitter /ˈbɪtə(r)/ adj **1** having a sharp unpleasant taste; not sweet **2** filled with anger and hatred: ~ enemies **3** causing unhappiness or anger for a long time: a ~ disappointment **4** very cold: a ~ wind ● bitter n [U] (GB) type of dark beer that is popular in Britain ▶ bitterly adv: ~ly disappointed/ cold ■ bitterness n [U]

bitumen /ˈbɪtʃəmən/ n [U] sticky black substance used in making roads

bivouac /ˈbɪvuæk/ n [C] temporary camp or shelter, built without using a tent ▶ bivouac v (-ck-) [I]

bizarre /bɪˈzɑː(r)/ adj very strange or unusual

blab /blæb/ v (-bb-) [I] (infml) tell a secret, usu through talking carelessly

black /blæk/ adj **1** of the darkest colour **2** of a dark-skinned race **3** (of coffee or tea) without milk or cream **4** very angry: give sb a ~ look **5** without hope; depressing: The future looks ~. **6** very dirty **7** (of humour) funny, but about unpleasant events: a ~ comedy ● black n **1** [U] the darkest colour **2** [C] person belonging to a race of people with dark skin ● black v [T] (GB) refuse to handle goods or do business with sb as a political protest: The strikers ~ed the cargo. [PV] **black out** lose consciousness **black sth out** switch off lights and cover windows ■ 'BlackBerry™ n [C] very small computer that can be used for sending and receiving emails ■ 'blackberry n [C] (pl -ies) small dark fruit growing wild on bushes ■ 'blackbird n [C] common European bird with black or brown feathers ■ 'blackboard n [C] board used in schools for writing on ■ black'currant n [C] small black fruit that grows on a bush ■ blacken v [I,T] become or make sth black **2** [T] say harmful things about sb ■ black 'eye n [C] dark-coloured bruise around the eye caused by a blow ■ 'blackhead n [C] small spot on the skin, with a black top ■ black 'ice n [U] clear thin layer of ice on a

road ■ **blackleg** n [C] (GB, disapprov) person who works when other workers are on strike
■ **blacklist** n [C] list of people considered dangerous or who are to be punished ▸ **blacklist** v [T]
▸ **blackly** adv ■ **black magic** n [U] magic used for evil purposes
■ **blackmail** n [U] 1 crime of demanding money from sb by threatening to tell sb else a secret about them 2 use of threats to influence sb: emotional/moral ~
■ **blackmail** n [T] ~ (into) force sb to give you money or do sth for you by threatening them ▸ **blackmailer** n [C] ■ **black market** n (C, usu sing) illegal buying and selling of goods ▸ **blackness** n [U] ■ **blackout** n [C] 1 period of darkness caused by electrical failure 2 period in a war when all lights must be switched off and windows covered 3 short loss of consciousness 4 prevention of the reporting of information: a news ~out ■ **black sheep** n [C] person who is different from the rest of their family or another group
■ **blacksmith** n [C] person whose job is to make things out of iron

bladder /'blædə(r)/ n [C] organ in the body in which urine collects

0̄ **blade** /bleɪd/ n [C] 1 sharp cutting edge of a knife, razor, etc 2 flat wide part of an oar, a propeller, etc 3 long narrow leaf of grass

0̄ **blame** /bleɪm/ v [T] consider sb/ sth to be responsible for sth bad [IDM] be to blame (for sth) be responsible for sth bad ■ **blame** n [U] responsibility for sth bad: lay/put the ~ on sb ▸ **blameless** adj not having done anything wrong ▸ **blameworthy** adj having done sth wrong

blanch /blɑːntʃ/ v 1 [I] become pale because you are shocked or frightened 2 [T] prepare food by putting it into boiling water for a short time

blancmange /blə'mɒnʒ/ n [C,U] jelly-like dessert made with milk

bland /blænd/ adj 1 ordinary or not very interesting 2 (of food) having little flavour 3 not showing any emotion ▸ **blandly** adv ▸ **blandness** n [U]

0̄ **blank** /blæŋk/ adj 1 (of paper) with nothing written on it 2 without expression; empty: a ~ look ■ **blank** n [C] 1 empty space in a document, etc 2 cartridge without a bullet ■ **blank cheque** n [C] cheque that is signed but which has a space so that the amount can be written in later ▸ **blankly** adv ■ **blank verse** n [U] (tech) poetry that has a regular rhythm but which does not rhyme

blanket /'blæŋkɪt/ n [C] 1 piece of thick cloth used as a warm covering on a bed 2 thin covering of sth: a ~ of snow ● **blanket** adj including all people or things in a group: a ~ ban on tobacco ● **blanket** v [T] cover sth

blare /bleə(r)/ v [I,T] make a loud unpleasant noise ● **blare** n [sing]

blasé /'blɑːzeɪ/ adj showing no excitement or interest in things because you have experienced them before

blaspheme /blæs'fiːm/ v [I,T] speak in a bad or disrespectful way about God or holy things ▸ **blasphemous** /'blæsfəməs/ adj ▸ **blasphemy** /'blæsfəmi/ n [U,C] (pl -ies)

blast /blɑːst/ n [C] 1 explosion, esp one caused by a bomb 2 sudden strong rush of air 3 loud sound made by a musical instrument, etc [IDM] (at) full blast at the greatest possible volume or power ● **blast** v [T] 1 break sth apart or destroy sth with explosives 2 direct water, air, etc at sb/sth with a lot of force [PV] **blast off** (of spacecraft) leave the ground ● **blast** exclam (infml) used for showing anger or annoyance ■ **blast furnace** n [C] large structure like an oven for melting iron ore (= rock containing iron) ■ **blast-off** n [U] moment when a spacecraft leaves the ground

blatant /'bleɪtnt/ adj very obvious; shameless ▸ **blatantly** adv

blaze /bleɪz/ n 1 [C] large dangerous fire 2 [sing] strong bright flames in a fire 3 [sing] ~ of bright show of light or colour; impressive show of sth: a ~ of publicity ● **blaze** v [I] 1 burn brightly 2 shine brightly 3 show strong feeling: blazing with anger ▸ **blazing** adj

blazer /'bleɪzə(r)/ n [C] jacket, often showing the colours of a school or team

bleach /bliːtʃ/ v [I,T] become or make sth white or lighter in colour by using a chemical or by leaving it in the sun ● **bleach** n [U] strong chemical used to bleach cloth or to clean sth well

bleak /bliːk/ adj 1 (of a situation) not hopeful or encouraging: The future looks ~. 2 cold and unpleasant: a ~ night ▸ **bleakly** adv

bleary /'blɪəri/ adj (-ier, -iest) (of eyes) sore and tired ▸ **blearily** adv

bleat /bliːt/ v [I], n [C] (make the) sound of a sheep or goat

bleed /bliːd/ v (pt, pp **bled** /bled/) 1 [I] lose blood 2 [T] draw liquid or air from sth

blemish /'blemɪʃ/ n [C] mark that spoils the good appearance of sth ● **blemish** v [T] spoil sth: The defeat has ~ed the team's record.

blend /blend/ v [I,T] mix together [PV] **blend in** mix well, so that you cannot notice separate parts ● **blend** n [C] mixture ▶ **blender** n [C] electric machine for mixing soft food or liquid

bless /bles/ v (pt, pp **~ed** /blest/) [T] **1** ask for God's favour for sb/sth **2** make sth holy ▶ **blessed** /'blesɪd/ adj **1** holy **2** giving pleasure ▶ **blessing** n [C] **1** something you are grateful for **2** [usu sing] approval **3** [usu sing] (prayer asking for) God's favour

blew pt of BLOW¹

blight /blaɪt/ n **1** [U,C] disease of plants **2** [U, sing] bad influence ▶ **blight** v [T] spoil or damage sth

0~ **blind**¹ /blaɪnd/ adj **1** unable to see **2 ~ (to)** unwilling to notice sth: ~ to the dangers involved **3** without reason or thought: ~ obedience [IDM] **(as) blind as a bat** unable to see well **blind drunk** (infml) very drunk ● **blind alley** n [C] course of action that does not produce satisfactory results ▶ **blindly** adv ▶ **blindness** n [U] ● **blind spot** n [C] **1** part of a road that a motorist cannot see **2** subject that sb is unwilling or unable to understand ▶ **blind** v [T] **1** make sb blind **2** take away sb's reason, judgement, etc: ~ed by love ● **the blind** n [pl] blind people

blind² /blaɪnd/ n [C] roll of cloth pulled down to cover a window

blindfold /'blaɪndfəʊld/ v [T] cover sb's eyes with a strip of cloth ● **blindfold** n [C] strip of cloth to cover the eyes ● **blindfold** adj, adv (as if) with the eyes covered

bling /blɪŋ/ **bling bling** (also **bling**) n [U] (infml) expensive shiny jewellery and fashionable clothes ▶ **bling-bling** (also **bling**) adj

blink /blɪŋk/ v **1** [I,T] shut and open your eyes quickly **2** [I] (of light) shine with an unsteady light ● **blink** n [C] act of blinking [IDM] **on the blink** (infml) (of a machine) not working properly

blinkers /'blɪŋkəz/ n [pl] leather pieces fixed at the side of a horse's eyes to stop it from looking sideways

bliss /blɪs/ n [U] perfect happiness ▶ **blissful** adj ▶ **blissfully** adv

blister /'blɪstə(r)/ n [C] **1** swelling on the surface of the skin, containing watery liquid **2** swelling on the surface of paint, etc ● **blister** v [I,T] (cause sth to) form blisters

blithe /blaɪð/ adj happy and carefree

blitz /blɪts/ n [C] **~ (on)** sudden attack: (fig) have a ~ on the house (= clean it very thoroughly)

blizzard /'blɪzəd/ n [C] severe snowstorm

bloated /'bləʊtɪd/ adj swollen

blob /blɒb/ n [C] **1** drop of liquid; small round mass

bloc /blɒk/ n [C] group of countries, etc united by a common interest

0~ **block** /blɒk/ n [C] **1** large solid piece: a ~ of ice/stone **2** large building divided into separate parts: a ~ of flats **3** group of buildings with streets on four sides: walk round the ~ **4** quantity of things considered as a unit: a ~ of shares **5** obstruction: a ~ to progress ● **block** v [T] **1** make movement on or in sth difficult or impossible: roads ~ed by snow **2** prevent sth from moving ■ **block capitals** (also **block letters**) n [pl] separate capital letters

blockade /blɒ'keɪd/ n [C] action of surrounding a place to prevent goods or people from coming in or out ● **blockade** v [T]

blockage /'blɒkɪdʒ/ n [C] thing that blocks; obstruction: a ~ in a pipe

blog /blɒg/ n (also **weblog**) n [C] personal record that sb puts on their website: Gloria is keeping a ~ about her swim round Ireland. ● **blog** v [I] (-**gg**-) ▶ **blogger** n [C]

blogosphere /'blɒgəʊsfɪə(r)/ n [sing] (infml) all the blogs that exist on the Internet

bloke /bləʊk/ n [C] (GB, infml) man

0~ **blonde** (also **blond**) /blɒnd/ n [C], adj (person) having golden or pale-coloured hair

0~ **blood** /blʌd/ n [U] **1** red liquid that flows through your body **2** (fml) family origins: a woman of noble ~ [IDM] **make sb's blood boil** make sb very angry **make sb's blood run cold** make sb very frightened **new/fresh blood** new members or employees with new ideas, etc ■ **bloodbath** n [C] violent killing of many people ■ **blood-curdling** adj filling you with horror ■ **blood donor** n [C] person who gives their blood for transfusions ■ **blood group** (esp US **blood type**) n [C] class of human blood ■ **bloodhound** n [C] large dog, used for tracking people ▶ **bloodless** adj **1** without any killing **2** very pale ■ **blood poisoning** n [U] infection of the blood with harmful bacteria ■ **blood pressure** n [U] measured force of blood as it travels round the body ■ **bloodshed** n [U] killing or wounding of people ■ **bloodshot** adj (of eyes) red ■ **blood sport** n [C,us,infml] sport in which animals or birds are killed ■ **bloodstained** adj covered with blood ■ **bloodstream** n [C] blood flowing through the body ■ **bloodsucker** **1** n animal or insect that sucks blood from people or animals **2** (infml, disapprov) person who takes advantage of other people to gain financial benefit ■ **bloodthirsty** adj wanting to kill or wound; showing interest in violence ■ **blood vessel** n [C] tube in the body through which blood flows

bloody /ˈblʌdi/ *adj, adv* (GB, spoken, ⚠) swear word that is used for adding emphasis: *You ~ idiot!*
● **bloody** *adj* (-ier, -iest) **1** covered with blood **2** with a lot of violence and killing ▸ **bloodily** *adv*
■ **bloody-minded** *adj* (GB, *infml*) deliberately unhelpful

bloom /bluːm/ *n* [C] flower [IDM] in (full) bloom with the flowers fully open ● **bloom** *v* [I] **1** produce flowers **2** become healthy, happy or confident

blossom /ˈblɒsəm/ *n* [C,U] flower, esp of a fruit tree: *The trees are in ~.*
● **blossom** *v* [I] **1** produce blossom **2** become more healthy, confident or successful

blot /blɒt/ *n* [C] **1** spot of ink, mark **2** fault: *a ~ on his character* ● **blot** *v* (-tt-) [T] **1** make a blot on sth **2** dry wet ink with blotting paper [PV] **blot sth out** cover or hide sth: *Thick cloud ~ted out the view.* ■ **blotter** *n* [C] large piece of blotting paper ■ **blotting paper** *n* [U] absorbent paper for drying wet ink

blotch /blɒtʃ/ *n* [C] irregular discoloured mark or spot

blouse /blaʊz/ *n* [C] piece of clothing like a shirt, worn by women

0﹢ **blow**[1] /bləʊ/ *v* (pt **blew** /bluː/ pp ~n /bləʊn/) **1** [I,T] send out air from the mouth **2** [I] (of the wind) be moving **3** [I,T] move sth or be moved by the wind, sb's breath, etc: *The wind blew my hat off.* ◊ *The door blew open.* **4** [I,T] produce sound from a brass instrument, whistle, etc **5** [T] clear your nose by forcing air out of it **6** [T] make or shape sth by blowing: *~ bubbles* **7** [I,T] (cause a fuse) melt because the electric current is too strong: *A fuse has ~n.* **8** [T] (*infml*) spend or waste a lot of money on sth [IDM] **blow your/sb's brains out** (*infml*) kill yourself/sb by shooting yourself/them through the head **blow your mind** (*infml*) produce a pleasant or shocking feeling **blow your own trumpet** (*infml*) praise your own abilities and achievements [PV] **blow (sth) out** (cause sth to) be extinguished by the wind, sb's breath, etc: *~ out a candle* **blow over** pass away without serious effect: *The argument will soon ~ over.* **blow up 1** explode **2** start suddenly and with force: *A storm is ~ing up.* **3** (*infml*) get angry with sb **blow sth up 1** destroy sth by an explosion **2** fill sth with air or gas **3** make a photograph bigger
■ **blowlamp** (*US* **blowtorch**) *n* [C] burner for directing a flame onto a surface, eg to remove old paint
■ **blowout** *n* [C] **1** bursting of a tyre

on a motor vehicle **2** sudden uncontrolled escape of oil or gas from a well **3** (*infml*) large meal
■ **blow-up** *n* [C] enlargement of a photograph

0﹢ **blow**[2] /bləʊ/ *n* [C] **1** hard hit with your hand or a weapon **2** sudden misfortune **3** action of blowing: *Give your nose a good ~.* [IDM] **come to blows** start fighting
■ **blow-by-blow** *adj* giving all the details of an event as they occur

blown *pp* of BLOW[1]

blubber /ˈblʌbə(r)/ *n* [U] fat of whales

bludgeon /ˈblʌdʒən/ *v* [T] (*written*) **1** hit sb several times with a heavy object **2** force sb to do sth, esp by arguing with them

0﹢ **blue** /bluː/ *adj* **1** having the colour of a clear sky on a sunny day **2** (*infml*) sad; depressed **3** (of films, jokes, etc) about sex: *a ~ film* ● **blue** *n* **1** [C,U] colour of a clear sky on a sunny day **2** (**the blues**) [U] slow sad music from the southern US (**the blues**) [pl] (*infml*) sadness [IDM] **out of the blue** unexpectedly
■ **bluebell** *n* [C] plant with blue bell-shaped flowers ■ **blue-blooded** *adj* from a royal or noble family ■ **bluebottle** *n* [C] large fly with a blue body ■ **blue-collar** *adj* of manual workers ■ **blueprint** *n* [C] detailed description of a plan
■ **blue-sky** *adj* involving new and interesting ideas: *~-sky thinking* ■ **Bluetooth**™ *n* [U] radio technology that makes it possible for electronic devices to be linked over short distances without wires: *B~tooth-enabled devices* ▸ **bluish** *adj* fairly blue

bluff[1] /blʌf/ *v* [I,T] try to make sb believe that you will do sth that you do not really intend to do ● **bluff** *n* [U,C] (act of) bluffing ● **bluff** *adj* (of a person) very direct and cheerful

blunder /ˈblʌndə(r)/ *n* [C] stupid or careless mistake ● **blunder** *v* [I] **1** make a mistake **2** move clumsily or uncertainly

blunt /blʌnt/ *adj* **1** without a sharp edge or point **2** (of a person) very direct; not trying to be polite
● **blunt** *v* [T] make sth less sharp ▸ **bluntness** *n* [U]

blur /blɜː(r)/ *n* [C] something that cannot be seen clearly ● **blur** *v* (-rr-) [I,T] become or make sth unclear

blurb /blɜːb/ *n* [C] short description of the contents of a book

blurt /blɜːt/ *v* [PV] **blurt sth out** say sth suddenly and thoughtlessly

blush /blʌʃ/ *v* [I] become red in the face because of embarrassment or shame ▸ **blush** *n* [C]

bluster /ˈblʌstə(r)/ *v* [I] **1** talk in a noisy, angry way but with little effect **2** (of the wind) blow violently

▶ **bluster** n [U] ▶ **blustery** adj (of the weather) with strong winds

boa constrictor /ˈbəʊə kənstrɪktə(r)/ (also **boa**) n [C] large South American snake that crushes animals to death

boar /bɔː(r)/ n [C] **1** male pig **2** wild pig

0-¬ **board¹** /bɔːd/ n [C] **1** long thin flat piece of wood: a floor- **2** [C] flat piece of wood, etc used for a special purpose: a notice- **3** [C] surface marked with patterns on which certain games are played: Chess is a ~ game. **4** [C] group of people controlling a business: the ~ of directors **5** [U] food in rented accommodation: pay for ~ and lodging [IDM] **across the board** affecting or including all members, groups, etc: an across-the-~ wage increase **be above board** be honest and open **go by the board** be rejected or ignored **on board** on or in a ship, an aircraft or a train **take sth on board** (infml) accept sth

0-¬ **board²** /bɔːd/ v **1** [T] get on a ship, plane, train, etc **2** (be boarding) [I] (of a plane, train, etc) be ready for passengers to get on **3** [I] live and take meals in sb's home, in return for payment **4** [I] live at a school during the term [PV] **board sth up** cover a window, door, etc with wooden boards ■ **boarder** n [C] pupil who lives at a boarding school during the term ■ **boarding card** n [C] card allowing a person to board a ship or an aircraft ■ **boarding house** n [C] private house providing meals and accommodation ■ **boarding school** n [C] school where pupils live during the term

boast /bəʊst/ v [I,T] ~ (about/of) talk about your own achievements, possessions, etc with too much pride: ~ about your new car **2** [T] possess sth that you are proud of: The hotel ~s a fine swimming pool. ● **boast** n [C] ■ **boastful** adj (disapprov) talking about yourself in a very proud way ▶ **boastfully** adv

0-¬ **boat** /bəʊt/ n [C] **1** vehicle (smaller than a ship) for travelling on water: a rowing ~ **2** any ship ■ **boathouse** n [C] building beside a river in which boats are stored ▶ **boating** n [U] activity of using a small boat for pleasure: go ~ing on the lake ■ **boat train** n [C] train that takes people to or from a passenger ship

bob /bɒb/ v (**-bb-**) **1** [I] move up and down, esp in water: a cork ~bing on the water **2** [T] cut sb's hair so that it is the same length all the way around ● **bob** n [C] woman's hairstyle in which the hair is cut the same length all the way around

bobbin /ˈbɒbɪn/ n [C] small device on

which you wind thread, used eg on a sewing machine

bobsleigh /ˈbɒbsleɪ/ (also **bobsled** /ˈbɒbsled/) n [C] sledge for racing on snow

bode /bəʊd/ v [IDM] **bode well/ill (for sb/sth)** (written) be a good/bad sign for sb/sth

bodice /ˈbɒdɪs/ n [C] upper part of a woman's dress

bodily /ˈbɒdɪli/ adj of the human body; physical ● **bodily** adv **1** by moving the whole of sb's body; by force **2** in one piece; completely

0-¬ **body** /ˈbɒdi/ n [C] (pl **-ies**) **1** whole physical structure of a person or an animal **2** main part of a human body without the head, arms or legs **3** dead body **4** main part of sth: the ~ of a car **5** group of people doing sth together: a parliamentary ~ **6** large amount of sth; mass: a ~ of water **7** (fml) object: heavenly bodies (= stars and planets) ■ **bodyboard** n [C] short light surfboard that you ride lying on your front ▶ **bodyboarding** n [U] ■ **bodyguard** n [C] person or group of people who protect sb important ■ **bodywork** n [U] main outside structure of a motor vehicle

bog /bɒg/ n [C] **1** area of soft wet ground **2** (GB, sl) toilet ● **bog** v (**-gg-**) [IDM] **be/get bogged down (in sth)** be/get stuck so that you cannot make progress: get ~ged down in small details ▶ **boggy** adj (of land) soft and wet

bogey (also **bogy**) /ˈbəʊgi/ n (pl **-ies**) thing that causes fear, often without reason

boggle /ˈbɒgl/ v [I] ~ (at) (infml) find sth difficult to imagine or accept: The mind ~s (at the idea).

BOGOF /ˈbɒgɒf/ n [C] Buy one, get one free; used in a shop to tell customers that they can buy two of a particular item and only pay for one

bogus /ˈbəʊgəs/ adj not real

bogy → BOGEY

0-¬ **boil** /bɔɪl/ v [I,T] **1** (of a liquid) (cause sth to) bubble and change into steam or vapour by being heated: The kettle (= the water in the kettle) is ~ing. ◊ She left the gas on and the pan ~ed dry (= the water boiled until there was none left). **2** [T] cook sth in boiling water: ~ an egg **3** [I] (written) be very angry [PV] **boil away** (of a liquid) boil until there is none left **boil down to sth** have to what you really want. **boil over 1** (of a liquid) rise and flow over the side of a pan **2** (of a situation, an emotion, etc) change into sth more dangerous or violent ● **boil** n

boiler

1 [sing] period of boiling; point at which liquid boils: *Bring the soup to the* ~, *then allow it to simmer.* **2** [C] red infected swelling under the skin ▶ **boiling** (*also* **boiling 'hot**) *adj* very hot ■ **'boiling point** *n* [C] temperature at which a liquid begins to boil

boiler /'bɔɪlə(r)/ *n* [C] device in which water is heated, eg for the central heating in a house ■ **'boiler suit** *n* [C] one-piece garment worn for doing dirty work

boisterous /'bɔɪstərəs/ *adj* (of a person) noisy and full of life and energy

bold /bəʊld/ *adj* **1** (of a person) brave and confident; not afraid to take risks **2** (of shape, colour, lines, etc) that can be clearly seen: ~ *designs* ▶ **boldly** *adv* ● **boldness** *n* [U]

bollard /'bɒlɑːd/ *n* [C] short thick post used to stop motor vehicles from going on to a road

bolster /'bəʊlstə(r)/ *n* [C] long pillow ● **bolster** *v* [T] ~ **(up)** improve sth or make it stronger

bolt /bəʊlt/ *n* [C] **1** metal bar that slides into a socket to lock a door, etc **2** metal screw used with a nut for holding things together **3** flash of lightning **4** act of running away quickly: *make a* ~ *for it* ● **bolt** *v* **1** [I,T] fasten sth with a bolt **2** [I] (esp of a horse) run away quickly **3** [T] ~ **(down)** swallow food quickly ● **bolt** *adv* [IDM] **sit/stand bolt upright** sit or stand with your back straight

0▬ **bomb** /bɒm/ *n* **1** [C] weapon designed to explode when it is thrown or dropped **2** (**the bomb**) [sing] nuclear weapons (atomic or hydrogen bombs) **3** (*a bomb*) (*GB*, *infml*) [sing] a lot of money: *This dress cost a* ~. ● **bomb** *v* [T] attack sb/ sth with bombs ● **bomber** *n* [C] **1** aircraft that drops bombs **2** person who puts a bomb somewhere illegally ■ **'bombshell** *n* [C] (*infml*) great shock

bombard /bɒm'bɑːd/ *v* [T] **1** attack sb/sth with bombs or shells from big guns **2** attack sb with a lot of questions, criticism, etc ▶ **bombardment** *n* [U,C]

bona fide /ˌbəʊnə 'faɪdi/ *adj*, *adv* genuine(ly)

bond /bɒnd/ *n* **1** [C] something that unites people or groups: ~*s of friendship* **2** [C] (*fml*) written agreement that has legal force **3** [C] certificate stating that money has been lent to a government, etc and will be paid back with interest **4** (**bonds**) [pl] (*fml*) ropes or chains used for tying up a prisoner ● **bond** *v* **1** [T] join sth together **2** [I,T]

develop a relationship of trust and affection with sb

0▬ **bone** /bəʊn/ *n* [C,U] any of the hard parts that form the skeleton of an animal's body [IDM] **feel (it) in your bones (that...)** feel certain about sth have **a bone to pick with sb** have sth to complain about to sb **make no bones about (doing) sth** not hesitate to do sth ● **bone** *v* [T] take bones out of sth ■ **bone 'dry** *adj* completely dry ■ **bone 'idle** *adj* (*GB*) very lazy ■ **'bone marrow** *n* [U] soft substance that fills the hollow parts of bones: *a* ~ *marrow transplant*

bonfire /'bɒnfaɪə(r)/ *n* [C] large outdoor fire

bonnet /'bɒnɪt/ *n* [C] **1** cover over the engine of a motor vehicle **2** baby's or woman's hat tied under the chin

bonus /'bəʊnəs/ *n* [C] **1** payment in addition to what is usual **2** anything pleasant in addition to what is usual

bony /'bəʊni/ *adj* (**-ier, -iest**) **1** full of bones: *This fish is* ~. **2** very thin; having bones that are clearly seen

boo /buː/ *exclam*, *n* [C] (*pl* ~**s**) sound made to show disapproval ● **boo** *v* [I,T] shout 'boo' at sb/sth

booby prize /'buːbi praɪz/ *n* [C] prize given to sb who comes last in a competition

booby trap /'buːbi træp/ *n* [C] object that looks harmless but that will kill or injure sb when touched ● **booby-trap** *v* (**-pp-**) [T] place a booby trap in sth

0▬ **book**[1] /bʊk/ *n* **1** [C] number of printed sheets of paper fastened together in a cover **2** [C] set of things fastened together like a book: *a* ~ *of stamps* **3** (**books**) [pl] business accounts **4** [C] main division of a large written work, eg the Bible [IDM] **be in sb's good/bad books** (*infml*) used to say that sb is pleased/ annoyed with you ■ **'bookcase** *n* [C] piece of furniture with shelves for books ■ **'book club** *n* [C] organization that sells books cheaply to its members ■ **'bookkeeper** *n* [C] person whose job is to keep an accurate record of the accounts of a business ▶ **'bookkeeping** *n* [U] ■ **'bookmaker** (*also infml* **'bookie**) *n* [C] person whose job is to take bets on horse races ■ **'bookmark** *n* [C] **1** something put in a book to mark the reader's place **2** (*computing*) record of the address of a file, a web page, etc that enables you to find it quickly ▶ **'bookmark** *v*: [T] *Do you want to* ~ *this site?* ■ **'bookshop** *n* [C] shop that sells mainly books ■ **'bookstall** *n* [C] small shop that is

botany

open at the front and which sells books, newspapers, etc ■ **book token** n [C] card with a voucher, usu given as a gift, that can be exchanged for books ■ **bookworm** n [C] person who is very fond of reading

0-π **book**[2] /bʊk/ v [I,T] order tickets, etc in advance; reserve sth **2** [T] write down the name of sb when bringing a legal charge: be ~ed for speeding ▸ **bookable** adj that can be reserved ■ **booking** n [C,U] arrangement that is made in advance to buy a ticket to travel somewhere, etc: No advance ~ is necessary. ■ **'booking office** n [C] office where tickets are sold

bookie /'bʊki/ n [C] (infml) short for BOOKMAKER (BOOK[1])

booklet /'bʊklət/ n [C] small thin book with paper covers

boom /buːm/ n [C] **1 ~ (in)** sudden increase in trade and economic activity **2** long pole that the bottom of a boat's sail is attached to **3** long pole that carries a microphone ● **boom** v **1** [I] make a loud deep sound **2** [I,T] **~ (out)** say sth in a loud deep voice **3** [I] (of business or the economy) have a period of rapid growth: Sales are ~ing.

boomerang /'buːməræŋ/ n [C] curved wooden stick (used by Australian Aborigines) that returns to the thrower

boon /buːn/ n [C] something that is helpful and makes life easier for you

boost /buːst/ v [T] increase the strength or value of sth ● **boost** n [C] ▸ **booster** n [C] **1** something that gives extra strength or power to sth **2** additional injection of a drug: a polio/tetanus ~er

0-π **boot** /buːt/ n [C] **1** shoe that covers the foot and ankle, and sometimes the lower leg **2** space for luggage at the back of a car [IDM] **be given/get the boot** (infml) be told that you must leave your job **put the boot in** (infml) kick sb hard, esp when they are on the ground ● **boot** v **1** [T] kick sb/sth **2** [I,T] (computing) prepare a computer for use by loading its operating system [PV] **boot sb out (of sth)** (infml) force sb to leave a job or place

booth /buːð/ n [C] **1** small stall where goods are sold **2** small enclosed area: a telephone ~

booze /buːz/ n [U] (infml) alcoholic drink ● **booze** v [I] (infml) drink alcohol, esp in large quantities ▸ **boozer** n [C] (infml) **1** person who boozes **2** (GB) pub ■ **'booze-up** n [C] (GB, infml) party, event, etc at which a lot of alcohol is drunk

bop /bɒp/ n [C, U] (GB, infml) dance to

pop music ● **bop** v **(-pp-)** [I] (infml) dance to pop music

0-π **border** /'bɔːdə(r)/ n [C] **1** (land near the) dividing line between two countries **2** edge of sth **3** (in a garden) strip of soil along the edge of the grass for planting flowers ● **border** v [I,T] **~ (on)** be next to another country or area [PV] **border on sth** come very close to being sth: a state of excitement ~ing on madness ■ **'borderline** n [C] division between two qualities or conditions ▸ **borderline** adj not clearly belonging to a particular condition or group: a ~line candidate (= one that may or may not pass an exam)

0-π **bore**[1] /bɔː(r)/ v **1** [T] make sb feel tired and uninterested, esp by talking too much **2** [I,T] **~ into/ through** make a long deep hole in sth with a special tool ● **bore** n [C] **1** person or thing that bores or annoys sb **2** (diameter of the) hollow part inside a tube, eg a pipe or gun **3** deep hole made in the ground, esp to find water or oil ▸ **boredom** /'bɔːdəm/ n [U] state of being bored ▸ **boring** adj dull; uninteresting

bore[2] pt of BEAR[1]

0-π **born** /bɔːn/ v **(be born)** (used only in the passive, without by) come out of your mother's body at the beginning of your life: He was ~ in 1954. ● **born** adj having a particular natural ability: a ~ leader ▸ **-born** (in compounds) born in the order, way, place, etc mentioned: Dutch-~ ■ **born-a'gain** adj having renewed and very strong faith in sth, esp a religion: a ~-again Christian

borne pp of BEAR[1]

0-π **borough** /'bʌrə/ n [C] town or part of a city that has its own local government

0-π **borrow** /'bɒrəʊ/ v [I,T] have or use sth that belongs to sb else, with the promise that it will be returned ▸ **borrower** n [C]

bosom /'bʊzəm/ n [C] a woman's chest or breasts ● (the ~ of sth) [sing] loving care and protection of sth: in the ~ of your family ■ **bosom 'friend** n [C] very close friend

0-π **boss** /bɒs/ n [C] person who is in charge of others at work and tells them what to do ● **boss** v [T] **~ (about/around)** (infml) tell sb what to do in an aggressive or annoying way ▸ **bossy** adj (-ier, -iest) always telling people what to do

botany /'bɒtəni/ n [U] scientific study of plants ▸ **botanical** /bə'tænɪkl/ adj ▸ **botanist** n [C] scientist who studies botany

botch

botch /bɒtʃ/ v [T] spoil sth by doing it badly • **botch** n [C] piece of badly-done work

both /bəʊθ/ adj, pron the two; the one as well as the other: *B~ (the) books are expensive. ◇ His parents are ~ dead.* • **both** adv with equal truth in two cases: *She has houses in ~ London and Paris.*

bother /ˈbɒðə(r)/ v 1 [T] cause trouble or annoyance to sb: *Is something ~ing you?* 2 [I,T] take the time or trouble to do sth: *Don't ~ to stand up.* • **bother** n [U] trouble or difficulty: *I don't want to put you to any ~ (= cause you any trouble).*

bottle /ˈbɒtl/ n 1 [C] container with a narrow neck, for liquids 2 [C] amount contained in this 3 [C, usu sing] baby's feeding bottle; milk from this: *It's time for her ~.* 4 [U] (*GB, infml*) courage: *She didn't have the ~ to ask him.* • **bottle** v [T] put sth in bottles [PV] **bottle sth up** not allow your feelings to be shown ■ **'bottleneck** n [C] 1 narrow or restricted stretch of road that causes traffic to slow down 2 anything that slows down movement or progress

bottom /ˈbɒtəm/ n 1 [C, usu sing] ~ (of) lowest part of sth 2 [C] (*esp GB*) part of the body that you sit on 3 [sing] ground under a sea, lake, etc 4 [usu sing] part that is furthest from you, your house, etc: *at the ~ of the garden* 5 [sing] lowest position in a class, organization, etc [IDM] **be/lie at the bottom of sth** be the original cause of sth **get to the bottom of sth** discover the real cause of sth • **bottom** v [PV] **bottom out (of** prices, a bad situation, etc) stop getting worse ■ **bottomless** adj very deep; unlimited ■ **the bottom 'line** n 1 [sing] most important or deciding point 2 (*business*) amount of money that is profit or loss after everything has been calculated

bough /baʊ/ n [C] large branch of a tree

bought pt, pp of BUY

boulder /ˈbəʊldə(r)/ n [C] large rock

bounce /baʊns/ v 1 [I,T] (cause eg a ball to) move quickly back from a surface it has just hit 2 [I,T] (cause sb/sth to) move up and down in a lively way: *She ~d the child on her lap.* 3 [I] move in the direction that is mentioned in a lively way: *She ~d into the room.* 4 [I,T] (*infml*) (of a cheque) be returned by a bank because there is not enough money in an account 5 [I,T] (of an email) be returned to the sender because the system could not deliver it • **bounce** n [C] action of bouncing ■ **bouncer** n [C] person employed by a club, pub, etc to throw out

troublemakers ► **bouncing** adj strong and healthy: *a ~ baby boy*

bound¹ pt, pp of BIND

bound² /baʊnd/ adj 1 ~ **to** certain or likely to happen, or to do or be sth: *He is ~ to win.* 2 forced to do sth by law or duty 3 ~ **(for)** travelling to a place: *a ship ~ for Rotterdam* [IDM] **bound up in sth** very busy with sth **bound up with sth** closely connected with sth

bound³ /baʊnd/ v 1 [I] jump; run with jumping movements 2 [T] (usu passive) (*fml*) form the boundary of sth: *an airfield ~ed by woods* • **bound** n [C] high or long jump

boundary /ˈbaʊndri/ n [C] (pl -ies) line that marks a limit

boundless /ˈbaʊndləs/ adj without limits

bounds /baʊndz/ n [pl] limits [IDM] **out of bounds (to sb)** (of a place) not allowed to be entered by sb

bounty /ˈbaʊnti/ n (pl -ies) 1 [U,C] (*lit*) generous actions 2 [C] money given as a reward ► **bountiful** adj giving generously

bouquet /buˈkeɪ/ n 1 [C] bunch of flowers 2 [C,U] smell of wine

bourgeois /ˈbʊəʒwɑː, ˌbʊəʒˈwɑː/ n [C], adj 1 (person) belonging to the middle class 2 (*disapprov*) (person who is) concerned with material possessions and social status ► **bourgeoisie** /ˌbʊəʒwɑːˈziː/ n [sing, with sing or pl verb] (the bourgeoisie) middle classes

bout /baʊt/ n [C] short period of activity or an illness

boutique /buːˈtiːk/ n [C] small shop, esp one that sells fashionable clothes

bow¹ /baʊ/ v [I,T] bend your head or the upper part of your body forward as a sign of respect or as a greeting [PV] **bow out (of sth)** stop taking part in sth **bow to sth** agree unwillingly to do sth because other people want you to • **bow** n [C] 1 act of bending your head or body forward as a sign of respect or as a greeting 2 (*also* bows [pl]) front part of a boat or ship

bow² /bəʊ/ n [C] 1 weapon used for shooting arrows, consisting of a long piece of wood curved by a tight string 2 long thin piece of wood with thin string stretched along it, used for playing the violin, etc 3 knot with two loops, often in ribbon, for decoration: *Her hair was tied back in a neat ~.* ■ **bow-legged** /ˌbəʊ ˈleɡd/ adj having legs that curve outward at the knees ■ **bow 'tie** n [C] man's tie formed as a bow (3)

bowel /ˈbaʊəl/ n [C, usu pl] 1 intestine 2 deepest part: *in the ~s of the earth*

bowl¹ /bəʊl/ n 1 [C] deep round container for food or liquid 2 [C] amount contained in this **3** [C] part of some objects that is shaped like a bowl **4** [C] heavy ball used in the game of bowls or tenpin bowling **5** (bowls) [U] game played on an area of very smooth grass, in which players try to roll bowls as near as possible to a small ball

bowl² /bəʊl/ v [I,T] roll a ball in the game of bowls or bowling **2** [I,T] throw a ball to the batsman in cricket **3** [T] ~ (**out**) get a batsman out of a game of cricket by hitting the wicket behind them with the ball [PV] **bowl sb over 1** run into sb and knock them down **2** surprise or impress sb a lot

bowler /ˈbəʊlə(r)/ n [C] (in cricket) person who bowls **2** (also **bowler hat**) man's hard round hat

bowling /ˈbəʊlɪŋ/ n [U] game in which heavy balls (bowls) are rolled along a track towards a group of bottle-shaped objects (pins) to knock them down

0-- **box** /bɒks/ n **1** [C] container made of wood, cardboard, etc, usu with a lid, used for holding solid things **2** [C] box and its contents: a ~ of chocolates **3** [C] separate enclosed area or compartment: a ~ in a theatre **4** [C] small hut used for a particular purpose: a telephone ~ **5** [C] small square on a form, to be filled in **6** (the box) [sing] (infml) television ● **box** v **1** [T] put sth into a box **2** [I,T] fight sb with the fists, wearing tough gloves, as a sport [PV] **box sb/sth in** prevent sb/sth from being able to move to surrounding them with people, vehicles, etc ▶ **boxer** n [C] **1** person who boxes (2) **2** breed of bulldog ● **boxing** n [U] sport in which two people fight each other with their fists ■ **box number** n [C] number used as an address in a newspaper advertisement, to which replies may be sent ■ **box office** n [C] office at a theatre, etc where tickets are sold

Boxing Day /ˈbɒksɪŋ deɪ/ n [U,C] (GB) the first weekday after Christmas Day

0-- **boy** /bɔɪ/ n [C] male child; young man ▶ **boyfriend** n [C] man or boy with whom sb has a romantic and/ or sexual relationship ▶ **boyhood** n [U] the time of being a boy ▶ **boyish** adj looking or behaving like a boy

boycott /ˈbɔɪkɒt/ v [T] refuse to be involved with or take part in sth as a way of protesting ● **boycott** n [C] act of boycotting sth

bra /brɑː/ n [C] (also fml **brassière**) piece of women's underwear worn to support the breasts

brace /breɪs/ v **1** ~ **sb/yourself** (for) prepare sb/yourself for sth difficult or unpleasant **2** [T] tighten the muscles in your body or part of your body before doing sth that is

physically difficult **3** [T] (tech) make sth stronger or more solid ● **brace** n **1** [C] wire device worn esp by children to straighten the teeth **2** [C] device that straightens or supports sth **3** (braces) [pl] (GB) straps that pass over the shoulders to hold trousers up ▶ **bracing** adj giving energy: the bracing sea air

bracelet /ˈbreɪslət/ n [C] piece of jewellery worn around the wrist

bracken /ˈbrækən/ n [U] wild plant with large leaves that grows on hills and in woods

bracket /ˈbrækɪt/ n [C] **1** (usu pl) either of a pair of marks, (), placed around extra information in a piece of writing **2** wood or metal support for a shelf **3** group within particular limits: the 20-30 age ~ ● **bracket** v [T] **1** put sth in brackets **2** group sb/sth together

brackish /ˈbrækɪʃ/ adj (of water) slightly salty

brag /bræg/ v (-gg-) [I] talk with too much pride about sth

braid /breɪd/ n **1** [U] thin coloured rope that is used to decorate furniture and military uniforms **2** [C] (esp US) = PLAIT ● **braid** v [T] (US) plait

Braille /breɪl/ n [U] system of writing for blind people, using raised dots

0-- **brain** /breɪn/ n **1** [C] organ in the body that controls thought, feeling, etc **2** [U,C, usu pl] mind; intelligence: have a good ~ **3** [C, usu pl] (infml) clever person [IDM] **have sth on the brain** (infml) think about sth constantly ● **brain** v [T] kill sb with a heavy blow on the head ■ **brainchild** n [sing] person's original idea or invention ■ **brain drain** n [sing] (infml) movement of skilled clever people to other countries where they can earn more money ▶ **brainless** adj stupid ■ **brainstorm** n [C] sudden mental disturbance ■ **brainstorming** n [U] way of making a group of people all think about sth at the same time, esp in order to solve a problem or to create good ideas ■ **brainwash** v [T] force sb to accept new beliefs by use of extreme mental pressure ■ **brainwave** n [C] sudden clever idea ▶ **brainy** adj (-ier, -iest) (infml) clever

braise /breɪz/ v [T] cook meat or vegetables slowly in a covered container

brake /breɪk/ n [C] device for reducing the speed of or stopping a vehicle ● **brake** v [I,T] slow down or stop a vehicle using a brake

bramble /ˈbræmbl/ n [C] prickly wild bush on which blackberries grow

bran /bræn/ n [U] outer covering of grain which is left when the grain is made into flour

o─ **branch** /brɑːntʃ/ n [C] **1** part of a tree growing out from a trunk **2** local office or shop belonging to a large company or organization: *a ~ office* **3** smaller or less important part of a river, road, railway, etc ● **branch** v [I] divide into two or more parts [PV] **branch off** turn from one road into a smaller one **branch out (into sth)** start to do an activity that you have not done before, esp in your work or business

o─ **brand** /brænd/ n [C] **1** type of product made by a particular company: *the cheapest ~ of soap ◇ Sportswear manufacturers owe their success to ~ image.* **2** particular kind: *a strange ~ of humour* **3** mark burnt onto the skin of an animal to show ownership ● **brand** v [T] **1** mark an animal with hot metal to show who owns it **2** give a bad name to sb: *He was ~ed (as) a thief.* ● **branding** n [U] activity of giving a particular name and image to goods and services to attract buyers ■ **brand name** (also 'trade name) [C] name given to a product by the company that produces it ■ **brand new** adj completely new

brandish /ˈbrændɪʃ/ v [T] wave sth, esp a weapon, threateningly in the air

brandy /ˈbrændi/ n [U,C] (pl -**ies**) strong alcoholic drink made from wine

brash /bræʃ/ adj confident in a rude or aggressive way

brass /brɑːs/ n **1** [U] bright yellow metal; objects made of brass **2** (the brass) [U, with sing or pl verb] (people who play) musical instruments of metal that form a band or a section of an orchestra ■ **brass band** n [C] group of musicians who play brass instruments

brassière /ˈbræziə(r)/ n [C] (fml) = BRA

brat /bræt/ n [C] (disapprov) badly-behaved child

bravado /brəˈvɑːdəʊ/ n [U] unnecessary or false show of courage

o─ **brave** /breɪv/ adj (~r, ~st) **1** (of a person) willing to do things which are dangerous or painful; not afraid **2** (of an action) requiring or showing courage ● **brave** v [T] have to deal with sth difficult or unpleasant in order to achieve sth ▶ **bravely** adv **bravery** /ˈbreɪvəri/ n [U]: *an award for outstanding ~*

bravo /ˌbrɑːˈvəʊ/ exclam, n [C] (pl -**s**) shout meaning 'Well done!'

brawl /brɔːl/ n [C] noisy argument, usu in a public place ▶ **brawl** v [I]

brawny /ˈbrɔːni/ adj (infml) strong and muscular

bray /breɪ/ v [I] **1** (of a donkey) make a loud harsh sound **2** (of a person) talk or laugh in a loud unpleasant voice ▶ **bray** n [C]

brazen /ˈbreɪzn/ adj open and without shame, usu about sth that people find shocking

brazier /ˈbreɪziə(r)/ n [C] metal container for holding a charcoal or coal fire

breach /briːtʃ/ n **1** [C,U] breaking or neglect of a law, an agreement, etc: *a ~ of contract ◇ a ~ of the peace* (= the crime of fighting in a public place) **2** [C] break in a friendly relationship **3** [C] (fml) opening, eg in a wall ● **breach** v [T] **1** not keep to an agreement or not keep a promise **2** (fml) make a hole in a wall, fence, etc, so that sb/sth can go through it ■ **breach of the 'peace** n [C, usu sing] (law) fighting in a public place

o─ **bread** /bred/ n [U] food made of flour, water and usu yeast, baked in an oven: *a loaf of brown ~* ■ **breadcrumbs** n [pl] tiny pieces of bread ■ **breadline** n [IDM] **on the breadline** very poor ■ **breadwinner** n [C] person who supports their family with the money they earn

breadth /bredθ/ n [U,C] **1** distance from side to side; width **2** wide range of (knowledge, interests, etc)

o─ **break¹** /breɪk/ v (pt **broke** /brəʊk/ pp **broken** /ˈbrəʊkən/) **1** [I,T] (cause sth to) be damaged and separated into pieces: *Glass ~s easily. ◇ ~ a plate* **2** [I,T] (cause sth to) stop working as a result of being damaged: *My watch has broken.* **3** [T] do sth that is against the law; not keep a promise, etc **4** [I] ~ (**for**) stop doing sth for a while, esp when it is time to eat or have a drink: *Let's ~ for lunch.* **5** [T] interrupt sth: *~ your journey* (= stop somewhere on the way to your destination) *◇ the silence ◇ Her tree broke his fall* (= stopped him as he was falling). **6** [I,T] ~ **free** (of a person or an object) escape from a position in which they are trapped: *He broke free from his attacker.* **7** [I,T] (cause sb/sth to) be weakened or destroyed: *~ the power of the unions ◇ His wife's death broke him.* **8** [I] (of the weather) change suddenly after a settled period **9** [I] begin: *Day was ~ing.* **10** [I,T] become or make sth known: *~ the news* **11** [I] (of a boy's voice) become deeper **12** [T] do better than a previous record **13** [T] solve sth secret: *~ a code* [IDM] **break the back of sth** finish the largest or most difficult part of sth **break even** make neither a loss nor a profit **break**

fresh/new ground introduce or discover a new method, activity, etc **break the ice** make people feel friendly towards one another, eg at the beginning of a party **break wind** let out air from the bowels **make or break sb/sth** cause sth to either succeed or fail [PV] **break away (from sb/sth)** go away from sb/sth; leave sth eg a political party **break down 1** (of machinery) stop working **2** fail; collapse: *Talks between the two sides have broken down.* **3** lose control of your feelings **break sth down 1** destroy sth: *~ down resistance* **2** analyse sth; classify: *~ down costs* **break in 1** enter a building by force **2 ~ in (on)** interrupt or disturb sth **break sb/sth in 1** train sb/sth in sth new that they must do **2** wear sth, esp new shoes, until they become comfortable **break into sth 1** enter a building or open a car, etc by force **2** suddenly begin sth: *~ into laughter/a run* start to use sth, eg money, that has been kept for an emergency **break off** stop speaking **break (sth) off** (cause to) separate by force **break sth off** end sth suddenly: *They've broken off their engagement.* **break out 1** (of sth bad) start suddenly: *Fire broke out.* **2 ~ out (of)** escape from a prison **3 ~ out (in)** suddenly become covered in sth: *~ out in spots* **break through (sth) 1** force a way through sth **2** (of the sun) appear from behind clouds **break up 1** (of a group of people) go away in different directions **2** (GB) (of a school or its pupils) begin the holidays **3 ~ up (with sb)** end a relationship with sb **break (sth) up 1** (cause sth to) separate into smaller pieces **2** (cause sth to) come to an end: *Their marriage is ~ing up.* ▶ **breakable** *adj* easily broken ■ **breakaway** *adj* (of a political group, or an organization) having separated from a larger group ■ **break-in** *n* [C] entry into a building by force, esp to steal sth ■ **breakout** *n* [C] escape from a prison ■ **breakthrough** *n* [C] important development or discovery ■ **break-up** *n* [C] end, esp of a relationship

break² /breɪk/ *n* [C] **1** rest; pause: *a lunch ~* **2** short holiday: *a weekend ~* **3** interruption or end of sth that has existed for a long time: *a ~ with tradition* **4** space or gap between two or more things **5** (*infml*) piece of luck that leads to success: *a lucky ~* **6** place where sth, esp a bone, is broken [IDM] **break of day/dawn** (*lit*) moment in the early hours of the morning when it begins to get light **make a break for sth/for it** run towards sth in order to try and escape

breakage /'breɪkɪdʒ/ *n* [C] object

that has been broken **2** [U,C] act of breaking sth

breakdown /'breɪkdaʊn/ *n* [C] **1** failure in machinery **2** failure of a relationship, discussion or system **3** analysis of statistics: *a ~ of expenses* **4** weakness or collapse of sb's mental health: *a nervous ~*

breaker /'breɪkə(r)/ *n* [C] large wave that breaks into foam

0️⃣ **breakfast** /'brekfəst/ *n* [C,U] first meal of the day ● **breakfast** *v* [I] eat breakfast

breakneck /'breɪknek/ *adj* dangerously fast: *at ~ speed*

breakwater /'breɪkwɔːtə(r)/ *n* [C] wall built out into the sea to protect a harbour

0️⃣ **breast** /brest/ *n* [C] **1** either of the two parts of a woman's body that produce milk **2** upper front part of the body ■ **breastbone** *n* [C] thin flat vertical bone in the chest between the ribs ■ **breaststroke** *n* [U, sing] kind of swimming style that you do on your front

0️⃣ **breath** /breθ/ *n* **1** [U] air taken into and sent out of the lungs **2** [C] amount of air that enters the lungs at one time: *Take a deep ~.* **3** [sing] slight movement of air [IDM] **get your breath (back)** breathe normally again after running, etc **out of breath** having difficulty breathing after exercise **take sb's breath away** be very surprising or beautiful **under your breath** quietly so that people cannot hear ▶ **breathless** *adj* **1** having difficulty breathing **2 ~ (with)** experiencing a strong emotional reaction: *~less with terror* ▶ **breathlessly** *adv* ■ **breathtaking** *adj* amazing

breathalyser /'breθəlaɪzə(r)/ (*US* **Breathalyzer**™) *n* [C] device used by the police for measuring the amount of alcohol in a driver's breath

0️⃣ **breathe** /briːð/ *v* [I,T] take air into the lungs and send it out again **2** [T] say sth very quietly; whisper sth **3** [T] (*fml*) be full of a particular feeling or quality [IDM] **breathe again** feel calm or relaxed after a difficult or anxious time **breathe down sb's neck** (*infml*) watch sb too closely ▶ **breather** *n* [C] (*infml*) short rest

0️⃣ **breed** /briːd/ *v* (pt, pp **bred** /bred/) **1** [T] keep animals for the purpose of producing young: *~ horses/cattle* **2** [I] (of animals) produce young **3** [T] bring sb up; educate sb in a particular way: *a well-bred child* **4** [T] be the cause of sth: *Dirt ~s disease.* ● **breed** *n* [C] **1** particular type of animal: *a ~ of cattle/dog* **2** particular kind of person: *a new ~ of businessman* ▶ **breeder** *n* [C] person who breeds

breeze

animals ▶ **breeding** n [U] **1** keeping or producing of animals or plants **2** good manners: *a man of good ~ing*

breeze /briːz/ n [C,U] light wind ● **breeze** v [I] move in a cheerful and confident way in a particular direction: *She just ~d into the office and sat down.* ▶ **breezily** adv ▶ **breezy** adj **1** windy **2** having a cheerful and relaxed manner

brevity /ˈbrevəti/ n [U] (fml) fact of lasting a short time: *the ~ of life*

brew /bruː/ v [I,T] prepare tea, coffee or beer **2** [I] (of sth unpleasant) develop ● **brew** n [C] result of brewing ▶ **brewer** n [C] ▶ **brewery** /ˈbruːəri/ n [C] (pl -ies) place where beer is brewed

bribe /braɪb/ n [C] something (esp money) given to sb to persuade them to help, usu by doing sth dishonest ● **bribe** v [T] give a bribe to sb ▶ **bribery** /ˈbraɪbəri/ n [U] the giving or taking of bribes

bric-a-brac /ˈbrɪkəbræk/ n [U] small ornaments of little value

O‑ **brick** /brɪk/ n [C,U] (block of) baked clay used for building ● **brick** v [PV] **brick sth in/up** fill or block an opening with bricks ▶ **bricklayer** n [C] person whose job is to build walls, etc with bricks ■ **brickwork** n [U] bricks in a wall, building, etc

bridal /ˈbraɪdl/ adj of a bride or wedding

bride /braɪd/ n [C] woman on her wedding day; newly married woman ■ **bridegroom** n [C] man on his wedding day; newly married man ■ **bridesmaid** n [C] woman or girl helping the bride on her wedding day

O‑ **bridge** /brɪdʒ/ n **1** [C] structure providing a way across a river, etc **2** [C] thing which links two or more different things **3** [C] part of a ship where the captain and officers stand to control and steer it **4** [sing] upper part of the nose **5** [C] part on a violin, etc over which the strings are stretched **6** [U] card game for four players ● **bridge** v [T] build a bridge across sth ■ **bridgehead** n [C] strong position captured in enemy territory

bridle /ˈbraɪdl/ n [C] part of a horse's harness that goes on its head ● **bridle** v **1** [T] put a bridle on a horse **2** [I] show anger or annoyance by moving your head up and back

O‑ **brief**[1] /briːf/ adj **1** lasting only a short time **2** using few words **3** (of clothes) short [IDM] **in brief** in a few words ▶ **briefly** adv

brief[2] /briːf/ n [C] **1** instructions and information for a particular task **2** (GB, law) legal case given to a lawyer to argue in court; piece of

work for a barrister **3** (GB, infml) solicitor or defence lawyer: *I want to see my ~.* ● **brief** v [T] **1** give sb information about sth so that they are prepared to deal with it **2** (GB, law) give a barrister the main facts of a legal case so that it can be argued in a court of law ■ **briefcase** n [C] flat leather case for papers, etc

briefs /briːfs/ n [pl] pants or knickers

brigade /brɪˈɡeɪd/ n [C] **1** army unit usu of three battalions **2** organization for a particular purpose: *the fire ~* ▶ **brigadier** /ˌbrɪɡəˈdɪə(r)/ n [C] officer commanding a brigade (1)

O‑ **bright** /braɪt/ adj **1** giving out or reflecting a lot of light; shining **2** (of colour) strong **3** cheerful; happy **4** clever **5** likely to be successful: *The future looks ~.* ▶ **brighten** v [I,T] become or make sth brighter ▶ **brightly** adv ▶ **brightness** n [U]

O‑ **brilliant** /ˈbrɪliənt/ adj **1** very clever or impressive **2** (of light or colours) very bright **3** (spoken) very good ▶ **brilliance** /ˈbrɪliəns/ n [U] ▶ **brilliantly** adv

brim /brɪm/ n [C] **1** edge of a cup, etc **2** bottom edge of a hat ● **brim** v (-mm-) [I] ~ **(with)** be full of sth [PV] **brim over (with sth)** overflow

brine /braɪn/ n [U] salt water, esp for preserving food

O‑ **bring** /brɪŋ/ v (pt, pp **brought** /brɔːt/) [T] **1** come to a place with sb/sth: *Please ~ a dictionary to class.* ◊ *He brought his mother with him.* **2** cause sth: *The story brought tears to her eyes.* **3** cause sb/sth to be in a particular condition or place: *~ the water to the boil* (= boil it) ◊ *~ the meeting to a close* **4** ~ **(against)** (law) officially accuse sb of a crime: *~ a charge against sb* **5** force yourself to do sth: *I can't ~ myself to tell him.* [IDM] **bring sth to a head** → HEAD[1] **bring sth to mind** → MIND[1] **bring sth into the open** → OPEN[1] [PV] **bring sth about** cause sth to happen **bring sb/ sth back 1** return sth: *~ back a book* ◊ *I brought the children back* (= home). **2** cause sth to be remembered **3** introduce sth again: *~ back the death penalty* **bring sb/sth down 1** cause sb/sth to fall: *~ down the government* ◊ *I brought him down with a rugby tackle.* **2** lower or reduce sth: *~ prices down* **3** cause an aircraft to fall out of the sky or to land **bring sth forward 1** move sth to an earlier date or time: *~ the meeting forward* **2** propose sth for discussion **bring sth/sb in 1** introduce a new law: *~ in new legislation* **2** attract sb/sth to a place or business **3** use sb's services as an adviser, etc: *~ in a scientist to check pollution* **bring sth off** succeed in doing sth difficult **bring sth on** make sth develop, usu sth unpleasant: *The* rain brought on his cold. **bring sb out** cause sb to go on strike: *Union leaders brought out the workers.* **bring sb out of himself, herself, etc** help sb to feel more confident **bring sth out 1** make sth appear: *A crisis ~s out the best in him.* **2** make sth easy to see or understand **3** produce or publish sth: *~ out a new type of computer* **bring sb round 1** cause sb to regain consciousness **2** persuade sb to agree to sth **bring sb up 1** care for a child, teaching him or her how to behave, etc: *We were brought up to be polite.* **bring sth up 1** call attention to sth; mention sth: *~ up the subject of salaries* **2** vomit sth **3** make sth appear on a computer screen

brink /brɪŋk/ n [sing] edge of a steep or dangerous place: (fig) on the ~ of war

brisk /brɪsk/ adj moving quickly; lively: *walk at a ~ pace* ▸ **briskly** adv

bristle /ˈbrɪsl/ n [C, U] short stiff hair, esp on a brush ● **bristle** v [I] **1** suddenly become annoyed or offended at what sb says or does **2** (of animal's fur) stand up stiffly [PV] **bristle with sth** have a large number of sth

brittle /ˈbrɪtl/ adj hard but easily broken

broach /brəʊtʃ/ v [T] begin a discussion of a subject

0— **broad** /brɔːd/ adj **1** measuring a large amount from one side to the other; wide: *~ shoulders* including a great variety of people or things: *a ~ range of subjects* **3** not detailed; general: *a ~ outline of a speech* **4** (of speech) with a strong accent **5** clear; obvious: *a ~ hint* [IDM] **in broad daylight** in the full light of day ■ **broadband** n [U] communications network that allows several channels of information to pass through a single cable at the same time, eg cable TV and Internet access ■ **broadband** adj (in telecommunications) of or using signals over a wide range of frequencies ▸ **broaden** v [I, T] become or make sth wider ▸ **broadly** adv generally: *~ly speaking* ■ **broad-minded** adj liberal and tolerant

0— **broadcast** /ˈbrɔːdkɑːst/ n [C] radio or television programme ● **broadcast** v (pt, pp **broadcast**) [I, T] send out radio or television programmes ▸ **broadcaster** n [C] ▸ **broadcasting** n [U]

broadside /ˈbrɔːdsaɪd/ n [C] fierce attack in words ● **broadside** adv sideways

broccoli /ˈbrɒkəli/ n [U] kind of cauliflower with dark green or purple flower heads

brochure /ˈbrəʊʃə(r)/ n [C] booklet

containing information or advertisements

broil /brɔɪl/ v [T] (US) grill meat or fish

broke¹ pt of BREAK¹

broke² /brəʊk/ adj (infml) having no money: *flat/stony ~* (= completely broke)

broken¹ pp of BREAK¹

0— **broken²** /ˈbrəʊkən/ adj **1** that has been damaged or injured; no longer whole or working correctly: *a ~ leg/arm* ◇ *a ~ marriage* **2** not continuous; interrupted: *~ sleep* **3** (of a person) weakened by illness or difficulties **4** (of a foreign language) spoken slowly and with a lot of mistakes ■ **broken home** n [C] family in which the parents have divorced or separated

broker /ˈbrəʊkə(r)/ n [C] person who buys and sells eg business shares for others

brolly /ˈbrɒli/ n [C] (pl -ies) (GB, infml) = UMBRELLA

bronchial /ˈbrɒŋkiəl/ adj of the tubes of the windpipe

bronchitis /brɒŋˈkaɪtɪs/ n [U] illness that affects the bronchial tubes

bronze /brɒnz/ n **1** [U] metal that is a mixture of copper and tin **2** [U] dark reddish-brown colour **3** [C] something made of bronze; bronze medal ▸ **bronze** v [T] make bronze in colour ■ **bronze medal** n [C] medal awarded as third prize in a competition, esp a sports contest

brooch /brəʊtʃ/ n [C] piece of jewellery with a pin on the back of it, that can be fastened to your clothes

brood /bruːd/ n **1** young birds produced at one hatching or birth **2** (hum) large family of children ● **brood** v [I] **1** think a lot about sth that makes you annoyed, anxious or upset: *~ing over her problems* **2** sit on eggs to hatch them ▸ **broody** adj **1** (of a woman) wanting very much to have babies **2** (of a hen) wanting to brood **3** sad and very quiet

brook /brʊk/ n [C] small stream

broom /bruːm/ n [C] brush with a long handle for sweeping floors

broth /brɒθ/ n [U] kind of soup

brothel /ˈbrɒθl/ n [C] house of prostitutes

0— **brother** /ˈbrʌðə(r)/ n [C] **1** son of the same parents as yourself or another person mentioned **2** man who is a member of the same society, profession, etc **3** (also Brother) (pl **brethren** /ˈbreðrən/ or **brothers**) male member of a religious group, esp a monk ▸ **brotherhood** n **1** [U] (feeling of) friendship and understanding between people **2** [C] organization formed for a particular purpose, esp a religious or political one **3** [U] relationship between brothers ■ 'brother-in-law n [C] (pl **-s-in-law**) brother of your husband or wife; your sister's husband ▶ **brotherly** adj

brought pt, pp of BRING

brow /braʊ/ n [C] **1** forehead **2** = EYEBROW **3** top part of a hill

browbeat /'braʊbiːt/ v (pt browbeat pp **-en** /-biːtn/) [T] frighten sb into doing sth

0-π **brown** /braʊn/ adj, n [C,U] (having) the colour of earth or coffee with milk ● **brown** v [I,U] become or make sth brown

browse /braʊz/ v [I] **1** look at a lot of things in a shop rather than looking for one particular thing **2** look through a book, newspaper, etc without reading everything **3** (computing) look for information on a computer **4** (of cows, goats, etc) feed on grass, leaves, etc ● **browse** n [sing]: The gift shop is well worth a ~. ● **browser** n [C] **1** (computing) program that lets you look at or read documents on the Internet: a web ~ **2** person who browses

bruise /bruːz/ n [C] blue, brown or purple mark caused by a blow to the body ● **bruise** v [I,I] develop a bruise, or make a bruise appear on the skin of sb/sth

brunette /bruːˈnet/ n [C] white-skinned woman with dark brown hair

brunt /brʌnt/ n [IDM] bear the brunt of sth ▶ BEAR

bruschetta /bruˈsketə/ n [U] Italian dish consisting of pieces of warm bread covered with oil and chopped tomatoes

0-π **brush¹** /brʌʃ/ n [C] **1** tool with bristles for cleaning, painting, etc: a tooth~ **2** [sing] act of brushing **3** [C] short unfriendly meeting with sb; unpleasant experience of sth: a nasty ~ with his boss **4** [C] land covered by small trees and bushes

0-π **brush²** /brʌʃ/ v [I] **1** clean sth with a brush **2** touch sb/sth lightly when passing [PV] brush sth aside pay little or no attention to sth brush sth up/ brush up on sth study or practise sth forgotten: ~ up (on) your French

brusque /bruːsk/ adj using few words and sounding rude ▶ **brusquely** adv ▶ **brusqueness** n [U]

Brussels sprout /ˌbrʌslz ˈspraʊt/ n [C] kind of vegetable that looks like a very small cabbage

brutal /ˈbruːtl/ adj violent and cruel ▶ **brutality** /bruːˈtæləti/ n [U,C] (pl **-ies**) ▶ **brutally** adv

brute /bruːt/ n [C] **1** cruel insensitive man **2** large strong animal ● **brute** adj involving physical strength only and not thought or intelligence: ~ force ▶ **brutish** adj of or like a brute

BSE /ˌbiː es ˈiː/ (also infml mad 'cow disease) n [U] bovine spongiform encephalopathy; brain disease of cows that causes death

0-π **bubble** /ˈbʌbl/ n [C] **1** (in the air) floating ball of liquid containing air or gas **2** (in a liquid) ball of air or gas ● **bubble** v [I] **1** send up, rise in or make the sound of bubbles **2** ~ with be full of a particular feeling ■ 'bubblegum n [U] chewing gum that can be blown into bubbles ● **bubbly** adj (**-ier, -iest**) **1** full of bubbles **2** happy and lively

buck /bʌk/ n **1** [C] (esp US, infml) US or Australian dollar **2** [C] male deer, hare or rabbit **3** (the buck) [sing] (infml) responsibility: pass the ~ (= make sb else responsible) ● **buck** v [I] (of a horse) jump into the air with all four feet together [PV] buck up hurry buck (sb) up (cause sb to) become more cheerful

bucket /ˈbʌkɪt/ n [C] **1** round open container with a handle, for carrying liquids **2** (also 'bucketful) amount a bucket contains ● **bucket down** v [PV] (GB, infml) rain heavily

buckle /ˈbʌkl/ n [C] metal or plastic fastener for a belt, etc ● **buckle** v [I,T] **1** fasten with a buckle **2** (cause sth to) become bent, esp because of force or heat [PV] buckle down (to sth) (infml) start to do sth seriously

bud /bʌd/ n [C] flower or leaf before it opens ● **bud** v (**-dd-**) [I] produce buds ▶ **budding** adj beginning to develop or become successful

Buddhism /ˈbʊdɪzəm/ n [U] Asian religion based on the teaching of Gautama Siddhartha (or Buddha) ▶ **Buddhist** /ˈbʊdɪst/ n [C], adj

buddy /ˈbʌdi/ n [C] (pl **-ies**) (infml) friend

budge /bʌdʒ/ v [I,T] (cause sb/sth to) move slightly: The stone won't ~.

budgerigar /ˈbʌdʒərɪɡɑː(r)/ n [C] (also infml **budgie**) small brightly-coloured bird, often kept as a pet

0-π **budget** /ˈbʌdʒɪt/ n [C,U] amount of money that is available to a person or an organization and a plan of how it will be spent over a period of time: The work was finished within ~ (= did not cost more money than was planned). ● **budget** v [I] ~ (for) plan the amount of money to be spent on sth ● **budget** adj cheap: ~ holidays

buff /bʌf/ n **1** [C] person who knows a lot about the subject that is mentioned: a computer ~ **2** [U] pale yellowish-brown colour ● **buff** v [T] polish sth with a soft cloth

buffalo /'bʌfələʊ/ n [C] (pl **buffalo** or **~es**) kind of large wild ox

buffer /'bʌfə(r)/ n [C] **1** device on a railway engine, etc to reduce the effect of a collision **2** (computing) area in a computer's memory where data can be stored for a short time ● **buffer** v [T] (computing) (of a computer) hold data for a short time before using it

buffet¹ /'bʊfeɪ/ n [C] **1** counter where food and drink may be bought and eaten, eg at a railway station **2** meal at which guests serve themselves from a number of dishes

buffet² /'bʌfɪt/ v [T] push or knock sb/sth roughly from side to side: ~ed by the wind

bug /bʌg/ n [C] **1** any small insect **2** (infml) infectious illness that is usu fairly mild: a stomach ~ **3** (infml) great interest in sth mentioned: He's got the travel ~ **4** (infml) small hidden microphone **5** (infml) fault in a machine, esp a computer ● **bug** v (-gg-) [T] **1** fit sb/sth with a bug (4) **2** (infml) annoy sb constantly

bugbear /'bʌgbeə(r)/ n [C] thing that is disliked or causes annoyance

bugger /'bʌgə(r)/ n [C] (GB, ⚠, sl) **1** annoying person or thing **2** person that you feel sorry for ● **bugger** exclam (GB, ⚠, infml) used for expressing anger or annoyance

bugle /'bjuːgl/ n [C] musical instrument like a small trumpet, used in the army for giving signals ▸ **bugler** n [C]

0‒ **build** /bɪld/ v (pt, pp **built** /bɪlt/) [T] **1** make sth by putting parts, etc together **2** create or develop sth: ~ a better future [PV] **build on sth** use sth as a basis for further progress **build sth on sth** base sth on sth **build (sth) up** (cause sth to) become greater; increase: Traffic is ~ing up. ◇ ~ up a business **build sb/sth up** speak with great praise about sb/sth ▸ **builder** n [C] ■ **build-up** n [C] **1** gradual increase **2** favourable description of sb/sth that is going to happen, which is intended to make people excited about it ■ **built-'in** adj included to form part of a structure: ~ wardrobes ■ **built-'up** adj (of an area of land) covered with buildings

build² /bɪld/ n [U, C] shape and size of the human body

0‒ **building** /'bɪldɪŋ/ n **1** [C] structure with a roof and walls **2** [U] (business of) constructing houses, etc ■ **'building society** n [C] (GB) organization that accepts money to be invested and lends money to people who want to buy houses

bulb /bʌlb/ n [C] **1** (also **light bulb**) glass part that fits into an electric lamp **2** thick rounded underground stem of certain plants ▸ **bulbous** adj round and fat

---

53   **bum**

bulge /bʌldʒ/ n [I] stick out from sth in a round shape ● **bulge** n [C] round lump that sticks out from sth

bulimia /bu'lɪmiə; -'liːmiə/ n (also **bulimia nervosa** /bu,lɪmiə nɜː'vəʊsə/) n [U] illness in which a person eats too much and then forces himself or herself to vomit ▸ **bulimic** /bu'lɪmɪk; -'liːmɪk/ adj

bulk /bʌlk/ n **1** (the bulk of sth) [sing] the main part of sth **2** [U] (large) size or quantity of sth: It's cheaper to buy in ~. **3** [sing] large shape or mass ▸ **bulky** adj (-ier, -iest) large; difficult to move

bull /bʊl/ n [C] **1** the male of any animal in the cow family **2** male of the elephant, whale and some other large animals [IDM] **a bull in a china shop** person who is clumsy where skill or care is needed **take the bull by the horns** face difficulty or danger directly and with courage ■ **bulldog** n [C] strong dog with a large head and a short thick neck ■ **bullseye** n [C] centre of the target used in archery and darts ■ **bullshit** n [U] (⚠, sl) nonsense

bulldoze /'bʊldəʊz/ v [T] **1** destroy buildings, trees, etc with a bulldozer **2** force sb to do sth ▸ **bulldozer** n [C] powerful tractor for moving large quantities of earth

0‒ **bullet** /'bʊlɪt/ n [C] round or pointed piece of metal shot from a gun ■ **bullet point** n [C] item in a list in a document that is printed with a mark, also called a bullet point, to show that it is important ■ **'bulletproof** adj that can stop bullets passing through it: a ~proof vest

bulletin /'bʊlətɪn/ n [C] short official news report

bullion /'bʊliən/ n [U] gold or silver in large amounts or in the form of bars

bullock /'bʊlək/ n [C] young bull that has been castrated

bully /'bʊli/ n (pl **-ies**) person who uses their strength to frighten or hurt weaker people: the school ~ ● **bully** v (pt, pp **-ied**) [T] frighten or hurt a weaker person; use your strength or power to make sb do sth

bulrush /'bʊlrʌʃ/ n [C] tall strong plant that grows in or near water

bulwark /'bʊlwək/ n [C] **1** person or thing that defends or protects sth **2** wall built as a defence

bum /bʌm/ n [C] (infml) **1** (GB) the part of the body that you sit on; buttocks **2** (esp US) homeless person who asks either for money or food **3** lazy person ● **bum** v [PV] **bum around** (infml) spend your time doing nothing in particular

bumblebee /'bʌmblbiː/ n [C] large hairy bee that makes a loud noise as it flies

bump /bʌmp/ v **1** [I] hit sth accidentally: I ~ed into the chair in the dark. **2** [T] hit sth against or on sth by accident: I ~ed my head on the door frame. **3** [I] move across a rough surface: The bus ~ed along the mountain road. [PV] **bump into sb** (infml) meet sb by chance **bump sb off** (infml) kill sb **bump sth up** (infml) increase sth ● **bump** n [C] **1** action or sound of sth hitting a hard surface **2** swelling on the body **3** uneven area on a road surface ▸ **bumpy** adj (-ier, -iest) not smooth; uneven

bumper /'bʌmpə(r)/ n [C] bar on the front and back of a motor vehicle to protect it from damage ● **bumper** adj unusually large: a ~ harvest

bun /bʌn/ n [C] **1** small round sweet cake (esp woman's) hair twisted round into a tight knot at the back of the head

0~ bunch /bʌntʃ/ n [C] **1** number of similar things fastened or growing together: a ~ of flowers/grapes **2** (infml) group of people ● **bunch** v [PV] **bunch (sb/sth) up/together** (cause sb/sth to) move closer and form into a group

bundle /'bʌndl/ n [C] number of things fastened or wrapped together: old clothes tied into a ~ **2** (sing) ~ **of** a mass of sth: He's a ~ of nerves (= he is very nervous). ● **bundle** v [T] **1** ~ **(up/together)** make or tie sth into a bundle **2** push or send sb somewhere quickly and roughly: They ~d him into a taxi. **3** ~ **(with)** supply extra equipment, esp software when selling a new computer, at no extra cost

bung /bʌŋ/ n v [T] (GB, infml) throw or put sth somewhere carelessly and quickly [PV] **bung sth up (with sth)** block sth: My nose is all ~ed up. ● **bung** n [C] stopper for closing the hole in a barrel or jar

bungalow /'bʌŋɡələʊ/ n [C] house built all on one level

bungee jumping /'bʌndʒi dʒʌmpɪŋ/ n [U] sport in which a person jumps from a high place, eg a bridge, with a long elastic rope (a bungee) tied to their feet

bungle /'bʌŋɡl/ v [I,T] do sth badly or clumsily; fail at sth

bunion /'bʌnjən/ n [C] painful swelling on the foot, usu on the big toe

bunk /bʌŋk/ n [C] **1** narrow bed fixed to a wall, eg on a ship or train **2** (also 'bunk bed) one of a pair of beds fixed one above the other, usu for children [IDM] **do a bunk** (GB, infml) run away

bunker /'bʌŋkə(r)/ n [C] **1** strongly built underground shelter for soldiers or guns **2** container for storing coal **3** small area filled with sand on a golf course

bunny /'bʌni/ n [C] (pl -ies) child's word for a rabbit

buoy /bɔɪ/ n [C] floating object attached to the sea bottom to show danger, rocks, etc ● **buoy** v [T] ~ **(up) 1** make sb feel cheerful or confident **2** keep sb/sth afloat **3** keep prices at a high level

buoyant /'bɔɪənt/ adj **1** (of prices, business activity, etc) tending to increase or stay at a high level, usu showing financial success: a ~ economy **2** cheerful and optimistic **3** able to float or keep things afloat ▸ **buoyancy** /-ənsi/ n [U] ▸ **buoyantly** adv

burden /'bɜːdn/ n [C] **1** responsibility or duty that causes worry or is hard to deal with: the ~ of taxation **2** (fml) heavy load ● **burden** v [T] **1** put a burden on sb **2** ~ **be ~ed with** be carrying sth heavy ▸ **burdensome** /'bɜːdnsəm/ adj (fml) causing worry

bureau /'bjʊərəʊ/ n [C] (pl -x or -s /-rəʊz/) **1** (GB) writing desk with drawers **2** (US) = CHEST OF DRAWERS **3** office or organization that provides information on a particular subject (esp US) government department

bureaucracy /bjʊə'rɒkrəsi/ n (pl -ies) **1** [U] (disapprov) unnecessary and complicated official rules **2** [U,C] (country with a) system of government in which there are a large number of state officials who are not elected ▸ **bureaucrat** /'bjʊərəkræt/ n [C] (usu disapprov) official who works in a government department ▸ **bureaucratic** /ˌbjʊərə'krætɪk/ adj

burger /'bɜːɡə(r)/ n [C] = HAMBURGER

burglar /'bɜːɡlə(r)/ n [C] person who breaks into a building to steal things ▸ **burglary** n [U,C] (pl -ies) crime of entering a building in order to steal things ▸ **burgle** /US burglarize/ /'bɜːɡləraɪz/ v [T] break into a building to steal things

burial /'beriəl/ n [C,U] act or ceremony of burying a dead body

burka (also **burkha**) /'bʊəkə; 'bɜːkə/ n [C] garment that covers the whole body, worn by some Muslim women

burly /'bɜːli/ adj (-ier, -iest) (of a man) having a strong heavy body

0~ burn /bɜːn/ v (pt, pp ~t /bɜːnt/ or ~ed /bɜːnd/) **1** [I] be on fire; produce flames and heat **2** [I,T] (cause sb/sth to) be destroyed, damaged, injured or killed by fire: ~ old papers ◇ The house ~ed to the ground. **3** [T] use sth for heating or lighting: ~ coal in a fire **4** [I,T] (cause food to) become spoilt because it gets too hot: Sorry, I've ~t *the toast.* **5** [I,T] (cause sb/sth to) be damaged or injured by the sun, heat, acid, etc: *My skin ~s easily* (= in the sun). **6** [I] (of part of the body) feel hot and painful **7** [I] ~ **with** (written) feel a strong emotion or desire **8** [T] put information onto a CD, etc. [PV] **burn (sth) down** (cause sth to) be completely destroyed by fire **burn (itself) out** (of a fire) stop burning because there is no more fuel **burn (yourself) out** exhaust yourself or ruin your health by working too hard **burn sth out** destroy sth completely by burning so that only the frame remains: *the ~t-out wreck of a car* ● **burn** *n* [C] injury or mark caused by fire, heat or acid ▸ **burner** *n* [C] part of a cooker, etc that produces a flame ▸ **burning** *adj* **1** intense: *a ~ing thirst/desire* **2** very important; urgent: *the ~ing question*

burnish /'bɜːnɪʃ/ *v* [T] (fml) polish metal by rubbing it

burp /bɜːp/ *v* [I] (infml) let out air from the stomach through the mouth, making a noise ▸ **burp** *n* [C]

burrow /'bʌrəʊ/ *n* [C] hole made in the ground by rabbits, etc ● **burrow** *v* [I,T] dig a hole

bursar /'bɜːsə(r)/ *n* [C] person who manages the money in a school or college ▸ **bursary** *n* [C] (pl **-ies**) money given to sb so that they can study, usu at a college or university

0─ **burst** /bɜːst/ *v* (pt, pp **burst**) **1** [I,T] (cause sth to) break open or apart, esp because of pressure from inside: *The tyre ~ suddenly.* ◇ *The river ~ its banks.* **2** [I] ~ **with** be full of sth to the point of breaking open: (fig) *She was ~ing with pride.* [IDM] **be bursting to do sth** be very eager to do sth **burst (sth) open** open (sth) suddenly or violently: *The door ~ open.* [PV] **burst in on/in sth** interrupt sb/sth by entering a place suddenly **burst into sth** suddenly start producing sth: *~ into tears/laughter* **burst into, out of, etc sth** move suddenly and forcefully in the direction that is mentioned **burst out 1** speak suddenly and loudly **2** begin doing sth suddenly: *~ out crying* ● **burst** *n* [C] **1** short period of an activity or a strong emotion: *a ~ of energy* **2** occasion when sth has burst **3** short series of shots from a gun

0─ **bury** /'beri/ *v* (pt, pp **-ied**) [T] **1** put a dead body in a grave **2** put sth underground; hide sth from view: *buried treasure* ◇ *She buried* (= hid) *her face in her hands.* **3** ~ **yourself** in give all your attention to sth [IDM] **bury the hatchet** | **bury your differences** stop arguing and become friends again

0─ **bus** /bʌs/ *n* [C] large motor vehicle that carries passengers ● **bus** *v* (**-s-** *also* **-ss-**) [I,T] go or take sb/sth by bus ■ **'bus stop** *n* [C] regular stopping place for a bus

0─ **bush** /bʊʃ/ *n* **1** [C] low plant that grows thickly: *a rose ~* **2** (the bush) [U] wild uncultivated land, esp in Africa and Australia ▸ **bushy** *adj* (**-ier, -iest**) growing thickly: *~y eyebrows*

0─ **business** /'bɪznəs/ *n* **1** [U] activity of buying and selling; commerce or trade **2** [U] work that is part of your job: *He's away on ~.* **3** [U] amount of work done by a company, etc; the rate or quality of this: *How's ~?* **4** [C] organization that sells goods or provides a service **5** [U] something that concerns a particular person or organization: *My private life is none of your ~* (= does not concern you)*!* **6** [U] important matters that need to be dealt with **7** [sing] matter; affair: *Let's forget the whole ~.* [IDM] **get down to business** start the work that must be done **go out of business** become bankrupt **have no business to do sth** have no right to do sth ■ **'businesslike** *adj* well organized; efficient: *a ~like manner* ■ **'businessman** | **'businesswoman** (pl **-men** pl **-women**) *n* [C] person who works in business

busker /'bʌskə(r)/ *n* [C] (infml) person who plays music in the street, etc to try to earn money

bust /bʌst/ *v* (pt, pp **bust** *or* **~ed**) [T] (infml) **1** break sth **2** (of the police) enter a place and search it or arrest sb: *He's been ~ed for drugs.* ● **bust** *n* [C] **1** sculpture of a person's head and shoulders **2** woman's breasts ● **bust** *adj* (infml) broken [IDM] **go bust** (of a business) become bankrupt

bustle /'bʌsl/ *v* [I] move busily and energetically ▸ **bustle** *n* [U]

0─ **busy** /'bɪzi/ *adj* (**-ier, -iest**) **1** having a lot to do; already working on sth: *I'm ~ all day so I won't be able to help you.* **2** full of activity: *a ~ day* **3** (of a telephone line) being used ▸ **busily** *adv* ● **busy** *v* (pt, pp **-ied**) [T] ~ **yourself** fill your time doing an activity

0─ **but** /bət, *strong form* bʌt/ *conj* used for showing a contrast: *Tom went to the party, ~ his brother didn't.* ● **but** *prep* apart from; except; nothing to eat ~ *bread and cheese* ◇ *I came last ~ one in the race* (= I wasn't last but next to last). ● **but** *adv* only: *We can ~ try.*

butcher /'bʊtʃə(r)/ *n* [C] **1** person whose job is to cut up and sell meat in a shop or to kill animals for this purpose **2** cruel murderer ● **butcher** *v* [T] **1** kill sb/sth cruelly and violently **2** kill and prepare animals for meat ■ **butchery** n [U] unnecessary cruel killing

butler /'bʌtlə(r)/ n [C] chief male servant in a house

butt /bʌt/ n [C] **1** thick end of a weapon or tool **2** end of a cigarette or cigar that is not burned **3** large barrel for storing liquids **4** person who is often joked about or criticized: *She's always the ~ of their jokes.* ● **butt** v [T] hit or push sb/sth hard with your head **[PV] butt in (on sb/sth)** interrupt sb's conversation rudely

0━ **butter** /'bʌtə(r)/ n [U] yellow fatty food made from cream, used on bread, etc ● **butter** v [T] spread butter on sth **[PV] butter sb up** flatter sb ■ **buttercup** n [C] wild plant with small yellow flowers ■ **butternut squash** /ˌbʌtənʌt ˈskwɒʃ/ n [C,U] large vegetable with yellow skin and orange flesh that is shaped like a pear ■ **butterscotch** n [U] hard pale brown sweet made by boiling sugar and butter together

butterfly /'bʌtəflaɪ/ n [C] (pl **-ies**) insect with a long thin body and large colourful wings

buttock /'bʌtək/ n [C, usu pl] either of the two round soft parts at the top of a person's legs

0━ **button** /'bʌtn/ n [C] **1** small round piece of metal, plastic, etc that is sewn onto a piece of clothing as a fastener: *Your top ~'s undone.* **2** small knob that is pressed to operate a machine, bell, etc ● **button** v [I,T] fasten sth or be fastened with buttons ■ **buttonhole** n [C] **1** hole through which a button is passed **2** flower worn on a coat or jacket ■ **buttonhole** v [T] stop sb and make them listen to you

buttress /'bʌtrəs/ n [C] support built against a wall ● **buttress** v [T] support or strengthen sth

buxom /'bʌksəm/ adj (of a woman) large in an attractive way, and with large breasts

0━ **buy** /baɪ/ v (pt, pp **bought** /bɔːt/) [T] **1** get sth by paying money for it **2** (*infml*) believe that sth is true **[PV] buy sb out** pay sb to give up a share in a business so that you can gain control ● **buy** n [C] thing bought: *a good ~* ■ **buyer** n [C] person who buys sth, esp sb who chooses goods to be sold in a large shop

buzz /bʌz/ v **1** [I] (of a bee) make a low sound **2** [I] make a sound like a bee buzzing: *The doorbell ~ed.* **3** [I] ~ **(with)** be full of excited talk **4** [T] call sb with a buzzer: *The doctor ~ed for her next patient.* **[PV] buzz off** (*infml*) go away ● **buzz** n **1** continuous

buzzing sound **2** [sing] (*infml*) feeling of pleasure or excitement **[IDM] give sb a buzz** (*infml*) telephone sb ■ **buzzer** n [C] electrical device that produces a buzzing sound as a signal

buzzard /'bʌzəd/ n [C] large European bird of prey of the hawk family

0━ **by** /baɪ/ prep **1** at the side of sb/ sth; near sb/sth: *Sit by me.* **2** used, usu after a passive verb, to show who or what does, creates or causes sth: *The soldiers were shot by terrorists.* ◇ *a play by Shaw* **3** used for showing how or in what way sth is done: *pay by cheque* ◇ *travel by train* ◇ *Switch it on by pressing this button.* **4** as a result of sth; because of sth: *meet by chance* **5** not later than the time mentioned; before: *finish the work by tomorrow* **6** during sth: *She walked by me.* **7** during sth: *travel by day/night* **8** used to show the degree or amount of sth: *The bullet missed him by ten millimetres.* **9** according to sth: *By law, his parents should be informed.* **10** used to show the part of sb/sth that sb touches, holds, etc: *take sb by the hand* **11** using sth as a standard or unit: *get paid by the hour* ◇ *sell material by the metre* **12** used to state the rate at which sth happens: *He did it bit by bit.* **13** used to show the measurements of sth: *The room measures 18 metres by 20 metres.* ● **by** adv past: *Let me get by.*

0━ **bye** /baɪ/ (*also* **bye-bye** /ˌbaɪ ˈbaɪ/) exclam (*infml*) goodbye

by-election /'baɪ ɪlekʃn/ n [C] election of a new Member of Parliament in a place when the member has died or resigned

bygone /'baɪɡɒn/ adj past: *in ~ days* ▶ **bygones** n [pl] **[IDM] let bygones be bygones** forgive and forget past quarrels

by-law (*also* **bye-law**) /'baɪ lɔː/ n [C] (*GB*) law made by a local authority

bypass /'baɪpɑːs/ n [C] **1** main road that goes round a town instead of through it **2** medical operation on the heart to redirect the flow of blood in order to avoid a part that is damaged or blocked ● **bypass** v [T] **1** go around or avoid a place **2** ignore a rule, an official system, etc, esp in order to get sth done quickly

by-product /'baɪ prɒdʌkt/ n [C] substance produced during the process of making or destroying sth else

bystander /'baɪstændə(r)/ n [C] person who sees sth that is happening but is not involved

byte /baɪt/ n [C] (*computing*) unit of information stored in a computer, equal to 8 bits. A computer's memory is measured in bytes.

A **B** C D E F G H I J K L M N O P Q R S T U V W X Y Z

byword /ˈbaɪwɜːd/ n [C] **1 ~ for** person or thing that is well known for a particular quality **2** common word or expression

Cc

C, c /siː/ n [C,U] (pl **C's, c's** /siːz/) the third letter of the English alphabet ● **C** abbr **1** Celsius; Centigrade **2** (also **c**) Roman numeral for 100

c (also **c.**) abbr **1** cent(s) **2** (also **C**) century **3** (also **ca**) (esp before dates) about

cab /kæb/ n [C] **1** taxi **2** place where the driver sits in a bus, train or lorry

cabaret /ˈkæbəreɪ/ n [U,C] singing and dancing provided in a restaurant or nightclub

cabbage /ˈkæbɪdʒ/ n [C,U] vegetable with a round head of thick green leaves

cabin /ˈkæbɪn/ n [C] **1** small room or compartment in a ship or an aircraft **2** small wooden hut ■ **cabin cruiser** n [C] = CRUISER(2)

0━ **cabinet** /ˈkæbɪnət/ n [C] **1** piece of furniture with drawers or shelves for storing things **2** (**the Cabinet**) [with sing or pl verb] group of chief ministers of a government

0━ **cable** /ˈkeɪbl/ n **1** [U,C] thick strong metal rope, used on ships, for supporting bridges, etc **2** [C,U] set of wires for carrying electricity, telephone signals, etc **3** [C] = CABLE TELEVISION ■ **cable car** n [U] **1** vehicle like a box that hangs on a moving cable and carries passengers up and down a mountain **2** (esp US) vehicle that runs on tracks and is pulled by a moving cable ■ **cable television** n [U] system of broadcasting television programmes along wires rather than by radio waves

cache /kæʃ/ n [C] **1** hidden store of things such as weapons **2** (computing) part of a computer's memory that stores copies of data that can be accessed very quickly

cackle /ˈkækl/ n **1** [U] loud clucking noise that a hen makes **2** [C] loud laugh ● **cackle** v [I] **1** (of a chicken) make a loud unpleasant noise **2** (of a person) laugh noisily

cactus /ˈkæktəs/ n [C] (pl **~es** or **-ti** /-taɪ/) plant that grows in hot dry regions, esp one with thick stems and prickles

cadet /kəˈdet/ n [C] young person training to become an officer in the police or armed forces

cadge /kædʒ/ v [I,T] (infml) ask sb for food, money, etc, esp because you do not want to pay for it yourself

cafe /ˈkæfeɪ/ n [C] place where you can buy drinks and simple meals

cafeteria /ˌkæfəˈtɪəriə/ n [C] restaurant where you choose and pay for your meal at a counter and carry it to your table

caffeine /ˈkæfiːn/ n [U] stimulating drug found in tea and coffee

cage /keɪdʒ/ n [C] structure of bars or wires in which birds or animals are kept ● **cage** v [T] put or keep an animal in a cage

cagey /ˈkeɪdʒi/ adj (infml) secretive

cagoule /kəˈɡuːl/ n [C] (GB) light long waterproof jacket with a hood

cairn /keən/ n [C] pile of stones as a landmark (1) or memorial

cajole /kəˈdʒəʊl/ v [T] make sb do sth by saying nice things to them

0━ **cake** /keɪk/ n **1** [C,U] sweet food made from a mixture of flour, eggs, butter, etc baked in an oven **2** [C] other food mixture cooked in a round flat shape: fish~s ● **cake** v [T] cover sth thickly with mud, etc

calamity /kəˈlæməti/ n [C] (pl **-ies**) great disaster

calcium /ˈkælsiəm/ n [U] (symb **Ca**) chemical element which is found as a compound in bones, teeth and chalk

calculable /ˈkælkjələbl/ adj that can be calculated

0━ **calculate** /ˈkælkjuleɪt/ v [I,T] use numbers to find out a total number, amount, etc: ~ the cost **[IDM] be calculated to do sth** be intended to do sth: ~d to attract attention ▶ **calculating** adj (disapprov) using deceit or trickery to get what you want ▶ **calculation** /ˌkælkjuˈleɪʃn/ n [C,U] ▶ **calculator** n [C] small electronic device for making calculations

calendar /ˈkælɪndə(r)/ n [C] **1** chart showing the days, weeks and months of a particular year **2** system by which time is divided: the Islamic

calf /kɑːf/ n (pl **calves** /kɑːvz/) **1** [C] back part of the leg, between the knee and the ankle **2** [C] young cow **3** [C] young of the seal, whale and certain other animals **4** (also **'calfskin**) [U] leather made from the skin of calves (2)

calibre (US **-ber**) /ˈkælɪbə(r)/ n **1** [U] quality; ability: His work is of the highest ~. **2** [C] diameter of the inside of a tube or gun

caliper = CALLIPER

0━ **call¹** /kɔːl/ v **1** [T] give sb/sth a name; use a particular name when talking to sb: name His name's Hiroshi but everyone ~s him Hiro. **2** [T] describe sb/sth in a particular way; consider sb/sth to be sth: I wouldn't ~ it a great film. **3** [I,T] say sth loudly; shout **4** [T] order or ask sb to come by telephoning, shouting, etc: ~ the

call

police 5 [I,T] telephone sb **6** [I] make a short visit to a person or place: *Let's ~ on Jane.* **7** [T] order sth to happen; announce sth: *~ a meeting/an election/a strike* **|IDM|** **call sb's bluff** invite sb to do what they are threatening to do **call it a day** (*infml*) decide to stop doing sth **call sb names** insult sb **call the shots/tune** (*infml*) be the person who controls a situation **call sb/sth to mind** → MIND¹ **[PV]** **call for sb/sth 1** visit a house, etc to collect sb/sth **2** demand or need sth: *The problem ~s for immediate action.* **call sb in** ask for the services of sb: *~ in the experts* **call sb/sth off** order a dog or person to stop attacking, searching, etc **call sth off** cancel a planned event **call on/upon sb** formally ask or invite sb to do sth **call sb out 1** ask sb to come, esp in an emergency: *~ out the fire brigade* **2** order a group of workers to go on strike **call sb up 1** (*esp US*) telephone sb **2** order sb to join the armed forces ▶ **caller** *n* [C] person who makes a telephone call or a short visit ● **'call-up** *n* [U,C] order to join the armed forces

0-¬ **call²** /kɔːl/ *n* **1** [C] (also **'phone call**) telephone conversation **2** [C] loud sound made by a bird or an animal, or by a person to attract attention **3** [C] short visit **4** [C] request, order or demand for sb to do sth or to go somewhere: *~s for the minister to resign* **5** [U] (no ~ for sth) no need or demand for sth **6** [C] (*infml*) decision: *It's your ~.* **|IDM|** **(be) on call** (of a doctor, etc) available for work if needed ● **'call box** *n* [C] = TELEPHONE BOX ● **'call girl** *n* [C] prostitute who makes appointments by telephone

calligraphy /kəˈlɪɡrəfi/ *n* [U] (art of) beautiful handwriting

calling /ˈkɔːlɪŋ/ *n* [C] strong desire or feeling of duty to do a certain job

calliper (also **caliper**) /ˈkælɪpə/ *n* **1** (**callipers**) [pl] instrument for measuring the diameter of round objects **2** (*GB*) [C, usu pl] metal support for weak or injured legs

callous /ˈkæləs/ *adj* cruelly unkind and insensitive

callow /ˈkæləʊ/ *adj* (*disapprov*) young and inexperienced

callus /ˈkæləs/ *n* [C] area of thick hardened skin

0-¬ **calm** /kɑːm/ *adj* **1** not excited, nervous or upset **2** (of the sea) without large waves **3** (of the weather) not windy ● **calm** *n* [U,C] calm state or period ● **calm** *v* [I,T] ~ (**down**) become or make sb/sth calm ▶ **calmly** *adv* ● **calmness** *n* [U]

calorie /ˈkæləri/ *n* [C] **1** unit of heat **2** unit of the energy value of food

calve /kɑːv/ *v* [I] (of a cow) give birth to a calf

calves *plural of* CALF

calypso /kəˈlɪpsəʊ/ *n* [C,U] (pl **~s**) Caribbean song; this type of music

camber /ˈkæmbə(r)/ *n* [C] slight rise in the middle of a road surface

came *pt of* COME

camel /ˈkæml/ *n* [C] animal with a long neck and one or two humps on its back

cameo /ˈkæmiəʊ/ *n* [C] (pl **~s**) **1** short part in a film or play by a famous actor: *a ~ role* **2** short piece of descriptive writing **3** piece of jewellery with a raised design, usu of a head

0-¬ **camera** /ˈkæmərə/ *n* [C] piece of equipment for taking photographs or moving pictures

camouflage /ˈkæməflɑːʒ/ *n* [C,U] (use of) colour, nets, branches, etc that help to hide sb/sth: *soldiers in ~* ● **camouflage** *v* [T] hide sb/sth by camouflage

0-¬ **camp** /kæmp/ *n* [C] **1** place where people live in tents or huts for a short time **2** group of people with the same, esp political, ideas ● **camp** *v* [I] put up a tent; spend a holiday in a tent: *We go ~ing every summer.* ▶ **camper** *n* [C] person who camps

0-¬ **campaign** /kæmˈpeɪn/ *n* [C] **1** series of planned activities with a particular aim: *an advertising ~* **2** series of military operations in a war ● **campaign** *v* [I] take part in a campaign ▶ **campaigner** *n* [C]

campus /ˈkæmpəs/ *n* [C] grounds of a university, college or school

0-¬ **can¹** /kən; strong form kæn/ *modal v* (neg **cannot** /ˈkænɒt/ short form **can't** /kɑːnt/ pt **could** /kəd; strong form kʊd/ neg **could not** short form **couldn't** /ˈkʊdnt/) **1** used to say that it is possible for sb/sth to do sth, or for sth to happen: *The building ~ be emptied in 2 minutes.* **2** be able to or know how to do sth: *C~ you ski?* **3** used with the verbs 'feel', 'hear', 'see', 'smell', 'taste': *C~ you hear a funny noise?* **4** used to show that sb is allowed to do sth: *You ~ borrow my car if you want.* **5** (*spoken*) used ask permission to do sth: *C~ I use your phone?* **6** (*spoken*) used to ask sb to do sth for you: *C~ you close the door, please?* **7** used in the negative for saying that you are sure sth is not true: *That ~'t be Dan – he's in Chicago.*

0-¬ **can²** /kæn/ *n* [C] **1** metal container for food or liquids: *a ~ of beans* **2** contents of such a container ● **can** *v* (**-nn-**) [T] put food, etc in a can ► **cannery** n [C] (pl **-ies**) factory where food is canned

canal /kəˈnæl/ n [C] **1** man-made waterway for boats to travel along or for irrigation

canary /kəˈneəri/ n [C] (pl **-ies**) small yellow bird, often kept in a cage as a pet

0━ **cancel** /ˈkænsl/ v (**-ll-** US **-l-**) [T] **1** say that sth already arranged will not be done or happen: *The meeting was~led.* **2** mark a ticket or stamp so that it cannot be used again [PV] **cancel (sth) out** be equal to sth in effect; balance: *Recent losses have ~led out any profits made earlier.* ► **cancellation** /ˌkænsəˈleɪʃn/ n [C, U]

0━ **cancer** /ˈkænsə(r)/ n [U, C] very serious disease in which lumps form in the body and kill normal cells ► **cancerous** adj: ~ **cells**

candid /ˈkændɪd/ adj saying what you think openly: *a ~ discussion* ► **candidly** adv

0━ **candidate** /ˈkændɪdət/ n [C] **1** person being considered for a job or in an election **2** person taking an exam

candle /ˈkændl/ n [C] stick of wax with a string (wick) through it, which gives out light when it burns ■ **candlestick** n [C] holder for a candle

candour (US **-dor**) /ˈkændə(r)/ n [U] quality of being candid

0━ **candy** /ˈkændi/ n [U, C] (pl **-ies**) (US) (piece of) sweet food made of sugar and/or chocolate, eaten between meals

cane /keɪn/ n **1** [C] hollow stem of certain plants, eg bamboo or sugar **2** [U] such stems used as a material for making furniture **3** [C] length of cane, etc, used as a support, for a plant or as a walking stick **4** [sing] punishment of children by being hit with a cane ● **cane** v [T] hit a child with a cane as a punishment

canine /ˈkeɪnaɪn/ adj of or like a dog

canister /ˈkænɪstə(r)/ n [C] **1** small (usu metal) box with a lid **2** cylinder fired from a gun

canker /ˈkæŋkə(r)/ n **1** [U] disease of trees **2** [U] disease that causes ulcers **3** [C] bad influence that spreads

cannabis /ˈkænəbɪs/ n [U] drug made from the hemp plant, smoked for its relaxing effect

cannery → CAN²

cannibal /ˈkænɪbl/ n [C] **1** person who eats human flesh **2** animal that eats its own kind ► **cannibalism** /ˈkænɪbəlɪzəm/ n [U] ► **cannibalize** (also **-ise**) /ˈkænɪbəlaɪz/ v [T] use a machine, vehicle, etc to provide spare parts for another

cannon /ˈkænən/ n [C] (pl **cannon**) **1** old type of large heavy gun firing

solid metal balls **2** automatic gun firing shells (2) from an aircraft

0━ **cannot** → CAN¹

canoe /kəˈnuː/ n [C] light narrow boat which you move along in the water with a paddle ● **canoe** v [I] travel by canoe ► **canoeist** n [C] person travelling in a canoe

canon /ˈkænən/ n [C] **1** priest with special duties in a cathedral **2** (fml) generally accepted standard or principle: *offend the ~s of good taste* ► **canonical** /kəˈnɒnɪkl/ adj according to the law of the Christian Church ► **canonize** (also **-ise**) /ˈkænənaɪz/ v [T] (of the Pope) officially declare sb to be a saint ■ **canon law** n [U] law of the Christian Church

canopy /ˈkænəpi/ n [C] (pl **-ies**) **1** cover that hangs above a bed, throne, etc **2** cover for the cockpit of an aircraft

can't cannot → CAN¹

cant /kænt/ n [U] insincere talk

cantankerous /kænˈtæŋkərəs/ adj bad-tempered and always complaining

canteen /kænˈtiːn/ n [C] **1** place, eg in a factory, an office or a school, where food is served **2** (GB) box containing a set of knives, forks and spoons

canter /ˈkæntə(r)/ n [C, usu sing] horse's movement that is faster than a trot but slower than a gallop ● **canter** v [I, T] (cause a horse to) move at a canter

cantilever /ˈkæntɪliːvə(r)/ n [C] long piece of metal or wood that sticks out from a wall to support the end of a bridge

canvas /ˈkænvəs/ n **1** [U] strong coarse cloth used for making tents, sails, etc and by artists for painting on **2** [C] piece of canvas used for painting on; an oil painting

canvass /ˈkænvəs/ v [I, T] go round an area asking people for their political support or opinions ► **canvasser** n [C]

canyon /ˈkænjən/ n [C] deep valley ► **canyoning** n [U] sport of jumping into a fast-flowing mountain stream and being carried downstream

0━ **cap** /kæp/ n [C] **1** soft flat hat with a peak (= hard curved part sticking out at the front) **2** top covering eg on a bottle or tube of toothpaste ● **cap** v (**-pp-**) [T] **1** cover the top or end of sth **2** do or say sth better than sth previously done or said **3** choose a player for a national team

capability /ˌkeɪpəˈbɪləti/ n (pl **-ies**) **1** ability or qualities necessary to do sth **2** the power or weapons that a country has for war or for military action: *Britain's nuclear ~*

0‑w **capable** /'keɪpəbl/ *adj* **1 ~ of** having the ability necessary for sth: *You are ~ of producing better work than this.* **2** having the ability to do things well ▸ **capably** *adv*

0‑w **capacity** /kə'pæsəti/ *n* (pl **-ies**) **1** [U,C, usu sing] number of people or things that a container or space can hold: *a hall with a seating ~ of 750* **2** [C,U] power or ability **3** [C] official position that sb has: *in my ~ as manager*

cape /keɪp/ *n* [C] **1** loose sleeveless garment like a short cloak **2** piece of land that sticks out into the sea

capillary /kə'pɪləri/ *n* [C] (pl **-ies**) (*anat*) any of the smallest tubes in the body that carry blood

0‑w **capital** /'kæpɪtl/ *n* **1** [C] town or city that is the centre of government of a country, etc **2** [U] wealth or property owned by a person or business; money with which a business is started **3** [C] (*also* **capital letter**) large letter, eg A, B, C, etc [IDM] **make capital (out) of sth** use a situation for your advantage ● **capital** *adj* involving punishment by death

capitalism /'kæpɪtəlɪzəm/ *n* [U] economic system in which a country's trade and industry are controlled by private owners and not the state ▸ **capitalist** /'kæpɪtəlɪst/ *n* **1** person who supports capitalism **2** person who owns capital (2) ▸ **capitalist** *adj*

capitalize (*also* **-ise**) /'kæpɪtəlaɪz/ *v* [T] **1** write a letter of the alphabet as a capital; begin a word with a capital letter **2** (*business*) sell possessions in order to change them into money **3** (*business*) provide a company, etc with the money it needs to function [PV] **capitalize on/upon sth** gain a further advantage for yourself from a situation

capitulate /kə'pɪtʃuleɪt/ *v* [I] **~ (to)** surrender to sb ▸ **capitulation** /kə,pɪtʃu'leɪʃn/ *n* [U]

capsize /kæp'saɪz/ *v* [I,T] (cause a boat to) turn over in the water

capsule /'kæpsjuːl/ *n* [C] **1** very small container of medicine that is swallowed **2** compartment for people or instruments in a spacecraft

0‑w **captain** /'kæptɪn/ *n* [C] **1** person in charge of a ship or an aircraft **2** officer in the army **3** leader of a sports team ● **captain** *v* [T] be captain of a sports team or a ship

caption /'kæpʃn/ *n* [C] words printed underneath a picture or cartoon in order to explain it

captivate /'kæptɪveɪt/ *v* [T] fascinate sb: *~d by her beauty*

captive /'kæptɪv/ *n* [C], *adj* (person

or animal) taken prisoner ▸ **captivity** /kæp'tɪvəti/ *n* [U] state of being kept as a prisoner

captor /'kæptə(r)/ *n* [C] person who captures a person or an animal

0‑w **capture** /'kæptʃə(r)/ *v* [T] **1** catch a person or an animal and keep them as a prisoner **2** take control of a place, building, etc using force **3** succeed in accurately expressing a feeling, etc in a picture, film, etc ● **capture** *n* [U] act of capturing sb/sth or of being captured: *data ~*

0‑w **car** /kɑː(r)/ *n* [C] **1** motor vehicle for carrying passengers **2** railway carriage of a particular type: *a dining ~* **3** **car 'boot sale** *n* [C] (GB) outdoor sale at which people sell unwanted goods from the backs of their cars ■ **car park** *n* [C] (GB) area where cars may be parked

carafe /kə'ræf/ *n* [C] glass container in which water or wine is served

caramel /'kærəml/ *n* **1** [U] burnt sugar used for colouring and flavouring food **2** [C] chewy sweet of boiled sugar

carat /'kærət/ *n* [C] **1** unit of weight for precious stones **2** unit for measuring the purity of gold

caravan /'kærəvæn/ *n* [C] **1** small home on wheels, pulled by a car **2** covered cart for living in **3** group of people and animals travelling across a desert

carbohydrate /,kɑːbəʊ'haɪdreɪt/ *n* [C,U] substance found in food, eg sugar and potatoes, that provides energy

carbon /'kɑːbən/ *n* [U] (*symb* **C**) non-metallic element found in diamonds, coal and all living matter ■ **carbon 'copy** (*also* **carbon**) *n* [C] copy of a document, etc made with carbon paper ■ **carbon dioxide** /,kɑːbən daɪ'ɒksaɪd/ *n* [U] gas breathed out by people and animals from the lungs, or produced by burning carbon ■ **carbon 'footprint** *n* [C] measure of the amount of carbon dioxide that is produced by the daily activities of a person or an organization, such as driving a vehicle, using electricity, etc: *a ~ footprint calculator* ■ **carbon monoxide** /,kɑːbən mə'nɒksaɪd/ *n* [U] poisonous gas formed when carbon burns partly but not completely. It is produced when petrol is burnt in car engines. ■ **carbon 'offset** *n* [C,U] way for sb to reduce the level of carbon dioxide for which they are responsible, by paying a company to reduce the amount produced in the world, for example by planting trees ■ **'carbon paper** *n* [C,U] (sheet of) thin paper coated with a dark substance, used for making copies

carbuncle /'kɑːbʌŋkl/ n [C] large painful swelling under the skin

carburettor /ˌkɑːbəˈretə(r)/ (US -t-) n [C] part of a car engine in which petrol and air are mixed

carcass /'kɑːkəs/ n [C] dead body of an animal

0─ **card** /kɑːd/ n 1 [U] thick stiff paper 2 [C] piece of stiff paper or plastic with information on it: *an identity ~ ◇ a business/credit ~* 3 [C] piece of card with a picture on it that you use for sending a greeting to sb: *a Christmas/birthday ~* 4 [C] = PLAYING CARD (PLAY¹) 5 [C] (computing) small device containing an electronic circuit that is part of a computer, enabling it to perform certain functions: *a sound ~* [IDM] **lay/ put your cards on the table** be honest about your intentions **on the cards** (*infml*) likely

0─ **cardboard** /'kɑːdbɔːd/ n [U] thick stiff kind of paper: *a ~ box*

cardiac /'kɑːdiæk/ adj of the heart

cardigan /'kɑːdɪɡən/ n [C] knitted woollen jacket with buttons or a zip at the front

cardinal /'kɑːdɪnl/ n [C] 1 senior Roman Catholic priest 2 (*also* ˌcardinal 'number*) number, eg 1, 2, or 5, used to show quantity rather than order ● **cardinal** adj (*fml*) most important

0─ **care¹** /keə(r)/ n 1 [U] protection: *The child was left in his sister's ~.* 2 [U] serious attention or thought: *She arranged the flowers with ~. ◇ Take ~ when crossing the road.* 3 [C, usu pl, U] feeling of worry or anxiety: *without a ~ in the world* [IDM] **in care** (*GB*) (of children) living in an institution run by the local authority rather than with their parents: *The boys were taken into ~ when their mother died.* **take care of yourself/ sb/sth** keep yourself/sb/sth safe from injury, illness, damage, etc; look after sb/sth/yourself 2 be responsible for sth ▸ **'carefree** adj without worries ▸ **careful** adj 1 (of a person) cautious; thinking about what you are doing 2 giving a lot of attention to details: *a ~ful piece of work* ▸ **carefulness** n [U] ▸ **careless** adj 1 not taking care; thoughtless 2 resulting from lack of attention and thought: *a ~less mistake* 3 ~ **of** (*fml*) not at all worried about sth ▸ **carelessly** adv ▸ **carelessness** n [U]

0─ **care²** /keə(r)/ v [I] 1 ~ **(about)** feel that sth is important and worth worrying about: *I ~ about this country's future.* 2 ~ **(about)** like or love sb and worry about what happens to them 3 ~ ~ **for/to** (*fml*) like to have sth or do sth: *Would you ~ for a drink?* [PV] **care for sb** 1 look after sb who is ill, very old, etc 2 love or like sb very much

0─ **career** /kəˈrɪə(r)/ n [C] 1 series of jobs that a person has in a particular area of work 2 the period of time that you spend in your life working ● **career** v [I] rush wildly: *~ down the mountain*

caress /kəˈres/ n [C] loving touch ● **caress** v [T] give a caress to sb/sth

caretaker /'keəteɪkə(r)/ n [C] person whose job is to look after a building

cargo /'kɑːɡəʊ/ n [C, U] (pl *-es* US also *~s*) goods carried in a ship or an aircraft

caricature /'kærɪkətʃʊə(r)/ n [C] picture or description of a person that emphasizes certain features to cause amusement or ridicule ● **caricature** v [T] produce a caricature of sb

carnage /'kɑːnɪdʒ/ n [U] killing of a lot of people

carnal /'kɑːnl/ adj (*fml*) connected with the body or with sex

carnation /kɑːˈneɪʃn/ n [C] white, pink or red flower, often worn as a decoration

carnival /'kɑːnɪvl/ n [C] public festival

carnivore /'kɑːnɪvɔː(r)/ n [C] any animal that eats meat ▸ **carnivorous** /kɑːˈnɪvərəs/ adj

carol /'kærəl/ n [C] Christian religious song sung at Christmas

carp /kɑːp/ n [C] large freshwater fish ● **carp** v [I] 1 ~ **(at/ about)** complain continually about sb/sth in an annoying way

carpenter /'kɑːpəntə(r)/ n [C] person whose job is to make and repair wooden objects ▸ **carpentry** /'kɑːpəntri/ n [U] work of a carpenter

0─ **carpet** /'kɑːpɪt/ n [U, C] (piece of) thick woollen or artificial fabric for covering floors ● **carpet** v [T] cover sth with or as if with a carpet

carriage /'kærɪdʒ/ n [C] 1 separate section of a train for carrying passengers 2 [C] vehicle pulled by a horse 3 [U] act or cost of transporting goods 4 [C] moving part of a machine: *a typewriter ~* ▪ **'carriageway** n [C] one of the two sides of a motorway, etc, intended for traffic moving in one direction

carrier /'kæriə(r)/ n [C] 1 person or company that carries goods 2 person or animal that can pass a disease to others without suffering from it ▪ **'carrier bag** n [C] paper or plastic bag for carrying shopping

0─ **carrot** /'kærət/ n [C] long pointed orange root vegetable

0─ **carry** /'kæri/ v (pt, pp *-ied*) 1 [T] support the weight of sb/sth and take them or it from place to place: *~ the boxes upstairs* 2 [T] have sth with you as you take it wherever you go: *I never ~ much money.* 3 [T] (of

carry

61

A B C D E F G H I J K L M N O P Q R S T U V W X Y Z

pipes, wires, etc) contain and direct the flow of water, electricity, etc **4** [T] support the weight of sth: *The pillars ~ the whole roof.* **5** [T] have sth as a result: *Power carries great responsibility.* **6** [I] (of a sound) be able to be heard at a distance: *His voice doesn't ~ very far.* **7** [T] (usu passive) approve of sth in a vote: *The proposal was carried.* **8** [T] (of a newspaper) include or contain a particular story [IDM] **be/get carried away** become so excited that you lose self control [PV] **carry sth off 1** win sth **2** succeed in doing sth difficult **carry on (with/doing sth)** continue doing sth: *~ with/doing sth* **carry on (with sb)** (*infml*) have an affair (3) with sb **carry sth on** take part in sth; conduct **carry sth out 1** do sth that you have said you will do or have been asked to do: *~ out a promise/threat* **2** do and complete a task: *~ out a survey* **carry sth through** complete sth successfully **carry sth through sth** help sb to survive a difficult period

cart /kɑːt/ *n* [C] vehicle for carrying loads, usu pulled by a horse [IDM] **put the cart before the horse** do things in the wrong order [PV] **cart** *v* [T] **1** carry sth in a cart or other vehicle **2** (*infml*) carry sth large, heavy or awkward ■ **'carthorse** *n* [C] large strong horse used for heavy work ■ **'cartwheel** *n* [C] sideways somersault with arms and legs stretched out

carte blanche /ˌkɑːt ˈblɑːnʃ/ *n* [U] complete freedom to do whatever you like

cartilage /ˈkɑːtɪlɪdʒ/ *n* [U,C] strong white flexible tissue found between the joints in the body

carton /ˈkɑːtn/ *n* [C] cardboard or plastic box for holding esp food or liquid

cartoon /kɑːˈtuːn/ *n* [C] **1** amusing drawing or series of drawings in a newspaper, etc **2** film made by photographing a series of drawings: *a Walt Disney ~* ► **cartoonist** *n* [C] person who draws cartoons

cartridge /ˈkɑːtrɪdʒ/ *n* [C] **1** tube or case containing explosive and a bullet, for firing from a gun **2** case containing sth that is used in a machine, eg photographic film for a camera, ink for a printer, etc **3** thin tube containing ink which you put in a pen

carve /kɑːv/ *v* [I,T] **1** make objects, patterns, etc by cutting away material from stone or wood: *~ your initials on a tree* **2** cut cooked meat into slices for eating [PV] **carve sth out (for yourself)** work hard in order to have a successful career, reputation, etc ► **carving** *n* [C] object or pattern carved in stone, etc ► **carving knife**

n [C] large sharp knife used for carving meat

cascade /kæˈskeɪd/ *n* [C] small waterfall ● **cascade** *v* [I] fall downwards in large amounts

0━ **case** /keɪs/ *n* **1** [C] particular situation or a situation of a particular type: *In most ~s, no extra charge is made.* **2** (**the case**) [sing] the true situation: *If that is the ~, we need more staff.* **3** [C] matter being investigated by the police **4** [C] matter to be decided in a law court: *a court ~* **5** [C, usu sing] set of facts, etc that support one side in a law court, discussion, etc **6** [C] box or other container for storing things: *a pencil ~* **7** [C] = SUITCASE **8** [C] instance of a disease or injury **9** [C,U] (in some languages) form of a word that shows its relationship to another word [IDM] **a case in point** clear example that is relevant to the matter being discussed **in any case** whatever happens **(just) in case (...)** because of the possibility of sth happening: *Take an umbrella in ~ it rains.* **in case of sth** if sth happens: *In ~ of emergency, phone the police.* **in that case** if that is the situation ■ **case history** *n* [C] record of a person's background, health, etc

casement /ˈkeɪsmənt/ *n* [C] window that opens like a door

0━ **cash** /kæʃ/ *n* [U] **1** money in coins or notes **2** (*infml*) money in any form ● **cash** *v* [T] exchange a cheque for cash [PV] **cash in (on sth)** take advantage of sth; profit from sth ■ **'cashback** *n* [U] sum of money from your bank account that you can ask for at the same time as you pay for sth in a shop with a debit card ■ **'cash cow** *n* [C] (*business*) part of a business that always makes a profit and that provides money for the rest of the business ■ **'cash crop** *n* [C] crop grown for selling ■ **'cash machine** (*also* **cash dispenser**, **'Cashpoint**™) *n* [C] machine outside a bank from which you can get money from your bank account using a special plastic card ■ **'cash register** *n* [C] machine in a shop for recording and storing cash received

cashew /ˈkæʃuː; kæˈʃuː/ *n* [C] (tropical American tree with a) small curved nut, used in cooking

cashier /kæˈʃɪə(r)/ *n* [C] person whose job is to receive and pay out money in a bank, shop, etc

cashmere /ˈkæʃmɪə(r); ˌkæʃ'm-/ *n* [U] fine soft wool

casing /ˈkeɪsɪŋ/ *n* [C] covering that protects sth

casino /kəˈsiːnəʊ/ *n* [C] (pl **~s**) public building or room where people play gambling games for money

cask /kɑːsk/ *n* [C] barrel for storing liquids

casket /'kɑːskɪt/ n [C] **1** small box for holding jewellery, letters, etc **2** (US) = COFFIN

cassava /kə'sɑːvə/ n [U] type of flour made from the thick roots of a tropical plant

casserole /'kæsərəʊl/ n **1** [C,U] hot dish made with meat, vegetables, etc that are cooked slowly in liquid in an oven **2** [C] container in which such food is cooked

cassette /kə'set/ n [C] small sealed case containing magnetic tape or film: a ~ recorder/player

cassock /'kæsək/ n [C] long outer garment worn by some Christian priests

0–w **cast¹** /kɑːst/ v (pt, pp **cast**) [T] **1** throw sth; allow sth to fall: ~ a net ◇ The tree ~ a long shadow. ◇ ~ a glance at sb ◇ ~ doubt on his claims ◇ ~ aspersions on his reputation **2** give an actor a part in a play **3** make an object by pouring metal into a mould (= a specially shaped container): a statue ~ in bronze [IDM] **cast an eye/your eyes over sth** look at or examine sth quickly **cast light on/upon sth** → LIGHT¹ **cast lots (for sth/to do sth)** → LOT³ [PV] **cast sth aside** (fml) get rid of sth **cast sth off** untie the ropes of a boat **cast sth off** (written) get rid of sth ▶ **casting** n **1** [U] process of choosing actors for a play or film **2** [C] object made by pouring metal into a mould ■ **casting vote** n [C] vote given to decide a matter when votes on each side are equal ■ **cast iron** n [U] hard alloy of iron made by pouring hot liquid metal into a mould ▶ **cast-iron** adj **1** made of cast iron **2** very strong or certain: a ~-iron excuse ■ **cast-off** (GB) n [C, usu pl] adj (piece of clothing) no longer wanted by its original owner

0–w **cast²** /kɑːst/ n [with sing or pl verb] **1** all the actors in a play, etc **2** object made by pouring hot liquid metal, etc into a mould (= a specially shaped container) **3** act of throwing sth, esp a fishing line

castanets /ˌkæstə'nets/ n [pl] musical instrument, consisting of two small round pieces of wood, hit together with the fingers, used esp in Spanish dances

castaway /'kɑːstəweɪ/ n [C] shipwrecked person

caste /kɑːst/ n [C] any one of the Hindu social classes

caster sugar (also **castor sugar** /ˌkɑːstə 'ʃʊɡə(r)/) n [U] very fine white sugar

castigate /'kæstɪɡeɪt/ v [T] (fml) criticize sth severely

0–w **castle** /'kɑːsl/ n [C] **1** old large building with thick walls, used for protection from enemies **2** chess piece

castor (US **caster**) /'kɑːstə(r)/ n [C] small wheel fixed to a chair, etc

castor oil /ˌkɑːstər 'ɔɪl/ n [U] thick yellowish oil used as a medicine

castor sugar n [U] = CASTER SUGAR

castrate /kæ'streɪt/ v [T] remove the testicles of a male animal ▶ **castration** /kæ'streɪʃn/ n [U,C]

casual /'kæʒuəl/ adj **1** not showing much care or thought; seeming not to be worried **2** informal: ~ clothes **3** not permanent or regular: ~ work **4** happening by chance: a ~ meeting ▶ **casually** adv

casualty /'kæʒuəlti/ n (pl **-ies**) [C] **1** person injured or killed in a war or an accident **2** [U] (GB also **casualty department**) part of a hospital where people who are most urgent treatment are taken

0–w **cat** /kæt/ n [C] **1** small furry animal often kept as a pet **2** wild animal of the cat family, eg lion or tiger ■ **cat burglar** n [C] burglar who enters buildings by climbing up walls, etc ■ **catcall** n [C] loud shrill whistle expressing disapproval ■ **catnap** n [C] short sleep

catacombs /'kætəkuːmz/ n [pl] series of underground tunnels for burying dead bodies

catalogue (US also **-log**) /'kætəlɒɡ/ n [C] list of items, eg goods for sale ● **catalogue** v [T] list sth in a catalogue

catalyst /'kætəlɪst/ n [C] something that speeds up or causes a change without itself changing

catalytic converter /ˌkætəˌlɪtɪk kən'vɜːtə(r)/ n [C] device used in the exhaust system of motor vehicles to reduce the damage caused to the environment

catapult /'kætəpʌlt/ n [C] Y-shaped stick with a piece of elastic, for shooting stones, etc ● **catapult** v [I,T] throw sb/sth or be thrown suddenly and violently through the air

cataract /'kætərækt/ n [C] **1** disease of the eye, causing blindness **2** (lit) large steep waterfall

catarrh /kə'tɑː(r)/ n [U] thick liquid (called phlegm) in the nose and throat, caused by a cold

catastrophe /kə'tæstrəfi/ n [C] sudden great disaster or misfortune ▶ **catastrophic** /ˌkætə'strɒfɪk/ adj

0–w **catch¹** /kætʃ/ v (pt, pp **caught** /kɔːt/) **1** [T] stop and hold sth moving, esp in the hands: ~ a ball **2** [T] capture a person or an animal: ~ a thief **3** [T] discover sb doing sth: ~ sb stealing **4** [T] be in time for and get on a train, etc **5** [I,t]

(cause sb/sth to) become trapped: *I caught my fingers in the door.* **6** [T] become ill with sth: ~ *a cold* **7** [T] hear sth; understand sth: *I didn't quite* ~ *your name.* **8** [T] hit sb/sth: *The stone caught him on the head.* [IDM] **catch sb's eye** attract sb's attention **catch sb's fancy → FANCY** **catch fire** begin to burn **catch sb napping** (*infml*) find sb not paying attention **catch sb red-handed** discover sb in the act of doing wrong **catch sight of sb/sth** see sb/ sth for a moment [PV] **catch on** (*infml*) become popular **catch on** (**to sth**) (*infml*) understand sth **catch sb out** show that sb is ignorant or is doing sth wrong **catch up** (**with sb**) (*GB also*) **catch sb up** reach the same level as sb **catch up on sth** do some extra time doing sth **be/get caught up in sth** be/get involved in sth
▶ **catching** *adj* (of a disease) infectious ■ **catchment area** *n* [C] area from which people are sent to a particular school, hospital, etc
■ **catchphrase** *n* [C] popular word or phrase connected with the politician or entertainer who made it famous ▶ **catchy** *adj* (-ier, -iest) (of music or the words of an advertisement) easy to remember

catch² /kætʃ/ *n* [C] **1** act of catching sth, esp a ball **2** (amount of) fish caught: *a huge* ~ *of fish* **3** device for fastening sth **4** hidden difficulty: *There must be a* ~ *somewhere.*

categorical /ˌkætəˈgɒrɪkl/ *adj* (of a statement) unconditional; absolute ▶ **categorically** /-kli/ *adv*

0₋ **category** /ˈkætəgəri/ *n* [C] (*pl* -ies) group in a complete system; class ▶ **categorize** (*also* -ise) /ˈkætəgəraɪz/ *v* [T] put sb/sth in a category

cater /ˈkeɪtə(r)/ *v* [I] ~ (**for**) **1** provide food and services for sb, esp at social functions **2** provide what is needed or desired by sb: *videos* ~*ing for all tastes* ● **caterer** *n* [C]

caterpillar /ˈkætəpɪlə(r)/ *n* [C] small creature like a worm with legs which develops into a butterfly or moth

catgut /ˈkætgʌt/ *n* [U] thin strong cord used in making the strings of musical instruments

cathedral /kəˈθiːdrəl/ *n* [C] main church of a district, under the care of a bishop

cathode /ˈkæθəʊd/ *n* [C] (*tech*) negative electrode in a battery, etc

catholic /ˈkæθlɪk/ *adj* **1** (Catholic) = ROMAN CATHOLIC (ROMAN) **2** (*fml*) including many things; general: *have* ~ *tastes* ● **Catholic** *n* [C] = ROMAN CATHOLIC (ROMAN) ▶ **Catholicism** /kəˈθɒlɪsɪzəm/ *n* [U]

teaching, beliefs, etc of the Roman Catholic Church

cattle /ˈkætl/ *n* [pl] cows and bulls that are kept as farm animals

catty /ˈkæti/ *adj* (-ier, -iest) (*infml*) (of a woman) saying unkind things about others

caught *pt*, *pp* of CATCH¹

cauldron /ˈkɔːldrən/ *n* [C] large deep pot for boiling things: *a witch's* ~

cauliflower /ˈkɒliflaʊə(r)/ *n* [C,U] vegetable with a large white flower head

0₋ **cause** /kɔːz/ *n* **1** [C] person or thing that makes sth happen: *the* ~ *of the fire* **2** [U] ~ (**for**) reason: *There's no* ~ *for concern.* ◇ *have* ~ *for complaint* **3** [C] organization or idea that is strongly supported: *the* ~ *of world peace* ● **cause** *v* [T] make sth happen, esp sth bad: *What* ~*d his death?*

causeway /ˈkɔːzweɪ/ *n* [C] raised road or path across water or wet ground

caustic /ˈkɔːstɪk/ *adj* **1** able to burn by chemical action: ~ *soda* **2** (of remarks) very bitter or critical ▶ **caustically** /-kli/ *adv*

caution /ˈkɔːʃn/ *n* **1** [U] great care **2** [C] (*GB*) warning given by the police to sb who has committed a minor crime **3** [U,C] warning words ● **caution** *v* [T] **1** warn sb of possible danger **2** (*GB, law*) warn sb that anything they say may be used in evidence against them in a law court ▶ **cautionary** /ˈkɔːʃənəri/ *adj* giving a warning: *a* ~*ary tale*

cautious /ˈkɔːʃəs/ *adj* very careful about what you do, esp to avoid danger ▶ **cautiously** *adv*

cavalcade /ˌkævlˈkeɪd/ *n* [C] procession of people on horseback, in cars, etc

cavalry /ˈkævlri/ *n* [C, with sing or pl verb] (*pl* -ies) soldiers fighting on horseback (esp in the past), or in armoured vehicles

cave /keɪv/ *n* [C] large hole in the side of a hill, or under the ground ● **cave** *v* [PV] **cave in** (**on sb/sth**) (of a roof, wall, etc) fall inwards; collapse

cavern /ˈkævən/ *n* [C] large cave ▶ **cavernous** *adj* (*written*) (of a room or space) large and often empty and/or dark

caviar (*also* **caviare**) /ˈkæviɑː(r)/ *n* [U] salted eggs of certain types of large fish, eaten as food

caving /ˈkeɪvɪŋ/ *n* [U] sport or activity of going into caves under the ground

cavity /ˈkævəti/ *n* [C] (*pl* -ies) (*fml*) small hole in sth solid, eg a tooth

cayenne /keɪˈen/ (*also* **cayenne 'pepper**) *n* [U] kind of hot red powdered pepper

CB /ˌsiː ˈbiː/ *abbr* Citizens' Band; range of waves on a radio on which people can talk to each other, esp when driving

cc /ˌsiː ˈsiː/ abbr cubic centimetre, as a measure of the power of an engine

CCTV /ˌsiː siː tiː ˈviː/ abbr = CLOSED-CIRCUIT TELEVISION (CLOSE[1])

0━ **CD** /ˌsiː ˈdiː/ abbr compact disc; small disc on which information or sound is recorded and reproduced by laser action. CDs are played on a special machine called a CD player.

CD-ROM /ˌsiː diː ˈrɒm/ n [C,U] compact disc read-only memory; CD on which large amounts of information, sound and pictures can be stored, for use on a computer: *The encyclopedia is available on ~.* ◇ a ~ drive (= in a computer)

0━ **cease** /siːs/ v [I,T] (fml) (cause sth to) stop happening or existing
■ **ceasefire** n [C] agreement to stop fighting ▸ **ceaseless** adj (fml) not stopping ▸ **ceaselessly** adv

cedar /ˈsiːdə(r)/ n 1 [C] tall evergreen tree with wide spreading branches 2 [U] hard sweet-smelling wood of this tree

0━ **ceiling** /ˈsiːlɪŋ/ n [C] 1 top inside surface of a room 2 official upper limit: *a price/wage ~*

0━ **celebrate** /ˈselɪbreɪt/ v 1 [I,T] mark a special occasion by enjoying yourself 2 [T] (fml) praise sb/sth ▸ **celebrated** adj famous ▸ **celebration** /ˌselɪˈbreɪʃn/ n [C,U]

celebrity /səˈlebrəti/ n (pl -ies) 1 [C] famous person 2 [U] fame

celery /ˈseləri/ n [U] plant whose white stems are eaten raw

celestial /səˈlestiəl/ adj (fml) of the sky; of heaven

celibate /ˈselɪbət/ adj not married and not having sex, esp for religious reasons ● **celibacy** /-bəsi/ n [U] ● **celibate** n [C] celibate person

0━ **cell** /sel/ n [C] 1 small room: *a prison ~* 2 smallest unit of living matter that can exist on its own: *red blood ~* 3 device for producing electric current by chemical action 4 small group of people, eg in a secret organization

cellar /ˈselə(r)/ n [C] underground room for storing things: *a wine ~*

cello /ˈtʃeləʊ/ n [C] (pl -s) kind of large violin, held between the knees ▸ **cellist** /ˈtʃelɪst/ n [C] person who plays a cello

Cellophane™ /ˈseləfeɪn/ n [U] thin transparent plastic material used for wrapping things

0━ **cellphone** /ˈselfəʊn/ n [C] (esp US) = MOBILE PHONE (MOBILE)

cellular /ˈseljələ(r)/ adj 1 connected with or consisting of plant or animal cells 2 connected with a telephone system that works by radio instead of wires 3 (GB) (of blankets, etc) loosely woven ■ **cellular 'phone** n

[C] (esp US) = MOBILE PHONE (MOBILE)

cellulite /ˈseljulaɪt/ n [U] type of fat just below the skin which stops the surface of the skin being smooth

Celsius /ˈselsiəs/ (also **centigrade**) (abbr C) adj, n [U] (of or using the) temperature scale in which water freezes at 0° and boils at 100°

cement /sɪˈment/ n [U] 1 grey powder that when mixed with water becomes hard like stone, used in building 2 kind of glue ● **cement** v [T] 1 join sth with cement 2 make a relationship, agreement, etc stronger

cemetery /ˈsemətri/ n [C] (pl -ies) place where dead people are buried

cenotaph /ˈsenətɑːf/ n [C] monument built in memory of soldiers killed in war

censor /ˈsensə(r)/ n [C] person whose job is to examine books, films, etc and remove parts considered indecent, offensive, etc ● **censor** v [T] examine or remove parts of a book, film, etc ▸ **censorship** n [U] act or policy of censoring books, etc

censure /ˈsenʃə(r)/ v [T] (fml) criticize sb strongly for sth they have done ● **censure** n [U]

census /ˈsensəs/ n [C] official counting of sth, esp of the population of a country

0━ **cent** /sent/ n [C] one 100th part of a main unit of money, eg a dollar

centaur /ˈsentɔː(r)/ n [C] (in Greek mythology) creature that is half man and half horse

centenarian /ˌsentɪˈneəriən/ n [C] person who is 100 years old or more

centenary /senˈtiːnəri/ n [C] (pl -ies) 100th anniversary

centennial /senˈteniəl/ adj [C] (esp US) centenary

center (US) = CENTRE

centigrade /ˈsentɪɡreɪd/ adj, n [U] = CELSIUS

0━ **centimetre** (US -meter) /ˈsentɪmiːtə(r)/ n [C] metric unit of length; 100th part of a metre

centipede /ˈsentɪpiːd/ n [C] small crawling creature with many legs

0━ **central** /ˈsentrəl/ adj 1 most important; main 2 at or of the centre ■ **central 'heating** n [U] system of heating a building from one main source through pipes and radiators ▸ **centrally** adv ■ **central 'processing unit** n [C] → CPU

centralize (also -ise) /ˈsentrəlaɪz/ v [I,T] (cause sth to) come under the control of one central authority ▸ **centralization** (also -isation) /ˌsentrəlaɪˈzeɪʃn/ n [U]

0— **centre** (US center) /'sentə(r)/
1 [C] middle point or part of sth **2** [C]
building or place for a particular
activity: *a shopping ~* **3** [C, usu sing]
point towards which people direct
their attention: *the ~ of attention*
4 (usu the centre) [sing] moderate
political position, between the
extremes of left and right ● **centre** v
[T] move sth so that it is in the centre
of sth else [PV] **centre (sth) around/
on/round/upon sb/sth** (cause sth to)
have sb/sth as its main concern

centrifugal /ˌsentrɪ'fjuːgl;
sen'trɪfjəgl/ *adj* (tech) moving away
from a centre: *~ force*

0— **century** /'sentʃəri/ n [C] (pl -ies)
1 period of 100 years **2** (in cricket)
100 runs by one player

ceramic /sə'ræmɪk/ n **1** [C, usu pl]
object made of clay that has been
made permanently hard by heat
2 (ceramics) [U] art of making and
decorating ceramics ► **ceramic** *adj*:
~ tiles

cereal /'sɪəriəl/ n [U, C] **1** (edible
grain produced by a) kind of grass,
eg wheat or barley **2** food made
from cereal grain: *breakfast ~s*

ceremonial /ˌserɪ'məʊniəl/ *adj*
relating to a ceremony:
a ~ occasion ● **ceremonial** [C, U]
system of rules, etc for ceremonies
► **ceremonially** /-niəli/ *adv*

ceremonious /ˌserə'məʊniəs/ *adj*
(written) very formal and polite
► **ceremoniously** *adv*

0— **ceremony** /'serəməni/ n (pl -ies)
1 [C] formal act(s), religious service,
etc on a special occasion: *a wedding
~* **2** [U] formal behaviour

0— **certain** /'sɜːtn/ *adj* **1** having no
doubts; sure **2** ~ (to) sure to happen:
They're ~ to win the game.
3 particular, but not named: *on ~
conditions* **4** slight; some: *a ~
coldness in his attitude* [IDM] **make
certain (that...)** find out whether sth
is definitely true: *Make ~ that no
bones are broken.* ► **certainly** *adv*
1 without doubt **2** (in answer to
questions) of course; yes
► **certainty** n (pl -ies) **1** [C] thing
that is certain **2** [U] state of being
sure

0— **certificate** /sə'tɪfɪkət/ n [C]
official paper that states certain
facts: *a birth ~*

certify /'sɜːtɪfaɪ/ v (pt, pp **-ied**) [T]
state officially, esp in writing, that
sth is true

cessation /se'seɪʃn/ n [U, C] (fml) the
stopping of sth

cesspit /'sespɪt/ (also cesspool
/'sespuːl/) n [C] underground hole
for collecting waste from a building,
esp the toilets

CFC /ˌsiː efˈsiː/ n [C, U]

chlorofluorocarbon; type of gas
used esp in aerosols. CFCs are
harmful to the layer of the gas ozone
in the earth's atmosphere

chador /'tʃɑːdɔː(r)/ n [C] large piece
of cloth that covers the head and
upper body, worn by some Muslim
women

chafe /tʃeɪf/ v [I, T] (cause sth to)
become sore by rubbing: *The rope
~d her wrists.* **2** [I] ~ **(at/under)**
become impatient because of sth

chaff /tʃɑːf/ n [U] outer covering of
grain, removed before the grain is
used as food

chagrin /'ʃægrɪn/ n [U] (fml)
disappointment or annoyance

0— **chain** /tʃeɪn/ n **1** [C, U] length of
metal rings joined together **2** [C]
series of connected things: *a ~ of
mountains/shops/events* ● **chain** v
[T] fasten sb/sth to another person
or thing with a chain ■ **chain
re'action** n [C] series of events, each
of which causes the next ■ **chain-
smoke** v [I, T] smoke cigarettes
continuously ► **chain-smoker** n [C]
■ **chain store** n [C] one of several
similar shops owned by the same
company

0— **chair** /tʃeə(r)/ n **1** [C] moveable
seat with a back, for one person
2 (the chair) [sing] (position of the)
person in charge of a meeting or
committee **3** [C] position of a
professor at a university ● **chair** v [T]
be in charge of a meeting
■ **'chairman** | **'chairperson** |
'chairwoman n [C] person in charge
of a meeting, committee, etc

chalet /'ʃæleɪ/ n [C] **1** Swiss
mountain hut built of wood **2** (GB)
small house in a holiday camp

chalk /tʃɔːk/ n [U] **1** kind of soft white
rock **2** [U, C] substance similar to
chalk made into white or coloured
sticks for writing or drawing ● **chalk**
v [I, T] write or draw with chalk [PV]
chalk up sth (infml) achieve a
success, points in a game, etc
► **chalky** *adj* (-ier, -iest) containing
or like chalk

0— **challenge** /'tʃælɪndʒ/ n [C]
1 difficult or demanding task
2 invitation to take part in a game,
fight, etc ● **challenge** v [T] **1** invite
sb to take part in a game, fight, etc
2 question the truth, rightness, etc
of sth ► **challenger** n [C]
► **challenging** *adj* difficult and
demanding

0— **chamber** /'tʃeɪmbə(r)/ n **1** [C]
large room in a public building used
for formal meetings: *the council ~*
2 (chambers) [pl] set of rooms used
by judges and barristers **3** [C, with
sing or pl verb] one of the parts of a
parliament **4** [C] room used for the
particular purpose mentioned: *a
burial ~* **5** [C] enclosed space: *the ~s
of the heart* ■ **'chambermaid** n [C]

woman whose job is to clean bedrooms in a hotel ■ **'chamber music** n [U] classical music written for a small group of instruments ■ **,Chamber of 'Commerce** n [C] group of business people organized to improve local trade interests

chameleon /kəˈmiːliən/ n [C] small lizard whose skin colour changes to match its surroundings

chamois /ˈʃæmwɑː/ n [C] (pl **chamois** /ˈʃæmwɑː/) animal like a small deer, that lives in the mountains of Europe and Asia ● **chamois** /ˈʃæmi/ n [C,U] (piece of) soft leather cloth from the skin of goats, etc, used esp for cleaning windows

champ /tʃæmp/ v [I] **1** (esp of horses) bite noisily **2** be impatient ■ **champ** n [C] (infml) = CHAMPION

champagne /ʃæmˈpeɪn/ n [U] sparkling white French wine

champion /ˈtʃæmpiən/ n [C] **1** person, team, etc that wins a competition **2** ~ (of) person who supports or defends sb or a principle: *a ~ of women's rights* ● **champion** v [T] fight or speak in support of a group of people or a belief ▶ **championship** n [C] **1** (also **championships** [pl]) competition to find the best player or team in a particular sport **2** position of being a champion

0— **chance** /tʃɑːns/ n **1** [C,U] possibility of sth happening, esp sth that you want: *no ~ of winning* **2** [C] suitable time when you have the opportunity to do sth: *have a ~ to apologize* **3** [C] unpleasant or dangerous possibility: *Don't take any ~s.* **4** [U] way in which things happen without any cause that can be seen; luck: *I met her by ~ at the station.* [IDM] **on the off chance (that)** because of the possibility of sth happening, although it is unlikely **take a chance (on sth)** decide to do sth, though it may not be the right choice ● **chance** v **1** [T] (infml) take a risk **2** [I] (written or fml) happen by chance ● **chance** adj not expected: *a ~ meeting* ● **chancy** adj (infml) risky

chancel /ˈtʃɑːnsl/ n [C] eastern part of a church, containing the altar

chancellor (also **Chancellor**) /ˈtʃɑːnsələ(r)/ n [C] **1** head of government in Germany or Austria **2** honorary head of a university in Britain ■ **Chancellor of the Ex'chequer** n [C] (GB) government minister responsible for finance

chandelier /ˌʃændəˈlɪə(r)/ n [C] decorative hanging light with branches for several bulbs or candles

0— **change¹** /tʃeɪndʒ/ v [I,T] become or make sth/sb different: *Our plans have ~d.* ◇ *Water ~s into steam.* ◇ *your attitude* **2** [T] replace one thing or person with another: *~ a light bulb* **3** [I,T] take off your clothes and put others on **4** [I,T] go from one train, bus, etc to another **5** [T] give and receive money in exchange for money of smaller value or in a foreign currency [IDM] **change hands** pass to another owner **change your/sb's mind** change a decision or opinion **change your tune** (infml) express a different opinion or behave differently when your situation changes [PV] **change over (from sth) (to sth)** change from one system or position to another ▶ **changeable** adj likely to change ■ **'changeover** n [C] change from one system or method of working to another

0— **change²** /tʃeɪndʒ/ n **1** [C,U] act or result of sth becoming different **2** (a change) [sing] fact of a situation, place, etc being different and therefore likely to be interesting, enjoyable, etc: *Let's stay in for a ~.* **3** [C] something used in place of another: *~ of name/clothes* **4** [U] money returned when the price of sth is less than the amount given **5** [U] coins of low value

0— **channel** /ˈtʃænl/ n [C] **1** television station **2** way by which news or information, may travel: *Your complaint must be made through the proper ~s.* **3** passage along which a liquid flows **4** narrow passage of water: *the English C~* ● **channel** v (-ll-; *US* -l-) **1** ~ **(into)** direct money, feelings, ideas, etc towards a particular thing or purpose: *~ all our resources into the new scheme* **2** carry or send water, light, etc through a passage

chant /tʃɑːnt/ n [C] **1** sing one or more words many times **2** sing a religious song or prayer using very few notes that are repeated many times ▶ **chant** n [C]

chaos /ˈkeɪɒs/ n [U] complete disorder or confusion ▶ **chaotic** /keɪˈɒtɪk/ adj

chap /tʃæp/ n [C] (GB, infml) man or boy ● **chap** v (-pp-) [I,T] (of the skin) (cause sth to) become cracked, rough and sore: *~ped lips*

chapel /ˈtʃæpl/ n [C] **1** place used for Christian worship, eg in a school or hospital **2** separate part of a church or cathedral, with its own altar

chaplain /ˈtʃæplɪn/ n [C] priest or Christian minister in the armed forces, a hospital, prison, etc

0— **chapter** /ˈtʃæptə(r)/ n [C] **1** (usu numbered) main division of a book **2** period of time

char /tʃɑː(r)/ v (-rr-) [I,T] (cause sth to) become black by burning ■ **'chargrill** v [T] to cook sth over a very high heat so that the outside is slightly burnt

0-w **character** /'kærəktə(r)/ n 1 [C] qualities that make sb, a country, etc different from others: *The ~ of the town has changed over the years.* **2** [U] particular quality of sth: *buildings that were simple in ~* **3** [C] interesting or unusual quality that a person or place has: *houses with no ~* **4** [U] moral strength: *a woman of ~* **5** [C] person in a play, novel, etc **6** [C] (*infml*) person, esp an unpleasant or a strange one **7** [C] letter or sign used in writing or printing: *Chinese ~s* [IDM] **in/out of character** typical/ not typical of sb's character
▶ **characterless** *adj* uninteresting; ordinary

0-w **characteristic** /ˌkærəktə'rɪstɪk/ *adj* typical of sth or sb's character
● **characteristic** *n* [C] typical quality or feature ▶ **characteristically** /-kli/ *adv*

characterize (*also* -ise) /'kærəktəraɪz/ v [T] (*fml*) **1** be typical of sb/sth **2** describe the qualities of sb/sth

charade /ʃə'rɑːd/ n **1** [C] absurd and obvious pretence **2** (**charades**) [U] party game in which one team acts a word that has to be guessed by the other team

charcoal /'tʃɑːkəʊl/ n [U] black substance of burnt wood, used as a fuel, for drawing, etc

0-w **charge¹** /tʃɑːdʒ/ n **1** [C, U] ask an amount of money for goods or a service: *They ~d me £50 for the repair.* **2** [T] to record sth as a debt to be paid by sb/sth: *C~ it to his account.* **3** [C] (*infml*) accuse sb of sth, esp in a law court: *He was ~d with murder.* **4** [U, T] rush forward and attack sb/sth **5** [C] put electricity into a battery **6** [T] ~ **with** (*esp passive*) (*written*) fill sb with an emotion: *a voice ~d with tension* **7** [U] ~ **with** (*fml*) give sb a duty or responsibility

0-w **charge²** /tʃɑːdʒ/ n **1** [C] price asked for goods or services **2** [C] formal claim that sb has done wrong: *a ~ of murder* **3** [U] responsibility and control: *She's in ~ of the accounts.* ◇ *take ~ of the department* **4** [C] sudden rush or violent attack **5** [C, U] amount of electricity put into a battery or carried by a substance [IDM] **in charge (of sb/sth)** having responsibility for and control of sb/ sth **bring/press/prefer charges against sb** (*law*) accuse sb formally of a crime so that there can be a trial in a court of law

chariot /'tʃæriət/ n [C] open vehicle with two wheels, pulled by horses, used in ancient times in battle and for racing ▶ **charioteer** /ˌtʃæriə'tɪə(r)/ n [C] driver of a chariot

charisma /kə'rɪzmə/ n [U] power to inspire devotion and enthusiasm ▶ **charismatic** /ˌkærɪz'mætɪk/ *adj*: *a ~tic politician*

charitable /'tʃærətəbl/ *adj* **1** kind in your attitude to others **2** of or connected with a charity (1) ▶ **charitably** /-bli/ *adv*

0-w **charity** /'tʃærəti/ n (pl -**ies**) **1** [C] organization that helps people in need **2** [U] money, food, etc given to people in need **3** [U] kindness towards others

charlatan /'ʃɑːlətən/ n [C] person who falsely claims to have a special skill or knowledge

charm /tʃɑːm/ n **1** [U] power of pleasing or attracting people **2** [C] pleasing quality **3** [C] object worn for good luck **4** [C] magic spell
● **charm** v [T] **1** please or attract sb **2** influence sb/sth (as if) using magic ▶ **charming** *adj* very pleasant or attractive

0-w **chart** /tʃɑːt/ n **1** [C] diagram, graph, etc giving information **2** [C] map of the sea **3** (**the charts**) [pl] (*esp GB*) weekly list of the best-selling pop music records ● **chart** v [T] **1** record or follow the progress or development of sb/sth **2** plan a course of action **3** make a map of an area

charter /'tʃɑːtə(r)/ n **1** [C] official written statement giving certain rights, privileges, principles, etc **2** [U] hiring of an aircraft or a ship ● **charter** v [T] hire an aircraft, a boat, etc for a particular purpose ▶ **chartered** *adj* qualified according to the rules of a certain profession: *'charter flight* n [C] flight in an aircraft in which all the seats are paid for by a travel company and then sold to their customers at a low price

0-w **chase** /tʃeɪs/ v [I, T] ~ **(after sb)** run, drive, etc after sb in order to catch them or make them go away ● **chase** n [C] act of chasing sb/sth

chasm /'kæzəm/ n [C] **1** deep opening in the ground **2** (*fml*) very big difference in attitude, etc between two people

chassis /'ʃæsi/ n [C] (pl **chassis** /-siz/) frame that a vehicle is built on

chaste /tʃeɪst/ *adj* **1** (*old-fash*) avoiding sexual activity **2** not expressing sexual feeling **3** (*fml*) simple and plain in style

chasten /'tʃeɪsn/ v [T] (*usu passive*) (*fml*) make sb feel sorry for sth they have done

chastise /tʃæ'staɪz/ v [T] (*fml*) criticize sb for doing sth wrong ▶ **chastisement** n [U]

chastity /'tʃæstəti/ n [U] state of not having sex with anyone or only with the person you are married to

chat /tʃæt/ n [C,U] friendly informal talk ● **chat** v (**-tt-**) [I] talk to sb in an informal way [PV] **chat sb up** (GB, infml) talk in a friendly way to sb you are sexually attracted to ■ '**chatline** n [C] telephone service which allows a number of people who call in separately to have a conversation, esp for fun ■ '**chat room** n [C] area on the Internet where people can communicate with each other ▶ **chatty** adj (**-ier, -iest**) talking a lot in a friendly way

chateau (also **château**) /ˈʃætəʊ/ n (pl **~x** /-təʊz/) castle or large country house in France

chatter /ˈtʃætə(r)/ v [I] 1 talk quickly and continuously about unimportant things 2 (of birds or monkeys) make short repeated high-pitched noises 3 (of the teeth) strike together from cold or fear ● **chatter** n [C] 1 continuous quick talk 2 series of high sounds that some animals make ■ '**chatterbox** n [C] person who talks a lot

chauffeur /ˈʃəʊfə(r)/ n [C] person whose job is to drive a car, esp for sb rich ● **chauffeur** v [T] drive sb in a car, usu as your job

chauvinism /ˈʃəʊvɪnɪzəm/ n [U] 1 excessive and unreasonable belief that your own country is the best 2 = MALE CHAUVINISM(MALE) ▶ **chauvinist** n [C] ▶ **chauvinistic** /ˌʃəʊvɪˈnɪstɪk/ adj

cheap /tʃiːp/ adj 1 costing little money 2 of poor quality: ~ and nasty 3 unkind and unfair: a ~ joke ▶ **cheapen** v [T] 1 make sb lose respect for himself or herself 2 lower the price of sth 3 make sth appear to have less value ▶ **cheaply** adv ▶ **cheapness** n [U]

cheat /tʃiːt/ v [I] act dishonestly: ~ in an examination [PV] **cheat sb (out) of sth** prevent sb from having sth by dishonest behaviour ● **cheat** n [C] person who cheats

check¹ /tʃek/ v 1 [T] examine sth to make sure it is correct, safe, satisfactory, etc 2 [T] find out if sth is correct or true, or if sth is how you think it is 3 [T] cause sb/sth to stop; control sth: ~ the enemy's progress [PV] **check in** inform sb of your arrival at an airport, a hotel, etc **check sth in** leave bags or cases with an official to be put on a plane **check out (of ...)** pay your bill and leave a hotel **check sth out** 1 find out if sth is correct, true or acceptable 2 (infml) look at or examine sth that seems interesting or attractive **check up on sb** make sure that sb is doing what they should be doing **check up on sth** examine sth to discover if it is true, safe, correct, etc ■ '**check-in** n 1 [C] place where you go first when you arrive at an airport 2 [U] act of showing your ticket, etc when you arrive at an airport: the ~-in desk ■ **checkout** n 1 [C] place where customers pay for goods in a supermarket 2 [U] time when you leave a hotel at the end of your stay ■ **checkpoint** n [C] place, eg on a frontier, where travellers and vehicles are inspected ■ '**check-up** n [C] medical examination to make sure that you are healthy

check² /tʃek/ n 1 [C] ~ (on) examination to make sure that sth is correct, safe, satisfactory, etc 2 [U] (fml) control: hold/keep your emotions in ~ 3 [U,C] pattern of squares, usu two colours: a ~ shirt 4 [C] (US) = CHEQUE 5 [C] (US) bill in a restaurant 6 [U] (in chess) position in which a player's king can be directly attacked 7 [C] (US) = TICK(1)

checkered (esp US) = CHEQUERED

checkers /ˈtʃekəz/ n [U] (US) = DRAUGHTS(3)

checkmate /ˈtʃekmeɪt/ n [U] 1 (in chess) situation in which one player cannot prevent the capture of his/her king and therefore loses the game 2 total defeat

cheek /tʃiːk/ n 1 [C] either side of the face below the eyes 2 [U] rude and disrespectful behaviour or talk ● **cheek** v [T] (GB, infml) speak to sb in a rude way that shows a lack of respect ▶ **cheeky** adj (**-ier, -iest**) (GB) rude and disrespectful ▶ **cheekily** adv

cheer /tʃɪə(r)/ v [I,T] give shouts of praise, support, etc to sb 2 [T] give hope, comfort or encouragement to sb: ~ing news [PV] **cheer (sb/sth) up** (cause sb/sth) to become more cheerful ● **cheer** n 1 [C] shout of praise, support, etc 2 (old-fash) happiness

cheerful /ˈtʃɪəfl/ adj 1 happy 2 giving you a feeling of happiness: a bright, ~ restaurant ▶ **cheerfully** adv: to laugh/nod/whistle ~ ▶ **cheerless** adj sad; gloomy

cheerio /ˌtʃɪəriˈəʊ/ exclam (GB, infml) goodbye

cheers /tʃɪəz/ exclam 1 word that people say to each other as they lift up their glasses to drink 2 (GB, infml) thank you

cheery /ˈtʃɪəri/ adj (**-ier, -iest**) lively and happy ▶ **cheerily** adv

cheese /tʃiːz/ n [U,C] solid food made from milk ■ '**cheesecake** n [C,U] cold sweet dish made with cream cheese on a base of crushed biscuits ■ '**cheesecloth** n [U] loosely woven cotton cloth ■ '**cheesed 'off** adj (GB, infml) annoyed, bored or frustrated

cheetah /ˈtʃiːtə/ n [C] spotted African wild animal of the cat family, able to run very fast

chef /ʃef/ n [C] chief cook in a restaurant, hotel, etc

0⇉ **chemical** /ˈkemɪkl/ adj 1 of or relating to chemistry 2 produced by or using processes which involve changes to atoms or molecules: a ~ reaction ● **chemical** n [C] substance obtained by or used in a chemical process ▸ **chemically** /-kli/ adv ■ **chemical 'warfare** n [U] use of poisonous gases and chemicals as weapons in a war ■ **chemical 'weapon** n [C] weapon that uses poisonous gases and chemicals to kill and injure people

0⇉ **chemist** /ˈkemɪst/ n [C] 1 person whose job is to prepare and sell medicines, and who works in a shop 2 student or expert in chemistry

0⇉ **chemistry** /ˈkemɪstri/ n [U] scientific study of the structure of substances and how they combine together

0⇉ **cheque** (US **check**) /tʃek/ n [C] written order to a bank to pay money ■ **chequebook** (US **checkbook**) n [C] book of printed cheques ■ **cheque card** n [C] card issued by a bank to sb who has an account with it, guaranteeing payment of his/her cheques up to a stated amount

chequered (US **checkered**) /ˈtʃekəd/ adj having good and bad parts: a ~ history

cherish /ˈtʃerɪʃ/ v [T] (written) 1 love sb/sth very much and want to protect them if 2 keep an idea, a hope, etc in your mind for a long time: ~ed memories

cherry /ˈtʃeri/ n [C] (pl **-ies**) small round red or black fruit with a stone inside

cherub /ˈtʃerəb/ n [C] 1 (in art) kind of angel 2 (infml) pretty young child; child who behaves well

chess /tʃes/ n [U] board game for two players

0⇉ **chest** /tʃest/ n 1 [C] upper front part of the body 2 [C] large strong box [IDM] **get sth off your chest** (infml) say sth that you have wanted to say for a long time ■ **chest of 'drawers** n [C] (pl **~s of drawers**) piece of furniture with drawers for keeping clothes in

chestnut /ˈtʃesnʌt/ n [C] (tree producing a) smooth reddish-brown nut ● **chestnut** adj reddish-brown in colour

0⇉ **chew** /tʃuː/ v [I,T] 1 bite food into small pieces in your mouth with your teeth 2 bite sth continuously, eg because you are nervous: Don't ~ your nails. [PV] **chew sth over** think

about sth slowly and carefully ● **chew** n [C] ■ **chewing gum** n [U] type of sweet that you chew but do not swallow ▸ **chewy** adj (**-ier, -iest**) (of food) needing to be chewed a lot

chic /ʃiːk/ adj fashionable; elegant

chick /tʃɪk/ n [C] young bird, esp a young chicken

0⇉ **chicken** /ˈtʃɪkɪn/ n 1 [C] large bird, often kept for its eggs or meat 2 [U] meat from a chicken ● **chicken** adj (sl) not brave; cowardly ● **chicken** v [PV] **chicken out (of sth/ doing sth)** (infml) decide not to do sth because you are afraid ■ **chicken flu** n [C] = BIRD FLU ■ **chickenpox** n [U] disease, esp of children, causing red spots on the skin

chicory /ˈtʃɪkəri/ n [U] small pale green plant with bitter leaves that can be eaten raw in salads. The root can be dried and used with coffee.

0⇉ **chief** /tʃiːf/ n [C] highest official; leader or ruler ● **chief** adj 1 most important; main 2 having the highest rank ■ **chief 'constable** n [C] (GB) head of the police force in a particular area ▸ **chiefly** adv mainly ■ **-in-'chief** (in compound nouns) highest in rank

chieftain /ˈtʃiːftən/ n [C] leader of a tribe

0⇉ **child** /tʃaɪld/ n [C] (pl **children** /ˈtʃɪldrən/) 1 young human being 2 son or daughter of any age ■ **childbirth** n [U] act of giving birth to a child ▸ **childhood** n [U,C] state or time of being a child ■ **childish** adj (of an adult) behaving like a child ▸ **childless** adj having no children ■ **childlike** adj simple; innocent ■ **childminder** n [C] (GB) person whose job is to care for children while their parents are at work

0⇉ **chill** /tʃɪl/ v 1 [I,T] become or make sb/sth cold 2 [T] (lit) frighten sb 3 (also **chill out**) [I] (infml) to spend time relaxing: to ~ in front of the TV ● **chill** n 1 [sing] feeling of being cold 2 [C] illness caused by cold and damp 3 [sing] feeling of fear: sent a ~ down my spine. ▸ **chilly** adj (**-ier, -iest**) 1 too cold to be comfortable 2 unfriendly

0⇉ **chilli** (US **chili**) /ˈtʃɪli/ n [C,U] (pl **~es**) small green or red fruit of a type of pepper plant used in cooking to give a hot taste to food, often dried or made into powder (**chilli powder**) ■ **chilli con carne** /ˌtʃɪli kɒn ˈkɑːni/ n [U] hot spicy Mexican dish made with meat, beans and chillies

chime /tʃaɪm/ n [C] ringing sound, esp one made by a bell ● **chime** v [I,T] (of a bell or clock) ring; show the time by making a ringing sound

chimney /ˈtʃɪmni/ n [C] structure through which smoke is carried away from a fire and through the roof of a building ■ **chimney pot** n [C] (GB) short pipe fitted to the top of a chimney ■ **chimney stack** n [C] part of the chimney that is above the roof of a building ■ **chimney sweep** n [C] person whose job is to clean the inside of chimneys

chimpanzee /ˌtʃɪmpænˈziː/ (also infml chimp) n [C] small intelligent African ape

0➔ **chin** /tʃɪn/ n [C] part of the face below the mouth

0➔ **china** /ˈtʃaɪnə/ n [U] **1** white clay which is baked and used for making delicate cups, plates, etc **2** cups and plates, etc that are made from china

chink /tʃɪŋk/ n [C] **1** narrow opening in sth **2** small area of light shining through a narrow opening **3** light ringing sound that is made when glass objects or coins touch ● **chink** [i] make a ringing sound when glass objects, coins, etc hit together

0➔ **chip** /tʃɪp/ n [C] **1** (GB) [usu pl] long thin piece of potato fried in oil or fat: fish and ~s **2** place from which a small piece of wood, glass, etc has broken from an object: a cup with a ~ in it **3** small piece of wood, glass, etc which has broken from an object **4** (US) = CRISP **5** = MICROCHIP **6** flat piece of plastic used in gambling to represent an amount of money [IDM] **have a chip on your shoulder** (about sth) (infml) be sensitive about sth that happened in the past because you think you were treated unfairly ● **chip** (-pp-) v [I,T] (cause sth to) become damaged by breaking a small piece off the edge of sth [PV] **chip in** (with sth) (infml) **1** join in or interrupt a conversation: She ~ped in with a couple of useful comments. **2** give money so a group of people can buy sth together ■ **chip card** n [C] plastic card on which information is stored in the form of a microchip ■ **chip and pin** n [U] system of paying for sth with a chip card. You prove your identity by typing a number (your PIN) rather than by signing your name.

chiropodist /kɪˈrɒpədɪst/ n [C] person whose job is to treat minor problems people have with their feet ▶ **chiropody** /kɪˈrɒpədi/ n [U]

chirp /tʃɜːp/ v [I], n [C] (make the short sharp sound of small birds ▶ **chirpy** adj (-ier, -iest) (infml) lively and happy

chisel /ˈtʃɪzl/ n [C] tool with a sharp end for cutting wood or stone ● **chisel** v (-ll-) (US also -l-) [T] cut or shape sth with a chisel

chit /tʃɪt/ n [C] note showing an amount of money owed

chivalry /ˈʃɪvəlri/ n [U] **1** rules and customs of knights in the Middle Ages **2** good manners, eg honour and politeness, esp as shown by

men towards women ▶ **chivalrous** /ˈʃɪvlrəs/ adj

chlorine /ˈklɔːriːn/ n [U] (symb Cl) strong-smelling greenish-yellow gas often used in swimming pools to keep the water clean

chlorofluorocarbon /ˌklɔːrəˌflʊərəʊˈkɑːbɒn/ n [C] → CFC

chlorophyll /ˈklɒrəfɪl/ n [U] green substance in plants that absorbs energy from sunlight to help them grow

0➔ **chocolate** /ˈtʃɒklət/ n **1** [U] hard brown sweet food made from cocoa beans **2** [C] sweet made of or covered with chocolate **3** [U] hot drink made from chocolate ● **chocolate** n [U] adj (of a) dark brown colour

0➔ **choice** /tʃɔɪs/ n **1** [C] act of choosing between two or more possibilities **2** [U] right or possibility of choosing: I had no ~ but to leave. **3** [C] variety from which to choose: a large ~ of restaurants **4** [C] person or thing chosen: She was the right ~ for the job. ● **choice** adj of high quality: ~ fruit

choir /ˈkwaɪə(r)/ n [C] **1** [with sing or pl verb] group of singers **2** part of a church where the choir sits

choke /tʃəʊk/ v **1** [I,T] (cause sb to) be unable to breathe because the windpipe is blocked **2** [T] block or fill a passage, space, etc: The drains are ~d with dead leaves. [PV] **choke sth back** prevent your feelings from showing: He ~d back the tears. ● **choke** n [C] device that controls the amount of air flowing into the engine of a vehicle

cholera /ˈkɒlərə/ n [U] infectious and often fatal disease caught from infected water

cholesterol /kəˈlestərɒl/ n [U] fatty substance found in blood, fat and most tissues of the body

0➔ **choose** /tʃuːz/ v (pt **chose** /tʃəʊz/ pp **chosen** /ˈtʃəʊzn/) **1** [I,T] decide which thing or person you want out of the ones available: You can't have all of the sweets, you must ~ one. **2** [T] prefer or decide to do sth: She chose to become a doctor.

0➔ **chop** /tʃɒp/ v [T] (-pp-) cut sth into pieces with an axe, a knife, etc ● **chop** n [C] **1** thick slice of meat, esp pork or lamb, with a bone attached to it **2** act of chopping sth

chopper /ˈtʃɒpə(r)/ n [C] **1** (infml) = HELICOPTER **2** heavy knife or small axe

choppy /ˈtʃɒpi/ adj (-ier, -iest) (of the sea) with a lot of small waves; not calm

chopstick /ˈtʃɒpstɪk/ n [usu pl] either of a pair of thin sticks used for eating with, esp in Asian countries

choral

choral /ˈkɔːrəl/ adj of or for a choir

chord /kɔːd/ n [C] **1** musical notes played together **2** (maths) straight line that joins two points on a curve

chore /tʃɔː(r)/ n [C] ordinary or boring task

choreography /ˌkɒriˈɒɡrəfi/ n [U] art of designing and arranging steps for dances on stage ► **choreographer** /ˌkɒriˈɒɡrəfə(r)/ n [C]

chorister /ˈkɒrɪstə(r)/ n [C] person, esp a boy, who sings in a church choir

chorus /ˈkɔːrəs/ n **1** [C] part of a song that is sung after each verse **2** [C] (piece of music for a) large group of singers **3** [sing] ~ of something said by many people together: *a ~ of approval* ● **chorus** v [T] sing or say sth all together

chose pt of CHOOSE

chosen pp of CHOOSE

Christ /kraɪst/ (also **Jesus, Jesus Christ**) n [sing] founder of the Christian religion

christen /ˈkrɪsn/ v [T] **1** give a name to a baby at his/her baptism to welcome him/her into the Christian church **2** give a name to sb/sth **3** (infml) use sth for the first time ► **christening** n [C]

Christian /ˈkrɪstʃən/ n [C] person who believes in the Christian religion ● **Christian** adj **1** of Christianity **2** showing the qualities of a Christian; kind ► **Christianity** /ˌkrɪstiˈænəti/ n [U] religion based on the belief that Christ was the son of God, and on his teachings ■ **Christian name** n [C] (GB) first name

Christmas /ˈkrɪsməs/ (also **Christmas Day**) n [U,C] yearly celebration of the birth of Christ; 25 December

chrome /krəʊm/ n [U] hard shiny metal used esp as a protective covering on other metals; chromium

chromium /ˈkrəʊmiəm/ n [U] (symb **Cr**) metallic element used esp as a shiny protective covering on other metals

chromosome /ˈkrəʊməsəʊm/ n [C] (biol) one of the fine threads in animal and plant cells, carrying genes

chronic /ˈkrɒnɪk/ adj **1** (of an illness) lasting a long time **2** (GB, infml) very bad ► **chronically** /-kli/ adv

chronicle /ˈkrɒnɪkl/ n [C] written record of events in the order in which they happened ● **chronicle** v [T] record events in the order in which they happened

chronology /krəˈnɒlədʒi/ n [U,C] (pl **-ies**) order in which a series of events

happened; list of these events in order ► **chronological** /ˌkrɒnəˈlɒdʒɪkl/ adj (of a number of events) arranged in the order in which they happened: *Present the facts in chronological order.* ► **chronologically** /-kli/ adv

chronometer /krəˈnɒmɪtə(r)/ n [C] very accurate clock

chrysalis /ˈkrɪsəlɪs/ n [C] form of an insect, esp a butterfly or moth, while it is changing into an adult inside a hard case

chrysanthemum /krɪˈsænθəməm/ n [C] garden plant with brightly coloured flowers

chubby /ˈtʃʌbi/ adj (**-ier, -iest**) slightly fat

chuck /tʃʌk/ v [T] (esp GB, infml) **1** throw sth carelessly **2** give up or stop doing sth **3** leave your boyfriend/girlfriend and stop having a relationship with him/her **4** (spoken) throw sth away ● **chuck** n [C] part of a tool such as a drill that can be adjusted to hold sth tightly

chuckle /ˈtʃʌkl/ v [I] laugh quietly ● **chuckle** n [C]

chum /tʃʌm/ n [C] (infml) friend ► **chummy** adj (**-ier, -iest**) friendly

chunk /tʃʌŋk/ n [C] **1** thick piece or lump: *a ~ of cheese* **2** (infml) fairly large amount of sth ► **chunky** adj (**-ier, -iest**) **1** thick and heavy: *~y jewellery* **2** having a short strong body **3** (of food) containing thick pieces

0➡ **church** /tʃɜːtʃ/ n **1** [C] building for public Christian worship **2** (**Church**) [C] particular group of Christians: *the Anglican C~* **3** ((the) **Church**) [sing] ministers of the Christian religion; the institution of the Christian religion: *go into/enter the C~* (= become a Christian minister) ■ **churchyard** n [C] enclosed area of land around a church, often used for burying people

churn /tʃɜːn/ n [C] **1** container in which milk or cream is shaken to make butter **2** (GB) large metal container in which milk is carried ● **churn** v **1** [T] beat milk or cream to make butter **2** [I,T] move (sth) around violently [PV] **churn sth out** (infml) produce sth in large amounts

chute /ʃuːt/ n [C] tube or passage down which people or things can slide

chutney /ˈtʃʌtni/ n [U] cold thick sauce made from fruit, spices, sugar and vinegar, eaten with cheese, etc

ciabatta /tʃəˈbætə/ n [U,C] type of Italian bread made in a long flat shape

cider /ˈsaɪdə(r)/ n [U,C] alcoholic drink made from apples

cigar /sɪˈɡɑː(r)/ n [C] roll of dried

tobacco leaves that people smoke, like a *cigarette* but bigger

0-w **cigarette** /ˌsɪgə'ret/ n [C] thin tube of paper filled with tobacco for smoking

cinder /'sɪndə(r)/ n [C, usu pl] small piece of partly burnt coal, etc

0-w **cinema** /'sɪnəmə/ n (GB) **1** [C] place where films are shown **2** (the cinema) [sing] films as an art or industry

cinnamon /'sɪnəmən/ n [U] yellowish-brown spice used in cooking

cipher (also **cypher**) /'saɪfə(r)/ n **1** [C,U] secret system of writing in which symbols or letters represent other letters **2** [C] (fml, disapprov) person or thing of no importance

circa /'sɜːkə/ prep (abbr **c**) (used with dates) about: born ~ 150 BC

0-w **circle** /'sɜːkl/ n [C] **1** (space enclosed by a) curved line, every point on which is the same distance from the centre **2** ring **3** group of people: our ~ of friends **4** upstairs seats in a theatre, etc ● **circle** v **1** [I,T] move in a circle, esp in the air **2** [T] draw a circle around sth

circuit /'sɜːkɪt/ n [C] **1** line or journey round a place: a racing ~ **2** complete path around which an electric current flows **3** series of places or events: a lecture ~ ► **circuitous** /sɜː'kjuːɪtəs/ adj (fml) long and indirect: a ~ous route

circular /'sɜːkjələ(r)/ adj **1** shaped like a circle; round **2** moving around in a circle: a ~ route ● **circular** n [C] printed letter, advertisement, etc sent to a large number of people

circulate /'sɜːkjəleɪt/ v [I,T] **1** (cause sth to) go around continuously; move about freely **2** pass (sth) from one person to another ► **circulation** /ˌsɜːkjə'leɪʃn/ n [U] **1** movement of blood round the body **2** [U] passing of sth from one person to another: the circulation of money **3** [U] fact that sb takes part in social activities at a particular time: He's been out of circulation for months with a bad back. **4** [C, usu sing] usual number of copies of a newspaper or magazine that are sold each day, week, etc

circumcise /'sɜːkəmsaɪz/ v [T] cut off the skin at the end of the penis of a man or boy ► **circumcision** /ˌsɜːkəm'sɪʒn/ n [C,U]

circumference /sə'kʌmfərəns/ n [C,U] (length of the) line that goes around a circle or any other curved shape: the earth's ~

circumflex /'sɜːkəmfleks/ n [C] mark over a vowel, as in French: rôle

circumnavigate /ˌsɜːkəm'nævɪgeɪt/ v [T] (fml) sail all the way around sth, esp the world ► **circumnavigation** /ˌsɜːkəmˌnævɪ'geɪʃn/ n [C,U]

circumspect /'sɜːkəmspekt/ adj (fml) cautious

0-w **circumstance** /'sɜːkəmstəns/ n **1** [C, usu pl] condition connected with an event or action: the ~s of his death **2** (circumstances) [pl] conditions of a person's life, esp the money they have **3** [U] situations and events that affect you but are not in your control: a victim of ~ **[IDM]** in/under the circumstances this being the case **in/under no circumstances** never

circumstantial /ˌsɜːkəm'stænʃl/ adj **1** (law) (of evidence) having details that strongly suggest sth but do not prove it **2** (fml) connected with particular circumstances

circus /'sɜːkəs/ n **1** [C] group of entertainers, sometimes with trained animals, who perform in a show that travels around to different places **2** (the circus) [sing] show performed by circus entertainers, usu in a large tent: We took the children to the ~. **3** (GB) (in some place names) open space in a town where several streets meet: Piccadilly C~

cistern /'sɪstən/ n [C] water tank, eg above a toilet

cite /saɪt/ v [T] (fml) **1** mention sth as an example or to support an argument **2** quote sth **3** (law) order sb to appear in court; name sb officially in a legal case ► **citation** /saɪ'teɪʃn/ n [C] **1** quotation **2** [U] act of citing sb/sth

0-w **citizen** /'sɪtɪzn/ n [C] **1** person who has full rights as a member of a country **2** person who lives in a town or city ■ **Citizens' Band** n [U] = CB ► **citizenship** n [U] legal rights, duties and state of being a citizen

citric acid /ˌsɪtrɪk 'æsɪd/ n [U] kind of weak acid from such fruits as oranges and lemons

citrus /'sɪtrəs/ n [C] any of a group of related trees including the lemon, lime and orange: ~ fruit

0-w **city** /'sɪti/ n (pl -ies) **1** [C] large important town **2** [C, with sing or pl verb] all the people living in a city **3** (the City) [sing] financial and business centre of London

civic /'sɪvɪk/ adj of a town or city or its citizens

0-w **civil** /'sɪvl/ adj **1** of the citizens of a country **2** connected with the state rather than with religion or with the armed forces: a ~ marriage ceremony **3** polite in a formal way ■ **civil engineering** n [U] design and building of roads, bridges, etc ■ **civility** /sə'vɪləti/ n (fml) **1** [U] polite behaviour **2** [C] (civilities) [pl] polite remarks ► **civilly** /'sɪvəli/ adv ■ **civil rights** n [pl] rights of each

civil (top right header)

A B **C** D E F G H I J K L M N O P Q R S T U V W X Y Z

citizen to freedom and equality
■ civil 'servant n [C] person who works in the civil service ■ the civil 'service n [sing] all government departments in a country, except the armed forces, and the people who work for them ■ civil 'war n [C,U] war between groups of people in the same country

civilian /sə'vɪliən/ n [C], adj (person) not of the armed forces

civilization (also -isation) /ˌsɪvəlaɪ'zeɪʃn/ n 1 [U] (esp advanced) state of human social development and organization 2 [C,U] culture and way of life of a society at a particular time and place: the history of western ~

civilize (also -ise) /'sɪvəlaɪz/ v [T] educate and improve a person or society; make sb's behaviour or manners better: the ~d world

CJD /ˌsiː dʒeɪ 'diː/ abbr = CREUTZFELDT-JAKOB DISEASE

clad /klæd/ adj (written) ~ (in) wearing a particular type of clothing

0━ claim /kleɪm/ v [T] 1 say that sth is true, without being able to prove it: He ~s to be a British citizen. 2 ask for or demand sth as your legal right 3 (written) (of a disaster, etc) cause sb's death: The earthquake ~ed thousands of lives. ● claim n 1 [C] statement that sth is true, without being able to prove it 2 [C,U] legal right that sb believes they have to sth, esp land or property 3 [C] request for money that you believe you have a right to, esp from the government, a company, etc: an insurance ~ ▶ claimant n [C] person who claims sth as their legal right

clairvoyance /kleə'vɔɪəns/ n [U] supposed power of seeing future events in the mind ▶ clairvoyant n [C], adj (person) having such power

clam /klæm/ n [C] large edible shellfish that has a shell in two parts that can open and close ● clam v (-mm-) [PV] clam up (on sb) (infml) refuse to speak

clamber /'klæmbə(r)/ v [I] climb with difficulty

clammy /'klæmi/ adj (-ier, -iest) unpleasantly damp and sticky

clamour (US -or) /'klæmə(r)/ n [C,U] (fml) loud confused noise ● clamour [I] ~ (for) demand sth noisily

clamp /klæmp/ n [C] tool for holding things tightly together, usu with a screw ● clamp v [T] fasten two things together with a clamp [PV] clamp down on sb/sth take strict action in order to prevent sth, esp crime ■ clampdown n [usu sing] sudden action taken to stop an illegal activity

clan /klæn/ n [C] large family group, esp in Scotland

clandestine /klæn'destɪn/ adj (fml) secret: a ~ organization

clang /klæŋ/ v [I,T] (cause sth to) make a loud ringing sound like that of metal being hit ▶ clang n [C]

clank /klæŋk/ v [I,T] (cause sth to) make a sound like pieces of metal hitting each other ▶ clank n [C]

0━ clap /klæp/ v (-pp-) [T] 1 hit your open hands together several times to show your approval of sth 2 [T] hit sb lightly with your open hand: ~ sb on the back/shoulder 3 [T] (infml) put sth/sb somewhere quickly and suddenly: She ~ped her hand over her mouth. ● clap n [C] 1 act or sound of clapping 2 sudden loud noise, esp of thunder ■ clapped 'out adj (GB, infml) (of a car or machine) old and in bad condition

claret /'klærət/ n [U,C] kind of red French wine ● claret adj dark red

clarify /'klærəfaɪ/ v (pt, pp -ied) [T] make sth clearer and easier to understand ▶ clarification /ˌklærəfɪ'keɪʃn/ n [U,C]

clarinet /ˌklærə'net/ n [C] kind of woodwind musical instrument ▶ clarinettist (also clarinetist) n [C] person who plays the clarinet

clarity /'klærəti/ n [U] 1 quality of being expressed clearly 2 ability to think about or understand sth clearly

clash /klæʃ/ v 1 [I] fight or argue with sb 2 [I] (of ideas, personalities, etc) be very different and opposed to one another 3 [I] (of events) happen at the same time so that you cannot go to or see them both 4 [I] (of colours, patterns, etc) look ugly when put together 5 [I,T] hit sth together with a harsh ringing noise ● clash n [C] 1 short fight, argument or disagreement 2 difference between two opposing things: a personality ~ with his boss 3 loud noise made by two metal objects being hit together: a ~ of cymbals

clasp /klɑːsp/ n [C] 1 device for fastening things together: the ~ of a necklace 2 firm hold with your hand ● clasp v [T] 1 hold sb/sth tightly 2 fasten sth with a clasp

0━ class /klɑːs/ n 1 [C, with sing or pl verb] group of students taught together 2 [C,U] period of time when a group of students meets to be taught 3 [C, with sing or pl verb] social group at a particular level: the working/middle/upper ~ 4 [C] way that people are divided into different social and economic groups 5 [C] group of people, animals or things with similar qualities 6 [U] (infml) elegance ● class v [T] think or decide that sb/sth is a particular type of person or thing: *Immigrant workers are ~ed as aliens.* ■ **classroom** *n* [C] room in a school in which a class of students is taught ■ **classy** *adj* (**-ier, -iest**) (*infml*) fashionable; stylish

0—w **classic** /'klæsɪk/ *adj* 1 typical: *a ~ example* 2 of very high quality: *a ~ film/novel* ● **classic** *n* 1 [C] book, film or song of high quality and lasting value: *The novel will become a modern ~.* 2 (**Classics**) [U] (study of the) languages and literature of ancient Greece and Rome

classical /'klæsɪkl/ *adj* 1 traditional 2 of the style of ancient Greece and Rome 3 (of music) serious and having a value that lasts
▸ **classically** /-kli/ *adv*

classify /'klæsɪfaɪ/ *v* (pt, pp **-ied**) [T] arrange sth into groups according to the features that they have in common ▸ **classification** /ˌklæsɪfɪ'keɪʃn/ *n* [C, U] ▸ **classified** *adj* officially secret: *classified information*

clatter /'klætə(r)/ *n* [sing] loud noise made by hard objects hitting each other: *the ~ of horses' hoofs* ● **clatter** *v* [I]

clause /klɔːz/ *n* [C] 1 (*gram*) group of words that contains a subject and a verb 2 (*law*) section of a legal document

claustrophobia /ˌklɔːstrə'fəʊbiə/ *n* [U] extreme fear of being in an enclosed space

claw /klɔː/ *n* [C] 1 hard curved nail at the end of the foot of an animal or a bird 2 long, sharp curved part of the body of some shellfish 3 device like a claw for gripping and lifting things ● **claw** *v* [I,T] ~ (**at**) tear or scratch sb/ sth with claws or with your fingernails [PV] **claw sth back 1** get sth back that you have lost, usu by using a lot of effort 2 (of a government) get back money that has been paid to people, usu by taxing them ■ **clawback** *n* [C] (*GB, business*) act of getting money back from people it has been paid to; money that is paid back

clay /kleɪ/ *n* [U] stiff sticky earth that becomes hard when baked, used for making bricks, pots, etc

0—w **clean**[1] /kliːn/ *adj* 1 not dirty 2 (of paper) with nothing written on it 3 not offensive or referring to sex: *a ~ joke* 4 not having any record of doing sth that is against the law: *a ~ driving licence* 5 smooth; regular: *a ~ cut* [IDM] **make a clean breast of sth** make a full confession of sth ● **clean** *adv* (*infml*) completely: *I ~ forgot about it.* ■ **come clean (with sb) (about sth)** make a full and honest confession ■ **clean-'cut** *adj* (esp of a man) looking neat and clean and therefore socially acceptable ■ **clean-'shaven** *adj* not having a beard or moustache

0—w **clean**[2] /kliːn/ *v* [T] make sth clean [PV] **clean sb out** (*infml*) take all sb's money **clean sth out** clean the inside of sth thoroughly: *He ~ed out the fish tank.* **clean (sth) up 1** remove dirt, rubbish, etc from a place 2 (*infml*) make or win a lot of money **clean sth up** remove crime and immoral behaviour from a place or an activity ● **clean** *n* [sing]: *The car needs a good ~.* ▸ **cleaner** *n* [C] 1 person whose job is to clean other people's houses, offices, etc 2 machine or substance that cleans: *a vacuum ~ ◊ window ~* 3 (**cleaner's**) (also **dry-'cleaner's**) shop where clothes, etc are cleaned with chemicals, not water

cleanliness /'klenlinəs/ *n* [U] state of being clean

cleanly /'kliːnli/ *adv* easily; smoothly

cleanse /klenz/ *v* [T] clean your skin or a wound ▸ **cleanser** *n* [C] substance that cleanses

0—w **clear**[1] /klɪə(r)/ *adj* 1 easy to understand, see or hear: *glass ~* 2 easy to understand, see or hear: *a ~ explanation of the problems* 3 obvious; definite: *a ~ case of cheating* 4 without doubt or confusion; certain: *I'm not ~ about what I should do.* 5 free from obstructions 6 ~ (**of**) not touching sth 7 without cloud or mist: *a ~ sky* 8 without spots: *~ skin* 9 free from guilt: *a ~ conscience* 10 (of a sum of money) with nothing to be taken away: *~ profit* [IDM] **make sth/ yourself clear** express sth/yourself in such a way that your wishes, etc are fully understood ● **clear** *n* [IDM] **in the clear** (*infml*) no longer in danger or suspected of sth ● **clear** *adv* 1 away from sth; not near or touching sth: *Stand ~ of the doors.* 2 (*esp US*) all the way to sth that is far away [IDM] **keep/stay/steer clear (of sb/sth)** avoid a person or thing because they/it may cause problems ■ **clear-'cut** *adj* definite and easy to see or identify ■ **clear-'headed** *n* able to think clearly ▸ **clearly** *adv* in a way that is easy to see, hear or understand; obviously ■ **clear-'sighted** *adj* understanding or thinking clearly

0—w **clear**[2] /klɪə(r)/ *v* 1 [T] remove sth unwanted from a place 2 [I] move freely again; no longer be blocked: *The traffic took ages to ~ after the accident.* 3 [I] (of sky or the weather) become brighter and free of cloud, fog or rain 4 [T] approve sth officially 5 [T] ~ (**of**) declare sb to be not guilty of a crime 6 [T] get past or over sth without touching it: *The horse ~ed the fence.* [IDM] **clear the air** remove fears, suspicions, etc by talking about them openly [PV] **clear (sth)**

away remove objects in order to leave a place tidy **clear off** (*infml*) go away **clear out (of...)** (*infml*) leave a place quickly **clear sth out** make sth empty or tidy by removing unwanted things: ~ *out the cupboards* **clear up** (of the weather) become bright or fine **clear sth up** make sth clean and tidy **clear sth up** remove doubt about sth; solve: ~ *a mystery*

clearance /ˈklɪərəns/ n 1 [C,U] removal of unwanted things 2 [C,U] clear space between two things: *There's not much ~ for vehicles passing under the bridge.* 3 [U] official approval or permission

clearing /ˈklɪərɪŋ/ n [C] open space from which trees have been cleared in a forest

cleavage /ˈkliːvɪdʒ/ n [C] 1 space between a woman's breasts 2 (*fml*) division or split

clef /klef/ n [C] musical symbol showing the pitch of the notes

clemency /ˈklemənsi/ n [U] (*fml*) kindness shown to sb when they are being punished; mercy

clench /klentʃ/ v [T] close sth tightly; press sth firmly together: ~ *your fists*

clergy /ˈklɜːdʒi/ n [pl] (often the **clergy**) priests and ministers of a religion, esp of the Christian Church ▪ **clergyman** /ˈklɜːdʒimən/ n [C] (pl **-men** /-mən/) Christian priest or minister

clerical /ˈklerɪkl/ adj 1 connected with office work 2 of or for the clergy

0—ᵣ **clerk** /klɑːk/ n [C] 1 person whose job is to keep the records or accounts in an office, a shop, etc 2 (*US*) (also **ˈsales clerk**) = SHOP ASSISTANT

0—ᵣ **clever** /ˈklevə(r)/ adj 1 quick at learning and understanding; intelligent 2 showing skill; effective: *a ~ scheme* ▸ **cleverly** adv ▸ **cleverness** n [U]

cliché /ˈkliːʃeɪ/ n [C] idea or expression that is used so often that it no longer has any meaning

0—ᵣ **click** /klɪk/ v 1 [I,T] (cause sth to) make a sharp sound: *He ~ed his fingers at the waiter.* 2 ~ **(on)** [I,T] choose a particular function or item on a computer screen, etc by pressing one of the buttons on the mouse: *Just ~ on the link to visit our website.* 3 [I] (*infml*) suddenly become understood ● **click** n [C]

0—ᵣ **client** /ˈklaɪənt/ n [C] 1 person who receives help or advice from a professional person: *a well-known lawyer with many famous ~s* 2 (*computing*) computer that is linked to a server

clientele /ˌkliːɒnˈtel/ n [sing, with

sing or pl verb] all the customers or clients of a shop, a restaurant, an organization, etc

cliff /klɪf/ n [C] steep rock face, esp by the sea

climactic /klaɪˈmæktɪk/ adj (*written*) (of an event or a point in time) very exciting, most important

0—ᵣ **climate** /ˈklaɪmət/ n 1 [C,U] general weather conditions of a place 2 [C] general attitude or feeling ▸ **climatic** /klaɪˈmætɪk/ adj

climax /ˈklaɪmæks/ n [C] most exciting or interesting moment in a story, etc, usu near the end ● **climax** v [I] reach a climax

0—ᵣ **climb** /klaɪm/ v 1 [I,T] go up sth, esp using your hands and feet 2 [I] move in the direction mentioned, with difficulty: ~ *out of the lorry* 3 [I] (of aircraft) go higher in the sky 4 [I] (of plants) grow up a wall or frame **[IDM] climb on the bandwagon** → BAND **[PV] climb down (over sth)** (*infml*) admit that you have made a mistake or were wrong ● **climb** n [C] 1 act of climbing 2 mountain or rock which people climb for sport ▪ **climber** n [C] act of admitting you were wrong ▸ **climber** n [C] 1 person who climbs 2 climbing plant

clinch /klɪntʃ/ v [T] 1 succeed in achieving or winning sth: ~ *an argument/a deal* 2 provide the answer to sth; settle sth that was not certain ● **clinch** n [C] (*infml*) tight embrace

cling /klɪŋ/ v (pt, pp **clung** /klʌŋ/) [I] ~ **(on)** hold on tightly to sth/sb ▪ **ˈcling film** n [U] clear thin plastic material used for wrapping food

clinic /ˈklɪnɪk/ n [C] building or part of a hospital where people go for special medical treatment or advice: *a children's ~* ▸ **clinical** adj 1 of clinics or medical treatment 2 cold and unfeeling 3 (of a room or building) very plain and undecorated

clink /klɪŋk/ n [C] sound of coins, small pieces of glass, etc knocking together ● **clink** v [I,T] (cause sth to) make this sound

clip /klɪp/ v (**-pp-**) 1 [I,T] fasten sth to sth else with a clip 2 [T] cut sth with scissors, etc 3 [T] hit the edge or side of sth ● **clip** n [C] 1 small metal or plastic object used for holding things together: *a hair/paper ~* 2 [sing] act of cutting sth to make it shorter 3 [C] short part of a film that is shown separately: *Here's a ~ from her latest film.* 4 [C] (*infml*) a quick hit with your hand: *She gave him a ~ round the ear.* ▪ **ˈclipboard** n [C] 1 portable board with a clip at the top for holding papers 2 (*computing*) place where information from a computer file is stored temporarily before it is added to another file ▶ clippers n [pl] tool for cutting small pieces off things: nail ~pers ■ clipping n [C] 1 [usu pl] piece cut off from sth 2 (esp US) = CUTTING(1)

clique /kliːk/ n [C] often (disapprov) closely united group of people

cloak /kləʊk/ n 1 [C] type of loose coat that has no sleeves and fastens at the neck 2 [sing] (lit) thing that hides or covers sth: a ~ of secrecy ● cloak v [T] (lit) cover or hide sth ■ 'cloakroom n [C] 1 (esp GB) place in a public building where coats, bags, etc may be left 2 (GB) room in a public building where there are toilets

0— clock /klɒk/ n [C] instrument for measuring and showing the time [IDM] around/round the clock all day and all night put/turn the clock back 1 return to a situation that existed in the past 2 return to old-fashioned ideas, etc ● clock v [T] reach a particular time or speed [PV] clock in/on record the time that you arrive at work, esp by putting a card into a machine clock out/off record the time that you leave work, esp by putting a card into a machine clock sth up win or achieve a particular number or amount ■ 'clockwise adv, adj in the direction of the movement of the hands of a clock ■ 'clockwork n [U] machinery wound up with a key [IDM] go/run like clockwork happen according to plan and without problems

clod /klɒd/ n [C] lump of earth or clay

clog /klɒɡ/ v (-gg-) [I, T] ~ (up) (cause sth to) become blocked ● clog n [C] wooden shoe

cloister /ˈklɔɪstə(r)/ n [C] covered passage round a square in a convent, college, cathedral, etc ▶ cloistered adj protected from the dangers and problems of normal life

clone /kləʊn/ n [C] 1 (biol) exact copy of a plant or animal, which is produced artificially from the cells of another plant or animal 2 (computing) computer designed to work in exactly the same way as another, usu one made by a different company ● clone v [T] 1 produce an exact copy of an animal or a plant from its cells 2 copy information illegally from a person's credit card or mobile phone so that you can use it but the owner receives the bill

0— close¹ /kləʊz/ v [I, T] 1 (cause sth to) shut: ~ the door ◇ The shop ~s at 5pm. 2 (cause sth to) come to an end: ~ a meeting/an investigation [IDM] close your eyes to sth pretend you have not noticed sth so that you do not have to deal with it [PV] close down (of a radio or television station) stop broadcasting at the end of the day close (sth) down (of a

factory, business, etc) stop (sth) operating as a business close in (on sb/sth) move nearer to sb/sth, esp in order to attack them ● close n [sing] (fml) end of a period of time or activity: I brought the meeting to a ~. ■ closed-'circuit 'television (abbr CCTV) n [U] television system that works within a limited area, eg a public building, to protect it from crime ■ 'close-down n [U, sing] stopping of work, esp permanently, in an office, a factory, etc ■ closed 'shop n [C] place of work where the employees must all be members of a particular trade union

0— close² /kləʊs/ adj (~r, ~st) 1 ~ (to) near 2 knowing sb very well and liking them very much: a ~ friend 3 near in a family relationship: ~ relatives 4 careful and thorough: on ~ inspection 5 won by a small difference: a ~ race 6 uncomfortably hot and without fresh air [IDM] a close call/shave (infml) situation in which a disaster or failure is only just avoided ● close adv near; not far away: follow ~ behind ■ close-'fitting adj (of clothes) fitting tightly to the body ■ close-'knit adj (of a group of people) joined together closely by shared beliefs, activities, etc ▶ closely adv closeness n [U] ■ close-'set adj situated very close together: ~-set eyes ■ 'close-up n [C] photograph taken very near to sb/sth

close³ /kləʊs/ n [C] 1 (GB) (esp in street names) street closed at one end 2 grounds of a cathedral

0— closet /ˈklɒzɪt/ n [C] (esp US) small room or space in a wall, used for storing things ● closet adj secret ● closet v [T] shut sb in a room away from other people

closure /ˈkləʊʒə(r)/ n [C, U] situation when a factory, school, etc shuts permanently

clot /klɒt/ n [C] lump formed from a liquid, esp blood ● clot v (-tt-) [I, T] (cause sth to) form into clots

0— cloth /klɒθ/ n 1 [U] material made by weaving cotton, wool, etc 2 [C] piece of cloth used for a special purpose: a table~ ◇ Wipe the table with a damp ~.

clothe /kləʊð/ v [T] provide clothes for sb

0— clothes /kləʊðz/ n [pl] things that you wear, eg trousers, dresses, etc ■ 'clothes hanger n [C] = HANGER ■ 'clothes horse n [C] frame on which clothes are hung to dry, esp indoors ■ 'clothes line n [C] rope stretched between posts on which washed clothes are hung to dry ■ 'clothes peg n [C] (GB) wooden or plastic clip for fastening clothes to a clothes line

A B C D E F G H I J K L M N O P Q R S T U V W X Y Z

0—̄ **clothing** /ˈkləʊðɪŋ/ n [U] clothes

0—̄ **cloud** /klaʊd/ n **1** [C,U] (mass of) visible water vapour floating in the sky **2** [C] mass of sth, eg dust or smoke, in the air **3** [C] thing that makes you feel sad or anxious [IDM] **under a cloud** in disgrace; under suspicion ● **cloud** v **1** [T] confuse sth: *His judgement was ~ed by jealousy.* **2** [I,T] ~ **(over)** (of the sky) to fill with clouds ● **cloudy** adj **(-ier, -iest) 1** covered with clouds **2** (of liquids) not clear

clout /klaʊt/ v [T] (infml) hit sb, esp with your hand ● **clout** n (infml) **1** [C] heavy blow, esp with the hand **2** [U] power and influence

clove /kləʊv/ n [C] **1** dried flower of a tropical tree, used in cooking as a spice **2** one of the small separate sections of a bulb of garlic: *Crush two ~s of garlic.*

clover /ˈkləʊvə(r)/ n [U,C] small wild plant with (usu) three leaves on each stalk

clown /klaʊn/ n [C] **1** performer in a circus who does silly things to make people laugh **2** (disapprov) person who acts in a stupid way ● **clown** v [I] ~ **(around)** behave foolishly

0—̄ **club** /klʌb/ n [C] **1** group of people who meet for sport, social entertainment, etc **2** building that a particular club uses **3** place where esp young people go to listen to music, dance, etc **4** thick heavy stick used as a weapon **5** stick for hitting the ball in golf **6** (clubs) [pl,U] one of the four sets of playing cards (suits) with black three-leaved shapes: *the queen of ~s* ● **club (-bb-) 1** [T] hit sb with a heavy stick: *The victim was ~bed to death with a baseball bat.* **2** [I] (go clubbing) (GB, infml) spend time dancing and drinking in a club (3) [PV] **club together** (GB) join together to give money for sth

cluck /klʌk/ v [I], n [C] (make the) noise of a hen

clue /kluː/ n [C] something that gives help in finding an answer to a problem: *The police are looking for ~s.* [IDM] **not have a clue** (infml) not know anything ● **clueless** adj (infml, disapprov) stupid

clump /klʌmp/ n [C] small group (esp of trees or plants) ● **clump** v **1** [I] walk heavily and awkwardly **2** [I,T] (cause sth to) come together to form a tight group

clumsy /ˈklʌmzi/ adj (-ier, -iest) **1** lacking in skill and not graceful in movement **2** (of actions and statements) tactless **3** difficult to use ▶ **clumsily** adv ▶ **clumsiness** n [U]

clung pt, pp of CLING

cluster /ˈklʌstə(r)/ n [C] group of

things close together ● **cluster** v [I] ~ **together** form a close group

clutch /klʌtʃ/ v [I,T] (try to) hold sb/ sth tightly, esp with the hands ● **clutch** n **1** [C] pedal in a car, etc that you press with your foot in order to change gear **2** [C] device in a machine that connects and disconnects the engine and the gears **3** (clutches) [pl] (infml) power of control: *be in sb's ~es* **4** [C] tight hold of sb/sth **5** [C] group of bird's eggs that hatch together

clutter /ˈklʌtə(r)/ n [U] (esp unnecessary or unwanted) things lying about untidily ● **clutter** v [T] fill a place with too many things so that it is untidy

cm abbr (pl **cm** or **~s**) centimetre

CND /ˌsiː en ˈdiː/ abbr Campaign for Nuclear Disarmament; (British organization whose aim is to persuade countries to get rid of their nuclear weapons)

Co. abbr company (1)

c/o /ˌsiː ˈəʊ/ abbr (on letters, etc addressed to sb staying at sb else's house) care of

0—̄ **coach** /kəʊtʃ/ n **1** [C] person who trains sb or a team in sport **2** [C] (GB) bus for carrying passengers on long journeys **3** [C] (GB) railway carriage **4** [C] large carriage with four wheels, pulled by horses **5** [U] (US) cheapest seats in a plane ● **coach** v [T] teach sb, esp for an examination or for a sport

coagulate /kəʊˈæɡjuleɪt/ v [I,T] (cause sth to) change from a liquid to a thick semi-solid state

0—̄ **coal** /kəʊl/ n [C,U] (piece of) black mineral that is burnt as a fuel ■ **coalface** n [C] surface in a coal mine from which coal is cut ■ **coalfield** n [C] district in which coal is mined ■ **coal mine** n [C] place underground where coal is dug ▶ **coal miner** n [C] person whose job is digging coal in a coal mine

coalesce /ˌkəʊəˈles/ v [I] (fml) come together to form one larger group, substance, etc

coalition /ˌkəʊəˈlɪʃn/ n [C] union of political parties for a special purpose

coarse /kɔːs/ adj (-r, -st) **1** rough; not fine **2** rude and offensive ▶ **coarsely** adv ▶ **coarsen** /ˈkɔːsn/ v [I,T] become or make sb/sth coarse ▶ **coarseness** n [U]

0—̄ **coast** /kəʊst/ n [C] land next to the sea [IDM] **the coast is clear** (infml) there is no danger of being seen or caught ● **coast** v [I] move, esp downhill, without using power ▶ **coastal** adj ■ **coastguard** n [C, with sing or pl verb] (one of a) group of people on police duty on the coast ■ **coastline** n [C] shape or outline of a coast

coat /kəʊt/ n [C] **1** piece of outdoor clothing worn over other clothes to keep warm or dry **2** fur or hair on an animal **3** layer on a surface: a ~ of paint ● **coat** v [T] cover sth with a layer of sth ■ '**coat hanger** n [C] = HANGER ▶ **coating** n [C] thin layer ■ **coat of arms** n [C] design on a shield used as a sign by a noble family, town, etc

coax /kəʊks/ v [T] persuade sb gently or gradually [PV] **coax sth out of/from sb** obtain sth from sb by persuading

cob /kɒb/ n [C] **1** = CORNCOB (CORN) **2** strong short-legged horse **3** male swan

cobble /ˈkɒbl/ v [PV] **cobble sth together** put sth together quickly or roughly

cobbles /ˈkɒblz/ (also **cobblestones**) n [pl] small round stones used to make the surfaces of roads, esp in the past ▶ **cobbled** adj

cobra /ˈkəʊbrə/ n [C] poisonous snake of India and Africa

cobweb /ˈkɒbweb/ n [C] spider's web

cocaine /kəʊˈkeɪn/ n [U] powerful, illegal drug taken for pleasure by some people

cock /kɒk/ n [C] **1** male bird, esp an adult male chicken **2** = STOPCOCK ● **cock** /kɒk/ v [T] **1** raise or turn part of the body upwards: The horse ~ed its ears. **2** raise the hammer of a gun ready for firing [PV] **cock sth up** (GB, sl) spoil or ruin sth ■ '**cock-up** n [C] (GB, spoken) bad mistake that spoils people's arrangements

cockatoo /ˌkɒkəˈtuː/ n [C] (pl ~s) kind of parrot with a large crest

cockerel /ˈkɒkərəl/ n [C] young male chicken

cockeyed /ˈkɒkaɪd/ adj (infml) **1** not straight or level; crooked **2** not practical: a ~ scheme

cockle /ˈkɒkl/ n [C] small edible shellfish

cockney /ˈkɒkni/ n **1** [C] person from the East End of London **2** [U] way of speaking that is typical of cockneys: a ~ accent

cockpit /ˈkɒkpɪt/ n [C] part of a plane, boat or racing car where the pilot or driver sits

cockroach /ˈkɒkrəʊtʃ/ n [C] large brown insect that lives esp in damp or dirty rooms

cocktail /ˈkɒkteɪl/ n **1** mixed alcoholic drink **2** mixture of fruit or shellfish: a prawn ~

cocky /ˈkɒki/ adj (-ier, -iest) (infml) too self-confident

cocoa /ˈkəʊkəʊ/ n **1** [U] brown powder tasting like bitter chocolate **2** [U,C] hot drink made from this

coconut /ˈkəʊkənʌt/ n [C] large nut with a hard hairy shell and an edible white lining and filled with milky juice

---

cohere

cocoon /kəˈkuːn/ n [C] silky covering made by an insect larva to protect itself while it is a chrysalis

cod /kɒd/ n [C,U] (pl **cod**) large sea fish with white flesh that is used for food

coddle /ˈkɒdl/ v [T] treat sb with too much care and attention

code /kəʊd/ n **1** [C,U] system of words, letters, numbers or symbols that represent a message or record information secretly or in a shorter form: break the ~ the enemy use to send messages **2** [U] (computing) system of computer programming instructions **3** [C] system of rules and principles: a ~ of behaviour ● **code** v [T] **1** put sth into code **2** (computing) write a computer program by putting one system of numbers, words and symbols into another system

coerce /kəʊˈɜːs/ v [T] (fml) force sb to do sth ▶ **coercion** /kəʊˈɜːʃn/ n [U] ▶ **coercive** /-ˈɜːsɪv/ adj

coexist /ˌkəʊɪɡˈzɪst/ v [i] (fml) exist together at the same time or in the same place ▶ **coexistence** n [U] state of being together in the same place at the same time: peaceful ~ence

coffee /ˈkɒfi/ n **1** [U,C] drink obtained from grinding the roasted seeds of the coffee tree **2** [U,C] hot drink made from coffee powder and boiling water

coffer /ˈkɒfə(r)/ n **1** [C] large strong box used in the past for holding money, etc **2** (**coffers**) [pl] (written) money that a government, etc has available to spend

coffin /ˈkɒfɪn/ n [C] (esp GB) box in which a dead body is buried or cremated

cog /kɒɡ/ n [C] **1** one of the teeth on a wheel that moves the teeth of a similar wheel **2** = COGWHEEL [IDM] **a cog in the machine** unimportant but necessary person in a large organization ■ '**cogwheel** (also **cog**) n [C] wheel with teeth round the edge

cogent /ˈkəʊdʒənt/ adj (fml) strongly and clearly convincing; convincing

cognac /ˈkɒnjæk/ n [U,C] kind of brandy

cohabit /kəʊˈhæbɪt/ v [i] (fml) (usu of an unmarried couple) live together as husband and wife ▶ **cohabitation** /ˌkəʊˌhæbɪˈteɪʃn/ n [U]

cohere /kəʊˈhɪə(r)/ v [i] (fml) (of ideas, etc) be connected logically **2** (of people) work closely together ▶ **coherent** /kəʊˈhɪərənt/ adj (of ideas, arguments, etc) connected

---

logically; clear and easy to understand ▶ **coherence** /kəʊˈhɪərəns/ n [U] ▶ **coherently** adv

cohesion /kəʊˈhiːʒn/ n [U] tendency to stick together; unity ▶ **cohesive** /kəʊˈhiːsɪv/ adj

coil /kɔɪl/ v [I,T] (cause sth to) wind into a series of circles ● **coil** n [C] **1** series of circles formed by winding up a length of rope, wire, etc **2** one circle of rope, wire, etc in a series

0─**coin** /kɔɪn/ n [C] piece of metal used as money ● **coin** v [T] **1** invent a new word or phrase **2** make coins ▶ **coinage** /ˈkɔɪnɪdʒ/ n [U] coins in use in a country

coincide /ˌkəʊɪnˈsaɪd/ v [I] **1** (of events) happen at the same time **2** (of opinions or ideas) agree **3** (fml) (of objects) meet; share the same space

coincidence /kəʊˈɪnsɪdəns/ n [C, U] fact of two or more things happening at the same time by chance: It was pure ~ that we were both travelling on the same plane. ▶ **coincidental** /kəʊˌɪnsɪˈdentl/ adj happening by chance ▶ **coincidentally** adv

coke /kəʊk/ n [U] **1** (infml) = COCAINE **2** black substance produced from coal and used as a fuel

colander /ˈkʌləndə(r)/ n [C] bowl with many small holes in it, used to drain water from food

0─**cold**[1] /kəʊld/ adj **1** of low temperature (of food) not heated; having cooled after being warm **3** unfriendly; unfeeling: a ~ stare/ welcome **4** unconscious: knock sb out ~ [IDM] **get/have cold feet** (infml) become/be afraid to do sth you had planned to do **give sb the cold shoulder** (infml) treat sb in an unfriendly way **in cold blood** deliberately cruel and without feeling: kill sb in ~ blood **pour/throw cold water on sth** be discouraging or not enthusiastic about sth ■ **cold-blooded** adj **1** (of people and their actions) without pity; cruel **2** (biol) (of animals) having a blood temperature that varies with the surroundings ■ **cold ˈcash** n [U] (US) = HARD CASH (HARD[1]) ■ **cold-hearted** adj not showing any love or sympathy for other people ▶ **coldly** adv ▶ **coldness** n [U] ■ **cold ˈwar** n [sing] very unfriendly relationship between two countries who are not actually fighting each other

0─**cold**[2] /kəʊld/ n **1** [U] lack of heat or warmth; low temperature **2** [C] common illness of the nose or throat [IDM] **leave sb out in the cold** not include sb in a group or an activity

coleslaw /ˈkəʊlslɔː/ n [U] finely chopped raw cabbage, carrots, etc mixed with mayonnaise

colic /ˈkɒlɪk/ n [U] severe pain in the stomach and bowels

collaborate /kəˈlæbəreɪt/ v [I] **1 ~ (with)** work together **2 ~ (with)** help the enemy ▶ **collaboration** /kəˌlæbəˈreɪʃn/ n [U] ▶ **collaborator** n [C]

collage /ˈkɒlɑːʒ/ n [C] picture made by sticking pieces of paper, cloth, etc onto a surface

collagen /ˈkɒlədʒən/ n [U] protein found in skin and bone, sometimes injected into the body to improve its appearance: ~ injections

0─**collapse** /kəˈlæps/ v **1** [I] fall down suddenly: The building ~d in the earthquake. **2** [I] fall down (and become unconscious) because of illness or tiredness **3** [I] fail suddenly and completely **4** [I,T] fold sth into a flat compact shape: The table ~s to fit into the cupboard. ● **collapse** n [C, usu sing, U]: the ~ of the company ▶ **collapsible** adj that can be folded for packing, etc: a collapsible chair/ table

collar /ˈkɒlə(r)/ n [C] **1** part around the neck of a shirt, jacket or coat **2** band of leather, etc put round the neck of a dog or other animal ● **collar** v [T] seize or catch sb ■ **collarbone** n [C] either of the two bones that go from the base of the neck to the shoulders

collate /kəˈleɪt/ v [T] gather information to examine and compare it

collateral /kəˈlætərəl/ n [U] (business) property or money used as security for a loan

0─**colleague** /ˈkɒliːɡ/ n [C] person that you work with

0─**collect** /kəˈlekt/ v [I,T] **1** come together; bring sb/sth together: A crowd ~ed at the scene of the accident. ◊ ~ the empty glasses **2** [T] save stamps, etc as a hobby **3** [I,T] ~ (for) obtain money from a number of people for sb/sth: ~ money for charity **4** [T] fetch sb/sth: ~ a child from school [IDM] **collect yourself/ your thoughts** control your emotions; prepare yourself mentally for sth ● **collect** adj, adv (US) (of a phone call) paid for by the person who receives the call ▶ **collected** adj calm and self-controlled ▶ **collection** /kəˈlekʃn/ n **1** [C] group of objects collected **2** [C, U] act of collecting sb/sth **3** [C] sum of money collected ● **collective** adj of a group or society as a whole; shared ▶ **collectively** adv ▶ **collector** n [C] person who collects sth, either as a hobby, or as a job: a stamp/ticket ~or

college /'kɒlɪdʒ/ n [C]
1 institution for higher education; part of a university **2** (GB) organized group of professional people

collide /kə'laɪd/ v [I] **~ (with) 1** (of moving objects or people) hit each other or against sb/sth **2** (of people, their opinions, etc) disagree strongly

collier /'kɒlɪə(r)/ n [C] person whose job is digging coal in a coal mine
colliery /'kɒlɪəri/ n [C] (pl **-ies**) (GB) coal mine

collision /kə'lɪʒn/ n [C,U] **1** accident in which two vehicles or people crash into each other **2** (written) strong disagreement

colloquial /kə'ləʊkwɪəl/ adj (of words and language) used in conversation but not in formal speech or writing ▸ **colloquialism** n [C] colloquial word or phrase ▸ **colloquially** adv

collude /kə'luːd/ v [I] **~ (with)** (fml) work with sb secretly and dishonestly ▸ **collusion** /kə'luːʒn/ n [U]

colon /'kəʊlən/ n [C] **1** punctuation mark (:) **2** (anat) lower part of the large intestine (= part of the bowels)

colonel /'kɜːnl/ n [C] high-ranking officer in the army or US air force

colonial /kə'ləʊnɪəl/ adj connected with or belonging to a colony **●** colonial n [C] person living in a colony (1) ▸ **colonialism** n [U] policy of having colonies ▸ **colonialist** n [C], adj

colonist /'kɒlənɪst/ n [C] person who settles in an area and colonizes it
colonize (also -ise) /'kɒlənaɪz/ v [T] establish an area as a colony (1) ▸ **colonization** (also -isation) /-'zeɪʃn/ n [U]

colonnade /ˌkɒlə'neɪd/ n [C] row of columns (1)

colony /'kɒləni/ n [C] (pl **-ies**) **1** country lived in and controlled by people from another country **2** group of people with the same interests, etc living in the same place

color (US) = COLOUR

colossal /kə'lɒsl/ adj very large

0— **colour¹** /'kʌlə(r)/ n [C,U] appearance that things have that results from the way in which they reflect light. Red, green and orange are colours. **2** colour (1) of the skin on sb's face: *The fresh air brought some ~ to her cheeks.* **3** [U,C] colour of a person's skin, when it shows the race they belong to **4** [C] interesting details or qualities **5** (colours) [pl] flag, badge, etc worn to show that sb is a member of a particular team, school, etc [IDM] **off colour** (infml) unwell; ill **with flying colours** with great success **■ colour-blind** adj unable to distinguish between colours (1) ▸ **colourful** adj

---

81

combine

1 brightly coloured **2** interesting or exciting ▸ **colourless** adj **1** without colour (1) **2** dull and uninteresting **■ colour supplement** n [C] (GB) magazine printed in colour, given free esp with a Sunday newspaper

0— **colour²** /'kʌlə(r)/ v **1** [T] give colour to sth, using paint, coloured pens, etc **2** [I] become red with embarrassment; blush **3** [T] affect sth, esp in a negative way [PV] **colour sth in** fill a picture, etc with colour ▸ **coloured** adj having a particular colour or different colours ▸ **colouring** n **1** [U,C] substance used to give a particular colour to food **2** [U] colours of sb's skin, eyes and hair **3** [U] colours that exist in sth, eg a plant or an animal

colt /kəʊlt/ n [C] young male horse

0— **column** /'kɒləm/ n [C] **1** tall vertical post supporting part of a building or standing alone **2** something shaped like a column: *a ~ of smoke* **3** (abbr **col.**) vertical division of a printed page **4** part of a newspaper or magazine which appears regularly: *a gossip ~* **5** long moving line of people or vehicles ▸ **columnist** /'kɒləmnɪst/ n [C] person who writes regular articles for a newspaper

coma /'kəʊmə/ n [C] state of deep unconsciousness

comb /kəʊm/ n [C] **1** piece of plastic or metal with teeth, used for tidying your hair **2** [usu sing] act of using a comb on your hair: *give your hair a ~* **3** n [C,U] = HONEYCOMB **●** comb v [T] **1** tidy your hair with a comb **2** search sth carefully in order to find sb/sth

combat /'kɒmbæt/ n [U,C] fighting or a fight, esp during a time of war **●** combat v (**-t-** or **-tt-**) [T] **1** stop sth unpleasant or harmful from happening or getting worse **2** (fml) fight against an enemy ▸ **combatant** /'kɒmbətənt/ n [C] person who fights ▸ **combatant** adj fighting

0— **combination** /ˌkɒmbɪ'neɪʃn/ n **1** [C] number of things or people joined or mixed together: *a ~ of traditional and modern architecture* **2** [U] act of joining two or more things together to form a single unit **3** [C] series of numbers or letters needed to open the lock of a safe, etc

0— **combine¹** /kəm'baɪn/ v [I,T] join two or more things together

combine² /'kɒmbaɪn/ n [C] **1** (GB also **combine 'harvester**) machine that both cuts and threshes grain **2** group of people or organizations acting together in business

A B **C** D E F G H I J K L M N O P Q R S T U V W X Y Z

combustible /kəmˈbʌstəbl/ *adj* that can catch fire and burn easily

combustion /kəmˈbʌstʃən/ *n* [U] process of burning

○━ **come** /kʌm/ *v* (pt **came** /keɪm/ pp **come**) [I] **1** move towards the speaker or the place towards which he/she is referring: *C~ and talk to me.* **2** arrive at or reach a place **3** reach; extend: *The path ~s right up to the gate.* **4** travel a specified distance: *We've ~ thirty miles since lunch.* **5** happen; take place: *Christmas ~s once a year.* **6** ~ **to/into** reach a particular state: *~ to an end* **7** ~ **(in)** (of goods, products, etc) exist; be available: *This dress ~s in several different colours.* **8** become: *The button came undone.* **9** ~ **to** + inf: *to realize the truth* [IDM] **come to grips with sth** → GRIP **come to a head** → HEAD¹ **come loose** → LOOSE **come to nothing | not come to anything** be unsuccessful **come what may** in spite of any problems or difficulties you may have **how come (...)?** (spoken) why? **to come** in the future: *for several years to ~* [PV] **come about** happen **come across/over 1** be understood: *He spoke for ages but his meaning didn't really ~ across.* **2** make a particular impression: *She ~s across well in interviews.* **come across/with** find sth or meet sb by chance **come along 1** arrive; appear: *When the right job ~s along, she'll take it.* **2** progress, develop or improve: *Her work is coming along nicely.* **3** = COME ON(3) **come apart** fall to pieces **come around/round/to 1** become conscious again **2** occur again: *Christmas seems to ~ round quicker every year.* **come around/round (to...)** visit for a short time: *C~ round to my place for the evening.* **come around/round (to sth)** change your mood or your opinion **come at sb** move towards sb to attack them: *He came at me with a knife.* **come back** return **come back (to sb)** return to sb's memory **come before sb/sth** (fml) be presented to sb/sth for discussion or a decision: *The case ~s before the court next week.* **come between A and B** interfere **come by sth** obtain or receive: *Good jobs are hard to ~ by these days.* **come down 1** collapse **2** (of rain, prices, etc) fall **3** decide and say publicly that you support or oppose sth **4** reach down to a particular point: *Her hair ~s down to her waist.* **come down (to sb)** have come from a long time in the past **come down to sth** be able to be explained by a single important point: *What it ~s down to is that if your work doesn't improve you'll have to leave.* **come in 1** (of the tide) move towards the land **2** become

fashionable **3** arrive somewhere; be received **4** have a part to play: *Where do I ~ in?* **come in for sth** be the object of punishment, criticism, etc **come into sth** inherit sth **come off/from sth** be the result of sth **come off 1** be able to be removed: *Will these dirty marks ~ off?* **2** (infml) take place; happen **3** (infml) (of plans, etc) be successful: *The experiment did not ~ off.* **come off (sth) 1** fall from sth: *~ off your bicycle/horse* **2** become separated from sth: *The button has ~ off my coat.* **come on 1** (of an actor) walk onto the stage **2** improve or develop in the way you want **3** used in orders to tell sb to hurry or to try harder: *C~ on, if we don't hurry we'll be late.* **4** (of rain, night, illness, etc) begin: *I think he has a cold coming on.* **come on/upon sb/sth** (fml) meet or find sb/sth by chance **come out 1** become visible; appear: *The rain stopped and the sun came out.* **2** become known; be published: *The truth came out eventually.* **3** (of workers) strike **4** be clearly revealed, esp in a photograph **come out (of sth)** be removed from sth: *Will the stains ~ out?* **come out in sth** become (partly) covered in spots, etc: *~ out in a rash* **come out with sth** say sth: *He ~s out with the strangest remarks.* **come over 1** (GB, infml) suddenly become sth: *She came over all shy.* **2** = COME ACROSS **come over (to...)** move from one place to another, esp for a visit: *~ over to Scotland for a holiday* **come over sb** (of feelings, etc) affect sb: *A feeling of dizziness came over him.* **come round (to sth)** = COME AROUND **come through (sth)** (of a message, signal, etc) arrive **come through (sth)** recover from a serious illness or escape injury **come to** = COME AROUND(1) **come to sb** (of an idea) enter your mind: *The idea came to me in a dream.* **come to sth 1** add up to sth: *The bill came to £20.* **2** reach a particular situation, esp a bad one: *The doctors could operate, but it might not ~ to that.* **come under sth 1** be in a certain category, etc **2** be subjected to sth: *~ under her influence* **come up 1** (of plants, etc) appear above the soil **2** happen: *Something urgent has ~ up so I'll be late home.* **3** be mentioned: *The question hasn't ~ up yet.* **come up against sb/sth** be faced with or opposed by sb/sth **come up to sth** reach sth: *The water came up to my waist.* **come up with sth** produce or find: *~ up with a solution* **come upon sb/sth** = COME ON SB/STH

■ **comeback** *n* [C, usu sing] return to a previous successful position: *an ageing pop star trying to make a ~back* ■ **comedown** *n* [C, usu sing] situation in which a person is not as important as before, or does not get as much respect from others ▶ **coming** adj future: in the coming months ▶ **coming** n [sing] arrival: the coming of spring **IDM** **comings and goings** arrivals and departures

comedian /kə'mi:diən/ n [C] (old-fash fem **comedienne** /kə,mi:di'en/) entertainer who makes people laugh by telling jokes, etc

0-r **comedy** /'kɒmədi/ n (pl -ies) **1** [C,U] amusing play, film, etc **2** [U] amusing aspect of sth

comet /'kɒmɪt/ n [C] bright object, like a star with a long tail, that moves round the sun

0-r **comfort** /'kʌmfət/ n **1** [U] state of being relaxed and free from pain or worry: They had enough money to live in ~ for the rest of their lives. **2** [U] feeling of not suffering or worrying so much; feeling of being less unhappy: take ~ from sb's words **3** [sing] person or thing that brings you help or relief **4** [C, usu pl] things that give physical ease and makes life more pleasant ● **comfort** v [T] make sb feel less unhappy or worried ▶ **comfortable** /'kʌmftəbl/ adj **1** (of clothes, furniture, etc) pleasant to sit on, wear, etc: a ~able chair **2** feeling pleasantly relaxed; warm enough, without pain, etc: Make yourself ~able while I make some coffee. **3** (infml) fairly rich **4** quite large; allowing you to win easily ▶ **comfortably** adv

comic /'kɒmɪk/ adj **1** amusing and making you laugh **2** connected with comedy ● **comic** n [C] **1** comedian **2** magazine, esp for children, with stories told in pictures ▶ **comical** adj (old-fash) funny or amusing because of being strange or unusual ■ **comic strip** (also **cartoon**) n [C] series of drawings that tell a story and are often printed in newspapers

comma /'kɒmə/ n [C] punctuation mark (,)

0-r **command** /kə'mɑːnd/ v **1** [I,T] order sb to do sth **2** [T] be in charge of a group of people in the army, navy or air force: ~ a regiment **3** [T] deserve and get sth: ~ respect **4** [T] (fml) have a clear view of a place: a ~ing position over the valley ● **command** n **1** [C] order given to a person or an animal **2** [C] instruction given to a computer **3** [U] control; authority over a situation or group of people: in ~ of a ship **4** (Command) [C] part of an army, air force, etc **5** [U, sing] ~ (of) ability to use sth: a good ~ of French

commandant /'kɒməndænt/ n [C] officer in command of a military group or an institution

commandeer /,kɒmən'dɪə(r)/ v [T] take possession or control of sth for official, esp military, purposes

commander /kə'mɑːndə(r)/ n **1** person who is in charge of sth, esp

an officer in charge of a group of soldiers or a military operation **2** (abbr **Cdr**) officer of fairly high rank in the British or American navy

commandment /kə'mɑːndmənt/ n [C] law given by God

commando /kə'mɑːndəʊ/ n [C] (pl ~s or -es) member of a) group of soldiers trained to make quick attacks in enemy areas

commemorate /kə'meməreɪt/ v [T] honour the memory of sb, an event, etc ▶ **commemoration** /kə,memə'reɪʃn/ n [C,U] ▶ **commemorative** /kə'memərətɪv/ adj

commence /kə'mens/ v [I,T] (fml) begin; start ▶ **commencement** n [U]

commend /kə'mend/ v [T] (fml) **1** praise sb/sth, esp publicly; recommend sb/sth **2** be approved of by sb: His outspoken behaviour did not ~ itself to his colleagues. ▶ **commendable** adj deserving praise ▶ **commendation** /-'deɪʃn/ n [U,C]

commensurate /kə'menʃərət/ adj ~ **with** (fml) matching sth in size, importance, etc: pay ~ with the importance of the job

0-r **comment** /'kɒment/ n [C,U] written or spoken statement which gives an opinion on or explains sb/ sth ● **comment** v [I] ~ **(on)** give your opinion on sth

commentary /'kɒməntri/ n (pl -ies) **1** [C,U] spoken description of an event given as it happens, esp on the radio or television: a sports ~ **2** [C] written explanation of a book, play, etc

commentate /'kɒmənteɪt/ v [I] ~ **(on)** give a commentary (1) ▶ **commentator** n [C]

commerce /'kɒmɜːs/ n [U] trade, esp between countries; the buying and selling of goods

0-r **commercial** /kə'mɜːʃl/ adj **1** of or relating to commerce **2** making a profit **3** (of television or radio) paid for by advertisements ● **commercial** n [C] advertisement on television or radio ▶ **commercialized** (also -ised) adj concerned mainly with making a profit: Their music has become very ~ized in recent years. ▶ **commercially** /-ʃəli/ adv ■ **com mercial 'traveller** n [C] person whose job is to go to different shops, etc to sell a company's products and get orders for them

commiserate /kə'mɪzəreɪt/ v [I] ~ **(with)** (fml) show sympathy to sb: I ~d with her on the loss of her job. ▶ **commiseration** /kə,mɪzə'reɪʃn/ n [C,U]

0━ **commission** /kəˈmɪʃn/ n **1** [C] (often Commission) official group of people asked to find out about sth and to report on it **2** [U,C] amount of money paid to sb who sells goods for making a sale **3** [C] formal request to sb to design a piece of work such as a building or painting **4** [C] officer's position in the armed forces ● **commission** v [T] **1** officially ask sb to do a piece of work for you **2** choose sb as an officer in one of the armed forces

commissioner /kəˈmɪʃənə(r)/ n [C] **1** (usu Commissioner) member of a commission (1) **2** (esp US po'lice commissioner) head of a particular police force in some countries **3** head of a government department in some countries

0━ **commit** /kəˈmɪt/ v (-tt-) [T] **1** do sth wrong or illegal: ~ murder/ adultery/suicide **2** ~ (to) promise sincerely that you will do sth: The government has ~ted itself to fighting inflation. **3** ~ yourself give your opinion openly so that it is then difficult to change it **4** be completely loyal to one person, organization, etc **5** ~ to order sb to be sent to a prison or hospital ▸ **commitment** n **1** [C] something that you have promised to do **2** [U] loyalty

0━ **committee** /kəˈmɪti/ n [C, with sing or pl verb] group of people chosen to deal with a particular matter

commodity /kəˈmɒdəti/ n [C] (pl -ies) useful thing, esp an article of trade; product

0━ **common¹** /ˈkɒmən/ adj **1** happening or found often and in many places; usual **2** shared or used by two or more people: a ~ interest ◊ ~ knowledge **3** (GB, disapprov) typical of sb from a low social class and not having good manners [IDM] **have sth in common** share interests, ideas, etc **in common with sb/sth** together with sb/sth ■ **common 'ground** n [U] shared opinions or aims ■ **common 'law** n [U] (in England) system of laws developed from customs and decisions made by judges, not created by Parliament ▸ **'common-law** adj ▸ **commonly** adv ■ **'commonplace** adj done very often or existing in many places ■ **common 'sense** n [U] ability to think about things in a practical way and make sensible decisions

common² /ˈkɒmən/ n [C] area of open land which everyone may use

commoner /ˈkɒmənə(r)/ n [C] person who does not come from a noble family

Commons /ˈkɒmənz/ n [sing] (the Commons) = THE HOUSE OF COMMONS (HOUSE¹)

commonwealth /ˈkɒmənwelθ/ n **1** (the Commonwealth) [sing] organization consisting of the UK and most of the countries that used to be part of the British Empire **2** (usu Commonwealth) [C] used in the names of some groups of countries or states that have chosen to be politically linked

commotion /kəˈmoʊʃn; kɒˈmɒʃn/ n [sing,U] noisy confusion

communal /kəˈmjuːnl; ˈkɒmjənl/ adj shared by a group of people

commune¹ /ˈkɒmjuːn/ n [C] **1** group of people who live together and share property and responsibilities **2** (in France, etc) smallest division of local government

commune² /kəˈmjuːn/ v [PV] **commune with sb/sth** (fml) share your emotions and feelings with sb/ sth without speaking: He spent his time communing with nature.

0━ **communicate** /kəˈmjuːnɪkeɪt/ v **1** [I,T] make your ideas, feelings, etc known to other people **2** [T] pass on a disease **3** [I] (of rooms) be connected: a communicating door ▸ **communication** /kəˌmjuːnɪˈkeɪʃn/ n **1** [U] activity of expressing ideas and feelings or of giving people information **2** [U] (also communications [pl]) methods of sending information, esp telephones, radio, computers, etc or roads and railways **3** [C] (fml) message, letter or telephone call ▸ **communicative** /kəˈmjuːnɪkətɪv/ adj willing to talk or to give information

communion /kəˈmjuːniən/ n **1** (also Communion, Holy Com'munion) Christian ceremony of sharing bread and wine **2** (fml) state of sharing thoughts, feelings, etc

communiqué /kəˈmjuːnɪkeɪ/ n [C] official announcement

communism /ˈkɒmjunɪzəm/ n [U] **1** social and economic system in which there is no private ownership and the means of production belongs to all members of society **2** (Communism) system of government by a ruling Communist Party, such as in the former Soviet Union ▸ **communist** (also Communist) /ˈkɒmjənɪst/ n [C], adj

0━ **community** /kəˈmjuːnəti/ n (pl -ies) **1** [sing] all the people living in one place **2** [C, with sing or pl verb] group of people who share the same religion, race, job, etc **3** [U] feeling of sharing or having things in common

commute /kəˈmjuːt/ v **1** [I] travel regularly by car, train, etc between your place of work and home **2** [T] (law) replace a punishment with one that is less severe ▸ **commuter** n [C] person who travels into a town to work each day, usu from quite far away

compact[1] /kəmˈpækt/ adj closely packed together; neatly fitted in a small space ▸ **compactly** adv ▸ **compactness** n [U]

compact[2] /ˈkɒmpækt/ n [C] small flat box with a mirror, containing face powder

compact disc n [C] = CD

companion /kəmˈpæniən/ n [C] person who spends time or travels with another ▸ **companionship** n [U] relationship between friends or companions

0-w **company** /ˈkʌmpəni/ n (pl -ies) 1 [C] (abbr Co.) business organization 2 [C] group of people who work or perform together: a film opera ~ 3 [U] fact of being with sb else and not alone: He is good/bad ~ (= he is pleasant/unpleasant to be with). 4 [U] (fml) guests in your house 5 [U] (fml) group of people together 6 [C] group of soldiers that forms part of a battalion [IDM] **keep sb company** stay with sb so that they are not alone

comparable /ˈkɒmpərəbl/ adj that can be compared; similar

comparative /kəmˈpærətɪv/ adj 1 connected with studying things to find out how similar or different they are 2 measured by comparing; relative: living in ~ comfort 3 (gram) (of adjectives and adverbs expressing a greater degree or 'more', eg better, worse: 'Better' is the ~ form of 'good'. ● **comparative** n [C] (gram) comparative form of an adjective or adverb ▸ **comparatively** adv

0-w **compare** /kəmˈpeə(r)/ v 1 [T] ~ (with/to) (abbr cf.) examine things to see how they are alike and how they are different: ~ the results of one test with the results of another 2 [I] ~ with/to be similar to sb/sth else, either better or worse 3 [T] ~ A to B show the similarity between sb/sth and sb/sth else [IDM] **compare notes (with sb)** exchange opinions with sb

0-w **comparison** /kəmˈpærɪsn/ n 1 [C,U] ~ (with) process of comparing sb/sth: There is no ~ between them. 2 [C] ~ (of A and/to/ with B);~ (between A and B) occasion when two or more people or things are compared [IDM] **by/in comparison (with sb/sth)** when compared with sb/sth

compartment /kəmˈpɑːtmənt/ n [C] 1 section of a railway carriage 2 separate section in a piece of furniture, etc for keeping things in

compass /ˈkʌmpəs/ n 1 device for finding direction, with a needle that points north 2 (also **compasses** [pl]) V-shaped instrument for

drawing circles 3 [C] (fml) range; scope

compassion /kəmˈpæʃn/ n [U] feeling of pity for the suffering of others ▸ **compassionate** /kəmˈpæʃənət/ adj showing or feeling compassion ▸ **compassionately** adv

compatible /kəmˈpætəbl/ adj ~ (with) 1 (of machines, esp computers) able to be used together 2 (eg of people, ideas or principles) able to exist together ▸ **compatibility** /kəmˌpætəˈbɪləti/ n [U]

compatriot /kəmˈpætriət/ n [C] person from the same country as sb else

compel /kəmˈpel/ v (-ll-) [T] (fml) force sb to do sth ▸ **compelling** adj convincing

compensate /ˈkɒmpenseɪt/ v [I,U] ~ (for) pay or give sb sth to balance or lessen the bad effect of damage, loss, etc ▸ **compensation** /ˌkɒmpenˈseɪʃn/ n [U,C] ~ (for) something, esp money, that sb gives you because they have hurt you, or damaged sth of yours; act of giving this to sb 2 [C, usu pl] things that make a bad situation better

compère /ˈkɒmpeə(r)/ n [C] person who introduces the performers or guests in a radio or television show ● **compère** v [T] act as a compère for a show

0-w **compete** /kəmˈpiːt/ v [I] take part in a race, contest, etc; try to win by defeating others: ~ against/with others

competence /ˈkɒmpɪtəns/ n [U] 1 ability to do sth well 2 (law) legal authority ▸ **competent** /ˈkɒmpɪtənt/ adj having the ability, skill, knowledge, etc to do sth well ▸ **competently** adv

0-w **competition** /ˌkɒmpəˈtɪʃn/ n 1 situation in which people compete for sth that not everyone can have 2 [C] event in which people compete to find out who is the best at sth: a photography ~ 3 (the competition) [sing, with sing or pl verb] people who are competing against sb ▸ **competitive** /kəmˈpetətɪv/ adj 1 of or involving competition 2 (of a person) trying hard to be better than others

competitor /kəmˈpetɪtə(r)/ n [C] person who competes

compile /kəmˈpaɪl/ v [T] 1 produce a book, report, etc by collecting information 2 (computing) translate a set of instructions into a language that a computer will understand ▸ **compilation** /ˌkɒmpɪˈleɪʃn/ n 1 [C] collection of items taken from different places and put together

A B **C** D E F G H I J K L M N O P Q R S T U V W X Y Z

2 [U] process of compiling
▶ **compiler** n [C]

complacent /kəm'pleɪsnt/ adj
(disapprov) calmly satisfied
▶ **complacency** /kəm'pleɪsnsi/ n [U]
▶ **complacently** adv

0━ **complain** /kəm'pleɪn/ v [I] say
that you are dissatisfied or unhappy
about sth/sth: ~ about the food

0━ **complaint** /kəm'pleɪnt/ n
1 [C, U] (statement of) complaining
2 [C] illness; disease

complement /'kɒmplɪmənt/ n [C]
1 something that goes well with sth
else, making it complete: Wine is the
perfect ~ to a meal. **2** total number
needed **3** (gram) word(s), esp
adjectives and nouns, used after a
verb such as be or become describing
the subject of the verb: In '1'm
unhappy', 'unhappy' is the ~.
● **complement** /'kɒmplɪmənt/ v [T]
go well with sth to form a whole
▶ **complementary**
/ˌkɒmplɪ'mentri/ adj going well
with each other to form a whole

0━ **complete** /kəm'pli:t/ adj
1 having all its parts; whole
2 finished; ended **3** in every way;
total: a ~ surprise ● **complete** v [T]
1 finish sth; make sth whole **2** fill in a
form ▶ **completely** adv in every
way ▶ **completeness** n [U]
▶ **completion** /kəm'pli:ʃn/ n [U] act
of finishing sth; state of being
complete

0━ **complex** /'kɒmpleks/ adj made
up of many different parts; difficult
to understand or explain
● **complex** n [C] **1** group of similar
buildings or things that are
connected: a sports ~ **2** abnormal
mental state: suffer from a guilt ~
▶ **complexity** /kəm'pleksəti/ n [C, U]
(pl -ies)

complexion /kəm'plekʃn/ n
1 natural colour and condition of
the skin on a person's face: a spotty ~
2 [usu sing] general character of sth

compliance /kəm'plaɪəns/ n [U]
(written) practice of obeying rules
made by those in authority
▶ **compliant** /kəm'plaɪənt/ adj
obedient

0━ **complicate** /'kɒmplɪkeɪt/ v [T]
make sth difficult to do, understand
or deal with ▶ **complicated** adj
difficult to understand or explain
because there are many different
parts ▶ **complication**
/ˌkɒmplɪ'keɪʃn/ n [C] something
that makes a situation more difficult

complicity /kəm'plɪsəti/ n [U] (fml)
taking part with another person in a
crime

compliment /'kɒmplɪmənt/ n **1** [C]
remark that expresses praise,
admiration, etc **2** (compliments) [pl]

(fml) greetings or good wishes
● **compliment** /'kɒmplɪmənt/ v [T]
express praise or admiration of sb/
sth ▶ **complimentary** /-'mentri/ adj
1 expressing admiration **2** given
free of charge: ~ tickets

comply /kəm'plaɪ/ v (pt, pp -ied) [I]
~ (with) (fml) obey a rule, an order,
etc

component /kəm'pəʊnənt/ n [C] any
of the parts of which sth is made
▶ **component** adj

compose /kəm'pəʊz/ v **1** [I, T] write
music, a poem, a letter, etc **2** [T]
(fml) manage to control your
feelings or expression: She made a
real effort to ~ herself. ▶ **composed**
adj **1** (be composed of sth) made or
formed from several parts, things or
people **2** calm ▶ **composer** n [C]
person who writes music

composite /'kɒmpəzɪt/ n [C], adj
(thing) made up of different parts or
materials

composition /ˌkɒmpə'zɪʃn/ n **1** [C]
sth, eg a piece of music, that is
composed **2** [U] action of
composing sth **3** [C] short piece of
written work done at school **4** [U]
parts of which sth is made: the
chemical ~ of the soil

compost /'kɒmpɒst/ n [U] mixture of
decayed plants, manure, etc, added
to soil to help plants grow

composure /kəm'pəʊʒə(r)/ n [U]
(fml) calmness

compound[1] /'kɒmpaʊnd/ n [C]
1 thing made up of two or more
parts **2** (chem) substance formed by
a chemical reaction of two or more
elements **3** (gram) word made up of
two or more words, eg travel agent,
dark-haired **4** enclosed area with
buildings, etc: a prison ~
● **compound** adj (tech) formed of
two or more parts ■ **compound
'interest** n [U] interest paid on both
the original amount of money and
on the interest added to it

compound[2] /kəm'paʊnd/ v [T] (fml)
1 make sth bad become even worse
2 (tech) mix sth together

comprehend /ˌkɒmprɪ'hend/ v [T]
(fml) understand sth fully

comprehension /ˌkɒmprɪ'henʃn/ n
1 [U] ability to understand sth **2** [C]
exercise that trains students to
understand a language: a reading/
listening ~ ▶ **comprehensible**
/-'hensəbl/ adj that can be
understood by sb

comprehensive /ˌkɒmprɪ'hensɪv/
adj **1** including (nearly) everything:
a ~ description **2** (GB) (of education)
for pupils of all abilities in the same
school ● **comprehensive** (also
compre'hensive school) n [C] (in
Britain) large secondary school
which teaches pupils of all abilities

compress /kəm'pres/ v [T] **1** force

sth into a small(er) space; press sth together **2** put ideas, etc into fewer words ▸ **compression** /-'preʃn/ n [U]

comprise /kəm'praɪz/ v [T] have sb/sth as parts or members; be composed of sb/sth

compromise /'kɒmprəmaɪz/ n [C,U] settling of an argument by which each side gives up sth it had asked for ● **compromise** v **1** [I] make a compromise **2** [T] put sb/sth into a dangerous or embarrassing position

compulsion /kəm'pʌlʃn/ n **1** [U,C] strong pressure that makes sb do sth they do not want to do **2** [C] strong desire to do sth

compulsive /kəm'pʌlsɪv/ adj **1** (of behaviour) that is difficult to stop or control: ~ eating/spending **2** (of people) not being able to control their behaviour: a ~ liar **3** that makes you pay attention to it because it is so interesting and exciting: The programme makes ~ viewing.

compulsory /kəm'pʌlsəri/ adj that must be done; required by the law, etc

compunction /kəm'pʌŋkʃn/ n [U] (fml) feeling of guilt

compute /kəm'pjuːt/ v [T] (fml) calculate sth ▸ **computation** /ˌkɒmpjuˈteɪʃn/ n [C,U] act or process of calculating sth

0-ᵣ **computer** /kəm'pjuːtə(r)/ n [C] electronic device that can store, organize and find information, do calculations and control other machines ▸ **computerize** (also -ise) v [T] **1** provide a computer to do the work of sth **2** store information on a computer: ~ized records ▸ **computerization** (also -isation) /kəmˌpjuːtəraɪˈzeɪʃn/ n [U] ◼ **computer-literate** adj able to use computers well

comrade /'kɒmreɪd/ n [C] person who is a member of the same communist or socialist political party as the speaker

Con abbr (in British politics) Conservative

con /kɒn/ v (-nn-) [T] (infml) trick sb ● **con** n [C] (infml) trick: He's a real ~ artist (= person who regularly cheats others). ◼ **con man** n [C] (infml) man who tricks others into giving him their money, etc

concave /kɒn'keɪv/ adj curved inwards

conceal /kən'siːl/ v [T] hide sb/sth ▸ **concealment** n [U] (fml)

concede /kən'siːd/ v **1** [T] admit that sth is true **2** [T] give sth away, esp unwillingly; allow sb to have sth **3** [I,T] admit that you have lost a game, etc

conceit /kən'siːt/ n [U] too high an opinion of yourself ▸ **conceited** adj

conceive /kən'siːv/ v [I,T] **1** ~ (of) form an idea, etc in your mind;

| 87 | **concession** |

imagine sth **2** become pregnant ▸ **conceivable** adj that you can imagine ▸ **conceivably** adv

0-ᵣ **concentrate** /'kɒnsntreɪt/ v **1** [I] ~ (on) give your full attention to sth: ~ on your work **2** [T] bring sth together in one place **3** [T] (tech) increase the strength of a substance by reducing its volume ● **concentrate** n [C,U] substance or liquid that is made stronger because water or other substances have been removed

concentration /ˌkɒnsnˈtreɪʃn/ n **1** [U] ability to give your full attention to sth **2** [U] ~ (on) process of people directing their full attention on a particular thing **3** [C] ~ (of) a lot of sth in one place ◼ **concentration camp** n [C] prison for political prisoners

concentric /kən'sentrɪk/ adj (of circles) having the same centre

0-ᵣ **concept** /'kɒnsept/ n [C] general idea

conception /kən'sepʃn/ n **1** [U] process of forming an idea or a plan **2** [U] understanding or belief of what sth is **3** [U,C] act of conceiving (2)

0-ᵣ **concern** /kən'sɜːn/ v [T] **1** involve sb; affect sb **2** be about sth **3** worry sb: I'm ~ed about her safety. **4** ~ yourself with/about take an interest in sth [IDM] as/so far as I am concerned → FAR¹ ▸ **concerning** prep (fml) about sth; involving sb/sth ● **concern** n **1** [U,C] worry **2** [C] something that is important to sb **3** [C] business or company: a profitable ~

0-ᵣ **concert** /'kɒnsət/ n [C] musical performance: Oasis in ~ at Wembley Arena [IDM] in concert with sb/sth (fml) working together with sb/sth

concerted /kən'sɜːtɪd/ adj arranged or done by people working together: make a ~ effort

concertina /ˌkɒnsəˈtiːnə/ n [C] musical instrument like a small accordion ▸ **concertina** v [I] fold up by being pressed together from each end

concerto /kən'tʃɜːtəʊ/ n [C] (pl ~s) musical composition for one instrument supported by an orchestra

concession /kən'seʃn/ n **1** [C,U] something that you allow or do, or allow sb to have, in order to end an argument, etc **2** [U] act of conceding **3** [C, usu pl] (GB) reduction in the amount of money that has to be paid; ticket sold at a reduced price to a particular group of people: Adults £2.50, ~ £2, family £5 **4** [C] special right given to sb to do sth: a ~ to drill for oil

conciliate /kən'sɪlɪeɪt/ v [T] (fml) make sb less angry or more pleasant ▸ **conciliation** /kən‚sɪlɪ'eɪʃn/ n [U] ▸ **conciliatory** /kən'sɪlɪətəri/ adj having the intention or effect of making angry people calm

concise /kən'saɪs/ adj giving a lot of information in a few words ▸ **concisely** adv ▸ **conciseness** n [U]

0▬ **conclude** /kən'kluːd/ v 1 [T] come to believe sth as a result of what you have heard or seen: The report ~d that the road should be closed to traffic. 2 [I,T] (fml) come or bring sth to an end 3 [T] arrange and settle an agreement with sb formally ▸ **conclusion** /kən'kluːʒn/ n [C] 1 decision; settlement 2 end of sth ▸ **conclusive** /kən'kluːsɪv/ proving sth and allowing no doubt: ~ evidence ▸ **conclusively** adv

concoct /kən'kɒkt/ v [T] 1 make sth, esp food or drink, by mixing several things together 2 invent a story, an excuse, etc ▸ **concoction** /kən'kɒkʃn/ n [C] strange or unusual mixture of things, esp drinks or medicines

concord /'kɒŋkɔːd/ n [U] (fml) agreement or harmony

concourse /'kɒŋkɔːs/ n [C] large open part of a public building, esp an airport or a train station

0▬ **concrete** /'kɒŋkriːt/ adj 1 made of concrete: a ~ wall/floor 2 based on facts, not on ideas or guesses 3 existing in material form; that can be touched, etc ● **concrete** n [U] building material made by mixing cement with sand, gravel, etc ● **concrete** v [T] cover sth with concrete

concur /kən'kɜː(r)/ v (-rr-) [I] (fml) agree ▸ **concurrence** /kən'kʌrəns/ n 1 [U,sing] agreement 2 [sing] example of two or more things happening at the same time ▸ **concurrent** /kən'kʌrənt/ adj existing or happening at the same time ▸ **concurrently** adv

concuss /kən'kʌs/ v [T] hit sb on the head, making them unconscious or confused for a short time ▸ **concussion** /kən'kʌʃn/ n [U]

condemn /kən'dem/ v [T] 1 say that you disapprove of sb/sth 2 ~ to (law) say what sb's punishment will be: He was ~ed to death. 3 ~ to make sb accept sth unpleasant: ~ed to a job she hates 4 say officially that a building, etc is unfit for use ▸ **condemnation** /‚kɒndem'neɪʃn/ n [U,C]

condense /kən'dens/ v 1 [I,T] (cause a gas to) change into a liquid 2 [I,T] (cause a liquid to) become thicker and stronger because it has lost

some of its water 3 [T] put sth into fewer words: ~ a speech ▸ **condensation** /‚kɒnden'seɪʃn/ n [U] 1 drops of liquid formed on a cool surface when warm water vapour condenses 2 process of a gas changing to a liquid ▸ **condenser** n [C]

condescend /‚kɒndɪ'send/ v [T] ~ (to) (disapprov) do sth that you think is below your social or professional position to do ▸ **condescending** adj ▸ **condescension** /‚kɒndɪ'senʃn/ n [U]

condiment /'kɒndɪmənt/ n [C] seasoning, eg salt or pepper

0▬ **condition** /kən'dɪʃn/ n 1 [U,sing] what sth is like; state of sth: a car in good~ 2 [U,sing] state of sb's health or physical fitness: be out of ~ 3 [C] illness or medical problem: He has a heart ~. 4 (conditions) [pl] circumstances 5 [C] rule or decision that you must agree to, esp as part of an agreement or contract: They agreed to lend us the car on ~ that (= only if) we returned it the next day. 6 [C] situation that must exist in order for sth else to happen: One of the ~s of the job is that you can drive. ● **condition** v [T] 1 train sb/sth to behave or think in a certain way 2 have an important effect on sb/sth; influence the way sth happens ▸ **conditioner** n [C,U] liquid that makes hair healthy and shiny after washing ▸ **conditioning** n [U]

conditional /kən'dɪʃənl/ adj 1 ~ (on) depending on sth: Payment is ~ on satisfactory completion of the work. 2 (gram) (of a clause) beginning with if or unless ▸ **conditionally** /-ʃənəli/ adv

condolence /kən'dəʊləns/ n [C, usu pl, U] expression of sympathy

condom /'kɒndɒm/ n [C] rubber covering worn by a man on his penis during sex, as a contraceptive

condone /kən'dəʊn/ v [T] accept behaviour that is morally wrong as if it were not serious

conducive /kən'djuːsɪv/ adj ~ to (written) allowing or helping sth to happen

0▬ **conduct¹** /kən'dʌkt/ v 1 [T] organize and do a particular activity: ~ a survey 2 [I,T] direct a group of people who are singing or playing music 3 [T] lead or guide sb through or around a place 4 ~ yourself (fml) behave in a certain way 5 [T] allow heat, electricity, etc to pass along or through sth ▸ **conduction** /kən'dʌkʃn/ n [U] conducting of heat or electricity ▸ **conductor** n [C] 1 person who conducts an orchestra, etc 2 (GB) person who sells tickets on a bus 3 substance that conducts heat or electricity

conduct² /ˈkɒndʌkt/ n [U]
1 behaviour: *The sport has a strict code of ~.* **2** way in which a business or an activity is organized and managed

cone /kəʊn/ n [C] **1** solid body that narrows to a point from a circular flat base **2** solid or hollow object that is shaped like a cone: *an ice-cream ~* **3** fruit of certain evergreen trees, eg fir or pine

confection /kənˈfekʃn/ n [C] cake or other sweet food that looks very attractive ▶ **confectioner** /kənˈfekʃənə(r)/ n [C] person who makes and sells sweets and cakes ▶ **confectionery** n [U] (*written*) sweets, cakes, etc

confederacy /kənˈfedərəsi/ n [sing] union of states, groups of people or political parties with the same aim

confederate /kənˈfedərət/ n [C] person who helps sb, esp to do sth illegal or secret

confederation /kənˌfedəˈreɪʃn/ n [C] organization of countries, businesses, etc that have joined together to help each other

confer /kənˈfɜː(r)/ v (-rr-) (*fml*) **1** [I] ~ (**with**) discuss sth with sb **2** [T] ~ (**on**) give sb an award, a university degree or a particular honour or right

0—**conference** /ˈkɒnfərəns/ n [C] **1** large official meeting, usu lasting for a few days, at which people with the same work or interests come together for discussion or exchange of opinions **2** meeting at which people have formal discussions: *He was in ~ with his lawyers all day.*

confess /kənˈfes/ v [I,T] **1** admit, esp formally or to the police, that you have done sth wrong or illegal **2** admit sth that you feel ashamed or embarrassed about **3** (esp in the Roman Catholic Church) tell your sins formally to a priest ▶ **confession** /kənˈfeʃn/ n [C,U] **1** statement admitting that you have done sth wrong **2** telling of your sins to a priest ▶ **confessional** /kənˈfeʃənl/ n [C] private enclosed place in a church where a priest hears confessions

confetti /kənˈfeti/ n [U] small pieces of coloured paper thrown at weddings

confidant (*fem* **confidante**) /ˌkɒnfɪˈdɑːnt; ˌkɒnfɪˈdænt/ n [C] person that you trust and who you talk to about private or secret things

confide /kənˈfaɪd/ v [I] tell sb secrets and personal information that you do not want others to know [**PV**] **confide in sb** tell sb secrets, etc because you feel you can trust them

0—**confidence** /ˈkɒnfɪdəns/ n **1** [U] ~ (**in**) firm trust in the abilities or good qualities of sb/sth: *I have every*

~ in her ability. **2** [U] belief in your own ability to do things and be successful **3** [U] feeling that you are certain about sth **4** [U] feeling of trust that sb will keep information private: *He told me this in the strictest ~.* **5** [C] (*fml*) secret that you tell sb [**IDM**] **take sb into your confidence** tell sb a secret ▶ **confident** /ˈkɒnfɪdənt/ *adj* very sure ▶ **confidently** *adv*

confidential /ˌkɒnfɪˈdenʃl/ *adj* **1** meant to be kept secret **2** trusted with secrets ▶ **confidentiality** /ˌkɒnfɪˌdenʃiˈæləti/ n [U] ▶ **confidentially** /-ʃəli/ *adv*

configuration /kənˌfɪɡəˈreɪʃn/ n **1** (*fml*) arrangement of the parts of sth **2** (*computing*) equipment and programs that form a computer system and the way these are set up to run

0—**confine** /kənˈfaɪn/ v [T] **1** ~ (**to**) keep sb/sth within certain limits: *The illness was ~d to the village.* **2** keep sb shut in: *~d to bed with a fever* ▶ **confined** *adj* (of space) limited; restricted ▶ **confinement** n [U] state of being shut in a closed space, prison, etc; act of putting sb there ▶ **confines** /ˈkɒnfaɪnz/ n [pl] (*fml*) limits; borders

0—**confirm** /kənˈfɜːm/ v [T] **1** show or say that sth is true: *The announcement ~ed my suspicions.* **2** say or write that sth is definite: *Please write to ~ the details.* **3** (usu passive) make sb a full member of the Christian Church ▶ **confirmation** /ˌkɒnfəˈmeɪʃn/ n [C,U] ▶ **confirmed** *adj* unlikely to change: *a ~ed bachelor*

confiscate /ˈkɒnfɪskeɪt/ v [T] officially take sth away from sb, esp as a punishment ▶ **confiscation** /ˌkɒnfɪˈskeɪʃn/ n [C,U]

conflagration /ˌkɒnfləˈɡreɪʃn/ n [C] (*fml*) large and destructive fire

0—**conflict** /ˈkɒnflɪkt/ n [C,U] **1** struggle, fight or serious disagreement **2** (of opinions, etc) opposition; difference ▶ **conflict** /kənˈflɪkt/ v [I] be in opposition

conform /kənˈfɔːm/ v [I] **1** ~ (**to**) keep to generally accepted rules, standards, etc **2** ~ **with/to** agree with sth ▶ **conformist** n [C] person who conforms ▶ **conformity** n [U]

confound /kənˈfaʊnd/ v [T] (*old-fash, fml*) puzzle and surprise sb

0—**confront** /kənˈfrʌnt/ v [T] **1** ~ (**with**) make sb face sth unpleasant or difficult **2** meet sb face to face; oppose sb ▶ **confrontation** /ˌkɒnfrʌnˈteɪʃn/ n [U,C] (instance of) angry opposition between two or more people

0—**confuse** /kənˈfjuːz/ v [T] **1** make sb unable to think clearly **2** mistake

---

A B **C** D E F G H I J K L M N O P Q R S T U V W X Y Z

sb/sth for sb/sth else: *Don't ~ quality with quantity.* **3** make sth unclear ▸ **confusion** /kənˈfjuːʒn/ n [U]

congeal /kənˈdʒiːl/ v [I] (of blood, fat, etc) become thick and solid

congenial /kənˈdʒiːniəl/ adj **1** pleasant: *a ~ atmosphere* **2** having similar interests ▸ **congenially** adv

congenital /kənˈdʒenɪtl/ adj (of a disease or medical condition) present from or before birth

congested /kənˈdʒestɪd/ adj too full; overcrowded: *streets ~ with traffic* ▸ **congestion** /kənˈdʒestʃən/ n [U]

conglomerate /kənˈɡlɒmərət/ n [C] (business) large business organization consisting of several different firms ▸ **conglomeration** /kənˌɡlɒməˈreɪʃn/ n [C] mixture of different things that are found all together

congratulate /kənˈɡrætʃuleɪt/ v [T] tell sb you are pleased about their success or achievements: *~ sb on good exam results*

0━ **congratulations** /kənˌɡrætʃuˈleɪʃnz/ exclam used for congratulating sb

congregate /ˈkɒŋɡrɪɡeɪt/ v [I] come together in a group ▸ **congregation** /ˌkɒŋɡrɪˈɡeɪʃn/ n [C] group of people who regularly attend a church ▸ **congregational** adj

0━ **congress** /ˈkɒŋɡres/ n [C, with sing or pl verb] **1** large formal meeting for discussion **2** (Congress) (in the US, etc) group of people elected to make laws ▸ **congressional** /kənˈɡreʃənl/ adj ■ **'Congressman | 'Congresswoman** n [C] member of the US Congress

congruent /ˈkɒŋɡruənt/ adj (of triangles) having the same size and shape

conical /ˈkɒnɪkl/ adj shaped like a cone

conifer /ˈkɒnɪfə(r); ˈkəʊn-/ n [C] tree, eg pine or fir, that produces hard dry fruit (cones) ▸ **coniferous** /kəˈnɪfərəs/ adj

conjecture /kənˈdʒektʃə(r)/ v [I,T] (fml) guess sth ● **conjecture** n [U,C] (fml) guessing ▸ **conjectural** adj

conjugal /ˈkɒndʒəɡl/ adj (fml) of the relationship between a husband and wife

conjunction /kənˈdʒʌŋkʃn/ n [C] **1** (gram) word, eg and, but or that joins words, phrases or sentences **2** [C] combination of events, etc that causes a particular result [IDM] **in conjunction with** (fml) together with

conjure /ˈkʌndʒə(r)/ v [I] do clever tricks that appear magical [PV] **conjure sth up** cause sth to appear as a picture in the mind ▸ **conjuror** (also -er) n [C] person who performs conjuring tricks

conk /kɒŋk/ [PV] **conk out** (infml) **1** (of a machine) stop working: *His old car has ~ed out.* **2** (esp US) (of a person) fall asleep

0━ **connect** /kəˈnekt/ v [I,T] come or bring two or more things together; join sth: *~ two wires* **2** [I,T] (cause sb/sth to) have a link with sth: *be ~ed by marriage* ◇ *There's nothing to ~ him with the crime.* **3** [I,T] join a computer to the Internet or a network: *Click 'Continue' to ~ to the Internet.*

0━ **connection** (GB also connexion) /kəˈnekʃn/ n **1** [C] something that connects two facts, ideas, etc **2** [U,C] act of connecting or state of being connected: *I'm having problems with my Internet ~.* **3** [C] train, coach, etc that takes passengers on the next stage of their journey **4** [C, usu pl] person you know who can help or advise you in your social or professional life: *He's one of my business ~s.* [IDM] **in connection with sb/sth** for reasons connected with sb/sth

connive /kəˈnaɪv/ v [I] (disapprov) **1 ~ at** seem to allow sth wrong to happen **2** work with sb to do sth wrong or illegal ▸ **connivance** n [U]

connoisseur /ˌkɒnəˈsɜː(r)/ n [C] expert, eg on food or art

connotation /ˌkɒnəˈteɪʃn/ n idea or quality suggested by a word in addition to its main meaning: *negative ~s*

conquer /ˈkɒŋkə(r)/ v [T] **1** take control of a country, city, etc by force **2** defeat sb or overcome sth ▸ **conqueror** n [C]

conquest /ˈkɒŋkwest/ n **1** [U] conquering, eg of a country or people **2** [C] something gained by conquering

conscience /ˈkɒnʃəns/ n [C, U] sense of right and wrong: *have a clear/ guilty ~* (= feel that you have done right/wrong) [IDM] **on your conscience** making you feel guilty for doing or failing to do sth

conscientious /ˌkɒnʃiˈenʃəs/ adj (of a person or their actions) very careful ▸ **conscientiously** adv ▸ **conscientiousness** n [U]

0━ **conscious** /ˈkɒnʃəs/ adj **1** awake **2 ~ (of)** aware of sth **3** intentional: *make a ~ effort* ▸ **consciously** adv ▸ **consciousness** n [U]: *regain ~ness after an accident*

conscript /kənˈskrɪpt/ v [T] force sb by law to serve in the armed forces ▸ **conscript** /ˈkɒnskrɪpt/ n [C] person who has been conscripted ▸ **conscription** /kənˈskrɪpʃn/ n [U]

consecrate /ˈkɒnsɪkreɪt/ v [T] **1** officially declare sth to be holy or sb to be a priest: *~ a church* **2** reserve sth for a special (esp religious) purpose ▶ consecration /ˌkɒnsɪˈkreɪʃn/ n [U]

consecutive /kənˈsekjʊtɪv/ adj coming one after the other without interruption ▶ consecutively adv

consensus /kənˈsensəs/ n [C, U] general opinion

consent /kənˈsent/ v [I] ~ (to) give agreement to or permission for sth ▶ consent n [U] agreement; permission

0━ consequence /ˈkɒnsɪkwəns/ n 1 [C] result or effect: the political ~s of the decision 2 [U] (fml) importance: It is of no ~.

consequent /ˈkɒnsɪkwənt/ adj (fml) following as a result ▶ consequently adv therefore

consequential /ˌkɒnsɪˈkwenʃl/ adj (fml) 1 consequent 2 important

conservation /ˌkɒnsəˈveɪʃn/ n [U] 1 (fml) protection of the natural environment 2 prevention of loss, waste, etc: ~ of energy ▶ conservationist n [C] person interested in protecting the natural environment

0━ conservative /kənˈsɜːvətɪv/ adj 1 opposed to great or sudden change 2 (Conservative) of the Conservative Party 3 cautious; moderate: a ~ estimate ● conservative n [C] 1 conservative person 2 (Conservative) member of the Conservative Party ▶ conservatively adv ■ the Conservative Party n [sing, with sing or pl verb] one of the main British political parties, on the political right, which supports capitalism ▶ conservatism /kənˈsɜːvətɪzəm/ n [U]

conservatory /kənˈsɜːvətri/ n [C] (pl -ies) 1 (GB) room with glass walls and roof that is built at the side of a house for growing plants in, etc 2 (esp US) school of music, drama, etc

conserve /kənˈsɜːv/ v [T] prevent sth from being changed, lost or destroyed ● conserve /ˈkɒnsɜːv/ n [C, U] (fml) jam, with quite large pieces of fruit

0━ consider /kənˈsɪdə(r)/ v [T] 1 think about sth carefully 2 think of sb/sth in a particular way: We ~ this (to be) very important. 3 take sth into account: ~ the feelings of others ▶ considered adj as a result of careful thought: a ~ed opinion

0━ considerable /kənˈsɪdərəbl/ adj great in amount or size ▶ considerably /kənˈsɪdərəbli/ adv (fml) much; a lot: It's considerably colder today.

considerate /kənˈsɪdərət/ adj kind and thinking of the needs of others ▶ considerately adv

0━ consideration /kənˌsɪdəˈreɪʃn/ n 1 [U] careful thought 2 [C]

consortium

something that must be thought about, esp when deciding sth: Cost is just one of the ~s. 3 [U] quality of being thoughtful towards others 4 [C] (fml) reward; payment [IDM] take sth into consideration think about and include a particular fact or fact when forming an opinion or making a decision

considering /kənˈsɪdərɪŋ/ prep, conj used to show that you are thinking about and are influenced by a particular fact when you make a statement about sth: She's very active, ~ her age.

consign /kənˈsaɪn/ v (fml) [T] 1 put sth/sb somewhere in order to get rid of them: ~ the letter to the waste-paper basket 2 give or send sth to sb ▶ consignment n 1 [C] quantity of goods sent or delivered somewhere 2 [U] act of sending or delivering sth

0━ consist /kənˈsɪst/ v [I] [PV] consist in sth have sth as the main or only part consist of sth be made up of sth: a meal ~ing of soup and bread

consistency /kənˈsɪstənsi/ (pl -ies) n 1 [U] quality of being consistent (1) 2 [C, U] degree of thickness, smoothness, etc, esp of a liquid

consistent /kənˈsɪstənt/ adj 1 (approv) always behaving in the same way, having the same opinions, standards, etc 2 ~ (with) in agreement: injuries ~ with the accident ▶ consistently adv

consolation /ˌkɒnsəˈleɪʃn/ n [U, C] person or thing that makes you feel better when you are unhappy

console¹ /kənˈsəʊl/ v [T] give sb comfort or sympathy

console² /ˈkɒnsəʊl/ n [C] panel for the controls of electronic equipment

consolidate /kənˈsɒlɪdeɪt/ v [I, T] 1 become or make sth stronger, more secure, etc 2 (tech) join things together or become joined into one: ~ all his debts ▶ consolidation /kənˌsɒlɪˈdeɪʃn/ n [U]

consommé /kənˈsɒmeɪ/ n [U] clear meat soup

consonant /ˈkɒnsənənt/ n [C] 1 speech sound made by (partly) stopping the breath with the tongue, lips, etc 2 letter of the alphabet that represents a consonant sound, eg b, c and d

consort /ˈkɒnsɔːt/ n [C] husband or wife, esp of a ruler ● consort /kənˈsɔːt/ v [I] ~ with (fml) spend time with sb that others disapprove of: ~ing with criminals

consortium /kənˈsɔːtiəm/ n (pl -s, -tia /-tiə/) [C, with sing or pl verb] group of businesses, banks, etc with a common purpose

conspicuous /kənˈspɪkjuəs/ *adj* easily seen; noticeable ▸ **conspicuously** *adv*

conspiracy /kənˈspɪrəsi/ *n* (pl **-ies**) [C,U] secret plan by a group of people to do sth harmful or illegal

conspire /kənˈspaɪə(r)/ *v* [I]
1 ~ (with; against) secretly plan with other people to do sth harmful or illegal: *He ~d with others against the government.* **2 ~ against** (*written*) (of events) seem to work together to make sth bad happen: *Circumstances ~d against them.* ▸ **conspirator** /kənˈspɪrətə(r)/ *n* [C] person who conspires

constable /ˈkʌnstəbl/ *n* [C] = POLICE CONSTABLE ▸ **constabulary** /kənˈstæbjələri/ *n* [C, with sing or pl verb] (pl **-ies**) (in Britain) police force of a particular area

0—**constant** /ˈkɒnstənt/ *adj*
1 continuing all the time: ~ *noise* **2** not changing: *a ~ temperature* ▸ **constancy** *n* [U] state of being constant (2)

constellation /ˌkɒnstəˈleɪʃn/ *n* [C] group of stars with a name

consternation /ˌkɒnstəˈneɪʃn/ *n* [U] feeling of surprise, fear and worry

constipated /ˈkɒnstɪpeɪtɪd/ *adj* not able to empty waste matter from the bowels easily ▸ **constipation** /ˌkɒnstɪˈpeɪʃn/ *n* [U]

constituency /kənˈstɪtjuənsi/ *n* [C, with sing or pl verb] (pl **-ies**) (in Britain) (voters living in an) area that sends a representative to Parliament

constituent /kənˈstɪtjuənt/ *adj*
1 being part of a whole **2** (of an assembly, etc) having the power or right to alter a political constitution ● **constituent** *n* [C] **1** member of a constituency **2** part of a whole

constitute /ˈkɒnstɪtjuːt/ *v* linking verb
1 be considered to be sth: *The decision to build the road ~s a real threat to the countryside.* **2** be the parts that together form sth: *Twelve months ~ a year.*

constitution /ˌkɒnstɪˈtjuːʃn/ *n* [C] **1** set of laws and principles according to which a country is governed **2** person's physical structure and condition: *a strong ~* **3** general structure of sth ▸ **constitutional** *adj* conforming to the laws, etc by which a country is governed ▸ **constitutionally** /-ʃənəli/ *adv*

constrain /kənˈstreɪn/ *v* [T] (*fml*)
1 make sb do sth by force or strong persuasion: *I felt ~ed to obey.* **2** restrict or limit sth/sb

constraint /kənˈstreɪnt/ *n* [C] thing that limits or restricts sth, or your freedom to do sth: *One of the ~s on the project will be the money*

available. **2** [U] strict control over the way you behave

constrict /kənˈstrɪkt/ *v* [I,T] become or make sth tighter, smaller or narrower: *Her throat ~ed and she swallowed hard.* **2** [T] limit or restrict what sb is allowed to do ▸ **constriction** /kənˈstrɪkʃn/ *n* [U,C]

0—**construct** /kənˈstrʌkt/ *v* [T] build sth or put sth together

0—**construction** /kənˈstrʌkʃn/ *n* **1** [U] way or act of building sth: *The new bridge is still under ~.* **2** [C] (*fml*) structure; building **3** [C] way in which words are used together and arranged to form a sentence, phrase, etc: *grammatical ~s* ▸ **constructive** /kənˈstrʌktɪv/ *adj* helpful; useful: ~ *suggestions* ▸ **constructively** *adv*

consul /ˈkɒnsl/ *n* [C] official sent by his/her government to live in a foreign country and help people from his/her own country who are living there ▸ **consular** /ˈkɒnsjələ(r)/ *adj* of a consul or his/ her work ▸ **consulate** /ˈkɒnsjələt/ *n* [C] consul's office

0—**consult** /kənˈsʌlt/ *v* [I,T] go to a person, book, etc for information, advice or help: ~ *the doctor about a sore throat* [I,T] ~ **with** discuss sth with sb to get their permission for sth or to help you make a decision: *You should have ~ed me before going ahead.*

consultant /kənˈsʌltənt/ *n* [C]
1 person who is paid to give expert advice **2** (*GB*) senior hospital doctor who specializes in a particular branch of medicine

consultation /ˌkɒnslˈteɪʃn/ *n* [U] act of discussing sth with sb before making a decision about it **2** [C] meeting with an expert, esp a doctor, to get advice or treatment

consume /kənˈsjuːm/ *v* [T] use sth: *Some types of car ~ less petrol than others.* **2** (*fml*) eat or drink sth **3 ~ (with)** fill sb with a strong feeling: *She was ~d with guilt.* **4** (of fire, etc) destroy sth ▸ **consuming** *adj* very strong

0—**consumer** /kənˈsjuːmə(r)/ *n* [C] person who buys goods ● con**sumer durables** *n* [pl] (*business*) goods expected to last for a long time, such as cars, televisions, etc ● con**sumer goods** *n* [pl] goods bought by individual customers, such as food, clothes, etc

consummate[1] /ˈkɒnsəmət; kənˈsʌmət/ *adj* (*fml*) very skilled; perfect

consummate[2] /ˈkɒnsəmeɪt/ *v* [T] (*fml*) **1** make a marriage or relationship complete by having sex **2** make sth perfect ▸ **consummation** /ˌkɒnsəˈmeɪʃn/ *n* [C,U]

consumption /kən'sʌmpʃn/ n [U] act of using food, resources, etc; amount used: *This food is not fit for human ~.* ◇ *measure a car's fuel ~*

0-ᴡ **contact** /'kɒntækt/ n **1** [U] act of communicating with sb, esp communicating with sb, esp regularly: *Stay in ~ with your parents.* **2** [U] state of touching sth: *This substance should not come into ~ with food.* **3** [C, usu pl] instance of meeting or communicating with sb: *a job involving ~s with other companies* **4** [C] person that you know, esp sb who can be helpful to you in your work: *He has several ~s in the building trade.* **5** [C] electrical connection ● **contact** v [T] communicate with sb, esp by telephone or letter: *Where can I ~ you next week?* ■ **'contact lens** n [C] thin piece of plastic that you put on your eye to help you see better

contagion /kən'teɪdʒən/ n [U] spreading of disease by being close to or touching other people ▸ **contagious** /kən'teɪdʒəs/ adj **1** (of a disease) spread by people touching each other: *Scarlet fever is highly ~.* ◇ *(fig) a laugh* **2** (of a person) having a disease that can be spread to others by touch

0-ᴡ **contain** /kən'teɪn/ v [T] **1** have or hold sth inside: *a bottle ~ing two litres of milk* **2** (written) keep your feelings under control **3** (written) prevent sth harmful from spreading or getting worse: ~ *an epidemic*

0-ᴡ **container** /kən'teɪnə(r)/ n [C] **1** bottle, box, etc for holding sth: *a ~ for sugar* **2** large metal box, etc for transporting goods

contaminate /kən'tæmɪneɪt/ v [T] make sth dirty or impure: *~d food* ▸ **contamination** /-'neɪʃn/ n [U]

0-ᴡ **contemplate** /'kɒntəmpleɪt/ v [T] **1** think carefully about sth; consider doing sth: ~ *visiting London* **2** (fml) look at sth thoughtfully: ~ *a picture* ▸ **contemplation** /ˌkɒntəm'pleɪʃn/ n [U] act of contemplating sth; deep thought ▸ **contemplative** /kən'templətɪv/ adj thoughtful

0-ᴡ **contemporary** /kən'temprəri/ adj **1** belonging to the same time: *a play by Shakespeare accompanied by ~ music* **2** of the present time; modern ● **contemporary** n [C] (pl **-ies**) person who lived or lives at the same time as another person: *Shakespeare and his contemporaries*

contempt /kən'tempt/ n [U] ~ **(for)** **1** feeling that sb/sth is of no value and cannot be respected: *feel ~ for people who are cruel to animals* **2** lack of respect for rules, danger, etc: *her ~ for the risks* ▸ **contemptible** /kən'temptəbl/ adj not deserving any respect at all ■ **con'tempt of 'court** n [U] crime of not obeying a court or judge: *He was in ~ of court.*

▸ **contemptuous** /kən'temptʃuəs/ adj feeling or showing contempt

contend /kən'tend/ v **1** [I, T] say that sth is true, esp in an argument: *He ~ed that the theory was wrong.* **2** [I] compete against sb in order to gain sth [PV] **contend with sth** have to deal with a problem or difficult situation ▸ **contender** n [C] person who tries to win sth in competition with others

content¹ /kən'tent/ adj satisfied; happy: ~ *to stay at home* ● **content** v [T] ~ **yourself** with accept and be satisfied with sth ▸ **contented** adj satisfied ▸ **contentedly** adv ▸ **contentment** (also **content**) n [U] state of being content

0-ᴡ **content²** /'kɒntent/ n **1** (contents) [pl] what is contained in sth: *the ~s of her bag* **2** (contents) [pl] list of chapters in a book **3** [sing] subject written or spoken about in a book, programme, etc **4** [sing] amount of sth contained in a substance, etc: *the silver ~ of a coin*

contention /kən'tenʃn/ n **1** [U] (fml) angry disagreement between people **2** [C] opinion expressed, esp in an argument ▸ **contentious** /kən'tenʃəs/ adj liking or causing argument

contest¹ /'kɒntest/ n [C] fight; competition

contest² /kən'test/ v [T] **1** take part in and try to win a competition, etc: ~ *an election* **2** formally oppose a decision, etc because you think it is wrong ▸ **contestant** n [C] person who takes part in a competition

0-ᴡ **context** /'kɒntekst/ n [C, U] **1** situation in which an event happens **2** sentence, phrase, etc in which a word appears

0-ᴡ **continent** /'kɒntɪnənt/ n **1** [C] one of the main land masses (Europe, Asia, Africa, etc) **2** (the Continent) [sing] (GB) the main part of the continent of Europe, not including Britain and Ireland ▸ **continental** /ˌkɒntɪ'nentl/ adj **1** (also **Continental**) (GB) of or in the continent of Europe, not including Britain and Ireland: *a ~al holiday* **2** of or typical of a continent

contingency /kən'tɪndʒənsi/ n [C] (pl **-ies**) event that may or may not happen: *make ~ plans*

contingent /kən'tɪndʒənt/ n [C, with sing or pl verb] **1** group of people at a meeting or an event who have sth in common **2** group of soldiers that are part of a larger force ● **contingent** adj ~ **(on/upon)** (fml) dependent on chance

continual /kən'tɪnjuəl/ adj happening all the time or very frequently: ~ *rain* ◇ ~ *interruptions*

continuation

▶ **continually** *adv* again and again; without stopping

continuation /kənˌtɪnjuˈeɪʃn/ *n*
1 [U,sing] act of continuing **2** [C] thing that continues beyond or extends sth else: *This road is a ~ of the motorway.*

0━ **continue** /kənˈtɪnjuː/ *v* [I,T] (cause sth to) keep existing or happening without stopping: ~ *running* ◊ *She ~d her visits to the hospital.* **2** [I] go or move further in the same direction: ~ *up the hill* **3** [I] remain in a particular job or condition **4** [I,T] start (sth) again after stopping

continuity /ˌkɒntɪˈnjuːəti/ *n* [U]
1 state of being continuous **2** logical connection between parts of a whole: *The story lacks ~.*

0━ **continuous** /kənˈtɪnjuəs/ *adj* going on without stopping: *a ~ line/noise/flow* ▶ **continuously** *adv* ■ **con·tinuous tense** *n* [C] (*gram*) phrase formed from part of the verb *be* and a verb ending in *-ing*, used to show an action that continues over a period of time, as in *I am singing*

contort /kənˈtɔːt/ *v* [I,T] (cause sth to) become twisted out of its normal shape: *a face ~ed with pain* ▶ **contortion** /kənˈtɔːʃn/ *n* [C,U]

contour /ˈkɒntʊə(r)/ *n* [C] **1** outline of a coast, a human figure, etc **2** (*also* **contour line**) line on a map showing points that are the same height above sea level

contraband /ˈkɒntrəbænd/ *n* [U] goods brought illegally into or out of a country

contraception /ˌkɒntrəˈsepʃn/ *n* [U] preventing of pregnancy ▶ **contraceptive** /ˌkɒntrəˈseptɪv/ *n* [C], *adj* (device, drug, etc for) preventing pregnancy

0━ **contract¹** /ˈkɒntrækt/ *n* [C,U] official written agreement: *a ~ between buyer and seller* ◊ *The builder is under ~ to finish the house by the end of June.* ▶ **contractual** /kənˈtræktʃuəl/ *adj* of or in a contract

0━ **contract²** /kənˈtrækt/ *v* [I,T] (cause sth to) become less or smaller: *Metal ~s as it cools.* **2** [T] (*written*) catch a disease **3** [I,T] make a legal agreement with sb: *She's ~ed to work 35 hours a week.* [PV] **contract out (of sth)** (*GB*) agree not to take part in sth ▶ **contraction** /kənˈtrækʃn/ *n* [U] process of becoming smaller **2** [C] tightening of the muscles around a woman's womb before birth **3** [C] (*ling*) short form of a word: *'Can't' is a ~ion of 'cannot'.*

contradict /ˌkɒntrəˈdɪkt/ *v* [T] **1** say that what a person has said is wrong

and that the opposite is true: *Don't ~ your mother.* **2** (of statements or pieces of evidence) be so different from each other that one of them must be wrong: *Her account ~s what you said.* ▶ **contradiction** *n* [C,U] ▶ **contradictory** *adj* not agreeing: *~ory accounts of the accident*

contraflow /ˈkɒntrəfləʊ/ *n* [C] (*GB*) system used when one half of a large road is closed for repairs, and the traffic going in both directions has to use the other half

contralto /kənˈtræltəʊ/ *n* [C,U] (*pl* **-os**) = ALTO(1)

contraption /kənˈtræpʃn/ *n* [C] (*infml*) strange or complicated device

contrary¹ /ˈkɒntrəri/ *adj* **(to)** opposite; quite different: *~ to what you believe* ● **contrary** *n* (*the contrary*) [sing] the opposite: *The ~ is true.* [IDM] **on the contrary** used to introduce a statement that says the opposite of the last one: *'It must have been awful.' 'On the ~, I loved every minute.'* **to the contrary** showing or proving the opposite: *I shall continue to believe this until I get evidence to the ~.*

contrary² /kənˈtreəri/ *adj* (*fml*) (of children) behaving badly; doing the opposite of what is expected ▶ **contrariness** *n* [U]

0━ **contrast** /kənˈtrɑːst/ *v* **1** [T] compare two things so that differences are made clear **2** [I] show a clear difference: *bright, ~ing colours* ● **contrast** /ˈkɒntrɑːst/ *n* [C,U] clear difference between two or more people or things

contravene /ˌkɒntrəˈviːn/ *v* [T] break a law, rule, etc ▶ **contravention** /ˌkɒntrəˈvenʃn/ *n* [C,U]

contretemps /ˈkɒntrətɒ̃/ (*pl* **contretemps**) *n* [C] unfortunate event or embarrassing disagreement with sb

0━ **contribute** /kənˈtrɪbjuːt, *GB also* ˈkɒntrɪbjuːt/ *v* **1** [I,T] ~ **(to/towards)** join with others in giving help, money, ideas, etc **2** [I] ~ **to** help to cause sth: *~ to her success* **3** [I,T] write articles, etc for newspapers, etc ▶ **contribution** /ˌkɒntrɪˈbjuːʃn/ *n* [C,U] ▶ **contributor** /kənˈtrɪbjətə(r)/ *n* [C] person who contributes ▶ **contributory** /kənˈtrɪbjətəri/ *adj*

contrite /ˈkɒntraɪt; kənˈtraɪt/ *adj* (*fml*) very sorry for sth bad that you have done ▶ **contritely** *adv* ▶ **contrition** /kənˈtrɪʃn/ *n* [U]

contrive /kənˈtraɪv/ *v* [T] (*fml*) **1** find a way of doing sth: *~ to live on a small income* **2** invent, plan or design sth: *~ a way of avoiding paying tax* ▶ **contrivance** *n* [C,U] something that sb has done or written that does not seem natural; fact of seeming artificial **2** [C] clever or complicated device or tool

0☞ **control** /kən'trəʊl/ n **1** [U] power to make decisions about how a country, an organization, etc is run: *A military junta took ~ of the country.* **2** [U] ability to make sb/sth do what you want: *She lost ~ of the car on the ice.* **3** [U,C] act of restricting, limiting or managing sth: *traffic ~* **4** [usu pl] means by which a machine, etc is operated or regulated **5** [C] (*tech*) standard of comparison for the results of an experiment [IDM] **be in control (of sth)** manage, direct or rule sth **be/get/run/etc out of control** be or become impossible to manage or to control: *The children are out of ~ since their father left.* **bring/get/keep sth under control** succeed in dealing with sth so that it does not cause any harm: *The fire was brought under ~.* ● **control** v (-ll-) [T] **1** have power or authority over sb/sth: *~ your temper* **2** limit sth or make it happen in a particular way: *drugs to ~ the pain* **3** make a machine or system work in the way that you want it to: *Dial dial ~s the volume.* ▶ **controller** n [C] person who manages or directs sth, esp part of a large organization

controversy /'kɒntrəvɜːsi, *GB also* kən'trɒvəsi/ n (pl -**ies**) [C,U] public argument or debate about sth many people do not agree with: *~ over the site of the new airport* ▶ **controversial** /ˌkɒntrə'vɜːʃl/ adj causing controversy: *a ~ scheme* ▶ **controversially** adv

conundrum /kə'nʌndrəm/ n [C, usu sing] **1** confusing problem **2** question, usu involving a trick with words, asked for fun

conurbation /ˌkɒnɜː'beɪʃn/ n [C] large urban area formed by several towns which have spread towards each other

convalesce /ˌkɒnvə'les/ v [I] become healthy and strong again after an illness ▶ **convalescence** n [sing, U] (period of) recovery from an illness ▶ **convalescent** n [C], adj (person who is) recovering from illness

convene /kən'viːn/ v [I,T] (arrange for people to) come together for a meeting, etc ▶ **convener** (*also* -**or**) n [C] person who arranges meetings

convenience /kən'viːniəns/ n **1** [U] quality of being useful, easy or suitable for sb **2** [C] device, tool, etc that is useful, suitable, etc: *Central heating is one of the ~s of modern houses.*

0☞ **convenient** /kən'viːniənt/ adj fitting in well with sb's needs; suitable: *a ~ place to stay* ▶ **conveniently** adv

convent /'kɒnvənt/ n [C] building where a community of nuns lives

0☞ **convention** /kən'venʃn/ n **1** [C,U] general, usually unspoken, agreement on how people should behave: *social ~s* **2** [C] meeting of the members of a profession, political party, etc: *a scientists' ~* **3** [C] official agreement between countries or leaders ▶ **conventional** adj based on or following convention (1); normal and ordinary, and perhaps not very interesting ▶ **conventionally** adv

converge /kən'vɜːdʒ/ v [I] (of lines, moving objects) come towards each other and meet at a point: *a village where two roads ~* ▶ **convergence** n [U] ▶ **convergent** adj

conversant /kən'vɜːsnt/ adj ~ **with** having knowledge and experience of sth: *~ with modern methods*

0☞ **conversation** /ˌkɒnvə'seɪʃn/ n [C,U] informal talk involving a small group of people or only two; activity or talking in this way: *I had a long ~ with her yesterday.* ◇ *He was deep in ~ with his boss.* ▶ **conversational** adj not formal; as used in conversation: *a ~ tone/style*

converse[1] /kən'vɜːs/ v [I] ~ **(with)** (*fml*) have a conversation with sb

converse[2] /'kɒnvɜːs/ n (**the converse**) n [sing] the opposite or reverse of a fact or statement ● **converse** adj ▶ **conversely** adv

conversion /kən'vɜːʃn/ n [C,U] (instance of) converting sb/sth: *the ~ of the barn into a house*

0☞ **convert**[1] /kən'vɜːt/ v [I,T] **1** (cause sth to) change from one form, use, etc to another: *~ a house into flats* **2** change or make sb change their religion or beliefs: *He ~ed to Islam.* ▶ **convertible** /kən'vɜːtəbl/ adj that can be changed to a different form or use ▶ **convertible** n [C] car with a roof that can be folded down or removed

convert[2] /'kɒnvɜːt/ n [C] person who has converted, esp to a different religion

convex /'kɒnveks/ adj curved outwards: *~ mirror*

convey /kən'veɪ/ v [T] **1** ~ **(to)** make feelings, ideas, etc known to sb: *She ~ed her fears to her friends.* **2** take, carry or transport sb/sth from one place to another: *goods ~ed by rail* ▶ **conveyance** n [C] (vehicle for) transporting ▶ **conveyancing** n [U] (*law*) branch of law concerned with moving property from one owner to another ▶ **conveyor** (*also* -**er**) n [C] person or thing that conveys sth ■ **con'veyor belt** n [C] (eg in a factory) continuous moving band used for transporting products, etc

convict /kən'vɪkt/ v [T] (of a judge, court, etc) declare that sb is guilty of

a crime: She was ~ed of theft.
● **convict** /'kɒnvɪkt/ n [C] person who has been convicted and sent to prison

conviction /kən'vɪkʃn/ n [C, U]
1 (instance of the) convicting of a person for a crime **2** firm belief: a ~ that what she said was true

0━ **convince** /kən'vɪns/ v [T] **1** ~ (of) make sb/yourself believe that sth is true: You'll need to ~ them of your enthusiasm for the job. **2** persuade sb to do sth ▸ **convincing** adj that makes sb believe that sth is true: a convincing argument ▸ **convincingly** adv

convivial /kən'vɪviəl/ adj cheerful and friendly: a ~ person/evening ▸ **conviviality** /kən,vɪvi'æləti/ n [U]

convoluted /'kɒnvəluːtɪd/ adj **1** extremely complicated and difficult to follow **2** having many twists or curves

convolution /,kɒnvə'luːʃn/ n [C, usu pl] (fml) **1** thing that is very complicated and difficult to follow: the ~s of the plot **2** twist; curve

convoy /'kɒnvɔɪ/ n [C] group of vehicles or ships travelling together, esp when soldiers, etc travel with them for protection [IDM] **in convoy** (of travelling vehicles) as a group; together: to drive in ~

convulse /kən'vʌls/ v [I, T] (cause sb to) make a violent shaking movement: A violent shiver ~d him. ▸ **convulsion** /kən'vʌlʃn/ n [C] **1** [usu pl] sudden uncontrollable and violent body movement **2** sudden important change ▸ **convulsive** adj

coo /kuː/ v **1** [I] make a soft quiet sound like that of a dove **2** [T] say sth in a soft quiet voice ● **coo** n [C]

0━ **cook** /kʊk/ v **1** [I, T] prepare food by heating it: ~ breakfast/dinner **2** (of food) be prepared by boiling, baking, frying, etc [IDM] **cook the books** (infml) change facts or figures dishonestly ● **cook** n [C] person who cooks food ▸ **cooker** n [C] device for cooking food by heating it ▸ **cookery** n [U] art or activity of preparing and cooking food ▸ **cooking** n [U] process of preparing food

0━ **cookie** /'kʊki/ n [C] **1** (esp US) biscuit **2** (US, infml) person: a tough ~ **3** (computing) computer file with information in it that is sent to the central server each time sb uses a network or the Internet

0━ **cool¹** /kuːl/ adj **1** not hot or cold; fairly cold: It feels ~ in the shade. **2** calm; not excited: stay ~ in spite of danger **3** showing no interest, enthusiasm, etc: He was ~ about the suggestion. **4** used about a sum of

money to emphasize how large it is **5** (infml) very good; fine ● **cool** n (the cool) [sing] cool air or place; coolness: sitting in the ~ [IDM] **keep/lose your cool** (infml) remain/not remain calm ● **cool-headed** adj not easily excited or worried; calm ▸ **coolly** adv ▸ **coolness** n [U]

0━ **cool²** /kuːl/ v [I, T] ~ (down/off) become or make sth cooler: Have a drink to ~ down. [PV] **cool down/off** become calm or less excited

coop /kuːp/ n [C] cage, esp for hens ● **coop** v [PV] **coop sb/sth up** confine sb/sth in a small space: prisoners ~ed up in cells

cooperate (also co-operate) /kəʊ'ɒpəreɪt/ v [I] **1** work or act together to achieve sth: They ~d on the project. **2** be helpful by doing what sb asks you to do ▸ **cooperation** (also co-operation) /kəʊ,ɒpə'reɪʃn/ n [U] **1** acting or working together with a common purpose **2** willingness to be helpful ▸ **cooperative** (also co-operative) /kəʊ'ɒpərətɪv/ adj **1** joint **2** willing to co-operate ● **cooperative** (also co-operative) n [C] business that is owned and run by the people involved, and they share the profits

co-opt /kəʊ'ɒpt/ v [T] make sb a member of a committee, etc, by voting for them

coordinate¹ (also co-ordinate) /kəʊ'ɔːdɪneɪt/ v [I, T] ~ **(with)** make actions, limbs, etc work together: ~ efforts to get the project finished ▸ **coordination** (also co-ordination) /kəʊ,ɔːdɪ'neɪʃn/ n [U] ▸ **coordinator** (also co-ordinator)

coordinate² (also co-ordinate) /kəʊ'ɔːdɪnət/ n **1** [C] either of the two numbers or letters used to fix the position of a point on a map, etc **2** (coordinates) [pl] pieces of clothing in matching colours for wearing together

cop /kɒp/ n [C] (infml) police officer ● **cop** v (-pp-) [T] (sl) receive sth unpleasant: ~ a bang on the head [PV] **cop out (of sth)** (infml) avoid or stop doing sth because you are afraid, lazy, etc ● **'cop-out** n [C] (infml, disapprov) act of or excuse for not doing sth

0━ **cope** /kəʊp/ v [I] ~ **(with)** deal successfully with sth difficult: She couldn't ~ with all her work.

copier → COPY²

copious /'kəʊpiəs/ adj (fml) in large amounts: I took ~ notes. ▸ **copiously** adv

copper /'kɒpə(r)/ n **1** [U] (symb Cu) a chemical element. Copper is a soft reddish-brown metal: ~-coloured hair ◇ ~ wire **2** (coppers) [pl] (GB) brown coins, of very low value **3** [C] (GB, infml) police officer

copse /kɒps/ n [C] small area of shrubs and trees

copulate /ˈkɒpjuleɪt/ v [I] ~ **(with)** (tech) have sex ● **copulation** /ˌkɒpjuˈleɪʃn/ n [U]

0-m **copy¹** /ˈkɒpi/ n [C] (pl **-ies**)
1 thing made to be like another, esp a reproduction of a letter, pictures, etc: Put a ~ of the letter in the file.
2 one example of a book, newspaper, etc of which many have been made: The library has two copies of this book. ● **copycat** n [C] (infml, disapprov) person who imitates another's behaviour, clothes, etc

0-m **copy²** /ˈkɒpi/ v (pt, pp **-ied**) **1** [T] make sth that is exactly like sth else: ~ a document on the photocopier **2** [T] write sth exactly as it is written somewhere else: I copied out several poems. **3** [T] behave or do sth in the same way as sb else: She copies everything her sister does. **4** [I] cheat in an exam, etc by copying what sb else has done, written, etc ▶ **copier** n [C] machine that copies documents

copyright /ˈkɒpiraɪt/ n [U, C] author's legal right to print, publish and sell his/her work ▶ **copyright** v [T] get the copyright for sth

coral /ˈkɒrəl/ n [U] hard red, pink or white substance formed on the sea bed by small creatures: a ~ reef ● **coral** adj made of coral

cord /kɔːd/ n **1** [C,U] (piece of) strong thick string or thin rope **2** [C,U] (esp US) = FLEX **3** [U] = CORDUROY

cordial /ˈkɔːdiəl/ adj (fml) warm and friendly ▶ **cordially** adv ● **cordial** n [U] (GB) non-alcoholic sweet drink: lime ~

cordon /ˈkɔːdn/ n [C] ring or line of police officers, soldiers, etc guarding sth or stopping people entering or leaving an area: a police ~ ● **cordon** v [PV] **cordon sth off** stop people getting into an area by surrounding it with police, soldiers, etc: The army ~ed off the area.

corduroy /ˈkɔːdərɔɪ/ n [U] thick cotton cloth with soft raised ridges

0-m **core** /kɔː(r)/ n **1** [C] usu hard centre of some fruits, eg the apple **2** central or most important part of anything: the ~ of the problem [IDM] **to the core** completely: shocked to the ~ ● **core** v [T] take the core out of sth, eg an apple

cork /kɔːk/ n **1** [U] light springy bark from a type of oak tree: ~ table mats **2** [C] round piece of this used to seal bottles, esp wine bottles ● **cork** v [T] seal a bottle with a cork ■ **corkscrew** n [C] tool for pulling corks from bottles

corn /kɔːn/ n **1** [U] (GB) grain (of) any plant that is grown for its grain, such as wheat **2** [U] (US) = MAIZE

---

3 [C] small painful area of hard skin on the foot ■ **corncob** n [C] hard part at the top of a maize stalk on which the grains grow ■ **cornflour** n [U] flour made from maize ■ **corn on the cob** n [C] corn that is cooked with all the grains still attached to the inner part and eaten as a vegetable

cornea /ˈkɔːniə/ n [C] (anat) transparent protective covering of the eyeball

corned beef /ˌkɔːnd ˈbiːf/ n [U] beef preserved in salt

0-m **corner** /ˈkɔːnə(r)/ n [C] **1** place where two lines or surfaces meet **2** place where two streets join **3** region: from all ~s of the earth **4** (infml) difficult or awkward situation: get out of a tight ~ **5** (in sports such as football) free kick taken from the corner of your opponent's end of the field [IDM] **turn the corner** pass a very important point in an illness or a difficult situation and start to improve ● **corner** v **1** [T] trap a person or an animal: ~ed by the police **2** [I] turn a corner on a road, etc: a car designed for fast ~ing

cornet /ˈkɔːnɪt/ n [C] small musical instrument like a trumpet

cornice /ˈkɔːnɪs/ n [C] ornamental border around a ceiling or at the top of a column

corny /ˈkɔːni/ adj (-ier, -iest) (infml) not original; used too often to sound interesting or sincere

coronary /ˈkɒrənri/ adj (med) of the arteries carrying blood to the heart ■ **coronary thrombosis** (also infml **coronary**) n [C] (med) blocking of an artery in the heart by a clot of blood, often damaging the heart or causing death

coronation /ˌkɒrəˈneɪʃn/ n [C] ceremony of crowning a king or queen

coroner /ˈkɒrənə(r)/ n [C] (GB) official whose job is to find the cause of any accidental or suspicious death by holding an inquest

coronet /ˈkɒrənet/ n [C] small crown worn by princes, princesses, etc

corporal /ˈkɔːpərəl/ n [C] (abbr **Cpl**) non-commissioned officer below the rank of sergeant in the army ● **corporal** adj involving physical punishment: ~ punishment

corporate /ˈkɔːpərət/ adj **1** of or belonging to a corporation (1) **2** shared by all the members of a group: ~ responsibility

corporation /ˌkɔːpəˈreɪʃn/ n [C, with sing or pl verb] **1** large business or company **2** (GB) group of people elected to govern a town

---

A B **C** D E F G H I J K L M N O P Q R S T U V W X Y Z

corps /kɔː(r)/ n [C] (pl **corps** /kɔːz/)
1 military force formed from part of
the full army, etc **2** one of the
technical branches of an army
3 group of people involved in a
particular activity: *the diplomatic ~*

corpse /kɔːps/ n [C] dead body, esp
of a human being

corpulent /ˈkɔːpjələnt/ adj (fml) fat

corpuscle /ˈkɔːpʌsl/ n [C] (anat) one
of the red or white cells in the blood

corral /kəˈrɑːl/ n [C] (in N America)
fenced area for horses, cattle, etc on
a farm or ranch ▸ **corral** v (-ll- US -l-)
[T] force horses or cattle into a corral

0━ **correct¹** /kəˈrekt/ adj **1** true;
right; accurate: *the ~ answer* ◇ *the ~
way to do it* **2** (of manners, dress,
etc) proper; decent ▸ **correctly** adv
▸ **correctness** n [U]

0━ **correct²** /kəˈrekt/ v [T] **1** make
sth correct; remove the mistakes
from sth: *~ sb's spelling* **2** change sth
so that it is accurate: *glasses to ~ my
eyesight* ▸ **correction** /kəˈrekʃn/ n
1 [C] change that corrects sth: *~ions
written in red ink* **2** [U] act of
correcting sth ▸ **corrective** n [C], adj
(something) that makes sth right

correlate /ˈkɒrəleɪt/ v [I,T] **~ (with)**
(of two things) be closely related or
connected; show such a relation
between two things: *The results of
the two tests do not ~.* ▸ **correlation**
/ˌkɒrəˈleɪʃn/ n [C,U] connection
between two things in which one
thing changes as the other does

correspond /ˌkɒrəˈspɒnd/ v [I]
1 **~ (to/with)** be the same or similar;
be in agreement with: *Your account
doesn't ~ with hers.* **2** **~ (with)** (fml)
exchange letters with sb
▸ **corresponding** adj **~ (to)**
matching or connected with sth
that you have just mentioned
▸ **correspondingly** adv

correspondence /ˌkɒrəˈspɒndəns/
n [C,U] agreement; similarity: *a
close ~ between the two texts* **2** [U]
letter writing; letters
▸ **correspondent** n [C] **1** person who
reports for a newspaper, radio or TV
station, usu from abroad **2** person
who writes letters to another person

corridor /ˈkɒrɪdɔː(r)/ n [C] long
narrow passage from which doors
open into rooms

corroborate /kəˈrɒbəreɪt/ v [T] (fml)
confirm the correctness of a belief,
statement, etc: *I can ~ what she
said.* ▸ **corroboration**
/kəˌrɒbəˈreɪʃn/ n [U]

corrode /kəˈrəʊd/ v [I,T] be
destroyed or destroy sth slowly, esp
by chemical action: *Acid ~s metal.*
▸ **corrosion** /kəˈrəʊʒn/ n [U]
▸ **corrosive** /kəˈrəʊsɪv/ n [C], adj

(substance) that corrodes sth:
corrosive acid

corrugated /ˈkɒrəɡeɪtɪd/ adj
shaped into a series of regular folds
that look like waves: *~ iron*

corrupt /kəˈrʌpt/ adj **1** immoral:
a ~ society/mind **2** dishonest, esp
because of taking bribes: *~ business
deals* **3** (computing) containing
changes or faults, and no longer in
the original state: *~ software*
● **corrupt** v [I,T] become or make sb/
sth corrupt: *~ing young people*
▸ **corruption** /kəˈrʌpʃn/ n [U]
▸ **corruptly** adv

corset /ˈkɔːsɪt/ n [C] piece of
women's underwear worn esp in the
past to make the waist look smaller

cortège (esp US cortege) /kɔːˈteʒ;
-ˈteɪʒ/ n [C] funeral procession

cosh /kɒʃ/ n [C] (GB) length of pipe,
rubber tubing filled with metal, etc
used as a weapon

cosmetic /kɒzˈmetɪk/ n [C, usu pl]
substance put on the body, esp the
face, to make it beautiful
● **cosmetic** adj **1** improving only the
outside appearance of sth and not
its basic character: *These reforms are
not merely ~.* **2** of medical treatment
that is intended to improve a
person's appearance: *~ surgery*

cosmic /ˈkɒzmɪk/ adj of the whole
universe or cosmos

cosmonaut /ˈkɒzmənɔːt/ n [C]
astronaut from the former Soviet
Union

cosmopolitan /ˌkɒzməˈpɒlɪtən/ adj
1 of or from all parts of the world:
a ~ city **2** having or showing a wide
experience of many different people
and things from many different
countries

cosmos /ˈkɒzmɒs/ (the cosmos) n
[sing] the universe

0━ **cost¹** /kɒst/ n **1** [C,U] price paid
for a thing: *the high ~ of repairs*
2 (costs) [pl] total amount of money
that needs to be spent by a business
3 [U, sing] effort, loss or damage that
is involved in order to do or achieve
sth: *the ~ of victory* **4** (costs) [pl] sum
of money that sb is ordered to pay
for lawyers, etc in a court case [IDM]
at all cost/costs whatever is needed
to achieve sth **to your cost** to your
loss or disadvantage ▸ **costly** adj
(-ier, -iest) **1** costing a lot of money
2 causing problems or the loss of
sth: *a ~ly mistake*

0━ **cost²** /kɒst/ v (pt, pp **cost**, in
sense 3 **~ed**) [T] **1** have as a price; be
obtainable at the price of: *shoes ~ing
£20* **2** cause the loss of sth; require
sth: *a mistake that ~ him his life* ◇ *~ a
great deal of effort* **3** (business)
estimate the cost of sth ▸ **costing** n
[C,U] (business) estimate of how
much money will be needed for sth

co-star /ˈkəʊ stɑː(r)/ n [C] well-
known actor who appears in a film,

etc with other actors of the same status ● **co-star** v (-rr-) [I] appear as a co-star

costume /'kɒstjuːm/ n [C,U]
1 clothes worn by people from a particular place or during a particular historical period: *Welsh national* ~ **2** clothes worn by actors on stage or worn by sb to make them look like sth else

cosy (US **cozy**) /'kəʊzi/ adj (-ier, -iest)
1 warm and comfortable: *a ~ room/ feeling* **2** friendly and private: *have a ~ chat* ▸ **cosily** (US **cozily**) adv ▸ **cosiness** (US **coziness**) n [U] ● **cosy** n [C] (pl **-ies**) cover to keep a teapot warm

cot /kɒt/ n [C] **1** (GB) small bed for a young child **2** (US) simple narrow bed, eg on a ship

0━ **cottage** /'kɒtɪdʒ/ n [C] small house, esp in the country

0━ **cotton** /'kɒtn/ n [U] **1** plant grown in warm countries for the soft, white hairs around its seeds that are used to make fabric and thread **2** fabric made from the cotton plant: *a ~ dress* **3** thread used for sewing: *a reel of* ~ ● **cotton** [PV] **cotton on (to sth)** (infml) begin to understand or realize sth without being told ■ **cotton 'wool** n [U] soft mass of white material used for cleaning the skin or a wound

couch /kaʊtʃ/ n [C] long comfortable seat like a bed ● **couch** v [T] ~ **(in)** (fml) say or write sth in a particular style or manner: *a reply* ~*ed in friendly terms*

couchette /kuːˈʃet/ n [C] narrow folding bed on a train

cougar /'kuːɡə(r)/ n [C] (esp US) = PUMA

0━ **cough** /kɒf/ v [I] force out air from the lungs violently and noisily: *The smoke made me* ~. **2** [T] ~ **(up)** force sth out of your lungs or throat by coughing ● **cough** n **1** [C] act or sound of coughing **2** [sing] illness that makes you cough

0━ **could** /kəd; strong form kʊd/ modal v (neg **could not**, short form **couldn't** /'kʊdnt/.) **1** used as the past tense of 'can': *I* ~ *hear him crying.* **2** used in requests: *C~ I use your phone?* ◇ *C~ you babysit on Friday?* **3** used to show that sth is or might be possible: *You* ~ *be right.* **4** used to suggest sth: *You* ~ *ask her to go with you.* [IDM] **could do with sth** (spoken) need sth: *I* ~ *do with a cold drink!*

0━ **council** /'kaʊnsl/ n [C, with sing or pl verb] group of people elected to manage the affairs of a city, town etc, give advice, make rules, etc: *a* ~ *meeting* ■ **'council house**, **'council flat** n [C] (GB) house or flat rented from the local council ■ **'council tax** n [sing,U] (in Britain) tax charged by local councils, based on the value of

a person's home ▸ **councillor** (US **councilor**) /'kaʊnsələ(r)/ n [C] member of a council

0━ **counsel** /'kaʊnsl/ n **1** [U] (fml) advice **2** [C] (pl **counsel**) (law) barrister acting in a law case ● **counsel** v (-ll- US -l-) [T] **1** listen to and give support to sb who needs help: *Therapists were brought in to* ~ *the victims.* **2** (fml) advise sb ▸ **counselling** (US **counseling**) n [U] professional advice about a problem: *marriage guidance* ~ ▸ **counsellor** (US -l-) n [C] **1** person who has been trained to advise people with problems **2** (US) lawyer

0━ **count¹** /kaʊnt/ v **1** [I] say numbers in order: *C~ from 1 to 10.* **2** [T] ~ **(up)** find the total number of people, things etc in a particular group: ~ *the people in the room* **3** [T] include sb/sth: *ten people,* ~*ing me* **4** [T] consider sb to be sth: ~ *yourself lucky* **5** [I] be important: *Every minute* ~*s.* **6** [I,T] be officially accepted: *That goal didn't* ~ *because the game was over.* [PV] **count (sth) against sb** be to the disadvantage of sb: *Will my past mistakes* ~ *against me?* **count on sb/ sth** rely or depend on sb/sth: *I'm* ~*ing on you to help.* **count sth/sb out 1** count things one after the other as you put them somewhere **2** not include sb: *C~ me out, I'm not going.* ▸ **countable** adj that can be counted: *'House' is a* ~*able noun.* ■ **'countdown** n [C] action of counting seconds backwards to zero, eg before a rocket is launched

count² /kaʊnt/ n [C] **1** (usu sing) act of counting; total number reached by counting: *There were 50 at the last* ~. **2** (law) crime that sb is accused of: *He is guilty on all* ~*s.* **3** (in some European countries) nobleman of high rank [IDM] **keep/ lose count (of sth)** know/not know how many there are of sth

countenance /'kaʊntənəns/ n (fml) **1** [C] person's face or expression **2** [U] support; approval: *give/lend* ~ *to a plan* ● **countenance** v [T] support sth or agree to sth happening: *I cannot* ~ *violence.*

0━ **counter** /'kaʊntə(r)/ n [C] **1** flat surface where goods are shown, items sold, etc in a shop, bank, etc **2** small disc used for counting games, etc **3** thing that can be exchanged for sth else: *a bargaining* ~ ● **counter** v [I,T] ~ **(with)** respond to an attack, etc with an opposing view, etc: ~ *his arguments with her own opinion* ● **counter** adv ~ **to** in the opposite direction; against sth: *Her theories ran* ~ *to the evidence.*

counter- /'kaʊntə(r)/ prefix (in compounds) **1** against; opposite: ~*productive* **2** corresponding: ~*part*

counteract /ˌkaʊntərˈækt/ v [T] do sth to reduce the bad or harmful effects of sth

counter-attack /ˈkaʊntər ətæk/ n [C], v [I] (make an) attack in response to an enemy's attack

counterbalance /ˌkaʊntəˈbæləns/ v [T] (fml) have an equal but opposite effect to sth else ● **counterbalance** /ˈkaʊntəbæləns/ n [C] thing that has an equal but opposite effect to sth else and can be used to limit the bad effects of sth

counter-espionage /ˌkaʊntər ˈespiənɑːʒ/ n [U] secret action taken by a country to prevent an enemy country from finding out its secrets

counterfeit /ˈkaʊntəfɪt/ adj (of money and goods for sale) made to look exactly like sth else in order to deceive people: ~ banknotes ▶ **counterfeit** n [C] ● **counterfeit** v [T] make an exact copy of sth in order to deceive people ▶ **counterfeiter** n [C] person who counterfeits money

counterfoil /ˈkaʊntəfɔɪl/ n [C] detachable part of a cheque, etc that can be kept as a record

countermand /ˌkaʊntəˈmɑːnd/ v [T] cancel or change a command you have already given

counterpart /ˈkaʊntəpɑːt/ n [C] person or thing similar or corresponding to another

counterproductive /ˌkaʊntəprəˈdʌktɪv/ adj producing the opposite effect to what is intended: Increasing taxes would be ~.

countersign /ˈkaʊntəsaɪn/ v [T] (tech) sign a document, etc that has already been signed, esp to make it valid

countess /ˈkaʊntəs; -es/ n [C] 1 woman who has the rank of a count or an earl 2 wife of a count or an earl

countless /ˈkaʊntləs/ adj very many: I've been there ~ times.

0~ **country** /ˈkʌntri/ n (pl -ies) 1 [C] area of land that forms a politically independent unit; nation 2 (the country) [sing] the people of a country: a politician loved by the whole ~ 3 (the country) [sing] land outside towns; fields, woods, etc used for farming, etc: ~ life/people [IDM] **go to the country** (of a government) call a general election

countryman /ˈkʌntrimən/ (fem **countrywoman** /ˈkʌntriwʊmən/) n [C] 1 person born or living in the same country as sb else 2 person who lives in the country (3)

0~ **countryside** /ˈkʌntrisaɪd/ n [U] land outside towns and cities, with fields, woods, etc

0~ **county** /ˈkaʊnti/ n [C] (pl -ies) (abbr Co.) area of Britain, Ireland or the US that has its own local government

coup /kuː/ n [C] (pl ~s /kuːz/) 1 (also **coup d'état** /ˌkuː deɪˈtɑː/) illegal seizing of power in a state, often by violence 2 fact of achieving sth that was difficult to do: This deal was a ~ for her.

0~ **couple**¹ /ˈkʌpl/ n [C] 1 two people or things, seen together or associated: a married ~ 2 ~ (of) a few: a ~ of drinks/days

couple² /ˈkʌpl/ v 1 [T] fasten or join two parts of sth, eg two vehicles or pieces of equipment 2 [I] (fml) (of two people or animals) have sex [PV] **couple sb/sth with sb/sth** link one thing, situation, etc to another: His illness, ~d with his lack of money, prevented him leaving.

coupon /ˈkuːpɒn/ n [C] 1 ticket which gives the holder the right to receive or do sth 2 printed form, often cut out from a newspaper, used to obtain a competition, order goods, etc

0~ **courage** /ˈkʌrɪdʒ/ n [U] ability to face danger, pain, etc without showing fear; bravery: show ~ in a battle ▶ **courageous** /kəˈreɪdʒəs/ adj ▶ **courageously** adv

courgette /kɔːˈʒet/ n [C] small green marrow (2), eaten as a vegetable

courier /ˈkʊriə(r)/ n [C] 1 person or company whose job is to take packages, documents, etc somewhere 2 (GB) person employed by a travel company to give help and advice to groups of tourists on holiday

0~ **course** /kɔːs/ n 1 [C] series of lessons, lectures, etc: a French ~ ◇ a degree ~ 2 [C] path or direction followed by sth: the ~ of a river/aircraft 3 [sing] way sth develops: the ~ of history 4 [C] one of several parts of a meal: the fish ~ 5 [C] (often in compounds) area where sports events, esp races, are held: a golf ~ ◇ a race~ 6 [C] (med) series of treatments, etc: a ~ of injections [IDM] **(as) a matter of course** (as) sth that is quite normal and expected in sth **in due course** at the right time **of course** naturally; certainly **run/take its course** develop and end in the usual way ● **course** v [I] (fml) (of liquids) move quickly: The blood ~d through his veins.

0~ **court**¹ /kɔːt/ n 1 [C,U] place where legal cases are heard 2 (the court) [sing] those present in a court, esp the judges, etc. 3 [C] (often in compounds) space marked out for certain ball games: a tennis ~ 4 [C,U] (residence of a) king or queen, their family and the people who work for them 5 [C] = COURTYARD

court² /kɔːt/ v **1** [T] try to gain the favour or support of sb: ~ sb's favour **2** [T] (fml) risk trouble, etc: ~ disaster **3** (old-fash) [T] try to win sb's affection, esp when hoping to marry them ▸ **courtship** [C,U] (old-fash) (period of) courting (3) sb

courteous /ˈkɜːtiəs/ adj having good manners; polite: a ~ person/request ▸ **courteously** adv

courtesy /ˈkɜːtəsi/ n (pl -ies) **1** [U] polite behaviour **2** [C] polite remark, action, etc [IDM] **(by) courtesy of sb/ sth** with the permission of sb/sth and as a favour

courtier /ˈkɔːtiə(r)/ n [C] (esp in the past) follower of a king or queen's court¹(4)

court martial /ˌkɔːt ˈmɑːʃl/ n [C] (pl **courts martial**) court for trying crimes against military law; trial in such a court ▸ **court-martial** v (-ll US -l-) [T] ~ (for) try sb in a court martial

courtyard /ˈkɔːtjɑːd/ n [C] open space surrounded by walls but with no roof: the central/inner ~

0-- **cousin** /ˈkʌzn/ n [C] child of your uncle or aunt

cove /kəʊv/ n [C] small bay

0-- **cover¹** /ˈkʌvə(r)/ v **1** [T] ~ (up/ over) place one thing over or in front of another; hide or protect sth in this way: ~ a table with a cloth ◇ ~ your face ◇ ~ (up) the body **2** [T] ~ (in/ with) (esp passive) spread, etc a layer of sth on the surface of sth: hills ~ed with snow ◇ boots ~ed in mud **3** [T] travel a certain distance: ~ 100 miles in a day **4** [T] (of money) be enough for sth: Will £20 ~ be enough for sth: Will £20 ~ your expenses? **5** [T] include sth; deal with sth: The survey ~s all aspects of the business. **6** [T] (of a journalist) report an event: I've been asked to ~ the election. **7** [I] ~ **for** do sb's work, etc while they are away **8** [I] ~ for have a lie or an excuse that will stop sb from getting into trouble **9** [T] keep a gun aimed at sb: We've got him ~ed. [IDM] **cover your tracks** leave no evidence of where you have been or what you have been doing [PV] **cover sth up** (disapprov) keep a scandal, an embarrassment, etc secret ▸ **coverage** n [U] reporting of news and sport in the media ▸ **covered** adj ~ **in/with** having a layer or amount of sth on it: His face was ~ed in blood. ■ **'cover-up** n [usu sing] act of hiding a mistake or crime from the public

0-- **cover²** /ˈkʌvə(r)/ n **1** [C] thing that is put over or on another thing, usu to protect or decorate it: a cushion ~ **2** [U] place or area giving shelter: We ran for ~ under some trees. **3** [C] thick outside pages of a book, magazine, etc **4** [U] insurance against loss, damage, etc **5** [U] protection from attack: Aircraft gave

the infantry ~. **6** (the covers) [pl] sheets, blankets, etc on a bed **7** [C, usu sing] ~ **(for)** means of keeping sth secret: a business that is a ~ for drug dealing [IDM] **under (the) cover of** hidden or protected by sth: ~ of darkness

covert /ˈkʌvət/ adj half-hidden; not open; secret: a ~ glance/threat ▸ **covertly** adv

0-- **cow¹** /kaʊ/ n [C] **1** large female animal kept on farms to produce milk or beef **2** female of the elephant, whale and some other large animals **3** (disapprov, sl) offensive word for a woman: You silly ~! ■ **'cowboy** n [C] **1** man who looks after cattle in the western parts of the US **2** (GB, infml) dishonest person in business, esp sb whose work is of bad quality

cow² /kaʊ/ v [T] frighten sb into doing what you want: He was ~ed into giving them all his money.

coward /ˈkaʊəd/ n [C] (disapprov) person who is not brave or does not have the courage to do things that other people do not consider very difficult ▸ **cowardly** adj ▸ **cowardice** /ˈkaʊədɪs/ n [U] (disapprov) fear or lack of courage

cower /ˈkaʊə(r)/ v [I] lower the body or move back from fear, cold, etc

cowl /kaʊl/ n [C] **1** large loose covering for the head, worn esp by monks **2** metal cover for a chimney, etc

cox /kɒks/ (also **formal coxswain** /ˈkɒksn/) n [C] person who controls the direction of a rowing boat while other people are rowing ● **cox** v [I,T] act as a cox

coy /kɔɪ/ adj **1** (pretending to be) shy, modest, etc: a ~ smile **2** not willing to give information, answer questions, etc: She was ~ about her past. ▸ **coyly** adv ▸ **coyness** n [U]

coyote /kaɪˈəʊti; kɔɪ-/ n [C] small wolf of western N America

cozy (US) = COSY

CPU /ˌsiː piː ˈjuː/ abbr (computing) central processing unit; part of a computer that controls all the other parts of the system

crab /kræb/ n [C] **1** shellfish with eight legs and two pincers that moves sideways on land **2** [U] meat from a crab, eaten as food

crabby /ˈkræbi/ adj (-ier, -iest) (infml) bad-tempered; irritable

0-- **crack¹** /kræk/ v [I,T] **1** (cause sth to) break without dividing into separate parts: ~ a plate ◇ The ice ~ed. **2** [T] break sth open or into pieces: ~ a safe ◇ ~ nuts **3** [T] hit sth/ sb sharply: ~ your head on the door **4** [I,T] (cause sth to) make a sharp sound: ~ a whip **5** [I] (of the voice) suddenly change in depth, volume, etc in a way that you cannot control: *in a voice ~ing with emotion* **6** [I] no longer be able to function normally because of pressure: *She finally ~ed and told the truth.* **7** [T] solve a problem, etc: *~ a code* **8** [T] (*infml*) tell a joke [IDM] **get cracking** [PV] start work immediately [PV] **crack down (on sb/sth)** become more severe in preventing illegal activity: *~ down on crime* **crack up** (*infml*) **1** become ill because of pressure **2** start laughing ■ **'crackdown** *n* [C] sudden strict or severe measures: *a police ~down on vandalism* ▶ **cracked** *adj* **1** damaged with lines in its surface: *a ~ed mirror* **2** (*infml*) slightly mad

0— **crack²** /kræk/ *n* **1** [C] ~ **(in)** line where sth has broken, but not into separate parts: *a ~ in a cup/the ice* **2** [C] narrow space or opening: *a ~ in the curtains* **3** [C] sudden loud noise: *the ~ of a whip/rifle* **4** [C] sharp blow: *a ~ on the head* **5** [C] ~ **(at)** (*infml*) attempt to do sth: *to have a ~ at the world record* **6** (also **,crack 'cocaine**) [U] very strong pure form of cocaine **7** [C] (*infml*) joke, esp a critical one: *She made a ~ about his baldness.* [IDM] **at the crack of dawn** (*infml*) very early in the morning ● **crack** *adj* excellent; very skilful: *She's a ~ shot.*

cracker /'krækə(r)/ *n* [C] **1** thin dry biscuit, often eaten with cheese **2** (also **,Christmas 'cracker**) tube of coloured paper that makes a cracking noise when pulled apart by two people and has toys, presents, etc inside it

crackers /'krækəz/ *adj* (*GB, infml*) mad; crazy

crackle /'krækl/ *v* [I] make a series of short sharp sounds, as when dry sticks burn: *Dry leaves ~d under our feet.* ● **crackle** *n* [U,C] series of short sharp sounds

crackpot /'krækpɒt/ *n* [C] (*infml*) eccentric or mad person: *a ~ idea/ person*

0— **cradle** /'kreɪdl/ *n* [C] **1** small bed for a baby which can be pushed from side to side **2** (*usu sing*) ~ **of** place where sth begins: *the ~ of Western culture* **3** any framework like a cradle ● **cradle** *v* [T] hold sb/sth gently in your arms or hands

0— **craft** /krɑːft/ *n* **1** [C] (*activity needing*) skill at making things with your hands: *traditional ~s such as basket-weaving* **2** [U] (*fml, disapprov*) skill in deceiving people **3** [C] (*pl* **craft**) ship, boat, aircraft or spacecraft ▶ **-craft** (in compounds): *handi~/needle~* ■ **'craftsman** *n* (*pl* **-men**) skilled worker who

practises a craft ■ **'craftsmanship** *n* [U] skill as a craftsman

crafty /'krɑːfti/ *adj* (**-ier, -iest**) clever at getting what you want, esp by dishonest methods ▶ **craftily** *adv* ▶ **craftiness** *n* [U]

crag /kræg/ *n* [C] high steep mass of rock ▶ **craggy** *adj* (**-ier, -iest**) **1** having many crags **2** (of sb's face) having strong features and deep lines

cram /kræm/ *v* (**-mm-**) [T] ~ **(in/into/ onto)** push too much of sth into sth: *~ the clothes into the suitcase* ▶ **crammed** *adj* ~ **(with)** full of things or people: *shelves ~med with books*

cramp /kræmp/ *n* **1** [U,C] sudden and painful tightening of the muscles **2** (**cramps**) [pl] severe pain in the stomach ● **cramp** *v* [T] (*usu passive*) give too little space to; prevent the movement or development of: *feel ~ed by the rules* [IDM] **cramp sb's style** (*infml*) stop sb doing things in the way they want to ▶ **cramped** *adj* having too little space: *~ conditions*

crampon /'kræmpɒn/ *n* [C] iron plate with spikes, worn over shoes for climbing on ice

cranberry /'krænbəri/ *n* [C] (*pl* **-ies**) small red slightly sour berry, used for making jelly and sauce

crane /kreɪn/ *n* [C] **1** machine with a long arm, used for lifting heavy weights **2** large wading bird with long legs and neck ● **crane** *v* [I,T] stretch your neck, eg to see better: *He ~d his neck to see over the crowd.*

cranium /'kreɪniəm/ *n* [C] (*pl* **-s** or **crania** /'kreɪniə/) (*anat*) bone structure that forms the head and protects the brain ▶ **cranial** *adj*

crank /kræŋk/ *n* [C] **1** (*disapprov*) person with fixed strange ideas **2** L-shaped handle for turning things ● **crank** *v* [T] ~ **(up)** make sth move by turning a crank: *~ the engine* (= start it with a crank) ■ **'crankshaft** *n* [C] (*tech*) metal rod in a vehicle that helps turn the engine's power into movement ▶ **cranky** *adj* (**-ier, -iest**) (*infml*) **1** strange; eccentric **2** (*esp US*) bad-tempered

cranny /'kræni/ *n* [C] very small hole or opening in a wall [IDM] **every nook and cranny** → NOOK

crap /kræp/ *v* (**-pp-**) [I] (*sl*, ⚠) empty solid waste from the bowels ● **crap** *n* (⚠) **1** [U] nonsense; rubbish **2** [U] excrement **3** [sing] act of emptying the bowels ▶ **crappy** *adj* (**-ier, -iest**) (*sl*) of very bad quality

0— **crash¹** /kræʃ/ *n* [C] **1** accident involving a vehicle in collision with sth: *a car ~* **2** [sing] sudden loud noise made by sth falling: *The dishes fell with a ~ to the floor.* **3** sudden fall in the price or value of sth;

collapse of a business, etc: *the 1987 stock market* ~ **4** sudden failure of a computer or system ● **crash** *adj* done to achieve quick results: *a ~ course in French* ▸ **crash** *adv* with a crash ■ **'crash helmet** *n* [C] hard hat worn by a motorcyclist to protect the head ■ **crash-'land** *v* [I,T] land an aircraft in an emergency ■ **crash 'landing** *n* [C] emergency landing

0= **crash²** /kræʃ/ *v* **1** [I,T] (cause sth to) collide with sth: ~ *the car (into a wall)* **2** [I,T] (cause sb/sth to) hit sth hard while moving, causing noise and/or damage: *The tree ~ed through the window.* **3** [I] make a loud noise: *The thunder ~ed.* **4** [I] (of prices, business, shares, etc) lose value or fail suddenly **5** [I,T] (cause a computer to) stop working

crass /kræs/ *adj* very stupid and showing no sympathy or understanding: ~ *question*

crate /kreɪt/ *n* [C] large wooden container for goods ● **crate** *v* [T] pack sth in a crate

crater /'kreɪtə(r)/ *n* [C] **1** opening at the top of a volcano **2** hole made by a bomb

cravat /krə'væt/ *n* [C] piece of cloth worn by men round the neck

crave /kreɪv/ *v* [T] ~ **(for)** have a strong desire for sth: ~ *for a cigarette* ▸ **craving** *n* [C]

crawl /krɔːl/ *v* [I] **1** move slowly along the ground or on the hands and knees: *The baby ~ed along the floor.* **2** move very slowly: *traffic ~ing into London* **3** ~ **with** (esp in the continuous tense) be covered with or full of things that crawl, etc: *a floor ~ing with ants* **4** ~ **to** (infml) try to gain sb's favour by doing what they want, flattering them, etc **IDM** **make your skin crawl** → SKIN ● **crawl** *n* **1** [sing] very slow speed **2** (the crawl) [sing,U] fast swimming stroke ▸ **crawler** *n* (infml, disapprov) person who crawls (4)

crayon /'kreɪən/ *n* [C] pencil of soft coloured chalk or wax ● **crayon** *v* [I,T] draw sth with crayons

craze /kreɪz/ *n* [C] enthusiastic, usu brief, popular interest in sth; object of such an interest

crazed /kreɪzd/ *adj* ~ **(with)** (fml, written) full of strong feelings and lacking control

0= **crazy** /'kreɪzi/ *adj* (-ier, -iest) (infml) **1** foolish; not sensible: *a ~ idea* **2** very angry: *The noise is driving me ~!* **3** wildly excited or enthusiastic: ~ *about football* **4** ~ **about** in love with sb: *He's ~ about you!* **5** mentally ill; insane ▸ **crazily** *adv* ▸ **craziness** *n* [U]

creak /kriːk/ *v* [I] make a sound like a door that needs oil: *a ~ing door/floorboard* ▸ **creaky** *adj* (-ier, -iest) making creaks

credit

0= **cream** /kriːm/ *n* **1** [U] thick yellowish fatty liquid that rises to the top of milk: *strawberries and* ~ **2** [C] a sweet that has a soft substance like cream inside **3** [U,C] any soft substance used on your skin to protect it, etc or used for cleaning things: *hand* ~ **4** [U] pale yellowish-white colour **5** (the cream) [sing] the best part: *the* ~ *of society* ● **cream** *adj* yellowish-white ● **cream** *v* [T] mix things together into a soft paste **[PV]** **cream sb/sth off** take the best part away ▸ **creamy** *adj* (-ier, -iest) like cream; containing cream

crease /kriːs/ *n* [C] **1** line made on cloth, paper, etc by crushing, folding or pressing **2** wrinkle on the skin **3** white line near the wicket on a cricket pitch ● **crease** *v* [I,T] (cause sth to) develop creases

0= **create** /kri'eɪt/ *v* [T] **1** make sth happen or exist **2** produce a particular feeling or impression: *The company wants to ~ a younger image.*

creation /kri'eɪʃn/ *n* **1** [U] act of making sth new or of causing sth to exist **2** (usu the Creation) [sing] making of the world, esp by God as described in the Bible **3** [U] the world and all the living things in it ▸ **creationism** /kri'eɪʃənɪzəm/ *n* [U] belief that the universe was made by God exactly as described in the Bible

0= **creative** /kri'eɪtɪv/ *adj* able to produce sth new or a work of art: *a ~ person who writes and paints* **2** involving the use of skill and the imagination to produce sth new: *the ~ act* ▸ **creatively** *adv* ▸ **creativity** /ˌkriːeɪ'tɪvəti/ *n* [U]

creator /kri'eɪtə(r)/ *n* **1** [C] person who creates: *the ~ of this novel* **2** (the Creator) [sing] God

0= **creature** /'kriːtʃə(r)/ *n* [C] living animal or person

crèche (also **creche**) /kreʃ/ *n* [C] (GB) place where babies are cared for while their parents are at work, etc

credentials /krə'denʃlz/ *n* [pl] **1** qualities, etc that make you suitable to do sth **2** documents showing that you are who you claim to be

credible /'kredəbl/ *adj* that can be believed or trusted: *a ~ story/ explanation* ▸ **credibility** /ˌkredə'bɪləti/ *n* [U] quality of being credible: *to gain/lose credibility* ▸ **credibly** /-əbli/ *adv*

0= **credit¹** /'kredɪt/ *n* **1** [U] agreement to buy sth and pay later: *buy a car on* ~ **2** [U] belief of others that a person, company, etc can pay debts: *have good/poor* ~ **3** [U] sum of money in a bank account **4** [U] sum of money lent by a bank, etc **5** [C] entry in an account of money received **6** [U] belief; trust: *give ~ to her story* **7** [U] praise; approval: *get/ be given all the ~ for sth* **8** [sing] ~ to person or thing that makes a reputation better: *She's a ~ to her family.* **9** [C] unit of study at a college or university |**IDM**| **to sb's credit** making sb deserve praise or respect ■ '**creditworthy** *adj* able to be trusted to repay money owed ▶ '**creditworthiness** *n* [U]

credit[2] /'kredit/ *v* [T] **1** ~ **(with)** think that sb has sth: *I ~ed you with more sense.* **2** add an amount of money to sb's bank account **3** believe sth: *Would you ~ it?*

creditable /'kreditəbl/ *adj* deserving praise (although not perfect): *a ~ piece of work* ▶ **creditably** *adv*

⊶ '**credit card** *n* [C] card allowing the holder to buy goods on credit (1)

creditor /'kreditə(r)/ *n* [C] person, company, etc that sb owes money to

credulous /'kredjələs/ *adj* too willing to believe things ▶ **credulity** /krɪ'dju:ləti/ *n* [U]

creed /kri:d/ *n* [C] set of beliefs, esp religious ones

creek /kri:k/ *n* [C] **1** (*GB*) narrow stretch of river cutting into a coast or river bank **2** (*US*) small river

creep /kri:p/ *v* [I] (pt, pp **crept** /krept/) **1** move along slowly or quietly, esp keeping the body close to the ground: *The thief crept along the corridor.* **2** (of plants, etc) grow over the surface of a wall, etc **3** ~ **(to)** (*GB, infml, disapprov*) try to gain sb's favour by doing what they want, flattering them, etc |**IDM**| **make your flesh creep** → FLESH |**PV**| **creep up on sb** move slowly nearer to sb, usu from behind, without being seen or heard: (*fig*) *Old age is ~ing up on me.* ● **creep** *n* [C] (*infml, disapprov*) unpleasant person, esp one who tries to gain sb's favour by doing what they want, flattering them, etc |**IDM**| **give sb the creeps** (*infml*) make sb feel fear or dislike ▶ **creeper** *n* [C] plant that grows along the ground, up walls, etc

creepy /'kri:pi/ *adj* (-**ier**, -**iest**) (*infml*) causing or feeling fear: *a ~ house/ atmosphere*

creepy-crawly /,kri:pi 'krɔ:li/ *n* [C] (*infml*) insect, worm, etc when you think of it as unpleasant

cremate /krə'meɪt/ *v* [T] burn the body of a dead person esp as part of a funeral ceremony ▶ **cremation** /krə'meɪʃn/ *n* [C, U] (act of) cremating sb ▶ **crematorium** /,kremə'tɔ:riəm/ *n* [C] (pl ~**s** or -**oria** /-ɔ:riə/) place where bodies are burned

creosote /'kri:əsəʊt/ *n* [U] brown oily liquid used for preserving wood

crêpe (*also* **crepe**) /kreɪp/ *n* **1** [U] any of various types of wrinkled cloth or paper **2** [U] rubber with a wrinkled surface, used for making the soles of shoes **3** [C] thin pancake

crept *pt, pp* of CREEP

crescendo /krə'ʃendəʊ/ *n* [C] (pl ~**s**) **1** (*music*) gradual increase in loudness **2** gradual increase in intensity, noise, etc to a climax ● **crescendo** *adj, adv* of with increasing loudness: *a ~ passage*

crescent /'kresnt; 'kreznt/ *n* [C] **1** (something shaped like the) curve of the new moon **2** row of houses built in a curve

cress /kres/ *n* [U] small plant with very small leaves, used in salads

crest /krest/ *n* [C] **1** top of a hill or wave **2** design used as the symbol of a particular family, organization, etc, esp one with a long history **3** group of feathers that stand up on top of a bird's head ● **crest** *v* [T] (*written*) reach the top of a hill, etc

crestfallen /'krestfɔ:lən/ *adj* very sad or disappointed

Creutzfeldt-Jakob disease /,krɔɪtsfelt 'jækɒb dɪzi:z/ *n* [U] (*abbr* **CJD**) fatal disease of the brain and nervous system, thought to be linked to BSE in cows.

crevasse /krə'væs/ *n* [C] deep open crack in thin ice

crevice /'krevɪs/ *n* [C] narrow opening or crack in a rock, wall, etc

crew /kru:/ *n* [with sing or pl verb] **1** all the people working on a ship or aircraft; these people, except the officers **2** group of people working together: *a film/camera ~* ● **crew** *v* [I, T] be part of a crew, esp on a ship

crib /krɪb/ *n* [C] **1** (*US*) small bed for a small child **2** long open box for holding an animal's food **3** (*infml*) written information such as answers to questions, often used dishonestly by students in tests: *a ~ sheet*

crick /krɪk/ *n* [sing] painful stiff feeling in your neck

cricket /'krɪkɪt/ *n* **1** [U] ball game played on grass by two teams of eleven players, in which a ball is bowled at a wicket and a batsman tries to hit it: *a ~ match/club/ball* **2** [C] small brown jumping insect that makes a shrill noise ▶ **cricketer** *n* [C] cricket player

cried *pt, pp* of CRY[1]

cries **1** *third pers sing pres tense* CRY[1] **2** *plural of* CRY[2]

⊶ '**crime** /kraɪm/ *n* **1** [U] activities that involve breaking the law **2** [C] ~ **(against)** illegal act for which there is a punishment by law: *commit a ~* **3** (a crime) [sing] act that you think is immoral or foolish: *It's a ~ to waste money like that.*

criminal /ˈkrɪmɪnl/ *adj* **1** of or concerning crime or the laws that deal with it: *a ~ offence* ◇ *~ law* **2** morally wrong: *a ~ waste of resources* ● **criminal** *n* [C] person who commits a crime or crimes ▸ **criminally** /-nəli/ *adv*

crimson /ˈkrɪmzn/ *adj, n* [U] (of a) deep red

cringe /krɪndʒ/ *v* [I] **1** move back and away from sb/sth in fear **2** feel very embarrassed about sth: *I ~ when I think of the poems I wrote then.*

crinkle /ˈkrɪŋkl/ *n* [C] very thin fold or line made on paper, fabric or skin ▸ **crinkle** *v* [I,T] (cause sth to) form crinkles: *~d paper*

cripple /ˈkrɪpl/ *v* [T] (usu passive) **1** damage sb's body so that they are no longer able to walk or move normally: *~d by a back injury* **2** seriously damage or harm sb/sth: *~d by debt* ● **cripple** *n* [C] (old-fash) person unable to move properly because of injury or disease, esp the spine or legs

0̸ **crisis** /ˈkraɪsɪs/ *n* [C,U] (pl **crises** /-siːz/) time of difficulty, danger, etc; decisive moment: *an economic ~* ◇ *a country in ~*

0̸ **crisp** /krɪsp/ *adj* **1** (*also* **crispy**) (of food) pleasantly hard and dry: *a ~ biscuit* **2** (*also* **crispy**) (of fruit and vegetables) fresh and firm: *a ~ lettuce* **3** (of paper or fabric) new and slightly stiff: *~ banknotes* **4** (of the weather) frosty, cold: *a ~ winter morning* **5** (of sb's way of speaking) quick and confident and not very friendly: *a ~ reply* ● **crisp** (*GB also* **po.tato ˈcrisp**) *n* [C, usu pl] thin slice of potato, fried and dried and sold in packets ● **crisp** *v* [I,T] become or make sth crisp ▸ **crisply** *adv* ▸ **crispness** *n* [U] ▸ **crispy** *adj* (**-ier, -iest**) (*infml*) = CRISP(1),(2)

criss-cross /ˈkrɪs krɒs/ *adj* with crossed lines: *a ~ pattern* ● **criss-cross** *v* [I,T] form or make a criss-cross pattern on sth: *roads ~ing the country*

0̸ **criterion** /kraɪˈtɪəriən/ *n* [C] (pl **-ria** /-riə/) standard by which sb/sth is judged

critic /ˈkrɪtɪk/ *n* [C] **1** person who gives opinions about the good and bad qualities of books, music, etc: *The ~s liked the play.* **2** person who expresses disapproval sth publicly

0̸ **critical** /ˈkrɪtɪkl/ *adj* **1** expressing disapproval of sb/sth publicly: *a ~ remark* **2** extremely important for the future: *a ~ decision* **3** serious, uncertain and possibly dangerous: *The fire victim is in a ~ condition.* **4** giving fair, careful judgements, esp about art, literature, etc: *a ~ review* ▸ **critically** /-kli/ *adv*: *to be ~ly ill*

0̸ **criticism** /ˈkrɪtɪsɪzəm/ *n* [U,C] **1** ~ (**of**) act of expressing disapproval of sb/sth and opinions about their bad qualities; statement showing disapproval: *I can't stand her constant ~.* **2** [U] work or activity of making fair, careful judgements about the good and bad qualities of sb/sth, esp books, music, etc: *literary ~*

0̸ **criticize** (*also* -ise) /ˈkrɪtɪsaɪz/ *v* **1** [I,T] point out the faults of sb/sth; express disapproval of sb/sth: *Don't ~ my work.* **2** [T] (*GB*) judge the good and bad qualities of sth

critique /krɪˈtiːk/ *n* [C] piece of written criticism of a set of ideas, work of art, etc

croak /krəʊk/ *n* [C] deep, hoarse sound as made by a frog ● **croak** *v* **1** [I] make a deep hoarse sound **2** [I,T] speak or say sth in a croaking voice

crockery /ˈkrɒkəri/ *n* [U] plates, cups, bowls, etc

crocodile /ˈkrɒkədaɪl/ *n* **1** [C] large river reptile with a long body and tail, found in hot countries **2** [U] crocodile skin made into leather **3** [C] (*GB*) long line of people, esp children, walking in pairs [IDM] **crocodile tears** insincere sorrow

crocus /ˈkrəʊkəs/ *n* [C] small plant with white, yellow or purple flowers appearing early in spring

croissant /ˈkrwæsɒ̃/ *n* [C] small sweet roll with a curved shape, eaten esp at breakfast

crony /ˈkrəʊni/ *n* [C] (pl **-ies**) (*disapprov*) friend or companion

crook /krʊk/ *n* [C] **1** (*infml*) criminal **2** bend in sth: *the ~ of your arm* (= the place where it bends at the elbow) **3** stick with a hook at one end, esp as used by a shepherd ● **crook** *v* [T] bend your finger or arm

crooked /ˈkrʊkɪd/ *adj* **1** not straight: *a ~ line* **2** (*infml*) dishonest: *a ~ politician* ▸ **crookedly** *adv*

0̸ **crop**[1] /krɒp/ *n* **1** [C] plant that is grown in large quantities, esp as food **2** [C] amount of grain, grass, fruit, etc produced in a year or season: *a good ~ of wheat* [sing] *~ of* people or things

crop[2] /krɒp/ *v* (**-pp-**) [T] **1** cut sb's hair very short **2** (of animals) bite off and eat the tops of plants, esp grass [PV] **crop up** appear or happen, esp unexpectedly: *A new problem has ~ped up.*

croquet /ˈkrəʊkeɪ/ *n* [U] game played on grass with balls that are knocked through hoops

0̸ **cross**[1] /krɒs/ *n* **1** [C] mark made by drawing one line across another, (x or +) **2** [C] long upright piece of wood with a shorter piece across it

---

near the top. In the past people were hung on crosses and left to die as a punishment. **3** (the Cross) [sing] the cross that Jesus Christ died on, used as a symbol of Christianity **4** [C] piece of jewellery, etc in the shape of a cross, used as a symbol of Christianity **5** (usu Cross) [C] small cross-shaped decoration awarded to sb for doing sth very brave **6** [C] mixture of two different things, breeds of animal, etc **7** [C] (in football or hockey) kick or hit of the ball across the field **[IDM] have a (heavy) cross to bear** have a difficult problem to deal with

O— **cross²** /krɒs/ v **1** [I,T] go across sth; extend from one side to the other of sth: *a bridge ~ing the road* **2** [I] pass across each other: *The letters ~ed in the post.* **3** [T] put or place sth across or over sth else: ~ *your arms/legs* (= place one arm or leg over the other) **4** [T] oppose sb or speak against them or their plans, etc: *You shouldn't ~ her in business.* **5** [T] ~ **(with)** cause two different types of animal or plant to produce young: *A mule is the product of a horse ~ed with a donkey.* **6** [I] (in football or hockey) kick or hit the ball sideways across the field **7** [T] draw a line across sth: ~ *a cheque* (= draw two lines on it to show that it must be paid into a bank account) **8** ~ **yourself** make the sign of a cross (= the Christian symbol) on your chest **[IDM] cross your mind** (of ideas, etc) come into your mind **[PV] cross sb/ sth off** draw a line through a person's name or an item on a list because they/it is no longer required: *C~ her off the list; she's not coming.* **cross sth out/through** draw a line through a word, usu because it is wrong

cross³ /krɒs/ adj annoyed; angry: *I was ~ with him for being so late.* ◇ *She's ~ about this.* ▶ **crossly** adv ▶ **crossness** n [U]

crossbow /ˈkrɒsbəʊ/ n [C] weapon consisting of a bow²(1) that is fixed onto a larger piece of wood, and that shoots short heavy arrows (bolts)

cross-breed /ˈkrɒs briːd/ v [I,T] (cause an animal or plant to) breed with an animal or plant of a different breed: *cross-bred sheep* ● **cross-breed** n [C] animal or plant that is the result of cross-breeding

cross-check /ˌkrɒs ˈtʃek/ v [I,T] make sure that information, figures, etc are correct by using a different method or system to check them ▶ **cross-check** /ˈkrɒs tʃek/ n [C]

cross-country /ˌkrɒs ˈkʌntri/ adj, adv across the country or fields, not on roads: *a ~ race*

cross-examine /ˌkrɒs ɪɡˈzæmɪn/ v [T] question sb closely, esp to test answers already given, in a law court ▶ **cross-examination** /ˌkrɒs ɪɡˌzæmɪˈneɪʃn/ n [C,U]

cross-eyed /ˌkrɒs ˈaɪd/ adj with one or both eyes turned towards the nose

crossfire /ˈkrɒsfaɪə(r)/ n [U] firing of guns from two or more points, so that the bullets cross

crossing /ˈkrɒsɪŋ/ n [C] **1** place where you can safely cross a road, river, etc or from one country to another **2** place where two roads, railways, etc meet **3** journey across the sea or a wide river: *an eleven-hour ferry ~*

cross-legged /ˌkrɒs ˈleɡd; -ˈleɡɪd/ adv, adj with one leg over the other

crosspiece /ˈkrɒspiːs/ n [C] (tech) piece of a structure or tool that lies or is fixed across another piece

cross purposes /ˌkrɒs ˈpɜːrpəsɪz/ n [IDM] **at cross purposes** (of two people or groups) misunderstanding what the other is talking about

cross reference /ˌkrɒs ˈrefrəns/ n [C] note directing the reader to another part of the book, file, etc

crossroads /ˈkrɒsrəʊdz/ n [C] (pl **crossroads**) place where two roads meet and cross each other **[IDM] at a/ the crossroads** at a point where an important decision is to be taken

cross section /ˈkrɒs sekʃn/ n **1** [C,U] (drawing of a) surface formed by cutting or slicing through sth **2** [C, usu sing] group of people or things that are typical of a larger group: *a ~ of society*

crosswind /ˈkrɒswɪnd/ n [C] wind blowing across the direction you are moving in

crossword /ˈkrɒswɜːd/ n [C] puzzle in which words have to be guessed from clues and written in spaces in a grid

crotch /krɒtʃ/ n (also **crutch**) n [C] place where a person's legs, or trouser legs, join

crouch /kraʊtʃ/ v [I] lower your body by bending your knees: ~ *down on the floor* ● **crouch** n [sing] crouching position

croupier /ˈkruːpieɪ/ n [C] person in charge of a table where people gamble money on cards, etc

crow /krəʊ/ n [C] **1** large black bird with a harsh cry **2** sound like that of a cock crowing **[IDM] as the crow flies** in a straight line: *It's ten miles away, as the ~ flies.* ● **crow** v **1** (of a cock) make loud high sounds, esp early in the morning **2** ~ **(about/ over)** talk too proudly about your own success or achievements: ~*ing over her profits* ■ **crow's feet** n [pl] lines on the skin near the corner of the eye ■ **'crow's nest** n [C] lookout platform at the top of a ship's mast

crowbar /ˈkrəʊbɑː(r)/ n [C] straight iron bar used as a lever for opening crates, moving heavy objects, etc

0━ **crowd** /kraʊd/ n [C, with sing or pl verb] **1** large number of people together: *a ~ of tourists* ○ (*infml*) particular group of people: *the usual ~* (= people who often meet each other) ● **crowd** v **1** [I] come together in a crowd: *~ around the stage* **2** [T] fill a place so there is little room to move: *Tourists ~ed the beach.* **3** [T] (*infml*) stand close to sb so that they feel nervous ▶ **crowded** adj (too) full of people: *a ~ room*

0━ **crown**¹ /kraʊn/ n **1** [C] circular ornamental headdress of a king or queen (**the Crown**) [sing] royal power **3** [C] top of a hill, head, hat, etc

crown² /kraʊn/ v [T] **1** put a crown on a new king or queen **2** ~ (**with**) (usu *passive*) (*written*) form or cover the top of sth: *His head was ~ed with a mop of curly hair.* **3** ~ (**with**) (usu *passive*) make sth complete or perfect: *a project ~ed with success* (**IDM**) **to crown it all** (*GB*) to be the last in a series of bad events ▶ **crowning** adj making sth perfect or complete: *a ~ achievement*

0━ **crucial** /ˈkruːʃl/ adj of decisive importance: *a ~ decision* ▶ **crucially** /-ʃəli/ adv

crucifix /ˈkruːsəfɪks/ n [C] model of the Cross with a figure of Christ on it

crucifixion /ˌkruːsəˈfɪkʃn/ n [C, U] (act of) crucifying sb

crucify /ˈkruːsɪfaɪ/ v (pt, pp **-ied**) [T] **1** kill sb as a punishment by nailing them to a cross **2** (*infml*) criticize or punish sb very severely

crude /kruːd/ adj **1** simple and not very accurate but giving a general idea of sth **2** (of objects or works of art) simply made: *~ tools* **3** rude and vulgar: *~ jokes* **4** (of materials) in a natural state and not refined: *~ oil* ▶ **crudely** adv

0━ **cruel** /ˈkruːəl/ adj (**-ler**, **-lest**) **1** (of people) enjoying the suffering of others **2** causing suffering: *~ treatment* ▶ **cruelly** adv **cruelty** n **1** [U] behaviour that causes pain and suffering to others **2** [C, usu pl] (pl **-ies**) cruel action

cruet /ˈkruːɪt/ n [C] small stand for salt and pepper, oil and vinegar, etc on a table

cruise /kruːz/ v **1** [I] travel in a ship visiting different places, esp as a holiday **2** (of cars, aircraft, etc) travel at a steady speed: *~ along at 50 miles per hour* ● **cruise** n [C] journey by sea, visiting different places: *go on a round-the-world ~* ▶ **cruiser** n [C] **1** fast warship **2** motor boat with sleeping accommodation ■ **'cruise**

missile n [C] missile that flies low and can guide itself

crumb /krʌm/ n [C] **1** very small piece of dry food, esp bread **2** very small amount

crumble /ˈkrʌmbl/ v **1** [I, T] (cause sth to) break into very small pieces **2** [I] begin to fail or come to an end: *Their marriage ~d.* ▶ **crumbly** adj (**-ier**, **-iest**) that breaks easily into small pieces: *~ cheese/soil*

crumple /ˈkrʌmpl/ v ~ (**up**) **1** [I, T] (cause sth to) be crushed into folds: *material that ~s easily* **2** [I] fall down; collapse

crunch /krʌntʃ/ v **1** [T] ~ (**up**) crush sth noisily between your teeth when eating **2** [I, T] crush sth or be crushed noisily: *The snow ~ed under our feet.* ● **crunch** n [C, usu sing] **1** noise like the sound of sth firm being crushed **2** (**the crunch**) [sing] important, often unpleasant situation: *when the ~ comes*

crusade /kruːˈseɪd/ n [C] ~ (**for/against**) long struggle for sth good or against sth bad: *a moral ~* ● **crusade** v [I] take part in a crusade ▶ **crusader** n

0━ **crush**¹ /krʌʃ/ v **1** [T] press sth so hard that there is breakage or injury: *Some people were ~ed to death in the accident.* **2** [I] push or press sb/sth into a small space: *Crowds ~ed into the theatre.* **3** [T] break sth into small pieces or powder by pressing hard **4** [T] (cause sth to) become full of creases: *clothes ~ed in a suitcase* **5** [T] defeat sb completely ▶ **crushing** adj used to emphasize how bad or severe sth is: *a ~ing defeat/blow*

crush² /krʌʃ/ n **1** [sing] crowd of people pressed together **2** [C] ~ (**on**) strong feeling of love, that usu does not last very long: *She's got a ~ on her teacher.*

crust /krʌst/ n [C, U] **1** hard outer surface of bread, pastry, etc **2** hard layer or surface: *the earth's ~* ▶ **crusty** adj (**-ier**, **-iest**) **1** having a crust; like a crust: *~y bread* **2** (*infml*) bad-tempered

crustacean /krʌˈsteɪʃn/ n [C] (*tech*) shellfish

crutch /krʌtʃ/ n [C] **1** stick used as a support under the arm to help an injured person walk **2** (*disapprov*) person or thing that you depend on for help and support **3** = CROTCH

crux /krʌks/ n [C] most important or difficult part of a problem

0━ **cry**¹ /kraɪ/ v (pt, pp **-ied**) **1** [I] ~ (**for; about/over; with**) produce tears from the eyes because you are unhappy or hurt: *The baby was ~ing for his mother.* ○ *~ with pain* [I, T] **2** [I] ~ (**for that**) shout loudly: *~ for help* ○ *'Get out!' he cried.* **3** [I] (of animals)

make a loud harsh noise [PV] **cry off**
(GB) cancel an appointment, etc **cry
out for sth** need sth urgently
■ 'crybaby n [C] person who cries
too easily or for no good reason

0~ **cry²** /kraɪ/ n (pl -ies) **1** [C] loud
sound expressing a strong feeling:
a ~ of anguish/despair **2** [C] sound
made by a bird or animal: the ~ of the
thrush **3** [sing] act or period of
crying: have a good ~ **4** [C] ~ (for)
urgent demand or request for sth:
a ~ for help [IDM] **a far cry from** very
different experience from

crypt /krɪpt/ n [C] room under a
church

cryptic /'krɪptɪk/ adj having a
hidden meaning

crystal /'krɪstl/ n **1** [C] regular shape
taken naturally by certain
substances: salt ~s **2** [U,C]
transparent colourless mineral, eg
quartz, used in making jewellery, etc
3 [U] high quality glass **4** [C] (US)
glass or plastic cover on the face of a
watch ▶ **crystalline** /'krɪstəlaɪn/ adj
1 made of crystal(s); like crystal
2 (fml) very clear: ~ water
▶ **crystallize** (also -ise) /'krɪstəlaɪz/ v
1 [I,T] (cause ideas, plans, etc to)
become clear and definite **2** [I,T]
(cause sth to) form into crystals

cub /kʌb/ n [C] young lion, bear, fox,
etc

cubbyhole /'kʌbɪhəʊl/ n [C] small
enclosed space or room

cube /kjuːb/ n **1** [C] solid figure with
six equal square sides **2** (maths)
result of multiplying a number by
itself twice ● **cube** v [T] (usu passive)
(maths) multiply a number by itself
twice: 3 ~d is 27. ▶ **cubic** /'kjuːbɪk/
adj **1** (abbr **cu**) produced by
multiplying length, width and
height: a ~ metre **2** having the shape
of a cube; of a cube

cubicle /'kjuːbɪkl/ n [C] small space
formed by dividing a larger room

cuckoo /'kʊkuː/ n [C] (pl **-os**) bird
whose call is like its name, and which
lays its eggs in the nests of other
birds

cucumber /'kjuːkʌmbə(r)/ n [C,U]
long green vegetable, eaten raw,
esp in salads

cud /kʌd/ n [U] food which cows, etc
bring back from the stomach and
chew again

cuddle /'kʌdl/ v [T] hold sb close and
lovingly in your arms: ~ a child [PV]
**cuddle up (to/against sb/sth)/ cuddle
up (together)** sit or lie very close to
sb/sth: She ~d up to her father.
● **cuddle** n [usu sing] act of cuddling
sb to show love or affection
▶ **cuddly** adj (**-ier, -iest**) (infml)
pleasant to cuddle: a ~ toy

cudgel /'kʌdʒl/ n [C] short thick stick

used as a weapon ● **cudgel** v (**-ll-** US
-l-) [T] hit sb with a cudgel

cue /kjuː/ n [C] **1** ~ (for) action or
event that is a signal to do sth: Jon's
arrival was the ~ for more drinks.
2 few words or an action in a play
that is a signal for another actor to
do sth **3** long thin stick used for
hitting the ball in games of snooker,
billiards, or pool

cuff¹ /kʌf/ n [C] **1** end of a coat or
shirt sleeve at the wrist **2** light hit
with an open hand [IDM] **off the cuff**
(of a remark, etc) said without
previous thought or preparation
● **cuff** v [T] hit sb quickly and lightly
with an open hand ■ 'cufflink n [C]
decorative object for fastening shirt
cuffs

cuisine /kwɪ'ziːn/ n [U] (style of)
cooking

cul-de-sac /'kʌl də sæk/ n [C] street
that is closed at one end

culinary /'kʌlɪnəri/ adj (fml) of or for
cooking

culminate /'kʌlmɪneɪt/ v [I] ~ in/
with have as a final result or highest
point: ~ in success ▶ **culmination**
/ˌkʌlmɪ'neɪʃn/ n [sing] final result or
highest point

culpable /'kʌlpəbl/ adj deserving
blame ▶ **culpability** /ˌkʌlpə'bɪləti/ n
[U] ▶ **culpably** adv

culprit /'kʌlprɪt/ n [C] person who
has done sth wrong

cult /kʌlt/ n [C] **1** system of religious
worship **2** devotion to a person,
thing, practice, etc **3** popular
fashion: a ~ film

cultivate /'kʌltɪveɪt/ v [T] **1** prepare
and use land for growing plants or
crops **2** grow plants and crops **3** try
to get sb's friendship or support
4 develop a way of talking,
behaving, etc: ~ her interest in
literature ▶ **cultivated** adj showing a
high level of education and good
manners ▶ **cultivation**
/ˌkʌltɪ'veɪʃn/ n [U]

0~ **culture** /'kʌltʃə(r)/ n **1** [U]
customs, beliefs, art, way of life, etc
of a particular country or group:
Greek ~ **2** [C] country, group, etc
with its own beliefs, etc **3** [U] art,
music, literature, etc thought of as a
group **4** [U] (tech) cultivating of
crops, etc **5** [C] (biol, med) group of
cells grown for study ▶ **cultural** adj
concerning culture ▶ **cultured** adj
(of people) able to appreciate art,
literature, etc ■ 'culture shock n [C]
feeling of confusion and anxiety that
sb may feel when they go to live in or
visit another country

cumbersome /'kʌmbəsəm/ adj
1 heavy and awkward to carry
2 slow and inefficient

cumulative /'kjuːmjələtɪv/ adj
increasing in amount, force, etc by
one addition after another

cunning /ˈkʌnɪŋ/ *adj* having or showing skill in deceiving people: *a ~ trick* ● **cunning** *n* [U] quality of being cunning ▸ **cunningly** *adv*

cunt /kʌnt/ *n* [C] (⚠, *offens*) (*sl*) **1** female sexual organs **2** very offensive word used to insult sb

cup¹ /kʌp/ *n* [C] **1** small bowl with a handle for drinking tea, coffee, etc **2** contents of a cup **3** gold or silver vessel given as a prize in a competition **4** something shaped like a cup [IDM] **not sb's cup of tea** (*infml, spoken*) not what sb likes ▸ **cupful** *n* [C] amount that a cup will hold

cup² /kʌp/ *v* (**-pp-**) [T] put your hands in the shape of a cup; hold sth as if in a cup: *~ your chin in your hands*

cupboard /ˈkʌbəd/ *n* [C] set of shelves with doors in the front

curable /ˈkjʊərəbl/ *adj* (of an illness) that can be cured

curate /ˈkjʊərət/ *n* [C] clergyman who helps a parish priest ● **curate** /kjʊˈreɪt/ *v* [T] select, organize and look after the items in a collection or exhibition: *The Palmer exhibition was ~d by Tim Wilcox.* ▸ **curator** /kjʊˈreɪtə(r)/ *n* [C] person in charge of a museum, art gallery, etc

curative /ˈkjʊərətɪv/ *adj* (*fml*) able to cure illness

curb /kɜːb/ *n* [C] **1** ~ (**on**) something that controls or limits sth (*esp US*) = KERB ● **curb** *v* [T] control or limit sth, esp sth bad: *Try to ~ your temper.*

curd /kɜːd/ *n* [U] (*also* **curds** [pl]) thick soft substance formed when milk turns sour

curdle /ˈkɜːdl/ *v* [I,T] (cause a liquid to) separate into solid and liquid parts

cure /kjʊə(r)/ *v* **1** ~ (**of**) bring sb back to health: *~d of a serious illness* **2** put an end to sth: *a policy to ~ inflation* **3** stop sb doing sth unpleasant, foolish, etc: *~ sb of an obsession* **4** treat meat, fish, etc in order to preserve it ● **cure** *n* [C] **1** ~ (**for**) medicine or medical treatment that cures an illness: *a new ~ for arthritis* **2** return to health

curfew /ˈkɜːfjuː/ *n* [C] time or signal for people to stay indoors

curio /ˈkjʊəriəʊ/ *n* [C] (*pl* ~**s**) rare or unusual small object

curiosity /ˌkjʊəriˈɒsəti/ *n* (*pl* -**ies**) **1** [U, sing] strong desire to know about sth **2** [C] strange or rare object

curious /ˈkjʊəriəs/ *adj* **1** eager to know about sth: *~ about how a machine works* **2** strange and unusual ▸ **curiously** *adv*

curl /kɜːl/ *n* [C] something that forms a curved or round shape, esp a small bunch of hair ● **curl** *v* [I,T] form into a curl or curls **2** [I] grow into curls; coil: *a plant ~ing round a*

109

post [PV] **curl up** lie or sit with a curved back and legs close to the body ▸ **curly** *adj* (-**ier**, -**iest**) having curls

currant /ˈkʌrənt/ *n* [C] **1** small dried grape used in cakes, etc **2** (used in compounds) (bush with) small black, red or white fruit: *black~s*

currency /ˈkʌrənsi/ *n* (*pl* -**ies**) **1** [U,C] money in use in a country **2** [U] state of being generally used or believed

current¹ /ˈkʌrənt/ *adj* **1** of the present time; happening now: *~ affairs* **2** in general use; generally accepted ● **current ac'count** *n* [C] bank account from which money can be drawn without notice ▸ **currently** *adv* at the present time; now

current² /ˈkʌrənt/ *n* [C] **1** movement of water or air in a particular direction **2** flow of electricity **3** fact of particular feelings, opinions, etc being present

curriculum /kəˈrɪkjələm/ *n* [C] (*pl* ~**s** or -**la** /-lə/) subjects included in a course of study or taught in a school, college, etc ▸ **curriculum vitae** /kəˌrɪkjələm ˈviːtaɪ/ (*abbr* **CV**) (*GB*) *n* [C] written record of your education and employment used when you apply for jobs

curry /ˈkʌri/ *n* [C,U] (*pl* -**ies**) Indian dish of meat, fish, vegetables, etc cooked with hot spices ● **curry** *v* (*pt, pp* -**ied**) [T] make curry out of meat or vegetables [IDM] **curry favour (with sb)** (*disapprov*) try to get sb to like or support you by praising or helping them a lot ▸ **curried** *adj* cooked with hot spices

curse /kɜːs/ *n* [C] **1** offensive word or phrase used to express anger, etc **2** word or phrase that has a magic power to make sth bad happen: *The witch put a ~ on him.* **3** sth that causes harm or evil ● **curse** *v* **1** [I] swear: *cursing her bad luck* **2** [T] say rude things to sb or think rude things about sb **3** [T] use a magic word or phrase against sb to harm them [PV] **be cursed with sth** continuously suffer from or be affected by sth bad ▸ **cursed** /ˈkɜːsɪd/ *adj* very bad: *a ~d nuisance*

cursor /ˈkɜːsə(r)/ *n* [C] (*computing*) small movable mark on a computer screen that shows the position you are at

cursory /ˈkɜːsəri/ *adj* (*usu disapprov*) done quickly and without much attention to detail ▸ **cursorily** *adv*

curt /kɜːt/ *adj* (of a speaker or sth spoken) abrupt; brief: *a ~ refusal* ▸ **curtly** *adv* ▸ **curtness** *n* [U]

curtail /kɜːˈteɪl/ *v* [T] (*fml*) shorten or limit sth: *~ sb's spending* ▸ **curtailment** *n* [U]

curtail

O━ **curtain** /'kɜːtn/ n **1** [C] piece of cloth, etc hung up to cover a window, divide a room, etc: draw the ~s **2** [sing] sheet of heavy material across the front of a stage in a theatre **3** [C, usu sing] anything that screens, covers, protects, etc: a ~ of mist [IDM] be curtains (for sb) (infml) be hopeless situation or one that you cannot escape from
● **curtain** v [T] provide curtains for a window or room

curtsy (also **curtsey**) /'kɜːtsɪ/ n [C] (pl -ies or ~s) act of bending the knees (by a woman) to show respect
● **curtsy** v (pt, pp -ied): [I] She ~ied to the Queen.

O━ **curve** /kɜːv/ n [C] **1** line or surface that bends gradually; smooth bend
● **curve** v **1** [I,T] (cause sth to) move in a curve **2** [I] be in the shape of a curve

cushion /'kʊʃn/ n [C] **1** small bag filled with soft material, to make a seat more comfortable, to kneel on, etc **2** something like a cushion: a ~ of air ● **cushion** v [T] **1** reduce the force of a blow, etc **2** ~ (from) protect sb from sth unpleasant

cushy /'kʊʃi/ adj (-ier, -iest) (usu disapprov) (of a job, etc) not needing much effort; easy

custard /'kʌstəd/ n [U] sweet yellow sauce made from eggs, sugar, flour and milk

custodian /kʌ'stəʊdiən/ n [C] person who is in charge of sth, esp a public building

custody /'kʌstədi/ n [U] **1** (legal right or duty of) caring for or keeping sb/sth: ~ of her child **2** imprisonment while waiting for trial: be in ~

O━ **custom** /'kʌstəm/ n **1** [U] generally accepted behaviour among members of a social group: ancient ~s **2** [sing] (fml) way a person usually behaves; habit **3** [U] (GB, fml) regular use of a shop, etc: We've lost a lot of ~ since prices went up. ▸ **customary** /'kʌstəməri/ adj according to custom, usual ■ **custom-built** (also **custom-made**) adj designed and made for a particular person

O━ **customer** /'kʌstəmə(r)/ n [C] person who buys sth in a shop, etc or uses a service

O━ **customs** /'kʌstəmz/ n [pl] **1** (Customs) government department that collects taxes on goods brought into the country, etc **2** place at an airport, etc where your bags are checked as you come into a country **3** taxes payable on imported goods

O━ **cut¹** /kʌt/ v (-tt- pt, pp **cut**) **1** [I,T] make an opening or wound in sth with sth sharp: I ~ my hand with a

knife. **2** [T] remove sth from sth larger with a knife, etc; divide sth into two or more pieces: ~ a piece of cake ◇ ~ the cake into four **3** [T] shorten sth by cutting it: ~ sb's hair **4** [I] be capable of cutting or being cut: This knife won't ~. ◇ Sandstone ~s easily **5** [T] reduce sth: ~ prices/ taxes **6** [T] remove sth from sth: ~ some scenes from a film **7** [I,T] remove part of a text on a computer screen in order to place it elsewhere: You can ~ and paste between different programs. **8** [T] prepare a film or tape by removing parts of it, etc; edit sth **9** [I] stop filming or recording **10** [I] (in films, radio or television) move quickly from one scene to another **11** [T] (infml, esp US) stay away from a class that you should go to **12** [T] (written) hurt sb emotionally: His remarks ~ me deeply. **13** [T] (of a line) cross another line [IDM] cut and dried decided in a way that cannot be changed or argued about cut both/ two ways have two opposite effects or results cut corners do things in the easiest and quickest way, often by being careless cut sb dead (GB) pretend not to have seen sb; refuse to greet sb cut it/things fine (infml) leave yourself just enough time to do sth cut loose (infml) act, speak, etc freely and without restraint cut your losses stop doing sth that is not successful before the situation gets even worse cut no ice (with sb) not impress or influence sb cut sb to the quick hurt sb's feelings cut sb/sth short stop sb speaking; interrupt sth [PV] cut across sth **1** affect different groups that usu remain separate: ~ across social barriers **2** go across a field, etc to shorten your route cut sth back| cut back (on sth) **1** reduce sth: ~ back on the number of workers **2** cut shrubs, etc close to the stem cut sth down cause sth to fall by cutting it at the base: ~ down a tree cut sth down| cut down (on sth) reduce the size, amount or number of sth: ~ down on your smoking cut in (on sb/sth) **1** interrupt a conversation, etc **2** move in front of another vehicle, leaving too little space cut sb off **1** interrupt sb: be ~ off while talking on the phone cut sb/sth off stop the supply of sth to sb: ~ off the gas cut sth off **1** remove sth by cutting: He ~ off his finger. **2** block or obstruct sth: ~ off their retreat cut out (of an engine, etc) stop working cut sth out **1** remove sth by cutting **2** make or shape sth by cutting: ~ out a dress **3** leave sth out of a piece of writing, etc **4** (infml) stop doing or using sth: ~ out cigarettes (not) be cut out for sth/to be sth (not) have the abilities needed for sth: I'm not ~ out to be a teacher. cut sb up (infml) upset sb emotionally cut sth up cut sth into small pieces ■ **cutback** n [C] reduction in sth ■ **cut-out** n [C] **1** shape cut out of paper, wood, etc **2** safety device that stops the flow of electric current through sth ■ **cut-price** adj reduced in price; cheap

0— **cut²** /kʌt/ n [C] **1** wound caused by sth sharp **2** hole or opening made with a knife, etc **3 ~ (in)** reduction in amount, size, supply, etc: a ~ in taxes **4** act of cutting sth: Your hair needs a ~. **5** style in which clothes, hair, etc is cut: a suit with a loose ~ **6** share in sth: a ~ of the profits **7** act of removing part of sth: make some ~s in the film **8** part that is cut from sth larger: a ~ of beef [IDM] **a cut above sb** better than sb

cute /kjuːt/ adj **1** attractive, pretty or charming **2** (infml, esp US) (too) clever; sharp-witted ▸ **cutely** adv ▸ **cuteness** n [U]

cuticle /ˈkjuːtɪkl/ n [C] layer of skin at the base of a fingernail or toenail

cutlery /ˈkʌtləri/ n [U] knives, forks, etc used for eating

cutlet /ˈkʌtlət/ n [C] slice of meat or fish

cutter /ˈkʌtə(r)/ n **1** [C] person or thing that cuts **2** (cutters) [pl] (used esp in compounds) tool for cutting **3** [C] type of small sailing boat

cut-throat /ˈkʌt θrəʊt/ adj (of an activity) in which people compete in aggressive and unfair ways

cutting /ˈkʌtɪŋ/ n [C] **1** article or a story cut from a newspaper or magazine **2** short piece of the stem of a plant, used for growing a new plant **3** (GB) narrow open passage cut in high ground for a road, railway or canal ● **cutting** adj (of remarks, etc) unkind; hurtful

CV /ˌsiː ˈviː/ abbr curriculum vitae

cyanide /ˈsaɪənaɪd/ n [U] strong poison

cyber- /ˈsaɪbə(r)/ prefix connected with electronic communication networks, esp the Internet

cybercafe /ˈsaɪbəkæfeɪ/ n [C] a cafe with computers on which customers can use the Internet, send emails, etc

cyberspace /ˈsaɪbəspeɪs/ n [U] imaginary place where electronic messages, pictures, etc exist while they are being sent between computers

cybersquatting /ˈsaɪbəskwɒtɪŋ/ n [U] illegal activity of buying and officially recording an address on the Internet that is the name of an existing company, with the intention of selling it to the owner in order to make money

0— **cycle** /ˈsaɪkl/ n [C] **1** (infml) bicycle or motorcycle: go for a ~ ride **2** series of events in a regularly repeated order: the ~ of the seasons ● **cycle** v [I] ride a bicycle ▸ **cyclical**

/ˈsaɪklɪkl; ˈsɪk-/ adj repeated many times and always happening in the same order ● **cyclist** n [C] person who cycles

cyclone /ˈsaɪkləʊn/ n [C] violent tropical storm in which strong winds move in a circle ▸ **cyclonic** /saɪˈklɒnɪk/ adj

cygnet /ˈsɪɡnət/ n [C] young swan

cylinder /ˈsɪlɪndə(r)/ n [C] **1** long solid or hollow body with circular ends and straight sides **2** hollow tube in an engine, shaped like a cylinder, inside which the piston moves ▸ **cylindrical** /səˈlɪndrɪkl/ adj cylinder-shaped

cymbal /ˈsɪmbl/ n [C] musical instrument in the form of a round metal plate, which is hit with a stick or against another cymbal to make a ringing sound

cynic /ˈsɪnɪk/ n [C] person who believes that people only do things to help themselves, rather than for good or sincere reasons ▸ **cynical** adj or like a cynic: a ~al remark ▸ **cynically** /-kli/ adv ▸ **cynicism** /ˈsɪnɪsɪzəm/ n [U]

cypher = CIPHER

cypress /ˈsaɪprəs/ n [C] any of various types of evergreen tree with dark leaves and hard wood

cyst /sɪst/ n [C] swelling or lump filled with liquid in the body or under the skin

cystitis /sɪˈstaɪtɪs/ n [U] infection of the bladder

czar, czarina = TSAR, TSARINA

Dd

D, d /diː/ n [C,U] (pl **D's, d's** /diːz/) **1** the fourth letter of the English alphabet **2** Roman numeral for 500

d. abbr died: d. 1924

dab /dæb/ v (-**bb**-) [T] touch sth lightly or gently: ~ your face dry ● **dab** n [C] small quantity of paint, etc put on a surface

dabble /ˈdæbl/ v **1** [I] ~ **(in)** be interested in a subject in a way that is not serious **2** [T] move your hands or feet gently about in water

dachshund /ˈdæksnd/ n [C] small dog with very short legs

0— **dad** /dæd/ n [C] (infml) father

daddy /ˈdædi/ n [C] (pl -**ies**) (used by children) father

daffodil /ˈdæfədɪl/ n [C] yellow trumpet-shaped flower that grows in spring

daft /dɑːft/ adj (infml) silly

dagger /ˈdæɡə(r)/ n [C] short sharp knife used as a weapon

0— **daily** /ˈdeɪli/ adj, adv happening or appearing every day or every weekday ● **daily** n [C] (pl **-ies**) newspaper that is published every day

dainty /'deɪnti/ adj (**-ier, -iest**) pretty and delicate ▶ **daintily** adv

dairy /'deəri/ n [C] (pl **-ies**) **1** building on a farm where butter and cheese are made **2** company that sells milk, butter, eggs, etc ● **dairy** adj **1** made from milk: ~ *products* **2** connected with the production of milk: ~ *cattle*

daisy /'deɪzi/ n [C] (pl **-ies**) small flower with a yellow centre and white petals

dale /deɪl/ n [C] (lit) valley

dam /dæm/ n [C] wall built to keep back water ● **dam** v (**-mm-**) build a dam across sth

0━ **damage** /'dæmɪdʒ/ n **1** [U] harm; loss: *The fire caused great* ~. **2** (**damages**) [pl] (law) money claimed from a person who has caused loss or injury ● **damage** v [T] harm or spoil sb/sth

dame /deɪm/ n [C] (**Dame**) title given to a woman as a special honour because of the work she has done

damn /dæm/ exclam (infml) used for showing anger or annoyance ● **damn** (also **damned**) adj, adv (infml) **1** swear word people use to show anger or annoyance: *You know* ~ *well what I mean!* **2** swear word people use to emphasize what they are saying: *He was ~ lucky to survive.* ● **damn** v [T] **1** used when swearing at sb/sth to show that you are angry **2** (of God) decide sb must suffer in hell **3** criticize sb/sth very strongly ● **damn** n [IDM] **not care/give a damn (about sb/sth)** (infml) not care at all about sb/sth ▶ **damnation** /dæm'neɪʃn/ n [U] state of being in hell; act of sending sb to hell

0━ **damp**¹ /dæmp/ adj slightly wet: *a* ~ *cloth* ● **damp** n [U] state of being damp; areas on a wall, etc that are damp ▶ **dampness** n [U]

damp² /dæmp/ v = DAMPEN [PV] **damp sth down** make a fire burn more slowly

dampen /'dæmpən/ v [T] **1** make sth slightly wet **2** make a feeling or a reaction less strong: ~ *his enthusiasm*

damper /'dæmpə(r)/ n [C] small flat piece of metal that controls the flow of air into a fire [IDM] **put a damper on sth** (infml) make sth less enjoyable, successful, etc

damson /'dæmzn/ n [C] (tree producing a) small purple plum

0━ **dance** /dɑːns/ n **1** [C] movements and steps in time to music **2** [U] art of dancing **3** [C] act of dancing: *He asked her for a* ~. **4** [C] social event at which people dance ● **dance** v [I] move with steps in time to music

2 [T] do a particular type of dance ▶ **dancer** n [C] ▶ **dancing** n [U]: *dancing classes/shoes*

dandelion /'dændilaɪən/ n [C] small wild plant with yellow flowers

dandruff /'dændrʌf/ n [U] small pieces of dead skin in a person's hair

0━ **danger** /'deɪndʒə(r)/ n **1** [U] possibility of being hurt or killed **2** [C] thing or person that may cause danger [IDM] **in danger** likely to be hurt or killed **out of danger** no longer seriously ill ▶ **dangerous** adj likely to cause danger: ~ *driving* ▶ **dangerously** adv

dangle /'dæŋgl/ v [I,T] hang or swing loosely

dank /dæŋk/ adj unpleasantly damp and cold: *a* ~ *cellar/cave*

0━ **dare** /deə(r)/ v **1** (pres tense, all persons dare, neg **dare not**, short form **daren't** /deənt/ or **do not/does not dare**, short form **don't/doesn't dare**) [I] ~ **(to)** (usu in negative sentences) have enough courage to do sth: *No one* ~*d speak.* ◇ *I* ~*n't ask him.* ◇ *We didn't* ~ *(to) go into the room.* **2** [T] ~ **(to)** challenge sb to do sth dangerous or difficult: *I* ~ *you to jump off the tree.* ● **dare** n [usu sing] something dangerous, difficult, etc that you try to persuade sb to do, to see if they will do it: *He climbed onto the roof for a* ~. ▶ **daredevil** n [C] person who likes to do dangerous things

daring /'deərɪŋ/ adj brave; willing to take risks ▶ **daringly** adv

0━ **dark**¹ /dɑːk/ adj **1** with no or very little light: *a* ~ *night/room* **2** (of colour) nearer black than white: ~ *blue* **3** (of the skin) not fair **4** hopeless; sad: *look on the* ~ *side of things* [IDM] **a dark horse** person who hides special abilities ▶ **darken** /v [I,T] become or make sth dark ▶ **darkly** adv ▶ **darkness** n [U]

0━ **dark**² /dɑːk/ n [U] lack of light: *sit in the* ~ [IDM] **after/before dark** after/before the sun goes down **in the dark (about sth)** knowing nothing about sth

darling /'dɑːlɪŋ/ n [C] person who is loved very much

darmstadtium /dɑːm'ʃtætiəm/ n [U] (symb Ds) radioactive chemical element that is produced artificially

darn /dɑːn/ v [T] repair a hole in sth by sewing: ~ *sb's socks* ● **darn** n [C] hole repaired by darning

dart /dɑːt/ n **1** [C] small pointed object used in the game of darts **2** (**darts**) [U] game in which darts are thrown at a target ● **dart** v [I] move suddenly and quickly

dash /dæʃ/ n [C] **1** sudden quick movement: *make a* ~ *for the bus* **2** small amount of sth added: *a* ~ *of pepper* **3** punctuation mark (—) ● **dash** v **1** [I] go somewhere quickly:

~ across the road **2** [T] throw sth violently onto a hard surface [IDM] **dash sb's hopes** destroy sb's hopes ▶ **dashing** *adj* (*written*) attractive and confident ■ **'dashboard** *n* [C] part of a car in front of the driver that has instruments and controls in it

0-**¬ data** /'deɪtə/ *n* [U] information or facts, eg to be analysed by a computer ■ **'database** *n* [C] organized store of computer data ■ **'data processing** *n* [U] (*computing*) series of actions that a computer performs on data to produce an output (= information that has been analysed)

0-**¬ date¹** /deɪt/ *n* **1** [C] particular day of the month or year: *Her ~ of birth is 24 April 1983.* **2** [sing] a particular time: *We'll discuss this at a later ~.* **3** [C] arrangement to meet sb, esp a boyfriend or girlfriend **4** [C] (*esp US*) boyfriend or girlfriend with whom you have arranged a date **5** [C] sweet sticky brown fruit that grows on a tree [IDM] **out of date 1** old-fashioned; no longer useful: *out-of-~ methods/machinery* **2** no longer valid: *My passport's out of ~.* **to date** until now up to date **1** completely modern **2** with all the latest information: *I'll bring you up to ~ with the latest news.*

0-**¬ date²** /deɪt/ *v* **1** [T] write a date on sth: *The letter was ~d 23 July.* **2** say when sth did existed or was made **3** [I] become old-fashioned **4** [T] (*US*) have a romantic relationship with sb [PV] **date back (to...)**| **date from...** have existed since...: *The Church ~s from the twelfth century.* ▶ **dated** /'deɪtɪd/ *adj* old-fashioned

daub /dɔːb/ *v* [T] put paint, plaster, etc roughly on a surface

0-**¬ daughter** /'dɔːtə(r)/ *n* [C] person's female child ■ **'daughter-in-law** *n* [C] (*pl* **~s-in-law**) wife of your son

daunting /'dɔːntɪŋ/ *adj* making you feel nervous and less confident

dawdle /'dɔːdl/ *v* [I] go somewhere very slowly

0-**¬ dawn** /dɔːn/ *n* **1** [C,U] first light of day **2** [sing] beginning of sth ● **dawn** *v* [I] begin to become light [PV] **dawn on sb** begin to become clear to sb: *The truth began to ~ on him.*

0-**¬ day** /deɪ/ *n* **1** [C] period of 24 hours **2** [U] time between sunrise and sunset: *It rained all ~ long.* **3** [C, usu sing] hours of the day when you are awake, working, etc **4** [C, usu pl] period of time or history: *in the ~s of the Roman Empire* [IDM] **any day (now)** (*spoken*) very soon **day after day** | **day in, day out** every day for a long time **day and night** → NIGHT **sb's/sth's days are numbered** the person or thing will soon die, fail, etc **make sb's day** (*infml*) make sb very

happy **one day** at some time in the future or at a particular time in the past ■ **daybreak** *n* [U] first light of day; dawn ■ **'daydream** *v* [I], *n* [C] (have) pleasant thoughts that make you forget about the present ■ **'daylight** *n* [U] light from the sun during the day ■ **'daytime** *n* [U] time between sunrise and sunset

daze /deɪz/ *n* [IDM] **in a daze** unable to think clearly

dazed /deɪzd/ *adj* unable to think or react normally

dazzle /'dæzl/ *v* [T] **1** make sb unable to see clearly because of too much strong light **2** impress sb with your beauty, skill, etc

DDT /ˌdiː diː 'tiː/ *n* [U] powerful dangerous insecticide

0-**¬ dead** /ded/ *adj* **1** (of people, animals or plants) no longer alive **2** belonging to the past; no longer used or believed in **3** (of machines, etc) not working: *The phone suddenly went ~.* **4** without activity: *The town is ~ after 10 o'clock.* **5** (*infml*) extremely tired; not well **6** (of part of the body) unable to feel because of cold, etc **7** complete; absolute: *a ~ silence/calm* ● **dead** *adv* completely; absolutely: *~ certain/accurate* ▶ **the dead** *n* [pl] people who have died ■ **dead end** *n* [C] place or situation where more progress is impossible ■ **'deadline** *n* [C] fixed date for completing a task: *meet/miss a ~line* ■ **dead loss** *n* [usu sing] (*GB, infml*) person or thing that is not useful or helpful

deaden /'dedn/ *v* [T] make a sound, feeling, etc less strong

deadlock /'dedlɒk/ *n* [C, U] total failure to reach agreement

deadly /'dedli/ *adj* (**-ier, -iest**) **1** causing or likely to cause death: *a ~ poison* **2** extreme; complete: *I'm in ~ earnest.* **3** (*GB, infml*) boring ● **deadly** *adv* (*infml*) extremely: *~ serious*

0-**¬ deaf** /def/ *adj* **1** unable to hear **2** ~ **to** unwilling to listen ▶ **the deaf** *n* [pl] deaf people ■ **deaf mute** *n* [C] somebody who is deaf and dumb ▶ **deafness** *n* [U]

deafen /'defn/ *v* [T] make it difficult for sb to hear sth: *~ed by the noise*

0-**¬ deal¹** /diːl/ *v* (*pt, pp* ~**t** /delt/) [I, T] **1** give out playing cards to a number of players **2** buy and sell illegal drugs [IDM] **deal sb/sth a blow** | **deal a blow to sb/sth** (*fml*) be very shocking or harmful to sb/sth [PV] **deal in sth** buy and sell goods; trade in sth: *~ in second-hand cars* **deal with sb/sth** **1** take appropriate action in a particular situation: *She has to ~ with difficult customers in her job.* **2** do business with a person, a company

or an organization **deal with sth**
1 solve a problem, carry out a task,
etc **2** be about sth: *poems that ~ with*
the subject of death ▸ **dealer** *n* [C]
1 person whose business is buying
and selling a particular product: *an*
antiques/art ~ **2** person who sells
illegal drugs **3** person who deals out
playing cards ▸ **dealings** *n* [pl]
business activities: *have ~ings with sb*

○━ **deal²** /diːl/ *n* **1** [sing] (a good/
great ~) much; a lot: *a good ~ of*
money ◇ I see a great ~ of him. **2** [C]
(business) agreement **3** [C, usu sing]
way that sb/sth is treated: *They'd*
had a rough/raw ~ (= been treated
unfairly). **4** [C] action of giving out
playing cards in a card game

dean /diːn/ *n* [C] **1** Anglican priest of
high rank in charge of other priests
2 head of a university department

○━ **dear** /dɪə(r)/ *adj* **1 ~ (to)** loved by
or important to sb **2** (**Dear**) used at
the beginning of letters: *D~ Madam/*
Sir (CB) expensive ● **dear** *exclam*
used for expressing surprise,
impatience, etc: *Oh ~! ◇ D~ me!*
● **dear** *n* [C] **1** (GB, spoken) kind
person **2** used when speaking kindly
to sb: *Yes, ~.* ● **dear** *adv* (GB) at a
high price ▸ **dearly** *adv* **1** very much
2 with great loss, damage, etc

dearth /dɜːθ/ *n* [sing ~ (of)] (*fml*)
shortage of sth

○━ **death** /deθ/ *n* **1** [C] dying; being
killed **2** [U] end of life; state of being
dead **3** [U] ~ **of** permanent end or
destruction of sth [IDM] **put sb to**
death kill sb; execute sb ● **to death**
extremely; very much: *be bored/*
frightened to ~ ▸ **deathly** *adj, adv*
like death ■ **'death penalty** *n* [sing]
punishment of being killed for a
crime ■ **'death trap** *n* [C] (*infml*)
road, vehicle, etc that is dangerous
and could cause sb's death ■ **'death**
warrant *n* [C] official order for sb to
be killed as punishment for a crime

debacle /deɪˈbɑːkl/ *n* [C] event or
situation that is a complete failure

debase /dɪˈbeɪs/ *v* [T] lower the value
or quality of sth ▸ **debasement** *n* [U]

○━ **debate** /dɪˈbeɪt/ *n* [C, U] formal
discussion at a public meeting or in
Parliament ● **debate** *v* [I, T] discuss
sth formally; consider ▸ **debatable**
adj not certain; open to
question

debauched /dɪˈbɔːtʃt/ *adj* (*fml*)
immoral ▸ **debauchery** /dɪˈbɔːtʃəri/
n [U] wild immoral behaviour

debilitating /dɪˈbɪlɪteɪtɪŋ/ *adj*
making sb weak: *a ~ illness*

debit /ˈdebɪt/ *n* [C] written note in a
bank account of money owed or
spent ● **debit** *v* [T] take money from
an account to pay for sth ■ **'debit**
card *n* [C] plastic card you can use to

take money directly from your bank
account when you pay for sth

debris /ˈdebriː; ˈdeɪ-/ *n* [U] pieces of
metal, wood, etc left after sth has
been destroyed

○━ **debt** /det/ *n* **1** [C] sum of money
owed to sb **2** [U] state of owing
money: *be in/out of ~* **3** [C, usu sing]
fact of feeling grateful to sb for their
help or kindness: *owe a ~ of gratitude*
to sb ▸ **debtor** *n* [C] person who
owes money to sb

debut (*also* **début**) /ˈdeɪbjuː/ *n* [C]
first public appearance of an actor,
musician, etc: *make your ~*

○━ **decade** /ˈdekeɪd; dɪˈkeɪd/ *n*
period of ten years

decadent /ˈdekədənt/ *adj*
(*disapprov*) showing a fall in moral
standards: *~ behaviour/society*
▸ **decadence** /ˈdekədəns/ *n* [U]

decaffeinated /diːˈkæfɪneɪtɪd/ *adj*
(of coffee) with the caffeine
removed

decant /dɪˈkænt/ *v* [T] pour wine, etc
from a bottle into another
container ▸ **decanter** *n* [C] glass
bottle with a stopper, for wine

decapitate /dɪˈkæpɪteɪt/ *v* [T] cut off
sb's head

○━ **decay** /dɪˈkeɪ/ *v* [I, T] (cause sth
to) be destroyed gradually by
natural processes: *~ing teeth/food*
2 [I] lose strength, power, etc;
deteriorate ▸ **decay** *n* [U]

deceased /dɪˈsiːst/ ▸ **the deceased**
n [C] (*pl* **the deceased**) (*fml*) person
who has recently died

deceit /dɪˈsiːt/ *n* [U, C] dishonest
behaviour that causes sb to believe
sth that is false ▸ **deceitful** *adj*
behaving dishonestly by making
people believe things which are
false ▸ **deceitfully** *adv*
▸ **deceitfulness** *n* [U]

deceive /dɪˈsiːv/ *v* [T] make sb
believe sth that is false ▸ **deceiver**
n [C]

○━ **December** /dɪˈsembə(r)/ *n* [U, C]
twelfth month of the year (See
examples of use at *April*.)

decent /ˈdiːsnt/ *adj* **1** of a good
enough standard or quality: *a ~ meal*
2 (of people) honest and fair
3 acceptable to people in a
particular situation: *That dress isn't*
~. ▸ **decency** /-nsi/ *n* [U] ▸ **decently**
adv

deception /dɪˈsepʃn/ *n* **1** [U] act of
deceiving sth: *obtain sth by ~* **2** [C]
trick intended to make sb believe sth
that is false

deceptive /dɪˈseptɪv/ *adj*
misleading: *a ~ appearance*
▸ **deceptively** *adv*

decibel /ˈdesɪbel/ *n* [C] unit for
measuring the loudness of sounds

○━ **decide** /dɪˈsaɪd/ *v* **1** [I] think
about sth and choose between the
possibilities available: *I ~d to leave.*

2 [T] (*law*) make an official or legal judgement **3** affect the result of sth **4** [T] be the reason why sb does sth
▶ **decided** *adj* obvious and definite
▶ **decidedly** *adv* definitely

deciduous /dɪˈsɪdʒuəs; -dju-/ *adj* (of trees) losing their leaves every autumn

decimal /ˈdesɪml/ *adj* based on or counted in tens or tenths: *the ~ system* ● **decimal** *n* [C] fraction expressed in tenths, hundredths, etc, eg 0.25 ▶ **decimalize** (*also* -ise) /-məlaɪz/ *v* [I,T] change to a decimal system ▶ **decimalization** /ˌdesɪməlaɪˈzeɪʃn/ (*also* -isation) /ˌdesɪməlaɪˈzeɪʃn/ *n* [U] ■ **decimal point** *n* [C] dot placed after the unit figure in decimals: *10.25*

decimate /ˈdesɪmeɪt/ *v* [T] **1** kill large numbers of animals, plants or people **2** (*infml*) severely damage or weaken sth

decipher /dɪˈsaɪfə(r)/ *v* [T] succeed in finding the meaning of sth that is difficult to read: *~ a code*

0━ **decision** /dɪˈsɪʒn/ *n* **1** [C] choice or judgement made after careful thought: *come to/reach/make a ~* **2** [U] ability to decide sth quickly **3** [U] process of deciding sth
▶ **decisive** /dɪˈsaɪsɪv/ *adj*
1 important for the final result of sth: *a ~ factor/victory* **2** able to decide sth quickly and with confidence
▶ **decisively** *adv*: *act ~*
▶ **decisiveness** *n* [U]

deck /dek/ *n* [C] **1** floor in a ship, bus, etc **2** (*esp US*) pack of playing cards **3** (*esp US*) wooden floor that is built outside the back of a house where you can sit and relax **4** part of a music system that records and/or plays sounds on a disc or tape
● **deck** *v* [T] ~ (**out**) decorate sb/sth: *streets ~ed out with flags*
■ **deckchair** *n* [C] folding canvas chair, used outside ▶ **decking** *n* [U] wood used to build a terrace outside the back of a house

0━ **declare** /dɪˈkleə(r)/ *v* [T] **1** say sth officially or publicly **2** state sth firmly and clearly **3** tell the authorities about money you have earned or goods you have imported, on which you have to pay tax ▶ **declaration** /ˌdekləˈreɪʃn/ *n* [C,U]

0━ **decline** /dɪˈklaɪn/ *n* [C,U] gradual and continuous loss of quality, importance, power, etc: *a ~ in population* ● **decline** *v* **1** [I] become smaller, fewer, weaker, etc **2** [I,T] (*fml*) refuse politely to do or accept sth

declutter (*also* **de-clutter**) /ˌdiːˈklʌtə(r)/ *v* [I,T] remove things you do not use so that you have more space: *Moving house is a good opportunity to ~.*

decode /ˌdiːˈkəʊd/ *v* [T] find the

---

115   **deed**

meaning of a message written in code

decompose /ˌdiːkəmˈpəʊz/ *v* [I,T] be destroyed gradually by natural chemical processes: *a ~d body*
▶ **decomposition** /-ˌpəˈzɪʃn/ *n* [U]

decor /ˈdeɪkɔː(r)/ *n* [U, C, usu sing] style in which the inside of a room is decorated

0━ **decorate** /ˈdekəreɪt/ *v* **1** [T] make sth more attractive by putting things on it: *The room was ~d with flowers and balloons.* **2** [I,T] put paint or wallpaper on the walls of a room or building **3** [T] give a medal to sb: *~d for bravery* ▶ **decoration** /ˌdekəˈreɪʃn/ *n* **1** [C, usu pl] thing used for decorating sth: *Christmas ~s* **2** [U] pattern or style in which sth is decorated **3** [C] medal, etc given to sb as an honour ▶ **decorative** /ˈdekərətɪv/ *adj* intended to look attractive: *purely ~ arches*
▶ **decorator** *n* [C] person whose job is painting and decorating houses

decoy /ˈdiːkɔɪ/ *n* [C] **1** real or imitation) bird used to attract others so that they can be caught or shot **2** person or thing that is used to tempt sb into a trap

0━ **decrease** /dɪˈkriːs/ *v* [I,T] become or make sth smaller in size, number, etc: *Sales are decreasing.* ● **decrease** /ˈdiːkriːs/ *n* [C,U] process of reducing sth or the amount that sth is reduced by: *a small ~ in exports*

decree /dɪˈkriː/ *n* [C] **1** official order that has the force of the law: *by royal ~* **2** decision made in a law court
● **decree** *v* [T] order, judge or decide sth officially

decrepit /dɪˈkrepɪt/ *adj* very old and not in good condition

dedicate /ˈdedɪkeɪt/ *v* [T] ~ **to 1** give a lot of your time, energy, etc to an activity because you think it is important **2** (of an author) write sb's name at the beginning of a book as a sign of friendship or respect
▶ **dedicated** *adj* working hard at sth because it is important to you
▶ **dedication** /ˌdedɪˈkeɪʃn/ *n* [U,C]

deduce /dɪˈdjuːs/ *v* [T] reach a conclusion, theory, etc by reasoning

deduct /dɪˈdʌkt/ *v* [T] take away an amount or part from sth: *~ £50 from her salary* ▶ **deductible** /dɪˈdʌktəbl/ *adj* that can be taken away from an amount of money you earn, from tax, etc ▶ **deductible** *n* [C] (*US*) = EXCESS(2)

deduction /dɪˈdʌkʃn/ *n* [U,C] **1** conclusion reached by reasoning **2** process of deducting sth; amount deducted: *tax ~s*

deed /diːd/ *n* [C] **1** (*fml*) something done; act **2** (*law*) signed agreement, esp about ownership

deem

deem /di:m/ v [T] consider sth to be sth: *The party was ~ed a great success.*

deep¹ /di:p/ adj **1** going a long way down from the top or surface: *a ~ river ◇ a hole one metre ~* **2** (of sounds) low **3** (of colours or feelings) strong; intense: *~ hatred* **4** (of sleep) from which it is difficult to wake **5** serious; profound: *a ~ book* **6** ~ **in** absorbed in sth: *~ in thought/a book* [IDM] **go off the deep end** (infml) become very angry ■ **in deep water(s)** (infml) in trouble ▶ **deeply** adv very much; intensely: *~ly hurt by your remarks* ■ **deep vein thrombosis** n [C,U] (abbr **DVT**) (med) serious condition caused by a blood clot forming in a vein

deep² /di:p/ adv far down or in sth ■ **deep 'freeze** n [C] = FREEZER ■ **deep-rooted** (also **deep-'seated**) adj (of feelings and beliefs) very fixed and strong; difficult to change or destroy: *~-rooted suspicions*

deepen /ˈdi:pən/ v [I,T] become or make sth deep, deeper or more intense

deer /dɪə(r)/ n [C] (pl **deer**) fast graceful animal, the male of which has branching horns (antlers)

deface /dɪˈfeɪs/ v [T] damage the appearance of sth, esp by drawing or writing on it

defame /dɪˈfeɪm/ v [T] (fml) attack the good reputation of sth ▶ **defamation** /ˌdefəˈmeɪʃn/ n [U]

default /dɪˈfɔ:lt/ v [I] **1** fail to pay a debt, perform a duty or appear (eg in a law court) when required **2** (computing) ~ **(to)** happen when you do not make any other choice or change ● **default** n [U,C] **1** failure to do sth, appear, etc: *win a game by ~* **2** (computing) what happens if you do not make any other choice or change ▶ **defaulter** n [C]

defeat /dɪˈfi:t/ v [T] **1** win a victory over sb **2** stop sth from being successful: *Looking at the answers ~s the object of the exercise!* ● **defeat** n [C,U] instance of defeating sb/sth or being defeated

defect¹ /ˈdi:fekt/ n [C] fault; imperfection ▶ **defective** /dɪˈfektɪv/ adj

defect² /dɪˈfekt/ v [I] leave your country, political party, etc and join an opposing one ▶ **defection** /dɪˈfekʃn/ n [C,U] ▶ **defector** n [C] person who defects

defence (US **defense**) /dɪˈfens/ n **1** [U] act of protecting sb/sth from attack, criticism, etc **2** [C] something that provides protection against attack: *the country's ~s* **3** [C,U] (law) (act of presenting an)

argument used in a law court to prove that a person did not commit a crime **4** (**the defence**) [sing, with sing or pl verb] the lawyer(s) acting in court for an accused person ▶ **defenceless** adj unable to defend yourself

defend /dɪˈfend/ v **1** [T] ~ **(from/against)** protect sth from attack **2** [T] speak or write in support of sb/sth: *a decision* **3** [I,T] act as a lawyer for sb who has been charged with a crime ▶ **defendant** n [C] person against whom a case is brought in a law court ▶ **defender** n [C] **1** person who defends sb/sth **2** (in sport) player who guards the goal area ▶ **defensible** /dɪˈfensəbl/ adj able to be defended

defensive /dɪˈfensɪv/ adj **1** protecting sb/sth against attack **2** behaving in a way that shows that you feel that people are criticizing you ● **defensive** n [IDM] **on/onto the defensive** ready to protect yourself against criticism ▶ **defensively** adv

defer /dɪˈfɜ:(r)/ v (**-rr-**) **1** [I] ~ **to** accept sb's decision, opinion, etc, because you respect him or her: *I ~ to her experience.* **2** [T] delay sth until a later time: *~ payment* ▶ **deference** /ˈdefərəns/ n [U] behaviour that shows you respect sb/sth

defiance /dɪˈfaɪəns/ n [U] open refusal to obey sb/sth: *in ~ of my orders* ▶ **defiant** /dɪˈfaɪənt/ adj openly and aggressively disobedient ▶ **defiantly** adv

defibrillator /di:ˈfɪbrɪleɪtə(r)/ n [C] (med) piece of equipment used to return the heart to its natural rhythm by giving a controlled electric shock

deficiency /dɪˈfɪʃnsi/ n [C,U] (pl **-ies**) state of not having, or not having enough of, sth that is essential ▶ **deficient** /dɪˈfɪʃnt/ adj not having enough of sth

deficit /ˈdefɪsɪt/ n [C] amount by which sth, esp a sum of money, is too small

defile /dɪˈfaɪl/ v [T] (fml) make sth dirty or impure

define /dɪˈfaɪn/ v [T] **1** say or explain what the meaning of a word or phrase is **2** describe or show sth clearly ▶ **definable** adj

definite /ˈdefɪnət/ adj **1** sure or certain; not likely to change **2** easily seen or understood; obvious ■ **definite 'article** n [C] (gram) the word *the* ▶ **definitely** adv **1** without doubt: *~ly not true* **2** (infml) (used in answer to a question) yes; certainly

definition /ˌdefɪˈnɪʃn/ n **1** [C] explanation of the meaning of a word or phrase, esp in a dictionary **2** [U] quality of being clear and easy to see: *The photograph lacks ~.*

definitive /dɪˈfɪnətɪv/ *adj* final; not able to be changed

deflate *v* [I,T] **1** /dɪˈfleɪt, ˌdiː-/ make a tyre, etc smaller by letting out air or gas **2** /dɪˈfleɪt/ make sb feel less important or confident **3** /dɪˈfleɪt/ reduce the amount of money in circulation in an economy ▶ **deflation** /ˌdiːˈfleɪʃn/ *n* [U]

deflect /dɪˈflekt/ *v* [I,T] (cause sth to) change direction, esp after hitting sth: *~ a bullet/criticism* ▶ **deflection** /dɪˈflekʃn/ *n* [C,U]

deform /dɪˈfɔːm/ *v* [T] change or spoil the natural shape of sth: *a ~ed foot* ▶ **deformity** *n* [C, U] (pl **-ies**)

defraud /dɪˈfrɔːd/ *v* [T] (*~ of*) get money illegally by tricking sb: *~ him of £100*

defrost /ˌdiːˈfrɒst/ *v* [T] remove ice from a refrigerator, frozen food, etc

deft /deft/ *adj* (*~ at*) quick and skilful, esp with your hands ▶ **deftly** *adv* ▶ **deftness** *n* [U]

defunct /dɪˈfʌŋkt/ *adj* (*fml*) no longer existing or being used

defuse /ˌdiːˈfjuːz/ *v* [T] **1** reduce the dangerous tension in a difficult situation **2** remove the fuse from a bomb

defy /dɪˈfaɪ/ *v* (pt, pp **-ied**) [T] **1** refuse to obey or respect sb in authority, a law, a rule, etc **2** be (almost) impossible to believe, explain, describe, etc: *~ description* **3** challenge sb to do sth

degenerate¹ /dɪˈdʒenəreɪt/ *v* [I] become worse in quality or strength, etc ● **degenerate** /dɪˈdʒenərət/ *adj* having lost good moral or mental qualities ● **degenerate** /dɪˈdʒenərət/ *n* [C]

degrade /dɪˈɡreɪd/ *v* [T] show or treat sb in a way that makes them seem unworthy of respect: *This poster ~s women.* ▶ **degradation** /ˌdeɡrəˈdeɪʃn/ *n* [U]

0━ **degree** /dɪˈɡriː/ *n* **1** [C] unit for measuring angles: *an angle of 30 ~s (30°)* **2** [C] unit for measuring temperature: *ten ~s Celsius (10°C)* **3** [C,U] amount or level of sth: *a high ~ of accuracy* ◇ *I agree with you to a certain ~.* **4** [C] qualification given by a university or college to sb who has completed a course [IDM] **by degrees** gradually

dehydrate /ˌdiːˈhaɪdreɪt/ *v* **1** [T] remove water from sth, esp food, in order to preserve it **2** [I,T] (cause sb to) lose too much water from the body

de-ice /ˌdiː ˈaɪs/ *v* [T] remove the ice from sth

deign /deɪn/ *v* [T] (*disapprov*) do sth in a way that shows you think you are too important to do it: *She didn't ~ to speak to me.*

deity /ˈdeɪəti/ *n* [C] (pl **-ies**) god or goddess

dejected /dɪˈdʒektɪd/ *adj* sad and disappointed ▶ **dejection** /-kʃn/ *n* [U]

0━ **delay** /dɪˈleɪ/ *v* **1** [I,T] not do sth until a later time or make sth happen at a later time **2** [T] be or make sb slow or late: *I was ~ed by the traffic.* ● **delay** *n* [C,U] (instance of) delaying sth or being delayed

delectable /dɪˈlektəbl/ *adj* (*written*) (of food) extremely pleasant to taste, look at, etc

delegate /ˈdelɪɡət/ *n* [C] person chosen by others to express their views at a meeting ● **delegate** /ˈdelɪɡeɪt/ *v* **1** [I,T] give part of your work, power, etc to sb in a lower position than you **2** [T] choose sb to do sth ▶ **delegation** /ˌdelɪˈɡeɪʃn/ *n* **1** [C] group of representatives of an organization, a country, etc **2** [U] process of delegating

delete /dɪˈliːt/ *v* [T] remove sth written, printed or stored in a computer ▶ **deletion** /dɪˈliːʃn/ *n* [C,U]

0━ **deliberate**¹ /dɪˈlɪbərət/ *adj* **1** intentional: *a ~ insult* **2** (of a movement or an action) slow and cautious ▶ **deliberately** *adv*

deliberate² /dɪˈlɪbəreɪt/ *v* [I,T] (*~ about/on*) (*fml*) think very carefully about sth

deliberation /dɪˌlɪbəˈreɪʃn/ *n* **1** [U,C, usu pl] careful thought **2** [U] slowness of action or speech

delicacy /ˈdelɪkəsi/ *n* (pl **-ies**) **1** [U] quality of being delicate **2** [C] tasty food: *a local ~*

0━ **delicate** /ˈdelɪkət/ *adj* **1** needing careful handling or treatment: *a ~ vase/situation* **2** (of a person) becoming ill easily: *in ~ health* **3** small and pretty **4** able to show very small changes or differences: *a ~ instrument* **5** (of colours, flavours and smells) light and pleasant; not strong ▶ **delicately** *adv*

delicatessen /ˌdelɪkəˈtesn/ *n* [C] shop selling prepared, esp unusual or imported, food

0━ **delicious** /dɪˈlɪʃəs/ *adj* having a very pleasant taste or smell

0━ **delight**¹ /dɪˈlaɪt/ *n* **1** [U] great pleasure: *take ~ in being a parent* **2** [C] cause or source of great pleasure ▶ **delightful** *adj* ▶ **delightfully** *adv*

0━ **delight**² /dɪˈlaɪt/ *v* [T] give sb a lot of pleasure [PV] **delight in sth/doing sth** enjoy doing sth very much ▶ **delighted** *adj* very pleased

delineate /dɪˈlɪnieɪt/ *v* [T] (*fml*) describe, draw or explain sth in detail

delinquent /dɪˈlɪŋkwənt/ *n* [C], *adj* (person) behaving badly or committing crimes ▶ **delinquency**

/dɪˈlɪŋkwənsi/ n [C, U] (pl **-ies**) bad or criminal behaviour, usu of young people

delirious /dɪˈlɪriəs; -ˈlɪəriəs/ adj 1 in a confused and excited state, usu because of fever 2 very excited and happy ▶ **deliriously** adv

delirium /dɪˈlɪriəm; -ˈlɪəriəm/ n [U] mental disturbance, esp during illness

0→ **deliver** /dɪˈlɪvə(r)/ v [I, T] take letters, goods, etc to houses or buyers: ~ milk/newspapers 2 [T] give a speech in public: ~ a lecture 3 [T] help a woman in the birth of a baby [IDM] **deliver the goods** → GOODS

0→ **delivery** /dɪˈlɪvəri/ n (pl **-ies**) 1 [U, C] act of delivering letters, goods, etc: When can you take ~ of (= be available to receive) the car? 2 [C] process of giving birth to a child: The mother had an easy ~. 3 [sing] way sb speaks, sings a song, etc in public

delta /ˈdeltə/ n [C] land in the shape of a triangle where a river separates into branches

delude /dɪˈluːd/ v [T] deceive sb

deluge /ˈdeljuːdʒ/ n [C] 1 heavy fall of rain 2 great quantity of sth: a ~ of letters ● **deluge** v [T] send or give sb/ sth a lot of things at once: We were ~d with applications.

delusion /dɪˈluːʒn/ n [C, U] false belief: ~s of grandeur (= a belief that you are more important than you really are)

de luxe /də ˈlʌks; ˈlʊks/ adj of very high quality: a ~ hotel

delve /delv/ v [I] search for sth inside a bag, container, etc [PV] **delve into sth** try hard to find out more information about sth

Dem. abbr (in politics in the US) Democrat(ic)

0→ **demand¹** /dɪˈmɑːnd/ n 1 [C] very firm request for sth; sth that sb needs: ~s for higher pay 2 [U, C] people's desire for sth/sb that they want to buy/employ: Our goods are in great ~. (= many people want them) [IDM] **on demand** when asked for

0→ **demand²** /dɪˈmɑːnd/ v [T] 1 ask for sth very firmly 2 need sth: work ~ing great care ▶ **demanding** adj 1 needing much skill, effort, etc: a ~ing job 2 making others work hard: a ~ing boss

demarcate /ˈdiːmɑːkeɪt/ v [T] (fml) fix the limits of sth ▶ **demarcation** /ˌdiːmɑːˈkeɪʃn/ n [U, C]

demean /dɪˈmiːn/ v [T] (fml) 1 ~ yourself do sth that makes people have less respect for you 2 make people have less respect for sb/sth

demeanour (US **-or**) /dɪˈmiːnə(r)/ n

[C, U, usu sing] (fml) way sb looks or behaves

demented /dɪˈmentɪd/ adj mad

demerara sugar /ˌdeməreərə ˈʃʊgə(r)/ n [U] (GB) type of rough brown sugar

demilitarize (also **-ise**) /ˌdiːˈmɪlɪtəraɪz/ v [T] remove military forces from an area

demise /dɪˈmaɪz/ n [sing] 1 end or failure of an institution, an idea, etc 2 (fml) death

demist /ˌdiːˈmɪst/ v [T] remove the condensation from a car's windows

democracy /dɪˈmɒkrəsi/ n (pl **-ies**) 1 [C, U] (country with a) system of government in which all the people of a country can vote to elect their representatives 2 [U] fair and equal treatment of everyone in an organization, etc

democrat /ˈdeməkræt/ n [C] 1 person who favours or supports democracy 2 (Democrat) (US) member of the Democratic Party ▶ **democratic** /ˌdeməˈkrætɪk/ adj of or supporting democracy ▶ **democratically** adv

demographics /ˌdeməˈɡræfɪks/ n [pl] data relating to the population and different groups within it

demography /dɪˈmɒɡrəfi/ n [U] changing number of births, deaths, diseases, etc. in a community over a period of time; scientific study of these changes: the social ~ of Africa ▶ **demographer** /dɪˈmɒɡrəfə(r)/ n [C] ▶ **demographic** /ˌdeməˈɡræfɪk/ adj: ~ changes/trends

demolish /dɪˈmɒlɪʃ/ v [T] 1 pull or knock down a building 2 destroy an argument, theory, etc ▶ **demolition** /ˌdeməˈlɪʃn/ n [C, U]

demon /ˈdiːmən/ n [C] 1 evil spirit 2 (infml) person with great skill or energy ▶ **demonic** /diːˈmɒnɪk/ adj

demonstrable /ˈdemənstrəbl/ adj that can be shown or proved ▶ **demonstrably** adv

0→ **demonstrate** /ˈdemənstreɪt/ v 1 show sth clearly by giving proof or evidence 2 [T] show and explain how sth works or how to do sth 3 [I] take part in a public meeting or march, usu as a protest ▶ **demonstrator** n [C] 1 person who demonstrates (3) 2 person whose job is to show or explain how sth works or is done

demonstration /ˌdemənˈstreɪʃn/ n 1 [C] public meeting or march at which people show that they are protesting against or supporting sth 2 [C, U] (also infml **demo**) act of showing how sth works or is done **3** [C,U] act of giving proof or evidence for sth ► **demonstrative** /dɪ'mɒnstrətɪv/ *adj* **1** showing feelings openly **2** (*gram*) used to identify the person or thing being referred to, eg *this, those*

demoralize (*also -ise*) /dɪ'mɒrəlaɪz/ *v* [T] destroy sb's courage, confidence, etc: ~*d students*

demote /ˌdiː'məʊt/ *v* [T] move sb to a lower position or rank

demure /dɪ'mjʊə(r)/ *adj* (of a woman) quiet, serious and shy ► **demurely** *adv*

den /den/ *n* [C] **1** a wild animal's hidden home: *a lion's ~* **2** (*disapprov*) place where people meet in secret, esp for some illegal or immoral activity: *a ~ of thieves*

denationalize (*also -ise*) /ˌdiː'næʃnəlaɪz/ *v* [T] sell a company so that it is no longer owned by the government; privatize sth ► **denationalization** (*also -isation*) /ˌdiː'næʃnəlaɪ'zeɪʃn/ *n* [U]

denial /dɪ'naɪəl/ *n* **1** statement that sth is not true **2** [C,U] refusal to allow sb to have sth they have a right to expect

denigrate /'denɪɡreɪt/ *v* [T] claim unfairly that sb/sth is inferior, worthless, etc

denim /'denɪm/ *n* [U] strong cotton cloth, that is usu blue and used for making clothes, esp jeans: *a ~ jacket*

denomination /dɪˌnɒmɪ'neɪʃn/ *n* [C] **1** religious group **2** unit of money or measurement ► **denominational** *adj* of religious groups

denominator /dɪ'nɒmɪneɪtə(r)/ *n* [C] number below the line in a fraction, eg 4 in ¾

denote /dɪ'nəʊt/ *v* [T] **1** be a sign of sth: *Red ~s danger.* **2** mean sth

denounce /dɪ'naʊns/ *v* [T] ~ (**as**) speak publicly against sb/sth

dense /dens/ *adj* (**~r, ~st**) **1** (of people and things) crowded together: ~ *traffic* **2** difficult to see through: ~ *fog* **3** (*infml*) stupid ► **densely** *adv*

density /'densəti/ *n* (*pl -ies*) **1** [U] the quality of being dense **2** [C,U] (*physics*) relation of mass to volume **3** [U] (*computing*) amount of space available on a disk: *a high ~ floppy*

dent /dent/ *n* hollow place in a hard surface made by sth hitting it ● **dent** *v* [T] make a dent in sth

dental /'dentl/ *adj* of or for the teeth

0— **dentist** /'dentɪst/ *n* [C] person whose job is to take care of people's teeth ► **dentistry** *n* [U] work of a dentist

denunciation /dɪˌnʌnsi'eɪʃn/ *n* [C,U] act of publicly criticizing sth

0— **deny** /dɪ'naɪ/ *v* (*pt, pp -ied*) [T] **1** say that sth is not true **2** refuse to give sth asked for or needed by sb

deodorant /di'əʊdərənt/ *n* [C,U] substance that hides or removes body odours

dep. *abbr* (in writing) depart(s); departure

depart /dɪ'pɑːt/ *v* [I] (*fml*) go away; leave: *The train ~s from platform 3.*

0— **department** /dɪ'pɑːtmənt/ *n* [C] (*abbr* **dept.**) one of several divisions of a government, business, shop, university, etc ■ **de'partment store** *n* [C] large shop where many kinds of goods are sold in different departments

0— **departure** /dɪ'pɑːtʃə(r)/ *n* [C,U] **1** act of leaving a place **2** plane, train, etc leaving at a particular time: *the ~s board*

0— **depend** /dɪ'pend/ *v* [I] [IDM] **that depends** | **it (all) depends** used to say that you are not certain about sth because other things must be considered [PV] **depend on/upon sb/ sth 1** rely on sb/sth; be certain about sth: *You can ~ on John not to be late.* **2** need the support of sb/sth in order to survive: *Children ~ on their parents.* **3** be affected or decided by sth: *Our success ~s on how hard we work.* ► **dependable** *adj* that can be relied on: *a ~able friend*

dependant (*esp US -ent*) /dɪ'pendənt/ *n* [C] person who depends on another for a home, food, etc

dependence /dɪ'pendəns/ *n* [U] state of needing sb/sth in order to survive, esp when this is not normal or necessary: ~ *on drugs*

dependent /dɪ'pendənt/ *adj* **1** ~ **(on/upon)** needing sb/sth for support: ~ *on her parents* **2** ~ **on/ upon** affected or decided by sth: ~ *on your passing the exam* ● **dependent** *n* [C] (*esp US*) = DEPENDANT

depict /dɪ'pɪkt/ *v* [T] show an image of sb/sth in a picture; describe sth in words ► **depiction** /-kʃn/ *n* [U,C]

deplete /dɪ'pliːt/ *v* [T] reduce sth by a large amount: *Our supplies are badly ~d.* ► **depletion** /dɪ'pliːʃn/ *n* [U]

deplore /dɪ'plɔː(r)/ *v* [T] express strong disapproval of sth ► **deplorable** *adj* very bad; deserving strong disapproval

deploy /dɪ'plɔɪ/ *v* [T] (*tech*) move soldiers or weapons into position for battle

deport /dɪ'pɔːt/ *v* [T] force sb unwanted to leave a country ► **deportation** /ˌdiːpɔː'teɪʃn/ *n* [C,U]

depose /dɪ'pəʊz/ *v* [T] remove a ruler from power

0— **deposit¹** /dɪ'pɒzɪt/ *n* [C] **1** payment of part of a larger sum, the rest of which is to be paid later **2** amount of money that sb pays when beginning to rent sth **3** amount of money paid into a bank account **4** layer of a substance left by a river, etc ■ de'posit account *n* [C] account at a bank, etc in which the money earns interest

0-■ **deposit²** /dɪ'pɒzɪt/ *v* [T] **1** (*fml*) lay or put sb/sth down **2** (eg of a river) leave mud, etc on sth **3** put money in to a bank, esp to earn interest; put sth valuable in a safe place

depot /'depəʊ/ *n* **1** storehouse; warehouse **2** (*GB*) place where vehicles, eg buses, are kept **3** (*US*) small railway or bus station

depraved /dɪ'preɪvd/ *adj* (*fml*) morally bad ▶ **depravity** /dɪ'prævəti/ *n* [U]

deprecate /'deprəkeɪt/ *v* [T] (*fml*) feel and show disapproval of

depreciate /dɪ'priːʃieɪt/ *v* [I] become less valuable over a period of time ▶ **depreciation** /dɪ,priːʃi'eɪʃn/ *n* [U]

0-■ **depress** /dɪ'pres/ *v* [T] **1** make sb sad: *feel very ~ed* **2** make trade, business, etc less active: *The recession has ~ed the housing market.* **3** lower the value of prices or wages **4** (*fml*) press or push sth down ▶ **depressing** *adj* making you feel sad: *a ~ing film*

depression /dɪ'preʃn/ *n* **1** [U,C] state of feeling very sad and anxious: *clinical ~* **2** [C] period of little economic activity with poverty and unemployment **3** [C] (*written*) part of a surface that is lower than the parts around it **4** [C] (*tech*) weather condition in which the air pressure becomes lower

deprive /dɪ'praɪv/ *v* [PV] **deprive sb/ sth of sth** prevent sb from having or doing sth: *~ people of freedom* ▶ **deprivation** /,deprɪ'veɪʃn/ *n* [U] ▶ **deprived** *adj* without enough food, housing, health care, etc

Dept *abbr* Department

0-■ **depth** /depθ/ *n* **1** [C,U] distance from the top to the bottom or from the front to the back **2** [U] deep thought, feeling, etc: *a writer of great ~* [IDM] **in depth** in detail; thoroughly **out of your depth 1** in water that is deeper than your height **2** in a situation that is beyond your understanding or control

deputation /,depju'teɪʃn/ *n* [C, with sing or pl verb] group of people with the right to act or speak for others

deputize (*also* -ise) /'depjutaɪz/ *v* [I] ~ (**for**) act as deputy: *~ for the manager*

deputy /'depjuti/ *n* [C] (*pl* -ies) person immediately below a business manager, a head of a school, a political leader, etc and

who does the person's job when he or she is away

derail /dɪ'reɪl/ *v* [T] cause a train to leave the track ▶ **derailment** *n* [C,U]

deranged /dɪ'reɪndʒd/ *adj* unable to act and think normally, esp because of mental illness

derelict /'derəlɪkt/ *adj* left to fall into ruin: *a ~ house* ▶ **dereliction** /,derə'lɪkʃn/ *n* [U]

derision /dɪ'rɪʒn/ *n* [U] unkind laughter or remarks

derisory /dɪ'raɪsəri/ *adj* (*fml*) too small to be considered seriously

derivation /,derɪ'veɪʃn/ *n* [C,U] origin or development of a word ▶ **derivative** /dɪ'rɪvətɪv/ *adj, n* [C] (something, esp a word) derived from

0-■ **derive** /dɪ'raɪv/ *v* [PV] **derive sth from sth** (*fml*) get sth from sth: *~ pleasure from sth* **derive from sth| be derived from sth** develop from sth: *words ~d from Latin*

derogatory /dɪ'rɒgətri/ *adj* showing a lack of respect for sb/sth

derrick /'derɪk/ *n* [C] **1** large crane for moving cargo on a ship **2** framework over an oil well to hold the drilling machinery, etc

descend /dɪ'send/ *v* [I,T] (*fml*) come or go down sth [IDM] **be descended from sb** be related to sb who lived a long time ago [PV] **descend on/upon sb/sth** visit sb/sth in large numbers, usu unexpectedly ▶ **descendant** *n* person or animal that is descended from another

descent /dɪ'sent/ *n* **1** [C, usu sing] action of coming or going down **2** [C] downward slope **3** [U] family; origin: *of French ~*

0-■ **describe** /dɪ'skraɪb/ *v* [T] **1** say what sb/sth is like **2** (*fml* or *tech*) form a particular shape: *~ a circle*

0-■ **description** /dɪ'skrɪpʃn/ *n* **1** [C,U] (giving a) statement of what sb/sth is like **2** [C] kind or type: *boats of every ~* ▶ **descriptive** /dɪ'skrɪptɪv/ *adj* saying what sb/sth is like

desecrate /'desɪkreɪt/ *v* [T] spoil or damage a sacred thing or place ▶ **desecration** /,desɪ'kreɪʃn/ *n* [U]

0-■ **desert¹** /dɪ'zɜːt/ *v* **1** [T] leave sb without help or support: *~ your family* **2** [T] go away from a place and leave it empty **3** [I] leave the armed forces without permission ▶ **deserter** *n* person who deserts (3) ▶ **desertion** /dɪ'zɜːʃn/ *n* [U,C]

desert² /'dezət/ *n* [C,U] large area of land, without water and trees, often covered with sand ■ **desert 'island** *n* [C] tropical island where no people live

deserts /dɪ'zɜːts/ *n* [pl] [IDM] **sb's (just) deserts** sb deserves, esp sth bad

0→ **deserve** /dɪ'zɜ:v/ v [T] earn sth, either good or bad, because of sth you have done: *She ~d to win.*

0→ **design** /dɪ'zaɪn/ n **1** [U] general arrangement of the parts of a machine, building, etc **2** [U] art of deciding how sth will look, work, etc by drawing plans **3** [C] drawing from which sth may be made **4** [C] decorative pattern of lines, shapes, etc **5** [U,C] plant; intention ● **design** v [T] **1** prepare a plan or drawing of sth to be made **2** make, plan or intend sth for a particular purpose or use: *a room ~ed for children* ▸ **designer** n [C] person whose job is to decide how clothes, buildings, etc will look by making drawings, plans, etc

designate /'dezɪgneɪt/ v [T] **1** choose sb for a particular job or purpose **2** mark sb/sth out clearly

desirable /dɪ'zaɪərəbl/ adj worth having or doing ▸ **desirability** /dɪ,zaɪərə'bɪləti/ n [U]

0→ **desire** /dɪ'zaɪə(r)/ n [C,U] strong wish to have or get sth: *no ~ to be rich/for wealth* **2** [C, sing] person or thing that is wished for ● **desire** v [T] (fml) want sb/sth very much

desist /dɪ'zɪst/ v [I] ~ (from) (fml) stop doing sth

0→ **desk** /desk/ n [C] table, usu with drawers in it, that you sit at to read, write or work ■ **desktop** n [C] screen on a computer that shows which programs can be used ■ **desktop com'puter** (also **desktop**) n [C] computer with a keyboard, screen and main processing unit, that fits on a desk ■ **desktop 'publishing** n [U] (abbr **DTP**) use of a small computer and a printer to produce a small book, a magazine, etc

desolate /'desələt/ adj **1** (of a place) empty and without people **2** lonely and sad ▸ **desolation** /,desə'leɪʃn/ n [U]

despair /dɪ'speə(r)/ n [U] feeling of having lost all hope ● **despair** v [I] ~ (of) stop having any hope: *~ of ever getting better*

despatch = DISPATCH

0→ **desperate** /'despərət/ adj **1** having little hope and ready to do anything without caring about danger to yourself and others: *The prisoners grew increasingly ~.* **2** (of an action) tried when everything else has failed: *a ~ attempt to save her* **3** in great need: *~ for money* **4** extremely serious or dangerous: *a ~ situation* ▸ **desperately** adv ▸ **desperation** /,despə'reɪʃn/ n [U]

despicable /dɪ'spɪkəbl/ adj very unpleasant or evil

despise /dɪ'spaɪz/ v [T] dislike and have no respect for sb/sth

0→ **despite** /dɪ'spaɪt/ prep used to introduce a contrast: *still a clear thinker, ~ his old age*

despondent /dɪ'spɒndənt/ adj sad, without hope ▸ **despondency** /-dənsi/ n [U] ▸ **despondently** adv

despot /'despɒt/ n [C] ruler with great power, esp one who rules unfairly ▸ **despotic** /dɪ'spɒtɪk/ adj: *~ rule*

dessert /dɪ'zɜ:t/ n [C,U] sweet food eaten at the end of a meal ■ **des'sertspoon** n [C] medium-sized spoon

destination /,destɪ'neɪʃn/ n [C] place to which sb/sth is going

destined /'destɪnd/ adj **1** intended or certain: *~ to become famous* **2** ~ **for** on the way to a place

destiny /'destəni/ n (pl -ies) **1** [C] what happens to sb, or what will happen to them in the future, esp things beyond their control **2** [U] fate

destitute /'destɪtju:t/ adj without food, money, shelter, etc ▸ **destitution** /,destɪ'tju:ʃn/ n [U]

0→ **destroy** /dɪ'strɔɪ/ v [T] **1** break or damage sth so badly it no longer exists, works, etc **2** kill an animal, usu because it is sick ▸ **destroyer** n [C] **1** small fast warship **2** person or thing that destroys

0→ **destruction** /dɪ'strʌkʃn/ n [U] act of destroying sth or of being destroyed ▸ **destructive** /dɪ'strʌktɪv/ adj causing destruction or damage

detach /dɪ'tætʃ/ v [I,t] remove sth from sth larger; become separated from sth ▸ **detached** adj **1** (of a house) not joined to another **2** not involved; unemotional ▸ **detachment** n [U] **1** state of not being emotionally involved **2** [C] group of soldiers sent away from the main group

0→ **detail** /'di:teɪl/ n **1** [C,U] small particular fact or item: *describe sth in ~* **2** (details) [pl] information about sth: *Further ~s are available on request.* ● **detail** v [T] **1** give a list of facts or information about sth **2** appoint a soldier for special duty

detain /dɪ'teɪn/ v [T] **1** keep sb in an official place, eg a police station, and prevent them from leaving **2** (fml) delay sb ▸ **detainee** /,di:teɪ'ni:/ n [C] person who is kept in prison, esp for political reasons

detect /dɪ'tekt/ v [T] discover the existence or presence of sth ▸ **detection** n [U] ▸ **detective** n [C] person, esp a police officer, whose job is to investigate crimes ▸ **detector** n [C] device for detecting sth: *a metal/smoke ~*

detention /dɪˈtenʃn/ n **1** [U] act of detaining sb, esp for political reasons **2** [U,C] punishment of being kept at school after school hours

deter /dɪˈtɜː(r)/ v (-rr-) [T] ~ (**from**) prevent or discourage sb from doing sth

detergent /dɪˈtɜːdʒənt/ n [C, U] liquid or powder used for washing clothes or plates, etc

deteriorate /dɪˈtɪəriəreɪt/ v [I] become worse: *My health* ~*d*. ▶ **deterioration** /dɪˌtɪəriəˈreɪʃn/ n [U]

0━ **determination** /dɪˌtɜːmɪˈneɪʃn/ n [U] **1** quality that makes you continue trying to do sth even when this is difficult: *a* ~ *to win* **2** process of deciding sth officially

0━ **determine** /dɪˈtɜːmɪn/ v [T] (*fml*) **1** discover the facts about sth: ~ *what happened* **2** control sth or cause sth to happen: *Our living standards are* ~*d by our income*. **3** officially decide sth: ~ *party policy* **4** decide firmly to do sth ▶ **determined** *adj* showing a serious wish to do sth successfully: ~*d to improve your English*

deterrent /dɪˈterənt/ n [C] something that makes sb less likely to do sth: *the nuclear* ~ (= nuclear weapons that are intended to stop an enemy from attacking)

detest /dɪˈtest/ v [T] hate sb/sth very much ▶ **detestable** *adj* that deserves to be hated

dethrone /ˌdiːˈθrəʊn/ v [T] remove a king, queen or ruler from power

detonate /ˈdetəneɪt/ v [I,T] (cause a bomb, etc to) explode ▶ **detonation** /ˌdetəˈneɪʃn/ n [C,U] ▶ **detonator** /-tə(r)/ n [C] device that makes a bomb explode

detour /ˈdiːtʊə(r)/ n [C] longer way round sth: *make a* ~ *round the floods*

detoxification /ˌdiːˌtɒksɪfɪˈkeɪʃn/ (*also infml* **detox** /ˈdiːtɒks/) n [U] **1** process of removing harmful substances from your body by only eating and drinking particular things: *a 28-day* ~ *plan* **2** treatment given to people to help them stop drinking alcohol or taking drugs: *a* ~ *unit*

detract /dɪˈtrækt/ v [PV] **detract (sth) from sth** make sth seem less good or enjoyable

detriment /ˈdetrɪmənt/ n [U] damage; harm: *to the* ~ *of her health* ▶ **detrimental** /ˌdetrɪˈmentl/ *adj* ~ (**to**) harmful

deuce /djuːs/ n [C] (in tennis) score of 40 points to each player

devalue /ˌdiːˈvæljuː/ v [I,T] make the value of a currency less ▶ **devaluation** /ˌdiːˌvæljuˈeɪʃn/ n [C,U]

devastate /ˈdevəsteɪt/ v [T] **1** completely destroy a place or an area **2** make sb very shocked and sad ▶ **devastation** /ˌdevəˈsteɪʃn/ n [U]

0━ **develop** /dɪˈveləp/ v **1** [I,T] become or make sth larger, more advanced, stronger, etc: *The argument* ~*ed into a fight*. **2** [I,T] begin to have sth, eg a disease or a problem; start to affect sb/sth: *a cough* **3** [T] build houses, etc on an area of land and so increase its value **4** [T] treat an exposed film so that the photograph can be seen ▶ **developer** n [C] person or company that develops land ▶ **development** n **1** [U] gradual growth of sth **2** [C] new event or situation **3** [C] area of land with new buildings on it

deviate /ˈdiːvieɪt/ v [I] ~ **from** turn away from what is usual, accepted, etc ▶ **deviation** /ˌdiːviˈeɪʃn/ n [C,U]

0━ **device** /dɪˈvaɪs/ n [C] **1** object designed to do a particular job **2** plan or trick

devil /ˈdevl/ n [C] **1** (**the Devil**) most powerful evil being; Satan **2** evil spirit **3** (*infml*) person who behaves badly, esp a child ■ **devil's ˈadvocate** n [C] person who speaks against sth/sb to encourage discussion

devious /ˈdiːviəs/ *adj* behaving in a dishonest or indirect way in order to get sth

devise /dɪˈvaɪz/ v [T] invent sth new

devoid /dɪˈvɔɪd/ *adj* ~ **of** without sth: ~ *of any ability*

devolution /ˌdiːvəˈluːʃn/ n [U] transfer of power from central to regional government

0━ **devote** /dɪˈvəʊt/ v [T] [PV] **devote sth to sth** give an amount of time, attention, etc to sth: *D*~ *an hour a day to the project*. **devote yourself to sb/sth** give most of your time, energy, etc to sb/sth ▶ **devoted** *adj* ~ (**to**) very loving or loyal to sb/sth ▶ **devotee** /ˌdevəˈtiː/ n [C] person who admires and is enthusiastic about sb/sth ▶ **devotion** /dɪˈvəʊʃn/ n **1** [U] great love, care and support for sb/sth **2** [pl] prayers

devour /dɪˈvaʊə(r)/ v [T] **1** eat all of sth quickly and hungrily **2** (*fml*) destroy sb/sth: *forests* ~*ed by fire*

devout /dɪˈvaʊt/ *adj* (of a person) believing strongly in a particular religion and obeying its laws

dew /djuː/ n [U] tiny drops of water that form on the ground during the night ▶ **dewy** *adj* ■ **ˈdewdrop** n [C] drop of dew

dexterity /dekˈsterəti/ n [U] skill, esp with your hands ▶ **dexterous** (*also* **dextrous**) /ˈdekstrəs/ *adj*

diabetes /ˌdaɪəˈbiːtiːz/ n [U] disease in which the body cannot control the level of sugar in the blood ▶ **diabetic** /ˌdaɪə'betɪk/ adj, n [C] (of or for a) person with diabetes

diabolical /ˌdaɪə'bɒlɪkl/ adj **1** (infml, esp GB) very bad: ~ weather **2** evil and wicked

diagnose /'daɪəgnəʊz/ v [T] say exactly what an illness or the cause of a problem is ▶ **diagnosis** /ˌdaɪəg'nəʊsɪs/ n [C, U] (pl -noses /-siːz/) act of identifying the exact cause of an illness or problem ▶ **diagnostic** /ˌdaɪəg'nɒstɪk/ adj

diagonal /daɪ'ægənl/ n [C], adj (straight line) joining two opposite sides of sth at an angle ▶ **diagonally** adv /-nəli/

0━ diagram /'daɪəgræm/ n [C] drawing, design or plan used for explaining or illustrating sth ▶ **diagrammatic** /ˌdaɪəgrə'mætɪk/ adj

dial /'daɪəl/ n [C] **1** marked face of a clock, watch or measuring instrument **2** round part on older telephones, that you move round to call a number ● **dial** v (-ll- US -l-) [I,T] use a telephone by turning the dial or pushing buttons to call a number ■ **dialling tone** n [C] sound heard on the telephone before you dial the number

dialect /'daɪəlekt/ n [C, U] form of a language used in part of a country

dialogue (US -log) /'daɪəlɒg/ n [C,U] **1** conversations in a book, play or film **2** formal discussion between two groups or countries ■ **dialogue box** (US, GB also **dialog box**) n [C] box that appears on a computer screen asking the user to choose what they want to do next

diameter /daɪ'æmɪtə(r)/ n [C] length of a straight line drawn from side to side through the centre of a circle

diametrically /ˌdaɪə'metrɪkli/ adv completely: ~ opposed

0━ diamond /'daɪəmənd/ n [U,C] very hard clear colourless precious stone: a ~ ring **2** [C] shape with four equal sides whose angles are not right angles **3** (diamonds) [pl] one of the four suits in a pack of cards, marked with red or black diamond shapes ■ **diamond jubilee** n [C] 60th anniversary of an important event

diaper /'daɪpə(r)/ (US) = NAPPY

diaphragm /'daɪəfræm/ n [C] **1** (anat) muscle between the lungs and the stomach **2** (tech) thin vibrating disc or plate in an instrument

diarrhoea (US diarrhea) /ˌdaɪə'rɪə/ n [U] too frequent and too watery emptying of the bowels

0━ diary /'daɪəri/ n [C] (pl -ies) book used for a daily record of events,

future appointments, etc: keep (= write regularly in) a ~ ◇ a desk ~

dice /daɪs/ n [C] (pl **dice**) small cube marked with spots to indicate numbers, used in games ● **dice** v [T] cut food into small cubes [IDM] **dice with death** (infml) risk your life

dictate /dɪk'teɪt/ v [I,T] **1** say words aloud for sb else to write down **2** order sb to do sth **3** control or influence how sth happens ▶ **dictation** /dɪk'teɪʃn/ n **1** [U] act of saying words aloud so that sb can write it down **2** [C,U] test in which students write down what is being read aloud to them

dictator /dɪk'teɪtə(r)/ n (disapprov) ruler who has complete power over a country ▶ **dictatorial** /ˌdɪktə'tɔːriəl/ adj ▶ **dictatorship** n [C,U] (country with) government by a dictator

diction /'dɪkʃn/ n [U] way that sb pronounces words

0━ dictionary /'dɪkʃənri/ n [C] (pl -ies) book containing the words of a language, with their meanings, arranged in alphabetical order

did pt of DO

didn't short for DID NOT

0━ die /daɪ/ v (pres pt **dying** /'daɪɪŋ/) [I] **1** stop living **2** stop existing; disappear: love that will never ~ [IDM] **be dying for sth/to do sth** (infml) want (to do) sth very much: I'm dying for a drink. ◇ I'm dying to tell her. **die laughing** (infml) find sth very funny [PV] **die away** become weaker and disappear **die down** become less strong **die out** disappear completely ● **die** n [C] metal block used to stamp designs on coins, medals, etc

diesel /'diːzl/ n **1** [U] (also **diesel oil** [U]) type of heavy oil used as a fuel instead of petrol **2** [C] vehicle that uses diesel: Our new car's a ~. ■ '**diesel engine** n [C] internal-combustion engine in buses, trains, lorries, etc

0━ diet /'daɪət/ n **1** [C,U] food that you eat and drink regularly **2** [C] limited variety or amount of food that you eat to lose weight or for medical reasons: be/go on a ~ ● **diet** v [I] eat less food or special food in order to lose weight

differ /'dɪfə(r)/ v [I] **1** ~ (from) be different from sb/sth else **2** disagree with sb

0━ difference /'dɪfrəns/ n **1** [C,U] way in which two people or things are not like each other; way in which sb/sth has changed: the ~ in their ages **2** [sing, U] amount that sth is greater or smaller than sth else: The ~ between 7 and 18 is 11. **3** [C] disagreement between people: It's

different

time to settle your ~s. **IDM** **make a, no, some, etc difference (to/in sb/sth)** have an effect/no ~ effect on sb/sth: *The rain made no ~ to the game.*

⊶ **different** /'dɪfrənt/ *adj* **1** ~ **(from/to/than)** not the same as sb/sth; not like sb/sth **2** separate and individual: *several ~ people*

differentiate /ˌdɪfə'renʃieɪt/ *v* [I,T] ~ **between A and B,** ~ **A from B** show the difference between two or more things; distinguish one thing from others

⊶ **difficult** /'dɪfɪkəlt/ *adj* **1** not easy; needing effort or skill: *find sth ~ to understand* **2** full of problems; causing trouble: *be in a ~ position/ situation* **3** (of people) not easy to please; not helpful ▪ **difficulty** *n* (*pl* -**ies**) **1** [C, usu *pl*, U] problem, thing or situation that causes problems: *We've run into ~ies with the project.* **2** [U] state or quality of being difficult to do or understand; effort that sth involves: *He stood up with great ~.*

diffident /'dɪfɪdənt/ *adj* lacking confidence; shy ▪ **diffidence** /-dəns/ *n* [U]

diffuse /dɪ'fjuːz/ *v* [I,T] (cause sth to) spread widely in all directions ▪ **diffuse** /dɪ'fjuːs/ *adj* **1** spread over a wide area: *~ light* **2** not clear or easy to understand; using a lot of words ▪ **diffusion** /dɪ'fjuːʒn/ *n* [U]

⊶ **dig**¹ /dɪg/ *v* (-**gg**-, *pt, pp* **dug** /dʌg/) **1** [I,T] make a hole in the ground or move soil from one place to another using your hands, a tool or a machine **2** [T] remove sth from the ground with a tool: *potatoes* **[PV]** **dig sth/sb out (of sth)** **1** remove sb/sth from sth by digging the ground around them/it **2** find sth that has been hidden or forgotten for a long time: *I dug these old photo albums out of the attic.* **dig sth up** remove or find sth by digging or careful searching

dig² /dɪg/ *n* [C] **1** small push with your fingers or elbow: *a ~ in the ribs* **2** ~ **(at)** critical remark: *That was a ~ at Ray.* **3** archaeological excavation

digest /daɪ'dʒest; dɪ-/ *v* **1** [T] change food in your stomach so that it can be used by your body **2** [I] (of food) be changed in this way **3** [T] understand sth fully ● **digest** /'daɪdʒest/ *n* [C] short concise report; summary

digit /'dɪdʒɪt/ *n* [C] **1** any of the ten numbers from 0 to 9 **2** (*anat*) finger or toe ▪ **digital** *adj* **1** using an electronic system that uses the numbers 0 and 1 to record sound or store information, and that gives high-quality results **2** (of clocks, watches, etc) showing information

by using numbers ▪ **digitize** (*also* -**ise**) /'dɪdʒɪtaɪz/ (*also* **digitalize** /'dɪdʒɪtəlaɪz/) (*also* -**ise**) *v* [T] change data into a digital form that can be easily read and processed by a computer

dignified /'dɪgnɪfaɪd/ *adj* calm and serious and deserving respect

dignitary /'dɪgnɪtəri/ *n* [C] (*pl* -**ies**) (*fml*) person with an important official position

dignity /'dɪgnəti/ *n* [U] **1** calm serious manner, that deserves respect **2** fact of being given honour and respect by people **IDM** **beneath your dignity** below what you see as your own importance or worth

digress /daɪ'gres/ *v* [I] ~ **(from)** turn from the main topic of discussion ▪ **digression** /daɪ'greʃn/ *n* [U,C]

dike *n* [C] = DYKE

dilapidated /dɪ'læpɪdeɪtɪd/ *adj* (of buildings) old and falling to pieces

dilate /daɪ'leɪt/ *v* [I,T] become or make sth wider, larger or more open

dilemma /dɪ'lemə/ *n* [C] difficult situation in which you have to choose between two things

diligent /'dɪlɪdʒənt/ *adj* hardworking; showing care and effort: *a ~ worker* ▪ **diligence** /'dɪlɪdʒəns/ *n* [U] ▪ **diligently** *adv*

dilute /daɪ'luːt, GB also -'ljuːt/ *v* [T] ~ **(with)** make a liquid weaker by adding water or another liquid ▪ **dilution** /daɪ'luːʃn, GB also -'ljuːʃn/ *n* [U]

dim /dɪm/ *adj* (-**mer**, -**mest**) **1** not bright: *in a ~ light* **2** not easy to see **3** unclear; vague: *~ memories* **4** (*infml*) not intelligent **IDM** **take a dim view of sb/sth** disapprove of sb/ sth ● **dim** *v* (-**mm**-) [I,T] become or make sth less bright or strong ▪ **dimly** *adv* ▪ **dimness** *n* [U]

dime /daɪm/ *n* [C] coin of USA and Canada worth ten cents

dimension /daɪ'menʃn/ *n* [C] **1** measurement of length, width or height of sth **2** [usu *pl*] size and extent of a situation: *the ~s of the problem* **3** aspect or way of looking at sth **4** (-**dimensional**) /-ʃənəl/ (in compound adjectives) having the number of dimensions that is mentioned: *two-~al*

diminish /dɪ'mɪnɪʃ/ *v* [I,T] become or make sth smaller, weaker, etc

diminutive /dɪ'mɪnjətɪv/ *adj* (*fml*) very small

dimple /'dɪmpl/ *n* [C] small natural hollow in sb's cheek or chin

din /dɪn/ *n* [U, sing] loud unpleasant noise ▪ **din** *v* (-**nn**-) **[PV]** **din sth into sb** tell sth to sb again and again

dine /daɪn/ *v* [I] (*fml*) eat dinner **[PV]** **dine out** eat dinner in a restaurant, hotel, etc ▪ **'dining car** *n* [C] railway carriage in which meals are served

■ '**dining room** n [C] room in which meals are eaten

dinghy /'dɪŋi; 'dɪŋgi/ n [C] (pl **-ies**) small open boat

dingy /'dɪndʒi/ adj (**-ier**, **-iest**) dark and dirty ▶ **dinginess** n [U]

dining → DINE

0⟶ **dinner** /'dɪnə(r)/ n [U,C] main meal of the day, eaten either at midday or in the evening ■ '**dinner jacket** n [C] (GB) man's black jacket worn at formal evening events

dinosaur /'daɪnəsɔ:(r)/ n [C] large prehistoric reptile that no longer exists

diocese /'daɪəsɪs/ n [C] area for which a bishop is responsible

dip /dɪp/ v (**-pp-**) **1** [T] put sth into a liquid for a short time: D~ your hand in to test the water. **2** [I,T] (cause sth to) go downwards or to a lower level: The sun ~ped below the horizon. **3** [T] (GB) lower a beam of light: Motorists should ~ their headlights. [**PV**] **dip into sth 1** put your hand into a container to take sth out **2** read parts of sth **3** take an amount from money you have saved ● **dip** n **1** [C] (infml) quick swim **2** [C] decrease in the amount or success of sth **3** [C] downward slope **4** [U,C] creamy sauce into which food is dipped

diphtheria /dɪf'θɪəriə/ n [U] serious disease of the throat

diphthong /'dɪfθɒŋ/ n [C] union of two vowels, eg /aɪ/ in pipe /paɪp/

diploma /dɪ'pləʊmə/ n [C] official paper showing that a student has passed an examination, etc

diplomacy /dɪ'pləʊməsi/ n [U] **1** management of relations between countries **2** skill in dealing with people; tact

diplomat /'dɪpləmæt/ n [C] person whose job is to represent his or her country in a foreign country ▶ **diplomatic** /ˌdɪplə'mætɪk/ adj **1** of diplomacy (1): work in the ~ic service **2** having or showing diplomacy (2); tactful ▶ **diplomatically** adv

dire /'daɪə(r)/ adj terrible

0⟶ **direct¹** /də'rekt; dɪ-; daɪ-/ adj **1** with nothing or nobody in between: a ~ result ◇ Avoid ~ sunlight. **2** going straight between two places without stopping: a ~ route **3** exact: the ~ opposite **4** frank and honest ● **direct** adv without interrupting a journey: fly ~ to Hong Kong ■ di**rect 'current** n [U] (abbr **DC**) electric current that flows in one direction only ■ di**rect 'debit** n [C] (in Britain) instruction to your bank that allows sb to take money from your account ▶ **directness** n [U] ■ di**rect 'object** n [C] (gram) noun, noun phrase or pronoun that is affected by the action of the verb, eg the money in He took the money.

■ di**rect 'speech** n [U] speaker's actual words

0⟶ **direct²** /də'rekt; dɪ-; daɪ-/ v [T] **1** aim sth in a particular direction or at a particular person: Was that remark ~ed at me? **2** control or be in charge of sb/sth: ~ a project/film **3** tell sb how to get somewhere: Can you ~ me to the station, please? **4** (fml) give an official order

0⟶ **direction** /də'rekʃn; dɪ-; daɪ-/ n **1** [C] general position a person or thing moves or points towards: run off in the opposite ~ **2** [C, usu pl] instructions about where to go, etc **3** [U] organization or management of sb/sth: under my ~

directive /də'rektɪv; dɪ-; daɪ-/ n [C] (fml) official instruction

0⟶ **directly** /də'rektli; dɪ-; daɪ-/ adv **1** in a direct manner; exactly **2** immediately ● **directly** conj as soon as: (GB) I came ~ I knew.

0⟶ **director** /də'rektə(r)/ n [C] **1** person who manages sth, esp a company **2** person who directs a play or a film ▶ **directorship** n [C] position of a company director

directory /də'rektəri; dɪ-; daɪ-/ n (pl **-ies**) **1** book with a list of names, addresses and telephone numbers **2** file containing a group of other files or programs on a computer

0⟶ **dirt** /dɜ:t/ n [U] **1** unclean matter, eg dust or mud **2** (infml) scandal **3** (infml) = EXCREMENT ■ ˌdirt 'cheap adj, adv (infml) very cheap

0⟶ **dirty** /'dɜ:ti/ adj (**-ier**, **-iest**) **1** not clean: ~ water **2** unpleasant or dishonest: a ~ trick **3** connected with sex in an offensive way: a ~ joke [**IDM**] **give sb a dirty look** look at sb in a way that shows you are annoyed with them ● **dirty** v (pt, pp **-ied**) [T] make sth dirty

disable /dɪs'eɪbl/ v [T] **1** injure or affect sb permanently so that they cannot walk or use a part of their body **2** to make sth unable to work so that it cannot be used: The burglars ~d the alarm. ▶ **disability** /ˌdɪsə'bɪləti/ n (pl **-ies**) **1** [C] physical or mental condition that disables sb **2** [U] state of being disabled

0⟶ **disabled** /dɪs'eɪbld/ adj unable to use a part of your body completely or easily because of an illness, injury, etc.; unable to learn easily: facilities for ~ people ● the **disabled** n [pl] people who are disabled: caring for the sick, elderly and ~ ▶ **disablement** n [U]

disabuse /ˌdɪsə'bju:z/ v [T] ~ of tell sb that what they think is true is, in fact, false

0⟶ **disadvantage** /ˌdɪsəd'vɑ:ntɪdʒ/ n [C] something that causes problems: I hope my lack of

experience won't be to my ~.
▶ **disadvantaged** adj not having the things, eg education or money, that people need to succeed in life
▶ **disadvantageous**
/ˌdɪsædvænˈteɪdʒəs/ adj

O⁓ disagree /ˌdɪsəˈɡriː/ v [I] **1** have different opinions: I ~ with you/with what you say. **2** be different [PV] **disagree with sb** (of food) make sb feel ill ▶ **disagreeable** adj unpleasant ▶ **disagreeably** adv
▶ **disagreement** n [C, U] difference of opinion

O⁓ disappear /ˌdɪsəˈpɪə(r)/ v [I]
1 go out of sight **2** stop existing
▶ **disappearance** n [U, C]

O⁓ disappoint /ˌdɪsəˈpɔɪnt/ v [I, T] fail to do or be what sb hoped for
▶ **disappointed** adj sad at not getting what was hoped for: He was bitterly ~ed by the result.
▶ **disappointing** adj: a ~ing result
▶ **disappointingly** adv
▶ **disappointment** n **1** [U] state of being disappointed **2** [C] person or thing that disappoints sb

O⁓ disapprove /ˌdɪsəˈpruːv/ v [I] ~ (of) say or think that sb/sth is bad
▶ **disapproval** n [U]

disarm /dɪsˈɑːm/ v **1** [T] take away all weapons from sb **2** [I] (of a country) give up all or some (esp nuclear) weapons **3** [T] (written) make sb feel less angry or critical ▶ **disarmament** n [U] act of disarming (2)

disarray /ˌdɪsəˈreɪ/ n [U] (fml) state of confusion and a lack of organization

disassociate /ˌdɪsəˈsəʊʃieɪt; -ˈsəʊs-/
= DISSOCIATE

O⁓ disaster /dɪˈzɑːstə(r)/ n [C] serious sudden misfortune; terrible accident ▶ **disastrous** /dɪˈzɑːstrəs/ adj ▶ **disastrously** adv

disband /dɪsˈbænd/ v [I, T] break up a group of people or an organization

disbelieve /ˌdɪsbɪˈliːv/ v [T] refuse to believe sb/sth ▶ **disbelief** /ˌdɪsbɪˈliːf/ n [U] feeling of not being able to believe sb/sth

O⁓ disc (US disk) /dɪsk/ n [C]
1 thin flat circular object **2** = CD
3 (GB, old-fash) = RECORD¹(2) **4** one of the layers of cartilage between the bones of the back: a slipped ~
▪ **disc jockey** n [C] (abbr DJ) person whose job is to introduce and play popular recorded music on the radio or at a club

discard /dɪsˈkɑːd/ v [T] get rid of sth; throw away

discern /dɪˈsɜːn/ v [T] (fml) **1** know, recognize or understand sth, esp sth that is not obvious **2** see or hear sth, but not very clearly ▶ **discernible** adj ▶ **discerning** adj (approv) showing good judgement about the quality of sth ▶ **discernment** n [U]

ability to judge the quality of sb/sth well

discharge /dɪsˈtʃɑːdʒ/ v **1** [T] give sb official permission to leave a place or a job; make sb leave a job **2** [I, T] send out a liquid or gas **3** [T] (fml) do everything necessary to perform and complete a particular duty: ~ a debt (= pay it) ● **discharge** /ˈdɪstʃɑːdʒ/ n **1** [U, C] action of releasing a gas, liquid, etc; substance that comes out of inside somewhere **2** [U, C] act of officially allowing sb to leave a place, etc **3** [U] (fml) act of performing a duty or paying money owed

disciple /dɪˈsaɪpl/ n [C] follower of a religious, political, etc leader

O⁓ discipline /ˈdɪsəplɪn/ n **1** [U] practice of training people to obey rules and punishing them if they do not; controlled behaviour that results from such training **2** [U] ability to control your behaviour or the way you live, work, etc **3** [C] (fml) area of knowledge ● **discipline** v [T] **1** punish sb for sth they have done **2** train sb to be obedient

disclaim /dɪsˈkleɪm/ v [T] (fml) say that you have no knowledge or responsibility for sth

disclose /dɪsˈkləʊz/ v [T] **1** make sth known **2** allow sth that was hidden to be seen ▶ **disclosure** /dɪsˈkləʊʒə(r)/ n [U, C]

disco /ˈdɪskəʊ/ (pl ~s) (also old-fash **discotheque** /ˈdɪskətek/) n [C] club, party, etc where people dance to pop records

discolour (US -or) /dɪsˈkʌlə(r)/ v [I, T] (cause sth to) change colour in an unpleasant way ▶ **discoloration** /ˌdɪsˌkʌləˈreɪʃn/ n [U, C]

discomfort /dɪsˈkʌmfət/ n **1** [U] lack of comfort; slight pain **2** [U] feeling of worry or embarrassment **3** [C] (fml) something that causes slight pain or lack of comfort

disconcert /ˌdɪskənˈsɜːt/ v [T] embarrass, upset or worry sb

disconnect /ˌdɪskəˈnekt/ v [T] ~ A (from B) detach sth from sth; undo a connection: My computer crashes every time I ~ from the Internet.
▶ **disconnected** adj **1** not related to the things or people around **2** (of speech or writing) badly ordered

disconsolate /dɪsˈkɒnsələt/ adj (fml) very unhappy and disappointed ▶ **disconsolately** adv

discontent /ˌdɪskənˈtent/ (also **discontentment** /ˌdɪskənˈtentmənt/) n [U, C] ~ (with) lack of satisfaction ▶ **discontented** adj not satisfied

discontinue /ˌdɪskənˈtɪnjuː/ v [T] (fml) put an end to sth; stop doing sth

discord /ˈdɪskɔːd/ n **1** [U] (fml) disagreement; quarrelling **2** [C, U] *(music)* combination of musical notes that sound harsh together ▶ **discordant** /dɪsˈkɔːdənt/ *adj*

discotheque /ˈdɪskətek/ *n* = DISCO

0─ **discount** /ˈdɪskaʊnt/ *n* [C] reduction in price ● **discount** /dɪsˈkaʊnt/ *v* [T] consider sth to be unimportant or untrue

discourage /dɪsˈkʌrɪdʒ/ *v* [T] **1** take away sb's hope or enthusiasm: ~*d by failure* **2** persuade sb not to do sth: ~ *children from smoking* ▶ **discouragement** *n* [U,C]

discourse /ˈdɪskɔːs/ *n* [C,U] *(fml)* long and serious speech

discourteous /dɪsˈkɜːtiəs/ *adj (fml)* impolite; rude ▶ **discourteously** *adv* ▶ **discourtesy** /dɪsˈkɜːtəsi/ *n* [U,C]

0─ **discover** /dɪsˈkʌvə(r)/ *v* [T] **1** find or learn about sth for the first time **2** come to know or realize sth; find out about sth ▶ **discoverer** *n* [C]: *the ~er of penicillin* ● **discovery** /dɪsˈkʌvəri/ *n* (*pl* -**ies**) **1** [C,U] act of finding sth/sb or learning sth that was unknown before **2** [C] something that is found or learned about for the first time

discredit /dɪsˈkredɪt/ *v* [T] **1** cause people to stop respecting sb/sth **2** cause to appear untrue or doubtful ● **discredit** *n* [U] *(fml)* loss of respect; damage to sb's reputation

discreet /dɪsˈkriːt/ *adj* careful in what you say or do, eg in order to keep sth secret ▶ **discreetly** *adv*

discrepancy /dɪsˈkrepənsi/ *n* [C] (*pl* -**ies**) difference between two things that should be the same

discretion /dɪsˈkreʃn/ *n* [U] **1** freedom to decide what should be done: *use your ~* **2** care in what you say and do, eg in order to keep sth secret

discriminate /dɪsˈkrɪmɪneɪt/ *v* [I] **1** ~ **(between)** see or show a difference between things or people **2** ~ **against/in favour of** treat sb worse/better than another in an unfair way ▶ **discriminating** *adj* ▶ **discrimination** /-ˈneɪʃn/ *n* [U]

discus /ˈdɪskəs/ *n* [C] heavy round disc thrown as a sport

0─ **discuss** /dɪsˈkʌs/ *v* [T] talk or write about sth ▶ **discussion** *n* [C,U]

disdain /dɪsˈdeɪn/ *n* [U] feeling that sb/sth is not good enough to deserve respect ● **disdain** *v* [I,T] **1** think that sb/sth does not deserve your respect **2** refuse to do sth because you think you are too important to do it ▶ **disdainful** *adj*

0─ **disease** /dɪˈziːz/ *n* [C,U] illness ▶ **diseased** *adj* having a disease

disembark /ˌdɪsɪmˈbɑːk/ *v* [I] leave a ship or an aircraft ▶ **disembarkation** /ˌdɪsˌembɑːˈkeɪʃn/ *n* [U]

disenchanted /ˌdɪsɪnˈtʃɑːntɪd/ *adj* ~ **(with)** having lost your good opinion of sth

disengage /ˌdɪsɪnˈgeɪdʒ/ *v* [T] **1** ~ **(from)** free sb/sth from the person or thing that is holding them or it **2** [I] *(tech)* (of an army) stop fighting

disentangle /ˌdɪsɪnˈtæŋgl/ *v* [T] **1** ~ **(from)** free sb/sth from sth complicated or confused **2** make string, etc free of knots

disfigure /dɪsˈfɪgə(r)/ *v* [T] spoil the appearance of sb/sth ▶ **disfigurement** *n* [C,U]

disgorge /dɪsˈgɔːdʒ/ *v* [I,T] *(written)* (cause sth to) flow or pour out of sth

disgrace /dɪsˈgreɪs/ *n* **1** [U] loss of other people's respect because of sb's bad behaviour **2** [sing] person or thing that is so bad that it causes shame to others: *He's a ~ to the legal profession.* ● **disgrace** *v* [T] behave badly in a way that makes you or other people feel ashamed ▶ **disgraceful** *adj* very bad; that people should feel ashamed about

disgruntled /dɪsˈgrʌntld/ *adj* annoyed and dissatisfied

disguise /dɪsˈgaɪz/ *v* [T] **1** change your appearance so that people cannot recognize you **2** hide sth or change it, so that it cannot be recognized: ~ *your anger* ● **disguise** *n* [C,U] thing you wear in order to disguise yourself **2** [U] art of changing your appearance

0─ **disgust** /dɪsˈgʌst/ *n* [U] strong dislike or disapproval of sth ● **disgust** *v* [T] make sb feel shocked and almost ill ▶ **disgusted** *adj* feeling disgust ▶ **disgusting** *adj* causing disgust

0─ **dish** /dɪʃ/ *n* **1** [C] flat shallow container for serving food **2** [C] particular kind of food in a meal **3** (**the dishes**) [pl] plates, bowls, cups, etc used for a meal ● **dish** *v* [PV] **dish sth out** *(infml)* give away a lot of sth: ~ *out leaflets/compliments* **dish (sth) up** serve food onto plates ■ **dishcloth** *n* [C] cloth for washing dishes ■ **dishwasher** *n* [C] machine that washes plates, bowls, etc

dishearten /dɪsˈhɑːtn/ *v* [T] *(written)* make sb lose hope or confidence

dishevelled (*US* -**l-**) /dɪˈʃevld/ *adj* (of clothes or hair) very untidy

0─ **dishonest** /dɪsˈɒnɪst/ *adj* not honest; intending to deceive people ▶ **dishonestly** *adv* ▶ **dishonesty** *n* [U]

dishonour (*US* -**or**) /dɪsˈɒnə(r)/ *n* [U] *(fml)* loss of respect because you have done sth immoral or unacceptable ● **dishonour** *v* [T] *(fml)* **1** make sb/sth lose people's respect **2** refuse to keep an agreement or promise

▶ **dishonourable** adj immoral or unacceptable

disillusion /ˌdɪsɪˈluːʒn/ v [T] destroy sb's belief in or good opinion of sb/ sth ▶ **disillusioned** adj
▶ **disillusionment** n [U]

disinclined /ˌdɪsɪnˈklaɪnd/ adj ~ (to) (fml) not willing

disinfect /ˌdɪsɪnˈfekt/ v [T] clean sth with a substance that kills bacteria: ~ a wound ▶ **disinfectant** n [U,C] substance that disinfects

disinformation /ˌdɪsˌɪnfəˈmeɪʃn/ n [U] false information, esp from a government

disinherit /ˌdɪsɪnˈherɪt/ v [T] prevent sb from inheriting your property

disintegrate /dɪsˈɪntɪɡreɪt/ v [I] break into small pieces
▶ **disintegration** /dɪsˌɪntɪˈɡreɪʃn/ n [U]

disinterested /dɪsˈɪntrəstɪd/ adj not influenced by personal interests

disjointed /dɪsˈdʒɔɪntɪd/ adj not communicated in a logical way; not connected

0─ **disk** /dɪsk/ n [C] **1** (esp US) = DISC **2** (computing) device for storing information on a computer, with a magnetic surface that records information received in electronic form: a floppy ~ ■ **'disk drive** n [C] device in a computer that transfers information to and from a disk (2)
▶ **diskette** n [C] = FLOPPY DISK (FLOP)

0─ **dislike** /dɪsˈlaɪk/ v [T] not like sb/ sth ● **dislike** n **1** [U] feeling of not liking sb/sth **2** [C] something that you dislike

dislocate /ˈdɪsləkeɪt/ v [T] **1** put a bone out of its usual position **2** stop a system, plan, etc from working
▶ **dislocation** /ˌdɪsləˈkeɪʃn/ n [C,U]

dislodge /dɪsˈlɒdʒ/ v [T] force or knock sth out of its position

disloyal /dɪsˈlɔɪəl/ adj not loyal
▶ **disloyally** adv ▶ **disloyalty** n [U]

dismal /ˈdɪzməl/ adj sad; miserable
▶ **dismally** adv

dismantle /dɪsˈmæntl/ v [T] take sth to pieces: ~ a machine/an engine

dismay /dɪsˈmeɪ/ n [U] worried, sad feeling after you have received an unpleasant surprise ● **dismay** v [T] shock and disappoint sb

dismember /dɪsˈmembə(r)/ v [T] **1** cut or tear the arms and legs off a dead body **2** divide a country, etc into smaller parts

0─ **dismiss** /dɪsˈmɪs/ v [T] **1** decide that sb/sth is not important and not worth thinking about **2** put thoughts and feelings out of your mind **3** officially remove sb from their job **4** send sb away or allow them to leave **5** (law) end a court case ▶ **dismissal** n [U,C]

disobedient /ˌdɪsəˈbiːdiənt/ adj failing or refusing to obey
▶ **disobedience** /ˌdɪsəˈbiːdiəns/ n [U] ▶ **disobediently** adv

disobey /ˌdɪsəˈbeɪ/ v [I,T] refuse to do what a person, law, etc tells you to do

disorder /dɪsˈɔːdə(r)/ n **1** [U] lack of order; confusion **2** [U] violent behaviour of large groups of people **3** [C,U] illness of the mind or body
▶ **disorder** v [T] put into disorder
▶ **disorderly** adj

disorganized (also -ised) /dɪsˈɔːɡənaɪzd/ adj badly planned; not able to organize well
▶ **disorganization** /dɪsˌɔːɡənaɪˈzeɪʃn/ n [U]

disorientate /dɪsˈɔːriənteɪt/ (esp US **disorient** /dɪsˈɔːrient/) v [T] cause sb to lose all sense of direction; confuse sb ▶ **disorientation** /dɪsˌɔːriənˈteɪʃn/ n [U]

disown /dɪsˈəʊn/ v [T] say that you no longer want to be connected with sb/sth

disparaging /dɪˈspærɪdʒɪŋ/ adj suggesting that sb/sth is not important; scornful

disparate /ˈdɪspərət/ adj (fml) **1** made up of parts or people that are very different from each other **2** (of two things) so different that they cannot be compared
▶ **disparity** /dɪˈspærəti/ n [U,C] (pl -ies) difference

dispassionate /dɪsˈpæʃənət/ adj not influenced by emotion; fair
▶ **dispassionately** adv

dispatch (GB also **despatch**) /dɪˈspætʃ/ v [T] (fml) **1** send sb/sth somewhere **2** finish sth quickly ● **dispatch** n **1** [U] (fml) act of dispatching sb/sth **2** [C] message or report that is sent

dispel /dɪˈspel/ v (-ll-) [T] cause sth to disappear: ~ doubts

dispense /dɪˈspens/ v [T] **1** (fml) give sth out to people; provide sth **2** prepare medicine and give it to people, as a job [PV] **dispense with sb/sth** get rid of sth/sb that is not necessary ▶ **dispensary** /dɪˈspensəri/ n (pl -ies) place where medicines are dispensed
▶ **dispensation** /ˌdɪspenˈseɪʃn/ n **1** [C,U] special permission to do sth usu forbidden **2** [U] (fml) act of dispensing sth

disperse /dɪˈspɜːs/ v [I,T] (cause sth to) move away and spread out
▶ **dispersal** n [U]

dispirited /dɪˈspɪrɪtɪd/ adj without enthusiasm; discouraged

displace /dɪsˈpleɪs/ v [T] **1** take the place of sb/sth **2** move sth from its usual position ▶ **displacement** n [U]

0─ **display** /dɪˈspleɪ/ v [T] show sth; exhibit sth ● **display** n [C] **1** act of being displayed; something displayed **2** words, pictures, etc shown on a computer screen

displease /dɪsˈpliːz/ v [T] annoy sb ▸ **displeasure** /dɪsˈpleʒə(r)/ n [U] annoyance

dispose /dɪsˈpəʊz/ v [PV] **dispose of sb/sth** get rid of sb/sth unwanted ▸ **disposable** /dɪsˈpəʊzəbl/ adj **1** made to be thrown away after use: ~ nappies **2** available for use: ~ income ▸ **disposal** n **1** [U] action of getting rid of sth **2** [C] (business) sale of part of a business, property, etc [IDM] **at your/sb's disposal** available for use as you prefer/sb prefers ▸ **disposed** adj ~ **(to)** willing to do sth: She seems favourably ~d to the move. ▸ **disposition** /ˌdɪspəˈzɪʃn/ n [U] (fml) person's natural character

dispossess /ˌdɪspəˈzes/ v [T] ~ **(of)** take sb's property, etc away from them

disproportionate /ˌdɪsprəˈpɔːʃənət/ adj too large or too small ▸ **disproportionately** adv

disprove /ˌdɪsˈpruːv/ v [T] show sth to be wrong or false

dispute /dɪˈspjuːt/ n [C,U] disagreement or argument ● **dispute** /dɪˈspjuːt/ v [T] **1** question whether sth is true and valid **2** [I,T] ~ **(with)** argue with sb, esp about who owns sth

disqualify /dɪsˈkwɒlɪfaɪ/ v (pt, pp **-ied**) [T] ~ **(from)** prevent sb from doing sth because they have broken a rule ▸ **disqualification** /dɪsˌkwɒlɪfɪˈkeɪʃn/ n [C,U]

disquiet /dɪsˈkwaɪət/ n [U] (fml) worry or anxiety ▸ **disquiet** v [T] (fml) make anxious

disregard /ˌdɪsrɪˈɡɑːd/ v [T] not consider sth; treat sth as unimportant ▸ **disregard** n [U] lack of attention or care

disrepair /ˌdɪsrɪˈpeə(r)/ n [U] state of needing repair

disrepute /ˌdɪsrɪˈpjuːt/ n [U] state of having lost the good opinion of people: bring the sport into ~ ▸ **disreputable** /dɪsˈrepjətəbl/ adj not respectable: a disreputable nightclub

disrespect /ˌdɪsrɪˈspekt/ n [U] lack of respect for sb/sth ▸ **disrespectful** adj

disrupt /dɪsˈrʌpt/ v [T] cause disorder in sth: ~ a public meeting ▸ **disruption** /dɪsˈrʌpʃn/ n [C,U] ▸ **disruptive** adj causing disruption: a ~ive influence

dissatisfied /dɪsˈsætɪsfaɪd; dɪˈsæt-/ adj ~ **(with)** not happy or satisfied with sth ▸ **dissatisfaction** /ˌdɪsˌsætɪsˈfækʃn/ n [U]

dissect /dɪˈsekt; daɪ-/ v [T] cut up a dead body to examine it ▸ **dissection** /dɪˈsekʃn/ n [U,C]

disseminate /dɪˈsemɪneɪt/ v [T] (fml) spread information, etc widely

▸ **dissemination** /dɪˌsemɪˈneɪʃn/ n [U]

dissension /dɪˈsenʃn/ n [U] disagreement

dissent /dɪˈsent/ n [U] fact of having opinions that differ from those that are officially accepted ● **dissent** v [I] ~ **(from)** (fml) disagree with an opinion ▸ **dissenter** n [C] person who dissents

dissertation /ˌdɪsəˈteɪʃn/ n [C] ~ **(on)** long piece of writing

disservice /dɪsˈsɜːvɪs/ n [sing] [IDM] **do sb a disservice** do sth that harms sb

dissident /ˈdɪsɪdənt/ n [C] person who disagrees with official government views

dissimilar /dɪˈsɪmɪlə(r)/ adj not the same ▸ **dissimilarity** /ˌdɪsɪmɪˈlærəti/ n [C,U] (pl **-ies**)

dissipated /ˈdɪsɪpeɪtɪd/ adj (disapprov) enjoying activities that are harmful, eg drinking too much

dissociate /dɪˈsəʊʃieɪt; -ˈsəʊs-/ (also **disassociate**) v [T] **1** ~ **yourself/sb from sb/sth** say that you do not support sb/sth **2** ~ **(from)** separate two people or things in your mind ▸ **dissociation** /dɪˌsəʊʃiˈeɪʃn; -ˌsəʊs-/ n [U]

0‑w **dissolve** /dɪˈzɒlv/ v **1** [I] (of a solid) become liquid: Salt ~s in water. **2** [T] make a solid become liquid: D~ the salt in water. **3** [T] bring an end to sth: ~ parliament [IDM] **dissolve into tears/laughter** suddenly start crying/laughing ▸ **dissolution** /ˌdɪsəˈluːʃn/ n [U] (written) act of officially ending a marriage, parliament, etc

dissuade /dɪˈsweɪd/ v [T] ~ **(from)** advise sb not to do sth

0‑w **distance** /ˈdɪstəns/ n **1** [C,U] amount of space between two points or places **2** [U] being far away in space or time **3** [C,U] distant place or point: listen from a ~ [IDM] **go the (full) distance** continue to run, fight, etc until the end of the contest ● **distance** v [I,T] ~ **yourself/sb/sth (from sb/sth)** become less involved or connected with sb/sth

■ **'distance learning** n [U] system of education in which people study at home with the help of special Internet sites and television and radio programmes

distant /ˈdɪstənt/ adj **1** far away **2** (of people) not closely related: a ~ cousin **3** unfriendly ▸ **distantly** adv

distaste /dɪsˈteɪst/ n [U,sing] dislike ▸ **distasteful** adj unpleasant or offensive

distil (US **distill**) /dɪˈstɪl/ v (**-ll-**) [T] **1** ~ **(from)** change a liquid to gas by heating it, and then cool the gas and collect drops of liquid **2** make

whisky, etc in this way **3 ~ (from/ into)** get the essential meaning from thoughts, information, etc
▸ **distillation** /ˌdɪstɪˈleɪʃn/ n [C, U]
▸ **distillery** /dɪˈstɪləri/ n [C] factory where whisky, etc is distilled

distinct /dɪˈstɪŋkt/ adj **1** clearly different; separate **2** easily heard or seen ▸ **distinctly** adv

distinction /dɪˈstɪŋkʃn/ n **1** [C] **~ (between two people or things** **2** [U] excellence **3** separation of people or things into different groups **4** [C, U] mark of honour or high achievement

distinctive /dɪˈstɪŋktɪv/ adj marking sth as clearly different
▸ **distinctively** adv

0━ **distinguish** /dɪˈstɪŋgwɪʃ/ v **1** [I, T] **~ (between)** A and B, **~** A from B recognize the difference between two people or things **2** [T] **~** A (**from B**) be a characteristic that makes two people or things different **3** [T] be able to see or hear sth well **4 ~** yourself do sth very well ▸ **distinguishable** adj ▸ **distinguished** adj successful and admired

distort /dɪˈstɔːt/ v **1** [T] pull or twist sth out of its usual shape **2** give a false account of sth: ~ the facts ▸ **distortion** /dɪˈstɔːʃn/ n [C, U]

distract /dɪˈstrækt/ v [T] take sb's attention away from sth
▸ **distracted** adj unable to pay attention to sb/sth because you are worried, etc ▸ **distraction** /dɪˈstrækʃn/ n **1** [C, U] something, eg noise, that distracts sb's attention **2** [C] activity that amuses or entertains you

distraught /dɪˈstrɔːt/ adj very upset and worried

distress /dɪˈstres/ n [U] **1** great worry, suffering or unhappiness **2** state of danger: a ship in ~ ● **distress** v [T] make sb feel very worried or unhappy ▸ **distressing** adj making you feel upset: ~ing news

0━ **distribute** /dɪˈstrɪbjuːt/ v [T] **1** give sth out **2** send goods to shops and businesses to be sold **3** spread sth over an area ▸ **distribution** /ˌdɪstrɪˈbjuːʃn/ n [U, C] ▸ **distributor** /dɪˈstrɪbjətə(r)/ n [C] **1** person or company that supplies goods to shops, etc **2** device in an engine that sends electric current to the spark plugs

0━ **district** /ˈdɪstrɪkt/ n [C] part of a town or country

distrust /dɪsˈtrʌst/ v [T] have no trust in sb ▸ **distrust** n [U, sing] lack of trust; suspicion ▸ **distrustful** adj

0━ **disturb** /dɪˈstɜːb/ v [T] **1** interrupt sb when they are working, etc **2** move sth or change its position

3 worry sb ▸ **disturbance** n **1** [U, C] act of disturbing sb/sth **2** [C] violent public disorder ▸ **disturbed** adj emotionally or mentally ill

disunity /dɪsˈjuːnəti/ n [U] (fml) lack of agreement between people

disuse /dɪsˈjuːs/ n [U] state of not being used: fall into ~ ▸ **disused** /ˌdɪsˈjuːzd/ adj

ditch /dɪtʃ/ n [C] long channel dug at the side of a road to hold or take away water ● **ditch** v [T] (infml) get rid of sb/sth unwanted: She ~ed her boyfriend.

dither /ˈdɪðə(r)/ v [I] be unable to decide what to do

ditto /ˈdɪtəʊ/ n [C] (symb ") (used in lists to avoid repeating a word)

ditty /ˈdɪti/ n [C] (pl -ies) short simple song

divan /dɪˈvæn/ n [C] long low seat without a back

dive /daɪv/ v (pt, pp **dived**, US also pt **dove** /dəʊv/) [I] **1** go head first into water **2** go under water **3** (of an aircraft) go steeply downwards **4** move quickly in the direction that is mentioned: ~ under the bed [PV] **dive into sth** (infml) put your hand quickly into sth such as a bag or pocket ● **dive** n [C] **1** act of diving into water **2** (infml) bar, club, etc that is cheap, and perhaps dark or dirty ▸ **diver** n [C] person who dives, esp one who works under water ■ **'diving board** n [C] board from which people dive into a swimming pool

diverge /daɪˈvɜːdʒ/ v [I] separate; differ ▸ **divergence** /-dʒəns/ n [C, U] ▸ **divergent** /-dʒənt/ adj

diverse /daɪˈvɜːs/ adj of different kinds: ~ interests ▸ **diversity** n [U, C, usu sing] range; variety

diversify /daɪˈvɜːsɪfaɪ/ v (pt, pp -ied) [I, T] (esp of a business) develop a wider range of products, interests, etc ▸ **diversification** /-fɪˈkeɪʃn/ n [C, U]

diversion /daɪˈvɜːʃn/ n **1** [C, U] act of changing direction: the ~ of a river **2** [C] something that draws attention away from sth that you do not want to be noticed: create a ~ **3** [C] different route for traffic ▸ **diversionary** adj: ~ary tactics

divert /daɪˈvɜːt/ v [T] **~ (from, to)** **1** turn sth from one direction, use, etc to another: ~ traffic **2** take sb's attention away from sth

0━ **divide** /dɪˈvaɪd/ v **1** [I, T] separate; break sth into parts **2** [T] cause people to disagree **3** [T] **~ by** find out how many times one number is contained in another: 30 ~d by 6 is 5. ● **divide** n [usu sing] something that divides sth/sth ▸ **dividers** n [pl] instrument for measuring lines, angles, etc

dividend /ˈdɪvɪdend/ n [C] part of the

profits paid to people who have shares in a company

divine /dɪ'vaɪn/ adj **1** of or like God or a god **2** (infml) wonderful ▶ **divinely** adv ▷ **divinity** /dɪ'vɪnəti/ n **1** [U] quality of being a god or like God **2** [C] god or goddess **3** [U] study of religion ● **divine** v [T] (fml) discover by guessing

divisible /dɪ'vɪzəbl/ adj that can be divided: 4 is ~ by 2.

0-**division** /dɪ'vɪʒn/ n **1** [U, sing] process or result of dividing or being divided **2** [U] process of dividing numbers **3** [C, U] disagreement **4** [C] big part of an organization: the sales ~ **5** [C] group of sports teams **6** [C] (tech) (in British Parliament) vote ▶ **divisional** /dɪ'vɪʒənl/ adj

0-**divorce** /dɪ'vɔːs/ n **1** [C, U] legal ending of a marriage **2** [C] (fml) ending of a relationship between two things ● **divorce** v **1** [T] end your marriage to sb by law: get ~d **2** [T] ~ from separate sth from sth else ▶ **divorcee** /dɪˌvɔː'siː/ n [C] (GB) divorced person

divulge /daɪ'vʌldʒ/ v [T] (fml) give sb secret information

DIY /ˌdiː aɪ 'waɪ/ n [U] (GB) abbreviation for 'do it yourself'; activity of doing house repairs, decorating rooms, etc yourself

dizzy /'dɪzi/ adj (-ier, -iest) **1** (of a person) feeling as if everything is turning round and round; unable to balance **2** causing this feeling ▶ **dizzily** adv ▷ **dizziness** n [U]

DJ /'diː dʒeɪ/ n [C] = DISC JOCKEY

DNA /ˌdiː en 'eɪ/ n [U] (chem) deoxyribonucleic acid; chemical in the cells of animals and plants that carries genetic information and is a type of nucleic acid: a ~ test ■ DNA 'fingerprinting n [U] = GENETIC FINGERPRINTING

0-**do¹** /duː/ v (third pers sing pres tense **does** /dʌz/, pt **did** /dɪd/, pp **done** /dʌn/) **1** [T] perform an action, activity or job: What are you doing now? ◇ What do you do (= What's your job)? ◇ do your hair ◇ do the cooking **2** [I] progress or develop; improve: She's doing well at school. **3** [T] produce or make sth: do a drawing **4** [T] provide a service: Do you do eye tests here? **5** [T] study sth or find the answer to sth: do a puzzle ◇ do French/a course/a degree **6** [T] travel a certain distance or at a certain speed: How many miles did you do? **7** [T] have a particular effect: The fresh air will do you good. ◇ do a lot of damage **8** [I, T] be enough or suitable: If you haven't got a pen, a pencil will do. **[IDM] be/have to do with sb/sth** be connected with sb/ sth: The letter is to do with the trip to

France. **how do you do?** (fml) used when meeting sb for the first time **what do you do (for a living)?** what is your job? **[PV] do away with yourself/ sb** (infml) kill yourself/sb **do away with sth** (infml) get rid of sth; abolish **do sb/sth down** (GB, infml) criticize sb/sth unfairly **do for sb** do housework for sb **do for sb/sth** (infml) (usu passive) ruin or kill sb/ sth: If we can't borrow the money, we're done for. **do for sth** (infml) manage to get sth: What will you do for lunch? **do sb/yourself in** (infml) **1** kill sb/yourself **2** make sb very tired: You look done in! **do sth in** (infml) injure a part of the body: do your back in **do sth out** (infml) make (a room, cupboard, etc) clean and tidy **do sb out of sth** (infml) stop sb having sth, esp by cheating **do sb over** (infml, esp GB) attack and beat sb severely **do sth up** be fastened: The skirt does up at the back. **do sth up 1** fasten a coat, skirt, etc **2** repair and decorate an old house, etc **do sth with sb/sth** (used in negative sentences and questions with what): What does he do with himself? (= how does he pass the time) at weekends? ◇ What have you done with (= where have you put) my keys? **do without (sb/sth)** manage without sb/sth: She can't do without a secretary. ■ **do-gooder** n [C] (infml, disapprov) person who tries too hard to help other people

0-**do²** /də; strong form duː/ aux v (neg **do not**, short form **don't** /dəʊnt/, third pers sing pres tense **does** /dəz; strong form dʌz/, neg **does not**, short form **doesn't** /'dʌznt/, pt **did** /dɪd/, neg **did not**, short form **didn't** /'dɪdnt/, pp **done** /dʌn/) **1** used before a full verb to form negative sentences and questions: I don't like fish. ◇ Do you believe him? **2** used at the end of a sentence to form a question tag: You live in Hastings, don't you? **3** used to avoid repeating a full verb: She runs faster than I do. **4** used for emphasizing that a verb is positive: He 'does look tired. ◇ 'Do shut up!

do³ /duː/ n [C] (pl **dos** or **do's** /duːz/) (GB, infml) party **[IDM] do's and don'ts** (infml) rules that you should follow

docile /'dəʊsaɪl/ adj quiet and easy to control

dock /dɒk/ n [C] **1** part of a port where ships are loaded and unloaded, or repaired **2** (US) = JETTY **3** part of a law court where the prisoner stands ● **dock** v **1** [I, T] (of a ship) come or be brought into a dock **2** [I, T] (of two spacecraft) join or be joined together in space **3** [T] take away part of sb's wages, etc

ABCD**D**EFGHIJKLMNOPQRSTUVWXYZ

4 [T] cut an animal's tail short
▶ **docker** n [C] person who loads and unloads ships ■ **dockland** n [U] (also **docklands** [pl]) (GB) district near docks ■ **dockyard** n [C] place where ships are built or repaired

docket /ˈdɒkɪt/ n [C] (business) document or label showing what is in a package, which goods have been delivered, etc

0➡ **doctor** /ˈdɒktə(r)/ n [C] (abbr Dr)
1 person who has been trained in medicine **2** person who has received the highest university degree ● **doctor** v [T] **1** change sth in order to deceive people: ~ the figures **2** (infml) remove part of the sex organs of an animal ▶ **doctorate** /ˈdɒktərət/ n [C] highest university degree

doctrinaire /ˌdɒktrɪˈneə(r)/ adj (disapprov) strictly applying a theory without thinking about practical problems: ~ attitudes

doctrine /ˈdɒktrɪn/ n [C,U] set of teachings; belief(s) ▶ **doctrinal** /dɒkˈtraɪnl/ adj

0➡ **document** /ˈdɒkjumənt/ n [C]
1 official paper giving information, evidence, etc **2** computer file that contains text and has a name that identifies it ● **document** v [T] record the details of sth; prove or support sth with documents ▶ **documentation** /ˌdɒkjumenˈteɪʃn/ n [U] documents used as evidence or proof

documentary /ˌdɒkjuˈmentri/ n [C] (pl -ies) film, radio or television programme that gives information and facts ▶ **documentary** adj of documents: ~ evidence

docusoap /ˈdɒkjusəʊp/ n [C] television programme about the lives of real people, presented as entertainment

dodge /dɒdʒ/ v [I,T] **1** move suddenly to one side in order to avoid sb/sth **2** [T] avoid sth by dishonesty: tax dodging ● **dodge** n [C] **1** sudden movement to avoid sb/sth **2** clever trick ▶ **dodger** n [C] (infml) person who dishonestly avoids doing sth ▶ **dodgy** /ˈdɒdʒi/ adj (infml, GB) dishonest; risky

doe /dəʊ/ n [C] adult female deer, reindeer, rabbit or hare

does /dʌz/ → DO

doesn't /ˈdʌznt/ short for DOES NOT

0➡ **dog¹** /dɒg/ n [C] **1** common animal kept by people for hunting, guarding, etc or as a pet **2** male dog, fox or wolf **3** (the dogs) [pl] (GB, infml) greyhound racing [IDM] (a case of) dog eat dog situation in business, politics, etc where people are willing to harm each other in order to succeed **a dog in the**

manger person who stops others enjoying sth even though he/she does not need or want it **a dog's life** an unhappy life **go to the dogs** (infml) get into a very bad state ■ **ˈdog collar** n [C] **1** collar for a dog **2** (infml) stiff white collar worn by a clergyman ■ **ˈdog-eared** adj (of a book) used so much that the corners of many pages are turned down ■ **ˈdoghouse** n [C] (US) = KENNEL [IDM] **be in the doghouse** (infml) be in disgrace because of sth bad you have done ■ **ˌdog-ˈtired** adj (infml) very tired

dog² /dɒg/ v (-gg-) [T] **1** (of a problem or bad luck) cause you trouble for a long time: ~ged by illness **2** follow sb/sth closely

dogged /ˈdɒgɪd/ adj (approv) not giving up easily; determined ▶ **doggedly** adv

dogma /ˈdɒgmə/ n [U, C] (esp religious) belief(s) to be accepted without questioning ▶ **dogmatic** /dɒgˈmætɪk/ adj giving opinions forcefully, without thinking that different opinions might be right ▶ **dogmatically** /-kli/ adv

do-gooder → DO¹

dogsbody /ˈdɒgzbɒdi/ n [C] (pl -ies) (GB, infml) person who does boring and unpleasant jobs for others

doldrums /ˈdɒldrəmz/ n [pl] (the doldrums) **1** state of feeling sad or depressed: He's been in the ~ since she left him. **2** lack of activity or improvement

dole /dəʊl/ n (the dole) [sing] (GB, infml) money paid regularly by the government to people without jobs: be/go on the ~ (= receive such money) ● **dole** v [PV] **dole sth out** give out an amount of food, money, etc to a group of people

doleful /ˈdəʊlfl/ adj sad; unhappy ▶ **dolefully** adv

doll /dɒl/ n [C] child's toy in the shape of a person, esp a baby or a child ● **doll** v [PV] **doll yourself up** (infml) make yourself look attractive for a party, etc

0➡ **dollar** /ˈdɒlə(r)/ n [C] **1** (symb $) unit of money in the USA, Canada, Australia, etc **2** banknote or coin worth one dollar

dollop /ˈdɒləp/ n [C] soft shapeless mass of sth, esp food

dolphin /ˈdɒlfɪn/ n [C] intelligent animal that looks like a large fish and lives in the sea

domain /dəʊˈmeɪn/ n [C] (fml) **1** area of activity or knowledge **2** (computing) set of Internet addresses that end with the same group of letters **3** area under sb's control ■ **doˈmain name** n [C] (computing) name which identifies a website or group of websites

dome /dəʊm/ n [C] round roof with a

circular base ▸ **domed** *adj* shaped like a dome

0🔊 **domestic** /də'mestɪk/ *adj* **1** of the home, house or family: ~ *duties* **2** within a particular country; not foreign: ~ *policies/flights* **3** (of animals) not wild; kept in a house or on a farm ▸ **domestic** *n* [C] (also **domestic 'help**) *n* [C] person who is paid to do housework ▸ **domesticated** *adj* (of animals) tame **2** (of people) enjoying housework and home life ■ **domestic 'science** *n* [U] (old-fash, GB) = HOME ECONOMICS

dominant /'dɒmɪnənt/ *adj* most important or powerful: *a ~ position* ▸ **dominance** /-nəns/ *n* [U]

0🔊 **dominate** /'dɒmɪneɪt/ *v* **1** [I,T] have control or power over sb/sth, esp in an unpleasant way **2** [T] be the most important feature of sth **3** [T] be most noticeable thing in a place: *The castle ~s the whole city.* ▸ **domination** /ˌdɒmɪ'neɪʃn/ *n* [U]

domineering /ˌdɒmɪ'nɪərɪŋ/ *adj* trying to control other people in an unpleasant way

dominion /də'mɪniən/ *n* **1** [U] (fml) authority to rule; control **2** [C] land controlled by a ruler

domino /'dɒmɪnəʊ/ *n* (pl **-es**) **1** [C] small flat piece of wood marked with spots, used for playing games **2** (**dominoes**) [U] game played with a set of dominoes

don /dɒn/ *n* [C] (GB) teacher at a university

donate /dəʊ'neɪt/ *v* [T] ~ (**to**) give money, clothes, etc to sb, esp a charity ▸ **donation** /dəʊ'neɪʃn/ *n* [C,U]

done[1] /dʌn/ *pt* of DO[1]

done[2] /dʌn/ *adj* **1** finished **2** (of food) cooked enough **3** socially correct

donkey /'dɒŋki/ *n* [C] animal like a small horse, but with longer ears [IDM] **donkey's years** (GB, *infml*) a very long time

donor /'dəʊnə(r)/ *n* [C] **1** person who gives sth to charity **2** person who gives blood or part of his/her body to help sick people: *a blood ~*

don't *short for* DO NOT

doodle /'duːdl/ *v* [I] do small drawings while you are thinking about sth else ▸ **doodle** *n* [C]

0🔊 **doom** /duːm/ *n* [U] death or destruction; any terrible event that you cannot avoid ▸ **doomed** *adj* certain to fail, suffer, die, etc ■ **'doomsday** *n* [sing] the end of the world

0🔊 **door** /dɔː(r)/ *n* [C] **1** piece of wood, etc used for closing the entrance to a building, room, etc **2** = DOORWAY [IDM] **be on the door** work at the entrance to a theatre, club, etc, eg collecting tickets (**from**)

door to door from building to building: *The journey takes an hour,* ~ *to* ~. **next door** (**to sb/sth**) to/in the next building, room, etc: *go next* ~ *to borrow some milk* **out of doors** in the open air ■ **'doorbell** *n* [C] bell that is rung by visitors to a house ■ **'doorstep** *n* [C] step in front of a door ■ **'doorway** *n* [C] opening of a door

dope /dəʊp/ *n* **1** [U] (*infml*) harmful drug **2** [C] stupid person ▸ **dope** *v* [T] give a drug to a person or an animal ▸ **dopey** *adj* (*infml*) **1** stupid **2** sleepy, as if drugged

dormant /'dɔːmənt/ *adj* not active: *a* ~ *volcano*

dormitory /'dɔːmətri/ *n* (pl **-ies**) large bedroom where several people sleep

dormouse /'dɔːmaʊs/ *n* [C] (pl **dormice** /-maɪs/) small animal like a mouse

dosage /'dəʊsɪdʒ/ *n* [C, usu sing] amount of medicine

dose /dəʊs/ *n* [C] **1** amount of medicine to be taken at one time **2** experience of sth unpleasant: *a ~ of flu* ▸ **dose** *v* [T] ~ (**with**) give sb/ yourself a medicine

doss /dɒs/ *v* [I] (GB, *sl*) ~ (**down**) sleep somewhere, esp somewhere uncomfortable or not in a proper bed ▸ **'dosshouse** *n* [C] (GB, *sl*) cheap place to stay for homeless people

dossier /'dɒsieɪ/ *n* [C] ~ (**on**) set of papers containing information about a person or event

0🔊 **dot** /dɒt/ *n* [C] **1** small round mark, esp one that is printed **2** (*computing*) symbol like a full stop used to separate parts of a domain name, a URL or an email address [IDM] **on the dot** at the exact time mentioned ▸ **dot** *v* (**-tt-**) [T] **1** put a dot above or next to a letter or word **2** (usu passive) spread things or people all over an area: *The sky was ~ted with stars.* ■ **dot·com** (also **dot.com**) *n* [C] company that sells goods and services on the Internet

dotage /'dəʊtɪdʒ/ *n* [IDM] **be in your dotage** be old and not able to think clearly

dote /dəʊt/ *v* [PV] **dote on/upon sb** show too much love for sb, ignoring their faults

0🔊 **double**[1] /'dʌbl/ *adj* **1** twice as much, big, good, etc: *Her income is* ~ *what it was a year ago.* **2** having two parts or uses: ~ *doors* ◇ *'Otter' is spelt with a* ~ *t.* **3** made for two people: *a* ~ *bed* ■ **double 'bass** *n* [C] largest instrument of the violin family, that plays very low notes ■ **double 'chin** *n* [C] fold of fat below the chin ■ **double-'dealing** *n* [U] deceitful behaviour ■ **double-'decker** n [C] bus with two floors ■ **double 'Dutch** n [U] (GB, infml) speech or writing that is impossible to understand

0-r **double**² /'dʌbl/ det twice as much or as many as: *He earns ~ what I do.* ● **double** adv in twos or in two parts: *I had to bend ~ to get under the table.* ■ **double-'barrelled** adj (of a gun) having two barrels ■ **double-book** v [T] promise the same ticket, hotel room, etc to two different people at the same time ■ **double-'breasted** adj (of a coat) made to cross over at the front with two rows of buttons ■ **double-'check** v [I,T] check sth for a second time or with great care ■ **double-'click** v [I,T] (computing) **~ (on)** choose a particular function or item on a computer screen, etc, by pressing one of the mouse buttons twice quickly ■ **double-'cross** v [T] cheat or deceive sb who trusts you ■ **double-'edged** adj (of a comment) having two possible meanings ■ **double 'glazing** n [U] windows that have two layers of glass, designed to reduce noise, heat loss, etc ■ **double-'jointed** adj having joints in your fingers, arms, etc that can bend backwards as well as forwards ■ **double 'quick** adv (infml) very quickly ■ **double-'quick** adj

0-r **double**³ /'dʌbl/ n **1** [U] twice the quantity: *He's paid ~ for the same job.* **2** [C] person who looks exactly like another **3** (doubles) [pl] game with two players on each side [IDM] **at the double** (infml) quickly

0-r **double**⁴ /'dʌbl/ v **1** [I,T] become or make sth become twice as much or as many: *The price has ~d.* **2** [T] bend or fold sth to make two layers [PV] **double (up) as sth** have a second use or function **double back** turn back in the opposite direction **double (sb) up/over** (cause sb to) bend the body over quickly: *be ~d up with laughter/pain*

doubly /'dʌbli/ adv (used before an adj) more than usual: *make ~ sure*

0-r **doubt** /daʊt/ n [U,C] feeling of uncertainty or not believing sb [IDM] **be in doubt** be uncertain **no doubt** very probably **without/beyond doubt** certainly ● **doubt** v [I,T] feel uncertain about sth; not believe sb/sth ▸ **doubtful** adj **1** uncertain **2** unlikely ▸ **doubtless** adv almost certainly, probably

dough /dəʊ/ n **1** [U, sing] mixture of flour, water, etc for making bread ■ **doughnut** n [C] small round cake made of fried dough

douse (also **dowse**) /daʊs/ v [T] **1** put out a fire by pouring water over it; put out a light **2** pour a lot of liquid

over sb/sth: *The car was ~d in petrol and set alight.*

dove¹ /dʌv/ n [C] **1** kind of pigeon. The white dove is a symbol of peace. **2** person in favour of peace ■ **dovecote** /'dʌvkɒt/ n [C] small building for doves to live in

dove² /dəʊv/ (US) pt of DIVE

dovetail /'dʌvteɪl/ v [I,T] fit together well ● **dovetail** n [C] joint for fixing two pieces of wood together

dowdy /'daʊdi/ adj (-ier, -iest) **1** (of a woman) not attractive or fashionable **2** (of a thing) dull or boring

0-r **down**¹ /daʊn/ adv, prep **1** to or at a lower level or place; from the top towards the bottom of sth: *jump ~* ◇ *roll ~ the hill* **2** (of flat objects) along: *live ~ the street* **3** to a sitting or horizontal position: *I think I'll lie ~.* **4** to or in the south: *We went ~ to London.* **5** used to show a reduction in level, amount, strength, etc: *Turn the heating ~.* ◇ *calm/settle ~* **6** (written) on paper: *Copy/Take this ~.* [IDM] **be down to sb** (infml) be the responsibility of sb **be/go down with sth** have or catch an illness **down under** (infml) in Australia **down with sb/sth** used to say you are opposed to sb/sth: *D~ with fascism!* ■ **down-and-out** n [C] person with no job, money or home ■ **down to'earth** adj (of a person) practical; sensible

down² /daʊn/ adj **1** sad: *feel ~* **2** lower than before: *Interest rates are ~.* **3** (of a computer or computer system) not working: *Our computers have been ~ all day.* ■ **down 'payment** n [C] part of the total cost of sth paid at the time of buying, with the rest to be paid later

down³ /daʊn/ v [T] (infml) **1** finish a drink quickly **2** force sb/sth to the ground

down⁴ /daʊn/ n [U] very soft feathers or hair: *duck ~*

downcast /'daʊnkɑːst/ adj **1** sad; depressed **2** (of eyes) looking down

downfall /'daʊnfɔːl/ n [sing] fall from power or success; cause of such a fall

downgrade /ˌdaʊn'greɪd/ v [T] **1** move sb/sth down to a lower rank or level **2** make sth/sb seem less important or valuable

downhearted /ˌdaʊn'hɑːtɪd/ adj sad; depressed

downhill /ˌdaʊn'hɪl/ adv towards the bottom of a hill: *run/walk ~* [IDM] **go downhill** get worse in quality, health, etc ● **downhill** adj going down a slope

Downing Street /'daʊnɪŋ striːt/ n [sing] way of referring to the British Prime Minister and government, taken from the name of the street where the Prime Minister lives

download /ˌdaʊn'ləʊd/ v [T]

(computing) copy a file or files from one computer to another
● **download** /ˈdaʊnləʊd/ n (computing) **1** [U] act of copying data from one computer to another **2** [C] computer file that is copied in this way ▸ **downloadable** /ˌdaʊnˈləʊdəbl/ adj

downpour /ˈdaʊnpɔ:(r)/ n [C] heavy fall of rain

downright /ˈdaʊnraɪt/ adj (of sth bad) complete: a ~ lie ● **downright** adv thoroughly: ~ rude

downs /daʊnz/ n (the downs) [pl] area of low hills

downspout /ˈdaʊnspaʊt/ (US) = DRAINPIPE

Down's syndrome (esp US **Down syndrome**) n [U] medical condition in which a person is born with a wide flat face, sloping eyes and a mental ability below average

0~ **downstairs** /ˌdaʊnˈsteəz/ adv, adj to or on a lower floor

downstream /ˌdaʊnˈstriːm/ adv in the direction in which a river flows

downtown /ˌdaʊnˈtaʊn/ adv, adj (esp US) to or in the centre of a city, esp its main business area

downtrodden /ˈdaʊntrɒdn/ adj treated badly: ~ workers

0~ **downward** /ˈdaʊnwəd/ adj moving or pointing towards a lower level ▸ **downwards** (esp US **downward**) adv towards the ground or a lower level: He lay face~ on the grass.

dowry /ˈdaʊri/ n [C] (pl -ies) property or money that a bride's father gives to her husband

dowse = DOUSE

doz. abbr dozen

doze /dəʊz/ v [I] sleep lightly for a short time ● **doze** n [sing] light sleep ▸ **dozy** adj (-ier, -iest) (infml) **1** sleepy **2** (GB) stupid; not intelligent

0~ **dozen** /ˈdʌzn/ n, det (pl dozen) **1** [C] (abbr **doz.**) set of twelve of the same thing: two ~ eggs **2** [C] group of approximately twelve people or things: a couple of ~ workers **3** (dozens) [pl] ~ (of) (infml) a lot of people or things: I've told her ~s of times. [IDM] talk, etc nineteen to the dozen → NINETEEN

Dr (also **Dr.**) abbr **1** Doctor: Dr (John) Waters **2** (in street names) Drive

drab /dræb/ adj (~ber, ~best) without interest or colour; dull ▸ **drabness** n [U]

0~ **draft** /drɑːft/ n **1** rough written plan of sth **2** [C] written order for payment of money by a bank **3** (the draft) [sing] (esp US) = CALL-UP (CALL[1]) **4** [C] (US) = DRAUGHT ● **draft** v [T] **1** write the first rough version of sth **2** send people somewhere for a special task **3** (US) = CONSCRIPT: He was ~ed

into the army. ● **draftsman**, **draftswoman** n [C] (pl **-men**, **-women**) **1** (US) = DRAUGHTSMAN, DRAUGHTSWOMAN **2** person who writes official or legal documents

drafty /ˈdrɑːfti/ adj (US) = DRAUGHTY (DRAUGHT)

0~ **drag** /dræg/ v (-gg-) **1** [T] pull sb/ sth along with effort and difficulty **2** [I] move yourself slowly and with effort: I ~ged myself out of bed. **3** [T] force sb to go somewhere: I'm going to ~ you all this way. **4** [I] (of time) pass slowly **5** [T] search the bottom of a river, lake, etc with nets, etc **6** (computing) [T] move some text, an icon, etc across a computer screen using the mouse [IDM] **drag your feet/heels** deliberately do sth slowly [PV] **drag on** (disapprov) go on for too long **drag sth out** cause a meeting, etc to last longer than necessary **drag sth out of sb** force sb to say sth they do not want to say **drag sth up** mention an unpleasant or embarrassing event ● **drag** n **1** [sing] (infml) boring thing or person **2** [sing] ~ **on** (infml) person or thing that makes progress difficult **3** [C] (infml) act of breathing in smoke from a cigarette, etc **4** [U] (infml) women's clothes worn by a man: in ~

dragon /ˈdrægən/ n [C] **1** (in stories) large animal with wings and claws, able to breathe out fire **2** fierce unpleasant old woman

drain /dreɪn/ n [C] **1** pipe or channel for carrying away water or sewage **2** [sing] ~ **on** sth that uses a lot of money, time, etc that could be used for sth else: a ~ on the country's resources [IDM] **(go) down the drain** | **(go) down the plughole** (infml) (be) wasted; (get) very much worse ● **drain** v **1** [I,T] become or make sth dry and empty by removing all the liquid from it: Leave the dishes to ~. ◊ D~ the pasta. **2** [I,T] ~ **(away/off)**, **(from)** (cause liquid to) flow away: The water ~ed away. **3** [T] empty a glass or cup by drinking everything in it **4** [T] make sb/sth weaker or poorer: The experience left him emotionally ~ed. ▸ **drainage** n [U] **1** process by which water, etc is drained from an area **2** system of drains ■ **draining board** (US **drainboard**) n [C] surface next to a sink, on which dishes, etc drain ■ **drainpipe** n [C] pipe for carrying water from the roof of a building to the ground

drake /dreɪk/ n [C] male duck

0~ **drama** /ˈdrɑːmə/ n **1** [C] play for the theatre, radio or television **2** [U] plays in general: Elizabethan ~ **3** [C, U] series of exciting events ▸ **dramatic** /drəˈmætɪk/ adj

1 exciting or impressive: *a ~tic rise/fall* ◇ *~tic developments* **2** of the theatre **3** exaggerated in order to attract people's attention: *Don't be so ~tic!* ▸ **dramatically** /-kli/ *adv* ▸ **dramatics** /drə'mætɪks/ *n* [pl] exaggerated behaviour that does not seem sincere ▸ **dramatist** /'dræmətɪst/ *n* [C] writer of plays ▸ **dramatize** (*also* -ise) /'dræmətaɪz/ *v* [T] **1** present a book, an event, etc as a play or film **2** make sth seem more exciting or important than it really is ▸ **dramatization** (*also* -isation) /-'zeɪʃn/ *n* [U,C]: *a ~tization of the novel*

drank *pt* of DRINK

drape /dreɪp/ *v* [T] **1** hang clothes, fabric, etc loosely on sb/sth **2** ~ (in/with) cover or decorate sb/sth with material **3** ~ round/over allow part of your body to rest loosely on sth: *His arm was ~d round her shoulders.* ● **drape** *n* [usu pl] (*esp US*) long thick curtain ▸ **drapery** /'dreɪpəri/ *n* (*pl* -ies) **1** [U] (*also* **draperies** [pl]) cloth, etc hanging in loose folds **2** [C, usu pl] (*US*) = DRAPE

drastic /'dræstɪk/ *adj* extreme; very significant: *a ~ shortage of food* ▸ **drastically** /-kli/ *adv*

draught /drɑːft/ (*US* **draft** /dræft/) *n* **1** [C] current of cool air in a room: *to sit in a ~* **2** [C] (*fml*) amount of liquid swallowed at one time **3** (**draughts**) (*GB*) [U] game for two players using 24 round pieces on a board [IDM] **on draught** (*GB*) (of beer) taken from a barrel ● **draught** *adj* **1** served from a barrel rather than a bottle: *~ beer* **2** used for pulling heavy loads: *a ~ horse* ▪ **draughtsman**, **draughtswoman** (*US* **drafts-**) *n* [C] (*pl* -**men**, -**women**) **1** person whose job is to draw detailed plans of machinery, buildings, etc **2** person who is skilled at drawing ▸ **draughty** *adj* (-**ier**, -**iest**) with currents of cold air blowing through

0̅⊏ **draw¹** /drɔː/ *v* (*pt* **drew** /druː/ *pp* **~n** /drɔːn/) **1** [I,T] make a picture with a pen, pencil, etc **2** [T] move sb/sth by pulling it/them: *The horses drew the coach along.* ◇ *~ the curtains* (= pull them across a window to cover or uncover it) **3** [I] (*written*) move in the direction mentioned: *The train drew into the station.* **4** [T] ~ **from/out of** take or pull sth out of sth: *~ a gun from your pocket* **5** [T] attract or interest sb: *~ a crowd* **6** [T] make or obtain sth by drawing, reasoning, etc: *~ a conclusion/comparison* **7** [I,T] decide sth by picking cards, tickets, numbers, etc by chance: *~ the winning ticket* **8** [I,T] finish a game with neither side winning: *They drew 3–3.* **9** [T] obtain sth from a source: *~ water from a well*

◇ *I drew £100 out of my account.* **10** [I,T] breathe in smoke or air [IDM] **draw a blank** see BLANK **draw sth/sb together** bring people or result **draw the line (at sth/doing sth)** refuse to do sth [IDM] **draw lots** → LOT³ [PV] **draw back (from sth/doing sth)** not take action, esp because you feel nervous **draw in** (of the day) become shorter **draw sb in|draw sb into sth/doing sth** make sb take part in sth, esp when they do not want to **draw on** (*written*) (of time) pass **draw on/upon sth** use a supply of sth: *~ on sb's experience* **draw out** (of the day) become longer **draw sb out** encourage sb to talk **draw sth out** make sth last longer than usual or necessary **draw up** (of a vehicle) arrive and stop **draw yourself up** stand up very straight **draw sth up** write out a list, etc

draw² /drɔː/ *n* [C] **1** (*usu sing*) ~ **(for)** act of drawing tickets, etc by chance; lottery or raffle **2** result of a game in which neither side wins **3** person or thing that attracts many people

drawback /'drɔːbæk/ *n* [C] disadvantage; problem

0̅⊏ **drawer** /drɔː(r)/ *n* [C] box-like container that slides in and out of a desk, chest, etc

0̅⊏ **drawing** /'drɔːɪŋ/ *n* **1** [C] picture **2** [U] art or skill of making pictures, plans, etc using a pen or pencil ▪ **drawing pin** *n* [C] (*GB*) short pin with a flat top ▪ **drawing room** *n* [C] (*fml*) room in which guests are received

drawl /drɔːl/ *v* [I,T] speak or say sth slowly, making the vowels longer ▸ **drawl** *n* [sing]

drawn¹ *pp* of DRAW¹

drawn² /drɔːn/ *adj* (of a person or their face) looking very tired or worried

dread /dred/ *v* [T] be very afraid of sth ● **dread** *n* [U] great fear and anxiety: *live like a ~.* ▸ **dreaded** *adj* causing fear ▸ **dreadful** *adj* very bad; terrible ▸ **dreadfully** *adv* terribly; very

0̅⊏ **dream** /driːm/ *n* **1** [C] series of images and events that happen in your mind while you are asleep **2** [C] wish to have or be sth, esp one that seems difficult to achieve: *his ~ of becoming president* **3** [sing] (*infml*) wonderful person or thing: *The car goes like a ~.* ● **dream** *v* (*pt, pp* **~t** /dremt/ *~ed*) [I,T] **1** ~ **(of/about)** have a dream; experience sth in a dream **2** ~ **(of/about)** imagine sth that you would like to happen [IDM] **not dream of sth/doing sth** (*spoken*) not consider doing sth; never do sth: *I wouldn't ~ of allowing you to pay* [PV] **dream sth up** (*infml*) have an idea, esp a silly one ● **dream** *adj* (*infml*) wonderful: *a ~ house* ▸ **dreamer** *n* [C] **1** person with impractical ideas **2** person who dreams ▸ **dreamless** *adj* (of sleep) without dreams ▶ **dreamlike** *adj* like a dream; strange and unreal ▶ **dreamy** *adj* (**-ier, -iest**) **1** thinking about other things and not paying attention to what is happening **2** imaginative, but not realistic **3** pleasant and peaceful ▶ **dreamily** *adv*

dreary /'drɪəri/ *adj* (**-ier, -iest**) dull or boring; making you feel depressed ▶ **drearily** /'drɪərəli/ *adv* ▶ **dreariness** *n* [U]

dredge /dredʒ/ *v* [I] clear mud, stones, etc from the bottom of a river, etc using a dredger [PV] **dredge sth up** mention sth unpleasant that has been forgotten ▶ **dredger** *n* [C] boat that can clear mud, etc from the bottom of rivers, canals, etc

dregs /dregz/ *n* [pl] **1** little bits of solid material that sink to the bottom of liquid: *coffee ~* **2** (*disapprov*) worst and most useless parts of sth: *the ~ of society*

drench /drentʃ/ *v* [T] make sb/sth completely wet

0→ **dress¹** /dres/ *n* [C] **1** piece of woman's clothing made in one piece that covers the body down to the legs **2** [U] clothes: *formal ~* ■ **dressmaker** *n* [C] person who makes women's clothes, esp as a job ■ **dress re'hearsal** *n* [C] final practice of a play, with costumes, lighting, etc

0→ **dress²** /dres/ *v* [I,T] put clothes on yourself/sb **2** [I] ~ (**for/in/as**) wear a particular type or style of clothes: *~ for dinner* ◇ *She was ~ed in black.* **3** [T] clean, treat and cover a wound **4** [T] prepare food for cooking or eating: *~ a salad* (= put oil or vinegar, etc on it) **5** [T] decorate or arrange sth: *~ a shop window* [IDM] **dressed to kill** (*infml*) wearing clothes that will make you noticed and admired [PV] **dress sb down** criticize sb angrily **dress up 1** put on your best clothes **2** put on special clothes for fun: *Children love ~ing up.*

dresser /'dresə(r)/ *n* [C] **1** (*esp GB*) piece of kitchen furniture with shelves for dishes, and cupboards below **2** (*US*) = CHEST OF DRAWERS

dressing /'dresɪŋ/ *n* [C,U] **1** sauce of oil, vinegar, etc put on salads **2** [U] (*US*) = STUFFING(2) **3** [C] bandage for protecting a wound ■ **'dressing gown** *n* [C] long loose piece of clothing worn indoors over your night clothes ■ **'dressing table** *n* [C] table with drawers and a mirror, in a bedroom

drew *pt* of DRAW¹

dribble /'drɪbl/ *v* [I,T] **1** let saliva or another liquid come out of your mouth **2** [I] (cause a liquid to) fall in small drops or a thin stream **3** [I,T] (in football, etc) move the ball along

---

with many short kicks ▶ **dribble** *n* [C,U]

dried *pt, pp* of DRY

drier → DRY

drift /drɪft/ *v* [I] **1** move along in a current of air or water **2** (of people) live or move somewhere without purpose ● **drift** *n* **1** [sing, U] slow steady movement from one place to another; a gradual change or development **2** [C] mass of snow piled up by the wind **3** [sing] general meaning: *the ~ of her argument* ▶ **drifter** *n* [C] person who moves from one place or job to another with no real purpose

drill /drɪl/ *n* **1** [C] tool for making holes **2** [C,U] way of learning sth by means of repeated exercises: *pronunciation ~s* **3** [C,U] practice of what to do in an emergency: *a fire ~* **4** [U] method of training soldiers ● **drill** *v* [I,T] **1** make a hole in sth, using a drill **2** train or teach sb with drills

drily *adv* = DRYLY

0→ **drink** /drɪŋk/ *v* (*pt* **drank** /dræŋk/ *pp* **drunk** /drʌŋk/) **1** [I,T] take liquid into your mouth and swallow it **2** [I] drink alcohol [IDM] **drink sb's health** (GB) wish sb good health as you lift your glass to drink from it **drink like a fish** (*infml*) drink a lot of alcohol regularly [PV] **drink sth in** watch or listen to sth with great interest **drink to sb/sth** wish sb happiness, etc as you lift your glass to drink from it ● **drink** *n* [C,U] **1** liquid for drinking; amount of liquid that you drink **2** alcohol or an alcoholic drink; sth that you drink on a social occasion: *Let's go for a ~.* ▶ **drinkable** *adj* ▶ **drinker** *n* [C] person who drinks too much alcohol

drip /drɪp/ *v* (**-pp-**) [I,T] (allow liquid to) fall in small drops [IDM] **dripping wet** very wet ● **drip** *n* [C] **1** series of drops of falling liquid **2** (*med*) device that puts liquid food, etc directly into a patient's veins **3** (*infml*) dull weak person ■ **drip-'dry** *adj* (of clothes) made of fabric that will dry easily when you hang it up ▶ **dripping** *n* [U] fat from roasted meat

0→ **drive¹** /draɪv/ *n* (*pt* **drove** /drəʊv/ *pp* ~**n** /drɪvn/) **1** [I,T] operate and control a vehicle **2** [T] take sb somewhere in a car, etc **3** [T] force animals or people to move somewhere **4** [T] be the power for a machine **5** [T] hit a ball with force **6** [T] force sth to go into sth mentioned: *~ a nail into wood* **7** [T] force sb to be in a certain state: *You're driving me mad!* [IDM] **what sb is driving at** the thing sb is trying to say **drive a hard bargain** argue aggressively and force sb to agree

on the best possible price, etc
■ **'drive-by** adj (esp US) done from a moving car: a ~-by shooting
■ **'drive-in** n [C] place where you can watch films, eat, etc without leaving your car ▶ **driver** n [C] **1** person who drives a vehicle **2** (computing) software that controls the sending of data between a computer and a piece of equipment attached to it, eg a printer ■ **'driving licence** (US **'driver's license**) n [C] official document that shows you are qualified to drive ■ **'driving test** (US **'driver's test**) n [C] test that you must pass before you are qualified to drive

0─▪ **drive²** /draɪv/ n **1** [C] journey in a car or other vehicle **2** [C] (also **'driveway**) private road leading to a house **3** [C] organized effort by a group of people: an export/economy ~ **4** [C,U] strong desire or need **5** [U] energy **6** [C] hard stroke in golf, tennis, etc

drivel /ˈdrɪvl/ n [U] silly nonsense

drizzle /ˈdrɪzl/ n [sing] fine light rain
● **drizzle** v [I] rain lightly

drone /drəʊn/ v [I] make a continuous low noise [PV] **drone on (about sth)** talk for a long time in a boring way ● **drone** n [C] **1** [usu sing] continuous low noise **2** male bee

drool /druːl/ v [I] **1** let saliva come out of your mouth **2** ~ **(over)** (disapprov) show how much you like sb/sth: teenagers ~ing over photos of movie stars

droop /druːp/ v [I] hang or bend downwards because of weakness

0─▪ **drop¹** /drɒp/ v (-pp-) **1** [I,T] fall or allow sth to fall **2** [I,T] become or make sth weaker or less **3** [T] ~ **(off)** stop so that sb can get out of a car, etc; deliver sth **4** [T] ~ **(from)** leave sb/sth out: He's been ~ped from the team. **5** [T] stop doing or discussing sth [IDM] **drop sb a line** (infml) write a short letter to sb [PV] **drop back/ behind| drop behind sb** move slowly and so get behind other people **drop by/in/round| drop in on sb** visit sb informally **drop off** (GB, infml) fall asleep **2** become fewer or less **drop out (of sth) 1** no longer take part in sth **2** leave college, etc without finishing your course ■ **'drop-down 'menu** n [C] (computing) = PULL-DOWN MENU (PULL¹) ■ **'dropout** n [C] **1** person who leaves college, etc without finishing their course **2** person who rejects the ideas, behaviour, etc accepted by the rest of society ▶ **droppings** n [pl] solid waste matter of animals and birds

0─▪ **drop²** /drɒp/ n **1** [C] small round mass of liquid **2** [C, usu sing] fall or reduction in sth: a ~ in prices **3** [sing]

steep or vertical distance: a ~ of 500 metres **4** (drops) [pl] liquid medicine taken in drops **5** [C] small round sweet [IDM] **at the drop of a hat** immediately; without hesitating

drought /draʊt/ n [C,U] long period of very dry weather

drove¹ pt of DRIVE¹

drove² /drəʊv/ n [usu pl] very large group: ~s of visitors

drown /draʊn/ v **1** [I,T] die in water because you cannot breathe; kill sb in this way **2** [T] ~ **(out)** (of a sound) be louder than other sounds so that you cannot hear them [IDM] **drown your sorrows** get drunk in order to forget your problems

drowsy /ˈdraʊzi/ adj (-ier, -iest) feeling sleepy ▶ **drowsily** /-əli/ adv ▶ **drowsiness** n [U]

drudge /drʌdʒ/ n [C] person who does hard boring work ▶ **drudgery** /ˈdrʌdʒəri/ n [U] hard boring work

0─▪ **drug** /drʌg/ n [C] **1** illegal substance, eg cocaine or heroin, used for pleasure: He's on ~s. ◇ She's a ~ addict (= cannot stop taking drugs). **2** substance used as a medicine ● **drug** v (-gg-) [T] **1** give drugs to a person or an animal, esp to make them unconscious **2** add a drug to sb's food or drink ■ **'drugstore** n [C] (US) chemist's shop that sells medicines and other types of goods, eg cosmetics

0─▪ **drum** /drʌm/ n [C] **1** musical instrument made of skin stretched tightly across a hollow round frame **2** large round metal container: an oil ~ ● **drum** v (-mm-) **1** [I] play a drum **2** [I,T] make a sound by hitting a surface again and again: Don't ~ your fingers on the table! [PV] **drum sth into sb** make sb remember sth by repeating it often **drum sth up** try hard to get support, customers, etc ▶ **drummer** n [C] person who plays a drum ■ **'drumstick** n [C] stick used for beating a drum

drunk¹ pp of DRINK

0─▪ **drunk²** /drʌŋk/ adj excited or confused by alcoholic drink
● **drunk** (also old-fash **drunkard** /ˈdrʌŋkəd/) n [C] person who often gets drunk ▶ **drunken** adj

1 showing the effects of too much alcohol **2** drunk or often getting drunk: a ~ driver ▶ **drunkenly** adv ▶ **drunkenness** n [U]

0─▪ **dry** /draɪ/ adj (**drier, driest**) **1** not wet: a ~ cloth ◇ ~ paint/weather **2** (of wine) not sweet **3** (of humour) pretending to be serious; ironic **4** boring; dull: a ~ speech ● **dry** v (pt, pp **dried**) [I,T] become or make sth dry [PV] **dry (sth) out** (cause sth to) become dry, in a way that is not wanted **dry up 1** (of a supply) come to an end **2** suddenly stop talking because you do not know what to say next **dry (sth) up** your dishes, etc with a cloth after washing them ■ **dry-'clean** v [T] clean clothes using chemicals instead of water ■ **dry-'cleaner's** n [C] = CLEANER'S (CLEAN²) ■ **dry-'cleaning** n [U] ■ **dry 'dock** n [C] part of a port from which water is removed, so that a ship may be repaired ▶ **dryer** (also **drier**) /'draɪə(r)/ n [C] machine that dries sth: a hair ~er ▶ **dryly** (also **drily**) /'draɪli/ adv ▶ **dryness** n [U] ■ **dry 'rot** n [U] fungus that causes wood to decay and turn to powder

dual /'djuːəl/ adj having two parts; double ■ **dual 'carriageway** n [C] road divided down the centre by a barrier or grass

dub /dʌb/ v (**-bb-**) [T] **1** give sb/sth a particular name **2** replace the original speech in a film with words in another language

dubious /'djuːbiəs/ adj causing or feeling doubt ▶ **dubiously** adv

duchess /'dʌtʃəs/ n [C] wife of a duke **2** woman who has the rank of a duke

duchy /'dʌtʃi/ n [C] (pl **-ies**) land owned by a duke or duchess

duck /dʌk/ n (pl **duck** or ~**s**) [C] **1** common bird that lives on or near water **2** [C] female duck **3** [U] meat from a duck **4** (a **duck**) [sing] (in cricket) batsman's score of 0 ● **duck** /dʌk/ v **1** [I,T] move your head or body down quickly **2** [T] push sb underwater for a short time **3** [I,T] ~ (**out of**) try to avoid a responsibility

duckling /'dʌklɪŋ/ n [C] young duck

duct /dʌkt/ n [C] tube or channel carrying liquids or air

dud /dʌd/ n [C], adj (infml) (something) that is useless: a ~ cheque

0—**due** /djuː/ adj **1** ~ **to** because of sb/sth; caused by sth: Her success is ~ to hard work. **2** arranged or expected: The train is ~ (to arrive) at 1.30. **3** needing to be paid; owed **4** suitable; right ● **due** adv (of points of the compass) exactly: ~ east ● **due** n [U] thing that should be given to sb by right **2** (dues) [pl] charges, eg for membership of a club

duel /'djuːəl/ n [C] **1** (in the past) formal fight with weapons between two people **2** contest between two people or groups ● **duel** v (**-ll-** US **-l-**) [I] fight a duel

duet /dju'et/ n [C] piece of music for two players or singers

duffle coat (also **duffle coat**) /'dʌfl kəʊt/ n [C] coat made of a heavy woollen fabric, usu with a hood

dug pt, pp of DIG¹

dugout /'dʌɡaʊt/ n [C] **1** rough shelter for soldiers, made by digging a hole in the ground **2** canoe made

by cutting out the inside of a tree trunk

duke /djuːk/ n [C] nobleman of the highest rank ▶ **dukedom** n [C] **1** position or rank of a duke **2** = DUCHY

0—**dull** /dʌl/ adj **1** not exciting; boring **2** not bright or shiny **3** (of pain) not severe, but continuous: a ~ ache **4** slow in understanding ● **dull** v [I,T] become or make sth/sb dull ▶ **dullness** n [U] ▶ **dully** /'dʌlli/ adv

duly /'djuːli/ adv in the correct manner; at the proper time

dumb /dʌm/ adj **1** (old-fash) unable to speak **2** temporarily not speaking: struck ~ with amazement **3** (infml, esp US) stupid ▶ **dumbly** adv ▶ **dumbness** n [U]

dumbfounded /dʌm'faʊndɪd/ adj unable to speak because of surprise

dummy /'dʌmi/ n (pl **-ies**) **1** model of a person, used esp for showing clothes in a shop **2** (GB) rubber or plastic object for a baby to suck ■ **dummy 'run** n [C] (GB) practice attempt before the real performance

0—**dump** /dʌmp/ v [T] **1** get rid of sth unwanted: ~ rubbish in the river **2** put sth down carelessly **3** (business) get rid of goods by selling them at a very low price, often abroad **4** (computing) copy information and move it somewhere to store it ● **dump** n [C] **1** place where rubbish may be left **2** (infml, disapprov) dirty unattractive place **3** store of military supplies **4** (computing) (act of making a) copy of data stored in a computer: a ~ screen ~ (= a copy of what is on the screen) [IDM] **down in the dumps** (infml) unhappy ■ **dumper truck** n [C] vehicle for carrying earth, etc

dumpling /'dʌmplɪŋ/ n [C] ball of cooked dough, eaten with meat

dumpy /'dʌmpi/ adj (**-ier**, **-iest**) short and fat

dunce /dʌns/ n [C] (disapprov) person, esp at school, who is slow to learn

dune /djuːn/ (also **'sand dune**) n [C] small hill of sand formed by the wind

dung /dʌŋ/ n [U] solid waste matter from animals

dungarees /ˌdʌŋɡə'riːz/ n [pl] trousers with an extra piece of fabric covering the chest, held up by straps

dungeon /'dʌndʒən/ n [C] dark underground prison

dunk /dʌŋk/ v [T] dip food into liquid before eating it

duo /'djuːəʊ/ n [C] (pl ~**s**) pair of performers

dupe /djuːp/ v [T] trick or cheat sb ● **dupe** n [C] (fml) person who is duped

duplex /'dju:pleks/ n [C] (esp US)
1 semi-detached house **2** flat on
two floors

duplicate¹ /'dju:plɪkeɪt/ v [T] make
an exact copy of sth ▸ **duplication**
/ˌdju:plɪ'keɪʃn/ n [U,C] ▸ **duplicator**
n [C] machine that copies
documents

duplicate² /'dju:plɪkət/ adj exactly
like sth else; made as a copy of sth
else ● **duplicate** n [C] something
that is exactly the same as sth else
[IDM] **in duplicate** (of documents,
etc) as two copies that are exactly
the same

durable /'djʊərəbl/ adj lasting for a
long time ▸ **durable goods** n [pl]
(US) = CONSUMER DURABLES

duration /dju'reɪʃn/ n [U] time
during which sth lasts

duress /dju'res/ n [U] (fml) threats or
force: under ~

0─w **during** /'djʊərɪŋ/ prep **1** all
through a period of time **2** at some
point in a period of time: He died ~
the night.

dusk /dʌsk/ n [U] time just before
night ▸ **dusky** adj (-ier, -iest) (lit) not
very bright; dark in colour

0─w **dust** /dʌst/ n [U] fine dry powder
of earth or other matter ● **dust** v
1 [I,T] clean furniture, etc by
removing dust from surfaces with a
cloth **2** [T] cover sth with fine
powder ■ **dustbin** n [C] container
for household rubbish ■ **dust bowl**
n [C] area that has no vegetation
because of drought, etc ■ **dustcart**
n [C] lorry for collecting rubbish from
dustbins ■ **duster** n [C] cloth for
removing dust from furniture
■ **dust jacket** n [C] loose paper
cover for a book ■ **dustman** n [C] (pl
-men) person whose job is to empty
dustbins ■ **dustpan** n [C] small flat
container into which dust is swept
■ **dust sheet** n [C] large sheet for
covering furniture, to protect it from
dust ▸ **dusty** adj (-ier, -iest) covered
with dust

Dutch /dʌtʃ/ adj of the Netherlands
(Holland), its people or their
language [IDM] **go Dutch (with sb)**
share the cost of sth

0─w **duty** /'dju:ti/ n [C,U] (pl -ies)
1 something that you must do
2 tax: customs duties [IDM] **on/off
duty** (of nurses, police officers, etc)
working/not working ▸ **dutiful** adj
showing respect and obedience
▸ **dutifully** adv ■ **duty-free** adj, adv
(of goods) able to be taken into a
country without payment of tax

duvet /'du:veɪ/ n [C] large bag filled
with soft feathers used as a bed
covering

0─w **DVD** /ˌdi: vi: 'di:/ n [C] 'digital
versatile disc'; disk on which large

amounts of information, esp
photographs and video, can be
stored, for use on a computer: a ~
player ◇ a ~-ROM drive

DVT /ˌdi: vi: 'ti:/ abbr = DEEP VEIN
THROMBOSIS

dwarf /dwɔ:f/ n [C] (pl -s or -ves)
person, animal or plant that is much
smaller than usual ● **dwarf** v [T]
make sb/sth seem small

dwell /dwel/ v (pt, pp **dwelt** or
dwelled) [I] (fml, lit) live somewhere
[PV] **dwell on/upon sth** think or talk a
lot about sth that it would be better
to forget ▸ **dweller** n [C] (in
compound nouns) person who lives
in the place mentioned: city ~ers
▸ **dwelling** n [C] (fml) home

dwindle /'dwɪndl/ v [I] become
gradually less, fewer or smaller

dye /daɪ/ v (pres pt **-ing**) [T] change
the colour of sth by dipping it in a
liquid ● **dye** n [C,U] substance used
to dye cloth, etc ■ **dyed in the
wool** adj totally fixed in your
opinions

0─w **dying** pres part DIE

dyke (also **dike**) /daɪk/ n [C] **1** long
wall of earth, for holding back water
2 (esp GB) channel that carries water
away from the land

dynamic /daɪ'næmɪk/ adj
1 energetic and forceful **2** (physics)
(of a force or power) producing
movement ▸ **dynamically**
/daɪ'næmɪkli/ adv ▸ **dynamics** n
1 [pl] way in which people or things
react to each other **2** [U] branch of
physics dealing with movement and
force ▸ **dynamism** /'daɪnəmɪzəm/ n
[U] energy and enthusiasm

dynamite /'daɪnəmaɪt/ n [U]
1 powerful explosive **2** person or
thing that is likely to shock or excite
● **dynamite** v [T] blow sth up with
dynamite

dynamo /'daɪnəməʊ/ n [C] (pl -s)
machine that uses the movement of
sth, eg water, to produce electricity

dynasty /'dɪnəsti/ n [C] (pl -ies) series
of rulers belonging to the same
family

dysentery /'dɪsəntri/ n [U] painful
disease of the bowels

dyslexia /dɪs'leksiə/ n [U] abnormal
difficulty in reading and spelling
▸ **dyslexic** /dɪs'leksɪk/ n [C], adj
(person) with dyslexia

Ee

E abbr **1** East(ern): E Sussex **2** (sl)
the illegal drug Ecstasy

E, e /i:/ n [C,U] (pl **E's, e's** /i:z/) the fifth
letter of the English alphabet ■ '**E-
number** n [C] number used for
showing an artificial substance
added to food

e- /iː/ *prefix* connected with electronic communication, esp the Internet, for sending information, doing business, etc: *e-commerce*

0→ **each** /iːtʃ/ *det, pron* used to refer to every one of two or more things or things, when you are thinking about them separately: *a ring on ~ finger* ◇ *~ of the girls* ◇ *The books cost £10 ~.*

0→ **each 'other** (*also* one another) *pron* used as the object of a v or a prep to show that each member of a group does sth to or for the other members: *Paul and Sue helped each other* (= Paul helped Sue and Sue helped Paul).

eager /ˈiːɡə(r)/ *adj* ~ (for), (to) wanting to have sth or to do sth very much: *~ for success* ▶ **eagerly** *adv* ▶ **eagerness** *n* [U, sing]

eagle /ˈiːɡl/ *n* [C] large strong bird that eats small animals ■ **eagle-'eyed** *adj* good at noticing small details

0→ **ear** /ɪə(r)/ *n* **1** [C] part of the body on each side of the head used for hearing **2** [sing] ability to recognize and copy sounds well: *She has a good ~ for music.* **3** [C] top part of wheat, barley, etc that contains the seeds [IDM] **be all ears** be listening with great interest **be up to your ears in sth** have a lot of sth to deal with ■ **'earache** *n* [U, C] pain inside the ear ■ **'eardrum** *n* [C] tightly stretched skin inside the ear which vibrates when sounds reach it ■ **'ear lobe** *n* [C] soft part at the bottom of the ear ■ **'earring** *n* [C] piece of jewellery fastened on or in the ear ■ **earshot** *n* [U] [IDM] **out of/within earshot (of sb/sth)** not close/close enough to hear sb/sth or be heard

earl /ɜːl/ *n* [C] nobleman of high rank ▶ **earldom** *n* [C] rank or lands of an earl

0→ **early** /ˈɜːli/ *adj, adv* (-ier, -iest) **1** near to the beginning of sth: *in the ~ morning* **2** before the usual or expected time: *The bus arrived ~.* [IDM] **an early bird** (*hum*) person who gets up or arrives early at the earliest time before which sth cannot happen **at your earliest convenience** (*written, business*) as soon as possible ■ **early 'warning** *n* [U, sing] thing that tells you that sth dangerous is going to happen: *an ~ warning system* (= of enemy attack)

earmark /ˈɪəmɑːk/ *v* [T] decide sth will be used for a special purpose

0→ **earn** /ɜːn/ *v* **1** [T] get money by working **2** [T] get sth you deserve because of sth good you have done ▶ **earner** *n* [C] ▶ **earnings** *n* [pl] money earned

earnest /ˈɜːnɪst/ *adj* serious and sincere ● **earnest** *n* [U] [IDM] **in earnest** serious(ly) ▶ **earnestly** *adv* ▶ **earnestness** *n*

0→ **earth** /ɜːθ/ *n* **1** (*also* Earth, the Earth) [U, sing] the world; the planet we live on **2** [U, sing] the surface of the world; land **3** [U] soil **4** [C] hole where an animal, esp a fox, lives **5** [C, usu sing] (GB) wire for electrical contact with the ground [IDM] **charge, cost, pay, etc the earth** (*infml*) charge, etc a lot of money **how, why, etc on earth** (*infml*) used to emphasize the question: *What on ~ are you doing?* ● **earth** *v* [T] (GB) (usu passive) make electrical equipment safe by connecting it to the ground with a wire ▶ **earthly** *adj* **1** (*written*) of this world; not spiritual **2** possible: *no ~ly use* ■ **earthquake** /ˈɜːθkweɪk/ *n* [C] sudden violent movement of the earth's surface ■ **earthworm** *n* [C] worm that lives in the soil ▶ **earthy** *adj* (-ier, -iest) **1** connected with the body, sex, etc, in a way some people find rude: *an ~y sense of humour* **2** of, or like soil

earthenware /ˈɜːθnweə(r)/ *n* [U] (bowls, etc) made of very hard baked clay

0→ **ease** /iːz/ *n* [U] **1** lack of difficulty: *do sth with ~* **2** comfort [IDM] **at (your) ease** comfortable and relaxed ● **ease** *v* **1** [I, T] make sth less unpleasant, painful, severe, etc **2** [T] move sb/sth slowly and carefully: *~ the injured man out of the car* [PV] **ease off/up** become less intense or severe

easel /ˈiːzl/ *n* [C] wooden frame to hold a picture while it is being painted

0→ **east** /iːst/ *n* [U, sing] (*abbr* E) **1** (the east) direction you look towards to see the sun rise; one of the four main points of a compass **2** (*also* East) eastern part of a country, region or city **3** (the East) countries of Asia, esp China, Japan and India ● **east** *adj, adv* **1** (*also* East) (*abbr* E) in or towards the east; the ~ *coast* ◇ *The house faces ~.* **2** (of winds) blowing from the east ■ **eastbound** *adj* travelling towards the east ▶ **easterly** *adj* **1** in or towards the east **2** (of winds) blowing from the east ▶ **eastern** (*also* Eastern) (*abbr* E) *adj* situated in the east or facing east: *E~ Europe* ▶ **eastward** *adj* towards the east ▶ **eastward(s)** *adv*

Easter /ˈiːstə(r)/ *n* [U] day when Christians celebrate the resurrection of Christ

0→ **easy** /ˈiːzi/ *adj* (-ier, -iest) **1** not difficult **2** free from anxiety, pain or trouble ▶ **easily** *adv* **1** without problems or difficulty **2** without doubt: *easily the best* ● **easy** *adv* [IDM] **go easy on sb** (*infml*) be less severe with sb **go easy on/with sth** (*infml*) used to tell sb not to use too much of sth **take it/things easy** relax and not work too hard ■ **easy 'chair** n [C] large comfortable armchair ■ **easy-going** adj relaxed and happy to accept things without worrying

0➡ **eat** /iːt/ v (pt ate /et/ pp **~en** /ˈiːtn/) **1** [I,T] put food into your mouth and swallow it **2** [I] have a meal: *Where shall we ~ tonight?* [IDM] **eat your heart out!** (*spoken*) used to compare two things and say that one of them is better: *Look at him dance. E~ your heart out John Travolta!* (= he dances even better than John Travolta) **eat your words** admit that you were wrong [PV] **eat sth away** destroy sth gradually **eat into sth 1** use up money, time, etc **2** destroy or damage the surface of sth ▶ **eatable** adj that can be eaten ▶ **eater** n [C] person who eats in a particular way: *a big ~er* (= a person who eats a lot)

eaves /iːvz/ n [pl] overhanging edges of a roof

eavesdrop /ˈiːvzdrɒp/ v (**-pp-**) [I] ~ (**on**) listen secretly to a private conversation ▶ **eavesdropper** n [C]

ebb /eb/ v [I] **1** (of the tide in the sea) move away from the land **2** become less or weaker ● **ebb** n (**the ebb**) [usu sing] flowing out of the tide

ebony /ˈebəni/ n [U] hard black wood ● **ebony** adj black in colour

eccentric /ɪkˈsentrɪk/ adj considered by other people to be strange or unusual ▶ **eccentric** n [C] ▶ **eccentricity** /ˌeksenˈtrɪsəti/ n [C,U] (pl **-ies**) (example of) eccentric behaviour

ecclesiastical /ɪˌkliːziˈæstɪkl/ adj of the Christian Church

echo /ˈekəʊ/ n (pl **-es**) sound reflected off a surface so that it seems to be repeated ● **echo** v **1** [I] be sent back as an echo **2** [T] (*written*) repeat or agree with sb's words

eclair /ɪˈkleə(r)/ n [C] long thin cream-filled cake with chocolate on top

eclipse /ɪˈklɪps/ n [C] **1** (of the sun) blocking of the sun's light by the moon **2** (of the moon) blocking of the moon's light when the earth's shadow falls on the moon ● **eclipse** v [T] make sb/sth seem less important by comparison

eco- /ˈiːkəʊ/ prefix (in nouns, adjectives and adverbs) connected with the environment

eco-friendly adj not harmful to the environment: *~ products*

ecology /ɪˈkɒlədʒi/ n [U] (study of the) relations of living things to their surroundings ▶ **ecological**

/ˌiːkəˈlɒdʒɪkl/ adj ▶ **ecologist** /ɪˈkɒlədʒɪst/ n [C] expert in ecology

0➡ **economic** /ˌiːkəˈnɒmɪk; ˌekə-/ adj **1** connected with trade and industry; of economics **2** (of a business, etc) profitable ▶ **economical** /ˌiːkəˈnɒmɪkl; ˌekə-/ adj careful in using money, time, etc ▶ **economically** /-kli/ adv

economics /ˌiːkəˈnɒmɪks; ˌekə-/ n [U] study of how a society organizes its money, trade and industry ▶ **economist** /ɪˈkɒnəmɪst/ n [C] student of or expert in economics

economize (also **-ise**) /ɪˈkɒnəmaɪz/ v [I] save money; spend less than before

0➡ **economy** /ɪˈkɒnəmi/ n (pl **-ies**) **1** (often **the economy**) [C] economic system of a country **2** [C,U] use of money, time, etc available in a way that avoids waste: *fly ~ class* (= by the cheapest class of air travel)

ecotourism /ˈiːkəʊtʊərɪzəm/ n [U] organized travel to unspoiled natural environments, when some of the money paid by the tourists is used to protect the area and the animals that live there ▶ **ecotourist** n [C]

ecstasy /ˈekstəsi/ n [U,C] (pl **-ies**) feeling of great happiness ▶ **ecstatic** /ɪkˈstætɪk/ adj ▶ **ecstatically** /-kli/ adv

ectopic /ekˈtɒpɪk/ adj (*med*) in an ectopic pregnancy, the baby starts to develop outside the mother's womb

eddy /ˈedi/ n [C] (pl **-ies**) circular movement of water or air ● **eddy** v (pt, pp **-ied**) [I] move around in a circle

0➡ **edge** /edʒ/ n [C] **1** outer limit of an object or surface: *the ~ of the bed* **2** sharp cutting part of a knife, etc **3** [sing] ~ (**on/over**) slight advantage over sb/sth [IDM] **be on edge** be nervous or tense **take the edge off sth** make sth less strong, bad, etc ● **edge** v **1** [I,T] move (sth) slowly and carefully in a particular direction: *She ~d (her way) along the cliff.* **2** [T] put sth round the edge of sth ▶ **edging** n [C,U] narrow border ▶ **edgy** adj (*infml*) nervous

edible /ˈedəbl/ adj that can be eaten

edit /ˈedɪt/ v [T] **1** prepare sb else's writing for publication **2** (*computing*) make changes to text or data on screen **3** prepare a film, television programme, etc by choosing and putting together different parts **4** direct the publishing of a newspaper, magazine, etc

0➡ **edition** /ɪˈdɪʃn/ n [C] **1** form in which a book is printed: *a paperback ~* **2** total number of copies of a book, etc published at one time

editor n [C] person who edits a newspaper, book, etc: *the ~ of The Times*

editorial /ˌedɪˈtɔːriəl/ adj of an editor ● **editorial** n [C] article in a newspaper giving the editor's opinion

0—**educate** /ˈedʒukeɪt/ v [T] teach sb ▶ **education** /ˌedʒuˈkeɪʃn/ n [U] **1** process of teaching, training and learning **2** (usu Education) institutions or people involved in teaching or training ▶ **educational** /ˌedʒuˈkeɪʃənl/ adj

eel /iːl/ n [C] long fish like a snake

eerie /ˈɪəri/ adj (~r, ~st) strange and frightening ▶ **eerily** /ˈɪərɪli/ adv

0—**effect** /ɪˈfekt/ n **1** [C,U] change that sb/sth causes in sb/sth else; result **2** [C,U] particular look, sound or impression that sb, eg an artist, wants to create **3** (effects) [pl] (fml, written) personal possessions [IDM] **bring/put sth into effect** put sth into use or operation **in effect 1** in fact; really **2** (of a law or rule) in use **take effect 1** start to produce the results that are intended: *The aspirin finally took~.* **2** come into use ● **effect** v [T] (fml) make sth happen

0—**effective** /ɪˈfektɪv/ adj **1** producing the result that is wanted or intended: *the most~ method* **2** (fml) (of laws, etc) coming into use ▶ **effectively** adv ▶ **effectiveness** n [U]

effectual /ɪˈfektʃuəl/ adj (fml) (of things) producing the result that was intended: *an ~ remedy*

effeminate /ɪˈfemɪnət/ adj (disapprov) (of a man) like a woman

effervescent /ˌefəˈvesnt/ adj **1** (of a person) excited and full of energy; bubbly **2** (of a liquid) having or producing small bubbles of gas ▶ **effervescence** /ˌefəˈvesns/ n [U]

0—**efficient** /ɪˈfɪʃnt/ adj able to work well: *an ~ manager* ● (of a machine, etc) producing good results ▶ **efficiency** /-ʃnsi/ n [U] ▶ **efficiently** adv

effigy /ˈefɪdʒi/ n [C] (pl **-ies**) figure or model of a person

0—**effort** /ˈefət/ n **1** [U] use of strength: *a waste of time and~* **2** [C] attempt ▶ **effortless** adj done easily, without effort ▶ **effortlessly** adv

effrontery /ɪˈfrʌntəri/ n [U] (fml) behaviour that is confident and rude without shame

effusive /ɪˈfjuːsɪv/ adj showing too much feeling ▶ **effusively** adv

EFL /ˌiː ef ˈel/ abbr (GB) English as a Foreign Language

0—**eg** /ˌiː ˈdʒiː/ abbr for example

0—**egg¹** /eg/ n **1** [C] round object with a hard shell, containing a baby bird **2** [C,U] hen's egg used as food **3** [C] female reproductive cell [IDM]

---

put all your eggs in one basket risk all your money, time, etc on one single opportunity ■ **egg cup** n [C] small container for a boiled egg ■ **egghead** n [C] (infml, disapprov) very intellectual person ■ **eggplant** n [C,U] (US) = AUBERGINE

egg² /eg/ v [PV] **egg sb on** encourage sb to do sth, esp sth bad

ego /ˈiːgəʊ; ˈegəʊ/ n [C] (pl **~s**) sense of your own value and importance

egocentric /ˌegəʊˈsentrɪk; ˌiːg-/ adj thinking only about yourself

egoism /ˈegəʊɪzəm; ˈiːg-/ (also **egotism** /ˈegətɪzəm; ˈiːg-/) n [U] self-centredness; selfishness ▶ **egoist** /ˈegəʊɪst; ˈiːg-/ (also **egotist** /ˈegətɪst; ˈiːg-/) n [C] (disapprov) person who thinks they are better than other people and who talks too much about himself / herself

eiderdown /ˈaɪdədaʊn/ n [C] thick, warm bed covering

0—**eight** /eɪt/ number **8** ▶ **eighth** /eɪtθ/ ordinal number, n [C] **1** 8th; the fraction ⅛; each of eight equal parts of sth

0—**eighteen** /ˌeɪˈtiːn/ number **18** ▶ **eighteenth** /ˌeɪˈtiːnθ/ ordinal number

0—**eighty** /ˈeɪti/ number **1** number **80 2** (the eighties) n [pl] numbers, years or temperatures from 80 to 89 ▶ **eightieth** ordinal number

0—**either** /ˈaɪðə(r); ˈiːðə(r)/ det, pron **1** one or the other of two: *park on ~ side of the road* **2** each of two: *The offices on ~ side are empty.* ● **either** adv, conj **1** used after negative verbs: *Jo can't go and I can't ~.* **2** (either...or...) used to show a choice of two things: *E~ you go or she does.*

eject /iˈdʒekt/ v [T] **~ (from)** push or send sb/sth out of a place, usu with force ▶ **ejection** /iˈdʒekʃn/ n [U] ■ **e**'**jector seat** n [C] seat that throws the pilot out of an aircraft in an emergency

eke /iːk/ v [PV] **eke sth out** make a small supply of sth last as long as possible

elaborate /ɪˈlæbərət/ adj complicated; very detailed ▶ **elaborately** adv ● **elaborate** /ɪˈlæbəreɪt/ v [I,T] **~ (on)** explain or describe sth in more detail ▶ **elaboration** /ɪˌlæbəˈreɪʃn/ n [U,C]

elapse /ɪˈlæps/ v [I] (fml) (of time) pass

elastic /ɪˈlæstɪk/ n [U] material made with rubber that can stretch and then return to its original size ● **elastic** adj **1** made with elastic **2** able to stretch and then return to its original size **3** not fixed: *Our plans are fairly ~.* ■ e,lastic 'band n [C]

---

elated

(*GB*) = RUBBER BAND ▸ **elasticity** /ˌiːlæˈstɪsəti/ *n* [U]

elated /iˈleɪtɪd/ *adj* ~ **(at/by)** very happy and excited ▸ **elation** /iˈleɪʃn/ *n* [U]

0─ **elbow** /ˈelbəʊ/ *n* [C] **1** joint where the arm bends **2** part of a piece of clothing that covers the elbow ● **elbow** *v* [T] push sb with your elbow, usu in order to get past them: *He ~ed his way through the crowd.* ■ **'elbow grease** *n* [U] (*infml*) effort used in physical work ■ **'elbow room** *n* [U] (*infml*) enough space to move in

elder /ˈeldə(r)/ *adj* (of two members of a family) older: *my ~ brother* ● **elder** *n* **1** (**elders**) [pl] people of greater age and authority **2** (**my, the elder**) [sing] (*fml*) person older than me, etc **3** [C] official in some Christian churches **4** [C] small tree with white flowers and black berries ■ **elder 'statesman** *n* [C] old and respected politician

0─ **elderly** *adj* (of people) used as a polite word for 'old': *an ~ couple*

0─ **eldest** /ˈeldɪst/ *adj, n* [C] (of three or more people) oldest (person)

0─ **elect** /iˈlekt/ *v* [T] **1** choose sb by voting **2** (*fml*) choose to do sth: *They ~ed to stay.* ● **elect** *adj* (*fml*) chosen but not yet doing the job: *the president ~* ▸ **elector** *n* [C] person with the right to vote in an election ▸ **electoral** /iˈlektərəl/ *adj* of elections ▸ **electorate** /iˈlektərət/ *n* [C, with sing or pl verb] all the electors

0─ **election** /iˈlekʃn/ *n* [C, U] process of choosing representatives by voting

0─ **electric** /iˈlektrɪk/ *adj* **1** using, produced by or producing electricity: *an ~ fire* **2** exciting ▸ **electrical** *adj* using, producing or connected with electricity ▸ **electrically** /-kli/ *adv* ■ **the e,lectric 'chair** *n* [sing] (esp in the US) chair in which criminals are killed by passing a strong electric current through their bodies ■ **e,lectric 'shock** *n* [C] sudden pain caused by electricity passing through your body

electrician /ɪˌlekˈtrɪʃn/ *n* [C] person whose job is to fit and repair electrical equipment

0─ **electricity** /ɪˌlekˈtrɪsəti/ *n* [U] **1** form of energy used for heating, lighting, driving machines, etc **2** supply of such energy: *We shouldn't waste ~.*

electrify /iˈlektrɪfaɪ/ *v* (*pt, pp* -**ied**) [T] **1** (usu passive) provide sth with electricity **2** (*written*) make sb excited

electrocute /iˈlektrəkjuːt/ *v* [T]

injure or kill sb using an electric current ▸ **electrocution** /ɪˌlektrəˈkjuːʃn/ *n* [U]

electrode /iˈlektrəʊd/ *n* [C] point by which an electric current enters or leaves a battery, etc

electromagnetic /ɪˌlektrəʊmæɡˈnetɪk/ *adj* (*physics*) having both electrical and magnetic characteristics (properties): *an ~ wave/field*

electron /iˈlektrɒn/ *n* [C] tiny particle of matter inside an atom, with a negative electric charge

0─ **electronic** /ɪˌlekˈtrɒnɪk/ *adj* **1** (of a device) having many small parts, eg microchips, that control and direct a small electric current: *an ~ calculator* **2** concerned with electronic equipment, eg computers: *an ~ engineer* ▸ **electronically** /-kli/ *adv* ▸ **electronics** *n* [U] science and development of electronic technology

0─ **elegant** /ˈelɪɡənt/ *adj* showing good taste; graceful and attractive ▸ **elegance** /ˈelɪɡəns/ *n* [U] ▸ **elegantly** *adv*

0─ **element** /ˈelɪmənt/ *n* **1** ~ (**in/of**) necessary or typical part of sth: *Justice is only one ~ in good government.* **2** [C, usu sing] small amount of sth: *an ~ of truth in her story* **3** [C] chemical substance that cannot be divided into simpler substances **4** [C] one of the four substances: earth, air, fire and water **5** (**the elements**) [pl] bad weather **6** (**elements**) [pl] basic principles of a subject **7** [C] part of a piece of electrical equipment that gives out heat [IDM] **in/out of your element** doing/not doing what you do best and enjoy

elementary /ˌelɪˈmentri/ *adj* **1** of the basic and first stages of sth: *an ~ maths class* **2** simple; not advanced ■ **ele'mentary school** *n* [C] (*US*) school for children aged about 6 to 12

elephant /ˈelɪfənt/ *n* [C] very large animal with thick grey skin, two tusks and a trunk

elevate /ˈelɪveɪt/ *v* [T] **1** (*fml or tech*) raise sb/sth; lift sb/sth up to a higher position **2** (*fml*) improve sb's mind or morals

elevation /ˌelɪˈveɪʃn/ *n* **1** [U] (*fml*) process of raising sb/sth to a higher position **2** [C, usu sing] (*tech*) height of a place above sea level **3** [C] (*fml*) piece of land that is higher than the area around **4** [C] (in architecture) (drawing of) one side of a building

0─ **elevator** /ˈelɪveɪtə(r)/ *n* [C] (*US*) = LIFT

0─ **eleven** /iˈlevn/ *number* 11 ▸ **elevenses** /iˈlevnzɪz/ *n* [U] (*GB, infml*) a mid-morning snack, often coffee and biscuits ▶ **eleventh** /ɪˈlevnθ/ ordinal number, n [C]

elf /elf/ n [C] (pl **elves** /elvz/) (in stories) creature with pointed ears and magic powers

elicit /ɪˈlɪsɪt/ v [T] ~ **(from)** (written) get information or a reaction from sb

eligible /ˈelɪdʒəbl/ adj ~ **(for), (to)** suitable; having the right qualifications: ~ for a job ▶ **eligibility** /ˌelɪdʒəˈbɪləti/ n [U]

eliminate /ɪˈlɪmɪneɪt/ v [T] remove or get rid of sb/sth ▶ **elimination** /ɪˌlɪmɪˈneɪʃn/ n [U, C]

elite /eɪˈliːt, ɪˈliːt/ n [C, with sing or pl verb] group of powerful important people in society ▶ **elitism** /-tɪzəm/ n [U] (usu disapprov) (belief in a system that aims to develop an elite ▶ **elitist** /-tɪst/ n [C], adj

elk /elk/ n [C] very large deer

ellipse /ɪˈlɪps/ n [C] (tech) regular oval shape ▶ **elliptical** /ɪˈlɪptɪkl/ adj

elm /elm/ n **1** [C] tall tree with broad leaves **2** [U] hard wood of the elm tree

elocution /ˌeləˈkjuːʃn/ n [U] art of speaking clearly

elongate /ˈiːlɒŋɡeɪt/ v [I, T] become or make sth longer

elope /ɪˈləʊp/ v [I] run away secretly to get married ▶ **elopement** /ɪ-/ n [C, U]

eloquence /ˈeləkwəns/ n [U] skilful use of language to express yourself or to persuade others ▶ **eloquent** /ˈeləkwənt/ adj ▶ **eloquently** adv

0━ **else** /els/ adv in addition to sth already mentioned; different: Have you got anything ~ to do? ∘ I saw Bob and no one ~. [IDM] **or else** otherwise; if not: Run or ~ you'll be late.
■ **else'where** adv in, at or to another place

ELT /ˌiː ˌel ˈtiː/ abbr (GB) English Language Teaching

elucidate /iˈluːsɪdeɪt/ v [T] (fml) make sth clearer by explaining it ▶ **elucidation** /iˌluːsɪˈdeɪʃn/ n [U, C]

elude /iˈluːd/ v [T] **1** avoid or escape from sb/sth **2** be difficult for sb to achieve, remember or understand: Sleep ~d him. ▶ **elusive** /iˈluːsɪv/ adj hard to find, describe or achieve

elves plural of ELF

emaciated /ɪˈmeɪʃieɪtɪd/ adj very thin and weak ▶ **emaciation** /ɪˌmeɪsiˈeɪʃn/ n [U]

0━ **email** (also **e-mail**) n **1** [U] way of sending electronic messages or data from one computer to another **2** [C, U] message(s) sent by email ● **email** v [T] send a message to sb by email

emanate /ˈeməneɪt/ v [I] ~ **from** (fml) come or flow from sb/sth

emancipate /ɪˈmænsɪpeɪt/ v [T] set sb free, esp politically or socially

---

▶ **emancipation** /ɪˌmænsɪˈpeɪʃn/ n [U]: the ~ of slaves

embalm /ɪmˈbɑːm/ v [T] preserve a dead body with chemicals, etc

embankment /ɪmˈbæŋkmənt/ n [C] wall of earth, etc that holds back water or supports a railway or road

embargo /ɪmˈbɑːɡəʊ/ n [C], (pl **-es**) ~ **(on)** official order that forbids trade with another country ● **embargo** v (pt, pp **-ed**) [T] put an embargo on sth

embark /ɪmˈbɑːk/ v [I] go on board a ship [PV] **embark on/upon sth** start sth new or difficult ▶ **embarkation** /ˌembɑːˈkeɪʃn/ n [C, U]

0━ **embarrass** /ɪmˈbærəs/ v [T] make sb feel shy, awkward or ashamed: His behaviour ~ed her. ▶ **embarrassing** adj: an ~ing mistake ▶ **embarrassingly** adv ▶ **embarrassment** n [U, C]

embassy /ˈembəsi/ n [C] (pl **-ies**) office of an ambassador and his/her staff

embed /ɪmˈbed/ v (**-dd-**) [T] ~ **(in)** (usu passive) fix sth firmly into a substance or solid object

embellish /ɪmˈbelɪʃ/ v [T] **1** ~ **(with)** (usu passive) make sth attractive by adding decorations **2** add details to a story to make it more interesting ▶ **embellishment** n [C, U]

ember /ˈembə(r)/ n [C, usu pl] piece of hot coal, etc in a dying fire

embezzle /ɪmˈbezl/ v [I, T] steal money that you are responsible for or that belongs to your employer

embitter /ɪmˈbɪtə(r)/ v [T] (usu passive) make sb feel angry and disappointed about sth

emblem /ˈembləm/ n [C] design or symbol that represents sth: The dove is an ~ of peace.

embody /ɪmˈbɒdi/ v (pt, pp **-ied**) [T] ~ **(in)** (fml) express an idea or feature; include ▶ **embodiment** n [usu sing]: She is the embodiment of honesty.

emboss /ɪmˈbɒs/ v [T] put a raised design or piece of writing on paper, leather, etc ▶ **embossed** adj: ~ed stationery

embrace /ɪmˈbreɪs/ v **1** [I, T] (written) take sb into your arms as a sign of affection **2** [T] (fml) accept an idea, religion willingly **3** [T] (fml) include sth ▶ **embrace** n [C, U]

embroider /ɪmˈbrɔɪdə(r)/ v **1** [I, T] decorate fabric with needlework **2** [T] add untrue details to a story to make it more interesting ▶ **embroidery** n [U, C]

embryo /ˈembriəʊ/ n [C] (pl **-s**) young animal before birth [IDM] **in embryo** existing but not yet fully developed ▶ **embryonic** /ˌembriˈɒnɪk/ adj

---

A B C D **E** F G H I J K L M N O P Q R S T U V W X Y Z

emerald /ˈemərəld/ n [C] bright green precious stone ▶ **emerald** (also **emerald green**) adj bright green in colour

0━ **emerge** /iˈmɜːdʒ/ v [I] **1** come out; come into view **2** (of facts) become known ▶ **emergence** /iˈmɜːdʒəns/ n [U] ▶ **emergent** /iˈmɜːdʒənt/ adj beginning to develop; new

0━ **emergency** /iˈmɜːdʒənsi/ n [C, U] (pl -**ies**) sudden serious and dangerous situation needing quick action ■ e'**mergency room** (abbr **ER**) (US) = CASUALTY.

emigrate /ˈemɪɡreɪt/ v [I] leave your own country to go and live in another ▶ **emigrant** /ˈemɪɡrənt/ n [C] person who emigrates ▶ **emigration** /ˌemɪˈɡreɪʃn/ n [U]

eminent /ˈemɪnənt/ adj (of a person) famous and respected ▶ **eminence** /ˈemɪnəns/ n [U] ▶ **eminently** adv (fml) very; extremely: ~ly qualified

emir /eˈmɪə(r); ˈemɪə(r)/ n [C] Muslim ruler ▶ **emirate** /ˈemɪərət; ˈemɪrət/ n [C] lands, etc ruled by an emir

emit /iˈmɪt/ v (-tt-) [T] (fml) send out sth such as light, heat, sound, gas, etc: ~ heat ▶ **emission** /iˈmɪʃn/ n [U, C]: the ~ of carbon dioxide into the atmosphere

emoticon /iˈməʊtɪkɒn/ n [C] group of keyboard symbols that represent the expression on sb's face, used in email, etc. to show the feelings of the person sending the message, eg:-) represents a smiling face

0━ **emotion** /iˈməʊʃn/ n [C, U] strong feeling, eg love, joy, fear or hate ▶ **emotional** /iˈməʊʃənl/ adj **1** of the emotions **2** causing emotion: an ~al speech **3** showing (too much) emotion ▶ **emotionally** adv

emotive /iˈməʊtɪv/ adj causing strong feelings

emperor /ˈempərə(r)/ n [C] ruler of an empire

0━ **emphasis** /ˈemfəsɪs/ n [U, C] (pl -**ases** /-əsiːz/) **1** special importance given to sth **2** extra force given to a word or words, esp to show that it is important ▶ **emphasize** (also -**ise**) /ˈemfəsaɪz/ v [T] put emphasis on sth ▶ **emphatic** /ɪmˈfætɪk/ adj having or using emphasis ▶ **emphatically** /-kli/ adv

0━ **empire** /ˈempaɪə(r)/ n [C] group of countries controlled by one ruler or government

empirical /ɪmˈpɪrɪkl/ adj (of knowledge) based on experiments or experience rather than theory

0━ **employ** /ɪmˈplɔɪ/ v [T] **1** give work to sb for payment **2** (fml) use sth ▶ **employable** adj having the skills that will make sb want to

employ you ▶ **employee** /ɪmˈplɔɪiː/ n [C] person who is paid to work for sb ▶ **employer** n [C] person or company that employs people ▶ **employment** n **1** [U, C] regular paid work; state of being employed **2** [U] act of employing sb

empower /ɪmˈpaʊə(r)/ v [T] (fml) (usu passive) give sb the power or authority to do sth

empress /ˈempres/ n [C] female ruler of an empire; wife of an emperor

0━ **empty** /ˈempti/ adj (-ier, -iest) **1** containing nothing or no one **2** having no value or meaning: ~ promises ▶ **empties** n [pl] empty bottles or glasses ▶ **emptiness** /ˈemptinəs/ n [U, sing] ● **empty** v (pt, pp -**ied**) [I, T] become or make sth empty ■ **empty-'handed** adj bringing or taking nothing ■ **empty-'headed** adj foolish; silly

emu /ˈiːmjuː/ n [C] large Australian bird that cannot fly

emulate /ˈemjuleɪt/ v [T] (fml) try to do sth as well as sb because you admire them ▶ **emulation** /ˌemjuˈleɪʃn/ n [U]

emulsifier /ɪˈmʌlsɪfaɪə(r)/ n [C] (chem) substance that is added to food to make the different substances combine to form a smooth mixture

emulsion /ɪˈmʌlʃn/ n [U, C] creamy liquid mixture, esp paint

0━ **enable** /ɪˈneɪbl/ v [T] ~ **to** make sb able to do sth ▶ -**enabled** adj (in compound adjectives) (computing) that can be used with a particular system or technology, esp the Internet: web~d phones

enamel /ɪˈnæml/ n [U] **1** shiny substance that is melted onto metal, pots, etc **2** hard covering of the teeth ▶ **enamelled** (US -**l-**) adj covered or decorated with enamel

enamoured (US -ored) /ɪˈnæməd/ adj ~ **of/with** liking sth a lot

enchant /ɪnˈtʃɑːnt/ v [T] (fml) attract sb strongly ▶ **enchanted** /ɪnˈtʃɑːntɪd/ adj placed under a magic spell ▶ **enchanting** adj attractive and pleasing ▶ **enchantment** n [C, U]

encircle /ɪnˈsɜːkl/ v [T] surround sb/ sth completely

encl. abbr (business) enclosed; used on business letters to show that another document is being sent in the same envelope

enclave /ˈenkleɪv/ n [C] part of a country or a city surrounded by another

enclose /ɪnˈkləʊz/ v [T] **1** build a wall, etc round sth **2** put sth in the same envelope as sth else ▶ **enclosure** /ɪnˈkləʊʒə(r)/ n [C] **1** area of land surrounded by a fence or wall **2** something put in the same envelope as a letter

encode /ɪnˈkəʊd/ v [T] **1** change ordinary language into letters, symbols, etc in order to send secret messages **2** (computing) change information into a form that can be processed by a computer

encore /ˈɒŋkɔː(r)/ exclam, n [C] (used by an audience to ask for a) repeated performance

0━ **encounter** /ɪnˈkaʊntə(r)/ v [T] (fml) meet sth/sb difficult or unexpected ● **encounter** n [C] unexpected (esp unpleasant) meeting

0━ **encourage** /ɪnˈkʌrɪdʒ/ v [T] give sb support, confidence or hope: *They ~d him to come.* ▶ **encouragement** n [U, C] ▶ **encouraging** adj

encroach /ɪnˈkrəʊtʃ/ v [I] ~ **(on)** (fml) go beyond what is right or natural: *~ on sb's rights*

encyclopedia (also -paedia) /ɪnˌsaɪkləˈpiːdiə/ n [C] book(s) or a CD-ROM giving information on all subjects or on one subject, usu in alphabetical order ▶ **encyclopedic** (also -paedic) /-ˈpiːdɪk/ adj complete and thorough

0━ **end** /end/ n [C] **1** point where sth stops; last part of sth: *at the ~ of the street/war* **2** small piece that remains: *cigarette ~s* **3** aim or purpose: *with this ~ in view* [IDM] **in the end** at last; finally **make (both) ends meet** earn just enough money to live on **no end of sth** (spoken) a lot of sth **on end 1** upright **2** continuously: *rain for days on ~* ● **end** n [I, T] (cause sth to) finish [PV] **end up** reach a certain place or state finally ▶ **ending** /ˈendɪŋ/ n [C] last part of a word, story, etc ▶ **endless** /ˈendləs/ adj having no end ▶ **endlessly** adv

endanger /ɪnˈdeɪndʒə(r)/ v [T] cause danger to sb/sth

endear /ɪnˈdɪə(r)/ v [T] [PV] **endear sb/yourself to sb** make yourself/sb popular ▶ **endearment** n [C, U] expression of affection

endeavour (US -or) /ɪnˈdevə(r)/ v [I] ~ **to** (fml) try to do sth ● **endeavour** n [U, C] (fml) attempt to do sth, esp sth new or difficult

endemic /enˈdemɪk/ adj often found in a particular place: *Malaria is ~ in many hot countries.*

endive /ˈendaɪv, -dɪv/ (US) = CHICORY

endorse /ɪnˈdɔːs/ v [T] **1** approve of or support sth/sb publicly **2** write your name on the back of a cheque **3** (GB) (usu passive) record a driving offence on a driving licence ▶ **endorsement** n [C, U]

endow /ɪnˈdaʊ/ v [T] give money that provides a regular income for a school, etc [PV] **be endowed with sth**

147

engrave

naturally have a particular feature, quality, etc ▶ **endowment** n [C, U]

endure /ɪnˈdjʊə(r)/ v **1** (written) [T] suffer pain, etc patiently **2** [I] (fml) continue to exist for a long time ▶ **endurance** n [U] ability to endure sth ▶ **enduring** adj lasting

0━ **enemy** /ˈenəmi/ n (pl -ies) **1** [C] person who hates sb or who acts against sb/sth **2** (the enemy) [sing, with sing or pl verb] (armed forces of a) country that you are fighting against

0━ **energy** /ˈenədʒi/ n **1** [U] ability to act or work with strength or enthusiasm **2** (energies) [pl] physical and mental effort you use to do sth **3** [U] power used for operating machinery, etc: *atomic ~* ▶ **energetic** /ˌenəˈdʒetɪk/ adj having or needing a lot of energy and enthusiasm ▶ **energetically** /-kli/ adv

enfold /ɪnˈfəʊld/ v [T] (fml) hold sb in your arms

enforce /ɪnˈfɔːs/ v [T] force people to obey a law, etc ▶ **enforceable** adj ▶ **enforcement** n [U]

0━ **engage** /ɪnˈɡeɪdʒ/ v **1** (fml) succeed in keeping your attention and interest **2** [T] (fml) employ sb **3** [I, T] (of parts of a machine) fit (sth) together [PV] **engage (sb) in sth** (make sb) take part in sth ▶ **engaged** adj having agreed to marry sb being used; busy ▶ **engagement** n [C] **1** agreement to marry sb **2** arrangement to do sth at a particular time **3** (fml) battle ▶ **engaging** adj pleasant; charming

0━ **engine** /ˈendʒɪn/ n [C] **1** machine that changes energy into movement **2** vehicle that pulls a train ● **engine driver** n [C] person who drives a railway engine

0━ **engineer** /ˌendʒɪˈnɪə(r)/ n [C] **1** person who designs machines, bridges, railways, etc **2** person whose job is to control and repair engines ● **engineer** v [T] arrange sth, esp secretly or indirectly ▶ **engineering** n [U] work of an engineer; study of engineering as a subject

English /ˈɪŋɡlɪʃ/ n **1** [U] the English language **2** (the English) [pl] the people of England ● **English** adj

engrave /ɪnˈɡreɪv/ v [T] ~ **A on B/B (with A)** cut words or designs on a hard surface [IDM] **be engraved on/in your heart, memory, mind, etc** be sth that you will never forget because it affected you so strongly ▶ **engraver** n [C] person whose job is to cut words or designs on wood, metal, etc ▶ **engraving** n **1** [C] picture printed from an engraved metal plate **2** [U] work of an engraver

engross /ɪnˈgrəʊs/ v [T] (usu passive) take all sb's attention: ~ed in her work

engulf /ɪnˈgʌlf/ v [T] (written) surround or cover sb/sth completely: The hotel was ~ed in flames.

enhance /ɪnˈhɑːns/ v [T] improve the good qualities of sth ▸ **enhancement** n [U,C]

enigma /ɪˈnɪgmə/ n [C] mystery ▸ **enigmatic** /ˌenɪgˈmætɪk/ adj ▸ **enigmatically** /-kli/ adv

0̶➔ **enjoy** /ɪnˈdʒɔɪ/ v [T] **1** get pleasure from sth **2 ~ yourself** be happy **3** (written) be lucky to have sth: ~ good health ▸ **enjoyable** adj pleasant ▸ **enjoyably** adv ▸ **enjoyment** n [U,C]

enlarge /ɪnˈlɑːdʒ/ v [I,T] become or make sth bigger [PV] **enlarge on/ upon sth** (fml) say or write more about sth ▸ **enlargement** n [C,U]

enlighten /ɪnˈlaɪtn/ v [T] give sb more knowledge or understanding of sth ▸ **enlightenment** n [U]

enlist /ɪnˈlɪst/ v **1** persuade sb to help you or join you in doing sth **2** [I,T] (make sb) join the armed forces ▸ **enlistment** n [U,C]

enormity /ɪˈnɔːməti/ n (pl -**ies**) **1** [U] very great size, effect, etc of sth **2** [C, usu pl] (fml) very serious crime

0̶➔ **enormous** /ɪˈnɔːməs/ adj very large ▸ **enormously** adv very; very much

0̶➔ **enough** /ɪˈnʌf/ det, pron as many or as much as sb needs or wants: Is £100 ~? ● **enough** adv sufficiently: not old ~ ● [IDM] **funnily, oddly, strangely, etc enough** used to show that sth is very surprising

enquire (also inquire) /ɪnˈkwaɪə(r)/ v [I,T] ~ (**about**) ask sb for information about sth: ~ about trains to Oxford [PV] **enquire after sb** ask about sb's health **enquire into sth** investigate sth ▸ **enquiring** adj showing an interest in learning: an enquiring mind

0̶➔ **enquiry** (also inquiry) /ɪnˈkwaɪəri/ n (pl -**ies**) **1** [C] request for information about sth; investigation **2** [U] act of asking questions or collecting information about sth/sth

enrage /ɪnˈreɪdʒ/ v [T] (written) make sb very angry

enrich /ɪnˈrɪtʃ/ v [T] **1 ~ (with)** improve sth by adding sth to it: soil ~ed with fertilizer **2** make sb/sth richer ▸ **enrichment** n [U]

enrol (esp US enroll) /ɪnˈrəʊl/ v (-**ll**-) [I,T] become or make sb a member of a college or course ▸ **enrolment** (US enrollment) n [U,C]

en route /ˌɒn ˈruːt; ˌɒn/ adv (GB) (from French) on the way

ensemble /ɒnˈsɒmbl/ n [C] **1** group of things considered as a whole **2** small group of musicians who often play together

ensign /ˈensən/ n [C] **1** ship's flag **2** junior officer in the US navy

ensue /ɪnˈsjuː/ v [I] (written) happen after or as a result of another event

en suite /ˌɒ̃ ˈswiːt/ adj, adv (GB) (of a bathroom) joined onto a bedroom and for use only by people in that bedroom

0̶➔ **ensure** (esp US insure) /ɪnˈʃʊə(r); -ˈʃɔː(r)/ v [T] make certain of sth

entail /ɪnˈteɪl/ v [T] involve sth that cannot be avoided: Your plan ~s a lot of work.

entangled /ɪnˈtæŋgld/ adj ~ (**in**) twisted or caught in sth ▸ **entanglement** n [C,U]

0̶➔ **enter** /ˈentə(r)/ v **1** [I,T] (fml) come or go into sth **2** [T] become a member of an institution; join a profession: ~ university **3** [T] write details of sb/sth in a book or list **4** [I,T] take part in a competition, examination, etc [PV] **enter into sth 1** begin to deal with sth **2** take an active part in sth; form part of sth **enter on/upon sth** (fml) begin sth

0̶➔ **enterprise** /ˈentəpraɪz/ n **1** [C] company or business **2** [C] large (esp difficult) project **3** [U] business activity: private ~ **4** [U] ability to think of new projects ▸ **enterprising** adj having or showing enterprise (4)

0̶➔ **entertain** /ˌentəˈteɪn/ v **1** [I,T] invite people to eat or drink with you in your home **2** [I,T] amuse and interest sb **3** [T] (fml) consider an idea, a hope, feeling, etc ▸ **entertainer** n [C] person whose job is to amuse or interest people, eg by singing ▸ **entertaining** adj amusing ▸ **entertainment** n **1** [U,C] films, music, etc used to entertain people **2** [U] act of entertaining sb

enthral (esp US enthrall) /ɪnˈθrɔːl/ v (-**ll**-) [T] capture sb's complete attention

enthuse /ɪnˈθjuːz/ v [I] ~ (**about/ over**) talk about sth with great enthusiasm

0̶➔ **enthusiasm** /ɪnˈθjuːziæzəm/ n [U] great excitement or interest in sth and a desire to become involved in it ▸ **enthusiast** /ɪnˈθjuːziæst/ n [C] person with a strong interest in sth ▸ **enthusiastic** /ɪnˌθjuːziˈæstɪk/ adj full of enthusiasm ▸ **enthusiastically** /-kli/ adv

entice /ɪnˈtaɪs/ v [T] persuade sb/sth to go somewhere or do sth, by offering them sth ▸ **enticement** n [C,U]

0̶➔ **entire** /ɪnˈtaɪə(r)/ adj complete ▸ **entirely** adv ▸ **entirety** /-ˈtaɪərəti/ n [U]

0̶➔ **entitle** /ɪnˈtaɪtl/ v **1 ~ to** give sb the right to have or do sth **2** give

equate

a title to a book, etc ▸ **entitlement** n [U, C]

entity /'entəti/ n [C] (pl -ies) (fml) something that has a separate existence

entourage /'ɒntʊrɑːʒ/ n [C, with sing or pl verb] people who travel with an important person

0— **entrance**¹ /'entrəns/ n **1** [C] door, gate etc used for entering a room, building or place **2** [C, usu sing] act of entering **3** [U] right to enter a building or place

entrance² /ɪn'trɑːns/ v [T] make sb feel great pleasure and give sb/sth all their attention: ~d by the music

entrant /'entrənt/ n [C] person who enters a competition, profession, etc

entreat /ɪn'triːt/ v [T] (fml) ask sb to do sth in a serious way ▸ **entreaty** n [C, U] (pl -ies) serious, often emotional, request

entrenched /ɪn'trentʃt/ adj (of ideas, etc) firmly fixed

entrepreneur /,ɒntrəprə'nɜː(r)/ n [C] person who starts a business

entrust /ɪn'trʌst/ v [T] ~ **with**, to give sth to sb to look after: ~ the job to him ◇ ~ him with the job

0— **entry** /'entri/ n (pl -ies) **1** [C] act of coming or going in a place **2** [U] right to take part in or join sth **3** [C] item written in a dictionary, diary, etc **4** [C] door, gate or passage where you enter a building

enumerate /ɪ'njuːməreɪt/ v [T] name things on a list one by one: to ~ the main points

enunciate /ɪ'nʌnsieɪt/ v [I, T] say words clearly ▸ **enunciation** /ɪ,nʌnsi'eɪʃn/ n [U]

envelop /ɪn'veləp/ v [T] wrap sb/sth up or cover them or it completely ▸ **envelopment** n [U]

0— **envelope** /'envələʊp; 'ɒn-/ n [C] paper covering for a letter

enviable /'enviəbl/ adj desirable; causing envy

envious /'enviəs/ adj feeling or showing envy ▸ **enviously** adv

0— **environment** /ɪn'vaɪrənmənt/ n **1** [C, U] physical conditions that sb/ sth exists in **2** (the environment) [sing] the natural world in which people, plants and animals live ▸ **environmental** /ɪn,vaɪrən'mentl/ adj ▸ **environmentalist** /ɪn,vaɪrən'mentəlɪst/ n [C] person who wants to protect the environment (2) ▸ **environmentally** /-təli/ adv: ~ally damaging ● **environmentally friendly** (also **environment-friendly**) adj (of products) not harming the environment: They use ~ally-friendly packaging.

envisage /ɪn'vɪzɪdʒ/ v [T] have an idea of sth as a future possibility

envoy /'envɔɪ/ n [C] messenger or representative of a government or an organization

envy /'envi/ n [U] feeling of wanting sth that sb else has [IDM] **be the envy of sb/sth** be a person or thing that others admire and that causes envy ● **envy** v (pt, pp **-ied**) [T] wish you had the same qualities, possessions, etc, as sb else

enzyme /'enzaɪm/ n [C] chemical substance formed in living cells that causes chemical change

epaulette (esp US **-let**) /'epəlet/ n [C] decoration on the shoulder of a uniform

ephemeral /ɪ'femərəl/ adj lasting for a very short time

epic /'epɪk/ n [C] long poem, film, etc about the actions of great heroes ● **epic** adj impressive; grand

epidemic /,epɪ'demɪk/ n [C] disease that spreads quickly among many people

epilepsy /'epɪlepsi/ n [U] disease that causes sb to become unconscious and to have violent fits ▸ **epileptic** /,epɪ'leptɪk/ adj, n [C]

epilogue (US **-log**) /'epɪlɒg/ n [C] last part of a book or play

episode /'epɪsəʊd/ n [C] **1** one important event or period of time in sb's life **2** one of several parts of a story on television, etc

epitaph /'epɪtɑːf/ n [C] words on a tombstone

epithet /'epɪθet/ n [C] adjective used to describe sb

epitome /ɪ'pɪtəmi/ n [C] person or thing that is the perfect example of a quality or type: She is the ~ of kindness. ▸ **epitomize** (also **-ise**) /ɪ'pɪtəmaɪz/ v [T] be a perfect example of sth

epoch /'iːpɒk/ n [C] period of time marked by important events or characteristics

equable /'ekwəbl/ adj moderate; not changing much: an ~ climate/ temper

0— **equal** /'iːkwəl/ adj **1** the same in size, number, value, etc **2** ~ **to** having the ability or strength for sth: ~ to the task ● **equal** n [C] person or thing equal to another ● **equal** v (-ll-; US **-l-**) [T] be equal to sb/sth ▸ **equality** /ɪ'kwɒləti/ n [U] fact of being equal in rights, status, advantages, etc ▸ **equalize** (also **-ise**) /ɪ,kwɒl/ v [I, T] become or make sb/sth equal ▸ **equally** adv **1** to the same degree; in the same way **2** in equal parts, amounts, etc

equate /ɪ'kweɪt/ v [T] consider sth to be the same or as important as sth else: You cannot ~ these two systems of government.

equation

150

equation /ɪˈkweɪʒn/ n [C] (maths) statement that two amounts or values are equal: $2x + 5 = 11$ is an ~.

equator /ɪˈkweɪtə(r)/ n (the equator) [sing] imaginary line round the earth, halfway between the North and South Poles ▶ **equatorial** /ˌekwəˈtɔːriəl/ adj

equestrian /ɪˈkwestriən/ adj connected with horse riding

equilibrium /ˌiːkwɪˈlɪbriəm/; ˌek- / n [U, sing] (fml) state of being balanced

equinox /ˈiːkwɪnɒks; ˈek- / n [C] one of the two times in the year when day and night are of equal length: the spring/autumn ~

equip /ɪˈkwɪp/ v (-pp-) [T] ~ (with) supply sb with sth needed for a particular purpose

0━ **equipment** /ɪˈkwɪpmənt/ n [U] things needed for a particular purpose: office ~

equitable /ˈekwɪtəbl/ adj fair and reasonable ▶ **equitably** adv

equity /ˈekwəti/ n **1** value of a company's shares; value of a property after all debts have been paid **2** (equities) [pl] shares in a company on which fixed interest is not paid **3** [U] (fml) fairness

0━ **equivalent** /ɪˈkwɪvələnt/ adj, n [C] (thing) that is equal in value, amount, importance, etc to sth else

equivocal /ɪˈkwɪvəkl/ adj (fml) not having one clear or definite meaning: an ~ answer ▶ **equivocate** /ɪˈkwɪvəkeɪt/ v [I] (fml) speak about sth in a way that is not clear in order to hide the truth

era /ˈɪərə/ n [C] period in history marked by an important event or development

eradicate /ɪˈrædɪkeɪt/ v [T] destroy sth bad ▶ **eradication** /-ˈkeɪʃn/ n [U]

erase /ɪˈreɪz/ v [T] remove sth completely: ~ the event from his memory ▶ **eraser** n [C] (esp US) = RUBBER(2)

erect /ɪˈrekt/ v [T] **1** (fml) build sth **2** fix or set sth upright: ~ a tent
● **erect** adj in an upright position: stand ~ ▶ **erection** /ɪˈrekʃn/ n [C] **1** swelling and hardening of a man's penis **2** [U] (fml) act of erecting sth **3** [C] (fml) building ▶ **erectness** n [U]

erode /ɪˈrəʊd/ v [T] (of the sea, wind, etc) gradually destroy the surface of sth ▶ **erosion** /ɪˈrəʊʒn/ n [U]

erotic /ɪˈrɒtɪk/ adj causing sexual excitement

err /ɜː(r)/ v [I] (old-fash, fml) make a mistake

errand /ˈerənd/ n [C] short journey, eg to buy goods from a shop

erratic /ɪˈrætɪk/ adj not regular or reliable ▶ **erratically** /-kli/ adv

erroneous /ɪˈrəʊniəs/ adj (fml) (of beliefs, etc) incorrect

0━ **error** /ˈerə(r)/ n [C, U] mistake: The accident was due to human ~.

erudite /ˈeruːdaɪt/ adj (fml) having or showing great knowledge

erupt /ɪˈrʌpt/ v [I] **1** (of a volcano) throw out lava **2** break out violently: Fighting ~ed on the streets. ▶ **eruption** /ɪˈrʌpʃn/ n [C, U]

escalate /ˈeskəleɪt/ v [I, T] become or make sth bigger or more serious ▶ **escalation** /ˌeskəˈleɪʃn/ n [C, U]

escalator /ˈeskəleɪtə(r)/ n [C] moving staircase for carrying people up or down

escapade /ˈeskəpeɪd/ n [C] exciting and possibly dangerous adventure

0━ **escape** /ɪˈskeɪp/ v **1** [I] ~ (from) get free from prison or sb's control **2** [I, T] get away from sth unpleasant **3** [I] ~ (from) (of gases, liquids, etc) find a way out **4** [T] be forgotten or not noticed: Her name ~s me (= I can't remember it). ● **escape** n **1** [C, U] act or method of escaping from somewhere **2** [C] leaking of a gas or liquid ▶ **escapism** n [U] activity that helps you forget your problems, etc ▶ **escapist** n

escort /ˈeskɔːt/ n [C] person or group of people or vehicles that travel with sb to protect them ● **escort** /ɪˈskɔːt/ v [T] go with sb as an escort

esophagus (US) = OESOPHAGUS

esoteric /ˌesəˈterɪk; ˌiːsə-/ adj understood by only a small group of people

0━ **especially** /ɪˈspeʃəli/ adj (abbr **esp.**) **1** in particular: I love Paris, ~ in spring. **2** for a particular purpose, person, etc **3** very much; to a great degree: This is ~ true of the old.

espionage /ˈespiənɑːʒ/ n [U] activity of spying

0━ **essay** /ˈeseɪ/ n [C] short piece of writing on one subject ▶ **essayist** n [C] writer of essays

essence /ˈesns/ n **1** [U] most important quality of sth **2** [C, U] flavouring in concentrated liquid form **IDM** in essence really

0━ **essential** /ɪˈsenʃl/ adj **1** extremely important; completely necessary **2** fundamental: an ~ part of the English character ● **essential** n [C, usu pl] most important or necessary thing: Pack the bare ~s. ▶ **essentially** /ɪˈsenʃəli/ adv basically or really

0━ **establish** /ɪˈstæblɪʃ/ v [T] **1** start or create a business, system, etc meant to last for a long time **2** settle yourself firmly in a position or activity **3** show a fact, etc to be true; prove ▶ **establishment** n [C] **1** (fml) organization, large institution or a hotel **2** (usu the Establishment) [sing, with sing or pl verb] often (disapprov) people in positions of power **3** [U] act of starting or creating sth

0~ **estate** /ɪˈsteɪt/ n [C] **1** land in the country, with one owner **2** (GB) large area of land with factories or houses on it: *a housing ~* **3** (law) all of a person's money and property, esp after their death ■ e'state agent n [C] person who buys and sells houses for others ■ e'state car n [C] car with an area for luggage behind the back seats and a door at the back

esteem /ɪˈstiːm/ n [U] (fml) good opinion; respect ▶ **esteem** v [T] (fml) respect sb/sth greatly

esthetic (US) = AESTHETIC

0~ **estimate** /ˈestɪmeɪt/ v [T] form an idea of the cost, size, value, etc of sth, but without calculating it exactly ● **estimate** /ˈestɪmət/ n [C] approximate calculation of the cost, size, etc of sth ▶ **estimation** /ˌestɪˈmeɪʃn/ n [U] judgement or opinion about value or quality of sb/ sth

estuary /ˈestʃuəri/ n [C] (pl -ies) mouth of a river into which the tide flows

0~ **etc** /ˌet ˈsetərə/ ˌɪt-/ abbr (short for 'et cetera') and other similar things; and the rest

etch /etʃ/ v [I,T] cut lines into a piece of glass, metal, etc in order to make words or a picture ▶ **etching** n [C,U] picture printed from an etched metal plate; art of making these pictures

eternal /ɪˈtɜːnl/ adj **1** lasting for ever **2** (disapprov) seeming never to stop ▶ **eternally** /ɪˈtɜːnəli/ adv

eternity /ɪˈtɜːnəti/ n **1** [U] (fml) time without end, esp after death **2** (an eternity) [sing] (infml) a very long time

ether /ˈiːθə(r)/ n [U] colourless liquid made from alcohol ▶ **ethereal** /iˈθɪəriəl/ adj very delicate and light

Ethernet /ˈiːθənet/ n [U] system for connecting a number of computer systems to form a network

ethic /ˈeθɪk/ n **1** (ethics) [pl] moral principles **2** [sing] system of moral principles: *the Christian ~* **3** (ethics) [U] study of moral principles ▶ **ethical** /-kl/ adj **1** of morals **2** morally correct ▶ **ethically** /-kli/ adv

ethnic /ˈeθnɪk/ adj of a national, racial or tribal group ▶ **ethnically** /-kli/ adv

etiquette /ˈetɪket/ n [U] rules for polite behaviour in society

etymology /ˌetɪˈmɒlədʒi/ n [U] study of the history of words

eucalyptus /ˌjuːkəˈlɪptəs/ n [C] tall evergreen tree from which an oil, used as medicine, is obtained

euphemism /ˈjuːfəmɪzəm/ n [C,U] use of a pleasant or indirect word or phrase to express sth unpleasant: *'Pass away'* is a ~ for 'die'. ▶ **euphemistic** /ˌjuːfəˈmɪstɪk/ adj

euphoria /juːˈfɔːriə/ n [U] feeling of great happiness and excitement ▶ **euphoric** /juːˈfɒrɪk/ adj

Euro- /ˈjʊərəʊ/ prefix of Europe or the European Union

0~ **euro** /ˈjʊərəʊ/ (pl ~**s**) n [C] (symb €) (since 1999) unit of money of many countries of the European Union

European /ˌjʊərəˈpiːən/ adj of or connected with Europe: ~ *languages* ■ the European Union n [sing] (abbr **EU**) economic and political organization that many European countries belong to

euthanasia /ˌjuːθəˈneɪziə/ n [U] painless killing of people who have a painful incurable disease

evacuate /ɪˈvækjueɪt/ v [T] move people from a place of danger to a safer place: ~ *the building* ▶ **evacuation** /ɪˌvækjuˈeɪʃn/ n [C,U]

evade /ɪˈveɪd/ v [T] **1** escape from or avoid meeting sb/sth **2** find a way of not doing or dealing with sth: ~ (answering) a question

evaluate /ɪˈvæljueɪt/ v [T] decide on the value or quality of sth ▶ **evaluation** /ɪˌvæljuˈeɪʃn/ n [C,U]

evangelical /ˌiːvænˈdʒelɪkl/ adj of a Christian group that emphasizes salvation by belief in Christ

evangelist /ɪˈvændʒəlɪst/ n [C] **1** person who travels around holding meetings to persuade people to become Christians **2** one of the four writers of the Gospels in the Bible ▶ **evangelistic** /ɪˌvændʒəˈlɪstɪk/ adj

evaporate /ɪˈvæpəreɪt/ v **1** [I,T] (cause a liquid to) change into gas, esp steam, and disappear **2** [i] gradually disappear ▶ **evaporation** /ɪˌvæpəˈreɪʃn/ n [U]

evasion /ɪˈveɪʒn/ n [C,U] act of avoiding sb/sth ▶ **evasive** /ɪˈveɪsɪv/ adj not willing to give clear answers to a question ▶ **evasively** adv

eve /iːv/ n [C, usu sing] day before an event, esp a religious festival: *Christmas E~*

0~ **even**[1] /ˈiːvn/ adv **1** used for emphasizing sth unexpected or surprising: *E~ a child can understand it* (= so adults certainly can). **2** used to make a comparison between two things stronger: *You know ~ less than I do.* **IDM** even if/though in spite of the fact that: *I'll get there ~ if I have to walk.* even now/so/then in spite of what (had) happened: *I told him, but ~ then he didn't believe me.*

even[2] /ˈiːvn/ adj **1** level and smooth: *an ~ surface* **2** not changing much in amount, speed, etc: *an ~ temperature* **3** (of amounts) equal or the same for each person, team, etc **4** (of two people or teams) equally balanced: *The two teams are very* ~. **5** (of numbers) that can be divided by two **[IDM] be/get even (with sb)** (*infml*) cause sb the same amount of harm as they have caused you on **an even keel** calm, with no sudden changes ■ **even** *v* **[PV] even (sth) out/up** become or make sth level, equal or balanced ■ **even-handed** *adj* fair ▶ **evenly** *adv* ▶ **evenness** *n* [U] ■ **even-tempered** *adj* not easily made angry

0━ **evening** /'iːvnɪŋ/ *n* [C,U] part of the day between the afternoon and bedtime ■ **evening dress** *n* **1** [U] clothes worn for formal occasions in the evening **2** [C] woman's long formal dress

0━ **event** /ɪ'vent/ *n* [C] **1** something that happens, esp sth important **2** one race, competition, etc in a sports programme **[IDM] at all events** whatever happens **in the event of sth** (*fml*) if sth happens ▶ **eventful** /ɪ'ventfl/ *adj* full of interesting or important events

eventual /ɪ'ventʃuəl/ *adj* happening at the end of a period of time or a process ▶ **eventuality** /ɪ,ventʃu'æləti/ *n* [C] (*pl* -ies) (*fml*) possible event or result

0━ **eventually** /ɪ'ventʃuəli/ *adv* in the end: *They* ~ *agreed to pay.*

0━ **ever** /'evə(r)/ *adv* **1** at any time: *Nothing* ~ *happens here.* ◇ *Do you* ~ *wish you were rich?* ◇ *the best work you've* ~ *done* **2** all the time or every time; always: *the* ~ *increasing number of students* ◇ *He said he'd love her for* ~. **3** (used for showing surprise in questions): *What* ~ *do you mean?* **[IDM] ever since (...)** continuously since the time mentioned: *She's liked reading* ~ *since she was a child.* **ever so/such a** (*spoken, esp GB*) very; really: ~ *so rich*

evergreen /'evəɡriːn/ *n* [C] (tree or bush) that has green leaves throughout the year ■ **evergreen** *adj*

everlasting /,evə'lɑːstɪŋ/ *adj* lasting for ever

0━ **every** /'evri/ *adj* **1** each (one): *E— child passed the exam.* **2** all possible: *You have* ~ *reason to be satisfied.* **3** used for showing that sth happens regularly: *Change* ~ *week.* **[IDM] every other** each alternate one: ~ *other day* (= Monday, Wednesday and Friday, etc) ■ **everybody** (*also* '**everyone**') *pron* every person; all people ■ **everyday** *adj* ordinary; daily ■ **everything** *pron* all things: *E—thing was destroyed.* ■ **everywhere** *adv* in or to every place

evict /ɪ'vɪkt/ *v* [T] force sb to leave a

house or land, esp by official authority of the law ▶ **eviction** /ɪ'vɪkʃn/ *n* [C,U]

0━ **evidence** /'evɪdəns/ *n* [U] **1** facts, signs or objects that make you believe sth is true **2** information used in a law court to try to prove sth: *I was asked to give* ~. **[IDM] in evidence** (be) present and clearly seen

evident /'evɪdənt/ *adj* plain and clear; obvious ▶ **evidently** *adv*

0━ **evil** /'iːvl/ *adj* wicked; cruel ■ **evil** *n* (*fml*) **1** [U] force that causes wicked things to happen **2** [C, usu pl] very bad or harmful thing: *the* ~*s of alcohol* ▶ **evilly** /'iːvəli/ *adv*

evocative /ɪ'vɒkətɪv/ *adj* that brings memories, feelings, etc of sth: *an* ~ *picture*

evoke /ɪ'vəʊk/ *v* [T] produce a memory, feeling, etc

evolution /,iːvə'luːʃn/ *n* [U] (theory of) gradual development, of animals and plants from earlier simpler forms

evolve /ɪ'vɒlv/ *v* [I,T] (cause sth to) develop gradually

ewe /juː/ *n* [C] female sheep

exacerbate /ɪɡ'zæsəbeɪt/ *v* [T] (*fml*) make sth worse, esp a disease or problem

exact¹ /ɪɡ'zækt/ *adj* correct in every detail; precise: *the* ~ *time* ▶ **exactitude** /-tɪtjuːd/ *n* [U] (*fml*) correctness ▶ **exactly** *adv* **1** precisely **2** used to agree with what sb has just said ▶ **exactness** *n* [U]

exact² /ɪɡ'zækt/ *v* [T] (*fml*) demand and obtain sth from sb: *He* ~*ed a promise from her.* ▶ **exacting** *adj* requiring or demanding hard work and care

0━ **exaggerate** /ɪɡ'zædʒəreɪt/ *v* [I,T] make sth seem better, larger, etc than it really is ▶ **exaggeration** /ɪɡ,zædʒə'reɪʃn/ *n* [C,U]

0━ **exam** /ɪɡ'zæm/ *n* [C] short for EXAMINATION(1)

0━ **examination** /ɪɡ,zæmɪ'neɪʃn/ *n* **1** [C] (*fml*) formal test of knowledge or ability, esp at school: *take/sit/do an* ~ **2** [U,C] action of looking at or considering sth carefully

0━ **examine** /ɪɡ'zæmɪn/ *v* [T] **1** consider or study an idea, subject, etc carefully **2** look at sb/sth to see if there is anything wrong **3** question sb in order to test their knowledge or ability ▶ **examiner** *n* [C] person who tests knowledge or ability

0━ **example** /ɪɡ'zɑːmpl/ *n* [C] **1** fact, thing, etc that shows a general rule or represents a group: *a fine* ~ *of Norman architecture* **2** person or quality to be copied: *His bravery is an* ~ *to us all.* **[IDM] for example** (*abbr* eg) used to emphasize sth that explains or supports what you are saying:

There is a similar word in many languages, for ~ French and Italian. **make an example of sb** punish sb as a warning to others

exasperate /ɪgˈzæspəreɪt/ v [T] annoy sb very much ▸ **exasperation** /ɪgˌzæspəˈreɪʃn/ n [U]

excavate /ˈekskəveɪt/ v [T] make or uncover sth by digging in the ground: ~ *a buried city* ▸ **excavation** /ˌekskəˈveɪʃn/ n [C,U] ▸ **excavator** n [C] person or machine that excavates sth

exceed /ɪkˈsiːd/ v [T] (fml) **1** be greater than a particular number or amount **2** go beyond a limit or rule: ~ *the speed limit* (= drive faster than is allowed) ▸ **exceedingly** adv (fml) extremely

excel /ɪkˈsel/ v (-ll-) [I] ~ **at/in** be very good at sth

Excellency /ˈeksələnsi/ n [C] (pl -ies) title of some officials, eg ambassadors or governors

0— **excellent** /ˈeksələnt/ adj very good ▸ **excellence** /-ləns/ n [U] ▸ **excellently** adv

0— **except** /ɪkˈsept/ prep not including; apart from: *The shop is open every day* ~ *Sunday.* ◆ **except** v [T] (fml) (usu passive) not include sb/sth

0— **exception** /ɪkˈsepʃn/ n [C] person, thing, etc that is not included [IDM] **make an exception (of sb/sth)** treat sb/sth as a special case **take exception to sth** be annoyed by sth **with the exception of** except; not including ▸ **exceptional** /-ʃənl/ adj very good; unusual ▸ **exceptionally** /-ʃənəli/ adv

excerpt /ˈeksɜːpt/ n [C] piece taken from a book, film, etc

excess /ɪkˈses/ n **1** [sing] ~ **of** more than is necessary, reasonable or acceptable: *an increase in* ~ *of* (= more than) 2%. ◇ *drink to* ~ (= too much) **2** [usu sing] (US **deductible**) part of an insurance claim that a person has to pay while the insurance company pays the rest: *There is an* ~ *of £100 on each claim under this policy.* **3** (**excesses**) [pl] (fml) unacceptable, illegal or immoral behaviour ◆ **excess** /ˈekses/ adj in addition to the usual or legal amount: ~ *baggage* ▸ **excessive** adj too much ▸ **excessively** adv

0— **exchange** /ɪksˈtʃeɪndʒ/ v [T] give and receive sth in return: ~ *euros for dollars* ◆ **exchange** n **1** [C,U] act of exchanging sth **2** [C] (angry) conversation **3** [U] process of changing an amount of one currency for an equal value of another: *the* ~ *rate* ◇ *get a good rate of* ~ **4** [C] place where people meet

for business: *the London Stock E~* **5** = TELEPHONE EXCHANGE

exchequer /ɪksˈtʃekə(r)/ n (the Exchequer) [sing] (GB) government department in charge of public money: *the Chancellor of the E~* (= the minister at the head of this department)

excise /ˈeksaɪz/ n [U] tax on certain goods produced inside a country

0— **excite** /ɪkˈsaɪt/ v [T] **1** cause strong, esp pleasant feelings in sb **2** cause a particular feeling or response in sb ▸ **excitable** adj easily excited ▸ **excited** adj full of strong happy feelings ▸ **excitedly** adv ▸ **excitement** n [U,C] ▸ **exciting** adj causing great interest and excitement

exclaim /ɪkˈskleɪm/ v [I,T] (written) say sth suddenly or loudly, esp because of strong emotion or pain ▸ **exclamation** /ˌekskləˈmeɪʃn/ n [C] sound(s) or word(s) exclaimed ■ **excla'mation mark** (US **excla'mation point**) n [C] mark (!) written after an exclamation

0— **exclude** /ɪkˈskluːd/ v [T] **1** deliberately not include sb/sth; keep sb/sth out of sth **2** decide that sth is not possible: *Police have* ~*d theft as a possible motive.* ▸ **exclusion** /ɪkˈskluːʒn/ n [U,C]

exclusive /ɪkˈskluːsɪv/ adj **1** only to be used by or given to one particular person or group **2** (of a group) admitting only carefully chosen people **3** of a high quality and expensive and therefore not used by many people ◆ **exclusive** n [C] report published by only one newspaper ▸ **exclusively** adv only

excommunicate /ˌekskəˈmjuːnɪkeɪt/ v [T] exclude sb from the Christian church ▸ **excommunication** /ˌekskəˌmjuːnɪˈkeɪʃn/ n [U,C]

excrement /ˈekskrɪmənt/ n [U] (fml) solid waste matter from the body

excrete /ɪkˈskriːt/ v [T] pass solid waste matter from the body

excruciating /ɪkˈskruːʃieɪtɪŋ/ adj very painful ▸ **excruciatingly** adv

excursion /ɪkˈskɜːʃn/ n [C] short journey, esp for pleasure

0— **excuse** /ɪkˈskjuːs/ n [C] reason given to explain or defend your behaviour ▸ **excusable** /ɪkˈskjuːzəbl/ adj forgivable ◆ **excuse** /ɪkˈskjuːz/ v [T] **1** ~ **(for)** forgive sb for sth they have done **2** justify sb's behaviour: *Nothing can* ~ *such rudeness.* **3** ~ **(from)** set sb free from a duty [IDM] **excuse me 1** used as an apology when you interrupt sb, disagree, etc **2** (US) used to ask sb to repeat sth they said

execute /'eksɪkjuːt/ v [T] **1** kill sb, esp as a legal punishment **2** (fml) do a piece of work, perform a duty, etc: ~ a plan ▸ **execution** /ˌeksɪ'kjuːʃn/ n **1** [U,C] act of killing sb, esp as a legal punishment **2** [U] (fml) act of carrying out of a plan, doing a piece of work, etc ▸ **executioner** /ˌeksɪ'kjuːʃənə(r)/ n [C] official who executes criminals

0─ **executive** /ɪg'zekjətɪv/ adj concerned with managing, and putting laws and decisions into effect ● **executive** n **1** [C] person with an important job as a manager of a company or an organization **2** (the executive) [sing, with sing or pl verb] branch of government responsible for putting laws into effect

executor /ɪg'zekjətə(r)/ n [C] (tech) person chosen to carry out the instructions in sb's will

exemplify /ɪg'zemplɪfaɪ/ v (pt, pp **-ied**) [T] be or give an example of sth ▸ **exemplification** /ɪgˌzemplɪfɪ'keɪʃn/ n [U, C]

exempt /ɪg'zempt/ adj ~ (from) free from a duty or obligation ● **exempt** v [T] ~ (from) give sb's official permission not to do or pay sth ▸ **exemption** /ɪg'zempʃn/ n [U, C]

0─ **exercise** /'eksəsaɪz/ n **1** [U] physical or mental activity that keeps you healthy: Jogging is good ~. **2** [C] activity intended for training or testing sb: relaxation ~s ◊ maths ~s **3** [U] careful use or practice: the ~ of power ● **exercise** v **1** [T] use your power, authority or a right in order to achieve sth **2** [I,T] keep your body healthy by doing sports, etc ■ **'exercise book** n [C] small book for students to write in

exert /ɪg'zɜːt/ v [T] **1** use power or influence to affect sth/sb: ~ pressure on sb to do sth **2** ~ yourself make a big effort ▸ **exertion** /ɪg'zɜːʃn/ n [C,U]

exhale /eks'heɪl/ v [I,T] breathe out the air, smoke, etc in your lungs ▸ **exhalation** /ˌekshə'leɪʃn/ n [U, C]

exhaust /ɪg'zɔːst/ v [T] **1** make sb very tired **2** use all of sth ● **exhaust** n **1** [U] waste gases that come out of a vehicle, engine, etc **2** [C] (also **ex'haust pipe**) pipe through which exhaust gases come out ▸ **exhausted** adj very tired ▸ **exhaustion** /ɪg'zɔːstʃən/ n [U] ▸ **exhaustive** adj thorough

0─ **exhibit** /ɪg'zɪbɪt/ v **1** [I,T] show sth publicly for people to enjoy or to give them information **2** [T] (written) show clearly that you have a particular feeling, quality or ability ● **exhibit** n [C] **1** something shown in a museum, etc **2** something shown as evidence in a law court ▸ **exhibitor** n [C] person who shows their works or products to the public

0─ **exhibition** /ˌeksɪ'bɪʃn/ n **1** [C] (US exhibit) public show of pictures, etc **2** [C] (usu sing) act of showing a skill, a feeling or kind of behaviour ▸ **exhibitionism** /-ʃənɪzəm/ n [U] behaviour intended to attract attention to yourself ▸ **exhibitionist** n [C]

exhilarate /ɪg'zɪləreɪt/ v [T] (usu passive) make sb feel happy and excited ▸ **exhilaration** /-'reɪʃn/ n [U]

exhort /ɪg'zɔːt/ v [T] (fml) urge sb to do sth: ~ them to try harder ▸ **exhortation** /ˌegzɔː'teɪʃn/ n [C,U]

exile /'eksaɪl/ n **1** [U] being sent to live in a country that is not your own, esp for political reasons: live in ~ **2** [C] person who is sent away from his/her own country ● **exile** v [T] send sb into exile

0─ **exist** /ɪg'zɪst/ v [T] **1** be real; continue living ▸ **existence** n **1** [U] state of existing: believe in the ~ence of God **2** [C] way of life: a miserable ~ence ▸ **existent** adj (fml) living; real

exit /'eksɪt/ n [C] **1** way out of a public building or vehicle **2** act of leaving a place, esp of an actor from the stage ● **exit** v [I] **1** go out; leave a building, stage, etc **2** finish using a computer program

exonerate /ɪg'zɒnəreɪt/ v [T] (fml) free sb from blame ▸ **exoneration** /ɪgˌzɒnə'reɪʃn/ n [U]

exorbitant /ɪg'zɔːbɪtənt/ adj (of a price) much too high ▸ **exorbitantly** adv

exorcize (also **-ise**) /'eksɔːsaɪz/ v [T] drive out an evil spirit by prayer ▸ **exorcism** /'eksɔːsɪzəm/ n [U,C] ▸ **exorcist** n [C]

exotic /ɪg'zɒtɪk/ adj **1** from another country, esp a tropical one: ~ fruits **2** attractive or pleasing because unusual

0─ **expand** /ɪk'spænd/ v [I,T] become or make sth greater in size, number or importance: Metals ~ when heated. ◊ ~ a business [PV] **expand on/upon sth** give more information about sth

expanse /ɪk'spæns/ n [C] wide open area (of land, sea, etc)

expansion /ɪk'spænʃn/ n [U] action of expanding ▸ **expansionism** /ɪk'spænʃənɪzəm/ n [U] (usu disapprov) policy of expanding your land or business ▸ **expansionist** adj

expansive /ɪk'spænsɪv/ adj **1** covering a large area **2** (of people) willing to talk a lot

expatriate /ˌeks'pætriət/ (also infml **expat**) n [C], adj (person) living outside his/her own country

0─ **expect** /ɪk'spekt/ v [T] **1** think or believe that sth will happen [IDM] **be**

expecting a baby/child be pregnant ▶ **expectancy** n [U] state of expecting sth to happen, esp sth good ▶ **expectant** adj **1** expecting sth to happen, esp sth good **2** pregnant ▶ **expectation** /ˌekspekˈteɪʃn/ n [C,U] strong hope or belief that sth will happen

expedient /ɪkˈspiːdiənt/ adj, n [C] (fml) (action that is) useful for a particular purpose, but not always fair or moral ▶ **expediency** /-ənsi/ n [U]

expedition /ˌekspəˈdɪʃn/ n [C] **1** organized journey for a purpose, eg exploration **2** people who go on an expedition ■ **expe'ditionary force** n [C] group of soldiers sent to another country to fight

expel /ɪkˈspel/ v (-ll-) [T] **1** force sb to leave a school or an organization **2** (tech) force air or water out of a part of the body or a container

expend /ɪkˈspend/ v [T] (fml) spend or use a lot of money, time or energy ▶ **expendable** adj (fml) that may be got rid of or destroyed when no longer needed

expenditure /ɪkˈspendɪtʃə(r)/ n [U,C] **1** amount of money spent on sth **2** act of spending or using money, energy, etc

O━ **expense** /ɪkˈspens/ n [U,C] **1** thing that makes you spend money; amount of money spent on sth **2** (expenses) [pl] money used for a particular purpose: travelling ~s [IDM] **at sb's expense 1** paid for by sb **2** (of a joke) intended to make sb look foolish

O━ **expensive** /ɪkˈspensɪv/ adj costing a lot of money ▶ **expensively** adv

O━ **experience** /ɪkˈspɪəriəns/ n **1** [U] knowledge or skill gained by doing or seeing things: learn by ~ **2** [C] event or activity that affects you in some way: a happy ~ ● **experience** v [T] have an experience of sth; feel a particular emotion or physical sensation: ~ difficulty/pain ▶ **experienced** adj having a lot of experience (1)

O━ **experiment** /ɪkˈsperɪmənt/ n [C,U] (esp in science) test done carefully to find out what happens ● **experiment** v [I] do a scientific experiment; try or test new ideas, methods, etc ▶ **experimental** /ɪkˌsperɪˈmentl/ adj of or using experiments ▶ **experimentation** /ɪkˌsperɪmenˈteɪʃn/ n [U]

O━ **expert** /ˈekspɜːt/ n [C] ~ (at/in) person with special knowledge or skill ● **expert** adj ~ (at/in) having or involving great knowledge or skill ▶ **expertly** adv

expertise /ˌekspɜːˈtiːz/ n [U] special knowledge or skill in a particular subject or job

expire /ɪkˈspaɪə(r)/ v [I] **1** (of a document, an agreement, etc) be no longer valid: My passport has ~d. **2** (lit) die ▶ **expiry** /ɪkˈspaɪəri/ n [U] ending of the period when a contract, etc is valid

O━ **explain** /ɪkˈspleɪn/ v [I,T] make sth clear, give the meaning of sth **2** [T] give reasons for sth: ~ your behaviour [PV] **explain sth away** give reasons why sth is not your fault or not important ▶ **explanation** /ˌekspləˈneɪʃn/ n **1** [C] statement that explains sth **2** [U] act of explaining sth ▶ **explanatory** /ɪkˈsplænətri/ adj giving the reasons for sth; intended to explain sth

explicit /ɪkˈsplɪsɪt/ adj **1** (of statements) clear and easy to understand **2** (of people) saying sth clearly and openly ▶ **explicitly** adv ▶ **explicitness** n [U]

O━ **explode** /ɪkˈspləʊd/ v **1** [I,T] (cause sth to) burst loudly and violently, usu causing damage **2** [I] (of people) show strong feelings suddenly

exploit /ɪkˈsplɔɪt/ v [T] **1** treat sb selfishly and unfairly, for profit **2** use or develop sth, esp for profit: ~ oil reserves ● **exploit** /ˈeksplɔɪt/ n [C] brave or exciting act ▶ **exploitation** /ˌeksplɔɪˈteɪʃn/ n [U] use of sb or sth, often in an unfair way

O━ **explore** /ɪkˈsplɔː(r)/ v [T] **1** travel through a country to learn about it **2** examine sth carefully: ~ different possibilities ▶ **exploration** /ˌekspləˈreɪʃn/ n [U,C] ▶ **exploratory** /ɪkˈsplɒrətri/ adj done in order to find out sth ▶ **explorer** n [C] person who travels to unknown places to find out more about them

O━ **explosion** /ɪkˈspləʊʒn/ n [C] **1** sudden loud noise caused by sth exploding; act of causing sth to explode **2** sudden burst of anger **3** great and sudden increase: the population ~

explosive /ɪkˈspləʊsɪv/ n [C], adj (substance) that can explode: an ~ device (= a bomb) ▶ **explosively** adv

exponent /ɪkˈspəʊnənt/ n [C] person who supports and explains a belief, etc

O━ **export** /ɪkˈspɔːt/ v [I,T] **1** sell and send goods to another country **2** [T] (computing) send data to another program ● **export** /ˈekspɔːt/ n **1** [U] (business of) exporting goods **2** [C, usu pl] product sold to another country ▶ **exporter** n [C] person, company or country that exports goods

O━ **expose** /ɪkˈspəʊz/ v [T] **1** show sth that is usu hidden **2** tell the true

A B C D **E** F G H I J K L M N O P Q R S T U V W X Y Z

facts about sb/sth and show them/it to be immoral, illegal, etc **3** put sb/sth in a place or situation where they are unprotected against harm or danger **4** (in photography) allow light to reach film ▶ **exposure** /ɪkˈspəʊʒə(r)/ n [C]

expound /ɪkˈspaʊnd/ v [I, T] (*fml*) ~ (**on**) explain sth by talking about it in detail: ~ *a theory*

0─ **express**[1] /ɪkˈspres/ v [T] **1** make known a feeling, an opinion, etc by words or looks: ~ *an opinion* **2** ~ **yourself** speak or write clearly your thoughts or feelings

0─ **express**[2] /ɪkˈspres/ adj **1** going quickly: *an ~ letter* **2** (*fml*) clearly stated: *his ~ wish* ● **express** adv (*esp GB*) by express post: *send a letter ~* ● **express** (*also* ex'press train) n [C] fast train ▶ **expressly** adv definitely; clearly ● ex'**pressway** n [C] (*US*) = MOTORWAY

0─ **expression** /ɪkˈspreʃn/ n **1** [C, U] things that people say, write or do to show their feelings, opinions or ideas **2** [C] look on sb's face that shows a feeling: *an angry* ~ **3** [C] word or phrase: *a polite* ~ **4** [U] feeling shown when singing, acting, etc ▶ **expressionless** adj not showing your feelings, thoughts, etc

expressive /ɪkˈspresɪv/ adj showing your feelings or thoughts
▶ **expressively** adv
▶ **expressiveness** n [U]

expropriate /eksˈprəʊprieɪt/ v [T] **1** (*fml or law*) (of a government) take away private property for public use **2** (*fml*) take sb's property and use it without permission

expulsion /ɪkˈspʌlʃn/ n [C, U] (act of) expelling sb

exquisite /ɪkˈskwɪzɪt; ˈekskwɪzɪt/ adj very beautiful; skilfully made
▶ **exquisitely** adv

0─ **extend** /ɪkˈstend/ v **1** [T] make sth longer or larger: ~ *the house* **2** [I] cover a particular area, distance or length of time: *The park ~s to the river.* **3** [T] stretch out part of your body fully **4** [T] (*fml*) offer or give sth to sb: ~ *an invitation*

0─ **extension** /ɪkˈstenʃn/ n **1** [U, C] act of extending sth **2** [C] new part that is added to a building: *a new ~ to the hospital* **3** [C] extra telephone line inside a house or an organization

0─ **extensive** /ɪkˈstensɪv/ adj large in area or amount ▶ **extensively** adv

0─ **extent** /ɪkˈstent/ n [sing, U] **1** how large, important, serious, etc sth is: *the ~ of the damage* **2** degree: *to some* ~

extenuating /ɪkˈstenjueɪtɪŋ/ adj (*fml*) making bad behaviour less

serious by giving reasons for it: ~ *circumstances*

exterior /ɪkˈstɪəriə(r)/ n [C] outside surface of sth or appearance of sb ● **exterior** adj on the outside of sth; done outdoors

exterminate /ɪkˈstɜːmɪneɪt/ v [T] kill all the members of a group of people or animals ▶ **extermination** /ɪkˌstɜːmɪˈneɪʃn/ n [U]

external /ɪkˈstɜːnl/ adj outside: ~ *injuries* (= not inside the body) ▶ **externally** /ɪkˈstɜːnəli/ adv

extinct /ɪkˈstɪŋkt/ adj **1** (of a kind of animal) no longer existing **2** (of a volcano) no longer active ▶ **extinction** /ɪkˈstɪŋkʃn/ n [U] situation in which a plant, animal, etc stops existing

extinguish /ɪkˈstɪŋgwɪʃ/ v [T] (*fml*) **1** cause a fire, etc to stop burning **2** destroy hope, love, etc ▶ **extinguisher** n = FIRE EXTINGUISHER (FIRE[1])

extol /ɪkˈstəʊl/ v (-ll-) [T] (*fml*) praise sb/sth greatly

extort /ɪkˈstɔːt/ v [T] obtain sth from sb using violence, threats, etc ▶ **extortion** /ɪkˈstɔːʃn/ n [U, C] ▶ **extortionate** /ɪkˈstɔːʃənət/ adj (*disapprov*) (of prices, etc) much too high

0─ **extra** /ˈekstrə/ adj more than usual or necessary; additional: ~ *pay* ● **extra** adv **1** more than usually: *an* ~ *strong box* **2** in addition: *price £1.75, postage* ~ ● **extra** n [C] **1** additional thing **2** person employed for a small part in a film

extract /ɪkˈstrækt/ v [T] **1** remove or obtain a substance from sth, eg by using an industrial process **2** obtain sth by force: ~ *money from sb* **3** pull sth out, esp with effort ● **extract** /ˈekstrækt/ n [C] **1** short part of a book, film, etc **2** substance obtained by extracting: *beef* ~ ▶ **extraction** /ɪkˈstrækʃn/ n **1** [U, C] act of removing or obtaining sth from sth else: *the* ~ *ion of information/a tooth* **2** [U] having a particular family origin: *of French* ~ *ion*

extra-curricular /ˌekstrə kəˈrɪkjələ(r)/ adj outside the regular course of work at a school or college

extradite /ˈekstrədaɪt/ v [T] send sb accused of a crime to the country where the crime was said to have been committed ▶ **extradition** /ˌekstrəˈdɪʃn/ n [U, C]

extramarital /ˌekstrəˈmærɪtl/ adj happening outside marriage: *an* ~ *affair*

extraneous /ɪkˈstreɪniəs/ adj (*fml*) not directly connected with what is being dealt with

0─ **extraordinary** /ɪkˈstrɔːdnri/ adj **1** beyond what is usual or ordinary;

remarkable: ~ **beauty 2** very strange ▸ **extraordinarily** adv

extrapolate /ɪkˈstræpəleɪt/ v [I,T] (fml) estimate sth unknown from facts that are already known ▸ **extrapolation** /ɪkˌstræpəˈleɪʃn/ n [U]

extraterrestrial /ˌekstrətəˈrestriəl/ adj of or from outside the planet Earth

extravagant /ɪkˈstrævəɡənt/ adj **1** wasting money, etc **2** (of ideas or behaviour) impressive but not reasonable ▸ **extravagance** /-ɡəns/ n [U,C] ▸ **extravagantly** adv

extravaganza /ɪkˌstrævəˈɡænzə/ n [C] large expensive and impressive entertainment

0ᴍ **extreme** /ɪkˈstriːm/ adj **1** very great in degree: in ~ pain **2** not ordinary or usual; serious or severe: ~ sports (= dangerous sports, eg bungee jumping) **3** far from what people consider normal; not moderate: ~ opinions **4** furthest possible: the ~ north of the country ● **extreme** n [C] **1** opposite feeling or condition: Love and hate are ~s. **2** greatest degree of sth: the ~s of heat in the desert ▸ **extremely** adv very ■ ex,treme 'sports n [pl] sports that are extremely exciting to do and often dangerous, for example skydiving and bungee jumping

extremist /ɪkˈstriːmɪst/ n [C], adj (disapprov) (a person) holding extreme (3) political opinions

extremity /ɪkˈstreməti/ n (pl -ies) **1** [C] furthest point, end or limit of sth **2** [C,U] degree to which a situation, feeling, action, etc is extreme **3** extremities [pl] (fml) parts of your body furthest from the centre, esp the hands and feet

extricate /ˈekstrɪkeɪt/ v [T] ~ (from) (enable sb to) escape from a difficult situation

extrovert /ˈekstrəvɜːt/ n [C] lively cheerful person

exuberant /ɪɡˈzjuːbərənt/ adj full of energy and excitement; lively ▸ **exuberance** /-rəns/ n [U] ▸ **exuberantly** adv

exude /ɪɡˈzjuːd/ v (fml) **1** [T] express a feeling strongly: ~ happiness **2** [I,T] (of drops of liquid, etc) (cause sth to) come out slowly

exult /ɪɡˈzʌlt/ v [I] (fml) show great happiness ▸ **exultant** adj ▸ **exultation** /ˌeɡzʌlˈteɪʃn/ n [U]

0ᴍ **eye** /aɪ/ n [C] **1** either of the two organs of sight **2** [C, usu sing] a particular way of seeing sth: She can do no wrong in his ~s. **3** [C] hole in a needle **4** [C] calm area in the centre of a storm [IDM] **be all eyes** be watching with all eyes all your attention **have an eye for sth** be able to judge if things look attractive, valuable, etc: have a good ~ for detail

---

in the eyes of the law, world, etc according to the law, most people in the world, etc **make eyes at sb | give sb the eye** look at sb in a way that shows you find them attractive **with your eyes open** fully aware of what you are doing ● **eye** n [T] look at sb/ sth carefully ■ **eyeball** n [C] the whole of the eye, including the part inside the head that cannot be seen ■ **eyebrow** n [C] line of hair above each eye ■ **eyelash** (also **lash**) n [C] one of the hairs growing on the edge of the eyelid ■ **eyelid** n [C] either of two folds of skin that cover the eyes when they close ■ **eye-opener** n [usu sing] surprising or revealing event or experience ■ **eyesight** n [U] ability to see ■ **eyesore** n [C] something that is ugly, eg a building ■ **eyewitness** n = WITNESS(1)

Ff

F, f /ef/ n [C,U] (pl **F's, f's** /efs/) the sixth letter of the English alphabet

F abbr Fahrenheit

fable /ˈfeɪbl/ n **1** [C] traditional short story, esp with animals as characters, that teaches a moral lesson **2** [U,C] statement or account of sth that is not true ▸ **fabled** adj famous and often talked about

fabric /ˈfæbrɪk/ n **1** [C,U] woven cloth **2** (the fabric (of sth)) [sing] the basic structure of sth: the ~ of society/a building

fabricate /ˈfæbrɪkeɪt/ v [T] **1** invent a false story **2** (tech) make or manufacture sth ▸ **fabrication** /ˌfæbrɪˈkeɪʃn/ n [C,U]

fabulous /ˈfæbjələs/ adj **1** (infml) wonderful **2** (written) very great: ~ wealth ▸ **fabulously** adv extremely: ~ly rich

facade /fəˈsɑːd/ n [C] **1** front of a building **2** false appearance: behind a ~ of respectability

0ᴍ **face** /feɪs/ n [C] **1** front part of the head **2** expression shown on sb's face **3** surface or (front) side of sth: the north ~ of the mountain [IDM] **face to face (with sb)** close to and looking at sb **face to face with sb** in a situation where you have to accept that sth is true and deal with it **lose face** → LOSE **make/pull faces/a face (at sb)** produce an expression on your face to show your dislike of sb/ sth or to make sb laugh **to sb's face** openly and directly in sb's presence ● **face** v [I,T] **1** be opposite sb/sth; have or turn the face towards sb/sth **2** [T] accept and deal with a difficult situation: ~ danger ◊ the problems that ~ the government **3** [T] cover a

---

surface with another material [IDM]
face the music (*infml*) accept
criticism or punishment for sth you
have done [PV] **face up to sth** accept
and deal with sth bravely
■ **'facecloth** *n* [C] (*GB*) =
FLANNEL(2) ▶ **faceless** *adj* with no
clear character or identity ■ **'facelift**
n [C] **1** medical operation performed
to make the face look younger
2 improvement in the appearance
of a building, etc ■ **,face 'value** *n*
[U,sing] value shown on a coin or
postage stamp [IDM] **take sth at face
value** believe that sth is what it
appears to be

facet /ˈfæsɪt/ *n* [C] **1** particular part or
aspect of sth **2** any of the many sides
of a cut stone or jewel

facetious /fəˈsiːʃəs/ *adj* trying to be
amusing, esp cleverly or at the
wrong time ▶ **facetiously** *adv*

facial /ˈfeɪʃl/ *adj* of or for the face

facile /ˈfæsaɪl/ *adj* (*disapprov*)
produced easily but without careful
thought: ~ *comments*

0➔ **facilitate** /fəˈsɪlɪteɪt/ *v* [T] (*fml*) make
sth possible or easier

0➔ **facility** /fəˈsɪləti/ *n* **1** (**facilities**)
[pl] buildings, services and
equipment that are provided for a
particular purpose: *sports facilities*
2 [C] special feature of a
machine, service, etc: *a bank
account with an overdraft* ~
3 [sing,U] natural ability to do sth
easily

facsimile /fækˈsɪməli/ *n* **1** [C] exact
copy of sth **2** [C,U] (*fml*) = FAX

0➔ **fact** /fækt/ *n* **1** [sing] ~ (**that ...**)
used to refer to a particular situation
that exists: *Despite the* ~ *that he felt
ill, he went to work.* **2** [C] thing that is
known to be true, esp when it can be
proved **3** [U] truth; reality [IDM] **the
facts of life** details of sex and how
babies are born **in (actual) fact**
1 used to give extra details about sth
2 really

0➔ **faction** /ˈfækʃn/ *n* [C] small group in
a larger group, esp in politics

0➔ **factor** /ˈfæktə(r)/ *n* **1** fact,
circumstance, etc that helps to
produce a result: *a major* ~ *in the
decision*

0➔ **factory** /ˈfæktri, -təri/ *n* [C] (pl
-ies) building(s) where goods are
made

factual /ˈfæktʃuəl/ *adj* based on or
containing facts ▶ **factually** *adv*

faculty /ˈfæklti/ *n* (pl **-ies**) **1** [usu
pl] natural ability of the body or
mind: *mental faculties* **2** university
department **3** [with sing or pl verb]
all the teachers in a faculty

fade /feɪd/ *v* **1** [I,T] (cause sth to)
become paler and less bright **2** [I]
~ (**away**) disappear gradually [PV]

fade away (of people) become
weaker; die

faeces (*US* **feces**) /ˈfiːsiːz/ *n* [pl] (*fml*)
solid waste matter passed from the
bowels

fag /fæg/ *n* **1** [C] (*GB*, *infml*) =
CIGARETTE **2** [C] (*US*) (*also* **faggot**)
(⚠, *sl*) offensive word for a male
homosexual **3** [sing] (*GB*)
something that is boring and tiring
to do ▶ **fagged out** /ˌfægd ˈaʊt/ *adj*
(*GB*, *spoken*) very tired

faggot (*US* **fagot**) /ˈfægət/ *n* [C]
1 (*GB*) ball of chopped meat
2 bundle of sticks for burning

Fahrenheit /ˈfærənhaɪt/ *adj*, *n* [U]
(*abbr* F) (of or using a) temperature
scale in which water freezes at 32°
and boils at 212°

0➔ **fail** /feɪl/ *v* **1** [I,T] be unsuccessful:
I'm going to ~ *the exam.* **2** [I] not do
sth: ~ *to keep an appointment* **3** [T]
decide that sb/sth has not passed a
test or an exam **4** [I] (of health,
eyesight, etc) become weak **5** [I,T]
not be enough for sb/sth;
disappoint sb: *The crops* ~*ed because
of drought.* ◇ *He felt he had* ~*ed his
family.* **6** [I] become bankrupt: *The
company* ~*ed.* ● **fail** *n* [C] failure in
an examination [IDM] **without fail**
definitely

failing /ˈfeɪlɪŋ/ *n* **1** [C] fault or
weakness in sb/sth ● **failing** *prep*
used to make a suggestion that
could be considered if the one
mentioned first is not possible

0➔ **failure** /ˈfeɪljə(r)/ *n* **1** [U] lack of
success **2** [C] person or thing that
fails **3** [C,U] (instance of) not doing
sth: *His* ~ *to help us was
disappointing.* **4** [U,C] (instance of)
not operating normally: *engine/
heart* ~

0➔ **faint** /feɪnt/ *adj* **1** that cannot be
clearly seen, heard or smelt:
~ *sounds* **2** very small or weak;
possible but unlikely: *a* ~ *hope* **3** (of
people) about to lose consciousness
[IDM] **not have the faintest/foggiest
(idea)** (*infml*) not knowing anything at
all about sth: *I haven't got the* ~*est
idea where he is.* ● **faint** *v* [I] become
unconscious, usually because of the
heat, a shock, etc ● **faint** *n* [sing] act
of fainting ■ **faint-'hearted** *adj* not
brave or confident ▶ **faintly** *adv*
▶ **faintness** *n* [U]

0➔ **fair¹** /feə(r)/ *adj* **1** acceptable
and appropriate; just: *a* ~ *decision*
2 quite good: *a* ~ *chance of success*
3 (of the weather) dry and fine **4** (of
the skin or hair) light in colour: *a*
~-*haired boy* [IDM] **fair play** fact of
acting honestly and according to
the rules ● **fair** *adv* according to the
rules; in a way that is considered to
be acceptable [IDM] **fair enough** (*esp
GB*, *spoken*) used to say that an idea,
etc seems reasonable ▶ **fairly** *adv*
1 moderately: ~*ly easy* **2** honestly

► **fairness** *n* [U] ■ **fair-'trade** *adj* involving trade which supports producers in developing countries with fair prices and fair pay

fair² /feə(r)/ *n* [C] **1** (*also* **'funfair**) outdoor entertainment with machines to ride on, games, shows, etc **2** (*GB*) = FÊTE **3** large exhibition of goods: *a world trade ~* ◇ *a book ~* **4** (*GB*) (in the past) market at which animals were sold ■ **'fairground** *n* [C] open area where funfairs are held

fairy /'feəri/ *n* [C] (*pl* -ies) small imaginary creature with magical powers ■ **'fairy tale** | **'fairy story** *n* [C] **1** story about fairies, magic, etc usu for children **2** untrue story; lie

fait accompli /ˌfeɪt əˈkɒmpliː/ *n* [C] (from French) something that has already happened and cannot be changed

0—► **faith** /feɪθ/ *n* **1** [U] ~ (**in**) strong trust and confidence in sb/sth **2** [U, sing] strong religious belief **3** [C] religion: *the Muslim ~* **IDM in good faith** with honest intentions

0—► **faithful** /'feɪθfl/ *adj* **1** ~ (**to**) loyal to sb/sth **2** accurate: *a ~ description* ► **the faithful** *n* [pl] true believers in a religion or a political party ► **faithfully** /'feɪθfəli/ *adv* **IDM** **Yours faithfully** (*GB*) used to end a formal letter before you sign your name ► **faithfulness** *n* [U]

faithless /'feɪθləs/ *adj* not loyal; false

fake /feɪk/ *adj* **1** made to look like sth else: *a ~ fur jacket* ● **fake** *n* [C] **1** object, eg a work of art, made to appear genuine **2** person who pretends to be what they are not in order to deceive ● **fake** *v* [T] **1** make sth false appear to be genuine **2** pretend to have a particular feeling, illness, etc

falcon /'fɔːlkən/ *n* [C] small bird that can be trained to hunt and kill other birds and animals

0—► **fall¹** /fɔːl/ *v* (*pt* **fell** /fel/ *pp* **-en** /'fɔːlən/) [I] **1** drop down from a higher level to a lower level: *Leaves ~ in autumn.* ◇ *~ off a ladder* **2** suddenly stop standing: *I fell over and hurt my knee.* **3** hang down: *Her hair ~s over her shoulders.* **4** (of land) slope downwards **5** decrease in amount, number or strength: *The temperature fell sharply.* **6** be captured or defeated; die in battle **7** pass into the state that is mentioned; become sth: *~ asleep* ◇ *~ into disuse* **8** happen or occur at a date: *Christmas ~s on a Friday this year.* **IDM** **fall flat** (eg of a joke or act) fail to produce the effect that was wanted **fall foul of sb/sth** get into trouble with sb because of doing sth wrong or illegal **fall in love with sb** feel a sudden strong attraction for sb **fall on your feet** → FOOT **fall short of sth** fail to reach the necessary standard [PV] **fall apart**

break into pieces **fall back** retreat **fall back on sth** use sth, when other things have been tried without success **fall behind (sb/sth)** fail to keep level with sb/sth **fall behind with sth** not do or pay sth at the right time: *He's ~en behind with his school work.* **fall for sb** (*infml*) be attracted to sb **fall for sth** (*infml*) be tricked into believing sth **fall in** collapse: *The roof fell in.* **fall off** become less: *Attendance has ~en off.* **fall on/upon sb/sth** attack or take hold of sb/sth with great enthusiasm **fall out (with sb)** (*GB*) quarrel with sb **fall through** fail to be completed: *The business deal fell through.*

0—► **fall²** /fɔːl/ *n* [C] **1** act of falling **2** amount of sth that has fallen: *a heavy ~ of snow* **3** distance through which sth/sb falls **4** (*also* **falls** [pl]) waterfall **5** (*US*) = AUTUMN

fallacy /'fæləsi/ *n* [C, U] (*pl* -ies) false belief or argument ► **fallacious** /fə'leɪʃəs/ *adj* (*fml*) wrong; based on a false idea

fallen *pp* of FALL¹

fallible /'fæləbl/ *adj* liable to make mistakes ► **fallibility** /-'bɪləti/ *n* [U]

fallout /'fɔːlaʊt/ *n* [U] radioactive dust in the air after a nuclear explosion

fallow /'fæləʊ/ *adj* (of farm land) not used for growing crops, esp to improve the quality of the land

0—► **false** /fɔːls/ *adj* **1** wrong; incorrect **2** not real; artificial: *~ teeth* **3** deceitful; disloyal: *a ~ friend* **IDM** **by/on/under false pretences** by pretending to be sb else in order to gain an advantage for yourself ■ **false a'larm** *n* [C] warning about a danger that does not happen ► **falsehood** *n* [C, U] untrue statement; lie; lying ► **falsely** *adv* ■ **false 'start** **1** unsuccessful beginning to sth **2** (in a race) start before the signal has been given

falsify /'fɔːlsɪfaɪ/ *v* (*pt, pp* -**ied**) [T] alter a document, etc so it is untrue ► **falsification** /ˌfɔːlsɪfɪ'keɪʃn/ *n* [C, U]

falsity /'fɔːlsəti/ *n* (*pl* -ies) [U] state of not being true or genuine

falter /'fɔːltə(r)/ *v* [I] **1** become weaker or less effective **2** walk or speak in a way that shows you are not confident ► **falteringly** *adv*

0—► **fame** /feɪm/ *n* [U] state of being well known ► **famed** *adj* famous

0—► **familiar** /fə'mɪliə(r)/ *adj* **1** ~ (**to**) well known to sb; often seen or heard **2** ~ (**with**) having a good knowledge of sth **3** close and (too) friendly ► **familiarity** /fəˌmɪli'ærəti/ *n* [C, U] (*pl* -ies) ► **familiarly** *adv*

A B C D E **F** G H I J K L M N O P Q R S T U V W X Y Z

familiarize (also **-ise**) /fə'mɪliəraɪz/ v [T] **yourself/sb (with sth)** make yourself/sb well informed about sth in order to understand it

0⟶ **family** /'fæməli/ n (pl **-ies**) **1** [C, with sing or pl verb] group consisting of one or two parents and their children **2** [C, with sing or pl verb, U] group consisting of one or two parents, their children and close relations **3** [C, with sing or pl verb] all the people descended from the same ancestor: *This painting has been in our ~ for generations.* **4** [C, with sing or pl verb, U] couple's or person's children: *start a ~ (=* have children) **5** [C] group of related animals or plants: *the cat ~* ■ **IDM** **run in the family** be a common feature in a particular family: *Red hair runs in the ~.* ■ **family 'planning** n [U] controlling the number of children in a family by using contraception ■ **family 'tree** n [C] chart showing the relationship of family members over a long period of time

famine /'fæmɪn/ n [C, U] serious shortage of food

famished /'fæmɪʃt/ adj (infml) very hungry

0⟶ **famous** /'feɪməs/ adj known about by many people ▸ **famously** adv in a way that is famous

0⟶ **fan** /fæn/ n [C] **1** object for making a current of air, eg to cool a room **2** very keen supporter: *football ~s* ◇ ~ *mail* (= letters from fans to a famous person) ■ **fan** v (**-nn-**) [T] **1** send a current of air onto sb/sth [PV] **fan out** spread out from a central point: *The troops ~ned out across the field.* ■ **fan belt** n [C] rubber belt used to turn the fan that cools a car engine

fanatic /fə'nætɪk/ n [C] **1** (infml) person who is very enthusiastic about sth: *a fitness ~* **2** (disapprov) person holding extreme or dangerous opinions: *a religious ~* ▸ **fanatical** /-kl/ adj ▸ **fanatically** /-kli/ adv ▸ **fanaticism** /fə'nætɪsɪzəm/ n [U]

fanciful /'fænsɪfl/ adj (written) **1** based on imagination, not reason **2** (of things) unusually decorated ▸ **fancifully** /-fəli/ adv

0⟶ **fancy** /'fænsi/ v (pt, pp **-ied**) [T] **1** (GB, infml) want sth or want to do sth: *I ~ going out tonight.* **2** (infml) find sb sexually attractive: *I think she fancies you.* **3** (GB, infml) ~ **yourself** (as) think you are very popular, intelligent, etc; believe that you are sth: *They ~ themselves as serious actors.* **4** think or believe ● **fancy** n (pl **-ies**) **1** [C, U] something that you imagine; your imagination **2** [sing] liking or desire: *a ~ for some cake* ■ **IDM** **catch/take sb's fancy** please or

attract sb **take a fancy to sb/sth** start liking sb/sth

0⟶ **fancy²** /'fænsi/ adj (**-ier, -iest**) **1** unusually complicated, often in an unnecessary way: *a kitchen full of ~ gadgets* **2** decorated and colourful; not plain: *~ cakes* ■ **fancy 'dress** n [U] (GB) clothes worn for a party to make you appear to be a different character: *guests in ~ dress*

fanfare /'fænfeə(r)/ n [C] short piece of music played on trumpets

fang /fæŋ/ n [C] long sharp tooth

fanny /'fæni/ n [C] (pl **-ies**) **1** (GB, △, sl) female sex organs **2** (sl, esp US) person's bottom

fantasize (also **-ise**) /'fæntəsaɪz/ v [I, T] ~ **(about)** imagine that you are doing sth you would like to do

fantastic /fæn'tæstɪk/ adj **1** (infml) wonderful: *a ~ party* **2** (infml) very large **3** strange and imaginative **4** (of ideas) not practical ▸ **fantastically** /-kli/ adv

fantasy /'fæntəsi/ n [C, U] (pl **-ies**) (pleasant idea or dream of the) imagination: *childhood ~*

0⟶ **far¹** /fɑː(r)/ adv (**~ther** /'fɑːðə(r)/ or **further** /'fɜːðə(r)/ or **~thest** /'fɑːðɪst/ or **furthest** /'fɜːðɪst/) **1** at or to a great distance: *How~ is it to London?* **2** very much; to a great degree: *fallen ~ behind with his work* ◇ ~ *richer* **3** used to talk about how much progress has been made: *I got as ~ as chapter 4.* ■ **IDM** **as/so far as** | **in so far as** to the degree that: *As ~ as I know, they're still coming.* **as/so far as I am concerned** used to give your personal opinion on sth: *As ~ as I'm concerned, you can do what you like.* **far from sth/doing sth** almost the opposite of sth: *F~ from hating the music, I love it!* ◇ *The work is ~ from easy* (= it is very difficult). **go far** | **go a long way** (of people) be very successful in the future **go too far** behave in a way that is beyond reasonable limits **not go far** (of money) not be enough to buy many things **2** (of a supply of sth) not be enough **so far** | **thus far** until now ■ **faraway** /ˌ/ adj **1** distant **2** (of a look in sb's eyes) dreamy ■ **far-'fetched** adj difficult to believe ■ **far-off** /ˌ/ adj long distance away ■ **far-'reaching** adj having a wide influence: *He made a ~-reaching decision.* ■ **far-'sighted** adj seeing what may happen in the future and so making wise plans

0⟶ **far²** /fɑː(r)/ adj (**~ther** /'fɑːðə(r)/ or **further** /'fɜːðə(r)/ or **~thest** /'fɑːðɪst/ or **furthest** /'fɜːðɪst/) **1** more distant; at the furthest point in a particular direction: *the ~ end of the street* ◇ *on the ~ right of the party* (= with extreme right-wing political views) **2** (old-fash or lit) distant: *a ~ country* ■ **the Far East** n [sing] China, Japan and other countries of E and SE Asia

farce /fɑːs/ n **1** [C,U] funny play for the theatre, with unlikely ridiculous situations; this type of writing or performance **2** [C] series of actual ridiculous events: *The trial was a complete ~.* ▶ **farcical** adj

fare /feə(r)/ n [C,U] money charged for a journey by bus, train, etc: *bus ~s* ● **fare** v [I] (*fml*) progress; get on: *~ well/badly*

farewell /ˌfeəˈwel/ exclam, n [C] (*old-fash* or *fml*) goodbye

0━ **farm** /fɑːm/ n **1** area of land and buildings for growing crops and raising animals ● **farm** v [I,T] use land for growing crops and raising animals ■ **farmer** n [C] person who owns or manages a farm ■ **'farmers' market** n [C] place where farmers sell food directly to the public ■ **farmhand** n [C] person who works for a farmer ■ **'farmhouse** n [C] main house on a farm, where the farmer lives ■ **farmyard** n [C] area surrounded by farm buildings

fart /fɑːt/ v [I] (△, *sl*) let air from the bowels out through the anus ● **fart** n [C] (△, *sl*) **1** act of letting air out through the anus **2** unpleasant, boring or stupid person

farther, farthest adv, adj → FAR

fascinate /ˈfæsɪneɪt/ v [T] attract or interest sb greatly ▶ **fascinating** adj ▶ **fascination** /ˌfæsɪˈneɪʃn/ n [U, C]

fascism (*also* **Fascism**) /ˈfæʃɪzəm/ n [U] extreme right-wing political system ▶ **fascist** (*also* **Fascist**) adj, n [C]

0━ **fashion** /ˈfæʃn/ n **1** [U,C] popular style of clothes, hair, etc at a particular time: *Flared trousers are in ~ again.* ◇ *Some styles never go out of ~.* **2** [C] popular way of behaving, doing sth, etc **3** [U] business of making and selling clothes: *a ~ designer/show* [IDM] **after a fashion** not very well ● **fashion** v [T] make or shape sth, esp with your hands

0━ **fashionable** /ˈfæʃnəbl/ adj **1** following a style that is popular at a particular time **2** used by many (*esp rich*) people: *a ~ restaurant* ▶ **fashionably** adv

0━ **fast**[1] /fɑːst/ adj **1** quick: ~ *cars* **2** (of a watch or clock) showing a time later than the true time **3** (of a boat, etc) firmly fixed **4** (of colours) not likely to fade or spread when washed ● **fast** adv **1** quickly; without delay **2** firmly; completely: *She was ~ asleep* (= sleeping deeply). [IDM] **stand fast** → STAND▲ ■ **ˌfast 'food** n [U] hot food, that is served very quickly in special restaurants and is often taken away to be eaten in the street

0━ **fast**[2] /fɑːst/ v [I] go without food, esp for religious reasons ● **fast** n [C] period of fasting

fatten

0━ **fasten** /ˈfɑːsn/ v [I,T] become or make sth joined together, closed or fixed: ~ *your seat belt* [PV] **fasten on(to) sb/sth** choose or follow sb/sth in a determined way ▶ **fastener** (*also* **fastening**) n [C] device, eg a button or a zip, that fasten things together

fastidious /fæˈstɪdiəs/ adj difficult to please; not liking things to be dirty or untidy ▶ **fastidiously** adv

0━ **fat**[1] /fæt/ adj (**~ter, ~test**) **1** (of sb's body) large; weighing too much **2** thick or wide **3** (*infml*) large in quantity: ~ *profits* ▶ **fatness** n [U]

0━ **fat**[2] /fæt/ n **1** [U] substance in the body of animals and humans, stored under the skin **2** [C,U] substance from animals or plants used in cooking

fatal /ˈfeɪtl/ adj **1** causing or ending in death: *a ~ accident* **2** causing disaster: *a ~ mistake* ▶ **fatally** adv

fatalism /ˈfeɪtəlɪzəm/ n [U] belief that events are controlled by fate (2) ▶ **fatalist** n [C]

fatality /fəˈtæləti/ n (pl -**ies**) **1** [C] death caused by accident or violence **2** [U] fact that a particular disease will end in death: *the ~ rate of this type of cancer* **3** [U] belief that we have no control over what happens to us

fate /feɪt/ n **1** [C] person's future, esp death: *The ~ of the three men is unknown.* **2** [U] power believed to control all events ▶ **fateful** adj important: *that ~ day*

0━ **father** /ˈfɑːðə(r)/ n [C] **1** male parent n (**fathers**) [pl] (*lit*) person's ancestors **2** leader: *the ~ of modern British sculpture* ■ (**Father**) title of a priest **3** (**Father**) God ● **father** v [T] be the father of sb ■ **ˌFather 'Christmas** n [C] old man who is believed by children to bring presents at Christmas ■ **ˌfather-in-law** n [C] (pl **~s-in-law**) father of your wife or husband ■ **fatherland** n [C] country in which your were born ▶ **fatherly** adj or like a father

fathom /ˈfæðəm/ n [C] measurement of the depth of water (1.8 metres or 6 feet) ● **fathom** v [T] ~ (**out**) understand sth fully ▶ **fathomless** adj too deep to measure or understand

fatigue /fəˈtiːɡ/ n **1** [U] great tiredness **2** [U] weakness in metals, etc caused by constant stress **3** (**fatigues**) [pl] clothes worn by soldiers when cleaning, cooking, etc ● **fatigue** v [T] (*fml*) make (sb) very tired

fatten /ˈfætn/ v [I,T] become or make sb/sth fatter, esp an animal before killing it for food

fatty

fatty /ˈfæti/ adj (-ier, -iest) containing a lot of fat; consisting of fat ▸ **fatty** n [C] (pl **-ies**) (infml, disapprov) fat person

fatuous /ˈfætʃuəs/ adj silly: ~ remarks ▸ **fatuously** adv

○━ **faucet** /ˈfɔːsɪt/ n [C] (US) = TAP(1)

○━ **fault** /fɔːlt/ n **1** [sing] responsibility for sth wrong that has happened or been done: It's my ~. ◇ The owners are at ~ (= responsible) for this. **2** [C] mistake or imperfection: an electrical ~ **3** [C] crack in the surface of the earth ● **fault** v [T] find a weakness in sb/ sth: I cannot ~ her performance. ▸ **faultless** adj perfect ▸ **faultlessly** adv ▸ **faulty** adj (esp of a machine) not working properly

fauna /ˈfɔːnə/ n [U] all the animals living in an area or a period of history

faux pas /ˌfəʊ ˈpɑː/ n (pl **faux pas** /-ˈpɑːz/) (from French) embarrassing mistake

○━ **favour** (US **-or**) /ˈfeɪvə(r)/ n **1** [C] thing you do to help sb: Do me a ~ and lend me your pen. **2** [U] approval or support for sb/sth: She's back in ~ with the boss again (= the boss likes her again). **3** [U] treatment that is generous to one person or group in a way that seems unfair to others: show ~ to sb [IDM] in favour (of sb/ sth) supporting sb/sth in sb's favour to the advantage of sb ● **favour** v [T] **1** support sb/sth **2** treat sb more generously than others ▸ **favourable** adj **1** getting or showing approval **2** helpful ▸ **favourably** adv

○━ **favourite** (US **favor-**) /ˈfeɪvərɪt/ n [C] **1** person or thing liked more than others **2** horse, competitor, team, etc expected to win a race ● **favourite** adj liked more than any other ▸ **favouritism** /ˈfeɪvərɪtɪzəm/ n [U] practice of being unfairly generous to one person or group

fawn /fɔːn/ n **1** [C] young deer **2** [U] light yellowish-brown colour ● **fawn** adj light yellowish-brown in colour ● **fawn** v [PV] **fawn on/over sb** (disapprov) try to gain sb's favour by pretending to like them

fax /fæks/ n **1** [C] (also **'fax machine**) machine that sends and receives documents electronically along telephone wires and then prints them **2** [U] system for sending documents using a fax machine: What's your ~ number? **3** [C] letter or message sent by fax ● **fax** v [T] send sb a document, etc by fax

FBI /ˌef biː ˈaɪ/ abbr (US) Federal Bureau of Investigation

○━ **fear** /fɪə(r)/ n [C,U] bad feeling you have when you are in danger, when sth bad might happen or

when sb/sth frightens you [IDM] in fear of your life afraid that you might be killed ● **fear** v [T] **1** be afraid of sb/sth **2** feel that sth bad might have happened or will happen in the future [IDM] fear for sb/sth be worried about sb/sth: We began to ~ for his safety. ▸ **fearful** adj **1** (fml) nervous and afraid **2** (fml) terrible and frightening ▸ **fearless** adj not afraid ▸ **fearlessly** adv

feasible /ˈfiːzəbl/ adj that can be done ▸ **feasibility** /ˌfiːzəˈbɪləti/ n [U]

feast /fiːst/ n [C] **1** large or special meal, esp for a lot of people **2** religious festival **3** thing that brings great pleasure ● **feast** v [I] ~ (on) eat a lot of food, with great enjoyment [IDM] feast your eyes on sth look at sth with pleasure

feat /fiːt/ n [C] action that needs skill, strength or courage

○━ **feather** /ˈfeðə(r)/ n [C] one of the many light parts that cover a bird's body: a ~ pillow (= one containing feathers) [IDM] a feather in your cap an action that you can be proud of ● **feather** v [IDM] feather your (own) nest make yourself richer or more comfortable ▸ ˌ**feather-bed** n [C] mattress filled with feathers ▸ **feathery** adj light and soft

○━ **feature** /ˈfiːtʃə(r)/ n [C] **1** noticeable part: an important ~ of city life **2** parts of sb's face, eg the eyes and mouth **3** ~ (on) special article in a newspaper ● **feature** v **1** [T] include a particular person or thing as a special feature **2** [I] ~ in have an important part in sth ▸ **featureless** adj uninteresting

○━ **February** /ˈfebruəri/ n [U,C] second month of the year (See examples of use at **April**.)

feces (US) = FAECES

fed pt, pp of FEED

○━ **federal** /ˈfedərəl/ adj **1** of a system of government in which several states unite, eg for defence **2** of the central government, not the government of states

federation /ˌfedəˈreɪʃn/ n [C] **1** union of states with a central federal government **2** similar union of clubs, trade unions, etc

fed up /ˌfed ˈʌp/ adj (infml) ~ (with) bored or unhappy

○━ **fee** /fiː/ n [C] **1** money paid for professional advice or services: legal ~s **2** money paid to join an organization or to do sth: an entrance ~

feeble /ˈfiːbl/ adj (~r, ~st) weak ▸ **feebly** /-bli/ adv

○━ **feed** /fiːd/ v (pt, pp **fed** /fed/) **1** [T] give food to sb/sth **2** [I] ~ (on) (esp of animals) eat food **3** [T] ~ A (with B), B into A supply sth to sb/sth ● **feed** n [C] **1** meal for an animal or baby **2** [U] food for animals or plants

3 [C] pipe, channel, etc that carries material to a machine ■ **'feedback** n [U] advice, criticism, etc about how good or useful sth or sb's work is ■ **'feeding bottle** n [C] plastic bottle from which a baby is given milk

0➡ **feel** /fi:l/ v (pt, pp **felt** /felt/)
1 linking verb experience a particular feeling or emotion: ~ happy/tired **2** [T] notice or be aware of sth: ~ the sun on your face ◇~ the tension in the atmosphere **3** linking verb give you a particular feeling or impression: These shoes ~ tight. ◇ It ~s strange to come back here again. **4** linking verb have a particular physical quality which you discover by touching: The water ~s warm. **5** [T] move your fingers over sth to find sth or to find out what sth is like: Can you ~ the bump on my head? **6** [T] think or believe that sth is the case: He felt he would succeed. **7** [T] experience the effects of sth, often strongly: ~ the cold [IDM] **feel like (doing) sth** want (to do) sth: ~ like (having) a drink [PV] **feel for sb** have sympathy for sb ■ **feel** n [sing] **1** (the feel) sensation caused by touching sth or being touched **2** act of feeling or touching **3** general impression of a place, etc **feeler** /ˈfiːlə(r)/ n [C] long thin part of an insect's head, used for touching things [IDM] **put out feelers** ask questions, etc to test the opinions of others

0➡ **feeling** /ˈfiːlɪŋ/ n **1** [C] something felt through the mind or senses **2** [sing] belief; vague idea: a ~ that something awful is going to happen **3** [U, C] attitude or an opinion **4** (feelings) [pl] sb's emotions rather than thoughts **5** [U] sympathy or sensitivity **6** [U] ability to feel physically [IDM] **bad/ill feeling** anger between people, esp after an argument

feet plural of FOOT

feign /feɪn/ v [T] (written) pretend sth

feint /feɪnt/ n [C, U] (esp in sport) movement to make your opponent think you are going to do one thing instead of another ● **feint** v [I] make a feint

felicity /fəˈlɪsəti/ n [U] (fml) great happiness

feline /ˈfiːlaɪn/ adj of or like a cat

fell pt of FALL[1]

fell[2] /fel/ n [C] area of rocky moorland in N England

fell[3] /fel/ v [T] **1** cut down a tree **2** (written) knock sb down

0➡ **fellow** /ˈfeləʊ/ n [C] **1** (old-fash, infml) man **2** [C] senior member of a college or university ● **fellow** adj of the same group or kind: ~ workers ▶ **fellowship** n **1** [U] feeling of friendship **2** [C] group or society **3** [C] position of a college fellow

felony /ˈfeləni/ n [C, U] (pl **-ies**) (US or

law) serious crime, eg murder ▶ **felon** /ˈfelən/ n [C] person guilty of a felony

felt[1] pt, pp of FEEL

felt[2] /felt/ n [U] thick cloth made from pressed wool, hair or fur ■ **felt-tip 'pen** (also **'felt tip**) n [C] pen with a pointed tube made of felt

0➡ **female** /ˈfiːmeɪl/ adj **1** of the sex that produces young **2** (of a plant) producing fruit **3** (of part of a device) having a hollow part into which another part fits ● **female** n [C] female person or animal

feminine /ˈfemənɪn/ adj **1** of or like women **2** (gram) of a particular class of nouns, pronouns, etc ▶ **femininity** /ˌfeməˈnɪnəti/ n [U] quality of being feminine

feminism /ˈfemənɪzəm/ n [U] belief in the principle that women should have the same rights as men ▶ **feminist** n [C], adj

fen /fen/ n [C] area of low flat wet land

0➡ **fence** /fens/ n [C] wall made of wood or wire ● **fence** v [I] **1** ~ **in/ off** surround or divide sth with a fence **2** [I] fight with a long thin sword as a sport **3** [I] avoid giving a direct answer to a question ▶ **fencing** n [U] **1** sport of fighting with long thin swords **2** material for making fences

fend /fend/ v [PV] **fend for yourself** look after yourself **fend sb/sth off** defend yourself from sth

ferment[1] /fəˈment/ v [I, T] (make sth) change chemically so that glucose becomes alcohol, eg in beer ▶ **fermentation** /ˌfɜːmenˈteɪʃn/ n [U]

ferment[2] /ˈfɜːment/ n [U, sing] state of political and social excitement

fern /fɜːn/ n [C, U] plant with feathery green leaves and no flowers

ferocious /fəˈrəʊʃəs/ adj fierce or violent ▶ **ferociously** adv

ferocity /fəˈrɒsəti/ n [U] quality of being ferocious

ferret /ˈferɪt/ n [C] small animal of the weasel family that hunts rabbits and rats ● **ferret** v [I] ~ **(about/around)** (infml) search for sth [PV] **ferret sth out** (infml) find sb/sth by searching thoroughly

ferry /ˈferi/ (also **'ferry boat**) n [C] (pl **-ies**) boat that carries people and goods across a river or short stretch of sea ● **ferry** v (pt, pp **-ied**) [T] transport people or goods from one place to another

fertile /ˈfɜːtaɪl/ adj **1** (of land or soil) able to produce strong plants **2** (of a person's mind) full of new ideas **3** (of plants or animals) able to produce fruit or young ▶ **fertility** /fəˈtɪləti/ n [U]

fertilize (also **-ise**) /ˈfɜːtəlaɪz/ v [T] make sth/sb fertile ▶ **fertilization**

(also -isation) /ˌfɜːtəlaɪˈzeɪʃn/ n [U]
▶ **fertilizer** (also -iser) n [U,C]
substance added to soil to make it
more fertile

fervent /ˈfɜːvənt/ adj showing
strong feeling: ~ belief/supporter
▶ **fervently** adv

fervour (US -or) /ˈfɜːvə(r)/ n [U] very
strong feeling; enthusiasm

fester /ˈfestə(r)/ v [I] 1 (of a wound)
become infected 2 (of bad feelings
or thoughts) become more bitter
and angry

0─ **festival** /ˈfestɪvl/ n [C]
1 organized series of performances
of music, drama, etc 2 (day or time
for a) public, esp religious,
celebration

festive /ˈfestɪv/ adj joyous

festivity /feˈstɪvəti/ n [U,C] (pl -ies)
happy celebration

0─ **fetch** /fetʃ/ v [T] 1 collect sb/sth
from a place: ~ the children from
school 2 be sold for a particular
price: The vase ~ed £1000.

fête /feɪt/ n [C] outdoor
entertainment, usu to collect money
for a particular purpose ● **fête** v [T]
(usu passive) honour sb in a special
way

fetish /ˈfetɪʃ/ n [C] something to
which too much attention is given

fetter /ˈfetə(r)/ n [C] 1 (usu pl)
something that restricts sb's
freedom: the ~s of government
controls 2 chain for a prisoner's foot
● **fetter** v [T] 1 (usu passive) put
chains on a prisoner 2 restrict sb's
freedom

fetus (US) = FOETUS

feud /fjuːd/ n [C] long bitter quarrel
● **feud** v [I] carry on a feud

feudal /ˈfjuːdl/ adj of the system of
receiving land from a nobleman,
and working and fighting for him in
return, during the Middle Ages in
Europe ▶ **feudalism** /-dəlɪzəm/ n [U]

0─ **fever** /ˈfiːvə(r)/ n 1 [C,U] very
high temperature of the body 2 [U]
disease causing a high body
temperature 3 [sing] state of
excitement ▶ **feverish** adj
1 excited; very fast 2 having a fever
▶ **feverishly** adv

0─ **few** /fjuː/ det, adj, pron 1 not
many people, things or places:
F~ people live to be 100. 2 (a few) a
small number of people or things;
some [IDM] few and far between very
rare

fiancé /fiˈɒnseɪ/ n [C] (fem fiancée)
person you are engaged to (= have
agreed to marry)

fiasco /fiˈæskəʊ/ n [C] (pl ~s US also
~es) complete failure

fib /fɪb/ n [C] (infml) small lie, esp
about sth unimportant ● **fib** v (-bb-)
[I] tell a fib ▶ **fibber** n [C]

fibre (US fiber) /ˈfaɪbə(r)/ n 1 [U]
part of food that helps to keep a
person healthy by keeping the
bowels working: a high-~ diet 2 [U]
material, eg rope, formed from a
mass of fibres 3 [C] one of the many
thin threads that form body tissue
and other natural materials: muscle/
cotton ~s 4 [U] person's character:
strong moral ~ ■ **fibreglass** (US
'fiber-) n [U] material made from
glass fibres, used for making boats,
etc ■ **fibre optics** (US 'fiber-) n [U]
use of thin fibres of glass, etc to send
information in the form of light
signals ▶ **fibrous** /ˈfaɪbrəs/ adj made
of, or like, fibres

fickle /ˈfɪkl/ adj often changing

fiction /ˈfɪkʃn/ n 1 [U] writing that
describes invented people and
events, not real ones 2 [C] thing that
is invented or not true ▶ **fictional**
/-ʃənl/ adj

fictitious /fɪkˈtɪʃəs/ adj untrue;
invented

fiddle /ˈfɪdl/ v 1 [I] ~ with keep
touching or playing with sth in your
hands 2 [T] (infml) change accounts
dishonestly; get sth by cheating 3 [I]
(infml) play the violin ● **fiddle** n [C]
(infml) = VIOLIN 2 dishonest
action ▶ **fiddler** n [C] person who
plays a violin ▶ **fiddling** adj small
and unimportant ▶ **fiddly** adj
difficult to do or use because small
objects are involved

fidelity /fɪˈdeləti/ n [U] 1 faithfulness
2 accuracy of a translation, report,
etc

fidget /ˈfɪdʒɪt/ v [I] move your body
about restlessly ● **fidget** n [C]
person who fidgets ▶ **fidgety** adj

0─ **field**[1] /fiːld/ n 1 area of land
on which crops are grown or cattle
are kept 2 open area: a football/
landing ~ 3 area of study or activity
4 area in which a force can be felt: a
magnetic ~ 5 (computing) part of a
record that is a separate item of
data ■ **field day** n [IDM] have a field
day have great fun, success, etc
■ **field marshal** n [C] officer of the
highest rank in the British army

field[2] /fiːld/ v 1 [I,T] (in cricket, etc)
(stand ready to) catch or stop the
ball 2 [T] put a team into the field
3 [T] deal with a question skilfully
▶ **fielder** n [C] (in cricket, etc) person
who fields

fiend /fiːnd/ n [C] 1 very wicked
person 2 person who is very keen on
sth mentioned: a health ~ ▶ **fiendish**
adj ▶ **fiendishly** adv very

fierce /fɪəs/ adj (~r, ~st) 1 angry and
violent 2 intense; strong: ~ heat
▶ **fiercely** adv ▶ **fierceness** n [U]

fiery /ˈfaɪəri/ adj (-ier, -iest) 1 of or
like fire; flaming 2 (of a person)
quickly made angry ▶ **fierily** /-rəli/
adv

0–ᴡ **fifteen** /fɪf'tiːn/ *number* 15
▶ **fifteenth** /fɪf'tiːnθ/ *ordinal number*

0–ᴡ **fifth** /fɪfθ/ *ordinal number, n* [C] 5th; ⅕; each of five equal parts of sth

0–ᴡ **fifty** /'fɪfti/ **1** *number* 50 **2** (**the fifties**) *n* [pl] numbers, years or temperatures from 50 to 59
▶ **fiftieth** *ordinal number* ● **fifty-'fifty** *adj, adv* (*infml*) shared equally between two

fig /fɪg/ *n* [C] (tree with a) soft sweet fruit full of small seeds

fig. *abbr* (*written*) **1** figure; illustration: *See fig. 3.* **2** figurative(ly)

0–ᴡ **fight** /faɪt/ *v* (pt, pp **fought** /fɔːt/) **1** [I,T] use force with the hands or weapons against sb **2** [T] take part in a war or battle against sth **3** [I] try hard to stop sth bad or achieve sth: *~ against poverty* **4** [I] quarrel or argue with sb [PV] **fight back** (**against sb/sth**) resist strongly or attack sb who has attacked you [PV] **fight sb/sth off** resist or repel sb/sth: *~ off an attacker/a cold* **fight sth out** fight or argue until the argument is settled
● **fight** *n* **1** [C] act of fighting against sb/sth **2** [U] desire or ability to keep fighting for sth ▶ **fighter** *n* [C] **1** fast military aircraft **2** person who fights in war or in sport

figment /'fɪgmənt/ *n* [IDM] **a figment of sb's imagination** something not real

figurative /'fɪgərətɪv/ *adj* (of words) used not in the ordinary literal sense but in an imaginative way
▶ **figuratively** *adv*

0–ᴡ **figure** /'fɪgə(r)/ *n* **1** [C] symbol representing a number **2** [C] price **3** [C] human form or shape: *a ~ approaching in the darkness* ◇ *have a good ~* (= slim body) **4** [C] person: *important ~s in history* **5** [C] form of a person that is drawn, carved, etc **6** [C] diagram; illustration ● **figure** *v* **1** [I] *~* (**as/in**) be a part of a process, situation, etc, esp an important one **2** [T] think or decide that sth is true or will happen [IDM] **it/that figures** used to say that sth seems logical [PV] **figure on sth/doing sth** plan sth or to do sth; expect sth **figure sb/sth out 1** think about sb/sth until you understand them/it **2** calculate an amount ● **figurehead** *n* [C] person in a high position but with no real authority ● **figure of 'speech** *n* [C] figurative expression

filament /'fɪləmənt/ *n* [C] thin wire inside a light bulb; thin thread

0–ᴡ **file¹** /faɪl/ *n* [C] **1** holder, box, cover, etc for keeping papers **2** organized computer data: *create/ delete a ~* **3** papers and information contained in a file: *have a confidential ~ on sb* **4** metal tool with a rough surface for cutting or shaping hard substances **5** [C] line of

people or things one behind the other [IDM] **in file** kept in a file

file² /faɪl/ *v* **1** [T] put sth in a file **2** [I,T] *~* (**for**) (*law*) make a formal request, etc officially: *~ for divorce* **3** [I] walk in a line of people, one after the other: *~ out of the room* **4** [T] cut or shape sth with a file¹(4): *~ your nails*
▶ **filings** /'faɪlɪŋz/ *n* [pl] small pieces of metal removed by a file¹(4)
● **'filing cabinet** (*US* **'file cabinet**) *n* [C] piece of office furniture for holding files

0–ᴡ **fill** /fɪl/ *v* **1** [I,T] become or make sth full of sth **2** [T] do a job, have a role or position, etc; put sb into a job: *~ a vacancy* [PV] **fill in** (**for sb**) do sb's job when they are away **fill sth in** (*esp US*) fill sth out complete a form, etc by writing information on it **fill out** become larger or fatter **fill** (**sth**) **up** (**with sth**) become or make sth completely full ● **fill** *n* [IDM] **your fill of sth/sb** as much of sth/sb as you can bear: *I've had my ~ of your rudeness!* **2** as much as you can eat or drink ▶ **filler** *n* [C,U] material used to fill holes in walls, etc before painting ● **filling** *n* [C] material used to fill a hole in a tooth ● **'filling station** *n* [C] = PETROL STATION

fillet /'fɪlɪt/ *n* [C,U] piece of meat or fish without bones ● **fillet** *v* [T] cut fish or meat into fillets

0–ᴡ **film** /fɪlm/ *n* **1** [C] cinema picture; movie **2** [U,C] roll of thin plastic used in photography **3** [C, usu sing] thin layer of sth on sth: *a ~ of oil* ● **film** *v* [I,T] make a film (1) ● **film star** *n* [C] famous cinema actor

filter /'fɪltə(r)/ *n* [C] **1** device used for holding back solid material in a liquid passed through it **2** coloured glass that allows light only of certain wavelengths to pass through ● **filter** *v* **1** [I,T] (cause sth to) flow through a filter **2** [I] pass or flow slowly; become known gradually

filth /fɪlθ/ *n* [U] **1** disgusting dirt **2** very rude and offensive words, pictures, etc ▶ **filthy** *adj* (**-ier, -iest**)

fin /fɪn/ *n* [C] **1** wide thin wing-like part of a fish **2** thing shaped like this, eg on the back of an aircraft

0–ᴡ **final** /'faɪnl/ *adj* **1** coming at the end; last **2** (of a decision) that cannot be changed [IDM] **final straw** → STRAW ● **final** *n* [C] **1** last of a series of competitions: *the tennis ~s* **2** (**finals**) [pl] last set of university examinations ▶ **finalist** /'faɪnəlɪst/ *n* [C] player in a final competition ● **finalize** (*also* **-ise**) /'faɪnəlaɪz/ *v* [T] complete the last part of a plan, etc ▶ **finally** /'faɪnəli/ *adv* **1** eventually **2** conclusively: *settle the matter ~ly*

finale /fɪ'nɑːli/ *n* [C] last part of a piece of music or drama

finance

0─ **finance** /ˈfaɪnæns; faɪˈnæns; fə-/ n **1** [U] management of (esp public) money **2** [U] money needed to pay for a project: *obtain ~ from the bank* **3** (**finances**) [pl] money available to a person, company, etc ▸ **finance** v [T] provide money for a project, etc ▸ **financial** /faɪˈnænʃl; fə-/ adj ▸ **financially** adv ▸ **financier** /faɪˈnænsɪə(r); fə-/ n [C] person who finances businesses

finch /fɪntʃ/ n [C] small bird

0─ **find** /faɪnd/ v (pt, pp **found** /faʊnd/) [T] **1** discover sth/sb unexpectedly **2** get back sth/sb that was lost **3** discover sth by searching, studying or testing **4** have a particular feeling or opinion about sth: *I ~ it difficult to understand him.* **5** have sth available for you to use: *~ time to study* **6** arrive at sth naturally: *Water always ~s its own level.* **7** exist in a particular place: *Tigers are found in India.* **8** (*fml*) decide sth in a court of law: *~ her guilty* [IDM] **find fault (with sth/sb)** look for mistakes in sth/sb; complain about sth/sb [PV] **find out (sth) (about sth/sb)** learn sth by study or inquiry: *~ out when the next train leaves* ▸ **find** n [C] something interesting or valuable that is found ▸ **finder** n [C] ▸ **finding** n [C] **1** [usu pl] what is learnt by study or inquiry **2** (*law*) decision reached by a court

0─ **fine¹** /faɪn/ adj (*~r, ~st*) **1** enjoyable or pleasing: *a ~ view* **2** in good health **3** (of weather) bright; clear **4** made of very small particles: *~ powder* **5** delicate; carefully made **6** (able to be) seen or noticed only with difficulty or effort: *a ~ distinction* ▸ **fine** adv (*infml*) well: *We're all doing ~.* ■ **fine art** n [U] (also **fine arts** [pl]) paintings, sculptures, etc ▸ **finely** adv **1** into small pieces: *~ly cut meat* **2** beautifully; delicately ▸ **fineness** n [U]

fine² /faɪn/ n [C] money paid as a punishment for breaking the law ▸ **fine** v [T] officially punish sb by making them pay a fine

finery /ˈfaɪnəri/ n [U] beautiful clothes

finesse /fɪˈnes/ n [U] skilful way of dealing with a situation

0─ **finger** /ˈfɪŋɡə(r)/ n [C] **1** any of the five parts at the end of each hand **2** part of a glove that fits over a finger [IDM] **get, pull, etc your finger out** (*infml*) stop being lazy; start to work hard **not put your finger on** not be able to find exactly what is wrong ▸ **finger** v [T] touch or feel sth with your fingers ■ **fingernail** n [C] hard layer that covers the end of each finger ■ **fingerprint** n [C] mark made by a finger when pressed on a surface ■ **fingertip** n [C] end of a finger [IDM] **have sth at your fingertips** know sth very well

0─ **finish** /ˈfɪnɪʃ/ v **1** [I,T] come or bring sth to an end; reach the end of a task **2** [T] eat, drink or use what is left of sth **3** [T] make sth complete [PV] **finish sb/sth off** (*infml*) destroy sb/sth **finish with sb/sth** no longer be dealing with sb/sth; end a relationship with sb ▸ **finish** n **1** [C] last part of sth **2** [C,U] last covering of paint or polish: *a highly-polished ~*

finite /ˈfaɪnaɪt/ adj **1** limited **2** (*gram*) (of a verb form) showing a particular tense, person and number: *'Is' and 'was' are ~ forms of 'be'.*

fir (also **fir tree**) /fɜː(r)/ n [C] evergreen tree with leaves like needles ■ **fir cone** n [C] fruit of the fir tree

0─ **fire¹** /ˈfaɪə(r)/ n **1** [U] burning that produces light and heat **2** [U,C] burning that causes destruction: *forest ~s* **3** [C] pile of burning fuel for heating, cooking, etc: *light a ~* **4** [C] apparatus for heating a room: *a gas ~* **5** [U] shots from guns [IDM] **come under fire** being shot at ■ **fire alarm** n [C] bell that warns people of a fire ■ **firearm** n [C, usu pl] gun ■ **the fire brigade** n [sing] team of people who put out fires ■ **fire drill** n [C,U] practice of leaving a burning building, etc safely ■ **fire engine** n [C] vehicle that carries firefighters and equipment to put out fires ■ **fire escape** n [C] outside staircase for leaving a burning building ■ **fire extinguisher** n [C] metal cylinder containing water or chemicals for putting out a small fire ■ **firefighter** n [C] person whose job is to put out fires ■ **fireguard** n [C] protective metal framework round a fire in a room ■ **fireman** n [C] (pl **-men**) person whose job is to put out fires ■ **fireplace** n [C] open space in a wall for a fire in a room ■ **fireproof** adj unable to be damaged by fire ■ **fireside** n [C, usu sing] part of a room beside the fire ■ **fire station** n [C] building for a fire brigade ■ **firewall** n [C] (*computing*) part of a computer system designed to prevent people from without getting at information without authority but that still allows them to receive information that is sent to them ■ **firewood** n [U] wood used for lighting fires or as fuel ■ **firework** n [C] device containing chemicals that burn or explode with coloured flames

0─ **fire²** /ˈfaɪə(r)/ v **1** [I,T] shoot with a gun; shoot a bullet **2** [T] force sb to leave their job **3** [T] excite sb **4** [T] heat a clay object in a special oven ■ **firing line** n [sing] front line of battle, nearest the enemy ■ **firing** squad n [C, U] group of soldiers ordered to shoot a condemned person

0📺 **firm** /fɜːm/ adj **1** fairly hard **2** strongly fixed in place **3** not likely to change **4** (of a person's voice or movements) strong and steady [IDM] **stand firm** → STAND²(11) ■ **firm** v [I,T] become or make sth firm ■ **firm** n [C] business or company ■ **firm** adv firmly ▸ **firmly** adv in a strong or definite way ▸ **firmness** n [U]

0📺 **first** /fɜːst/ det, ordinal number coming before all others [IDM] **at first sight** when seen for the first time **first thing** as early as possible in the day ■ **first 'aid** n [U] treatment given immediately to an injured person before a doctor comes ■ **first 'class** n [U] adv (using) the best seats on a train, plane, etc or the fastest form of mail ■ **first-'class** adj of the best class ■ **first 'floor** n [C] **1** (GB) floor immediately above the ground floor **2** (US) = GROUND FLOOR (GROUND¹) ■ **first-'hand** adj, adv (of information) (obtained) directly from the origin ▸ **firstly** adv (in giving a list) to begin with ■ **first name** n [C] name that goes before your family name ■ the **first 'person** n [sing] (gram) set of pronouns, eg I, we, me, and the verb forms, eg am, used with them ■ **first-'rate** adj excellent

0📺 **first²** /fɜːst/ adv **1** before anyone or anything else: She spoke ~. **2** for the first time: when I ~ came to London **3** in preference to sth else [IDM] **at first** at or in the beginning

0📺 **first³** /fɜːst/ n **1** (the first) [C] the first person or thing: the ~ to leave [C, usu sing] (infml) important new achievement **3** [C] (GB) highest level of university degree

0📺 **fish** /fɪʃ/ n (pl fish or ~es) **1** [C] cold-blooded animal that lives in water **2** [U] flesh of a fish eaten as food: ~ and chips ■ **fish** v **1** [I] try to catch fish [PV] **fish for sth** try to obtain compliments, etc indirectly **fish sb/sth out (of sth)** take or pull sb/sth out of a place: He ~ed a coin out of his pocket. ■ **fisherman** n [C] (pl -men) person who catches fish, as a job or as a sport ■ **fishery** n [C, usu pl] (pl -ies) part of the sea where fish are caught ■ **fishing** n [U] sport or job of catching fish: go ~ing ■ **fishmonger** /ˈfɪʃmʌŋɡə(r)/ n [C] person who sells fish in a shop ▸ **fishy** adj (-ier, -iest) **1** (infml) causing doubt: a ~y story **2** like fish

fission /ˈfɪʃn/ n [U] splitting, esp of an atom: nuclear ~

fissure /ˈfɪʃə(r)/ n [C] deep crack in rock

fist /fɪst/ n [C] hand when tightly closed ▸ **fistful** n [C] number or quantity that can be held in a fist

---

167

fixture

0📺 **fit¹** /fɪt/ v (-tt-) **1** [I, T] be the right size and shape for sb/sth: These shoes don't ~ (me). **2** [T] (usu passive) put clothes on sb to have them the right size, shape, etc: have a new coat ~ted **3** [T] put or fix sth somewhere: ~ a new window **4** [I,T] (make sth) agree with, match or be suitable for sth: make the punishment ~ the crime [PV] **fit sb/sth in** find time or room for sb/sth **fit in (with sb/sth)** live, work, etc in an easy way with sb/sth **fit sb/sth out** equip sb/sth ▸ **fitted** adj fixed in place: ~ted carpets/cupboards ▸ **fitter** n [C] **1** person whose job is to put together and fit machinery **2** person who cuts and fits clothes, carpets, etc

0📺 **fit²** /fɪt/ adj (~ter, ~test) **1** healthy and strong: keep ~ by jogging **2** ~ for/, to suitable; good enough; right: not ~ to eat ∘ Do as you think ~. **3** ~ to ready to do sth extreme: laughing ~ to burst ▸ **fitness** n [U] **1** state of being physically fit **2** ~ for/, to suitability for sth

fit³ /fɪt/ n [C] **1** sudden attack of an illness, eg epilepsy, in which you become unconscious and make violent movements **2** sudden short period of intense feeling or activity: a ~ of enthusiasm **3** way in which sth, esp clothing, fits: a tight ~ [IDM] **by/in fits and starts** not continuously over a period of time **have/throw a fit** (infml) be very shocked or angry ▸ **fitful** /ˈfɪtfl/ adj occurring irregularly ▸ **fitfully** /-fəli/ adv

fitting /ˈfɪtɪŋ/ adj (fml) right; suitable ■ **fitting** n [C] **1** [usu pl] small part on a piece of equipment: electrical ~s **2** [usu pl] something, eg a cooker, that is fixed in a building but can be removed

0📺 **five** /faɪv/ number **5** ▸ **fiver** /ˈfaɪvə(r)/ n [C] (GB, infml) £5 (note)

0📺 **fix¹** /fɪks/ v [T] **1** fasten sth firmly to sth **2** arrange or organize sth: ~ a date for a meeting **3** (esp US) prepare food or drink **4** repair sth **5** put sth in order: ~ your hair **6** unfairly influence the result of sth **7** direct your eyes, thoughts, etc onto sth [IDM] **fix sb with a look, a stare, etc** look directly at sb for a long time [PV] **fix on sb/sth** choose sb/sth **fix sb up (with sth)** (infml) provide sb with sth ▸ **fixation** /fɪkˈseɪʃn/ n [C] unhealthy interest in sb/sth; obsession

fix² /fɪks/ n [C] **1** (infml) solution to a problem **2** [sing] (infml) injection of a narcotic drug **3** [sing] difficult situation **4** act of finding the position of a ship or aircraft

fixture /ˈfɪkstʃə(r)/ n [C] **1** [usu pl] something, eg a bath, that is fixed in a building and cannot be removed **2** sporting event on an agreed date

fizz /fɪz/ v [I] make a hissing sound of bubbles of gas in a liquid ● **fizz** n [U, sing] small bubbles of gas in a liquid ▸ **fizzy** adj (**-ier, -iest**)

fizzle /ˈfɪzl/ v [I] make a weak hissing sound [PV] **fizzle out** come to a weak disappointing end

flab /flæb/ n [U] (infml) soft loose flesh on a person's body ▸ **flabby** adj (**-ier, -iest**) **1** having soft loose flesh; fat **2** feeble and weak ▸ **flabbiness** n [U]

flabbergasted /ˈflæbəɡɑːstɪd/ adj (infml) very shocked and surprised

0-π **flag** /flæɡ/ n [C] piece of cloth used as a symbol of a country, or as a signal ● **flag** v (**-gg-**) **1** [T] mark information to show you think it is important **2** [I] become tired or weak: *Enthusiasm is ~ging.* [PV] **flag sb/sth down** signal to a vehicle to stop ■ **flagship** n [C] **1** main ship in a fleet of ships in the navy **2** most important product, service, etc that an organization owns

flagon /ˈflæɡən/ n [C] large round bottle for wine, cider, etc

flagrant /ˈfleɪɡrənt/ adj openly bad: *~ disobedience* ▸ **flagrantly** adv

flagstone /ˈflæɡstəʊn/ n [C] large flat stone for a floor, path or pavement

flair /fleə(r)/ n [U, sing] natural ability to do sth well: *She has a ~ for languages* (= is quick at learning them).

flake /fleɪk/ n [C] small thin layer; small piece of sth: *snow~s* ● **flake** v [I] fall off in flakes [PV] **flake out** (infml) collapse with exhaustion ▸ **flaky** adj (**-ier, -iest**) made of flakes; tending to flake

flamboyant /flæmˈbɔɪənt/ adj **1** (of a person) very confident and lively **2** brightly coloured ▸ **flamboyance** /-ˈbɔɪəns/ n [U] ▸ **flamboyantly** adv

0-π **flame** /fleɪm/ n [C, U] hot bright stream of burning gas coming from sth on fire: *The house was in ~s* (= was burning). ● **flame** v **1** [I] burn with a bright flame **2** have the colour of flames; blaze ▸ **flaming** adj violent: *a flaming argument*

flamingo /fləˈmɪŋɡəʊ/ n [C] (pl ~s) large bird with long legs, a long neck and pink feathers

flammable /ˈflæməbl/ adj that can burn easily

flan /flæn/ n [C] open pastry case with fruit, jam, etc in it

flank /flæŋk/ n [C] **1** left or right side of an army **2** side of an animal between the ribs and the hip ● **flank** v [T] place sb/sth on one or both sides of sb/sth

flannel /ˈflænl/ n **1** [U] soft light

---

fabric, containing cotton or wool **2** small piece of cloth used for washing yourself **3** (flannels) [pl] trousers made of flannel

flap /flæp/ n [C] **1** flat piece of material that covers an opening **2** action or sound of flapping **3** part of the wing of an aircraft that can be lifted [IDM] **be in/get into a flap** (infml) be/become excited or confused ● **flap** v (**-pp-**) **1** [I, T] (of a bird's wings) move or be made to move quickly up and down: *The bird ~ped its wings.* **2** [I, T] (cause sth to) move up and down or from side to side: *sails ~ping in the wind* **3** [I] (GB, infml) become excited and anxious

flare /fleə(r)/ v **1** [I] burn brightly, but only for a short time **2** [I] (of clothes) become wider at the bottom: *~d trousers* [PV] **flare up 1** burst into a bright flame **2** become more violent ● **flare** n [C] **1** [usu sing] bright unsteady light or flame that does not last **2** (device that produces a) flaring light used as a signal **3** shape that becomes gradually wider ■ **flare-up** n [usu sing] **1** sudden expression of violent feeling **2** (of illness) sudden attack

0-π **flash** /flæʃ/ n [C] **1** sudden bright burst of light: *a ~ of lightning* ◇ (fig) *a ~ of inspiration* **2** [C, U] (device that produces a) brief bright light for taking photographs indoors [IDM] **in/like a flash** very quickly ● **flash** adj (infml) expensive-looking; showy ● **flash** v **1** [I, T] (cause sth to) shine with a sudden bright light **2** [I] move quickly: *The train ~ed past us.* **3** [I] come suddenly into view or into the mind **4** [T] send information quickly by radio, computer, etc ■ **flashback** n [C] part of a film, etc that shows a scene in the past ■ **flashbulb** n [C] electric bulb in a flash (2) ■ **flashlight** n [C] (esp US) small electric torch ■ **flashmob** n [C] large group of people who arrange to gather together in a public place at exactly the same time, spend a short time doing sth there and then quickly all leave at the same time ▸ **flashy** adj (**-ier, -iest**) attractive, but not in good taste: *~y clothes* ▸ **flashily** adv

flask /flɑːsk/ n [C] **1** bottle with a narrow neck **2** (GB) = VACUUM FLASK **3** (esp US) = HIP FLASK (HIP)

0-π **flat¹** /flæt/ adj (**~ter, ~test**) **1** smooth and level, not curved or sloping **2** having a broad level surface but not high: *~ shoes* **3** dull; boring **4** absolute: *a ~ refusal* **5** (music) below the correct pitch **6** (of drinks) no longer fizzy **7** (of a battery) no longer producing electricity **8** (of a tyre) no longer having air inside ● **flat** adv **1** in or into a flat position: *Lie ~ and breathe deeply.* **2** exactly: *in 10 seconds ~*

3 (*music*) lower than the correct pitch [IDM] **flat out** (*infml*) as fast as or as hard as possible ● **flat-footed** *adj* having feet with flat soles

0-m **flat²** /flæt/ *n* **1** [C] (*esp GB*) (*esp US* **apartment**) set of rooms on one floor of a building, used as a home **2** [sing] flat level part of sth **3** [C, usu pl] area of low level ground **4** [C] (*music*) (*symb* ♭) note that is half a tone lower than the note named **5** [C] (*esp US*) flat tyre

flatten /'flætn/ *v* [I, T] become or make sth flat

flatter /'flætə(r)/ *v* [T] **1** praise sb too much or insincerely **2** make sb seem more attractive than they really are [IDM] **be/feel flattered** be pleased because sb has made you feel special ▸ **flatterer** *n* [C] ▸ **flattery** *n* [U] insincere praise

flaunt /flɔːnt/ *v* [T] (*disapprov*) show sth valuable or impressive in order to gain admiration: ~ *your wealth*

flautist /'flɔːtɪst/ *n* [C] flute player

0-m **flavour** (*US* **-or**) /'fleɪvə(r)/ *n* **1** [U] taste and smell of food: *add salt to improve the* ~ **2** [C] particular quality ● **flavour** *v* [T] give flavour to sth ▸ **flavouring** *n* [C, U] something added to food to give flavour ▸ **flavourless** *adj*

flaw /flɔː/ *n* [C] fault or mistake; imperfection ▸ **flawed** *adj* having a flaw; damaged ▸ **flawless** *adj* perfect ▸ **flawlessly** *adv*

flax /flæks/ *n* [U] plant grown for its fibres, used for making linen ▸ **flaxen** /'flæksn/ *adj* (*written*) (of hair) pale yellow

flea /fliː/ *n* [C] small jumping insect that feeds on blood

fleck /flek/ *n* [C] very small patch, spot or grain ● **fleck** *v* [T] cover or mark sth with flecks

flee /fliː/ *v* (*pt, pp* **fled** /fled/) [I, T] ~ (**from**) run or hurry away from sb/ sth; escape

fleece /fliːs/ *n* **1** [C] woolly coat of a sheep **2** [U, C] type of soft warm cloth that feels like wool; jacket that is made from this cloth ● **fleece** *v* [T] (*infml*) rob sb by trickery, esp by charging too much money ▸ **fleecy** *adj* like fleece; woolly

fleet /fliːt/ *n* [C] **1** group of ships under one commander **2** group of buses, cars, etc owned by one organization

fleeting /'fliːtɪŋ/ *adj* lasting only a short time: *a* ~ *glimpse*

0-m **flesh** /fleʃ/ *n* **1** [U] soft part between the skin and bones of animal bodies **2** [U] soft juicy part of a fruit **3** (**the flesh**) [sing] the body, contrasted with the mind or the soul [IDM] **in the flesh** in real life **make your flesh creep** make you feel afraid or uncomfortable **your (own) flesh**

and blood person you are related to ▸ **fleshy** *adj* fat

flew *pt* of FLY¹

flex /fleks/ *n* [C, U] wire for electric current, in a covering of plastic, etc ● **flex** *v* [T] bend or stretch your legs, muscles, etc

flexible /'fleksəbl/ *adj* **1** that can bend easily without breaking **2** easily changed: ~ *plans* ▸ **flexibility** /ˌfleksə'bɪləti/ *n* [U]

flick /flɪk/ *n* [C] **1** quick light blow **2** quick sharp movement: *with a* ~ *of his wrist* ● **flick** *v* [T] hit sth lightly with a sudden quick movement [PV] **flick through sth** turn over the pages of a book, etc quickly

flicker /'flɪkə(r)/ *v* [I] **1** (of a light or flame) keep going on and off **2** (of an emotion) appear briefly **3** move with small quick movements ● **flicker** *n* [C, usu sing] **1** flickering movement **2** feeling or emotion that only lasts for a short time: *a* ~ *of hope*

flier = FLYER

0-m **flight** /flaɪt/ *n* **1** [C] journey made by air **2** [C] plane making a particular journey: ~ *BA 4793 from London* **3** [U] act of flying **4** [C] set of stairs between two floors **5** [U] fleeing or running away **6** [C] group of aircraft or birds flying together [IDM] **a flight of fancy/imagination** unrealistic imaginative idea ● **flight path** *n* [C] course of an aircraft through the air

flimsy /'flɪmzi/ *adj* (**-ier, -iest**) **1** light and thin; easily destroyed **2** difficult to believe: *a* ~ *excuse* ▸ **flimsily** *adv*

flinch /flɪntʃ/ *v* [I] move back because of shock, fear or pain

fling /flɪŋ/ *v* (*pt, pp* **flung** /flʌŋ/) [T] throw sb/sth violently somewhere [PV] **fling yourself into sth** do sth with a lot of energy and enthusiasm ● **fling** *n* [C] short period of enjoyment and fun

flint /flɪnt/ *n* **1** [U, C] hard stone, used for making sparks **2** [C] piece of flint or hard metal that is used to make a spark

flip /flɪp/ *v* (**-pp-**) **1** [T] make sth move, esp through the air, by hitting it lightly: ~ *a coin* **2** [I] (*infml*) become very angry ● **flip** *n* [C] quick light blow

flippant /'flɪpənt/ *adj* not showing enough respect ▸ **flippancy** /-ənsi/ *n* [U] ▸ **flippantly** *adv*

flipper /'flɪpə(r)/ *n* [C] **1** broad flat limb of a seal, turtle, etc **2** large flat rubber shoe used when swimming underwater

flirt /flɜːt/ *v* [I] **1** ~ (**with**) behave towards sb in a romantic but not serious way **2** ~ **with** think about sth, but not seriously ● **flirt** *n* [C] person who flirts ▸ **flirtation** /-'eɪʃn/

n [C,U] ▸ **flirtatious** /-eɪʃəs/ *adj* fond of flirting

flit /flɪt/ *v* (**-tt-**) [I] fly or move lightly and quickly

◦▪ **float** /fləʊt/ *v* **1** [I,T] (cause sth to) stay on the surface of a liquid or up in the air **2** [T] suggest an idea or plan **3** [T] (*business*) sell shares in a business or company for the first time **4** [I,T] (of a currency) (allow its value) to change according to the value of foreign currencies ● **float** *n* [C] **1** large vehicle, esp one used in a procession: *a carnival ~* **2** light object that floats (often used to support a heavier object in water) **3** amount of money used, esp by a shopkeeper to provide change ▸ **floating** *adj* not fixed

flock /flɒk/ *n* [C] **1** group of sheep, birds or goats **2** large crowd of people **3** church congregation ● **flock** *v* [I] move in great numbers: *Crowds ~ed to the football match.*

flog /flɒg/ *v* (**-gg-**) [T] **1** beat sb severely as punishment **2** (*infml*) sell sth to sb [IDM] **flog a dead horse** (*infml*) waste your efforts doing sth that cannot succeed **flog sth to death** (*infml*) repeat a story, joke, etc too often ▸ **flogging** *n* [C,U] severe beating

◦▪ **flood** /flʌd/ *n* [C] **1** (coming of a) great quantity of water, esp over a place that is usu dry **2** large quantity: *a ~ of tears/letters* ● **flood** *v* [I,T] **1** fill or cover sth with water **2** (of a feeling) affect sb suddenly and strongly: *A sense of relief ~ed over her.* **3** **~ in/into/out of** arrive or go somewhere in large numbers ▪ **flood tide** *n* [C] rising tide

◦▪ **floodlight** /ˈflʌdlaɪt/ *n* [C, usu pl] large powerful light that produces a wide beam ● **floodlight** *v* (pt, pp **floodlit** /-lɪt/) [T] light sth with floodlights

◦▪ **floor** /flɔː(r)/ *n* **1** [C] surface of a room that you walk on **2** [C] number of rooms on the same level in a building: *I live on the fourth ~.* **3** [C, usu sing] ground at the bottom of the sea, a forest, etc **4** (**the floor**) [sing] part of a building, esp in a parliament, where debates are held **5** [C, usu sing] area in a building used for a particular activity: *the dance ~* ◇ *the factory/shop ~* (= where the ordinary workers, not the managers, work) ● **floor** *v* [T] **1** surprise or confuse sb so that they are not sure what to do **2** knock sb down **3** provide a building or room with a floor ▪ **floorboard** *n* [C] wooden plank for a floor ▪ **floor show** *n* [C] cabaret entertainment

flop /flɒp/ *v* (**-pp-**) [I] **1** move or fall clumsily or helplessly: *~ exhausted into a chair* **2** (*infml*) (of a book, film,

etc) fail ● **flop** *n* [C] **1** (usu sing) flopping movement or sound **2** (*infml*) failure of a book, film, etc ▸ **floppy** *adj* (**-ier, -iest**) hanging down loosely; soft and flexible: *a ~py hat* ▪ **floppy 'disk** (*also* **floppy**) (pl **-ies**) (*also* **diskette**) *n* [C] (*computing*) flexible disk used for storing data

flora /ˈflɔːrə/ *n* [U] (*tech*) all the plants of an area or period of time

floral /ˈflɔːrəl/ *adj* of flowers

florid /ˈflɒrɪd/ *adj* (*written*) **1** (of a person's face) red **2** (*disapprov*) decorated too much

florist /ˈflɒrɪst/ *n* [C] person who has a shop that sells flowers

flotation /fləʊˈteɪʃn/ *n* [C,U] (*business*) act of floating (3) a company

flotilla /fləˈtɪlə/ *n* [C] group of small, esp military, ships

flounce /flaʊns/ *v* [I] move in a quick angry manner: *She ~d out of the room.*

flounder /ˈflaʊndə(r)/ *v* [I] **1** struggle to know what to say or do or how to continue with sth **2** struggle to move through water, mud, etc

◦▪ **flour** /ˈflaʊə(r)/ *n* [U] fine powder made from grain, used for making bread, etc

flourish /ˈflʌrɪʃ/ *v* **1** [I] be successful: *Her business is ~ing.* **2** [I] grow healthily **3** [T] (*written*) wave sth about ● **flourish** *n* [C, usu sing] **1** exaggerated movement made to attract attention **2** short loud piece of music

flout /flaʊt/ *v* [T] disobey rules, etc openly and without respect

◦▪ **flow** /fləʊ/ *v* [I] **1** (of liquid, gas or electricity) move steadily and continuously: (fig) *Keep the traffic ~ing.* **2** (of hair or clothes) hang loosely **3** (of the tide) come in from the sea to the land [PV] **flow from sth** (*fml*) come or result from sth ● **flow** *n* [C, usu sing] **1** flowing movement; constant stream or supply **2** movement of the sea towards the land: *the ebb and ~ of the tide*

◦▪ **flower** /ˈflaʊə(r)/ *n* [C] part of a plant that produces seeds, often brightly coloured [IDM] **the flower of sth** (*lit*) finest part of sth ● **flower** *v* [I] produce flowers ▪ **flower bed** *n* [C] piece of ground where flowers are grown ▪ **flowerpot** *n* [C] pot in which a plant is grown ▸ **flowery** *adj* **1** having many flowers **2** (of language) too complicated

flown *pp* of FLY[1]

◦▪ **flu** /fluː/ *n* [U] (often **the flu**) (*also fml* **influenza**) infectious disease with fever, aches and a bad cold

fluctuate /ˈflʌktʃueɪt/ *v* [I] change frequently in size, amount, quality, etc ▸ **fluctuation** /-ˈeɪʃn/ *n* [C,U]

fluent /ˈfluːənt/ *adj* **1** (of a person) able to speak a language easily and well: *He's ~ in English.* **2** (of a language or an action) expressed in a smooth easy way: *speak ~ English* ▶ **fluency** /-ənsi/ *n* [U] ▶ **fluently** *adv*

fluff /flʌf/ *n* [U] **1** soft light pieces that come from woolly material **2** soft fur or hair on a young animal ● **fluff** *v* [I,T] (*infml*) do sth badly or fail at sth: *The actor ~ed his lines.* **2 ~ out/up** shake or brush sth so that it looks larger and/or softer: *~ up a pillow* ▶ **fluffy** *adj* (**-ier, -iest**) soft and light; covered with fluff: *a ~y cat*

fluid /ˈfluːɪd/ *adj* **1** (of movements, designs, music, etc) smooth, graceful and flowing **2** (of a situation) not fixed; likely to change ● **fluid** *n* [C,U] liquid

fluke /fluːk/ *n* [usu sing] (*infml*) accidental good luck

flung *pt, pp* of FLING

fluorescent /ˌflɔːˈresnt/ *adj* giving out a bright glowing light when exposed to natural or other light

fluoride /ˈflɔːraɪd/ *n* [U] chemical compound thought to prevent teeth from decaying

flurried /ˈflʌrɪd/ *adj* nervous and confused

flurry /ˈflʌri/ *n* [C] (*pl* **-ies**) **1** [usu sing] short burst of activity: *a ~ of activity/excitement* **2** sudden rush of wind, snow, etc

flush /flʌʃ/ *n* **1** [C, usu sing] redness of the face **2** [C, usu sing] sudden strong feeling: *a ~ of anger/ embarrassment* **3** [sing] act of cleaning a toilet with a sudden flow of water ● **flush** *v* [I,T] **1** (of the face) become red **2** clean sth with a rush of water: *~ the toilet* ▶ **flushed** *adj* (of a person) red; with a red face ● **flush** *adj* **1** (*infml*) having plenty of money *~ with* **2** (of two surfaces) level

fluster /ˈflʌstə(r)/ *v* [T] make sb nervous and confused ● **fluster** *n* [sing] nervous confused state

flute /fluːt/ *n* [C] musical instrument like a thin pipe, played by blowing across a hole at one end

flutter /ˈflʌtə(r)/ *v* **1** [I,T] (cause sth to) move about lightly and quickly: *curtains ~ing in the breeze* **2** [I,T] (of birds or insects) move the wings lightly and quickly up and down **3** [I] (of the heart) beat irregularly ● **flutter** *n* **1** [C, usu sing] quick light movement **2** [sing] state of nervous excitement

flux /flʌks/ *n* [U] continuous change: *in a state of ~*

0─ fly¹ /flaɪ/ *v* (*pt* **flew** /fluː/ *pp* **flown** /fləʊn/) **1** [I] move through the air as a bird does, or in an aircraft **2** [I,T] control an aircraft etc **3** [I] go or move quickly: *It's late. I must ~.* **4** [T] raise a flag [IDM] **fly in the face of sth** (written) oppose or be the opposite of sth **fly into a rage, temper, etc** become suddenly very angry ■ **flying saucer** *n* [C] spacecraft believed to have come from another planet ■ **flying squad** *n* [C] (GB) group of police officers who are ready to travel quickly to the scene of a serious crime ■ **flying start** *n* [sing] very good beginning ■ **flying visit** *n* [C] (GB) very short visit

0─ fly² /flaɪ/ *n* [C] (*pl* **flies**) **1** insect with two wings **2** natural or artificial fly used as a bait in fishing **3** (*usu pl*) (*pl* **flies**) zip or buttoned opening on the front of a pair of trousers

flyer (*also* **flier**) /ˈflaɪə(r)/ *n* [C] **1** (*infml*) pilot of an aircraft **2** person who travels in an aircraft **3** small sheet of paper that advertises sth

flyleaf /ˈflaɪliːf/ *n* [C] (*pl* **-leaves**) blank page at the beginning or end of a book

flyover /ˈflaɪəʊvə(r)/ *n* [C] bridge that carries road over another

foal /fəʊl/ *n* [C] young horse

foam /fəʊm/ *n* [U] **1** (*also* **foam rubber**) soft light rubber material used for seats, mattresses, etc **2** mass of small usu white air bubbles in a liquid ● **foam** *v* [I] (of a liquid) have or produce foam

fob /fɒb/ *v* (**-bb-**) [PV] **fob sb off (with sth)** trick sb into accepting sth of little or no value: *He ~bed me off with a weak excuse.*

0─ focus /ˈfəʊkəs/ *n* [C] **1** [usu sing] centre of interest: *the ~ of attention* **2** point at which rays of light, heat, etc meet [IDM] **in/out of focus** giving/ not giving a clear sharp picture ● **focus** *v* (**-s-** *or* **-ss-**) **1** [T] adjust a lens, etc to give a clear sharp image **2** [T] *~ (on)* give all your attention to sth/sb

fodder /ˈfɒdə(r)/ *n* [U] food for farm animals

foe /fəʊ/ *n* [C] (*old-fash* or *fml*) enemy

foetus /ˈfiːtəs/ *n* [C] young human or animal before it is born

fog /fɒɡ/ *n* [U,C] **1** thick cloud of tiny drops of water in the air: *I couldn't see through the ~.* **2** state of confusion ● **fog** *v* (**-gg-**) [I,T] **1** cover sth or become covered with fog: *The window has ~ged up.* **2** make sb/sth confused and less clear ■ **fogbound** *adj* unable to travel or operate because of fog ▶ **foggy** *adj* (**-ier, -iest**) not clear because of fog: *a ~gy night* ■ **foghorn** *n* [C] instrument used for warning ships in fog ■ **fog lamp** (*also* **fog light**) *n* [C] powerful light on the front of a car for use in fog

foil /fɔɪl/ *n* **1** [U] metal cut into thin sheets, used for covering food **2** [C] person or thing that contrasts with

foist

172

another ● **foil** v [T] prevent sb from doing sth, esp sth illegal

foist /fɔɪst/ v [PV] **foist sb/sth on/upon sb** force sb to accept sb/sth that they do not want

☞ **fold** /fəʊld/ v **1** [T] bend one part of sth back on itself: ~ *a letter* **2** [I] be able to be folded: *a ~ing bed* **3** [I] (of a business) come to an end; fail [IDM] **fold your arms** cross your arms over your chest ● **fold** n [C] **1** part of fabric, etc that is folded **2** line made by folding sth **3** area surrounded by a wall where sheep are kept ■ **folder** n [C] holder, usu made of cardboard, for papers

foliage /ˈfəʊliɪdʒ/ n [U] (*fml*) all the leaves of a tree or plant

☞ **folk** /fəʊk/ n **1** [pl] people in general **2** (folks) [pl] (*infml*) relatives **3** [U] (*also* **folk music**) music in the traditional style of a country or community ■ **folk dance** [C,U] (music for a) traditional popular dance ■ **folklore** /ˈfəʊkləː(r)/ n [U] traditions and stories of a country or community ■ **folk music** = FOLK(3) ■ **folk song** n [C] traditional popular song

☞ **follow** /ˈfɒləʊ/ v **1** [I] come or go after sb/sth **2** [I] be the logical result of sth: *It ~s from what you say that...* **3** [T] go along a road, etc **4** [T] act according to advice, instructions, etc **5** [I,T] understand sth: *I don't ~ (your meaning).* **6** [T] watch or listen to sb/sth carefully **7** [T] take an interest in sth: ~ *all the football news* [IDM] **as follows** used to introduce a list **follow in sb's footsteps** do what sb else has done earlier **follow your nose** act instinctively **follow suit** do what sb else has just done [PV] **follow sth through** carry out or continue sth to the end **follow sth up 1** add to sth you have just done by doing sth else **2** investigate sth: *Police are ~ing up a new lead.* ▶ **follower** n [C] supporter or admirer ■ **follow-up** n [C] something done to continue what has already been done: *a ~-up visit*

☞ **following** /ˈfɒləʊɪŋ/ adj (the following...) **1** next **2** about to be mentioned: *Answer the ~ questions.* ● **following** n [usu sing] group of supporters ● **following** prep after or as a result of a particular event

folly /ˈfɒli/ n (pl -ies) [U,C] (action that shows) lack of judgement; foolishness

fond /fɒnd/ adj **1** ~ **of** having a great liking for sb/sth **2** loving: *a ~ embrace* **3** hoped for but not likely to happen: ~ *hopes* ▶ **fondly** adv ■ **fondness** n [U]

fondle /ˈfɒndl/ v [T] touch sb/sth lovingly

font /fɒnt/ n [C] **1** basin in a church to hold water for baptism **2** (*tech*) size and style of a set of letters used for printing or computer documents

☞ **food** /fuːd/ n **1** [U] things that people or animals eat: *a shortage of ~* **2** [C,U] particular kind of food: *health ~s* [IDM] **food for thought** idea that makes you think seriously ■ **foodstuff** n [usu pl] any substance used as food

fool /fuːl/ n [C] person who you think lacks intelligence or good judgement [IDM] **act/play the fool** behave in a stupid way to make people laugh **make a fool of yourself** do sth stupid ● **fool** v **1** [T] trick sb into believing sth that is not true **2** [I] ~ **(about/around)** behave in a silly way, often in order to make people laugh: *Stop ~ing around!* ● **fool** adj (*infml*) stupid ■ **foolhardy** adj (*disapprov*) taking unnecessary risks ▶ **foolish** adj silly ▶ **foolishly** adv ▶ **foolishness** n [U] ■ **foolproof** adj that cannot go wrong: *a ~proof plan*

☞ **foot** /fʊt/ n (pl **feet** /fiːt/) **1** [C] lowest part of the leg, below the ankle **2** [sing] lowest part: *at the ~ of the stairs* **3** [C] (pl **feet** or **foot**) (*abbr* **ft**) measure of length equal to 12 inches (30.48 centimetres) [IDM] **fall/land on your feet** recover quickly esp through good luck, after being in difficulties **on foot** walking **put your feet up** rest **put your foot down** be firm in opposing sb/sth **put your foot in it** say or do sth that upsets or offends sb else ● **foot** v [IDM] **foot the bill** pay the bill ■ **foot-and-mouth disease** n [U] disease that cows, sheep, etc. can die from, which causes sore places on the mouth and feet ■ **football** n **1** [U] game played by two teams of 11 players. Each team tries to kick the ball into the other's goal. **2** [C] large round or oval ball ■ **footballer** n [C] (*GB*) person who plays football ■ **football pools** n [pl] system of betting money on the results of football matches ■ **footer** n [C] line of text that is automatically added to the bottom of every page that is printed from a computer ■ **foothill** n [usu pl] low hill at the base of a mountain ■ **foothold** n [C] **1** firm place for the foot when climbing **2** strong position in a business, etc from which progress can be made ■ **footnote** n [C] note at the bottom of a page ■ **footpath** n [C] path made for people to walk along ■ **footprint** n [usu sing] mark made by sb's foot ■ **footstep** n [usu pl] sound or mark made each time your foot touches the ground ■ **footwear** n [U] shoes, etc

footing /ˈfʊtɪŋ/ n [sing] **1** secure

A B C D E **F** G H I J K L M N O P Q R S T U V W X Y Z

placing of the feet **2** relationship with others: *on an equal ~*

for /fə(r); strong form fɔː(r)/ *prep* **1** used to show the person who is intended to have or use sth or where sth is intended to be put: *a letter ~ you* ◇ *a table ~ the kitchen* **2** in order to help sb/sth: *What can I do ~ you?* **3** concerning sb/sth: *anxious ~ his safety* **4** representing sb/sth; meaning: *Speak ~ yourself!* ◇ *Red is ~ danger.* **5** in support of sb/sth: *Are you ~ or against nuclear arms?* **6** used to show purpose or reason: *go ~ a walk* ◇ *What's this machine ~?* **7** used to show reason or cause: *famous ~ its church* **8** in order to obtain sth: *pray ~ peace* ◇ *buy a book — £15* ◇ *trade your car in ~ a new one* **10** considering what can be expected from sb/sth: *She's tall ~ her age.* **11** used to show when sb/sth is going: *Is this the train ~ York?* **12** used to show a distance or a length of time: *walk ~ three miles* ◇ *stay ~ a few days* **13** used to say how difficult, necessary, pleasant, etc sth is that sb might do or has done: *It's impossible ~ me to go.*

forage /ˈfɒrɪdʒ/ *v* [I] ~ **(for)** search for sth: *birds foraging for food*

foray /ˈfɒreɪ/ *n* sudden attack or rush: *(fig) the company's first ~ into the computer market*

forbear *n* [C] = FOREBEAR

forbearance /fɔːˈbeərəns/ *n* [U] (*fml*) quality of being patient and forgiving

forbid /fəˈbɪd/ *v* (*pt* **forbade** /fəˈbæd; fəˈbeɪd/ *pp* **-den** /fəˈbɪdn/) [T] ~ **(to)** order sb not to do sth; order that sth must not be done: *I ~ you to go.* ◇ *Smoking is ~den.* ▶ **forbidding** *adj* looking unfriendly; threatening

force /fɔːs/ *n* **1** [U] strength, power or violence **2** [C,U] power or influence: *the ~s of nature* ◇ *economic ~s* **3** [U] authority: *the ~ of the law* **4** [C] group of soldiers, etc: *the police ~* ◇ *a sales ~* **5** [C, U] power that causes movement: *the ~ of gravity* [IDM] **bring sth/come into force** (cause a law, rule, etc to) start being used in force **1** (of people) in large numbers **2** (of a law, etc) being used ● **force** *v* [T] **1** ~ **(to)** make sb do sth they do not want to do: ~ *him to talk* **2** use physical strength to move sb/sth into a particular position: ~ *a lock/door* (= break it open using force) **3** make yourself laugh, smile, etc ▶ **forceful** /ˈfɔːsfl/ *adj* (of a person or argument, etc) strong; convincing ▶ **forcefully** /-fəli/ *adv* ▶ **forcible** /ˈfɔːsəbl/ *adj* involving the use of physical force ▶ **forcibly** *adv*

forceps /ˈfɔːseps/ *n* [pl] medical instrument used for holding things

ford /fɔːd/ *n* [C] shallow place in a river where you can walk or drive across ● **ford** *v* [T] cross a river or a stream

fore /fɔː(r)/ *adj* front ● **fore** *n* [IDM] **be/come to the fore** be/become important

forearm /ˈfɔːrɑːm/ *n* [C] part of the arm from the elbow to the wrist

forebear (*also* **forbear**) /ˈfɔːbeə(r)/ *n* [C, usu pl] (*fml*) ancestor

foreboding /fɔːˈbəʊdɪŋ/ *n* [U,C] strong feeling that danger or trouble is coming

forecast /ˈfɔːkɑːst/ *v* (*pt, pp* ~ or **-ed**) [T] say in advance what is expected to happen ● **forecast** *n* [C] statement of expected future events: *weather ~*

forecourt /ˈfɔːkɔːt/ *n* [C] open area in front of a building

forefather /ˈfɔːfɑːðə(r)/ *n* [C, usu pl] (*fml or lit*) person in your family who lived a long time ago; ancestor

forefinger /ˈfɔːfɪŋɡə(r)/ *n* [C] finger next to the thumb

forefront /ˈfɔːfrʌnt/ *n* [sing] most forward or important position: *in the ~ of space research*

foregone /fɔːˈɡɒn/ *adj* [IDM] **a foregone conclusion** result that is certain to happen

foreground /ˈfɔːɡraʊnd/ *n* [sing] (**the foreground**) **1** nearest part of a view or picture: *in the ~* **2** most important and noticeable position

forehand /ˈfɔːhænd/ *n* [C], *adj* (stroke in tennis, etc) made with the palm of your hand turned forward

forehead /ˈfɔːhed; ˈfɒrɪd/ *n* [C] part of the face above the eyes

foreign /ˈfɒrən/ *adj* **1** of, in or from a country that is not your own **2** concerning other countries: ~ *policy* **3** ~ **to** (*fml*) not natural to sb/sth: ~ *to his nature* **4** (*fml*) having entered sth by accident: *a ~ body* (= eg a hair) *in the eye* ▶ **foreigner** *n* [C] foreign person ■ **foreign exchange** *n* [U] (system of buying and selling) foreign money

foreman /ˈfɔːmən/ *n* (*pl* **-men** /-mən/ *fem* **forewoman** /-wʊmən/ *pl* **-women** /-wɪmɪn/) **1** worker who is in charge of others **2** leader of a jury

foremost /ˈfɔːməʊst/ *adj* most important

forensic /fəˈrensɪk/ *adj* of or used in courts of law: ~ *medicine*

forerunner /ˈfɔːrʌnə(r)/ *n* [C] person or thing that prepares the way for the coming of another

foresee /fɔːˈsiː/ *v* (*pt* **foresaw** /fɔːˈsɔː/ *pp* ~**n** /fɔːˈsiːn/) [T] see in advance what is going to happen: ~ *difficulties* ▶ **foreseeable** /fɔːˈsiːəbl/ *adj* that can be foreseen [IDM] **in the foreseeable future** for the time being; fairly soon

forest

0─ forest /ˈfɒrɪst/ n [C,U] large area of land covered with trees ▶ **forestry** n [U] science and practice of planting and caring for forests

forestall /fɔːˈstɔːl/ v [T] (*written*) prevent sth from happening by doing sth first

foretell /fɔːˈtel/ v (pt, pp **foretold** /fɔːˈtəʊld/) [T] (*lit*) say what will happen in the future

forethought /ˈfɔːθɔːt/ n [U] careful planning for the future

0─ forever /fərˈevə(r)/ adv 1 (*also* **for ever**) always: I'll love you ~! ◇ (*infml*) It takes her ~ (= a very long time) to get dressed. 2 (*spoken*) constantly: He is ~ complaining.

forewarn /fɔːˈwɔːn/ v [T] ~ **(of)** warn sb of a possible danger or problem

foreword /ˈfɔːwɜːd/ n [C] short introduction to a book

forfeit /ˈfɔːfɪt/ v [T] lose sth as a punishment for or as a result of an action ● **forfeit** n [C] something forfeited

forgave pt of FORGIVE

forge /fɔːdʒ/ n [C] place where objects are made by heating and shaping metal ● **forge** v [T] 1 put a lot of effort into making sth successful: ~ a friendship/link 2 make an illegal copy of sth, in order to deceive people: ~ banknotes 3 shape metal by heating and hammering it [PV] **forge ahead (with sth)** advance or progress quickly ▶ **forger** n [C] person who forges money, documents, etc ▶ **forgery** /ˈfɔːdʒəri/ n (pl -ies) 1 [U] forging of money, documents, etc 2 [C] forged banknote, document, etc

0─ forget /fəˈget/ v (pt **forgot** /fəˈgɒt/ pp **forgotten** /fəˈgɒtn/) [I,T] 1 fail to remember sth: Don't ~ to post the letters. 2 stop thinking about sth: Let's ~ our differences. ▶ **forgetful** /fəˈgetfl/ adj in the habit of forgetting

0─ forgive /fəˈgɪv/ v (pt **forgave** /fəˈgeɪv/ pp **-n** /fəˈgɪvn/) [T] ~ **(for)** stop being angry with sb for sth they have done to you: She forgave him his rudeness. ▶ **forgivable** adj that can be forgiven ▶ **forgiveness** n [U] ▶ **forgiving** adj willing to forgive

forgo (*also* **forego**) /fɔːˈgəʊ/ v (pt **forwent** /fɔːˈwent/ pp **-gone** /-ˈgɒn/) [T] decide not to have or do sth that you would like

forgot pt of FORGET

forgotten pp of FORGET

0─ fork /fɔːk/ n [C] 1 tool with sharp points, used for lifting food to the mouth 2 gardening tool with metal points, used for digging 3 place where a road, tree, etc divides into two parts 4 thing shaped like a fork with two or more long parts ● **fork** v

1 [I] (of a road, etc) divide into two parts 2 [I] (of a person) turn left or right where a road, etc divides into two 3 [T] move, dig or carry sth with a fork [PV] **fork out (sth)** (*infml*) pay money unwillingly ▶ **forked** adj divided into two or more parts ■ **forklift truck** (*also* **fork-lift**) n [C] small powerful vehicle for lifting heavy goods

forlorn /fəˈlɔːn/ adj lonely and unhappy ▶ **forlornly** adv

0─ form¹ /fɔːm/ n 1 [C] kind or type: different ~s of government 2 [C,U] shape; appearance 3 [C] printed paper with spaces to be filled in: application ~s 4 [U] general way in which sth is made or put together: ~ and content 5 [C,U] (*gram*) spelling or pronunciation of a word: The plural ~ of 'goose' is 'geese'. 6 [C] (*GB, old-fash*) class in a school [IDM] **on/off form** fit/unfit; performing well/badly ▶ **formless** adj (*written*) without shape

0─ form² /fɔːm/ v 1 [I,T] (cause sth to) come into existence: ~ a government 2 [T] produce or give shape to sth 3 [I,T] be arranged or arrange sb/sth in a certain position or shape: ~ a line 4 linking verb be sth: It ~s part of the course.

0─ formal /ˈfɔːml/ adj 1 showing or expecting careful serious behaviour: a ~ dinner 2 (of clothes or words) used in formal situations 3 regular in design: ~ gardens 4 official: a ~ declaration of war ▶ **formality** /fɔːˈmæləti/ n (pl -ies) 1 [U] attention to rules 2 [C] action required by custom: a legal ~ity ▶ **formalize** (*also* -ise) v [T] make an arrangement, a plan, etc official ▶ **formally** adv

format /ˈfɔːmæt/ n [C] size, shape or general arrangement of sth ● **format** v (-tt-) [T] arrange sth in a particular format, usu for a computer

formation /fɔːˈmeɪʃn/ n 1 [U] forming or shaping of sth 2 [C,U] structure; arrangement

formative /ˈfɔːmətɪv/ adj influencing the development of sth or of sb's character: a child's ~ years

0─ former /ˈfɔːmə(r)/ adj of an earlier period: the ~ president ▶ **the former** pron the first of two people or things mentioned ▶ **formerly** adv in earlier times

formidable /ˈfɔːmɪdəbl/ adj (of people, things or situations) causing fear and respect because they are impressive or powerful or because they seem very difficult: a ~ opponent ▶ **formidably** /-əbli/ adv

0─ formula /ˈfɔːmjələ/ n (C) (pl -s or, in scientific use, **-mulae** /-mjuliː/) 1 rule, fact, etc shown in letters, signs or numbers: a chemical ~ 2 method or set of ideas to achieve sth: *a peace* ~ **3** list of things that sth is made from **4** fixed group of words used in a particular situation

formulate /'fɔːmjuleɪt/ v [T] **1** create or prepare sth carefully **2** express sth in carefully chosen words ▸ **formulation** /-'leɪʃn/ n [U,C]

forsake /fə'seɪk/ v (pt **forsook** /fə'sʊk/ pp ~**n** /fə'seɪkən/) [T] (fml) leave sb/sth

fort /fɔːt/ n [C] building for military defence

forte /'fɔːteɪ/ n [sing] something sb does well: *Singing is not my* ~.

forth /fɔːθ/ adv (lit) away from a place; out [IDM] **and (so on and) so forth** and other things of the same kind

forthcoming /ˌfɔːθ'kʌmɪŋ/ adj **1** about to happen, be published, etc very soon when needed: *The money was not* ~. **3** willing to give information about sth

fortieth → FORTY

fortify /'fɔːtɪfaɪ/ v (pt, pp **-ied**) [T] **1** ~ **(against)** strengthen a place against attack **2** make sb/sth stronger: *cereal fortified with extra vitamins* ▸ **fortification** /ˌfɔːtɪfɪ'keɪʃn/ n **1** [U] act of fortifying sth **2** [C, usu pl] tower, wall, etc built for defence

fortnight /'fɔːtnaɪt/ n [C] (esp GB) two weeks ▸ **fortnightly** adj, adv happening every fortnight

fortress /'fɔːtrəs/ n [C] large fort; castle

fortuitous /fɔː'tjuːɪtəs/ adj (fml) happening by chance

fortunate /'fɔːtʃənət/ adj lucky ▸ **fortunately** adv

0→ **fortune** /'fɔːtʃuːn/ n **1** [C,U] good or bad luck; chance **2** [C] what will happen to sb in the future: *tell sb's* ~ **3** [C] large amount of money: *cost a* ~ ■ **fortune-teller** [C] person who tells people's fortunes (2)

0→ **forty** /'fɔːti/ number **1** 40 **2** (**the forties**) n [pl] numbers, years or temperatures from 40 to 49 ▸ **fortieth** /'fɔːtiəθ/ ordinal number

forum /'fɔːrəm/ n [C] place for public discussion: *an internet* ~

0→ **forward**[1] /'fɔːwəd/ adj **1** directed towards the front; at the front: *movements* **2** (of the future: ~ *planning* **3** behaving in a way that is too confident or informal ● **forward** n [C] attacking player in football, etc ● **forward** v [T] **1** send or pass goods or information to sb **2** send on (a letter, etc to a new address **3** help to develop sth: ~ *his career* ▸ **forwardness** n [U] behaviour that is too confident or informal

0→ **forward**[2] /'fɔːwəd/ adv (also **forwards**) towards the front; towards the future ■ **forward-looking** adj (approv) having modern ideas

forwent pt of FORGO

fossil /'fɒsl/ n [C] remains of an animal or plant that have hardened and turned into rock ▸ **fossilize** (*also* -ise) /'fɒsəlaɪz/ v [I,T] **1** (cause sth to) become a fossil **2** (*disapprov*) (cause sth to) become fixed and unable to change

foster /'fɒstə(r)/ v [T] **1** encourage sth to develop **2** take care of a child without becoming his/her legal parent ● **foster** adj used with some nouns in connection with the fostering of a child: *a* ~ *mother*

fought pt, pp of FIGHT

foul /faʊl/ adj **1** dirty and smelling bad **2** very unpleasant; very bad: *a* ~ *temper* **3** (of language) obscene and offensive **4** (of weather) stormy ● **foul** n [C] (sport) action against the rules ● **foul** v [I,T] (sport) commit a foul against another player **2** [T] make sth dirty [PV] **foul sth up** (infml) spoil sth ■ **foul 'play** n [U] **1** criminal violence that leads to murder **2** (sport) unfair play

found[1] pt, pp of FIND

0→ **found**[2] /faʊnd/ v [T] **1** build or establish sth: ~ *a hospital* **2** (usu passive) base sth on sth: *a novel* ~*ed on facts*

0→ **foundation** /faʊn'deɪʃn/ n **1** [C, usu pl] layer of bricks, etc that form the strong base of a building **2** [C, U] an idea, etc on which sth is based **3** [C] organization that provides money for a charity, etc **4** [U] act of starting a new institution or organization

founder /'faʊndə(r)/ v [I] (written) **1** (of a plan, etc) fail **2** (of a ship) fill with water and sink ● **founder** n [C] person who establishes sth

foundry /'faʊndri/ n [C] (pl **-ies**) factory where metal or glass is melted and shaped into objects

fount /faʊnt/ n [C] ~ **(of)** (lit or num) place where sth important comes from: *the* ~ *of all knowledge*

fountain /'faʊntən/ n [C] **1** ornamental structure from which water is pumped into the air **2** powerful jet of liquid ■ **'fountain pen** n [C] pen with a container from which ink flows to the nib

0→ **four** /fɔː(r)/ number **4** [IDM] **on all fours** bent over with your hands and knees on the ground ▸ **fourth** /fɔːθ/ ordinal number [C] **1** 4th **2** (esp US) = QUARTER

0→ **fourteen** /ˌfɔː'tiːn/ number **14** ▸ **fourteenth** ordinal number

fowl /faʊl/ n (pl **fowl** or ~**s**) [C, U] bird, eg a chicken, kept for its meat or eggs

fox /fɒks/ n [C] wild animal of the dog family with red fur and a bushy tail ● **fox** v [T] (infml) confuse or trick sb

foyer

'fox-hunting n [U] sport in which a fox is hunted by hounds and people on horses

foyer /ˈfɔɪeɪ/ n [C] **1** large entrance hall in a theatre or hotel **2** (US) entrance hall in a private house or flat

fractal /ˈfræktl/ n [C] (maths, physics) pattern that includes a smaller pattern which has exactly the same shape

fraction /ˈfrækʃn/ n [C] **1** division of a number, eg ⅓ **2** small part: a ~ of a second ▸ **fractional** /-ʃənl/ adj very small

fracture /ˈfræktʃə(r)/ n [C, U] **1** breaking of sth, esp a bone ● **fracture** v [I, T] (cause sth to) break or crack

fragile /ˈfrædʒaɪl/ adj **1** easily broken or damaged **2** (infml) weak; not healthy ▸ **fragility** /frəˈdʒɪləti/ n [U]

fragment /ˈfrægmənt/ n [C] small part of sth that has broken off ● **fragment** /frægˈment/ v [I, T] (written) (cause sth to) break into pieces ▸ **fragmentary** adj incomplete ▸ **fragmentation** /ˌfrægmenˈteɪʃn/ n [U]

fragrance /ˈfreɪgrəns/ n [C, U] sweet smell ▸ **fragrant** /ˈfreɪgrənt/ adj sweet-smelling

frail /freɪl/ adj weak ▸ **frailty** n (pl -ies) **1** [U] quality of being frail **2** [U, C] fault in sb's character

0— **frame** /freɪm/ n [C] **1** border in which a picture, window, etc is set **2** main structure of a building, vehicle, etc that forms a support for its parts **3** [usu pl] structure that holds the lenses of a pair of glasses **4** [usu sing] human or animal body **5** single photograph on a cinema film [IDM] **a frame of mind** mood; way you feel about sth ● **frame** v [T] **1** put a frame ( ) round sth **2** (infml) make an innocent person appear guilty of a crime **3** express sth in words ■ **framework** n [C] **1** structure giving shape and support **2** set of principles or ideas

franchise /ˈfræntʃaɪz/ n [C, U] (fml) right to vote

frank /fræŋk/ adj showing thoughts and feelings openly ▸ **frankly** adv ▸ **frankness** n [U] ● **frank** v [T] mark a letter to show that postage has been paid

frankfurter /ˈfræŋkfɜːtə(r)/ n [C] kind of small smoked sausage

frantic /ˈfræntɪk/ adj **1** wildly afraid or anxious **2** hurried but disorganized ▸ **frantically** /-kli/ adv

fraternal /frəˈtɜːnl/ adj brotherly ▸ **fraternally** adv

fraternity /frəˈtɜːnəti/ n (pl -ies)

1 [C] group of people with the same interests or job **2** [C] (US) society of male university students **3** [U] brotherly feeling

fraternize (also **-ise**) /ˈfrætənaɪz/ v [I] ~ **(with)** become friendly with sb: ~ with the enemy ▸ **fraternization** (also **-isation**) /ˌfrætənaɪˈzeɪʃn/ n [U]

fraud /frɔːd/ n **1** [C, U] crime of deceiving sb in order to gain money illegally **2** [C] person who deceives others ▸ **fraudulent** /ˈfrɔːdjələnt/ adj intended to deceive sb

fraught /frɔːt/ adj **1** ~ **with** filled: ~ with danger **2** worried or anxious

fray /freɪ/ v [I, T] **1** (cause cloth, etc to) become worn, so that there are loose threads **2** (cause sth to) become strained: ~ed nerves

freak /friːk/ n [C] **1** very unusual act or event: a ~ storm **2** person thought to be very abnormal **3** (infml) person who is very interested in sth mentioned: a jazz ~ ▸ **freakish** adj strange; unusual

freckle /ˈfrekl/ n [C, usu pl] small brown spot on a person's skin ▸ **freckled** adj

0— **free** /friː/ adj (~**r**, ~**st**) **1** not in prison; allowed to go where you want **2** not controlled by sb else, rules, a government, etc: a ~ democracy with ~ speech and a ~ press **3** costing nothing **4** not blocked; clear: a ~ flow of water **5** ~ **from/of** without sth, usu sth unpleasant: ~ from pain/blame **6** without the thing mentioned: tax ~ **7** not fixed to sth: the ~ end of a rope **8** not being used: a ~ seat **9** (of a person) not busy **10** ~ **with** ready to give sth, esp sth not wanted: He's ~ with his opinions. [IDM] **free and easy** relaxed a free hand permission to do what you want: get/have a ~ hand ● **free** adv **1** without payment **2** no longer fixed or trapped [IDM] **make free with sth** use sth a lot, even though it does not belong to you ● **free** v [T] make sb/sth free ■ **free 'enterprise** n [U] operation of business and trade without government control ■ **'free-for-all** n [sing] quarrel, fight, etc in which everyone joins in ■ **'freehand** adj, adv (drawn) by hand, without instruments ■ **'freelance** adj, adv done by a writer, artist, etc who works for several employers ● **freelance** v [I] work in this way ▸ **freely** adv **1** in a free manner; readily ■ **free 'radical** n [C] (chem) atom or group of atoms that has an electron that is not part of a pair, causing it to take part easily in chemical reactions ■ **free-range** adj produced by hens kept in natural conditions ■ **free 'speech** n [U] right to express one's opinions in public ■ **free 'trade** n [U] system of international trade without taxes or

---

other controls ■ **freeway** *n* [C] (*US*) = MOTORWAY ■ **free 'will** *n* [U] power to make your own decisions independently of God or fate [IDM] **of your own free will** because you want to do sth

0—w **freedom** /ˈfriːdəm/ *n* **1** [C,U] ~ (of) right to do or say what you want without anyone stopping you: ~ *of speech* **2** [U] state of being free

0—w **freeze** /friːz/ *v* (*pt* **froze** /frəʊz/ *pp* **frozen** /ˈfrəʊzn/) **1** [I] (esp of water) change into ice **2** [I] (used with *it*) (of weather) be at or below 0° Celsius: *It's freezing today.* **3** [I] be very cold: be *so cold you could die: He froze to death on the mountain.* **4** [T] keep food, etc at a temperature below freezing point: *frozen peas* **5** [I] stop moving suddenly because of fear, etc: ~ *with terror* **6** [T] hold prices, wages, etc at a fixed level [IDM] **freeze the blood** of **COLD** [PV] **freeze over/up** become covered/blocked with ice ● **freeze** *n* [C] **1** period of freezing weather **2** fixing of wages, prices, etc ▸ **freezer** *n* [C] large refrigerator in which food is kept frozen ■ **'freezing point** *n* [U,C] temperature at which a liquid, esp water, freezes

freight /freɪt/ *n* [U] goods carried by ships, aircraft, etc ● **freight** *v* [T] send or carry goods by air, sea or train ▸ **freighter** *n* [C] ship or aircraft that carries freight

French /frentʃ/ *adj* of France, its people or their language ■ **French 'fry** *n* (*usu pl*) (*esp US*) = CHIP(1) ■ **French 'window** *n* [C, *usu pl*] glass door that opens onto a garden or balcony

frenzy /ˈfrenzi/ *n* [C, *usu sing*, U] violent excitement ▸ **frenzied** *adj*

frequency /ˈfriːkwənsi/ *n* (*pl* **-ies**) **1** [U] rate at which sth happens or is repeated **2** [C] rate at which a radio wave vibrates

0—w **frequent¹** /ˈfriːkwənt/ *adj* happening often ▸ **frequently** *adv*

frequent² /friˈkwent/ *v* [T] (*fml*) go to a place often

fresco /ˈfreskəʊ/ *n* [C] (*pl* ~**es** or ~**s**) picture painted on a wall before the plaster is dry

0—w **fresh** /freʃ/ *adj* **1** new or different: *make a ~ start* **2** newly made or produced; not stale: ~ *bread* **3** (of food) not tinned or frozen **4** (of water) not salty **5** (of weather) cool and windy **6** (of colours) clear and bright **7** full of energy **8** (*infml*) rude and too confident with sb ~ **from** having just left a place: *students ~ from college* ▸ **freshly** *adv* (*usu with a pp*) recently: ~*ly painted* ▸ **freshness** [U] ▸ **freshwater** *adj* living in or having water that is not salty

freshen /ˈfreʃn/ *v* **1** [T] make sth

fresh **2** [I] (of the wind) become stronger [PV] **freshen** (*yourself*) **up** wash and make yourself look clean and tidy

fret /fret/ *v* (-**tt**-) [I,T] ~ (**about**) (cause sb to) worry about sth ▸ **fretful** /ˈfretfl/ *adj* worried or complaining ▸ **fretfully** *adv* ● **fret** *n* [C] one of the metal bars across the neck of a guitar, etc

friar /ˈfraɪə(r)/ *n* [C] male member of a certain Christian group

friction /ˈfrɪkʃn/ *n* **1** [U] rubbing of one thing against another **2** [C, U] disagreement between people

0—w **Friday** /ˈfraɪdeɪ; -di/ *n* [C,U] the day of the week after Thursday and before Saturday (See examples of use at *Monday*.)

0—w **fridge** /frɪdʒ/ *n* [C] (*GB*) (*also fml* or *US* **refrigerator**) electrical appliance in which food is kept cold

fried *pt, pp* of FRY

0—w **friend** /frend/ *n* [C] **1** person you know well and like, but who is not a relative (*often distinct*): *a ~ of the arts* [IDM] **be/make friends** (**with sb**) become a friend of sb ▸ **friendless** *adj* without any friends ▸ **friendly** *adj* (**-ier, -iest**) **1** acting as a friend **2** (of an argument, game, etc) not as a serious competition ▸ **friendliness** *n* [U] ▸ **friendship** *n* [C, U] friendly relationship

frieze /friːz/ *n* [C] band of decoration along the top of a wall

frigate /ˈfrɪɡət/ *n* [C] small fast warship

fright /fraɪt/ *n* [U,C] feeling of sudden fear

0—w **frighten** /ˈfraɪtn/ *v* [T] make sb suddenly feel afraid ▸ **frightened** *adj* afraid ▸ **frightening** *adj* causing fear ▸ **frighteningly** *adv*

frightful /ˈfraɪtfl/ *adj* (*old-fash*) very unpleasant; very bad ▸ **frightfully** /-fli/ *adv* (*old-fash*) very

frigid /ˈfrɪdʒɪd/ *adj* **1** (of a woman) not able to enjoy sex **2** very cold ▸ **frigidity** /frɪˈdʒɪdəti/ *n* [U] ▸ **frigidly** *adv*

frill /frɪl/ *n* **1** [C] decorative border on a dress, etc **2** [*pl*] unnecessary additions ▸ **frilly** *adj*

fringe /frɪndʒ/ *n* **1** hair hanging over the forehead **2** decorative edge of loose threads on a rug, etc **3** outer edge: *on the ~ of the crowd*

frisk /frɪsk/ *v* **1** [T] pass your hands over sb's body to search for hidden weapons, etc **2** [I] (of animals) jump and run about playfully ▸ **frisky** *adj* (**-ier, -iest**) lively

fritter /ˈfrɪtə(r)/ *v* [PV] **fritter sth away** (**on sth**) waste money or time on unimportant things ● **fritter** *n* [C] piece of fried batter, with sliced fruit, meat, etc in it

frivolous

frivolous /ˈfrɪvələs/ *adj* not serious; silly ▶ **frivolity** /frɪˈvɒləti/ *n* (pl -ies) [U, C] silly behaviour, esp when this is not suitable ▶ **frivolously** *adv*

frizzy /ˈfrɪzi/ *adj* (of hair) having small tight curls

fro /frəʊ/ *adv* [IDM] **to and fro** → TO³

frog /frɒɡ/ *n* [C] small cold-blooded jumping animal that lives in water and on land ■ **frogman** *n* [C] (pl -men) (GB) person who works underwater, wearing a rubber suit and breathing apparatus

frolic /ˈfrɒlɪk/ *v* (pt, pp ~ked) [I] play about in a lively way ● **frolic** *n* [sing] (old-fash) lively and enjoyable activity

0— **from** /frəm; strong form frɒm/ *prep* **1** used to show where sb/sth starts: *the train ~ Leeds* **2** used to show when sth starts: *on holiday ~ 1 May* **3** used to show who sent or gave sth: *a letter ~ my brother* **4** used to show what the origin of sb/sth is: *quotations ~ Shakespeare* **5** used to show the material that sth is made of: *Wine is made ~ grapes.* **6** used to show the distance between two places: *10 miles ~ the sea* **7** used to show the range of sth: *Tickets cost ~ £3 to £12.* **8** used to show change: *~ bad to worse* **9** used to show that sb/ sth is separated or removed: *take the money ~ my purse* **10** used to show that sth is prevented: *save a boy ~ drowning* **11** used to show the reason for sth: *She felt sick ~ tiredness.* **12** used to show the reason for making a judgement: *reach a decision ~ the evidence*

0— **front** /frʌnt/ *n* **1** (usu the front) [C, sing] part or side of sth that faces forward: *the ~ of a building* **2** [sing] the part of sb's body that faces forward; the chest: *Lie on your ~.* **3** (the front) [sing] (GB) road beside the sea **4** (the front) [C, usu sing] (in war) area where fighting takes place **5** [C] particular area of activity: *on the financial ~* **6** [sing] (often fake) behaviour: *put on a brave ~* **7** [C, usu sing] ~ (for) person or organization that hides an illegal or secret activity **8** [C] where cold air meets warm air [IDM] **in front** in the most forward position; ahead **in front of 1** ahead of sb/sth **2** in the presence of sb ● **front** *v* [I, T] show the front facing sth: *hotels that ~ onto the sea* ▶ **frontage** /ˈfrʌntɪdʒ/ *n* [U] extent of a piece of land or building along its front ▶ **frontal** *adj* of, from or in the front ■ **the front line** *n* [sing] line of fighting that is nearest the enemy ■ **front-page** *adj* appearing on the front page of a newspaper

frontier /ˈfrʌntɪə(r)/ *n* [C] **1** (land near) the border between two countries **2** [usu pl] extreme limit: *the ~s of science*

frost /frɒst/ *n* [C, U] (period of) weather with the temperature below freezing point **2** [U] thin white layer of ice on the ground ● **frost** *v* [I, T] ~ **over/up** (cause sth to become covered with frost (C)) **2** [T] give a rough surface to glass to make it opaque: *~ed windows* **3** [T] (esp US) cover a cake with powdered sugar ■ **frostbite** *n* [U] injury to the fingers, toes, etc caused by extreme cold ▶ **frostbitten** *adj* ▶ **frosty** *adj* (-ier, -iest) **1** cold with frost **2** unfriendly: *a ~y welcome*

froth /frɒθ/ *n* [U] **1** mass of small bubbles, eg on beer **2** (disapprov) light but worthless talk, ideas, etc ● **froth** *v* [I] have or produce froth ▶ **frothy** *adj* (-ier, -iest) like or covered with froth

frown /fraʊn/ *v* [I] bring your eyebrows together to express anger, thought, etc [PV] **frown on/upon sth** disapprove of sth ▶ **frown** *n* [C]

froze *pt* of FREEZE

frozen *pp* of FREEZE

frugal /ˈfruːɡl/ *adj* **1** not wasteful; economical **2** costing little; small ▶ **frugality** /fruˈɡæləti/ *n* [U]

0— **fruit** /fruːt/ *n* **1** [C, U] part of a plant used as food, eg apple, banana **2** [C] (tech) part of a plant or tree which contains the seeds [IDM] **the fruit/fruits of sth** good results of hard work, etc ▶ **fruitful** *adj* producing useful results ▶ **fruitless** *adj* producing no useful results ▶ **fruity** *adj* (-ier, -iest) **1** of or like fruit **2** (infml) (of the voice) rich and deep

fruition /fruˈɪʃn/ *n* [U] (fml) successful result of a plan, process or activity: *Our plans finally came to ~.*

frustrate /frʌˈstreɪt/ *v* [T] **1** make sb feel annoyed because they cannot achieve what they want **2** prevent sb from doing sth or sth from happening ▶ **frustrated** *adj* annoyed; not satisfied ▶ **frustration** /frʌˈstreɪʃn/ *n* [U, C]

0— **fry** /fraɪ/ *v* (pt, pp **fried** /fraɪd/) [I, T] cook sth in hot fat or oil ■ **frying pan** (US **frypan**) *n* [C] shallow pan used for frying food [IDM] **out of the frying pan into the fire** from a bad situation to a worse one

ft (also **ft.**) *abbr* feet; foot

fuck /fʌk/ *v* [I, T] (△, sl) **1** have sex with sb **2** offensive swear word used to show anger or surprise [PV] **fuck off** go away ▶ **fuck** *n* [C] (△, sl) act of having sex ■ **fuck 'all** *n* [U] (△, sl) nothing ▶ **fucking** *adj, adv* (△, sl) offensive swear word used to emphasize a comment or angry remark

fudge /fʌdʒ/ *n* [U] soft brown sweet made of sugar, butter, milk, etc ● **fudge** *v* [T] (infml) avoid giving clear information or a clear answer

fuel /'fjuːəl/ n [U] material, eg coal or oil, burned to produce heat or power ● **fuel** v (-ll- US -l-) [T] **1** supply sth with fuel **2** make a bad situation worse: *to ~ inflation* ■ **'fuel injection** n [U] system of putting fuel into a car engine under pressure in order to improve its performance

fugitive /'fjuːdʒətɪv/ n [C] ~ (from) person who is escaping from sth

fulfil (US **fulfill**) /fʊl'fɪl/ v (-ll-) [T] **1** do or achieve what was hoped for, expected or required: *~ an ambition ◇ ~ a duty/promise* **2** make sb feel happy and satisfied with what they are doing or have done ▶ **fulfilment** n [U]

full /fʊl/ adj **1** holding as much or as many as possible: *a ~ bottle* **2** ~ of thinking or talking a lot about sth: (*disapprov*) *He's ~ of himself* (= thinking only of himself). **3** having eaten enough **4** complete: *give ~ details ◇ Write your name in ~.* **5** to the highest level or greatest amount possible: *He came round the corner at ~ speed. ◇ enjoy life to the ~* **6** plump: *a ~ figure/face* **7** (of clothes) wide and loose: *a ~ skirt* ● **full** adv **1** exactly; directly: *hit him ~ in the face* **2** very: *You knew ~ well that he was lying.* ■ **full 'board** n [U] hotel accommodation with all meals included ■ **full-length** adj **1** (of a picture, mirror, etc) showing the whole of a person **2** (of clothing) reaching the ankles ■ **full 'moon** n [C, usu sing] the moon appearing as a complete circle ▶ **fullness** n [U] ■ **full-scale** adj **1** (of drawings, plans, etc) of the same size as the object itself **2** complete: *a ~-scale inquiry* ■ **full 'stop** n [C] (*GB*) mark (.) used esp at the end of a sentence [IDM] **come to a full stop** stop completely ■ **full-'time** adj, adv working all the normal hours ▶ **fully** adv completely

fumble /'fʌmbl/ v [I] use your hands awkwardly

fume /fjuːm/ n [C, usu pl] strong-smelling smoke or gas ● **fume** v [I] **1** be very angry about sth **2** give off fumes

fun /fʌn/ n [U] **1** (source of) enjoyment; pleasure **2** playfulness [IDM] **for fun** for amusement in fun not seriously **make fun of sb/sth** laugh at sb/sth unkindly ■ **'funfair** n [C] = FAIR²(1)

function /'fʌŋkʃn/ n [C] **1** purpose of a thing or person **2** formal social event **3** (*computing*) part of a program, etc that carries out a basic operation ● **function** v [I] work in the correct way ▶ **functional** /-ʃənl/ adj **1** having a practical use, not decorative **2** working; able to work ▶ **functionality** /ˌfʌŋkʃəˈnæləti/ n **1** [U] quality in sth of being very

suitable for the purpose it was designed for **2** [U,C] (*computing*) range of functions that a computer or other electronic system can perform

fund /fʌnd/ n [C] **1** amount of money for a purpose **2** supply of sth: *a large ~ of experience* ● **fund** v [T] provide money for sth

fundamental /ˌfʌndəˈmentl/ adj very important; basic or essential ● **fundamental** n [C, usu pl] basic rule or principle ▶ **fundamentalism** /-təlɪzəm/ n [U] **1** practice of following very strictly the rules of any religion **2** (in Christianity) belief that everything written in the Bible is true ▶ **fundamentalist** n [C], adj ▶ **fundamentally** /-təli/ adv

funeral /'fjuːnərəl/ n [C] ceremony of burying or cremating (= burning) a dead person ■ **'funeral parlour** n [C] (*GB*) place where dead people are prepared for the funeral and where visitors can see the body

fungus /'fʌŋɡəs/ n [C, U] (pl **fungi** /'fʌŋɡiː; -ɡaɪ/) plant without leaves that grows on decaying matter, eg old wood

funnel /'fʌnl/ n [C] **1** tube that is wide at the top and narrow at the bottom, used for pouring liquids through **2** chimney on a steam engine or ship ● **funnel** v (-ll- US -l-) [I,T] pour sth through a funnel or narrow space

funny /'fʌni/ adj (-ier, -iest) **1** causing laughter; amusing **2** strange ▶ **funnily** adv ■ **'funny bone** n [C] sensitive part of the elbow

fur /fɜː(r)/ n **1** [U] soft thick hair covering a cat, rabbit, etc **2** [C] (coat, etc made from an) animal skin with the fur on it **3** [U] hard grey covering on the inside of kettles, pipes, etc ▶ **furry** adj (-ier, -iest) of, like or covered with fur

furious /'fjʊəriəs/ adj **1** very angry **2** very strong; wild: *a ~ storm* ▶ **furiously** adv

furlong /'fɜːlɒŋ/ n [C] distance of 220 yards (201 metres)

furnace /'fɜːnɪs/ n [C] enclosed fireplace used eg for heating metals

furnish /'fɜːnɪʃ/ v [T] **1** put furniture in a room, etc **2** (*fml*) provide sth with sth ▶ **furnishings** n [pl] furniture, carpets, curtains, etc in a room or house

furniture /'fɜːnɪtʃə(r)/ n [U] large movable things, eg tables, chairs, etc in a house or office

furrier /'fʌriə(r)/ n [C] person who prepares or sells fur clothing

furrow /'fʌrəʊ/ n [C] **1** long mark cut into the ground by a plough **2** deep

ABCDE **F** GHIJKLMNOPQRSTUVWXYZ

line in the skin of the face ▸ **furrow** v [T] make furrows in sth

furry → FUR

further /ˈfɜːðə(r)/ adv **1** at or to a greater distance in space or time: *It's not safe to go any ~.* **2** to a greater degree or extent **3** in addition ● **further** adj more; additional: *~ information* ● **further** v [T] help sb/sth to advance ▸ **furtherance** n [U] (fml) advancement ● **further edu'cation** n [U] (abbr **FE**) (GB) formal (but not university) education for people older than 16 ▸ **furthermore** adv (fml) in addition ▸ **furthermost** adj most distant

furthest /ˈfɜːðɪst/ *superlative of* FAR

furtive /ˈfɜːtɪv/ adj done or behaving secretly so as not to be noticed ▸ **furtively** adv ▸ **furtiveness** n [U]

fury /ˈfjʊəri/ n [U,C] violent anger

fuse /fjuːz/ n [C] **1** short wire in an electrical appliance that melts to break the circuit if the current is too strong **2** long piece of string or paper which is lit to make a bomb or firework explode **3** (US also **fuze**) device in a bomb that makes it explode ● **fuse** v [I,T] **1** (cause two things to) join together to form a single thing (GB) (cause sth to) stop functioning because a fuse melts: *~ the lights*

fuselage /ˈfjuːzəlɑːʒ/ n [C] body of an aircraft

fusion /ˈfjuːʒn/ n [C,U] mixing or joining of different things into one

fuss /fʌs/ n [U,sing] unnecessary excitement, worry or activity **IDM** **make a fuss of/over sb** pay a lot of loving attention to sb ● **fuss** v [I] be worried or excited esp about small things ▸ **fussy** adj (-ier, -iest) **1** ~ (about) too concerned about unimportant details **2** showing nervous excitement **3** (of dress or style) decorated too much ▸ **fussily** adv

futile /ˈfjuːtaɪl/ adj unsuccessful; useless ▸ **futility** /fjuːˈtɪləti/ n [U]

future /ˈfjuːtʃə(r)/ n **1** (the future) [sing] the time that will come after the present: *in the ~* **2** [C] what will happen to sb/sth: *The company's ~ is uncertain* **3** [C] possibility of success: *There is no ~ in this job.* **4** (futures) [pl] (business) goods or shares bought at agreed prices but to be delivered and paid for later **5** (the future) [sing] (also the **future 'tense**) [sing] (gram) form of a verb that expresses what will happen after the present **IDM** **in future** from now onwards ● **future** adj of or happening in the future

futuristic /ˌfjuːtʃəˈrɪstɪk/ adj looking very modern and strange

fuzz /fʌz/ n [U] fluff ▸ **fuzzy** adj (-ier,

-iest) **1** (of hair) tightly curled **2** (of cloth, etc) soft or fluffy **3** not clear in shape or sound ▸ **fuzzily** adv ▸ **fuzziness** n [U]

FYI abbr used in writing to mean 'for your information'

Gg

G, g /dʒiː/ n (pl **G's, g's** /dʒiːz/) the seventh letter of the English alphabet

g abbr gram(s): *500g*

gabble /ˈɡæbl/ v [I,T] talk or say sth too quickly to be understood ● **gabble** n [U] very fast talk

gable /ˈɡeɪbl/ n [C] triangular part of an outside wall, between the two sloping slides of the roof

gad /ɡæd/ v (-dd-) [PV] **gad about/around** (infml) visit different places and have fun

gadget /ˈɡædʒɪt/ n [C] small useful tool or device ▸ **gadgetry** n [U] gadgets

Gaelic n [U] adj **1** /ˈɡeɪlɪk/ (language) of the Celtic people of Ireland **2** /ˈɡælɪk; ˈɡeɪlɪk/ (language) of the Celtic people of Scotland

gaffe /ɡæf/ n [C] tactless remark or act

gag /ɡæɡ/ n [C] **1** something put over sb's mouth to prevent them from speaking **2** joke ● **gag** v (-gg-) [T] put a gag (1) on sb

gaga /ˈɡɑːɡɑː/ adj (infml) senile

gaggle /ˈɡæɡl/ n [C] **1** group of geese **2** group of noisy people

gaily /ˈɡeɪli/ adv happily; cheerfully

gain /ɡeɪn/ v [I,T] **1** obtain sth wanted or needed: *~ experience/an advantage* **2** increase in speed, weight, etc **3** (of a clock or watch) go too fast: *My watch ~s two minutes a day.* **IDM** **gain ground** → GROUND **gain time** obtain extra time by making excuses, thinking slowly, etc **PV** **gain on sb/sth** come closer to sb/sth, eg in a race ● **gain** n [C,U] increase in amount or wealth; advantage ▸ **gainful** /-fl/ adj useful work that you are paid for: *~ful employment*

gait /ɡeɪt/ n [C] way of walking

gala /ˈɡɑːlə/ n [C] special public celebration or entertainment

galaxy /ˈɡæləksi/ n (pl **-ies**) **1** [C] large group of stars (the Galaxy) [sing] the system of stars that contains our sun and planets, seen as a pale band in the sky **3** [C] (infml) group of people ▸ **galactic** /ɡəˈlæktɪk/ adj

gale /ɡeɪl/ n [C] **1** very strong wind **2** noisy outburst of laughter

gall /ɡɔːl/ n [U] **1** rude behaviour showing lack of respect **2** (fml) bitter feeling of hatred ■ 'gall bladder n [C] organ attached to the liver that stores bile • 'gallstone /n [C] hard painful mass that can form in the gall bladder • gall v [T] annoy sb

gallant /'gælənt/ adj 1 (old-fash or lit) brave 2 (of a man) giving polite attention to women ▶ gallantly adv ▶ gallantry n [U]

galleon /'gæliən/ n [C] Spanish sailing ship (15th to 17th centuries)

gallery /'gæləri/ n [C] (pl -ies) 1 room or building for showing works of art 2 raised area along an inner wall of a hall or theatre 3 highest seats in a theatre 4 passage in a mine

galley /'gæli/ n [C] 1 (in the past) long flat ship with sails and oars 2 kitchen on a ship or plane

gallivant /'gælivænt/ v [PV] gallivant about/around (old-fash, infml) travel for pleasure

0━ gallon /'gælən/ n [C] measure for liquids equal to 4.5 litres in the UK and 3.8 litres in the US

gallop /'gæləp/ n [C] fastest pace of a horse: at full ~ • gallop v 1 [I,T] (cause a horse to) go at a gallop 2 [I] (infml) hurry

gallows /'gæləʊz/ n [C] structure on which people, eg criminals are killed by hanging

galore /gə'lɔː(r)/ adv (infml) in large quantities: prizes ~

galvanize (also -ise) /'gælvənaɪz/ v [T] 1 ~ (into) shock sb into taking action 2 (tech) cover iron with zinc to protect it from rust

gambit /'gæmbɪt/ n [C] 1 thing said or done at the beginning of a conversation, etc, intended to give some advantage 2 opening move in chess, to produce an advantage later

0━ gamble /'gæmbl/ v [I] play games of chance for money [PV] gamble on sth take a risk with sth • gamble n [C] risky attempt to win money or to be successful ▶ gambler n [C] person who gambles ▶ gambling n [U]

gambol /'gæmbl/ v (-ll- US also -l-) [I] jump about playfully

0━ game /geɪm/ n 1 [C] form of play or sport with rules 2 (games) [pl] sports, esp athletics competitions 3 [C] single part of a match in tennis, etc 4 [C] children's activity when they play with toys, pretend to be sb else, etc 5 [C] activity or business: Politics is a power ~. 6 [C] (infml) secret plan or trick 7 [U] (flesh of) animals or birds hunted for food [IDM] give the game away carelessly reveal a secret (be) off one's game (be) unable to play as well as usual ■ 'gamekeeper n [C] man employed to breed and protect

game (7), eg pheasants • game adj willing to do sth risky ▶ gamely adv

gammon /'gæmən/ n [U] smoked or cured ham

gamut /'gæmət/ n (the gamut) [sing] complete range of sth

gander /'gændə(r)/ n [C] male goose

gang /gæŋ/ n [C, with sing or pl verb] 1 organized group of criminals or workers 2 group of young people, usu males, who often fight against other groups: a street ~ • gang v[PV] gang up (on/against sb) (infml) join together to hurt or frighten sb ■ 'gangmaster n [C] (GB) person who illegally employs foreign workers and pays them very low wages

gangling /'gæŋglɪŋ/ adj (of a person) tall, thin and awkward

gangrene /'gæŋgriːn/ n [U] decay of a part of the body because blood has stopped flowing to it ▶ gangrenous /'gæŋgrɪnəs/ adj

gangster /'gæŋstə(r)/ n [C] member of a gang of armed criminals

gangway /'gæŋweɪ/ n [C] 1 movable bridge from a ship to the land 2 passage between rows of seats

gaol (GB) = JAIL

0━ gap /gæp/ n [C] 1 empty space in sth or between two things 2 period of time when sth stops or between two things 3 space where sth is missing: ~s in your knowledge ■ 'gap year n [C] (GB) year when sb is working and/or travelling, usu between school and university: I went backpacking in India during my ~ year.

gape /geɪp/ v [I] 1 stare at sb/sth with your mouth open, usu in surprise 2 be or become wide open: a gaping hole ▶ gape n [C]

0━ garage /'gærɑːʒ; -rɑːdʒ; -rɪdʒ/ n [C] 1 building in which a car is kept 2 place where cars are repaired • garage v [T] put or keep a vehicle in a garage

0━ garbage /'gɑːbɪdʒ/ n [U] (esp US) rubbish ■ 'garbage can n [C] (US) = DUSTBIN

0━ garbled /'gɑːbld/ adj incomplete and confused: a ~ message

0━ garden /'gɑːdn/ n 1 [C, U] piece of land next to or around your house used for growing flowers, vegetables, etc 2 (usu gardens) [pl] public park • garden v [I] work in a garden ■ 'garden centre n [C] (GB) place that sells plants, seeds, garden equipment, etc ▶ gardener n [C] person who works in a garden ▶ gardening n [U] ■ 'garden party n [C] formal social party in a garden

gargle /'gɑːgl/ v [I] wash the throat with liquid without swallowing

gargle n **1** [C, U] liquid used for gargling **2** [sing] act of gargling

gargoyle /ˈɡɑːɡɔɪl/ n [C] stone figure of an ugly creature on the roof of a church, etc, through which rainwater is carried away

garish /ˈɡeərɪʃ/ adj unpleasantly bright ▸ **garishly** adv

garland /ˈɡɑːlənd/ n [C] circle of flowers or leaves as a decoration ● **garland** v [T] (lit) decorate sb/sth with a garland

garlic /ˈɡɑːlɪk/ n [U] strong-smelling plant of the onion family, used in cooking

garment /ˈɡɑːmənt/ n [C] (fml) piece of clothing

garnish /ˈɡɑːnɪʃ/ v [T] decorate a dish of food with a small amount of another food ● **garnish** n [C] small amount of food used to decorate a larger dish

garret /ˈɡærət/ n [C] small room at the top of a house

garrison /ˈɡærɪsn/ n [C, with sing or pl verb] group of soldiers living in a town or fort ● **garrison** v [T] defend a place with a garrison

garrulous /ˈɡærələs/ adj (fml) talking too much

garter /ˈɡɑːtə(r)/ n [C] elastic band worn round the leg to keep up a sock or stocking

0─ **gas** /ɡæs/ n (pl **~es** US also **~ses**) **1** [C, U] substance like air **2** [U] gas used for heating, cooking, etc **3** [U] (US) = PETROL ● **gas** v (**-ss-**) [T] kill sb with gas ■ **gasbag** n [C] (infml, disapprov) person who talks too much ■ **gaseous** /ˈɡæsiəs; ˈɡeɪsiəs/ adj or like gas ■ **gas fitter** n [C] worker who puts in gas pipes, heaters, cookers, etc ■ **gaslight** n [C, U] light from burning gas ■ **gasman** n [C] (pl **-men**) (infml) official who reads meters and checks gas heaters, etc ■ **gas mask** n [C] breathing apparatus to protect the wearer against poisonous gas ■ **gas station** n [C] (US) = PETROL STATION (PETROL) ■ **gassy** adj (**-ier**, **-iest**) of or like gas; full of gas: ~y beer ■ **gasworks** n [C] (pl **gasworks**) factory where coal is made into gas

gash /ɡæʃ/ n [C] ~ (in) long deep cut ● **gash** v [T] make a gash in sth

gasket /ˈɡæskɪt/ n [C] soft flat piece of material between two metal surfaces to prevent oil, steam, etc from escaping

0─ **gasoline** (also **gasolene**) /ˈɡæsəliːn/ n [U] (US) = PETROL

gasp /ɡɑːsp/ v **1** [I] breathe in quickly, because of surprise, pain, etc **2** [I, T] have difficulty breathing or speaking ● **gasp** n [C] quick deep breath

gastric /ˈɡæstrɪk/ adj of the stomach: ~ ulcers

gastro-enteritis /ˌɡæstrəʊ ˌentəˈraɪtɪs/ n [U] (med) illness of the stomach that causes diarrhoea and vomiting

gastropub /ˈɡæstrəʊpʌb/ n [C] (GB) pub which is well known for serving good food

0─ **gate** /ɡeɪt/ n **1** [C] movable barrier that closes an opening in a wall, fence, etc **2** [C] way out from an airport building to a plane **3** [C, U] (money paid for or by the number of people attending a sports event ■ **gatecrash** v [I, T] go to a party without being invited ▸ **gatecrasher** n [C] ■ **gatepost** n [C] post on which a gate is hung ■ **gateway** n [C] **1** opening with a gate **2** [usu sing] ~ to means of reaching sth: the ~way to success **3** (computing) device connecting two computer networks that cannot be connected in any other way

0─ **gather** /ˈɡæðə(r)/ v **1** [I, T] come or bring people or things together to form a group **2** [T] pick flowers, fruit, etc; cut and collect crops **3** [T] understand or believe sth: I ~ she's looking for a job. **4** [T] collect information from different sources **5** [T] increase in speed, force, etc **6** [T] pull a piece of clothing together in folds ▸ **gathering** n [C] meeting

gauche /ɡəʊʃ/ adj socially awkward

gaudy /ˈɡɔːdi/ adj (**-ier**, **-iest**) (disapprov) too bright and showy ▸ **gaudily** adv

gauge (US also **gage**) /ɡeɪdʒ/ n **1** instrument for measuring sth: a petrol ~ **2** measurement of the thickness of sth, esp sheet of metal or wire **3** distance between the rails on a railway **4** means of comparison; measure of sth: a ~ of her progress ● **gauge** v [T] **1** make a judgement about sth, esp people's feelings or attitudes **2** measure sth accurately **3** estimate sth

gaunt /ɡɔːnt/ adj (of a person) very thin, as from illness or hunger ▸ **gauntness** n [U]

gauntlet /ˈɡɔːntlət/ n [C] strong glove with a wide covering for the wrist

gauze /ɡɔːz/ n [U] thin net material, used eg on wounds

gave pt of GIVE[1]

gawky /ˈɡɔːki/ adj (**-ier**, **-iest**) (esp of a tall young person) awkward and clumsy: a ~ teenager ▸ **gawkiness** n [U]

gawp /ɡɔːp/ v [I] (infml) stare rudely or stupidly at sb/sth

gay /ɡeɪ/ adj **1** homosexual **2** (old-

fash) happy; cheerful ● **gay** *n* [C] homosexual person

gaze /geɪz/ *v* [I] ~ **(at)** look steadily at sb/sth for a long time ● **gaze** *n* [sing] long steady look

gazelle /ɡəˈzel/ *n* [C] small graceful antelope (= an African animal like a deer)

gazette /ɡəˈzet/ *n* [C] official newspaper with legal notices, news, etc

gazump /ɡəˈzʌmp/ *v* [T] (*GB, infml, disapprov*) (usu passive) increase the price of a house after accepting an offer from a buyer

GB /ˌdʒiː ˈbiː/ *abbr* Great Britain

GCSE /ˌdʒiː siː es ˈiː/ *n* [C] (*GB*) General Certificate of Secondary Education; examination in a particular subject taken by school pupils aged about 16

GDP /ˌdʒiː diː ˈpiː/ *abbr* gross domestic product; total value of all the goods and services produced in a country in one year

0—w **gear** /ɡɪə(r)/ *n* **1** [C, U] set of toothed wheels working together in a machine: *The car has five ~s.* ◇ *change* ~ **2** [U] equipment: *camping* ~ **3** [U] apparatus of wheels, levers, etc: *the landing* ~ *of an aircraft* ● **gear** *v* [PV] **gear sth to/towards sth** adapt or organize sth for a particular need: *The whole city is ~ed to the needs of tourists.* **gear (sb) up (for/to sth)** become or make sb ready for sth ■ **gearbox** *n* [C] case that contains the gears of a car or machine ■ **gear lever** /**gearstick** (*US* **gear shift**) *n* [C] handle used for changing gear (1)

geek /ɡiːk/ *n* [C] (*infml*) person who is not popular or fashionable: *a computer* ~ ▶ **geeky** *adj*

geese *plural of* GOOSE

gelatin /ˈdʒelətɪn/ (*also* **gelatine** /ˈdʒelətiːn/) *n* [U] clear tasteless substance, used for making jelly

gelding /ˈɡeldɪŋ/ *n* [C] male horse whose sexual organs have been removed

gelignite /ˈdʒelɪɡnaɪt/ *n* [U] powerful explosive

gem /dʒem/ *n* [C] **1** jewel **2** person, place or thing that is special or good

gender /ˈdʒendə(r)/ *n* [C, U] **1** fact of being male or female **2** (*gram*) grouping of nouns and pronouns into masculine, feminine and neuter

gene /dʒiːn/ *n* [C] (*biol*) unit in a cell that controls a particular quality in a living thing that has been passed on from its parents

genealogy /ˌdʒiːniˈælədʒi/ *n* (*pl* *-ies*) **1** [U] study of family history **2** [C] diagram showing the history of a family ▶ **genealogical** /ˌdʒiːniəˈlɒdʒɪkl/ *adj*

0—w **general** /ˈdʒenrəl/ *adj* **1** affecting all or most people, places

---

genetic

or things: *of* ~ *interest* ◇ *a* ~ *strike* **2** not exact or detailed: ~ *impressions* **3** not limited to a particular subject or use or to just one part or aspect of sb/sth: ~ *knowledge* ◇ *a* ~ *anaesthetic* **4** (in titles) chief [IDM] **in general** usually; mainly ● **general** *n* [C] army officer of very high rank ■ **general election** *n* [C] election in which all the people of a country vote to choose a government ▶ **generality** /ˌdʒenəˈræləti/ *n* (*pl* *-ies*) **1** [C] general statement **2** [U] quality of being general ▶ **generally** *adv* **1** by or to most people: *The plan was* ~*ly welcomed.* **2** usually; in most cases: *I* ~*ly get up early.* **3** without discussing the details of sth: ~*ly speaking* ■ **general practitioner** (*abbr* **GP**) *n* [C] (*esp GB*) doctor trained in general medicine who treats patients in the local community rather than at a hospital ■ **general strike** *n* [C] refusal to work by all or most workers

generalize (*also* **-ise**) /ˈdʒenrəlaɪz/ *v* [I] make a general statement about sth ▶ **generalization** (*also* **-isation**) /ˌdʒenrəlaɪˈzeɪʃn/ *n* [C, U] (statement based on) generalizing

0—w **generate** /ˈdʒenəreɪt/ *v* [T] produce sth: ~ *electricity* ▶ **generative** /ˈdʒenərətɪv/ *adj* (*fml*) able to produce sth ▶ **generator** *n* [C] machine that generates electricity

0—w **generation** /ˌdʒenəˈreɪʃn/ *n* **1** [C] all the people born at about the same time **2** [C] single stage in a family history **3** [U] act of generating sth

generic /dʒəˈnerɪk/ *adj* (*fml*) shared by a whole group; not specific ▶ **generically** /-kli/ *adv*

0—w **generous** /ˈdʒenərəs/ *adj* **1** giving freely; kind: *He's ~ with his money.* **2** larger than normal: *a ~ helping of food* ▶ **generosity** /ˌdʒenəˈrɒsəti/ *n* [U] ▶ **generously** *adv*

genetic /dʒəˈnetɪk/ *adj* of genes or genetics ▶ **genetically** /-kli/ *adv* ■ **genetically modified** *adj* (*abbr* **GM**) (of food, plants, etc) grown from cells whose genes have been changed artificially ■ **genetic engineering** *n* [U] science of changing the way a human, an animal or a plant develops by changing the information in its genes ■ **genetic fingerprinting** (*also* **DNA fingerprinting**) *n* [U] method of finding the particular pattern of genes in an individual person, particularly to identify sb or find out if sb has committed a crime ▶ **genetics** *n* [U] study of how

---

characteristics are passed from one
generation to the next

genial /ˈdʒiːniəl/ adj kind and
pleasant ▶ **genially** adv

genie /ˈdʒiːni/ n [C] (in stories) spirit
with magic powers, esp one that
lives in a bottle or a lamp

genital /ˈdʒenɪtl/ adj of the
reproductive organs of people or
animals ▶ **genitals** (also **genitalia**
/ˌdʒenɪˈteɪliə/) n [pl] (anat) person's
external sex organs

genius /ˈdʒiːniəs/ n 1 [U] very great
intelligence or artistic ability 2 [C]
unusually intelligent or artistic
person 3 [sing] special skill or ability:
have a ~ for languages

genocide /ˈdʒenəsaɪd/ n [U] killing of
a whole race or group of people

genome /ˈdʒiːnəʊm/ n [C] (biol)
complete set of genes in a cell or
living thing: the human ~

genre /ˈʒɑːnrə/ n [C] (fml) particular
style or type of literature, art, film or
music

gent /dʒent/ n [C] (GB) 1 [C] (old-fash or
hum) gentleman 2 (a/the **Gents**)
[sing] (infml) public toilet for men

genteel /dʒenˈtiːl/ adj quiet and
polite, esp in an exaggerated way

gentile /ˈdʒentaɪl/ n [C], adj (person
who is) not Jewish

0─ **gentle** /ˈdʒentl/ adj (~r /-lə(r)/ ~st
/-lɪst/) not rough or violent
▶ **gentleness** n [U] ▶ **gently** /-li/ adv

0─ **gentleman** /ˈdʒentlmən/ n [C]
(pl -**men** /-mən/) 1 [C] man who is
polite and behaves well 2 [C, usu pl]
(fml) used to address or refer to a
man, esp one you do not know:
Ladies and ~men... 3 (old-fash) man
of wealth and social position
▶ **gentlemanly** adv (fml or old-fash)
behaving like a gentleman (1)

gentry /ˈdʒentri/ n [pl] (old-fash)
(usu the **gentry**) people of high
social class

0─ **genuine** /ˈdʒenjuɪn/ adj real;
true ▶ **genuinely** adv
▶ **genuineness** n [U]

genus /ˈdʒiːnəs/ n [C] (pl **genera**
/ˈdʒenərə/) (biol) division of animals
or plants within a family (5)

0─ **geography** /dʒiˈɒɡrəfi/ n [U]
1 study of the earth's surface,
climate, countries, population, etc
2 arrangement of features in a
particular region ▶ **geographer**
/-fə(r)/ n [C] expert in geography
▶ **geographical** /ˌdʒiːəˈɡræfɪkl/ adj
▶ **geographically** /-kli/ adv

geology /dʒiˈɒlədʒi/ n [U]
scientific study of the earth's rocks,
crust, etc 2 [sing] structure of rocks,
etc, in a particular region
▶ **geological** /ˌdʒiːəˈlɒdʒɪkl/ adj
▶ **geologically** /-kli/ adv

▶ **geologist** /dʒiˈɒlədʒɪst/ n [C]
expert in geology

geometry /dʒiˈɒmətri/ n [U] study of
lines, angles and figures and their
relationships ▶ **geometric**
/ˌdʒiːəˈmetrɪk/ (also **geometrical**)
adj

geranium /dʒəˈreɪniəm/ n [C]
garden plant with red, pink or white
flowers

geriatrics /ˌdʒeriˈætrɪks/ n [U]
branch of medicine concerned with
the care of old people ▶ **geriatric**
adj

germ /dʒɜːm/ n 1 [C, usu pl] very
small living thing that can cause
disease 2 [sing] ~ of beginning: the
~ of an idea

German /ˈdʒɜːmən/ adj of Germany,
its people or their language
■ **German 'measles** /n [U] mild
infectious disease causing red spots
all over the body

germinate /ˈdʒɜːmɪneɪt/ v [I,T]
(cause seeds to) start growing
▶ **germination** /ˌdʒɜːmɪˈneɪʃn/ n [U]

gerund /ˈdʒerənd/ n [C] the -ing form
of a verb when used as a noun (as
in 'fond of swimming')

gestation /dʒeˈsteɪʃn/ n [U, sing]
process or period of a baby or young
animal being carried in the womb

gesticulate /dʒeˈstɪkjuleɪt/ v [I]
(fml) move your hands and arms
about to express yourself
▶ **gesticulation** /dʒeˌstɪkjuˈleɪʃn/ n
[C, U]

gesture /ˈdʒestʃə(r)/ n 1 [C, U]
movement of the hand or head to
show an idea, feeling, etc 2 [C]
action done to express a particular
feeling or intention: a ~ of support/
defiance

0─ **get** /get/ v (-**tt**- pt, pp **got** /ɡɒt/ US
pp **gotten** /ˈɡɒtn/) 1 [T] receive sth: ~
a letter 2 [T] obtain sth: ~ a new car
3 [T] fetch sth: G~ your coat. 4 [T]
receive sth as a punishment: ~ six
months (= six months in prison) 5 [T]
(begin to) suffer from an illness, etc:
~ flu/a headache 6 [I, T] (cause sb/
sth/yourself to) reach a particular
state or condition: ~ wet/dressed ◇ ~
the children ready for school ◇ ~ your
hair cut ◇ He got (= was) killed in a car
accident. 7 [I] reach the point at
which you feel, know, are, etc sth: ~
to know someone 8 [T] make or
persuade sb/sth to do sth: I can't ~
her to understand. ◇ He got me to help
him with his homework. 9 [I] start
doing sth: We soon got talking. 10 [I]
arrive at or reach a place or point: ~
home early ◇ What time did you ~ to
London? 11 [I, T] (cause sb/sth to)
move somewhere, sometimes with
difficulty: ~ off the bus ◇ We can't ~
the piano downstairs. ~ a message
to sb 12 [T] use a bus, train, etc: ~ a
plane to Rome 13 [T] prepare a meal

14 [T] (spoken) answer the telephone or a door when sb calls, knocks, etc: Can you ~ the phone? **15** [T] catch sb, esp in order to harm or punish them: The police got the robber. ◇ I'll ~ you for that! **16** [T] kill or wound sb: The bullet got him in the neck. **17** [T] (infml) understand sb/sth: I don't ~ you. ◇ She didn't ~ the joke. **18** [T] (spoken) confuse or puzzle sb: That's got you! **19** [T] (spoken) annoy sb: What ~s me is having to listen to his problems all the time. **[IDM]** **get (sb) anywhere/somewhere/nowhere** (infml) (cause sb to) achieve something/nothing: I tried to persuade him but I got nowhere (= I failed). **get to grips with sth → GRIP** **[PV]** **get (sth) across (to sb)** (cause sth to) be communicated or understood by sb: I couldn't ~ my point across to the others. **get ahead (of sb)** make progress (further than others have done) **get along (with sb)** = GET ON (WITH STH) **get along with sb** = GET ON WITH STH **get at sb** (infml) criticize sb: Stop ~ting at me! **get at sth 1** reach or gain access to sth **2** learn or find out sth: ~ at the truth **3** (only in the continuous tenses) suggest sth indirectly: What are you ~ting at? **get away 1** have a holiday: ~ away for two weeks in France **2** ~ (from...) escape from sb or a place: Two prisoners got away. **get away with sth 1** steal sth and escape with it **2** receive a relatively light punishment: ~ to ~ away with just a fine **3** do sth wrong and receive no punishment: ~ away with murder **get by (on/in/with sth)** survive: ~ by on a small salary **get sb down** (infml) make sb feel depressed **get sth down 1** swallow sth with difficulty **get down to sth** begin to do sth seriously: ~ down to work/business **get sb/sth into sth** arrive at a place: The train got in late. **get sb in 1** call sb to your house to do a job: ~ someone to fix the TV **get sb in 1** collect or gather sth **2** buy a supply of sth: ~ some coal in for the winter **3** manage to do or say sth: He talks so much I can't ~ a word in. **get in with sb** (infml) become friendly with sb, usu to gain an advantage **get into sth 1** put on a piece of clothing, esp with difficulty **2** start a career in a particular profession: ~ into journalism **3** become involved in sth; start sth: ~ into a fight ◇ ~ into conversation with sb **4** develop a habit: ~ into the habit of going to bed early ◇ Don't ~ into drugs (= Don't start taking them)! **5** (infml) become interested in sth: I can't ~ into this book. **get (yourself/sb) into sth** (cause yourself/sb to) reach a particular state or condition: ~ into trouble/difficulties **get off (sb/sth)** used to tell sb to stop touching you/sb/sth **get (sb) off** (help sb to) leave a place or start a journey: ~ the children off to

school **get (sb) off (with sth)** (help sb to) receive little or no punishment: She got off with just a fine. **get on 1** progress or become successful in life, in a career, etc **2** (only in the continuous tenses) be getting old **3** (only in the continuous tenses) be getting late **get on/along (with sb)** have a friendly relationship with sb: We don't ~ on. ◇ Do you ~ on with your boss? ◇ We ~ along just fine. **get on with sth 1** (also **get along with sth**) make progress: How are you ~ting on with your new job? **2** continue doing sth: G~ on with your work. **get out 1** become known: The secret got out. **2** ~ (of) leave a place **get out of sth** avoid a responsibility or duty: We can't ~ out of going to her wedding. **get over sth 1** recover from an illness, a shock, the end of a relationship, etc **2** deal with or gain control of sth: ~ over your fears **get sth over (to sb)** make sth clear to sb **get over (with)** (infml) finish sth unpleasant: I'm glad I've got my exams over with. **get round/around sb** persuade sb to agree or do what you want, often by flattery, etc: She knows how to ~ round her father. **get round/around sth** deal with a problem successfully **get round/around to** find the time to do sth: I didn't ~ round to phoning her. **get through sth 1** use up a large amount of sth: ~ through £100 a week **2** manage to do or complete sth (during an exam, etc) **get through (sth)** (GB) be successful in an exam, etc **get through (to sb)** reach sb: We must ~ the supplies through to the refugees. **2** contact sb, esp by telephone **get (sth) through to sb** succeed in making sb understand sth: I just can't ~ through to them (that this is wrong). **get together (with sb)** meet sb socially or to discuss sth: ~ together for a drink **get (sb) up 1** (cause sb to) get out of bed **2** stand up after sitting, kneeling, etc **get up to sth 1** reach a particular point: ~ up to page ten **2** be busy with sth, esp sth surprising or unpleasant: What have the kids been ~ting up to? ■ **getaway** n [C] escape: a fast ~away ■ **get-together** n [C] (old-fash, infml) informal social meeting ■ **get-up** n [C] (infml) set of clothes, esp an unusual one ■ **get-up-and-go** n [U] (infml) energy and determination to get things done

geyser /ˈɡiːzə(r)/ n [C] natural spring§(4) sending up a column of hot water or steam

ghastly /ˈɡɑːstli/ adj (-ier, -iest) **1** (of an event) causing horror: a ~ accident **2** (infml) very bad: a ~ mistake **3** very pale and ill

ghetto

ghetto /ˈɡetəʊ/ n [C] (pl **-s**) area of a city where many people of the same race or background live, separately from the rest of the population. Ghettos are often crowded, with bad living conditions. ■ **ghetto blaster** n [C] (infml) large, powerful, portable radio and cassette player

ghost /ɡəʊst/ n **1** [C] spirit of a dead person that appears to be living **2** [sing] very slight amount of sth that is left behind: the ~ of a (= very little) chance [IDM] **give up the ghost** die ▶ **ghostly** adj of or like a ghost ■ **ghost town** n [C] town that was once full of people but is now empty ■ **ghostwriter** n [C] person who writes material for sb else but does not use his/her own name

GI /ˌdʒiː ˈaɪ/ n [C] soldier in the US army

o͞— giant /ˈdʒaɪənt/ n [C] (fem **-ess**) (in stories) enormous and very strong person ▶ **giant** adj enormous

gibberish /ˈdʒɪbərɪʃ/ n [U] meaningless talk; nonsense

gibbon /ˈɡɪbən/ n [C] long-armed ape

gibe = JIBE

giblets /ˈdʒɪblɪts/ n [pl] heart, liver, etc of a chicken or other bird, usu taken out before it is cooked

giddy /ˈɡɪdi/ adj (**-ier, -iest**) feeling that everything is spinning around and that you are going to fall ▶ **giddiness** n [U]

o͞— gift /ɡɪft/ n [C] **1** something given freely; present **2** natural ability: a ~ for languages [IDM] **the gift of the gab** the ability to speak easily and persuasively ▶ **gifted** adj talented

gig /ɡɪɡ/ n [C] **1** live performance by pop or jazz musicians **2** (infml) = GIGABYTE

gigabyte /ˈɡɪɡəbaɪt/ n [C] (also infml **gig**) n [C] (abbr **Gb**) (computing) unit of computer memory, equal to about a billion bytes

gigantic /dʒaɪˈɡæntɪk/ adj very big

giggle /ˈɡɪɡl/ v [I] ~ (**at**) laugh in a silly way because you are amused, embarrassed, etc ● **giggle** n **1** [C] light silly laugh **2** [sing] (GB, infml) something done for amusement

gild /ɡɪld/ v [T] cover sth with gold leaf or gold paint

gill¹ /ɡɪl/ n [C, usu pl] organ through which a fish breathes

gill² /dʒɪl/ n [C] measure for liquids; one quarter of a pint (0.142 litre)

gilt /ɡɪlt/ n [U] thin layer of gold that is used as a surface for decoration ■ **gilt-edged** adj (business) very safe: ~-edged shares/stocks [C] = investments considered very safe because they have been sold by the government)

gimmick /ˈɡɪmɪk/ n [C] (usu disapprov) unusual trick or device used for attracting attention or persuading people to buy sth ▶ **gimmicky** adj

gin /dʒɪn/ n [C] strong colourless alcoholic drink

ginger /ˈdʒɪndʒə(r)/ n [U] **1** root of the ginger plant used in cooking as a spice **2** orange-brown colour ■ **ginger ale**, **ginger beer** n [U] non-alcoholic drink flavoured with ginger ■ **gingerbread** n [U] sweet cake flavoured with ginger

gingerly /ˈdʒɪndʒəli/ adv with great care; hesitantly

gingham /ˈɡɪŋəm/ n [U] cotton cloth with a pattern of squares or stripes

gipsy = GYPSY

giraffe /dʒəˈrɑːf/ n [C] African animal with a very long neck and legs

girder /ˈɡɜːdə(r)/ n [C] long strong piece of iron or steel used for supporting a floor, roof, bridge, etc

girdle /ˈɡɜːdl/ n [C] piece of women's underwear that fits closely around the body from the waist to the thigh ▶ **girdle** v [T] (lit) surround

o͞— girl /ɡɜːl/ n [C] female child; daughter; young woman ■ **girlfriend** n [C] **1** woman that sb is having a romantic relationship with **2** (esp US) woman's female friend ■ **Girl Guide** n [C] = GUIDE(5) ▶ **girlhood** n [U] (old-fash) time of being a girl ▶ **girlish** adj of or like a girl ■ **Girl Scout** (US) = GUIDE(5)

giro /ˈdʒaɪrəʊ/ n (pl **-s**) **1** [U,C] system for transferring money directly from one bank or post office account to another **2** [C] (GB) cheque issued by the government for a social security payment

girth /ɡɜːθ/ n **1** [U,C] measurement round sth, esp a person's waist **2** [C] leather strap fastened round the body of a horse to keep the saddle in place

gist /dʒɪst/ n (**the gist**) [sing] ~ (**of**) general meaning or main points: get (= understand) the ~ of an argument

o͞— give /ɡɪv/ v (pt **gave** /ɡeɪv/ pp **given** /ˈɡɪvn/) **1** [T] hand sth to sb so they can look at it, use it or keep it for a time: ~ her a cheque ◊ Have you been~n the books you need? **2** [T] let sb have sth as a present: What did he ~ you for your birthday? ◊ They both~ regularly to charity. **3** [T] provide sb with sth: They were thirsty so I gave them all a drink. ◊ I'll ~ you (= allow you to have) a week to decide. ◊ an account of your journey **4** [T] ~ **for** pay money in exchange for sth: I gave her £500 for the car. **5** [T] ~ **to** use time, energy, etc for sb/sth: I gave the matter a lot of thought. **6** [T] make sb suffer a particular punishment: The judge gave him a suspended sentence. **7** [T] infect

with an illness: *You've ~n me your cold.* **8** [T] provide a party, meal, etc as a host: *~ a dinner party* **9** [T] perform sth in public: *~ a poetry reading* **10** [T] used with a noun to describe an action, giving the same meaning as the related verb: *She gave a smile* (= smiled). ◊ *He gave her a kiss* (= kissed her). ◊ *~ a wave* **11** [T] bend or stretch under pressure: *The plank gave a little when I stepped on it.* [IDM] **give and take** be tolerant and willing to compromise: *You have to ~ and take in a marriage.* **give ground (to sb/sth)** → GROUND [give or take (sth)** (*infml*) plus or minus: *It takes an hour to get to Hastings, ~ take a few minutes.* [PV] **give sth away** give sth as a gift **give sth/sb away** betray sb or reveal a secret **give sb back sth/ give sth back (to sb)** return sth to sb: *~ the book back (to him)* ◊ *~ him back the book* **give in (to sb/sth) 1** admit that you have been defeated by sb/ sth **2** agree to do sth that you do not want to do **give sth off** produce sth, eg smoke, a smell, etc **give sth out 1** (of supplies, sb's strength, etc) come to an end **2** (of a motor, etc) stop working **give sth out** distribute sth to a lot of people: *~ out prizes/leaflets* **give over** (*GB, spoken*) used to tell sb to stop doing sth **give sb up 1** believe that sb is never going to arrive, get better, etc: *After so many years, they had ~n him up for dead.* **2** stop having a relationship with sb **give sth up 1** stop doing or having sth: *I've ~n up smoking.* ◊ *I gave up my job.* **2** allow sb else to have sth: *He gave up his seat to the old man.* **give yourself/sb up (to sb)** offer yourself/ sb to be captured: *He gave himself up to the police.* **give up on sb 1** stop believing that sb will change, get better, etc **2** (*esp US*) = GIVE SB UP
▶ **given** *adj* agreed: *at the ~n time*
▶ **given** *prep* considering sth: *G~n his size, he runs very fast.*
■ **giveaway** *n* [C] (*infml*) **1** something that a company gives free of charge **2** something that reveals a secret

give² /ɡɪv/ *n* [U] ability of sth to bend and stretch under pressure: *This rope has too much ~ in it.* [IDM] **give and take** willingness to be tolerant and make compromises in a relationship

glacial /ˈɡleɪʃl; ˈɡleɪsiəl/ *adj* (*geol*) very cold or covered with ice or the Ice Age

glacier /ˈɡlæsiə(r)/ *n* [C] mass of ice that moves slowly down a valley

0--w **glad** /ɡlæd/ *adj* (~**der**, ~**dest**) **1** pleased; happy: *~ to hear the news* ◊ *I'd be ~ to help you.* **2** grateful for sth: *He was ~ of the warm coat.*
▶ **gladden** /ˈɡlædn/ *v* [T] (*old-fash*) make sb feel pleased or happy
▶ **gladly** *adv* happily; willingly: *I will ~ly help you.* ▶ **gladness** *n* [U]

glade /ɡleɪd/ *n* [C] (*lit*) small open space in a forest

gladiator /ˈɡlædieɪtə(r)/ *n* [C] (in ancient Rome) man trained to fight at public shows in an arena

glamour (*US also* -**or**) /ˈɡlæmə(r)/ *n* [U] attractive and exciting quality: *the ~ of Hollywood* **2** physical beauty that suggests wealth and success
▶ **glamorize** (*also* -**ise**) *v* [T] make sth bad seem attractive and exciting
▶ **glamorous** *adj*

glance /ɡlɑːns/ *v* [I] take a quick look at sth/sb [PV] **glance off (sth)** hit sth and bounce off it at an angle
● **glance** *n* [C] quick look [IDM] **at a (single) glance** at once

gland /ɡlænd/ *n* [C] organ that produces a chemical substance for the body to use ▶ **glandular** /ˈɡlændjʊlə(r)/ *adj*

glare /ɡleə(r)/ *v* [I] **1** ~ **(at)** look at sb/ sth angrily **2** shine with a bright unpleasant light ● **glare** *n* **1** [U, sing] very bright unpleasant light **2** [C] angry look ▶ **glaring** *adj* **1** (of sth bad) very easily seen: *a glaring mistake* **2** (of light) very bright and unpleasant **3** angry; fierce

0--w **glass** /ɡlɑːs/ *n* **1** [U] hard transparent substance used in windows, etc: *a sheet/pane of ~* ◊ *I cut myself on a piece of ~.* **2** [C] drinking container made of glass; its contents: *a ~ of milk* **3** (**glasses**) [pl] two lenses in a frame worn in front of the eyes to help a person to see better: *a pair of ~es* ■ **glasshouse** *n* [C] type of greenhouse ▶ **glassware** /-weə(r)/ *n* [U] objects made of glass ▶ **glassy** *adj* (-**ier**, -**iest**) **1** smooth and shiny **2** showing no feeling or emotion

glaze /ɡleɪz/ *v* **1** ~ **(over)** [I] (of sb's eyes) become dull and lifeless because of boredom or tiredness **2** [T] fit sheets of glass into sth: *~ a window* **3** [T] cover sth with a thin shiny surface: *~ pottery* ● **glaze** *n* [C, U] thin shiny coating ▶ **glazier** /ˈɡleɪziə(r)/ *n* [C] person who fits glass into windows, etc

gleam /ɡliːm/ *n* [C, usu sing] **1** pale clear light, often reflected from sth **2** small amount of sth: *a ~ of hope* ● **gleam** *v* [I] **1** shine softly **2** look very clean or bright

glean /ɡliːn/ *v* [T] obtain information, etc in small quantities and with difficulty

glee /ɡliː/ *n* [U] ~ **(at)** feeling of happiness and satisfaction ▶ **gleeful** /-fl/ *adj* ▶ **gleefully** *adv*

glen /ɡlen/ *n* [C] narrow valley, esp in Scotland or Ireland

glib /ɡlɪb/ *adj* (~**ber**, ~**best**) (*disapprov*) speaking or spoken easily and confidently but not

sincerely: a ~ answer ▶ **glibly** adv
▶ **glibness** n [U]

glide /glaɪd/ v [I] **1** move along smoothly and quietly **2** fly without engine power ● **glide** n [C] continuous smooth movement
▶ **glider** n [C] light aircraft without an engine ● **gliding** n [U] sport of flying in a glider

glimmer /ˈglɪmə(r)/ v [I] shine with a weak unsteady light ● **glimmer** n [C] **1** weak unsteady light **2** (also **glimmering**) small sign of sth: a ~ of interest

glimpse /glɪmps/ n [C] quick incomplete look at sb/sth: He caught a ~ of her in the crowd. ● **glimpse** v [T] see sb/sth for a moment, but not very clearly

glint /glɪnt/ v [I] produce small bright flashes of light ● **glint** n [C] sudden flash of light or colour shining from a bright surface

glisten /ˈglɪsn/ v [I] (of sth wet) shine

glitter /ˈglɪtə(r)/ v [I] shine brightly with little flashes of light: ~ing jewels ● **glitter** n [U] **1** bright sparkling light **2** attractiveness; excitement: the ~ of show business

gloat /gləʊt/ v [I] ~ (about/at/over) show selfish happiness at your own success or at sb else's failure
▶ **gloatingly** adv

0—¬ **global** /ˈgləʊbl/ adj **1** covering or affecting the whole world **2** considering or including all parts of sth ▶ **globally** /-bəli/ adv ■ ,**global 'village** n [sing] the whole world, considered as a single community connected by electronic communication systems ■ ,**global 'warming** n [U] increase in temperature of the earth's atmosphere, caused by the increase of particular gases, esp carbon dioxide

globalize /ˈgləʊbəlaɪz/ v [I, T] (of business companies, etc) operate all around the world ▶ **globalization** n [U]: the globalization of world trade

globe /gləʊb/ n **1** [C] a model of the earth **2** (the globe) [sing] the world ■ **'globetrotter** n [C] person who travels in many countries around the world

globule /ˈglɒbjuːl/ n [C] (fml) tiny drop, esp of liquid

gloom /gluːm/ n **1** [U, sing] feeling of being sad and without hope **2** [U] (lit) almost total darkness ▶ **gloomy** adj (-ier, -iest) **1** almost dark **2** sad and without hope ▶ **gloomily** /-ɪli/ adv

glorify /ˈglɔːrɪfaɪ/ v (pt, pp -ied) [T] **1** (usu disapprov) make sth seem better or more important than it really is: His cottage is just a glorified barn. **2** (fml) praise and worship

God ▶ **glorification** /ˌglɔːrɪfɪˈkeɪʃn/ n [U].

glorious /ˈglɔːriəs/ adj (fml) **1** deserving or bringing great fame and success: a ~ victory **2** magnificent ▶ **gloriously** adv

glory /ˈglɔːri/ n (pl -ies) **1** [U] fame, praise or honour: I do all the work and he gets all the ~. **2** [U] praise and worship of God **3** [U] great beauty: The house was restored to its former ~. **4** [C] special cause for pride, respect or pleasure: Her hair is her crowning ~. ● **glory** v (pt, pp -ied) [I] ~ in take too much pleasure in sth

gloss /glɒs/ n **1** [U, sing] shine on a smooth surface **2** (also **gloss 'paint**) [U] paint that has a shiny surface when dry **3** [U, sing] deceptively good appearance **4** [C] ~ (on) explanation of a word or phrase in a text ● **gloss** v [T] give an explanation of a word or phrase in a text [PV] **gloss over sth** avoid talking about sth unpleasant or embarrassing ▶ **glossy** adj (-ier, -iest) smooth and shiny: ~y magazines (= magazines printed on shiny paper)

glossary /ˈglɒsəri/ n [C] (pl -ies) alphabetical list of explanations of words

0—¬ **glove** /glʌv/ n [C] covering for the hand

glow /gləʊ/ v [I] **1** (esp of sth hot or warm) produce a dull, steady light: ~ing coal **2** be warm or red in the face **3** appear a strong, warm colour ● **glow** n [sing] **1** glowing light: the ~ of a sunset **2** warm colour ▶ **glowing** adj giving enthusiastic praise: a ~ing report

glower /ˈglaʊə(r)/ v [I] ~ (at) look at sb angrily

glucose /ˈgluːkəʊs/ n [U] natural sugar found in fruit

0—¬ **glue** /gluː/ n [U, C] sticky substance used for joining things together ● **glue** v [T] join two things together with glue [IDM] **be glued to sth** (infml) give all your attention to sth; stay close to sth: They were ~d to the TV. ■ **'glue-sniffing** n [U] dangerous habit of breathing in the fumes of some kinds of glue as a drug

glum /glʌm/ adj (~mer, ~mest) sad; gloomy ▶ **glumly** adv

glut /glʌt/ v (-tt-) [T] supply sth with too much of sth: The market is ~ted with cheap apples. ● **glut** n [C, usu sing] ~ (of) situation in which there is more of sth than can be used

glutton /ˈglʌtn/ n [C] **1** (disapprov) person who eats too much **2** person who enjoys doing difficult or unpleasant tasks: a ~ for punishment ▶ **gluttonous** /-tənəs/ adj very greedy ▶ **gluttony** [U] habit of eating too much

glycerine /ˈglɪsəriːn/ (*US* **glycerin** /-rɪn/) *n* [U] thick colourless liquid used in eg medicines and explosives

GM /ˌdʒiː ˈem/ *abbr* (GB) genetically modified: *GM foods*

gm (*also* **gm.**) *abbr* gram(s)

gnarled /nɑːld/ *adj* **1** (of trees) rough and twisted **2** (of a person or part of the body) bent or twisted because of age or illness

gnash /næʃ/ *v* [PV] **gnash your teeth** feel very angry or upset about sth, esp because you cannot get what you want

gnat /næt/ *n* [C] small fly with two wings, that bites

gnaw /nɔː/ *v* [I, t] **1** keep biting or chewing sth so that it gradually disappears: *The dog was ~ing a bone.* ◇ (*fig*) *Self-doubt had begun to ~ away at her confidence.*

gnome /nəʊm/ *n* [C] **1** (in stories) small old man who lives under the ground **2** model of such a man used as a garden ornament

GNP /ˌdʒiː en ˈpiː/ *abbr* gross national product; total value of all the goods and services produced by a country in one year, including the total income from foreign countries

go¹ /ɡəʊ/ *v* (third pers sing pres tense **goes** /ɡəʊz/, pt **went** /went/ pp **gone** /ɡɒn/) [I] **1** move from one place to another: *go home/for a walk/on holiday/to the cinema* **2** move or travel: *go five miles to get a doctor* **3** leave a place: *It's time for us to go.* **4** ~ **to** visit or attend a place for a particular purpose: *go to school* **5** lead or extend from one place to another: *This road goes to London.* **6** have as a usual or correct position: *The book goes on the shelf.* **7** fit into a place or space: *This key won't go in the lock.* **8** make progress: *How are things going?* ◇ *The party went very well.* **9** used to show that sb/sth has reached a particular state/is no longer in a particular state: *go to sleep* ◇ *go out of fashion* **10** *linking verb* become different in a particular way, esp a bad way: *go bald/blind/mad* **11** live or move around in a particular state: *go barefoot/hungry* **12** have a certain wording or tune: *How does the poem/song go?* **13** make a certain sound: *The bell went at 3 p.m.* ◇ *The clock goes 'tick-tock'.* **14** (esp in commands) begin an activity: *One, two, three, go!* **15** (of a machine) work: *This clock doesn't go.* **16** get worse; stop working: *My sight is going.* ◇ *The car battery has gone.* **17** be given, lost, spent, used up, etc: *Supplies of coal went very quickly.* **18** ~ (**to, for**) be sold: *The car went to a dealer for £500.* **19** (of time) pass: *two hours to go before lunch* [IDM] **anything goes** (*infml*) anything is allowed **be going to do sth 1** intend; plan: *We're going*

to sell our house. **2** be likely or about to happen: *It's going to rain.* **go and do sth** used to show that you are angry that sb has done sth stupid: *That stupid girl went and lost her watch.* **go to seed** → SEED **go to waste** → WASTE² **there goes sth** (*infml*) used for showing regret that sth has been lost: *There goes my chance of getting the job* (= I will certainly not get it). [PV] **go about 1** move from place to place or spread **about sth** start working on sth: *How do you go about writing a novel?* **go after sb** chase or follow sb **go after sb/sth** try to get sb/sth **go against sb/sth 1** oppose sb/sth: *Don't go against my wishes.* **2** be unfavourable to sb: *The verdict went against him.* **go ahead 1** travel in front of other people in your group and arrive before them **2** happen; be done: *The tennis match went ahead in spite of the bad weather.* **go along 1** continue with an activity: *He made up the story as he went along.* **2** make progress; develop **go along with sb/sth 1** accompany sb **2** agree with sb/sth: *Will they go along with the plan?* **go around/round 1** spin or turn: *go round in a circle* **2** be enough for everyone: *There aren't enough apples to go round.* **3** often be in a particular state or behave in a certain way: *You can't go around criticizing people like that.* **go around/round (to...)** visit sb or a place that is near: *I'm going round to my sister's later.* **go around/round with sb** be often in the company of sb **go at sb/sth 1** attack sb **2** work hard at sth **go away 1** leave a person or place: *Go away and leave me alone!* **2** leave home for a period of time, esp for a holiday **3** disappear: *Has the pain gone away?* **go back 1** return **2** extend backwards in space or time: *Our family goes back 300 years.* **go back on sth** fail to keep a promise: *He went back on his word.* **go by** (of time) pass: *The days go by so slowly.* **go by sth** be guided by sth: *I always go by what my doctor says.* **go down 1** fall to the ground (of a ship, etc) sink **3** (of the sun, moon, etc) set **4** (of food) be swallowed **5** (of the sea, wind, etc) become calm **6** (of prices, the temperature, etc) become lower **7** (*computing*) stop working temporarily: *The system went down for over an hour.* **go down (in sth)** be written or recorded in sth: *Her name will go down in history.* **go down well/badly (with sb)** (of a comment, performance, etc) be well/badly received by sb **go down with sth** become ill with an illness: *go down with flu* **go for sb/sth 1** fetch sb/sth **2** attack sb: *The dog went for* him. **3** apply to sb/sth: *What she said goes for me too.* **4** (*infml*) like or prefer sth/sth **go in 1** enter a room, house, etc **2** (of the sun, moon, etc) disappear behind clouds **go in for sth 1** enter a competition, etc **2** have sth as an interest or hobby: *She doesn't go in for team games.* **go into sth 1** (of a car, etc) hit sth **2** join an organization, esp in order to have a career in it: *go into the Army* **3** examine sth carefully: *go into the details* **4** begin to do sth: *go into a long explanation* **go off 1** leave a place, esp in order to do sth: *She went off to get a drink.* **2** explode; be fired **3** (of an alarm, etc) suddenly make a loud noise **4** (of a light, the electricity, etc) stop working **5** (*GB*) (of food, etc) become unfit to eat: *The milk has gone off.* **6** proceed: *The party went off well.* **7** get worse in quality **go off sth** stop liking sth/sth **go on 1** (of time) pass **2** (of a light, the electricity, etc) start to work **3** continue: *The meeting went on for hours.* **4** happen: *What's going on here?* **5** used to encourage sb: *Go on! Have a cake.* **go on (about sb/sth)** talk about sb/sth for a long time **go on (at sb)** criticize sb **go on (with/doing sth)** continue an activity **go on to sth/to do sth** do or say sth next **go out 1** leave your house to go to a social event: *I don't go out much at weekends.* **2** (of a fire, light, etc) stop burning or shining **3** become unfashionable **go out (together)| go out with sb** have a romantic or sexual relationship with sb: *How long have they been going out together?* **go over sth** examine or check sth carefully **go round** = GO AROUND **go round (to)** = GO AROUND (TO) **go round with sb** = GO AROUND WITH SB **go through** to be officially accepted and completed: *The deal didn't go through.* **go through sth 1** study or consider sth in detail **2** examine sth carefully: *go through the papers* **3** experience or suffer sth **4** use up or finish sth completely **go through with sth** complete sth, esp sth unpleasant or difficult **go to/towards sth** be contributed to sth: *All profits go to charity.* **go under 1** sink **2** fail **go up 1** rise **2** be built **3** be destroyed by fire or in an explosion: *The petrol station went up in flames.* **4** (of prices, temperatures, etc) become higher **go up with sth** climb sth **go with sb** accompany sb **go together| go with sth** match: *Do green curtains go with a pink carpet?* **go without (sth)** manage without sth you usu have or need: *go without food for four days* ■ **go-ahead** n [sing] permission to start doing sth ■ **go-ahead** adj willing to

try new methods ■ **go-slow** n [C] industrial protest in which workers work more slowly than usual

go² /gəʊ/ n (pl **-es** /gəʊz/) **1** [C] (*GB*) person's turn to play in a game **2** [C] attempt: *'I can't lift this box.' 'Let me have a go.'* **3** [U] (*GB*, *infml*) energy and enthusiasm: *He's full of go.* [IDM] **be all go** (*GB*, *infml*) be very busy or full of activity **be on the go** (*infml*) be very active or busy **have a go (at sb)** criticize sb or attack sb **make a go of sth** (*infml*) make a success of sth

goad /gəʊd/ v [T] ~ (**into**) annoy sb continually: *He ~ed me into an angry reply.* [PV] **goad sb on** urge sb to do sth ■ **goad** n [C] pointed stick for making cattle move

0~ **goal** /gəʊl/ n [C] **1** (in football, hockey, etc) pair of posts between which the ball has to go in order to score **2** point scored when the ball goes into the goal **3** something that you hope to achieve ■ **goalkeeper** n [C] player who stands in the goal and tries to prevent the other team from scoring ■ **goalpost** n [C] either of the two posts which form a goal (1)

goat /gəʊt/ n [C] small horned animal with long hair that lives in mountain areas: *~'s milk/cheese* [IDM] **get sb's goat** (*infml*) annoy sb

gobble /ˈɡɒbl/ v [I,T] eat sth quickly and greedily **2** [I] (of a turkey) make a sound in the throat

go-between /ˈɡəʊ bɪtwiːn/ n [C] person who takes messages between one person or group and another

goblet /ˈɡɒblət/ n [C] cup for wine, usu made of glass or metal, with a stem but no handle

goblin /ˈɡɒblɪn/ n [C] (in fairy stories) small ugly mischievous creature

0~ **god** /ɡɒd/ n **1** (God) [sing] (in Christianity, Judaism and Islam) the maker and ruler of the universe **2** [C] (in some religions) being that is believed to have power over nature or to represent a particular quality **3** [C] person or thing that is greatly admired or loved **4** (the gods) [pl] (*GB*, *infml*) seats high up in a theatre [IDM] **God willing** (*spoken*) if everything goes as planned ■ **godchild | god-daughter** | **godson** n [C] person for whom sb takes responsibility as a godparent ▸ **goddess** /ˈɡɒdes/ n [C] female god ■ **godfather | godmother** | **godparent** n [C] person who promises when a child is baptized to see that he/she is brought up as a Christian ■ **God-fearing** adj (*old-fash*) sincerely religious ■ **godforsaken** adj (of places) boring, depressing and ugly ▸ **godless** adj not believing in God; wicked ■ **godlike** adj like God or a god in some quality ▸ **godly** adj

(-ier, -iest) (old-fash) deeply religious ▶ **godliness** n [U] ■ **godsend** n [sing] unexpected piece of good luck

goggle /'gɒgl/ v [I] (old-fash) ~ (at) look at sb/sth with wide round eyes ▶ **goggles** n [pl] glasses worn to protect the eyes from wind, dust, etc: a pair of swimming/safety ~s

going /'gəʊɪŋ/ n **1** [sing] (fml) departure **2** [U] (with an adjective) speed or difficulty involved in doing sth: It was good ~ to get to York so quickly. ● **going** adj [IDM] **a going concern** a profitable business the **going rate (for sth)** the usual price or cost of sth ■ **goings-on** n [pl] (infml) unusual events or dishonest activities

go-kart (also go-cart) /'gəʊ kɑːt/ n [C] small, low, open racing car

0~ **gold** /gəʊld/ n **1** (symb Au) [U] yellow precious metal **2** [U] jewellery, money, etc made of gold **3** [U,C] bright yellow colour of gold **4** [C] = GOLD MEDAL ■ **goldfish** n [C] (pl **goldfish**) small orange or red fish kept as a pet ■ **gold leaf** (also **gold foil**) n [U] very thin sheet of gold, used for decoration ■ **gold medal** n [C,U] (sport) prize given to the winner of a competition, esp a sports contest ■ **gold mine** n [C] **1** place where gold is dug out of the ground **2** profitable business activity ■ **gold rush** n [C] rush to a place where gold has been discovered in the ground ■ **goldsmith** n [C] person who makes or sells objects made of gold

golden /'gəʊldən/ adj **1** of or like gold **2** special; wonderful: a ~ opportunity ■ **golden handshake** n [C] large sum of money given to sb when they leave their job ■ **golden jubilee** n [C] 50th anniversary of an important event ■ **golden rule** n [C] very important rule of behaviour

golf /gɒlf/ n [U] outdoor game in which players hit a small ball into a series of 9 or 18 holes: play a round of ~ ■ **golf ball** n [C] ball used in golf ■ **golf club** n [C] **1** (also **club**) long metal stick used for hitting the ball in golf **2** organization whose members play golf; place where these people meet ■ **golf course** (also **course**) n [C] large area of land designed for playing golf on ▶ **golfer** n [C] person who plays golf

gone pp of GO[1]

gong /gɒŋ/ n [C] round piece of metal that makes a loud ringing sound when it is hit with a stick

gonorrhoea (US **gonorrhea**) /ˌgɒnə'rɪə/ n [U] sexually transmitted disease

0~ **good[1]** /gʊd/ adj (**better** /'betə(r)/ **best** /best/) **1** of a high quality: very ~ exam results **2** pleasant; that you

enjoy or want: ~ news/weather ◇ have a ~ time ◇ It's a ~ thing (= it is lucky) you are not a vegetarian. **3** able to do sth well; skilful: a ~ teacher ◇ ~ at languages **4** morally right or acceptable **5** kind: They were very ~ to her when she was ill. **6** (esp of a child) well behaved **7** beneficial; suitable: Milk is ~ for you. **8** (spoken) used as an expression of approval, agreement, etc: 'I've finished!' 'G~!' **9** (spoken) used in exclamations: G~ Heavens! **10** great in number, amount or degree: a ~ many people **11** not less than: a ~ three miles to the station **12** thorough: a ~ sleep **13** likely to provide sth: He's always ~ for a laugh. **14** used in greetings and farewells: G~ morning/afternoon. [IDM] **a good job** (spoken) used to show you are pleased about sth or that sb is lucky that sth happened **(all) in good time** (spoken) used to say that sth will happen or be done at the appropriate time and not before **as good as** very nearly: as ~ as finished **as good as gold** very well behaved **(do sb) a good turn** (do) sth useful or helpful for sb **for good measure** as an extra amount of sth in addition to what has already been given **good and...** (infml) completely: I won't go until I'm ~ and ready. **good for you, sb, them, etc** (infml) used to praise sb for doing sth well **good grief!** (infml) used to express surprise or shock about sth **good luck (with sth)** used to wish sb success with sth **have a good mind to do sth** be very willing to do sth **have a good night** → NIGHT **in good time** early **make good** become rich and successful ■ **good-for-nothing** n [C], adj (person who is) lazy and without any skills ■ **Good Friday** n [U,C] the Friday before Easter Sunday ■ **good-humoured** (US -humored) adj cheerful ■ **good-looking** adj handsome; beautiful ■ **good-natured** adj kind and friendly ■ **good sense** n [U] ability to act wisely ■ **good-tempered** adj not easily annoyed

0~ **good[2]** /gʊd/ n [U] **1** behaviour which is morally right or acceptable: ~ and evil **2** something that helps sb/sth: It's for your own ~. [IDM] **be no good | not be any/much good 1** not be useful; have no useful effect: It's no ~ talking to them. **2** not be interesting or enjoyable: His new film's not much ~. **do (sb) good** have a useful effect; help sb: A walk will do you ~. **for good** permanently; for ever **up to no good** (infml) doing sth wrong

0~ **goodbye** /ˌgʊd'baɪ/ exclam, n [C] used when you are leaving or when sb else is leaving

A B C D E F **G** H I J K L M N O P Q R S T U V W X Y Z

goodness /'gʊdnəs/ n [U] **1** (spoken) used to express surprise: My ~! **2** quality of being good **3** part of food that provides nourishment: Brown bread is full of ~.

o─ **goods** /gʊdz/ n [pl] **1** things for sale; movable property: electrical ~ **2** things carried by train: a ~ train [IDM] **come up with/deliver the goods** (infml) do what you have promised

goodwill /ˌgʊd'wɪl/ n [U] **1** friendly or helpful feeling towards other people or countries **2** financial value of the good reputation of a business, calculated when the business is sold

goody (also goodie) /'gʊdi/ n [C] (pl -ies) (infml) **1** [usu pl] something pleasant, esp to eat **2** hero of a book, film, etc

goose /guːs/ n (pl geese /giːs/) **1** [C] bird like a large duck with a long neck **2** [U] meat from a goose **3** [C] female goose ■ **'goose pimples** n [pl] (esp GB 'goose-flesh [U]) (esp US 'goosebumps) small raised spots on the skin, caused by cold or fear

gooseberry /'gʊzbəri/ n [C] (pl -ies) (bush with a) green hairy sour berry

gorge /gɔːdʒ/ n [C] narrow steep-sided valley ● **gorge v** [I,T] ~ (yourself) (on) eat a lot of sth until you cannot eat any more

gorgeous /'gɔːdʒəs/ adj very beautiful and attractive; giving pleasure and enjoyment ▶ **gorgeously** adv

gorilla /gə'rɪlə/ n [C] large powerful African ape

gorse /gɔːs/ n [U] bush with sharp thorns and yellow flowers

gory /'gɔːri/ adj (-ier, -iest) (infml) involving blood and violence

gosh /gɒʃ/ exclam (infml) used to express surprise

gosling /'gɒzlɪŋ/ n [C] young goose

gospel /'gɒspl/ n **1** (the Gospel) [sing] life and teaching of Jesus **2** (Gospel) [C] any one of the first four books of the New Testament **3** [U] (infml) the complete truth **4** (also 'gospel music) [U] style of religious singing popular among African Americans and other black people: a ~ choir

gossamer /'gɒsəmə(r)/ n [U] fine silky thread

gossip /'gɒsɪp/ n **1** [U,C] informal talk about other people, esp about their private lives **2** [C] (disapprov) person who likes gossip ■ **'gossip column** [C] piece of writing in a newspaper about the personal lives of famous people ● **gossip v** [I] talk gossip

got pt, pp of GET

gotten (US) pp of GET

gouge /gaʊdʒ/ n [C] tool with a sharp semicircular edge for cutting grooves in wood ● **gouge v** [T] make a hole in sth roughly [PV] **gouge sth out** force sth out with a sharp tool or your fingers

goulash /'guːlæʃ/ n [C,U] hot spicy Hungarian dish of meat cooked slowly in liquid with paprika

gourd /gʊəd; gɔːd/ n [C] type of large fruit, not usu eaten, with hard skin and soft flesh. Gourds are often dried and used as containers.

gourmet /'gʊəmeɪ/ n [C] expert in good food and drink

gout /gaʊt/ n [U] disease that causes painful swellings in joints, esp toes and fingers

o─ **govern** /'gʌvn/ v [I,T] **1** legally control and run a country, city, etc **2** [T] control or influence sth/sb: The law of supply and demand ~s the prices of goods. ▶ **governing** /'gʌvənɪŋ/ adj having the power or right to govern sth: the ~ing body of a school

governess /'gʌvənəs/ n [C] (esp in the past) woman employed to teach the children of a rich family and to live with them

o─ **government** /'gʌvənmənt/ n **1** (the Government) (also abbr **govt**) [C, with sing or pl verb] group of people who govern a country or state **2** [U] (method or system of) governing a country: democratic ~

o─ **governor** /'gʌvənə(r)/ n [C] **1** person who governs a province or (in the USA) a state **2** head of an institution; member of a governing body: a prison/school ~

gown /gaʊn/ n [C] **1** woman's long dress for special occasions **2** loose usu black garment worn by judges, members of a university, etc

GP /ˌdʒiː 'piː/ abbr = GENERAL PRACTITIONER (GENERAL)

GPS /ˌdʒiː piː 'es/ abbr global positioning system; system by which signals are sent from satellites to a device which shows the exact position of sb or sth

o─ **grab** /græb/ v (-bb-) [I,T] take sth in your hand suddenly or roughly ● **grab** n [C] sudden attempt to grab sth [IDM] **up for grabs** (infml) available for anyone to take

grace /greɪs/ n **1** [U] simple beauty, esp in movement **2** [U] polite and pleasant behaviour, deserving respect **3** [U] extra time allowed to complete sth, pay money, etc: give sb a week's ~ **4** [U,C] short prayer of thanks before or after a meal **5** [U] God's kindness towards people [IDM] **with (a) bad/good grace** unwillingly/ willingly ● **grace v** [T] (fml) **1** make sth more attractive **2** bring honour to sb/sth; be kind enough to attend sth: The Queen is gracing us with her presence. ▶ **graceful** /-fl/ adj having grace (1): a ~ful dancer ▶ **gracefully**

adv ▸ **graceless** *adj* without grace (2); rude

gracious /ˈɡreɪʃəs/ *adj* **1** polite; kind **2** showing the comfort that wealth can bring: ~ *living* ▸ **graciously** *adv* ▸ **graciousness** *n* [U]

0━ **grade** /ɡreɪd/ *n* [C] **1** step or degree in quality, rank, etc: *different* ~*s of pay* **2** mark given for work in school **3** (*US*) class in a school **4** (*US*) gradient [IDM] **make the grade** (*infml*) reach the required standard ● **grade** *v* [T] **1** arrange people or things in groups according to their ability, size, etc **2** (*esp US*) mark schoolwork ■ **grade school** *n* [C] (*US*) = ELEMENTARY SCHOOL

gradient /ˈɡreɪdiənt/ *n* [C] degree of slope of a road, railway, etc

0━ **gradual** /ˈɡrædʒuəl/ *adj* taking place slowly over a period of time; not sudden ▸ **gradually** /ˈɡrædʒuəli/ *adv*

graduate[1] /ˈɡrædʒuət/ *n* [C] **1** person with a university degree **2** (*US*) person who has completed their school studies

graduate[2] /ˈɡrædʒueɪt/ *v* [I] **1** get a degree, esp a first degree, from a university: ~ *in law* **2** (*US*) complete a course in education, esp at high school **3** start doing sth more difficult or important than what you were doing before ▸ **graduated** *adj* **1** divided into groups or levels on a scale **2** (of a container, etc) marked with lines to show measurements ▸ **graduation** /ˌɡrædʒuˈeɪʃn/ *n* **1** [U,C] (ceremony of) graduating at a university, etc **2** [C] mark showing a measurement

graffiti /ɡrəˈfiːti/ *n* [U, pl] drawings or writing on a wall in a public place

graft /ɡrɑːft/ *n* **1** [C] piece cut from a plant and fixed in another plant to form a new growth **2** [C] (*med*) piece of skin, bone, etc transplanted to another body or another part of the same body **3** [U] (*GB, infml*) hard work ● **graft** *v* [T] attach sth to sth else as a graft

0━ **grain** /ɡreɪn/ *n* **1** [U,C] seeds of food plants such as wheat and rice: *America's* ~ *exports* **2** [C] small hard piece of particular substances: ~*s of sand/sugar* **3** [C] very small amount: *a* ~ *of truth* **4** [U,C] pattern of the lines of fibres in wood, etc [IDM] **be/go against the grain** be or do sth different from what is normal or natural

0━ **gram** (*GB* **gramme**) /ɡræm/ *n* [C] metric unit of weight

0━ **grammar** /ˈɡræmə(r)/ *n* [C, U] (book that describes the) rules for forming words and making sentences ▸ **grammarian** /ɡrəˈmeəriən/ *n* [C] expert in grammar ■ **grammar school** *n* [C] kind of British secondary school that

grape

provides academic courses ▸ **grammatical** /ɡrəˈmætɪkl/ *adj* of or correct according to the rules of grammar ▸ **grammatically** /-kli/ *adv*

granary /ˈɡrænəri/ *n* [C] (*pl* **-ies**) building where grain is stored

0━ **grand** /ɡrænd/ *adj* **1** impressive and large or important: *a* ~ *palace* **2** full; final: *the* ~ *total* **3** proud; important **4** (*infml*) enjoyable ● **grand** *n* [C] **1** (*pl* **grand**) (*infml*) $1000; £1000 **2** = GRAND PIANO ▸ **grandly** *adv* ■ **grand piano** *n* [C] large piano with horizontal strings ■ **grandstand** *n* [C] large building with rows of seats for people watching sports

grand- *prefix* (used in compound nouns to show family relationships) ■ **grandchild** (*pl* **-children**) ■ **granddaughter** | **grandson** *n* [C] daughter or son of your child ■ **grandfather** | **grandmother** | **grandparent** *n* [C] father or mother of either of your parents ■ **grandfather clock** *n* [C] clock in a tall wooden case

grandad (*also* **granddad**) /ˈɡrændæd/ *n* (*infml*) grandfather

grandeur /ˈɡrændʒə(r); -dʒə(r)/ *n* [U] greatness; importance

grandiose /ˈɡrændiəus/ *adj* (*disapprov*) seeming impressive but not practical

grandma /ˈɡrænmɑː/ *n* (*infml*) grandmother

grandpa /ˈɡrænpɑː/ *n* (*infml*) grandfather

granite /ˈɡrænɪt/ *n* [U] hard grey or red stone used for building

granny (*also* **grannie**) /ˈɡræni/ *n* (*pl* **-ies**) (*infml*) grandmother ■ **granny flat** *n* [C] (*GB, infml*) flat for an old person in a relative's house

0━ **grant** /ɡrɑːnt/ *v* **1** (*fml*) agree to give sb what they ask for, esp formal or legal permission to do sth: ~ *sb's request* **2** (*fml*) admit that sth is true [IDM] **take it for granted (that...)** believe sth is true without first making sure that it is **take sb/sth for granted** be so familiar with sb/sth that you no longer value them/it ● **grant** *n* [C] sum of money given by the government for a particular purpose

granulated sugar /ˌɡrænjuleɪtɪd ˈʃuɡə(r)/ *n* [U] white sugar in the form of grains

granule /ˈɡrænjuːl/ *n* [C] small hard piece of sth; small grain

grape /ɡreɪp/ *n* [C] small green or purple fruit used for making wine ■ **grapevine** *n* [C] (*IDM*) **on/through the grapevine** by talking in an informal way to other people: *I heard it on the* ~*-vine.*

grapefruit /'greɪpfruːt/ n [C] (pl **grapefruit** or ~s) large yellow fruit like an orange but usu not so sweet

graph /grɑːf/ n [C] diagram showing the relationship of two or more sets of numbers ● **graph paper** n [U] paper with small squares of equal size

graphic /'græfɪk/ adj **1** connected with drawings and design: ~ *design* **2** (of descriptions) clear and detailed ▸ **graphically** /-kli/ adv clearly: ~*ally described* ▸ **graphics** n [pl] designs, drawings or pictures: *computer* ~*s*

graphite /'græfaɪt/ n [U] soft black substance used in pencils

grapple /'græpl/ v [I] ~ (**with**) **1** hold and struggle with sb/sth **2** try to deal with a problem

grasp /grɑːsp/ v [T] **1** take a firm hold of sb/sth **2** understand sth fully [PV] **grasp at sth 1** try to take hold of sth in your hands **2** try to take an opportunity ● **grasp** n [C, usu sing] **1** firm hold of sb/sth **2** understanding ▸ **grasping** adj (*disapprov*) greedy for money

0~ **grass** /grɑːs/ n **1** [U] common wild short green plant eaten by cattle, etc **2** [C] any type of grass **3** (usu the grass) [sing, U] ground covered with grass: *Don't walk on the* ~*.* **4** [U] (*sl*) marijuana **5** [C] (*GB, sl*) person who grasses on sb [IDM] **not let the grass grow under your feet** not delay in doing sth ● **grass** (*also* **grass sb up**) v [I] (*GB, infml*) ~ (**on**) tell the police about sb's criminal activities [PV] **grass sth over** cover an area with grass ● **grass roots** n [pl] ordinary people rather than leaders or decision makers: *the* ~ *roots of the party* ▸ **grassy** adj (**-ier, -iest**) covered with grass

grasshopper /'grɑːshɒpə(r)/ n [C] jumping insect that makes a sound with its legs

grate /greɪt/ n [C] metal frame in a fireplace ● **grate** v **1** [T] rub food against a grater to cut it into small pieces: ~*d cheese* **2** [I] ~ (**on/with**) irritate or annoy sb: *His voice* ~*s on me.* **3** [I] make a rough unpleasant noise by rubbing together or against sth ▸ **grater** n [C] kitchen utensil with a rough surface, used for grating food

0~ **grateful** /'greɪtfl/ adj **1** ~ (**to**) feeling or showing thanks: *I'm ~ to you for your help.* **2** used to make a request, esp in a letter: *I would be ~ if you could send me…* ▸ **gratefully** /-fəli/ adv

gratify /'grætɪfaɪ/ v (pt, pp **-ied**) [T] (*written*) please or satisfy sb/sth ▸ **gratification** /ˌgrætɪfɪ'keɪʃn/ n [U, C] (*fml*) feeling of pleasure or satisfaction ▸ **gratifying** adj (*fml*) pleasing

grating /'greɪtɪŋ/ n [C] framework of bars across an opening, eg a window ● **grating** (of a person's voice) harsh and unpleasant

gratis /'grætɪs/ adj, adv done or given without having to be paid for: *a ~ copy of a book*

gratitude /'grætɪtjuːd/ n [U] ~ (**to; for**) feeling of being grateful and wanting to express your thanks: *a deep sense of ~*

gratuitous /grə'tjuːɪtəs/ adj (fml, disapprov) done without any good reason and often having harmful effects: ~ *violence on television* ▸ **gratuitously** adv

gratuity /grə'tjuːəti/ n [C] (pl **-ies**) **1** (*fml*) money given for a service done; tip **2** (*GB*) money given to a retiring worker

0~ **grave** /greɪv/ n [C] hole in the ground for a dead body ■ **gravestone** n [C] stone over a grave ■ **graveyard** n [C] cemetery ● **grave** adj (~**r**, ~**st**) serious: *a ~ situation* ▸ **gravely** adv

gravel /'grævl/ n [U] small stones, used to make the surfaces of paths and roads ● **gravel** v (**-ll-** *US also* **-l-**) [T] cover sth with gravel ▸ **gravelly** /'grævəli/ adj **1** full of gravel **2** (of a voice) deep and rough

gravitate /'grævɪteɪt/ v (written) [PV] **gravitate to/toward(s) sb/sth** move towards sb/sth that you are attracted to ▸ **gravitation** /ˌgrævɪ'teɪʃn/ n [U] (*physics*) force of attraction that causes objects to move towards each other

gravity /'grævəti/ n [U] **1** (*abbr* **g**) force that attracts objects towards the centre of the earth **2** (*fml*) seriousness: *the ~ of the situation*

gravy /'greɪvi/ n [U] juice that comes from meat while it is cooking

gray (*esp US*) = GREY

graze /greɪz/ v **1** (of cattle, sheep, etc) eat grass **2** [T] put cattle, etc in a field to eat grass **3** [T] break the surface of your skin by rubbing it against sth rough **4** [T] touch sth lightly while passing it ● **graze** n [C] place where the surface of the skin has been broken

grease /griːs/ n [U] **1** thick oily substance **2** soft animal fat ● **grease** v [T] rub grease or fat on sth [IDM] **like greased lightning** (*infml*) very fast ▸ **greaseproof 'paper** n [U] paper used in cooking that does not let grease pass through it ▸ **greasy** adj (**-ier, -iest**) covered with grease ▸ **greasily** adv

0~ **great** /greɪt/ adj **1** very large in size, quantity or degree: *of ~ importance* **2** (*infml*) used for emphasis: *Look at that* ~ *big tree!* **3** very good in ability or quality: *a ~*

artist **4** (*infml*) very good or pleasant: *a ~ time on holiday* ◇ *What a ~ idea!* **5** important and impressive: *The wedding was a ~ occasion.* **6** healthy; fine: *I feel ~ today.* **7** used in compounds to show a further generation: *my ~-aunt* (= my father's or mother's aunt) ■ **Great Britain** *n* [*sing*] England, Wales and Scotland ▶ **greatly** *adv* (*fml*) very much: *Your help would be ~ly appreciated.* ▶ **greatness** *n* [U]

greed /griːd/ *n* [U] ~ **(for)** strong desire for too much food, money, etc ▶ **greedy** *adj* (*-ier, -iest*) ▶ **greedily** *adv*

0~ **green**[1] /griːn/ *adj* **1** having the colour of grass **2** covered with grass or other plants **3** (of fruit) not yet ripe **4** (*infml*) (of a person) young and inexperienced **5** (of a person) pale; looking ill **6** concerned about protecting the environment: *the G~ Party* [IDM] **give sb/get the green light** (*infml*) give sb/get permission to do sth **green with envy** very jealous ■ **green bean** *n* [C] long thin pod, cooked and eaten whole as a vegetable ■ **green belt** *n* [U,C, usu *sing*] (*GB*) area of open land round a city, where building is strictly controlled ■ **green fingers** *n* [pl] (*US* **green thumb** [*sing*]) (*infml*) skill in gardening ■ **greengrocer** *n* [C] (*esp GB*) shopkeeper who sells fruit and vegetables ■ **greenhouse** *n* [C] glass building used for growing plants ■ **greenhouse effect** *n* [*sing*] slow warming of the earth's atmosphere, caused by increased carbon dioxide ▶ **greenhouse gas** *n* [C] any of the gases thought to cause the greenhouse effect, esp carbon dioxide ▶ **greenness** *n* [U]

0~ **green**[2] /griːn/ *n* **1** [U, C] colour of grass **2** (**greens**) [pl] green vegetables **3** [C] area of grass, esp in the middle of a town or village **4** [C] (in golf) area of grass cut short around a hole on a golf course

greenery /ˈɡriːnəri/ *n* [U] attractive green leaves and plants

greet /griːt/ *v* [T] **1** say hello to sb or welcome sb **2** react to sb/sth in a particular way **3** (of sights and sounds) be the first thing you see or hear ▶ **greeting** *n* **1** [C,U] something you say or do to greet sb **2** (**greetings**) [pl] message of good wishes for sb: *Christmas ~s*

gregarious /ɡrɪˈɡeəriəs/ *adj* **1** liking to be with other people **2** (*biol*) (of animals and birds) living in groups

grenade /ɡrəˈneɪd/ *n* [C] small bomb thrown by hand

grew *pt* of GROW

0~ **grey** (*esp US* **gray**) /ɡreɪ/ *adj* **1** of the colour of black mixed with white **2** having grey hair ● **grey** *n* [U, C] grey colour ● **grey** *v* [I] (of hair)

become grey ■ **grey matter** *n* [U] (*infml*) person's intelligence

greyhound /ˈɡreɪhaʊnd/ *n* [C] thin dog able to run fast

grid /ɡrɪd/ *n* [C] **1** pattern of straight lines that cross each other to form squares **2** framework of bars: *a cattle ~* (= one placed at a gate to stop cattle from leaving a field) **3** pattern of squares on a map, marked with numbers or letters: *The ~ reference is C8.* **4** (*esp GB*) system of wires for supplying electricity: *the national ~* (= the electricity supply in a country)

grief /ɡriːf/ *n* [U] ~ **(over/at)** great sadness, esp when sb dies [C,U] thing that causes great sadness [IDM] **come to grief** (*infml*) **1** end in failure **2** be injured in an accident

grievance /ˈɡriːvəns/ *n* [C] ~ **(against)** real or imagined cause for complaint

grieve /ɡriːv/ *v* ~ **(for/over)** [I] feel very sad, esp because sb has died **2** [T] (*fml*) make you feel sad: *It ~d him that he could not help her.*

grill /ɡrɪl/ *n* [C] **1** shelf in a cooker where food is cooked below direct heat **2** food, esp meat, cooked in this way: *a mixed ~* ● **grill** *v* **1** [I,T] cook food under or over direct heat **2** [T] question sb severely

grille (*also* **grill**) /ɡrɪl/ *n* [C] screen of metal bars in front of a window, door, etc, to protect it

grim /ɡrɪm/ *adj* (**~mer, ~mest**) **1** looking or sounding serious: *~-faced* **2** unpleasant; depressing: *~ news* ▶ **grimly** *adv*

grimace /ɡrɪˈmeɪs; ˈɡrɪməs/ *n* [C] ugly expression on the face, to show pain, disgust, etc ● **grimace** *v* [I] make an ugly expression with your face to show pain, etc

grime /ɡraɪm/ *n* [U] dirt, esp on a surface ▶ **grimy** *adj* (**-ier, -iest**)

grin /ɡrɪn/ *v* (**-nn-**) [I] smile widely [IDM] **grin and bear it** accept pain, disappointment, etc without complaining ● **grin** *n* [C] wide smile

grind /ɡraɪnd/ *v* (*pt, pp* **ground** /ɡraʊnd/) [T] **1** crush sth into powder: *~ corn into flour* **2** make sth sharp or smooth by rubbing it against a hard surface: *~ a knife* **3** press or rub sth into a surface: *He ground the cigarette into the ashtray.* [IDM] **grind to a halt** stop slowly [PV] **grind sb down** treat sb very cruelly or unfairly over a long period of time ● **grind** *n* [*sing*] **1** (*infml*) hard boring task **2** harsh noise made by machines ▶ **grinder** *n* [C] person or thing that grinds sth ■ **grindstone** *n* [C] round stone used for sharpening tools

grip /ɡrɪp/ *v* (**-pp-**) [I,T] hold sth tightly **2** [T] interest or excite sb;

hold sb's attention: *a ~ping film*
● **grip** *n* **1** [C, usu sing] hold of sb/sth **2** [sing] ~ **(on)** control or power over sth; understanding of sth **3** [U] ability of sth to move over a surface without slipping **4** [C] part of sth that has a special surface so that it can be held without the hands slipping [IDM] **come/get to grips with sth** begin to understand and deal with sth difficult

grisly /'ɡrɪzli/ *adj* causing horror or terror

gristle /'ɡrɪsl/ *n* [U] tough tissue in meat

grit /ɡrɪt/ *n* [U] **1** very small pieces of stone or sand **2** courage and determination ● **grit** *v* (**-tt-**) [T] spread grit on an icy road **grit your teeth 1** bite your teeth tightly together **2** show courage and determination ▶ **gritty** *adj* (**-ier, -iest**)

groan /ɡrəʊn/ *v* [i], *n* [C] (make a) long deep sound of pain or distress: *She ~ed with pain.*

grocer /'ɡrəʊsə(r)/ *n* [C] shopkeeper who sells food and goods for the home

0━ **grocery** /'ɡrəʊsəri/ (US) (also **grocery store**) *n* **1** [C] shop that sells food and other goods **2** (**groceries**) [pl] food and other goods sold by a grocer or at a supermarket: *We need some ~ies for the weekend.*

groggy /'ɡrɒgi/ *adj* (**-ier, -iest**) (*infml*) weak and unsteady after illness, etc

groin /ɡrɔɪn/ *n* [C] part of the body where the legs meet

groom /ɡruːm/ *n* [C] **1** person who looks after horses **2** bridegroom ● **groom** *v* [T] **1** clean and brush an animal **2** prepare sb for an important job or position ▶ **groomed** *adj* neat and tidy: *a well-~ed young man*

groove /ɡruːv/ *n* [C] long narrow cut in a surface [IDM] **be (stuck) in a groove** (GB) become set in a particular way of life which has become boring ▶ **grooved** *adj* having grooves

grope /ɡrəʊp/ *v* [i] try and find sth that you cannot see, by feeling with your hands: *~ for the light switch* **2** (*infml, disapprov*) touch sb sexually, esp when they do not want you to

gross /ɡrəʊs/ *adj* **1** being the total amount before anything is taken away: *~ income* (= before tax has been deducted) **2** (*fml or law*) (of a crime etc) very obvious and unacceptable: *~ injustice* **3** (*spoken*) very unpleasant **4** very fat and ugly ● **gross** *v* [C] earn sth or a total amount before tax is deducted ● **gross** *n* [C] (pl **gross**)

group of 144 things ▶ **grossly** *adv* (*disapprov*) very ▶ **grossness** *n* [U]

grotesque /ɡrəʊ'tesk/ *adj* strange, ugly and unnatural: *a ~ building/ figure* ▶ **grotesquely** *adv*

grotto /'ɡrɒtəʊ/ *n* [C] (pl **~es** or **~s**) small cave

0━ **ground**[1] /ɡraʊnd/ *n* **1** (often the ground) [sing] solid surface of the earth: *fall to the ~* **2** [U] soil: *stony/ marshy ~* **3** [U] area of open land: *piece of waste ~* **4** [C] piece of land used for a particular purpose: *a football/sports ~* **5** (**grounds**) [pl] land or gardens round a building: *the palace ~s* **6** [U] area of interest, knowledge or ideas: *common ~ between the two sides* (= points on which they can agree) **7** [C, usu pl] reason: *~s for divorce* **8** (**grounds**) [pl] small solid bits at the bottom of a liquid: *coffee ~s* [IDM] **gain/make up ground (on sb/sth)** gradually get closer to sb/sth who is ahead of you: *gain ~ on your competitors* **get off the ground** (of a project) make a successful start **give/lose ground (to sb/sth)** lose an advantage over sb/ sth **hold/stand your ground** not change your position, opinion, etc; not yield ■ **ground floor** (US **first floor**) *n* [sing] (GB) floor of a building at ground level ▶ **groundless** *adj* without good reason: *~less fears* ■ **groundsheet** *n* [C] large waterproof piece of material to spread on the ground in a tent, etc ■ **groundwork** *n* [U] preparation for further study or work

ground[2] /ɡraʊnd/ *v* **1** [i,t] (cause a ship to) touch the sea bottom and be unable to move **2** [T] prevent an aircraft from taking off **3** [T] punish a child by not allowing them to go out with their friends: *You're ~ed for a week!* [IDM] **(be) grounded in/on sth** (be) based on sth [PV] **ground sb in sth** teach sb the basic principles of a subject **ground sth on sth** base beliefs, ground etc on sth ▶ **grounding** *n* [sing] teaching of the basic principles of a subject

ground[3] *pt, pp of* GRIND

0━ **group** /ɡruːp/ *n* [C, with sing or pl verb] **1** number of people or things together **2** (*business*) number of companies owned by the same person or organization ● **group** *v* [i,t] (cause sb/sth to) form into a group

grouse /ɡraʊs/ *v* [i] (*infml*) complain about sb/sth in a way that people find annoying ● **grouse** *n* [C] **1** (pl **grouse**) small fat bird, shot for sport and food **2** (*infml*) complaint

grove /ɡrəʊv/ *n* [C] group of trees

grovel /'ɡrɒvl/ *v* (**-ll-** *US* **-l-**) [i] **1** (*disapprov*) show humility and respect towards sb, trying to gain his/her favour **2** move along the ground on your hands and knees ▶ **grovelling** adj: a ~ling letter of apology

0─ **grow** /ɡrəʊ/ v (pt **grew** /ɡruː/ pp ~n /ɡrəʊn/) **1** [I] increase in size, number, strength or quality **2** [I, T] (cause sth to) develop: *Plants ~ from seeds.* ◇ ~ *a beard* **3** (usu used with an adj) become: ~ *old/bored/calm* **[PV] grow on sb** become more attractive to sb: *The picture will ~ on you.* **grow out of sth 1** become too big to wear sth **2** stop doing sth as you become older: ~ *out of playing with toys* **grow up 1** (of a person) develop into an adult **2** develop gradually: *A warm friendship grew up between them.*

growl /ɡraʊl/ v [I], n [C] (make a) low threatening sound: *The dog ~ed at the burglars.*

grown /ɡrəʊn/ adj mentally and physically an adult ■ **grown-'up** adj adult; mature ■ **grown-up** n [C] adult person

0─ **growth** /ɡrəʊθ/ n **1** [U] process of growing; development **2** [U] increase in the size, amount or degree of sth **3** [C] lump caused by a disease that forms in or on the body **4** [U, C] something that has grown: *three days' ~ of beard*

grub /ɡrʌb/ n **1** [C] young form of an insect **2** [U] (*infml*) food ● **grub** v (**-bb-**) [I] look for sth, esp by digging

grubby /'ɡrʌbi/ adj (**-ier, -iest**) dirty

grudge /ɡrʌdʒ/ v [T] do or give sth unwillingly: *I ~ paying so much tax.* ● **grudge** n [C] feeling of anger towards sb because of sth bad they have done to you in the past: *bear/have a ~ against sb* ▶ **grudging** adj unwilling ▶ **grudgingly** adv

gruelling (*US* **grueling**) /'ɡruːəlɪŋ/ adj very tiring

gruesome /'ɡruːsəm/ adj causing horror and disgust: *a ~ murder* ▶ **gruesomely** adv

gruff /ɡrʌf/ adj rough and unfriendly ▶ **gruffly** adv ▶ **gruffness** n [U]

grumble /'ɡrʌmbl/ v [I] complain about sth/sth in a bad-tempered way ● **grumble** n [C] complaint

grumpy /'ɡrʌmpi/ adj (**-ier, -iest**) (*infml*) bad-tempered ▶ **grumpily** adv

grunt /ɡrʌnt/ v [I] **1** (esp of pigs) make a low sound in the throat **2** (of people) make a similar sound to show you are annoyed, bored, etc ● **grunt** n [C] low sound made by a person or an animal

0─ **guarantee** /ˌɡærənˈtiː/ n [C] **1** firm promise that you will do sth or that sth will happen **2** written promise given by a company that sth you buy will be repaired without payment if it goes wrong: *The watch is still under ~.* **3** promise to be

responsible for the payment of a debt ● **guarantee** v [T] **1** promise sth: *We cannot ~ that trains will arrive on time.* **2** give a guarantee for sth

guarantor /ˌɡærənˈtɔː(r)/ n [C] (*fml* or *law*) person who agrees to be responsible for sb or for making sure that sth happens

0─ **guard** /ɡɑːd/ n **1** [C] person, eg a soldier or police officer, who watches over sb or sth: *a security ~* **2** [C, with sing or pl verb] group of people, eg soldiers or police officers, who protect sb/sth: *a ~ of honour* **3** [U] act or duty of protecting sb/sth from attack or danger, or of preventing prisoners from escaping: *a soldier on ~* **4** (esp in compounds) article designed to protect sb/sth: *fire~* **5** [C] (*GB*) official in charge of a train ● **guard** v **1** [T] protect sb/sth **2** [T] prevent prisoners from escaping **[PV] guard against sth** take care to prevent sth: ~ *against disease* ▶ **guarded** adj not showing or saying too much

guardian /'ɡɑːdiən/ n [C] **1** person who protects sb **2** person legally responsible for the care of a child ▶ **guardianship** n [U] position of being responsible for sb/sth

guerrilla (*also* **guerilla**) /ɡəˈrɪlə/ n [C] fighter in an unofficial army that attacks in small groups

0─ **guess** /ɡes/ v [I, T] try and give an answer or form an opinion about sth without being sure of all the facts **2** [T] (*infml, esp US*) suppose sth to be true or likely ● **guess** n [C] ~ **(at)** attempt to give an answer or opinion when you cannot be certain you are right ▶ **guesstimate** (*also* **guestimate**) /'ɡestɪmət/ n [C] (*infml*) calculation that is based on guessing ■ **guesswork** n [U] process of guessing sth

0─ **guest** /ɡest/ n [C] **1** person invited to your house or an event that you are paying for **2** person staying at a hotel, etc **3** famous person who takes part in a television show **[IDM] be my guest** (*infml*) used to give sb permission to do sth ■ **guest house** n [C] small hotel

guffaw /ɡəˈfɔː/ v [I], n [C] (give a) noisy laugh

0─ **guidance** /'ɡaɪdns/ n [U] help or advice

0─ **guide** /ɡaɪd/ n [C] **1** book, magazine, etc that gives information about sth: *a ~ to plants* **2** (*also* **guidebook**) book with information about a place for travellers **3** person who shows other people the way to a place, esp sb employed to show tourists around: *a tour ~* **4** something that gives you enough information to be able to

guild

form an opinion about sth: *As a rough ~, allow 1 cup of rice per person.* **5** (Guide) (*GB old-fash*, **Girl Guide**) (*US*, **Girl Scout**) member of an organization for girls that aims to develop practical skills ● **guide** v [T] act as a guide to sb ▸ **guided missile** n [C] missile that can be guided in flight ▸ **guideline** n [C, usu pl] advice on how to do sth

guild /gɪld/ n [C] society of people with similar jobs or interests

guile /gaɪl/ n [U] (*fml*) use of clever but dishonest behaviour to deceive people

guillotine /ˈɡɪlətiːn/ n [C] **1** machine for cutting off the heads of criminals **2** machine for cutting sheets of paper **3** (*GB, pol*) time limit for a discussion in Parliament ● **guillotine** v [T] use a guillotine on sb/sth

guilt /gɪlt/ n [U] **1** feeling of shame for having done wrong **2** fact that sb has done sth illegal: *an admission of ~* **3** blame or responsibility for wrongdoing ▸ **guiltily** adv

0─ **guilty** /ˈɡɪlti/ adj (**-ier, -iest**) **1** feeling shame for having done wrong: *She had a ~ conscience and could not sleep.* **2** having done sth illegal; being responsible for sth bad that has happened

guinea /ˈɡɪni/ n [C] old British gold coin worth 21 shillings (= £1.05)

guinea pig /ˈɡɪni pɪg/ n [C] **1** small animal with short ears and no tail, often kept as a pet **2** person used in an experiment

guise /gaɪz/ n [C] (*fml*) outward appearance

guitar /ɡɪˈtɑː(r)/ n [C] musical instrument with six strings played with the fingers ▸ **guitarist** n [C]

gulf /ɡʌlf/ n [C] **1** part of the sea almost surrounded by land: *the G~ of Mexico* **2 ~ (between)** big difference in opinion, lifestyle, etc

gull /ɡʌl/ n [C] large seabird with long wings

gullet /ˈɡʌlɪt/ n [C] food passage from the mouth to the stomach

gullible /ˈɡʌləbl/ adj easily deceived

gulp /ɡʌlp/ v [I,T] **1** swallow food or drink quickly **2** swallow because of a strong emotion, eg fear **3** breathe deeply because you need air ● **gulp** n [C] act of gulping

gum /ɡʌm/ n **1** [C, usu pl] either of the firm areas of pink flesh around the teeth **2** [U] sticky substance produced by certain trees **3** [U] type of glue **4** [U] = CHEWING GUM (CHEW) **5** [C] fruit-flavoured sweet that you chew ● **gum** v (**-mm-**) [T] (*old-fash*) spread glue on sth; stick two things together with glue ■ **gumboot** n [C] (*old-fash*) =

WELLINGTON ▸ **gummy** adj (**-ier, -iest**) sticky ■ **gum tree** n [C] eucalyptus tree

0─ **gun** /ɡʌn/ n [C] weapon that fires bullets or shells from a metal tube ● **gun** v (**-nn-**) [PV] **be gunning for sb** (*infml*) be looking for an opportunity to blame or attack sb **gun sb down** (*infml*) shoot sb, esp so as to kill them ■ **gunboat** n [C] small warship with heavy guns ■ **gunfire** n [U] shooting of guns ■ **gunman** n [C] (pl **-men**) man who uses a gun to rob or kill ▸ **gunner** n [C] soldier who uses large guns ■ **gunpoint** n [IDM] **at gunpoint** under the threat of being shot ■ **gunpowder** n [U] explosive powder ■ **gunshot** n **1** [C] shot fired from a gun **2** [U] distance that a bullet from a gun can travel ■ **gunsmith** n [C] person who makes and repairs guns

gurgle /ˈɡɜːɡl/ v [I], n [C] (make the) bubbling sound of flowing water

guru /ˈɡuːruː/ n [C] **1** Hindu or Sikh religious teacher or leader **2** (*infml*) person who is an expert on a particular subject or who is very good at doing sth: *a management/fashion ~*

gush /ɡʌʃ/ v [I] **1** flow out of sth suddenly and in large amounts: *blood ~ing from a wound* **2** (*disapprov*) talk with too much enthusiasm ● **gush** n [sing] sudden outburst ▸ **gushing** adj

gust /ɡʌst/ n [C] sudden rush of wind ▸ **gusty** adj (**-ier, -iest**)

gut /ɡʌt/ n **1** [C] intestine **2** (**guts**) [pl] organs in and around the stomach **3** (**guts**) [pl] (*infml*) courage and determination necessary to do sth difficult **4** (**guts**) [pl] most important part of sth: *the ~s of the problem/argument* **5** [U] = CATGUT ● **gut** v (**-tt-**) [T] **1** destroy the inside of a building or room: *a house~ted by fire* **2** take the guts out of a fish, etc ■ **gut** adj based on feelings rather than thought: *a ~ reaction*

gutter /ˈɡʌtə(r)/ n **1** [C] channel under the edge of a roof, or at the side of a road, to carry away rainwater **2** (**the gutter**) [sing] bad social conditions or lack of morals ■ **the gutter 'press** n [sing] (*disapprov*) newspapers that contain a lot of gossip and scandal

0─ **guy** /gaɪ/ n [C] **1** (*infml*) man **2** (in Britain) figure of a man dressed in old clothes burned on a bonfire on 5 November **3** (*also* **guy rope**) rope used to keep a tent or a pole firmly in place

guzzle /ˈɡʌzl/ v [I,T] (*infml*) eat or drink sth greedily

gym /dʒɪm/ n (*infml*) **1** (*also fml* **gymnasium**) [C] room or hall with apparatus for physical exercise **2** [U] physical exercises done in a gym, esp at school ■ **gym shoe** n [C] (GB) = PLIMSOLL

gymkhana /dʒɪmˈkɑːnə/ n [C] public competition of horse riding

gymnasium /dʒɪmˈneɪziəm/ n [C] (pl ~s or **gymnasia** /-ziə/) (fml) = GYM

gymnast /ˈdʒɪmnæst/ n [C] expert in gymnastics

gymnastics /dʒɪmˈnæstɪks/ n [pl] physical exercises to train the body or show how agile it is ▶ **gymnastic** adj

gynaecology (US **gynec-**) /ˌɡaɪnəˈkɒlədʒi/ n [U] study and treatment of disorders of the female reproductive system
▶ **gynaecological** (US **gynec-**) /ˌɡaɪnəkəˈlɒdʒɪkl/ adj
▶ **gynaecologist** (US **gynec-**) n [C] expert in gynaecology

gypsy (also gipsy) /ˈdʒɪpsi/ n [C] (pl **-ies**) sometimes (offens) member of a race of people who travel around and traditionally live in caravans

gyrate /dʒaɪˈreɪt/ v [I,T] (cause sth to) move around in circles ▶ **gyration** /dʒaɪˈreɪʃn/ n [C,U]

Hh

H, h /eɪtʃ/ n [C,U] (pl **H's, h's** /ˈeɪtʃɪz/) the eighth letter of the English alphabet

haberdasher /ˈhæbədæʃə(r)/ n [C] **1** (GB, old-fash) shopkeeper who sells small articles for sewing, eg needles **2** (US) shopkeeper who sells men's clothing ▶ **haberdashery** n [U] (old-fash) goods sold by a haberdasher

o—**habit** /ˈhæbɪt/ n **1** [C,U] thing that you do often and almost without thinking: Smoking is a bad~. **2** [C] long garment worn by a monk or nun [IDM] **make a habit of (doing) sth** do sth regularly: Don't make a ~ of borrowing money.

habitable /ˈhæbɪtəbl/ adj fit to be lived in

habitat /ˈhæbɪtæt/ n [C] natural home of an animal or plant

habitation /ˌhæbɪˈteɪʃn/ n [U] act of living in a place: houses unfit for human~

habitual /həˈbɪtʃuəl/ adj **1** usual or typical of sb/sth **2** doing sth by habit: a ~ criminal/drinker ▶ **habitually** adv

hack /hæk/ v [I,T] **1** cut sth roughly **2** ~ (into) (computing) secretly look at and/or change information on sb else's computer system ■ **hacksaw** n [C] tool for cutting metal ● **hack** n [C] (disapprov) writer, esp of newspaper articles, who does a lot of low quality work for little money

hacker /ˈhækə(r)/ n [C] person who

looks at computer data without permission

hackneyed /ˈhæknid/ adj (of a phrase, etc) meaninglessly because used too often

had /həd; əd; strong form hæd/ pt, pp of HAVE

haddock /ˈhædək/ n [C,U] (pl **haddock**) sea fish used for food

hadn't /ˈhædnt/ short for HAD NOT

haemophilia (US **hem-**) /ˌhiːməˈfɪliə/ n [U] medical condition that causes a person to bleed badly from even a small injury
▶ **haemophiliac** (US **hem-**) /-ˈfɪliæk/ n [C] person with haemophilia

haemorrhage (US **hem-**) /ˈhemərɪdʒ/ n [C,U] great flow of blood

haemorrhoids (US **hem-**) /ˈhemərɔɪdz/ n [pl] (med) swollen veins inside the anus

hag /hæg/ n [C] (offens) ugly old woman

haggard /ˈhægəd/ adj looking tired, esp from worry

haggis /ˈhægɪs/ n [C,U] Scottish food made from parts of a sheep and cooked in a sheep's stomach

haggle /ˈhægl/ v [I] ~ (over/about) argue about a price

hail /heɪl/ n **1** [U] small balls of ice that fall like rain **2** [sing] large number or amount of sth that is aimed at sb to harm them: a ~ of bullets ● **hail** v **1** [T] describe sb/sth as being very good or special, esp in newspapers, etc: They ~ed him as their hero. **2** [T] signal to a taxi or a bus to stop **3** [T] (lit) call out to sb, in order to attract attention **4** [I] (of small balls of ice) fall like rain [PV] **hail from...** (fml) come from a particular place ■ **hailstone** n [C] small ball of ice that falls like rain ■ **hailstorm** n [C] storm with hail

o—**hair** /heə(r)/ n [U,C] substance that looks like a mass of fine threads growing esp on the head; one of these threads [IDM] **(by) a hair's breadth** (by) a very small distance **make sb's hair stand on end** shock or frighten sb ■ **haircut** n [C] act or style of cutting the hair ■ **hairdo** n [C] (pl **-dos**) (infml, old-fash) act or style of arranging a woman's hair ■ **hairdresser** n [C] person who cuts and styles hair ■ **hairgrip** n [C] clip for holding the hair in place ■ **hairline** n [C] **1** edge of the hair above the forehead **2** (used as an adjective) very thin line: a ~ line crack/fracture ■ **hairpin** n [C] bent pin used for keeping the hair in place ■ **hairpin 'bend** n [C] very sharp bend in a road ■ **hair-raising** adj very frightening ■ **hairstyle** n [C] way of arranging or cutting the

hale

hair ▶ **hairy** adj (-ier, -iest)
1 covered with hair **2** (infml)
exciting but frightening ▶ **hairiness**
n [U]

hale /heɪl/ adj [IDM] **hale and hearty**
strong and healthy

0—ᴡ **half¹** /hɑːf/ n [C] (pl halves
/hɑːvz/) **1** one of two equal parts; ½
2 either of two periods of time into
which a sports match, concert, etc is
divided **3** a ticket or drink that is half
the usual price or size: *Two halves to
the station, please.* [IDM] **go half and half | go
halves (with sb)** share the cost of sth
equally

0—ᴡ **half²** /hɑːf/ det, pron **1** amount
equal to half of sth/sb: ~ *an hour*
2 the largest part of sth: *H~ the time,
you don't listen to what I say.* [IDM]
half past one, two, etc (US also) **half
after one, two, etc** thirty minutes
after any hour on the clock ■ **half-
and-half** adj being half one thing
and half another ■ **half 'board** n [U]
(GB) hotel accommodation with
breakfast and evening meal
included ■ **half 'mast** n [IDM] **at half
mast** (of a flag) flown halfway up a
mast, as a sign of respect for a dead
person ■ **half-term** n [C] (GB) short
holiday in the middle of a school
term ■ **half-time** n [U] interval
between the two halves of a sports
match ■ **half'way** adj, adv between
and at an equal distance from two
places ■ **halfwit** n [C] (infml) stupid
person ▶ **half-'witted** adj

0—ᴡ **half³** /hɑːf/ adv **1** to the extent of
half: ~ *full* **2** partly: ~ *cooked* [IDM] **not
half** (GB, infml) used to emphasize a
statement or opinion: *It wasn't ~
good* (= it was very good). ■ **half-
baked** adj (infml) not well planned
■ **half-'hearted** adj showing little
enthusiasm

0—ᴡ **hall** /hɔːl/ n [C] **1** space or
passage inside the entrance of a
house **2** building or large room for
meetings, concerts, meals, etc
3 building for university students to
live in: *a ~ of residence*

hallmark /'hɔːlmɑːk/ n [C] **1** feature
that is typical of sb/sth **2** mark
stamped on gold or silver objects to
show the quality of the metal
● **hallmark** v [T] put a hallmark on
metal goods

hallo (GB) = HELLO

Halloween (also Hallowe'en)
/ˌhæləʊˈiːn/ n [U] 31 October, when
children dress up as ghosts and
witches

hallucination /həˌluːsɪˈneɪʃn/ n
[C, U] seeing sth that is not really
there

halo /'heɪləʊ/ n [C] (pl **~es**) **1** circle of
light round the head of a holy

person in a picture **2** circle of light
round the sun or moon

halt /hɔːlt/ v [I, T] (cause sb/sth to)
stop ● **halt** n [sing] stop: *The train
came to a ~ outside the station.*

halter /'hɔːltə(r)/ n [C] rope or
leather strap put round a horse's
head, for leading the horse

halting /'hɔːltɪŋ/ adj slow and
hesitating ▶ **haltingly** adv

halve /hɑːv/ v **1** [T] divide sth into
two equal parts **2** [I, T] (cause sth to)
reduce by a half: ~ *the cost*

halves plural of HALF¹

ham /hæm/ n **1** [C, U] (meat from the
top part of a pig's leg, that has been
salted or smoked to be eaten as food
2 [C] (infml) amateur radio operator
3 [C] (infml) bad actor ● **ham** v
(**-mm-**) [PV] **ham it up** (infml) (esp of
actors) to act in an exaggerated
way ■ **ham-'fisted** (US **ham-
handed**) adj (infml) lacking skill
when using your hands or dealing
with people

hamburger /'hæmbɜːgə(r)/ n [C] flat
round cake of minced meat, usu
fried and eaten in a bread roll

hamlet /'hæmlət/ n [C] small village

0—ᴡ **hammer** /'hæmə(r)/ n **1** [C] tool
with a heavy metal head, used for
hitting nails, etc **2** [C] (in a piano)
part that hits the strings ● **hammer**
v **1** [I, T] hit sth with a hammer **2** [T]
(infml) defeat sb completely [PV]
hammer away at sth work hard at sth
hammer out sth reach an agreement
about sth after long discussion

hammock /'hæmək/ n [C] bed made
of cloth or rope net hung between
two posts

hamper /'hæmpə(r)/ v [T] (written)
prevent sb from easily doing or
achieving sth ● **hamper** n [C] large
basket with a lid, used for carrying
food

hamster /'hæmstə(r)/ n [C] small
animal like a mouse, kept as a pet

0—ᴡ **hand¹** /hænd/ n **1** [C] part of the
human arm below the wrist **2** (a
hand) [sing] (infml) help in doing
sth: *Can you give me a ~ with the
washing-up?* **3** [sing] ~ **in** role or
influence that sb/sth has in a
particular situation: *She had a ~ in his
downfall.* **4** [C] pointer on a clock,
dial, etc: *hour-* ~ **5** [C] worker: *a farm
~* **6** [C] set of cards dealt to a player
in a game [IDM] **(close/near) at hand**
close to you **by hand 1** by a person,
not a machine **2** (of a letter)
brought by a person, not sent by
post **give sb/sth a big hand** show
your approval of sb by clapping your
hands; be applauded in this way
hand in hand 1 (of people) holding
each other's hand **2** (of things)
closely connected **have/take a hand
in sth** be partly responsible for sth
have your hands full be very busy in

hand 1 available to be used 2 in control: *The situation is well in ~.* 3 that is being dealt with: *the job in ~* **in/out of sb's hands** in/no longer in sb's control or care **off/on your hands** no longer being/being your responsibility **on hand** available **on the one hand...on the other (hand)...** used for showing two opposite points of view **out of hand** 1 out of control 2 without further thought: *All our suggestions were dismissed out of ~.* **(at) second, third, etc hand** being told about sth by sb else who has seen it, heard about it, etc, rather than experiencing it yourself ■ **handbag** (*US* **purse**) *n* [C] woman's bag for money, keys, etc ■ **handbook** *n* [C] book giving facts and instructions ■ **handbrake** *n* [C] brake in a car, van, etc operated by the driver's hand ■ **handcuff** *v* [T] put handcuffs on sb ■ **handcuffs** *n* [pl] metal rings joined by a chain, for fastening round a prisoner's wrists ▶ **handful** *n* 1 [C] as much as can be held in one hand 2 [sing] small number 3 [sing] (*infml*) person or animal that is difficult to control ■ **hand-held** *adj* small enough to be held in the hand while being used ▶ **hand-held** *n* [C] ■ **hand-picked** *adj* carefully chosen ■ **hands-free** *adj* (esp of a telephone) that can be operated without using your hands ■ **handshake** *n* [C] shaking of sb's hand with your own, as a greeting, etc ■ **handstand** *n* [C] movement in which you balance yourself on your hands, with your feet in the air ■ **handwriting** *n* [U] (style of) writing by hand

0─ **hand²** /hænd/ *v* [T] pass or give sth to sb: *Please ~ me that book.* **IDM hand sth to sb on a plate** → PLATE **[PV] hand sth down (to sb)** give or leave sth to sb who is younger than you **hand sth in (to sb)** give sth to a person in authority, esp a piece of work: *~ in homework* **hand sth on (to sb)** give sth to another person to use or deal with **hand sth out (to sb)** 1 give a number of things to members of a group 2 give advice, punishment, etc **hand sb/sth over (to sb)** give the responsibility for sb/ sth to sb: *~ a prisoner over to the authorities* ■ **handout** *n* [C] 1 something, eg food or money, given freely 2 sheet of information given out, eg by a teacher

handicap /'hændikæp/ *n* [C] 1 (*old-fash*) disability in a person's body or mind 2 condition that makes it difficult to do sth 3 disadvantage given to a skilled competitor in a sport ▶ **handicap** *v* (-pp-) [T] make sth more difficult for sb to do ▶ **handicapped** *adj* (*old-fash*) having a handicap (1)

handicraft /'hændikrɑːft/ *n* [C]

---

work, eg pottery, that needs skill with the hands

handiwork /'hændiwɜːk/ *n* [U] 1 work done or something made using artistic skill 2 thing done by a particular person, esp sth bad

handkerchief /'hæŋkətʃɪf, -tʃiːf/ *n* [C] square piece of cloth used for blowing your nose

0─ **handle** /'hændl/ *n* [C] part of a cup, door, tool, etc, by which it is held ● **handle** *v* 1 [T] deal with or control sb/sth 2 [T] touch, hold or move sth with your hands 3 [I,T] (esp of a vehicle) operate or control sth in the way that is mentioned: *This car ~s well.* ■ **handlebars** *n* [pl] bar with a handle at each end for steering a bicycle or motorcycle ▶ **handler** *n* [C] person who trains an animal, eg a police dog

handsome /'hænsəm/ *adj* 1 (esp of men) good-looking 2 (of gifts, behaviour, etc) generous ▶ **handsomely** *adv*

handy /'hændi/ *adj* (-ier, -iest) 1 useful; easy to use or do 2 easily reached; near 3 clever with your hands **[IDM] come in handy** be useful ▶ **handily** *adv* ■ **handyman** *n* [C] (pl -men) person skilled at doing small repairs

0─ **hang¹** /hæŋ/ *v* (pt, pp hung /hʌŋ/, in sense 2 ~ed) 1 [I,T] attach sth or be attached at the top so that the lower part is free or loose: *~ the washing out to dry* 2 [T] kill sb by tying a rope around their neck and allowing them to drop 3 [T] stick wallpaper to a wall 4 [I] **hang about/ around** wait or stay near a place, not doing very much **hang back (from sth)** hesitate because you are nervous about doing sth **hang on** 1 hold sth tightly 2 (*spoken*) wait for a short time **hang on to sth** 1 hold sth tightly 2 (*infml*) keep sth **hang up** put down a telephone receiver **(be/get) hung up (on/about sth/sb)** (*infml*) (feel) very worried about sth/ sb; (be) thinking about sth/sb too much ■ **hang-gliding** *n* [U] sport of flying while hanging from a frame like a large kite ■ **hang-glider** *n* 1 frame used in hang-gliding 2 person who goes hang-gliding ▶ **hanging** *n* 1 [U, C] death by hanging 2 [C, usu pl] large piece of material hung on a wall for decoration: *wall ~s* ■ **hangman** *n* [C] (pl -men) man whose job is to hang criminals ■ **hang-up** *n* [C] (*infml*) emotional problem about sth

hang² /hæŋ/ *n* **[IDM] get the hang of sth** (*infml*) understand sth or learn how to do sth

hangar /'hæŋə(r)/ *n* [C] building in which aircraft are kept

---

A B C D E F G **H** I J K L M N O P Q R S T U V W X Y Z

hanger /'hæŋə(r)/ (also ˌcoat
ˈhanger, ˈclothes hanger) n [C] piece
of wood, wire, etc with a hook, used
for hanging up clothes
▶ **hanger-ˈon** n [C] (pl **~s-on**)
(disapprov) person who tries to be
friendly, in the hope of personal gain

hangover /'hæŋəʊvə(r)/ n [C]
1 unpleasant feeling after drinking
too much alcohol on the previous
night **2** something left from an
earlier time

hanker /'hæŋkə(r)/ v [I] **~ after/for**
have a strong desire for sth
▶ **hankering** n [C]

hanky (also hankie) /'hæŋki/ n [C] (pl
-ies) (infml) = HANDKERCHIEF

haphazard /,hæp'hæzəd/ adj with no
particular plan or order
▶ **haphazardly** adv

0̶ **happen** /'hæpən/ v [I] **1** (of an
event) take place, usu by chance
2 do or be sth by chance: I ~ed to be
out when he called. **[PV] happen on
sb/sth** (old-fash) find sb/sth by
chance ▶ **happening** n [C] event

0̶ **happy** /'hæpi/ adj (**-ier, -iest**)
1 feeling, giving or expressing
pleasure; pleased: I'm very ~ for you.
◇ a ~ marriage ◇ a ~ smile **2** used in
greetings to express good wishes:
H~ birthday! **3** satisfied that sth is
good or right; not anxious **4** willing
or pleased to do sth **[IDM] a/the
happy medium** a balance between
two extremes ▶ **happily** adv ▶ **happiness** n [U] ▶ **happy-go-
lucky** adj not worrying about the
future

harangue /hə'ræŋ/ n [C] long loud
angry speech ● **harangue** v [T]
speak loudly and angrily to sb in a
way that criticizes them

harass /'hærəs/ v [T] worry or annoy
sb by putting pressure on them
▶ **harassment** n [U]

harbour (US **-or**) /'hɑːbə(r)/ n [C]
place of shelter for ships ● **harbour**
v [T] **1** hide and protect sb who is
hiding from the police **2** (written)
keep feelings in your mind for a long
time: ~ secret fears

0̶ **hard¹** /hɑːd/ adj **1** firm and solid;
not easy to bend, cut, etc: as ~ as
rock **2** difficult: a ~ exam **3** needing
or showing great effort: ~ work ◇ a ~
worker **4** (of a person) showing no
kindness; harsh **5** (infml) (of people)
ready to fight and showing no fear
6 that can be proved to be definitely
true: ~ evidence/facts **7** (of the
weather) very cold and severe: a ~
winter **[IDM] hard and fast** (of rules,
etc) fixed and not able to be changed
hard luck (GB) used to tell sb you feel
sorry for them **hard of hearing** rather
deaf ■ **hardback** n [C] book with a
stiff cover ■ **hardboard** n [U] thin

board made of very small pieces of
wood pressed together ■ **hard
ˈcash** (US ˌcold ˈcash) n [U] money in
the form of coins and notes ■ **hard
ˈcopy** n [U] (computing) information
from a computer that has been
printed on paper ■ **hard ˈcore** n
[sing] central most involved
members of a group ■ **hard
ˈcurrency** n [U,C] money that is not
likely to fall suddenly in value
■ **hard ˈdisk** n [C] disk inside a
computer that stores data and
programs ■ **hard ˈdrug** n [C] strong
dangerous drug that is likely to lead
to addiction ■ **hard-ˈheaded** adj
determined; not influenced by your
emotions ■ **hard-ˈhearted** adj not
kind or caring ■ **hard ˈlabour** (US
ˌhard ˈlabor) n [U] punishment in
prison that involves hard physical
work ■ **hard-ˈline** adj fixed in your
beliefs ■ **hard ˈshoulder** n [sing]
hard surface at the side of a
motorway, used in an emergency
■ **hardware** n [U] **1** (computing)
machinery and electronic parts of a
computer system **2** tools and
equipment used in the house and
garden ■ **hard ˈwater** n [U] water
that contains calcium and other
minerals that make mixing with
soap difficult ■ **hardwood** n [U]
hard heavy wood, eg oak or beech

0̶ **hard²** /hɑːd/ adv **1** with great
effort; with difficulty: try/work ◇ my
~-earned money **2** carefully and
thoroughly: think/listen ~ **3** heavily;
a lot: raining ~ **[IDM] be/feel hard
done by** be or feel unfairly treated **be
hard pressed/pushed to do sth | be
hard put (to it) (to do sth)** find it very
difficult to do sth **be hard to say** be
difficult to estimate the size, etc of sth
be hard up for sth have too few or too
little of sth **hard on sth** (fml) soon after
sth **take sth hard** be very upset by sth
■ **hard-ˈboiled** adj (of eggs) boiled
until the yellow part (yolk) is hard
■ **hard-ˈpressed** adj in difficulties,
because of lack of time or money
■ **hard ˈup** adj (infml) having little
money ■ **hard-ˈwearing** adj (GB)
(of cloth) tough and lasting for a
long time

0̶ **harden** /'hɑːdn/ v **1** [I,T] become or
make sth firm, solid, etc **2** [T] ~ (to)
make sb less sensitive to sth

0̶ **hardly** /'hɑːdli/ adv **1** almost no;
almost not: ~ ever **2** used to
emphasize that it is difficult to do
sth: I could ~ keep my eyes open.

hardship /'hɑːdʃɪp/ n [U,C] (cause of)
severe suffering

hardy /'hɑːdi/ adj (**-ier, -iest**) able to
endure cold, difficult conditions,
etc ▶ **hardiness** n [U]

hare /heə(r)/ n [C] animal like a large
rabbit with strong back legs that can
run very fast ● **hare** v [I] run fast

hare-brained adj crazy and unlikely to succeed

harem /'hɑ:ri:m/ n [C] (women living in the) separate women's part of a Muslim house

hark /hɑ:k/ v [I] (old-fash) listen [PV] **hark back (to sth)** mention again an earlier subject or event

0— **harm** /hɑ:m/ n [U] damage; injury [IDM] **out of harm's way** safe ● **harm** v [T] cause harm to sb/sth ▸ **harmful** adj causing harm ▸ **harmless** adj **1** not dangerous **2** unlikely to upset or offend people: ~less fun

harmonica /hɑ:'mɒnɪkə/ n [C] = MOUTH ORGAN (MOUTH¹)

harmonize (also -ise) /'hɑ:mənaɪz/ v [I,T] **1** (cause two or more things to) match and look attractive together: colours that ~ well **2** (music) sing or play in harmony

harmony /'hɑ:məni/ n (pl -ies) **1** [U] state of peaceful existence and agreement: live together in perfect ~ **2** [U,C] (music) pleasing combination of musical notes **3** [C,U] pleasing combination of related things: the ~ of colours ▸ **harmonious** /hɑ:'məʊniəs/ adj

harness /'hɑ:nɪs/ n [C] **1** set of leather straps for fastening a horse to a cart, etc **2** set of straps for fastening sth to a person's body or to keep them from moving off or falling: a safety ~ ● **harness** v [T] **1** put a harness on a horse or other animal **2** use the force or strength of sth to produce power: ~ the sun's rays as a source of energy

harp /hɑ:p/ n [C] large upright musical instrument with vertical strings played with the fingers ● **harp** v [PV] **harp on (about) sth** keep talking about sth in a boring way ▸ **harpist** n [C] person who plays the harp

harpoon /hɑ:'pu:n/ n [C] spear on a rope, used for catching whales ● **harpoon** v [T] hit sth with a harpoon

harpsichord /'hɑ:psɪkɔ:d/ n [C] musical instrument like a piano, but with strings that are plucked mechanically

harrowing /'hærəʊɪŋ/ adj very shocking or frightening

harsh /hɑ:ʃ/ adj **1** unpleasantly rough or sharp **2** cruel; severe: a ~ punishment ▸ **harshly** adv ▸ **harshness** n [U]

harvest /'hɑ:vɪst/ n **1** [C,U] (season for) cutting and gathering of crops on a farm, etc **2** [C] crops, amount of crops gathered: a good wheat ~ ● **harvest** v [T] cut and gather a crop

has /həz, əz/ → HAVE

hash /hæʃ/ n **1** [U] cooked chopped meat **2** (infml) = HASHISH **3** (also 'hash sign) (GB) [C] symbol (#), esp

one on a telephone [IDM] **make a hash of sth** (infml) do sth badly

hashish /'hæʃiːʃ; hæˈʃiːʃ/ n [U] drug from the hemp plant

hasn't /'hæznt/ has not → HAVE

hassle /'hæsl/ n [C,U] (infml) difficulty; trouble ● **hassle** v [T] (infml) annoy sb by continually asking them to do sth

haste /heɪst/ n [U] speed in doing sth, esp because there is not much time

hasten /'heɪsn/ v [I] be quick to do or say sth: I ~ to add that your child is safe. **2** [T] (written) cause sth to happen sooner

hasty /'heɪsti/ adj **1** made or done too quickly: a ~ meal **2** (of a person) acting too quickly ▸ **hastily** adv

0— **hat** /hæt/ n [C] covering for the head [IDM] **I take my hat off to sb | hats off to sb** (esp GB) used to show admiration for sb ● **hat-trick** n [C] three similar successes made one after the other by one person

hatch /hætʃ/ v **1** [I,T] ~ (**out**) (cause a young bird, fish, insect, etc to) come out of an egg: The chicks have ~ed (out). **2** [T] prepare a plan, etc, esp in secret ● **hatch** n [C] (movable cover over an) opening in a floor, wall, etc: an escape ~

hatchback /'hætʃbæk/ n [C] car with a sloping door at the back that opens upwards

hatchet /'hætʃɪt/ n [C] small axe

hatchway /'hætʃweɪ/ n [C] = HATCH

hate /heɪt/ v [T] **1** have a great dislike for sb/sth **2** be sorry: I ~ to trouble you. [IDM] **hate sb's guts** (infml) dislike sb very much ● **hate** n [U] great dislike ▸ **hateful** adj very unpleasant

0— **hatred** /'heɪtrɪd/ n [U] ~ (**for/of**) hate

haughty /'hɔ:ti/ adj (-ier, -iest) unfriendly and too proud; arrogant ▸ **haughtily** adv ▸ **haughtiness** n [U]

haul /hɔ:l/ v [I,T] pull sth/sb with a lot of effort ● **haul** n [C] **1** large amount of sth stolen or illegal: a ~ of weapons/drugs **2** distance covered in a particular journey: a long~ flight **3** quantity of fish caught at one time ▸ **haulage** n [U] (GB) business of transporting goods by road or railway

haunch /hɔ:ntʃ/ n [C, usu pl] part of the body between the waist and the thighs

haunt /hɔ:nt/ v [T] **1** (of ghosts) appear in a place: a ~ed house **2** (of sth unpleasant) return repeatedly to your mind: The memory still ~s me. **3** continue to cause problems for sth ● **haunt** n [C] place visited often

0— **have**¹ /həv/ av; strong form hæv/ (third pers sing pres tense **has** pt **had** pp **had**) (GB have got) v [T]

---

have

A B C D E F G **H** I J K L M N O P Q R S T U V W X Y Z

have

1 (also **have got**) own, hold or possess sth: *He has/has got a house in London. ◇ Has she (got)/Does she ~ blue eyes?* **2** (also **have got**) let a feeling or thought come into your mind: *I ~ no doubt (= that you are right. ◇ H~ you (got) any idea where he lives?* **3** (also **have got**) suffer from an illness: *~ a headache* **4** experience sth: *~ a good holiday* **5** eat, drink or smoke sth: *~ breakfast/a cigarette* **6** give birth to sb/sth: *to ~ a baby* **8** produce a particular effect: *~ a strong influence on sb* **9** receive sth from sb: *I've had a letter from my aunt.* **10** suffer the effects of what sb does to you: *They had their house burgled.* **11** cause sth to be done for sb by sb else: *You should ~ your hair cut.* **12** allow sth: *I won't ~ such behaviour here!* **13** (*infml*) trick or deceive sb: *You've been had!* **14** entertain sb in your home: *We're having friends to dinner.* [IDM] **have had it** (*infml*) **1** be in very bad condition; be unable to be repaired **2** be unable to accept a situation any longer: *I've had it (up to here) with his problems.* **have it in for sb** (*infml*) not like sb and be unpleasant to them **have it (that)** claim that it is a fact that...: *Rumour has it that...* **have (got) to (do sth)** (showing obligation) must (do sth) [PV] **have sb on** (*infml*) play a trick on sb **have (got) sth on** be wearing sth **have sth on sb** (*infml*) have information to show that sb has done sth wrong **have sth out** cause sth, esp part of the body, to be removed: *~ a tooth out* **have sth out (with sb)** settle a disagreement with sb by arguing about it openly **have sb up (for sth)** (*infml*) (*esp passive*) cause sb to appear in court for a crime: *He was had up for robbery.*

9 (*infml*) trick: *You've been had!* [IDM] **have had it** (*infml*) not be able to continue doing sth **have it (that)** claim or say that: *Rumour has it that...* [PV] **have sb on** (*infml*) play a trick on sb **have sth out (with sb)** to be removed: *~ a tooth out* **have sth out (with sb)** settle a disagreement with sb by argument **have sb up (for sth)** (*infml*) (*esp passive*) cause sb to appear in court for a crime: *He was had up for robbery.*

haven /ˈheɪvn/ *n* [C] place of safety or rest

haven't /ˈhævnt/ *short for* HAVE NOT

0➡ **have to** /ˈhæv tə; ˈhæf tə; *strong form* ˈhæv tu; ˈhæf tu:/ (*also* **have got to** /ˈhæv; ˈhæf tu:/) *modal v* used for saying that sb must do sth or that sb must happen: *I've got to go now. ◇ You don't have to (= it is not necessary to) go out.*

havoc /ˈhævək/ *n* [U] widespread damage

hawk /hɔːk/ *n* [C] **1** large bird that catches and eats small birds and animals **2** person, esp a politician, who favours the use of military force

hay /heɪ/ *n* [U] grass cut and dried for use as animal food ■ **hay fever** /*n* [U] illness of the nose and throat, caused by pollen from plants ■ **haystack** /*n* large pile of hay firmly packed for storing ■ **haywire** /*adj* [IDM] **go haywire** become disorganized or out of control

hazard /ˈhæzəd/ *n* [C] **1** ~ **(to)** danger; risk ● **hazard** *v* [T] **1** suggest or guess at sth that you know may be wrong **2** (*fml*) risk sth or put it in danger ▸ **hazardous** *adj* dangerous; risky

haze /heɪz/ *n* [U] **1** thin mist **2** confused mental state

hazel /ˈheɪzl/ *n* [C] small tree that produces small edible nuts (hazelnuts) ● **hazel** *adj* (of eyes) greenish-brown or reddish-brown in colour

hazy /ˈheɪzi/ *adj* (-**ier**, -**iest**) **1** misty **2** not clear; vague: *~ memories* ▸ **hazily** *adv* ▸ **haziness** *n* [U]

H-bomb /ˈeɪtʃ bɒm/ *n* [C] = HYDROGEN BOMB (HYDROGEN)

0➡ **have²** /hæv; əv; *strong form* hæv/ *aux v* used to form perfect tenses: *I ~/I've finished. ◇ She has/she's gone. ◇ (fml) Had I known that (= if I had known that) I would never have come.* [IDM] **had I, he, she, etc** if I, etc had: *Had I known,...*

0➡ **he** /hiː/ *pron* (used as the subject of a *v*) **1** male person or animal mentioned earlier: *I spoke to John before he left.* **2** (*old-fash*) (male or female) person: *Every child needs to know that he is loved.*

0➡ **have³** /hæv/ *v* [T] (always used in the negative and interrogative with *do*) **1** perform; take: *~ a swim/walk* **2** eat, drink, smoke, etc: *~ breakfast/a cigarette* **3** receive; experience: *I've had a letter from my aunt. ◇ ~ a good holiday* **4** give birth to; produce: *to ~ a baby ◇ (fig) ~ a good effect* **5** cause (sth to be done): *You should ~ your hair cut.* **6** suffer the results of: *They had their house burgled.* **7** allow: *I won't ~ such behaviour here!* **8** cause (sb) to come as a visitor: *We're having friends round for dinner.*

0➡ **head¹** /hed/ *n* **1** [C] part of the body that contains the eyes, nose, brain, etc **2** [C] mind or brain: *The thought never entered my ~.* **3** (heads) [U] side of a coin with the head of a person on it **4** [C, usu sing] wider end of a long narrow object: *the ~ of a pin/hammer* **5** [sing] top: *at the ~ of the page* **6** [sing] most important end: *at the ~ of the table ◇*

the ~ of a bed (= where your head rests) **7** [sing] front: *at the ~ of the queue* **8** [C] person in charge of a group of people or an organization: *~s of government* **9** [sing] pressure produced by steam [IDM] **a/per head** for each person: *dinner at £15 a ~* ▪ be **banging, etc your head against a brick wall** keep trying to do sth without any success **bring sth/come to a head** bring sth to/reach the point at which action is essential **go to your head 1** make you slightly drunk **2** (of success) make you too confident **have a head for sth** be good at sth: *to have a ~ for business/figures* **have your head screwed on (the right way)** (*infml*) be sensible **head first 1** with your head before the rest of your body: *fall ~ first down the stairs* **2** without thinking before acting **head over heels in love** love sb very much **keep/lose your head** stay calm/fail to stay calm in a crisis **laugh, scream, etc your head off** (*infml*) laugh, etc a lot and very loudly **over sb's head 1** too difficult to understand **2** to a higher position of authority than sb **put our/your/their heads together** discuss a plan, etc as a group ▸ **headache** *n* [C] **1** pain in the head **2** problem ▸ **header** *n* [C] **1** (in football) act of hitting the ball with your head **2** line of text that is automatically added to the top of every page printed from a computer ▪ **headland** *n* [C] high piece of land that sticks out into the sea ▪ **headlight** (*also* **headlamp**) *n* [C] bright light on the front of a vehicle ▪ **headline** *n* [C] **1** words printed in large letters above a newspaper story **2** (**the headlines**) [pl] summary of the main points of the news on radio or television ▪ **headmaster** (*fem* **headmistress**) *n* [C] teacher who is in charge of a school ▪ **head-on** *adj, adv* with the front parts hitting each other: *The cars crashed ~-on.* ▪ **headphones** *n* [pl] receivers that fit over the ears, for listening to music, etc ▪ **headquarters** *n* [U, with sing or pl verb] (*abbr* **HQ**) place from which an organization is controlled ▪ **headrest** *n* [C] part of a seat that supports a person's head, esp in a car ▪ **headroom** *n* [U] clear space above a vehicle ▪ **headstone** *n* [C] stone that marks the head of a grave ▪ **headway** *n* [U] [IDM] **make headway** make progress

0— **head²** /hed/ *v* [T, I] move in the direction that is mentioned: *~ south/for home* **2** [T] (*also* **head sth up**) lead or be in charge of sth: *She'll ~ the research team.* **3** [T] be at the front of a line of people or top of a list of names: *~ a procession* **4** [T] hit a football with your head [PV] **head sb off** get in front of sb and make them change direction **head sth off**

take action to prevent sth from happening

heading /ˈhedɪŋ/ *n* [C] words at the top of a page, as a title

headlong /ˈhedlɒŋ/ *adv, adj* **1** with the head first **2** quickly and without thinking: *rush ~ into a decision*

headstrong /ˈhedstrɒŋ/ *adj* determined to do things your own way, refusing to listen to advice

heady /ˈhedi/ *adj* (**-ier, -iest**) having a strong effect on your senses, making you feel excited

0— **heal** /hiːl/ *v* [I,T] become or make sth healthy again: *The cut was ~ed.*

0— **health** /helθ/ *n* [U] **1** condition of a person's body or mind: *be in good/poor ~* **2** state of being physically and mentally healthy **3** work of providing medical services: *the Department of H~* ▪ **health farm** (*US* **health spa**) *n* [C] place where people can stay for short periods of time in order to improve their health by dieting, doing physical exercises, etc ▸ **healthy** *adj* (**-ier, -iest**) **1** having good health **2** good for your health: *a ~y diet* **3** showing that you are in good health: *a ~y appetite* **4** large and showing success: *~y profits* ▸ **healthily** *adv*

0— **heap** /hiːp/ *n* [C] **1** pile or mass of things or material: *a ~ of books/sand* **2** (**heaps**) [pl] (*infml*) large quantity of sth: *~s of time* ▸ **heap** *v* [T] put sth in a large pile: *~ food on your plate*

0— **hear** /hɪə(r)/ *v* (*pt, pp* **-d** /hɜːd/) **1** [I,T] be aware of sounds with your ears **2** [T] pay attention to sb: *You're not to go, do you ~ me?* **3** [T] be told about sth: *I ~ she's leaving.* **4** [T] listen and judge a case in a law court [IDM] **hear! hear!** used for expressing agreement at a meeting [PV] **hear from sb** receive a letter, news, etc from sb **hear of sb/sth** know about: *I've never ~d of the place.* **not hear of sth** refuse to allow sth: *He wouldn't ~ of my walking home alone.* **hear sb out** listen to sb until they finish speaking

0— **hearing** /ˈhɪərɪŋ/ *n* **1** [U] ability to hear **2** [C] official meeting at which the facts of a crime, complaint, etc are presented to a group of people and a course of action is decided **3** [sing] opportunity to defend your opinion, actions, etc: *get a fair ~* [IDM] **in/within (sb's) hearing** near enough to sb so that they can hear what is said ▪ **hearing aid** *n* [C] small device used for improving hearing

hearsay /ˈhɪəseɪ/ *n* [U] rumour

hearse /hɜːs/ *n* [C] car used for carrying the coffin to a funeral

0— **heart** /hɑːt/ *n* [C] **1** organ that pumps blood around the body

2 centre of a person's feelings, esp love **3** centre or most important part of sth **4** something shaped like a heart **5** (**hearts**) [pl] one of the four sets of playing cards (suits), with red heart symbols on them [IDM] **break sb's heart** make sb feel very sad **by heart** from memory: *learn/know a poem by ~* **from the (bottom of your) heart** sincerely **not have the heart (to do sth)** not be cruel enough to do sth **take/lose heart** become encouraged/discouraged **take sth to heart** be very upset by sth that says or does ■ **heartache** n [U,C] great sadness ■ **heart attack** n [C] sudden serious illness in which the heart stops working ■ **heartbeat** n [C] movement or sound of the heart as it pumps blood ■ **heartbreaking** *adj* causing deep sadness ■ **heartbroken** *adj* feeling great sadness ■ **heartburn** n [U] burning feeling in the chest, caused by indigestion ■ **heartfelt** *adj* sincere ▶ **heartless** *adj* without pity ▶ **heartlessly** *adv* ■ **heart-rending** *adj* causing deep sadness ■ **heart-to-heart** n [C] open honest talk about personal matters

hearten /ˈhɑːtn/ v [T] make sb feel encouraged and more hopeful

hearth /hɑːθ/ n [C] (area in front of the) fireplace

hearty /ˈhɑːti/ *adj* (**-ier, -iest**) **1** friendly: *a ~ welcome* **2** loud and (too) cheerful **3** (of a meal or appetite) big **4** showing that you feel strongly about sth: *a ~ dislike of sb* ▶ **heartily** *adv* in a hearty way **2** very: *I'm heartily sick of this rain.*

heat¹ /hiːt/ n **1** [U, sing] quality of being hot **2** [U, C, usu sing] level of temperature: *increase/reduce the ~* **3** [U] hot weather **4** [U] great anger or excitement **5** [C] early stage in a competition [IDM] **be on heat** (US) **be in heat** (of female dogs, etc) be in a period of sexual excitement ■ **heatwave** n [C] period of unusually hot weather

heat² /hiːt/ v [I,T] become or make sth hot ▶ **heated** *adj* angry; excited: *a ~ed argument* ■ **heater** n [C] machine used for heating a room or water ■ **heating** n [U] system for heating a building

heath /hiːθ/ n [C] area of open land covered with rough grass and heather

heathen /ˈhiːðn/ n [C] (*old-fash, offens*) person who does not believe in one of the world's main religions

heather /ˈheðə(r)/ n [U] low wild plant with small purple, pink or white flowers

heave /hiːv/ v [I,T] **1** lift, pull or throw sth heavy with great effort **2** [I] rise

and fall regularly: *Her shoulders ~d with laughter.* **3** [T] make a sound slowly: *~ a sigh of relief* **4** [I] get a tight feeling in your throat as though you are about to vomit [PV] **heave to** (pt, pp **hove** /həʊv/) (of a ship) stop moving ● **heave** n [C] act of heaving

heaven /ˈhevn/ n **1** (also **Heaven**) [U] place believed to be the home of God and of good people after death **2** [U, C] (*infml*) place or state of great happiness **3** (**Heaven**) [U] (*fml*) God **4** (**the heavens**) [pl] (*lit*) the sky [IDM] **(Good) Heavens!** (spoken) used for showing surprise ▶ **heavenly** *adj* **1** of or from heaven or the sky: *~ bodies* (= the sun, moon, stars and planets) **2** (*infml*) very pleasant ■ **heavenly body** n [C] the sun or moon or a planet, etc

heavy /ˈhevi/ *adj* (**-ier, -iest**) **1** weighing a lot; difficult to lift or move **2** of more than the usual amount, force, etc: *~ rain ◇ a ~ smoker* (= a person who smokes a lot) **3** busy: *a ~ day/schedule* **4** (of work) hard; needing a lot of effort **5** (of food) large in amount or very solid **6** (of writing, music, etc) difficult and serious [IDM] **heavy going** difficult or boring **a heavy heart** feeling of great sadness **make heavy weather of sth** make sth more difficult than it really is ▶ **heavily** *adv*: *drink/sleep heavily* ▶ **heaviness** n [U] ● **heavy** n [C] (pl **-ies**) (*infml*) big strong man employed as a bodyguard, etc ■ **heavy-duty** *adj* strong enough for rough use, bad weather, etc ■ **heavy industry** n [U,C] industry that produces metal, large machines, etc ■ **heavyweight** n [C] **1** boxer weighing 79.5 kilograms or more **2** important person

heckle /ˈhekl/ v [I,T] shout out rude remarks at a speaker in a meeting ▶ **heckler** /ˈheklə(r)/ n [C]

hectare /ˈhekteə(r)/ n [C] (*abbr* **ha**) metric measure of area; 10000 square metres

hectic /ˈhektɪk/ *adj* very busy; full of activity: *lead a ~ life*

he'd /hiːd/ = HE HAD; HE WOULD

hedge /hedʒ/ n [C] **1** row of bushes between fields, gardens, etc **2** ~ (**against**) defence: *a ~ against inflation* ● **hedge** v **1** [I] avoid giving a direct answer to a question **2** [T] put a hedge around a field, etc [IDM] **hedge your bets** protect yourself against loss by supporting more than one side in an argument, etc ■ **hedgerow** n [C] row of bushes, etc, planted along the edge of a road or field

hedgehog /ˈhedʒhɒg/ n [C] small animal covered with spines

heed /hiːd/ v [T] (*fml*) pay careful attention to sb's advice or a warning ● **heed** n [U] [IDM] **give/pay heed (to sb/sth) | take heed (of sb/ sth)** (fml) pay careful attention to sb/ sth ► **heedless** adj ~ **(of)** (fml) not paying attention to sb/sth

0━ **heel** /hiːl/ n [C] **1** back part of the human foot **2** part of a sock or shoe that covers this **3** raised part of a shoe under the back of the foot [IDM] **at/on sb's heels** following closely behind sb **come to heel 1** agree to obey sb **2** (of a dog) come close behind its owner **down at heel** untidy and poorly dressed ► **heel** v **1** [T] repair the heel of a shoe **2** [I] ~ **(over)** (of a ship) lean over to one side

hefty /'hefti/ adj (-ier, -iest) (infml) big; powerful

heifer /'hefə(r)/ n [C] young female cow

0━ **height** /haɪt/ n **1** [U,C] measurement of how tall a person or thing is **2** [U] quality of being tall **3** [C,U] particular distance above the ground: gain/lose ~ **4** [C, usu pl] high place or position **5** [sing] highest degree or main point of sth: the ~ of folly/summer

heighten /'haɪtn/ v [I,T] become or make a feeling or effect greater or more intense

heir /eə(r)/ n [C] ~ **(to; of)** person with the legal right to receive property, etc when the owner dies ► **heiress** /'eəres/ n [C] female heir ► **heirloom** /'eəluːm/ n [C] valuable object that has belonged to the same family for many years

held pt, pp of HOLD[1]

helicopter /'helɪkɒptə(r)/ n [C] aircraft with horizontal revolving blades (rotors) on the top

helium /'hiːliəm/ n [U] (symb He) light colourless gas, used in balloons and airships

he'll /hiːl/ short for HE WILL

0━ **hell** /hel/ n **1** (usu Hell) [sing] place believed to be the home of wicked people after death **2** [U,sing] very unpleasant situation or experience causing great suffering **3** [U] (sl) swear word used to show anger or for emphasis: Who the ~ is he? [IDM] **(just) for the hell of it** (infml) just for fun **give sb hell** (infml) make life unpleasant for sb **like hell 1** (infml) used for emphasis: drive like ~ (= very fast) **2** (spoken) used when you are refusing permission or denying sth ► **hellish** adj (infml, esp GB) very unpleasant

0━ **hello** (GB hallo, hullo) /hə'ləʊ/ n [C], exclam (pl ~s) used as a greeting, to attract sb's attention or to express surprise

helm /helm/ n [C] handle or wheel for steering a boat or ship [IDM] **at the helm** in control

helmet /'helmɪt/ n [C] protective covering for the head

0━ **help**[1] /help/ v **1** [I,T] do part of the work of sb; be of use or service to sb: They ~ed me (to) lift the boxes. ◇ H~! I'm stuck! **2** [T] ~ **yourself/sb (to)** serve yourself/sb with food, drink, etc [IDM] **can (not) help (doing) sth | can not help but do sth** can not prevent or avoid sth: She couldn't ~ laughing. [PV] **help (sb) out** help sb in a difficult situation ► **helper** n [C] person who helps ► **helping** n [C] serving of food

0━ **help**[2] /help/ n **1** [U] act of helping sb to do sth; fact of being useful **2** [U] advice, money, etc given to sb to solve their problems: medical ~ ◇ a ~ key/screen (= function on a computer that gives information on how to use the computer) **3** [sing] person or thing that helps sb: She's a great ~ to me. ■ **help desk** n [C] service in a business company that gives people information and help, esp if they are having problems with a computer ► **helpful** adj useful ► **helpfully** /-fəli/ adv ► **helpfulness** n [U] ► **helpless** adj needing the help of others; powerless ► **helplessly** adv ► **helplessness** n [U] ■ **helpline** n [C] (GB) telephone service that provides advice and information about particular problems

hem /hem/ n [C] edge of a piece of cloth, turned under and sewn, esp on a piece of clothing ● **hem** v (-mm-) [T] make a hem on sth [PV] **hem sb/sth in** surround sb/sth, so that they cannot move easily ■ **hemline** n [C] lower edge of a skirt or dress

hemisphere /'hemɪsfɪə(r)/ n [C] **1** one half of the earth: the northern ~ **2** (anat) either half of the brain **3** one half of a sphere

hemo- → HAEMO-

hemp /hemp/ n [U] plant used for making rope and cloth, and also to make the drug cannabis

hen /hen/ n [C] **1** adult female chicken **2** female of any bird ■ **hen party** (also **hen night**) (GB) n [C] party for women only which is held for a woman who will soon get married ■ **henpecked** adj (infml) (of a man) ruled by his wife

0━ **hence** /hens/ adv **1** for this reason **2** from now on ► **hence'forth** (also -**forward**) adv (fml) from now on

henchman /'hentʃmən/ n [C] (pl -**men**) faithful supporter who always obeys his leader's orders

henna /'henə/ n [U] (plant producing a) reddish-brown dye, used esp on the hair and skin

O─ **her** /hɜ:(r)/ *pron* (used as the object of a v or prep) female person or animal mentioned earlier: *I love ~.* ◇ *Give it to ~.* ● **her** *det* of or belonging to her: *That's ~ book, not yours.* ▸ **hers** /hɜ:z/ *pron* of or belonging to her: *Is that ~?*

herald /ˈherəld/ *n* [C] **1** sign that sth else is going to happen soon **2** (in the past) person who carried messages from a ruler ● **herald** *v* [T] (*written*) be a sign that sth is going to happen ▸ **heraldry** /ˈherəldri/ *n* [U] study of coats of arms

herb /hɜ:b/ *n* [C] plant whose leaves or seeds are used in medicine or to add flavour to food ▸ **herbal** *adj* of herbs ▸ **herbalist** *n* [C] person who grows or sells herbs for medical use

herbaceous /hɜːˈbeɪʃəs/ *adj* (*tech*) (of a plant) having a soft stem ■ **her,baceous 'border** *n* [C] flower bed with plants that flower every year

herd /hɜ:d/ *n* [C] group of animals, esp cattle, together ● **herd** *v* [T] move sb/sth in a particular direction: *The prisoners were ~ed onto a train.* ▸ **herdsman** /ˈhɜ:dzmən/ *n* [C] (*pl* **-men**) man who looks after a herd

O─ **here** /hɪə(r)/ *adv* **1** in, at or to this place: *I live ~.* ◇ *Come ~.* **2** now; at this point: *H~ the speaker paused.* [IDM] **here and there** in various places **here's to sb/sth** used when drinking to the health or success of sb/sth **neither here nor there** not important or relevant ■ **,here'abouts** *adv* (*fml*) near this place ■ **,here'in** *adv* (*fml* or *law*) in this place or document ■ **,here'with** *adv* (*written*) with this letter, book or document

hereafter /ˌhɪərˈɑ:ftə(r)/ *adv* (*fml*) **1** (in legal documents, etc) in the rest of this document **2** from this time; in future ● **the hereafter** *n* [sing] life after death

hereditary /həˈredɪtri/ *adj* (esp of illness) passed on from parent to child

heredity /həˈredəti/ *n* [U] passing of characteristics from parents to children

heresy /ˈherəsi/ *n* [U,C] (*pl* **-ies**) (holding of) a belief that is completely different from what is generally accepted, esp in a religion ▸ **heretic** /ˈherətɪk/ *n* [C] person guilty of heresy ▸ **heretical** /həˈretɪkl/ *adj*

heritage /ˈherɪtɪdʒ/ *n* [C, usu sing] all the things that have been passed on over many years in a country

hermit /ˈhɜ:mɪt/ *n* [C] person who lives a simple life alone for religious reasons

hernia /ˈhɜ:niə/ *n* [C,U] medical condition in which the bowel pushes through the wall of the abdomen

O─ **hero** /ˈhɪərəʊ/ *n* [C] (*pl* **-es**) **1** person admired for bravery or other good qualities **2** main male character in a story, play, etc ▸ **heroic** /həˈrəʊɪk/ *adj* of heroes; very brave ▸ **heroically** /-kli/ *adv* ▸ **heroics** *n* [pl] (*disapprov*) talk or behaviour that is too brave or dramatic ▸ **heroine** /ˈherəʊɪn/ *n* [C] female hero ▸ **heroism** /ˈherəʊɪzəm/ *n* [U] very great courage

heroin /ˈherəʊɪn/ *n* [U] drug made from morphine

herpes /ˈhɜ:pi:z/ *n* [U] infectious disease that causes painful spots on the skin

herring /ˈherɪŋ/ *n* [C] sea fish used for food ■ **'herringbone** *n* [U] V-shaped pattern

O─ **hers** → HER

O─ **herself** /hɜːˈself/ *pron* **1** used as a reflexive when the female doer of an action is also affected by it: *She hurt ~.* **2** used for emphasis: *She told me the news ~.* [IDM] **(all) by herself 1** alone **2** without help

he's /hi:z/ *short for* HE IS; HE HAS

hesitant /ˈhezɪtənt/ *adj* slow to speak or act because you are unsure ▸ **hesitancy** *n* [U]

O─ **hesitate** /ˈhezɪteɪt/ *v* [I] be slow to speak or act because you are uncertain or nervous ▸ **hesitation** /ˌhezɪˈteɪʃn/ *n* [U,C]

heterogeneous /ˌhetərəˈdʒi:niəs/ *adj* (*fml*) made up of different kinds

heterosexual /ˌhetərəˈsekʃuəl/ *adj, n* [C] (person who is) sexually attracted to people of the opposite sex

het up /ˌhet ˈʌp/ *adj* (*infml*, GB) upset

hexagon /ˈheksəgən/ *n* [C] (*geom*) shape with six sides

heyday /ˈheɪdeɪ/ *n* [sing] time of greatest success

O─ **hi** /haɪ/ *exclam* (*infml*) used as a greeting: *Hi guys!*

hiatus /haɪˈeɪtəs/ *n* [usu sing] space or pause when nothing happens or where something is missing

hibernate /ˈhaɪbəneɪt/ *v* [I] (of animals) sleep during the winter ▸ **hibernation** /ˌhaɪbəˈneɪʃn/ *n* [U]

hiccup (also **hiccough**) /ˈhɪkʌp/ *n* [C] **1** sudden repeated stopping of the breath with a sound that you cannot control **2** (*infml*) small problem ● **hiccup** *v* [I] give a hiccup (1)

O─ **hide¹** /haɪd/ *v* (*pt* **hid** /hɪd/ *pp* **hidden** /ˈhɪdn/) **1** [T] put or keep sb/ sth out of sight **2** [I] get out of sight ■ **'hideaway** *n* [C] place where you can go to hide or be alone ■ **'hideout** *n* [C] place where sb goes when they do not want anyone to

A B C D E F G **H** I J K L M N O P Q R S T U V W X Y Z

find them ■ **'hiding place** n [C] place where sb/sth can be hidden

hide² /haɪd/ n [C] animal's skin

hideous /ˈhɪdiəs/ adj very ugly; horrible ■ **hideously** adv

hiding /ˈhaɪdɪŋ/ n **1** [U] state of being hidden [sing] (infml, esp GB) physical punishment of being beaten

hierarchy /ˈhaɪərɑːki/ n [C] (pl **-ies**) organization with ranks of authority from lowest to highest

hi-fi /ˈhaɪ faɪ/ adj, n [C, U] (of) equipment that reproduces recorded sound almost perfectly

0─ **high¹** /haɪ/ adj **1** measuring a long distance from the bottom to the top: a ~ fence **2** having the distance that is mentioned from the bottom to the top: The wall is six feet ~. **3** greater than normal in quantity, size or degree: a ~ price ◇ a ~ degree of accuracy **4** important: a ~ official **5** morally good: have ~ ideals **6** very favourable: have a ~ opinion of her **7** (of a sound) not deep **8** middle or most attractive part of a period of time: ~ summer **9** (of food) beginning to go bad and having a strong smell **10** ~ (on) (infml) under the influence of drugs [IDM] be/get on your high horse (infml) act proudly, thinking that you know best **high and dry** without help or support **it's high time** → TIME¹
■ **'highbrow** adj knowing a lot about or concerned with intellectual matters ■ **high-'class** adj of good quality ■ **High Com'missioner** n [C] representative of one Commonwealth country in another ■ **High 'Court** n [C] highest court of law for civil cases in England and Wales ■ **higher edu'cation** n [U] (abbr **HE**) education at college and university, esp to degree level ■ **high fi'delity** adj, n [C] (old-fash) = HI-FI ■ **high-'flyer** (also **high-'flier**) n [C] person with the ambition and ability to be very successful ■ **high-'grade** adj of high quality ■ **high-'handed** adj using power without consideration for others ■ **the 'high jump** n [sing] sport of jumping over a high bar ■ **'highland** /ˈhaɪlənd/ n [pl] mountainous part of a country ■ **high-'level** adj **1** (of meetings, etc) involving senior people **2** advanced ■ **the 'high life** n [sing] fashionable luxurious way of living ■ **high-'minded** adj having strong moral principles ■ **high-'powered** adj having great power and influence; full of energy ■ **high-'profile** adj receiving a lot of media attention ■ **high-'rise** adj (of a building) very tall ■ **high school** n [C] (esp US) secondary school, for pupils aged about 14–18 ■ **the high 'seas** n [pl] (fml) areas of the sea that do not belong to any particular country

■ **high 'season** n [U, sing] (esp GB) time of year when a hotel, resort, etc has most visitors ■ **high-'spirited** adj lively; excited ■ **high spot** n [C] most enjoyable or important part of sth ■ **'high street** n [C] main street of a town ■ **high 'tea** n [C] (GB) early evening meal ■ **high-'tech** (also **hi-'tech**) adj (infml) **1** using the most modern methods and machines, esp electronic ones **2** (of designs, objects, etc) very modern in appearance ■ **high tech'nology** n [U] use of the most modern methods and machines, esp electronic ones, in industry, etc ■ **high-'tension** adj carrying a powerful electrical current: ~-tension cables ■ **'highway** n [C] **1** (esp US) main road, usu connecting large towns **2** (GB, fml) public road ■ **'highwayman** n [C] (pl **-men**) (in the past) man who robbed travellers on roads

0─ **high²** /haɪ/ n [C] **1** highest level or number: Profits reached a new ~. **2** (infml) feeling of intense pleasure: He was on a real ~ after winning. ■ **high** adv at or to a high position: a desk piled ~ with papers

0─ **highlight** /ˈhaɪlaɪt/ n [C] **1** most interesting part of sth **2** [pl] areas of the hair which are lighter than the rest, usu because they have been dyed **3** [pl] (tech) light part of a picture ■ **highlight** n [T] give special attention to sth

0─ **highly** /ˈhaɪli/ adv **1** very; to a great extent: a ~ amusing film **2** very favourably: think ~ of sb ■ **highly-'strung** (US **high-'strung**) adj easily upset

Highness /ˈhaɪnəs/ n [C] title of a member of the royal family: His/Her (Royal) ~

hijab /hɪˈdʒɑːb/ n **1** head covering worn in public by some Muslim women **2** [U] religious system which controls the wearing of such clothing

hijack /ˈhaɪdʒæk/ v [T] take control of a vehicle, esp an aircraft, by force ■ **hijacker** n [C]

hike /haɪk/ n [C], v [I] (go for a) long walk in the country ■ **hiker** n [C]

hilarious /hɪˈleəriəs/ adj very amusing ■ **hilariously** adv ■ **hilarity** /hɪˈlærəti/ n [U] loud happy laughter

0─ **hill** /hɪl/ n [C] **1** area of high land, not as high as a mountain **2** slope on a road, etc ■ **hillside** n [C] side of a hill ■ **hilltop** n [C] top of a hill ■ **hilly** adj having many hills

hilt /hɪlt/ n [C] handle of a sword [IDM] (up) to the hilt as much as possible

0─ **him** /hɪm/ pron (used as the object of a v or prep) male person or animal mentioned earlier: I love ~.

A B C D E F G **H** I J K L M N O P Q R S T U V W X Y Z

0→ **himself** /hɪmˈself/ pron **1** used as a reflexive when the male doer of an action is affected by it: *He cut ~.* **2** used for emphasis: *He told me the news ~.* [IDM] **(all) by himself 1** alone **2** without help

hind /haɪnd/ adj at the back: *the ~ legs of a horse* ■ **hind′quarters** n [pl] back parts of an animal with four legs ■ **hind** n [C] female deer

hinder /ˈhɪndə(r)/ v [T] make it difficult for sb to do sth or for sth to happen: *~ sb from working* ► **hindrance** /ˈhɪndrəns/ n [C] person or thing that hinders sb/sth

hindsight /ˈhaɪndsaɪt/ n [U] understanding of an event after it has happened

Hindu /ˌhɪmˈduː/ n [C] person whose religion is Hinduism ● **Hindu** adj of the Hindus ► **Hinduism** /ˈhɪnduːɪzəm/ n [U] Indian religion involving the worship of several gods and belief in reincarnation

hinge /hɪndʒ/ n [C] piece of metal on which a door, gate, etc swings ● **hinge** v [T] attach sth with a hinge [PV] **hinge on/upon sth** depend on sth completely: *Everything ~s on the result of these talks.*

hint /hɪnt/ n [C] **1** indirect suggestion: *Should I drop a ~ (= give a hint) to her?* **2** slight trace of sth: *a ~ of envy in his voice* **3** [usa pl] practical piece of advice: *helpful ~s* ● **hint** v [I,T] ~ **at** suggest sth indirectly

0→ **hip** /hɪp/ n [C] part on either side of the body above the legs and below the waist ■ **hip flask** n [C] small flat bottle used for carrying alcohol

hippie (also **hippy**) /ˈhɪpi/ n [C] (pl **-ies**) person who rejects usual social standards

hippo /ˈhɪpəʊ/ n [C] (pl **~s**) (infml) short for HIPPOPOTAMUS

hippopotamus /ˌhɪpəˈpɒtəməs/ n [C] (pl **-muses** or **-mi** /-maɪ/) large African river animal with thick skin

0→ **hire** /ˈhaɪə(r)/ v [T] **1** obtain the use of sth in return for payment: *~ a car for a week* **2** employ sb for a job [PV] **hire sth out** allow the use of sth for a short time, in return for payment ● **hire** n [U] act of hiring sth for a short time: *bicycles for ~* ■ **hire′purchase** n [U] (GB) agreement to pay small regular amounts for sth, having the use of it immediately

0→ **his** /hɪz/ det of or belonging to him: *That's ~ book, not yours.* ● **his** pron of or belonging to him: *Is that ~?*

hiss /hɪs/ v [I,T] make a sound like that of a long 's', esp to show

disapproval of sb/sth ● **hiss** n [C] hissing sound

historian /hɪˈstɔːriən/ n [C] student of, or expert in, history

historic /hɪˈstɒrɪk/ adj important in history: *a ~ event*

0→ **historical** /hɪˈstɒrɪkl/ adj of or concerning history: *~ studies/novels* ► **historically** /-kli/ adv

0→ **history** /ˈhɪstri/ n (pl **-ies**) **1** [U] study of past events **2** [C] description of past events **3** [sing] past events or experiences of sb/sth: *his medical ~* [IDM] **go down in/make history** do or be sth so important that it will be remembered

0→ **hit¹** /hɪt/ v (**-tt-** pt, pp **hit**) [T] **1** bring sth forcefully against sb/sth: *He ~ me with a stick.* **2** come against sth/sb with force: *The car ~ a tree.* **3** have a bad effect on sb/sth: *The new law will ~ the poor.* **4** reach a place or level; find sth: *~ the right road* [IDM] **hit it off (with sb)** (infml) have a good relationship with sb **hit the hay/sack** (infml) go to bed **hit the nail on the head** say sth that is exactly right **hit the roof** (infml) suddenly become very angry [PV] **hit back (at sb/sth)** reply forcefully to an attack **hit on/upon sth** think of a plan, solution, etc unexpectedly **hit out (at sb/sth)** attack sb/sth forcefully, esp with words ■ **hit-and-run** adj (of a road accident) caused by a driver who does not stop to help

0→ **hit²** /hɪt/ n [C] **1** act of hitting sb/ sth **2** person or thing that is very popular: *Her new play is a great ~.* **3** result of a search on a computer, esp on the Internet ■ **hit list** n [C] (infml) list of people to be killed or against whom an action is planned ■ **hit man** n [C] (infml) criminal who is paid to kill sb ■ **hit parade** n [C] list of best-selling popular records

hitch /hɪtʃ/ v **1** [I,T] get free rides in other people's cars; travel around in this way: *~ round Europe* **2** [T] ~ **(up)** pull up a piece of your clothing **3** [T] fasten sth to sth with a loop or hook ● **hitch** n [C] **1** small problem that causes a delay **2** kind of knot ■ **hitchhike** v [I] travel around by obtaining free rides in other people's cars ■ **hitchhiker** n [C]

hitherto /ˌhɪðəˈtuː/ adv (fml) until now

HIV /ˌeɪtʃ aɪ ˈviː/ abbr virus that causes AIDS: *to be ~ positive*

hive /haɪv/ n [C] **1** box for bees to live in **2** place full of busy people: *a ~ of activity* ● **hive** v [PV] **hive sth off (to/ into sth)** separate one part of a group from the rest; sell part of a business

HMS /ˌeɪtʃ em ˈes/ abbr (used before the name of British warships) Her/ His Majesty's Ship

hoard /hɔːd/ n [C] often secret store of money, food, etc ● **hoard** v [T] save and store food, money, etc, esp secretly

hoarding /'hɔːdɪŋ/ n [C] (GB) large board on which advertisements are stuck

hoarse /hɔːs/ adj (~r, ~st) (of a voice) sounding rough ▸ **hoarsely** adv ▸ **hoarseness** n [U]

hoax /həʊks/ n [C] trick played on sb for a joke: a bomb ~ ● **hoax** v [T] deceive sb with a hoax

hob /hɒb/ n [C] (GB) flat heating surface on a cooker

hobble /'hɒbl/ v [I] walk awkwardly, eg because your feet hurt

0━ **hobby** /'hɒbi/ n [C] (pl -ies) activity you do for pleasure in your free time

hobnail boot /ˌhɒbneɪl 'buːt/ n [C] heavy boot with short nails in the sole

hockey /'hɒki/ n [U] **1** (GB) team game played on a field with curved sticks and a small hard ball **2** (US = ICE HOCKEY (ICE¹)

hod /hɒd/ n [C] box with a long handle, used for carrying bricks

hoe /həʊ/ n [C] garden tool with a long handle, used for breaking up the soil ● **hoe** v [I,T] break up soil, remove plants, etc with a hoe

hog /hɒg/ n [C] castrated male pig, kept for its meat ● **hog** v (-gg-) [T] take more than your fair share of sth and stop others from having it

Hogmanay /'hɒgməneɪ/ n [U] (in Scotland) New Year's Eve (31 December)

hoist /hɔɪst/ v [T] lift sth up, esp with ropes ● **hoist** n [C] piece of equipment with ropes and pulleys for lifting heavy things

0━ **hold¹** /həʊld/ v (pt, pp **held** /held/) **1** [T] carry sth; have sth in your hands **2** [T] keep sb/sth in a particular position: H~ your head up! **3** [T] support the weight of sb/sth: That branch won't ~ you. **4** [T] have enough room for sth/sb: This barrel ~s 25 litres. **5** [T] not allow sb to leave: H~ the thief until the police come. **6** [T] defend sth against attack **7** [T] remain firm or unchanged: How long will this fine weather ~? **8** [T] keep sb's attention or interest **9** [T] own or have sth: ~ shares **10** [T] have a particular job or position: ~ the post of Prime Minister **11** [T] have a belief, opinion, etc **12** [T] (fml) consider that sth is true: I ~ you responsible for the accident. **13** [T] cause a meeting, conversation, etc to take place **14** [T] (of a car, etc) keep a grip on a road [IDM] hold sb/sth at bay → BAY **hold your breath** stop breathing for a short time **hold the fort** look after sth while others are away **hold good**

---

be true **hold your ground** → GROUND¹ **hold it** (spoken) used for asking sb to wait, or not to move **hold the line** keep a telephone connection open **hold your own (against sb)** not be defeated by sb **hold your tongue** not say anything **there's no holding sb** sb cannot be prevented from doing sth [PV] **hold sth against sb** allow sth bad to influence your opinion of sb **hold back** be unwilling to act **hold sb/sth back 1** control sb/sth: ~ back the crowd **2** keep sth secret **hold sb down** control the freedom of sb **hold sth down 1** keep sth at a low level: ~ down prices **2** keep a job for some time **hold forth (on sth)** speak for a long time about sth **hold off (of rain, etc)** be delayed **hold sb/sth off** resist an attack **hold off (doing) sth** delay doing sth **hold on 1** (spoken) used to tell sb to wait or stop **2** survive, even in a difficult situation **hold sth on** keep sth in position **hold on to sb/sth** keep sth **hold out 1** last **2** resist an attack or survive in a dangerous situation **hold sth out** offer sth **hold out for sth** refuse to accept an offer, and continue to demand sth **better hold sth over** postpone sth **hold sb to sth** make sb keep a promise **hold sb/sth up 1** delay sb/sth: Our flight was held up by fog. **2** use sth/sb as an example **hold up sth** rob a bank, etc by force ● **hold-up** n [C] **1** delay, eg in traffic **2** robbery by armed robbers

0━ **hold²** /həʊld/ n **1** [sing] act of holding sth **2** [C] way of holding an opponent, eg in wrestling **3** [sing] ~ (on/over) influence or power over sb/sth **4** [C] place where you can put your hands or feet when climbing **5** [C] part of a ship or plane where goods or luggage is stored [IDM] **catch, grab, take, etc (a) hold of sb/sth** take sth in your hands **get hold of sth** (infml) **1** contact or find sb **2** find and use sth

holdall /'həʊldɔːl/ n [C] (GB) large soft bag, used when travelling

holder /'həʊldə(r)/ n [C] **1** person who owns or possesses sth: ticket ~ **2** thing that supports or holds sth: a cigarette ~

holding /'həʊldɪŋ/ n [C] **1** ~ (in) number of shares that sb has in a company **2** something, eg land, that is owned

0━ **hole** /həʊl/ n **1** [C] hollow space or gap in sth solid or in the surface of sth: a ~ in the road/wall **2** [C] small animal's home **3** [C] (infml) unpleasant place to live or be in **4** [sing] (infml) difficult situation: be in a ~ **5** [C] place into which a ball must be hit in golf, etc [IDM] **make a hole in sth** (infml) use up a large part of your money, etc ● **hole** v **1**

A B C D E F G **H** I J K L M N O P Q R S T U V W X Y Z

make a hole in sth **2** [I,T] ~ **(out)** hit a golf ball into the hole [PV] **hole up**; **be holed up** (infml) hide in a place

0-π **holiday** /ˈhɒlədeɪ/ n [C] **1** day(s) of rest from work: be/go on ~ **2** period of time spent travelling away from home: a camping ~ ● **holiday** v [I] spend a holiday somewhere ■ **'holidaymaker** n [C] person visiting a place on holiday

holiness /ˈhəʊlinəs/ n **1** [U] quality of being holy **2** [C] (His/Your Holiness) title of the Pope

0-π **hollow** /ˈhɒləʊ/ adj **1** having a hole or empty space inside **2** curving inwards; sunken: ~ cheeks **3** (of sounds) echoing, as if coming from a hollow place **4** not sincere; false: ~ words ● **hollow** n [C] area that is lower than the surface around it ● **hollow** v [PV] **hollow sth out** make a hole in sth by removing part of it: ~ out a tree trunk

holly /ˈhɒli/ n [C,U] small evergreen tree with sharp-pointed leaves and red berries

holocaust /ˈhɒləkɔːst/ n [C] large-scale destruction and the killing of many people, esp because of a war

holster /ˈhəʊlstə(r)/ n [C] leather holder for a small gun

0-π **holy** /ˈhəʊli/ adj (-ier, -iest) **1** associated with God or religion **2** pure and good: live a ~ life ■ the **Holy 'Spirit** (also the **Holy 'Ghost**) n [sing] (in Christianity) God in the form of a spirit

homage /ˈhɒmɪdʒ/ n [U,C, usu sing] (fml) ~ **(to)** something said or done to show respect for sb

0-π **home** [1] /həʊm/ n **1** [C,U] place where you live, esp with your family **2** [C] place for the care of old people or children **3** [C] place where an animal or plant lives naturally **4** [sing] place in which sth was first discovered, made or invented: Greece is the ~ of democracy. [IDM] at **home 1** in a person's own house, office **2** comfortable and relaxed: Make yourself at ~! ■ the **Home 'Counties** n [pl] the counties around London ■ **home eco'nomics** n [U] cooking and other skills needed at home, taught as a school subject ■ **home-'grown** adj (of food, etc) produced in your own country, garden, etc ■ **home 'help** n [C] (GB) person whose job is to help old or sick people with cooking, cleaning, etc ■ **'homeland** n [C] country where a person was born ▸ **homeless** adj having no home ■ **home-'made** adj made at home ■ the **Home Office** n [sing] British government department dealing with the police, immigration, etc ■ **'home page** n [C] (computing) main page created by a

company, an organization, etc on the World Wide Web from which connections to other pages can be made ■ **homesick** adj sad because you are away from home ■ **'homesickness** n [U] ■ **'homestay** n [U,C] accommodation in a family home for an international student in the country where he/she is studying ■ **home 'truth** n [usu pl] true but unpleasant fact about sb ▸ **homeward** adj going towards home ▸ **homewards** adv towards home ■ **'homework** n [U] **1** work that a pupil does away from school **2** (infml) work sb does to prepare for sth

0-π **home** [2] /həʊm/ adj **1** of or connected with the place where you live **2** connected with your own country rather than foreign countries: ~ news **3** (sport) played on the team's own ground: a ~ match ● **home** adv **1** to or at your home: on her way ~ **2** into the correct position: drive a nail ~ [IDM] **be home and dry** have done sth difficult successfully **bring sth/come home to sb** make sth/become fully understood ■ **'homecoming** n [C,U] act of returning to your home after being away for a long time ● **home** v [PV] **home in on sth** aim at sth and move straight towards it

homely /ˈhəʊmli/ adj (-ier, -iest) **1** (approv, esp GB) comfortable; simple and good **2** (US, disapprov) (of a person's appearance) unattractive ▸ **homeliness** n [U]

homeopathy /ˌhəʊmiˈɒpəθi/ n [U] treatment of disease by giving small doses of drugs which in larger amounts would cause the same disease ▸ **homeopathic** /ˌhəʊmiəˈpæθɪk/ adj

homicide /ˈhɒmɪsaɪd/ n [C,U] (esp US, law) crime of killing sb deliberately ▸ **homicidal** /ˌhɒmɪˈsaɪdl/ adj

homing /ˈhəʊmɪŋ/ adj **1** (of a pigeon, etc) having the ability to find its way home **2** (of a missile, etc) fitted with a device that guides it to the target

homogeneous /ˌhɒməˈdʒiːniəs/ adj (fml) consisting of things or people that are the same or of the same type

homogenized (also -ised) /həˈmɒdʒənaɪzd/ adj (of milk) treated so that the cream is mixed in with the rest

homonym /ˈhɒmənɪm/ n [C] word spelt and pronounced like another word but with a different meaning, eg can meaning 'be able' and can meaning 'container'

homophobia /ˌhɒməˈfəʊbiə/ n [U] strong dislike and fear of homosexual people ▸ **homophobic** /ˌhɒməˈfəʊbɪk/ adj

homosexual /ˌhəʊmə'sekʃuəl, ˌhɒm-/ n [C], adj (person who is) sexually attracted to people of their own sex ▸ **homosexuality** /ˌhəʊmə,sekʃu'ælətɪ, ˌhɒm-/ n [U]

0━ **honest** /'ɒnɪst/ adj 1 (of a person) telling the truth; not cheating or stealing 2 not hiding the truth about sth: an ~ opinion ▸ **honestly** adv 1 in an honest way 2 (used for emphasis) really ▸ **honesty** n [U]

honey /'hʌnɪ/ n 1 [U] sweet sticky substance made by bees 2 [C] (spoken, esp US) way of addressing sb that you like or love ■ **'honeycomb** n [U] wax structure made by bees for holding their honey and eggs ■ **'honeysuckle** n [U] climbing plant with sweet-smelling flowers

honeymoon /'hʌnɪmuːn/ n [C] 1 holiday taken by a couple who have just got married 2 pleasant time at the start of a new job, etc: The ~ period for the government is now over. ● **honeymoon** v [I] spend your honeymoon somewhere

honk /hɒŋk/ v [I], n [C] (make the) sound of a car horn

honorary /'ɒnərəri/ adj 1 (of a degree or rank) given as an honour 2 (of a person or organization) unpaid: ~ president

0━ **honour** (US -or) /'ɒnə(r)/ n 1 [U] great respect and admiration for sb: the guest of ~ (= the most important one) 2 [sing] (fml) something you are pleased and proud to do because of people's respect for you: a great ~ to be invited 3 [U] strong sense of right; reputation for good behaviour: a man of ~ 4 [sing] person or thing that brings respect: You are an ~ to your school. 5 (honours) [pl] (abbr Hons) university course of a higher level than a basic course; high mark obtained on such a course: an ~ degree 6 (His/Her/Your Honour) [C] title of respect to a judge or a US mayor ● **honour** v [T] 1 do sth which shows great respect or praise for sb 2 do what you have agreed or promised to do

honourable (US -nor-) /'ɒnərəbl/ adj 1 deserving or showing honour 2 (the Honourable) title given to certain high officials, etc ▸ **honourably** adv

hood /hʊd/ n [C] 1 covering for the head and neck, fastened to a coat 2 folding cover of a car, pram, etc 3 (US) = BONNET(1) ▸ **hooded** adj having a hood

hoodwink /'hʊdwɪŋk/ v [T] trick sb

hoody (also **hoodie**) /'hʊdi/ n [C] (pl -**ies**) (GB, infml) jacket with a hood

hoof /huːf/ n [C] (pl -s or **hooves** /huːvz/) hard bony part of the foot of a horse, etc

0━ **hook** /hʊk/ n [C] 1 curved piece of metal, plastic, etc used for catching hold of sth or for hanging sth on 2 (in boxing) short blow with the elbow bent [IDM] **off the hook** 1 (of a telephone receiver) not resting on the main part of the telephone 2 (infml) no longer in a difficult situation: let/get sb off the ~ ● **hook** v [T] 1 fasten or catch sth with a hook 2 make sth into the form of a hook: ~ your foot round sth ▸ **hooked** adj 1 curved; shaped like a hook 2 ~ (on) (infml) dependent on sth bad, esp a drug 3 enjoying sth very much so that you want to do it, see it, etc as much as possible

hooligan /'huːlɪgən/ n [C] noisy violent young person: football ~s ▸ **hooliganism** n [U]

hoop /huːp/ n [C] circular band of wood or metal: gold ~ earrings

hooray /hu'reɪ/ exclam used to show happiness or approval of sth

hoot /huːt/ n [C] 1 short loud laugh or shout 2 [sing] very funny situation or person 3 sound of a car horn 4 cry of an owl [IDM] **not care/ give a hoot/two hoots** (infml) not care at all ● **hoot** v [I] make a loud noise 2 [T] sound a car horn ▸ **hooter** n [C] (esp GB) horn, siren, etc

Hoover™ /'huːvə(r)/ n [C] = VACUUM CLEANER ● **hoover** n [C] (GB) clean sth with a vacuum cleaner

hooves plural of HOOF

hop /hɒp/ v (-pp-) [I] 1 jump on one foot 2 (of an animal or bird) jump with all or both feet together 3 (infml) move quickly or easily: ~ on a bus [IDM] **hop it** (old-fash, infml) go away ● **hop** n [C] 1 short jump 2 (infml) short journey, esp by plane 3 climbing plant used to flavour beer

0━ **hope** /həʊp/ n 1 [C, U] desire and expectation that sth good will happen 2 [C, sing] person or thing that will help you get what you want: You're my last ~. [IDM] **be beyond hope (of sth)** have no chance of succeeding or recovering ● **hope** v [I, T] want sth to happen and think that it is possible: I ~ (that) you win. ▸ **hopeful** adj having or giving hope ▸ **hopefully** adv 1 used for expressing hope that sth will happen: H~fully, she'll be here soon. 2 in a hopeful way ▸ **hopeless** adj 1 giving no hope 2 ~ (at) (infml) very bad at sth; with no ability or skill: ~less at maths ▸ **hopelessly** adv ▸ **hopelessness** n [U]

horde /hɔːd/ n [C] very large crowd

horizon

horizon /həˈraɪzn/ n **1** (the horizon) [sing] the line at which the earth and sky seem to meet **2** [C] limit of your knowledge, experience, etc: *Travel broadens your ~s.*

☞ **horizontal** /ˌhɒrɪˈzɒntl/ *adj* flat and level: *~ and vertical lines* ● **horizontal** n [sing] horizontal line or position ► **horizontally** /-təli/ *adv*

hormone /ˈhɔːməʊn/ n [C] substance produced in the body that encourages growth, etc

☞ **horn** /hɔːn/ n **1** [C] hard pointed usu curved growth on the heads of cattle, deer, etc **2** [U] hard substance of which animal horns are made **3** [C] musical instrument with a trumpet-shaped end: *a French ~* **4** [C] device in a vehicle for making a warning sound ► **horny** *adj* (**-ier, -iest**) **1** (*infml*) sexually excited or exciting **2** made of or like horn

hornet /ˈhɔːnɪt/ n [C] large wasp

horoscope /ˈhɒrəskəʊp/ n [C] statement about sb's future based on the position of the stars and planets at the time of their birth

horrendous /hɒˈrendəs/ *adj* very unpleasant or shocking: *~ injuries*

horrible /ˈhɒrəbl/ *adj* **1** (*spoken*) very bad or unpleasant: *~ weather* **2** causing horror: *a ~ crime* ► **horribly** *adv*

horrid /ˈhɒrɪd/ *adj* (*old-fash* or *infml*) very unpleasant; nasty

horrific /həˈrɪfɪk/ *adj* extremely bad and shocking or frightening ► **horrifically** *adv*

horrify /ˈhɒrɪfaɪ/ v (*pt, pp* -**ied**) [T] fill sb with horror

☞ **horror** /ˈhɒrə(r)/ n **1** [C, U] (something causing a) feeling of great shock, fear or disgust **2** [U] type of book, film, etc that is designed to frighten people: *a ~ story/film* **3** [C] (*infml*) naughty child ■ **'horror-struck** (*also* -**stricken**) *adj* very shocked

hors d'oeuvre /ˌɔː ˈdɜːv/ n [C, U] small amount of food served at the beginning of a meal

☞ **horse** /hɔːs/ n [C] large four-legged animal that people ride on or use for pulling carts, etc [IDM] (**straight**) **from the horse's mouth** (*infml*) directly from the person concerned ● **horse** v [PV] **horse about/around** (*infml*) behave in a noisy playful way ■ **horseplay** n [U] rough noisy fun or play ■ **'horsepower** n [U] unit for measuring the power of an engine ■ **'horseshoe** n [C] U-shaped metal shoe for a horse

horseback /ˈhɔːsbæk/ n [IDM] **on horseback** sitting on a horse ► **horseback** *adv, adj* (*US*): *~ riding*

horticulture /ˈhɔːtɪkʌltʃə(r)/ n [U]

science of growing flowers, fruit, and vegetables ► **horticultural** /ˌhɔːtɪˈkʌltʃərəl/ *adj*

hose /həʊz/ n **1** [C, U] flexible tube used for directing water onto a garden or a fire **2** [pl] stockings, socks, etc ● **hose** v [T] ~ (**down**) wash sth with a hose

hosiery /ˈhəʊziəri/ n [U] used esp in shops as a word for tights, stockings and socks: *the ~ department*

hospice /ˈhɒspɪs/ n [C] hospital for people who are dying

hospitable /hɒˈspɪtəbl; ˈhɒspɪtəbl/ *adj* **1** ~ (**to/towards**) giving a kind welcome to guests **2** (*of places*) pleasant to be in ► **hospitably** *adv*

☞ **hospital** /ˈhɒspɪtl/ n [C] place where people are treated for illness or injuries ► **hospitalize** (*also* -ise) v [T] send sb to hospital for treatment

hospitality /ˌhɒspɪˈtæləti/ n [U] **1** friendly and kind behaviour towards guests **2** food, drink or services provided by an organization for guests, customers, etc: *the ~ industry* (= hotels, restaurants, etc)

☞ **host** /həʊst/ n [C] **1** person who entertains guests in their house **2** country, city or organization that holds a special event **3** person who introduces guests on a radio or television programme **4** ~ of large number of people or things: *a ~ of different reasons* ● **host** v [T] act as a host at sth or to sb

hostage /ˈhɒstɪdʒ/ n [C] prisoner kept by a person who threatens to hurt or kill them unless their demands are obeyed

hostel /ˈhɒstl/ n [C] **1** building providing cheap accommodation for students, travellers, etc **2** building where homeless people can stay

hostess /ˈhəʊstəs; -es/ n [C] **1** female host **2** woman employed to welcome and entertain men at a nightclub

hostile /ˈhɒstaɪl/ *adj* ~ (**to/towards**) **1** unfriendly **2** belonging to a military enemy: *~ aircraft* **3** (*business*) (of an offer to buy a company, etc) not wanted by the company that is to be bought: *a ~ takeover bid*

hostility /hɒˈstɪləti/ n **1** [U] unfriendly behaviour **2** (**hostilities**) [pl] (acts of) war

☞ **hot** /hɒt/ *adj* (~**ter**, ~**test**) **1** having a high temperature **2** (of food) producing a burning taste: *~ spices/curry* **3** (*infml*) new, exciting and very popular **4** (of news) very recent and usu exciting **5** strong; fierce: *He has a ~ temper* (= gets angry quickly). [IDM] **be in/get into hot water** (*infml*) be in/get into trouble ■ **hot air** (*infml*) meaningless talk ■ **(be) hot on sb's/sth's heels/ tracks/trail** following sb/sth closely ■ **not so hot** (*infml*) not good ● **hot** *v* (**-tt-**) [PV] **hot up** (*infml*) become more exciting or intense ■ **hot-blooded** *adj* easily angered; passionate ■ **hot-desking** *n* [U] practice in an office of giving desks to workers when they are required, rather than giving each worker their own desk ■ **hot dog** *n* [C] hot sausage served in a long bread roll ■ **hotfoot** *adv* (*written*) quickly and eagerly ■ **hothead** *n* [C] person who acts too quickly, without thinking ■ **hot-headed** *adj* ■ **hothouse** *n* [C] heated glass building, for growing plants ■ **hotline** *n* [C] **1** special telephone line that people can use to get information or to talk about sth **2** direct telephone connection between heads of government ▸ **hotly** *adv* **1** passionately **2** closely: *~ly pursued* ■ **hot spot** *n* [C] **1** place where fighting is common, esp for political reasons **2** place where there is a lot of activity or entertainment **3** (*computing*) area on a computer screen that you click on to start an operation, eg to load a file ■ **hot-tempered** *adj* easily angered

0━ **hotel** /həʊˈtel/ *n* [C] building where rooms and meals are provided for travellers ▸ **hotelier** /həʊˈteliə(r); -liˈeɪ/ *n* [C] person who owns or manages a hotel

hound /haʊnd/ *n* [C] hunting or racing dog ● **hound** *v* [T] keep following sb and not leave them alone: *~ed by newspaper reporters*

0━ **hour** /ˈaʊə(r)/ *n* **1** [C] period of 60 minutes: *London is only two ~s away* (= it takes two hours to get there). **2** [C, usu sing] period of about an hour: *a long lunch ~* **3** [hours] [pl] fixed period of time for work, etc: *Office ~s are from 9 a.m. to 5 p.m.* **4** (**the hour**) [sing] time when it is exactly 1 o'clock, 2 o'clock, etc: *Trains leave on the ~.* [IDM] **at the eleventh hour** at the last possible moment

hourly /ˈaʊəli/ *adj* **1** done or happening every hour: *an ~ bus service* **2** calculated by the hour: *an ~ rate of £20* ● **hourly** *adv* every hour

0━ **house¹** /haʊs/ *n* [C] (*pl ~s* /ˈhaʊzɪz/) **1** building made for people to live in, usu for one family **2** [usu sing] people living in a house: *Be quiet or you'll wake the whole ~!* **3** building made for a purpose that is mentioned: *an opera ~ ◇ a hen ~* **4** business firm: *a publishing ~* **5** (usu **House**) (building used by) people who discuss or pass laws: *the H~s of Parliament ◇ the H~ of Representatives* **6** part of a theatre where the audience sits; the

audience at a particular performance: *a full ~* (= (a large audience) **7** division of a school for competitions in sport, etc **8** (usu **the House of...**) old and famous family [IDM] **bring the house down** make an audience laugh or clap loudly ■ **on the house** paid for by the pub, firm, etc ■ **housebound** *adj* not able to leave your house because of illness, etc ■ **housebreaking** *n* [U] (*esp GB*) crime of entering a building by force ■ **housekeeper** *n* [C] person (esp a woman) whose job is to manage a household ■ **housekeeping** *n* [U] **1** work of managing a household **2** money allowed for this ■ **housemaster** (*fem* **housemistress**) *n* [C] (*esp GB*) teacher in charge of a group of children (a house) in a school ■ **the House of 'Commons** (*also* **the Commons**) (*GB*) *n* [sing, with sing or pl verb] (members of) the part of Parliament which is elected ■ **the House of 'Lords** (*also* **the Lords**) (*GB*) *n* [sing, with sing or pl verb] (members of) the non-elected part of Parliament ■ **house music** (*also* **house**) *n* [U] type of popular dance music with a fast beat, played on electronic instruments ■ **house-proud** *adj* giving great attention to the appearance of your home ■ **housewife** *n* [C] (*pl* **-wives** /-waɪvz/) woman who works at home looking after her family, cleaning, cooking, etc ■ **housework** *n* [U] work done in a house, eg cleaning and cooking

house² /haʊz/ *v* [T] provide sb with a place to live

0━ **household** /ˈhaʊshəʊld/ *n* [C] all the people living in a house [IDM] **a household name/word** name of sb/ sth that is very well known

0━ **housing** /ˈhaʊzɪŋ/ *n* **1** [U] houses, flats, etc considered as a group: *poor ~ conditions* **2** [U] job of providing houses, flats, etc for people to live in: *a ~ committee/officer* **3** [C] cover that protects a machine

hove → HEAVE

hovel /ˈhɒvl/ *n* [C] (*disapprov*) small dirty house or hut

hover /ˈhɒvə(r)/ *v* [I] **1** (of birds, helicopters, etc) stay in the air in one place **2** (of a person) wait about, in an uncertain manner ■ **hovercraft** *n* [C] (*pl* **hovercraft**) vehicle that moves over land or water supported by a cushion of air underneath it

0━ **how** /haʊ/ *adv* **1** (used in questions) in what way or manner: *H~ is this word spelt?* **2** used to ask about sb's health: *H~ are you?* **3** used to ask whether sth is successful or enjoyable: *H~ was your* trip? **4** (used with an adj or adv) used to ask about the amount, degree, etc of sth or about sb's age: H~ much are those earrings? ◇ H~ old is he? **5** used to express surprise, pleasure, etc: H~ kind of you to help! ● how conj the way in which: He told me ~ to get to the station.

O━ **however** /haʊˈevə(r)/ adv **1** to whatever degree: He'll never succeed, ~ hard he tries. **2** (used for adding a comment to what you have just said) although sth is true: Sales are poor. H~, there may be an increase next month. **3** (used in questions for showing surprise) in what way; how: H~ did you get here without a car? ● however conj in any way: H~ you look at it, it's going to cost a lot.

howl /haʊl/ n [C] (make a) long loud cry

HQ /ˌeɪtʃ ˈkjuː/ abbr = HEADQUARTERS

hr abbr (pl **hrs**) = HOUR

HRH /ˌeɪtʃ ɑːr ˈeɪtʃ/ abbr His/Her Royal Highness

hub /hʌb/ n [C] **1** central point of an activity **2** central part of a wheel
 ■ **hubcap** n [C] round metal cover over the hub of a car wheel

hubbub /ˈhʌbʌb/ n [sing] loud noise made by a lot of people talking at the same time

huddle /ˈhʌdl/ v [I,T] **1** ~ (**up**) crowd together, usu because of cold or fear **2** hold your arms and legs close to your body: I ~d under a blanket.
 ● **huddle** n [C] number of people or things close together

hue /hjuː/ n [C] (fml) (shade of) colour
 [IDM] **hue** and [IDM] **hue and cry** loud angry public protest

huff /hʌf/ n [IDM] **in a huff** (infml) in a bad mood, esp because sb has upset you

hug /hʌɡ/ v (**-gg-**) [T] **1** put your arms round sb tightly, esp to show love **2** keep close to sth: The boat ~ged the shore. ● **hug** n [C] act of hugging sb: give sb a ~

O━ **huge** /hjuːdʒ/ adj very large
 ► **hugely** adv very much

hulk /hʌlk/ n [C] **1** broken old ship **2** large awkward person or thing
 ► **hulking** adj large and awkward

hull /hʌl/ n [C] body of a ship

hullo = HELLO

hum /hʌm/ v (**-mm-**) **1** [I,T] sing a tune with your lips closed: ~ a tune **2** [I] make a low continuous sound **3** [I] (infml) be full of activity ● **hum** n [C] humming sound

O━ **human** /ˈhjuːmən/ adj **1** of people **2** showing the better qualities of people; kind ● **human** (also **human being**) n [C] person ► **humanly** adv within human ability: do all that is ~ly possible

■ **human ˈrights** n [pl] basic rights of freedom, equality, justice, etc

humane /hjuːˈmeɪn/ adj showing kindness towards people and animals by making sure they do not suffer more than is necessary: the ~ killing of animals ► **humanely** adv

humanity /hjuːˈmænəti/ n **1** [U] people in general **2** [U] quality of being kind to people and animals **3** (**the humanities**) [pl] subjects of study concerned with the way people think and behave, eg literature, philosophy, etc

humble /ˈhʌmbl/ adj (~**r**, ~**st**) **1** having a modest opinion of yourself **2** low in rank; unimportant **3** (of things) not large or special in any way: a ~ farmhouse ● **humble** v [T] make sb feel humble ► **humbly** adv

humdrum /ˈhʌmdrʌm/ adj boring and always the same

humid /ˈhjuːmɪd/ adj (of the air) warm and damp ► **humidity** /hjuːˈmɪdəti/ n [U] (amount of) water in the air

humiliate /hjuːˈmɪlieɪt/ v [T] make sb feel ashamed or foolish ► **humiliating** adj: a humiliating defeat ► **humiliation** /-ˈeɪʃn/ n [C,U]

humility /hjuːˈmɪləti/ n [U] quality of being humble (1)

humorist /ˈhjuːmərɪst/ n [C] person who writes or tells jokes

O━ **humorous** /ˈhjuːmərəs/ adj funny; amusing ► **humorously** adv

O━ **humour** (US **-or**) /ˈhjuːmə(r)/ n [U] (ability to cause or feel) amusement: have a sense of ~ ● **humour** v [T] keep sb happy by doing what they want

O━ **hundred** /ˈhʌndrəd/ number **1** 100: one, two, etc ~ **2** (**a hundred** or **hundreds** (of...)) large amount: ~s of people ► **hundredth** /ˈhʌndrədθ; -ətθ/ ordinal number 100th; the fraction ¹⁄₁₀₀; one of a hundred equal parts of sth

hundredweight /ˈhʌndrədweɪt/ n [C] (pl **hundredweight**) measure of weight; one twentieth of one ton (50.8 kilograms)

hung pt, pp of HANG¹

hunger /ˈhʌŋɡə(r)/ n **1** [U] need or desire for food **2** [sing] ~ **for** (fml) strong desire ● **hunger** v [PV] **hunger for/after sth/sb** have a strong desire for sth/sb ■ **ˈhunger strike** n [C] refusal to eat food as a protest

human /ˈhjuːmən/ adj

humane /hjuːˈmeɪn/ adj

humble /ˈhʌmbl/ adj

humid /ˈhjuːmɪd/ adj

humanity /hjuːˈmænəti/ n

humiliate /hjuːˈmɪlieɪt/ v

hungry /ˈhʌŋgri/ adj (-ier, -iest) feeling hunger ▶ **hungrily** adv

hunk /hʌŋk/ n [C] thick piece cut off sth: a ~ of bread/cheese

hunt /hʌnt/ v [I,T] **1** chase wild animals to catch or kill them for food or sport **2** ~ (for) try to find sb/sth [PV] **hunt sb down** search for and find sb • **hunt** n **1** [sing] act of hunting **2** [C] group of people who hunt foxes ▶ **hunter** n [C] person who hunts

hurdle /ˈhɜːdl/ n [C] **1** frame to be jumped over in a race **2** difficulty to be overcome

hurl /hɜːl/ v [T] throw sth/sb violently in a particular direction: (fig) ~ insults at sb

hurly-burly /ˈhɜːli ˈbɜːli/ n [U] noisy busy activity

hurrah /həˈrɑː/ (also **hurray** /huˈreɪ/) exclam = HOORAY

hurricane /ˈhʌrɪkən/ n [C] violent storm with very strong winds

hurry /ˈhʌri/ v (pt, pp **-ied**) [I,T] (make sb) move or do sth (too) quickly [PV] **hurry (sb) up** (make sb) do sth more quickly: H~ up! It's late. ▶ **hurried** adj done (too) quickly ▶ **hurriedly** adv • **hurry** n [U] need to do sth quickly [IDM] **in a hurry 1** very quickly **2** impatient to do sth

hurt /hɜːt/ v (pt, pp **hurt**) **1** [I,T] cause injury or pain to sb/yourself: He ~ himself. ◇ I ~ my hand. **2** [I,T] cause pain to a person or their feelings: My feet ~. ◇ It ~ his pride. [IDM] **it won't/wouldn't hurt (sb/sth) (to do sth)** used to say that sb should do a particular thing: It wouldn't ~ (you) to say sorry. • **hurt** n [U, sing] unhappiness because sb has been unkind to you ▶ **hurtful** adj ▶ **hurtfully** adv

hurtle /ˈhɜːtl/ v [I] move violently or quickly

husband /ˈhʌzbənd/ n [C] man that a woman is married to

hush /hʌʃ/ v [I,T] become or make sb/sth quiet [PV] **hush sth up** keep sth secret • **hush** n [U,sing] silence

husk /hʌsk/ n [C] dry outer covering of seeds, esp grain • **husk** v [T] remove the husks from grain, seeds, etc

husky /ˈhʌski/ adj (-ier, -iest) (of a voice) dry and rough ▶ **huskily** adv • **husky** n [C] (pl **-ies**) dog used for pulling sledges across snow

hustle /ˈhʌsl/ v [T] **1** make sb move by pushing them roughly **2** ~ (into) make sb act quickly: ~ sb into a decision • **hustle** n [U] busy lively activity ▶ **hustler** /ˈhʌslə(r)/ n **1** (US) (infml, esp US) person who tries to trick sb into giving them their money **2** (sl) prostitute

hut /hʌt/ n [C] small roughly-built house or shelter

hutch /hʌtʃ/ n [C] cage for rabbits, etc

hyacinth /ˈhaɪəsɪnθ/ n [C] plant with sweet-smelling flowers, growing from a bulb

hyaena = HYENA

hybrid /ˈhaɪbrɪd/ n [C] animal or plant produced from two different species

hydrant /ˈhaɪdrənt/ n [C] pipe connected to a water supply, esp in a street

hydraulic /haɪˈdrɔːlɪk/ adj worked by the pressure of a liquid, esp water

hydroelectric /ˌhaɪdrəʊˈlektrɪk/ adj using the power of water to produce electricity: a ~ dam

hydrofoil /ˈhaɪdrəfɔɪl/ n [C] boat which rises above the surface of the water when travelling fast

hydrogen /ˈhaɪdrədʒən/ n [U] (symb H) light colourless gas that combines with oxygen to form water • **hydrogen bomb** (also **H-bomb**) n [C] extremely powerful bomb that explodes when the central parts (nuclei) of hydrogen atoms join together

hyena (also **hyaena**) /haɪˈiːnə/ n [C] wild animal with a laughing cry

hygiene /ˈhaɪdʒiːn/ n [U] keeping yourself and your living area clean, in order to prevent disease ▶ **hygienic** /haɪˈdʒiːnɪk/ adj of hygiene; clean ▶ **hygienically** adv

hymn /hɪm/ n [C] song of praise to God

hyperactive /ˌhaɪpərˈæktɪv/ adj (esp of children) too active; unable to rest ▶ **hyperactivity** /ˌhaɪpəræktɪˈvɪti/ n [U]

hyperlink /ˈhaɪpəlɪŋk/ n [C] place in an electronic document on a computer that is linked to another electronic document: Click on the ~.

hypermarket /ˈhaɪpəmɑːkɪt/ n [C] (GB) very large supermarket

hyphen /ˈhaɪfn/ n [C] mark (-) used for joining two words or parts of words ▶ **hyphenate** /ˈhaɪfəneɪt/ v [T] join two words with a hyphen

hypnosis /hɪpˈnəʊsɪs/ n [U] state like deep sleep in which a person's actions may be controlled by another person ▶ **hypnotic** /hɪpˈnɒtɪk/ adj **1** making you feel sleepy **2** produced by hypnosis ▶ **hypnotism** /ˈhɪpnətɪzəm/ n [U] practice of hypnotizing sb ▶ **hypnotist** /ˈhɪpnətɪst/ n [C] ▶ **hypnotize** (also **-ise**) /ˈhɪpnətaɪz/ v [T] produce a state of hypnosis in sb

hypo- /ˈhaɪpəʊ/ prefix (in adjectives and nouns) under; below normal: hypodermic ◇ hypothermia

hypo-allergenic /ˌhaɪpəʊˌæləˈdʒenɪk/ adj unlikely to cause an allergic reaction

hypochondriac /ˌhaɪpəˈkɒndriæk/ n [C] person who worries too much about their health

hypocrisy /hɪˈpɒkrəsi/ n [U,C] (pl -ies) (disapprov) making yourself appear more moral, etc than you really are ▸ **hypocrite** /ˈhɪpəkrɪt/ n [C] person who makes himself or herself appear better than they really are ▸ **hypocritical** /ˌhɪpəˈkrɪtɪkl/ adj

hypodermic /ˌhaɪpəˈdɜːmɪk/ adj, n [C] (of a needle) used for injecting a drug into a person: a ~ syringe

hypotenuse /haɪˈpɒtənjuːz/ n [C] longest side of a right-angled triangle

hypothesis /haɪˈpɒθəsɪs/ n [C] (pl -theses /-siːz/) idea that is suggested as a possible explanation of facts ▸ **hypothetical** /ˌhaɪpəˈθetɪkl/ adj based on ideas or situations which are possible but not real

hysteria /hɪˈstɪəriə/ n [U] state of extreme excitement, fear or anger, which causes loss of control **2** uncontrolled excitement ▸ **hysterical** /hɪˈsterɪkl/ adj ▸ **hysterics** /hɪˈsterɪks/ n [pl] attack(s) of hysteria

I i

0ᵐ **I** /aɪ/ pron (used as the subject of a v) person who is the speaker or writer

I, i /aɪ/ n [C,U] (pl **I's, i's** /aɪz/) **1** the ninth letter of the English alphabet **2** Roman numeral for 1

0ᵐ **ice¹** /aɪs/ n [U] **1** water that has frozen and become solid **2** pieces of ice used to keep food and drinks cold **IDM on ice 1** (of wine, etc) kept cold by being surrounded with ice **2** (of a plan, etc) waiting to be dealt with at a later time ■ **iceberg** /ˈaɪsbɜːɡ/ n [C] large mass of ice floating in the sea ■ **icebox** [C] **1** box with ice in, for keeping food cool **2** (esp US) refrigerator ■ **ice cap** n [C] layer of ice permanently covering parts of the earth, esp around the North and South Poles ■ **ice hockey** n [U] team game played on ice with sticks and a hard rubber disc ■ **ice lolly** n [C] flavoured ice on a stick ■ **ice skate** n [C] boot with a thin metal blade on the bottom, for skating on ice ■ **ice-skate** v [I] skate on ice

ice² /aɪs/ v [T] cover a cake with icing **[PV] ice (sth) over/up** cover sth with ice; become covered with ice

0ᵐ **ice cream** (esp US 'ice cream) n [U,C] (portion of) frozen flavoured creamy mixture: Desserts are served with ice cream.

icicle /ˈaɪsɪkl/ n [C] pointed piece of ice, formed when water freezes as it drips from a roof, etc

icing /ˈaɪsɪŋ/ n [U] mixture of powdered sugar, flavouring, etc, used for decorating cakes

icy /ˈaɪsi/ adj (-ier, -iest) **1** very cold **2** covered with ice **3** unfriendly: an ~ stare ▸ **icily** adv

I'd /aɪd/ short for I HAD; I WOULD

0ᵐ **idea** /aɪˈdɪə/ n **1** [C] plan or thought: That's a good ~! **2** [U,sing] picture in the mind **3** [C] opinion or belief **4** [U,sing] feeling that sth is possible: I've an ~ it will rain. **5** (the idea) [sing] the aim or purpose of doing sth: You'll soon get the ~ (= understand). **IDM have no idea | not have the faintest, first, etc idea** (spoken) used to emphasize that you do not know sth: He has no ~ how to manage people.

0ᵐ **ideal** /aɪˈdɪəl/ adj **1** perfect: ~ weather **2** existing only in the imagination: in an ~ world ● **ideal** n [C] **1** idea or standard that seems perfect **2** [usu sing] person or thing considered perfect ▸ **ideally** adv **1** in an ideal way: ~ly suited to the job **2** if conditions were perfect

idealist /aɪˈdɪəlɪst/ n [C] person who has (often impractical) ideals (1) and who tries to achieve them ▸ **idealism** /-ɪzəm/ n [U] ▸ **idealistic** /ˌaɪdɪəˈlɪstɪk/ adj

idealize (also -ise) /aɪˈdɪəlaɪz/ v [T] think of sb/sth as perfect ▸ **idealization** (also -isation) /-ˈzeɪʃn/ n [U,C]

identical /aɪˈdentɪkl/ adj **1** the same **2** ~ (to/with) exactly alike: ~ twins ▸ **identically** adv

0ᵐ **identify** /aɪˈdentɪfaɪ/ v (pt, pp -ied) [T] show or prove who or what sb/sth is: Can you ~ the man who attacked you? **[PV] identify with sb** understand the feelings of sb **identify yourself with sb/sth** support sb/sth; be closely connected with sb/sth ▸ **identification** /aɪˌdentɪfɪˈkeɪʃn/ (abbr **ID**) n [U,C] act of identifying sb/sth **2** [U] official papers that can prove who you are

0ᵐ **identity** /aɪˈdentəti/ n (pl -ies) **1** [C,U] who or what sb/sth is: the ~ of the thief **2** [U] state of being very similar to and able to understand sb/sth ■ **identity card** (also **I'D card**) n [C] card with your name, photograph, etc. on it that proves who you are ■ **identity theft** n [U] using sb else's name and details in order to obtain credit cards and other goods or to take money out of the person's bank accounts

ideology /ˌaɪdiˈɒlədʒi/ n (pl -ies)

-ies set of (political) beliefs
▸ **ideological** /ˌaɪdɪə'lɒdʒɪkl/ *adj*

idiocy /'ɪdɪəsɪ/ *n* (pl **-ies**) **1** [U] extreme stupidity **2** [C] very stupid act, remark, etc

idiom /'ɪdɪəm/ *n* [C] group of words with a meaning that is different from the meaning of all the individual words: *'Pull your socks up' is an ~ meaning 'improve your behaviour'.* ▸ **idiomatic** /ˌɪdɪə'mætɪk/ *adj* (of language) natural and correct

idiosyncrasy /ˌɪdɪə'sɪŋkrəsɪ/ *n* (pl **-ies**) way of behaving that is particular to a person
▸ **idiosyncratic** /ˌɪdɪəsɪŋ'krætɪk/ *adj*

idiot /'ɪdɪət/ *n* [C] (*infml*) very stupid person ▸ **idiotic** /ˌɪdɪ'ɒtɪk/ *adj*

idle /'aɪdl/ *adj* (~r, ~st) **1** (of people) lazy; not working hard **2** (of machines, etc) not in use **3** (of people) unemployed **4** useless: *~ gossip/promises* ● **idle** *v* [I,T] waste time: *He ~d the days away, watching TV.* [i] (of an engine) run slowly in neutral gear [PV] **idle sth away** waste (time) ▸ **idleness** *n* [U] ▸ **idly** *adv*

idol /'aɪdl/ *n* [C] **1** person or thing that is greatly loved or admired **2** statue that is worshipped as a god ▸ **idolize** (*also* **-ise**) /'aɪdəlaɪz/ *v* [T] admire or love sb very much

idyllic /ɪ'dɪlɪk/ *adj* peaceful and beautiful; perfect

O~ ie /ˌaɪ 'i:/ *abbr* That is: *They arrived on the next day, ie Monday.*

O~ if /ɪf/ *conj* **1** on condition that: *She will help you if you ask her.* **2** whether: *Do you know if he's working today?* **3** when; whenever; every time: *If you mix yellow and blue, you get green.* **4** used after verbs or adjectives expressing feelings: *I'm sorry if I'm disturbing you.* **5** used before an adjective to introduce a contrast: *The hotel was good value, if a little expensive.* [IDM] **if I were you** used to give sb advice: *If I were you, I'd look for a new job.* **if only** used for expressing a strong wish: *If only I were rich!* ● **if** *n* [C] (*infml*) uncertainty [IDM] **ifs and buts** reasons for delay; uncertainty: *No more ifs and buts—you're going to the party.*

igloo /'ɪglu:/ *n* [C] (pl **~s**) small round house made of blocks of snow by the Inuit people

ignite /ɪg'naɪt/ *v* [I,T] (*written*) (cause sth to) start to burn ▸ **ignition** /ɪg'nɪʃn/ *n* **1** [C] electrical apparatus that starts the engine of a car, etc **2** [U] (*tech*) process of igniting sth

ignorant /'ɪgnərənt/ *adj* lacking knowledge about sth ▸ **ignorance** /'ɪgnərəns/ *n* [U] ▸ **ignorantly** *adv*

O~ ignore /ɪg'nɔ:(r)/ *v* [T] take no notice of sb/sth

I'll /aɪl/ *short for* I WILL

O~ ill /ɪl/ *adj* **1** sick; suffering from an illness or disease: *She was taken ~ suddenly.* **2** bad: *~ health/luck* ● *~ feeling* (= anger, jealousy, etc) [IDM] **be taken ill** become ill ● **ill** *n* **1** [C, usu pl] (*fml*) problem **2** [U] (*lit*) harm; bad luck ● **ill** *adv* **1** badly: *an ~-written book* **2** only with difficulty: *We can ~ afford the time.* [IDM] **ill at ease** uncomfortable; embarrassed **speak/think ill of sb** say or think bad things about sb ■ **ill-advised** *adj* unwise ■ **ill-bred** *adj* badly brought up ■ **ill-natured** *adj* bad-tempered ■ **ill-treat** *v* [T] treat sb cruelly ■ **ill-treatment** *n* [U] ■ **ill will** *n* [U] unkind feelings towards sb

illegal /ɪ'li:gl/ *adj* against the law; not legal ▸ **illegality** /ˌɪlɪ'gæləti/ *n* [U,C] ▸ **illegally** /-gəli/ *adv*

illegible /ɪ'ledʒəbl/ *adj* difficult or impossible to read

illegitimate /ˌɪlə'dʒɪtəmət/ *adj* **1** born to parents not married to each other **2** not allowed by the law ▸ **illegitimately** *adv*

illicit /ɪ'lɪsɪt/ *adj* not allowed by the law ▸ **illicitly** *adv*

illiterate /ɪ'lɪtərət/ *n* [C], *adj* (person who is) unable to read or write ▸ **illiteracy** /ɪ'lɪtərəsi/ *n* [U]

illness /'ɪlnəs/ *n* **1** [U] state of being ill **2** [C] specific kind of illness

illogical /ɪ'lɒdʒɪkl/ *adj* not logical; not reasonable ▸ **illogicality** /ˌɪlɒdʒɪ'kæləti/ *n* [C,U] ▸ **illogically** *adv*

illuminate /ɪ'lu:mɪneɪt/ *v* [T] **1** shine light on sth **2** (*fml*) make sth clearer or easier to understand **3** decorate sth with lights ▸ **illuminated** *adj* (of books, etc) decorated with gold, silver and bright colours ▸ **illuminating** *adj* explaining sth clearly: *an illuminating lecture* ▸ **illumination** /ɪˌlu:mɪ'neɪʃn/ *n* **1** [U] lighting **2** (**illuminations**) [pl] (*GB*) bright colourful lights to decorate a town

illusion /ɪ'lu:ʒn/ *n* [C] **1** false idea or belief **2** something that seems to exist but in fact does not: *an optical ~* ▸ **illusory** /ɪ'lu:səri/ *adj* not real, though seeming to be

O~ illustrate /'ɪləstreɪt/ *v* [T] **1** use pictures, diagrams, etc in a book, etc: *~ a book* **2** explain sth by using examples, diagrams, etc ▸ **illustration** /ˌɪlə'streɪʃn/ *n* **1** [C] picture or drawing in a book, etc **2** [C,U] example of sth **3** [U] process of illustrating sth ▸ **illustrative** /'ɪləstrətɪv/ *adj* helping to explain sth ▸ **illustrator** *n* [C] person who draws pictures for books, etc

illustrious /ɪˈlʌstriəs/ *adj* (fml) very famous and much admired
▶ **illustriously** *adv*

I'm /aɪm/ *short for* I AM (BE)

0━▪ **image** /ˈɪmɪdʒ/ *n* 1 [C,U] impression that a person, company, product etc gives to the public 2 [C] mental picture of sb/sth 3 [C] copy of sth, esp in wood or stone 4 [C] picture of sb/sth seen in a mirror, through a camera, etc [IDM] **be the (living/spitting) image of sb** (infml) look exactly like sb ▶ **imagery** /ˈɪmɪdʒri/ *n* [U] use of figurative language to produce pictures in the mind

0━▪ **imaginary** /ɪˈmædʒɪnəri/ *adj* unreal

0━▪ **imagine** /ɪˈmædʒɪn/ *v* [T] 1 form a picture of sth in your mind: *Can you ~ life without electricity?* 2 suppose sth: *I ~ he'll be there.* ▶ **imaginable** *adj* that can be imagined ▶ **imaginable** *adj*
imagination /ɪˌmædʒɪˈneɪʃn/ *n* 1 [U,C] ability to form pictures or ideas in the mind, esp of interesting things 2 [C] something experienced in the mind, not in real life ▶ **imaginative** /ɪˈmædʒɪnətɪv/ *adj* having or showing imagination (1)

imaging /ˈɪmɪdʒɪŋ/ *n* [U] (computing) process of capturing, storing and showing an image on a computer screen: *~ software*

imbalance /ɪmˈbæləns/ *n* [C] lack of equality or balance

imbecile /ˈɪmbəsiːl/ *n* [C] stupid person ▶ **imbecile** *adj*

imbue /ɪmˈbjuː/ *v* [T] ~ **with** (fml) fill sb with a feeling, etc

imitate /ˈɪmɪteɪt/ *v* [T] 1 copy sb/sth 2 copy the way a person speaks or behaves ▶ **imitative** /ˈɪmɪtətɪv/ *adj* (fml) that copies sb/sth ▶ **imitator** *n* [C]

imitation /ˌɪmɪˈteɪʃn/ *n* 1 [C] copy of sth, esp sth expensive: *~ leather* 2 [C,U] act of copying sth

immaculate /ɪˈmækjələt/ *adj* clean; perfect ▶ **immaculately** *adv*

immaterial /ˌɪməˈtɪəriəl/ *adj* ~ **(to)** 1 not important 2 (fml) not having a physical form

immature /ˌɪməˈtjʊə(r)/ *adj* 1 not sensible in behaviour 2 not fully developed ▶ **immaturity** *n* [U]

immeasurable /ɪˈmeʒərəbl/ *adj* too large to be measured

0━▪ **immediate** /ɪˈmiːdiət/ *adj* 1 happening or done at once: *take ~ action* 2 nearest: *in the ~ future*

0━▪ **immediately** /ɪˈmiːdiətli/ *adv* 1 at once; without delay 2 being nearest; closest: *the years ~ after the war* ● **immediately** *conj* (esp GB) as soon as: *I recognized her ~ I saw her.*

immense /ɪˈmens/ *adj* very large ▶ **immensely** *adv* very much: *I*

enjoyed the film *~ly.* ▶ **immensity** *n* [U]

immerse /ɪˈmɜːs/ *v* [T] 1 ~ **(in)** put sth under the surface of a liquid 2 ~ **yourself (in)** involve yourself deeply in sth: *~ yourself in your work* ▶ **immersion** /ɪˈmɜːʃn/ *n* [U] ▶ **im'mersion heater** *n* [C] (GB) electric heater in a water tank

immigrant /ˈɪmɪɡrənt/ *n* [C] person who has come to live in a country that is not their own ▶ **immigration** /ˌɪmɪˈɡreɪʃn/ *n* [U] moving of people from one country to come to live in another country

imminent /ˈɪmɪnənt/ *adj* likely to happen very soon ▶ **imminently** *adv*

immobile /ɪˈməʊbaɪl/ *adj* not moving; unable to move ▶ **immobility** /ˌɪməʊˈbɪləti/ *n* [U] ▶ **immobilize** (also *-ise*) /ɪˈməʊbəlaɪz/ *v* [T] prevent sb/sth from moving or working properly

0━▪ **immoral** /ɪˈmɒrəl/ *adj* 1 not moral; wrong 2 against usual standards of sexual behaviour ▶ **immorality** /ˌɪməˈræləti/ *n* [U,C]

immortal /ɪˈmɔːtl/ *adj* 1 living or lasting for ever 2 famous and likely to be remembered for ever ● **immortal** *n* [C] immortal being ▶ **immortality** /ˌɪmɔːˈtæləti/ *n* [U] ▶ **immortalize** (also *-ise*) /ɪˈmɔːtəlaɪz/ *v* [T] prevent sth from being forgotten in the future: *~ized in a novel*

immune /ɪˈmjuːn/ *adj* 1 ~ **(to/ against)** that cannot be harmed by a disease: *~ to smallpox* 2 ~ **(to)** not affected by sth: *~ to criticism* 3 ~ **(from)** protected from sth: *~ from tax* ▶ **immunity** *n* [U] ▶ **immunize** (also *-ise*) /ˈɪmjunaɪz/ *v* [T] ~ **(against)** make sb immune to a disease, esp by giving them an injection of a vaccine ▶ **immunization** (also *-isation*) /ˌɪmjunaɪˈzeɪʃn/ *n* [U,C]

imp /ɪmp/ *n* [C] 1 (in stories) little devil 2 mischievous child

0━▪ **impact** /ˈɪmpækt/ *n* 1 [C, usu sing] ~ **(on)** strong effect that sth has on sb/sth: *the ~ of computers on industry* 2 [U] (force of the) hitting of one object against another: *The bomb exploded on ~* (= when it hit sth). ● **impact** /ɪmˈpækt/ *v* [T] have an effect on sth 2 [I,T] hit sth with great force

impair /ɪmˈpeə(r)/ *v* [T] damage sth or make sth worse: *Loud noise can ~ your hearing.*

impale /ɪmˈpeɪl/ *v* [T] ~ **(on)** push a sharp pointed object through sth/ sb: *~d on a spear*

impart /ɪmˈpɑːt/ *v* [T] (fml) pass information, etc to other people

impartial /ɪmˈpɑːʃl/ *adj* just; fair: *A judge must be ~.* ▶ **impartiality** /ˌɪmˌpɑːʃiˈæləti/ *n* [U]

impassable /ɪmˈpɑːsəbl/ *adj* (of a road, etc) impossible to travel on

impassioned /ɪmˈpæʃnd/ *adj* showing strong deep feeling: *an ~ appeal*

impassive /ɪmˈpæsɪv/ *adj* showing no sign of feeling ▶ **impassively** *adv*

0─ impatient /ɪmˈpeɪʃnt/ *adj*
1 showing a lack of patience **2** very eager: *~ to leave school*
▶ **impatience** /-ʃns/ *n* [U]
▶ **impatiently** *adv*

impeccable /ɪmˈpekəbl/ *adj* faultless ▶ **impeccably** *adv*

impede /ɪmˈpiːd/ *v* [T] delay or stop the progress of sth

impediment /ɪmˈpedɪmənt/ *n* [C]
1 something that makes progress difficult **2** physical defect, esp in speech

impending /ɪmˈpendɪŋ/ *adj* about to happen: *~ disaster*

impenetrable /ɪmˈpenɪtrəbl/ *adj*
1 that cannot be passed through
2 impossible to understand

imperative /ɪmˈperətɪv/ *adj* very urgent or important ● **imperative** *n* [C] (*gram*) verb form that expresses a command, eg *Go!* ▶ **imperatively** *adv*

imperfect /ɪmˈpɜːfɪkt/ *adj* not perfect ● **imperfect** *n* (**the imperfect**) [sing] (*gram*) verb tense that shows incomplete action in the past, eg *was speaking*
▶ **imperfection** /ˌɪmpəˈfekʃn/ *n* [C, U] fault or weakness in sb/sth
▶ **imperfectly** *adv*

imperial /ɪmˈpɪəriəl/ *adj* of an empire or its ruler ▶ **imperialism** *n* [U] (belief in a) political system of gaining economic or political control over other countries
▶ **imperialist** *n* [C], *adj* ▶ **imperially** *adv*

impersonal /ɪmˈpɜːsənl/ *adj*
1 lacking friendly human feelings: *a large ~ organization* **2** not referring to any particular person
▶ **impersonally** /-nəli/ *adv*

impersonate /ɪmˈpɜːsəneɪt/ *v* [T] pretend to be another person
▶ **impersonation** /-ˈneɪʃn/ *n* [C, U]

impertinent /ɪmˈpɜːtɪnənt/ *adj* not showing proper respect
▶ **impertinence** /-əns/ *n* [U, sing]
▶ **impertinently** *adv*

impervious /ɪmˈpɜːviəs/ *adj* **1** not influenced by sth: *~ to criticism*
2 (*tech*) not allowing a liquid or gas to pass through

impetuous /ɪmˈpetʃuəs/ *adj* acting quickly and without thinking

impetus /ˈɪmpɪtəs/ *n* **1** [U, sing] something that encourages a process to develop more quickly: *give a fresh ~ to trade* **2** [U] (*tech*) force with which sth moves

impinge /ɪmˈpɪndʒ/ *v* [I] ~ **(on)** (*fml*)

have an effect on sb/sth, esp a bad one

implacable /ɪmˈplækəbl/ *adj* that cannot be changed or satisfied

implant /ɪmˈplɑːnt/ *v* [T] ~ **(in/into)** (*written*) **1** fix an idea, attitude, etc firmly in sb's mind **2** put sth, usu sth artificial, into a part of the body for medical purposes ● **implant** /ˈɪmplɑːnt/ *n* [C] something that is put into sb's body during a medical operation

implement[1] /ˈɪmplɪment/ *v* [T] carry out a plan, idea, etc
▶ **implementation** /ˌɪmplɪmenˈteɪʃn/ *n* [U]

implement[2] /ˈɪmplɪmənt/ *n* [C] tool or instrument

implicate /ˈɪmplɪkeɪt/ *v* [T] ~ **(in)** show or suggest that sb is involved in a crime, etc

0─ implication /ˌɪmplɪˈkeɪʃn/ *n*
1 [C, usu pl] possible effect of an action or decision **2** [C, U] something suggested or implied **3** [U] act of implicating sb, esp in a crime

implicit /ɪmˈplɪsɪt/ *adj* **1** implied, but not expressed directly
2 unquestioning; complete: *~ trust*
▶ **implicitly** *adv*

implore /ɪmˈplɔː(r)/ *v* [T] ask or beg sb strongly: *They ~d her to stay.*
▶ **imploringly** *adv*

0─ imply /ɪmˈplaɪ/ *v* (*pt, pp* -**ied**) [T]
1 suggest that sth is true without actually saying it: *Are you ~ing that I stole your watch?* **2** suggest sth as a necessary result

impolite /ˌɪmpəˈlaɪt/ *adj* not polite; rude ▶ **impolitely** *adv*
▶ **impoliteness** *n* [U]

import /ɪmˈpɔːt/ *v* [T] bring in goods, etc from another country
● **import** /ˈɪmpɔːt/ *n* **1** [C, usu pl] product or service that is imported
2 [U] (business of) importing goods
3 [U] (*fml*) importance
▶ **importation** /ˌɪmpɔːˈteɪʃn/ *n* [U, C]
▶ **importer** *n* [C] person, company, etc that imports goods to sell

0─ important /ɪmˈpɔːtnt/ *adj*
1 having a great effect or value: *an ~ decision* **2** (of a person) having great influence or authority ▶ **importance** /ɪmˈpɔːtns/ *n* [U] ▶ **importantly** *adv*

0─ impose /ɪmˈpəʊz/ *v* **1** ~ **(on/upon)** [T] put a tax, penalty, etc on sb/sth **2** [T] try to make sb accept an opinion, etc **3** expect sb to do sth for you when it may be inconvenient [PV] **impose on/upon sb** take advantage of sb unfairly ▶ **imposing** *adj* large and impressive
▶ **imposition** /ˌɪmpəˈzɪʃn/ *n* [U, C]

0─ impossible /ɪmˈpɒsəbl/ *adj*
1 not possible **2** very difficult to deal with: *an ~ situation* ▶ **impossibility**

/ɪmˌpɒsəˈbɪləti/ n [U, C] ▶ **impossibly** adv

impostor /ɪmˈpɒstə(r)/ n [C] person who pretends to be sb else, esp to deceive others

impotent /ˈɪmpətənt/ adj **1** powerless or helpless **2** (of a man) unable to have sex ▶ **impotence** /-əns/ n [U]

impound /ɪmˈpaʊnd/ v [T] take possession of sth by law

impoverish /ɪmˈpɒvərɪʃ/ v [T] make sb/sth poor

impracticable /ɪmˈpræktɪkəbl/ adj impossible to put into practice

impractical /ɪmˈpræktɪkl/ adj not sensible, useful or realistic

imprecise /ˌɪmprɪˈsaɪs/ adj not exact or accurate

impregnable /ɪmˈpregnəbl/ adj that cannot be entered by attack

impregnate /ˈɪmpregneɪt/ v [T] **1** cause one substance to be filled in every part with another substance: cloth ~d with perfume **2** (fml) make a woman or female animal pregnant

impresario /ˌɪmprəˈsɑːriəʊ/ n [C] (pl ~s) manager of a theatre or music company

0─ **impress** /ɪmˈpres/ v [T] **1** cause sb to feel admiration: Her honesty ~ed me. **2** ~ on/upon (fml) fix sth in sb's mind: ~ on him the importance of hard work

0─ **impression** /ɪmˈpreʃn/ n [C] **1** idea, feeling or opinion that you get about sb/sth: My general ~ was that she seemed a nice woman. **2** lasting effect on sb's mind or feelings: create a good ~ **3** funny imitation of sb's behaviour or way of talking **4** mark left when an object is pressed hard into a surface [IDM] **be under the impression that...** have the (usu wrong) idea that... ▶ **impressionable** /ɪmˈpreʃənəbl/ adj easily influenced ▶ **Impressionism** /ɪmˈpreʃənɪzəm/ n [U] style in painting that gives a general impression (1) of sth by using the effects of colour and light

0─ **impressive** /ɪmˈpresɪv/ adj causing admiration: an ~ building ▶ **impressively** adv

imprint /ɪmˈprɪnt/ v [T] print or press a mark or design onto a surface: (fig) details ~ed on his memory ● **imprint** /ˈɪmprɪnt/ n [C] **1** mark made by pressing sth onto a surface **2** lasting effect

imprison /ɪmˈprɪzn/ v [T] put sb in prison ▶ **imprisonment** n [U]

improbable /ɪmˈprɒbəbl/ adj not likely to be true or to happen ▶ **improbability** /ɪmˌprɒbəˈbɪləti/ n [U, C] (pl -ies) ▶ **improbably** adv

impromptu /ɪmˈprɒmptjuː/ adj, adv (done) without preparation: an ~ speech

improper /ɪmˈprɒpə(r)/ adj **1** dishonest or morally wrong: ~ business practices **2** (fml) not suitable for the purpose, situation, etc: ~ behaviour/dress **3** wrong or incorrect: ~ use of the drug ▶ **improperly** adv

0─ **improve** /ɪmˈpruːv/ v [I,T] become or make sth/sb better ▶ **improvement** n **1** [U] process of becoming or making sth better **2** [C] change that improves sth: home ~ments

improvise /ˈɪmprəvaɪz/ v [I,T] **1** make sth from whatever is available, without preparation **2** compose music or speak or act without preparation ▶ **improvisation** /ˌɪmprəvaɪˈzeɪʃn/ n [U, C]

impudent /ˈɪmpjədənt/ adj very rude and disrespectful ▶ **impudence** /-əns/ n [U] ▶ **impudently** adv

impulse /ˈɪmpʌls/ n **1** [C,U] sudden desire to do sth **2** [C] (tech) force or movement of energy: an electrical ~ [IDM] **on impulse** suddenly and without thought

impulsive /ɪmˈpʌlsɪv/ adj acting suddenly without thinking carefully about the results of your actions ▶ **impulsively** adv ▶ **impulsiveness** n [U]

impunity /ɪmˈpjuːnəti/ n [IDM] **with impunity** (fml, disapprov) without being punished

impure /ɪmˈpjʊə(r)/ adj **1** mixed with sth else; not clean **2** (old-fash) morally wrong ▶ **impurity** n [U,C] (pl -ies)

0─ **in¹** /ɪn/ adv **1** (to a position) within a particular area or space: He opened the bedroom door and went in. **2** at home or at a place of work: Nobody was in when we called. **3** (of trains, buses, etc) at the station **4** (of letters) received: Competition entries should be in by 31 May. **5** (of the tide) at or towards its highest point on land **6** elected: Labour came in after the war. **7** (sport) batting **8** (sport) (of a ball) inside the line [IDM] **be in for sth** (infml) be about to experience sth, esp sth unpleasant **be/get in on sth** (infml) be/become involved in sth; share or know about sth **be (well) in with sb** (infml) be (very) friendly with sb **have it in for sb** (infml) not like sb and be unpleasant to them ● **in** adj **1** (infml) popular and fashionable **2** shared by a small group: Exotic pets are the thing.

0─ **in²** /ɪn/ prep **1** at a point within an area or a space; surrounded by sth: Rome is in Italy. ◇ play in the street ◇ lying in bed ◇ a pen in his pocket **2** used for showing movement into sth: Throw it in the fire. **3** forming the whole or part of sth/sb: *seven days in a week* **4** during a period of time: *in June* **5** after a particular length of time: *Lunch will be ready in an hour.* **6** wearing sth: *the woman in white* **7** used to show physical surroundings: *go out in the cold* **8** used to show a state or condition: *in a mess* ◇ *in love* **9** used to show sb's job or profession: *a career in journalism* **10** used to show form or arrangement of sth: *a story in three parts* **11** used to show the language, material, etc used: *speak in English* ◇ *write in ink* **12** concerning sth: *lacking in courage* ◇ *3 metres in length* **13** used to show a rate or relative amount: *a slope of 1 in 5 (= 20%)* **[IDM] in that** (*written*) for the reason that; because: *The chemical is dangerous in that it can kill.*

in³ /ɪn/ n **[IDM] the ins and outs (of sth)** all the details, esp the complicated ones

0→ **inability** /ˌɪnəˈbɪləti/ n [U,sing] ~ **(to)** fact of not being able to do sth

inaccessible /ˌɪnækˈsesəbl/ adj impossible to reach

inaccurate /ɪnˈækjərət/ adj not correct ▸ **inaccuracy** /ɪnˈækjərəsi/ n [U,C] (pl -ies) ▸ **inaccurately** adv

inadequate /ɪnˈædɪkwət/ adj not (good) enough ▸ **inadequately** adv

inadmissible /ˌɪnədˈmɪsəbl/ adj that cannot be allowed in a court of law: ~ *evidence*

inadvertent /ˌɪnədˈvɜːtənt/ adj done without thinking or accidentally ▸ **inadvertently** adv

inalienable /ɪnˈeɪliənəbl/ adj (*fml*) that cannot be taken away from you: *the ~ right to decide your own future*

inane /ɪˈneɪn/ adj silly ▸ **inanely** adv

inanimate /ɪnˈænɪmət/ adj not living: *A rock is an ~ object.*

inapplicable /ˌɪnəˈplɪkəbl; ɪnˈæplɪkəbl/ adj ~ **(to)** not applicable to sth

inappropriate /ˌɪnəˈprəʊpriət/ adj ~ **(to/for)** not suitable for sb/sth ▸ **inappropriately** adv

inarticulate /ˌɪnɑːˈtɪkjələt/ adj **1** unable to express yourself clearly **2** (of speech) not clear

inasmuch as /ˌɪnəzˈmʌtʃ əz/ conj (*fml*) to the extent that; since

inaudible /ɪnˈɔːdəbl/ adj not loud enough to be heard

inaugural /ɪˈnɔːɡjərəl/ adj (of an official speech, meeting, etc) first, and marking the beginning of sth important: *the President's ~ speech*

inaugurate /ɪˈnɔːɡjəreɪt/ v [T] **1** introduce a new official or leader at a special ceremony **2** start or open an organization, exhibition, etc with a special ceremony **3** (*fml*) introduce a new development or

important change ▸ **inauguration** /ɪˌnɔːɡjəˈreɪʃn/ n [U,C]

inborn /ˌɪnˈbɔːn/ adj (of a quality) existing in a person from birth

inbred /ˌɪnˈbred/ adj **1** having ancestors closely related to one another **2** = INBORN ▸ **inbreeding** /ˈɪnbriːdɪŋ/ n [U] breeding among closely related people or animals

inbuilt /ˈɪnbɪlt/ adj (of a quality) existing as an essential part of sth/sb

Inc. (*also* **inc**) /ɪŋk/ abbr Incorporated (used after the name of a company in the US)

incalculable /ɪnˈkælkjələbl/ adj too great to be calculated

incapable /ɪnˈkeɪpəbl/ adj ~ **of** not able to do sth: ~ *of telling a lie*

incapacitate /ˌɪnkəˈpæsɪteɪt/ v [T] (*fml*) make sb unable to live or work normally ▸ **incapacity** /ˌɪnkəˈpæsəti/ n [U] inability

incarcerate /ɪnˈkɑːsəreɪt/ v [T] (*fml*) put sb in prison ▸ **incarceration** /ɪnˌkɑːsəˈreɪʃn/ n [U]

incarnation /ˌɪnkɑːˈneɪʃn/ n [C] **1** period of life in a particular form **2** [C] person who represents a particular quality in human form: *the ~ of evil*

incendiary /ɪnˈsendiəri/ adj **1** designed to cause fires: *an ~ device* **2** causing strong feeling: *an ~ speech* ▸ **incendiary** n [C] (pl -ies) incendiary bomb

incense¹ /ˈɪnsens/ n [U] substance that produces a pleasant smell when burnt

incense² /ɪnˈsens/ v [T] make sb very angry

incentive /ɪnˈsentɪv/ n [C,U] ~ **(to)** something that encourages you to do sth

incessant /ɪnˈsesnt/ adj not stopping; continual: *his ~ complaints* ▸ **incessantly** adv

incest /ˈɪnsest/ n [U] sexual activity between close relatives ▸ **incestuous** /ɪnˈsestjuəs/ adj

0→ **inch** /ɪntʃ/ n [C] **1** measure of length; one twelfth of a foot (2.54 cm) **2** small amount: *escaped death by an ~.* **[IDM] every inch** all; completely within **an inch of sth** very close to sth ● **inch** v [I,T] move or make sth move slowly and carefully in the direction mentioned: *He ~ed his way through the tunnel.*

incidence /ˈɪnsɪdəns/ n [C, usu sing] number of times or way in which sth happens: *a high ~ of crime*

0→ **incident** /ˈɪnsɪdənt/ n **1** [C] event, esp sth unusual or unpleasant **2** [C,U] serious or violent event, eg a crime or an accident: *a shooting ~.*

incidental /ˌɪnsɪˈdentl/ adj happening in connection with sth else, but not as important as it, or not intended: ~ *expenses* ◇ ~ *music for a film* ▶ **incidentally** /ˌɪnsɪˈdentli/ *adv* used for introducing sth extra that you have just thought of

incinerate /ɪnˈsɪnəreɪt/ *v* [T] burn sth completely ▶ **incineration** /ɪnˌsɪnəˈreɪʃn/ *n* [U] ▶ **incinerator** *n* [C] furnace, etc for burning rubbish

incipient /ɪnˈsɪpiənt/ *adj* (fml) just beginning

incision /ɪnˈsɪʒn/ *n* [C, U] (act of making a) sharp cut in sth, esp during a medical operation

incisive /ɪnˈsaɪsɪv/ *adj* clear and direct: ~ *comments* ▶ **incisively** *adv*

incisor /ɪnˈsaɪzə(r)/ *n* [C] any one of the front cutting teeth

incite /ɪnˈsaɪt/ *v* [T] encourage sb to do sth violent, illegal or unpleasant: ~ *workers to riot* ▶ **incitement** *n* [U,C]

inclination /ˌɪnklɪˈneɪʃn/ *n* 1 [U,C] feeling that makes you want to do sth: *I have no* ~ *to leave.* 2 [C] tendency to do sth 3 [C, usu sing, U] (tech) angle of a slope

incline¹ /ɪnˈklaɪn/ *v* (fml) 1 [I,T] ~ *to/ towards* (persuade sb to) tend to think or behave in a particular way: *He* ~*s to laziness.* 2 [T] bend your head forward, sideways, etc as a sign of agreement, etc 3 [I,T] ~ **(towards)** (cause sth to) lean or slope in a particular direction ▶ **inclined** *adj* ~ **(to)** 1 wanting to do sth 2 tending to do sth; likely to do sth: *I'm* ~*d to believe him.*

incline² /ˈɪnklaɪn/ *n* [C] (fml) slope

0⊷ **include** /ɪnˈkluːd/ *v* [T] 1 have sth as part of a whole: *Prices* ~ *delivery.* 2 make sb/sth part of a larger group: ~ *Chris in the team* ▶ **inclusion** /ɪnˈkluːʒn/ *n* [U] ▶ **inclusive** /ɪnˈkluːsɪv/ *adj* including everything

incognito /ˌɪnkɒɡˈniːtəʊ/ *adv, adj* in a way that prevents other people from finding out who you are: *Famous people often travel* ~.

incoherent /ˌɪnkəʊˈhɪərənt/ *adj* not clear; not expressed clearly ▶ **incoherence** /-əns/ *n* [U] ▶ **incoherently** *adv*

0⊷ **income** /ˈɪnkʌm; ˈɪnkəm/ *n* [C,U] money received during a month, year, etc, esp as payment for work ■ **income tax** *n* [U] money that you pay to the government according to how much you earn

incoming /ˈɪnkʌmɪŋ/ *adj* 1 recently elected or appointed: *the* ~ *president* 2 arriving or being received: ~ *mail*

incomparable /ɪnˈkɒmprəbl/ *adj* so good or impressive that nothing can be compared to it

incompatible /ˌɪnkəmˈpætəbl/ *adj* not able or suitable to exist together: *The hours of the job are* ~ *with family*

life. ▶ **incompatibility** /ˌɪnkəmˌpætəˈbɪləti/ *n* [U]

incompetent /ɪnˈkɒmpɪtənt/ *adj* not skilful enough to do your job or a task as it should be done ▶ **incompetence** /ɪnˈkɒmpɪtəns/ *n* [U]

incomplete /ˌɪnkəmˈpliːt/ *adj* not complete ▶ **incompletely** *adv*

incomprehensible /ɪnˌkɒmprɪˈhensəbl/ *adj* impossible to understand ▶ **incomprehension** /ɪnˌkɒmprɪˈhenʃn/ *n* [U] failure to understand sth

inconceivable /ˌɪnkənˈsiːvəbl/ *adj* impossible to imagine or believe

inconclusive /ˌɪnkənˈkluːsɪv/ *adj* not leading to a definite decision or result: ~ *evidence*

incongruous /ɪnˈkɒŋɡruəs/ *adj* out of place: *Modern buildings look* ~ *in an old village.* ▶ **incongruity** /ˌɪnkɒnˈɡruːəti/ *n* [U,C] (pl -**ies**)

inconsiderate /ˌɪnkənˈsɪdərət/ *adj* not caring about the feelings of other people ▶ **inconsiderately** *adv*

inconsistent /ˌɪnkənˈsɪstənt/ *adj* ~ **(with)** not in harmony with sth; likely to change ▶ **inconsistency** /-ənsi/ *n* [U,C] (pl -**ies**) ▶ **inconsistently** *adv*

inconspicuous /ˌɪnkənˈspɪkjuəs/ *adj* not attracting attention; not easy to notice ▶ **inconspicuously** *adv*

incontinent /-ənt/ *adj* unable to control the bladder or bowels ▶ **incontinence** /ɪnˈkɒntɪnəns/ *n* [U]

incontrovertible /ˌɪnkɒntrəˈvɜːtəbl/ *adj* that is true and cannot be denied

inconvenience /ˌɪnkənˈviːniəns/ *n* [C,U] (cause of) trouble, difficulty or discomfort ● **inconvenience** *v* [T] cause trouble or difficulty for sb ▶ **inconvenient** /ˌɪnkənˈviːniənt/ *adj* causing inconvenience ▶ **inconveniently** *adv*

incorporate /ɪnˈkɔːpəreɪt/ *v* [T] include sth so that it forms part of sth: ~ *your ideas in the new plan* ▶ **incorporated** *adj* (business) (abbr **Inc.**) formed into a business company with legal status ▶ **incorporation** /ɪnˌkɔːpəˈreɪʃn/ *n* [U]

incorrect /ˌɪnkəˈrekt/ *adj* not correct; wrong ▶ **incorrectly** *adv* ▶ **incorrectness** *n* [U]

incorrigible /ɪnˈkɒrɪdʒəbl/ *adj* (of a person or bad behaviour) that cannot be corrected or improved

0⊷ **increase¹** /ɪnˈkriːs/ *v* [I,T] become or make sth greater in amount, number, value, etc ▶ **increasingly** *adv* more and more: *increasingly difficult*

0⊷ **increase²** /ˈɪnkriːs/ *n* [C,U] ~ **(in)** rise in the amount, number or value of sth

incredible /ɪnˈkredəbl/ adj **1** impossible to believe **2** (infml) wonderful; amazing ▸ **incredibly** adv

incredulous /ɪnˈkredjələs/ adj not believing sth; showing disbelief ▸ **incredulity** /ˌɪnkrəˈdjuːləti/ n [U] ▸ **incredulously** adv

increment /ˈɪŋkrəmənt/ n [C] increase in money or value

incriminate /ɪnˈkrɪmɪneɪt/ v [T] make sb appear to be guilty of doing sth wrong or illegal

incubate /ˈɪŋkjubeɪt/ v [I,T] keep eggs warm until they hatch ▸ **incubation** /ˌɪŋkjuˈbeɪʃn/ n **1** [U] hatching of eggs **2** [C] (med) (also incuˈbation period) period between infection and the first appearance of a disease ▸ **incubator** n [C] **1** piece of hospital equipment for keeping alive weak or premature babies **2** machine for hatching eggs by artificial warmth

incumbent /ɪnˈkʌmbənt/ adj ~ on (fml) necessary as part of sb's duty ● **incumbent** n [C] person holding an official position

incur /ɪnˈkɜː(r)/ v (-rr-) [T] cause yourself to suffer sth, esp sth bad: ~ large debts

incurable /ɪnˈkjʊərəbl/ adj that cannot be cured ▸ **incurable** n [C] person with an incurable disease ▸ **incurably** /-əbli/ adv

incursion /ɪnˈkɜːʃn/ n [C] (fml) sudden attack; invasion

indebted /ɪnˈdetɪd/ adj very grateful: ~ to him for his help

indecent /ɪnˈdiːsnt/ adj **1** likely to shock people; obscene **2** unsuitable; not right ▸ **indecency** /-nsi/ n [U] ▸ **indecently** adv

indecision /ˌɪndɪˈsɪʒn/ n [U] state of being unable to decide

indecisive /ˌɪndɪˈsaɪsɪv/ adj **1** unable to make decisions **2** not giving a clear answer or result ▸ **indecisively** adv

0‑ **indeed** /ɪnˈdiːd/ adv **1** used to emphasize a positive statement or answer: 'Did he complain?' 'I~ he did.' **2** used after very to emphasize a statement: Thank you very much ~. **3** used to show that you are surprised at sth or that you find sth ridiculous: 'She thinks she got the job.' 'Does she ~!'

indefensible /ˌɪndɪˈfensəbl/ adj impossible to defend: ~ rudeness

indefinable /ˌɪndɪˈfaɪnəbl/ adj impossible to define or put in words

indefinite /ɪnˈdefɪnət/ adj **1** lasting for a period of time with no fixed end: an ~ period of time **2** not clearly defined ■ inˌdefinite ˈarticle n [C] (gram) a or an ▸ **indefinitely** adv: The meeting was postponed ~ly.

indelible /ɪnˈdeləbl/ adj impossible to forget or remove ▸ **indelibly** adv

indelicate /ɪnˈdelɪkət/ adj (fml) rude or embarrassing

indemnify /ɪnˈdemnɪfaɪ/ v (pt, pp -ied) [T] (promise to) pay sb for loss, damage, etc

indemnity /ɪnˈdemnəti/ n (pl -ies) (fml or law) **1** [U] protection against damage or loss **2** [C] payment for damage or loss

indent /ɪnˈdent/ v [T] start a line of writing further in from the margin than the other lines ● **indent** /ˈɪndent/ n [C] (business) official order for goods or equipment ▸ **indentation** /ˌɪndenˈteɪʃn/ n **1** [C] cut or mark on the edge of sth: the ~ations of the coastline **2** (also indent) [C,U] (act of) indenting sth

0‑ **independent** /ˌɪndɪˈpendənt/ adj **1** (of countries) having their own government: an ~ nation **2** able to work alone; self-confident **3** ~ (of) not needing money, etc from other people to live ● **independent** n [C] politician who does not belong to a particular political party ▸ **independence** /ˌɪndɪˈpendəns/ n [U]: a woman's financial independence ▸ **independently** adv

indescribable /ˌɪndɪˈskraɪbəbl/ adj impossible to describe ▸ **indescribably** adv

indestructible /ˌɪndɪˈstrʌktəbl/ adj impossible to destroy

0‑ **index** /ˈɪndeks/ n [C] (pl -es in sense 3 -es or indices /ˈɪndɪsiːz/) **1** list of names, subjects, etc in alphabetical order at the end of a book **2** (also ˈcard index) (GB) box of cards with information on them, arranged in alphabetical order **3** system that compares the level of prices, etc with that of a former time: the cost-of-living ~ ◇ the Dow Jones ~ ● **index** v [T] make an index of documents, the contents of a book, etc; add sth to an index ■ ˈindex finger n [C] finger next to the thumb

0‑ **indicate** /ˈɪndɪkeɪt/ v **1** [T] show sth, esp by pointing; be a sign of sth **2** [I,T] (GB) signal that your vehicle is about to change direction ▸ **indication** /ˌɪndɪˈkeɪʃn/ n [C,U] remark or sign that shows that sth is happening or what sb is thinking ▸ **indicative** /ɪnˈdɪkətɪv/ adj ~ (of) (fml) showing or suggesting sth ▸ **indicator** n [C] **1** something that gives information, eg a pointer on a machine **2** flashing light on a vehicle showing that it is about to change direction

indict /ɪnˈdaɪt/ v [T] ~ (for) (esp US, law) officially charge sb with a crime: ~ed for murder ▸ **indictable** (esp US, law) for which you can be indicted: an ~able offence

indie 226

indictment *n* **1** [C, usu sing] sign that a system, a society, etc is very bad or wrong **2** [C,U] (*esp US*) (act of making a) written statement accusing sb of a crime

indie /'ɪndi/ *adj* not belonging to, working for or produced by a large organization; independent: *an ~ band/record label*

indifferent /ɪn'dɪfrənt/ *adj* **1** ~ (**to**) not interested in sth **2** not very good: *an ~ meal* ▶ **indifference** /ɪn'dɪfrəns/ *n* [U] ▶ **indifferently** *adv*

indigenous /ɪn'dɪdʒənəs/ *adj* ~ (**to**) belonging naturally to a place; native: *Kangaroos are ~ to Australia.*

indigestion /ˌɪndɪ'dʒestʃən/ *n* [U] (pain from) difficulty in digesting food

indignant /ɪn'dɪgnənt/ *adj* angry, esp at injustice ▶ **indignantly** *adv* ▶ **indignation** /ˌɪndɪg'neɪʃn/ *n* [U]

indignity /ɪn'dɪgnəti/ *n* [C, U] (*pl* -**ies**) treatment causing shame or loss of respect

indirect /ˌɪndə'rekt, -daɪ'r-/ *adj* **1** not immediate; secondary: *an ~ cause* **2** avoiding saying sth in a clear way: *an ~ answer* **3** not going in a straight line: *an ~ route* ▶ **indirectly** *adv* ■ **indirect 'object** *n* [C] (*gram*) person or thing to whom or to which an action is done: *In 'Give him the book', 'him' is the ~ object.* ■ **indirect 'speech** *n* [U] (*gram*) reporting of what sb has said, without using their actual words: *In ~ speech, 'I'll come later' becomes 'He said he'd come later'.* ■ **indirect tax** *n* [C, U] tax that is included in the price of certain goods

indiscreet /ˌɪndɪ'skri:t/ *adj* not careful about what you say and do ▶ **indiscreetly** *adv* ▶ **indiscretion** /ˌɪndɪ'skreʃn/ *n* **1** [U] indiscreet behaviour **2** [C] indiscreet remark or act

indiscriminate /ˌɪndɪ'skrɪmɪnət/ *adj* acting or done without careful thought ▶ **indiscriminately** *adv*

indispensable /ˌɪndɪ'spensəbl/ *adj* absolutely necessary

indisposed /ˌɪndɪ'spəʊzd/ *adj* (*fml*) **1** ill **2** unwilling to do sth: ~ *to help*

indisputable /ˌɪndɪ'spju:təbl/ *adj* that is true and cannot be denied ▶ **indisputably** *adv*

indistinguishable /ˌɪndɪ'stɪŋgwɪʃəbl/ *adj* ~ (**from**) impossible to identify as different: ~ *from her sister*

individual /ˌɪndɪ'vɪdʒuəl/ *adj* **1** single; separate **2** of or for one person ▶ **individual** *n* [C] any one human being ▶ **individuality** /ˌɪndɪˌvɪdʒu'æləti/ *n* [U] all the characteristics that make a person

different from others ▶ **individually** *adv*

indoctrinate /ɪn'dɒktrɪneɪt/ *v* [T] ~ (**with**) (*disapprov*) fill sb's mind with fixed beliefs or ideas ▶ **indoctrination** /ɪnˌdɒktrɪ'neɪʃn/ *n* [U]

indolent /'ɪndələnt/ *adj* (*fml*) lazy ▶ **indolence** /-əns/ *n* [U]

indoor /'ɪndɔ:(r)/ *adj* done or situated inside a building: *an ~ swimming pool* ▶ **indoors** /ˌɪn'dɔ:z/ *adv* inside or into a building

induce /ɪn'dju:s/ *v* [T] **1** (*fml*) persuade or influence sb to do sth **2** (*fml*) cause sth **3** (*med*) cause a woman to begin childbirth by giving her drugs ▶ **inducement** *n* [C, U] something, eg money, that encourages sb to do sth: *a pay rise as an ~ment to work harder*

induction /ɪn'dʌkʃn/ *n* **1** [U, C] act of introducing sb to a new job **2** [U] (*tech*) method of reasoning in which general laws are produced from particular facts **3** [U, C] inducing of a pregnant woman

indulge /ɪn'dʌldʒ/ *v* [I] ~ (**in**) allow yourself to enjoy sth **2** [T] satisfy a desire **3** [T] allow sb to have whatever they like or want ▶ **indulgence** *n* **1** [C] something pleasant in which sb indulges **2** [U] indulging ▶ **indulgent** *adj* tending to indulge (3) sb

industrial /ɪn'dʌstriəl/ *adj* of industry ■ **in,dustrial 'action** *n* [U] refusing to work normally; striking ▶ **industrialism** /-ɪzəm/ *n* [U] system in which large industries have an important part ▶ **industrialist** *n* [C] owner of a large industrial company ▶ **industrialize** (*also* -**ise**) *v* [I, T] develop a country with many industries ▶ **industrially** *adv*

industrious /ɪn'dʌstriəs/ *adj* hard-working; busy

industry /'ɪndəstri/ *n* (*pl* -**ies**) **1** [C, U] (branch of) manufacture or production of goods from raw materials: *the steel ~* **2** [U] (*fml*) quality of being hard-working

inebriated /ɪ'ni:brieɪtɪd/ *adj* (*fml* or *hum*) drunk

inedible /ɪn'edəbl/ *adj* (*fml*) not suitable to be eaten

ineffective /ˌɪnɪ'fektɪv/ *adj* not producing the results that you want ▶ **ineffectively** *adv* ▶ **ineffectiveness** *n* [U]

ineffectual /ˌɪnɪ'fektʃuəl/ *adj* (*written*) without the ability to achieve much; weak: *an ~ teacher* ▶ **ineffectually** *adv*

inefficient /ˌɪnɪ'fɪʃnt/ *adj* not doing a job well and not making the best use of time, money, energy etc ▶ **inefficiency** /-ənsi/ *n* [U] ▶ **inefficiently** *adv*

ineligible /ɪn'elɪdʒəbl/ *adj* ~ (**for**)

A B C D E F G H **I** J K L M N O P Q R S T U V W X Y Z

inept /ɪ'nept/ *adj* acting or done with no skill ▶ **ineptitude** /ɪ'neptɪtjuːd/ *n* [U]

inequality /ˌɪnɪ'kwɒləti/ *n* [U,C] (pl **-ies**) unfair difference between groups of people in society

inert /ɪ'nɜːt/ *adj* **1** (*fml*) without power to move or act **2** (*tech*) without active chemical or other properties (= characteristics): ~ *gases*

inertia /ɪ'nɜːʃə/ *n* [U] **1** lack of energy; lack of desire to move or change **2** (*physics*) tendency of an object to remain still or to continue moving unless another force acts on it

inescapable /ˌɪnɪ'skeɪpəbl/ *adj* impossible to avoid or ignore

0‒ **inevitable** /ɪn'evɪtəbl/ *adj* **1** that you cannot avoid or prevent **2** (*infml*) familiar and expected ▶ **inevitability** /ɪnˌevɪtə'bɪləti/ *n* [U] ▶ **inevitably** *adv*

inexact /ˌɪnɪg'zækt/ *adj* not exact or precise

inexcusable /ˌɪnɪk'skjuːzəbl/ *adj* too bad to accept or forgive

inexpensive /ˌɪnɪk'spensɪv/ *adj* not costing a lot of money

inexperience /ˌɪnɪk'spɪəriəns/ *n* [U] lack of experience ▶ **inexperienced** *adj*

inexplicable /ˌɪnɪk'splɪkəbl/ *adj* that cannot be explained ▶ **inexplicably** *adv*

inextricable /ˌɪnɪk'strɪkəbl; ɪn'ekstrɪkəbl/ *adj* (*fml*) too closely linked to be separated

infallible /ɪn'fæləbl/ *adj* **1** never wrong: *Nobody is* ~. **2** that never fails: *an* ~ *method* ▶ **infallibility** /ɪnˌfælə'bɪləti/ *n* [U]

infamous /'ɪnfəməs/ *adj* well known for being bad or evil ▶ **infamy** /'ɪnfəmi/ *n* [C,U] (pl **-ies**) (instance of) infamous behaviour

infancy /'ɪnfənsi/ *n* [U] **1** state or period of being a young child **2** early stage of development: *The project is still in its* ~.

infant /'ɪnfənt/ *n* [C] baby or very young child

infantile /'ɪnfəntaɪl/ *adj* of an infant; childish: ~ *behaviour*

infantry /'ɪnfəntri/ *n* [U, with sing or pl verb] soldiers who fight on foot

infatuated /ɪn'fætʃueɪtɪd/ *adj* ~ (**with**) having a very strong feeling of love or attraction for sb so that you cannot think clearly ▶ **infatuation** /ɪnˌfætʃu'eɪʃn/ *n* [U,C]

0‒ **infect** /ɪn'fekt/ *v* [T] ~ (**with**) **1** make a disease or an illness spread to another person, animal or plant **2** make sb share a particular feeling ▶ **infection** /ɪn'fekʃn/ *n* **1** [U] act or process of causing or getting a disease: *danger of* ~*ion* **2** [C] illness caused by bacteria or a virus: *an ear* ~ ▶ **infectious** /ɪn'fekʃəs/ *adj* **1** (of a disease) caused by bacteria, etc that are passed from one person to another: (*fig*) ~*ious laughter* **2** (of a person or an animal) having a disease that can be spread to others

infer /ɪn'fɜː(r)/ *v* (**-rr-**) [T] ~ (**from**) reach an opinion from facts: *What can be* ~*red from the election results?* ▶ **inference** /'ɪnfərəns/ *n* [C,U]

inferior /ɪn'fɪəriə(r)/ *adj* ~ (**to**) not as good as sb/sth else ● **inferior** *n* [C] inferior person ▶ **inferiority** /ɪnˌfɪəri'ɒrəti/ *n* [U] ■ **inferi'ority complex** *n* [C] feeling that you are not as good, important, etc as other people

inferno /ɪn'fɜːnəʊ/ *n* [C] (pl **~s**) large destructive fire

infertile /ɪn'fɜːtaɪl/ *adj* **1** (of people, animals and plants) not able to have babies or produce young **2** (of land) not able to produce good crops: ~ *land*

infest /ɪn'fest/ *v* [T] ~ (**with**) (of rats, insects, etc) live in large numbers in a particular place: *shark~ed waters*

infidelity /ˌɪnfɪ'deləti/ *n* [C,U] (pl **-ies**) (*fml*) (act of) being unfaithful to your wife, husband or partner by having sex with someone else

infighting /'ɪnfaɪtɪŋ/ *n* [U] fierce competition between colleagues or rivals in an organization

infiltrate /'ɪnfɪltreɪt/ *v* [T] enter a place or an organization secretly to get information, etc ▶ **infiltration** /ˌɪnfɪl'treɪʃn/ *n* [U] ▶ **infiltrator** *n* [C]

infinite /'ɪnfɪnət/ *adj* without limits; endless ▶ **infinitely** *adv*

infinitive /ɪn'fɪnətɪv/ *n* [C] (*gram*) basic form of a verb, without inflections, etc (in English used with or without *to*, eg *'let him go'*, *'allow him to go'*)

infinity /ɪn'fɪnəti/ *n* [U] endless distance, space or quantity

infirm /ɪn'fɜːm/ *adj* weak, esp from old age or illness ▶ **infirmity** *n* [U,C] (pl **-ies**)

infirmary /ɪn'fɜːməri/ *n* [C] (pl **-ies**) hospital

inflame /ɪn'fleɪm/ *v* [T] make sb/sth very angry or overexcited ▶ **inflamed** *adj* (of a part of the body) red, hot and sore

inflammable /ɪn'flæməbl/ *adj* easily set on fire; that can burn easily

inflammation /ˌɪnflə'meɪʃn/ *n* [C,U] condition in which a part of the body is red, swollen and sore

inflammatory /ɪn'flæmətri/ *adj* likely to make people angry or overexcited: ~ *remarks*

inflate /ɪn'fleɪt/ *v* **1** [I,T] fill sth or become filled with gas or air **2** [T]

make sth appear to be more important than it really is **3** [I,T] (cause sth to) increase in price ▶ **inflation** /ɪnˈfleɪʃn/ n [U]
1 general rise in prices in a particular country, resulting in a fall in the value of money; rate at which this happens **2** process of filling sth with air or gas ▶ **inflationary** /ɪnˈfleɪʃənri/ adj of or causing inflation (1)

inflection (also **inflexion**) /ɪnˈflekʃn/ n [C,U] **1** (gram) change in the form of a word to show a past tense, plural, etc **2** rise and fall of the voice in speaking

inflexible 1 refusing to change or be influenced **2** (of a material) impossible to bend or turn ▶ **inflexibility** /ˌɪnˌfleksəˈbɪləti/ n [U] ▶ **inflexibly** adv

inflict /ɪnˈflɪkt/ v [T] ~ **(on)** make sb/ sth suffer sth unpleasant: *a defeat on the enemy* ▶ **infliction** /ɪnˈflɪkʃn/ n [U]

in-flight adj provided or happening during a journey on a plane: *an ~ magazine/movie*

0▬ **influence** /ˈɪnfluəns/ n **1** effect that sb/sth has on the way sb thinks or behaves or on the way sth develops **2** [C] power to produce an effect on sb/sth **3** [C] somebody or something that affects the way people behave or think: *She's a bad ~ on me.* [IDM] **under the influence** drunk ● **influence** v [T] have an effect on sb/sth

influential /ˌɪnfluˈenʃl/ adj having a lot of influence on sb/sth

influenza /ˌɪnfluˈenzə/ n [U] = FLU

influx /ˈɪnflʌks/ n [C] arrival, esp in large numbers or quantities

0▬ **inform** /ɪnˈfɔːm/ v **1** tell sb about sth, esp in an official way **2** ~ **yourself (of/about)** find out information about sth [PV] **inform on sb** give information about sb's illegal activities to the police ▶ **informant** /ɪnˈfɔːmənt/ n [C] person who gives secret information about sb/sth to the police or a newspaper ▶ **informed** adj having or showing knowledge ● **informer** n [C] criminal who gives information to the police about other criminals

0▬ **informal** /ɪnˈfɔːml/ adj **1** not formal or serious: ~ *clothes* (= those worn when you are relaxing) **2** (of words) used when you can be friendly and relaxed ▶ **informality** /ˌɪnfɔːˈmæləti/ n [U] ▶ **informally** adv

0▬ **information** /ˌɪnfəˈmeɪʃn/ n [U] ~ **(on/about)** facts or details about sb/sth ▶ **informative** /ɪnˈfɔːmətɪv/ adj giving a lot of information

infrared /ˌɪnfrəˈred/ adj (physics) of the invisible, heat-giving rays below red in the spectrum

infrastructure /ˈɪnfrəstrʌktʃə(r)/ n [C,U] basic systems and services necessary for a country or an organization, eg transport, power supplies, etc

infrequent /ɪnˈfriːkwənt/ adj not happening often; rare ▶ **infrequency** /-kwənsi/ n [U] ▶ **infrequently** adv

infringe /ɪnˈfrɪndʒ/ v **1** [T] break a law or a rule **2** [I,T] ~ **(on)** limit sb's legal rights: ~ *on the rights of other people* ▶ **infringement** n [U,C]

infuriate /ɪnˈfjʊərieɪt/ v [T] make sb very angry

infuse /ɪnˈfjuːz/ v **1** [T] (fml) fill sb with a quality: ~ *the workers with energy* ○ ~ *energy into the workers* **2** [I,T] (of tea or herbs) soak in hot water to make a drink ▶ **infusion** /ɪnˈfjuːʒn/ n [C,U] (liquid made by) soaking herbs, etc in hot water

ingenious /ɪnˈdʒiːniəs/ adj **1** (of an object, plan, idea, etc) original and well designed **2** (of a person) having a lot of clever new ideas ▶ **ingeniously** adv ▶ **ingenuity** /ˌɪndʒəˈnjuːəti/ n [U]

ingot /ˈɪŋɡət/ n [C] (usu brick-shaped) piece of metal, esp gold or silver

ingrained /ɪnˈɡreɪnd/ adj (of habits, etc) deeply fixed

ingratiate /ɪnˈɡreɪʃieɪt/ v [T] (fml, disapprov) ~ **yourself (with)** try to make sb like you, esp sb who will be useful to you ▶ **ingratiating** adj

ingratitude /ɪnˈɡrætɪtjuːd/ n [U] not feeling or showing that you are grateful for sth

ingredient /ɪnˈɡriːdiənt/ n [C] one of the parts of a mixture: *the ~s of a cake*

inhabit /ɪnˈhæbɪt/ v [T] live in a particular place ▶ **inhabitant** /ɪnˈhæbɪtənt/ n [C] person living in a place

inhale /ɪnˈheɪl/ v [I,T] breathe in ▶ **inhaler** n [C] device that produces a vapour to make breathing easier

inherent /ɪnˈhɪərənt/ adj ~ **(in)** that is a basic or permanent part of sb/ sth: ~ *weaknesses in a design*

inherit /ɪnˈherɪt/ v [T] **1** receive property, money, etc from sb when they die **2** receive qualities, etc from your parents, grandparents, etc ▶ **inheritance** n [C,U sing, U] money, etc that you inherit; fact of inheriting sth ▶ **inheritor** n [C] person who inherits sth

inhibit /ɪnˈhɪbɪt/ v [T] **1** prevent sth from happening **2** ~ **(from)** make sb nervous or embarrassed so that they are unable to do sth ▶ **inhibited** adj unable to relax and express your feelings naturally ▶ **inhibition**

/ˌɪnhɪˈbɪʃn/ n [C, U] feeling of being unable to behave naturally

inhospitable /ˌɪnhɒˈspɪtəbl/ adj not hospitable: an ~ climate

inhuman /ɪnˈhjuːmən/ adj without kindness, pity etc ► **inhumanity** /ˌɪnhjuːˈmænəti/ n [U]

inhumane /ˌɪnhjuːˈmeɪn/ adj not caring about the suffering of other people; cruel ► **inhumanely** adv

inimitable /ɪˈnɪmɪtəbl/ adj too good or individual for anyone else to copy

0━ **initial** /ɪˈnɪʃl/ adj happening at the beginning; first ● initial n [C, usu pl] first letter of a person's name ● initial v (-ll- US -l-) [I, T] sign sth with your initials ► **initially** /ɪˈnɪʃəli/ adv at the beginning

initiate /ɪˈnɪʃieɪt/ v [T] 1 (fml) make sth begin 2 ~ (into) introduce sb into a club, group, etc ● initiate /ɪˈnɪʃiət/ n [C] person who has just been initiated into a group ► **initiation** /ɪˌnɪʃiˈeɪʃn/ n [U]

0━ **initiative** /ɪˈnɪʃətɪv/ n 1 [C] action taken to solve a difficulty 2 [U] ability to act without help: do sth on your own ~ 3 (the initiative) (sing) power or opportunity to take action: It's up to you to take the ~ and make a plan. [IDM] **take the initiative** take the first step in a task

inject /ɪnˈdʒekt/ v [T] 1 put sth into sb with a syringe: ~ a drug into sb ◇ ~ sb with a drug 2 ~ (into) add a particular quality to sth: ~ new life into the team ► **injection** /ɪnˈdʒekʃn/ n [C, U]

injunction /ɪnˈdʒʌŋkʃn/ n [C] (fml) ~ (against) official order from a court of law

0━ **injure** /ˈɪndʒə(r)/ v [T] hurt or damage sb/sth physically ► **injured** adj physically hurt; offended ► the injured n [pl] injured people

0━ **injury** /ˈɪndʒəri/ n (pl -ies) ~ (to) 1 [C, U] harm done to a person's or an animal's body, eg in an accident 2 [U] damage to a person's feelings

injustice /ɪnˈdʒʌstɪs/ n 1 [U] fact of a situation being unfair 2 [C] unfair act [IDM] **do yourself/sb an injustice** judge yourself/sb unfairly

0━ **ink** /ɪŋk/ n [U, C] coloured liquid for writing, printing, etc ► **inky** adj black

inkling /ˈɪŋklɪŋ/ n [usu sing] vague idea

inland /ˈɪnlənd/ adj in or near the middle of a country: ~ lakes ● inland /ˌɪnˈlænd/ adv towards the middle of a country; away from the coast ■ **the Inland Revenue** n [sing] (in Britain) government department that collects taxes

in-laws /ˈɪn lɔːz/ n [pl] (infml) relatives by marriage

inlet /ˈɪnlet/ n [C] strip of water reaching into the land

inmate /ˈɪnmeɪt/ n [C] person living in a prison, mental hospital, etc

inmost /ˈɪnməʊst/ adj = INNERMOST (INNER)

inn /ɪn/ n [C] (GB, old-fash) small old hotel or pub, usu in the country ■ **innkeeper** /ˈɪnkiːpə(r)/ n [C] (old-fash) person who manages an inn

innards /ˈɪnədz/ n [pl] 1 organs inside the body, esp the stomach 2 parts inside a machine

innate /ɪˈneɪt/ adj (of a quality, etc) existing in a person from birth ► **innately** adv

0━ **inner** /ˈɪnə(r)/ adj 1 inside; near to the middle 2 (of feelings) private and secret ► **innermost** /ˈɪnəməʊst/ adj 1 most private and secret: ~ thoughts 2 furthest inside

innings /ˈɪnɪŋz/ n [C] (pl innings) (in cricket) time during which a team or player is batting [IDM] **sb had a good innings** (GB, infml) used about sb who has died to say that they had a long happy life ► **inning** n [C] (in baseball) part of a game in which both teams bat

0━ **innocent** /ˈɪnəsnt/ adj 1 not guilty 2 harmless: ~ fun 3 knowing nothing of evil ► **innocence** /ˈɪnəsns/ n [U] ► **innocently** adv

innocuous /ɪˈnɒkjuəs/ adj harmless: an ~ remark

innovate /ˈɪnəveɪt/ v [I] introduce new things, ideas or ways of doing sth ► **innovation** /ˌɪnəˈveɪʃn/ n 1 [U] introduction of new things, ideas, etc 2 [C] new idea, method, etc ► **innovative** /ˈɪnəveɪtɪv/, GB also /ˈɪnəvətɪv/ (also innovatory /ˌɪnəˈveɪtəri/) adj ► **innovator** n [C]

innuendo /ˌɪnjuˈendəʊ/ n [C, U] (pl ~es or ~s) indirect remark about sb/ sth, usu suggesting sth bad or rude

innumerable /ɪˈnjuːmərəbl/ adj too many to count

inoculate /ɪˈnɒkjuleɪt/ v [T] inject sb with a vaccine in order to prevent a disease: ~ sb against cholera ► **inoculation** /ɪˌnɒkjuˈleɪʃn/ n [C, U]

inoffensive /ˌɪnəˈfensɪv/ adj not likely to offend or upset anyone

inopportune /ɪnˈɒpətjuːn/ adj (fml) not suitable or convenient: an ~ remark/time ► **inopportunely** adv

inordinate /ɪnˈɔːdɪnət/ adj (fml) far more than is usual or expected ► **inordinately** adv

inorganic /ˌɪnɔːˈɡænɪk/ adj not made of living substances: Rocks and minerals are ~.

0━ **input** /ˈɪnpʊt/ n [C, U] time, knowledge, etc that you put into work, etc to make it succeed; act of putting sth in 2 [C] (computing) act of putting information into a computer; the information that you put into it: data ● input v (-tt- pt, pp

input or **~ted**) [T] put information into a computer

inquest /'ɪnkwest/ n [C] official investigation to find out the cause of sb's death

inquire, inquiry = ENQUIRE, ENQUIRY

inquisition /ˌɪnkwɪ'zɪʃn/ n [C] (fml) severe and detailed investigation

inquisitive /ɪn'kwɪzətɪv/ adj (too) fond of asking questions about other people's affairs ▶ **inquisitively** adv

inroad /'ɪnrəʊd/ n [C] something that is achieved, esp by reducing the power or success of sth else [IDM] **make inroads into/on sth** gradually use, eat, etc more and more of sth: make ~ into your savings

insane /ɪn'seɪn/ adj mad ▶ **insanely** adv ▶ **insanity** /ɪn'sænəti/ n [U]

insatiable /ɪn'seɪʃəbl/ adj impossible to satisfy

inscribe /ɪn'skraɪb/ v [T] write or cut words onto sth: ~ words on a tombstone ▶ **inscription** /ɪn'skrɪpʃn/ n [C] words written in the front of a book or cut in stone, etc

inscrutable /ɪn'skruːtəbl/ adj impossible to understand; mysterious

0→ **insect** /'ɪnsekt/ n [C] any small creature with six legs, eg an ant or a fly ▶ **insecticide** /ɪn'sektɪsaɪd/ n [C,U] chemical used for killing insects

insecure /ˌɪnsɪ'kjʊə(r)/ adj **1** lacking confidence **2** not safe ▶ **insecurely** adv ▶ **insecurity** n [U]

insensible /ɪn'sensəbl/ adj (fml) **1** ~ (to) not able to feel sth: ~ to pain **2** ~ (of) unaware of sth **3** unconscious ▶ **insensibility** /ɪnˌsensə'bɪləti/ n [U]

insensitive /ɪn'sensətɪv/ adj not realizing or caring how people feel ▶ **insensitively** adv ▶ **insensitivity** /ɪnˌsensə'tɪvəti/ n [U]

inseparable /ɪn'seprəbl/ adj impossible to separate: ~ friends

0→ **insert** /ɪn'sɜːt/ v [T] put or fit sth into sth: ~ a key in a lock ● **insert** /'ɪnsɜːt/ n [C] something put inside sth else, eg an advertisement put between the pages of a newspaper ▶ **insertion** /ɪn'sɜːʃn/ n [C,U]

inset /'ɪnset/ n [C] small picture, map, etc within a larger one

inshore /ˌɪn'ʃɔː(r)/ adj /ˌɪn'ʃɔː(r)/ adv (of sth at sea) close to the land

0→ **inside¹** /ɪn'saɪd/ n **1** [C, usu sing] part or surface nearest to the centre **2** [sing] (also **insides** [pl]) (infml) person's stomach and bowels [IDM] **inside out** with the part that is usu inside facing out **2** thoroughly: know sth ~ out on **the inside** in an organization so that you can find

out secret information ● **inside** adj **1** on or in the inside of sth **2** known or done by sb who is in an organization: The robbery was an ~ job. ▶ **insider** n [C] member of an organization who can obtain special information ▶ **insider dealing** (also **insider trading**) n [U] crime of buying or selling shares in a company with the help of information known only by people who work for the business

0→ **inside²** /ɪn'saɪd/ (esp US **inside of**) prep **1** on or to the inner side of sth/sb: come ~ the house **2** in less than the amount of time mentioned: ~ a year ● **inside** adv **1** on or to the inside: go ~ (= into the house) **2** (infml) in prison

insidious /ɪn'sɪdiəs/ adj doing harm secretly ▶ **insidiously** adv

insight /'ɪnsaɪt/ n [C,U] (instance of) understanding: ~s into his character

insignia /ɪn'sɪgniə/ n [U, with sing or pl verb] symbol, badge or sign that shows sb's rank or membership of a group

insignificant /ˌɪnsɪg'nɪfɪkənt/ adj having little importance or value ▶ **insignificance** /-kəns/ n [U] ▶ **insignificantly** adv

insincere /ˌɪnsɪn'sɪə(r)/ adj saying or doing sth that you do not really mean or believe ▶ **insincerely** adv ▶ **insincerity** /ˌɪnsɪn'serəti/ n [U]

insinuate /ɪn'sɪnjueɪt/ v [T] **1** suggest indirectly that sth unpleasant is true **2** ~ yourself into (fml) gain sb's respect, affection, etc so that you can use the situation to your own advantage ▶ **insinuation** /ɪnˌsɪnju'eɪʃn/ n [C,U]

insipid /ɪn'sɪpɪd/ adj (disapprov) **1** having almost no taste or flavour **2** not interesting or exciting ▶ **insipidly** adv

0→ **insist** /ɪn'sɪst/ v [I,T] ~ (on) **1** demand sth strongly: ~ on going with sb ◇ ~ that she (should) stay **2** declare sth firmly: He ~s that he is innocent. ▶ **insistent** adj strongly insisting ▶ **insistence** n [U]

insofar as /ˌɪnsə'fɑːr əz/ = IN SO FAR AS (FAR¹)

insolent /'ɪnsələnt/ adj ~ (to) very rude ▶ **insolence** /-əns/ n [U]

insoluble /ɪn'sɒljəbl/ adj **1** (of problems, etc) impossible to solve **2** (of substances) impossible to dissolve

insolvent /ɪn'sɒlvənt/ adj not having enough money to pay what you owe ▶ **insolvency** /-ənsi/ n [U,C] (pl **-ies**)

insomnia /ɪn'sɒmniə/ n [U] inability to sleep ▶ **insomniac** /ɪn'sɒmniæk/ n [C] person who cannot go to sleep easily

inspect /ɪn'spekt/ v [T] examine sth/sb carefully ▶ **inspection**

/ɪnˈspekʃn/ n [C, U] ▶ **inspector** n [C] **1** official who inspects sth, eg schools **2** (GB) police officer above a sergeant in rank

inspire /ɪnˈspaɪə(r)/ v [T] **1** fill sb with the ability or desire to do sth **2** fill sb with feelings: ~ sb with confidence ◇ ~ confidence in sb ▶ **inspiration** /ˌɪnspəˈreɪʃn/ n [U] influence producing creative ability; state of being inspired **2** [C, usu sing] person or thing that is the reason why sb creates or does sth **3** [C, U] (infml) sudden good idea ▶ **inspired** adj filled with or showing inspiration (1) ▶ **inspiring** adj

instability /ˌɪnstəˈbɪləti/ n [U] lack of stability

0-w **install** /ɪnˈstɔːl/ v [T] **1** fix machines, furniture, etc into position **2** (fml) put sb in a new position of authority **3** (fml) make sb/yourself comfortable in a particular place ▶ **installation** /ˌɪnstəˈleɪʃn/ n [U, C]

instalment (US -ll-) /ɪnˈstɔːlmənt/ n [C] **1** one of a number of payments spread over a period of time until sth has been paid for **2** one part of a story that appears over a period of time

0-w **instance** /ˈɪnstəns/ n [C] particular example or case of sth [IDM] **for instance** for example

instant /ˈɪnstənt/ n [C, usu sing] **1** moment: I'll be there in an ~. **2** particular point in time: Come here this ~ (= immediately). ● **instant** adj **1** happening immediately: an ~ success **2** (of food) that can be made very quickly and easily: ~ coffee ▶ **instantly** adv immediately

instantaneous /ˌɪnstənˈteɪniəs/ adj happening or done immediately ▶ **instantaneously** adv

0-w **instead** /ɪnˈsted/ adv in the place of sb/sth: Bill was ill so I went ~. ■ **instead of** prep in the place of sb/sth: drink tea ~ of coffee

instep /ˈɪnstep/ n [C] top part of the foot

instigate /ˈɪnstɪɡeɪt/ v [T] make sth start or happen: ~ a strike/riot ▶ **instigation** /ˌɪnstɪˈɡeɪʃn/ n [U] ▶ **instigator** n [C]

instil (US **instill**) /ɪnˈstɪl/ v (-ll-) [T] ~ (in/into) put ideas, etc into sb's mind

instinct /ˈɪnstɪŋkt/ n [C, U] natural tendency to behave in a certain way ▶ **instinctive** /ɪnˈstɪŋktɪv/ adj based on instinct: ~ive fear of fire ▶ **instinctively** adv

0-w **institute** /ˈɪnstɪtjuːt/ n [C] (building used by an) organization with a particular purpose ● **institute** v [T] (fml) introduce a system, policy, etc or start a process

0-w **institution** /ˌɪnstɪˈtjuːʃn/ n [C] (building used by an) organization

with a social purpose, eg a school or hospital **2** [C] established custom or practice: the ~ of marriage **3** [U] act of introducing a system, law, etc ▶ **institutional** /-ʃənl/ adj ▶ **institutionalize** (also -ise) /-ʃənəlaɪz/ v [T] **1** send sb who is not capable of living independently to live in an institution **2** make sth into an institution (2)

instruct /ɪnˈstrʌkt/ v [T] (fml) **1** tell sb to do sth: ~ the child not to go out **2** teach sb sth, esp a practical skill **3** (law) employ a lawyer to represent you in court ▶ **instructive** adj giving a lot of useful information ▶ **instructor** n [C] teacher or trainer

0-w **instruction** /ɪnˈstrʌkʃn/ n **1** (instructions) [pl] information on how to do sth: Follow the ~s on packet. **2** [C, usu pl] order **3** [U] act of teaching sth to sb

0-w **instrument** /ˈɪnstrəmənt/ n [C] **1** tool or device used for a particular task, esp delicate or scientific work: surgical ~s **2** = MUSICAL INSTRUMENT (MUSIC) ▶ **instrumental** /ˌɪnstrəˈmentl/ adj **1** ~ in important in making sth happen: You were ~al in her promotion. **2** made by or for musical instruments ▶ **instrumentalist** /ˌɪnstrəˈmentəlɪst/ n [C] person who plays a musical instrument

insubordinate /ˌɪnsəˈbɔːdɪnət/ adj disobedient ▶ **insubordination** /ˌɪnsəˌbɔːdɪˈneɪʃn/ n [U, C]

insufferable /ɪnˈsʌfrəbl/ adj unbearable: ~ behaviour

insufficient /ˌɪnsəˈfɪʃnt/ adj not enough ▶ **insufficiency** /-ʃənsi/ n [U] ▶ **insufficiently** adv

insular /ˈɪnsjələ(r)/ adj (disapprov) only interested in your own country, ideas, etc and not in those from outside ▶ **insularity** /-ˈlærəti/ n [U]

insulate /ˈɪnsjuleɪt/ v [T] **1** cover sth to prevent heat, electricity, etc from escaping: ~d wires **2** (written) protect sb/sth from unpleasant experiences ▶ **insulation** /ˌɪnsjuˈleɪʃn/ n [U] (materials used in) insulating sth

0-w **insult** /ɪnˈsʌlt/ v [T] be rude to sb ● **insult** /ˈɪnsʌlt/ n [C] rude remark or action ▶ **insulting** adj

0-w **insurance** /ɪnˈʃɔːrəns/ n [U, C] **1** agreement by a company or the state to pay money because of loss, illness, death, etc in return for regular payments **2** [U] money paid by or to an insurance company **3** [U, C] protection against loss, failure, etc

insure /ɪnˈʃɔː(r)/ v [T] **1** protect sb/sth by insurance: ~ a car against fire/theft **2** (esp US) = ENSURE

A B C D E F G H **I** J K L M N O P Q R S T U V W X Y Z

insurgent /ɪnˈsɜːdʒənt/ adj rebellious ► **insurgent** n (usu pl) (fml) rebel soldier

insurmountable /ˌɪnsəˈmaʊntəbl/ adj (fml) (of problems or difficulties) impossible to solve or overcome

insurrection /ˌɪnsəˈrekʃn/ n [C, U] rebellion

intact /ɪnˈtækt/ adj undamaged; complete

intake /ˈɪnteɪk/ n **1** [U, C] amount of food, drink, etc that you take into your body **2** [C] number of people taken in: last year's ~ of students **3** [C] place where liquid, air, etc enters a machine **4** [C] act of taking sth in, esp breath

intangible /ɪnˈtændʒəbl/ adj **1** that exists but is difficult to describe or understand: an ~ air of sadness **2** (business) that has no physical existence but is still valuable to a company: ~ assets/property

integer /ˈɪntɪdʒə(r)/ n [C] (maths) whole number, eg 1, 3, 11

integral /ˈɪntɪɡrəl/ adj necessary to make sth complete: an ~ part of the plan ► **integrally** adv

integrate /ˈɪntɪɡreɪt/ v [T] ~ (into/with) combine with so that it becomes fully a part of sth else **2** [I, T] (of people) mix or be together as one group ► **integration** /ˌɪntɪˈɡreɪʃn/ n [U]

integrity /ɪnˈteɡrəti/ n [U] **1** honesty and goodness **2** wholeness; unity

intellect /ˈɪntəlekt/ n [U] power of the mind to reason ► **intellectual** /ˌɪntəˈlektʃuəl/ adj **1** of the intellect **2** of or interested in ideas, the arts, etc rather than practical matters ► **intellectual** n [C] intellectual person ► **intellectually** adv

0━ **intelligence** /ɪnˈtelɪdʒəns/ n [U] **1** ability to learn, understand and think **2** secret information about a country's enemies; people who collect this information ► **intelligent** /ɪnˈtelɪdʒənt/ adj clever ► **intelligently** adv

intelligible /ɪnˈtelɪdʒəbl/ adj that can be understood ► **intelligibility** /-ˈbɪləti/ n [U] ► **intelligibly** adv

0━ **intend** /ɪnˈtend/ v [T] have a plan, result or purpose in your mind when you do sth; mean: I ~ to leave soon.

intense /ɪnˈtens/ adj **1** extreme; very strong: ~ heat/anger **2** (of a person) serious and very emotional ► **intensely** adv ► **intensify** /-sɪfaɪ/ (pt, pp **-ied**) [I, T] become or make sth greater or stronger ► **intensification** /ɪnˌtensɪfɪˈkeɪʃn/ n [U] ► **intensity** n [U] state of being intense; strength of feeling, etc

intensive /ɪnˈtensɪv/ adj concentrating effort, work, etc on

one task; very thorough: an ~ search ► **intensively** adv

intent /ɪnˈtent/ adj **1** showing strong interest and attention: an ~ look/ gaze **2** ~ on determined to do sth: ~ on becoming manager ● **intent** n [C] (law) what you intend to do: shoot with ~ to kill [IDM] to all intents and purposes in the important details; almost completely ► **intently** adv

0━ **intention** /ɪnˈtenʃn/ n [C, U] aim; purpose ► **intentional** /-ʃənl/ adj done on purpose ► **intentionally** adv

inter /ɪnˈtɜː(r)/ v (**-rr-**) [T] (fml) bury a dead person

interact /ˌɪntərˈækt/ v [I] ~ **(with) 1** have an effect on each other **2** (of people) communicate and work together ► **interaction** /-ˈækʃn/ n [U, C] ► **interactive** /-ˈæktɪv/ adj **1** involving people working together and influencing each other **2** (computing) allowing a continuous exchange of information between a computer and a user: an ~ive whiteboard (= large board in a classroom that allows information to be passed in both directions between a computer and the teacher or student who writes on it)

intercept /ˌɪntəˈsept/ v [T] stop sb/ sth that is moving between two places ► **interception** /-ˈsepʃn/ n [U]

interchange /ˌɪntəˈtʃeɪndʒ/ v [I, T] (cause two people or things to) change places with each other ● **interchange** n **1** [C, U] act of sharing or exchanging sth, esp ideas or information **2** [C] place where a main road joins a motorway ► **interchangeable** adj

intercity /ˌɪntəˈsɪti/ adj (of transport) travelling between cities

intercom /ˈɪntəkɒm/ n [C] system of communication using a microphone and loudspeaker, used eg in a building

intercontinental /ˌɪntəˌkɒntɪˈnentl/ adj between continents: ~ flights

intercourse /ˈɪntəkɔːs/ n [U] (fml) **1** = SEXUAL INTERCOURSE (SEXUAL) **2** (old-fash) communication between people, nations, etc

0━ **interest** /ˈɪntrəst/ n **1** [sing, U] ~ **(in)** desire to learn or know about sb/sth: lose ~ o take an ~ in art **2** [U] quality that attracts attention or curiosity: an idea of ~ to us **3** [C] activity or subject which you enjoy doing or learning about: Her great ~ is football. **4** [U] ~ **(on)** money paid for the use of money: borrow money at a high rate of ~ **5** [C, usu pl] advantage for sb/sth: It is in your ~s (= It is to your advantage) to work hard. **6** [C, usu pl] share in a business **7** [C, usu pl] group of people in the same business, etc [IDM] in the

interest(s) of sth in order to help or achieve sth ● **interest** v [T] attract your attention and make you feel interested ▶ **interested** adj 1 ~ (in) showing interest (1) in sth: be ~ed in history 2 personally involved ▶ **interesting** adj holding your attention

interface /'ɪntəfeɪs/ n [C] (computing) 1 way a computer program presents information to a user, esp the layout of the screen and the menus: the user~ 2 electrical circuit, connection or program that joins one device or system to another

interfere /ˌɪntə'fɪə(r)/ v [I] ~ (in) get involved in a situation that does not concern you, in a way that annoys other people [PV] **interfere with sb** (GB) touch a child in a sexual way **interfere with sth** 1 prevent sth from succeeding or happening as planned 2 touch, use or change sth so that it is damaged or no longer works correctly ▶ **interference** n [U] 1 act of interfering 2 interruption of a radio signal by another signal, causing unwanted extra noise

interim /'ɪntərɪm/ adj intended to last for only a short time: ~ arrangements ● **interim** n [IDM] **in the interim** in the time between two events

0— **interior** /ɪn'tɪəriə(r)/ n 1 [C] inside part of sth 2 (the interior) [sing] inland part of a country or continent 3 (the Interior) [sing] a country's own affairs rather than those involving other countries: the Minister of the I~ ● **interior** adj connected with the inside part of sth

interjection /ˌɪntə'dʒekʃn/ n [C] (gram) word or phrase, eg Ow! spoken suddenly to express an emotion

interlock /ˌɪntə'lɒk/ v [I, T] lock or join together

interlude /'ɪntəluːd/ n [C] short period of time between two parts of a play, etc or two events

intermarry /ˌɪntə'mæri/ v (pt, pp -ied) [I] marry sb of a different race or from a different country or religious group ▶ **intermarriage** /ˌɪntə'mærɪdʒ/ n [U]

intermediary /ˌɪntə'miːdiəri/ n [C] (-ies) person who passes information between two groups, esp to get agreement

intermediate /ˌɪntə'miːdiət/ adj 1 between two points or stages 2 between elementary and advanced: an ~ course

interminable /ɪn'tɜːmɪnəbl/ adj (disapprov) lasting too long and therefore boring ▶ **interminably** adv

intermission /ˌɪntə'mɪʃn/ n [C, U] (esp US) interval in a play, etc; pause

intermittent /ˌɪntə'mɪtənt/ adj stopping and starting often over a period of time: ~ rain ▶ **intermittently** adv

intern[1] /ɪn'tɜːn/ v [T] put sb in prison during a war or for political reasons ▶ **internment** n [U]

intern[2] (also **interne**) /'ɪntɜːn/ n [C] (US) 1 junior doctor at a hospital 2 student or graduate getting practical experience of a job ▶ **internship** n [C]

0— **internal** /ɪn'tɜːnl/ adj 1 of or on the inside: ~ injuries (= inside the body) 2 not foreign; domestic: ~ trade ▶ **internally** adv

0— **international** /ˌɪntə'næʃnəl/ adj of or existing between two or more countries ● **international** n [C] 1 sports match with teams from two countries 2 player who takes part in a match against another country ▶ **internationally** adv

0— **Internet** /'ɪntənet/ n [sing] (usu the Internet) (also infml the Net) international computer network connecting other networks from companies, universities, etc

interplay /'ɪntəpleɪ/ n [U] way in which two or more things affect each other

interpose /ˌɪntə'pəʊz/ v (fml) 1 [I] add a question or remark into a conversation 2 [T] place sth between two people or things

0— **interpret** /ɪn'tɜːprɪt/ v 1 [T] ~ as explain the meaning of sth 2 [T] ~ as understand sth in a particular way: ~ his silence as an expression of guilt 3 [I] translate one language into another as you hear it ▶ **interpretation** /ɪnˌtɜːprɪ'teɪʃn/ n [U, C] explanation or understanding of sth ▶ **interpreter** n [C] person whose job is to translate what sb is saying into another language

interrogate /ɪn'terəgeɪt/ v [T] question sb closely and for a long time ▶ **interrogation** /ɪnˌterə'geɪʃn/ n [C, U] ▶ **interrogator** n [C]

interrogative /ˌɪntə'rɒgətɪv/ adj (gram) used in questions: ~ pronouns (= eg who, why) ● **interrogative** n [C] question word

0— **interrupt** /ˌɪntə'rʌpt/ v 1 [I, T] say or do sth that stops sb speaking 2 [T] break the continuity of sth: ~ a journey ▶ **interruption** /-'rʌpʃn/ n [C, U]

intersect /ˌɪntə'sekt/ v 1 [I, T] (of lines, roads, etc) meet or cross each other 2 [T] (usu passive) divide an area by crossing it ▶ **intersection** /ˌɪntə'sekʃn/ n 1 [C] place where roads, lines, etc meet or cross each other 2 [U] act of intersecting sth

intersperse /ˌɪntəˈspɜːs/ v [T] (written) put sth between or among other things

0— **interval** /ˈɪntəvl/ n [C] **1** time between two events **2** (GB) short period of time between the parts of a play, etc **3** short period during which sth different happens: It'll be cloudy with sunny ~s.

intervene /ˌɪntəˈviːn/ v [I] (fml) **1** ~ (in) become involved in a situation to improve or help it **2** happen in a way that delays sth **3** (fml) exist between two events or places ▶ **intervening** adj coming between: in the intervening years ▶ **intervention** /-ˈvenʃn/ n [U,C]

0— **interview** /ˈɪntəvjuː/ n [C] ~ (with) meeting at which sb, eg sb applying for a job, is asked questions ● **interview** v [T] ask sb questions in an interview ▶ **interviewer** n [C] person who interviews sb

intestate /ɪnˈtesteɪt/ adj (law) not having made a will: die ~

intestine /ɪnˈtestɪn/ n [C, usu pl] long tube from the stomach to the anus ▶ **intestinal** adj

intimacy /ˈɪntɪməsi/ n **1** [U] state of having a close personal relationship with sb **2** [C, usu pl] thing a person says or does to sb they know very well

intimate¹ /ˈɪntɪmət/ adj **1** having a very close relationship: They are ~ friends. **2** private and personal: ~ details of her life **3** (of knowledge) very detailed and thorough ▶ **intimately** adv

intimate² /ˈɪntɪmeɪt/ v [T] (fml) let sb know what you mean in an indirect way ▶ **intimation** /ˌɪntɪˈmeɪʃn/ n [C,U]

intimidate /ɪnˈtɪmɪdeɪt/ v [T] frighten or threaten sb ▶ **intimidation** /ɪnˌtɪmɪˈdeɪʃn/ n [U]

0— **into** /ˈɪntə; before vowels ˈɪntu:/ prep **1** to a position in or inside sth: Come ~ the house. **2** to a point at which you hit sb/sth: A lorry drove ~ a line of cars. **3** to a point during a period of time: work long ~ the night **4** used to show a change in state: The fruit can be made ~ jam. **5** used to show the result of an action: frighten sb ~ submission **6** used for expressing division in mathematics: 5 ~ 25 is 5. **IDM be into sth** (infml) be very interested in sth

intolerable /ɪnˈtɒlərəbl/ adj too bad to be endured ▶ **intolerably** adv

intolerant /ɪnˈtɒlərənt/ adj not willing to accept ideas, etc that are different from your own ▶ **intolerance** /-əns/ n [U]

intonation /ˌɪntəˈneɪʃn/ n [C,U] rise and fall of the voice in speaking

intoxicated /ɪnˈtɒksɪkeɪtɪd/ adj (fml) **1** under the influence of alcohol or drugs **2** very excited by sth ▶ **intoxication** /ɪnˌtɒksɪˈkeɪʃn/ n [U]

intranet /ˈɪntrənet/ n [C] (computing) computer network that is private to a company, organization, etc but is connected to and uses the same software as the Internet

intransitive /ɪnˈtrænsətɪv/ adj (gram) (of a verb) used without an object, eg rise in 'Smoke rises.'

in tray /ˈɪn treɪ/ n [C] container on your desk for holding letters, etc that are waiting to be read or answered

intrepid /ɪnˈtrepɪd/ adj (fml) brave: ~ explorers ▶ **intrepidly** adv

intricate /ˈɪntrɪkət/ adj with many small parts put together in a complicated way ▶ **intricacy** /-kəsi/ n (pl -ies) **1** [pl] complicated parts or details of sth **2** [U] fact of being intricate ▶ **intricately** adv

intrigue /ɪnˈtriːg/ v **1** [T] make sb interested or curious: ~ sb with a story **2** [I] secretly plan with other people to harm sb ● **intrigue** /ˈɪntriːg/ n **1** [U] activity of making secret plans to do sth bad **2** [C] secret plan or relationship ▶ **intriguing** adj very interesting, esp because unusual

intrinsic /ɪnˈtrɪnsɪk; -zɪk/ adj belonging to the real nature of sth/ sb ▶ **intrinsically** /-kli/ adv

0— **introduce** /ˌɪntrəˈdjuːs/ v [T] **1** ~ (to) make sth known to sb else by giving each person's name to the other: I ~d Mark to Emma. **2** be the main speaker in a television or radio show, giving details about the show and the people in it **3** make sth available for use, discussion, etc for the first time: ~ computers into schools

0— **introduction** /ˌɪntrəˈdʌkʃn/ n **1** [U] act of bringing sth into use for the first time **2** [C,U] act of introducing one person to another **3** [C] first part of a book or speech **4** [C] textbook for people beginning to study a subject

introductory /ˌɪntrəˈdʌktəri/ adj written or said at the beginning of sth as an introduction to what follows

introspection /ˌɪntrəˈspekʃn/ n [U] careful examination of your own thoughts, feelings, etc ▶ **introspective** /ˌɪntrəˈspektɪv/ adj

introvert /ˈɪntrəvɜːt/ n [C] quiet person who is more interested in their own thoughts than in spending time with other people ▶ **introverted** adj

intrude /ɪnˈtruːd/ v [I] ~ **on** go or be somewhere where you are not invited or wanted ▶ **intruder** n [C] person who enters a building or an area illegally ▶ **intrusion** /ɪnˈtruːʒn/ n [U,C] ▶ **intrusive** /ɪnˈtruːsɪv/ adj too noticeable, direct, etc in a way that is annoying

intuition /ˌɪntjuˈɪʃn/ n **1** [U] ability to understand sth quickly without conscious thought **2** [C] idea that sth is true although you cannot explain why ▶ **intuitive** /ɪnˈtjuːɪtɪv/ adj ▶ **intuitively** adv

inundate /ˈɪnʌndeɪt/ v [T] **1** give or send sb so many things that they cannot deal with them all: ~d with replies **2** (fml) flood an area of land

invade /ɪnˈveɪd/ v [T] **1** enter a country with armed forces in order to attack or occupy it **2** enter a place in large numbers: Fans ~d the football pitch. ▶ **invader** n [C] ▶ **invasion** /ɪnˈveɪʒn/ n [C,U]

invalid[1] /ˈɪnvəlɪd/ adj **1** not legally or officially acceptable: an ~ passport **2** not based on all the facts and therefore not correct: an ~ argument **3** (computing) of a type that the computer cannot recognize: ~ characters ▶ **invalidate** v [T] prove that sth is wrong ▶ **invalidation** /ɪnˌvælɪˈdeɪʃn/ n [U]

invalid[2] /ˈɪnvəlɪd, -liːd/ n [C] person who is weak or disabled because of illness or injury ● **invalid** v [T] (GB) ~ (out) force sb to leave the armed forces because of illness or injury

invaluable /ɪnˈvæljuəbl/ adj having a value that is too high to be measured

invariable /ɪnˈveəriəbl/ adj never changing ▶ **invariably** adv always

invasion → INVADE

invective /ɪnˈvektɪv/ n [U] (fml) rude language sb uses when they are very angry

0–ᴡ **invent** /ɪnˈvent/ v [T] **1** make or design sth that did not exist before: Who ~ed television? **2** think of sth untrue: ~ an excuse ▶ **invention** /ɪnˈvenʃn/ n **1** [C] something invented **2** [U] act of inventing sth ▶ **inventive** adj having the ability to invent things ▶ **inventor** n [C]

inventory /ˈɪnvəntri/ n [C] (pl -ies) detailed list of all goods or furniture in a building

inverse /ˌɪnˈvɜːs/ adj opposite in amount or position to sth else ● **inverse** /ˈɪnvɜːs/ n (the inverse) [sing] (tech) the direct opposite of sth

invert /ɪnˈvɜːt/ v [T] turn sth upside down or arrange sth in the opposite order ▶ **inversion** /ɪnˈvɜːʃn/ n [U,C] ■ in‚verted 'commas n [pl] (GB) = QUOTATION MARKS (QUOTATION)

0–ᴡ **invest** /ɪnˈvest/ v [I,T] ~ (in) use money to buy business shares, property, etc in order to make more money: ~ (money) in shares **2** [T] ~ in give time, effort, etc to sth you think

is good or useful: ~ your time in learning French **3** [T] ~ **with** (of) give sb power or authority [PV] **invest in sth** (infml) buy sth expensive but useful: ~ in a new car ▶ **investment** n **1** [U] act of investing money in sth **2** [C] money that you invest, or the thing that you invest in ▶ **investor** n [C]

0–ᴡ **investigate** /ɪnˈvestɪgeɪt/ v [I,T] examine the facts about sth in order to discover the truth: ~ a murder ▶ **investigation** /ɪnˌvestɪˈgeɪʃn/ n [C,U] ▶ **investigative** /-gətɪv/ adj of or concerned with investigating ▶ **investigator** n [C]

investiture /ɪnˈvestɪtʃə(r)/ n [C] ceremony at which sb receives an official title or special powers

inveterate /ɪnˈvetərət/ adj (disapprov) firmly fixed in a bad habit: ~ liar/smoker

invigilate /ɪnˈvɪdʒɪleɪt/ v [I,T] (GB) watch over students in an examination ▶ **invigilation** /ɪnˌvɪdʒɪˈleɪʃn/ n [U] ▶ **invigilator** n [C]

invigorate /ɪnˈvɪgəreɪt/ v [T] make sb feel more lively and healthy ▶ **invigorating** adj

invincible /ɪnˈvɪnsəbl/ adj too strong to be defeated

inviolable /ɪnˈvaɪələbl/ adj (fml) that must be respected and not attacked or destroyed: ~ rights

inviolate /ɪnˈvaɪələt/ adj (fml) that has been, or must be, respected and cannot be attacked

invisible /ɪnˈvɪzəbl/ adj ~ **(to)** that cannot be seen ▶ **invisibility** /ɪnˌvɪzəˈbɪləti/ n [U] ▶ **invisibly** adv

0–ᴡ **invite** /ɪnˈvaɪt/ v [T] **1** ~ **(to/for)** ask sb to go somewhere or to do sth: ~ sb to/for dinner **2** make sth, esp sth bad, likely to happen: ~ criticism ▶ **invitation** /ˌɪnvɪˈteɪʃn/ n **1** [C] ~ **(to)** request to do sth or go somewhere: an invitation to a party **2** [U] act of inviting sb or being invited: Admission is by invitation only. ▶ **inviting** adj attractive ▶ **invitingly** adv

invoice /ˈɪnvɔɪs/ n [C] list of goods sold, work done, etc showing what you must pay ● **invoice** v [T] (business) write or send sb a bill for work you have done or goods you have provided

invoke /ɪnˈvəʊk/ v [T] (fml) **1** mention or use a law, rule, etc as a reason for doing sth **2** make a request (for help) to sb, esp a god **3** make sth appear by magic ▶ **invocation** /ˌɪnvəˈkeɪʃn/ n [C,U] prayer or appeal for help

involuntary /ɪnˈvɒləntri/ adj done without intention: an ~ movement ▶ **involuntarily** /-trəli/ adv

involve /ɪnˈvɒlv/ v [T] **1** make sth a necessary condition or result: *The job ~d me/my living in London.* **2** include or affect sb > ~ **in** make sb/ sth take part in sth ▸ **involved** adj **1** ~ **(in)** taking part in sth; being connected with sth **2** ~ **(with)** having a close personal relationship with sb **3** complicated ▸ **involvement** n [U, C]

invulnerable /ɪnˈvʌlnərəbl/ adj that cannot be hurt or damaged

inward /ˈɪnwəd/ adj **1** inside your mind: ~ *thoughts* **2** towards the inside or centre of sth ▪ **inward** (also **inwards**) adv **1** towards the inside or centre **2** towards yourself and your interests ▸ **inwardly** adv in your mind; secretly

iodine /ˈaɪədiːn/ n [U] dark blue liquid used in medicine and photography

ion /ˈaɪən/ n [C] electrically charged particle ▸ **ionize** (also -**ise**) v [I, T] (tech) change sth or be changed into ions

iota /aɪˈəʊtə/ n [sing] very small amount

IOU /ˌaɪ əʊ ˈjuː/ n [C] (infml) 'I owe you'; written promise to pay sb the money you owe them

IQ /ˌaɪ ˈkjuː/ n [C] measure of sb's intelligence: *have a high/low IQ*

irate /aɪˈreɪt/ adj (fml) angry ▸ **irately** adv

iridescent /ˌɪrɪˈdesnt/ adj (fml) changing colour as light falls on it from different directions

iris /ˈaɪrɪs/ n [C] **1** coloured part round the pupil of the eye **2** tall plant with large bright flowers

irk /ɜːk/ v [T] (fml or lit) annoy sb ▸ **irksome** /ˈɜːksəm/ adj annoying

iron[1] /ˈaɪən/ n **1** (symb Fe) hard strong metal, used in manufacturing and building: *an ~ bridge/gate* ◇ (fig) *She had a will of ~* (= it was very strong).* **2** [C] tool with a flat metal base that can be heated to smooth clothes: *a steam ~* **3** (**irons**) [pl] chains for a prisoner [IDM] **have several, etc irons in the fire** be involved in many different activities at the same time ▪ the **Iron Curtain** n [sing] frontier separating the eastern European communist countries from the West ▪ **ironmonger** /ˈaɪənmʌŋgə(r)/ n [C] (GB) shopkeeper who sells tools and household goods

iron[2] /ˈaɪən/ v [I, T] make clothes, etc smooth by using an iron (2) [PV] **iron out sth** remove any difficulties, etc affecting sth ▸ **ironing** n [U] **1** action of ironing clothes **2** clothes that need to be ironed: *a pile of ~ing*

▪ **ironing board** n [C] long narrow board on which clothes are ironed

ironic /aɪˈrɒnɪk/ (also **ironical** /-kl/) adj using or expressing irony ▸ **ironically** /-kli/ adv

irony /ˈaɪrəni/ n (pl -**ies**) **1** [U, C] amusing or strange aspect of an unexpected event or situation **2** [U] saying the opposite of what you really mean, often as joke

irrational /ɪˈræʃənl/ adj not guided by reason: *an ~ fear of water* ▸ **irrationally** /-nəli/ adv

irreconcilable /ɪˌrekənˈsaɪləbl/ adj (fml) (of differences or disagreements) impossible to settle

irregular /ɪˈregjələ(r)/ adj **1** uneven: ~ *teeth* **2** against the normal rules **3** (gram) not formed in the normal way: ~ *verbs* ▸ **irregularity** /ɪˌregjəˈlærəti/ n [C, U] (pl -**ies**) ▸ **irregularly** adv

irrelevant /ɪˈreləvənt/ adj not important to the situation ▸ **irrelevance** /-əns/ n [U]

irreparable /ɪˈreprəbl/ adj (of damage, an injury, etc) too bad to be put right

irreplaceable /ˌɪrɪˈpleɪsəbl/ adj impossible to replace if lost or damaged

irrepressible /ˌɪrɪˈpresəbl/ adj impossible to hold back or control

irreproachable /ˌɪrɪˈprəʊtʃəbl/ adj (fml) without fault or blame

irresistible /ˌɪrɪˈzɪstəbl/ adj too strong, attractive, etc to be resisted ▸ **irresistibly** adv

irrespective /ˌɪrɪˈspektɪv əv/ prep (written) without considering sth: *Buy it now, ~ the cost.*

irresponsible /ˌɪrɪˈspɒnsəbl/ adj (disapprov) (of a person) not thinking enough about the effects of what they do ▸ **irresponsibility** /-ˈbɪləti/ n [U] ▸ **irresponsibly** adv

irreverent /ɪˈrevərənt/ adj not showing respect, esp for holy things ▸ **irreverence** /-əns/ n [U] ▸ **irreverently** adv

irrevocable /ɪˈrevəkəbl/ adj (fml) impossible to change; final: *an ~ decision*

irrigate /ˈɪrɪgeɪt/ v [T] supply land with water so that crops will grow ▸ **irrigation** /ˌɪrɪˈgeɪʃn/ n [U]

irritable /ˈɪrɪtəbl/ adj easily annoyed ▸ **irritability** /ˌɪrɪtəˈbɪləti/ n [U] ▸ **irritably** adv

irritate /ˈɪrɪteɪt/ v [T] **1** annoy sb **2** make part of the body sore ▸ **irritation** /ˌɪrɪˈteɪʃn/ n [U, C]

is /ɪz/ → BE

Islam /ˈɪzlɑːm/ n **1** [U] Muslim religion, based on the teaching of the Prophet Muhammad **2** [sing] all Muslims ▸ **Islamic** /ɪzˈlæmɪk/ adj

island /ˈaɪlənd/ n **1** [C] piece of land surrounded by water **2** =

▶ **islander** n [C] person living on an island

isle /aɪl/ n [C] (esp in poetry and proper names) island

isn't /'ɪznt/ is not → BE

isolate /'aɪsəleɪt/ v [T] separate sb/ sth from other people or things ▶ **isolated** adj far from others: an ~d cottage ▶ **isolation** /,aɪsə'leɪʃn/ n [U]

ISP /,aɪ es 'pi:/ abbr Internet service provider; company that provides you with an Internet connection and services such as email, etc

0━ **issue** /'ɪʃu:, GB also 'ɪsju:/ n 1 [C] important topic for discussion 2 [C] (infml) problem or worry that sb has with sth 3 [C] one of a regular series of a magazine, etc 4 [U] supply and distribution of sth 5 [U] (law) children of your own [IDM] (the matter, point, etc) at issue (the matter, etc) being discussed ● **issue** v [T] (fml) 1 make sth known formally: ~ a statement 2 give sth to sb, esp officially: ~ a passport/visa 3 produce sth, such as a magazine

0━ **it** /ɪt/ pron (used as the subject or object of a v or after a prep) 1 animal or thing mentioned earlier: Where's my book? Have you seen it? 2 baby, esp one whose sex is not known 3 used to identify a person: 'Who's that?' 'It's the postman.' 4 used when the subject or object comes at the end of a sentence: It's nice to see you. 5 used when you are talking about time, distance or weather: It's 12 o'clock. ◊ It's raining. 6 used to emphasize any part of a sentence: It was work that exhausted him. [IDM] **that is it 1** this/that is the important point, reason, etc **2** this/that is the end: That's it, then—we've lost the match. **this is it** the expected event is going to happen: Well, this is it! Wish me luck. **2** this is the main point ▶ **its** /ɪts/ det of or belonging to a thing, animal or baby: its tail

italic /ɪ'tælɪk/ adj (of printed letters) sloping forwards: This is ~ type. ▶ **italics** n [pl] italic letters

itch /ɪtʃ/ n 1 [C, usu sing] feeling of irritation on the skin, causing a desire to scratch 2 [sing] (fml) strong desire to do sth: have an ~ to travel ● **itch** v 1 [I] have an itch (1) **2** [I] ~ for/to (infml) want to do sth very much: pupils ~ing for the lesson to end ◊ ~ing to tell her the news ▶ **itchy** adj having or producing irritation on the skin: my ~ shirt [IDM] (get/have) itchy feet (infml) want to travel or move to a different place

it'd /'ɪtəd/ short for IT HAD; IT WOULD

0━ **item** /'aɪtəm/ n [C] 1 single thing or unit in a list, etc 2 single piece of news ▶ **itemize** (also -ise) v [T] produce a detailed list of sth: an ~ized bill

itinerant /aɪ'tɪnərənt/ adj (fml) travelling from place to place: ~ workers

itinerary /aɪ'tɪnərəri/ n [C] (pl -ies) plan for a journey

it'll /'ɪtl/ short for IT WILL

it's /ɪts/ short for IT IS; IT HAS

0━ **its** → IT

0━ **itself** /ɪt'self/ pron 1 used as a reflexive when the animal, thing, etc causing the action is also affected by it: My dog hurt ~. **2** used to emphasize an animal, a thing, etc: The name ~ sounds foreign. [IDM] **(all) by itself 1** automatically **2** alone

IVF /,aɪ vi: 'ef/ n [U] (tech) in vitro fertilization; process which helps a woman's egg outside her body

ivory /'aɪvəri/ n [U] **1** creamy-white bone-like substance forming the tusks (= long teeth) of elephants **2** colour of ivory [IDM] **an ivory tower** (disapprov) place where people stay away from the unpleasant realities of everyday life

ivy /'aɪvi/ n [C] climbing evergreen plant with dark shiny leaves

Jj

J, j /dʒeɪ/ n [C, U] (pl **J's, j's** /dʒeɪz/) the tenth letter of the English alphabet

jab /dʒæb/ v (**-bb-**) [T] 1 push a pointed object into sb/sth with sudden force: She ~bed him in the ribs with her finger. ● **jab** n [C] **1** sudden strong hit with sth pointed **2** (GB, infml) injection

jabber /'dʒæbə(r)/ v [I, T] (disapprov) talk or say sth quickly and excitedly ▶ **jabber** n [U]

jack /dʒæk/ n [C] 1 device for lifting sth heavy, esp a car **2** playing card between the ten and the queen ● **jack** v [PV] **jack sth in** (GB, infml) decide to stop doing sth, esp your job **jack sth up** lift sth, esp a vehicle, using a jack

0━ **jacket** /'dʒækɪt/ n [C] **1** short coat with sleeves **2** loose paper cover for a book **3** outer cover round a tank, pipe, etc **4** (GB) skin of a baked potato

jackknife /'dʒæknaɪf/ n [C] (pl **-knives**) large knife with a folding blade ● **jackknife** v [i] (esp of an articulated lorry) bend sharply in the middle

jackpot /'dʒækpɒt/ n [C] largest money prize to be won in a game of chance

Jacuzzi™ /dʒə'ku:zi/ n [C] bath with fast underwater currents of water

jade

jade /dʒeɪd/ n [U] hard, usu green, stone from which ornaments, etc are carved

jaded /ˈdʒeɪdɪd/ adj tired and lacking energy, usu after too much of sth

jagged /ˈdʒægɪd/ adj with rough, pointed, often sharp edges: ~ rocks

jaguar /ˈdʒæɡjuə(r)/ n [C] large spotted animal of the cat family, found in central America

jail /dʒeɪl/ n [C,U] prison ● **jail** v [T] put sb in prison ► **jailer** n [C] (old-fash) person in charge of prisoners

0̶ⁿ jam /dʒæm/ n [C,U] **1** [C] sweet food made by boiling fruit with sugar, eaten on bread **2** [C] number of people, things, etc crowded together and preventing movement: a traffic ~ **[IDM] be in a jam** (infml) be in a difficult situation ● **jam** v (-mm-) **1** [T] push sb/sth somewhere with force or squeeze sb/sth into a small space: ~ clothes into a suitcase **2** [I,T] (cause sth to) become unable to move or to work: The photocopier has ~med. **3** [T] (tech) send out radio signals to prevent another radio broadcast from being heard **[IDM] jam on the brake(s) | jam the brake(s) on** operate the brakes on a vehicle suddenly and with force

jangle /ˈdʒæŋɡl/ v [I,T] (cause sth to) make a harsh sound like two pieces of metal hitting each other ● **jangle** n [sing] hard noise like that of metal hitting metal

janitor /ˈdʒænɪtə(r)/ n [C] (US) = CARETAKER

0̶ⁿ January /ˈdʒænjuəri/ n [U,C] the first month of the year (See examples of use at **April**.)

jar /dʒɑː(r)/ n [C] **1** round glass container with a lid, used for storing food **2** a jar and what it contains: a ~ of coffee/jam ● **jar** v (-rr-) [I,T] give or receive a sudden sharp painful knock **2** [I] ~ **(on)** have an unpleasant effect on sb: Her moaning really ~s on my nerves. **3** [I] ~ **(with)** be different from sth in a strange or unpleasant way ► **jarring** adj

jargon /ˈdʒɑːɡən/ n [U] technical words or expressions used by a particular profession or group of people: medical/legal ~

jaundice /ˈdʒɔːndɪs/ n [U] medical condition that makes the skin and whites of the eyes yellow ► **jaundiced** adj suspicious; bitter: a ~d opinion

jaunt /dʒɔːnt/ n [C] (old-fash or hum) short journey, made for pleasure ► **jaunty** adj (-ier, -iest) cheerful and self-confident ► **jauntily** adv

javelin /ˈdʒævlɪn/ n [C] light spear which is thrown in a sporting event

jaw /dʒɔː/ n **1** [C] either of the bone structures containing the teeth: the lower/upper ~ **2** [sing] lower part of the face **3** (jaws) [pl] mouth with its bones and teeth **4** (jaws) [pl] part of a tool or machine that holds things tightly **[IDM] the jaws of death, defeat, etc** (lit) used to describe an unpleasant situation that almost happens ■ **jawbone** n [C] bone that forms the lower jaw

jazz /dʒæz/ n [U] type of music with strong rhythms, created by African American musicians ● **jazz** v **[PV] jazz sth up** (infml) make sth more lively, interesting or attractive ► **jazzy** adj (-ier, -iest) (infml) **1** in the style of jazz **2** brightly coloured or showy: a ~y tie

0̶ⁿ jealous /ˈdʒeləs/ adj **1** feeling angry or unhappy because sb you like or love is showing interest in sb else: a ~ husband **2** ~ **(of)** feeling angry or unhappy because you wish you had what sb else has **3** determined to keep and protect what you have: They're very ~ of their good reputation (= they do not want to lose it). ► **jealously** adv ► **jealousy** n [U,C] (pl -ies)

0̶ⁿ jeans /dʒiːnz/ n [pl] trousers made of strong cotton, esp denim

Jeep™ /dʒiːp/ n [C] motor vehicle for driving over rough ground

jeer /dʒɪə(r)/ v [I,T] ~ **(at)** laugh rudely at sb; mock ● **jeer** n [C] jeering remark

0̶ⁿ jelly /ˈdʒeli/ n (pl -ies) **1** [U,C] (US **jello, Jell-O™** [U]) clear sweet soft fruit-flavoured food **2** [U] type of clear jam: blackcurrant ~ ■ **jellyfish** n [C] (pl **jellyfish**) sea creature with a soft clear body which can sting

jeopardize (also -ise) /ˈdʒepədaɪz/ v [T] put sb/sth in danger ► **jeopardy** /ˈdʒepədi/ n **[IDM] in jeopardy** in a dangerous position and likely to be lost or harmed: The success of our plan has been put in jeopardy.

jerk /dʒɜːk/ n [C] **1** sudden quick sharp movement **2** (infml) stupid person ● **jerk** v [I,T] (cause sth to) move with a jerk ► **jerky** adj (-ier, -iest) with sudden starts and stops

jersey /ˈdʒɜːzi/ n [C] knitted woollen or cotton piece of clothing for the upper body, with long sleeves

Jerusalem artichoke /dʒəˌruːsələm ˈɑːtɪtʃəʊk/ n [C] light brown root vegetable that looks like a potato

jest /dʒest/ n [C] (old-fash or fml) something done or said to amuse people **[IDM] in jest** as a joke ● **jest** v [I] (fml) joke

jet /dʒet/ n **1** [C] aircraft powered by a jet engine **2** [C] strong narrow stream of gas, liquid, etc forced out of a small opening, which is also called a jet **3** [U] black highly-polished mineral, used in jewellery ● **jet** v (**-tt-**) [I] (*infml*) fly somewhere in a plane ■ **jet-black** *adj* of a deep shiny black colour ■ **jet engine** n [C] engine that drives an aircraft forward by pushing out a stream of gases behind it ■ **jet lag** n [U] tiredness felt after a long flight to a place where the time is different ■ **the jet set** n [sing] rich fashionable people who travel a lot ■ **'Jet Ski**™ n [C] vehicle with an engine, like a motorbike, for riding across water ▶ **jet-skiing** n [U]

jettison /'dʒetɪsn/ v [T] throw away sth unwanted

jetty /'dʒeti/ n [C] (pl **-ies**) wall or platform built out into the sea, a river, etc as a landing place for boats

Jew /dʒuː/ n [C] person of the Hebrew people or religion ▶ **Jewish** *adj*

jewel /'dʒuːəl/ n [C] **1** precious stone, eg a diamond **2** small precious stone used in a watch **3** (*infml*) person or thing that is greatly valued ▶ **jewelled** (*US* **-l-**) n [C] person who sells, makes or repairs jewellery

0━ **jewellery** (also **jewelry**) /'dʒuːəlri/ n [U] objects such as rings and necklaces that people wear as decoration: silver/gold ~

jibe (also **gibe**) /dʒaɪb/ v [I] ~ (**at**) make fun of sb/sth ● **jibe** n [C] comment that makes fun of sb/sth

jiffy /'dʒɪfi/ n [C, usu sing] (*infml*) moment: *I'll be with you in a ~.*

jig /dʒɪg/ n [C] (music for a) quick lively dance ● **jig** v (**-gg-**) [I, T] (cause sb/sth to) move up and down with short quick movements

jiggle /'dʒɪɡl/ v [I, T] (*infml*) (make sth) move quickly from side to side or up and down: *He ~d the car keys in his hands.*

jigsaw /'dʒɪɡsɔː/ n [C] (also **'jigsaw puzzle**) picture on cardboard or wood cut into irregular shapes that has to be fitted together again

jihad /dʒɪˈhɑːd/ n [C] holy war fought by Muslims against those who reject Islam

jilt /dʒɪlt/ v [T] end a romantic relationship with sb suddenly and unkindly

jingle /'dʒɪŋɡl/ n **1** [sing] gentle ringing sound of small bells, keys, etc **2** [C] short simple rhyme or song, esp used in advertising ● **jingle** v [I, T] (cause sth to) make a gentle ringing sound

jinx /dʒɪŋks/ n [C, sing] ~ (**on**) (person or thing thought to bring) bad luck

jive /dʒaɪv/ n [sing] fast dance to music with a strong beat, esp popular in the 1950s ● **jive** v [I] dance to jazz or rock and roll music

0━ **job** /dʒɒb/ n [C] **1** work for which you receive regular payment **2** particular task or piece of work:

Finding a flat to rent was quite a ~. **3** [usu sing] responsibility or duty: *It's not my ~ to do this.* **4** (*infml*) criminal act, esp theft **5** item of work processed by a computer as a single unit [IDM] **just the job** (*infml*) exactly what is wanted or needed **make a bad, good, etc job of sth** do sth badly, well, etc ▶ **jobless** *adj* unemployed ■ **job-sharing** n [U] arrangement by which two people are employed part-time to share a full-time job

jockey /'dʒɒki/ n [C] professional rider in horse races ● **jockey** v [I] ~ (**for**) try all possible ways to gain an advantage over other people: ~ *for position*

jog /dʒɒɡ/ v (**-gg-**) **1** [I] run slowly, esp for exercise **2** [T] hit sth lightly and accidentally [IDM] **jog sb's memory** help sb to remember sth [PV] **jog along** (*GB, infml*) continue as usual with little or no excitement ● **jog** n [sing] **1** slow run, esp for exercise **2** light push or knock ▶ **jogger** n [C] person who jogs regularly for exercise

0━ **join** /dʒɔɪn/ v **1** [T] fix or connect two or more things together **2** [I, T] (of two things or groups) come together to form one: *The two roads ~ here.* **3** [T] become a member of an organization, a company, a club, etc **4** [T] take part in sth that sb else is doing: *Please ~ us for a drink.* [IDM] **join forces (with sb)** work together to achieve a shared aim [PV] **join in (sth)** take part in an activity ● **join** n [C] place where two things are fixed together

joiner /'dʒɔɪnə(r)/ n [C] skilled worker who makes wooden window frames, doors, etc of buildings ▶ **joinery** n [U] work of a joiner

0━ **joint** /dʒɔɪnt/ n [C] **1** place where two bones are joined together **2** place where two or more things are joined: *the ~s of a pipe* **3** large piece of meat **4** (*infml*) place where people meet to eat, drink, dance, etc **5** (*infml*) cigarette containing marijuana ● **joint** *adj* shared or done by two or more people: ~ *responsibility* ◇ a ~ *account* (= a bank account in the name of more than one person) ▶ **jointly** *adv* ■ **joint-stock company** (*business*) company that is owned by all the people who have shares in it

joist /dʒɔɪst/ n [C] wood or steel beam supporting a floor or ceiling

0━ **joke** /dʒəʊk/ n [C] something said or done to make people laugh ● **joke** v [I] tell funny stories ▶ **joker** n [C] **1** person who likes making jokes **2** extra playing card used in certain card games ▶ **jokingly** *adv* in a joking manner

jolly

jolly /'dʒɒli/ adj (**-ier, -iest**) happy and cheerful ● **jolly** adv (GB, oldfash, spoken) very: a ~ good idea

jolt /dʒəʊlt/ v [I,T] (make sth) move suddenly and roughly ● **jolt** n [C, usu sing] sudden rough movement

jostle /'dʒɒsl/ v [I,T] push roughly against sb, usu in a crowd

jot /dʒɒt/ v (**-tt-**) [PV] **jot sth down** write sth quickly ▶ **jotter** n [C] small notebook

journal /'dʒɜːnl/ n [C] **1** magazine or newspaper that deals with a particular subject: a medical/ scientific ~ **2** daily written record of events ▶ **journalism** /-nəlɪzəm/ n [U] work of writing for newspapers, magazines, television or radio

0–**journalist** /'dʒɜːnəlɪst/ n [C] person whose profession is journalism

0–**journey** /'dʒɜːni/ n [C] act of travelling from one place to another ● **journey** v [I] (fml) travel

jovial /'dʒəʊviəl/ adj (written) cheerful and friendly

0–**joy** /dʒɔɪ/ n **1** [U] great happiness **2** [C] person or thing that causes you to feel very happy ▶ **joyful** adj (written) very happy; causing people to be happy ▶ **joyfully** adv▶ **joyous** adj (lit) very happy; causing people to be happy ▶ **joyously** adv

joypad /'dʒɔɪpæd/ n [C] device used with some computer games, with buttons for moving images on the screen

JP /ˌdʒeɪ 'piː/ abbr = JUSTICE OF THE PEACE (JUSTICE)

jubilant /'dʒuːbɪlənt/ adj (fml) very happy, esp because of a success ▶ **jubilation** /ˌdʒuːbɪ'leɪʃn/ n [U] great happiness, esp because of a success

jubilee /'dʒuːbɪliː/ n [C] (celebration of a) special anniversary

Judaism /'dʒuːdeɪɪzəm/ n [U] religion of the Jewish people; their culture

0–**judge** /dʒʌdʒ/ n [C] **1** public officer with authority to decide cases in a law court **2** person that decides who has won a competition **3** person able to give an opinion on the value of sth: She's a good ~ of character. ● **judge** v [I,T] **1** form an opinion about sb/sth **2** act as a judge in sth

0–**judgement** (also esp law judgment) /'dʒʌdʒmənt/ n **1** [U] ability to make sensible decisions **2** [C,U] opinion that you form after careful thought; act of making this opinion known to others: make a fair ~ of his character **3** [C,U] decision of a law court or judge: The court has yet to pass ~ (= give its decision).

judicial /dʒu'dɪʃl/ adj of or by a law court; of a judge or judgement

judiciary /dʒu'dɪʃəri/ n [C,with sing or pl verb] (pl **-ies**) all the judges of a country

judicious /dʒu'dɪʃəs/ adj (fml) showing or having good sense ▶ **judiciously** adv

judo /'dʒuːdəʊ/ n [U] sport in which two people fight and try to throw each other to the ground

jug /dʒʌɡ/ n [C] (GB) **1** deep container for liquids, with a handle and a lip **2** amount of liquid contained in a jug: a ~ of milk

juggernaut /'dʒʌɡənɔːt/ n [C] (GB) very large lorry

juggle /'dʒʌɡl/ v [I,T] **1** keep objects, esp balls, in the air by throwing and catching them **2** organize information, figures, etc in the most useful or effective way ▶ **juggler** n [C]

0–**juice** /dʒuːs/ n [U,C] liquid obtained from fruit, vegetables or meat ▶ **juicy** adj (**-ier, -iest**) **1** containing a lot of juice **2** (infml) interesting, esp because scandalous

jukebox /'dʒuːkbɒks/ n [C] machine in a pub, etc that plays music when you put coins in it

0–**July** /dʒu'laɪ/ n [U,C] the seventh month of the year (See examples of use at April.)

jumble /'dʒʌmbl/ v [T] ~ (**together/ up**) mix things together in an untidy or confused way ● **jumble** n **1** [sing] confused or untidy group of things **2** [U] (GB) goods for a jumble sale ■ **jumble sale** n [C] (GB) sale of old unwanted things to get money for a charity

jumbo /'dʒʌmbəʊ/ adj (infml) very large ● **jumbo** n [C] (pl **-s**) (also **jumbo 'jet**) large plane that can carry several hundred passengers, esp a Boeing 747

0–**jump¹** /dʒʌmp/ v **1** [I] move quickly off the ground by pushing yourself with your legs and feet: ~ up in the air **2** [T] pass over sth by jumping: ~ a wall **3** [T] move quickly and suddenly: The loud bang made me ~. **4** [I] rise suddenly by a large amount: Prices ~ed by 60% last year. **5** [T] (infml) attack sb suddenly [IDM] **jump on the bandwagon** → BAND **jump the gun** do sth too soon **jump the queue** (US) **jump the line** go to the front of a queue without waiting for your turn **jump to conclusions** come to a decision about sth too quickly [PV] **jump at sth** accept an opportunity, chance, etc eagerly

0–**jump²** /dʒʌmp/ n [C] **1** act of jumping **2** thing to be jumped over **3** ~ (**in**) sudden rise in amount: a huge ~ in profits ▶ **jumpy** adj (**-ier, -iest**) (infml) nervous; anxious

A B C D E F G H I **J** K L M N O P Q R S T U V W X Y Z

jumper /ˈdʒʌmpə(r)/ n [C] **1** (GB) = JERSEY **2** person, an animal or an insect that jumps

junction /ˈdʒʌŋkʃn/ n [C] place where roads or railway lines meet

juncture /ˈdʒʌŋktʃə(r)/ n [C] (fml) particular point in an activity or series of events

0~ **June** /dʒuːn/ n [U, C] the sixth month of the year (See examples of use at April.)

jungle /ˈdʒʌŋgl/ n [C, U] land in a tropical country, covered with thick forest

0~ **junior** /ˈdʒuːniə(r)/ adj **1** ~ (to) lower in rank than sb **2** (Junior) (esp US) used after the name of a man who has the same name as his father **3** (GB) (of a school or part of a school) for children under the age of 11 or 13 • **junior** n **1** (C) person with a low level job within an organization **2** [sing] person who is a certain number of years younger than sb else: He is three years her ~.

junk /dʒʌŋk/ n [U] old or unwanted things, usu of little value: The chair came from a ~ shop. • **junk bond** n [C] (business) type of bond that pays a high rate of interest because of the risk involved • **junk food** n [U] (infml, disapprov) food that is thought to be bad for your health

jurisdiction /ˌdʒʊərɪsˈdɪkʃn/ n [U] (fml) legal authority

juror /ˈdʒʊərə(r)/ n [C] member of a jury

jury /ˈdʒʊəri/ n [C, with sing or pl verb] (pl -ies) **1** group of people in a law court who decide whether the accused person is guilty or not guilty **2** group of people who decide the winner of a competition

just¹ /dʒʌst/ adj according to what is right and proper; fair: a ~ decision ▸ **justly** adv

0~ **just²** /dʒʌst/ adv **1** exactly: This jacket is ~ my size. ◇ You're ~ in time. ◇ Leave everything ~ as you find it. **2** ~ as at the same moment as: She arrived ~ as I did. **3** no less than; equally: It's ~ as cheap to go by plane. **4** by a small amount: I arrive ~ after nine. **5** used to say that you did sth very recently: I've ~ had dinner. **6** at this/that moment: We're ~ leaving. **7** ~ about/going to do sth used to refer to the immediate future: The water's ~ about to boil. ◇ Why not ~ wait and see? **8** only: There is ~ one way of saving him. **10** used in orders to catch sb's attention: J~ listen to me! [IDM] **just about** (infml) almost: We're ~ there. **just now 1** at this moment: I can't do it ~ now. **2** only a short time ago

0~ **justice** /ˈdʒʌstɪs/ n **1** [U] quality of being right and fair **2** [U] the law and its administration: a court of ~ **3** [C] judge in a court of law: the Lord

| 241 | **keep** |

Chief /~ ■ **Justice of the Peace** n [C] judge in the lowest courts of law

0~ **justify** /ˈdʒʌstɪfaɪ/ v (pt, pp -**ied**) [T] **1** show that sb/sth is right or reasonable **2** be a good reason for sth ▸ **justifiable** /ˌdʒʌstɪˈfaɪəbl/ adj that can be justified ▸ **justifiably** adv ▸ **justification** /ˌdʒʌstɪfɪˈkeɪʃn/ n [U, C] ~ (for) acceptable reason

jut /dʒʌt/ v (-**tt**-) [I, T] ~ (out) (cause sth to) stick out further than the surrounding surface

juvenile /ˈdʒuːvənaɪl/ n [C] (fml or law) young person • **juvenile** adj **1** (fml or law) of or suitable for young people **2** (disapprov) silly and childish • **juvenile delinquent** n [C] young person who is guilty of a crime, eg vandalism

juxtapose /ˌdʒʌkstəˈpəʊz/ v [T] put people or things side by side, esp to show a contrast ▸ **juxtaposition** /ˌdʒʌkstəpəˈzɪʃn/ n [U, C]

K k

K /keɪ/ abbr (pl **K**) **1** (infml) one thousand **2** kilometre(s) **3** (computing) = KILOBYTE(S)

K, k /keɪ/ n [C, U] (pl **K's, k's** /keɪz/) the eleventh letter of the English alphabet

kaleidoscope /kəˈlaɪdəskəʊp/ n **1** [C] tube containing mirrors and small pieces of coloured glass, turned to produce changing patterns **2** [sing] constantly and quickly changing pattern

kangaroo /ˌkæŋgəˈruː/ n [C] (pl -**s**) Australian animal that jumps along and carries its baby in a pouch

karaoke /ˌkæriˈəʊki/ n [U] type of entertainment in which a machine plays only the music of popular songs while people sing the words themselves

karate /kəˈrɑːti/ n [U] Japanese system of fighting, using the hands and feet

kebab /kɪˈbæb/ n [C] small pieces of meat cooked on a metal stick

keel /kiːl/ n [C] wood or steel structure along the bottom of a ship • **keel** v [I, T] (of a ship) fall over onto its side [PV] **keel over** fall over sideways

0~ **keen** /kiːn/ adj **1** ~ **on** having a strong interest in sth; enthusiastic or eager: He's very ~ on tennis. **2** ~ **on** fond of sb **3** (of the senses, mind or feelings) strong; quick (lit) (of the wind) very cold ▸ **keenly** adv

0~ **keep¹** /kiːp/ v (pt, pp **kept** /kept/) **1** [I, T] (cause sb/sth to) remain in a state or position: K~ (them) quiet! ◇ K~ off the grass! **2** [I] ~ (**on**) doing

keep

continue doing sth; do sth repeatedly: *He ~s (on) interrupting me.* **3** [T] delay sb: *You're late—what kept you?* **4** [T] (used to have sth of): *Here's £5—you can ~ the change.* **5** [T] put or store sth in a particular place: *Where do you ~ the sugar?* **6** [T] own or manage a shop **7** [I] (spoken) used to ask or talk about sb's health: *How's she ~ing?* **8** [I] (of food) remain in good condition: *Milk doesn't ~ in hot weather.* **9** [T] not tell sb a secret **10** [T] do what you have promised to do; go where you have agreed to go: *~ a promise/ an appointment* **11** [T] write down sth as a record: *~ a diary* **12** [T] support sb financially [IDM] **keep abreast of sth** → ABREAST **keep sb at arm's length** avoid having a close relationship with sb **keep the ball rolling** → BALL **keep sb/sth at bay** → BAY **keep sb company** stay with sb so that they are not alone **keep count of sth** → COUNT² **keep your distance (from sb/sth)** **1** not go too near to sb/sth **2** avoid getting too friendly or involved with sb/sth **keep an eye on sb/sth** make sure that sb/ sth is safe **keep your fingers crossed** hope that sb will be successful: *Good luck with your exam—we're ~ing our fingers crossed for you.* **keep your hair on** (GB, spoken) used to tell sb not to be angry **keep your head** → HEAD¹ **keep your head above water** deal with problems, esp financial worries, and just manage to survive **keep sth in mind** → MIND¹ **keep sb in the dark** → DARK² **keep it up** continue to do good work **keep your mouth shut** (infml) not talk about sth because it is a secret **keep an open mind** → OPEN¹ **keep pace (with sb/sth)** move forward at the same speed as sb/sth **keep the peace 1** stop people fighting **2** not make a disturbance in public **keep quiet about sth | keep sth quiet** say nothing about sth; keep sth secret **keep a straight face** → STRAIGHT² **keep a tight rein on sb/ sth** control sb/sth firmly **keep your wits about you** → WIT [PV] **keep away (from sb/sth)** avoid going near sb/sth **keep sb/sth away (from sb/sth)** prevent sb/sth from coming somewhere **keep sth back (from sb)** refuse to tell sb about sth **keep sb down** prevent a person, group, etc from expressing themselves freely **keep sth down** not allow sth to grow or increase **keep sb from sth** prevent sb from doing sth: *~ him from leaving* **keep sb in with sb** remain friendly with sb **keep on about sth** → ON¹ **keep on (at sb) (about sb/sth)** (esp GB) speak to sb often and in an annoying way

about sb/sth **keep out (of sth)** not enter a place **keep out of sth** avoid sth **keep to sth 1** avoid leaving a path or road **2** talk or write only about the subject that you are supposed to discuss: *~ to the point* **3** do what you have promised or agreed to do: *~ to an agreement* **keep yourself to yourself** avoid meeting people socially **keep sth to yourself** not tell other people about sth **keep sth up 1** make sth stay at a high level: *~ prices up* ◇ *your spirits up* **2** continue sth at the same, usu high, level: *K~ up the good work/K~ it up!* **3** continue to use or practise sth: *Do you still ~ up your French?* **4** maintain a house, garden, etc in good condition **keep up (with sb/ sth)** move at the same speed as sb/ sth

keep² /kiːp/ *n* [U] (cost of) food, clothes and all the other things a person needs to live: *earn your ~* [IDM] **keep sth** (infml) for ever

keeper /ˈkiːpə(r)/ *n* [C] **1** (esp in compounds) person whose job is to look after a building and its contents: *a shop~* **2** person whose job is to look after animals in a zoo

keeping /ˈkiːpɪŋ/ *n* [IDM] **in sb's keeping** in sb's care: *The keys are in his ~.* **in/out of keeping (with sth)** in/ not in harmony with sth

keepsake /ˈkiːpseɪk/ *n* [C] small object that sb gives you so that you will remember them

kennel /ˈkenl/ *n* [C] **1** small hut for a dog **2** (kennels) [with sing or pl verb] place where dogs are bred, looked after when the owner is away, etc

kept *pt, pp of* KEEP¹

kerb (US curb) /kɜːb/ *n* [C] stone edge of a pavement

kernel /ˈkɜːnl/ *n* [C] **1** inner part of a nut or seed **2** most important part of an idea, a subject, etc

kestrel /ˈkestrəl/ *n* [C] small bird of prey of the falcon family

ketchup /ˈketʃəp/ *n* [U] thick cold sauce made from tomatoes

kettle /ˈketl/ *n* [C] container with a spout, used for boiling water

0━ key¹ /kiː/ *n* [C] **1** piece of metal that locks or unlocks a door, etc **2** [usu sing] **~ (to)** something that makes you able to understand sth or achieve sth: *Diet and exercise are the ~ to good health.* **3** any of the buttons that you press to operate a computer or typewriter **4** any of the parts that you press to play a piano and some other musical instruments **5** (music) set of related notes: *in the ~ of G* **6** set of answers to exercises ● **key** *adj* most important; essential: *a ~ position* ■ **keyboard** *n* [C] set of keys on a computer, typewriter, piano or other musical instrument

▶ **keyboard** v [T] type information into a computer ■ **keyhole** n [C] hole in a lock that you put a key in ■ **keynote** n [C] central idea of a speech, book, etc ■ **key ring** n [C] small ring on which keys are kept ■ **keyword** n [C] **1** word that tells you the central idea or subject of sth **2** word that you type into a computer to search for information about a particular subject

0➡ **key²** /kiː/ v [T] ~ (**in**) (*computing*) type information into a computer using a keyboard ■ **keyed up** adj excited or nervous

kg abbr kilogram(s)

khaki /ˈkɑːki/ adj greenish or yellowish-brown colour

kibbutz /kɪˈbʊts/ n [C] (pl ~**im** /kɪbʊtˈsiːm/) communal farm or factory in Israel

0➡ **kick¹** /kɪk/ v **1** [T] hit sb/sth with your foot **2** [I] move your legs as if you were kicking sth **3** ~ **yourself** [T] (*infml*) be annoyed with yourself because you have done sth stupid [IDM] **kick the bucket** (*infml*) die **kick the habit** (*infml*) stop smoking, drinking alcohol, etc [PV] **kick against sth** protest about or resist sth **kick off** start **kick sb out (of sth)** (*infml*) make sb leave a place ■ **kick-off** n [C, U] start of a football match

0➡ **kick²** /kɪk/ n **1** [C] act of kicking sb/sth: *give sb a ~* **2** [C] (*infml*) strong feeling of pleasure **3** [U, sing] (*infml*) strength of a drug or alcoholic drink

0➡ **kid** /kɪd/ n **1** [C] (*infml*) child or young person **2** [C] young goat **3** [U] leather made from the skin of a young goat ● **kid** v (-**dd**-) [I, T] (*infml*) **1** tell sb sth that is not true, esp as a joke **2** ~ **sb/yourself** allow sb/yourself to believe sth that is not true

kidnap /ˈkɪdnæp/ v (-**pp**- *US also* -**p**-) [T] take sb away illegally and keep them prisoner, esp in order to demand money ▶ **kidnapper** n [C]

kidney /ˈkɪdni/ n **1** [C] organ that removes waste products from the blood and produces urine **2** [U, C] kidney(s) of certain animals used as food

0➡ **kill** /kɪl/ v [I, T] make sb/sth die: (*infml*) *He'll ~ me* (= be very angry with me) *if he finds me here.* **2** [T] destroy or spoil sth or make it stop: *a rumour/story* **3** [T] (*infml*) hurt: *My feet are ~ing me.* [IDM] **kill two birds with one stone** achieve two aims with one action ● **kill** n **1** [C] act of killing, esp when an animal is killed **2** [usu sing] animal(s) killed ▶ **killer** n [C] ▶ **killing** n [C] act of killing sb deliberately [IDM] **make a killing** (*infml*) make a large profit quickly ▶ **killjoy** n [C] (*disapprov*) person who stops others enjoying themselves

kiln /kɪln/ n [C] oven for baking pottery, bricks, etc

kilo /ˈkiːləʊ/ n [C] (pl ~**s**) kilogram

kilobyte /ˈkɪləbaɪt/ n [C] (abbr **K**) 1024 bytes of computer memory or information

0➡ **kilogram** (*GB also* -**gramme**) /ˈkɪləɡræm/ n [C] metric unit of weight; 1000 grams

0➡ **kilometre** (*US* -**meter**) /ˈkɪləmiːtə(r), *GB also* kɪˈlɒmɪtə(r)/ n [C] metric unit of length; 1000 metres

kilowatt /ˈkɪləwɒt/ n [C] unit of electrical power; 1000 watts

kilt /kɪlt/ n [C] tartan skirt sometimes worn by Scottish men

0➡ **kind¹** /kaɪnd/ n [C] group of people or things with similar features; sort; type: *two ~s of fruit* [IDM] **in kind 1** (of payment) in goods, not money **2** (*fml*) with the same thing **a kind of** (*infml*) used to show that sth you are saying is not exact

0➡ **kind²** /kaɪnd/ adj friendly and thoughtful to others ■ **kind-hearted** adj kind and generous ▶ **kindly** adj (-**ier, -iest**) (*infml*) kind ▶ **kindly** adv **1** in a kind way **2** (*old-fash, fml*) used to ask or tell sb to do sth, esp when you are annoyed [IDM] **not take kindly to sth/sb** not like sth/sb ▶ **kindness** n **1** [U] quality of being kind **2** [C] kind act

kindergarten /ˈkɪndəɡɑːtn/ n [C] school for very young children

kindle /ˈkɪndl/ v **1** [I, T] (cause a fire to) start burning **2** [T] arouse or stimulate an interest, emotion, etc

kindred /ˈkɪndrəd/ adj [IDM] **a kindred spirit** person whose interests, beliefs, etc are similar to your own

0➡ **king** /kɪŋ/ n [C] **1** male ruler of an independent state that has a royal family **2** ~ (**of**) the most important member of a group **3** (in chess) the most important piece **4** playing card with the picture of a king on it ■ **king-size** (*also* -**sized**) adj larger than normal: *a ~-size bed*

kingdom /ˈkɪŋdəm/ n [C] **1** country ruled by a king or queen **2** one of the three traditional divisions of the natural world: *the animal, plant and mineral ~s*

kink /kɪŋk/ n **1** bend or twist in sth that is usu straight **2** (*infml, disapprov*) something strange or abnormal in sb's character ● **kink** v [I, T] (cause sth to) develop a bend or twist ▶ **kinky** adj (-**ier, -iest**) (*infml*) strange or abnormal sexual behaviour

kiosk /ˈkiːɒsk/ n [C] small open-fronted shop where newspapers, sweets, etc are sold

kipper /'kɪpə(r)/ n [C] salted herring (= a type of fish), dried or smoked

0━ **kiss** /kɪs/ v [I,T] touch sb with your lips to show affection or as a greeting ● **kiss** n [C] touch given with the lips **IDM the kiss of life** (GB) mouth-to-mouth method of helping sb to start breathing again

kit /kɪt/ n **1** [C] set of pieces to be put together to make sth **2** [C] set of tools or equipment: *a first-aid ~* **3** [U] (GB) set of clothes and equipment that you use for a particular activity ● **kit** v (-tt-) [PV] **kit sb out/up (in/with sth)** provide sb with the correct clothes and equipment for an activity

0━ **kitchen** /'kɪtʃɪn/ n [C] room in which meals are cooked

kite /kaɪt/ n [C] light framework covered with paper, cloth, etc, which flies in the wind

kitten /'kɪtn/ n [C] young cat

kitty /'kɪti/ n (pl **-ies**) (infml) money collected by several people for an agreed use

kiwi /'kiːwiː/ n [C] **1** (Kiwi) (infml) person from New Zealand **2** New Zealand bird that cannot fly ■ **kiwi fruit** n [C] (pl **kiwi fruit**) (also **kiwi**) small fruit with thin hairy brown skin and soft green flesh with black seeds

km abbr (pl **km** or **~s**) kilometre(s)

knack /næk/ n [sing] skill at doing a task

knackered /'nækəd/ adj (GB, sl) very tired

knead /niːd/ v [T] press and stretch bread dough with your hands **2** rub and press muscles

0━ **knee** /niː/ n [C] **1** joint in the middle of the leg **2** part of a piece of clothing that covers the knee **IDM bring sb to their knees** force sb to give in ■ **kneecap** n [C] small flat bone at the front of the knee ■ **knee-deep** adj up to your knees

kneel /niːl/ v (pt, pp **knelt** /nelt/ or US also **~ed**) [I] **~ (down)** go down on your knees

knew pt of KNOW

knickers /'nɪkəz/ n [pl] (GB) piece of women's underwear that covers the body from the waist to the top of the legs

knick-knack /'nɪk næk/ n [C, usu pl] small ornament

0━ **knife** /naɪf/ n [C] (pl **knives** /naɪvz/) sharp blade with a handle, used for cutting ● **knife** v [T] injure sb with a knife ■ **knife-edge** n [usu sing] sharp edge of a knife **IDM on a knife-edge** (of an important situation or result) very uncertain

knight /naɪt/ n [C] **1** (in the Middle Ages) soldier of noble birth **2** (in Britain) man to whom the title 'Sir' has been given **3** chess piece

● **knight** v [T] give sb the rank or title of a knight ▸ **knighthood** /'naɪthʊd/ n [C] rank or title of a knight

0━ **knit** /nɪt/ v (-tt-, pt, pp **~ted** in sense 2, usu **knit**) [I,T] **1** make clothes, etc from wool or cotton thread using two long needles **2** (cause people or things to) join closely together: *a closely- ~ family* ▸ **knitting** n [U] item being knitted ■ **knitting needle** n [C] long thin stick, used for knitting

knives plural of KNIFE

0━ **knob** /nɒb/ n [C] **1** round control button on a machine such as a television **2** round handle of a door, drawer, etc **3** small lump of sth, eg butter ▸ **knobbly** /'nɒbli/ adj (**-ier, -iest**) having small hard lumps: *~bly knees*

0━ **knock¹** /nɒk/ v **1** [I] hit a door, etc firmly to attract attention: *~ on the door* **2** [T] hit sb/sth, often accidentally, with a short, hard blow **3** [T] (infml) criticize sb/sth **PV knock about with sb** spend a lot of time with sb **knock sb/sth about** hit sth/sth roughly **knock sth back** (infml) drink sth quickly **knock sb down/over** hit sb and make them fall to the ground: *She was ~ed down by a bus.* **knock sb down** demolish a building **knock sb/sth down (from sth) (to sth)** (infml) persuade sb to reduce the price of sth **knock off (sth)** stop work: *When do you ~ off?* **knock sth off** **1** reduce the price of sth **2** (sl) steal sth **knock sb out** **1** make sb fall asleep or become unconscious **2** make sb/yourself very tired **knock sb out (of sth)** defeat sb so that they cannot continue competing **knock sth up** make sth quickly: *~ up a meal* ▸ **knocker** n [C] metal object on the outside of a door, used for knocking (1) ■ **knock-kneed** adj having legs that turn inwards at the knees ■ **knock-'on effect** n [C] indirect result of an action ■ **knockout** n [C] **1** (in boxing) blow that makes a boxer unable to get up **2** competition from which losers are eliminated **3** (infml) person or thing that is very impressive

0━ **knock²** /nɒk/ n [C] **1** sound of sb knocking on a door, etc **2** (infml) unfortunate experience

0━ **knot** /nɒt/ n [C] **1** fastening made by tying together pieces of string, rope, etc **2** twisted piece; tangle **3** hard round spot in a piece of wood **4** small group of people **5** unit of speed used by ships; one nautical mile per hour ● **knot** v (-tt-) [T] fasten sth with a knot **2** [I,T] make or form knots in sth ▸ **knotty** adj (**-ier, -iest**) **1** difficult to solve: *a ~ty problem* **2** (of wood) full of knots

0━ **know** /nəʊ/ v (pt **knew** /njuː/ pp **~n** /nəʊn/) **1** have information in your mind: *Do you ~ his address?* ◊ *I ~ of at least two people who did the same thing.* **2** [I,T] realize, understand or be aware of sth **3** [I,T] feel certain about sth **4** [T] be familiar with a person, place, thing, etc **5** [T] be able to recognize sb/sth: *I'll ~ her when I see her.* **6** [T] understand and be able to use a language, skill, etc **7** [T] have personal experience of sth: *a man who has ~n poverty* [IDM] **be known as sth** be called or regarded as sth **know sb by sight** recognize sb without knowing them personally **know your own mind** know what you want [PV] **know about sth** have information about sth **know of sb/ sth** have (only a little) information about sb/sth: *I ~ of the book but I've not read it.* ■ **know-how** *n* [U, *infml*] practical knowledge or ability

knowing /'nəʊɪŋ/ *adj* showing that you have information which is secret: *a ~ look* ▸ **knowingly** *adv* **1** deliberately **2** in a knowing way

0━ **knowledge** /'nɒlɪdʒ/ *n* **1** [U, sing] information, understanding and skills gained through education or experience **2** [U] state of knowing about a particular fact or situation: *done without my ~* ▸ **knowledgeable** /-əbl/ *adj* knowing a lot

known *pp* of KNOW

knuckle /'nʌkl/ *n* [C] any of the joints in the fingers ■ **knuckle** *v* [PV] **knuckle under (to sb/sth)** (*infml*) accept sb else's authority

koala /kəʊˈɑːlə/ *n* [C] Australian tree-climbing animal like a small bear

Koran /kəˈrɑːn/ *n* (the Koran) [sing] the holy book of Muslims

kosher /'kəʊʃə(r)/ *adj* (of food) prepared according to the rules of Jewish law

kowtow /ˌkaʊˈtaʊ/ *v* [I] ~ (to) (*infml, disapprov*) show sb in authority too much respect and be too willing to obey them

kph /ˌkeɪ piː 'eɪtʃ/ *abbr* kilometres per hour

Ll

L *abbr* **1** (esp on maps) Lake **2** (esp for sizes of clothes) large

L, l /el/ *n* [C, U] (pl **L's, l's** /elz/) **1** the twelfth letter of the English alphabet **2** Roman numeral for 50

l *abbr* **1** litre(s) **2** line

Lab *abbr* (in British politics) Labour

0━ **lab** /læb/ *n* [C] (*infml*) = LABORATORY

0━ **label** /'leɪbl/ *n* [C] **1** piece of paper, cloth, etc fixed to sth to describe what it is, who owns it, etc

2 (*disapprov*) word(s) describing sb/ sth in a way that is too general or unfair ■ **label** *v* (-**ll-** *US* -**l-**) [T] **1** put a label on sth **2** describe sb/sth in a particular way, esp unfairly: *They ~led her (as) a liar.*

labor (*US*) = LABOUR ■ **labor union** (*US*) = TRADE UNION (TRADE¹)

0━ **laboratory** /ləˈbɒrətri/ *n* [C] (pl **-ies**) room or building used for scientific experiments

laborious /ləˈbɔːriəs/ *adj* needing great effort ▸ **laboriously** *adv*

0━ **labour¹** (*US* -**or**) /'leɪbə(r)/ *n* **1** [U] (esp physical) work **2** [U, usu pl] (*fml*) task or period of work **3** [U, usu pl] workers as a group **4** [U, C, usu sing] process of childbirth: *a woman in ~* **5** (Labour) [sing] = THE LABOUR PARTY ■ **the Labour Party** *n* [sing, with sing or pl verb] (*GB, pol*) major political party, representing esp the interests of workers

labour² (*US* -**or**) /'leɪbə(r)/ *v* [I] **1** try hard to do sth difficult **2** do hard physical work [IDM] **labour the point** continue to repeat or explain sth already understood [PV] **labour under sth** (*fml*) believe sth that is not true ▸ **labourer** (*US* -**bor-**) *n* [C] person who does heavy unskilled work

labyrinth /'læbərɪnθ/ *n* [C] complicated series of paths, which it is difficult to find your way through

lace /leɪs/ *n* **1** [U] delicate decorative cloth with an open-work design of threads **2** [C] = SHOELACE (SHOE) ■ **lace** *v* **1** [I,T] fasten sth or be fastened with laces **2** [T] ~ **with** add a small amount of alcohol, a drug, etc to a drink

lacerate /'læsəreɪt/ *v* [T] (*fml*) cut skin or flesh with sth sharp ▸ **laceration** /ˌlæsəˈreɪʃn/ *n* [C, U]

0━ **lack** /læk/ *v* [T] have none or not enough of sth: *He ~s confidence.* [IDM] **be lacking in** sth have not enough of sth ▸ **lacking** *adj* **1** ~ (**in**) having none or not enough of sth: *The book is completely ~ing in originality.* **2** not present or not available ■ **lack** *n* [U, sing] ~ (**of**) absence or shortage of sth: *a ~ of food/money/skills*

lackadaisical /ˌlækəˈdeɪzɪkl/ *adj* (*written*) not showing enough care or attention

laconic /ləˈkɒnɪk/ *adj* (*fml*) using few words ▸ **laconically** /-kli/ *adv*

lacquer /'lækə(r)/ *n* [U] liquid used on metal or wood to give it a hard shiny surface ■ **lacquer** *v* [T] cover sth with lacquer

lacy /'leɪsi/ *adj* (-**ier**, -**iest**) of or like lace (1)

lad /læd/ *n* [C] **1** (*old-fash*) boy; young man **2** (the lads) [pl] (*GB*,

A B C D E F G H I J K **L** M N O P Q R S T U V W X Y Z

spoken) group of male friends: *He's gone out with the ~s.* **3** (*GB, infml*) lively young man ▶ **the lads** [pl] (*infml*) group of male friends

ladder /'lædə(r)/ n [C] **1** two lengths of wood or metal, joined together with steps or rungs, used for climbing **2** series of stages of progress in a career or an organization: *climb up the social ~* **3** (*GB*) long thin hole in women's tights or stockings ● **ladder** v [I,T] (cause tights or stockings to) develop a ladder

laden /'leɪdn/ adj ~ (**with**) heavily loaded with

ladle /'leɪdl/ n [C] large deep spoon for serving liquids ● **ladle** v [T] serve sth with a ladle

0🔊 **lady** /'leɪdi/ n [C] (pl -ies) **1** (esp in polite use) woman **2** woman who has good manners **3** (*old-fash*) (in Britain) woman of good family and social position **4** (**Lady**) (in Britain) title of a woman of noble rank **5** (a/ the ladies) [U, sing] (*GB*) public toilet for women ■ **ladylike** adj like or suitable for a lady; polite ■ **ladyship** n [C] (Her/Your Ladyship) title used when speaking to or about a Lady (4)

lag /læg/ v (**-gg-**) **1** [I] ~ (**behind**) move or develop slowly or more slowly than others **2** [T] cover pipes, etc with material to prevent heat from escaping

lager /'lɑːgə(r)/ n [C, U] (glass or bottle of) light pale beer

lagoon /lə'guːn/ n [C] saltwater lake separated from the sea by sandbanks or coral reefs

laid pt, pp of LAY¹

lain pp of LIE²

lair /leə(r)/ n [C] home of a wild animal

0🔊 **laity** /'leɪəti/ n [sing, with sing or pl verb] (the laity) all the members of a Church who are not clergy

0🔊 **lake** /leɪk/ n [C] large area of water surrounded by land

lamb /læm/ n **1** [C] young sheep **2** [U] meat from a young sheep

lame /leɪm/ adj **1** (of people or animals) unable to walk well because of injury to the leg or foot **2** (of an excuse, etc) weak and hard to believe ■ **lame 'duck** n [C] **1** person, organization, etc that is in difficulties and needs help **2** (*infml, esp US*) elected official in his/her final period of office ▶ **lame** v [T] make lame ■ **lameness** n [U]

lament /lə'ment/ v [I,T] express great sadness about sth/sth ● **lament** n [C] song or poem expressing great sadness for sb/sth ▶ **lamentable** /'læməntəbl/ adj unsatisfactory; regrettable ▶ **lamentably** adv

laminated /'læmɪneɪtɪd/ adj made by joining several thin layers together

0🔊 **lamp** /læmp/ n [C] device that uses electricity, oil or gas to produce light ■ **lamp post** n [C] (esp GB) tall post in the street with a lamp at the top ■ **lampshade** n [C] cover placed round or over a lamp

LAN /læn/ n [C] (*computing*) local area network; system that connects computers inside a single building or group of nearby buildings

lance /lɑːns/ n [C] long weapon with a pointed metal end used by people fighting on horses in the past ■ **lance** v [T] cut open an infected place on sb's body with a knife in order to let out the liquid inside

0🔊 **land**¹ /lænd/ n **1** [U] solid dry part of the earth's surface **2** [U] area of ground used for farming, etc: *work on the ~* **3** [U] property in the form of land **4** (the land) [U] used to refer to the countryside as opposed to cities: *His family had always farmed the ~.* **5** [C] (*lit*) country or nation [IDM] see, etc how the land lies (*GB*) find out about a situation ▶ **landed** adj owning a lot of land ■ **landline** n [C] telephone connection that uses wires, carried on poles or under the ground, in contrast to a mobile phone ■ **landlocked** adj almost or completely surrounded by land ■ **landmark** n [C] **1** object easily seen and recognized from a distance **2** ~ (**in**) important event, discovery, etc ■ **landowner** n [C] person who owns an area of land, esp a large area ■ **landslide** n [C] **1** mass of earth, rock, etc that falls down the side of a mountain or cliff **2** victory by a very large majority in an election

0🔊 **land**² /lænd/ v **1** [I] come down through the air onto the ground or another surface: *The plane ~ed safely.* **2** [T] bring an aircraft down to the ground in a controlled way **3** [T] put sb/sth on land from an aircraft, a boat, etc **4** [T] (*infml*) succeed in getting sth: ~ *a job* [IDM] **land on your feet → FOOT** [PV] **land sb/yourself in sth** (*infml*) get sb/yourself into difficulties **land up in, at...** (*infml*) reach a final position or situation: ~ *up in jail* **land yourself with sth/sb** (*infml*) give yourself/sb sth unpleasant to do

landing /'lændɪŋ/ n **1** [C] level area at the top of a set of stairs **2** [C, U] act of bringing an aircraft to the ground after a journey: *a crash ~* **3** [C] act of bringing soldiers to land in an area controlled by the enemy ■ **landing craft** n [C] flat-bottomed boat that brings soldiers, vehicles, etc to the shore ■ **landing gear** n [U] = UNDERCARRIAGE ■ **'landing stage** n

[C] platform on which people and goods are landed from a boat

landlady /ˈlændleɪdi/ n [C] (pl **-ies**) **1** woman from whom you rent a room, house, etc **2** (GB) woman who owns or manages a pub or guest house

landlord /ˈlændlɔːd/ n [C] **1** man from whom you rent a room, house, etc **2** (GB) man who owns or manages a pub or guest house

0–◉ **landscape** /ˈlændskeɪp/ n [C] **1** everything you see when you look across a large area of land **2** painting of a view of the countryside ● **landscape** v [T] improve the appearance of an area of land by changing the design and planting trees, etc: ~d gardens ● **landscape** adj (computing) (of a document) printed so that the writing at the top of the page is one of the longer sides

0–◉ **lane** /leɪn/ n [C] **1** narrow country road **2** (in place names) narrow street: Mill Lane **3** part of a road that is marked for a single line of traffic: a four-~ motorway **4** route regularly used by ships or aircraft **5** marked part of track or water for each competitor in a race

0–◉ **language** /ˈlæŋgwɪdʒ/ n **1** [C] system of communication in speech and writing used by people of a particular country: the English ~ **2** [U] the use by humans of a system of sounds and words to communicate **3** [U] particular style of speaking or writing: bad/strong ~ (= words that people may consider offensive) **4** [C,U] way of expressing ideas and feelings using movements, symbols and sounds: body ~ ◇ sign ~ **5** [C,U] system of symbols and rules used to operate a computer ■ **language laboratory** n [C] room where foreign languages are learned by listening to tapes, etc

languid /ˈlæŋgwɪd/ adj (written) (of a person) having no energy ▸ **languidly** adv

languish /ˈlæŋgwɪʃ/ v [I] (fml) **1** ~ in be forced to live and suffer in unpleasant conditions: ~ in prison **2** become weaker or fail to make progress

lank /læŋk/ adj (of hair) straight, dull and unattractive

lanky /ˈlæŋki/ adj (**-ier, -iest**) unattractively tall and thin

lantern /ˈlæntən/ n [C] portable lamp with a transparent case for a candle or flame

lanyard /ˈlænjəd/ n [C] rope or cord worn around the neck or wrist in order to carry sth, such as an electronic device

lap /læp/ n [C] **1** top part of your legs that forms a flat surface when you sit down: a baby on his ~ **2** one complete journey round a track or

racecourse ● **lap** v (**-pp-**) **1** [I] (of water) make gentle splashing sounds **2** [T] (animals) drink sth with quick movements of the tongue **3** [T] (in a race) pass another competitor on a track to be one lap ahead [PV] **lap sth up** (infml) receive praise, news, etc eagerly

lapel /ləˈpel/ n [C] front part of the collar of a coat that is folded back

lapse /læps/ n [C] **1** small error in behaviour, memory, etc **2** passing of a period of time ● **lapse** v [I] (of a contract, an agreement, etc) be no longer valid because the period of time it lasts has come to an end **2** gradually become weaker or come to an end: His concentration soon ~d. **3** ~ (**from**) stop believing in or practising your religion: a ~d Catholic [PV] **lapse into sth** gradually pass into a worse or weaker state

laptop /ˈlæptɒp/ n [C] small computer that can work with a battery and be easily carried

larch /lɑːtʃ/ n [C] tall deciduous tree of the pine family with small cones

lard /lɑːd/ n [U] fat of pigs, used in cooking

larder /ˈlɑːdə(r)/ n [C] cupboard or small room for storing food

0–◉ **large** /lɑːdʒ/ adj (**~r, ~st**) more than average or usual in size; big [IDM] **at large 1** as a whole; in general: the country at ~ **2** (of a dangerous person or animal) not captured; free **by and large** (infml) on the whole; generally **(as) large as life** (hum) used to show surprise at seeing sb/sth ▸ **largely** adv to a great extent; mainly ■ **large-scale** adj **1** extensive: a ~-scale search **2** drawn or made to a large scale

lark /lɑːk/ n [C] **1** small brown songbird **2** [usu sing] (infml) thing that you do for fun or a joke

larva /ˈlɑːvə/ n [C] (pl **-ae** /-viː/) insect in the first stage of its life

larynx /ˈlærɪŋks/ n [C] (pl **larynges** /ləˈrɪndʒiːz/) (anat) area at the top of the throat that contains the vocal cords ▸ **laryngitis** /ˌlærɪnˈdʒaɪtɪs/ n [U] infection of the larynx

lascivious /ləˈsɪviəs/ adj (fml, disapprov) feeling or showing sexual desire

laser /ˈleɪzə(r)/ n [C] device that makes a very strong beam of controlled light (= with rays that are parallel and of the same wavelength): a ~ beam ■ **laser printer** n [C] printer that produces good quality printed material by means of a laser beam

lash /læʃ/ v [I,T] **1** hit sb/sth with great force **2** [T] hit a person or an animal with a whip, rope, stick, etc **3** [T] fasten sth tightly to sth else with

A B C D E F G H I J K **L** M N O P Q R S T U V W X Y Z

ropes, etc **4** [I, T] (cause sth to) move violently from side to side: *The crocodile's tail was ~ing furiously from side to side.* [PV] **lash out (at sb/sth) 1** suddenly try to hit sb **2** criticize sb/sth in an angry way ● **lash** n [C] **1** = EYELASH (EYE) **2** hit with a whip, given as a form of punishment

lashings /ˈlæʃɪŋz/ n [pl] (GB, infml) large amount of sth, esp food and drink

lass /læs/ n [C] girl; young woman

lasso /læˈsuː/ n [C] (pl ~s or ~es) looped rope used for catching horses and cattle ● **lasso** v [T] catch an animal with a lasso

0ⁿ **last**[1] /lɑːst/ det **1** coming after all others: *Friday is the ~ day of the week.* **2** most recent; latest: ~ *night* **3** only remaining; final: *This is our ~ bottle of milk.* **4** least likely or suitable: *She's the ~ person to trust with a secret.* [IDM] **be on your/its last legs** be very weak or in bad condition **have the last laugh** be successful over your critics, rivals, etc in the end **have the last word (on sth)** make the final remark that ends an argument in the **as a last resort** when there are no other possible courses of action **last-ditch** the final effort to be made to avoid defeat: *a ~ ditch attempt* **the last straw** → STRAW **the last word (in sth)** the most fashionable, modern, best thing: *This car is the ~ word in luxury.* ● **last** n (the) (pl **the last)** **1** person or thing that comes or happens after all others **2** ~ **of** only remaining part or items of sth: *the ~ of the apples* [IDM] **at (long) last** after much delay, effort, etc ▶ **lastly** adv in the last place; finally

0ⁿ **last**[2] /lɑːst/ adv **1** after all others **2** most recently

0ⁿ **last**[3] /lɑːst/ v **1** [I] continue for a period of time **2** [I, T] be enough for sb to use over a period of time: *enough food to ~ two days* ▶ **lasting** adj continuing for a long time

latch /lætʃ/ n [C] **1** small metal bar for fastening a door or gate **2** type of lock on a door that can only be opened from the outside with a key ● **latch** v [T] fasten sth with a latch [PV] **latch on to sb** (infml) join sb and refuse to leave them

0ⁿ **late** /leɪt/ adj (~r, ~st) **1** near the end of a period of time, a person's life, etc: *in the ~ afternoon* ◇ *She's in her ~ twenties* (= she is 28 or 29). **2** after the expected or usual time: *The train is ~.* **3** near the end of the day: *It's getting ~.* **4** no longer alive: *her ~ husband* ● **late** adv **1** after the expected or usual time: *get up ~* **2** near the end of a period of time: *as ~ as the 1990s* ▶ **lately** adv recently ▶ **latest** adj most recent or newest:

the ~st fashion ▶ **the latest** n (infml) the most recent or the newest thing or piece of news: *This is the ~st in robot technology.* [IDM] **at the latest** no later than the time mentioned

latent /ˈleɪtnt/ adj existing but not yet active or developed: ~ *talent*

lateral /ˈlætərəl/ adj of or to the side of sth

lathe /leɪð/ n [C] machine that shapes pieces of wood, metal, etc by turning them against a cutting tool

lather /ˈlɑːðə(r)/ n [U] white foam produced by soap mixed with water ● **lather** v **1** [T] cover sth with lather **2** [I] produce lather

Latin /ˈlætɪn/ adj, n [U] (of the) language of ancient Rome ■ **Latin A'merica** n [U] Mexico and parts of Central and South America in which Spanish or Portuguese is the official language ▶ **Latin A'merican** n [C], adj

latitude /ˈlætɪtjuːd/ n [U] **1** distance north or south of the equator, measured in degrees **2** (fml) freedom to choose what you do

0ⁿ **latter** /ˈlætə(r)/ adj near to the end of a period of time: *the ~ part of her life* ▶ **the latter** the second mentioned of two things, people or groups ■ **'latter-day** adj modern ▶ **latterly** adv most recently

lattice /ˈlætɪs/ n [C] framework of crossed wooden or metal strips

0ⁿ **laugh** /lɑːf/ v [I] make the sounds and movements of your face that show you are happy or think sth is funny [IDM] **be no laughing matter** be sth serious that you should not joke about **laugh your head off** → HEAD[1] [PV] **laugh at sb/sth** make sb/sth seem stupid by making jokes about them/it ● **laugh** n [C] **1** act or sound of laughing **2** (a laugh) (infml) amusing situation or person who is fun to be with ▶ **laughable** adj ridiculous ▶ **laughably** adv ■ **'laughing stock** n [C, usu sing] person who is made to appear foolish ▶ **laughter** n [U] act or sound of laughing

0ⁿ **launch** /lɔːntʃ/ v [T] **1** begin an activity, esp an organized one: ~ *a new business* **2** make a product available to the public for the first time **3** put a ship or boat into the water, esp one that has just been built **4** send a rocket, weapon, etc into space or through water [PV] **launch out (into sth)** do sth new in your career ● **launch** n [C] **1** action of launching sth; event at which sth is launched **2** large motor boat ■ **'launch pad** (also **'launching pad)** n [C] base from which spacecraft, etc are launched

launder /ˈlɔːndə(r)/ v [T] **1** (fml) wash and iron clothes **2** move illegally-obtained money into foreign bank accounts or legal businesses

launderette (*also* **laundrette**) /lɔːnˈdret/ (*US* **Laundromat**™ /ˈlɔːndrəmæt/) *n* [C] place where you can wash and dry your clothes in coin-operated machines

laundry /ˈlɔːndri/ *n* (*pl* **-ies**) **1** [U] clothes, etc that need washing, or that are being washed: *a ~ basket/room* **2** [C] place where you send clothes, etc to be washed

laurel /ˈlɒrəl/ *n* [C] evergreen bush with dark smooth shiny leaves

lava /ˈlɑːvə/ *n* [U] hot liquid rock that comes out of a volcano

lavatory /ˈlævətri/ *n* [C] (*pl* **-ies**) (*fml*, *GB*) toilet

lavender /ˈlævəndə(r)/ *n* [U] **1** plant with sweet-smelling pale purple flowers **2** pale purple colour

lavish /ˈlævɪʃ/ *adj* **1** large in amount, or impressive and expensive: *a ~ meal* **2** generous ► **lavish** *v* [PV] **lavish sth on/upon sb/sth** give a lot of sth to sb/sth ► **lavishly** *adv*

0━ **law** /lɔː/ *n* **1** (*also* **the law**) [U] whole system of rules that everyone in a country must obey: *Murder is against the ~.* **2** [C] rule that deals with a particular crime, agreement, etc **3** (**the law**) [sing] the police **4** [C] basic rule of action, eg in science: *the ~s of physics* [IDM] **be a law unto yourself** ignore the usual rules and conventions of behaviour ■ **law and order** respect for the law ■ **law-abiding** *adj* obeying the law ■ **law court** *n* [C] (*GB*) place where legal cases are heard and judged ► **lawful** *adj* (*fml*) allowed or recognized by law; legal ► **lawfully** *adv* ■ **lawless** *adj* not controlled by the law ► **lawlessness** *n* [U] ■ **lawsuit** *n* [C] non-criminal case in a law court

lawn /lɔːn/ *n* [C] area of short grass ■ **lawnmower** *n* [C] machine for cutting grass ■ **lawn tennis** (*fml*) = TENNIS

0━ **lawyer** /ˈlɔːjə(r)/ *n* [C] person who is trained and qualified to advise people about the law

lax /læks/ *adj* not strict enough; careless ► **laxity** *n* [U]

laxative /ˈlæksətɪv/ *n* [C], *adj* (medicine, food or drink) that helps sb empty their bowels easily

0━ **lay¹** /leɪ/ *v* (*pt*, *pp* **laid** /leɪd/) **1** [T] put sth in a particular position: *She laid the baby down on the bed.* **2** [T] put sth down, esp on the floor, ready to be used: *a ~ carpet/cable* **3** [I,T] (of birds, insects, etc) produce eggs **4** [T] (*GB*) arrange knives, forks, plates, etc on a table ready for a meal: *to ~ the table* **5** [T] (△, *sl*) (esp passive) have sex with sb [IDM] **lay sth bare** (*written*) reveal sth that was secret or hidden: *~ bare your feelings* **lay the blame on sb** say that sb is

responsible for a mistake, etc **lay claim to sth** state that you have a right to own sth **lay down the law** tell sb what they should or should not do **lay down your life (for sb/sth)** (*lit*) die in order to save sb/sth **lay a finger on sb** harm sb **lay it on (thick)** (*infml*) make one's feelings or experiences seem greater than they really are **lay sb low** make sb ill or weak **lay yourself open to sth** behave so that one is likely to receive (criticism, etc) **lay sth waste** (*fml*) destroy sth completely [PV] **lay into sb/sth** (*infml*) attack sb/sth with words or blows **lay off (sth)** (*infml*) stop doing or using sth harmful **lay sb off** stop employing sb because there is not enough work for them to do **lay sth on** (*GB*, *infml*) provide sth for sb, esp food or entertainment: *~ on a party* **lay sb out** knock sb unconscious **lay sth out 1** spread sth out to be seen easily **2** arrange sth in a planned way: *a well laid out garden* **lay sb up** cause sb to stay in bed: *be laid up with flu* ■ **laid-back** *adj* (*sl*) happily relaxed and unworried ■ **lay-off** *n* [C] act of dismissing a worker from a job ■ **layout** *n* [C] way in which parts of sth are arranged according to a plan ■ **layover** *n* [C] (*US*) = STOPOVER (STOP²)

lay² *pt* of LIE²

lay³ /leɪ/ *adj* **1** not having expert knowledge of a particular subject **2** not in an official position in the Church: *a ~ preacher* ■ **layman** (*also* **layperson**) *n* [C] person who does not have expert knowledge of a subject

layabout /ˈleɪəbaʊt/ *n* [C] (*old-fash*, *GB*, *infml*) lazy person

lay-by /ˈleɪ baɪ/ *n* [C] (*GB*) area at the side of a road where vehicles may stop

0━ **layer** /ˈleɪə(r)/ *n* [C] thickness of some substance or material, often one of many, on a surface: *a ~ of dust*

layman → LAY³

laze /leɪz/ *v* [I] **~ (about/around)** relax and do very little

0━ **lazy** /ˈleɪzi/ *adj* (**-ier**, **-iest**) **1** (*disapprov*) unwilling to work **2** showing a lack of activity ► **lazily** *adv* ► **laziness** *n* [U]

lb *abbr* (*pl* **lb**, **lbs**) one pound in weight (454 grams)

0━ **lead¹** /liːd/ *v* (*pt*, *pp* **led** /led/) **1** [I,T] go with or in front of a person or an animal to show the way: *The receptionist led the way to the boardroom.* **2** [I] **~ from/to** connect one object or place to another: *the pipe ~s from the top of the water tank* **3** [I,T] (of a road, etc) go somewhere or in a particular

lead

direction **4** [I] ~ to have sth as its result: *a mistake that led to his downfall* **5** [T] ~ **(to)** be the reason why sb does sth or thinks sth: *What led you to this conclusion?* **6** [T] have a certain kind of life: ~ *a miserable existence* **7** [I,T] be the best at sth; be in first place **8** [I,T] control or direct sb/sth: ~ *a team of scientists* [IDM] **lead sb astray** encourage sb to do wrong **lead the way** go first; show the way [PV] **lead sb on** persuade sb to believe or do sth by making false promises, etc **lead up to sth** prepare or introduce sth ▸ **leader** *n* [C] person who leads ▸ **leadership** *n* [U] position of being a leader; qualities of a leader ▸ **leading** *adj* most important ■ **leading 'article** (*also* **leader**) *n* [C] (GB) newspaper article giving the editor's opinion ■ **leading 'question** *n* [C] question that you ask in a particular way to get the answer you want

lead² /liːd/ *n* **1** (**the lead**) [sing] first place or position in a race or competition: *take the* ~ **2** [sing] distance by which sb/sth is in front of sb/sth else: *a* ~ *of ten metres* **3** [sing] example or action for people to copy: *follow sb's* ~ **4** [C] piece of information that might solve a crime or other problem: *The police will follow up all possible* ~*s.* **5** [C] (person playing the) main part in a play, etc **6** [C] strap or rope for holding and controlling a dog **7** [C] (GB) wire that connects a piece of electrical equipment to a source of electricity

lead³ /led/ *n* **1** [U] heavy soft greyish metal, used for water pipes, in roofing, etc **2** [C,U] thin black part of a pencil which marks paper ▸ **leaden** *adj* **1** dull, heavy or slow **2** dull grey in colour

leaf /liːf/ *n* (*pl* **leaves** /liːvz/) **1** [C] one of the usu green and flat parts of a plant growing from a stem **2** [C] sheet of paper **3** [U] metal, esp gold or silver, in the form of very thin sheets: *gold*-~ **4** [C] part of a table that can be lifted up to make the table bigger [IDM] **take a leaf from/out of sb's book** copy the way sb does things, because they are successful ● **leaf** *v* [PV] **leaf through sth** turn over the pages of a book, etc quickly, without reading them closely ▸ **leafy** *adj* (**-ier, -iest**)

leaflet /ˈliːflət/ *n* [C] printed sheet of paper

league /liːɡ/ *n* [C] **1** group of people or countries who have combined for a particular purpose **2** group of sports teams that play against each other **3** (*infml*) level of quality, ability, etc: *They're not in the*

same ~. [IDM] **in league (with sb)** making secret plans with sb

leak /liːk/ *n* [C] **1** small hole or crack through which liquid or gas escapes **2** liquid or gas that escapes through a hole in sth **3** deliberate act of giving secret information to the newspapers, etc: *a security* ~ ● **leak** *v* [I] **1** allow liquid or gas to pass through a small hole or crack **2** [I] (of liquid or gas) escape through a hole in sth **3** [T] make secret information publicly known ▸ **leakage** /ˈliːkɪdʒ/ *n* [C,U] process of leaking; amount that leaks ▸ **leaky** *adj* (**-ier, -iest**)

lean¹ /liːn/ *v* (*pt, pp* ~**ed** *adj* (GB *also* ~**t** /lent/) **1** [I] bend or move from an upright position **2** [I,T] ~ **against/on** (cause sth to) rest on or against sth for support: *~ a ladder against a wall* [PV] **lean on sb/sth 1** depend on sb/sth for help and support **2** try to influence sb by threatening them **lean to/toward/towards sth** have a tendency to prefer sth, esp an opinion ▸ **leaning** *n* [C] tendency; inclination: *political* ~*ings*

lean² /liːn/ *adj* **1** (of a person or animal) thin and healthy **2** (of meat) containing little fat **3** (of a period of time) not productive: ~ *years* **4** (of organizations, etc) strong and more efficient, because the number of employees has been reduced

leap /liːp/ *v* (*pt, pp* ~**t** /lept/ *or* ~**ed**) [I] **1** jump high or a long way **2** move quickly in the direction that is mentioned: ~ *into the car* [PV] **leap at sth** accept sth eagerly: *She* ~*t at the chance.* ● **leap** *n* [C] **1** long or high jump **2** sudden large increase or change [IDM] **by/in leaps and bounds** very quickly; in large amounts ■ **leapfrog** *n* [U] game in which players jump over others' bent backs ● **leapfrog** *v* (**-gg-**) [I,T] jump over sb in this way ■ **leap year** *n* [C] one year in every four years, with an extra day (29 February)

learn /lɜːn/ *v* (*pt, pp* ~**t** /lɜːnt/ *or* ~**ed**) **1** [I,T] gain knowledge or skill in a subject or activity: ~ *Dutch* ◇ ~ *(how) to swim* **2** [I,T] ~ **(of/about)** become aware of sth by hearing about it from sb else: ~ *of his death* **3** [T] study and repeat sth in order to be able to remember it: ~ *a poem* ▸ **learned** /ˈlɜːnɪd/ *adj* having a lot of knowledge ▸ **learner** *n* [C] ▸ **learning** *n* [U] knowledge gained by study

lease /liːs/ *n* [C] contract for the use of land, a building, etc in return for rent ● **lease** *v* [T] give or obtain the use of sth in this way ▸ **leasehold** *n* [U] *adj* (land, etc) held on a lease

leash /liːʃ/ *n* [C] = LEAD²(6)

least /liːst/ *det, pron* (usu the least) smallest in size, amount, degree, etc: *She gave (the)* ~ *of all towards the present.* [IDM] **not in the**

least not at all: *I'm not in the ~ tired.*
● **least** *adv* to the smallest degree: *the ~ expensive hotel* [**IDM**] **at least 1** not less than: *at ~ three months* **2** even if nothing else is true: *at ~ she's reliable* **not least** especially

0➡ **leather** /'leðə(r)/ *n* [U] material from animal skins, used for making shoes, etc ▶ **leathery** *adj* as tough as leather

0➡ **leave**[1] /liːv/ *v* (pt, pp **left** /left/) **1** [I,T] go away from a person or place **2** [T] cause or allow sb/sth to remain in a certain condition: *~ the window open* **3** [T] cause sth to happen or remain as a result: *Blood ~s a stain.* **4** (be left) [T] remain to be used, sold, etc: *Is there any coffee left?* **5** [T] forget or fail to take or bring sth/sb with you: *I left my book at home.* **6** [T] (*maths*) have a certain amount remaining: *7 from 10 ~s 3* **7** [T] give sth to sb when you die **8** [T] allow sb to take care of sth: *We left him to do the cooking.* [**IDM**] **leave/ let sb/sth alone** not interfere with or disturb sb/sth **leave sb/sth alone** not interfere with or disturb sb/sth **leave go (of sth)** (*GB, infml*) stop holding on to sth **leave it at that** (*infml*) say or do nothing more about sth **leave sb in the lurch** (*infml*) fail to help sb when they are relying on you to do so **leave well alone** → WELL[1] [**PV**] **leave sb/sth behind 1** (*usu passive*) make much better progress than sb **2** leave a person, place or state permanently **leave off** (*infml*) stop doing sth: *Start reading where you left off last time.* **leave sb/sth out (of sth)** not include sb/sth in sth

leave[2] /liːv/ *n* [U] **1** time when you are allowed to be away from work for a holiday or a special reason: *maternity ~* **2** (*fml*) official permission to do sth

leaves *plural of* LEAF

lecherous /'letʃərəs/ *adj* (*disapprov*) having or showing strong sexual desire

lectern /'lektən/ *n* [C] stand for holding a book, notes, etc when you are giving a talk, etc

0➡ **lecture** /'lektʃə(r)/ *n* [C] **1** talk given for the purposes of teaching **2** long angry talk given to sb because they have done wrong ● **lecture** *v* [I] give a lecture on a particular subject **2** [T] criticize sb, or tell them how you think they should behave ▶ **lecturer** *n* [C] **1** person who gives a lecture **2** (*esp GB*) person who teaches at a college or university ▶ **lectureship** *n* [C] position as a lecturer

led *pt, pp of* LEAD[1]

ledge /ledʒ/ *n* [C] narrow shelf coming out from a wall, cliff, etc

ledger /'ledʒə(r)/ *n* [C] book in which a company's accounts are kept

lee /liː/ *n* [sing] (*fml*) part of sth providing shelter against the wind

leech /liːtʃ/ *n* [C] **1** small bloodsucking worm **2** (*disapprov*) person who depends on sb else for money

leek /liːk/ *n* [C] vegetable with a white stem and long green leaves

leer /lɪə(r)/ *n* [C] unpleasant look that suggests sexual desire ● **leer** *v* [I] *~ (at)* look at sb with a leer

0➡ **left**[1] *pt, pp of* LEAVE[1] ▪ **left-luggage office** *n* [C] (*GB*) place at a railway station, etc where you can pay to leave bags or suitcases for a short time ▪ **leftovers** *n* [pl] food that has not been eaten at the end of a meal

0➡ **left**[2] /left/ *adj, adv* on or towards the side of your body that is towards the west when you are facing north ● **left** *n* **1** (the/sb's left) [sing] left side or direction **2** (the Left, the Left) [sing, with sing or pl verb] political groups who support the ideas and beliefs of socialism ▪ **left-hand** *adj* of or on the left side of sth/sb ▪ **left-handed** *adj* (of a person) using the left hand more easily or usually than the right ▶ **leftist** *n* [C], *adj* (supporter) of socialism ▪ the **left wing** *n* [sing, with sing or pl verb] supporters of a more extreme form of socialism than others in their party ▶ **left-wing** *adj*: *~-wing policies*

0➡ **leg** /leg/ *n* [C] **1** one of the long parts that connect the feet to the rest of the body **2** the leg of an animal, cooked and eaten **3** part of a pair of trousers that covers the leg: *a trouser ~* **4** support of a chair, table, etc **5** one section of a journey or race [**IDM**] **not have a leg to stand on** (*infml*) have no evidence or reason for your opinion or behaviour

legacy /'legəsi/ *n* [C] (pl -ies) **1** money or property given to you by sb when they die **2** situation that exists now as a result of sth that happened in the past

0➡ **legal** /'liːɡl/ *adj* **1** of or based on the law: *my ~ adviser* **2** allowed or required by law ▶ **legality** /liːˈɡæləti/ *n* [U] fact of being legal ▶ **legally** /'liːɡəli/ *adv*

legalistic /ˌliːɡəˈlɪstɪk/ *adj* (*disapprov*) obeying the law very strictly

legalize (*also* -ise) /'liːɡəlaɪz/ *v* [T] make sth legal

legend /'ledʒənd/ *n* [C,U] (type of) story from ancient times that may or may not be true: *the ~ of Robin Hood* **2** [C] famous person, esp in a particular field, who is admired by other people: *He has become a ~ in his own lifetime.* **3** [C] (*tech*) explanation of a map or diagram in a book ► **legendary** /ˈledʒəndri/ adj famous; known only in legends

legible /ˈledʒəbl/ adj clear enough to be read easily ► **legibly** adv

legion /ˈliːdʒən/ n [C] **1** division of an army, esp of the ancient Roman army **2** large number of people ● **legion** adj (fml) very many ► **legionary** /ˈliːdʒənəri/ n [C] (pl **-ies**) soldier who is part of a legion

legislate /ˈledʒɪsleɪt/ v [I] (fml) make a law affecting sth ► **legislation** /ˌledʒɪsˈleɪʃn/ n [U] **1** law or set of laws passed by a parliament **2** process of making laws ► **legislator** n [C] (fml)

legislative /ˈledʒɪslətɪv/ adj connected with the act of making and passing laws: a ~ assembly

legislature /ˈledʒɪsleɪtʃə(r)/ n [C] (fml) group of people with the power to make and change laws

legitimate /lɪˈdʒɪtɪmət/ adj **1** reasonable: a ~ excuse **2** allowed by law **3** (of a child) born of parents married to each other ► **legitimacy** /-məsi/ n [U]

legless /ˈleɡləs/ adj (infml, GB) very drunk

leisure /ˈleʒə(r)/ n [U] free time [IDM] **at your leisure** when you are free and not in a hurry ● **leisure centre** n [C] (GB) public building where people can go to do sports, etc in their free time ► **leisured** adj not having to work and therefore having a lot of free time ► **leisurely** adj, adv without hurrying: a ~ly walk

0─ **lemon** /ˈlemən/ n **1** [C,U] yellow citrus fruit with a sour juice: a ~ tree **2** [U] pale yellow colour

lemonade /ˌleməˈneɪd/ n [C,U] sweet fizzy drink with a lemon flavour

0─ **lend** /lend/ v (pt, pp **lent** /lent/) [T] **1** ~ (to sb) give the use of sth to sb for a short time: He lent him the money. ◇ He lent it to him. **2** ~ (to) (written) contribute or add sth to sth: Her presence lent dignity to the occasion. **3** lend itself to be suitable for sth [IDM] lend (sb) a (helping) hand (with sth) (infml) help sb with sth

0─ **length** /leŋθ/ n **1** [U,C] size or measurement of sth from one end to the other **2** [U,C] amount of time that sth lasts **3** [C] extent of sth used as a measurement: swim two ~s of the pool **4** [C] long thin piece of sth: a ~ of rope [IDM] at length **1** for a long time and in great detail (lit) eventually **go to any, some, great, etc lengths (to do sth)** put a lot of effort into sth, esp when this seems extreme ► **lengthen** v [I,T] (cause sth to) become longer ► **lengthways** (also **lengthwise**) adv along the length of sth: Cut the banana in half

~ways ► **lengthy** adj (**-ier**, **-iest**) very long

lenient /ˈliːniənt/ adj not strict when punishing people ► **leniency** /-ənsi/ n [U] ► **leniently** adv

lens /lenz/ n [C] **1** curved piece of glass or plastic that makes things look larger, smaller or clearer when you look through it: a pair of glasses with tinted ~es **2** = CONTACT LENS (CONTACT) **3** (anat) transparent part of the eye used for focusing light

lent pt, pp of LEND

lentil /ˈlentl/ n [C] small green, orange or brown seed that is usu dried and eaten as food

leopard /ˈlepəd/ n [C] large animal of the cat family with yellow fur and dark spots ► **leopardess** /ˌlepəˈdes/ n [C] female leopard

leotard /ˈliːətɑːd/ n [C] close-fitting piece of clothing worn by acrobats, dancers, etc

leper /ˈlepə(r)/ n [C] **1** person suffering from leprosy **2** person who is rejected and avoided by other people

leprosy /ˈleprəsi/ n [U] infectious disease that causes loss of feeling and which can lead to the loss of fingers, toes, etc

lesbian /ˈlezbiən/ n [C] woman who is sexually attracted to other women ► **lesbian** adj

0─ **less** /les/ det, pron a smaller amount of: ~ to do than I thought ● **less** adv to a smaller degree; not so much: It rains ~ here. [IDM] **even/much/still less** and certainly not less **and less** smaller and smaller amounts **no less than...** used to emphasize a large amount ● **less** prep used before a particular amount that must be taken away from the amount just mentioned: £1000 a month ~ tax

lessen /ˈlesn/ v [I,T] (cause sth to) become smaller, weaker, less important, etc

lesser /ˈlesə(r)/ adj smaller [IDM] **the lesser of two evils** the less important of two bad choices

0─ **lesson** /ˈlesn/ n [C] **1** period of time in which sb is taught sth: piano ~s **2** experience that sb can learn from: Let this be a ~ to you!

lest /lest/ conj (fml) in order to prevent sth from happening

0─ **let** /let/ v (**-tt-** pt, pp **let**) [T] **1** allow sb to do sth or sth to happen: We ~ him leave. **2** allow sb/ sth to go somewhere: ~ sb into the house **3** used for making suggestions or offers: L~'s go! ◇ Here, ~ me do it. **4** allow sb to use a house, room, etc in return for regular payments [IDM] **let alone** and certainly not: We cannot even pay our bills, ~ alone make a profit. **let sb/sth**

alone → LEAVE [1] **let the cat out of the bag** tell a secret carelessly or by mistake **let sth drop** do or say nothing more about sth **let fly (at sb/sth) (with sth)** attack sb/sth physically or with words **let sb/sth go | let go (of sb/sth)** stop holding sb/sth physically or with words **let yourself go 1** no longer hold back your feelings **2** stop being careful about how you look, dress, etc **let your hair down** (*infml*) relax and enjoy yourself **let sb have it** (*spoken, infml*) attack sb physically or with words **let sb know** tell sb about sth **let off steam** (*infml*) release energy or anger and become less excited **let the side down** fail to give your friends, family, etc the help, support, etc they expect **let sleeping dogs lie** leave sth alone **let sth slide** allow sth to become neglected, less organized, etc **let slip sth** accidentally reveal secret information **let sth slip (through your fingers)** miss or fail to use an opportunity **let us say** used when giving an example **let well alone → WELL**[2] **[PV] let sb down** disappoint sb **let sth down 1** lower sth **2** make clothes longer **3** (*GB*) allow air to escape from sth deliberately **let sb/ yourself in for sth** involve sb/ yourself in sth that is likely to be unpleasant or difficult **let sb in on sth | let sb into sth** (*infml*) allow sb to share a secret or private plan **let sb off (with sth)** not punish sb severely for sth they have done wrong **let sb off sth** allow sb not to do an unpleasant task **let sth off** fire a gun or make a bomb, etc. explode **let on (to sb)** (*infml*) tell a secret: *Don't ~ on that you know.* **let sth out 1** give a cry, etc **2** make a piece of clothing looser or larger **let up** become less strong; stop: *The rain began to ~ up.* ■ **'let-down** *n* [C] disappointment ■ **'let-up** *n* [C, U] reduction in strength, intensity, etc

lethal /ˈliːθl/ *adj* causing death

lethargy /ˈleθədʒi/ *n* [U] lack of energy or interest ▶ **lethargic** /ləˈθɑːdʒɪk/ *adj*

let's short for LET US

letter /ˈletə(r)/ *n* **1** [C] written message sent to sb **2** [C] written or printed sign representing a sound ■ **'letter bomb** *n* [C] small bomb sent to sb in an envelope ■ **'letter box** *n* [C] (*GB*) hole in a door for letters **2** boxes in the street or at a post office into which letters are posted ▶ **lettering** *n* [U] letters or words, esp with reference to their style and size

lettuce /ˈletɪs/ *n* [C, U] plant with green leaves, eaten in salads

leukaemia (*US* **-kem-**) /luːˈkiːmiə/ *n* [U] serious disease in which there are too many white blood cells

0— **level**[1] /ˈlevl/ *adj* **1** having a flat surface that does not slope **2** ~ (**with**) at the same height,

---

253

---

libel

position, etc as another; equal: *Wales drew* ~ (= made the score equal) *early in the game.* (**IDM**) **do/try your level best (to do sth)** do all that you can to achieve sth ■ **level 'crossing** *n* [C] place where a road crosses a railway ■ **level-'headed** *adj* sensible; calm

0— **level**[2] /ˈlevl/ *n* **1** [C] amount of sth that exists in a particular situation at one time: *a high ~ of unemployment* **2** [C, U] standard or quality: *He studied French to degree~.* **3** [U, C] position or rank in a scale of size or importance: *talks at management ~* **4** [C, U] height of sth in relation to the ground or to what it used to be: *below ground ~*

level[3] /ˈlevl/ *v* (*-ll- US -l-*) [T] **1** make sth flat or smooth **2** demolish a building **3** ~ (**at**) aim a weapon or criticism at sb [PV] **level off/out 1** stop rising and falling and become horizontal **2** stay at a steady level of development after a period of sharp rises and falls: *Sales ~led off.* **level with sb** (*infml*) speak honestly to sb

lever /ˈliːvə(r)/ *n* [C] **1** handle used to operate a vehicle or a machine **2** bar that turns on a fixed point used to lift things **3** action used to put pressure on sb to do sth ● **lever** *v* [T] move sth with a lever: *L~ it into position.* ▶ **leverage** /ˈliːvərɪdʒ/ *n* [U] **1** (*fml*) power to influence what people do **2** (*tech*) force of a lever

levity /ˈlevəti/ *n* [U] (*written*) lack of respect for sth serious

levy /ˈlevi/ *v* (*pt, pp* **-ied**) [T] demand and collect a payment, tax etc by authority: *~ a tax* ● **levy** *n* [C] (*pl* **-ies**) sum of money that has to be paid, esp as a tax to the government

lewd /ljuːd/ *adj* referring to sex in a rude way: *~ jokes*

liability /ˌlaɪəˈbɪləti/ *n* (*pl* **-ies**) **1** [U] state of being legally responsible for sb/sth **2** [C, usu sing] (*infml*) person or thing that causes you difficulties or problems: *An old car is a ~.* **3** [C, usu pl] debt that must be paid

liable /ˈlaɪəbl/ *adj* **1** ~ (**for**) legally responsible for paying the cost of sth: *~ for debts* **2** ~ **to** likely to do sth: *~ to make mistakes* **3** ~ **to** likely to be affected by sth: *be ~ to injury*

liaise /liˈeɪz/ *v* [I] work together with sb and exchange information

liaison /liˈeɪzn/ *n* **1** [U] working association between different groups **2** [C] secret sexual relationship

liar /ˈlaɪə(r)/ *n* [C] person who tells lies

libel /ˈlaɪbl/ *n* [U, C] act of printing a statement about sb that is not true and that damages their reputation ● **libel** *v* (*-ll- US -l-*) [T] publish a

---

written statement about sb that is not true ▸ **libellous** (US **libelous**) /-bələs/ adj

liberal /ˈlɪbərəl/ adj **1** tolerant of the beliefs or behaviour of others **2** giving or given generously: a ~ supply **3** (of education) giving a wide general knowledge ▸ the **Liberal Democrats** (abbr **Lib Dems**) n [pl] one of the main British political parties, in favour of some political and social change but not extreme ▸ **liberalism** n [U] liberal opinions, esp in politics ▸ **liberalize** (also -ise) /ˈlɪbrəlaɪz/ v [T] make a law or a political or religious system less strict ▸ **liberally** adv

liberate /ˈlɪbəreɪt/ v [T] (fml) set sb/ sth free ▸ **liberated** adj free in social and sexual matters ▸ **liberation** /ˌlɪbəˈreɪʃn/ n [U]

liberty /ˈlɪbəti/ n (pl **-ies**) **1** [C,U] (fml) right or freedom to do as you choose **2** [U] (fml) state of not being a prisoner or a slave [IDM] be at liberty free **take the liberty of doing sth** do sth without permission

0— **library** /ˈlaɪbrəri; ˈlaɪbri/ n [C] (pl **-ies**) (room or building for a) collection of books, records, etc ▸ **librarian** /laɪˈbreəriən/ n [C] person in charge of a library

lice plural of LOUSE

0— **licence** (US **license**) /ˈlaɪsns/ n [C,U] (official paper giving) permission to do, own, etc sth: a driving ~

0— **license** /ˈlaɪsns/ v [T] give sb official permission to do, own, etc sth ▸ **licensee** /ˌlaɪsənˈsiː/ n [C] person who has a licence, esp to sell alcohol ■ **license number** n (US = REGISTRATION NUMBER (REGISTRATION)

lick /lɪk/ v [T] **1** move your tongue over the surface of sth in order to eat it, make it wet or clean it: The dog ~ed its paw. **2** (of flames) touch sth lightly **3** (infml) easily defeat sb [IDM] **lick your lips** → LIP ● **lick** n [C] act of licking sth **2** [sing] small amount of paint, etc

licorice (esp US) = LIQUORICE

0— **lid** /lɪd/ n [C] **1** cover over a container that can be removed: a dustbin ~ **2** = EYELID (EYE)

0— **lie**[1] /laɪ/ v (pt, pp ~**d** pres pt **lying**) [I] say or write sth that you know is not true ● **lie** n [C] statement that you know to be untrue: to tell a ~

0— **lie**[2] /laɪ/ v (pt **lay** /leɪ/ pp **lain** /leɪn/ pres pt **lying**) [I] **1** (of a person or an animal) be or put yourself in a flat or horizontal position so that you are not standing or sitting **2** (of a thing) be or remain in a flat position on a surface: Clothes lay all over the floor. **3** be or remain in a

particular state: machines lying idle **4** be situated: The town ~s on the coast. **5** be spread out in a particular place **6** (of abstract things) be found: It does not ~ within my power to help you. [IDM] **lie in wait (for sb)** be hidden, waiting to surprise sb **lie low** (infml) keep quiet or hidden **take sth lying down** accept an insult, unfair treatment, etc without protesting [PV] **lie behind sth** be the real reason for sth **lie down** be or get into a horizontal position, esp on a bed, in order to sleep or rest **lie with sb (to do sth)** (fml) be sb's duty or responsibility: The final decision ~s with you. ● **lie** n [IDM] **the lie of the land 1** natural features of an area **2** the way a situation is now and how it is likely to develop ■ **lie-down** n [sing] (GB, infml) short rest ■ **lie-in** n [C] (GB, infml) stay in bed later than your usual time in the morning: have a ~-in

lieutenant /lefˈtenənt/ (abbr **Lieut., Lt**) n [C] officer of middle rank in the army, navy or air force

0— **life** /laɪf/ n (pl **lives** /laɪvz/) **1** [U] ability to breathe, grow, reproduce, etc which makes people, animals and plants different from objects **2** [U,C] state of being alive as a human being; an individual person's existence: He expects a lot from ~. ◇ Many lives were lost. **3** [U] living things: Is there ~ on Mars? **4** [C] period between birth and death: She spent her whole ~ in Canada. **5** [C] period during which sth continues to exist or function: a battery with a ~ of three years **6** [U] punishment of being sent to prison for life: The judge gave him ~. **7** [U] experience and activities that are typical of all people's existences: The dishwasher makes ~ easier for us. **8** [U] particular way of living: city/country ~ **9** [U] quality of being lively and exciting: full of ~ **10** [U] living model, used as the subject in art: a portrait drawn from ~ **11** [C] story of sb's life: a ~ of Dante [IDM] **come to life** become lively or active **for the life of you** (infml) however hard you try **the life and soul of the party, etc** (GB, infml) the most lively and amusing person at a party, etc **not on your life** (spoken) certainly not **take sb's life** kill sb **take your life in your hands** risk being killed ■ **lifebelt** (also **lifebuoy**) n [C] floating ring for sb who has fallen into the water to hold onto ■ **lifeboat** n [C] boat built to save people in danger at sea ■ **life cycle** n [C] (biol) series of forms into which a living thing changes as it develops: the ~ cycle of a frog ■ **lifeguard** n [C] expert swimmer employed to rescue other swimmers in danger ■ **life jacket** n [C] jacket worn to keep a person afloat in water ▶ **lifeless** adj **1** dead **2** not lively; dull ■ **lifelike** adj exactly like a real person or thing: *a ~like painting* ● **lifeline** n [C] **1** rope used for rescuing sb who has fallen into the water **2** something that is very important for sb and that they depend on ■ **lifelong** adj lasting all through your life ■ **life-size(d)** adj the same size as the person or thing really is ■ **lifespan** n [C] length of time that sth is likely to live, continue, or function ■ **lifestyle** n [C] way a person or group of people lives and works ■ **lifetime** n [C] length of time that sb is alive

0─ **lift** /lɪft/ v **1** [I,T] raise sb/sth or be raised to a higher level or position **2** [T] remove or end restrictions: *a ~ ban* **3** [T] make sb more cheerful: *The news ~ed her spirits.* **4** [I] (of clouds, fog, etc) rise and disappear **5** [T] (*infml*) steal sth [IDM] **not lift a finger** (*infml*) do nothing to help sb [PV] **lift off** (of a spacecraft) leave the ground and rise up into the air ● **lift** n **1** [C] (*GB*) machine that carries people or goods from one floor of a building to another **2** [C] (*GB*) free ride in a vehicle: *a ~ to the station* **3** [sing] feeling of being happier than before **4** [sing] act of lifting sth ■ **lift-off** n [C,U] act of launching a spacecraft into the air

ligament /ˈlɪɡəmənt/ n [C] band of strong tissue that holds bones together

0─ **light**¹ /laɪt/ n **1** [U] energy from the sun, a lamp, etc that makes it possible to see things: *bright/dim ~* **2** [C] something, esp an electric lamp, that produces light: *turn the ~s on* **3** [sing] match or device with which you can light a cigarette: (*GB*) *Have you got a ~?* **4** [sing] expression in sb's eyes which shows what they are thinking **5** [sing] way in which sb/sth is thought about: *see things in a good ~* (= favourably): [IDM] **bring sth/come to light** make sth/become known to people **cast/shed/throw light on sth** make sth clearer **in the light of sth** considering sth: *in the ~ of this news* **light at the end of the tunnel** something that shows you are nearly at the end of a long and difficult time ■ **light bulb** = BULB(1) ■ **lighthouse** n [C] tower containing a powerful light to warn and guide ships ■ **light year** n [C] **1** distance that light travels in one year **2** (**light years**) [pl] (*infml*) a very long time

0─ **light²** /laɪt/ adj **1** full of light; having the natural light of day: *a ~ room* **2** pale in colour: *~-blue eyes* **3** easy to lift or move; not heavy **4** of less than the usual weight, amount, force, etc: *~ rain* **5** gentle: *a ~ touch* **6** easy to do; not tiring: *~ work* **7** entertaining rather than serious or

difficult: *~ reading* **8** not serious or severe: *a ~ sentence* **9** (of a meal) small in quantity and easy to digest: *a ~ snack* **10** (of drinks) low in alcohol **11** (of sleep) not deep [IDM] **make light of sth** treat sth as unimportant ■ **light-fingered** adj (*infml*) likely to steal things ■ **light-headed** adj feeling slightly faint ■ **light-hearted** adj **1** intended to be amusing rather than serious **2** cheerful ■ **light industry** n [C] industry that produces small consumer goods or parts ▶ **lightly** adv **1** gently; with little force or effort **2** to a small degree; not much **3** not seriously [IDM] **get off/be let off lightly** (*infml*) manage to avoid severe punishment ■ **lightness** n [U] ■ **lightweight** n [C] **1** boxer weighing between 57 and 61 kilograms **2** (*infml*) person of little importance or influence

0─ **light³** /laɪt/ v (pt, pp **lit** /lɪt/ or **lighted**) **1** [I,T] (cause sth to) start to burn **2** [T] give light to sth or to a place: *a stage lit by spotlights* ◇ *well/badly lit streets* [PV] **light on/upon sth** (*lit*) see or find sth by chance **light (sth) up 1** (*infml*) begin to smoke a cigarette **2** cause light to shine on sth: *The fire lit up the whole sky.* **3** (cause sb's face or eyes to) show happiness and excitement ▶ **lighting** n [U] arrangement or type of light in a place

lighten /ˈlaɪtn/ v **1** [T] reduce the amount of work, debt, worry, etc that sb has: *gadgets to ~ the load of domestic work* **2** [I,T] (cause sth to) become brighter or lighter in colour **3** ~ (up) [I,T] (cause sb to) feel less sad, worried or serious **4** [T] make sth lighter in weight

lighter /ˈlaɪtə(r)/ n [C] device for lighting cigarettes, etc

lightning /ˈlaɪtnɪŋ/ n [U] flash of bright light in the sky, produced by electricity ● **lightning** adj very quick, brief or sudden: *at ~ speed* ■ **lightning conductor** (*US* **lightning rod**) n [C] metal wire that goes from the top of a building to the ground, to prevent damage by lightning

0─ **like¹** /laɪk/ v [T] **1** find sb/sth pleasant, attractive or satisfactory; enjoy sth **2** want: *Do what you ~.* **3** used in negative sentences to mean 'be unwilling to do sth': *I didn't ~ to stop you.* **4** used with *should* or *would* to express a wish or choice politely: *would you ~ a cup of tea?* ◇ *I'd ~ to think about it.* [IDM] **if you like** (*spoken*) used to politely agree to sth or to suggest sth **not like the look/sound of sb/sth** have a bad impression based on what you have seen/heard of sb/sth ● **like** n

like 256

1 (likes) [pl] the things that you like: *We all have different ~s and dislikes.* **2** [sing] person or thing that is similar to another: *Music, painting and the ~.* ▸ **likeable** (*also* **likable**) *adj* pleasant

0‒ **like²** /laɪk/ *prep* **1** similar to sb/ sth: *a hat ~ mine* **2** used to ask sb's opinion of sb/sth: *What's his new girlfriend ~?* **3** typical of sb/sth: *It's just ~ him to be rude.* **4** in the same way as sb/sth: *behave ~ children* ◇ *drink ~ a fish* **5** for example: *sports, football and hockey* **IDM** **like anything** (*GB, infml*) very much ● **like** *conj* (*infml*) **1** in the same way as **2** as if: *She acts ~ she owns the place.*

0‒ **like³** /laɪk/ *adj* (*fml*) similar to another person or thing ■ **like-minded** *adj* having similar ideas and interests

likelihood /ˈlaɪklihʊd/ *n* [U, sing] probability

0‒ **likely** /ˈlaɪkli/ *adj* (**-ier, -iest**) probable or expected: *~ to rain* **IDM** **a likely story** (*spoken*) used to show that you do not believe what sb has said ● **likely** *adv* **IDM** **as likely as not** | **most/very likely** very probably **not likely!** (*spoken, esp GB*) used to disagree strongly with a statement or suggestion

liken /ˈlaɪkən/ *v* **PV** **liken sth/sb to sth/sb** (*fml*) compare one thing or person to another and say they are similar

likeness /ˈlaɪknəs/ *n* [C, U] (instance of) being similar in appearance: *a family ~*

likewise /ˈlaɪkwaɪz/ *adv* (*fml*) similarly; also

liking /ˈlaɪkɪŋ/ *n* [sing] **~ (for)** feeling that you like sb/sth: *He has a ~ for fast cars.* ◇ *She's taken a real ~ to him.* **IDM** **to sb's liking** (*fml*) satisfactory

lilac /ˈlaɪlək/ *n* **1** [C] bush with sweet-smelling pale purple or white flowers **2** [U] pale purple colour

lilt /lɪlt/ *n* [sing] pleasant rise and fall of the voice ▸ **lilting** *adj*

lily /ˈlɪli/ *n* (*pl* **-ies**) plant that grows from a bulb and has large usu white flowers

limb /lɪm/ *n* [C] **1** leg, arm or wing **2** large branch of a tree **IDM** **out on a limb** (*infml*) not supported by other people

limber /ˈlɪmbə(r)/ *v* **PV** **limber up** exercise your muscles before a race, etc

limbo /ˈlɪmbəʊ/ *n* **IDM** **in limbo** in an uncertain state

lime /laɪm/ *n* **1** [U] white substance used in making cement **2** [C, U] (juice of a) small green fruit like a lemon but more acid **3** (*also* **lime tree**) [C] tree with sweet-smelling yellow flowers ■ **limestone** *n* [U] type of white stone that contains calcium, used in building

limelight /ˈlaɪmlaɪt/ *n* (**the limelight**) [U] centre of public attention

limerick /ˈlɪmərɪk/ *n* [C] humorous poem with five lines

0‒ **limit** /ˈlɪmɪt/ *n* [C] **1** point or line that may not or cannot be passed **2** greatest or smallest amount allowed or possible **IDM** **be the limit** (*old-fash, spoken*) be extremely annoying **off limits** (*esp US*) = OUT OF BOUNDS (BOUNDS) **within limits** to some extent; with some restrictions: *I'm willing to help, within ~s.* ● **limit** *v* [T] keep sb/sth within a limit ▸ **limitation** /ˌlɪmɪˈteɪʃn/ *n* **1** [U] act of limiting or controlling sb/sth **2** [C] rule, fact or condition that limits sb/sth; weakness ▸ **limited** *adj* restricted; few or small ■ **limited ˈcompany** *n* [C] (in Britain) company whose owners only have to pay a limited amount of its debts ▸ **limitless** *adj* without limits

limousine /ˈlɪməziːn/ *n* [C] large luxurious car with the driver's seat separated from the passengers in the back

limp /lɪmp/ *v* [i] walk with difficulty because one leg is injured ● **limp** *n* [sing] limping walk: *to walk with a ~* ● **limp** *adj* not stiff or firm ▸ **limply** *adv* ▸ **limpness** *n* [U]

linchpin /ˈlɪntʃpɪn/ *n* [C] person or thing that is essential to an organization, plan, etc

0‒ **line¹** /laɪn/ *n* **1** [C] long thin mark on a surface **2** [C] long thin mark on the ground to show the limit or border of sth: *~ marking a tennis court* **3** [C] mark like a line on sb's skin that people get as they get older: *the ~s on his face* **4** [C] an imaginary limit or border between one thing and another: *There's a fine ~ between showing interest and interfering.* **5** [C] overall shape; outline **6** [C] row of people or things: *customers standing in a* (~) **7** [C, usu sing] series of people, things or events that follow one another in time: *She came from a long ~ of doctors.* **8** [C] row of words on a page **9** [C] words spoken by an actor **10** [C] length of thread, rope or wire: *a fishing ~* **11** [C] telephone connection: *I was talking to John when the ~ went dead.* **12** [C] railway track or section of a railway system **13** [C, usu sing] direction or course: *the ~ of fire* (= the direction sb is shooting in) **14** [C] course of action, behaviour or thought: *a new ~ of research* **15** [sing] type or area of business, activity or interest: *My ~ of work pays pretty well.* **16** [C] type of product: *a new ~ in coats* **17** [C]

A B C D E F G H I J K **L** M N O P Q R S T U V W X Y Z

company that provides transport for people or goods: *a shipping ~* **18** [C] series of military defences where the soldiers are fighting during a war: *He was sent to fight in the front ~.* IDM **be on line 1** be working or functioning **2** using a computer; communicating with other people by computer **drop sb a line → DROP**[1] **in line for sth** likely to get sth **in line with sth** similar to sth; in accordance with sth **(put sth) on the line** (*infml*) (put sth) at risk **on the right lines** following a way that is likely to succeed **out of line (with sb/sth)** **1** not forming a straight line **2** unacceptably different from others **3** (*US*) = OUT OF ORDER(3) ORDER[1] ■ **'line drawing** *n* drawing done with a pen, pencil, etc ■ **line printer** *n* [C] machine that prints very quickly, producing a complete line of text at a time

line[2] /laɪn/ *v* [T] **1** cover the inside surface of sth with another material: *fur~d gloves* **2** form a layer on the inside of sth **3** form lines or rows along sth: *a road ~d with trees* **4** mark sth with lines: *a ~d paper* IDM **line your/sb's (own) pocket(s)** make yourself or sb richer, esp by being dishonest [PV] **line (sb) up** (cause people to) form a line **line sth up** (*infml*) arrange or organize sth ■ **'line-up** *n* [C] **1** line of people formed for inspection, etc **2** set of people or things arranged for a purpose

linear /ˈlɪniə(r)/ *adj* **1** of or in lines **2** of length: *~ measurement*

linen /ˈlɪnɪn/ *n* [U] (cloth for making) sheets, tablecloths, etc

liner /ˈlaɪnə(r)/ *n* [C] **1** large passenger ship **2** (in compounds) something put inside sth to protect it: *bin~s*

linesman /ˈlaɪnzmən/ *n* [C] (pl **-men**) (*sport*) official who says whether a ball has gone outside the limits during a game

linger /ˈlɪŋɡə(r)/ *v* [I] stay somewhere for a long time; be slow to leave or disappear ▶ **lingering** *adj* slow to end or disappear: *a ~ illness*

lingerie /ˈlænʒəri/ *n* [U] women's underwear

linguist /ˈlɪŋɡwɪst/ *n* [C] **1** person who knows several foreign languages well **2** person who studies language or linguistics ▶ **linguistic** /lɪŋˈɡwɪstɪk/ *adj* of language or linguistics ▶ **linguistics** *n* [U] study of language

liniment /ˈlɪnɪmənt/ *n* [C,U] liquid for rubbing on parts of the body which ache

lining /ˈlaɪnɪŋ/ *n* [C,U] layer of material to cover the inside surface of sth: *a fur ~*

○━ **link** /lɪŋk/ *n* [C] **1** connection or relationship between two or more people or things **2** each ring of a chain ● *v* [C] **1** make a connection between two or more people or things [PV] **link up (with sb/sth)** join or become joined with sb/sth

linoleum /lɪˈnəʊliəm/ (*GB also* **lino** /ˈlaɪnəʊ/) *n* [U] type of strong material with a hard shiny surface, used for covering floors

lint /lɪnt/ *n* [U] soft cotton material, used for putting on wounds

lion /ˈlaɪən/ *n* [C] large powerful animal of the cat family IDM **the lion's share (of sth)** (*GB*) the largest or best part of sth ■ **lioness** *n* [C] female lion

○━ **lip** /lɪp/ *n* [C] **1** either of the two soft edges of the mouth **2** [C] edge of a jug, cup, etc **3** [U] (*infml*) rude disrespectful talk IDM **lick/smack your lips** (*infml*) show that you are looking forward eagerly to sth enjoyable **my lips are sealed** used to say that you will not repeat sb's secret to other people ■ **'lip-read** *v* (pt, pp) **'lip,read** /-red/) [I,T] understand sb's speech by watching the movements of their lips ▶ **'lip-reading** *n* [U] ■ **'lip service** *n* [U] IDM **pay lip service to sth** say that you support sb while not doing so in reality ■ **lipstick** *n* [C,U] (stick of) colouring for the lips

liqueur /lɪˈkjʊə(r)/ *n* [U,C] strong sweet alcoholic drink

○━ **liquid** /ˈlɪkwɪd/ *n* [C,U] substance, eg water or oil, that flows freely but which is not a gas ● **liquid** *adj* **1** in the form of a liquid **2** easily changed into cash: *~ assets* **3** (*lit*) clear and looking wet: *~ blue eyes* **4** (*lit*) (of sounds) clear and flowing

liquidate /ˈlɪkwɪdeɪt/ *v* [T] **1** close down an unsuccessful business company **2** sell sth in order to get money, esp to pay a debt **3** destroy or remove sb/sth that causes problems ▶ **liquidation** /ˌlɪkwɪˈdeɪʃn/ *n* [U]

liquidize (*also* **-ise**) /ˈlɪkwɪdaɪz/ *v* [T] crush fruit, vegetables, etc into liquid ▶ **liquidizer** (*also* **-iser**) *n* [C] electric machine for liquidizing food

liquor /ˈlɪkə(r)/ *n* [U] (*esp US*) strong alcoholic drink ■ **'liquor store** *n* [C] (*US*) = OFF-LICENCE

liquorice /ˈlɪkərɪʃ; -rɪs/ *n* [U] black substance with a strong flavour, used as a sweet or in medicine

lisp /lɪsp/ *n* [sing] speech fault in which the sound 's' is pronounced 'th' ● **lisp** *v* [I,T] speak with a lisp

○━ **list**[1] /lɪst/ *n* [C] **1** set of names, things, etc written down in order **2** [sing] fact of a ship leaning to one

listen

side ■ **'list price** n [usu sing] (business) price at which goods are advertised for sale, eg in a catalogue ● **list** v **1** [T] write a list of things in a particular order **2** [T] mention or include sth in a list **3** [I] (of a ship) lean over to one side

0— **listen** /'lɪsn/ v [I] ~ **(to sb/sth) 1** pay attention to sb/sth that you can hear: to ~ to music ◇ L~! What's that noise? Can you hear it? **2** take notice or believe what sb says: None of this would have happened if you'd ~ed to me. **[PV] listen (out) for sth** be prepared to hear a particular sound: Can you ~ out for the doorbell? **listen in (on/to sth)** listen to a conversation that you are not supposed to hear ▶ **listener** n [C]

listeria /lɪ'stɪəriə/ n [U] type of bacteria that makes people sick if they eat infected food

listless /'lɪstləs/ adj too tired to show interest ▶ **listlessly** adv ▶ **listlessness** n [U]

lit pt, pp of LIGHT³

liter (US) = LITRE

literacy /'lɪtərəsi/ n [U] ability to read and write

literal /'lɪtərəl/ adj **1** being the basic or usual meaning of a word **2** that follows the original words exactly: a ~ translation ▶ **literally** adv **1** in a literal way; exactly: The word 'planet'—ly means 'wandering body'. **2** (infml) used to emphasize the truth of sth that may seem surprising: I was —ly bored to tears.

literary /'lɪtərəri/ adj of literature or authors

literate /'lɪtərət/ adj **1** able to read and write **2** well educated; cultured

0— **literature** /'lɪtrətʃə(r)/ n [U] **1** writings valued as works of art, eg novels, plays and poems **2** ~ **(on)** pieces of writing on a particular subject

lithe /laɪð/ adj (fml) (of a person or their body) able to bend easily

litigation /ˌlɪtɪ'ɡeɪʃn/ n [U] (law) process of making or defending a claim in a law court

0— **litre** /'liːtə(r)/ n [C] (abbr **l**) metric unit of capacity, used for measuring liquids

litter /'lɪtə(r)/ n **1** [U] bits of paper, bottles, etc that people have left lying in a public place **2** [C] all the young born to an animal at one time ● **litter** v [T] make a place untidy with litter ■ **'litter bin** n [C] container for rubbish

0— **little¹** /'lɪtl/ adj **1** small: ~ cups **2** young: a ~ boy **3** (of distance or time) short: wait a ~ while **4** not important: a ~ mistake

0— **little²** /'lɪtl/ det, pron **1** used with uncountable nouns to mean 'not

much': There was ~ doubt in my mind. **2** (a little) used with uncountable nouns to mean 'a small amount' or 'some': a ~ milk ● **little** adv (**less, least**) **1** not much; only slightly: I slept very ~ last night. ◇ (written) L~ does he know (= He doesn't know) what trouble he's in. **2** (a little) (a little bit) to a small degree: She seemed a ~ (bit) afraid of going outside. **[IDM] little by little** gradually **little wonder (that...)** → WONDER

0— **live¹** /lɪv/ v **1** [I] have your home: ~ in Leeds **2** [I] remain alive: Doctors say he has six months to ~. **3** [I] be alive **4** [I,T] spend your life in a particular way: ~ happily **5** [I] enjoy life fully **[IDM] live beyond/within your means** spend more/less money than you earn or can afford **live (from) hand to mouth** spend all the money you earn on basic needs such as food, without being able to save any money **live it up** (infml) involve yourself in an exciting way **[PV] live sth down** be able to make people forget about sth embarrassing you have done **live for sb/sth** think that sb/sth is the main purpose of or the most important thing in your life **live in/out** (of a worker or student) live at/away from the place where you work or study **live off sb/sth** receive the money you need to live from sb/ sth because you do not have any money **live on** continue to live or exist live on sth **1** have sth as your main food **2** have enough money for the basic things you need to live **live through sth** experience sth and survive: ~ through two wars **live together** (also **live with sb**) live with sb as if you are married **live up to sth** do as well as or be as good as other people expect you to be: ~d up to my expectations **live with sth** accept sth unpleasant

0— **live²** /laɪv/ adj **1** living; not dead **2** (of a broadcast) sent out while the event is actually happening, not recorded first and broadcast later **3** (of a performance) given or made when people are watching, not recorded: ~ music **4** (of a wire) carrying electricity **5** still able to explode or catch fire; ready for use: ~ ammunition **6** burning or glowing: ~ coals **7** (of a question or subject) of great interest at the present time

liveable /'lɪvəbl/ adj fit to live in; tolerable

livelihood /'laɪvlihʊd/ n [C, usu sing] means of earning money in order to live

0— **lively** /'laɪvli/ adj (**-ier, -iest**) **1** full of life and energy **2** (of colours) bright ▶ **liveliness** n [U]

liven /'laɪvn/ v **[PV] liven (sb/sth) up** (cause sb/sth) to become more interesting and exciting

liver /'lɪvə(r)/ n **1** [C] large organ in

the body that cleans the blood **2** [U] animal's liver as food

lives plural of LIFE

livestock /'laɪvstɒk/ n [U] farm animals

livid /'lɪvɪd/ adj **1** (infml) extremely angry **2** dark bluish-grey in colour

0‑ **living** /'lɪvɪŋ/ adj **1** alive now **2** used or practised now: a ~ language [**IDM**] **be the living image of sb** ≡ IMAGE **within/in living memory** at a time remembered by people still alive ● **living** n [sing] money to buy the things you need in life: What do you do for a ~? **2** [U] way or style of life: a low standard of ~ **3** (the living) [pl] people who are alive now ● **living room** n [C] room in a house where people sit together, watch TV, etc

lizard /'lɪzəd/ n [C] small four-legged reptile with a long tail

0‑ **load** /ləʊd/ n **1** [C] thing that is carried by a person, vehicle, etc **2** [C] (esp in compounds) quantity that can be carried: bus~s of furniture **3** [sing] (GB also **loads (of sth)** [pl]) (infml) a large number or amount of sb/sth; plenty: ~s of money **4** [C] amount of work that a person or a machine has to do **5** [C] feeling of responsibility or worry: Hearing they had arrived safely took a ~ off my mind. ● **load** v **1** [I,T] put a load onto or into sth; receive a load: ~ cargo onto a ship **2** [T] give sb a lot of things to carry **3** [T] put sth into a weapon, a camera or other piece of equipment so that it can be used **4** [I,T] put data or a program into the memory of a computer: Wait for the game to ~. ▶ **loaded** adj **1** ~ (with) carrying a load; full and heavy **2** (infml) very rich **3** acting either as an advantage or a disadvantage to sb in a way which is unfair **4** having more meaning than you realize at first and intended to trap you: It was a ~ed question. **5** containing bullets, camera film, etc

loaf /ləʊf/ n (pl **loaves** /ləʊvz/) [C] mass of shaped and baked bread ● **loaf** v [I] ~ (about/around) (infml) spend your time not doing anything

0‑ **loan** /ləʊn/ n **1** [C] money that an organization such as a bank lends and sb borrows **2** [sing] act of lending; state of being lent: This painting is on loan. ● **loan** v [T] (esp US) lend sth to sb, esp money

loath (also **loth**) /ləʊθ/ adj ~ **to** (fml) unwilling to do sth

loathe /ləʊð/ v [T] dislike sb/sth very much ▶ **loathing** n [U] disgust ▶ **loathsome** /'ləʊðsəm/ adj disgusting

loaves plural of LOAF

lob /lɒb/ v (**-bb-**) [I,T] throw or hit a ball, etc in a high curve ▶ **lob** n [C]

lobby /'lɒbi/ n (pl **-ies**) **1** [C] entrance

259

locust

hall of a hotel, theatre, etc **2** [C, with sing or pl verb] group of people who try to influence politicians ● **lobby** v (pt, pp **-ied**) [I,T] try to persuade a politician to support or oppose a proposed law, etc

lobe /ləʊb/ n [C] **1** = EAR LOBE (EAR) **2** part of an organ in the body, esp the lungs or brain

lobster /'lɒbstə(r)/ n **1** [C] shellfish with eight legs and two claws **2** [U] meat from a lobster, eaten as food

0‑ **local** /'ləʊkl/ adj **1** of a particular place: ~ news **2** affecting only a part, not the whole, of the body: a ~ anaesthetic ■ **local area network** n [C] = LAN ● **local** n [C] **1** (usu pl) person who lives in a particular place **2** (GB, infml) pub near where you live ▶ **locally** adv

locality /ləʊ'kæləti/ n [C] (pl **-ies**) district; place

localize (also **-ise**) /'ləʊkəlaɪz/ v [T] limit sth to a particular area: ~ a disease

0‑ **locate** /ləʊ'keɪt/ v **1** [T] find out the exact position of sb/sth **2** [T] put or build sth in a particular place: Our offices are ~d in Paris. ▶ **location** /ləʊ'keɪʃn/ n [C] place or position [**IDM**] **on location** (of a film) photographed in natural surroundings, not in a studio

loch /lɒk/ n [C] (in Scotland) lake: L~ Ness

0‑ **lock**[1] /lɒk/ v [I,T] **1** fasten sth or be fastened with a lock **2** (cause sth to) become fixed in one position and unable to move [**PV**] **lock sb away/up** (infml) put sb in prison **lock sth away/up** put sth safely in a locked place **lock sb/yourself in/out** prevent sb/yourself from entering or leaving a place by locking the door **lock (sth) up** make a house, etc safe by locking the doors

0‑ **lock**[2] /lɒk/ n [C] **1** device for fastening a door, etc **2** enclosed section of a canal, in which the water level can be raised or lowered **3** portion of hair that naturally hangs together [**IDM**] **lock, stock and barrel** including everything ■ **locksmith** n [C] person who makes and mends locks

locker /'lɒkə(r)/ n [C] small cupboard that can be locked, used for storing clothes, luggage, etc

locket /'lɒkɪt/ n [C] piece of jewellery, worn on a chain around the neck, in which you can put a picture, piece of hair, etc

locomotive /,ləʊkə'məʊtɪv/ n [C] (fml) railway engine

locust /'ləʊkəst/ n [C] winged insect that flies in large groups and destroys crops

A B C D E F G H I J K **L** M N O P Q R S T U V W X Y Z

lodge

lodge /lɒdʒ/ *n* [C] **1** country house or cabin: *a hunting ~* **2** small house, esp at the entrance to the grounds of a large house • **lodge** *v* **1** [T] make a formal statement about sth to a public organization: *~ a complaint* **2** [I] (old-fash) pay to live in a room in sb's house **3** [T] provide sb with a place to sleep or live **4** [I,T] **~ in** (cause sth to) enter and become fixed in sth: *The bullet (was) ~d in his arm.* • **lodger** *n* [C] (esp GB) person who pays rent to live in sb's house

lodging /ˈlɒdʒɪŋ/ *n* **1** [U] temporary accommodation **2** [C, usu pl] (old-fash) room or rooms in sb else's house that you rent to live in

loft /lɒft/ *n* [C] room or space under the roof of a house, used for storing things

lofty /ˈlɒfti/ *adj* (**-ier, -iest**) (fml) **1** very high **2** (of thoughts, etc) noble **3** (disapprov) proud

log /lɒg/ *n* [C] **1** thick piece of wood that is cut from or has fallen from a tree (also **logbook**) official record of events during a period of time, esp a journey on a ship or plane • **log** *v* (**-gg-**) [T] **1** put information in an official record or write a record of events **2** travel a particular distance or for a particular length of time [IDM] **log in/on** (computing) perform the actions that allow you to start using a computer system **log sb in/on** (computing) allow sb to start using a computer system **log off/out** (computing) perform the actions that allow you to finish using a computer system **log sb off/out** (computing) cause sb to finish using a computer system

loggerheads /ˈlɒgəhedz/ *n* [IDM] at **loggerheads (with sb) (over sth)** in strong disagreement

logic /ˈlɒdʒɪk/ *n* [U] **1** science or method of organized reasoning **2** sensible reasoning: *There's no ~ in what he says.* ▸ **logical** /ˈlɒdʒɪkl/ *adj*, in accordance with logic ▸ **logically** /-kli/ *adv*

logo /ˈləʊgəʊ/ *n* [C] (pl **~s**) printed design or symbol that a company, organization, etc uses as its special sign

loin /lɔɪn/ *n* **1** [C, U] piece of meat from the back or sides of an animal: *~ of pork* **2** (**loins**) [pl] (lit) person's sex organs

loiter /ˈlɔɪtə(r)/ *v* [I] stand or wait somewhere, esp with no obvious reason

loll /lɒl/ *v* [I] **1** lie, stand or sit in a lazy or relaxed way **2** (of the head or tongue) hang loosely

lollipop /ˈlɒlipɒp/ (GB also infml **lolly** /ˈlɒli/) (pl **-ies**) *n* [C] large boiled sweet or piece of frozen fruit juice on a stick

lone /ləʊn/ *adj* without any other people or things

0━ **lonely** /ˈləʊnli/ *adj* (**-ier, -iest**) **1** sad because you have no friends or people to talk to **2** (of places) not often visited ▸ **loneliness** *n* [U]

lonesome /ˈləʊnsəm/ *adj* (esp US) = LONELY

0━ **long1** /lɒŋ/ *adj* (**~er** /ˈlɒŋgə(r)/ **~est** /ˈlɒŋgɪst/) having a great or a given extent in space or time: *a ~ journey ◇ 800 metres ~* [IDM] **go a long way** → FAR1 **in the long run** eventually; ultimately **the long and (the) short of it** all that need be said about it **long in the tooth** (hum) (of a person) old **not by a long chalk/shot** not nearly; not at all ■ **long-distance** *adj, adv* travelling or operating between distant places ■ **long drink** *n* [C] cold drink, served in a tall glass ■ **long-range** *adj* of or for a long period of time or distance: *a ~-range weather forecast* ■ **long-sighted** *adj* not able to see things that are close to you clearly ■ **long-term** *adj* of or for a long period of time ■ **long wave** *n* [U] (abbr **LW**) radio wave with a length of more than 1000 metres ■ **long-winded** *adj* (disapprov) (of talking or writing) too long and therefore boring

0━ **long2** /lɒŋ/ *adv* (**~er** /-ŋgə(r)/ **~est** /ŋgɪst/) **1** for a long time: *Were you in Rome ~? ◇ I shan't be ~* (= I will come soon). **2** at a distant time: *all day* ◇ (of duration) throughout: *all day* ━ [IDM] **as/so long as** on condition that; provided that **no/any longer** used to say that sth which was possible or true before, is not now: *I can't wait any ~er.* ■ **long-standing** *adj* that has existed for a long time ■ **long-standing arrangement** ■ **long-suffering** *adj* patiently bearing problems and difficulties

long3 /lɒŋ/ *v* [I] **~ for; to** want sth very much: *~ for the holidays* ▸ **longing** *n* [C, U] (having a) strong feeling of wanting sth/sb ▸ **longingly** *adv*

longitude /ˈlɒndʒɪtjuːd/ *n* [U] distance of a place east or west of Greenwich in Britain, measured in degrees

loo /luː/ *n* [C] (pl **~s**) (GB, infml) toilet

0━ **look1** /lʊk/ *v* **1** [I] **~ (at)** turn your eyes in a particular direction **2** [I] **~ (for)** try to find sb/sth **3** [I,T] pay attention to sth: *L~ where you're going!* **4** linking verb seem; appear: *~ sad/pale* **5** [I] **~ as if/as though; like** seem likely: *She ~ed as if she was asleep. ◇ It ~s like rain.* **6** [I] face a particular direction: *The house ~s out over the harbour.* [IDM] **look one's best** appear as beautiful, attractive, etc as possible **look daggers at sb** look very angrily at sb **look down**

your nose at sb/sth (*infml, esp GB*) behave in a way that suggests that you think you are better than sb or that sth is not good enough for you **look here** (*old-fash*) used for expressing a protest or for asking sb to pay attention **look like sb/sth** | **look as if** have the appearance of sb/ sth; seem probable: *She ~ed as if she was asleep.* ◇ *It ~s like rain.* **look sharp** (*GB*) hurry up **(not) look yourself** (not) have your usual healthy appearance **never/not look back** (*infml*) become more and more successful **not much to look at** (*infml*) not attractive **[PV] look after yourself/sb/sth** (*esp GB*) be responsible for or take care of sb/sth **look ahead (to sth)** think about what is going to happen in the future **look around/round (sth)** visit a place or building, walking around it to see what is there **look at sth** examine or consider sth: *I'll ~ at your proposal tomorrow.* **look back** think about sth in your past **look down on sb/sth** (*infml*) think that you are better than sb/sth **look for sth** hope for sth; expect sth **look forward to sth** think with pleasure about sth that is going to happen in the future **look in (on sb)** (*GB*) make a short visit to a place, esp sb's house **look into sth** examine sth without becoming involved in it yourself **look on/at sb as sb/sth** consider sb/sth to be sb/sth **look out** be careful **look out for sb/sth** **1** try to avoid sth bad happening or doing sth bad: *You should ~ out for pickpockets.* **2** keep trying to find sth or meet sb **look sth over** examine sth to see how good, big, etc it is **look through sth** examine or read sth quickly **look to sb for sth/to do sth** rely on sb to provide or do sth **look up** (*infml*) (of business, sb's situation, etc) become better **look sb up** (*infml*) visit sb, esp when you have not seen them for a long time **look sth up** look for information in a dictionary or reference book **look up to sb** admire or respect sb ● **look** *exclam* used to interrupt sb or make them listen to sth you are saying ■ '**look-in** *n* [C] (*infml*) (not) get a chance to take part or succeed in sth ■ '**lookout** *n* [C] **1** place for watching from, esp for danger **2** person who watches for danger **[IDM] be your (own) lookout** (*GB, infml*) used to say that you do not think sb's actions are sensible, but that it is their own responsibility: *If you want to waste your money, that's your ~out.*

0━ **look²** /lʊk/ *n* **1** [C, usu sing] act of looking at sb/sth: *Take a ~ at this.* **2** [C, usu sing] ~ **(for sth)** act of trying to find sth/sb **3** [C] expression or appearance: *I don't like the ~ of him.* **4** (looks) [pl] person's (attractive)

appearance: *She's got her father's good ~s.*

loom /luːm/ *v* [I] appear in an unclear, often threatening, way **[IDM] loom large** be worrying or frightening and seem hard to avoid ● **loom** *n* [C] machine for weaving cloth

loop /luːp/ *n* [C] **1** shape like a circle made by a line curving right round and crossing itself **2** piece of rope, wire, etc in the shape of a curve or circle ● **loop** *v* **1** [T] bend sth into a loop **2** [I] move in a way that makes the shape of a loop

loophole /'luːphəʊl/ *n* [C] way of escape from a legal restriction: *a legal/tax ~*

0━ **loose** /luːs/ *adj* (**-r, -st**) **1** not firmly fixed where it should be; able to become separated from sth: *a ~ button/tooth* **2** not tied or fastened together: *~ sheets of paper* **3** freed from control; not tied up or shut in somewhere: *The dog is too dangerous to be set ~*. **4** (of clothes) not tight **5** not exact: *a ~ translation* **6** (*old-fash*) immoral **[IDM] at a loose end** (*US also*) loose ends having nothing to do **come/work loose** (of a fastening, etc) become unfastened ▶ **loosely** *adv* ▶ **loosen** /'luːsn/ *v* [I,T] become or make sth loose or less tight

loot /luːt/ *n* [U] money and valuable objects taken from an enemy in war or stolen by thieves ● **loot** *v* [I,T] steal things from shops or buildings after a riot, fire, etc

lop /lɒp/ *v* (**-pp-**) [T] cut branches, etc off a tree

lopsided /ˌlɒp'saɪdɪd/ *adj* with one side lower, smaller, etc than the other

0━ **lord** /lɔːd/ *n* [C] **1** (in Britain) nobleman **2** (Lord) (in Britain) title used by some high ranks of noblemen (= men of high social class) **3** (Lord) (sing) (in Britain) title of certain high officials: *L~ Mayor* **4** ((the) Lord) [sing] God; Jesus **5** (the Lords) [sing, with sing or pl verb] = THE HOUSE OF LORDS (HOUSE¹) **[IDM] (good) Lord!** | **Oh Lord!** used to show that you are surprised, annoyed or worried about sth ▶ **lordly** *adj* too proud; arrogant ▶ **lordship** *n* [C] (His/Your Lordship) title of respect used when speaking to a judge, bishop or a lord

0━ **lorry** /'lɒri/ *n* [C] (pl **-ies**) large motor vehicle for carrying heavy loads by road

0━ **lose** /luːz/ *v* (pt, pp **lost** /lɒst/) **1** [T] become unable to find sth/sb: *~ your keys* **2** [T] have sth taken away from you by accident, death, etc.: *~ your job* **3** [T] have less and less of sth: ~ **interest in sth** ◇ ~ **weight** **4** [T] (*infml*) be no longer understood by sb: *I'm afraid you've lost me.* **5** [I,T] fail to win sth: ~ *a game* **6** [T] waste time or an opportunity **7** [I,T] (of a clock or watch) go too slowly or become a particular amount of time behind the correct time [IDM] **lose your bearings** become lost or confused **lose count of sth** → COUNT² **lose face** be less respected or look stupid because of sth you have done **lose ground (to sb/sth)** → GROUND¹ **lose your head** → HEAD¹ **lose heart** → HEART **lose your heart (to sb/sth)** (*written*) fall in love with sb/sth **lose sight of sb/sth 1** no longer be able to see sb/sth **2** fail to consider or remember sth **lose touch (with sb/sth)** no longer have any contact with sb/sth **lose your way** become lost **lose weight** → WEIGHT [PV] **lose out (on sth)** (*infml*) not get sth you wanted or feel you should have **lose yourself in sth** become so interested in sth that it takes all your attention ▸ **loser** *n* [C]

0━ **loss** /lɒs/ *n* **1** [U,C] state of no longer having sth or as much of sth; the process that leads to this: ~ *of blood/self-control* **2** [C] money lost in business [C,U] death of a person: *heavy* ~ *of life* [IDM] **at a loss** not knowing what to say or do

lost¹ *pt, pp of* LOSE

0━ **lost²** /lɒst/ *adj* **1** unable to find your way; not knowing where you are **2** that cannot be found or brought back [IDM] **a lost cause** something that has failed or that cannot succeed

0━ **lot¹** /lɒt/ *pron* (**a lot**) (*also infml* **lots**) large number or amount ◇ **a lot of** (*also infml* **lots of**) *det* a large number or amount of sb/sth: *a* ~ *of people*

0━ **lot²** /lɒt/ *adv* (**a lot**) (*infml*) **1** (used with an adj and adv) much: *I feel a* ~ *better.* **2** (used with a v) a great amount

0━ **lot³** /lɒt/ *n* **1** (**the lot, the whole lot**) [sing, with sing or pl verb] (*infml*) the whole number or amount of people or things **2** [C, with sing or pl verb] (*esp GB*) group or set of people or things: *the next* ~ *of students* **3** [C] object or a number of objects to be sold, esp at an auction **4** [C] area of land used for a particular purpose: *a parking* ~ **5** [sing] person's luck or situation in life [IDM] **cast/draw lots (for sth/to do sth)** choose sb to do sth or decide each person to do sth by asking each person to take a piece of paper, etc from a container and the person whose paper has a special mark is chosen

loth = LOATH

lotion /ˈləʊʃn/ *n* [C,U] liquid used for cleaning, protecting or treating the skin

lottery /ˈlɒtəri/ *n* [C] (*pl* **-ies**) way of giving prizes to the buyers of numbered tickets chosen by chance

0━ **loud** /laʊd/ *adj* **1** making a lot of noise **2** (of colours) too bright and lacking good taste ● **loud** *adv* in a way that makes a lot of noise or can be easily heard [IDM] **loud and clear** in a way that is easy to understand ▸ **loudly** *adv* ▸ **loudness** *n* [U] ■ **loud'speaker** *n* [C] part of a radio, etc that changes electrical signals into sound

lounge /laʊndʒ/ *v* [I] sit, stand or lie in a lazy way ● **lounge** *n* [C] **1** room for waiting in at an airport, etc **2** (*GB*) room in a private house for sitting and relaxing in ■ **'lounge bar** *n* [C] (*GB*) bar in a pub or hotel that is smarter and more expensive than other bars

louse /laʊs/ *n* [C] (*pl* **lice** /laɪs/) small insect that lives on the bodies of animals and human beings

lousy /ˈlaʊzi/ *adj* (**-ier, -iest**) (*infml*) very bad: ~ *weather*

lout /laʊt/ *n* [C] (*GB*) rude and aggressive man or boy ▸ **loutish** *adj*

lovable /ˈlʌvəbl/ *adj* easy to love; deserving love

0━ **love** /lʌv/ *n* **1** [U] strong feeling of deep affection for sb/sth **2** [U] strong feeling of affection and sexual attraction for sb: *He's fallen in* ~. **3** [U, sing] strong feeling of enjoyment that sth gives you: *a* ~ *of music* **4** [C] person or thing that you like very much **5** [U] (in tennis) score of zero points or games [IDM] **give/send my love to sb** (*infml*) used to send friendly greetings to sb **make love (to sb)** have sex **there's little/no love lost between A and B** they do not like each other ● **love** *v* [T] **1** have very strong feelings of affection for sb/sth **2** like or enjoy sth a lot: *I* ~ *cakes.* ■ **'love affair** *n* [C] romantic and/or sexual relationship between two people

0━ **lovely** /ˈlʌvli/ *adj* (**-ier, -iest**) **1** beautiful; attractive: *a* ~ *woman* **2** very enjoyable and pleasant: *a* ~ *holiday* ▸ **loveliness** *n* [U]

0━ **lover** /ˈlʌvə(r)/ *n* [C] **1** partner in a sexual relationship outside marriage **2** person who likes or enjoys a particular thing: *a* ~ *of music*

loving /ˈlʌvɪŋ/ *adj* feeling or showing love for sb/sth ▸ **lovingly** *adv*

0━ **low¹** /ləʊ/ *adj* **1** not high or tall: *a* ~ *wall* **2** below the usual level, value or amount: ~ *prices* **3** (of a sound) not high; not loud **4** below others in importance or quality **5** weak or depressed: ~ **6** not very good: *have a* ~ *opinion of him* **7** (of a person) dishonest **8** (of a gear) allowing a slower speed **[IDM] at a low ebb** in a poor or bad state **be/ run low (on sth)** (of supplies) be/ become almost finished ■ 'low-down *adj* (*infml*) not fair or honest ■ 'low-down *n* [sing] (the low-down) ~ **on sb/sth** (*infml*) the full facts about sb/sth: *She gave me the ~-down on the guests at the party.* ■ 'low-key *adj* not intended to attract a lot of attention ■ 'lowland *adj*, *n* [C, usu pl] (of a) fairly flat area of land that is not very high above sea level ▸ **lowness** *n* [U] ■ low-'profile *adj* receiving or involving very little attention: *a ~-profile campaign* ■ low-'spirited *adj* depressed

0➔ **low²** /ləʊ/ *adv* at or to a low level: *aim/shoot* ~ ● **low** *n* [C] low or lowest level or point: *Shares reached a new ~ yesterday.*

lower /ˈləʊə(r)/ *adj* at or being the bottom part of sth: *the ~ lip* ● **lower** *v* [T] let or make sb/sth go down: ~ *a flag* **2** [I,T] (cause sth to) become less in value, quality, etc: ~ *the price* **[PV] lower yourself (by doing sth)** behave in a way that makes people respect you less ■ the ,lower 'class *n* [C] social class below middle class ▸ **lower 'class** *n*

lowly /ˈləʊli/ *adj* (**-ier, -iest**) low in status or importance

0➔ **loyal** /ˈlɔɪəl/ *adj* ~ **(to)** faithful to sb/sth: ~ *supporters* ▸ **loyally** *adv* ▸ **loyalty** *n* (pl **-ies**) **1** [U] quality of being faithful to sb/sth **2** [C, usu pl] strong feeling that you want to be loyal to sb/sth

lozenge /ˈlɒzɪndʒ/ *n* [C] **1** diamond-shaped figure **2** small sweet containing medicine

LP /ˌel ˈpiː/ *abbr* long-playing record; a record that plays for about 25 minutes each side and turns 33 times per minute

Ltd *abbr* Limited = LIMITED COMPANY (LIMIT)

lubricate /ˈluːbrɪkeɪt/ *v* [T] put oil, etc on sth such as the parts of a machine, to help them move smoothly ▸ **lubrication** /ˌluːbrɪˈkeɪʃn/ *n* [U]

lucid /ˈluːsɪd/ *adj* (*fml*) **1** easy to understand; clear **2** able to think and speak clearly ▸ **lucidity** /luːˈsɪdəti/ *n* [U] ▸ **lucidly** *adv*

0➔ **luck** /lʌk/ *n* [U] **1** good things that happen to you by chance **2** chance; the force that causes good or bad things to happen to people **[IDM] be down on your luck** (*infml*) have no money because of a period of bad luck **be in/out of luck** be fortunate/unfortunate ▸ **lucky** *adj* (**-ier, -iest**) having, bringing or resulting from good luck ▸ **luckily** *adv*

lucrative /ˈluːkrətɪv/ *adj* producing

---

a large amount of money; making a large profit

ludicrous /ˈluːdɪkrəs/ *adj* ridiculous and unreasonable ▸ **ludicrously** *adv*

lug /lʌɡ/ *v* (**-gg-**) [T] carry or drag sth heavy with great effort

0➔ **luggage** /ˈlʌɡɪdʒ/ *n* [U] bags, suitcases, etc taken on a journey

lukewarm /ˌluːkˈwɔːm/ *adj* **1** slightly warm **2** not enthusiastic

lull /lʌl/ *n* [C, usu sing] quiet period between times of activity ● **lull** *v* [T] make sb relaxed and calm: ~ *a baby to sleep*

lullaby /ˈlʌləbaɪ/ *n* [C] (pl **-ies**) song sung to make a child go to sleep

lumbago /lʌmˈbeɪɡəʊ/ *n* [U] pain in the lower back

lumber /ˈlʌmbə(r)/ *n* [U] **1** (*esp US*) = TIMBER(1) **2** (*GB*) unwanted old furniture ● **lumber** *v* **1** [I] move in a slow, heavy and awkward way **2** [T] ~ **(with)** (*infml*) give sth/sb unwanted to sb: *They've ~ed me with the washing-up again.* ■ 'lumberjack *n* [C] person whose job is to cut down trees or produce timber

luminous /ˈluːmɪnəs/ *adj* giving out light; that can be seen in the dark

0➔ **lump** /lʌmp/ *n* [C] **1** piece of sth hard or solid, usu without a particular shape: *a ~ of coal* **2** swelling under the skin **[IDM] have, etc a lump in your throat** feel pressure in your throat because you are very angry or emotional ● **lump** *v* [T] ~ **(together)** put or consider different things together in the same group **[IDM] lump it** (*infml*) accept sth unpleasant because there is no other choice ■ ,lump 'sum *n* [C] amount of money paid at one time and not on separate occasions ▸ **lumpy** *adj* (**-ier, -iest**)

lunacy /ˈluːnəsi/ *n* [U] behaviour that is stupid or crazy

lunar /ˈluːnə(r)/ *adj* of the moon

lunatic /ˈluːnətɪk/ *n* [C] **1** person who does crazy things that are often dangerous **2** (*old-fash*) person who is mad ● **lunatic** *adj* crazy, ridiculous or extremely stupid ■ 'lunatic asylum *n* [C] (*old-fash, esp GB*) psychiatric hospital

0➔ **lunch** /lʌntʃ/ *n* [C, U] meal eaten in the middle of the day ● **lunch** *v* [I] (*fml*) have lunch, esp at a restaurant

luncheon /ˈlʌntʃən/ *n* [C, U] (*fml*) = LUNCH

0➔ **lung** /lʌŋ/ *n* [C] either of the two breathing organs in the chest

lunge /lʌndʒ/ *n* [C], *v* [I] (make a) sudden forward movement

lurch /lɜːtʃ/ *n* [C, usu sing] sudden unsteady movement ● **lurch** *v* [I] move along with a lurch

---

A B C D E F G H I J K **L** M N O P Q R S T U V W X Y Z

lure /lʊə(r)/ n [C, usu sing] attractive qualities of sth: *the ~ of adventure* ● **lure** v [T] persuade or trick sb to go somewhere or do sth by promising them a reward: *~ sb into a trap*

lurid /'lʊərɪd/ adj (disapprov) **1** having unpleasantly bright colours **2** (of a story or piece of writing) shocking and violent: *~ headlines*

lurk /lɜːk/ v [I] wait somewhere secretly, esp when you are going to do sth bad or illegal

luscious /'lʌʃəs/ adj having a very sweet pleasant taste

lush /lʌʃ/ adj **1** (of plants, trees, etc) growing thickly and strongly **2** beautiful and making you feel pleasure; seeming expensive

lust /lʌst/ n [U,C] **~ (for)** **1** strong sexual desire **2** strong desire for or enjoyment of sth: *his ~ for power* ● **lust** v [PV] **lust after/for sb/sth** feel an extremely strong, esp sexual, desire for sb/sth ► **lustful** adj

lustre (US **luster**) /'lʌstə(r)/ n [U] **1** shining quality of a surface **2** quality of being special in a way that is exciting

lusty /'lʌsti/ adj healthy and strong

luxuriant /lʌg'ʒʊəriənt/ adj (of plants or hair) growing thickly and strongly ► **luxuriance** /-əns/ n [U] ► **luxuriantly** adv

luxurious /lʌg'ʒʊəriəs/ adj very comfortable and expensive ► **luxuriously** adv

luxury /'lʌkʃəri/ n (pl **-ies**) **1** [U] great comfort, esp in expensive surroundings: *a life of ~* **2** [C] thing that is expensive and enjoyable, but not essential

LW abbr (esp GB) = LONG WAVE (LONG¹)

lying pres part LIE¹

lynch /lɪntʃ/ v [T] kill sb, usu by hanging, without giving them a lawful trial

lyric /'lɪrɪk/ adj **1** (of poetry) expressing direct personal feelings **2** of or for singing ● **lyric** n **1** lyric poem **2** (lyrics) [pl] words of a song ► **lyrical** /-kl/ adj expressing strong emotion in an imaginative way ► **lyrically** /-kli/ adv

Mm

M, m /em/ n [C,U] (pl **M's, m's** /emz/) **1** the thirteenth letter of the English alphabet **2** Roman numeral for 1000 **3** used with a number to show the name of a British motorway: *the M1*

m (also **m.**) abbr **1** married **2** metre(s) **3** million(s)

MA /em 'eɪ/ n [C] Master of Arts; a second university degree in an Arts subject, or, in Scotland, a first degree

ma /mɑː/ n [C] (infml) mother

ma'am /mæm; mɑːm/ n [sing] **1** (US) used as a polite way of addressing a woman **2** (GB) = MADAM

mac (also **mack**) /mæk/ n [C] (GB, infml) short for MACKINTOSH

macabre /mə'kɑːbrə/ adj unpleasant and strange because connected with death

macaroni /ˌmækə'rəʊni/ n [U] pasta in the form of hollow tubes

mace /meɪs/ n **1** [C] ornamental stick carried by an official as a sign of authority **2** [U] dried outer covering of nutmegs, used in cooking as a spice

Mach /mɑːk; mæk/ n [U] measurement of speed, used esp for aircraft: *M~ 2* (= twice the speed of sound)

machete /mə'ʃeti/ n [C] broad heavy knife

0ᵣ machine /mə'ʃiːn/ n [C] **1** piece of equipment with moving parts that uses power to perform a particular task **2** group of people that control an organization: *the party ~* ● **machine** v [T] (tech) make sth with a machine ■ **ma'chine-gun** n [C] gun that automatically fires many bullets one after the other very quickly ■ **ma,chine-'readable** adj (of data) in a form that a computer can understand ► **machinery** n [U] **1** machines as a group **2** moving parts of a machine **3** system of methods or organization of sth: *the ~ of government* ■ **ma'chine tool** n [C] tool for cutting or shaping metal, wood, etc, driven by a machine ► **machinist** n [C] person who operates a machine

macho /'mætʃəʊ/ adj (usu disapprov) male in an aggressive way

mackerel /'mækrəl/ n [C] (pl **mackerel**) striped sea fish, eaten as food

mackintosh /'mækɪntɒʃ/ n [C] (GB) coat made of rainproof material

0ᵣ mad /mæd/ adj (**~der, ~dest**) **1** mentally ill **2** (infml) very stupid; crazy **3 ~ (at)** (infml, esp US) angry with sb: *You're driving me ~!* **4 ~ (about/on)** liking sth/sb very much: *He's ~ about football.* **5** wild and excited: *in a ~ rush* [IDM] **like crazy/mad** (infml) very fast, hard, much, etc **mad keen (on sth/sb)** (infml) very enthusiastic about sth/sb ■ **mad 'cow disease** n [U] (infml) = BSE ► **madly** adv **1** in a way that shows a lack of control: *rush about ~ly* **2** (infml) extremely: *~ly in love* ■ **madman | 'madwoman** n person who is mentally ill ▸ **madness** *n* [U]

madam /ˈmædəm/ *n* [sing] (*fml*) used when speaking or writing to a woman in a formal or business situation

madden /ˈmædn/ *v* [T] make sb very angry

made *pt, pp* of MAKE¹

madonna /məˈdɒnə/ *n* **1 (the Madonna)** [sing] the Virgin Mary, mother of Jesus Christ **2 (madonna)** [C] picture or statue of the Virgin Mary

madrigal /ˈmædrɪgl/ *n* [C] song for several singers, usu without musical instruments, popular in the 16th century

maestro /ˈmaɪstrəʊ/ *n* [C] (*pl* **~s**) great performer, esp a musician

0━ magazine /ˌmægəˈziːn/ *n* [C] **1** weekly or monthly paper-covered publication with articles, stories, etc **2** part of a gun that holds the bullets

magenta /məˈdʒentə/ *adj* reddish-purple in colour ● **magenta** *n* [U]

maggot /ˈmægət/ *n* [C] creature like a short worm that is the young form of a fly

0━ magic /ˈmædʒɪk/ *n* [U] **1** secret power of appearing to make impossible things happen by saying special words, etc **2** art of doing tricks that seem impossible in order to entertain people **3** special quality that sb/sth has, that seems too wonderful to be real: *the ~ of the circus* ● **magic** *adj* **1** used in or using magic **2** (*infml*) wonderful ▸ **magical** /-kl/ *adj* containing or using magic; wonderful ▸ **magically** /-kli/ *adv* ▸ **magician** /məˈdʒɪʃn/ *n* [C] person who can do magic tricks

magistrate /ˈmædʒɪstreɪt/ *n* [C] official who acts as a judge in the lowest courts of law

magnanimous /mægˈnænɪməs/ *adj* (*fml*) generous ▸ **magnanimity** /ˌmægnəˈnɪməti/ *n* [U] ▸ **magnanimously** *adv*

magnate /ˈmægneɪt/ *n* [C] wealthy and powerful person, esp in business

magnesium /mægˈniːziəm/ *n* [U] (*symb* Mg) silver-white metal

magnet /ˈmægnət/ *n* [C] **1** piece of iron that attracts other metal objects towards it **2** [usu sing] person, place or thing that sb/sth is attracted to ▸ **magnetic** /mægˈnetɪk/ *adj* **1** having the qualities of a magnet **2** that people find very powerful and attractive ▸ **magnetically** /-kli/ *adv* ■ **mag‚netic ˈnorth** *n* [U] direction to which the needle on a compass points ■ **mag‚netic ˈtape** *n* [U] plastic tape on which sound, pictures or computer data can be recorded ▸ **magnetism**

/ˈmægnətɪzəm/ *n* **1** physical property (= characteristic) of some metals, eg iron, that causes forces between objects, either pulling them together or pushing them apart **2** great personal attraction ▸ **magnetize** (*also* -ise) *n* [T] make sth magnetic

magnificent /mægˈnɪfɪsnt/ *adj* extremely attractive and impressive ▸ **magnificence** /-sns/ *n* [U] ▸ **magnificently** *adv*

magnify /ˈmægnɪfaɪ/ *v* (*pt, pp* -**ied**) [T] **1** make sth look bigger than it really is **2** exaggerate sth: *~ the dangers* ▸ **magnification** /ˌmægnɪfɪˈkeɪʃn/ *n* [U] power or act of making sth look larger ■ **magnifying glass** *n* [C] lens for making objects look bigger than they really are

magnitude /ˈmægnɪtjuːd/ *n* [U] (*fml*) **1** great size of sth **2** (degree of) importance of sth

magpie /ˈmægpaɪ/ *n* [C] noisy black and white bird that likes to collect bright objects

mahogany /məˈhɒgəni/ *n* [U] dark brown wood used for making furniture

maid /meɪd/ *n* [C] female servant in a house or hotel

maiden /ˈmeɪdn/ *n* [C] (*lit*) young unmarried woman ● **maiden** *adj* being the first of its kind: *a ship's ~ voyage* ■ **maiden name** *n* [C] woman's family name before marriage

0━ mail /meɪl/ *n* [U] **1** official system used for sending and delivering letters, packages, etc **2** letters, packages, etc that are sent and delivered by post ● **mail** *v* [T] (*esp US*) send sth to sb by post ■ **mailbox** *n* [C] **1** (*US*) = LETTER BOX(2)(LETTER) **2** (*US*) = POSTBOX (POST¹) **3** area of a computer's memory where electronic mail messages are stored ■ **mailman** *n* [C] (*US*) = POSTMAN (POST¹) ■ **mail ‚order** *n* [U] system of buying and selling goods through the mail ■ **mailshot** *n* [C] advertising that is sent to a large number of people at the same time by mail

maim /meɪm/ *v* [T] injure sb so seriously that some part of the body cannot be used

0━ main¹ /meɪn/ *adj* being the largest or most important of its kind: *the ~ purpose of the meeting* ■ **mainframe** (*also* **mainframe com‚puter**) *n* [C] large powerful computer, usu the centre of a network and shared by many users ■ **mainland** *n* [sing] **(the mainland)** main area of land of a country, not including any islands near to it

265 **main**

A B C D E F G H I J K L **M** N O P Q R S T U V W X Y Z

▶ **mainly** adv chiefly ■ **mainspring** n [C] **1** (written) most important part of sth or influence on sth **2** most important spring in a clock or watch ■ **mainstay** n [C] chief support; foundation ■ **mainstream** n [sing] group of commonly accepted ideas and opinions about a subject

main² /meɪn/ n **1** [C] large pipe supplying water or gas, or large wire supplying electricity, to a building **2** (the mains) [pl] (GB) source of supply of water, gas, or electricity to a building [IDM] **in the main** generally

0━ **maintain** /meɪnˈteɪn/ v [T] **1** make sth continue at the same level, standard, etc: ~ peaceful relations **2** keep a building, machine, etc in good condition: ~ a car **3** keep stating that sth is true: ~ your innocence **4** support sb/sth with money ▶ **maintenance** /ˈmeɪntənəns/ n [U] **1** act of keeping sth in good condition **2** act of making a state or situation continue **3** (GB, law) money that you are legally required to pay to support sb

maisonette /ˌmeɪzəˈnet/ n [C] (GB) flat on two floors that is part of a larger building

maize /meɪz/ n [U] tall plant grown for its large yellow grains that are used for making flour or eaten as a vegetable

majesty /ˈmædʒəsti/ n (pl -ies) [U] **1** (written) impressive and attractive quality that sth has **2** (His/Her/Your Majesty) [C] title of respect used when speaking to or about a king or queen ▶ **majestic** /məˈdʒestɪk/ adj ▶ **majestically** /-kli/ adv

0━ **major** /ˈmeɪdʒə(r)/ adj very large or important: a ~ road ● **major** n [C] (abbr **Maj.**) officer of fairly high rank in the army or the US air force ● **major** v [PV] **major in** sth (US) study sth as your main subject at college or university

0━ **majority** /məˈdʒɒrəti/ n (pl -ies) **1** [sing, with sing or pl verb] ~ (of) largest part of a group of people or things **2** [C] number by which votes for one side are more than those for the other side: win by a ~ of 9 votes **3** [U] (law) age at which you are legally considered to be an adult

0━ **make¹** /meɪk/ v (pt, pp **made** /meɪd/) **1** [T] construct, produce or prepare sth; bring sth into existence: ~ bread **2** [T] cause sth to exist, happen or be done: ~ a lot of noise ◊ ~ trouble **3** [T] cause sb/sth to be or become sth: The news made her happy. **4** [T] cause sb to do sth: He ~s me laugh. ◊ ~ sb jump **5** [T] force sb to do sth: Her parents ~ her study hard. **6** [T] elect or choose sb as sth: They made me the manager.

7 linking verb become or develop into sth: She will ~ a brilliant doctor. **8** linking verb add up to or equal sth: Two and two ~ four. **9** [T] earn or gain money: ~ a profit **10** [T] think or calculate sth to be sth: What do you ~ the time? **11** [T] manage to reach or go to a place or position: We didn't ~ Dover by 12 o'clock. [IDM] **make as if to do sth** (written) make a movement that makes it seem that you are going to do sth: She made as if to hit him. **make do (with sth)** manage with sth which is really not adequate **make it** (infml) **1** be successful in your career **2** succeed in reaching a place in time, esp when this is difficult **3** be able to be present at a place: Thanks for inviting us, but I'm afraid we won't be able to ~ it on Saturday. **4** survive after an illness, accident or difficult situation: The doctors think he's going to ~ it. **make up ground (on sb/sth)** → GROUND¹ [PV] **make for sth** **1** move towards sth **2** help to make sth possible: Does exercise ~ for good health? **make sb/sth into sb/sth** change sb/sth into sb/sth: ~ the attic into a bedroom **make sth of sb/sth** understand sb/sth: What do you ~ of this sentence? **make off** hurry away, esp to escape **make off with sth** steal sth and escape with it **make out** (infml) **1** manage: How are you making out in your new job? **2** (US) kiss and touch sb in a sexual way **make sb/sth out 1** manage to see sb/sth or read or hear sth: I can't ~ out his writing. **2** understand sb/sth: I just can't ~ her out. **make sth out 1** say that sth is true when it may not be: He ~s himself out to be cleverer than he is. **2** write out or complete a form or document: ~ out a cheque **make (sb/yourself) up** put cosmetics on your/sb's face **make sth up 1** form sth: Women ~ up 56% of the student numbers. **2** put several things together from several different things **3** invent a story, esp in order to deceive: She made up an excuse. **4** complete a number or an amount required: We need £5 to ~ up the sum. **5** prepare a bed for use **make up (to sb) for sth** compensate for sth **make up to sb** (GB, infml, disapprov) be pleasant to sb in order to get sth **make up (with sb)** (GB also **make it up**) end a quarrel with sb and become friends again ■ **make-believe** n [U] (disapprov) imagining or pretending: a world of ~-believe

0━ **make²** /meɪk/ n [C] ~ (of) named kind of product: What ~ of car does he drive? [IDM] **on the make** (infml, disapprov) trying to gain money or an advantage for yourself

maker /ˈmeɪkə(r)/ n **1** [C] person, company, etc that makes or produces sth: a decision/law ~

2 (the, his, your, etc Maker) [sing] God

makeshift /ˈmeɪkʃɪft/ adj used for a time because there is nothing better

0‑**make-up** n **1** [U] cosmetics: *Lucy never wears ~.* **2** [sing] different qualities that combine to form a person's character **3** [sing] different things, people, etc that combine to form sth: *the ~ of the new committee*

making /ˈmeɪkɪŋ/ n [U] act or process of making or producing sth **IDM** **be the making of sb** cause sb to succeed or develop well **have the makings of sth** have the qualities needed to become sth

maladjusted /ˌmælə'dʒʌstɪd/ adj having mental and emotional problems that lead to unacceptable behaviour ▶ **maladjustment** /-mənt/ n

malaria /mə'leəriə/ n [U] serious fever caught from mosquito bites

0‑**male** /meɪl/ adj **1** belonging to the sex that does not give birth **2** (biol) (of a plant) having flowers with parts that produce pollen **3** (tech) (of electrical plugs, parts of tools, etc) having a part that sticks out and is designed to fit into a hole, socket, etc ● **male** n [C] male person or animal ■ **male ˈchauvinism** n [U] (disapprov) belief held by some men that men are superior to women ■ **male ˈchauvinist** n [C] (disapprov) man who believes men are superior to women

malevolent /mə'levələnt/ adj (fml) wishing to do evil or cause harm to others ▶ **malevolence** /-əns/ n [U] ▶ **malevolently** adv

malformation /ˌmælfɔː'meɪʃn/ n [U, C] (state of having a) part of the body that is not formed correctly ▶ **malformed** /ˌmælˈfɔːmd/ adj

malfunction /ˌmælˈfʌŋkʃn/ v [I] (fml) (of a machine) fail to work correctly ● **malfunction** n [C, U]

malice /ˈmælɪs/ n [U] desire to harm other people ▶ **malicious** /mə'lɪʃəs/ adj ▶ **maliciously** adv

malignant /mə'lɪgnənt/ adj **1** (of a tumour or disease) serious and likely to cause death **2** (fml) having a great desire to harm others ▶ **malignantly** adv

0‑**mall** /mɔːl, GB also mæl/ n [C] (esp US) = SHOPPING MALL (SHOP)

malleable /ˈmæliəbl/ adj **1** (tech) (of metals) that can be beaten or pressed into new shapes **2** (of people, ideas, etc) easily influenced or changed

mallet /ˈmælɪt/ n [C] hammer with a wooden head

malnourished /ˌmælˈnʌrɪʃt/ adj in bad health because of a lack of (the right kind of) food

malnutrition /ˌmælnjuːˈtrɪʃn/ n [U]

condition caused by a lack of (the right kind of) food

malt /mɔːlt/ n [U] grain, esp barley, used for making beer, whisky, etc

maltreat /ˌmælˈtriːt/ v [T] (written) be very cruel to a person or animal ▶ **maltreatment** n [U]

mama (also mamma) /ˈmæmə/ n [C] (US) mother

mamba /ˈmæmbə/ n [C] black or green poisonous snake

mammal /ˈmæml/ n [C] any animal that gives birth to live babies, not eggs, and feeds its young on milk

mammoth /ˈmæməθ/ n [C] large hairy kind of elephant, now extinct ● **mammoth** adj (infml) extremely large

0‑**man¹** /mæn/ n (pl **men** /men/) **1** [C] adult male human being **2** [U] human beings as a group: *the origins of ~* **3** [C] (lit, old-fash) person, either male or female: *All must die.* **4** [C] man who comes from the place mentioned or whose job or interest is connected with the thing mentioned: *a French- ◇ a business- ~* **5** [C, usu pl] soldier or male worker under the authority of sb of higher rank: *officers and men* **6** [sing] (infml spoken, esp US) used for addressing a male person **7** [C] husband or sexual partner: *What's her new ~ like?* **8** [C] male person with the qualities of strength, courage, etc associated with men: *Don't give up —be a ~!* **9** [C] piece used in a game such as chess **IDM** **be your own man/ woman** act or think independently, not following others **the man (and/ or woman) in the street** the average person **man to man** between two men who are treating each other honestly and equally **to a man | to the last man** (written) all, without exception ■ **ˈmanhole** n [C] hole in the street that is covered with a lid, through which sb enters an underground drain, etc ▶ **manhood** n [U] state or qualities of being a man ■ **ˌman-ˈmade** adj made by people; artificial ■ **ˈmanpower** n [U] number of people needed or available to do a job ■ **ˈmanslaughter** n [U] (law) crime of killing sb unintentionally

man² /mæn/ v (**-nn-**) [T] work at a place or in charge of a place or machine; supply people to work somewhere: *Soldiers ~ned barricades around the city.*

manacle /ˈmænəkl/ n [C, usu pl] one of a pair of chains for tying a prisoner's hands or feet ● **manacle** v [T] tie up sb with manacles

0‑**manage** /ˈmænɪdʒ/ v [I, T] succeed in doing sth, esp sth difficult: *How did the prisoners ~ to* *escape?* **2** [I] be able to solve your problems, deal with a difficult situation, etc **3** [I] be able to live without having much money: *I can only just ~ on my wages.* **4** [T] use money, time, information, etc in a sensible way **5** [T] control or be in charge of sth ▶ **manageable** *adj* that can be dealt with ■ **managing di'rector** *n* [C] (*abbr* **MD**) (*esp GB*) person who is in charge of a business

0━ **management** /'mænɪdʒmənt/ *n* **1** [U] act of running and controlling a business, etc: *problems caused by bad* ~ **2** [C, with sing or pl verb] people who manage a business, etc: *workers and* ~ **3** [U] (*fml*) act or skill of dealing with people or situations successfully

0━ **manager** /'mænɪdʒə(r)/ *n* [C] person who organizes a business, sports team, etc ▶ **manageress** /,mænɪdʒə'res/ *n* [C] woman who is in charge of a business, etc ▶ **managerial** /,mænə'dʒɪəriəl/ *adj* of managers

mandate /'mændeɪt/ *n* [C, usu sing] authority given to a government, trade union, etc by the people who support it ▶ **mandatory** /'mændətəri; mæn'deɪtəri/ *adj* (*fml*) required by law

mandolin /'mændəlɪn; ,mændə'lɪn/ *n* [C] musical instrument with eight metal strings

mane /meɪn/ *n* [C] long hair on the neck of a horse or lion

maneuver (*US*) = MANOEUVRE

manfully /'mænfəli/ *adv* using a lot of effort in a brave and determined way

manger /'meɪndʒə(r)/ *n* [C] long open box that horses or cattle can eat from

mangle /'mæŋgl/ *v* [T] (*usu passive*) cut or twist sth so that it is badly damaged

mango /'mæŋgəʊ/ *n* [C, U] (*pl* ~es) tropical fruit with soft orange flesh and a large stone inside

mangy /'meɪndʒi/ *adj* (-ier, -iest) with patches of hair, fur, etc missing; shabby

manhandle /'mænhændl/ *v* [T] **1** push, pull or handle sb roughly **2** move a heavy object using a lot of effort

mania /'meɪniə/ *n* **1** [C, usu sing, U] ~ **(for)** extremely strong desire or enthusiasm for sth **2** [U] mental illness ▶ **maniac** /'meɪnɪæk/ *n* [C] **1** (*infml*) mad person **2** person with an extremely strong desire or enthusiasm for sth ▶ **maniacal** /mə'naɪəkl/ *adj* wild or violent

manic /'mænɪk/ *adj* suffering from mania ■ **manic de'pression** *n* [U] =

BIPOLAR DISORDER ■ **manic-de'pressive** *adj* = BIPOLAR

manicure /'mænɪkjʊə(r)/ *n* [C, U] care and treatment of a person's hands and nails ● **manicure** *v* [T] care for and treat your hands and nails ▶ **manicurist** *n* [C]

manifest /'mænɪfest/ *adj* (*fml*) clear and obvious ● **manifest** *v* [T] (*fml*) show sth clearly: *The disease ~ed itself.* ▶ **manifestation** /,mænɪfe'steɪʃn/ *n* [C, U] ▶ **manifestly** *adv*

manifesto /,mænɪ'festəʊ/ *n* [C] (*pl* ~s) written statement of a group's beliefs and plans, esp of a political party

manifold /'mænɪfəʊld/ *adj* (*fml*) many; of many different types ● **manifold** *n* [C] (*tech*) pipe or enclosed space with several openings for taking gases in and out of a car engine

manipulate /mə'nɪpjuleɪt/ *v* [T] **1** control or influence sb/sth, esp in a dishonest way **2** control or use sth in a skilful way ▶ **manipulation** /mə,nɪpjʊ'leɪʃn/ *n* [C, U] ▶ **manipulative** /-lətɪv/ *adj*

mankind /mæn'kaɪnd/ *n* [U] the human race

manly /'mænli/ *adj* (-ier, -iest) (*approv*) (of a man) having the qualities or appearance expected of a man ▶ **manliness** *n* [U]

0━ **manner** /'mænə(r)/ *n* **1** [sing] (*fml*) way in which sth is done or happens: *in a friendly* ~ **2** [sing] person's way of behaving towards others: *I don't like your* ~. **3** (**manners**) [pl] polite social behaviour: *to have good* ~s [IDM] **all manner of sb/sth** (*fml*) many different types of people or things **in a manner of speaking** to some extent; if considered in a certain way ▶ **-mannered** (in compound adjectives) having manners of the kind stated: *well* ~ed

mannerism /'mænərɪzəm/ *n* [C] particular way of speaking or behaving that sb has

manoeuvre (*US* **maneuver**) /mə'nu:və(r)/ *n* **1** [C] movement performed with skill **2** [C, U] clever plan, action or movement, used to give sb an advantage **3** (**manoeuvres**) [pl] military exercises involving a large number of soldiers, ships, etc ● **manoeuvre** (*US* **maneuver**) *v* **1** [I, T] (*cause sth to*) move or turn skilfully **2** control or influence a situation in a skilful but sometimes dishonest way ▶ **manoeuvrable** (*US* **maneuverable**) *adj* that can easily be moved into different positions

manor /'mænə(r)/ (*also* '**manor house**) *n* [C] large country house surrounded by land that belongs to it

mansion /'mænʃn/ n [C] large grand house

mantelpiece /'mæntlpiːs/ n [C] shelf above a fireplace

mantle /'mæntl/ n **1** [sing] ~ of (lit) the responsibilities of an important job: take on the ~ of supreme power **2** [C] (lit) layer: a ~ of snow **3** [C] loose piece of clothing without sleeves, worn over other clothes, esp in the past

manual /'mænjuəl/ adj done with or controlled by the hands ● **manual** n [C] book giving practical information or instructions ▸ **manually** adv

0➡ **manufacture** /ˌmænjuˈfæktʃə(r)/ v [T] make or produce goods in large quantities, using machinery ● **manufacture** n [U] process of producing goods in large quantities ▸ **manufacturer** n [C]

manure /məˈnjʊə(r)/ n [U] animal waste matter spread over the soil to help plants to grow

manuscript /'mænjuskrɪpt/ n [C] **1** copy of a book, piece of music, etc before it has been printed **2** old handwritten book

0➡ **many** /'meni/ det, pron **1** a large number of people or things: ~ people ◇ not ~ of the students ◇ I've known him for a great ~ (= very many) years. **2** (many a) (used with a singular noun and v) a large number of: a ~ mother (= many mothers) **IDM** have had one too many (infml) to be slightly drunk

0➡ **map** /mæp/ n [C] drawing or plan of (part of) the earth's surface, showing countries, towns, rivers, etc **IDM** put sb/sth on the map make sb/sth famous or important ● **map** v (-pp-) [T] make a map of an area

mar /mɑː(r)/ v (-rr-) [T] (fml) damage or spoil sth good: a mistake that ~red his career

marathon /'mærəθən/ n [C] long running race of about 42 kilometres or 26 miles ● **marathon** adj very long and needing a lot of effort: a ~ task

0➡ **March** /mɑːtʃ/ n the third month of the year (See examples of use at April.)

0➡ **march** /mɑːtʃ/ v **1** [I] walk as soldiers do, with regular steps **2** [T] force sb to walk somewhere with you: They ~ed the prisoner away. ● **march** n **1** [C] organized walk by many people from one place to another, esp as a protest **2** [C] act of marching; journey made by marching **3** [sing] ~ of the steady progress of sth: the ~ of time **4** [C] piece of music for marching to: a funeral ~

marchioness /ˌmɑːʃəˈnes/ n [C] **1** woman with the same rank as a marquess **2** wife of a marquess

mare /meə(r)/ n [C] female horse or donkey

margarine /ˌmɑːdʒəˈriːn/ n [U] food like butter, made from animal or vegetable fats

margin /'mɑːdʒɪn/ n **1** [C] empty space at the side of a written or printed page **2** [C, usu sing] amount of votes, time, etc by which sb wins sth: He won by a narrow ~. **3** [C] (business) = PROFIT MARGIN (PROFIT): a gross ~ of 45% **4** [C] amount of space, time, etc allowed for success or safety ▸ **marginal** /-nl/ adj small and not important: a ~al increase ▸ **marginally** /-nəli/ adv

marijuana /ˌmærəˈwɑːnə/ n [U] drug (illegal in many countries) made from the dried leaves and flowers of the hemp plant, which is usu smoked

marina /məˈriːnə/ n [C] small harbour for yachts and small boats

marinade /ˌmærɪˈneɪd/ n [C, U] mixture of oil, wine, herbs, etc in which meat or fish is soaked before being cooked

marinate /'mærɪneɪt/ (also **marinade**) v [I, T] (leave food to) soak in a mixture of oil, wine, herbs, etc before cooking it

marine /məˈriːn/ adj **1** of the sea and the creatures and plants that live in it: ~ life **2** of ships or trade at sea ● **marine** n [C] soldier trained to fight on land or at sea

marionette /ˌmæriəˈnet/ n [C] puppet moved by strings

marital /'mærɪtl/ adj of marriage

maritime /'mærɪtaɪm/ adj **1** of the sea or ships **2** (fml) near the sea

0➡ **mark**[1] /mɑːk/ n **1** stain, spot, etc esp that spoils the appearance of sth: dirty ~s on my new shirt **2** spot or area on the body of a person or animal which helps you to recognize them: a birth~ **3** written or printed symbol: punctuation ~s **4** sign that a quality or feeling exists: a ~ of respect **5** (esp GB) number or letter given to show the standard of sb's work or performance: get top ~s **6** (Mark) model or type of a machine, etc: a

M~ II engine [IDM] **make your/a mark (on sth)** become famous and successful in sth **quick/slow off the mark** fast/slow in reacting to a situation **up to the mark** as good as it/they should be

0~ **mark²** /mɑːk/ v **1** [T] write or draw a symbol, line, etc on sth to give information about it: *documents ~ed 'secret'* **2** [I,T] (cause sth to) become spoilt or damaged: *You've ~ed the table.* ◇ *The carpet ~s easily.* **3** [T] show the position of sth or be a sign of sth: *This cross ~s the place where she died.* ◇ *His death ~ed the end of an era.* **4** [T] (*esp GB*) give marks to students' work **5** [T] give sb/sth a particular quality or character **6** [T] (*sport*) stay close to an opposing player to prevent them from getting the ball [IDM] **mark time** pass the time while you wait for sth more interesting [PV] **mark sth down/up** reduce/increase the price of sth **mark sth off** separate sth by drawing a line between it and sth else **mark sth out** show where the edges of sth are **mark sb out as/for sth** make people recognize sb as special in some way ▶ **marked** *adj* easy to see; noticeable: *a ~ed improvement* ▶ **markedly** /ˈmɑːkɪdli/ *adv*
▶ **marker** *n* [C] **1** object or sign that shows the position of sth or that sth exists **2** pen with a thick felt tip **3** (*GB*) person who marks examination, etc papers ▶ **marking** *n* **1** [usu pl] pattern of colours or marks on animals, birds or wood **2** [usu pl] lines, colours or shapes painted on roads, vehicles, etc **3** [U] activity of correcting students' exams or written work ▶ **markup** /ˈmɑːkʌp/ *n* [C, usu sing] amount that a seller adds to a price

0~ **market** /ˈmɑːkɪt/ *n* **1** [C] (public place for a) meeting of people in order to buy and sell goods **2** [sing] business or trade, or the amount of trade in a particular type of goods: *The coffee ~ was steady.* **3** [C] particular area or country in which goods might be sold: *the global/domestic ~* **4** [sing] ~ (**for**) demand: *a good ~ for cars* **5** (**the market**) [sing] people who buy and sell goods in competition with each other [IDM] **in the market for sth** interested in buying sth **on the market** available for people to buy: *a product not yet on the ~* ● **market** *v* [T] advertise and offer a product for sale ▶ **marketable** *adj* easy to sell; attractive to customers or employers ▶ **market 'garden** *n* [C] (*GB*) type of farm where vegetables are grown for sale ▶ **marketing** *n* [U] part of business concerned with the advertising, selling of a company's products ■ **'marketplace** *n* **1** (**the marketplace**) [sing] activity of buying and selling goods, services, etc **2** [C] open area in a town where a market is held ■ **market re'search** *n* [U] study of what people buy and why ■ **market 'share** *n* [U, sing] (*business*) amount that a company sells of its products or services compared with the competition

marksman /ˈmɑːksmən/ *n* [C] (pl **-men** /-mən/) person skilled in shooting accurately

marmalade /ˈmɑːməleɪd/ *n* [U] kind of jam made from oranges

maroon /məˈruːn/ *adj, n* [C] (of a) dark brownish-red colour
● **maroon** *v* [T] leave sb in a place that they cannot escape from

marquee /mɑːˈkiː/ *n* [C] very large tent

marquess (*also* **marquis**) /ˈmɑːkwɪs/ *n* [C] (in Britain) nobleman of high rank

0~ **marriage** /ˈmærɪdʒ/ *n* [U, C] legal union of a man and woman as husband and wife ▶ **marriageable** *adj* (*old-fash*) old enough or suitable for marriage

marrow /ˈmærəʊ/ *n* **1** [U] = BONE MARROW (BONE) **2** [C, U] (*GB*) very large oval vegetable with white flesh and stripy green skin

0~ **marry** /ˈmæri/ *v* (*pt, pp* **-ied**) **1** [I,T] become the husband or wife of sb; get married to sb **2** [T] perform a ceremony in which a man and woman become husband and wife: *Which priest is going to ~ them?* **3** [T] find a husband or wife for sb, esp your son or daughter ▶ **married** *adj* **1** (*abbr* **m**) **~ (to)** having a husband or wife of: of marriage: *married life*

marsh /mɑːʃ/ *n* [C, U] area of low land that is soft and wet ▶ **marshy** *adj* (**-ier, -iest**)

marshal /ˈmɑːʃl/ *n* [C] **1** officer of the highest rank in the British air force or army **2** official who organizes a public event, esp a sports event **3** (*US*) officer whose job is to carry out court orders ● **marshal** *v* (**-ll- *US* -l-**) [T] **1** gather together and organize the people or things that you need for a particular purpose **2** control or organize a large group of people

marsupial /mɑːˈsuːpiəl/ *adj, n* [C] (of an) Australian animal, eg a kangaroo, the female of which has a pouch on its body to hold its young

martial /ˈmɑːʃl/ *adj* (*fml*) of fighting or war ■ **martial 'art** *n* [usu pl] fighting sport such as judo and karate ■ **martial 'law** *n* [U] situation where the army of a country controls an area rather than the police

martyr /ˈmɑːtə(r)/ *n* [C] person who dies or suffers for their religious or political beliefs ● martyr v [T] kill sb because of their religious or political beliefs ▶ martyrdom /'mɑːtədəm/n [U, C] suffering or death of a martyr

marvel /'mɑːvl/ n [C] wonderful thing: the ~s of modern science ● marvel v (-ll- US -l-) [T] ~ at (fml) be very surprised at sth ▶ marvellous (US -velous) /'mɑːvələs/ adj excellent; wonderful ▶ marvellously (US -velously) adv

Marxism /'mɑːksɪzəm/ n [U] political and economic theories of Karl Marx, on which Communism is based ▶ Marxist /-sɪst/ n [C], adj

marzipan /'mɑːzɪpæn/ n [U] thick paste of crushed almonds, sugar, etc

mascara /mæ'skɑːrə/ n [U] colour for darkening the eyelashes

mascot /'mæskɒt; -skət/ n [C] thing, animal or person thought to bring good luck

masculine /'mæskjəlɪn/ adj 1 of or like men 2 (gram) belonging to a particular class of nouns, pronouns, etc ● n [U] quality of being masculine ▶ masculinity /,mæskjə'lɪnəti/ n [U]

mash /mæʃ/ v [T] ~ (up) crush food into a soft mass: M~ the banana with a fork. ● mash n [U] (GB) mashed potatoes

mask /mɑːsk/ n [C] covering for part or all of the face worn to hide or protect it: (fig) His behaviour is really a ~ for his shyness. ● mask v [T] hide a feeling, smell, fact, etc so that it cannot be easily seen or noticed ▶ masked adj wearing a mask

masochism /'mæsəkɪzəm/ n [U] practice of getting esp sexual pleasure from being physically hurt ▶ masochist /-kɪst/ n [C] ▶ masochistic /,mæsə'kɪstɪk/ adj

mason /'meɪsn/ n [C] person who builds in or works with stone ▶ masonry /-sənri/ n [U] the parts of a building that are made of stone

masquerade /,mɑːskə'reɪd/ v [I] ~ as pretend to be sth that you are not: ~ as a police officer ● masquerade n [C] (fml) false show

Mass (also mass) /mæs/ n [U, C, (esp in the Roman Catholic Church) service held in memory of the last meal of Jesus Christ

0─ mass /mæs/ n 1 [C] large amount of a substance that does not have a definite shape: a ~ of earth 2 [sing] large number: a ~ of tourists 3 (masses) [pl] ~ (of) (infml) large number or amount of sth 4 (the masses) [pl] ordinary working people 5 [U] (phys) amount of matter in an object ● mass v [I, T] come together or gather sth/sb together in large numbers: The general ~ed his troops. ● the mass media n [pl] television, newspapers, etc ■ mass-pro'duce v [T] produce

271

goods in very large quantities ■ mass pro'duction n [U]

massacre /'mæsəkə(r)/ n [C] cruel killing of a large number of people ● massacre v [T] kill a large number of people cruelly

massage /'mæsɑːʒ/ n [C, U] (act of) rubbing and pressing sb's body, esp to reduce pain in the muscles or joints ● massage v [T] give a massage to sb

masseur /mæ'sɜː(r)/ n (fem masseuse /mæ'sɜːz/) person whose job is to give people massage

0─ massive /'mæsɪv/ adj extremely large ▶ massively adv

mast /mɑːst/ n [C] 1 tall pole on a boat or ship that supports the sails 2 tall metal tower with an aerial that sends and receives radio or television signals

0─ master¹ /'mɑːstə(r)/ n [C] 1 (old-fash) man who has people working for him, esp as servants in his home 2 ~ of (written) person who is able to control sth 3 ~ of (fml) person who is very skilled in sth 4 male owner of a dog, horse, etc 5 (GB, old-fash) male schoolteacher 6 (master's) second university degree, or, in Scotland, a first degree, such as an MA 7 (Master) person who has a master's degree: a M~ of Arts/ Sciences 8 captain of a ship 9 great artist 10 film, tape, etc from which copies can be made: the ~ copy ● master adj 1 very skilled at the job mentioned: a ~ carpenter 2 largest and/or most important: the ~ bedroom ■ 'mastermind v [T] plan and direct a complicated project ■ mastermind n [C] intelligent person who plans and directs a complicated project ■ master of 'ceremonies (abbr MC) n [C] person who introduces guests or entertainers at a formal occasion ■ 'masterpiece n [C] work of art, eg a painting, that is the best example of the artist's work

master² /'mɑːstə(r)/ v [T] 1 learn or understand sth completely: ~ a foreign language 2 gain control of sth

masterful /'mɑːstəfl/ adj able to control people or situations confidently ▶ masterfully /-fəli/ adv

masterly /'mɑːstəli/ adj very skilful

mastery /'mɑːstəri/ n [U] 1 great skill or knowledge 2 control or power

masturbate /'mæstəbeɪt/ v [I] give yourself sexual pleasure by rubbing your sexual organs ▶ masturbation /,mæstə'beɪʃn/ n [U]

mat /mæt/ n [C] 1 piece of thick material or carpet used to cover part of a floor: Wipe your feet on the ~. 2 small piece of material put under a

vase, hot dish, etc to protect a table
● mat adj (US) = MATT

matador /'mætədɔː(r)/ n [C]
bullfighter whose task is to kill the
bull

0⇀ **match** /mætʃ/ n **1** [C] short piece
of wood or cardboard used for
lighting a fire, cigarette, etc **2** [C]
(esp GB) sports event where people
or teams compete against each
other: a football ~ **3** [sing] person
who is equal to sb else in skill,
strength, etc: He's no ~ for her at
tennis. **4** [sing] person or thing that
combines well with sth/sb else: The
carpets and curtains are a good ~.
● match v **1** [I,T] combine well with
sth: The door was painted blue to ~
the walls. **2** [T] be equal to sb/sth
3 [T] find sb/sth to go together with
another person or thing
■ **matchbox** n [C] box for holding
matches ▶ **matchless** adj (fml)
without an equal ■ **matchmaker** n
[C] person who likes trying to
arrange marriages or relationships
for others

0⇀ **mate** /meɪt/ n [C] **1** friend,
companion or person you work or
share accommodation with: He's
gone out with his ~s. ◇ a flat~ **2** (GB,
infml) used as a friendly way of
addressing sb, esp between men
3 either of a pair of birds or animals
4 (GB) person whose job is to help a
skilled worker: a plumber's ~
5 officer in a commercial ship below
the rank of captain ● mate v [I,T]
~ (with) (put birds or animals
together to) have sex in order to
produce young

0⇀ **material** /məˈtɪəriəl/ n [U,C]
cloth used for making clothes, etc
2 [C, U] substance that things can be
made from: building ~s (= bricks,
sand, etc) **3** [U] information or ideas
for a book, etc: ~ for a newspaper
article ● **material** adj **1** connected
with money, possessions, etc rather
than the needs of the mind or spirit:
~ comforts **2** of the physical world
rather than the mind or spirit: the ~
world **3** ~ (to) (law) important: ~
evidence

materialism /məˈtɪəriəlɪzəm/ n [U]
(disapprov) belief that only money,
possessions, etc are important
▶ **materialist** /-lɪst/ n [C]
▶ **materialistic** /məˌtɪəriəˈlɪstɪk/ adj

materialize (also -ise)
/məˈtɪəriəlaɪz/ v [I] **1** take place or
start to exist as expected or planned
2 appear suddenly and/or in a way
that cannot be explained: The train
failed to ~ (= it did not come).

maternal /məˈtɜːnl/ adj **1** of or like a
mother **2** related through the
mother's side of the family: a ~
grandfather

maternity /məˈtɜːnəti/ n [U] state of
being or becoming a mother: a ~
ward/hospital (= one where women
go to give birth) ■ **ma'ternity
leave** n [U] period of time when a
woman temporarily leaves her job to
have a baby

0⇀ **mathematics** /ˌmæθəˈmætɪks/
(GB also infml **maths** /mæθs/) (US
also infml **math** /mæθ/) n [U] science
of numbers and shapes
▶ **mathematical** /-ɪkl/ adj
▶ **mathematically** /-kli/ adv
▶ **mathematician** /ˌmæθəməˈtɪʃn/
[C] student of or expert in
mathematics

matinee (also **matinée**) /'mætɪneɪ/ n
[C] afternoon performance of a play
or film

matriarch /'meɪtriɑːk/ n [C] woman
who is the head of a family or social
group ▶ **matriarchal** /-'ɑːkl/ adj

matriculate /məˈtrɪkjuleɪt/ v [I]
(fml) officially become a student at a
university ▶ **matriculation**
/məˌtrɪkjuˈleɪʃn/ n

matrimony /'mætrɪməni/ n [U] (fml)
state of being married
▶ **matrimonial** /ˌmætrɪˈməʊniəl/
adj

matrix /'meɪtrɪks/ n [C] (pl **matrices**
/'meɪtrɪsiːz/) **1** (maths)
arrangement of numbers, symbols,
etc in rows and columns, treated as a
single quantity **2** (fml) formal social,
political, etc situation from which a
society or person grows or develops
3 (tech) mould in which sth is
shaped **4** (computing) group of
electronic circuit elements arranged
in rows and columns like a grid
5 (geol) mass of rock in which
minerals, etc are found in the
ground

matron /'meɪtrən/ n [C] **1** (GB)
woman who works as a nurse in a
school **2** (GB) (in the past) senior
female nurse in charge of other
nurses in a hospital **3** (old-fash)
older married woman ▶ **matronly**
adj (disapprov) (of a woman) no
longer young, and rather fat

matt (US **mat** also **matte**) /mæt/ adj
(of surfaces) not shiny

matted /'mætɪd/ adj (of hair, etc)
forming a thick mass, esp because it
is wet and dirty

0⇀ **matter¹** /'mætə(r)/ n **1** [C] affair
or subject: an important business ~
2 (matters) [pl] the present
situation: To make ~s worse, I
couldn't find my keys. **3** (the matter)
[sing] ~ (with) used to (ask) if sb is
upset, etc or if there is a problem:
What's the ~ with her? ◇ Is anything
the ~? **4** [sing] situation that
involves sth or depends on sth: It's
simply a ~ of letting people know in
time. ◇ Well, that's a ~ of opinion (=
others may think differently). **5** [U]
(tech) physical substance that

everything in the world is made of **6** [U] substance or material of the kind that is mentioned: *reading ~* (= books, newspapers, etc) **[IDM] as a matter of fact** (*spoken*) (used for emphasis) **for that matter** (*spoken*) used to add a comment on sth that you have just said **(as) a matter of course** the usual and correct thing that is done **a matter of hours, minutes, etc** only a few hours, minutes, etc **a matter of opinion** subject on which there is disagreement **(be) a matter of (doing) sth** (be) a question or situation that depends on sth else: *Teaching isn't just a ~ of good communication.* **no matter who, what, where, etc** used to say that sth is always true, whatever the situation is: *They don't last, no ~ how careful you are.* ■ **matter-of-fact** *adj* said or done without showing any emotion

○➤ **matter²** /ˈmætə(r)/ *v* [I] be important or have an important effect on sb/sth: *It doesn't ~.*

matting /ˈmætɪŋ/ *n* [U] rough woven material used as a floor covering

mattress /ˈmætrəs/ *n* [C] soft part of a bed, that you lie on

mature /məˈtjʊə(r)/ *adj* **1** (of a child or young person) behaving in a sensible way, like an adult **2** (of a person, a tree, a bird or an animal) fully grown and developed **3** (of wine or cheese) having reached its full flavour **4** (*business*) (of an insurance policy) ready to be paid ● **mature** *v* [I,T] become or make sth mature ▸ **maturity** *n* [U]

maul /mɔːl/ *v* [T] hurt sb by rough or cruel handling: *be ~ed by a lion*

mausoleum /ˌmɔːsəˈliːəm/ *n* [C] special building made to hold the dead body of an important person or a family

mauve /məʊv/ *adj, n* [U] (of a) pale purple colour

maxim /ˈmæksɪm/ *n* [C] saying that expresses a general truth or rule of behaviour

maximize (*also* -ise) /ˈmæksɪmaɪz/ [T] **1** increase sth as much as possible **2** make the best use of sth

○➤ **maximum** /ˈmæksɪməm/ *n* [C, usu sing] greatest possible amount: *the ~ load a lorry can carry* ● **maximum** *adj* as large, fast, etc as is possible or the most that is possible or allowed

○➤ **May** /meɪ/ *n* [U, C] the fifth month of the year (See examples of use at April.)

○➤ **may** /meɪ/ *modal v* (*neg* **may not**) (*pt* **might** /maɪt/ *neg* **might not** *short form* **mightn't** /ˈmaɪtnt/) **1** used to say that sth is possible: *This coat ~ be Sarah's.* ◇ *He ~ have* (= Perhaps he has) *forgotten to come.* **2** (*fml*) used

273

mean

to ask for or give permission: *M~ I sit down?* **3** (*fml*) used to express wishes and hopes: *M~ you both be very happy!*

○➤ **maybe** /ˈmeɪbi/ *adv* perhaps

mayonnaise /ˌmeɪəˈneɪz/ *n* [U] thick creamy sauce made from eggs, oil and vinegar, and eaten with salads

○➤ **mayor** /meə(r)/ *n* [C] head, usu elected yearly, of a city or town council ▸ **mayoress** /meəˈres/ *n* [C] **1** woman who has been elected mayor **2** wife of a mayor

maze /meɪz/ *n* [C] system of paths in a park or garden that is designed so that it is difficult to find your way through

MB (*also* Mb) *abbr* = MEGABYTE

MC /ˌem ˈsiː/ *abbr* **1** = MASTER OF CEREMONIES (MASTER¹) **2** (*M.C.*) (*US*) Member of Congress

MD /ˌem ˈdiː/ *abbr* **1** Doctor of Medicine **2** = MANAGING DIRECTOR (MANAGE)

○➤ **me** /miː/ *pron* (used as the object of a v or prep) person who is the speaker or writer: *Don't hit me.* ◇ *Give it to me.*

meadow /ˈmedəʊ/ *n* [C, U] field of grass

meagre (*US* meager) /ˈmiːgə(r)/ *adj* small in quantity and poor in quality: *a ~ income* ▸ **meagerly** *adv* ▸ **meagreness** *n* [U]

○➤ **meal** /miːl/ *n* **1** [C] occasion when food is eaten **2** [C] food that is eaten at a meal **3** [U] roughly crushed grain: *oat~*

○➤ **mean¹** /miːn/ *v* (*pt, pp* ~**t** /ment/) **1** (of words, sentences, etc) have sth as an explanation: *What does this word ~?* ◇ *A green light ~s 'go'.* **2** have sth as a purpose; intend: *What do you ~ by coming* (= Why did you come) *so late? ◇ Sorry, I ~t to tell you earlier. ◇ Don't laugh! I ~ it* (= I am serious)*! ◇ You're ~t to* (= You are supposed to) *pay before you come in.* **3** have sth as a result or a likely result: *This will ~ more work.* **4** ~ **to** be of value or importance to sb: *Your friendship ~s a lot to me.* **[IDM] be meant to do sth** be supposed to do sth **mean business** (*infml*) be serious in your intentions **mean well** have good intentions, although their effect may not be good ▸ **meaning** *n* [U, C] **1** thing or idea that a word, sentence, etc represents **2** [U,C] things or ideas that sb wishes to communicate to you **3** [U] purpose, value or importance: *My life has lost all ~ing.* ▸ **meaningful** *adj* serious and important; full of meaning ▸ **meaningless** *adj* without meaning

mean² /miːn/ *adj* **1** not willing to give or share things, esp money **2** unkind (*esp US*) likely to become

angry or violent **4** (*tech*) average: the ~ *temperature* [**IDM**] **be no mean ...** (*approv*) used to say that sb is very good at sth ▶ **meanness** *n* [U]
● **mean** *n* (*maths*) quantity between two extremes; average

meander /miˈændə(r)/ *v* [I] **1** (of a river, road, etc) curve a lot **2** wander about

0━ **means** /miːnz/ *n* (pl **means**) **1** [C] method: *find a ~ of improving the standard of education* **2** [pl] money that a person has: *a man of ~ (= a rich man)* ◇ *Are the repayments within your ~ (=* Can you afford them)*?* ◇ *Try not to live beyond your ~ (=* spend more money than you earn)*.* [**IDM**] **by all means** (*spoken*) yes, of course **by means of sth** (*fml*) with the help of sth **by no means** (*fml*) not at all
■ **means test** *n* [C] official check of sb's wealth or income to decide if they are poor enough to receive money from the government

meant *pt, pp* of MEAN¹

meantime /ˈmiːntaɪm/ *n* [**IDM**] **in the meantime** meanwhile ▶ **meantime** *adv* meanwhile

0━ **meanwhile** /ˈmiːnwaɪl/ *adv*
1 while sth else is happening **2** in the time between two events

measles /ˈmiːzlz/ *n* [U] infectious disease, esp of children, that causes small red spots on the skin

0━ **measure¹** /ˈmeʒə(r)/ *v* **1** [T] find the size, length, degree, etc of sth in standard units: ~ *a piece of wood* **2** linking verb be a particular size, length, etc: *The room ~ s 5 metres across.* [**PV**] **measure sth out** take the amount of sth you need from a larger amount **measure up (to sth/ sb)** be as good, successful, etc as expected or needed ▶ **measured** *adj* careful ▶ **measurement** *n* **1** [C] act of measuring sth **2** [C, usu pl] length, width, etc that is measured: *take sb's waist ~ment*

0━ **measure²** /ˈmeʒə(r)/ *n* **1** [C] official action done to achieve a particular purpose: *safety/security ~ s* **2** [sing] degree of sth; some: *a ~ of success* **3** [sing] sign of the size or strength of sth: *a ~ of his anger* **4** [C, U] unit used for stating the size, quantity or degree of sth; system or a scale of these units: *weights and ~ s* **5** [C] instrument, eg a ruler, marked with standard units: *a tape ~* [**IDM**] **get/take/have the measure of sb** (*fml*) form an opinion about sb's character or abilities **made-to-measure** (*GB*) specially made for one person according to particular measurements

0━ **meat** /miːt/ *n* [U,C] flesh of animals, used as food **2** [U]

important or interesting part of sth
▶ **meaty** *adj* (**-ier, -iest**)

mechanic /məˈkænɪk/ *n* [C] worker skilled in using or repairing machines, esp car engines
▶ **mechanical** *adj* **1** of, connected with or produced by machines **2** (*disapprov*) done without thought; automatic ▶ **mechanically** /-kli/ *adv*

mechanics /məˈkænɪks/ *n* [U] **1** science of movement and force; science of machinery **2** [pl] practical study of machinery **3** (**the mechanics**) [pl] way sth works or is done

mechanism /ˈmekənɪzəm/ *n* [C] **1** set of moving parts in a machine **2** way of getting sth done

mechanize (*also* -ise) /ˈmekənaɪz/ *v* [T] change a process, so that the work is done by machines rather than people ▶ **mechanization** (*also* -isation) /ˌmekənaɪˈzeɪʃn/ *n* [U]

medal /ˈmedl/ *n* [C] small round flat piece of metal, given as an honour for bravery or as a prize ▶ **medallist** (*US* medalist) /ˈmedəlɪst/ *n* [C] person who has won a medal, esp in sport

medallion /məˈdæliən/ *n* [C] piece of jewellery in the shape of a large flat coin worn on a chain around the neck

meddle /ˈmedl/ *v* [I] (*disapprov*) become involved in sth that does not concern you ▶ **meddler** *n* [C]

0━ **media** /ˈmiːdiə/ *n* (**the media**) [sing, with sing or pl verb] television, radio, newspapers, etc

mediaeval = MEDIEVAL

mediate /ˈmiːdieɪt/ *v* [I] ~ (**between**) take action to end a disagreement between two or more people or groups ▶ **mediation** /ˌmiːdiˈeɪʃn/ *n* [U] ▶ **mediator** *n* [C]

medic /ˈmedɪk/ *n* [C] (*infml*) medical student or doctor

0━ **medical** /ˈmedɪkl/ *adj* **1** of illness and injury and their treatment: *her ~ records* **2** of ways of treating illness that do not involve cutting the body ● **medical** *n* [C] thorough examination of your body done by a doctor, eg before you start a new job ▶ **medically** /-kli/ *adv*

Medicare /ˈmedɪkeə(r)/ *n* US government scheme providing free medical care for old people

medication /ˌmedɪˈkeɪʃn/ *n* [C, U] drug or medicine used to prevent or treat a disease

medicinal /məˈdɪsɪnl/ *adj* (used for) healing

0━ **medicine** /ˈmedsn/ *n* **1** [U] study and treatment of diseases and injuries **2** [U,C] substance, esp a liquid that is taken to cure an illness [**IDM**] **a dose/taste of your own medicine** the same bad treatment

that you have given to others
■ **'medicine man** *n* [C] = WITCH DOCTOR (WITCH)

medieval (*also* **mediaeval**) /ˌmedi'iːvl/ *adj* of the Middle Ages (about AD 1000 - 1450)

mediocre /ˌmiːdi'əʊkə(r)/ *adj* (*disapprov*) not very good ▶ **mediocrity** /ˈbkrɒti/ *n* [U,C] (pl **-ies**)

meditate /'mediteɪt/ *v* [I] ~ **(on)** think deeply, usu in silence, esp for religious reasons ● **meditation** /ˌmedi'teɪʃn/ *n* [U,C]

0━ **medium** /'miːdiəm/ *n* [C] (pl **media** /'miːdiə/ *or* **-s**) **1** way of communicating information, etc to people: *an effective advertising ~* **2** something that is used for a particular purpose: *Video is a good ~ for practising listening comprehension.* **3** substance or surroundings in which sth exists **4** (pl **-s**) person who claims to communicate with dead people ● **medium** *adj* in the middle between two sizes, amounts, etc: *a man of ~ height/build* ■ **'medium wave** (*abbr* **MW**) *n* [U] band of radio waves with a length of between 100 and 1000 metres

meek /miːk/ *adj* quiet, gentle and always willing to do what others want ▶ **meekly** *adv* **meekness** *n* [U]

0━ **meet**[1] /miːt/ *v* (pt, pp **met** /met/) **1** [I,T] come together with sb: *Let's ~ again soon.* **2** [T] go to a place and wait there for a particular person to arrive **3** [I,T] see and know sb for the first time; be introduced to sb: *Pleased to ~ you.* **4** [T] experience sth, esp sth unpleasant: ~ *your death* **5** [I,T] touch sth; join: *Their hands met.* **6** [T] do or satisfy what is needed or what sb asks for: ~ *sb's wishes* **7** [T] pay sth: ~ *all expenses* [IDM] **meet sb halfway** make a compromise with sb **there is more to sb/sth than meets the eye** sb/sth is more complicated, interesting, etc than you might think at first [PV] **meet with sb** (*esp US*) meet sb, esp for discussions **meet with sth** (*written*) **1** be received or treated by sb in a particular way: *to ~ with success/failure* **2** experience sth unpleasant: ~ *with an accident*

meet[2] /miːt/ *n* [C] **1** (*esp US*) sports competition **2** (*GB*) event at which horse riders and dogs hunt foxes

0━ **meeting** /'miːtɪŋ/ *n* [C] occasion when people come together, esp to discuss or decide sth

megabyte /'megəbaɪt/ *n* [C] (*abbr* **MB**) unit of computer memory, equal to 2²⁰ (or about 1 million) bytes

megaphone /'megəfəʊn/ *n* [C] device shaped like a cone, used to make your voice sound louder

melancholy /'melənkəli; -kɒli/ *n* [U] (*fml*) deep sadness that lasts for a long time ● **melancholy** *adj* sad ▶ **melancholic** /ˌmelən'kɒlɪk/ *adj*

mellow /'meləʊ/ *adj* **1** (of colour or sound) soft, rich and pleasant **2** (of a taste or flavour) smooth and pleasant **3** (of people) calm, wise and gentle because of age or experience ● **mellow** *v* [I,T] (cause sb/sth to) become mellow ▶ **mellowness** *n* [U]

melodrama /'melədrɑːmə/ *n* [U,C] **1** story, play, etc that is exciting and in which the characters and emotions seem too exaggerated to be real **2** events, behaviour, etc that are exaggerated or extreme ▶ **melodramatic** /ˌmelədrə'mætɪk/ *adj* ▶ **melodramatically** /-kli/ *adv*

melody /'melədi/ *n* [C] (pl **-ies**) tune or song ▶ **melodic** /mə'lɒdɪk/ *adj* of melody ▶ **melodious** /mə'ləʊdiəs/ *adj* having a pleasant tune

melon /'melən/ *n* [C] large round juicy fruit with a hard skin

0━ **melt** /melt/ *v* [I,T] **1** (cause sth to) become liquid as a result of heating: *The sun ~ed the snow.* **2** (cause a feeling, an emotion, etc to) become gentler and less strong [PV] **melt (sth) away** (cause sth to) disappear gradually **melt sth down** melt a metal object in order to use the metal again ■ **'meltdown** *n* [U,C] melting of the overheated centre of a nuclear reactor, causing the escape of radioactivity ■ **'melting pot** *n* [usu sing] place where large numbers of people from different countries live together [IDM] **in the melting pot** likely to change; in the process of changing

0━ **member** /'membə(r)/ *n* [C] **1** person belonging to a group, club, etc **2** (*fml*) part of the body; limb ■ **Member of 'Parliament** *n* [C] (*abbr* **MP**) elected representative in the House of Commons ▶ **membership** *n* **1** [U] state of being a member of a group, club, etc **2** [C, with sing or pl verb] (number of) members of a group, club, etc

membrane /'membreɪn/ *n* [C,U] layer of soft thin skin-like material

memento /mə'mentəʊ/ *n* [C] (pl **-es** *or* **-s**) thing that you keep to remind you of a person or place

memo /'meməʊ/ *n* [C] (pl **-s**) (*also fml* **memorandum**) official note from one person to another in the same organization

memoir /'memwɑː(r)/ *n* (**memoirs**) [pl] person's written account of their own life

memorable /'memərəbl/ *adj* deserving to be remembered; remarkable ▶ **memorably** *adv*

memorandum /ˌmeməˈrændəm/ *n* [C] (pl **-da** /-də/) (*fml*) = MEMO

memorial /məˈmɔːriəl/ *n* [C] statue, stone, etc that is built to remind people of a past event or a famous person: *a war ~.*

memorize (*also* -ise) /ˈmeməraɪz/ *v* [T] learn sth well enough to remember it exactly

0— **memory** /ˈmeməri/ *n* (pl **-ies**) **1** [C, U] your ability to remember things: *He's got a good ~.* **2** [U] period of time that sb is able to remember events **3** [C] thought of sth that you remember from the past: *memories of childhood* **4** [U] what is remembered about sb after their death **5** [C, U] part of a computer where information is stored; amount of space in a computer for storing information [IDM] **in memory of sb** in order that people will remember sb who has died

men plural of MAN¹

menace /ˈmenəs/ *n* **1** [C, U, sing] person or thing that will probably cause serious harm or danger **2** [U] atmosphere that makes you feel threatened **3** [C, U, sing] (*infml*) annoying person or thing ● **menace** *v* [T] threaten sth/sb ▸ **menacingly** *adv*

menagerie /məˈnædʒəri/ *n* [C] collection of wild animals; zoo

mend /mend/ *v* **1** [T] repair sth damaged or broken so that it can be used again **2** [I] return to good health [IDM] **mend your ways** stop behaving badly ● **mend** *n* [IDM] **on the mend** (*infml, esp GB*) recovering from an illness or injury

menial /ˈmiːniəl/ *adj* (*disapprov*) (of work) not skilled or important and often boring

meningitis /ˌmenɪnˈdʒaɪtɪs/ *n* [U] serious illness causing inflammation of the outer part of the brain and spinal cord

menopause /ˈmenəpɔːz/ *n* (the **menopause**) [sing] gradual stopping of a woman's menstruation usu at around the age of 50

menstruate /ˈmenstrueɪt/ *v* [I] (*fml*) (of a woman) have a flow of blood from her uterus every month ▸ **menstrual** /-struəl/ *adj* ▸ **menstruation** /ˌmenstruˈeɪʃn/ *n* [U]

0— **mental** /ˈmentl/ *adj* **1** of or in the mind: *a ~ illness* ◇ *make a ~ note of sth* (= try to remember sth) **2** of or concerned with illnesses of the mind: *a ~ patient/hospital* **3** (GB, sl) crazy ▸ **mentally** /-təli/ *adv* of or in the mind: *~ly ill*

mentality /menˈtæləti/ *n* [usu sing]

(pl **-ies**) particular attitude or way of thinking of a person or group

menthol /ˈmenθɒl/ *n* [U] substance that tastes and smells of mint, used in some medicines and as a flavouring

0— **mention** /ˈmenʃn/ *v* [T] speak or write about sth/sb briefly [IDM] **don't mention it** (*spoken*) used as a polite answer when sb has thanked you for sth **not to mention** sth used to introduce extra information and to emphasize what you are saying ● **mention** *n* [C, U] brief reference to sth/sb

0— **menu** /ˈmenjuː/ *n* [C] **1** list of food that can be ordered in a restaurant **2** (*computing*) list of possible choices that are shown on a computer screen: *a pull-down ~*

meow (*esp US*) = MIAOW

MEP /ˌem iː ˈpiː/ *abbr* Member of the European Parliament

mercantile /ˈmɜːkəntaɪl/ *adj* (*fml*) of trade and commercial affairs

mercenary /ˈmɜːsənəri/ *adj* (*disapprov*) interested only in making money ● **mercenary** *n* [C] (pl **-ies**) soldier who will fight for any country or group that offers payment

merchandise /ˈmɜːtʃəndaɪz/ *n* [U] (*fml*) goods bought and sold; goods for sale in a shop

merchant /ˈmɜːtʃənt/ *n* [C] person who buys and sells goods in large quantities ● **merchant** *adj* concerned with the transport of goods by sea: *~ ships* ● **merchant bank** *n* [C] bank that deals with large businesses ● **merchant** 'navy (US ˌmerchant ma'rine) *n* [C, with sing or pl verb] country's commercial ships and the people who work on them

mercury /ˈmɜːkjəri/ *n* [U] (*symb* Hg) heavy silver-coloured metal, usu in liquid form ● **mercurial** /mɜːˈkjʊəriəl/ *adj* (*lit*) (of a person or their moods) lively and often changing

mercy /ˈmɜːsi/ *n* (pl **-ies**) **1** [U] kindness or forgiveness shown to sb you have the power to punish **2** [C] event or situation to be grateful for [IDM] **at the mercy of sb/sth** powerless to prevent sb/sth from harming you ▸ **merciful** *adj* ready to forgive people ▸ **mercifully** /-fəli/ *adv* ▸ **merciless** *adj* showing no kindness or pity ▸ **mercilessly** *adv*

0— **mere** /mɪə(r)/ *adj* nothing more than; only: *She's a ~ child.* ▸ **merely** *adv* only; simply

merge /mɜːdʒ/ *v* **1** [I, T] (cause two or more things to) combine to make one thing: *The two companies ~d.* **2** [I] ~ **(into)** fade or change gradually into sth: *Day ~d into night.* ▸ **merger** *n* [C] joining together of two or more organizations or businesses

meridian /məˈrɪdiən/ n [C] one of the lines drawn from the North to the South Pole on a map of the world

meringue /məˈræŋ/ n [U,C] (small cake made from a) baked mixture of the whites of egg and sugar

merit /ˈmerɪt/ n **1** [U] (fml) quality of being good and deserving praise **2** [C, usu pl] good feature that deserves praise or reward ● **merit** v [T] (fml) deserve praise, attention, etc

mermaid /ˈmɜːmeɪd/ n [C] (in stories) woman with a fish's tail instead of legs

merry /ˈmeri/ adj (-ier, -iest) **1** happy and cheerful **2** (infml, esp GB) slightly drunk ▶ **merrily** adv ● **merriment** n [U] ■ **merry-go-round** n [C] revolving circular platform with wooden horses, etc on which children ride at a fairground

mesh /meʃ/ n [U,C] material made of threads of plastic rope or wire woven together like a net ● **mesh** v [I] (written) fit together or match in a satisfactory way: *Their opinions don't really ~.*

mesmerize (also -ise) /ˈmezməraɪz/ v [T] hold the attention of sb completely

0‑ **mess** /mes/ n **1** [C, usu sing] dirty or untidy state **2** [C, usu sing] difficult or confused situation: *My life's in a ~.* **3** [C] (esp US 'mess hall) room or building in which members of the armed forces eat their meals ● **mess** v [T] (infml) make sth untidy or dirty [PV] **mess about/around 1** behave in a silly and annoying way **2** spend time doing sth for pleasure in a relaxed way **mess sb about/around** treat sb in an annoying and unfair way **mess (sth) up** spoil sth or do it badly ▶ **messy** adj (-ier, -iest)

0‑ **message** /ˈmesɪdʒ/ n **1** [C] written or spoken piece of information to sb or left for sb **2** [sing] central idea that a book, speech, etc tries to communicate [IDM] **get the message** (infml) understand what sb has been trying to tell you ▶ **messenger** /ˈmesɪndʒə(r)/ n [C] person who takes a message to sb

Messiah /məˈsaɪə/ n **1** (the Messiah) [sing] (in Christianity) Jesus Christ **2** (the Messiah) [sing] (in Judaism) king sent by God who will save the Jewish people **3** (messiah) [C] leader who people believe will solve the problems of the world

met pt, pp of MEET[1]

metabolism /məˈtæbəlɪzəm/ n [U,sing] (biol) process in the body by which food is used to supply energy ▶ **metabolic** /ˌmetəˈbɒlɪk/ adj

0‑ **metal** /ˈmetl/ n [C,U] any of a kind of mineral substance such as tin, iron or gold ▶ **metallic** /məˈtælɪk/ adj

metaphor /ˈmetəfə(r)/ n [C,U] (example of the) use of words to show sth different from the literal meaning, as in 'She has a heart of stone' ▶ **metaphorical** /ˌmetəˈfɒrɪkl/ adj ▶ **metaphorically** /-kli/ adv

mete /miːt/ v [PV] **mete sth out (to sb)** (fml) give sb a punishment

meteor /ˈmiːtiə(r)/, -iɔː(r)/ n [C] piece of rock that moves through space into the earth's atmosphere, becoming bright as it burns ▶ **meteoric** /ˌmiːtiˈɒrɪk/ adj **1** achieving success very quickly: *a ~ic rise to fame* **2** of meteors ▶ **meteorite** /ˈmiːtiəraɪt/ n [C] meteor that has fallen to earth

meteorology /ˌmiːtiəˈrɒlədʒi/ n [U] study of the weather and the earth's atmosphere ▶ **meteorological** /ˌmiːtiərəˈlɒdʒɪkl/ adj ▶ **meteorologist** n [C] expert in meteorology

meter /ˈmiːtə(r)/ n [C] **1** device that measures sth: *a gas ~* **2** (US) = METRE

0‑ **method** /ˈmeθəd/ n **1** [C] way of doing sth **2** [U] quality of being well planned and organized ▶ **methodical** /məˈθɒdɪkl/ adj using an organized system; careful ▶ **methodically** /-kli/ adv

methodology /ˌmeθəˈdɒlədʒi/ n [C,U] (pl -ies) (fml) set of methods and principles used to perform a particular activity

meticulous /məˈtɪkjələs/ adj showing great care and attention to detail ▶ **meticulously** adv

0‑ **metre** (US **meter**) /ˈmiːtə(r)/ n **1** (abbr m) [C] metric unit of length **2** [U,C] pattern of stressed and unstressed syllables in poetry ▶ **metric** /ˈmetrɪk/ adj of the metric system ▶ **metrication** /ˌmetrɪˈkeɪʃn/ n [U] process of changing to the metric system ■ the 'metric system n [sing] system of measurement that uses the metre, kilogram and litre as basic units

metropolis /məˈtrɒpəlɪs/ n [C] main or capital city of a region or country ▶ **metropolitan** /ˌmetrəˈpɒlɪtən/ adj

mettle /ˈmetl/ n [U] ability and determination to do sth successfully [IDM] **on your mettle** prepared to do your best, because you are being tested

mews /mjuːz/ n [C] (pl **mews**) street of stables, converted into houses or flats

miaow (US, GB also **meow**) /miˈaʊ/ n [C] sound made by a cat ▶ **miaow** v [I] mice *plural of* MOUSE

mickey /'mɪkɪ/ *n* [IDM] **take the mickey (out of sb)** (*GB, infml*) tease sb

microbe /'maɪkrəʊb/ *n* [C] tiny living thing, esp one that causes disease

microchip /'maɪkrəʊtʃɪp/ *n* [C] very small piece of material that has a complicated electronic circuit on it

microcosm /'maɪkrəʊkɒzəm/ *n* [C] thing, place or group that has all the qualities and features of sth much larger

microfiche /'maɪkrəʊfiːʃ/ *n* [U,C] film on which written information is stored in very small print and which can only be read with a special machine

microfilm /'maɪkrəʊfɪlm/ *n* [U,C] film on which written information is stored in print of very small size

microlight /'maɪkrəʊlaɪt/ *n* [C] very small light aircraft for one or two people

microphone /'maɪkrəfəʊn/ *n* [C] device for recording sounds or for making your voice louder when you are speaking to an audience

microprocessor /ˌmaɪkrəʊ'prəʊsesə(r)/ *n* [C] (*computing*) small unit of a computer that contains all the functions of the central processing unit

microscope /'maɪkrəskəʊp/ *n* [C] instrument that makes very small objects appear larger ▶ **microscopic** /ˌmaɪkrə'skɒpɪk/ *adj* **1** very small **2** using a microscope

microwave /'maɪkrəweɪv/ (*also fml* ˌmicrowave 'oven) *n* [C] type of oven that cooks or heats food very quickly using electromagnetic waves rather than heat

0━ **mid-** /mɪd/ *prefix* in the middle of: ~*-morning* ◇ ~*-air* (= in the sky)

0━ **midday** /ˌmɪd'deɪ/ *n* [U] 12 o'clock in the middle of the day

0━ **middle** /'mɪdl/ *n* (the middle) [sing] position at an equal distance from all the edges or between the beginning and the end of sth ● **middle** *adj* position in the middle of an object, group of objects, people, etc, between the beginning and the end of sth ■ ˌmiddle 'age *n* [U] period of your life between the ages of about 45 and 60 ▶ ˌmiddle-'aged *adj* ■ the Middle 'Ages *n* [pl] in European history, the period from about AD 1000 to 1450 ■ ˌmiddle 'class *n* [C, with sing or pl verb] social class whose members are neither very rich nor very poor and that includes professional and business people ▶ ˌmiddle-'class *adj* ■ the Middle 'East *n* [sing] area that covers SW

Asia and NE Africa ■ 'middleman *n* [C] (pl **-men** /-men/) trader who buys goods from the company that makes them and sells them to sb else ■ ˌmiddle-of-the-'road *adj* (of people, policies, etc) not extreme; moderate

middling /'mɪdlɪŋ/ *adj* of average size, quality, etc

midge /mɪdʒ/ *n* [C] small flying insect that bites humans and animals

midget /'mɪdʒɪt/ *n* [C] (*offens*) very small person ● **midget** *adj* very small

Midlands /'mɪdləndz/ *n* (the Midlands) [sing, with sing or pl verb] central counties of England

0━ **midnight** /'mɪdnaɪt/ *n* [U] 12 o'clock in the middle of the night

midriff /'mɪdrɪf/ *n* [C] middle part of the body, between the waist and the chest

midst /mɪdst/ *n* [IDM] **in the midst of (doing) sth** in the middle of sth

midway /ˌmɪd'weɪ/ *adj, adv* halfway: ~ *between Paris and Rome*

midwife /'mɪdwaɪf/ *n* [C] (pl **-wives** /-waɪvz/) person, esp a woman, trained to help women in childbirth ▶ **midwifery** /ˌmɪd'wɪfəri/ *n* [U] profession and work of a midwife

0━ **might**[1] /maɪt/ *modal v* (neg **might not** short form **mightn't** /'maɪtnt/) **1** used as the past tense of *may* when reporting what sb has said **2** used when showing that sth is or was possible: *He ~ be at home, but I doubt it.* **3** used to make a polite suggestion: *You ~ try calling the help desk.* **4** (*GB*) used to ask permission politely **5** used to show that you are annoyed about sth that sb could or could have done: *They ~ at least offer to help!*

might[2] /maɪt/ *n* [U] (*fml or lit*) great strength or power ■ **mighty** *adj* (**-ier, -iest**) *esp* (*lit*) **1** powerful **2** large and impressive ● **mighty** *adv* (*infml, esp US*) very

migraine /'miːɡreɪn; 'maɪɡ-/ *n* [U,C] very painful headache

migrate /maɪˈɡreɪt/ *v* [I] ~ (**from, to**) **1** (of birds, etc) go from one part of the world to another regularly each year **2** (of a lot of people) move from one place to go to live in another ▶ **migrant** /'maɪɡrənt/ *n* [C] person or bird, etc that migrates ▶ **migration** /maɪˈɡreɪʃn/ *n* [U,C] ▶ **migratory** /'maɪɡrətri; maɪˈɡreɪtəri/ *adj*

mike /maɪk/ *n* [C] (*infml*) = MICROPHONE

0━ **mild** /maɪld/ *adj* **1** gentle; not severe: *a ~ climate* **2** not sharp or strong in flavour: *~ curry* ▶ **mildly** *adv* ▶ **mildness** *n* [U]

mildew /'mɪldjuː/ *n* [U] small white fungus that grows on walls, plants, food, etc in warm wet conditions

mind

mile /maɪl/ *n* [C] unit of distance; 1760 yards (1609 metres) ► **mileage** /-ɪdʒ/ *n* **1** [C, U] distance travelled, measured in miles **2** [U] (*infml*) amount of advantage or use that you can get from an event or a situation: *The press can't get any more ~ out of that story.* ■ **milestone** (*US* **milepost**) *n* [C] **1** important stage or event in the development of a road showing the distance to a place ■ **milometer** (*also* **mileometer**) /maɪˈlɒmɪtə(r)/ *n* [C] instrument in a vehicle that records the number of miles travelled

militant /ˈmɪlɪtənt/ *n* [C], *adj* (person) supporting the use of strong methods, esp force, to achieve your aims ► **militancy** /-ənsi/ *n* [U]

0▬ **military** /ˈmɪlətri/ *adj* of or for soldiers or war ■ **the military** *n* [sing, with sing or pl verb] soldiers; the armed forces

militate /ˈmɪlɪteɪt/ *v* [PV] **militate against sth** (*fml*) prevent sth; make it difficult for sth to happen or exist

militia /məˈlɪʃə/ *n* [sing, with sing or pl verb] group of people trained to act as soldiers in an emergency

0▬ **milk** /mɪlk/ *n* [U] **1** white liquid produced by female mammals as food for their young **2** white juice of some trees and plants: *coconut ~* ● **milk** *v* **1** [I,T] take milk from a cow, goat, etc **2** [T] obtain as much money, advantage, etc for yourself as you can from a situation, esp dishonestly ■ **milkman** *n* [C] (*esp in Britain*) person whose job is to deliver milk to customers each morning ■ **milkshake** *n* [C] drink made of milk and sometimes ice cream, with flavouring added to it ► **milky** *adj* (**-ier, -iest**) **1** of or like milk **2** made with a lot of milk: *~y coffee* ■ **the Milky Way** *n* [sing] = THE GALAXY(1)

mill /mɪl/ *n* [C] **1** building with machinery for grinding grain into flour **2** factory that produces a particular type of material: *a cotton/ paper ~* **3** small machine for crushing sth: *a pepper ~* [IDM] **put sb/ go through the mill** (cause sb to) have a difficult time ● **mill** *v* [T] crush or grind sth in a mill [PV] **mill about/ around** move around aimlessly in a disorganized group ■ **miller** *n* [C] person who owns or runs a mill ■ **millstone** *n* [C] either of a pair of flat circular stones used, esp in the past, to crush grain [IDM] **a millstone around/round your neck** difficult problem or responsibility that seems impossible to solve or get rid of

millennium /mɪˈleniəm/ *n* (*pl* **-nia** /-niə/ *or* **~s**) **1** [C] period of 1000 years **2** (**the millennium**) [sing] time when one period of 1000 years end

and another begins: *How did you celebrate the ~?*

millet /ˈmɪlɪt/ *n* [U] type of cereal plant producing very small grain

milli- /ˈmɪli/ *prefix* (in the metric system) one thousandth: *~gram* ◊ *~metre*

0▬ **million** /ˈmɪljən/ *number* **1** (*abbr* **m**) 1,000,000 **2** (**a million** *or* **millions (of...)**) (*infml*) a very large amount: *I have ~ s things to do.* ► **millionaire** /ˌmɪljəˈneə(r)/ *n* [C] (*fem* **millionairess** /-ˈneərəs/) person who has a million pounds, dollars, etc; very rich person ► **millionth** *ordinal number, n* [C] 1,000,000th; one of a million equal parts of sth

millipede /ˈmɪlɪpiːd/ *n* [C] small creature like an insect with many legs

milometer → MILE

mime /maɪm/ *n* [U,C] (performance involving) use of hand or body movements and facial expressions to act sth without speaking ● **mime** *v* [I,T] act sth using mime

mimic /ˈmɪmɪk/ *v* (*pt, pp* **~ked**) [T] **1** copy the way sb speaks, etc in an amusing way **2** look or behave like sth else ● **mimic** *n* [C] person or an animal that can copy the voice, movements, etc of others ► **mimicry** /-ri/ *n* [U] action or skill of mimicking sb

minaret /ˌmɪnəˈret/ *n* [C] tall thin tower of a mosque, from which people are called to prayer

mince /mɪns/ *v* **1** [T] cut food, esp meat into very small pieces using a special machine (a mincer) **2** [I] walk with quick short steps, in a way that is not natural [IDM] **not mince (your) words** say sth in a direct way, even though it may offend people ● **mince** *n* [U] minced meat ■ **mincemeat** *n* [U] (*esp GB*) mixture of dried fruit, used esp for making pies [IDM] **make mincemeat of sb** (*infml*) defeat sb completely in a fight or argument

0▬ **mind¹** /maɪnd/ *n* **1** [C, U] part of a person's brain where their thoughts are: *The idea never entered my ~.* ◊ *She has a brilliant ~* (= She is very clever). **2** [C] very intelligent person: *one of the greatest ~s of their generation* **3** [U] your ability to remember things: *My ~ has gone blank!* [IDM] **be in two minds about (doing) sth** (*US*) **be of two minds about (doing) sth** feel doubtful about sth **be/take a load/weight off sb's mind** remove a cause of worry from sb **be/go out of your mind** (*infml*) be/go mad **bear/keep sb/sth in mind** remember sb/sth **bring/call sb/sth to mind** (*fml*) 1 remember sb/ sth 2 remind you of sb/sth **have a good mind to do sth | have half a mind to do sth** have a strong desire to do sth **make up your mind** reach a decision **on your mind** making you worry about sth **put/set/turn your mind to sth** give your attention to sth **take your mind off sth** help you not to think about sth **to my mind** in my opinion **your mind's eye** your imagination

0~ **mind²** /maɪnd/ v [I,T] 1 be upset, annoyed or worried by sth: *I don't ~ the cold.* 2 [I,T] used to ask permission or request sth politely: *Do you ~ if I open the window?* 3 [I,T] used to tell sb to be careful or warn sb of danger: *M~ you don't fall!* 4 [T] take care of sb/sth: *~ the baby* [IDM] **mind your own business** not interfere in other people's affairs **mind your step** → STEP¹ **mind you** (*spoken*) used to add sth to what you have just said, esp sth that makes it less strong: *They're separated now. M~ you, I'm not surprised—they were always arguing.* **never mind 1** used to tell sb not to worry or be upset **2** used to suggest that sth is not important [PV] **mind out (for sb/sth)** (*GB, spoken*) be careful ▸ **minder** *n* [C] person whose job is to look after and protect sb: *a child~er*

mindful /'maɪndfl/ *adj* ~ **of** (*fml*) conscious of sb/sth when you do sth

mindless /'maɪndləs/ *adj* **1** (*disapprov*) done or acting without thought and for no particular reason: *~ violence* **2** not needing thought

0~ **mine¹** /maɪn/ *pron* of or belonging to me: *Is this book yours or ~?* ● **mine** *n* [C] **1** deep hole or holes under the ground where minerals such as coal, etc are dug **2** bomb that is hidden under the ground or in the sea [IDM] **a mine of information (about/on sth)** rich source of knowledge

0~ **mine²** /maɪn/ *v* [I,T] ~ **(for)** dig coal, etc from holes in the ground **2** [T] place mines below the surface of land or water ■ **mine-detector** *n* [C] device for finding mines¹(2) ■ **minefield** *n* [C] **1** area of land or sea where mines¹(2) have been hidden **2** situation that contains hidden dangers ▸ **miner** *n* [C] person who works in a mine taking out coal, etc ■ **minesweeper** *n* [C] ship used for finding and clearing away mines¹(2)

0~ **mineral** /'mɪnərəl/ *n* [C,u] natural substance (eg coal or gold) taken from the earth ■ **mineral water** *n* **1** [U,C] water from a spring

in the ground that contains mineral salts or gases **2** [C] glass or bottle of mineral water

mineralogy /ˌmɪnəˈrælədʒi/ *n* [U] scientific study of minerals ▸ **mineralogist** *n* [C] student of or expert in mineralogy

mingle /'mɪŋɡl/ *v* **1** [I,T] ~ **with** (*written*) (cause sth to) combine and mix with sth else **2** [I] move among people and talk to them

mini- /'mɪni/ *prefix* small: *a ~bus*

miniature /'mɪnətʃə(r)/ *adj* very small; much smaller than usual: *~ roses* ● **miniature** *n* [C] very small detailed painting, esp of a person ▸ **miniaturize** (*also* -**ise**) *v* [T] make a much smaller version of sth

minimal /'mɪnɪml/ *adj* smallest in amount or degree

minimize (*also* -**ise**) /'mɪnɪmaɪz/ *v* [T] reduce to the smallest possible amount, size or level

0~ **minimum** /'mɪnɪməm/ *n* [C, usu sing] smallest possible amount, degree, etc ● **minimum** *adj* as small as possible: *the ~ age*

mining /'maɪnɪŋ/ *n* [U] process of getting coal, metals, etc from the earth

minion /'mɪniən/ *n* [C] (*disapprov*) unimportant person in an organization who has to obey orders

0~ **minister** /'mɪnɪstə(r)/ *n* [C] **1** (*often* **Minister**) (*GB*) person at the head of a government department **2** Christian clergyman ● **minister** *v* [PV] **minister to sb** (*fml*) care for sb, esp sb who is sick or old ▸ **ministerial** /ˌmɪnɪˈstɪəriəl/ *adj*

0~ **ministry** /'mɪnɪstri/ *n* (*pl* -**ies**) **1** [C] (*GB*) government department **2** (**the Ministry**) [sing, with sing or pl verb] (*esp Protestant*) ministers of religion, considered as a group: *enter the ~* (= become a clergyman) **3** [C] work of a minister (2)

mink /mɪŋk/ *n* **1** [C] small fierce animal **2** [U] valuable shiny brown fur of the mink

0~ **minor** /'maɪnə(r)/ *adj* not very large, important or serious: *~ injuries* ◇ *a ~ road* ● **minor** *n* [C] (*law*) person below the age of full legal responsibility

0~ **minority** /maɪˈnɒrəti/ *n* (*pl* -**ies**) **1** [sing, with sing or pl verb] smaller part of a group; less than half of the people or things in a large group **2** [C] small group of people of a different race, religion, etc from the rest **3** [U] (*law*) state or time of being a minor

minster /'mɪnstə(r)/ *n* [C] large or important church

minstrel /'mɪnstrəl/ *n* [C] (in the Middle Ages) travelling singer

mint /mɪnt/ *n* **1** [U] plant whose leaves are used for flavouring **2** [U,C] *short for* PEPPERMINT **3** [C] place where money is made **4** (a mint) [sing] (*infml*) very large amount of money [IDM] **in mint condition** (as if) new ● **mint** *v* [T] make a coin from metal

minuet /ˌmɪnjuˈet/ *n* [C] (music for a) slow graceful dance

minus /ˈmaɪnəs/ *prep* **1** less: *15 − 6 equals 9* **2** below zero: *~ 3 degrees Celsius* **3** (*infml*) without ● **minus** (*also* **minus sign**) *n* [C] mathematical symbol (-) ● **minus** *adj* negative

0─ minute[1] /ˈmɪnɪt/ *n* **1** (*abbr* **min.**) [C] each of the 60 parts of an hour, equal to 60 seconds **2** [sing] (*spoken*) very short time: *I'll be with you in a ~.* **3** [C] each of the 60 parts of a degree, used in measuring angles **4** (*usu the minutes*) [pl] record of what is said and decided at a meeting: *Who is going to take (= write) the ~s?* [IDM] **the minute/ moment (that...)** as soon as... ● **minute** *v* [T] write sth down in the minutes (4)

minute[2] /maɪˈnjuːt/ *adj* (**-r, -st**) **1** extremely small **2** very detailed and thorough ▸ **minutely** *adv*

minutiae /maɪˈnjuːʃiiː/ *n* [pl] very small details

miracle /ˈmɪrəkl/ *n* **1** [C] act or event that does not follow the laws of nature and is believed to be caused by God **2** [sing] (*infml*) lucky thing that happens that you did not expect or think possible: *It's a ~ we weren't all killed.* **3** [C] ~ of wonderful example of sth: *a ~ of modern science* ▸ **miraculous** /mɪˈrækjələs/ *adj*

mirage /ˈmɪrɑːʒ; mɪˈrɑːʒ/ *n* [C] something that does not really exist, esp water in the desert

mire /ˈmaɪə(r)/ *n* [U] soft muddy ground

0─ mirror /ˈmɪrə(r)/ *n* [C] piece of glass that you can look in and see yourself ● **mirror** *v* [T] show sth/sth exactly as in a mirror

misadventure /ˌmɪsədˈventʃə(r)/ *n* **1** [U] (*GB, law*) death caused by accident, rather than as a result of a crime **2** [C,U] (*fml*) bad luck

misappropriate /ˌmɪsəˈprəʊprieɪt/ *v* [T] (*fml*) take sb else's money or property for yourself

misbehave /ˌmɪsbɪˈheɪv/ *v* [I] behave badly ▸ **misbehaviour** (*US* **-ior**) *n* [U]

miscalculate /ˌmɪsˈkælkjuleɪt/ *v* [I,T] estimate amounts, etc wrongly ▸ **miscalculation** /-ˈleɪʃn/ *n* [C,U]

miscarriage /ˈmɪskærɪdʒ; ˌmɪsˈk-/ *n* [C,U] process of giving birth to a baby before it has developed enough to stay alive ● **mis carriage of ˈjustice** *n* [U,C] (*law*) incorrect legal decision

miscarry /ˌmɪsˈkæri/ *v* (*pt, pp* **-ied**)

[i] **1** give birth to a baby before it has developed enough to stay alive **2** (of a plan) fail

miscellaneous /ˌmɪsəˈleɪniəs/ *adj* of various kinds

miscellany /mɪˈseləni/ *n* [C] (*pl* **-ies**) collection of things of various kinds

mischance /ˌmɪsˈtʃɑːns/ *n* [U,C] (*fml*) bad luck

mischief /ˈmɪstʃɪf/ *n* [U] behaviour (esp of children) that is bad, but not serious [IDM] **do yourself a mischief** (*GB, infml*) hurt yourself physically ▸ **mischievous** /-tʃɪvəs/ *adj* **1** enjoying playing tricks and annoying people **2** causing trouble ▸ **mischievously** *adv*

misconceived /ˌmɪskənˈsiːvd/ *adj* badly planned or judged

misconception /ˌmɪskənˈsepʃn/ *n* [C,U] ~ (**about**) belief or idea that is not based on correct information

misconduct /ˌmɪsˈkɒndʌkt/ *n* [U] (*fml*) unacceptable behaviour, esp by a professional person

misdeed /ˌmɪsˈdiːd/ *n* [C, usu pl] (*fml*) bad or evil act

miser /ˈmaɪzə(r)/ *n* [C] (*disapprov*) person who loves money and hates spending it ▸ **miserly** *adj*

miserable /ˈmɪzrəbl/ *adj* **1** very unhappy **2** causing unhappiness: *~ weather* **3** poor in quality: *earn a ~ wage* ▸ **miserably** *adv*

misery /ˈmɪzəri/ *n* (*pl* **-ies**) **1** [U,C] great suffering or unhappiness **2** [C] (*GB, infml*) person who is always complaining

misfire /ˌmɪsˈfaɪə(r)/ *v* [I] **1** (*infml*) (of a plan or joke) fail to have the intended effect **2** (of a gun, etc) fail to work properly

misfit /ˈmɪsfɪt/ *n* [C] person who is not accepted by a group of people: *a social ~*

misfortune /ˌmɪsˈfɔːtʃuːn/ *n* [C,U] (*written*) (instance of) bad luck

misgiving /ˌmɪsˈɡɪvɪŋ/ *n* [U,C, usu pl] feelings of doubt or anxiety

misguided /ˌmɪsˈɡaɪdɪd/ *adj* wrong because you have understood or judged a situation badly

mishap /ˈmɪshæp/ *n* [C,U] small accident or piece of bad luck

misjudge /ˌmɪsˈdʒʌdʒ/ *v* [T] **1** form a wrong opinion about a person or situation **2** estimate sth, eg time or distance, wrongly

mislay /ˌmɪsˈleɪ/ *v* (*pt, pp* **mislaid** /-ˈleɪd/) [T] put sth down and forget where it is

mislead /ˌmɪsˈliːd/ *v* (*pt, pp* **misled** /-ˈled/) [T] cause sb to have a wrong idea or impression about sth

mismanage /ˌmɪsˈmænɪdʒ/ *v* [T] deal with or manage sth badly ▸ **mismanagement** *n* [U]

misprint /ˈmɪsprɪnt/ n [C] mistake in printing

misrepresent /ˌmɪsˌreprɪˈzent/ v [T] give false information about sb/sth ▶ **misrepresentation** /-zenˈteɪʃn/ n [C, U]

○━ **miss** /mɪs/ v **1** [I, T] fail to hit, catch or reach, etc sb/sth: ~ *the ball/the train* **2** [T] fail to see, hear or notice sth **3** [T] feel sad because of the absence of sb/sth: *I'll ~ you when you go.* [PV] **miss sb/sth out** (GB) not include sb/sth ■ **miss out (on sth)** fail to benefit from sth useful or enjoyable by not taking part in it ● **miss** n [C] **1** (Miss) used before the family name when speaking to or of an unmarried woman: *M~ Smith* **2** failure to hit, catch or reach sth [IDM] **give sth a miss** (infml, esp GB) decide not to do sth, eat sth, etc ▶ **missing** adj that cannot be found; lost

missile /ˈmɪsaɪl/ n [C] **1** explosive weapon sent through the air: *nuclear ~s* **2** object or weapon thrown or fired

mission /ˈmɪʃn/ n **1** [C] important official job that a person or group of people is given to do, esp abroad: *a trade ~ to China* **2** [C, U] work of teaching people about Christianity, esp in a foreign country; group of people who do this work **3** [C] special work you feel it is your duty to do: *her ~ in life* ■ **missionary** /ˈmɪʃənri/ n [C] (pl **-ies**) person sent to a foreign country to teach people about Christianity ■ **mission statement** n [C] official statement of the aims of a company or organization

misspell /ˌmɪsˈspel/ v (pt, pp **~t** /-ˈspelt/ or *esp US* **~ed**) [T] spell a word wrongly ▶ **misspelling** n [C, U]

misspend /ˌmɪsˈspend/ v [T] (usu passive) spend time or money carelessly: *his misspent youth*

mist /mɪst/ n [U, C] cloud of very small drops of water in the air, making it difficult to see: *hills covered in a ~* ◇ (fig) *She gazed at him through a ~ of tears.* ● **mist** v [I, T] ~ **(over/up)** (cause sth to) become covered with small drops of water: *My glasses ~ed over.* ▶ **misty** adj (**-ier, -iest**) **1** with a lot of mist: *a ~y morning* **2** not clear or bright: *~y memories*

○━ **mistake** /mɪˈsteɪk/ n [C] wrong action, idea or opinion [IDM] **by mistake** accidentally ● **mistake** v (pt **mistook** /mɪˈstʊk/ pp **~n** /mɪˈsteɪkən/) [T] not understand or judge sb/sth correctly [PV] **mistake sb/sth for sb/sth** think wrongly that sb/sth is sb/sth else: *People often ~ me for my twin sister.* ▶ **mistaken** adj wrong; not correct: *~n beliefs* ▶ **mistakenly** adv

mistletoe /ˈmɪsltəʊ/ n [U] evergreen plant with white berries, used as a Christmas decoration

mistress /ˈmɪstrəs/ n [C] **1** woman that a married man is having a regular sexual relationship with and who is not his wife **2** (GB) female schoolteacher **3** woman in a position of authority **4** female owner of a dog, horse, etc

mistrust /ˌmɪsˈtrʌst/ v [T] have no confidence in sb/sth ● **mistrust** n [U] lack of confidence; suspicion ▶ **mistrustful** adj

misty → MIST

misunderstand /ˌmɪsʌndəˈstænd/ v (pt, pp **-stood** /-ˈstʊd/) [T] fail to understand sb/sth correctly: *He misunderstood the instructions and got lost.* ▶ **misunderstanding** n [C, U] failure to understand sb/sth correctly, esp when this causes argument

misuse /ˌmɪsˈjuːz/ v [T] **1** use sth in the wrong way or for the wrong purpose: *~ your time* **2** treat sb badly ● **misuse** /ˌmɪsˈjuːs/ n [U, C]: *~ of power*

mitigate /ˈmɪtɪgeɪt/ v [T] (fml) make sth less harmful, serious, etc ▶ **mitigating** adj (~ *circumstances/ factors*) (fml, law) circumstances or factors that explain sb's actions or a crime and make them easier to understand ▶ **mitigation** /-ˈgeɪʃn/ n [U]

mitre (US **miter**) /ˈmaɪtə(r)/ n [C] tall pointed hat worn by bishops

mitten /ˈmɪtn/ (also with /mɪt/) n [C] kind of glove that covers the four fingers together and the thumb separately

○━ **mix** /mɪks/ v **1** [I, T] (cause two or more substances to) combine, usu in a way that means they cannot easily be separated: *~ flour and water to make paste* ◇ *Oil and water don't ~.* **2** [I] meet and talk to different people, esp at social events: *He finds it hard to ~.* **3** [T] (tech, music) combine different recordings of voices and/or instruments to produce a single piece of music [IDM] **be/get mixed up in sth** (infml) be/ become involved in sth bad [PV] **mix sb/sth up (with sb/sth)** confuse sb/ sth with sb/sth else: *I got her ~ed up with her sister.* ● **mix** n [C, U] set of different substances to be mixed together: *a cake ~* ▶ **mixed** adj **1** of different kinds **2** or for people of both sexes: *a ~ed school* ▶ **mixer** n [C] machine used for mixing things ■ **mix-up** n [C] (infml) confused situation

○━ **mixture** /ˈmɪkstʃə(r)/ n [C] combination of different things: *a ~ of fear and sadness*

mm abbr millimetre(s)

moan /məʊn/ v [I] **1** make a long low sound of pain **2** ~ **(about)** (infml) complain: *He's always ~ing about having no money.* ▶ **moan** *n* [C]

moat /məʊt/ *n* [C] deep wide channel filled with water that was dug around a castle

mob /mɒb/ *n* [C, sing, with sing or pl verb] **1** noisy disorganized crowd **2** (*infml*) group of criminals ● **mob** *v* (**-bb-**) [T] gather round sb in great numbers in order to see them and get their attention: *a film star~bed by his fans*

0-w **mobile** /ˈməʊbaɪl/ *adj* that can move or be moved easily from place to place ● **mobile** *n* [C] **1** ornamental hanging structure with parts that move freely in currents of air **2** (*GB*) = MOBILE PHONE ▶ **mobility** /məʊˈbɪləti/ *n* [U]

0-w **mobile ˈphone** (*GB also* **mobile**) (*esp US* **cellphone**) *n* [C] telephone that does not have wires and works by radio, that you can carry around with you and use anywhere: *Please switch off your mobile phone.*

mobilize (*also* -ise) /ˈməʊbəlaɪz/ *v* [I, T] (cause sth/sb to) become organized or ready for service, eg in war

moccasin /ˈmɒkəsɪn/ *n* [C] soft leather shoe

mock /mɒk/ *v* [I, T] laugh at sb/sth unkindly, esp by copying what they say or do: *a mocking smile* ● **mock** *adj* **1** not sincere: *~ horror* **2** not real: *a ~ exam* ● **mockery** *n* **1** [U] comments or actions intended to make sb/sth seem ridiculous **2** [sing] (*disapprov*) decision, etc that is a failure and not as it should be: *a ~ of a trial* [IDM] **make a mockery of sth** make sth seem ridiculous

modal /ˈməʊdl/ (*also* **modal ˈverb**, **modal auˈxiliary**) *n* [C] (*gram*) verb that is used with another verb, eg *can, may* or *should* to express possibility, permission, etc

mode /məʊd/ *n* [C] (*fml*) way in which sth is done

0-w **model¹** /ˈmɒdl/ *n* [C] **1** small-scale copy of sth: *a ~ of the new airport* **2** design or kind of product: *This car is our latest ~.* **3** person or thing of the best kind: *a ~ student* **4** person who poses for an artist or photographer **5** person who wears and shows new clothes to possible buyers: *a fashion ~*

model² /ˈmɒdl/ *v* (**-ll-** *US* **-l-**) **1** [I, T] show clothes, etc to possible buyers by wearing them **2** [T] create a copy of an activity, etc so that you can study it before dealing with the real thing: *The program can ~ a typical home page for you.* **3** [I, T] shape clay, etc in order to make sth [PV] **model yourself on sb** copy the behaviour of sb you like and respect in order to be like them

modem /ˈməʊdem/ *n* [C] device that connects one computer system to another using a telephone line so that data can be sent

moderate¹ /ˈmɒdərət/ *adj* not extreme; limited ● **moderate** *n* [C] person who has moderate opinions, esp in politics ▶ **moderately** *adv* not very: *only ~ly successful*

moderate² /ˈmɒdəreɪt/ *v* [I] (cause sth to) become less extreme or severe

moderation /ˌmɒdəˈreɪʃn/ *n* [U] quality of being reasonable and not extreme: *Alcohol should only be taken in ~* (= in small quantities).

0-w **modern** /ˈmɒdn/ *adj* **1** of the present or recent times **2** new; up-to-date ▶ **modernize** (*also* -ise) /ˈmɒdənaɪz/ *v* [I, T] bring sth up to date ▶ **modernization** (*also* -isation) /ˌmɒdənaɪˈzeɪʃn/ *n* [U]

modest /ˈmɒdɪst/ *adj* **1** not very large, expensive, important, etc: *a ~ salary* **2** (*approv*) not talking much about your own abilities or possessions **3** (of people, esp women) shy about showing much of the body; not intended to attract attention, esp in a sexual way: *~ behaviour* ▶ **modestly** *adv* ▶ **modesty** *n* [U]

modify /ˈmɒdɪfaɪ/ *v* (*pt*, *pp* -**ied**) [T] **1** change sth slightly **2** make sth less extreme: *~ your behaviour* **3** (*gram*) (esp of an adj or adv) describe a word or restrict its meaning in some way: *In the phrase 'walk slowly', 'slowly' modifies 'walk'.* ▶ **modification** /ˌmɒdɪfɪˈkeɪʃn/ *n* [C, U]

module /ˈmɒdjuːl/ *n* [C] **1** independent unit in a course of study: *the biology ~ in the science course* **2** (*computing*) unit of a computer system or program that has a particular function **3** one of a set of parts or units that can be joined together to make a machine, a building, etc **4** independent unit of a spacecraft ▶ **modular** /-jələ(r)/ *adj*

mohair /ˈməʊheə(r)/ *n* [U] soft wool made from the fine hair of the angora goat

moist /mɔɪst/ *adj* slightly wet ▶ **moisten** /ˈmɔɪsn/ *v* [I, T] become or make sth moist ▶ **moisture** /ˈmɔɪstʃə(r)/ *n* [U] tiny drops of water on a surface, etc

molar /ˈməʊlə(r)/ *n* [C] large back tooth, used for grinding and chewing food

mold, molder, moldy (*US*) = MOULD, MOULDER, MOULDY

mole /məʊl/ *n* [C] **1** small grey furry animal that lives in tunnels **2** small dark brown spot on the skin **3** employee who secretly gives

molecule 284

information to another
organization, etc ■ **molehill** n [C]
small pile of earth thrown up by a
mole

molecule /ˈmɒlɪkjuːl/ n [C] smallest
group of atoms that a particular
substance can consist of
▶ **molecular** /məˈlekjələ(r)/ adj

molest /məˈlest/ v [T] attack sb, esp a
child, sexually

mollusc (US **mollusk**) /ˈmɒləsk/ n [C]
any of a class of animals, eg oysters
and snails, that have a soft body and
usu a hard shell

molt (US) = MOULT

molten /ˈməʊltən/ adj (of metal, rock
or glass) heated to a very high
temperature so that it becomes
liquid

0̶ᴡ **mom** /mɒm/ n [C] (US, infml) =
MUM

0̶ᴡ **moment** /ˈməʊmənt/ n **1** [C]
very short period of time **2** [sing]
exact point in time **3** [sing] particular
time for doing sth: *I'm waiting for the
right ~ to tell him.* [IDM] **the moment
(that …)** → MINUTE¹ ▶ **momentary**
/-mantri/ adj lasting for a very short
time ▶ **momentarily** /-trali/ adv
1 for a very short time **2** (US, spoken)
very soon

momentous /məˈmentəs/ adj very
important or serious

momentum /məˈmentəm/ n [U]
1 ability to keep increasing or
developing: *They lost ~ in the second
half.* **2** force that is gained by
movement **3** (tech) quantity of
movement of a moving object

mommy /ˈmɒmi/ n [C] (US) =
MUMMY

0̶ᴡ **monarch** /ˈmɒnək/ n [C] king, queen,
emperor or empress ▶ **monarchy** n
(pl -**ies**) **1** (the monarchy) [U] system
of rule by a monarch **2** [C] country
ruled by a monarch

monastery /ˈmɒnəstri/ n [C] (pl -**ies**)
building in which monks live

monastic /məˈnæstɪk/ adj of monks
or monasteries

0̶ᴡ **Monday** /ˈmʌndeɪ; -di/ n [C, U] the
day of the week after Sunday
and before Tuesday: *They're coming
on ~. ◇ last/next ~ ◇ The museum is
closed on ~s* (= every Monday).

0̶ᴡ **monetary** /ˈmʌnɪtri/ adj of money

0̶ᴡ **money** /ˈmʌni/ n [U] **1** what you
earn by working or selling things,
and use to buy things **2** coins
and printed paper accepted when
buying and selling [IDM] **get your
money's worth** get full value for the
money you have spent ■ **money
box** n [C] box used for saving coins

mongrel /ˈmʌŋɡrəl/ n [C] dog of
mixed breed

0̶ᴡ **monitor** /ˈmɒnɪtə(r)/ n [C]
1 television screen used to show

particular kinds of information
2 screen that shows information
from a computer: *a PC with a 17 inch
colour ~* **3** piece of equipment used
to check or record sth: *a heart ~*
4 pupil with certain duties in a
school **5** person whose job is to
check that sth is done fairly and
honestly ● **monitor** v [T] watch and
check sth over time to see how it
develops

monk /mʌŋk/ n [C] member of a
male religious community living in a
monastery

monkey /ˈmʌŋki/ n [C] **1** small long-
tailed tree-climbing animal **2** (infml)
lively mischievous child ▶ **monkey** v
[PV] **monkey about/around** (infml)
behave mischievously

mono /ˈmɒnəʊ/ adj, n [U] (system of)
recording or producing sound
which comes from only one
direction

monochrome /ˈmɒnəkrəʊm/ adj
having only one colour or black and
white

monocle /ˈmɒnəkl/ n [C] single glass
lens for one eye, used in the past

monogamy /məˈnɒɡəmi/ n [U] fact
or custom of being married to only
one person at a time
▶ **monogamous** /-məs/ adj

monogram /ˈmɒnəɡræm/ n [C] two
or more letters (esp a person's
initials) combined in one design

monologue (US also **monolog**)
/ˈmɒnəlɒɡ/ n [C] long speech by one
person, eg in a play

monopoly /məˈnɒpəli/ n [C] (pl -**ies**)
1 (business) complete control of
trade in particular goods or a
service; type of goods or a service
controlled in this way **2** complete
control, possession or use of sth: *A
good education should not be the ~ of
the rich.* ▶ **monopolize** (also -**ise**) v
[T] have or take complete control of
the largest part of sth so that other
people cannot share it

monorail /ˈmɒnəʊreɪl/ n [U] railway
system using a single rail

monosyllable /ˈmɒnəsɪləbl/ n [C]
word with only one syllable
▶ **monosyllabic** /ˌmɒnəsɪˈlæbɪk/ adj

monotonous /məˈnɒtənəs/ adj
never changing and therefore
boring: *a ~ voice* ▶ **monotonously**
adv ▶ **monotony** /-təni/ n [U]

monsoon /ˌmɒnˈsuːn/ n [C] wind
which blows in S Asia, bringing
heavy rains in the summer

monster /ˈmɒnstə(r)/ n [C] **1** large
ugly frightening (esp imaginary)
creature **2** cruel or evil person
3 animal or thing that is large and
ugly

monstrous /ˈmɒnstrəs/ adj **1** very
shocking and morally wrong **2** very
large, ugly and frightening
▶ **monstrosity** /mɒnˈstrɒsəti/ n [C]

A B C D E F G H I J K L **M** N O P Q R S T U V W X Y Z

(pl -ies) sth that is very large and ugly, esp a building ▶ **monstrously** adv

0—**month** /mʌnθ/ n [C] one of the twelve divisions of the year; period of about four weeks ▶ **monthly** adj, adv **1** done or happening once a month **2** paid, valid or calculated for one month ● **monthly** n (pl -ies) magazine published once a month

monument /ˈmɒnjumənt/ n [C] **1** building, statue, etc to remind people of a person or event **2** very old interesting building ▶ **monumental** /ˌmɒnjuˈmentl/ adj **1** very important and influential **2** very large, good, bad, stupid, etc: a ~ failure ∎ **monumentally** adv

moo /muː/ n [C] long deep sound made by a cow ● **moo** v [I]

0—**mood** /muːd/ n [C] **1** way you are feeling at a particular time: She's in a good ~ (= happy) today. **2** period of being angry or impatient **3** (gram) any of the sets of verb forms which show that sth is certain, possible, doubtful, etc: the indicative/subjunctive ~ ▶ **moody** adj (-ier, -iest) having moods that often change; bad-tempered ∎ **moodily** adv

0—**moon**[1] /muːn/ n **1** (the moon) [sing] the round object that moves round the earth and shines at night **2** [C] natural satellite that moves round a planet other than the earth [IDM] **over the moon** (infml, esp GB) extremely happy ∎ **moonbeam** n [C] ray of light from the moon ∎ **moonlight** n [U] light of the moon ∎ **moonlight** v (pt, pp -lighted) [I] (infml) have a second job, esp at night, in addition to your main job

moon[2] /muːn/ v [PV] **moon about/around** (GB, infml) spend time doing nothing or walking about with no particular purpose

moor /mɔː(r)/ n [C, usu pl] open uncultivated high land, esp covered with heather: walk on the ~ ● **moor** v [I, T] fasten a boat, etc to the land or a fixed object with ropes, etc ▶ **mooring** n **1** (moorings) [pl] ropes, anchors, etc, used to moor a boat **2** [C] place where a boat is moored ∎ **moorland** n [U, C] land consisting of moor

moose /muːs/ n [C] (pl **moose**) (US) kind of very large deer

mop /mɒp/ n [C] **1** tool for washing floors that has a long handle and a bunch of thick strings or cloth at the end **2** mass of thick untidy hair ● **mop** v (-pp-) [T] **1** clean sth with a mop **2** wipe liquid from the surface of sth using a cloth [PV] **mop sth up** remove the liquid from sth using cloth that absorbs it

mope /məʊp/ v [I] spend your time doing nothing and feeling sorry for yourself

moped /ˈməʊped/ n [C] kind of motorcycle with a small engine

0—**moral** /ˈmɒrəl/ adj **1** concerning principles of right and wrong: ~ standards **2** following the standards of behaviour considered acceptable and right by most people ▶ **morally** adv ∎ **moral support** n [U] encouragement or sympathy ● **moral** n (morals) [pl] principles or standards of good behaviour **2** [C] practical lesson that a story or experience teaches you

morale /məˈrɑːl/ n [U] amount of confidence, enthusiasm, etc that a person or group has

morality /məˈræləti/ n (pl -ies) **1** [U] principles of good or right behaviour **2** [C] system of moral principles followed by a group of people

moralize (also -ise) /ˈmɒrəlaɪz/ v [I] ~ (about/on) (usu disapprov) tell other people what is right or wrong

morbid /ˈmɔːbɪd/ adj having an unhealthy interest in death ▶ **morbidly** adv

0—**more** /mɔː(r)/ det, pron (used as the comparative of 'much', 'a lot of', 'many') a large number or amount of: I need ~ time. ◇ ~ people ◇ Please tell me ~. ● **more** adv **1** used to form comparatives of adjectives and adverbs: ~ expensive ◇ talk ~ quietly **2** to a greater extent than sth else; to a greater degree than usual: You need to sleep ~. ◇ I'll go there once ~ (= one more time). [IDM] **more and more** increasingly more or less **1** almost **2** approximately: £20, ~ or less

0—**moreover** /mɔːrˈəʊvə(r)/ adv (fml) in addition; besides

morgue /mɔːg/ n [C] (esp GB) building in which dead bodies are kept before a funeral

0—**morning** /ˈmɔːnɪŋ/ n [C, U] early part of the day from the time when people wake up until midday or before lunch [IDM] **in the morning** during the morning of the next day: see him in the ~ ∎ **morning dress** n [U] clothes worn by a man on very formal occasions, eg weddings

moron /ˈmɔːrɒn/ n [C] (infml) stupid person ▶ **moronic** /məˈrɒnɪk/ adj

morose /məˈrəʊs/ adj sad, bad-tempered and silent ▶ **morosely** adv

morphine /ˈmɔːfiːn/ n [U] powerful drug made from opium, used to reduce pain

Morse code /ˌmɔːs ˈkəʊd/ n [U] system of sending messages using short and long sounds, etc to represent letters

A B C D E F G H I J K L **M** N O P Q R S T U V W X Y Z

morsel /'mɔːsl/ n [C] ~ (of) small piece, esp of food

mortal /'mɔːtl/ adj **1** that must die **2** (lit) causing death: a ~ wound **3** extreme: in ~ fear ● mortal n [C] human being ► **mortality** /mɔː'tæləti/ n [U] **1** state of being human and not living for ever **2** number of deaths in a particular situation or period: the infant ~ rate (= the number of babies that die at or just after birth) ► **mortally** /'mɔːtəli/ adv (lit) **1** resulting in death: ~ly wounded **2** extremely: ~ly offended

mortar /'mɔːtə(r)/ n [U] **1** mixture of lime, sand and water, used to hold bricks, etc together in building **2** [C] heavy gun that fires bombs and shells high into the air **3** [C] strong bowl in which substances, eg seeds and grains, can be crushed with a special tool (pestle)

mortgage /'mɔːgɪdʒ/ n [C] **1** legal agreement by which a bank lends you money to buy a house, etc **2** sum of money borrowed ● **mortgage** v [T] give a bank, etc the right to own your house in return for money lent

mortify /'mɔːtɪfaɪ/ v (pt, pp -ied) [T] (usu passive) make sb feel very ashamed or embarrassed ► **mortification** /,mɔːtɪfɪ'keɪʃn/ n [U]

mortuary /'mɔːtʃəri/ n [C] (pl -ies) **1** building or room in which dead bodies are kept before a funeral **2** (US) = FUNERAL PARLOUR (FUNERAL)

mosaic /məʊ'zeɪɪk/ n [C, U] picture or pattern made by placing together small pieces of coloured glass or stone

Moslem = MUSLIM

mosque /mɒsk/ n [C] building in which Muslims worship

mosquito /məs'kiːtəʊ/ n [C] (pl -es) small flying insect that sucks blood

moss /mɒs/ n [U] (thick mass of a) small green or yellow plant that grows on damp surfaces ► **mossy** adj (-ier, -iest)

0̶ **most** /məʊst/ det, pron (used as the superlative of 'much', 'a lot of', 'many') **1** the largest in number or amount: Who will get the ~ votes? ◇ He ate the ~. **2** more than half of sb/sth; almost all of sb/sth: M~ people must pay the new tax. [IDM] at (the) most not more than ● **most** adv **1** used to form superlatives of adjectives and adverbs: the ~ expensive car **2** to the greatest degree: Children need ~ sleep. **3** (fml) very: a ~ interesting talk [IDM] most likely → LIKELY ► **mostly** adv mainly; generally

motel /məʊ'tel/ n [C] hotel for people travelling by car

moth /mɒθ/ n [C] winged insect, similar to the butterfly that flies mainly at night ■ **mothball** n [C] small ball of a strong-smelling substance, for keeping moths out of clothes ■ '**moth-eaten** adj **1** (of clothes) damaged by moths **2** (disapprov) old and in bad condition

0̶ **mother** /'mʌðə(r)/ n [C] **1** female parent **2** head of a female religious community ● **mother** v [T] care for sb/sth because you are their mother or as if you were their mother ■ **mother country** n [C] country where you were born ► **motherhood** n [U] ■ '**mother-in-law** n [C] (pl **~s-in-law**) mother of your wife or husband ► **motherly** adv or like a mother ■ '**mother tongue** n [C] language that you first learn to speak as a child

motif /məʊ'tiːf/ n [C] theme or pattern in music or art

0̶ **motion** /'məʊʃn/ n **1** [U] act or process of moving or the way sth moves **2** [C] particular movement: signal with a ~ of the hand **3** [C] formal proposal to be discussed and voted on at a meeting [IDM] **go through the motions (of doing sth)** (infml) do sth because you have to, not because you want to ● **set/put sth in motion** start sth moving ● **motion** v [I, T] ~ **to** signal to sb by making a movement of the hand or head ► **motionless** adj not moving

motivate /'məʊtɪveɪt/ v [T] **1** be the reason why sb does sth **2** make sb want to do sth ► **motivation** /,məʊtɪ'veɪʃn/ n [C, U]

motive /'məʊtɪv/ n [C] reason for doing sth: I'm suspicious of his ~s.

0̶ **motor** /'məʊtə(r)/ n [C] **1** device that changes power into movement: an electric ~ **2** (GB, old-fash) car ● **motor** adj **1** having an engine, using the power of an engine: ~ vehicles **2** of vehicles that have engines: ~ racing ● **motor** v [I] (old-fash, GB) travel by car ■ '**motorbike** n [C] = MOTORCYCLE ■ '**motorcade** /'məʊtəkeɪd/ n [C] procession of motor cars ■ '**motor car** n [C] (GB, fml) = CAR ■ '**motorcycle** n [C] road vehicle with two wheels, driven by an engine ► **motorcycling** n [U] sport of riding motorcycles ► **motorist** n [C] person who drives a car ► **motorized** (also -ised) adj having an engine: a ~ wheelchair ■ '**motor racing** n [U] sport of racing fast cars on a special track ■ '**motor scooter** n [C] (esp US) = SCOOTER(1) ■ '**motorway** n [C, U] (in Britain) wide road with at least two lanes in each direction, for fast traffic

motto /'mɒtəʊ/ n [C] (pl **~es** or **~s**)

short sentence that expresses the aims and beliefs of a person, a group, etc and is used as a rule of behaviour

mould /məʊld/ n **1** [C] shaped container, into which a soft or liquid substance is poured so that it sets in that shape **2** [U] fine soft grey or green substance like fur that grows on old food, etc ● **mould** v [T] **1** shape sth in a mould **2** strongly influence the way sth's character, etc develops ▶ **mouldy** adj (-ier, -iest) covered with or containing mould: ~y bread

moulder /'məʊldə(r)/ v [I] decay slowly and steadily

moult /məʊlt/ v [I] **1** (of a bird) lose feathers **2** (of a dog or cat) lose hair

mound /maʊnd/ n [C] **1** small hill **2** pile or heap

0— **mount** /maʊnt/ v [T] **1** organize and begin sth: ~ an exhibition **2** [I] increase gradually: ~ing costs **3** [I] go up sth or up on to sth raised: slowly ~ the stairs **4** [I,T] get on a bicycle, horse, etc in order to ride it **5** [T] fix sth in position: a diamond ~ed in gold ● **mount** n [C] **1** (Mount) (abbr Mt) (used in place names) mountain **2** (lit) horse that you ride on

0— **mountain** /'maʊntən/ n **1** [C] very high hill, often with rocks near the top **2** [usu pl] (infml) very large amount or number of sth: We made ~s of sandwiches. **IDM** make a **mountain out of a molehill** make an unimportant matter seem important ▶ **mountaineer** /ˌmaʊntə'nɪə(r)/ n [C] person who is skilled at climbing mountains ▶ **mountaineering** n [U] ▶ **mountainous** adj **1** having many mountains **2** huge: ~ous waves

mourn /mɔːn/ v [I, T] ~ (for) feel or show sadness for sb/sth, esp sb's death ▶ **mourner** n [C] ▶ **mournful** adj sad ▶ **mourning** n [U] **1** sadness that you show and feel because sb has died **2** black clothes, worn to show sadness at sb's death

0— **mouse** /maʊs/ n [C] (pl **mice** /maɪs/) **1** small furry animal with a long tail **2** (pl also ~s) (computing) small device moved by hand across a surface to control the movement of the cursor on a computer screen ▶ **mousy** (also mousey) /'maʊsi/ adj (-ier, -iest) (disapprov) **1** (of hair) of a dull brown colour **2** (of people) shy and quiet

mousse /muːs/ n [U, C] cold sweet dish made from cream and eggs, flavoured with fruit or chocolate

moustache /mə'stɑːʃ/ (US **mustache** /'mʌstæʃ/) n [C] hair allowed to grow on the upper lip

0— **mouth**[1] /maʊθ/ n [C] (pl ~s /maʊðz/) **1** opening in the face used

for speaking, eating, etc **2** entrance or opening of sth: the ~ of the cave ▶ **mouthful** n **1** [C] amount of food, etc put into the mouth at one time **2** [sing] (infml) word or phrase that is too long or difficult to say ■ '**mouth organ** n [C] musical instrument played by passing it along the lips while blowing or sucking air ▶ '**mouthpiece** n [C] **1** part of a musical instrument, telephone, etc that is placed in or near the mouth **2** person, newspaper, etc that expresses the opinions of others ■ '**mouth-watering** adj (approv) (of food) looking or smelling delicious

mouth[2] /maʊð/ v [I,T] say sth by moving your lips but not making any sound

movable /'muːvəbl/ adj that can be moved from one place to another

0— **move**[1] /muːv/ v **1** [I,T] (cause sb/ sth to) change place or position: Don't ~ while I'm taking the photo. **2** [I] make progress: The company has ~d ahead of the competition. **3** [I] ~ (from, to) change the place where you live, have your work, etc: They are ~ing (house) soon. **4** [T] cause sb to have strong feelings, esp pity: ~d by a sad film **5** [T] (fml) suggest sth formally so that it can be discussed and decided **PV** move in/out **PV** move in/out sell or leave your old house **move off** (esp of a vehicle) start moving and leave

0— **move**[2] /muːv/ n [C] **1** action done to achieve a purpose: ~s to end the strike **2** change of place or position, esp in a board game: It's your ~! **IDM** be on the move **1** be travelling between one place and another **2** be moving get a move on (spoken) hurry up make a move (GB, infml) begin a journey or task

0— **movement** /'muːvmənt/ n **1** [C,U] (act of) moving the body or part of the body [C, with sing or pl verb] group of people with a shared set of aims or principles: the peace ~ **3** [C] one of the main sections of a piece of music

0— **movie** /'muːvi/ n (esp US) **1** [C] cinema film **2** (the movies) [pl] the cinema

0— '**movie theater** (also **theater**) n [C] (US) = CINEMA: The documentary opens tomorrow in ~s nationwide.

mow /məʊ/ v (pt ~ed pp ~n /məʊn/ or ~ed) [T] cut grass, etc, esp with a lawnmower **PV** mow sb down kill people in large numbers, using a vehicle or a gun ▶ **mower** n [C] = LAWNMOWER (LAWN)

MP /ˌem piː/ abbr, n [C] (esp GB) Member of Parliament

A B C D E F G H I J K L **M** N O P Q R S T U V W X Y Z

MP3 player /,em pi: 'θri: pleɪə(r)/ n [C] piece of computer equipment that can open and play MP3 files (= sound files)

mpg /,em pi: 'dʒi:/ abbr miles per gallon

mph /,em pi: 'eɪtʃ/ abbr miles per hour

MPV /,em pi: 'vi:/ n [C] multi-purpose vehicle; large car like a van

O━ **Mr** /'mɪstə(r)/ abbr title for a man

O━ **Mrs** /'mɪsɪz/ abbr title for a married woman

O━ **Ms** /mɪz; məz/ abbr title for a married or unmarried woman

Mt abbr = MOUNT: Mt Everest

O━ **much** /mʌtʃ/ det, pron a large amount or quantity of sth: I haven't got ~ money. ◇ too ~ salt ◇ How ~ is it (= What does it cost)? [IDM] **not much of a...** not a good...: He's not ~ of a runner. ● **much** adj to a great degree: work ~ harder ◇ the ~ in the office (= often). ◇ My new job is ~ the same as the old one. [IDM] **much as** although: M~ as I want to stay, I must go.

muck /mʌk/ n [U] **1** waste matter from farm animals; manure **2** (infml) dirt or mud ● **muck** v [PV] **muck about/around** (GB, infml) behave in a silly way **muck in** (GB, infml) work with other people to complete a task: If we all ~ in we'll soon get the job done. **muck sth up** (infml, esp GB) **1** do sth badly; spoil sth **2** make sth dirty ▶ **mucky** adj (-ier, -iest)

mucous /'mju:kəs/ adj of or covered with mucus ● **mucous 'membrane** n [C] (anat) moist skin that lines parts of the body such as the nose and mouth

mucus /'mju:kəs/ n [U] sticky liquid produced by the mucous membrane eg in the nose

O━ **mud** /mʌd/ n [U] soft wet earth ▶ **muddy** adj (-ier, -iest) ■ **'mudguard** n [C] curved cover over a wheel of a bicycle

muddle /'mʌdl/ n [C, usu sing] state of confusion or untidiness ● **muddle** v [T] **1** put things in the wrong order or mix them up **2** confuse sb [PV] **muddle along** (esp GB) continue doing sth with no clear plan or purpose **muddle through** achieve your aims, even though you do not really know how to do things

muesli /'mju:zli/ n [U] breakfast food of grain, nuts, dried fruit, etc

muffle /'mʌfl/ v [T] **1** make sound quieter and less easily heard **2** wrap or cover sb/sth for warmth ▶ **muffler** n [C] **1** (old-fash) scarf worn round the neck for warmth **2** (US) = SILENCER (SILENCE)

mug /mʌɡ/ n [C] **1** tall cup for

drinking from, usu with straight sides and a handle **2** mug and what it contains **3** (sl) person's face **4** (infml) person who is stupid and easy to trick ● **mug** v (-gg-) [T] attack sb violently in order to steal their money ▶ **mugger** n [C] ▶ **mugging** n [C, U]

muggy /'mʌɡi/ adj (-ier, -iest) (of weather) unpleasantly warm and damp

Muhammad (also Mohammed) /mə'hæmɪd/ n Arab prophet and founder of Islam ▶ **Muhammadan** (also Muhammedan, Mohammedan) /-ən/ adj, n [C] Muslim

mulberry /'mʌlbəri/ n [C] (pl -ies) (purple or white) fruit of a(ny) tree with broad dark green leaves

mule /mju:l/ n [C] animal that is half donkey and half horse, used for carrying heavy loads ▶ **mulish** adj stubborn

mull /mʌl/ v [PV] **mull sth over** think about sth carefully: Give me time to ~ it over before deciding what to do.

mulled /mʌld/ adj (of wine) mixed with sugar and spices and heated

multi- /'mʌlti/ prefix (in nouns and adjectives) more than one; many: ~-ethnic society

multicultural /,mʌlti'kʌltʃərəl/ adj for or including people of different races, religions, languages, etc: We live in a ~ society. ▶ **multiculturalism** /,mʌlti'kʌltʃərəlɪzəm/ n [U] the practice of giving importance to all cultures in a society

multilateral /,mʌlti'lætərəl/ adj in which three or more countries, groups, etc take part

multimedia /,mʌlti'mi:diə/ adj (in computing) using sound, pictures and film in addition to text on a screen: the ~ industry (= producing CD-ROMs, etc)

multinational /,mʌlti'næʃnəl/ adj involving many countries ▶ **multinational** n [C] very large powerful company that operates in many countries

multiple /'mʌltɪpl/ adj many in number; involving many different people or things ● **multiple** n [C] (maths) quantity that contains another quantity an exact number of times: 28 is a ~ of 7. ■ **multiple-'choice** adj (of exam questions) with several possible answers shown from which you must choose the correct one ■ **multiple scle'rosis** /-sklə'rəʊsɪs/ n [U] (abbr MS) serious disease of the nervous system that causes loss of control of movement and speech

O━ **multiply** /'mʌltɪplaɪ/ v (pt, pp -ied) [I, T] **1** add a number to itself the number of times that is mentioned: 6 multiplied by 5 is 30.

2 (cause sth to) increase in number or amount **3** (biol) (cause sth to) reproduce or increase in large numbers: *Rabbits ~ quickly.* ▶ **multiplication** /ˌmʌltɪplɪˈkeɪʃn/ n [U, C]

multi-purpose /ˌmʌltiˈpɜːpəs/ adj able to be used for several different purposes

multi-skilling /ˌmʌltiˈskɪlɪŋ/ n [U] (business) fact of a person being trained in several different jobs requiring different skills

multitask /ˌmʌltiˈtɑːsk/ v [I]
1 (computing) (of a computer) operate several programs at the same time **2** do several things at the same time: *Women seem to be able to ~ better than men.* ▶ **multitasking** n [U] **1** (computing) ability of a computer to operate several programs at the same time **2** activity of doing several things at the same time

multitude /ˈmʌltɪtjuːd/ n [C] (fml) large number of people or things

0~ mum /mʌm/ (US mom) n [C] (infml) mother ● **mum** adj [IDM] **keep mum** (infml) say nothing about sth; keep silent **mum's the word!** (infml) used to tell sb to keep sth secret

mumble /ˈmʌmbl/ v [I, T] speak or say sth unclearly

mummify /ˈmʌmɪfaɪ/ v (pt, pp **-ied**) [T] preserve a dead body by treating it with oils and wrapping it in cloth

mummy /ˈmʌmi/ n [C] (pl **-ies**) **1** (US **mommy**) (infml) child's word for a mother **2** dead body that has been mummified: *an Egyptian ~*

mumps /mʌmps/ n [U] disease, esp of children, that causes painful swellings in the neck

munch /mʌntʃ/ v [I, T] eat sth steadily and often noisily

mundane /mʌnˈdeɪn/ adj not interesting or exciting

municipal /mjuːˈnɪsɪpl/ adj of a town or city with its own local government ▶ **municipality** /mjuːˌnɪsɪˈpæləti/ n [C] (pl **-ies**) town or city with its own local government

munitions /mjuːˈnɪʃnz/ n [pl] military supplies, esp bombs and guns

mural /ˈmjʊərəl/ n [C] picture painted on a wall

0~ murder /ˈmɜːdə(r)/ n **1** [U, C] crime of killing sb deliberately **2** [U] (spoken) used to describe sth difficult or unpleasant: *Climbing that hill was ~.* ● **murder** v [T] kill sb deliberately and illegally ▶ **murderer** n [C] person guilty of murder ▶ **murderess** n [C] (old-fash) woman guilty of murder ▶ **murderous** adj intending or likely to murder: *a ~ous attack*

murky /ˈmɜːki/ adj (**-ier, -iest**)

unpleasantly dark: *~ waters of the river*

murmur /ˈmɜːmə(r)/ v **1** [T] say sth in a low voice **1** [I] make a quiet continuous sound ● **murmur** n [C] **1** quietly spoken word(s) **2** quiet expression of feeling: *He paid the extra cost without a ~* (= without complaining at all). **3** low continuous sound in the background

0~ muscle /ˈmʌsl/ n [C, U] (one of the pieces of) elastic tissue in the body that you tighten to produce movement **2** [U] physical strength ● **muscle** v [PV] **muscle in (on sb/sth)** (infml, disapprov) join in sth when you have no right to do so, for your own advantage

muscular /ˈmʌskjələ(r)/ adj **1** of the muscles **2** having large strong muscles

0~ museum /mjuˈziːəm/ n [C] building in which objects of art, history or science are shown

mushroom /ˈmʌʃrʊm/ n [C] fungus of which some kinds can be eaten ● **mushroom** v [I] spread or grow in number quickly

0~ music /ˈmjuːzɪk/ n [U] **1** sounds arranged in a way that is pleasant or exciting to listen to: *listen to ~* **2** art of writing or playing music **3** written or printed signs representing the sounds to be played or sung in a piece of music ▶ **musical** /-kl/ adj **1** of music **2** fond of or skilled in music ▶ **musical** n [C] play or film with songs and usu dancing ■ **musical instrument** n [C] object used for producing musical sounds, eg a piano or a drum ▶ **musically** /-kli/ adv

0~ musician /mjuˈzɪʃn/ n [C] person skilled in playing music; writer of music

Muslim /ˈmʊzlɪm/ n [C] person whose religion is Islam ● **Muslim** adj of Muslims or Islam

muslin /ˈmʌzlɪn/ n [U] thin fine cotton cloth

mussel /ˈmʌsl/ n [C] kind of edible shellfish with a black shell

0~ must /məst; strong form mʌst/ modal v (neg **must not** short form **mustn't** /ˈmʌsnt/) **1** used to say that sth is necessary or very important (often involving a rule or law): *You ~ finish your work before you go.* ◇ *Visitors ~ not feed the birds.* **2** used to say sth is likely or logical: *You ~ be* (= I am sure that you are) *tired after your journey.* ● **must** n [C] (infml) thing that must be done, seen, etc: *Her new film is a ~.*

mustache (US) = MOUSTACHE

mustard /ˈmʌstəd/ n [U] yellow substance made from the seeds of a plant, used to flavour food

muster /ˈmʌstə(r)/ v **1** [T] find as much support, courage, etc as you can: *She left the room with all the dignity she could ~.* **2** [I,T] (cause people to) gather together

musty /ˈmʌsti/ adj (-ier, -iest) smelling damp and unpleasant because of a lack of fresh air

mutation /mjuːˈteɪʃn/ n [C,U] (biol) (instance of) change in a living thing that causes a new kind of thing to develop: *genetic ~s*

mute /mjuːt/ adj (written) not speaking ● **mute** n [C] **1** (music) device used to lessen the sound of a musical instrument **2** (old-fash) person who is unable to speak ▸ **muted** adj gentle; not bright: *~d colours*

mutilate /ˈmjuːtɪleɪt/ v [T] damage sb's body severely, esp by cutting or tearing off part of it ▸ **mutilation** /ˌmjuːtɪˈleɪʃn/ n [U,C]

mutiny /ˈmjuːtəni/ n [C,U,C] (pl -ies) rebellion against authority, esp by sailors ▸ **mutineer** /ˌmjuːtəˈnɪə(r)/ n [C] person who takes part in a mutiny ▸ **mutinous** /-nəs/ adj **1** refusing to obey sb in authority **2** taking part in a mutiny ● **mutiny** v (pt, pp **-ied**) [I] (esp of soldiers and sailors) refuse to obey sb in authority

mutter /ˈmʌtə(r)/ v [I,T] speak or say sth in a low quiet voice, esp because you are annoyed about sth ● **mutter** n [C, usu sing] quiet sound or words that are difficult to hear

mutton /ˈmʌtn/ n [U] meat from a sheep

mutual /ˈmjuːtʃuəl/ adj **1** felt or done by each towards the other: *~ affection/respect* **2** shared by two or more people: *a ~ friend* ▸ **mutually** /-əli/ adv

muzzle /ˈmʌzl/ n [C] **1** nose and mouth of an animal **2** guard placed over the nose and mouth of an animal to prevent it from biting people **3** open end of a gun, where the bullets come out ● **muzzle** v [T] **1** put a muzzle over a dog's mouth **2** prevent sb from expressing their opinions freely

MW abbr = MEDIUM WAVE (MEDIUM)

0̄**my** /maɪ/ det **1** of or belonging to me: *Where's my hat?* **2** used in exclamations to express surprise, etc: *My goodness!* **3** used when addressing sb to show affection: *my dear*

myopia /maɪˈəʊpiə/ n [U] (tech) inability to see clearly objects that are far away ▸ **myopic** /-ˈɒpɪk/ adj

0̄**myriad** /ˈmɪriəd/ n [C] (lit) extremely large number: *a ~ of stars*

myrrh /mɜː(r)/ n [U] sticky sweet-smelling substance that comes from trees, used for making incense and perfume

0̄**myself** /maɪˈself/ pron **1** (the reflexive form of *I*) used when the speaker or writer is also the person affected by the action: *I've cut ~.* **2** used to emphasize that the speaker is doing sth: *I'll speak to her ~.* [IDM] (all) by myself **1** alone; without anyone else **2** without any help

0̄**mysterious** /mɪˈstɪəriəs/ adj **1** hard to understand or explain: *her ~ disappearance* **2** keeping things secret: *He's been very ~ and not told anyone his plans.* ▸ **mysteriously** adv

0̄**mystery** /ˈmɪstri/ n (pl -ies) **1** [C] something that cannot be understood or explained: *Her disappearance is a real ~.* **2** [U] quality of being difficult to understand or explain

mystic /ˈmɪstɪk/ (also **mystical** /ˈmɪstɪkl/) adj having hidden meaning or spiritual powers ● **mystic** n [C] person who practises mysticism ▸ **mysticism** /ˈmɪstɪsɪzəm/ n [U] belief that knowledge of God and real truth can be found through prayer and meditation

mystify /ˈmɪstɪfaɪ/ v (pt, pp **-ied**) [T] make sb confused because they do not understand sth

mystique /mɪˈstiːk/ n [U, sing] quality of mystery associated with a person or thing: *The ~ surrounding the monarchy has gone for ever.*

myth /mɪθ/ n [C,U] **1** (type of) story from ancient times: *ancient Greek ~s* **2** something that many people believe but that does not exist or is false ▸ **mythical** /-ɪkl/ adj **1** existing only in myths **2** that does not exist or is not true

mythology /mɪˈθɒlədʒi/ n [U,C] **1** group of ancient myths: *Greek ~* **2** ideas or facts that many people believe but that are not true ▸ **mythological** /ˌmɪθəˈlɒdʒɪkl/ adj of ancient myths

Nn

N abbr north(ern): *N Yorkshire*

N, n /en/ n [C, U] (pl **N's, n's** /enz/) the fourteenth letter of the English alphabet

nab /næb/ v (**-bb-**) [T] (infml) **1** catch sb doing wrong **2** take or get sth: *Who ~bed my drink?*

nag /næg/ v (**-gg-**) [I,T] **~ (at)** **1** keep criticizing sb or asking them to do sth **2** worry or irritate you continuously

0̄**nail** /neɪl/ n [C] **1** thin hard layer covering the outer tip of the fingers or toes **2** small thin pointed piece of metal, hit with a hammer, eg to hold pieces of wood together • **nail** v [T] **1** fasten sth to sth with a nail or nails **2** (*infml*) catch sb and prove they are guilty of a crime [**PV**] **nail sb down (to sth)** force sb to say clearly what they plan to do

naive (*also* **naïve**) /naɪˈiːv/ *adj* **1** (*disapprov*) lacking experience of life and willing to believe that people always tell you the truth **2** (of people and their behaviour) innocent and simple ▶ **naively** *adv* ▪ **naivety** *n* [U]

0▬ **naked** /ˈneɪkɪd/ *adj* **1** not wearing any clothes **2** without the usual covering: *a ~ light* [**IDM**] **the naked eye** normal power of the eye without the help of an instrument ▶ **nakedly** *adv* ▪ **nakedness** *n* [U]

0▬ **name** /neɪm/ *n* **1** [C] word(s) by which a person or thing is known: *My ~ is Tim.* **2** [usu sing] general opinion that people have of sb/sth; reputation: *She made her ~ as a writer of children's books.* **3** [C] famous person: *the big ~s in show business* [**IDM**] **in the name of sb/sth 1** on behalf of sb/sth **2** by the authority of sth: *I arrest you in the ~ of the law.* **make a name for yourself** become well known **take sb's name in vain** talk disrespectfully about sb • **name** v [T] **1 ~ (after)|** (*US*) **(for)** give a name to sb/sth: *The child was ~d after his father.* **2** say the name(s) of sb/sth: *The victim has not been ~d.* **3** state sth exactly; choose sb/sth: *~ the day for the party* ▪ **name-dropping** *n* [U] (*disapprov*) mentioning the names of famous people that you know in order to impress others ▶ **nameless** *adj* **1** having no name **2** not to be mentioned or described: *~less horrors* ▪ **namesake** *n* [C] person or thing with the same name as sb/sth else

namely /ˈneɪmli/ *adv* that is to say: *Only one child was missing, ~ John.*

nanny /ˈnæni/ *n* [C] (pl **-ies**) woman employed to look after children

nanny goat /ˈnæni ɡəʊt/ *n* [C] female goat

nap /næp/ *n* **1** [C] short sleep, esp during the day **2** [sing] surface of cloth, etc made of soft hairs usu brushed in one direction • **nap** v (**-pp-**) [I] sleep for a short period, esp during the day

napalm /ˈneɪpɑːm/ *n* [U] petrol jelly used in bombs

nape /neɪp/ *n* [C, sing] back of the neck

napkin /ˈnæpkɪn/ *n* [C] piece of cloth or paper used at meals for protecting your clothes and wiping your hands and lips

nappy /ˈnæpi/ *n* [C] (pl **-ies**) piece of cloth or padding folded round a

baby's bottom to absorb waste matter

narcissus /nɑːˈsɪsəs/ *n* [C] (pl **narcissi** /nɑːˈsɪsaɪ/) one of several kinds of spring flower, eg daffodil

narcotic /nɑːˈkɒtɪk/ *n* [C], *adj* (kind of drug) producing sleep

narrate /nəˈreɪt/ v [T] (*fml*) tell a story ▶ **narration** /nəˈreɪʃn/ *n* [C, U] ▪ **narrator** *n* [C] person who narrates

narrative /ˈnærətɪv/ *n* **1** [C] description of events, esp in a novel **2** [U] act, process or skill of telling a story

0▬ **narrow** /ˈnærəʊ/ *adj* **1** small in width: *a ~ road* **2** only just achieved or avoided: *a ~ escape* **3** limited in a way that ignores important issues or the opinions of others: *a ~ view of the world* **4** limited in variety or numbers: *a ~ circle of friends* • **narrow** v [I,T] become or make sth narrower ▶ **narrowly** *adv* only by a small amount: *~ly escape* ▪ **narrow-minded** *adj* (*disapprov*) not willing to consider new ideas or the opinions of others ▶ **narrowness** *n* [U]

nasal /ˈneɪzl/ *adj* of or in the nose

nasturtium /nəˈstɜːʃəm/ *n* [C] garden plant with red, orange or yellow flowers

nasty /ˈnɑːsti/ *adj* (**-ier, -iest**) **1** very bad or unpleasant: *a ~ taste* **2** unkind; unpleasant: *make ~ remarks about sb* **3** dangerous or serious: *a ~ injury* ▶ **nastily** *adv* ▪ **nastiness** *n* [U]

0▬ **nation** /ˈneɪʃn/ *n* [C] large community of people living in a particular country under one government ▪ **nationwide** *adj, adv* over the whole of a nation

0▬ **national** /ˈnæʃnəl/ *adj* **1** of a particular nation; shared by a whole nation: *local and ~ news* **2** owned, controlled or supported by the federal government: *a ~ airline* • **national** *n* [C] (*tech*) citizen of a particular country ▪ **national anthem** *n* [C] official song of a nation ▪ **National Health Service** *n* [sing] (*abbr* **NHS**) (in Britain) public service that provides medical care, paid for by taxes ▪ **National Insurance** *n* [U] (*abbr* **NI**) (in Britain) system of compulsory payments made by workers to provide help for the sick, elderly or the unemployed ▶ **nationalism** *n* [U] **1** feeling that your country should be politically independent **2** love of and support for your own country ▶ **nationalist** *adj, n* [C] ▶ **nationally** *adv* ▪ **national service** *n* [U] period of compulsory service in the armed forces

nationality /ˌnæʃəˈnæləti/ n [U,C] (pl -ies) legal right belonging to a particular nation: *a person with French ~*

nationalize (also -ise) /ˈnæʃnəlaɪz/ v [T] transfer a company from private to government ownership ▸ **nationalization** (also -isation) /ˌnæʃnəlaɪˈzeɪʃn/ n [U,C]

native /ˈneɪtɪv/ n [C] **1** person born in a place or country **2** person who lives in a place, esp sb who has lived there a long time **3** animal or plant which occurs naturally in a place ● **native** adj **1** of the place of your birth: *my ~ city* **2** (of an animal or plant) found naturally in a certain area ■ Native American n [C], adj (of a) member of any of the races of people who were the original people living in America

nativity /nəˈtɪvəti/ n (the Nativity) [sing] birth of Jesus Christ

NATO /ˈneɪtəʊ/ n [sing] North Atlantic Treaty Organization; military association of several countries

0␣ **natural** /ˈnætʃrəl/ adj **1** existing in nature; not made or caused by humans: *the earth's ~ resources* (= its coal, oil, etc) **2** normal; as you would expect: *to die of ~ causes* (= of old age) **3** of the basic character of a living thing: *It's ~ for a bird to fly.* **4** born with a certain skill: *a ~ artist* **5** relaxed and not pretending to be sb/sth different ● **natural** n [C] person who is very good at sth without having to learn how to do it: *That dancer is a ~.* ■ natural 'history n [U] study of plants and animals

naturalist /ˈnætʃrəlɪst/ n [C] person who studies plants and animals

naturalize (also -ise) /ˈnætʃrəlaɪz/ v [T] make sb from another country a citizen of a country ▸ **naturalization** (also -isation) /-ˈzeɪʃn/ n [U]

0␣ **naturally** /ˈnætʃrəli/ adv **1** in a way that you would expect; of course: *N~, I'll help you.* **2** without artificial help **3** as a skill from birth: *She's ~ musical.* **4** in a relaxed and normal way: *behave ~*

0␣ **nature** /ˈneɪtʃə(r)/ n **1** (often Nature) [U] all the plants, animals and things that exist in the universe and are not made by people: *the beauties of ~* **2** (often Nature) [U] way that things happen in the physical world when it is not controlled by people: *the forces/laws of ~* **3** [C,U] typical qualities of sb/sth: *It's her ~ to be kind.* ■ [U] sort or kind of sth: *changes of that ~* [IDM] **(get, go, etc) back to nature** return to a simple life in the country, away from civilization ■ 'nature reserve n

[C] area of land where the animals and plants are protected

naught /nɔːt/ n [C] = NOUGHT(2)

naughty /ˈnɔːti/ adj (-ier, -iest) **1** (esp of a child) disobedient; bad **2** (infml) slightly rude; connected with sex ▸ **naughtily** adv ▸ **naughtiness** n [U]

nausea /ˈnɔːziə, -siə/ n [U] feeling of wanting to vomit ▸ **nauseate** /ˈnɔːzieɪt, -sieɪt/ v [T] make sb feel that they want to vomit ▸ **nauseous** adj

nautical /ˈnɔːtɪkl/ adj of ships, sailors or sailing ■ nautical 'mile n [C] measure of distance at sea; 1852 metres

naval /ˈneɪvl/ adj of a navy

nave /neɪv/ n [C] long central part of a church

navel /ˈneɪvl/ n [C] small hollow in the middle of the stomach

navigable /ˈnævɪɡəbl/ adj (of a river, etc) wide and deep enough for ships to travel on

navigate /ˈnævɪɡeɪt/ v [I,T] find your position or the position of your ship, plane, car, etc eg by using a map ▸ **navigation** /ˌnævɪˈɡeɪʃn/ n [U] ▸ **navigator** n [C]

0␣ **navy** /ˈneɪvi/ n [C, with sing or pl verb] part of a country's armed forces that fights at sea, and the ships that it uses ■ navy 'blue (also navy) adj dark blue

NB /ˌen ˈbiː/ abbr used in writing to make sb take notice of an important piece of information

0␣ **near**[1] /nɪə(r)/ adj **1** a short distance away in space or time: *Where's the ~est bank?* **2** used to describe a close family connection: *~ relations* [IDM] **a near thing** a situation in which failure or disaster is only just avoided ● **near** v [I,T] (fml) come closer to sth: *The ship is ~ing land.* ▸ **nearness** n [U] ■ nearside adj, n [sing] (GB) (for a driver) (on) the side nearest the edge of the road ■ near'sighted (esp US) = SHORT-SIGHTED (SHORT[1])

0␣ **near**[2] /nɪə(r)/ prep **1** at a short distance away from sb/sth: *Do you live ~ here?* **2** short period of time from sth ● **near** adv at a short distance away [IDM] **nowhere near** far from ■ near'by adv a short distance from sb/sth: *They live ~ by.* ■ near'by adj not far away ▸ **nearly** adv almost; not quite; not completely [IDM] **not nearly** much less than; not at all: *not ~ly enough money*

0␣ **neat** /niːt/ adj **1** tidy and in order; carefully done or arranged: *a ~ answer to the problem* **2** (of people) liking to keep things tidy and in order **3** simple but clever: *a ~ idea* **4** (esp of an alcoholic drink) not

mixed with water or anything else
▶ **neatly** adv ▶ **neatness** n [U]

0⁻ **necessary** /'nesəsəri/ adj that is needed for a purpose or reason: *Have you made the ~ arrangements?* ▶ **necessarily** /ˌnesə'serəli; 'nesəsərəli/ adv used to say that sth cannot be avoided [IDM] **not necessarily** used to say that sth is possibly true but not always

necessitate /nə'sesɪteɪt/ v [T] (fml) make sth necessary

necessity /nə'sesəti/ n (pl -ies) **1** [U] fact that sth must happen or be done; need for sth **2** [C] thing that you must have and cannot manage without: *Food is a ~ of life.*

0⁻ **neck** /nek/ n [C] **1** part of the body that joins the head to the shoulders **2** part of a piece of clothing that fits around the neck **3** long narrow part of sth: *the ~ of a bottle* [IDM] **be up to your neck in sth** be very deeply involved in sth **neck and neck (with sb/sth)** level with sb in a race or competition **risk/save your neck** risk/save your life ● **neck** v [I] (infml) (of couples) hug and kiss each other ■ **necklace** /'nekləs/ n [C] decorative string of beads, jewels, etc worn round the neck ■ **necktie** n [C] (old-fash or US) = TIE²(1)

nectar /'nektə(r)/ n [U] sweet liquid collected by bees from plants

née /neɪ/ adj used before the name of a woman to give her family name before she married: *Mrs Jane Smith, ~ Brown*

0⁻ **need¹** /niːd/ modal v (pres tense, all persons **need** neg **need not** short form **needn't** /'niːdnt/) used to show what is/was necessary: *You ~n't finish that work today.* ● **need** v [T] **1** require sth/sb: *That dog ~s a bath.* **2** used to show what you should or have to do

0⁻ **need²** /niːd/ n **1** [sing, U] situation when sth is necessary or must be done: *There's a ~ for more nurses. ◇ There's no ~ to start yet.* **2** [C, usu pl] things that sb requires in order to live comfortably: *financial/physical ~s* **3** [U] state of not having enough food, money or support: *people in ~* [IDM] **if need be** if necessary ▶ **needless** adj unnecessary [IDM] **needless to say** used to emphasize that the information you are giving is obvious ▶ **needlessly** adv ▶ **needy** adj (-ier, -iest) very poor

0⁻ **needle** /'niːdl/ n [C] **1** small pointed piece of steel, with a hole at the top for thread, used in sewing **2** = KNITTING NEEDLE (KNIT) **3** the thin pointed piece of steel on the end of a syringe used for giving injections: *a hypodermic ~* **4** small pointed piece of metal that touches a record that is being played

● **needle** v [T] (infml) deliberately annoy sb ■ **needlework** n [U] sewing; embroidery

negation /nɪ'geɪʃn/ n [U] (fml) act of denying or refusing sth

0⁻ **negative** /'negətɪv/ adj **1** bad or harmful: *have a ~ effect on sb* **2** lacking enthusiasm or hope **3** (of words, answers, etc) showing or meaning 'no' or 'not' **4** (tech) of the kind of electric charge carried by electrons: *a ~ charge/current* **5** less than zero ● **negative** n [C] **1** word or statement that means 'no' or 'not': *He answered in the ~ (=* said 'no'). **2** photographic film with light and dark areas reversed ▶ **negatively** adv

neglect /nɪ'glekt/ v [T] **1** fail to take care of sb/sth: *She denied ~ing her children.* **2** not give enough attention to sth: *~ your work* **3** fail or forget to do sth ● **neglect** n [U] fact of neglecting sb/sth or of being neglected ▶ **neglectful** adj (fml) not giving enough care or attention to sth

negligee (also **negligée**) /'neglɪʒeɪ/ n [C] woman's thin light dressing gown

negligent /'neglɪdʒənt/ adj (fml or law) failing to give sb/sth enough care or attention ▶ **negligence** /-dʒəns/ n [U] ▶ **negligently** adv

negligible /'neglɪdʒəbl/ adj of very little importance or size

negotiable /nɪ'gəʊʃiəbl/ adj **1** that can be discussed or changed before an agreement is reached **2** (business) that can be exchanged for money or given to sb else in exchange for money

negotiate /nɪ'gəʊʃieɪt/ v **1** [I, T] try to reach an agreement by formal discussion **2** [T] successfully get past or over an obstacle ▶ **negotiation** /nɪˌgəʊʃi'eɪʃn/ n [C, U] ▶ **negotiator** n [C] person who negotiates

neigh /neɪ/ v [I], n [C] (make the) long high sound of a horse

0⁻ **neighbour** (US -or) /'neɪbə(r)/ n [C] **1** person who lives in a house, etc near another **2** person, thing or country that is next to or near another ▶ **neighbourhood** n [C] district; nearby area [IDM] **in the neighbourhood of** approximately ▶ **neighbouring** adj near to sth: *~ing towns* ▶ **neighbourliness** n [U] friendliness ▶ **neighbourly** adj friendly

0⁻ **neither** /'naɪðə(r); 'niːðə(r)/ det, pron not one nor the other of two things or people: *N~ answer is correct.* ● **neither** adv **1** used to show that a negative statement is also true of sb/sth else: *She doesn't like Mozart and ~ do I. ◇ I've never*

been to Paris and ~ has she.
2 (neither...nor...) used to show that
a negative statement is true of two
things: N~ his sister nor his brother
was invited.

neo- /'niːəʊ/ *prefix* (in adjectives and
nouns) new; in a later form: ~
classical ○ ~ *con* (= conservative)

neon /'niːɒn/ *n* [U] (*symb* Ne)
colourless gas used in electric lights

0━ **nephew** /'nefjuː; 'nevjuː/ *n* [C]
son of your brother(-in-law) or
sister(-in-law)

nepotism /'nepətɪzəm/ *n* [U]
(*disapprov*) giving unfair advantages
to your own family if you are in a
position of power

0━ **nerve** /nɜːv/ *n* **1** [C] any of the
long thin threads that carry
messages between the brain and
parts of the body, enabling you to
move, feel pain, etc (**nerves**) [pl]
feelings of worry or anxiety: *I need
something to calm my ~s.* **3** [U]
courage to do sth difficult or
dangerous: *lose your* ~ **4** [sing, U]
(*infml*) way of behaving that people
think is rude or not appropriate: *He's
got a ~ asking us for money!* [**IDM**] **get
on sb's nerves** (*infml*) annoy sb
■ **'nerve-racking** *adj* causing great
worry

0━ **nervous** /'nɜːvəs/ *adj* **1** ~ **about/**
of anxious about sth or afraid of sth
2 easily worried or frightened: *a
thin, ~ woman* **3** of the body's
nerves: *a ~ disorder* ■ **nervous**
breakdown *n* [C] mental illness that
causes depression, tiredness and
weakness ▶ **nervously** *adv*
▶ **nervousness** *n* [U] ■ **nervous**
system *n* [C] system of all the nerves
in the body

nervy /'nɜːvi/ *adj* (*infml*) **1** (*GB*)
anxious and nervous **2** (*US*) rude
and disrespectful

0━ **nest** /nest/ *n* **1** place made by
a bird for its eggs **2** group of similar
things (esp tables) made to fit inside
each other ● **nest** *v* [I] make and use
a nest ■ **'nest egg** *n* [C] sum of
money saved for future use

nestle /'nesl/ *v* **1** [I] sit or lie down in
a warm or soft place: ~ (*down*)
among the cushions **2** [T] put or hold
sb/sth in a comfortable position in a
warm or soft place

nestling /'nestlɪŋ/ *n* [C] bird that is
too young to leave its nest

0━ **net** /net/ *n* **1** [C,U] (piece of) loose
open material made of knotted
string, wire, etc: *curtains* ○ *fishing
~s* **2** (**the Net**) [sing] (*infml*) = THE
INTERNET ● **net** (*GB also* **nett**) *adj*
remaining when nothing more is
to be taken away: ~ *income* (= after
tax has been paid) ● **net** *v* (-**tt**-) [T]
1 earn an amount of money as a

profit after you have paid tax on it
2 catch sth (as if) with a net
■ **netball** *n* [U] team game in which
a ball is thrown through a net on the
top of a post

netiquette /'netɪket/ *n* [U] (*infml*)
rules of correct or polite behaviour
among people using the Internet

netting /'netɪŋ/ *n* [U] material made
of string, wire, etc that is woven or
tied together

nettle /'netl/ *n* [C] common wild
plant with leaves that sting if you
touch them

0━ **network** /'netwɜːk/ *n* [C]
1 complex system of roads, lines,
nerves, etc crossing each other
2 closely linked group of people,
companies, etc **3** (*computing*)
number of computers, etc linked
together so that equipment and
information can be shared **4** group
of radio or television stations

neurology /njʊəˈrɒlədʒi/ *n* [U] study
of nerves and their diseases
▶ **neurologist** *n* [C] doctor who
studies and treats diseases of the
nerves

neurosis /njʊəˈrəʊsɪs/ *n* [C,U] (*pl*
-**oses** /-əʊsiːz/) (*med*) mental illness
causing feelings of fear or
worry

neurotic /njʊəˈrɒtɪk/ *adj* abnormally
sensitive and anxious ● **neurotic** *n*
[C] neurotic person

neuter /'njuːtə(r)/ *adj* (*gram*) neither
masculine nor feminine in gender
● **neuter** *v* [T] remove the sex organs
of an animal so that it cannot
produce young

neutral /'njuːtrəl/ *adj* **1** not
supporting either side in an
argument, war, etc **2** having no
clear or strong qualities: *a dull ~
colour* **3** (*chem*) neither acid nor
alkaline ● **neutral** *n* **1** [U] position of
the gears of a vehicle in which no
power is carried from the engine to
the wheels: *leave the car in* ~ **2** [C]
neutral person or country
▶ **neutrality** /njuːˈtræləti/ *n* [U]
state of not supporting either side in
an argument, etc ▶ **neutralize** (*also*
-**ise**) *v* [T] **1** stop sth from having any
effect **2** (*chem*) make a substance
neutral (3)

neutron /'njuːtrɒn/ *n* [C] (*physics*)
tiny particle of matter inside an
atom, with no electric charge

0━ **never** /'nevə(r)/ *adv* not at any
time; not on any occasion: *I ~ eat
meat.*

0━ **nevertheless** /ˌnevəðəˈles/ *adv*
(*fml*) in spite of sth you have just
mentioned: *Our defeat was expected
but it was disappointing ~.*

0━ **new** /njuː/ *adj* **1** not existing
before; recently made, introduced,
etc: *a ~ film* **2** different from the
previous one: *get a ~ job* **3** already

existing, but not seen, experienced, etc before: *learn ~ words* **4 ~ (to)** not yet familiar with sth: *I'm ~ to this town.* **5** used in compounds to describe sth that has recently happened: *enjoying his ~-found freedom* **6** just beginning or beginning again: *He went to Australia to start a ~ life.* **IDM** **new blood** → BLOOD **a new lease of life** new energy or desire to live ■ **newcomer** *n* [C] person who has recently arrived in a place ▶ **newly** *adv* recently: *a ~ly married couple* ■ **newly-wed** *n* [usu pl] person who has recently got married ■ **new 'moon** *n* [C] the moon appearing as a thin crescent ■ **newness** *n* [U] ■ **new 'year** (*also* **New Year**) *n* [U, sing] the beginning of the year: *Happy N~ Year!*

0━ **news** /njuːz/ *n* **1** [U] information about sth that has happened recently: *Here's some good ~!* **2** [U] reports of recent events in newspapers or on television or radio: *He's always in the ~.* **3** (**the news**) [sing] regular television or radio broadcast of the latest news ■ **newsagent** (*US* **'newsdealer**) *n* [C] shopkeeper who sells newspapers, etc ■ **'newsflash** *n* [C] short piece of important news on television or radio ■ **'newspaper** *n* [C] printed publication, issued daily or weekly, with news, advertisements, etc

newt /njuːt/ *n* [C] small lizard-like animal that can live in water or on land

0━ **next** /nekst/ *adj* **1** coming straight after sth in order, space or time: *the ~ name on the list* **2** the one immediately following: *~ Thursday* ● **next** *adv* after sth else; then; afterwards: *What are you going to do ~?* ■ **next 'door** *adv, adj* in or into the next house ■ **next of 'kin** *n* [C, U] your closest living relatives ■ **next to** *prep* **1** in or into a position right beside sb/sth: *Come and sit ~ to me.* **2** almost: *in ~ to no time*

NHS /ˌen eɪtʃ 'es/ *abbr* = NATIONAL HEALTH SERVICE → NATIONAL

nib /nɪb/ *n* [C] metal point of a pen

nibble /'nɪbl/ *v* [I,T] take small bites of sth ● **nibble** *n* [C] a small bite of sth

0━ **nice** /naɪs/ *adj* (**~r, ~st**) **1** pleasant, enjoyable or attractive: *a ~ day* **2** used before adjectives or adverbs to emphasize how pleasant sth is: *I had a ~ hot bath.* **3** kind; friendly: *~ neighbours* **4** nice or unpleasant: *You've got us into a ~ mess!* **5** (*fml*) involving a small detail or distinction **IDM** **nice and ...** (*infml*) (used before adjectives) pleasantly: *It's ~ and quiet here.* ▶ **nicely** *adv* in a nice way **IDM** **do nicely 1** (usu be doing nicely) be making good progress **2** be satisfactory:

295

nineteen

Tomorrow at ten will do ~ly. ▶ **niceness** *n* [U]

nicety /'naɪsəti/ *n* [C, usu pl] (pl **-ies**) (written) small distinction: *niceties of meaning*

niche /niːʃ; nɪtʃ/ *n* [C] **1** comfortable or suitable role, job, etc **2** (*business*) opportunity to sell a product to a particular group of people: *I spotted a ~ in the market.* **3** small hollow place in a wall, eg for a statue

nick /nɪk/ *n* **1** (**the nick**) [sing] (*GB, sl*) prison or police station **2** [C] small cut in the edge or surface of sth **IDM** **in good, etc nick** (*GB, infml*) in good, etc condition or health **in the nick of time** (*infml*) at the very last moment ● **nick** *v* [T] **1** make a small cut in sth: *He ~ed himself shaving.* **2** (*GB, infml*) steal sth **3** (*GB, infml*) arrest sb

nickel /'nɪkl/ *n* **1** [U] (*symb* Ni) hard silver-white metal **2** [C] coin of the US or Canada worth 5 cents

nickname /'nɪkneɪm/ *n* [C] informal name used instead of sb's real name ● **nickname** *v* [T] give a nickname to sb/sth

nicotine /'nɪkətiːn/ *n* [U] poisonous substance found in tobacco

0━ **niece** /niːs/ *n* [C] daughter of your brother(-in-law) or sister(-in-law)

0━ **night** /naɪt/ *n* [C, u] time of darkness between one day and the next: *These animals only come out at ~.* **IDM** **have a good/bad night** sleep well/badly **night and day** | **day and night** all the time; continuously ■ **'nightclub** *n* [C] place that is open until late in the evening where people can go to dance, drink, etc ■ **'nightdress** (*also infml* **nightie** /'naɪti/) *n* [C] long loose piece of clothing, worn by a woman or girl in bed ■ **'nightfall** *n* [U] (*fml or lit*) time in the evening when it gets dark ■ **'nightlife** *n* [U] entertainment that is available at night ▶ **nightly** *adj, adv* happening every night ■ **'nightmare** *n* [C] **1** frightening dream **2** (*infml*) very frightening or unpleasant experience ■ **'nightwatchman** *n* [C] (pl **-men**) man employed to guard a building at night

nightingale /'naɪtɪŋgeɪl/ *n* [C] small bird that sings sweetly

nil /nɪl/ *n* [U] **1** (*esp GB*) the number 0, esp as the score in some games **2** nothing

nimble /'nɪmbl/ *adj* (**~r, ~st**) **1** able to move quickly and easily **2** (of the mind) able to think and understand quickly ▶ **nimbly** *adv* /-bli/

0━ **nine** /naɪn/ *number* **9** ▶ **ninth** /naɪnθ/ *ordinal number, n* [C] **9**th; each of nine equal parts of sth

0━ **nineteen** /ˌnaɪn'tiːn/ *number* **19** **IDM** **talk, etc nineteen to the dozen**

A B C D E F G H I J K L M **N** O P Q R S T U V W X Y Z

(GB, infml) talk, etc without stopping ▶ **nineteenth** /-ˈtiːnθ/ ordinal 19th

0̄ **ninety** /ˈnaɪnti/ n *number* 90 **2** (the nineties) n [pl] numbers, years or temperatures from 90 to 99 ▶ **ninetieth** ordinal number [C] 90th

nip /nɪp/ v (**-pp-**) **1** [T] give a quick painful bite or pinch **2** [I] (GB, infml) go somewhere quickly and/or for only a short time: *I'll just ~ out to the shops.* [IDM] **nip sth in the bud** stop sth in its early development ● **nip** n [C] **1** [usu sing] sharp pinch or bite **2** (infml) a feeling of cold: *There's a ~ in the air.* **3** (infml) small drink of strong alcohol

nipple /ˈnɪpl/ n [C] **1** round point of the breast **2** something like a nipple, eg on a baby's bottle

nippy /ˈnɪpi/ adj (**-ier, -iest**) (infml) **1** quick: *a ~ little car* **2** (of the weather) cold

niqab /nɪˈkɑːb/ n [C] piece of cloth covering most of the face, worn by some Muslim women

nit /nɪt/ n [C] **1** egg of a parasitic insect that lives in human hair **2** (GB, infml) stupid person

nitrogen /ˈnaɪtrədʒən/ n [U] colourless gas that is found in large quantities in the earth's atmosphere

nitroglycerine (esp US **-glycerin**) /ˌnaɪtrəʊˈɡlɪsəriːn, -rɪn/ n [U] powerful liquid explosive

nitwit /ˈnɪtwɪt/ n [C] (infml) stupid person

No. (also **no.**) abbr (pl **~s**) number

0̄ **no** /nəʊ/ det not one; not any: *No child is to leave the room.* ◇ *She had no money.* **2** used, eg on notices, to say that sth is not allowed: *No smoking.* **3** used to express the opposite: *He's no fool* (= He's intelligent). ● **no** exclam **1** used to give a negative reply or statement: *'Would you like a drink?' 'No thanks.'* **2** used to express shock or surprise at what sb has said: *'I'm leaving.' 'No!'* ● **no** adv used before adjectives and adverbs to mean 'not': *He's feeling no better.* ● **no** n [C] (pl **~es**) **1** word or answer of 'no' **2** (the noes) [pl] total number of people voting 'no' in a formal debate ■ **no-brainer** n [C] (infml) decision or problem that does not need much thought because the answer is obvious ■ **no-claims bonus** n [C] reduction in the cost of your insurance because you made no claims in the previous year ■ **no-frills** adj (esp of a service or a product) including only the basic features, without anything unnecessary added to make sth more attractive, comfortable, etc: *a*

~ airline/supermarket ■ **no-go area** n [C] (esp GB) place, esp in a city, which it is dangerous for people to enter ■ **'no-man's-land** n [U, sing] (in war) ground between two opposing armies

nobility /nəʊˈbɪləti/ n **1** (the nobility) [sing, with sing or pl verb] people of high social position with titles such as that of duke or duchess **2** (fml) quality of being noble in character

noble /ˈnəʊbl/ adj (**~r, ~st**) **1** having personal qualities admired by others, eg courage and honesty: *a ~ leader* **2** impressive in appearance, size, etc **3** belonging to a family of high social rank ● **noble** n [C] person of noble rank or birth ■ **nobleman** (fem **noblewoman**) n [C] person of noble birth or rank ▶ **nobly** /-bli/ adv

0̄ **nobody** /ˈnəʊbədi/ (also **no one** /ˈnəʊ wʌn/) pron not anybody; no person: *N~ came to see me.* ● **nobody** n [C] (pl **-ies**) unimportant person

nocturnal /nɒkˈtɜːnl/ adj **1** (of animals) active at night **2** (written) happening during the night: *a ~ visit*

nod /nɒd/ v (**-dd-**) [I, T] move your head up and down to show agreement or as a greeting [PV] **nod off** (infml) fall asleep ● **nod** n [C] movement of the head down and up again

0̄ **noise** /nɔɪz/ n [C, U] sound, esp when loud or unpleasant ▶ **noisy** adj (**-ier, -iest**) making a lot of noise ▶ **noisily** adv

nomad /ˈnəʊmæd/ n [C] member of a tribe that moves from place to place ▶ **nomadic** /nəʊˈmædɪk/ adj

nominal /ˈnɒmɪnl/ adj **1** being in name only; not in reality: *the ~ ruler of the country* **2** (of a sum of money) very small: *a ~ rent* **3** (gram) of a noun ▶ **nominally** /-nəli/ adv

nominate /ˈnɒmɪneɪt/ v [T] suggest officially that sb should be chosen for a role, prize, position, etc ▶ **nomination** /ˌnɒmɪˈneɪʃn/ n [U, C]

nominee /ˌnɒmɪˈniː/ n [C] **1** person who has been formally suggested for a job, prize, etc **2** (business) person in whose name money is invested in a company, etc

0̄ **non-** /nɒn/ prefix not ■ **non-com'missioned** adj not having a high rank in the armed forces ■ **non-com'mittal** adj not expressing an opinion or decision clearly ■ **non-ex'ecutive** adj (GB, business) (of a company director) able to give advice at a high level but not having the power to make decisions about the company ■ **noncon'formist** n [C], adj (person) who does not think or behave like other people ■ **non-'fiction** n writing that describes real facts, people and events ■ **non-'stick** *adj* (of pans) covered with a material that prevents food from sticking during cooking ■ **non-'stop** *adj, adv* without any stops: *a ~-stop train*

nonchalant /'nɒnʃələnt/ *adj* behaving in a calm and relaxed way without showing any anxiety ► **nonchalance** /-ləns/ *n* [U] ► **nonchalantly** *adv*

nondescript /'nɒndɪskrɪpt/ *adj* ordinary; uninteresting

0➡ **none** /nʌn/ *pron* not one; not any: *N~ of them has/have come back yet.* [IDM] **none the less** = NONETHELESS ● **none** *adv* (before the) not at all: *He seems ~ the worse for the experience.* **2** (none too) not at all; not very: *He looked ~ too happy.*

nonentity /nɒ'nentəti/ *n* [C] (pl -ies) unimportant person

nonetheless (also **none the 'less**) /ˌnʌnðə'les/ *adv* (*written*) in spite of this fact: *She may be ill but she got the work done ~.*

nonplussed /ˌnɒn'plʌst/ *adj* very surprised and puzzled

0➡ **nonsense** /'nɒnsns/ *n* **1** [U,C, sing] foolish talk, ideas, etc **2** [U] meaningless words ► **nonsensical** /nɒn'sensɪkl/ *adj* ridiculous; meaningless

noodle /'nu:dl/ *n* [C, usu pl] long thin strip of pasta, used esp in Chinese and Italian cooking

nook /nʊk/ *n* [C] sheltered quiet place [IDM] **every nook and cranny** (*infml*) every part of a place

noon /nu:n/ *n* [U] 12 o'clock in the middle of the day

0➡ **no one** = NOBODY: *N~ was at home.*

noose /nu:s/ *n* [C] loop of a rope that becomes tighter when the rope is pulled

0➡ **nor** /nɔ:(r)/ *conj, adv* **1** (neither...nor..., not...nor...) and not: *Neither Chris ~ his sister wanted to come.* ◇ *He can't see, ~ can he hear.* **2** used before a positive verb to agree with sth negative that has just been said: *'I'm not going.' 'N~ am I.'*

0➡ **norm** /nɔ:m/ *n* [C] usual or expected way of behaving

0➡ **normal** /'nɔ:ml/ *adj* typical, usual or ordinary ● **normal** *n* [U] usual state or level ► **normality** /nɔ:'mæləti/ (*esp US* **normalcy** /'nɔ:mlsi/) *n* [U] situation where everything is normal or as you would expect ► **normally** /-məli/ *adv*

0➡ **north** /nɔ:θ/ *n* [U, sing] (*abbr* N) **1** (the north, the North) point of the compass, to the left of a person watching the sun rise **2** (the north, the North) northern part of a country, a region or the world ● **north** *adj* (*also* **North**) **1** in or towards the north **2** (of winds) blowing from the north

● **north** *adv* towards the north ■ **north-'east** *n* [sing] *adj, adv* (*abbr* NE) (direction or region) halfway between north and east ► **north-'eastern** *adj* ► **northerly** /'nɔ:ðəli/ *adj, adv* **1** in or towards the north **2** (of winds) blowing from the north ► **northern** (*also* **Northern**) /'nɔ:ðən/ *adj* (*abbr* N) of the north part of the world or of a particular country ► **northerner** *n* [C] person born or living in the northern part of a country ► **northwards** /'nɔ:θwədz/ (*also* **northward**) *adv, adj* towards the north ■ **north-'west** *n* [sing] *adj, adv* (*abbr* NW) (direction or region) halfway between north and west ► **north-'western** *adj*

0➡ **nose¹** /nəʊz/ *n* **1** [C] part of the face above the mouth for breathing and smelling **2** [C] front part of an aircraft, spacecraft, etc **3 ~ for** [sing] special ability for understanding or recognizing sth: *a ~ for a good story* **4** [sing] sense of smell [IDM] **get up sb's nose** (GB, *infml*) annoy sb **poke/ stick your nose into sth** (*infml*) interfere in sth that does not concern you **under sb's nose** (*infml*) directly in front of sb ■ **'nosebleed** *n* [C] flow of blood from the nose ■ **'nosedive** *n, v* [I] **1** (of prices, costs, etc) (make) a sudden steep fall or drop: *Oil prices took a ~dive during the crisis.* **2** (make) a sharp vertical drop in an aircraft

nose² /nəʊz/ *v* [I,T] (cause sth to) move forward slowly and carefully [PV] **nose about/around (for sth)** look for sb, esp information about sb: *He's been nosing around in my desk.*

nosey = NOSY

nostalgia /nɒ'stældʒə/ *n* [U] feeling of sadness and pleasure when you think of happy times in the past ► **nostalgic** /-dʒɪk/ *adj*

nostril /'nɒstrəl/ *n* [C] either of the two openings into the nose

nosy (*also* **nosey**) /'nəʊzi/ *adj* (-ier, -iest) (*infml, disapprov*) too interested in other people's private lives ■ **nosy 'parker** *n* [C] (GB, *infml*) nosy person

0➡ **not** /nɒt/ *adv* used to form the negative of the verbs *be, do, etc* and often shortened to *n't*: *She did ~ see him.* ◇ *He warned me ~ to be late.* ◇ *Don't be late!* [IDM] **not only... (but) also** used to emphasize that sth else is also true: *She's ~ only my sister but also my best friend.* **not that** used to state that you are not suggesting sth: *She hasn't written—— that she said she would.*

notable /'nəʊtəbl/ *adj* deserving to be noticed or to receive attention ● **notable** *n* [C] important person ► **notably** /-bli/ *adv* especially

notary /ˈnəʊtəri/ n [C] (pl -ies) (also tech ˌnotary ˈpublic) official, esp a lawyer, with authority to witness documents

notation /nəʊˈteɪʃn/ n [C, U] system of signs or symbols representing numbers, musical notes, etc

notch /nɒtʃ/ n [C] **1** level on a scale, marking quality, etc **2** V-shaped cut in a surface ● notch v [T] **1** ~ (up) achieve sth such as a win or high score: ~ up a victory **2** make a V-shaped cut in sth

0— **note** /nəʊt/ n **1** [C] short piece of writing to help you remember sth: take ~s at a lecture **2** [C] short informal letter: Leave a ~ about it on his desk. **3** [C] short comment on a word, etc in a book **4** [C] piece of paper money: a £5 ~ **5** [C] (written sign representing a) single musical sound **6** [sing] quality or tone, esp of sb's voice: a ~ of bitterness in his voice **7** [C] official document: a sick ~ from your doctor **[IDM]** of note of importance or interest take note (of sth) pay attention to sth ● note v [T] **1** notice or pay attention to sth **[PV]** note sth down write sth down important to sth that you will not forget it ■ ˈnotebook n [C] **1** small book for writing notes in **2** (also ˈnotebook comˈputer) small computer that you can carry with you and use anywhere ▶ noted adj well known ■ ˈnotepaper n [C] paper for writing letters on ■ ˈnoteworthy adj deserving to be noticed; remarkable

0— **nothing** /ˈnʌθɪŋ/ pron not anything; no single thing: I've had ~ to eat since lunch. ◊ You've hurt your arm.' 'It's ~' (= It is not important, serious, etc). **[IDM]** be/have nothing to do with sb/sth have no connection with sb/sth for nothing **1** without payment: He did the job for ~. **2** with no reward or result: All that effort was for ~! nothing but only; no more/less than: ~ but the best nothing like (infml) **1** not at all like: She's ~ like her sister. **2** not nearly: This is ~ like as good. there is/was nothing (else) for it (but to do sth) there is no other action to take except the one mentioned: There's ~ for it but to work late tonight.

0— **notice** /ˈnəʊtɪs/ n **1** [U] fact of sb paying attention to sb/sth or knowing about sth: Take no ~ of what he says ◊ It was Jo who brought the problem to my ~ (= told me about it). **2** [C] (written or printed) news or information **3** [U] warning: give her a month's ~ to leave **[IDM]** at short notice at a moment's notice not long in advance; without warning take no notice of sb/sth pay no attention to sb/sth ● notice v [I, t] see or hear sb/sth; pay attention to

sb/sth ▶ noticeable /ˈnəʊtɪsəbl/ adj easily noticed: a ~able improvement ▶ noticeably adv: Her hand was shaking ~ably.

notify /ˈnəʊtɪfaɪ/ v (pt, pp -ied) [T] ~ (of) formally tell sb about sth: ~ the police of the accident ▶ notification /ˌnəʊtɪfɪˈkeɪʃn/ n [U, c]

notion /ˈnəʊʃn/ n [C] idea; opinion

notorious /nəʊˈtɔːriəs/ adj well known for sth bad: a ~ murderer ▶ notoriety /ˌnəʊtəˈraɪəti/ n [U] fame for being bad in some way ▶ notoriously adv

nougat /ˈnuːgɑː/ n [U] hard sweet made of sugar, nuts, etc

nought /nɔːt/ n **1** [C, U] (esp US zero) the figure 0 **2** (also naught) [U] (lit) nothing: All our efforts have come to ~ (= have failed).

the Noughties /ˈnɔːtiz/ n [pl] (GB) the years from 2000 to 2009

noun /naʊn/ n [C] (gram) word that refers to a person, a place or a thing, a quality or an activity

nourish /ˈnʌrɪʃ/ v [T] **1** keep sb/sth alive and healthy with food **2** (fml) allow a feeling, etc to grow stronger ▶ nourishment n [U] (fml or tech) food

0— **novel** /ˈnɒvl/ adj new and unusual: a ~ idea ● novel n [C] long written story ▶ novelist /ˈnɒvəlɪst/ n [C] writer of novels

novelty /ˈnɒvlti/ n (pl -ies) **1** [U] quality of being new, different and interesting **2** [C] thing, person or situation that is unusual or new **3** [C] small cheap toy or decoration

0— **November** /nəʊˈvembə(r)/ n [U, C] the 11th month of the year (See examples of use at April.)

novice /ˈnɒvɪs/ n [C] **1** person who is new and inexperienced in a job, activity, etc **2** person training to become a monk or nun

0— **now** /naʊ/ adv **1** (at) the present time: Where are you living ~? ◊ From ~ on, I'll be more careful. **2** at or from this moment, but not before: Start writing ~. **3** (spoken) used to attract attention, etc: N~, listen to me! **[IDM]** (every) now and again/then occasionally: He visits me every ~ and then. ● now conj ~ (that) because the thing mentioned is happening or has happened: N~ (that) he's left, let's begin.

nowadays /ˈnaʊədeɪz/ adv at the present time: I don't go out much ~.

0— **nowhere** /ˈnəʊweə(r)/ adv not in or to any place: There is ~ interesting to visit in this town. **[IDM]** get (sb) nowhere → GET

noxious /ˈnɒkʃəs/ adj (fml) poisonous or harmful

nozzle /ˈnɒzl/ n [C] shaped end of a hose through which liquid is directed

nuance /ˈnjuːɑːns/ n [C] small difference in meaning, opinion, colour, etc

○┅ **nuclear** /ˈnjuːkliə(r)/ adj
1 using, producing or resulting from nuclear energy **2** (physics) of the nucleus of an atom ■ nuclear ˈenergy (also nuclear ˈpower) n [U] powerful form of energy produced by splitting the nuclei of atoms and used to produce electricity ■ nuclear reˈactor n [C] large structure used for the controlled production of nuclear energy

nucleus /ˈnjuːkliəs/ n [C] (pl **nuclei** /-kliaɪ/) **1** (physics) central part of an atom **2** (biol) central part of a cell **3** central part, around which other parts are grouped: These books form the ~ of the library.

nude /njuːd/ adj not wearing any clothes ● nude n [C] work of art consisting of a naked human figure [IDM] **in the nude** not wearing any clothes ▶ **nudist** n [C] person who does not wear any clothes because they believe this is more natural: a nudist beach ▶ **nudity** n [U]

nudge /nʌdʒ/ v [T] push sb gently, esp with your elbow ● nudge n [C] gentle push

nugget /ˈnʌɡɪt/ n [C] **1** lump of metal, esp gold **2** interesting piece of information

nuisance /ˈnjuːsns/ n [C, usu sing] annoying person, situation, etc

null /nʌl/ adj [IDM] **null and void** (law) (of an election, etc) having no legal force ▶ **nullify** /ˈnʌlɪfaɪ/ v (pt, pp -ied) [T] make sth, eg a legal agreement or order, have no effect

numb /nʌm/ adj unable to feel anything: ~ with cold/shock ● numb v [T] make sb or a part of sb's body numb ▶ **numbness** n [U]

○┅ **number** /ˈnʌmbə(r)/ n [C]
1 symbol or word representing a quantity: 3, 13 and 103 are ~s **2** quantity or amount: a large ~ of people ◇ A ~ of (= some) books are missing. **3** (GB) issue of a magazine **4** song or dance ● number v [T]
1 give a number to sth as part of a series or list: ~ the pages **2** amount to sth: The crowd ~ed over 3000 **3** ~ **among** (fml) include sb/sth in a group

numeracy /ˈnjuːmərəsi/ n [U] good basic knowledge of mathematics: standards of literacy and ~ ▶ **numerate** adj able to understand and work with numbers

numeral /ˈnjuːmərəl/ n [C] sign or symbol representing a number

numerical /njuːˈmerɪkl/ adj of or expressed in numbers ▶ **numerically** /-kli/ adv

numerous /ˈnjuːmərəs/ adj (fml) existing in large numbers: on ~ occasions

nun /nʌn/ n [C] member of a female religious community, living in a convent ▶ **nunnery** n [C] (pl -ies) (old-fash) = CONVENT

○┅ **nurse** /nɜːs/ n [C] person whose job is to take care of ill or injured people, usu in a hospital ● nurse v [T] **1** take care of people who are ill, etc **2** feed a baby with milk from the breast **3** have a strong feeling in your mind for a long time: ~ feelings of revenge **4** give special care to sb/sth: ~ young plants ▶ **nursing** n [U] job or skill of caring for the sick ■ ˈnursing home n [C] small private hospital, esp for old people

nursery /ˈnɜːsəri/ n [C] (pl -ies) **1** place where young children are cared for while their parents are at work **2** place where young plants are grown ■ ˈnursery rhyme n [C] poem or song for young children ■ ˈnursery school n [C] school for children from 2 to 5 years old

nurture /ˈnɜːtʃə(r)/ v [T] (fml) **1** care for and protect a child **2** encourage the development of sb/sth

○┅ **nut** /nʌt/ n [C] **1** small hard fruit with a hard shell that grows on some trees **2** small piece of metal with a hole through the centre for screwing onto a bolt **3** (GB, infml) (also nutter) crazy person [IDM] **off your nut** (GB, spoken) crazy ■ **nutcase** n [C] (infml) crazy person ■ **nutcracker** n (GB also nutcrackers) [pl] tool for cracking open the shells of nuts ■ **nutshell** n [IDM] **(put sth) in a nutshell** (say sth) in a very clear way, using few words ▶ **nutty** adj (-ier, -iest) **1** tasting of or containing nuts **2** (infml) crazy

nutmeg /ˈnʌtmeɡ/ n [U, C] hard seed of an E Indian tree used in cooking as a spice, esp to flavour cakes and sauces

nutrient /ˈnjuːtriənt/ n [C] (tech) substance needed to keep a living thing alive and help it to grow

nutrition /njuˈtrɪʃn/ n [U] process by which living things receive the food necessary for them to be healthy ▶ **nutritional** /-ʃənl/ adj ▶ **nutritious** /-ʃəs/ adj (of food) good for you

nuts /nʌts/ adj (infml) crazy; mad

nuzzle /ˈnʌzl/ v [I, T] touch or rub sb/sth gently with the nose, esp to show affection

nylon /ˈnaɪlɒn/ n [U] very strong artificial material, used in clothes, rope, etc

nymph /nɪmf/ n [C] (in ancient Greek and Roman stories) spirit of nature living in rivers, trees, etc

O o

O, o /əʊ/ n [C,U] (pl **O's, o's** /əʊz/) **1** the fifteenth letter of the English alphabet **2** (*spoken*) used to mean 'zero' when saying telephone numbers, etc

oaf /əʊf/ n [C] awkward or stupid person

oak /əʊk/ (*also* **oak tree**) n **1** [C] large tree that produces small nuts (acorns), often eaten by animals **2** [U] hard wood of the oak tree

OAP /ˌəʊ eɪ ˈpiː/ abbr (GB) old-age pensioner

oar /ɔː(r)/ n [C] long pole with a flat blade, used for rowing a boat [IDM] **put/stick your oar in** (*GB, infml*) give your opinion, advice, etc where it is not asked for

oasis /əʊˈeɪsɪs/ n [C] (pl **oases** /-siːz/) area in a desert with water and plants

oath /əʊθ/ n [C] (pl ~s /əʊðz/) **1** formal promise or statement **2** (*old-fash*) swear word [IDM] **on/under oath** (*law*) having made a formal promise to tell the truth in a court of law

oats /əʊts/ n [pl] (grain from a) cereal plant grown as food ■ **oatmeal** n [U] crushed oats

obedient /əˈbiːdiənt/ adj doing what you are told to do
▶ **obedience** /-əns/ n [U]
▶ **obediently** adv

obelisk /ˈɒbəlɪsk/ n [C] tall pointed stone column

obese /əʊˈbiːs/ adj (*fml*) (of people) very fat ▶ **obesity** n [U]

0— **obey** /əˈbeɪ/ v [I,T] do what you are told or expected to do

obituary /əˈbɪtʃuəri/ n [C] (pl **-ies**) article about sb's life, printed in a newspaper soon after they have died

0— **object**[1] /ˈɒbdʒɪkt/ n [C] **1** thing that can be seen or touched but is not alive **2** ~ **of** person or thing to which an action, feeling, etc is directed: an ~ of pity **3** aim or purpose: Our ~ is to win. **4** (*gram*) noun, phrase, etc towards which the action of a verb is directed, for example *him* and *the money* in: *Give him the money.* [IDM] **expense, money, etc is no object** used to say that you are willing to spend as much as you need to

0— **object**[2] /əbˈdʒekt/ v [I] ~ **(to)** say that you disagree with or oppose sth

objection /əbˈdʒekʃn/ n [C] ~ **(to)** (statement giving the) reason why you dislike or are opposed to sth

▶ **objectionable** /-ʃənəbl/ adj (*fml*) unpleasant or offensive
▶ **objectionably** adv

0— **objective** /əbˈdʒektɪv/ adj **1** not influenced by personal feelings: an ~ report **2** (*phil*) having existence outside the mind; real ● **objective** n [C] something that you are trying to achieve ▶ **objectively** adv
▶ **objectivity** /ˌɒbdʒekˈtɪvəti/ n [U]

obligation /ˌɒblɪˈɡeɪʃn/ n [C,U] something that ought to be done; duty [IDM] **be under no obligation to do sth** not have to do sth

obligatory /əˈblɪɡətri/ adj (*fml*) that is required by law or custom

oblige /əˈblaɪdʒ/ v [T] ~ **to** (usu passive) force sb to do sth, eg by law, because it is a duty, etc: *Parents are ~d to send their children to school.* **2** [I,T] help sb by doing what they ask or what they want: *If you need any help, I'd be happy to ~.* ● **obliged** adj (*fml*) used to show that you are grateful to sb: *I'm much ~d to you for helping us.* ● **obliging** adj willing to help ▶ **obligingly** adv

oblique /əˈbliːk/ adj **1** indirect: an ~ reference **2** (of a line) sloping
● **oblique** n [C] (GB) = SLASH(3)
▶ **obliquely** adv

obliterate /əˈblɪtəreɪt/ v [T] remove all signs of sth; destroy sth
▶ **obliteration** /əˌblɪtəˈreɪʃn/ n [U]

oblivion /əˈblɪviən/ n [U] state of being unaware of sth or being forgotten

oblivious /əˈblɪviəs/ adj ~ **of/to** not aware of sth: ~ of the news

oblong /ˈɒblɒŋ/ n [C], adj (figure) with four straight sides and angles of 90°, longer than it is wide

obnoxious /əbˈnɒkʃəs/ adj very unpleasant

oboe /ˈəʊbəʊ/ n [C] wooden instrument that you blow into to make sound ▶ **oboist** n [C] oboe player

obscene /əbˈsiːn/ adj shocking and offensive, esp sexually ▶ **obscenely** adv ▶ **obscenity** /əbˈsenəti/ n [C,U] (pl **-ies**) (instance of) obscene language or behaviour

obscure /əbˈskjʊə(r)/ adj **1** not well known: an ~ poet **3** difficult to understand ● **obscure** v [T] make it difficult to see, hear or understand sth: a hill ~d by fog ▶ **obscurely** adv ▶ **obscurity** n [U] state of being obscure

observance /əbˈzɜːvəns/ n **1** [U,sing] keeping of a law, custom, festival, etc **2** [C,usu pl] part of a religious ceremony

observant /əbˈzɜːvənt/ adj quick at noticing things

0— **observation** /ˌɒbzəˈveɪʃn/ n **1** [U,C] act of watching sb/sth carefully for a period of time: *The suspect is under ~* (= watched closely by the police). ◇ *She has keen powers of ~* (= the ability to notice things around her). **2** [C] comment

observatory /əbˈzɜːvətri/ *n* [C] (pl **-ies**) building in which scientists watch and study the stars, etc

0—**observe** /əbˈzɜːv/ *v* [T] **1** see or notice sth/sth **2** watch sth/sth carefully **3** (*fml*) make a remark **4** (*fml*) obey a rule, law, etc **5** (*fml*) celebrate a festival, birthday, etc ▸ **observer** *n* [C] **1** person who observes sth/sth **2** person who attends a meeting to listen and watch but not to take part

obsess /əbˈses/ *v* [T] (*usu passive*) completely fill your mind, so that you cannot think about anything else: *be ~ed by the fear of death* ▸ **obsession** /əbˈseʃn/ *n* **1** [U] state of being obsessed **2** [C] person or thing that sb thinks about too much ▸ **obsessive** *adj* thinking too much about one person or thing

obsolescent /ˌɒbsəˈlesnt/ *adj* becoming out of date ▸ **obsolescence** /ˌɒbsəˈlesns/ *n* [U]

obsolete /ˈɒbsəliːt/ *adj* no longer used; out of date

obstacle /ˈɒbstəkl/ *n* [C] something that stops progress or makes it difficult: *an ~ to world peace* ■ **'obstacle course 1** series of objects that competitors in a race have to jump over, through, etc **2** (*US*) = ASSAULT COURSE

obstetrics /əbˈstetrɪks/ *n* [U] branch of medicine concerned with childbirth ▸ **obstetrician** /ˌɒbstəˈtrɪʃn/ *n* [C] doctor trained in obstetrics

obstinate /ˈɒbstɪnət/ *adj* **1** refusing to change your opinions, way of behaving, etc **2** difficult to get rid of or deal with: *~ stains* ▸ **obstinacy** /-nəsi/ *n* [U] ▸ **obstinately** *adv*

obstreperous /əbˈstrepərəs/ *adj* (*fml*) noisy and difficult to control: *a class full of ~ children*

obstruct /əbˈstrʌkt/ *v* [T] **1** block a road, entrance, etc **2** prevent sth/sth from doing sth or progressing: *~ justice* ▸ **obstruction** /əbˈstrʌkʃn/ *n* **1** [U,C] fact of obstructing sth/sth **2** [C] something that blocks sth ▸ **obstructive** *adj* intending to obstruct sth/sth

0—**obtain** /əbˈteɪn/ *v* [T] (*fml*) get sth: *I finally managed to ~ a copy of the report.* ▸ **obtainable** *adj*

obtrusive /əbˈtruːsɪv/ *adj* very noticeable in an unpleasant way: *a modern house which is ~ in an old village* ▸ **obtrusively** *adv*

obtuse /əbˈtjuːs/ *adj* (*fml, disapprov*) slow or unwilling to understand sth ■ **ob'tuse 'angle** *n* [C] angle between 90° and 180° ▸ **obtusely** *adv* ▸ **obtuseness** *n* [U]

obverse /ˈɒbvɜːs/ *n* [sing] **1** (*fml*)

opposite of sth **2** (*tech*) side of a coin that has the head or main design on it

0—**obvious** /ˈɒbviəs/ *adj* easy to see or understand; clear ▸ **obviously** *adv*

0—**occasion** /əˈkeɪʒn/ *n* **1** [C] particular time when sth happens **2** [C] special event or celebration **3** [U,sing] (*fml*) time that provides a reason for sth to happen: *I have had no ~ to visit them recently.* [IDM] **on occasion(s)** sometimes but not often ▸ **occasion** *v* [T] (*fml*) cause sth

occasional /əˈkeɪʒənl/ *adj* happening sometimes, but not often

0—**occasionally** /əˈkeɪʒnəli/ *adv* sometimes but not often: *We ~ meet for a drink after work.*

Occident /ˈɒksɪdənt/ *n* (the Occident) [sing] (*fml*) the western part of the world, esp Europe and America ▸ **occidental** /ˌɒksɪˈdentl/ *adj*

occult /əˈkʌlt; ˈɒkʌlt/ *n* (the occult) [sing] supernatural or magical powers, practices, etc ▸ **occult** *adj*

occupant /ˈɒkjəpənt/ *n* [C] person who lives or works in a house or room ▸ **occupancy** /-pənsi/ *n* [U] (*fml*) act of living in or using a building, room, etc

occupation /ˌɒkjuˈpeɪʃn/ *n* **1** [C] job or profession **2** [C] activity that fills your time **3** [U] act of taking possession of a country ▸ **occupational** /-ʃənl/ *adj* of or connected with sb's job

0—**occupy** /ˈɒkjupaɪ/ *v* (*pt, pp* **-ied**) [T] **1** fill or use a space, an area or an amount of time **2** (*fml*) live or work in a room, house or building **3** take control of a country, town, etc, esp by military force **4 ~ yourself** keep yourself busy **5** have an official job or position ▸ **occupier** *n* [C] person who lives in a house or room

0—**occur** /əˈkɜː(r)/ *v* (*-rr-*) [I] **1** (*fml*) happen: *The accident ~red in the rain.* **2** be found somewhere; exist [PV] **occur to sb** (of an idea or thought) come into your mind: *It never ~red to me that he might be lying.* ▸ **occurrence** /əˈkʌrəns/ *n* [C] event **2** [U] fact of sth happening

0—**ocean** /ˈəʊʃn/ *n* (Ocean) [C] one of the very large areas of sea on the earth's surface: *the Pacific O~* ▸ **oceanic** /ˌəʊʃiˈænɪk/ *adj* (*tech*)

0—**o'clock** /əˈklɒk/ *adv* used with the numbers 1 to 12 when telling the time, to mean an exact hour: *It's 5 ~.*

octagon /ˈɒktəɡən/ *n* [C] (*geom*) flat shape with eight sides and eight angles ▸ **octagonal** /ɒkˈtæɡənl/ *adj*

octane /ˈɒkteɪn/ n [U] substance found in petrol used as a measure of its quality

octave /ˈɒktɪv/ n [C] (music) space between a note and the next one of the same name above or below it

☞ **October** /ɒkˈtəʊbə(r)/ n [U, C] the tenth month of the year (See examples of use at *April*.)

octopus /ˈɒktəpəs/ n [C] sea creature with a soft body and eight arms (tentacles)

☞ **odd** /ɒd/ adj **1** strange; unusual **2** missing its pair or set: *an ~ sock/ shoe* **3** (of numbers) that cannot be divided by 2: *1 and 5 are ~ numbers.* **4** a little more than the number mentioned: *30~ years* [IDM] **the odd man/one out** person or thing that is different from the others in a group ► **oddity** n (pl **-ies**) **1** strange or unusual thing or person **2** [U] quality of being strange ■ **odd ˈjobs** n [pl] small jobs of various types ■ **odd-job man** n [C] (esp GB) person paid to do odd jobs ► **oddly** adv strangely

oddments /ˈɒdmənts/ n [pl] small pieces of fabric, wood, etc that are left after a larger piece has been used

odds /ɒdz/ n [pl] probability or chance that sth will or will not happen: *The ~ are (= It is probable that) she'll win.* [IDM] **be at odds (with sb/sth)** disagree with sb; be different from sth ■ **it makes no odds** (spoken) it is not important ■ **odds and ˈends** n [pl] (GB, infml) small items of various types

ode /əʊd/ n [C] poem that speaks to a person or thing or celebrates an event

odious /ˈəʊdiəs/ adj (fml) extremely unpleasant

odour (US **odor**) /ˈəʊdə(r)/ n [C, U] (fml) smell

oesophagus /iˈsɒfəɡəs/ n [C] (anat) tube through which food passes from the mouth to the stomach

☞ **of** /əv/; strong form ɒv/ prep **1** belonging to sb; relating to sth: *a friend of mine* ◇ *the works of Shakespeare* ◇ *the support of the voters* **2** belonging to sth; being part of sth; relating to sth: *the lid of the box* ◇ *a member of the team* **3** coming from or living in a place: *the people of Wales* **4** concerning or showing sb/sth: *a picture of my cat* **5** used to say what sb/sth is, consists of or contains: *the city of Dublin* ◇ *a crowd of people* ◇ *a bottle of lemonade* **6** used with measurements and expressions of time, age, etc: *40 litres of petrol* ◇ *a girl of 12* ◇ *the first of May* **7** used to show the position of sth/sb in space or time: *just south of Paris* **8** used after nouns formed

from verbs: *the arrival of the police* ◇ *fear of the dark* **9** used after some verbs before mentioning sb/sth involved in the action: *rob sb of sth* ◇ *He was cleared of all blame.* **10** used to give your opinion of sb's behaviour: *It was kind of you to offer.*

☞ **off¹** /ɒf/ adv **1** away from a place; at a distance in space or time: *I must be ~ (= I must leave).* ◇ *The town is still 5 miles ~.* ◇ *He's to France today.* **2** used to say that sth has been removed: *take your hat ~* ◇ *He shaved his beard ~.* **3** starting a race: *They're ~ (= the race has begun).* **4** (infml) cancelled: *The wedding is ~.* **5** not connected or functioning: *The electricity is ~.* ◇ *Make sure the TV is ~.* **6** (esp GB) (of an item on a menu) no longer available: *The soup is ~.* **7** away from work: *take the day ~* [IDM] **off and on** and **on and off** from time to time: *It rained ~ and on all day.*

off² /ɒf/ adj **1** (of food) no longer fresh: *The milk is ~.* **2 ~ (with)** (infml, esp GB) impolite or unfriendly: *He can be a bit ~ sometimes.* **3** (infml) not acceptable: *It's a bit ~ expecting us to work on a Sunday.* [IDM] **do sth on the off chance** do sth even though there is only a slight possibility of success: *I went to his house on the ~ chance (that he'd be at home).* ■ **ˈoff day** n [C] (infml) day when you do not do things as well as usual ■ **ˈoff season** n [C] time of year that is less busy in business or travel

☞ **off³** /ɒf/ prep **1** down or away from a place or at a distance in space or time: *fall ~ a ladder* ◇ *take a packet ~ the shelf* ◇ *We're getting ~ the subject.* **2** leading away from sth: *a lane ~ the main road* **3** away from work: *He's had ten days ~.* **4** (infml) not wanting or liking sth that you usu eat or use: *He's ~ his food.* ◇ *He's ~ drugs now* (= he no longer takes them).

offal /ˈɒfl/ n [U] inside parts of an animal used as food

☞ **offence** (US **-ense**) /əˈfens/ n **1** [C] ~ **(against)** illegal act **2** [U] act of upsetting or insulting sb: *I didn't mean to give* ~ (= to upset you). ◇ *He's quick to take* ~ (= He is easily upset.).

☞ **offend** /əˈfend/ v **1** [T] upset or insult sb **2** [T] seem unpleasant to sb: *ugly buildings that ~ the eye* **3** [I] commit a crime **4** [I] ~ **against** (fml) be against what people believe is morally right ► **offender** n [C] person who breaks the law ► **offending** adj causing a problem or difficulty

☞ **offensive** /əˈfensɪv/ adj **1** very unpleasant; insulting: ~ *language* **2** (fml) used for attacking: ~ *weapons* ● **offensive** n [C] strong military attack [IDM] **go on (to) the**

offensive | **take the offensive** start attacking sb/sth ▶ **offensively** adv ▶ **offensiveness** n [U]

O━ **offer** /'ɒfə(r)/ v **1** [I,T] say that you are willing to do sth for sb or give sth to sb: *I ~ed to do first.* ◇ *They ~ed me the job.* **2** [T] make sth available or provide the opportunity for sth: *The job ~s good chances of promotion.* ● **offer** n [C] **1** act of offering to do sth or give sth to sb **2** something offered ▶ **offering** n [C] something offered, esp to God

offhand /,ɒf'hænd/ adj (disapprov) not showing any interest in sb/ sth ● **offhand** adv without being able to check sth or think about it: *I can't give you an answer ~.*

O━ **office** /'ɒfɪs/ n **1** [C] room or building where people work, usu sitting at desks **2** [C] room or building used for a particular purpose: *a tourist ~* **3** (**Office**) [C] used in the names of some British government departments: *The Foreign O~* **4** [U,C] (work of an) important position of authority: *the ~ of president*

O━ **officer** /'ɒfɪsə(r)/ n [C] **1** person in command in the armed forces: *an ~ in the navy* **2** person with authority: *a customs ~* **3** policeman or policewoman

O━ **official** /ə'fɪʃl/ adj **1** of a position of authority or trust **2** said, done, etc publicly and with authority: *an ~ statement* ● **official** n [C] person in a position of authority in a large organization ▶ **officialdom** /-dəm/ n [U] (disapprov) people in positions of authority when they seem more interested in following rules than in being helpful ▶ **officially** /-ʃəli/ adv publicly; formally

officiate /ə'fɪʃieɪt/ v [I] ~ (**at**) perform official duties at a ceremony

officious /ə'fɪʃəs/ adj (disapprov) too eager to give orders ▶ **officiously** adv ▶ **officiousness** n [U]

offing /'ɒfɪŋ/ n [IDM] **in the offing** (infml) likely to appear or happen soon

off-licence /'ɒf laɪsns/ n [C] (GB) shop where alcoholic drinks are sold to be taken away

offline /,ɒf'laɪn/ adj (computing) not directly controlled by or connected to a computer or the Internet

off-peak /,ɒf 'pi:k/ adj in or used at a time that is less busy: *~ travel*

off-putting /'ɒf pʊtɪŋ/ adj (esp GB, infml) causing dislike; unpleasant: *His manner is very ~.*

offset /'ɒfset/ v (**-tt-** pt, pp **offset**) [T] use one cost, payment or situation to cancel or reduce the effect of another: *increase prices to ~ higher costs*

offshoot /'ɒfʃuːt/ n [C] **1** thing that develops from sth, esp a small

organization that develops from a larger one **2** [C] new stem that grows on a plant

offshore /,ɒf'ʃɔː(r)/ adj, adv **1** at a distance out to sea: *an ~ oil rig* **2** away from the land towards the sea: *~ breezes* **3** (*business*) (of money, companies, etc) kept or situated in a country that has more generous tax laws than other places

offside /,ɒf'saɪd/ adj, n [U] **1** (*sport*) (fact of a player being) in a position in front of the ball, which is against the rules **2** (GB) (on the) side of a vehicle that is furthest from the edge of the road

offspring /'ɒfsprɪŋ/ n [C] (pl **offspring**) (fml) a person's child or children; young of animals

off-white /,ɒf 'waɪt/ adj very pale yellowish-white in colour

O━ **often** /'ɒfn; also 'ɒftən/ adv **1** many times; frequently: *We ~ go there.* **2** in many cases: *Old houses are ~ damp.* [IDM] **as often as not** | **more often than not** usually; typically **every so often** sometimes

ogle /'əʊgl/ v [I,T] look at sb with great sexual interest

ogre /'əʊgə(r)/ n **1** (in stories) cruel frightening giant who eats people **2** very frightening person

O━ **oh** /əʊ/ exclam used to show surprise, fear, etc: *Oh dear!*

O━ **oil** /ɔɪl/ n **1** [U] any of several thick slippery liquids that burn easily, used for fuel, food, etc **2** (*oils*) [pl] coloured paint containing oil used by artists ● **oil** v [T] put oil on or into sth: *He ~ed the bike and pumped up the tyres.* ■ **oilfield** n [C] area where oil is found in the ground or under the sea ■ **oil paint** (*also* **oil colour**) n [C,U] type of paint that contains oil ■ **oil painting** n [C] picture painted in oil paint ■ **oil rig** (*esp US* **oil platform**) n [C] large structure with equipment for getting oil from under the ground ■ **oilskin** n [C,U] (coat, etc made of) cloth treated with oil to make it waterproof ■ **oil slick** n [C] area of oil floating on the sea ■ **oil well** n [C] hole made in the ground to obtain oil ▶ **oily** adj (**-ier, -iest**) **1** of or like oil; covered with oil **2** (disapprov) trying to be too polite: *an ~y smile*

ointment /'ɔɪntmənt/ n [C,U] smooth substance rubbed on the skin to heal a wound

O━ **OK** (*also* **okay**) /,əʊ'keɪ/ adj, adv (spoken) **1** safe and well; in a calm or happy state: *Are you OK?* **2** all right; satisfactory: *Is it OK for me to go now?* ● **OK** exclam (infml) used for showing agreement: *OK, I'll do it.* ● **OK** v [T] (infml) officially agree to sth: *She filed in the claim and her* *manager OK'd it.* ● **OK** *n* [sing] (*infml*) permission: *wait for the OK*

○━ **old** /əʊld/ *adj* **1** of a particular age: *He's 40 years ~.* ◊ *How ~ are you?* **2** having lived for a long time: *an ~ man* **3** having existed or been used for a long time: *~ shoes* **4** belonging to past times or a past time in your life: *Things were different in the ~ days.* ◊ *my ~ school* **5** known for a long time: *an ~ friend* [IDM] **(be) an old hand (at (doing) sth)** be very experienced and skilled in sth **old hat** old-fashioned and no longer interesting **an old wives' tale** (*disapprov*) old belief that has been proved not to be scientific ▸ **the old** *n* [pl] old people ■ **old-age** **'pension** *n* [C] (*GB*) money paid regularly by the state to people above a certain age ■ **old-age** **'pensioner** (*abbr* **OAP**) *n* [C] person who receives an old-age pension ■ **old 'maid** *n* [C] (*old-fash*, *disapprov*) unmarried woman thought to be too old for marriage ■ **old 'master** *n* [C] (picture by an) important painter, esp of the 13th - 17th centuries

○━ **old-'fashioned** *adj* **1** not modern; out of date: *old-fashioned clothes/equipment* **2** believing in old ways, etc

olive /'ɒlɪv/ *n* **1** [C] (tree of S Europe with a) small green or black fruit, eaten raw or used for its oil **2** [U] yellowish-green colour ■ **'olive** **branch** *n* [C] symbol of a wish for peace

ombudsman /'ɒmbʊdzmən; -mæn/ *n* [C] (pl **-men** /-mən/) government official whose job is to consider complaints about organizations

omelette /'ɒmlət/ *n* [C] eggs beaten together and fried

omen /'əʊmen/ *n* [C] sign of what is going to happen in the future

ominous /'ɒmɪnəs/ *adj* suggesting that sth bad will happen ▸ **ominously** *adv*

omission /ə'mɪʃn/ *n* **1** [U] act of omitting sth/sb **2** [C] thing that has not been included or done

omit /ə'mɪt/ *v* (**-tt-**) [T] (*fml*) **1** not include sth/sb either deliberately or by accident **2** ~ to fail to do sth: *I ~ted to mention his age.*

omnibus /'ɒmnɪbəs/ *n* [C] **1** (*GB*) radio or television programme that combines several recent programmes in a series **2** large book containing a number of books, esp by the same writer

omnipotent /ɒm'nɪpətənt/ *adj* (*fml*) having unlimited power ▸ **omnipotence** /-təns/ *n* [U]

omniscient /ɒm'nɪsiənt/ *adj* (*fml*)

knowing everything ▸ **omniscience** /-sɪəns/ *n* [U]

omnivorous /ɒm'nɪvərəs/ *adj* (*tech*) (of animals) eating both meat and plants

○━ **on**[1] /ɒn/ *adv* **1** used to show that sth continues: *They wanted the band to play on.* **2** used to show that sth moves or is sent forward: *walk on to the bus stop* ◊ *from that day on* (= from then until now) **3** on sb's body; being worn: *Put your coat on.* ◊ *He had nothing on.* **4** covering, touching or forming part of sth: *Make sure the lid is on.* **5** connected or being used: *The electricity isn't on.* ◊ *The radio is on.* **6** happening: *There was a war on at the time* ◊ *What's on at the cinema?* **7** planned to take place in the future: *Have you got anything on* (= any plans for) *this weekend?* **8** on duty; working: *I'm on now until 8 in the morning.* **9** in or into a large vehicle: *get on the bus* [IDM] **be/go/keep on about sth** (*infml*) talk in a boring way about sth **it isn't on** (*infml*) used to say that sth is unacceptable **on and off** ⇨ OFF[1] **on and on** without stopping

○━ **on**[2] /ɒn/ *prep* **1** in or into a position covering, touching or forming part of a surface: *a picture on the wall* **2** supported by sb/sth: *She was standing on one foot.* ◊ *Hang your coat on the hook.* **3** used to show a means of transport: *He came on the train.* **4** used to show a day or a date: *on Sunday* ◊ *on 1 May* **5** immediately after sth: *On arriving home I discovered they had gone.* **6** about sb/sth: *a lecture on Bach* **7** being carried by sb; in the possession of sb: *Have you got any money on you?* **8** used to show membership of a group: *be on the staff* **9** eating, drinking or taking sth regularly: *She lives on a diet of junk food.* ◊ *He's on antibiotics.* **10** used to show direction: *on the left/right* **11** at or near a place: *a town on the coast* **12** used to show the reason for sth: *On her advice I applied for the job.* **13** supported financially by sb: *live on a student grant* **14** by means of sth; using sth: *Most cars run on petrol.* ◊ *speak on the phone* **15** used to say who or what is affected by sth: *a tax on beer* ◊ *He's hard on his kids.* **16** used to describe an activity or state: *be on business/holiday* ◊ *be on fire* (= burning)

○━ **once** /wʌns/ *adv* **1** on one occasion only; one time: *I've only been there ~.* **2** at some time in the past: *She ~ lived in Zambia.* [IDM] **at once 1** immediately; without delay **2** at the same time: *Don't all speak at ~!* **once again | once more** one more time; another time **once and for all** now and for the last time **once in a blue moon** (*infml*) very rarely **(every)**

once in a while occasionally **once upon a time** used at the beginning of stories to mean 'a long time ago' ● **once** *conj* as soon as; when: *It's easy ~ you know how.*

oncoming /ˈɒnkʌmɪŋ/ *adj* coming towards you: *~ traffic*

0— **one**[1] /wʌn/ *number, det* **1** the number 1 **2** a certain: *~ day* **3** used for emphasis to mean 'the only one' or 'the most important one': *She is the ~ person I can trust.* **4** the same: *They all went off in ~ direction.* [IDM] **(be) at one** (with sb/sth) in complete agreement with sb/sth **for one** used to emphasize that sb does sth and that you believe other people do too: *I for ~ don't like it.* **one or two** a few **one up** (on sb) (*infml*) having an advantage over sb ■ **one-off** *n* [C], *adj* (thing) made or happening only once ■ **one-sided** *adj* **1** (of an argument, etc) not balanced **2** (esp in sport) with opposing players of unequal abilities ■ **one-parent family** *n* [C] family in which the children live with one parent rather than two ■ **one-time** *adj* former: *her ~-time best friend, Anna* ■ **one-to-one** (*US* **one-on-one**) *adj, adv* between two people only: *a ~-to-~ relationship* ■ **one-way** *adj, adv* (allowing movement) in one direction only: *a ~-way street*

0— **one**[2] /wʌn/ *pron* **1** used to avoid repeating a noun: *I forgot to bring a pen. Can you lend me ~? ◊ The small car is just as fast as the big ~.* **2** used when you are identifying the person or thing you are talking about: *Our house is the ~ with the red door.* **3** **~ of** person or thing belonging to a particular group: *He is not ~ of my customers.* **4** person of the type mentioned: *He wanted to be at home with his loved ~.* **5** (*fml*) used to mean 'people in general' or 'I' when the speaker is referring to him/herself: *O~ should never criticize if ~ is not sure of the facts.*

0— **one another** *pron* each other: *They don't like ~.*

onerous /ˈəʊnərəs/ *adj* (*fml*) needing effort; difficult

oneself /wʌnˈself/ *pron* (*fml*) **1** used as a reflexive when people in general cause an action and are also affected by an action: *wash ~* **2** used to emphasize one: *One could arrange it all ~.* [IDM] **(all) by oneself** **1** alone **2** without help

ongoing /ˈɒnɡəʊɪŋ/ *adj* continuing: *~ research*

0— **onion** /ˈʌnjən/ *n* [C, U] round vegetable with a strong smell and flavour, used in cooking

online /ˌɒnˈlaɪn/ *adj* controlled by or connected to a computer or to the Internet: *an ~ ticket booking system* ▸ **online** *adv*

onlooker /ˈɒnlʊkə(r)/ *n* [C] person who watches sth happening

0— **only** /ˈəʊnli/ *adj* **1** with no other(s) of the same group: *Jane was the ~ person able to do it.* **2** best: *He's the ~ person for the job.* ● **only** *adv* **1** nobody or nothing except: *I ~ saw Mary.* **2** in no other situation, place, etc: *Children are admitted ~ if accompanied by an adult.* [IDM] **only just 1** not long ago/before: *We've ~ just arrived.* **2** almost not: *We ~ just caught the train.* **only too...** very: *~ too pleased to help* ● **only** *conj* (*infml*) except that; but: *I'd love to come, ~ I have to work.*

onrush /ˈɒnrʌʃ/ *n* [sing] (*written*) strong movement forward

onset /ˈɒnset/ *n* [sing] beginning, esp of sth unpleasant

onshore /ˈɒnʃɔː(r)/ *adj, adv* towards the shore: *~ winds*

onslaught /ˈɒnslɔːt/ *n* [C] **~ (against/on)** (*written*) strong or violent attack on sb/sth

0— **onto** (*also* **on to**) /ˈɒntə; before vowels ˈɒntu/ *prep* to a position on: *climb ~ a horse* [IDM] **be onto sb 1** (*infml*) know about what sb has done wrong **2** be talking to sb, usu in order to ask or tell them sth **be onto sth** have information that could lead to discovering sth important

onus /ˈəʊnəs/ *n* [sing] (*fml*) responsibility: *The ~ is on you.*

onward /ˈɒnwəd/ *adj* (*fml*) continuing or moving forward: *an ~ flight* ▸ **onwards** (*US* **onward**) *adv*: *The pool is open from 7am ~s.*

ooze /uːz/ *v* **1** [I] (of thick liquids) come or flow out slowly **2** [I, T] show a particular characteristic strongly: *He ~d charm.* ● **ooze** *n* [U] soft liquid mud

opacity /əʊˈpæsəti/ *n* [U] (*tech*) fact of being difficult to see through or opaque

opal /ˈəʊpl/ *n* [C] white or almost clear precious stone

opaque /əʊˈpeɪk/ *adj* **1** (of glass, liquid, etc) not clear enough to see through **2** (of speech or writing) difficult to understand; not clear

0— **open**[1] /ˈəʊpən/ *adj* **1** not closed: *leave the door ~* **2** spread out; with the edges apart: *The flowers were all ~.* **3** not fastened: *an ~ shirt* **4** not enclosed: *~ fields* **5** with no cover or roof: *people working in the ~ air* (= not in a building) **6** ready for business: *Are the shops ~ yet?* **7** public; free to all: *an ~ championship* **8** **~ to** likely to suffer sth such as criticism, injury, etc: *He has laid himself wide ~ to political attack.* **9** honest; not keeping your feelings hidden **10** **~ to** (of a person) willing to listen and think about new ideas **11** outdoors: in the countryside **12** not yet finally decided: *leave the matter* ~ **[IDM] have/keep an open mind (about/on sth)** be willing to consider new ideas in the open air outside (a building, etc) **with open arms** with great affection or enthusiasm ● **open door** *n* [sing] **1** outdoors; in the countryside **2** not hidden or secret: *bring the truth out into the* ~ ◇ *a problem which is out in the* ~ ■ **open-air** *adj* taking place outside ■ **open-and-shut 'case** *n* [C] legal case that is easy to decide or solve ■ **open 'cheque** *n* [C] cheque that is not crossed and can be exchanged for cash ■ **open-'ended** *adj* without any limits or dates set in advance ■ **open-'handed** *adj* generous ▸ **openly** *adv* not secretly ■ **open-'minded** *adj* willing to consider new ideas ■ **openness** *n* [U] honesty ■ **open-'plan** *adj* with no dividing walls ■ **open-work** *n* [U] pattern with spaces between threads, etc

0— **open²** /'əʊpən/ *v* [I,T] (cause sth to) move so that it is no longer closed: *The door* ~*ed.* ◇ *Please* ~ *your mouth.* **2** [T] remove the lid, undo the fastening, etc of a container to see what is inside **3** [I,T] (cause sth to) spread out or unfold: *The parachute didn't* ~. ◇ ~ *a book* **4** [T] make it possible for people, cars, etc to pass through a place: ~ *a new road through the forest* **5** [I,T] (cause sth to) be ready for business: *When does the bank* ~? **6** [T] start sth: ~ *a bank account* **[IDM] open your/sb's eyes (to sth)** make you/sb realize the truth about sth **open fire** start shooting **[PV] open up** talk freely about your feelings or ideas **open sth up** (cause sth to) be available for development, business, etc: ~ *up possibilities*

0— **opener** /'əʊpnə(r)/ *n* [C] (usu in compounds) tool that is used to open things: *a tin-~er*

0— **opening** /'əʊpnɪŋ/ *n* **1** [C] space or hole that sb/sth can pass through **2** [usu sing] beginning **3** [sing] process of becoming or making sth open: *the* ~ *of the new library* **4** [C] job that is available ● **opening** *adj* first: *her* ~ *words*

opera /'ɒprə/ *n* [C] musical play in which most of the words are sung ▸ **operatic** /ˌɒpə'rætɪk/ *adj*

0— **operate** /'ɒpəreɪt/ *v* **1** [I] work in a particular way **2** [I,T] use or control a machine or make it work: ~ *machinery* **3** [I,T] do business; direct sth: *They plan to* ~ *out of a new office in Leeds.* **4** [I] perform a surgical operation on sb's body ● **operable** /'ɒpərəbl/ *adj* (of a medical condition) that can be treated by an operation ■ **operating theatre** *n* [C] room in a hospital used for medical operations

0— **operation** /ˌɒpə'reɪʃn/ *n* **1** [C] (*med*) process of cutting open a part of the body to remove a diseased or injured part **2** [C] organized activity: *a rescue* ~ **3** [C] business or company **4** [C,U] act performed by a machine, esp a computer **5** [U] working of parts of a machine or system: *the* ~ *of the controls* **6** [C, usu pl] military activity **[IDM] in operation** working or being used: *Temporary traffic controls are in* ~. **come into operation** start working or having an effect ▸ **operational** /-ʃənl/ *adj* (*fml*) **1** connected with the way a business, machine, etc works **2** ready for use

operative /'ɒpərətɪv/ *adj* ready to be used; in use: *The law becomes* ~ *immediately.* ● **operative** *n* [C] (*tech*) worker

operator /'ɒpəreɪtə(r)/ *n* [C] person who works sth, esp a telephone switchboard

operetta /ˌɒpə'retə/ *n* [C] short light musical comedy

0— **opinion** /ə'pɪnjən/ *n* **1** [C] your feelings or thoughts about sb/sth: *In my* ~, *the price is too high.* ◇ *his* ~ *of the new manager* **2** [C] beliefs or views of a group of people: *public* ~ **3** [C] professional advice: *a doctor's* ~ ▸ **opinionated** /-eɪtɪd/ *adj* having opinions that you are not willing to change

opium /'əʊpiəm/ *n* [U] drug made from poppy seeds

0— **opponent** /ə'pəʊnənt/ *n* [C] person who is against another in a fight, argument or game

opportune /'ɒpətjuːn/ *adj* (*fml*) **1** (of time) suitable for a purpose **2** (of an action) coming at the right time

opportunism /ˌɒpə'tjuːnɪzəm/ *n* [U] (*disapprov*) practice of using situations unfairly to gain advantage for yourself ▸ **opportunist** *n* [C]

0— **opportunity** /ˌɒpə'tjuːnəti/ *n* [C,U] (pl **-ies**) favourable time or chance to do sth

0— **oppose** /ə'pəʊz/ *v* [T] disagree strongly with sb, a plan, policy, etc ▸ **opposed** *adj* ~ **to** disagreeing strongly with sth: *He is* ~*ed to our plans.* **[IDM] as opposed to** (*written*) in contrast to

0— **opposite** /'ɒpəzɪt/ *adj* **1** facing the speaker; the house ~ (*to*) *mine* **2** as different as possible from sth: *in the* ~ *direction* ● **opposite** *prep, adv* on the other side of an area from sb/sth and usu facing them: ~ *the station* ◇ *the person sitting* ~ ● **opposite** *n* [C] person or thing that is as different as possible from sb/sth else ■ **your opposite 'number** *n* [C] person who does the same job as you in an organization

307

order

0‑➤ **opposition** /ˌɒpəˈzɪʃn/ n [U] **1** ~ (to) act of strongly disagreeing with sb/sth: *strong ~ to the new law* **2** (the opposition) [sing, with sing or pl verb] people you are competing against in business, a competition, etc **3** [sing, with sing or pl verb] (the Opposition) main political party that is opposed to the government: *the leader of the O~*

oppress /əˈpres/ v [T] **1** treat sb in a cruel and unfair way, esp by not giving them the same freedom, rights, etc as others **2** make sb only able to think about sad or worrying things: *~ed by the gloomy atmosphere* ▸ **oppression** /əˈpreʃn/ n [U] ▸ **oppressive** adj **1** treating people in a cruel and unfair way **2** hard to bear; uncomfortable: *~ive heat* ▸ **oppressor** n [C] cruel or unjust leader or ruler

opt /ɒpt/ v [T] ~ **for/against** choose to take or not to take a particular course of action: *~ for a career in music.* [PV] **opt out (of sth)** choose not to take part in sth

optic /ˈɒptɪk/ adj (tech) of the eye: *the ~ nerve* (= from the eye to the brain) ▸ **optical** /-kl/ adj of the sense of sight ■ **optical illusion** n [C] something that tricks your eyes and makes you think you see sth that is not there ▸ **optician** /ɒpˈtɪʃn/ n [C] person who makes or sells glasses and contact lenses

optimism /ˈɒptɪmɪzəm/ n [U] belief that good things will happen ▸ **optimist** /-mɪst/ n [C] ▸ **optimistic** /-ˈmɪstɪk/ adj

optimize (also -ise) /ˈɒptɪmaɪz/ v [T] make sth as good as it can be; use sth in the best possible way

optimum /ˈɒptɪməm/ adj most favourable; best: *the ~ price*

0‑➤ **option** /ˈɒpʃn/ n **1** [U] freedom to choose what you do **2** [C] something that you can choose to have or do **3** [C] right to buy or sell sth at some time in the future: *share ~s* (= right to buy shares in a company) **4** [C] (computing) one of the choices you can make when using a computer program ▸ **optional** /-ʃənl/ adj that you can choose to do or have if you want to

opulent /ˈɒpjələnt/ adj (fml) showing signs of great wealth ▸ **opulence** /-ləns/ n [U]

0‑➤ **or** /ɔː(r)/ conj **1** used to introduce an alternative: *Is it green or blue? ◇ Do you want tea, coffee or milk?* (also or else) if not; otherwise: *Turn the heat down or it'll burn.* **3** in other words: *It weighs one pound, or about 450 grams.* [IDM] **or else** (infml) (used as a threat) or something bad will happen: *Do it, or else I'll hit you!* **or so** about: *We stayed there an hour or so.*

oral /ˈɔːrəl/ adj **1** spoken, not written: *an ~ test* **2** of, by or for the mouth: *~ medicine* ● **oral** n [C] a spoken exam, esp in a foreign language ▸ **orally** adv

0‑➤ **orange** /ˈɒrɪndʒ/ n [C,U] round thick-skinned juicy reddish-yellow fruit ● **orange** adj bright reddish-yellow in colour

orang-utan /ɔːˌræŋuːˈtæn; əˈræŋutæn/ n [C] large ape with long arms and reddish hair

oration /ɔːˈreɪʃn/ n [C] (fml) formal public speech

orator /ˈɒrətə(r)/ n [C] (fml) person who makes formal public speeches ▸ **oratory** /ˈɒrətri/ n [U] art of skilful public speaking

orbit /ˈɔːbɪt/ n [C] **1** curved path of a planet or satellite round the earth, sun, etc **2** area of influence ● **orbit** v [I,T] move in an orbit round sth: *The earth takes a year to ~ the sun.* ▸ **orbital** /-l/ adj

orchard /ˈɔːtʃəd/ n [C] piece of land on which fruit trees are grown

orchestra /ˈɔːkɪstrə/ n [C, with sing or pl verb] group of musicians playing different musical instruments together ▸ **orchestral** /ɔːˈkestrəl/ adj ▸ **orchestrate** /-streɪt/ v [T] **1** arrange a piece of music to be played by an orchestra **2** organize a complicated plan very carefully or secretly ▸ **orchestration** /ˌɔːkɪˈstreɪʃn/ n [C,U]

orchid /ˈɔːkɪd/ n [C] plant with flowers of brilliant colours and unusual shapes

ordain /ɔːˈdeɪn/ v [T] **1** make sb a member of the clergy **2** (fml) (of God, the law, etc) order or command sth

ordeal /ɔːˈdiːl; ˈɔːdiːl/ n [C] difficult or unpleasant experience

0‑➤ **order**¹ /ˈɔːdə(r)/ n **1** [U] way in which people or things are arranged in relation to one another: *names in alphabetical ~ ◇ arranged in ~ of size* **2** [U] state of being carefully arranged: *It was time she put her life in ~.* **3** [U] state that exists when people obey laws, rules or authority: *The army was sent in to restore ~. ◇ The chairman called them to ~* (= ordered them to obey the rules of the meeting). **4** [C] command given by sb in authority **5** [C,U] request to supply goods: *Send the shop your ~ for books* **6** [C] goods supplied in response to a particular order: *Your ~ will arrive tomorrow.* **7** [C] formal written instruction for sb to be paid money **8** [C] (badge, etc worn by) group of people who are specially honoured: *~s and medals* [IDM] **in order** as it should be; valid: *Your passport is in ~.* **in order that** (fml) so

A B C D E F G H I J K L M N **O** P Q R S T U V W X Y Z

that sth can happen **in order to do sth** with the purpose of doing sth **of/in the order of** (*fml*) about: *It will cost in the ~ of £60.* **of the highest/first order** of the highest quality or degree **on order** but not yet supplied: *The machines are still on ~.* **out of order 1** (of a machine, etc) not working properly **2** not arranged correctly or neatly: *The papers are all out of ~.* **3** (*infml*) behaving in a way that is not acceptable or right: *You were well out of ~ taking it without asking.* **4** (*fml*) not allowed by the rules of a formal meeting: *His objection was ruled out of ~.* **be in/take (holy) orders** be/become a priest

0— **order²** /ˈɔːdə(r)/ v [T] ask sb to do sth: *He ~ed the soldiers to attack.* **2** [I,T] ask for goods or services to be supplied: *to ~ a dessert* **3** [T] (*fml*) organize or arrange sth [PV] **order sb about/around** keep telling sb what to do in an unkind way

orderly /ˈɔːdəli/ *adj* **1** carefully arranged; tidy **2** well behaved; peaceful ▸ **orderliness** *n* [U] ▸ **orderly** *n* [C] (*pl* **-ies**) hospital worker

ordinal /ˈɔːdɪnl/ (*also* **ordinal number**) *n* [C] number, eg *first, second* and *third*, showing order in a series

0— **ordinary** /ˈɔːdnri/ *adj* normal; usual [IDM] **out of the ordinary** unusual ▸ **ordinarily** /-rəli/ *adv*

ordination /ˌɔːdɪˈneɪʃn/ *n* [C, U] ceremony of making a person a member of the clergy

ore /ɔː(r)/ *n* [U,C] rock or earth from which metal can be extracted

0— **organ** /ˈɔːgən/ *n* [C] **1** part of the body that has a particular purpose: *the sense ~s* (= the eyes, ears, etc) **2** large musical instrument from which sounds are produced by air forced through pipes **3** (*fml*) official organization which has a special purpose: *the ~s of government* **4** (*fml*) newspaper, etc that supplies information about a particular group or organization ▸ **organist** *n* [C] person who plays the organ

organic /ɔːˈgænɪk/ *adj* **1** (of food, farming etc) produced without using chemicals **2** produced by or from living things **3** (*fml*) consisting of related parts ▸ **organically** /-kli/ *adv*

organism /ˈɔːgənɪzəm/ *n* [C] **1** (usu very small) living thing **2** (*fml*) system with parts dependent on each other

0— **organization** (*also* **-isation**) /ˌɔːgənaɪˈzeɪʃn/ *n* **1** [C] group of people who form a business, club,

etc to achieve a particular aim **2** [U] act of making arrangements or preparations for sth

0— **organize** (*also* **-ise**) /ˈɔːgənaɪz/ v [T] **1** make preparations for sth: *~ a party* **2** arrange sth into a particular structure or order: *~ your time*

orgasm /ˈɔːgæzəm/ *n* [C] point of feeling greatest sexual pleasure

orgy /ˈɔːdʒi/ *n* [C] (*pl* **-ies**) wild party with a lot of drinking and sexual activity

Orient /ˈɔːrient/ *n* [sing] (*lit*) (the Orient) the eastern part of the world, esp China and Japan ▸ **oriental** /ˌɔːriˈentl/ *adj* of or from the eastern part of the world

orient /ˈɔːrient/ (*GB also* **orientate** /ˈɔːrienteɪt/) v [T] **1** ~ (**to/towards**) (usu passive) direct sb/sth towards a particular purpose: *Our company is ~ed towards exports.* **2** ~ **yourself** find your position in relation to your surroundings ▸ **orientation** /ˌɔːriənˈteɪʃn/ *n* [U,C]

orifice /ˈɒrɪfɪs/ *n* [C] (*fml*) hole or opening, esp in the body

0— **origin** /ˈɒrɪdʒɪn/ *n* [C,U] (*also* **origins** [pl]) **1** starting point or cause of sth **2** person's social and family background: *people of Polish ~*

0— **original** /əˈrɪdʒənl/ *adj* **1** existing at the beginning of a period, process or activity: *Go back to your ~ plan.* **2** newly created; fresh: *~ designs* **3** able to produce new and interesting ideas: *an ~ thinker* **4** painted, written, etc by the artist rather than copied ● **original** *n* [C] the earliest form of sth, from which copies can be made ▸ **originality** /əˌrɪdʒəˈnæləti/ *n* [U] quality of being new and interesting ▸ **originally** /-nəli/ *adv* used to describe the situation that existed at the beginning of a period or activity, esp before sth was changed: *His shirt was ~ly white.*

originate /əˈrɪdʒɪneɪt/ v (*fml*) **1** [I] begin **2** [T] create sth new ▸ **originator** *n* [C]

ornament /ˈɔːnəmənt/ *n* (*fml*) **1** [C] object that is beautiful rather than useful **2** [U] use of objects, designs, etc as decoration ● **ornament** /-ment/ v [T] (*fml*) add decoration to sth ▸ **ornamental** /ˌɔːnəˈmentl/ *adj*

ornate /ɔːˈneɪt/ *adj* having a lot of decoration ▸ **ornately** *adv*

ornithology /ˌɔːnɪˈθɒlədʒi/ *n* [U] study of birds ▸ **ornithologist** *n* [C]

orphan /ˈɔːfn/ *n* [C] child whose parents are dead ● **orphan** v [T] (usu passive) make a child an orphan ▸ **orphanage** /ˈɔːfənɪdʒ/ *n* [C] home for children whose parents are dead

orthodox /ˈɔːθədɒks/ *adj* (having opinions that are) generally accepted or approved ▸ **orthodoxy** *n* [U,C] (*pl* **-ies**)

orthography /ɔːˈθɒɡrəfi/ n [U] (fml) system of spelling in a language

orthopaedics (US **-pedics**) /ˌɔːθəˈpiːdɪks/ n [U] branch of medicine that deals with problems and diseases of bones ▶ **orthopaedic** (US **-pedic**) adj

oscillate /ˈɒsɪleɪt/ v [I] (fml) **1 ~ (between A and B)** keep changing between extremes of feeling or opinion: Her mood ~d between elation and depression. **2** (physics) keep moving from one position to another and back again ▶ **oscillation** /ˌɒsɪˈleɪʃn/ n [U, C] (fml)

ostensible /ɒˈstensəbl/ adj given as a reason, etc though perhaps not the real one ▶ **ostensibly** /-əbli/ adv

ostentation /ˌɒstenˈteɪʃn/ n [U] (disapprov) show of wealth, importance, etc in order to impress people ▶ **ostentatious** /ˌɒstenˈteɪʃəs/ adj

osteopath /ˈɒstiəpæθ/ n [C] person whose job is treating some diseases and physical problems by pressing and moving the bones and muscles ▶ **osteopathy** /ˌɒstiˈɒpəθi/ n [U]

ostracize (also **-ise**) /ˈɒstrəsaɪz/ v [T] (fml) exclude sb from a social group; refuse to meet or talk to sb

ostrich /ˈɒstrɪtʃ/ n [C] very large African bird with a long neck and long legs, that cannot fly

0-w **other** /ˈʌðə(r)/ adj, pron **1** used to refer to a person or thing additional to that already mentioned: Tim, John and two ~ students were there. **2** (the, my, your, etc **other**) used to refer to the second of two people or things: Pull the cork out with your ~ hand. **3** used to refer to the remaining people or things in a group: I went swimming while the ~s played tennis. ◇ The ~ teachers are from Brunei. **4** (the **other**) used to refer to a place, direction, etc that is the opposite to where you are, going, etc: He works on the ~ side of town. [IDM] **other than** except: We're away in June, but ~ than that we'll be around all summer.

0-w **otherwise** /ˈʌðəwaɪz/ adv **1** used to state what the result would be if the situation were different: Shut the window, ~ it'll get too cold in here. **2** apart from that: The rent is high, but ~ the room is satisfactory. **3** in a different way to the way mentioned; differently

otter /ˈɒtə(r)/ n [C] fur-covered animal that lives in rivers and eats fish

ouch /aʊtʃ/ exclam used to express sudden pain: Ouch! That hurt!

0-w **ought to** /ˈɔːt tə; before vowels and finally ˈɔːt tu/ modal v (neg **ought not to** or **oughtn't to**) **1** used to say what is the right thing to do: You ~ to apologize. **2** used to say

what you advise or recommend: You ~ to see a doctor about that cough. **3** used to say what has probably happened or is probably true: She started early, so she ~ to be here by now.

ounce /aʊns/ n **1** (abbr **oz**) [C] unit of weight; one sixteenth of a pound, equal to 28.35 grams **2** [sing] ~ (**of**) (infml) very small amount of sth

0-w **our** /ɑː(r); ˈaʊə(r)/ det of or belonging to us: ~ house ◇ **ours** /ɑːz; ˈaʊəz/ pron the one(s) that belong to us: He's a friend of ~s.

0-w **ourselves** /ɑːˈselvz; aʊəˈselvz/ pron **1** (the reflexive form of **we**) used when you and others cause and are affected by an action: We hurt ~. **2** used to emphasize we or us: We saw the crash ~. [IDM] (**all**) **by ourselves 1** alone **2** without help

0-w **oust** /aʊst/ v [T] ~ (**from**) (written) force sb to leave a job, etc

0-w **out** /aʊt/ adv, prep **1** ~ (**of**) away from the inside of a place or thing: go ~ for some fresh air ◇ walk ~ of the room ◇ He opened the box and ~ jumped a frog. **2** ~ (**of**) (of people) not at home or at a place of work: I phoned her but she was ~. ◇ He's ~ of the office this morning. **3** ~ (**of**) away from the edge of a place: Do not lean ~ of the window. **4** ~ (**of**) a long or particular distance away from a place or from land: The boats were all ~ at sea. ◇ a mile ~ of Hull **5** ~ (**of**) used to show that sth/sb is removed from a place, job, etc: This detergent is good for getting stains ~. **6** ~ (**of**) used to show that sth comes from or is obtained from sth/sb: made ~ of wood ◇ Drink ~ of the bottle. **7** ~ (**of**) without: He's been ~ of work for months. **8** ~ **of** not or no longer in the state or condition mentioned: Stay ~ of trouble. **9** ~ (**of**) no longer involved in sth: He'll be ~ (= of prison) on bail in no time. **10** ~ **of** used to show the reason why sth is done: I asked ~ of curiosity. **11** ~ **of** from a particular number or set: in nine cases ~ of ten **12** (of the tide) away from the shore **13** available to everyone; known by everyone: The secret is ~. **14** clearly and loudly: shout ~ **15** (sport) (in cricket, baseball, etc) no longer batting **16** (sport) (of a ball) outside the line **17** not correct or exact; wrong: I'm ~ in my calculations. **18** not fashionable: Short skirts are ~. **19** (of fire, lights, etc) no longer burning **20** (GB, infml) on strike **21** to the end; completely: I'm tired ~. [IDM] **be out for sth/to do sth** be trying to get or do sth: I'm not ~ to change the world! ▪ **out-and-ʹout** adj complete

outboard /ˈaʊtbɔːd/ adj (tech) on, towards or near the outside of a ship or aircraft ● **outboard** ˈmotor n [C] engine that you can fix to the back of a small boat

outbreak /ˈaʊtbreɪk/ n [C] sudden start of sth unpleasant: *the ~ of war*

outbuilding /ˈaʊtbɪldɪŋ/ n [C] building separate from the main building

outburst /ˈaʊtbɜːst/ n [C] sudden strong expression, esp of anger

outcast /ˈaʊtkɑːst/ n [C] person sent away from home or society

outcome /ˈaʊtkʌm/ n [C] effect or result

outcrop /ˈaʊtkrɒp/ n [C] (geol) large mass of rock that sticks out of the ground

outcry /ˈaʊtkraɪ/ n [C] (pl -ies) strong public protest

outdated /ˌaʊtˈdeɪtɪd/ adj no longer useful because of being old-fashioned

outdo /ˌaʊtˈduː/ v (third pers sing pres tense **-does** /-ˈdʌz/ pt **-did** /-ˈdɪd/ pp **-done** /-ˈdʌn/) [T] (written) do more or better than sb else else: *Not to be outdone, she tried again.*

0—▪ **outdoor** /ˈaʊtdɔː(r)/ adj done or situated outside rather than in a building ▸ **outdoors** /ˌaʊtˈdɔːz/ adv outside, rather than in a building

0—▪ **outer** /ˈaʊtə(r)/ adj 1 on the outside of sth: *~ walls* 2 furthest from the inside or centre of sth: *the ~ suburbs* ▸ **outermost** adj furthest from the inside or centre ● **outer ˈspace** = SPACE(4)

outfit /ˈaʊtfɪt/ n [C] 1 clothing or equipment needed for a particular occasion or purpose 2 [with sing or pl verb] (infml) organization or group of people ▸ **outfitter** n [C] (old-fash) shop or shopkeeper selling clothes

outflank /ˌaʊtˈflæŋk/ v [T] go round the side of an enemy in order to attack them

outgoing /ˈaʊtɡəʊɪŋ/ adj 1 friendly 2 leaving: *the ~ president* ▸ **outgoings** n [pl] (GB) amount of money that a person or business has to spend regularly, eg every month

outgrow /ˌaʊtˈɡrəʊ/ v (pt **-grew** /-ˈɡruː/ pp **-grown** /-ˈɡrəʊn/) [T] 1 grow too big to be able to wear or fit into sth 2 stop doing sth or lose interest in sth as you grow older

outhouse /ˈaʊthaʊs/ n [C] small building next to the main building

outing /ˈaʊtɪŋ/ n [C] trip made for pleasure

outlandish /aʊtˈlændɪʃ/ adj (usu disapprov) strange or extremely unusual: *~ clothes* ▸ **outlandishly** adv

outlaw /ˈaʊtlɔː/ v [T] make sth no longer legal: *~ the sale of guns*

● **outlaw** n [C] (esp in the past) person who has broken the law and is hiding to avoid being caught

outlay /ˈaʊtleɪ/ n [C] amount of money spent in order to start a new project, etc

outlet /ˈaʊtlet/ n [C] 1 way of expressing or making good use of strong feelings or energy: *sport is a good ~ for aggression* 2 (business) shop that sells goods made by a particular company or of a particular type: *The business has 34 retail ~s.* 3 (esp US) shop that sells goods of a particular make at reduced prices 4 pipe or hole through which liquid or gas can flow out

0—▪ **outline** /ˈaʊtlaɪn/ n [C] 1 description of the main facts involved in sth: *an ~ of the plan* 2 line that goes round the edge of sth, showing its main shape ● **outline** v [T] 1 give a short general description of sth 2 show or mark the outer edge of sth

outlive /ˌaʊtˈlɪv/ v [T] live longer than sb: *~ your children*

outlook /ˈaʊtlʊk/ n [C] 1 person's attitude to life and the world 2 what seems likely to happen

outlying /ˈaʊtlaɪɪŋ/ adj far from a centre or city: *~ villages*

outmoded /ˌaʊtˈməʊdɪd/ adj (disapprov) no longer fashionable

outnumber /ˌaʊtˈnʌmbə(r)/ v [T] be greater in number than sb/sth

out of date → DATE[1]

outpatient /ˈaʊtpeɪʃnt/ n [C] person who goes to a hospital for treatment, but does not stay there

outpost /ˈaʊtpəʊst/ n [C] 1 small military observation post far from the main army 2 small town in a lonely part of a country

0—▪ **output** /ˈaʊtpʊt/ n [sing] 1 quantity of goods, etc produced 2 (computing) information, results, etc produced by a computer 3 power, energy, etc produced by a piece of equipment

outrage /ˈaʊtreɪdʒ/ n 1 [U] strong feeling of shock and anger 2 [C] act or event of great violence and cruelty that shocks people and makes them angry ● **outrage** v [T] make sb very shocked and angry ▸ **outrageous** /aʊtˈreɪdʒəs/ adj 1 very shocking and unacceptable 2 very unusual ▸ **outrageously** adv

outright /ˈaʊtraɪt/ adv 1 openly and honestly: *I told him ~ what I thought.* 2 clearly and completely: *He won ~.* 3 not gradually; immediately: *be killed ~* ● **outright** /ˈaʊtraɪt/ adj complete and total: *an ~ ban/rejection*

outset /ˈaʊtset/ n [IDM] **at/from the outset (of sth)** at/from the beginning of sth

outshine /ˌaʊtˈʃaɪn/ v (pt, pp **outshone** /-ˈʃɒn/) [T] (written) be much better than sb/sth: *She ~s all her friends at games.*

○━ **outside** /ˌaʊtˈsaɪd/ *n* [C, usu sing] outer side or surface of sth: *the ~ of the house* ● **outside** /ˈaʊtsaɪd/ *adj* **1** of, on or facing the outer side **2** not included in or connected with your group, organization, etc: *~ help* **3** used to say that sth is very unlikely: *an ~ chance* ● **outside** /ˌaʊtˈsaɪd/ (*esp US* **outside of**) *prep* **1** on or to a place on the outside of sth: *~ the bank* **2** away from or not in a particular place: *We live in a village just ~ Bath.* **3** not part of sth: *my areas of responsibility* **4** (outside of) apart from: *no interests ~ of his work* ● **outside** /ˌaʊtˈsaɪd/ *adv* on or to the outside of sth; in the open air: *Please wait ~.*

outsider /ˌaʊtˈsaɪdə(r)/ *n* [C] **1** person who is not a member of or not accepted by a group of people **2** horse, team, etc that is not expected to win a competition

outsize /ˈaʊtsaɪz/ *adj* (esp of clothing) larger than the standard sizes

outskirts /ˈaʊtskɜːts/ *n* [pl] outer areas of a city or town

outsmart /ˌaʊtˈsmɑːt/ *v* [T] gain an advantage over sb by being cleverer than them

outsource /ˈaʊtsɔːs/ *v* [I,T] (business) arrange for sb outside a company to do work or provide goods for that company ▶ **outsourcing** *n* [U]

○━ **outspoken** /aʊtˈspəʊkən/ *adj* saying exactly what you think, even if this shocks people

○━ **outstanding** /aʊtˈstændɪŋ/ *adj* **1** extremely good; excellent **2** very obvious or important **3** (of payment, work, problems, etc) not yet paid, done or solved ▶ **outstandingly** *adv* **1** used to emphasize the good quality of sth **2** extremely well

outstay /ˌaʊtˈsteɪ/ *v* [IDM] **outstay your welcome** stay somewhere as a guest longer than you are wanted

outstrip /ˌaʊtˈstrɪp/ *v* (-pp-) [T] be or become better, larger, more important, etc than sb/sth: *Demand is ~ping production.*

outward /ˈaʊtwəd/ *adj* **1** of or on the outside: *an ~ appearance* **2** going away from a particular place: *the ~ journey* ▶ **outwardly** *adv* on the surface; in appearance ▶ **outwards** (*also* **outward**) *adv* towards the outside; away from the centre or a particular point

outweigh /ˌaʊtˈweɪ/ *v* [T] be greater or more important than sth

outwit /ˌaʊtˈwɪt/ *v* (-tt-) [T] defeat or gain an advantage over sb by doing sth clever

outwork /ˈaʊtwɜːk/ *n* [U] (GB,

business) work that is done by people at home ▶ **outworker** *n* [C]

oval /ˈəʊvl/ *n* [C], *adj* (shape) like an egg

ovary /ˈəʊvəri/ *n* [C] (pl -ies) either of the two organs in women and female animals that produce eggs

ovation /əʊˈveɪʃn/ *n* [C] enthusiastic clapping by an audience as a sign of their approval

○━ **oven** /ˈʌvn/ *n* [C] enclosed box-like space in which food is cooked

○━ **over¹** /ˈəʊvə(r)/ *prep* **1** resting on the surface of and partly or completely covering sb/sth: *She put a blanket ~ the sleeping child.* **2** in or to a position higher than but not touching sb/sth: *They held an umbrella ~ her.* **3** from one side of sth to the other: *a bridge ~ the river* **4** on the far or opposite side of sth: *I live ~ the road.* **5** so as to cross sth and be on the other side: *jump ~ the wall* **6** in or on all or most parts of sth: *travel all ~ the world ◇ books all ~ the floor* **7** more than a particular time, amount, etc: *wait for ~ an hour* **8** used to show that sb has control or authority: *rule ~ an empire* **9** during sth: *discuss it ~ lunch* **10** because of sth: *an argument ~ money* **11** using sth; by means of sth: *I tell her ~ the phone.* [IDM] **over and above** in addition to sth **over sb's head** → HEAD¹

○━ **over²** /ˈəʊvə(r)/ *adv* **1** outwards and downwards from an upright position: *knock a vase ~* **2** from one side to another side: *She turned ~ onto her front.* **3** across a road, open space, etc: *I went ~* (= across the room) *and asked his name.* **4** so as to cover sb/sth completely: *paint sth ~* **5** above; more: *children of 14 and ~* **6** remaining; not used or needed: *the food left ~* **7** again: (*esp US*) *do it ~* **8** ended: *The meeting is ~.* [IDM] **(all) over again** once more from the beginning **over and over (again)** many times

over³ /ˈəʊvə(r)/ *n* [C] (in cricket) series of six balls bowled in succession by the same bowler

over- *prefix* **1** more than usual; too much: *~work* **2** across; above: *~cast ◇ ~hang*

○━ **overall** /ˈəʊvərɔːl/ *adj, adv* including or considering everything: *the ~ cost* ● **overall** /ˈəʊvərɔːl/ *n* **1** [C] (GB) loose coat worn over other clothes to protect them from dirt, etc **2** (overalls) [pl] (GB) one-piece garment covering the body and legs, worn over other clothing by workers doing dirty work

overawe /ˌəʊvərˈɔː/ *v* [T] (usu passive) impress sb so much that they feel nervous or frightened

A B C D E F G H I J K L M N **O** P Q R S T U V W X Y Z

overbalance /ˌəʊvəˈbæləns/ v [I] fall over

overbearing /ˌəʊvəˈbeərɪŋ/ adj (disapprov) forcing others to do what you want ▸ **overbearingly** adv

overboard /ˈəʊvəbɔːd/ adv over the side of a ship into the water

overcast /ˌəʊvəˈkɑːst/ adj (of the sky) covered with cloud

overcharge /ˌəʊvəˈtʃɑːdʒ/ v [I, T] charge sb too high a price for sth

overcoat /ˈəʊvəkəʊt/ n [C] thick warm coat

0━ **overcome** /ˌəʊvəˈkʌm/ v (pt **-came** /-ˈkeɪm/ pp **-come** /-ˈkʌm/) [T] **1** succeed in dealing with a problem that has prevented you from achieving sth: *She overcame injury to win the race.* **2** (written) defeat sb **3** be strongly affected by sth: *be ~ with grief*

overcrowded /ˌəʊvəˈkraʊdɪd/ adj with too many people in a place ▸ **overcrowding** /-dɪŋ/ n [U]

overdo /ˌəʊvəˈduː/ v (third pers sing pres tense **-does** /-ˈdʌz/ ; pt **-did** /-ˈdɪd/ ; pp **-done** /-ˈdʌn/) [T] do sth too much; exaggerate sth [IDM] **overdo it/things** work, etc too hard or for too long

overdose /ˈəʊvədəʊs/ n [C, usu sing] too much of a drug taken at one time

overdraft /ˈəʊvədrɑːft/ n [C] amount of money by which a bank account is overdrawn

overdrawn /ˌəʊvəˈdrɔːn/ adj **1** (of a person) having taken money out of your bank account than you have in it **2** (of an account) with more money taken out than was paid in or left in

overdrive /ˈəʊvədraɪv/ n [C, U] extra high gear in a vehicle, used when driving at high speeds

overdue /ˌəʊvəˈdjuː/ adj not paid, arrived, returned, etc by the right or expected time

overflow /ˌəʊvəˈfləʊ/ v [I, T] **1** flow over the edges of sth: *The river was ~ed it banks.* **2** spread beyond the limits of a room, etc ● **overflow** /ˈəʊvəfləʊ/ [U, sing] **1** number of people or things that do not fit into the space available **2** action of liquid flowing out of a container that is already full; liquid that flows out

overgrown /ˌəʊvəˈɡrəʊn/ adj covered with plants that are growing thickly in an uncontrolled way

overhang /ˌəʊvəˈhæŋ/ v (pt, pp **-hung** /-ˈhʌŋ/) [I, T] stick out over and above sth else ● **overhang** /ˈəʊvəhæŋ/ n [C, usu sing] part of sth that overhangs

overhaul /ˌəʊvəˈhɔːl/ v [T] examine a machine, system, etc thoroughly

and repair any faults: *~ the engine* ● **overhaul** /ˈəʊvəhɔːl/ n [C] thorough examination of a machine or system

overhead /ˈəʊvəhed/ adj above your head; raised above the ground: *~ wires* ● **overhead** /ˌəʊvəˈhed/ adv above your head; in the sky: *aircraft flying~*

overheads /ˈəʊvəhedz/ n [pl] regular business expenses, eg rent, salaries and insurance

overhear /ˌəʊvəˈhɪə(r)/ v (pt, pp **-heard** /-ˈhɜːd/) [T] hear what sb is saying without them knowing

overjoyed /ˌəʊvəˈdʒɔɪd/ adj extremely happy

overland /ˈəʊvəlænd/ adj, adv across the land; by land, not by sea or air

overlap /ˌəʊvəˈlæp/ v (-pp-) [I, T] partly cover sth by going over its edge: (fig) *These two subjects ~.* ● **overlap** /ˈəʊvəlæp/ n [C, U] part that overlaps

overleaf /ˌəʊvəˈliːf/ adv (written) on the other side of the page

overload /ˌəʊvəˈləʊd/ v [T] **1** put too great a weight on sth **2** put too great a demand on a computer, an electrical system, etc, causing it to fail

overlook /ˌəʊvəˈlʊk/ v [T] **1** fail to see or notice sth **2** see sth wrong or bad but decide to ignore it: *~ a fault* **3** have a view of a place from above

overmanned /ˌəʊvəˈmænd/ adj (of a company, office, etc) having more workers than are needed ▸ **overmanning** n [U]

overnight /ˌəʊvəˈnaɪt/ adv **1** during or for the night: *stay ~* **2** (infml) suddenly or quickly: *become a success ~* ● **overnight** /ˈəʊvənaɪt/ adj an ~ bag

overpass /ˈəʊvəpɑːs/ n [C] (US) = FLYOVER

overpower /ˌəʊvəˈpaʊə(r)/ v [T] defeat sb by using greater strength ▸ **overpowering** adj very strong or powerful: *an ~ing smell*

overrate /ˌəʊvəˈreɪt/ v [T] have too high an opinion of sb/sth

overreach /ˌəʊvəˈriːtʃ/ v ~ **yourself** fail by trying to achieve more than is possible

overreact /ˌəʊvəriˈækt/ v [I] react too strongly, esp to sth unpleasant

override /ˌəʊvəˈraɪd/ v (pt **-rode** /-ˈrəʊd/ pp **-ridden** /-ˈrɪdn/) [T] **1** use your authority to reject sb's decision, order, etc **2** be more important than sth ▸ **overriding** adj more important than anything else

overrule /ˌəʊvəˈruːl/ v [T] decide against sth already decided by using your higher authority

overrun /ˌəʊvəˈrʌn/ v (pt **-ran** /-ˈræn/ pp **-run**) [T] spread over and occupy an area quickly: *a house ~ by*

insects 2 [I, T] take more time or money than was intended: *The meeting might* ~.

overseas /ˌəʊvəˈsiːz/ *adj, adv* to, of or in foreign countries, esp those separated from your country by the sea

oversee /ˌəʊvəˈsiː/ *v* (pt **-saw** /-ˈsɔː/ pp **-seen** /-ˈsiːn/) [T] watch over sb's work to see that it is done properly ▶ **overseer** /ˈəʊvəsɪə(r)/ *n* [C]

overshadow /ˌəʊvəˈʃædəʊ/ *v* [T] **1** make sb/sth seem less important or successful **2** throw a shadow over sth

overshoot /ˌəʊvəˈʃuːt/ *v* (pt, pp **-shot** /-ˈʃɒt/) [T] go further than a place where you intended to stop or turn

oversight /ˈəʊvəsaɪt/ *n* [C, U] careless failure to notice sth

oversleep /ˌəʊvəˈsliːp/ *v* (pt, pp **-slept** /-ˈslept/) [I] sleep longer than you intended

overspill /ˈəʊvəspɪl/ *n* [U, sing] (*GB*) people who move out of a crowded city to an area where there is more space

overstep /ˌəʊvəˈstep/ *v* (**-pp-**) [T] go beyond the normal accepted limits

overt /əʊˈvɜːt/ *adj* (*fml*) done or shown openly ▶ **overtly** *adv*

overtake /ˌəʊvəˈteɪk/ *v* (pt **-took** /-ˈtʊk/ pp **-taken** /-ˈteɪkən/) [I, T] **1** go past a moving vehicle or person ahead of you **2** [T] (of unpleasant events) affect sb suddenly and unexpectedly

overthrow /ˌəʊvəˈθrəʊ/ *v* (pt **-threw** /-ˈθruː/ pp **-thrown** /-ˈθrəʊn/) [T] remove a government, ruler, etc from power ▶ **overthrow** /ˈəʊvəθrəʊ/ *n* [C, usu sing]

overtime /ˈəʊvətaɪm/ *n* [U] time spent at work in addition to your usual working hours

overtone /ˈəʊvətəʊn/ *n* [C, usu pl] something suggested but not expressed openly

overture /ˈəʊvətjʊə(r)/ *n* [C] musical introduction to an opera or ballet [IDM] **make overtures (to sb)** try to begin a friendly or business relationship with sb

overturn /ˌəʊvəˈtɜːn/ *v* **1** [I, T] (cause sth to) turn upside down or on its side **2** [T] officially decide that a legal decision, etc is not correct, and make it no longer valid

overview /ˈəʊvəvjuː/ *n* [C] general description of sth

overweight /ˌəʊvəˈweɪt/ *adj* (of people) too heavy or fat

overwhelm /ˌəʊvəˈwelm/ *v* [T] **1** (usu passive) have such a strong emotional effect on sb that it is difficult for them to resist: *~ed by the beauty of the landscape* **2** defeat sb completely

---

overwork /ˌəʊvəˈwɜːk/ *v* [I, T] (cause sb to) work too hard ▶ **overwork** *n* [U]

overwrite /ˌəʊvəˈraɪt/ *v* (pt **-wrote** /-ˈrəʊt/ pp **-written** /-ˈrɪtn/) [T] (*computing*) replace information on the screen or in a file by putting new information over it

overwrought /ˌəʊvəˈrɔːt/ *adj* nervous, anxious and upset

ovulate /ˈɒvjuleɪt/ *v* [I] (of a woman or female animal) produce an egg (ovum) from an ovary ▶ **ovulation** /ˌɒvjuˈleɪʃn/ *n* [U]

ovum /ˈəʊvəm/ *n* [C] (pl **ova** /ˈəʊvə/) (*biol*) female cell that can develop into a new individual

ow /aʊ/ *exclam* used to express sudden pain: *Ow! That hurt!*

0▬ **owe** /əʊ/ *v* [T] **1** have to return money that you have borrowed or pay for sth you have already received: *I ~ him £10*. **2** ~ to feel that you ought to sb for sth or give them sth, esp because you are grateful to them: *I ~ a debt of gratitude to all my family.*

owing /ˈəʊɪŋ/ *adj* still to be paid ■ **owing to** *prep* because of

owl /aʊl/ *n* [C] bird of prey with large round eyes, that hunts at night

own¹ /əʊn/ *adj, pron* belonging to the person mentioned: *his ~ room* ◊ *a room of his ~* [IDM] **get your own back (on sb)** (*infml*) harm sb because they have harmed you **(all) on your own 1** alone **2** without help

0▬ **own²** /əʊn/ *v* [T] possess sth: *~ a house* [PV] **own up (to sth/to doing sth)** (*infml*) admit that you are to blame for sth ▶ **owner** *n* [C] ■ **ownership** *n* [U]

ox /ɒks/ *n* [C] (pl **-en** /ˈɒksn/) fully grown castrated bull

oxygen /ˈɒksɪdʒən/ *n* [U] gas without colour, taste or smell, present in the air and necessary for life

oyster /ˈɔɪstə(r)/ *n* [C] large flat shellfish ■ **oystercatcher** *n* [C] wading sea bird

oz *abbr* ounce(s)

ozone /ˈəʊzəʊn/ *n* [U] **1** (*chem*) poisonous form of oxygen **2** (*GB, infml*) fresh air at the seaside ■ **ozone-friendly** *adj* not containing substances that will damage the ozone layer ■ **ozone layer** *n* [sing] layer of ozone high above the earth's surface that helps to protect the earth from the sun's harmful rays

Pp

P, p /piː/ n [C, U] (pl **P's, p's** /piːz/) the sixteenth letter of the English alphabet

p abbr **1** (infml) penny; pence **2** (pl **pp**) page

PA /ˌpiː ˈeɪ/ n [C] (esp GB) personal assistant; person who works as a secretary for just one person

p.a. abbr per year (from Latin 'per annum')

0—̄ pace /peɪs/ n **1** [sing, U] speed at which sb/sth walks, runs or moves **2** [C] (length of a) single step in walking or running **3** [U] rate of progress ● **pace** v **1** [I,T] walk up and down in a small area many times **2** [T] set the speed at which sth happens or develops [PV] **pace sth off/out** measure sth by taking regular strides across it ■ **pacemaker** n [C] electronic device placed inside a person's body to help their heart beat regularly

pacifism /ˈpæsɪfɪzəm/ n [U] belief that all war is wrong ▸ **pacifist** /-ɪst/ n [C]

pacify /ˈpæsɪfaɪ/ v (pt, pp **-ied**) make sb who is angry calm ▸ **pacification** /ˌpæsɪfɪˈkeɪʃn/ n [U] ▸ **pacifier** n [C] (US) = DUMMY(2)

0—̄ pack[1] /pæk/ v **1** [T] put clothes, etc into a bag for a trip away from home: a suitcase ~ **2** [T] put sth into a container so that it can be transported, etc sold: I carefully ~ed the gifts. **3** [T] cover or protect sth with material, to prevent damage: plates ~ed in newspaper **4** [I,T] ~ (into) fill a space with a lot of people or things: Crowds ~ed (into) the theatre. [PV] **pack sth in** (infml) stop doing sth **pack sb off (to...)** (infml) send sb away **pack up** (infml, esp GB) (of a machine) stop working properly **pack (sth) up** **1** put your possessions into a bag, etc and leave **2** (GB, infml) stop doing sth, esp a job ● **packed** adj full of people

0—̄ pack[2] /pæk/ n [C] **1** (esp US) container that holds a number of things or an amount of sth, ready to be sold: a ~ of gum/cigarettes **2** number of things wrapped or tied together, esp for carrying **3** group of wild animals: a ~ of wolves **4** group of people or things: a ~ of fools/lies **5** complete set of playing cards

0—̄ package /ˈpækɪdʒ/ n [C] **1** (esp US) = PARCEL **2** (US) (contents of a) box, bag, etc, in which things are wrapped or packed **3** (also **'package deal**) set of items or ideas that must be bought or accepted

together: a benefits ~ **4** (also **'software package**) (computing) set of related programs, sold and used as a single unit: The system came with a database software ~. ● **package** v [T] put sth into a box, bag, etc to be sold or transported ■ **'package holiday/tour** n [C] holiday arranged by a company at a fixed price which includes the cost of travel, hotels, etc

0—̄ packet /ˈpækɪt/ n [C] **1** (GB) small container in which goods are packed for selling: a ~ of cigarettes/ crisps **2** [sing] (infml) large amount of money **3** (computing) piece of information that forms part of a message sent through a computer network

packing /ˈpækɪŋ/ n [U] **1** process of packing goods **2** material used for packing delicate objects, to protect them

pact /pækt/ n [C] agreement

pad /pæd/ n [C] **1** thick piece of soft material, used eg for absorbing liquid, protecting or cleaning sth: shin/shoulder ~s **2** number of sheets of paper fastened together: a sketch ~ **3** soft fleshy part under the foot of a dog, fox, etc **4** flat surface from which spacecraft are launched or helicopters take off ● **pad** v (**-dd-**) **1** [T] put a layer of soft material in or on sth to protect it or change its shape: a ~ded jacket **2** [I] walk with quiet steps [PV] **pad sth out** make sth, eg an article, longer by adding unnecessary parts ▸ **padding** n [U] **1** soft material used to pad sth **2** unnecessary material in a book, speech, etc

paddle /ˈpædl/ n [C] **1** short pole with a wide flat part at one or both ends, used to move a small boat through water **2** (a paddle) [sing] act of walking in shallow water with bare feet: Let's go for a ~. ● **paddle** v **1** [I,T] move a boat with a paddle **2** [I] walk with bare feet in shallow water

paddock /ˈpædək/ n [C] small field where horses are kept

paddy /ˈpædi/ n [C] (pl **-ies**) (also **'paddy field**) field in which rice is grown

padlock /ˈpædlɒk/ n [C] lock with a curved bar that forms a loop when closed ● **padlock** v [T] fasten a gate, bicycle, etc with a padlock

paediatrics /ˌpiːdiˈætrɪks/ n [U] branch of medicine concerned with children and their diseases ▸ **paediatrician** /ˌpiːdiəˈtrɪʃn/ n [C] doctor who specializes in paediatrics

pagan /ˈpeɪɡən/ n [C] person who holds religious beliefs that are not part of any of the world's main religions ▸ **pagan** adj: ~ festivals ▸ **paganism** n [U]

page /peɪdʒ/ n [C] **1** (abbr **p**) one side or both sides of a sheet of paper in a book, etc **2** section of data or information that can be shown on a computer screen at any one time **3** (GB) = PAGEBOY **4** (in the Middle Ages) boy who worked for a knight while training to be a knight himself

pageant /ˈpædʒənt/ n [C] **1** public entertainment in which historical events are acted **2** (US) competition for young women in which their beauty, personal qualities, etc are judged: a beauty ~ ▸ **pageantry** n [U] impressive and colourful events and ceremonies

pageboy /ˈpeɪdʒbɔɪ/ n [C] (GB) small boy who helps or follows a bride during a marriage ceremony

pagoda /pəˈɡəʊdə/ n [C] religious building in India or in E Asia, in the form of a tower with several levels

paid pt, pp of PAY¹

pail /peɪl/ n [C] (US) = BUCKET

pain /peɪn/ n **1** [C, U, C] feelings of suffering that you have in your body when you are hurt or ill: a ~ in her leg ◇ He was in a lot of ~. **2** [U, C] mental or emotional suffering: the ~ of separation **3** [C] (infml) very annoying person or thing **IDM be a pain in the neck** (infml) very annoying person or thing ● **pain** v [T] (fml) cause sb pain ▸ **pained** adj unhappy and upset: a ~ed look ▸ **painful** adj causing pain ▸ **painless** adj not causing pain

pains /peɪnz/ n [pl] **IDM take (great)/be at pains to do sth** make a great effort to do sth ■ **painstaking** adj very careful; thorough

paint /peɪnt/ n **1** [U] coloured liquid that is put on a surface **2** (paints) [pl] set of tubes of paint: oil ~s ● **paint** v **1** [T] cover a surface or an object with paint: ~ the door **2** [I,T] make a picture or design using paints: ~ flowers **3** [T] give a particular impression of sb/sth: The article ~s them as a gang of criminals. **IDM paint the town red** (infml) go out and enjoy yourself ▸ **painting** n **1** [C] picture that has been painted **2** [U] action or skill of painting ■ **paintwork** n [U] painted surface

painter /ˈpeɪntə(r)/ n [C] **1** person whose job is painting walls, buildings, etc: He's a ~ and decorator. **2** artist who paints pictures

pair /peə(r)/ n [C] **1** two things of the same kind: a ~ of shoes **2** [C] object made from two parts joined together: a ~ of trousers/scissors **3** [C, with sing or pl verb] two people closely connected, eg a married couple ● **pair** v [I,T] ~ (off) (cause people or things to) form groups of two

pajamas (US) = PYJAMAS

pal /pæl/ n [C] (infml) friend

palace /ˈpæləs/ n [C] large splendid house, esp the official home of a king, queen or president

palaeontology (esp US **paleo-**) /ˌpæliɒnˈtɒlədʒi; esp US ˌpeɪ-/ n [U] study of fossils ▸ **palaeontologist** (esp US **paleo-**) /-dʒɪst/ n [C]

palatable /ˈpælətəbl/ adj **1** having a pleasant taste **2** ~ (to) pleasant or acceptable to sb: The truth is not always very ~.

palate /ˈpælət/ n [C] **1** top part of the inside of the mouth **2** [usu sing] sense of taste

palatial /pəˈleɪʃl/ adj like a palace; very large and impressive: a ~ hotel

palaver /pəˈlɑːvə(r)/ n [U, sing] (infml) unnecessary trouble; fuss

pale /peɪl/ adj (~r, ~st) **1** (of a person or their face) having little colour; whiter than usual because of illness, shock, etc **2** light in colour; not bright: ~ blue eyes ● **pale** v [I] **1** become pale **2** seem less important when compared with sth else: Compared to your problems mine ~ into insignificance. ● **pale** n [IDM **beyond the pale** considered unacceptable ▸ **paleness** n [U]

paleo- (esp US) = PALAEO-

palette /ˈpælət/ n [C] board on which an artist mixes colours

paling /ˈpeɪlɪŋ/ n [C] fence made of pointed pieces of wood

pall /pɔːl/ v [I] ~ (on) become less interesting to sb over time because they have done or seen it too much ● **pall** n [C] **1** [usu sing] thick dark cloud of sth: a ~ of smoke **2** cloth spread over a coffin ■ **pall-bearer** n [C] person who walks beside or helps to carry the coffin at a funeral

pallet /ˈpælət/ n [C] large flat frame for carrying heavy goods, lifted by a forklift truck

pallid /ˈpælɪd/ adj pale; looking ill ▸ **pallor** /ˈpælə(r)/ n [U]

palm /pɑːm/ n [C] **1** inner surface of the hand **2** (also **palm tree**) tree growing in warm climates, with no branches and a mass of large leaves at the top ● **palm** v [PV **palm sth off (on/onto sb)** (infml) get rid of sth unwanted by persuading sb to accept it: She's always ~ing off the worst jobs on me.

palmist /ˈpɑːmɪst/ n [C] person who claims to be able to tell sb's future by looking at the palm of their hand ▸ **palmistry** /-ri/ n [U] skill of a palmist

palmtop /ˈpɑːmtɒp/ n [C] small computer that can be held in the palm of one hand

palpable /ˈpælpəbl/ adj (fml) clear to the mind; obvious ▸ **palpably** /-əbli/ adv

palpitate /ˈpælpɪteɪt/ v [I] (of the heart) beat very fast and/or irregularly, esp because of fear or excitement ▸ **palpitations** /ˌpælpɪˈteɪʃnz/ n [pl] physical condition in which your heart beats rapidly and irregularly

paltry /ˈpɔːltri/ adj (-ier, -iest) very small; worthless

pamper /ˈpæmpə(r)/ v [T] take care of sb very well

pamphlet /ˈpæmflət/ n [C] thin book with a paper cover

0-ᴡ **pan** /pæn/ n [C] **1** metal container with a handle, used for cooking: a frying ~ **2** amount contained in a pan: a ~ of boiling water **3** (GB) the bowl of a toilet ● **pan** v (-nn-) **1** [T] (infml) strongly criticize sth, eg a play or a film **2** [I,T] turn a television or video camera to follow a moving object or to film a wide area **3** [I] ~ (**for**) wash small stones in a dish in order to look for gold [PV] **pan out** (infml) (of events) develop in a particular way: How did things ~ out?

panacea /ˌpænəˈsiːə/ n [C] something that will solve all the problems of a situation

panache /pəˈnæʃ/ n [U] confident stylish manner

pancake /ˈpænkeɪk/ n [C] thin flat round cake of batter fried on both sides

pancreas /ˈpæŋkriəs/ n [C] part of the body that produces substances which help in the digestion of food

panda /ˈpændə/ n [C] large bear-like black and white animal from China

pandemonium /ˌpændəˈməʊniəm/ n [U] wild and noisy disorder

pander /ˈpændə(r)/ v [PV] **pander to sth/sb** (disapprov) try to satisfy a weak or bad desire or sb who has one: ~ to sb's whims/wishes

pane /peɪn/ n [C] sheet of glass in a window

0-ᴡ **panel** /ˈpænl/ n [C] **1** square or rectangular piece of wood, glass or metal that forms part of a door or wall **2** group of speakers who discuss topics of interest, esp on a radio or television programme **3** flat board in a vehicle or piece of machinery for controls and instruments: a control/display ~ ● **panel** v (-ll- US -l-) [T] cover or decorate a surface with panels: The walls were ~led in oak. ▸ **panelling** (US -l-) n [U] series of panels on a wall, etc

pang /pæŋ/ n [C] sudden strong feeling of pain, guilt, etc

panic /ˈpænɪk/ n [U,C] sudden uncontrollable feeling of great fear ● **panic** v (-ck-) [I,T] (cause sb to) feel panic ▸ **panicky** adj (infml) feeling

or showing panic ■ **panic-stricken** adj filled with panic

pannier /ˈpæniə(r)/ n [C] one of a pair of bags on either side of the back wheel of a bicycle or motorcycle

panorama /ˌpænəˈrɑːmə/ n [C] view of a wide area ▸ **panoramic** /-ˈræmɪk/ adj

pansy /ˈpænzi/ n [C] (pl -**ies**) small garden plant with bright flowers

pant /pænt/ v [I] breathe with short quick breaths ● **pant** n [C, usu pl] short quick breath

panther /ˈpænθə(r)/ n [C] **1** black leopard **2** (US) = PUMA

panties /ˈpæntiz/ n (esp US) = KNICKERS

pantomime /ˈpæntəmaɪm/ n [C,U] funny play for children, based on a fairy tale, with music and dancing, esp at Christmas

pantry /ˈpæntri/ n [C] (pl -**ies**) cupboard or small room in a house where food is kept

0-ᴡ **pants** /pænts/ n [pl] **1** (GB) men's underpants; women's knickers **2** (esp US) = trousers

papacy /ˈpeɪpəsi/ n (the papacy) [sing] position or authority of the Pope ▸ **papal** /ˈpeɪpl/ adj of the Pope

0-ᴡ **paper** /ˈpeɪpə(r)/ n **1** [U] substance in thin sheets used for writing, printing or drawing on or wrapping things in **2** [C] newspaper **3** (papers) [pl] official documents **4** [C] (GB) set of exam questions **5** [C] academic article **6** [C] (US) piece of written work done by a student ● **paper** v [T] cover the walls of a room with wallpaper ■ **paperback** n [C,U] book with a thick paper cover ■ **paper boy**, **paper girl** n [C] boy or girl who delivers newspapers to people's houses ■ **paper clip** n [C] piece of bent wire, used to hold sheets of paper together ■ **paperweight** n [C] small heavy object put on top of loose papers to keep them in place ■ **paperwork** n [U] writing letters and reports, filling in forms, etc

paprika /ˈpæprɪkə/ n [U] red powder of a sweet pepper, used in cooking

par /pɑː(r)/ n [U,C] **1** (in golf) average number of hits necessary to hit the ball into a hole or complete the course **2** (also **par value**) (business) value that a share in a company has originally [IDM] **below/under par** (infml) less well, good, etc than usual **on a par with sb/sth** equal in quality, importance, etc to sb/sth

parable /ˈpærəbl/ n [C] (esp in the Bible) simple story that teaches a moral lesson

parachute /ˈpærəʃuːt/ n [C] umbrella-shaped device by which sb may fall slowly and safely to the

ground from an aircraft
● **parachute** v [I,T] jump or drop sth from an aircraft using a parachute ▶ **parachutist** n [C] person who jumps from a plane using a parachute

parade /pə'reɪd/ n [C] **1** procession **2** formal gathering of soldiers in order to march in front of people ● **parade** v **1** [I] walk somewhere in a formal group of people, to celebrate or protest about sth **2** [I] walk around in a way that makes people notice you **3** [I,T] show sb/ sth in public so that people can see them/it: ~ *your wealth* **4** [I,T] (cause soldiers to) gather together to march in front of people

paradise /'pærədaɪs/ n **1** (often **Paradise**) [U] heaven **2** [U,C] place or state of perfect happiness

paradox /'pærədɒks/ n [C] **1** statement which seems to contain two opposite facts but is or may be true ▶ **paradoxical** /ˌpærə'dɒksɪkl/ *adj* ▶ **paradoxically** /-kli/ *adv*

paraffin /'pærəfɪn/ n [U] oil obtained from petroleum, used as a fuel

paragliding /'pærəɡlaɪdɪŋ/ n [U] sport in which you jump from a high place, wearing something like a parachute, and are carried along by the wind

paragon /'pærəɡən/ n [C] ~ (of) person who is a perfect example of a quality: *She is a ~ of virtue.*

paragraph /'pærəɡrɑːf/ n [C] division of a piece of writing, started on a new line

parakeet /'pærəkiːt/ n [C] small long-tailed parrot

0- **parallel** /'pærəlel/ *adj* **1** (of lines) always at the same distance from each other **2** very similar ● **parallel** n [C,U] person or thing that is exactly similar to another [C, usu pl] comparison or similarity: *draw a ~ between A and B* ● **parallel** v [T] be equal or similar to sth

parallelogram /ˌpærə'leləɡræm/ n [C] (geom) four-sided figure with its opposite sides parallel to each other

paralyse (US -**lyze**) /'pærəlaɪz/ v [T] **1** make sb unable to feel or move all or part of their body **2** prevent sth from functioning normally: *The city was ~d by the railway strike.*

paralysis /pə'ræləsɪs/ n [U] **1** loss of feeling in or control of part of the body **2** total inability to move, act or function, etc ▶ **paralytic** /ˌpærə'lɪtɪk/ *adj* **1** (GB, infml) very drunk **2** (fml) suffering from paralysis ▶ **paralytic** n [C] person suffering from paralysis

parameter /pə'ræmɪtə(r)/ n [C, usu pl] something that decides or limits how sth can be done

paramilitary /ˌpærə'mɪlətri/ *adj* (of

a military force) organized like but not part of an official army

paramount /'pærəmaʊnt/ *adj* (fml) more important than anything else

paranoia /ˌpærə'nɔɪə/ n [U] mental illness in which sb believes that other people want to harm them ▶ **paranoid** /'pærənɔɪd/ n [C], *adj* (person) suffering from paranoia

parapet /'pærəpɪt; -pet/ n [C] low protective wall at the edge of a roof, bridge, etc

paraphernalia /ˌpærəfə'neɪliə/ n [U] many small articles of different kinds

paraphrase /'pærəfreɪz/ v [T] express what sb has said or written using different words ▶ **paraphrase** n [C]

parascending /'pærəsendɪŋ/ n [U] sport in which you wear a parachute and are pulled along behind a boat so that you rise up into the air

parasite /'pærəsaɪt/ n [C] **1** animal or plant that lives on and gets food from another **2** person supported by others, giving nothing in return ▶ **parasitic** /ˌpærə'sɪtɪk/ *adj*

parasol /'pærəsɒl/ n [C] umbrella used for giving shade from the sun

paratroops /'pærətruːps/ n [pl] soldiers trained to drop from an aircraft using parachutes ▶ **paratrooper** /-pə(r)/ n [C]

parcel /'pɑːsl/ n [C] (esp GB) something wrapped up for carrying and sending by post ● **parcel** v (-**ll-** US -**l-**) [T] ~ (**up**) wrap sth up and make it into a parcel [PV] **parcel sth out** divide sth into parts

parched /pɑːtʃt/ *adj* **1** very dry, because of a lack of water **2** (infml) very thirsty

parchment /'pɑːtʃmənt/ n [U] **1** material made from animal skin for writing on **2** thick yellowish type of paper

pardon /'pɑːdn/ n **1** [C] official decision not to punish sb for a crime **2** [U] (fml) ~ (**for**) act of forgiving sb for sth: *He asked her ~ for deceiving her.* ● **pardon** v [T] **1** officially allow sb to leave prison and/or avoid punishment **2** forgive sb for sth ● **pardon** *exclam* (esp US ˌpardon 'me) used to ask sb to repeat sth because you did not hear or understand it ▶ **pardonable** *adj* that can be forgiven

pare /peə(r)/ v [T] **1** ~ (**off/away**) cut away the outer part, edge or skin of sth **2** ~ (**back/down**) gradually reduce the size or amount of sth

0- **parent** /'peərənt/ n [C] father or mother ▶ **parental** /pə'rentl/ *adj*

parenthesis /pə'renθəsɪs/ n [C] (pl **-eses** /-əsiːz/) **1** additional sentence or phrase within another sentence, separated off using brackets, commas or dashes **2** [usu pl] (*US*) or (*fml*) = BRACKET(1)

parish /ˈpærɪʃ/ n [C] area that has its own church and priest
▸ **parishioner** /pəˈrɪʃənə(r)/ n [C] person living in a parish, esp one who goes to church regularly

parity /ˈpærəti/ n [U] (*fml*) state of being equal

0━ **park** /pɑːk/ n [C] public garden or area of ground for public use ● **park** v [I,T] stop and leave a vehicle in a place for a time ■ **parking meter** n [C] machine beside the road that you put money into when you park your car near it ■ **parkland** n [U] open area of grass and trees

parkour (also **Parkour**) /pɑːˈkʊə(r)/ n [U] activity which involves running, jumping and climbing from one point to another as fast as possible

0━ **parliament** /ˈpɑːləmənt/ n [C, with sing or pl form] group of people that make the laws of a country ▸ **parliamentary** /ˌpɑːləˈmentri/ adj

parlour (*US* -lor) /ˈpɑːlə(r)/ n [C] **1** (*old-fash*) sitting room **2** (in compounds) (*esp US*) shop: *a beauty/an ice-cream ~*

parochial /pəˈrəʊkiəl/ adj **1** (*fml*) of a church parish **2** (*disapprov*) only concerned with small issues that happen in your local area
▸ **parochially** adv

parody /ˈpærədi/ n (pl -ies) [C,U] piece of writing intended to amuse by imitating the style of sb else **2** [C] (*disapprov*) something that is such a bad example of sth that it seems ridiculous: *The trial was a ~ of justice.* ● **parody** v (pt, pp -ied) [T] copy the style of sb/sth in order to make people laugh

parole /pəˈrəʊl/ n [U] permission given to a prisoner to leave prison before the end of their sentence on condition that they behave well: *She was released on ~.* ● **parole** v [T]

paroxysm /ˈpærəksɪzəm/ n [C] (*written*) sudden attack or burst of anger, pain, etc

parquet /ˈpɑːkeɪ/ n [U] floor covering made of flat pieces of wood fixed together

parrot /ˈpærət/ n [C] tropical bird with a curved beak and bright feathers ● **parrot** v [T] (*disapprov*) repeat what sb else has said without thinking about what it means

parry /ˈpæri/ v (pt, pp -ied) [T] turn aside or avoid a blow, question, etc
▸ **parry** n [C]

parsimonious /ˌpɑːsɪˈməʊniəs/ adj (*fml, disapprov*) extremely unwilling to spend money

parsley /ˈpɑːsli/ n [U] small plant with curly leaves used for flavouring and decorating food

parsnip /ˈpɑːsnɪp/ n [C,U] long pale yellow root vegetable

parson /ˈpɑːsn/ n [C] parish priest
▸ **parsonage** /-ɪdʒ/ n [C] parson's house

0━ **part1** /pɑːt/ n [C] **1** ~ (of) some but not all of something: *We spent (a) ~ of our holiday in Paris.* **2** piece of a machine: *spare ~s* **3** area of a country, town, etc **4** section of a book, television series, etc: *The final ~ will be shown next Sunday evening.* **5** person's share in an activity; actor's role in a play, film, etc **6** (*music*) melody for a particular voice or instrument **7** (*US*) = PARTING [IDM] **for the most part** mostly; usually **for my, his, their, etc part** speaking for myself, etc **in part** to some extent **on sb's part** made or done by sb **take part (in sth)** be involved in sth **take sb's part** (*GB*) support sb, eg in an argument ● **part** adv (often in compounds) consisting of two things; partly: *She's ~ French, ~ English.* ▸ **partly** adv to some extent; not completely ■ **part of speech** n [C] (*gram*) one of the classes of words, eg noun or verb ■ **part-time** adj, adv working only a part of the day or week

part2 /pɑːt/ v [I,T] (*fml*) separate; leave sb: *The clouds ~ed.* ◊ *He has ~ed from his wife.* **2** [T] prevent sb from being with sb else: *I hate being ~ed from the children.* **3** [T] divide your hair into two sections with a comb, creating a line on the top of your head [IDM] **part company (with/from sb) 1** leave sb; end a relationship with sb **2** disagree with sb about sth [PV] **part with sth** give sth to sb, esp sth you would prefer to keep: *Read the contract before ~ing with any money.* ▸ **parting** n [U,C] act of leaving a person or place **2** (*US* **part**) line where the hair is parted: *a side ~*

partake /pɑːˈteɪk/ v (pt -took /-ˈtʊk/ pp -taken /-ˈteɪkən/) [I] (*fml*) ~ of eat or drink sth

partial /ˈpɑːʃl/ adj **1** not complete or whole: *only a ~ success* **2** ~ to (*old-fash*) liking sth very much **3** ~ (towards) (*disapprov*) unfairly showing favour to one person or side ▸ **partiality** /ˌpɑːʃiˈæləti/ n **1** [U] (*disapprov*) unfair support of one person or side **2** [C, usu sing] fondness for sth ▸ **partially** /ˈpɑːʃəli/ adv not completely; partly

participate /pɑːˈtɪsɪpeɪt/ v [I] ~ (in) take part or become involved in an activity ▸ **participant** /-pənt/ n [C] person who participates in sth ▸ **participation** /pɑːˌtɪsɪˈpeɪʃn/ n [U]

participle /ˈpɑːtɪsɪpl/ n [C] (*gram*)

form of a verb: 'Sinking' and 'sunk' are the present and past ~s of 'sink'.

particle /ˈpɑːtɪkl/ n [C] **1** very small piece of sth: dust~s **2** (gram) adverb or preposition that can combine with a verb to make a phrasal verb

0-**particular** /pəˈtɪkjələ(r)/ adj **1** relating to one individual person or thing and not others: in this ~ case **2** greater than usual; special: of ~ interest **3** ~ (about) very definite about what you like and careful about what you choose [IDM] **in particular** especially: I like these flowers in ~. ● **particular** n [C, usu pl] (fml) fact or detail, esp one that is written down: The nurse asked me for my ~s (= my name, address, etc).
▸ **particularly** adv especially

partisan /ˌpɑːtɪˈzæn/ n [C] **1** strong supporter of a particular leader, group, etc **2** member of an unofficial armed force in a country occupied by enemy soldiers ● **partisan** adj showing too much support for one person, cause, etc

partition /pɑːˈtɪʃn/ n **1** [C] thin wall that separates one part of a room from another **2** [U] division of a country into two or more countries: the ~ of Germany after the war ● **partition** v [T] divide sth into two parts [PV] **partition sth off** separate sth with a partition

0-**partner** /ˈpɑːtnə(r)/ n [C] **1** person you are married to or have a sexual relationship with **2** one of the people who owns a business and shares the profits, etc **3** person you are doing an activity with, eg dancing or playing a game ● **partner** v [T] be sb's partner in a dance, game, etc ▸ **partnership** n **1** [U] state of being a partner in business: be in/go into ~ship **2** [C, U] (state of having a) relationship between two people, organizations, etc

partook pt of PARTAKE

partridge /ˈpɑːtrɪdʒ/ n [C] bird with brown feathers, a round body and a short tail that is hunted for food or sport

0-**party** /ˈpɑːti/ n [C] (pl -ies) (also Party) [with sing or pl verb] group of people with the same political aims: the Labour P~ **2** social occasion, often in sb's home: a birthday ~ **3** [with sing or pl verb] group of people doing sth together, eg travelling: a ~ of tourists **4** (fml) one of the people or groups involved in a legal agreement or dispute: the innocent ~ [IDM] **be (a) party to sth** (fml) be involved in or support sth ■ **party line** n [sing] official opinions of a political party

pashmina /pæʃˈmiːnə/ n [C] long piece of cloth made of fine soft wool from a type of goat and worn by a woman around the shoulders

0-**pass**¹ /pɑːs/ v [I, T] move past or to the other side of sb/sth: ~ the house **2** [I, T] (cause sb/sth to) go or move in the direction mentioned: He ~ed through Oxford on his way to London. **3** [T] give sth to sb: Please ~ me the butter. **4** [I, T] (sport) kick, hit, etc the ball, etc to a player on your own side **5** [I] ~ from; to/into change from one state or condition to another **6** [I] (of time) go by **7** [T] spend time **8** [I] come to an end: wait for the storm to ~ **9** [I, T] reach the required standard in an exam **10** [T] test sb and decide they have reached the required standard **11** [T] accept a proposal, law, etc by voting **12** [I] be allowed: I don't like it but I'll let it ~. **13** [T] say or state sth, esp officially: ~ sentence on a prisoner [IDM] **pass the time of day (with sb)** greet sb and have a short conversation with them **pass water** (fml) urinate [PV] **pass away** die **pass by (sb/sth)** go past **pass sth by** happen without affecting sb/sth **pass for/as sb/sth** be accepted as sb/sth: He could ~ for a Frenchman. **pass off** (GB) (of an event) take place and be completed **pass sb/yourself/sth off as sb/sth** pretend that sth is sth they are not **pass on** = PASS AWAY **pass sth on (to sb)** give sth to sb else **pass out** faint **pass sb over** not choose sb for a job **pass over sth** ignore or avoid sth **pass sth up** (infml) not take advantage of sth ■ **ˌpasser-ˈby** n [C] (pl passers-by) person who is going past sb/sth by chance

pass² /pɑːs/ n [C] **1** (esp GB) successful result in an exam **2** official document or ticket showing that you have the right to enter a building, travel on a train, etc **3** (sport) act of kicking, hitting, etc the ball to a player on your own side **4** road or way over or through mountains [IDM] **make a pass at sb** (infml) try to start a sexual relationship with sb ■ **password** n [C] secret word or phrase that you need to know to be allowed to enter a place, use a computer, etc

passable /ˈpɑːsəbl/ adj **1** fairly good, but not excellent **2** (of a road, etc) open to traffic ▸ **passably** /-əbli/ adv

0-**passage** /ˈpæsɪdʒ/ n **1** [C] (also **passageway** /ˈpæsɪdʒweɪ/) narrow way through sth; corridor: underground ~s **2** [C] short section from a book, piece of music, etc **3** [sing] (lit) process of time passing: ~ of time **4** [C] journey by ship **5** [C, usu sing] way through sth: clear a ~ through the crowd

0-**passenger** /ˈpæsɪndʒə(r)/ n [C] person travelling in a bus, train, plane, etc other than the crew

0━ **passing** /ˈpɑːsɪŋ/ *adj* lasting only for a short time and then disappearing: *a ~ thought* ● **passing** *n* [U] **1** process of time going by **2** (*fml*) fact of sth ending or of sb dying **3** ~ of act of making sth law [IDM] **in passing** done or said while giving your attention to sth else

passion /ˈpæʃn/ *n* **1** [C,U] strong feeling of love, hate, anger, etc **2** [U] ~ **(for)** very strong sexual love **3** [sing] ~ **for** strong liking for sth: *a ~ for books* ▶ **passionate** /ˈpæʃənət/ *adj* showing passion ▶ **passionately** *adv*

passive /ˈpæsɪv/ *adj* **1** accepting what happens or what people do without trying to change anything or oppose them **2** (*gram*) of the verb form which shows that the subject is affected by the action of the verb, as in 'She was bitten by a dog' ● **passive** (*also* ˌpassive ˈvoice) *n* [sing] (*gram*) form of a verb used when the subject is affected by the action of the verb ▶ **passively** *adv* ▶ **passiveness** /-nəs/ *n* [U]

Passover /ˈpɑːsəʊvə(r)/ *n* [U] Jewish religious festival

0━ **passport** /ˈpɑːspɔːt/ *n* [C] **1** official document to be carried by a traveller abroad **2** ~ **to** thing that makes sth possible: *a ~ to success*

0━ **past**[1] /pɑːst/ *adj* **1** gone by in time; of the time before the present: *in ~ years* **2** (*gram*) (of a verb form) showing a state or action in the past: *a ~ participle* ● **past** *n* **1** (the past) [sing] (things that happened in) the time before the present **2** [C] person's past life or career **3** (the past) (*also* ˌpast ˈtense) (*gram*) form of a verb used to describe actions in the past: *The ~ (tense) of 'take' is 'took'.* ■ ˌpast ˈperfect (*also* ˌpast ˈperfect ˈtense) *n* [sing] (*gram*) verb form which expresses an action completed before a particular time in the past, formed in English with *had* and a past participle

0━ **past**[2] /pɑːst/ *prep* **1** later than sth; after: *~ midnight* **2** on or to the other side of sth: *She walked ~ the church.* **3** above or further than a particular point or stage: *I'm ~ caring* (= I no longer care) *what happens.* [IDM] **past it** (GB, *infml*) too old to do what you used to be able to do ● **past** *adv* **1** from one side of sth to the other **2** used to describe time passing: *A week went ~ and nothing happened.*

pasta /ˈpæstə/ *n* [U] Italian food made from flour, eggs and water and cut into various shapes

paste /peɪst/ *n* **1** [U] soft wet mixture, usu made of powder and a liquid: *Mix the flour and water to a* smooth ~. **2** [C] (esp in compounds) mixture of meat or fish for spreading on bread: *fish ~* **3** [U] type of glue used for sticking paper to things: *wallpaper ~* ● **paste** *v* **1** [T] stick sth to sth else using glue or paste **2** [I,T] (*computing*) copy or move text into a document from another place: *It's quicker to cut and ~ than to retype it.*

pastel /ˈpæstl/ *n* **1** [U] soft coloured chalk, used for drawing pictures **2** (pastels) [pl] small sticks of chalk **3** [C] picture drawn with pastels **4** [C] pale delicate colour

pasteurize (*also* -ise) /ˈpɑːstʃəraɪz/ *v* [T] heat a liquid, esp milk, in order to remove bacteria: *~d milk*

pastille /ˈpæstəl/ *n* [C] small sweet that you suck, esp one containing medicine for a sore throat

pastime /ˈpɑːstaɪm/ *n* [C] something that you enjoy doing when you are not working

pastor /ˈpɑːstə(r)/ *n* [C] Christian clergyman in charge of a church

pastoral /ˈpɑːstərəl/ *adj* **1** of the work of a priest or teacher, giving advice on personal matters **2** of country life or the countryside

pastry /ˈpeɪstri/ *n* (*pl* -ies) **1** [U] mixture of flour, fat and water baked in an oven and used for pies, etc **2** [C] small cake made using pastry

pasture /ˈpɑːstʃə(r)/ *n* [C,U] (area of) land covered with grass for cattle

pasty[1] /ˈpeɪsti/ *adj* (-ier, -iest) pale; looking unhealthy: *a ~ white skin*

pasty[2] /ˈpæsti/ *n* (*pl* -ies) small pie containing meat and vegetables

pat /pæt/ *v* (-tt-) [T] touch sb/sth gently several times with your open hand, esp to show affection ● **pat** *n* [C] **1** gentle tap with your open hand **2** small soft lump of butter ● **pat** *adj* (*disapprov*) too quick, easy or simple: *a ~ answer*

patch /pætʃ/ *n* [C] **1** small area of sth that is different from the area around it: *a bald ~ on the top of his head* **2** small piece of material put over a hole or damaged place **3** piece of material worn to protect an injured eye **4** area of land, esp one used for growing vegetables or fruit: *a vegetable ~* [IDM] **be not a patch on sb/sth** (*infml*) be much less good, attractive, etc than sb/sth else ● **patch** *v* [T] cover a hole, esp in clothes, with a piece of material [PV] **patch sth/sb up 1** repair sth quickly **2** treat sb's injuries, esp quickly **3** settle a quarrel ■ **ˈpatchwork** *n* **1** [U] material in which small pieces of cloth are sewn together **2** [sing] thing that is made up of many different pieces or parts ▶ **patchy** *adj* (-ier, -iest) uneven in quality

pâté /ˈpæteɪ/ *n* [U] soft paste of meat or fish

patent /ˈpeɪtnt; ˈpætnt/ n [C,U] official right to be the only person to make or sell a new invention ● **patent** /ˈpeɪtnt/ adj **1** connected with a patent: ~ *laws* **2** (of a product) made or sold by a particular company: ~ *medicines* **3** (*fml*) used to emphasize that sth bad is very clear and obvious ● **patent** /ˈpeɪtnt; ˈpætnt/ v [T] obtain a patent for an invention ■ **patent 'leather** n [U] leather with a hard shiny surface ▶ **patently** adv (*fml*) without doubt; clearly

paternal /pəˈtɜːnl/ adj **1** of or like a father **2** related through the father's side of the family: *my ~ grandfather* ▶ **paternally** adv

paternity /pəˈtɜːnəti/ n [U] (*written*) fact of being the father of a child

0‑w **path** /pɑːθ/ n [C] **1** (also **'pathway**) way or track made for or by people walking **2** line along which sth moves

pathetic /pəˈθetɪk/ adj **1** making you feel pity or sadness: *a ~ sight* **2** (*infml, disapprov*) weak, useless and unsuccessful: *a ~ attempt* ▶ **pathetically** /-kli/ adv

pathology /pəˈθɒlədʒi/ n [U] study of diseases ▶ **pathological** /ˌpæθəˈlɒdʒɪkl/ adj **1** not reasonable or sensible; impossible to control: *pathological fear* **2** of or caused by disease or illness **3** (*tech*) of pathology ▶ **pathologist** n [C] expert in pathology

pathos /ˈpeɪθɒs/ n [U] (in writing, speech and plays) power to produce feelings of pity or sadness

0‑w **patience** /ˈpeɪʃns/ n [U] **1** ~ (**with**) ability to stay calm and accept delay or annoyance without complaining **2** ability to spend a lot of time doing sth difficult that needs a lot of attention **3** (*GB*) card game for one player

0‑w **patient** /ˈpeɪʃnt/ n [C] person receiving medical treatment ● **patient** adj having or showing patience ▶ **patiently** adv

patio /ˈpætiəʊ/ n [C] (pl **‑s**) paved area next to a house where people can sit, eat, etc outdoors

patriarch /ˈpeɪtriɑːk/ n [C] **1** male head of a family or tribe **2** (Patriarch) title of a most senior priest in the Orthodox or Roman Catholic Church ▶ **patriarchal** /ˌpeɪtriˈɑːkl/ adj

patriot /ˈpeɪtriət; ˈpæt-/ n [C] person who loves their country and is ready to defend it ▶ **patriotic** /ˌpeɪtriˈɒtɪk; ˌpæt-/ adj ▶ **patriotism** n [U] love of your country and willingness to defend it

patrol /pəˈtrəʊl/ v (-ll-) [I,T] go round an area or building at regular times to protect or guard it ● **patrol** n **1** [U] act of patrolling a place: *soldiers*

321

paw

on ~ **2** [C] group of soldiers, vehicles, etc that patrol an area

patron /ˈpeɪtrən/ n [C] **1** person who gives money and support to an artist, a writer or an organization: *a wealthy ~ of the arts* **2** (*fml*) regular customer at a shop, restaurant, etc ▶ **patronage** /ˈpætrənɪdʒ/ n [U] **1** support, esp financial, given by a patron: *her ~age of the arts* **2** system by which sb gives help or a job to sb in return for their support ■ **patron 'saint** n [C] Christian saint believed to protect a particular group of people or place

patronize (also **-ise**) /ˈpætrənaɪz/ v [T] **1** (*disapprov*) treat sb in a way that shows you think sb is not very intelligent, experienced, etc **2** (*fml*) be a regular customer of a shop, restaurant, etc ▶ **patronizing** (also **-ising**) adj

patter /ˈpætə(r)/ n **1** [sing] sound made by sth repeatedly hitting a surface quickly and lightly: *the ~ of rain on the roof* **2** [U, sing] fast talk, eg of entertainers or salespeople ● **patter** v [I] make quick light sounds

0‑w **pattern** /ˈpætn/ n [C] **1** regular way in which sth happens or is done: *the usual ~ of events* **2** regular arrangement of lines, shapes, etc, as a decorative design **3** design or instructions from which sth is to be made: *a knitting ~* ● **pattern** v [PV] **pattern sth on sth** (*US* **pattern sth after sth**) (usu passive) use sth as a model for sth; copy sth: *a new approach ~ed on Japanese ideas* ▶ **patterned** adj ~ (**with**) decorated with a pattern

paucity /ˈpɔːsəti/ n [sing] (*fml*) small amount; lack of sth

paunch /pɔːntʃ/ n [C] fat stomach

pauper /ˈpɔːpə(r)/ n [C] (in the past) very poor person

0‑w **pause** /pɔːz/ n [C] short stop or interval in action or speech: *a ~ in the conversation* ● **pause** v [I] stop talking or doing sth for a short time

pave /peɪv/ v [T] cover a path, etc with flat stones or bricks [IDM] **pave the way (for sb/sth)** create a situation in which sb will be able to do sth or sth can happen ■ **'paving stone** n [C] flat piece of stone used for making pavements

pavement /ˈpeɪvmənt/ n [C] paved path at the side of a road for people to walk on

pavilion /pəˈvɪliən/ n [C] **1** temporary building used at public events and exhibitions **2** (*GB*) building next to a sports ground, used by players and spectators

paw /pɔː/ n [C] animal's foot with claws ● **paw** v ~ (**at**) **1** [I,T] (of an animal) touch or scratch sth repeatedly with a paw **2** [T] touch sb in a rough sexual way

pawn /pɔːn/ *n* **1** least valuable chess piece **2** person whose actions are controlled by more powerful people ● **pawn** *v* [T] leave an object with a pawnbroker in exchange for money lent ■ **pawnbroker** *n* [C] person who lends money in exchange for articles left with them, which they can sell if you do not pay the money back

0━ **pay¹** /peɪ/ *v* (pt, pp **paid** /peɪd/) **1** [I,T] give money to sb for goods, services, etc: ~ *him for the bread* **2** [T] give sb money that you owe them: ~ *the rent* **3** [I,T] produce some advantage or profit for sb: *It's hard to make farming ~.* ◇ *It ~s to be honest.* **4** [I] suffer or be punished for your beliefs or actions: *You'll ~ for that remark!* **5** [T] used with some nouns to show that you are giving or doing the thing mentioned: ~ *attention to sth* ◇ ~ *a visit* [IDM] **pay lip service to sth ➙** LIP **pay through the nose (for sth)** (*infml*) pay too much money for sth **pay your respects (to sb)** (*fml*) visit sb or send greetings as a sign of respect for them: *Many came to ~ their last respects (= by attending sb's funeral).* **pay your way** pay for everything yourself without having to rely on anyone else's money **put paid to sth** destroy or ruin sth [PV] **pay sb back (sth)** return money to sb that you have borrowed from them **pay sb back (for sth)** punish sb for making you or sb else suffer **pay off** (*infml*) be successful **pay sb off 1** pay sb what they have earned and tell them to leave their job **2** (*infml*) give money to sb to prevent them from doing sth **pay sth off** finish paying money owed for sth **pay sth out 1** pay a large sum of money for sth **2** pass a length of rope through your hands **pay up** pay in full the money that is owed ■ **paid-up** *adj* having paid all the money necessary to be a member of a club or an organization ● **payable** *adj* that must or can be paid ▶ **payee** /ˌpeɪˈiː/ *n* [C] (*tech*) person that money or a cheque is paid to ▶ **payer** *n* [C] person who pays or has to pay for sth ▶ **payment** *n* **1** [U] act of paying sb/sth or being paid **2** [C] amount of money (to be) paid ■ **pay-as-you-go** *adj* connected with a system of paying for a service just before you use it rather than paying for it later: ~*-as-you-go mobile phones* ■ **pay-off** *n* [C] (*infml*) **1** payment of money to sb so that they will not cause you any trouble **2** advantage or reward from sth you have done

■ **pay-per-view** *n* [U] system in which you pay a sum of money to watch a particular television programme

0━ **pay²** /peɪ/ *n* [U] money paid for regular work ■ **payload** *n* [C] (*tech*) amount carried in an aircraft or other vehicle ■ **pay packet** *n* [C] envelope containing your wages; amount that sb earns ■ **payphone** *n* [C] coin-operated public telephone ■ **payroll** *n* [C] list of people employed and paid by a company

PC /ˌpiːˈsiː/ *abbr* **1** personal computer; a small computer designed for one person to use at work or home: *software for* ~ **2** (*GB*) Police Constable; police officer of the lowest rank **3** = POLITICALLY CORRECT (POLITICAL)

PDA /ˌpiː diː ˈeɪ/ *abbr* personal digital assistant; hand-held computer for storing information and accessing the Internet

PE /ˌpiː ˈiː/ *n* [U] physical education; sport and exercise taught in schools

pea /piː/ *n* [C] round green seed eaten as a vegetable

0━ **peace** /piːs/ *n* **1** [U, sing] situation or a period of time in which there is no war or violence in a country: ~ *talks* ◇ *A UN force has been sent in to keep the* ~ (= prevent people from fighting). **2** [U] state of being calm or quiet: *He just wants to be left in* ~. ◇ *I need some* ~ *and quiet.* **3** [U] state of living in friendship with sb without arguing [IDM] **make (your) peace with sth** end an argument with sb, esp by apologizing ▶ **peaceable** *adj* not involving or causing argument or violence ▶ **peaceful** *adj* **1** not involving war, violence or argument **2** quiet and calm ▶ **peacefully** *adv* ▶ **peacefulness** *n* [U] ■ **peacekeeping** *adj* intended to help stop people fighting and prevent war or violence in a place where this is likely: ~*keeping operations* ■ **peacetime** *n* [U] time when a country is not at war

peach /piːtʃ/ *n* [C] round juicy fruit with soft yellowish-red skin and a rough stone inside ● **peach** *adj* pinkish-orange in colour

peacock /ˈpiːkɒk/ *n* [C] large male bird with blue and green tail feathers

peahen /ˈpiːhen/ *n* [C] female of a peacock

0━ **peak** /piːk/ *n* **1** point when sb/sth is best, most successful, strongest, etc: *Traffic reaches a* ~ *between 8 and 9 in the morning.* **2** pointed top of a mountain **3** pointed front part of a cap ● **peak** *v* [I] reach the highest point or value ● **peak** *adj* at its highest level; busiest: *the ~ summer season* ▶ **peaked** *adj* having a peak

peal /piːl/ *n* [C] **1** loud sound or series

of sounds: ~s of laughter/thunder
2 loud ringing of bells ● **peal** v [I] (of
bells) ring loudly

peanut /'piːnʌt/ n [C] nut that
grows underground in a thin shell
2 (**peanuts**) [pl] (infml) very small
amount of money

pear /peə(r)/ n [C] yellow or green
fruit that is narrow at the top and
wide at the bottom ■ **pear-shaped**
adj shaped like a pear [IDM] **go pear-
shaped** (GB, infml) go wrong

pearl /pɜːl/ n [C] small hard shiny
white jewel that grows inside an
oyster

peasant /'peznt/ n [C] **1** (esp in the
past) person who works on the land
2 (infml, disapprov) person who is
rude or uneducated ► **peasantry** n
[sing, with sing or pl verb] the
peasants of a country

peat /piːt/ n [U] partly decayed plant
material, used in gardening or as a
fuel ► **peaty** adj

pebble /'pebl/ n [C] small stone made
smooth and round by water
► **pebbly** adj

peck /pek/ v **1** [I,T] (of a bird) hit sth
with the beak **2** [T] (infml) kiss sb
lightly and quickly: He ~ed her on the
cheek. ● **peck** n [C] **1** (infml) light
quick kiss **2** act of pecking sb/sth

peckish /'pekɪʃ/ adj (GB, infml)
slightly hungry

peculiar /pɪ'kjuːliə(r)/ adj **1** strange
or unusual, esp in a way that is
unpleasant or worrying **2** ~ (**to**)
belonging only to a particular
person, time, place, etc: an accent ~
to the West of the country **3** (GB,
infml) unwell ► **peculiarity**
/pɪˌkjuːli'ærəti/ n (pl **-ies**) **1** [C]
strange or unusual feature or habit
2 [C] feature belonging to a
particular person, thing, place, etc
3 [U] quality of being strange
► **peculiarly** adv **1** very; more than
usually **2** oddly

pedagogue /'pedəgɒg/ n [C] (old-
fash or fml) teacher ► **pedagogy**
/'pedəgɒdʒi/ n [U] (tech) study of
teaching methods ► **pedagogic**
/ˌpedə'gɒdʒɪk/ (also **pedagogical**
/-ɪkl/) adj ► **pedagogically** /-kli/ adv

pedal /'pedl/ n [C] flat bar that drives
or controls a machine (eg a bicycle)
when pressed down by the foot
● **pedal** v (**-ll-** US also **-l-**) [I,T] ride a
bicycle somewhere; turn or press the
pedals on a bicycle, etc

pedant /'pednt/ n [C] (disapprov)
person who is too concerned with
small details and rules ► **pedantic**
/pɪ'dæntɪk/ adj ► **pedantically** /-kli/
adv

peddle /'pedl/ v [I,T] go from house
to house trying to sell goods
► **peddler** n [C] **1** US = PEDLAR
2 person who sells illegal drugs

pedestal /'pedɪstl/ n [C] base of a

323

peg

pillar, for a statue [IDM] **put/place sb
on a pedestal** admire sb so much
that you do not notice their faults

pedestrian /pə'destriən/ n [C]
person who is walking in the street
and not travelling in a vehicle
● **pedestrian** adj **1** of or for
pedestrians **2** not interesting; dull
■ **pe destrian 'crossing** n [C] part of
a road where vehicles must stop to
allow people to cross

pediatrician (US) = PAEDIATRICIAN

pediatrics (US) = PAEDIATRICS

pedigree /'pedɪgriː/ n [C] official
record of the animals from which an
animal has been bred **2** [C,U]
person's (esp impressive) family
history or background ● **pedigree**
(US **pedigreed**) adj (of an animal)
descended from a known line of
ancestors of the same breed

pedlar /'pedlə(r)/ n [C] (in the past)
person who went from house to
house trying to sell small objects

pee /piː/ v [I] (infml) pass waste liquid
from your body ● **pee** n (infml)
1 [sing] act of urinating **2** [U] urine

peek /piːk/ v [I], n [C] ~ (**at**) (take a)
quick look at sth secretly

peel /piːl/ v **1** [T] take the skin off fruit
or vegetables: ~ the potatoes **2** [I,T]
(cause sth to) come off in layers: The
paint is ~ing. ◇ Carefully ~ away the
lining paper. [PV] **peel (sth) off**
remove some or all of your clothes
● **peel** n [U] skin of fruit, etc: lemon ~

peep /piːp/ v [I] ~ (**at**) look quickly
and secretly at sth, esp through a
small opening ● **peep** n **1** [C, usu
sing] quick or secret look at sth
2 [sing] (infml) sound made by sb,
esp in sth said: We didn't hear a ~ out of
him all night. **3** [C] short high sound

peer /pɪə(r)/ n [C] **1** [usu pl] person of
the same age or social status as you
2 (in Britain) member of the
nobility ● **peer** v [I] ~ (**at**) look
closely or carefully at sth, esp when
you cannot see it clearly ► **peerage**
/'pɪərɪdʒ/ n **1** [sing] all the peers (2)
as a group **2** [C] rank of a peer (2) or
peeress ► **peeress** /'pɪərəs/ n [C]
female peer (2) ■ **'peer group** n [C]
group of people of the same age or
social status

peeved /piːvd/ adj (infml) annoyed
► **peevish** /'piːvɪʃ/ adj easily
annoyed; bad-tempered
► **peevishly** adv

peg /peg/ n [C] **1** short thin piece of
wood, metal or plastic, used to hang
things on or for fastening sth **2** =
CLOTHES PEG (CLOTHES) ● **peg** v
(**-gg-**) **1** [T] fasten sth with pegs **2** [T]
(usu passive) fix or keep prices,
wages, etc at a particular level [PV]
peg out (GB, infml) die

pejorative /prɪˈdʒɒrətɪv/ adj (fml) expressing criticism

Pekinese /ˌpiːkɪˈniːz/ n [C] small dog with short legs and long silky hair

pelican /ˈpelɪkən/ n [C] large waterbird with a large beak for storing fish to eat ■ **pelican ˈcrossing** n [C] (in Britain) place on a road where you can stop the traffic and cross by operating a set of traffic lights

pellet /ˈpelɪt/ n [C] 1 small hard ball made from soft material 2 small metal ball, fired from a gun

pelmet /ˈpelmɪt/ n [C] strip of wood or fabric above a window to hide the curtain rail

pelt /pelt/ v 1 [T] ~ (with) attack sb by throwing things at them 2 [i] ~ (down) (of rain) fall very heavily 3 [i] (infml) run somewhere very fast ● pelt n [C] animal's skin with the fur on it [IDM] (at) full pelt as fast as possible

pelvis /ˈpelvɪs/ n [C] (anat) wide curved set of bones at the bottom of the body that the legs and spine are connected to ▶ **pelvic** /-vɪk/ adj

0‑ **pen** /pen/ n [C] 1 instrument for writing with ink 2 small enclosed piece of land for keeping farm animals ● pen v (-nn-) [T] 1 (fml) write sth 2 ~ (in/up) shut an animal or a person in a small space ■ **penfriend** (also ˈpen pal) n [C] person that you make friends with by writing letters, often sb you have never met ■ **penknife** /-naɪf/ n [C] (pl **-knives**) small knife with folding blades ■ **pen-name** n [C] name used by a writer instead of their real name

penal /ˈpiːnl/ adj of the punishment of criminals: reform of the ~ system

penalize (also ise) /ˈpiːnəlaɪz/ v [T] (usu passive) 1 ~ (for) punish sb for breaking a rule or law 2 cause sb to suffer a disadvantage

penalty /ˈpenəlti/ n [C] (pl **-ies**) 1 ~ (for) punishment for breaking a law, rule or contract: the death ~ 2 ~ (of) disadvantage suffered as a result of sth 3 (sport) advantage given to a player or team when the other side breaks a rule 4 (in football) free kick at the goal by the attackers

penance /ˈpenəns/ n [C,U] ~ (for) act that you give yourself to do to show that you are sorry for sth you have done wrong

pence plural of PENNY

penchant /ˈpɒ̃ʃɒ̃/ n [sing] ~ for (written) liking for sth

0‑ **pencil** /ˈpensl/ n [C,U] narrow piece of wood, containing a black or coloured substance, used for writing or drawing ● pencil v (-ll- US -l-) [T] write or draw sth with a pencil [PV] **pencil sth/sb in** write down details of

an arrangement with sb that you know may have to be changed later

pendant /ˈpendənt/ n [C] piece of jewellery that hangs from a chain worn round the neck

pending /ˈpendɪŋ/ adj (fml) 1 waiting to be decided 2 going to happen soon ● pending prep (fml) until sth happens

pendulum /ˈpendjələm/ n [C] weight hung so that it can swing freely, esp in a clock

penetrate /ˈpenɪtreɪt/ v 1 [i,T] go into or through sth: The snow ~d the holes in his shoes. 2 [T] see into or through sth: ~ the darkness ▶ **penetrating** adj 1 (of sb's eyes or the way they look at you) making you feel uncomfortable 2 (of a sound) loud and hard 3 showing that you have understood sth quickly ▶ **penetration** /ˌpenɪˈtreɪʃn/ n [U]

penguin /ˈpeŋgwɪn/ n [C] black and white Antarctic seabird that uses its wings for swimming

penicillin /ˌpenɪˈsɪlɪn/ n [U] antibiotic medicine

peninsula /pəˈnɪnsjələ/ n [C] area of land almost surrounded by water ▶ **peninsular** adj

penis /ˈpiːnɪs/ n [C] sex organ of a man or male animal

penitent /ˈpenɪtənt/ adj feeling or showing that you are sorry for having done sth wrong ▶ **penitence** /-təns/ n [U]

penitentiary /ˌpenɪˈtenʃəri/ n [C] (pl **-ies**) (US) prison

pennant /ˈpenənt/ n [C] long narrow pointed flag, used on a ship for signalling, etc

penniless /ˈpeniləs/ adj having no money

0‑ **penny** /ˈpeni/ n [C] (pl **pennies** or **pence** /pens/) 1 (abbr p) small British coin and unit of money. There are 100 pence in one pound (£1). 2 (before 1971) British coin worth one twelfth of a shilling [IDM] **the penny drops** (esp GB, infml) used to say that sb has finally realized or understood sth

0‑ **pension**[1] /ˈpenʃn/ n [C,U] money paid regularly by a government or company to sb who is too old or ill to work ● pension sth off [PV] **pension sb off** allow or force sb to retire and pay them a pension ▶ **pensionable** adj giving sb the right to receive a pension ▶ **pensioner** n [C] person receiving a pension, esp because they have retired from work

pension[2] /ˈpɒ̃sjɒ̃/ n [C] small, usu cheap, hotel in some European countries, esp France

pensive /ˈpensɪv/ adj thinking deeply about sth ▶ **pensively** adv

pentagon /ˈpentəgən/ n 1 [C] (geom) flat shape with five sides and five angles **2** (the Pentagon) [sing] the headquarters of the US Defense Department ▶ **pentagonal** /pen'tægənl/ adj

pentathlon /pen'tæθlən/ n [C] sports contest in which each competitor takes part in five events

penthouse /'penthaʊs/ n [C] expensive and comfortable flat or set of rooms at the top of a tall building

pent-up /ˌpent'ʌp/ adj (of feelings) that cannot be expressed: ~ *anger*

penultimate /pen'ʌltɪmət/ adj (written) just before the last one; last but one

penury /'penjəri/ n [U] (fml) state of being extremely poor ▶ **penurious** /pə'njʊəriəs/ adj

0-〒 **people** /'piːpl/ n **1** [pl] persons in general: *How many ~ were at the party?* **2** [C] nation; race: *the ~s of Asia* **3** [pl] persons who live in a particular place: *the ~ of London* **4** (the people) [pl] ordinary persons without special rank or position ● **people** v [T] (written) live in a place or fill it with people

pep /pep/ n [U] energy and enthusiasm ● **pep** v (-pp-) [PV] **pep sb/sth up** (infml) make sb/sth more interesting or full of energy ■ **'pep pill** n [C] (infml) pill taken to make you feel happier or livelier ■ **'pep talk** n [C] (infml) short speech intended to encourage you to work harder, try to win, etc

0-〒 **pepper** /'pepə(r)/ n **1** [U] grey powder made from dried berries (peppercorns), used for giving a hot flavour to food **2** [C] hollow fruit, usu red, green or yellow, eaten as a vegetable either raw or cooked: *green ~s* ● **pepper** v [T] put pepper on food [PV] **pepper sb/sth with sth** (usu passive) hit sb/sth with a series of small objects, esp bullets ■ **peppercorn** 'rent n [C] (GB) very low rent

peppermint /'pepəmɪnt/ n **1** [U] type of mint grown for its strong-tasting oil **2** [C] sweet flavoured with peppermint oil

0-〒 **per** /pə(r); strong form pɜː(r)/ prep for each: *£60 ~ person ~ day* ■ **per annum** /pər 'ænəm/ (abbr **p.a.**) adv for each year: *He earns over $80 000 ~ annum.* ■ **per se** /ˌpɜː 'seɪ/ adv by itself

perceive /pə'siːv/ v [T] (written) notice or become aware of sth; think of sth in a particular way

0-〒 **per 'cent** adv for or in each hundred: *a five ~ wage increase*

percentage /pə'sentɪdʒ/ n [C, with sing or pl verb] rate, number or amount of sth, expressed as if it is part of a total which is 100; part or share of a whole: *pay a ~ of your*

earnings in tax **2** [usu sing] share of the profits of sth

perceptible /pə'septəbl/ adj (fml) great enough to be noticed: *a ~ change in colour* ▶ **perceptibly** adv

perception /pə'sepʃn/ n (fml) **1** [U] ability to perceive sth **2** [C] way of seeing or understanding sth

perceptive /pə'septɪv/ adj (fml) quick to notice or understand things ▶ **perceptively** adv

perch /pɜːtʃ/ v **1** [I] ~ **(on)** (of a bird) land and stay on a branch, etc **2** [I,T] ~ **(on)** (cause sb) to sit on sth, esp on the edge of it: *I ~ed myself on a high stool at the bar.* **3** [I] be placed on the top or edge of sth ● **perch** n [C] **1** place, eg a branch, where a bird rests **2** (infml) high seat or position **3** (pl **perch**) freshwater fish, sometimes eaten as food

percolate /'pɜːkəleɪt/ v **1** [I] (of a liquid, gas, etc) move gradually through a surface that has very small holes in it **2** [I] gradually become known or spread through a group or society ▶ **percolator** n [C] coffee pot in which boiling water percolates through crushed coffee beans

percussion /pə'kʌʃn/ n [U] musical instruments, eg drums, that you play by hitting them

peremptory /pə'remptəri/ adj (fml, disapprov) showing that you expect to be obeyed immediately ▶ **peremptorily** /-trəli/ adv

perennial /pə'reniəl/ adj **1** continuing for a long time; happening again and again: *a ~ problem* **2** (of a plant) living for more than two years ● **perennial** n [C] perennial plant ▶ **perennially** adv

0-〒 **perfect**[1] /'pɜːfɪkt/ adj **1** having everything necessary; complete and without faults: *in ~ condition* **2** completely correct; exact: *The dress is a ~ fit.* **3** the best of its kind **4** excellent; very good: *~ weather* **5** total: *a ~ stranger* **6** (gram) of a tense formed with *have* and a past participle, eg *I have eaten* ▶ **perfectly** adv in a perfect way; completely

perfect[2] /pə'fekt/ v [T] make sth perfect or as good as you can ▶ **perfectible** adj that can be perfected

perfection /pə'fekʃn/ n [U, sing] **1** state of being perfect: *The fish was cooked to ~.* **2** act of making sth perfect ▶ **perfectionist** /-ʃənɪst/ n [C] person who is not satisfied with anything less than perfection

perfidious /pə'fɪdiəs/ adj (lit) that cannot be trusted

perforate /'pɜːfəreɪt/ v [T] make a hole or holes through sth ▶ **perforation** /ˌpɜːfə'reɪʃn/ n [C, U] small hole in a surface, often one of a series of small holes

O⃞ **perform** /pəˈfɔːm/ v [T] do sth, eg a piece of work: ~ a task **2** [I,T] entertain an audience by playing music, acting in a play, etc **3** [I] work or function in the way that is mentioned: *This new car ~s well.* ▸ **performance** n **1** [C] act of performing a play, concert, etc **2** [U] way of performing sth **3** how well or badly you do sth or sth works ▸ **performer** n [C] person who sings, acts, etc in front of an audience

perfume /ˈpɜːfjuːm/ n [C,U] liquid, often made from flowers, that you put on your skin to make yourself smell nice ▸ **perfume** v [T] (lit) give a sweet smell to sth

perfunctory /pəˈfʌŋktəri/ adj (fml) done as a duty or habit, without real care or interest ▸ **perfunctorily** /-trəli/ adv

O⃞ **perhaps** /pəˈhæps; præps/ adv possibly; it may be (that): *P~ the weather will improve tomorrow.*

peril /ˈperəl/ n (fml or lit) **1** [U] serious danger **2** [C, usu pl] fact of sth being dangerous or harmful: *warning about the ~s of drug abuse* ▸ **perilous** adj ▸ **perilously** adv

perimeter /pəˈrɪmɪtə(r)/ n **1** outside edge of an enclosed area of land **2** (maths) total length of the outside edge of a shape

O⃞ **period** /ˈpɪəriəd/ n **1** particular length of time **2** (time allowed for a) lesson at school, college, etc **3** monthly flow of blood from a woman's body **4** (US) = FULL STOP (FULL) ▸ **periodic** /ˌpɪəriˈɒdɪk/ adj happening fairly often and regularly ▸ **periodical** n [C] magazine that is published at regular intervals ▸ **periodically** /-kli/ adv fairly often

peripatetic /ˌperɪpəˈtetɪk/ adj (fml) going from place to place, esp to work: *a ~ music teacher*

periphery /pəˈrɪfəri/ n [usu sing] (pl -ies) (fml) outer edge of a particular area ▸ **peripheral** /-rəl/ adj **1** not as important as the main aim, part, etc of sth: *peripheral information* **2** (tech) of the outer edge of an area: *peripheral vision* **3** (computing) (of equipment) connected to a computer

periscope /ˈperɪskəʊp/ n [C] instrument with mirrors, for seeing things at a higher level, used esp in submarines

perish /ˈperɪʃ/ v [I] **1** (fml or lit) die; be destroyed **2** (of material such as rubber) rot ▸ **perishable** adj (of food) likely to go bad quickly ▸ **perishables** n [pl] (tech) types of food that go bad quickly

▸ **perishing** adj (GB, infml) extremely cold

perjure /ˈpɜːdʒə(r)/ v ~ **yourself** (law) tell a lie in a court of law ▸ **perjury** n [U]

perk /pɜːk/ n [C, usu pl] something you receive as well as your wages for doing a particular job: *Free health insurance and a car are the ~s of the job.* ● **perk** v [PV] **perk (sb/sth) up** become or make sb/sth more cheerful or lively ▸ **perky** adj (-ier, -iest) (infml) cheerful and full of energy

perm /pɜːm/ n [C] putting of artificial curls into the hair ● **perm** v [T] give sb's hair a perm

O⃞ **permanent** /ˈpɜːmənənt/ adj lasting for a long time or for ever ▸ **permanence** /-nəns/ n [U] ▸ **permanently** adv

permeate /ˈpɜːmieɪt/ v [I,T] (fml) enter and spread to every part of sth ▸ **permeable** /-miəbl/ adj (tech) (of) allowing a liquid or gas to pass through

permissible /pəˈmɪsəbl/ adj (fml) that is allowed ▸ **permissibly** /-əbli/ adv

O⃞ **permission** /pəˈmɪʃn/ n [U] act of allowing sb to do sth

permissive /pəˈmɪsɪv/ adj allowing great freedom of behaviour, esp in sexual matters: *the ~ society* ▸ **permissiveness** n [U]

O⃞ **permit** /pəˈmɪt/ v (-tt-) [T] (fml) allow sb to do sth or allow sth to happen ● **permit** /ˈpɜːmɪt/ n [C] official written paper that allows sb to do sth: *a work ~*

permutation /ˌpɜːmjuˈteɪʃn/ n [C, usu pl] any of the different ways in which a set of things can be ordered

pernicious /pəˈnɪʃəs/ adj (fml) very harmful

pernickety /pəˈnɪkəti/ adj (infml, disapprov) worrying too much about small unimportant details

perpendicular /ˌpɜːpənˈdɪkjələ(r)/ adj ~ **(to)** at an angle of 90° to another line or surface; upright ▸ **perpendicular** n [sing] (the perpendicular) line, position or direction that is exactly perpendicular

perpetrate /ˈpɜːpətreɪt/ v [T] (fml) commit a crime or do sth wrong or evil ▸ **perpetrator** n [C]

perpetual /pəˈpetʃuəl/ adj **1** continuous **2** frequently repeated, in a way which is annoying: *their ~ complaints* ▸ **perpetually** /-tʃuəli/ adv

perpetuate /pəˈpetʃueɪt/ v [T] (fml) make sth bad continue for a long time ▸ **perpetuation** /pəˌpetʃuˈeɪʃn/ n [U]

perplex /pəˈpleks/ v [T] (usu passive) make sb feel puzzled or confused, because they do not understand sth:

They were ~ed by her response. ▶ **perplexity** /-əti/ *n* [U] state of feeling perplexed

per se → PER

persecute /'pɜːsɪkjuːt/ *v* [T] treat sb cruelly or unfairly, esp because of their race, religion or political beliefs ▶ **persecution** /ˌpɜːsɪˈkjuːʃn/ *n* [U,C] ▶ **persecutor** *n* [C]

persevere /ˌpɜːsɪˈvɪə(r)/ *v* [I] (*approv*) ~ (**in/with**) continue doing sth in spite of difficulties: *You have to* ~ *with difficult students.* ▶ **perseverance** *n* [U]

persist /pəˈsɪst/ *v* [I] **1** ~ (**in/with**) continue to do sth in spite of opposition, in a way that can seem unreasonable: *He will* ~ *in thinking I don't like him.* **2** continue to exist: *If the symptoms* ~, *see a doctor.* ▶ **persistence** *n* [U] ▶ **persistent** *adj* **1** determined to do sth, esp when others are against you **2** continuing; repeated: *a* ~*ent cough* ▶ **persistently** *adv*

0—**person** /'pɜːsn/ *n* [C] (pl **people** /'piːpl/ or, esp in formal use **persons**) **1** human being: *They're just the* ~ *we need.* **2** (*gram*) any of the three classes of personal pronouns: *the first* ~ (= I, we) ◇ *the second* ~ (= you) ◇ *the third* ~ (= he, she, it, they) [IDM] **in person** actually present; yourself: *The actress will be there in* ~.

personable /'pɜːsənəbl/ *adj* having a pleasant appearance or manner: *a* ~ *young woman*

personage /'pɜːsənɪdʒ/ *n* [C] (*fml*) important or famous person

0—**personal** /'pɜːsənl/ *adj* **1** your own; not of or belonging to anyone else: ~ *belongings* **2** not of your professional life; private: *receive a* ~ *phone call at work* **3** critical of a person: ~ *remarks* **4** of the body: ~ *cleanliness* ▶ **personally** /'pɜːsənəli/ *adv* **1** used to show that you are giving your own opinion: *P~ly, I think you're crazy!* **2** doing sth yourself ■ **personal as'sistant** *n* [C] = PA ■ **personal com'puter** *n* [C] = PC(1) ■ **personal 'pronoun** *n* [C] (*gram*) pronoun *I, she, you,* etc

0—**personality** /ˌpɜːsəˈnæləti/ *n* (pl **-ies**) **1** [C, U] person's character: *a strong* ~ **2** [C] famous person, esp from entertainment, sport, etc

personify /pəˈsɒnɪfaɪ/ *v* (pt, pp **-ied**) [T] **1** be a good example of a quality: *She* ~ *kindness.* **2** show or think of an object, quality, etc as a person ▶ **personification** /pəˌsɒnɪfɪˈkeɪʃn/ *n* [U,C]

personnel /ˌpɜːsəˈnel/ *n* **1** [pl] all the people who work for an organization **2** [U, with sing or pl verb] department in a company, etc that deals with employees and their problems: *a* ~ *manager*

perspective /pəˈspektɪv/ *n* **1** [C] way of thinking about sth **2** [U] ability to think about problems, etc in a reasonable way without exaggerating their importance: *Try to keep these issues in* ~. **3** [U] art of drawing things so as to give the impression of depth and distance

Perspex™ /'pɜːspeks/ *n* [U] strong plastic often used instead of glass

perspire /pəˈspaɪə(r)/ *v* [I] (*fml*) sweat ▶ **perspiration** /ˌpɜːspəˈreɪʃn/ *n* [U]

0—**persuade** /pəˈsweɪd/ *v* [T] **1** make sb do sth by giving them good reasons for doing it: *They* ~*d him to try again.* **2** make sb believe sth that is true

persuasion /pəˈsweɪʒn/ *n* **1** [U] act of persuading sb to do sth or believe sth **2** [C, U] set of beliefs

persuasive /pəˈsweɪsɪv/ *adj* able to persuade sb to do sth: *She can be very* ~ *when she wants.* ▶ **persuasively** *adv*

pert /pɜːt/ *adj* cheeky; disrespectful: *a* ~ *reply* ▶ **pertly** *adv* ▶ **pertness** *n* [U]

pertain /pəˈteɪn/ *v* [I] (*fml*) ~ **to** be connected with or belong to sth

pertinent /'pɜːtɪnənt/ *adj* (*fml*) relevant

perturb /pəˈtɜːb/ *v* [T] (*fml*) make sb very worried

peruse /pəˈruːz/ *v* [T] (*fml*) read sth, esp carefully ▶ **perusal** *n* [U, sing]

pervade /pəˈveɪd/ *v* [T] (*fml*) spread through every part of sth

pervasive /pəˈveɪsɪv/ *adj* present or felt everywhere

perverse /pəˈvɜːs/ *adj* showing deliberate determination to behave in a way others think is unreasonable ▶ **perversely** *adv* ▶ **perversity** *n* [U]

perversion /pəˈvɜːʃn/ *n* **1** [U,C] behaviour, esp sexual behaviour, that people think is not normal or acceptable **2** [U] act of changing sth good into sth bad: *the* ~ *of justice*

pervert /pəˈvɜːt/ *v* [T] **1** change a system, etc in a bad way so that it is not what it should be: ~ *the course of justice* **2** affect sb in a way that makes them behave in an immoral way ▶ **pervert** /'pɜːvɜːt/ *n* [C] person whose sexual behaviour is considered to be unnatural

pessimism /'pesɪmɪzəm/ *n* [U] belief that bad things will happen ▶ **pessimist** /-mɪst/ *n* [C] ▶ **pessimistic** /ˌpesɪˈmɪstɪk/ *adj*

pest /pest/ *n* [C] **1** insect or animal that destroys plants, food, etc **2** (*infml*) annoying person

pester /'pestə(r)/ *v* [T] annoy or bother sb constantly

pesticide /'pestɪsaɪd/ n [C, U] chemical substance used for killing pests, esp insects

pestle /'pesl/ n [C] stick with a thick end used for crushing things in a bowl (mortar)

⚬━ **pet** /pet/ n [C] **1** animal, eg a cat or dog, that you keep at home as a companion **2** person treated as a favourite: *She's the teacher's ~*. ■ pet v (-tt-) **1** [T] (*esp US*) treat a child or an animal lovingly, esp by stroking them **2** [I] (*infml*) (of two people) kiss and touch each other in a sexual way ■ '**pet name** [C] name you use for sb instead of their real name, as a sign of affection

petal /'petl/ n [C] delicate coloured part of a flower

peter /'piːtə(r)/ v [PV] **peter out** gradually come to an end

petition /pə'tɪʃn/ n [C] **1** ~ (**against/ for**) written request to sb in authority that is signed by many people **2** (*law*) official document asking a court of law to take legal action ■ **petition** v [I,T] make a formal request to sb in authority

petrify /'petrɪfaɪ/ v (pt, pp -**ied**) **1** [T] (usu passive) frighten sb very much **2** [I,T] (cause sth to) change into stone

⚬━ **petrol** /'petrəl/ n [U] (*GB*) liquid obtained from petroleum, used as fuel in car engines, etc ■ '**petrol station** [C] (*GB*) place at the side of a road where you take your car to buy petrol, oil, etc

petroleum /pə'trəʊliəm/ n [U] mineral oil that forms underground

petticoat /'petɪkəʊt/ n [C] (*old-fash*) piece of women's underwear, worn under a dress or skirt

petty /'peti/ adj (-**ier**, -**iest**) (*disapprov*) **1** small and unimportant: *~ squabbles* ◇ *~ crime* (= that is not very serious) **2** concerned with unimportant matters; unkind ▶ **pettiness** n [U] ■ petty 'cash n [U] money kept in an office for small payments ■ petty 'officer n [C] sailor of middle rank in the navy

petulant /'petjʊlənt/ adj bad-tempered in a childish way ▶ **petulance** /-əns/ n [U] ▶ **petulantly** adv

pew /pjuː/ n [C] long wooden seat in a church

pewter /'pjuːtə(r)/ n [U] grey metal made by mixing tin with lead

phallus /'fæləs/ n [C] image of the penis ▶ **phallic** /'fælɪk/ adj

phantom /'fæntəm/ n [C] **1** ghost **2** unreal or imagined thing

pharaoh /'feərəʊ/ n [C] king of ancient Egypt

pharmaceutical /ˌfɑːmə'sjuːtɪkl/ adj of the making of drugs and medicines

pharmacist /'fɑːməsɪst/ n [C] person trained to prepare and sell medicines in a shop

pharmacy /'fɑːməsi/ n (pl -**ies**) **1** [C] (part of a) shop where medicines are sold **2** [U] study of the preparation of drugs and medicines

⚬━ **phase** /feɪz/ n [C] **1** stage of development **2** shape that the moon appears to have at a particular time ■ phase v [T] arrange to do sth in stages over a period of time [PV] **phase sth in/out** begin/stop using sth gradually

PhD /ˌpiː eɪtʃ 'diː/ abbr Doctor of Philosophy; university degree of a very high level

pheasant /'feznt/ n [C,U] large bird with a long tail, often shot for food; meat from this bird

phenomenal /fə'nɒmɪnl/ adj very great or impressive: *~ success* ▶ **phenomenally** /-nəli/ adv: *~ly successful*

phenomenon /fə'nɒmɪnən/ n [C] (pl -**mena** /-mɪnə/) **1** fact or event in nature or society, esp one that is not fully understood **2** person or thing that is very successful or impressive

philanthropy /fɪ'lænθrəpi/ n [U] giving of money and other help to people in need ▶ **philanthropic** /ˌfɪlən'θrɒpɪk/ adj ▶ **philanthropist** /fɪ'lænθrəpɪst/ n [C]

philately /fɪ'lætəli/ n [U] (*tech*) collection and study of postage stamps

philistine /'fɪlɪstaɪn/ n [C] (*disapprov*) person who does not like or understand art, literature, music, etc

philosopher /fə'lɒsəfə(r)/ n [C] **1** person who studies or writes about philosophy **2** person who thinks deeply about things

⚬━ **philosophy** /fə'lɒsəfi/ n (pl -**ies**) **1** [U] study of nature and the meaning of existence, how people should live, etc **2** [C] set or system of beliefs ▶ **philosophical** /ˌfɪlə'sɒfɪkl/ adj **1** of philosophy **2** (*approv*) ~ (**about**) having a calm attitude towards failure, disappointment, etc ▶ **philosophically** /-kli/ adv ▶ **philosophise** (*also* -**ise**) /-faɪz/ v [I] talk about sth in a serious way, esp when others find it boring

phishing /'fɪʃɪŋ/ n [U] activity of getting sb to give their personal details over the Internet, in order to steal money from them

phlegm /flem/ n [U] **1** thick yellowish-green substance that forms in the nose and throat, esp when you have a cold **2** (*written*) ability to remain calm in a difficult situation ▶ **phlegmatic** /fleg'mætɪk/ adj not easily made angry or upset ▶ **phlegmatically** /-klɪ/ adv

phobia /ˈfəʊbiə/ n [C] strong unreasonable fear or hatred of sth

0━ **phone** /fəʊn/ n **1** [U,C] (also **telephone**) (machine used in a) system for talking to sb else over long distances using wires or radio: *make a ~ call* **2** [C] the part of the telephone that you hold in your hand and speak into: *He put the ~ down.* [IDM] **be on the phone** use the telephone ● **phone** v [I,T] (GB also **phone up**) make a telephone call to sb ■ **'phone book** n [C] = TELEPHONE DIRECTORY (TELEPHONE) ■ **'phone booth** n [C] partly-enclosed place, containing a telephone, in a hotel, restaurant, etc ■ **'phone box** n [C] small enclosed unit, containing a public telephone, in the street, at a station, etc ■ **'phone-in** n [C] radio or television programme in which telephoned questions and answers from the public are broadcast ■ **'phone number** = TELEPHONE NUMBER (TELEPHONE)

phonetic /fəˈnetɪk/ adj **1** using special symbols to represent each different speech sound: *the International P~ Alphabet* **2** (of a spelling system) that closely matches the sounds represented **3** of the sounds of human speech ▶ **phonetically** /-klɪ/ adv ▶ **phonetician** /ˌfəʊnəˈtɪʃn; ˌfɒn-/ n [C] expert in phonetics ▶ **phonetics** n [U] study of speech sounds

phoney (esp US **phony**) /ˈfəʊni/ adj (**-ier, -iest**) (infml, disapprov) false, and trying to deceive people ● **phoney** (also **phony**) n [C] phoney person or thing

phonology /fəˈnɒlədʒi/ n [U] (ling) (study of) the speech sounds of a particular language: *English ~* ▶ **phonological** /ˌfəʊnəˈlɒdʒɪkl/ adj

phosphorescent /ˌfɒsfəˈresnt/ adj (tech) producing a faint light without heat, esp in the dark ▶ **phosphorescence** /-sns/ n [U]

phosphorus /ˈfɒsfərəs/ n [U] (symb P) poisonous, pale yellow substance that shines in the dark

0━ **photo** /ˈfəʊtəʊ/ n [C] (pl **~s**) = PHOTOGRAPH ■ **photo 'finish** n [C] end of a race in which the leading competitors are so close together that a photograph is needed to show the winner

0━ **photocopy** /ˈfəʊtəʊkɒpi/ n [C] (pl **-ies**) photographic copy of a document, etc ● **photocopy** v (pt, pp **-ied**) make a photocopy of sth ▶ **photocopier** /-piə(r)/ n [C] machine for photocopying documents, etc

photogenic /ˌfəʊtəʊˈdʒenɪk/ adj looking attractive in photographs

329

piano

0━ **photograph** /ˈfəʊtəɡrɑːf/ n [C] picture made by using a camera that has film sensitive to light inside it ● **photograph** v [T] take a photograph of sb/sth ▶ **photographer** /fəˈtɒɡrəfə(r)/ n [C] person who takes photographs, esp as a job ▶ **photographic** /ˌfəʊtəˈɡræfɪk/ adj ▶ **photography** /fəˈtɒɡrəfi/ n [U] art or process of taking photographs

phrasal /ˈfreɪzl/ adj of or connected with a phrase ■ **phrasal 'verb** n [C] (gram) verb combined with an adverb and/or preposition, to give a new meaning: *'Blow up' and 'look forward to' are ~ verbs.*

0━ **phrase** /freɪz/ n [C] **1** (gram) group of words without a finite verb, esp one that forms part of a sentence **2** group of words that have a particular meaning when used together ● **phrase** v [T] say or write sth in a particular way: *a badly ~d example* ■ **phrase book** n [C] book containing common expressions translated into another language, esp for people visiting a foreign country

phraseology /ˌfreɪziˈɒlədʒi/ n [U] (fml) choice or style of words

0━ **physical** /ˈfɪzɪkl/ adj **1** of the body: *~ exercise/fitness* **2** of things that can be touched or seen: *the ~ world* **3** of the laws of nature: *a ~ impossibility* ■ **physical edu'cation** n = PE ■ **physical ge'ography** n [U] study of the natural features on the surface of the earth ▶ **physically** /-klɪ/ adv

physician /fɪˈzɪʃn/ n [C] (fml, esp US) doctor, esp one specializing in general medicine

physicist /ˈfɪzɪsɪst/ n [C] scientist who studies physics

0━ **physics** /ˈfɪzɪks/ n [U] scientific study of matter and energy

physiology /ˌfɪziˈɒlədʒi/ n [U] scientific study of the normal functions of living things ▶ **physiological** /ˌfɪziəˈlɒdʒɪkl/ adj ▶ **physiologist** n [U] scientist who studies physiology

physiotherapy /ˌfɪziəʊˈθerəpi/ n [U] treatment of disease, etc in the joints or muscles by exercises, massage and the use of light and heat ▶ **physiotherapist** n [C]

physique /fɪˈziːk/ n [C] general appearance and size of a person's body

0━ **piano** /piˈænəʊ/ n [C] (pl **~s**) large musical instrument in which metal strings are struck by hammers operated by pressing black and white keys ▶ **pianist** /ˈpiːənɪst/ n [C] person who plays the piano

A B C D E F G H I J K L M N O **P** Q R S T U V W X Y Z

piccolo /ˈpɪkələʊ/ n [C] (pl **-s**) musical instrument like a small flute

0─ pick¹ /pɪk/ v [T] **1** choose sb/sth from a group of people or things: ~ *a number between 1 and 10.* **2** take flowers, fruit, etc from the plant or tree where they are growing: ~ *strawberries* **3** pull or remove sth or small pieces of sth from sth else, esp with your fingers: ~ *your teeth* [IDM] **pick and choose** choose only the things that you like or want very much **pick sb's brains** (*infml*) ask sb a lot of questions because they know more about the subject than you do **pick a fight/quarrel (with sb)** deliberately start a fight or argument with sb **pick holes in sth** find faults in sth such as a plan, suggestion, etc **pick a lock** open a lock without a key **pick sb's pocket** [PV] **pick at sth 1** eat food in very small amounts **2** pull or touch sth several times: *He tried to undo the knot by ~ing at it with his fingers.* **pick on sb** treat sb unfairly by criticizing or punishing them: *He's always ~ing on me.* **pick sb/sth out 1** choose sb/sth carefully from a group of people or things **2** recognize sb/sth clearly in a large group **pick up 1** get better, stronger, etc; improve **2** start again; continue: *Let's ~ up where we left off yesterday.* **pick sb up 1** go somewhere in your car to collect sb **2** allow sb to get into your vehicle and take them somewhere **3** take hold of sb and lift them up **4** (*infml, disapprov*) talk to sb you do not know, to try to start a sexual relationship **5** (*infml*) (of the police) arrest sb **pick sth up 1** learn a skill, foreign language, etc by chance rather than by making a deliberate effort **2** take hold of sth and lift it up **3** get or obtain sth **4** receive a radio signal ▸ **picker** n [C] person or machine that picks fruit, etc ▸ **pickings** n [pl] money or profits that can be easily or dishonestly obtained ■ **ˈpickpocket** n [C] person who steals from people's pockets ■ **ˈpickup** n [C] **1** (*also* **ˈpickup truck**) small van or truck with low sides and no roof at the back **2** (*disapprov*) person who meets sb for the first time **3** part of a record player that holds the needle

pick² /pɪk/ n **1** [sing] act of choosing sth: *take your* ~ **2** [sing] the pick (of sth) the best thing(s) in a group **3** [C] = PICKAXE

pickaxe (*US* **pickax**) /ˈpɪkæks/ n [C] large tool with a curved metal bar that has two sharp ends, used for breaking up roads, rocks, etc

picket /ˈpɪkɪt/ n [C] worker or group of workers standing outside a place of work esp during a strike to try to persuade others not to enter ● **picket** v [I,T] stand outside a place to protest about sth or to persuade people to join a strike: ~ *a factory*

pickle /ˈpɪkl/ n **1** [C, usu pl] vegetable that has been preserved in vinegar or salt water **2** [U] (*GB*) cold thick spicy sauce, often sold in jars, served with meat, cheese, etc [IDM] **in a pickle** (*infml*) in a difficult or unpleasant situation ● **pickle** v [T] preserve food in vinegar or salt water ▸ **pickled** *adj* (*old-fash, infml*) drunk

picnic /ˈpɪknɪk/ n [C] informal meal eaten outdoors ● **picnic** v (**-ck-**) [I] have a picnic ▸ **picnicker** n [C]

pictorial /pɪkˈtɔːriəl/ *adj* of or using pictures

0─ picture /ˈpɪktʃə(r)/ n [C] **1** painting, drawing, etc, that shows a scene, a person or thing **2** photograph **3** image on a television screen **4** description that gives you an idea of what sth is like **5** mental image or memory of sth **6** [sing] (the picture) the general situation concerning sb/sth **7** [C] film or movie: *The movie won nine awards, including Best P~.* **8** (the pictures) (*GB, old-fash*) [pl] cinema: *go to the ~s* [IDM] **be the picture of health, etc** look very healthy, etc **get the picture** (*spoken*) understand a situation **put/keep sb in the picture** (*infml*) give sb the information they need to be able to understand a situation ● **picture** v [T] **1** imagine sb/sth: *He ~d himself as a rich man* **2** show sb/sth in a photograph or picture

picturesque /ˌpɪktʃəˈresk/ *adj* **1** attractive to look at: *a ~ fishing village* **2** (of language) very descriptive

pidgin /ˈpɪdʒɪn/ n [C] simple form of a language, used together with words from a local language

pie /paɪ/ n [C,U] meat or fruit covered with pastry and baked in a dish

piebald /ˈpaɪbɔːld/ *adj* (of a horse) having black and white patches of irregular shape

0─ piece /piːs/ n **1** [C] ~ **(of)** amount of sth that has been cut or separated from the rest: *a ~ of cake/ paper* **2** [C, usu pl] one of the bits or parts that sth breaks into or is made of: *There were tiny ~s of glass on the floor.* ◇ *I took the clock to ~s.* **3** [C] single item or example of sth: *a ~ of furniture* ◇ *a ~ of news/advice* **4** [C] single item of writing, art, music, etc **5** [C] coin: *a ten-pence ~* **6** [C] small object used in a board game: *a chess ~* [IDM] **give sb a piece of your mind** (*infml*) tell sb that you disapprove of their behaviour or are angry with them **go to pieces** (*infml*) be so upset or afraid that you lose control of yourself (all) in one piece (*infml*) safe and unharmed, eg after a dangerous experience **a piece of cake** (*infml*) thing that is very easy to do ■ **piecework** *n* [U] work paid for by the amount done and not by the hours worked

piece² /piːs/ *v* [PV] **piece sth together** put the parts of sth together to make it complete

piecemeal /ˈpiːsmiːl/ *adj* (*usu disapprov*) done or happening gradually at different times rather than carefully planned ▶ **piecemeal** *adv*

pier /pɪə(r)/ *n* [C] **1** long structure built out into the sea, esp with places of entertainment on it **2** (*tech*) pillar supporting a bridge, etc

pierce /pɪəs/ *v* [I,T] make a small hole in sth or go through sth, with a sharp object **2** [T] ~ (**through**) (*lit*) (of light or sound) be suddenly seen or heard ▶ **piercing** *adj* **1** (of eyes) searching **2** (of sound) sharp and unpleasant **3** (of the wind) cold and very strong ▶ **piercingly** *adv*

piety /ˈpaɪəti/ *n* [U] strong religious beliefs and behaviour

0ᵐ pig /pɪg/ *n* [C] **1** fat short-legged animal with pink, black or brown skin, kept on farms for its meat **2** (*infml, disapprov*) greedy, dirty or rude person ▶ **piggy** *n* [C] (*pl* **-ies**) (*infml*) child's word for a pig ▶ **piggy bank** *n* [C] small container, esp one shaped like a pig, used by children for saving money in ■ **pig-headed** *adj* refusing to change your opinion or actions; stubborn ■ **pigsty** *n* (*pl* **-ies**) **1** [C] small building for pigs **2** [sing] (*infml*) very dirty or untidy room or house ■ **pigtail** *n* [C] length of plaited hair that hangs down from the back of the head

pigeon /ˈpɪdʒɪn/ *n* [C] fat grey bird of the dove family ■ **pigeonhole** *n* [C] one of a series of small open box-like sections for letters or messages ▶ **pigeonhole** *v* [T] decide that sth belongs to a particular class or group **2** decide to deal with sth later or to forget it ■ **pigeon-toed** *adj* having toes that turn inwards

piglet /ˈpɪglət/ *n* [C] young pig

pigment /ˈpɪgmənt/ *n* [U,C] **1** substance existing naturally in people, animals and plants that gives their skin, leaves, etc a particular colour **2** coloured powder that is mixed with a liquid to make paint, etc ▶ **pigmentation** /ˌpɪgmenˈteɪʃn/ *n* [U] natural colouring

pigmy = PYGMY

pike /paɪk/ *n* **1** (*pl* **pike**) large freshwater fish **2** long wooden spear, used by soldiers in the past

Pilates /pɪˈlɑːtiːz/ *n* [U] system of

---

stretching and pushing exercises which help make your muscles stronger

pilchard /ˈpɪltʃəd/ *n* [C] small sea fish eaten as food

0ᵐ pile /paɪl/ *n* [C] **1** number of things lying one upon another: *a ~ of papers* **2** [C, usu *pl*] (*infml*) a lot of sth: *~s of work to do* **3** [U, sing] soft surface of threads or loops on a carpet or some fabrics **4** [C] large wooden, metal or stone post that is fixed into the ground to support a building, etc [IDM] **make a/your pile** (*infml*) earn a lot of money ● **pile** *v* **1** [T] put things one on top of the other; form a pile: *~ the books on the table* **2** [T] load sth with sth: *The table was ~d high with boxes.* **3** [I] (*infml*) (of a number of people) go somewhere quickly without order or control: *When the bus finally arrived, we all ~d on.* [PV] **pile up** increase in quantity or amount: *The work is ~ing up.* ■ **pile-up** *n* [C] road crash involving several vehicles crashing into each other

piles /paɪlz/ *n* [pl] = HAEMORRHOIDS

pilfer /ˈpɪlfə(r)/ *v* [I,T] steal things of little value

pilgrim /ˈpɪlgrɪm/ *n* [C] person who makes a journey to a holy place ▶ **pilgrimage** /-ɪdʒ/ *n* [C, U] journey made by a pilgrim

0ᵐ pill /pɪl/ *n* **1** [C] small round piece of medicine that you swallow **2** (**the pill**) [sing] pill taken regularly as a form of birth control

pillage /ˈpɪlɪdʒ/ *v* [I,T] (*fml*) steal things from a place, esp in a war, using violence

pillar /ˈpɪlə(r)/ *n* [C] **1** tall upright post of stone, wood, etc as a support for part of a building **2** strong supporter of sth; important member of sth ■ **pillar box** *n* [C] (*GB, old-fash*) tall round container in the street, in which letters are posted

pillion /ˈpɪliən/ *n* [C] seat for a passenger behind the driver of a motor cycle

pillory /ˈpɪləri/ *v* (*pt, pp* **-ied**) [T] (*written*) criticize sb strongly in public

pillow /ˈpɪləʊ/ *n* [C] soft cushion used for supporting the head in bed ● **pillow** *v* [T] (*lit*) rest sth, esp your head, on an object ■ **pillowcase** (*also* **pillowslip**) *n* [C] fabric cover for a pillow

0ᵐ pilot /ˈpaɪlət/ *n* [C] **1** person who operates the controls of an aircraft, esp as a job **2** person who guides a ship into or out of a harbour ● **pilot** *v* [T] **1** act as a pilot of sth; drive/guide sb/sth somewhere **2** test a new product, idea, etc ● **pilot** *adj* used for testing sth: *a ~ scheme* ■ **pilot**

---

light n [C] small flame that burns all the time on a gas cooker, etc and lights a larger flame

pimp /pɪmp/ n [C] man who controls prostitutes, finds customers for them and makes a profit from them

pimple /'pɪmpl/ n [C] small sore spot on the skin ■ **pimply** adj

PIN /pɪn/ (also **'PIN number**) n [C] personal identification number; number given to you by a bank so that you can use a plastic card to take out money from a cash machine

0-m **pin**[1] /pɪn/ n [C] 1 short thin pointed piece of metal with a round head, used for fastening things together ■ **'pincushion** n [C] small cushion for sticking pins in when they are not being used ■ **'pinpoint** v [T] discover or describe sth exactly ■ **pins and 'needles** n [pl] uncomfortable feeling in a part of your body, esp when you have been sitting or lying in an awkward position ■ **'pinstripe** n [C] (of fabric) with very narrow stripes

0-m **pin**[2] /pɪn/ v (-nn-) [T] 1 fasten sth with a pin 2 make sb unable to move by holding them or pressing them against sth: *He ~ned him against a wall.* [IDM] **pin (all) your hopes on sb/sth** rely on sb/sth completely for success or help [PV] **pin sb down to (doing) sth** make sb make a decision or state their intentions clearly **pin sth down** explain or understand sth exactly: *The cause of the disease is difficult to ~ down.* ■ **'pin-up** n [C] picture of an attractive person, eg a film star, for pinning on a wall

pinafore /'pɪnəfɔː(r)/ n [C] loose sleeveless garment worn over a dress to keep it clean

pincer /'pɪnsə(r)/ n 1 (**pincers**) [pl] tool used for holding things tightly and pulling out nails 2 [C] curved claw of a shellfish

pinch /pɪntʃ/ v 1 [T] press sth tightly between your thumb and finger or two surfaces 2 [I] be too tight: *These shoes ~.* 3 [T] (infml) steal sth ● **pinch** n [C] 1 act of squeezing a part of sb's skin between your thumb and finger 2 amount that you can hold between your thumb and finger: *a ~ of salt* [IDM] **at a pinch** (US) **in a pinch** if necessary **feel the pinch** (infml) not have enough money **take sth with a pinch of salt** be careful about believing that sth is completely true

pine /paɪn/ n 1 (also **'pine tree**) [C,U] tall evergreen tree with leaves like needles (also **'pinewood**) [U] pale soft wood of the pine tree ● **pine** v [I] be very unhappy because sb has gone away or has died [PV] **pine for**

sb/sth want or miss sb/sth very much

pineapple /'paɪnæpl/ n [C,U] large juicy tropical fruit with sweet yellow flesh

ping /pɪŋ/ v [I], n [C] (make a) short high ringing noise

ping-pong /'pɪŋpɒŋ/ n [U] = TABLE TENNIS (TABLE)

pinion /'pɪnjən/ v [T] hold or tie sb, esp by their arms, so that they cannot move

0-m **pink** /pɪŋk/ adj of a pale red colour ● **pink** n [U,C] pale red colour [IDM] **in the pink** (old-fash, infml) in very good health

pinnacle /'pɪnəkl/ n [C] 1 [usu sing] **~ (of)** most important or successful part of sth: *the ~ of her career* 2 pointed stone decoration on a roof 3 high pointed piece of rock

pinpoint → PIN[1]

pinstripe → PIN[1]

0-m **pint** /paɪnt/ n [C] 1 measure for liquids; one eighth of a gallon (0.568 litre in the UK and 0.473 litre in the US) 2 (GB) pint of beer, esp in a pub

pioneer /ˌpaɪə'nɪə(r)/ n [C] 1 **~ in/of** person who is the first to study a new area of knowledge 2 one of the first people to go into a new land or area ● **pioneer** v [T] be one of the first people to do, discover or use sth new

pious /'paɪəs/ adj having or showing a deep respect for God and religion ▶ **piously** adv

pip /pɪp/ n [C] small seed, eg of an apple, orange or grape ● **pip** v (-pp-) [T] (GB, infml) beat sb in a race, etc by only a small amount: *He was ~ped at/to the post for the top award.*

0-m **pipe**[1] /paɪp/ n 1 [C] tube through which liquids or gases can flow 2 [C] narrow tube with a bowl at one end, used for smoking tobacco 3 [C] musical instrument consisting of a tube with holes 4 (**pipes**) [pl] = BAGPIPES ■ **'pipe dream** n [C] impossible idea or plan ■ **'pipeline** n [C] system of connected pipes, usu underground, for carrying oil or gas [IDM] **in the pipeline** being prepared; about to happen

pipe[2] /paɪp/ v 1 [T] carry water, gas, etc in pipes 2 [I,T] play music on a pipe or the bagpipes 3 speak or sing in a high voice [PV] **pipe down** (infml, spoken) be less noisy; stop talking **pipe up (with sth)** (infml) begin to speak ■ **piped 'music** n [U] recorded music played continuously in large shops, stations, etc

piper /'paɪpə(r)/ n [C] person who plays music on a pipe or the bagpipes

piping /'paɪpɪŋ/ n [U] pipe or system of pipes ● **piping** adj (of a person's voice) high ∎ **piping** *hot adj* (of liquids or food) very hot

piquant /ˈpiːkənt/ *adj* (written) **1** having a pleasantly strong or spicy taste **2** exciting and interesting ► **piquancy** /-ənsi/ *n* [U] (written) ► **piquantly** *adv*

pique /piːk/ *n* [U] annoyance and bitterness because your pride has been hurt ● **pique** *v* [T] (fml) make sb annoyed and upset

piracy /ˈpaɪrəsi/ *n* [U] **1** crime of attacking ships and stealing from them **2** act of making illegal copies of video tapes, CDs, etc

piranha /pɪˈrɑːnə/ *n* [C] small S American freshwater fish that eats live animals

pirate /ˈpaɪrət/ *n* [C] **1** (esp in the past) person who robs other ships at sea **2** person who makes illegal copies of video tapes, computer programs, etc ● **pirate** *v* [T] copy and sell sb's work or a product without permission

pirouette /ˌpɪruˈet/ *n* [C] ballet dancer's fast turn or spin on one foot ► **pirouette** *v*: [I] *She ~d across the stage.*

piss /pɪs/ *v* (▲, *sl*) [I] urinate [PV] **piss off** (*esp GB*) go away ● **piss** *n* (▲, *sl*) urine [IDM] **take the piss (out of sb/ sth)** make fun of sb ► **pissed** *adj* **1** (*GB*, ▲, *sl*) drunk **2** (*US*, *sl*) very angry or annoyed

pistol /ˈpɪstl/ *n* [C] small gun held in one hand

piston /ˈpɪstən/ *n* [C] round plate or short cylinder that moves up and down inside a tube, used in engines, pumps, etc

pit /pɪt/ *n* **1** [C] large deep hole in the ground **2** [C] large hole in the ground from which minerals are dug out: *a gravel ~* **3** [C] = COAL MINE (COAL) **4** [C] hollow mark left on the skin by some diseases, eg chickenpox **5** [C] (*esp US*) = STONE(4) **6** (**the pits**) [pl] (*US* **the pit** [C]) (in motor racing) place near a race track where cars stop for fuel, etc during a race **7** [C] space in front of the stage for the orchestra [IDM] **be the pits** (*infml*) be very bad or the worst example of sth **the pit of your/ the stomach** the bottom of the stomach where fear is thought to be felt ● **pit** *v* (-tt-) [T] (usu passive) make marks or holes in the surface of sth [PV] **pit sth against sb/sth** test sb or their strength, intelligence, etc in a contest against sb/sth else

0⌐ pitch¹ /pɪtʃ/ *n* **1** [C] area of ground with lines marked for playing football, cricket, etc **2** [sing, U] degree or strength of a feeling or activity; the highest point of sth: *a frenetic ~ of activity* **3** [sing, U] how high or low a sound

is, esp a musical note **4** [C, usu *sing*] talk or arguments used by a person trying to sell things or persuade people to do sth: *an aggressive sales ~* **5** [C] (in baseball) act of throwing a ball; way in which it is thrown **6** [U] black substance that is sticky when hot and hard when cold, used for making roofs, etc waterproof **7** [C] (*GB*) place where a street trader does business ∎ **pitch-black** *adj* completely black or dark

pitch² /pɪtʃ/ *v* **1** [T] throw sth/sth in the direction or way that is mentioned **2** [I] fall heavily in a particular direction **3** [I] (of a ship or aircraft) move up and down on the water or in the air **4** [T] set sth at a particular level **5** [I,T] try to persuade sb to buy sth, give you sth or make a business deal with you **6** [T] produce a sound or piece of music at a particular level **7** [T] set up a tent [PV] **pitch in (with sb/sth)** (*infml*) join in and help with an activity, by doing some of the work or by giving money, etc **pitch into sb** (*infml*) attack or criticize sb ∎ **pitched battle** *n* [C] intense violent fight ∎ **pitchfork** *n* [C] farm tool in the shape of a fork with a long handle, for lifting hay, etc

pitcher /ˈpɪtʃə(r)/ *n* [C] **1** (*US*) = JUG **2** (*GB*) large clay container with two handles, used esp in the past for holding liquids **3** (in baseball) player who throws the ball to the batter

piteous /ˈpɪtiəs/ *adj* (lit) deserving or causing pity: *a ~ cry* ► **piteously** *adv*

pitfall /ˈpɪtfɔːl/ *n* [C] hidden or unexpected difficulty or danger

pith /pɪθ/ *n* [U] soft white substance under the skin of oranges, etc and in the stems of some plants ► **pithy** *adj* (-ier, -iest) (approv) short, but full of meaning: *~ remarks* ► **pithily** *adv*

pitiable /ˈpɪtiəbl/ *adj* **1** deserving or causing you to feel pity **2** not deserving respect ► **pitiably** *adv*

pitiful /ˈpɪtɪfl/ *adj* **1** deserving or causing you to feel pity **2** not deserving respect: *a ~ excuse* ► **pitifully** *adv*

pitiless /ˈpɪtɪləs/ *adj* showing no pity or mercy; cruel ► **pitilessly** *adv*

pittance /ˈpɪtns/ *n* [usu *sing*] very small amount of money

0⌐ pity /ˈpɪti/ *n* **1** [U] feeling of sympathy and sadness for the sufferings or troubles of others: *I took ~ on her and lent her the money.* **2** [sing] something that is sad and unfortunate: *It's a ~ (that) the weather isn't better.* [IDM] **more's the pity** (*infml*) unfortunately ● **pity** *v* (pt, pp **-ied**) [T] feel pity for sb

pivot /ˈpɪvət/ *n* **1** central pin or point on which sth turns or balances

2 central or most important person or thing ● **pivot** v [I] (cause sth to) turn or balance on a central pivot ► **pivotal** adj (written) of great importance because other things depend on it

pixel /ˈpɪksl/ n [C] (computing) any of the small individual areas on a computer screen, which together form the whole display

pixie /ˈpɪksi/ n [C] (in stories) small creature with pointed ears that has magic powers

pizza /ˈpiːtsə/ n [C, U] flat round piece of dough covered with tomatoes, cheese, etc and baked in an oven

placard /ˈplækɑːd/ n [C] large notice that is shown publicly

placate /pləˈkeɪt/ v [T] make sb feel less angry about sth

0—w place[1] /pleɪs/ n [C] **1** particular position, point or area: Is this the ~ where it happened? **2** [C] particular city, town, building, etc: Canada is a big ~. **3** [C] building or area used for a particular purpose: a meeting ~ **4** [C] seat or position kept for or occupied by sb: I've saved you a ~ next to him. ◊ I laid a ~ for them at the table. **5** [sing] ~ (in) role or importance of sb/sth in a particular situation **6** [C] opportunity to take part in sth, esp to study at a school, etc: get a ~ at university **7** [C] natural or correct position for sth: Put everything away in the right ~. **8** [sing] house or flat; a person's home: What about dinner at my ~? **9** [C, usu sing] position among the winners in a race or competition **10** (Place) [sing] used as part of the name of a short street or square [IDM] **all over the place** (GB also) **all over the shop** (US also) **all over the lot** (infml) **1** everywhere **2** untidy; not well organized **in/out of place 1** in/ not in the correct position **2** suitable/unsuitable: His remarks were out of ~. **in place of sb/sth** instead of sb/sth **in the first, second, etc place** used to introduce the different points you are making in an argument **put sb in their place** make sb feel stupid or embarrassed for being too confident **take place** happen **take the place of sb/sth** replace sb/sth

0—w place[2] /pleɪs/ v [T] **1** put sth in a certain place **2** put sb/yourself in a particular situation: to ~ sb under arrest **3** recognize sb/sth and be able to identify them/it: I know her face, but I can't ~ her. **4** give instructions about sth or make a request for sth to happen: to ~ a bet/ an order ► **placement** n [U] **1** act of finding sb a job or place to live **2** act of placing sth/sb somewhere

placenta /pləˈsentə/ n [C] (anat)

material inside the womb during pregnancy, through which the baby is fed

placid /ˈplæsɪd/ adj calm; not easily angered ► **placidly** adv

plagiarize (also -ise) /ˈpleɪdʒəraɪz/ v [T] (disapprov) copy another person's work, words, ideas, etc and pretend that they are your own ► **plagiarism** /-rɪzəm/ n [U, C]

plague /pleɪg/ n **1** [C, U] infectious disease that kills a lot of people **2** [C] large numbers of an animal or insect that come into an area and cause great damage: a ~ of locusts ● **plague** v [T] ~ (**with**) **1** cause pain or trouble to sb/sth over a period of time: to be ~d by doubts **2** annoy sb continually with sth

plaice /pleɪs/ n [C, U] (pl **plaice**) flat sea fish eaten as food

plaid /plæd/ n [C, U] (long piece of) woollen cloth with a pattern of coloured stripes or squares

0—w plain[1] /pleɪn/ adj **1** easy to see or understand: I made it ~ that he should leave. **2** not trying to trick anyone; honest and direct: He has a reputation for ~ speaking. **3** not decorated or complicated: ~ food ◊ available in ~ or printed cotton **4** not beautiful or attractive: a ~ girl [IDM] **be plain sailing** be simple and free from trouble ● **plain** adv (infml) used to emphasize how bad, stupid, etc sth is: ~ stupid/wrong ■ plain-**clothes** adj (of a police officer) wearing ordinary clothes when on duty, not a uniform ► **plainly** adv ► **plainness** n [U] ■ 'plain-spoken adj very honest and direct in your speech

plain[2] /pleɪn/ n [C] large area of flat land

plaintiff /ˈpleɪntɪf/ n [C] (law) person who brings a legal action against sb

plaintive /ˈpleɪntɪv/ adj (written) sounding sad ► **plaintively** adv

plait /plæt/ v [T] twist three or more pieces of hair, rope, etc together to make one long piece ● **plait** n [C] length of hair, esp hair, that has been plaited

0—w plan /plæn/ n [C] **1** arrangement for doing sth, considered in advance; intention: make ~s for the holidays **2** detailed map of a building, town, etc: a street ~ **3** (tech) detailed drawing of a machine, building, etc ● diagram showing how sth will be arranged: a seating ~ ● **plan** v (-nn-) [I, T] make a plan of or for sth ► **planner** n [C] person who plans sth, esp how land is to be used in a town: a town ~ner

0—w plane /pleɪn/ n [C] **1** flying vehicle with wings and one or more engines **2** (geom) flat or level surface **3** level of thought, existence or development **4** tool with a blade set in a flat surface, used for making wood smooth **5** (*also* usu **plane tree**) tree with broad leaves and thin bark ● **plane** *adj* (*tech*) completely flat; level ● **plane** *v* [T] make a piece of wood smoother or flatter with a plane

0—┐ **planet** /'plænɪt/ *n* [C] large round object in space that moves around a star (eg the sun) and receives light from it ▸ **planetary** /-tri/ *adj*

plank /plæŋk/ *n* [C] long flat piece of wood ▸ **planking** [U] planks used to make a floor, etc

plankton /'plæŋktən/ *n* [U] very small plants and animals that live near the surface of the sea

0—┐ **plant¹** /plɑːnt/ *n* **1** [C] living thing that grows in the earth, with a stem, leaves and roots **2** [C] factory **3** [U] machinery used in an industrial process

0—┐ **plant²** /plɑːnt/ *v* [T] **1** put plants, seeds, etc in the ground to grow **2** place sth or yourself firmly in position **3** ~ **(on)** (*infml*) hide sth, esp sth illegal, in sb's possessions to make that person seem guilty of a crime **4** send sb to a place secretly, as a spy ▸ **planter** *n* [C] **1** attractive container to grow a plant in **2** person who owns or manages a plantation

plantation /plɑːn'teɪʃn/ *n* [C] large area of land, esp in a hot country, planted with trees or crops, eg sugar, coffee or rubber

plaque /plæk, *GB also* plɑːk/ *n* **1** [C] flat piece of stone, metal, etc fixed on a wall in memory of sb/sth **2** [U] harmful substance that forms on the teeth

plasma /'plæzmə/ *n* [U] (*med*) clear liquid part of blood, in which the blood cells, etc float

plaster /'plɑːstə(r)/ *n* **1** [U] mixture of lime, sand and water that is put on walls and ceilings to give them a smooth surface **2** [U] (*also* **plaster of Paris**) white powder mixed with water that becomes very hard when dry, used for holding broken bones in place: *Her leg is still in ~.* **3** [C,U] (*GB also* **sticking plaster**) (small strip) of fabric that can be stuck to the skin to protect a small wound or cut ● **plaster** *v* [T] **1** cover a wall, etc with plaster **2** cover sb/sth with a wet or sticky substance: *hair ~ed with oil* ■ **plaster cast** *n* [C] **1** case made of plaster of Paris, used to hold a broken bone in place **2** copy of sth that is made from plaster of Paris ▸ **plastered** *adj* (*infml*) drunk ▸ **plasterer** *n* [C] person whose job is to put plaster on walls and ceilings

0—┐ **plastic** /'plæstɪk/ *n* [U,C] light, chemically produced material that can be formed into shapes and is used to make different objects and fabrics ● **plastic** *adj* **1** made of

plastic: *a ~ bag/cup* **2** (of materials) easily formed into different shapes ▸ **plasticity** /plæ'strsəti/ *n* [U] ■ **plastic surgery** *n* [U] medical operations to repair injury to a person's skin, or to improve their appearance

Plasticine™ /'plæstəsiːn/ *n* [U] (*GB*) soft coloured substance like clay, used by children for making models

0—┐ **plate** /pleɪt/ *n* **1** [C] flat, usu round, dish that you put food on **2** [C] amount of food that you can put on a plate **3** [C] flat thin sheet of metal **4** [usu pl] pieces of metal or plastic at the front and back of a vehicle with numbers and letters on them **5** [U] gold or silver articles, eg spoons and dishes **6** [C] photograph used as a picture in a book, esp one that is printed separately **7** [C] sheet of metal from which the pages of a book are printed [IDM] **hand sth to sb on a plate** (*infml*) give sth to sb without the person concerned making any effort **have enough/a lot/too much on your plate** (*infml*) have a lot of work or problems, etc to deal with ● **plate** *v* [T] cover another metal with a thin layer of gold, silver, etc ■ **plate glass** *n* [U] clear glass made in large thick sheets

plateau /'plætəʊ/ *n* [C] (pl -eaux /-təʊz/) **1** large area of high level ground **2** time of little or no change after a period of growth: *Prices have reached a ~.*

0—┐ **platform** /'plætfɔːm/ *n* [C] **1** raised surface beside the track at a railway station **2** flat raised surface for speakers or performers **3** main aims and plans of a political party, esp as stated before an election **4** type of computer system or the software that is used: *a multimedia ~*

plating /'pleɪtɪŋ/ *n* [U] (esp thin) covering of gold, silver, etc

platinum /'plætɪnəm/ *n* [U] very valuable greyish white metal, used for jewellery, etc

platitude /'plætɪtjuːd/ *n* [C] (*fml*) statement that is obviously true but not at all new or interesting

platonic /plə'tɒnɪk/ *adj* (of love or friendship between two people) close and deep, but not sexual

platoon /plə'tuːn/ *n* [C] small group of soldiers, commanded by a lieutenant

platter /'plætə(r)/ *n* [C] large plate that is used for serving food

platypus /'plætɪpəs/ *n* [C] (duck-billed *platypus*) furry Australian animal with a beak like a duck, which lays eggs and feeds its young on milk

plausible /'plɔːzəbl/ *adj* reasonable; likely to be true ▸ **plausibly** *adv*

0⟿ **play**¹ /pleɪ/ *v* **1** [I,T] do things for pleasure, as children do; enjoy yourself, rather than work **2** [I,T] ~ **(at)** pretend to be or do sth for amusement **3** [I,T] take part in a game or sport; compete against sb in a game **4** [T] make contact with the ball and hit or kick it in the way mentioned **5** [T] move a piece in chess **6** [I,T] (in card games) put a card face upwards on the table **7** [I,T] perform on a musical instrument: *to ~ the piano* **8** [T] make a tape, CD, etc produce sound **9** [T] act in a play, film, etc; act the role of sb **10** [T] pretend to be sth you are not: *I decided it was safer to ~ dead.* **11** [T] (~ a part/role (in)) have an effect on sth **12** [I] move quickly and lightly: *sunlight ~ing on the lake* [IDM] **play ball (with sb)** (*infml*) be willing to work with other people in a helpful way **play your cards right** act in the most effective way to get sth that you want **play it by ear** (*infml*) deal with a situation calmly, without getting excited **play it by ear** (*fml*) decide how to deal with a situation as it develops rather than by making plans in advance: *We'll ~ it by ear depending on the weather.* **play for time** try to gain time by delaying **play the game** behave fairly and honestly **play gooseberry** (*GB*) be the unwanted third person when two lovers want to be alone together **play (merry) hell with sth** (*GB, infml*) affect sth badly **play into sb's hands** do sth that gives your opponent an advantage **play a part (in sth)** be involved in sth **play second fiddle (to sb/sth)** be treated as less important than sb/sth; have a less important position than sb/sth else **what is sb playing at?** used to ask angrily about what sb is doing [PV] **play along (with sb/sth)** pretend to agree with sb/sth **play at (doing) sth** (*disapprov*) do sth with little seriousness or interest **play sth back (to sb)** allow the material recorded on a tape, video, etc to be heard or seen **play sth down** try to make sth seem less important than it is **play A off against B** put two people in competition with each other, esp to get an advantage for yourself **play on/upon sth** take advantage of sb's feelings, etc: *The advert ~s on people's fears.* **play (sb) up** (*infml, esp GB*) cause sb pain or problems **play sth up** try to make sth seem more important than it is **play up to sb** behave so as to win the favour of sb **play with sth** consider an idea, etc with little seriousness ▸ **playback** *n* [U] act of playing music, showing a film or listening to a telephone message that has been recorded

before ▪ **'playing card** *n* [C] any of a set of 52 cards with numbers and pictures printed on one side, used for various games ▪ **'playing field** *n* [C] large area of grass on which people play sports ▪ **'playlist** *n* [C] list of the music that is played by a radio station or programme ▪ **'play-off** *n* [C] game or a series of games between two players who are level, to decide the winner

0⟿ **play²** /pleɪ/ *n* **1** [U] things that people, esp children, do for pleasure **2** [C] story written to be performed by actors in a theatre, on television or on the radio: *a Shakespeare ~* **3** [U] playing of a game or sport: *Rain stopped ~.* **4** [U] possibility of free and easy movement: *a lot of ~ in the rope* **5** [U] activity or operation of sth: *The crisis has brought new factors into ~.* **6** [U] (*lit*) light quick movement: *the ~ of sunlight on water* [IDM] **a play on words** = PUN ▪ **'play-acting** *n* [U] behaviour that seems sincere when in fact the person is pretending ▪ **'playboy** *n* [C] rich man who spends his time enjoying himself ▪ **'playground** *n* [C] outdoor area where children can play, esp at a school ▪ **'playgroup** *n* [C] place where children below school age go regularly to play together and to learn through playing ▪ **'playhouse** *n* [C] used in names of theatres ▪ **'playmate** *n* [C] friend with whom a child plays ▪ **'playpen** *n* [C] small portable enclosure in which a baby can play ▪ **'plaything** *n* [C] **1** person or thing that you treat like a toy, without really caring about them/it **2** (*old-fash*) toy ▪ **'playwright** /'pleɪraɪt/ *n* [C] person who writes plays

0⟿ **player** /'pleɪə(r)/ *n* [C] **1** person who plays a game **2** company or person involved in a particular area of business or politics **3** machine for reproducing sound or pictures that have been recorded on cassettes, discs, etc: *a CD/DVD ~* **4** person who plays a musical instrument: *a trumpet ~*

playful /'pleɪfl/ *adj* **1** full of fun; wanting to play **2** not serious ▸ **playfully** *adv* ▸ **playfulness** *n* [U]

plaza /'plɑːzə/ *n* [C] (*esp US*) small shopping centre, sometimes also with offices

plc (*also* **PLC**) /ˌpiː el ˈsiː/ *abbr* (*GB*) public limited company; (used after the name of a company or business)

plea /pliː/ *n* **1** (*fml*) ~ **(for)** urgent emotional request: *~s for mercy* **2** (*law*) statement made by sb or for sb who is accused of a crime: *a ~ of not guilty*

plead /pliːd/ *v* (*pt, pp* ~**ed** *US* **pled** /pled/) **1** [I] ~ **(with)** make repeated serious requests to sb **2** [T] (*law*) state officially in court that you are guilty or not guilty of a crime **3** [T] (*law*) present a case in a court of law **4** [T] ~ (**for**) offer sth as an excuse for sth

0━ **pleasant** /ˈpleznt/ *adj*
1 enjoyable, pleasing or attractive
2 friendly ▸ **pleasantly** *adv* ▸ **pleasantness** *n* [U]

pleasantry /ˈplezntri/ *n* [C] (pl **-ies**) (*fml*) polite friendly remark

0━ **please** /pliːz/ *exclam* used as a polite way of asking for sth or telling sb to do sth: Come in, ~. ● **please** *v* **1** [I,T] make sb happy **2** [I] choose or want to do sth: He does as he ~s. ▸ **pleased** *adj* happy or satisfied: She was very ~ with her exam results. ▸ **pleasing** *adj* ~ (**to**) giving pleasure or satisfaction

0━ **pleasure** /ˈpleʒə(r)/ *n* **1** [U] feeling of happiness or enjoyment **2** [C] thing that makes you happy or satisfied: It's a ~ helping you. ▸ **pleasurable** /-ərəbl/ *adj* (*fml*) giving enjoyment ▸ **pleasurably** *adv* ■ **pleasure boat** *n* [C] boat used for short pleasure trips

pleat /pliːt/ *n* [C] permanent fold in a piece of fabric, made by sewing the top or side of the fold ▸ **pleated** *adj* having pleats: a ~ed skirt

plebeian /pləˈbiːən/ *n* [C], *adj* (*disapprov*) (member) of the lower social classes

plectrum /ˈplektrəm/ *n* [C] (pl **-s** or **-tra** /-trə/) small piece of plastic, metal, etc for plucking the strings of a guitar, etc

pled (*US*) pt, pp of PLEAD

pledge /pledʒ/ *n* [C] **1** serious promise **2** sum of money or sth valuable that you leave with sb to prove that you will do sth or pay back money owed ● **pledge** *v* [T] **1** (make sb or yourself) formally promise to give or do sth: The government has ~d itself to fight poverty. **2** leave sth with sb as a pledge (2)

plenary /ˈpliːnəri/ *adj* (of a meeting) attended by all who have the right to attend: a ~ session

plentiful /ˈplentɪfl/ *adj* available or existing in large quantities: a ~ supply ▸ **plentifully** *adv*

0━ **plenty** /ˈplenti/ *pron*, *adv* ~ (**of**) as much as or more than is needed; a lot: There's ~ of time before we go.

holding small things or for bending or cutting wire

plight /plaɪt/ *n* [sing] serious and difficult situation

plimsoll /ˈplɪmsəl/ *n* [C] (*GB*) light rubber-soled canvas sports shoe

plinth /plɪnθ/ *n* [C] square base on which a column or statue stands

plod /plɒd/ *v* (**-dd-**) walk slowly with heavy steps, esp because you are tired ▸ **plodder** *n* [C] person who works steadily and slowly but with no imagination

plonk /plɒŋk/ (*US* **plunk**) *v* [T] ~ (**down**) (*infml*) **1** put sth down on sth, esp noisily or carelessly: P~ it (down) on the chair. **2** ~ **yourself** sit or lie down heavily or in a relaxed way ● **plonk** *n* [U] (*infml*, *esp GB*) cheap wine of poor quality

plop /plɒp/ *n* [C] short sound like that of a small object dropping into water ● **plop** *v* (**-pp-**) [I] fall or drop sth, making a plop

0━ **plot** /plɒt/ *n* **1** [C,U] series of events which form the story of a film, novel, etc **2** [C] secret plan made by several people, to do sth wrong or illegal **3** [C] small piece of land ● **plot** *v* (**-tt-**) **1** [I,T] make a secret plan to harm sb, esp a government or its leader **2** [T] mark sth on a map, eg the position or course of sth **3** [T] make a line by joining points on a graph ▸ **plotter** *n* [C]

plough (*US* **plow**) /plaʊ/ *n* [C] large farming tool for breaking and turning over soil ● **plough** (*US* **plow**) *v* [I,T] dig and turn over a field, etc with a plough [PV] **plough sth back** (**in/into sth**) put money made as profit back into a business in order to improve it **plough into sb/sth** crash violently into sb/sth **plough (your way) through sth** make slow and difficult progress through sth

ploy /plɔɪ/ *n* [C] something said or done to gain an advantage over sb else

pluck /plʌk/ *v* [T] **1** pull out hairs with your fingers or with tweezers: ~d eyebrows **2** pull the feathers off a dead bird, eg a chicken **3** play a musical instrument, esp the guitar, by pulling the strings with your fingers **4** (*lit*) remove sb from a dangerous place or situation: Survivors were ~ed to safety by helicopter. [IDM] **pluck up courage** (**to do sth**) make yourself do sth even though you are afraid [PV] **pluck at sth** hold sth with the fingers and pull it gently ● **pluck** *n* [U] (*old-fash*, *infml*) courage ▸ **plucky** *adj* (**-ier**, **-iest**) having a lot of courage and determination

plug

plug /plʌg/ n [C] **1** device with metal pins for connecting a piece of equipment to the electricity supply **2** piece of rubber or plastic that fits tightly into a hole in a bath or sink **3** (infml) piece of favourable publicity for a product on radio or television ● **plug** v (-gg-) [T] **1** fill a hole with sth **2** (infml) give praise or attention to a new book, film, etc, to encourage people to read it, see it, etc [PV] **plug away (at sth)** continue working hard at sth **plug sth in** connect sth to the electricity supply ■ **plughole** n [C] hole in a bath, sink, etc into which a plug fits

plum /plʌm/ n [C] round sweet smooth-skinned fruit with a stone in the middle ● **plum** adj (GB) considered good and desirable: a ~ job

plumage /ˈpluːmɪdʒ/ n [U] feathers on a bird's body

plumb /plʌm/ v (lit) try to understand sth completely [IDM] **plumb the depths of sth** be or experience an extreme example of sth unpleasant ● **plumb** adv exactly: ~ in the middle ■ **plumb line** n [C] piece of string with a weight tied to one end, used esp for testing whether a wall is vertical

plumber /ˈplʌmə(r)/ n [C] person whose job is to fit and repair water pipes

plumbing /ˈplʌmɪŋ/ n [U] **1** system of water pipes, tanks, etc in a building **2** work of a plumber

plume /pluːm/ n [C] cloud of sth that rises into the air **2** large feather

plummet /ˈplʌmɪt/ v [I] fall suddenly and quickly from a high level: House prices have ~ed.

plump /plʌmp/ adj having a soft, round body; slightly fat ● **plump** v [T] ~ **(up)** make sth larger, softer and rounder: ~ up the pillows [PV] **plump for sb/sth** (infml) choose sb/sth ▶ **plumpness** n [U]

plunder /ˈplʌndə(r)/ v [I,T] steal things from a place, esp during a war ● **plunder** n [U] **1** act of plundering **2** things that have been stolen, esp during a war

plunge /plʌndʒ/ v [I,T] (cause sb/sth to) move suddenly forwards and/or downwards: The car ~d into the river. ◇ He ~d his hands into his pockets. ● **plunge** n [C, usu sing] sudden movement downwards or away from sth; decrease [IDM] **take the plunge** (infml) finally decide to do sth important or difficult ▶ **plunger** n [C] part of a piece of equipment that can be pushed down

pluperfect /ˌpluːˈpɜːfɪkt/ n (gram) = THE PAST PERFECT (PAST¹)

plural /ˈplʊərəl/ n [usu sing] adj (gram) (form of a word) used for referring to more than one: The ~ of 'child' is 'children'.

plus /plʌs/ prep **1** used when the two numbers or amounts mentioned are being added together: One ~ two is three. **2** as well as sth/sb; and also ● **plus** n [C] **1** (infml) advantage; good thing **2** (also **plus sign**) mathematical symbol (+) ● **plus** adj above zero; positive

plush /plʌʃ/ adj (infml) smart, expensive and comfortable

plutonium /pluːˈtəʊniəm/ n [U] (chem) (symb Pu) radioactive element used in nuclear reactors and weapons

ply /plaɪ/ v (pt, pp **plied**) [I,T] (lit) (of ships, etc) go regularly along a route: ferries that ~ between the islands [IDM] **ply your trade** (written) do your work or business [PV] **ply sb with sth 1** keep giving sb large amounts of food and drink **2** keep asking sb questions ● **ply** n [U] (esp in compounds) measurement of wool, rope, wood, etc that tells you how thick it is ■ **plywood** n [U] board made by sticking thin layers of wood on top of each other

PM /ˌpiː ˈem/ abbr (infml, esp GB) Prime Minister

p.m. /ˌpiː ˈem/ abbr after 12 o'clock noon

pneumatic /njuːˈmætɪk/ adj **1** filled with air: a ~ tyre **2** worked by air under pressure: a ~ drill ▶ **pneumatically** /-kli/ adv

pneumonia /njuːˈməʊniə/ n [U] serious illness affecting the lungs

PO /ˌpiː ˈəʊ/ abbr **1** = POST OFFICE (POST¹) **2** = POSTAL ORDER (POSTAL) ■ **PO box** (also **post office box**) n [C] used as a kind of address, so that mail can be sent to a post office where it is kept until it is collected

poach /pəʊtʃ/ v **1** [T] cook fish or an egg without its shell in water that is boiling gently **2** [I,T] illegally hunt animals, birds or fish on sb else's property **3** [T] take from sb/sth dishonestly; steal sth ▶ **poacher** n [C] person who illegally hunts animals, birds or fish on sb else's property

pocket /ˈpɒkɪt/ n [C] **1** small bag sewn into a piece of clothing so that you can carry things in it **2** small bag or container fastened to sth so that you can put things in it, eg in a car door or handbag **3** [usu sing] amount of money that you have to spend: He had no intention of paying out of his own ~. **4** small separate group or area [IDM] **in/out of pocket** (esp GB) having gained/lost money as a result of sth ● **pocket** v [T] **1** put sth into your pocket **2** keep or take sth, esp money, that does not belong to you ∎ **'pocketbook** n [C] **1** (US) used to refer to the financial situation of a person or country **2** (esp GB) small notebook ∎ **'pocket money** n [U] small amount of money that parents give their children, usu every week

pockmark /'pɒkmɑːk/ n [C] hollow mark on the skin, often caused by disease or infection ● **'pock-marked** adj covered with hollow marks or holes: *a pock-marked face*

pod /pɒd/ n [C] long thin case filled with seeds that develops from the flowers of some plants, esp peas and beans

podcast /'pɒdkɑːst/ n [C] recording of sth that you can download from the Internet and listen to on a computer or MP3 player ● **podcast** v [T] (pt, pp ~): *Part two will be ~ next week.*

podgy /'pɒdʒi/ adj (-ier, -iest) (of a person) short and fat

0~ **poem** /'pəʊɪm/ n [C] piece of writing arranged in lines, usu with a regular rhythm and often with a pattern of rhymes

poet /'pəʊɪt/ n [C] writer of poems ● **Poet Laureate** /ˌpəʊɪt 'lɒriət/ n [C] (esp in Britain) poet officially chosen to write poems for the country's special occasions, paid by the government or the king or queen

poetic /pəʊ'etɪk/ (also **poetical** /-ɪkl/) adj **1** of poetry **2** like poetry, esp because it shows imagination and deep feeling ▸ **poetically** /-kli/ adv

0~ **poetry** /'pəʊətri/ n [U] **1** collection of poems; poems in general **2** graceful quality: *the ~ of dance*

poignant /'pɔɪnjənt/ adj causing deep sadness: *~ memories* ▸ **poignancy** /-jənsi/ n ▸ **poignantly** adv

0~ **point¹** /pɔɪnt/ n **1** [C] thing that sb says or writes giving their opinion or stating a fact: *OK, you've made your ~! ◊ I take your ~* = (understand and accept what you are saying). **2** (usu the point) [sing] main idea: *come to/get to the ~ ◊ see/miss the ~ of a joke ◊ That's beside the ~* = (not relevant). **3** [U, sing] purpose or aim of sth: *There's no ~ in going now.* **4** [C] particular quality or feature that sb/sth has: *Tidiness is not his strong ~.* **5** [C] particular time or stage of development: *We were on the ~ of giving up.* **6** [C] particular place or area: *No parking beyond this ~.* **7** [C] one of the marks of direction around a compass **8** [C] individual unit that adds to a score in a game or sports competition: *We won by six ~s.* **9** [C] mark or unit on a scale of measurement: *boiling ~* **10** [C] dot in writing or printing; full stop or

339

marker of decimals **11** [C] sharp end of sth: *the ~ of a pin/pencil* **12** [C] narrow piece of land that extends into the sea **13** [C] electrical socket in a wall, etc **14** (points) [pl] (GB) movable rails by which a train can move from one track to another [IDM] **beside the point** not relevant ∎ **make a point of doing sth** make a special effort to do sth ∎ **on the point of doing sth** just about to do sth ∎ **point of view** opinion that sb has about sth ∎ **take sb's point** understand and accept what sb is saying ∎ **to the point** expressed in a simple, clear way

0~ **point²** /pɔɪnt/ v [I, T] **1** ~ (**at/to/towards**) stretch out your finger or sth held in your hand to show sb where a person or thing is **2** [T] ~ **at** aim sth at sb/sth: *~ a gun at sb* **3** [T] put cement between the bricks of a wall [PV] **point sth out** (**to sb**) draw sb's attention to sth ▸ **pointed** adj **1** having a sharp end **2** directed in a clear, often critical way, against a particular person: *~ remarks* ▸ **pointedly** adv

point-blank /ˌpɔɪnt 'blæŋk/ adj, adv **1** (of a shot) fired with the gun (almost) touching the person or thing it is aimed at **2** directly and rather rudely: *He refused ~.*

pointer /'pɔɪntə(r)/ n [C] **1** (infml) piece of advice **2** thin piece of metal, plastic, etc that points to numbers on a dial or scale **3** stick used to point to things on a map or a picture on a wall **4** short-haired hunting dog

pointless /'pɔɪntləs/ adj having no purpose; not worth doing ▸ **pointlessly** adv

poise /pɔɪz/ n [U] **1** calm and confident manner and self-control **2** balanced control of movement ● **poise** v [I,T] be or hold sth steady in a particular position ▸ **poised** adj **1** in a position that is completely still but ready to move at any moment **2** ~ (**for/to**) ready for sth or to do sth

0~ **poison** /'pɔɪzn/ n [C,U] substance causing death or harm if absorbed by a living thing ● **poison** v [T] **1** give poison to sb; put poison on sth **2** (written) have a bad effect on sth ▸ **poisonous** adj

poke /pəʊk/ v [I,T] **1** quickly push your fingers or another object into sb/sth **2** put or move sth somewhere with a quick, sharp movement: *P~ your head out of the window.* [IDM] **poke fun at sb/sth** make sb appear foolish ∎ **poke your nose into sth** ➔ NOSE¹ ● **poke** n [C] action of poking sth to make sb

poker

move ∎ **poker** /'pəʊkə(r)/ n **1** [U] card game played for money **2** [C] metal stick used for moving coal in a fire

poky /ˈpəʊki/ *adj* (-ier, -iest) (*infml*) **1** (of a room or building) too small **2** (*also* pokey) (*US*) very slow and annoying

polar /ˈpəʊlə(r)/ *adj* **1** of or near the North or South Pole **2** (*fml*) directly opposite ● 'polar bear *n* [C] white bear that lives near the North Pole ▸ polarity /pəˈlærəti/ *n* [U] (*fml*) state of having two opposite qualities or tendencies

polarize (*also* -ise) /ˈpəʊləraɪz/ *v* [I,T] (cause people to) separate into two groups with completely opposite opinions: *an issue that ~d public opinion* ▸ polarization (*also* -isation) /ˌpəʊləraɪˈzeɪʃn/ *n* [U]

0— **pole** /pəʊl/ *n* [C] **1** long thin piece of wood or metal, used as a support **2** either of the two ends of the Earth's axis: *the North/South P~* **3** (*physics*) either of the ends of a magnet or the positive or negative points of an electric battery [IDM] be poles apart be widely separated; have no shared interests ● the 'pole vault *n* [sing] sporting event in which people try to jump over a high bar using a long pole to support them ▸ 'pole-vaulter *n* [C] ▸ 'pole-vaulting *n* [U]

polecat /ˈpəʊlkæt/ *n* [C] small European wild animal with an unpleasant smell *cf* = SKUNK

0— **police** /pəˈliːs/ *n* (the police) [pl] (members of an) official organization whose job is to keep public order, prevent and solve crime, etc ■ police *v* [T] keep order in a place ■ po'lice 'constable (*abbr* PC) *n* [C] (in Britain and some other countries) a police officer of the lowest rank ■ po'lice force *n* [C] police organization of a country or region ■ po'liceman | po'lice officer | po'licewoman *n* [C] member of a police force ■ po'lice station *n* [C] office of a local police force

0— **policy** /ˈpɒləsi/ *n* [C,U] (pl -ies) **1** plan of action agreed or chosen by a political party, a business, etc: *the Government's foreign ~* **2** written insurance contract

polio /ˈpəʊliəʊ/ *n* [U] serious infectious disease affecting the central nervous system, often causing paralysis

0— **polish** /ˈpɒlɪʃ/ *v* [T] **1** make sth smooth and shiny by rubbing it **2** ~ (up) improve sth [PV] polish sth off (*infml*) finish sth, esp food, quickly ● polish *n* **1** [U] substance used when rubbing a surface to make it smooth and shiny **2** [sing] act of polishing sth **3** [U] high quality of performance achieved with great skill ▸ polished *adj* **1** shiny as a

result of polishing **2** elegant, confident and/or highly skilled

0— **polite** /pəˈlaɪt/ *adj* having or showing good manners ▸ politely *adv* ▸ politeness *n* [U]

politic /ˈpɒlətɪk/ *adj* (*fml*) (of actions) sensible; wise

0— **political** /pəˈlɪtɪkl/ *adj* **1** of the state, government or public affairs: *~ prisoners* **2** of politics; of political parties **3** (of people) interested in politics ▸ politically /-kli/ *adv* ■ po litically cor'rect *adj* (*abbr* PC) used to describe language that deliberately tries to avoid offending particular groups of people

0— **politician** /ˌpɒləˈtɪʃn/ *n* [C] person whose job is connected with politics

0— **politics** /ˈpɒlətɪks/ *n* **1** [U, with sing or pl verb] activities of government; political affairs **2** [pl] person's political views **3** [U] study of government

polka /ˈpɒlkə/ *n* [C] (music for a) fast dance, popular in the 19th century

poll /pəʊl/ *n* **1** [C] survey of public opinion **2** [C] (*also* the polls [pl]) election: *The final result of the ~ will be known tomorrow.* ◇ *P~s close* (= voting ends) *at 9 p.m.* **3** [sing] number of votes given in an election ● poll *v* [T] **1** receive a certain number of votes in an election **2** ask a large number of members of the public what they think about sth ■ 'polling booth *n* [C] small, partly enclosed space in a polling station where people vote by marking a card, etc ■ 'polling station *n* [C] building where people go to vote in an election

pollen /ˈpɒlən/ *n* [U] fine usu yellow powder formed from flowers that fertilizes other flowers

pollinate /ˈpɒləneɪt/ *v* [T] put pollen into a flower or plant so that it produces seeds ▸ pollination /ˌpɒləˈneɪʃn/ *n* [U]

pollute /pəˈluːt/ *v* [T] add dirty or harmful substances to land, air, water, etc: *a river~d with toxic waste*

0— **pollution** /pəˈluːʃn/ *n* [U] the process of making air, water, soil, etc. dirty; the state of being dirty: *environmental ~*

polo /ˈpəʊləʊ/ *n* [U] ball game played on horseback with long-handled hammers ■ polo neck *n* [C] (piece of clothing with a) high round collar that is folded over

polyester /ˌpɒliˈestə(r)/ *n* [U,C] artificial fabric used for making clothes

polygamy /pəˈlɪɡəmi/ *n* [U] (*tech*) custom of having more than one wife at the same time ▸ polygamist /pəˈlɪɡəmɪst/ *n* [C] ▸ polygamous /pəˈlɪɡəməs/ *adj*: *a ~ society*

polygon /ˈpɒlɪɡən/ *n* [C] (*geom*)

figure with five or more straight sides

polystyrene /ˌpɒliˈstaɪriːn/ n [U] very light soft plastic, used for making containers, etc: ~ cups

polythene /ˈpɒliθiːn/ (US **polyethylene**) n [U] strong thin plastic, used esp for making bags or wrapping things

polyunsaturated /ˌpɒliʌnˈsætʃəreɪtɪd/ adj (esp of vegetable fats) having a chemical structure that does not help cholesterol to form in the blood

pomegranate /ˈpɒmɪɡrænɪt/ n [C] thick-skinned round fruit with a reddish centre full of seeds

pomp /pɒmp/ n [U] impressive clothes, decorations, music, etc at an official ceremony

pompous /ˈpɒmpəs/ adj (disapprov) full of self-importance ▶ **pomposity** /pɒmˈpɒsəti/ n [U] ▶ **pompously** adv

poncho /ˈpɒntʃəʊ/ n [C] (pl ~s) piece of cloth with a hole for the head, worn as a cloak

pond /pɒnd/ n [C] small area of water: a fish ~

ponder /ˈpɒndə(r)/ v [I,T] (written) think about sth carefully

ponderous /ˈpɒndərəs/ adj (written) **1** (disapprov) (of speech or writing) too slow; serious and dull **2** moving slowly and heavily ▶ **ponderously** adv

pong /pɒŋ/ v [I], n [C] (GB, infml) (make a) strong unpleasant smell

pontoon /pɒnˈtuːn/ n **1** [C] boat or structure, esp supporting a bridge **2** [U] (GB) kind of card game

pony /ˈpəʊni/ n [C] (pl **-ies**) small horse ■ **'ponytail** n [C] hair tied at the back of the head so that it hangs down

poodle /ˈpuːdl/ n [C] small dog with thick curly hair

0-ℼ **pool** /puːl/ n **1** [C] = SWIMMING POOL (SWIM) **2** [C] small area of water **3** [C] small amount of liquid or light lying on a surface: a ~ of blood **4** [C] common supply of goods, services or people, shared among many: a ~ of cars used by the firm's sales staff **5** [U] game for two people played with 16 coloured balls on a table, often in pubs and bars **6** (the pools) [pl] = FOOTBALL POOLS (FOOT) ● **pool** v [T] collect money, information, etc from different people so that it can be shared

0-ℼ **poor** /pɔː(r)/ adj **1** having very little money **2** deserving pity and sympathy: P~ Lisa is ill. **3** low in quality: be in ~ health **4** having very small amounts of sth: soil ~ in nutrients ▶ **poorness** n [U]

poorly /ˈpʊəli, ˈpɔːli/ adv **1** (GB, infml) ill ● **poorly** adv in a way that is not satisfactory

0-ℼ **pop¹** /pɒp/ n **1** [U] (also **'pop music**) modern popular music with a strong rhythm: rock, ~ and soul **2** [sing] (infml, esp US) used as a word for 'father' **3** [C] short sharp explosive sound ● **pop** adj of or in the style of modern popular music

0-ℼ **pop²** /pɒp/ v (**-pp-**) **1** [I,T] (cause sth to) make a short explosive sound **2** [I] (GB, infml) go somewhere quickly, suddenly or for a short time: She's just ~ped out to the shops. **3** [I] suddenly appear, esp when not expected: The menu ~s up when you double-click on the icon. ■ **'popcorn** n [U] type of food made from grains of maize, heated until they burst open ■ **pop-eyed** adj (infml) with eyes wide open with surprise ■ **'pop-up** adj (computing) that can be brought to the screen quickly, while you are working on another document: a ~-up menu/window

pope /pəʊp/ n [C] (the Pope) head of the Roman Catholic Church

poplar /ˈpɒplə(r)/ n [C] tall straight thin tree

poppy /ˈpɒpi/ n [C] (pl **-ies**) plant with large red flowers

populace /ˈpɒpjələs/ n (the populace) [sing] (fml) all the ordinary people in a country

0-ℼ **popular** /ˈpɒpjələ(r)/ adj **1** ~ (with) liked or enjoyed by many people **2** of or for ordinary people: ~ culture/fiction **3** (of beliefs, etc) shared by many people ▶ **popularity** /ˌpɒpjuˈlærəti/ n [U] ▶ **popularize** (also **-ise**) v [T] (written) make a lot of people know about sth and enjoy it ▶ **popularly** adv

populate /ˈpɒpjuleɪt/ v [T] (usu passive) live in an area and form its population

0-ℼ **population** /ˌpɒpjuˈleɪʃn/ n [C] (number of) people living in a particular country, city, etc

porcelain /ˈpɔːsəlɪn/ n [U] (articles made of) fine china

porch /pɔːtʃ/ n [C] covered entrance to a building

porcupine /ˈpɔːkjupaɪn/ n [C] animal with long pointed spikes on its back

pore /pɔː(r)/ n [C] tiny hole in your skin, that sweat can pass through ● **pore v [PV] pore over sth** look at or read sth carefully

pork /pɔːk/ n [U] meat from a pig

pornography /pɔːˈnɒɡrəfi/ (also infml porn) n [U] (disapprov) books, films, etc that show sexual activity in order to cause sexual excitement ▶ **pornographic** /ˌpɔːnəˈɡræfɪk/ (also infml porno) adj

porous /ˈpɔːrəs/ adj allowing liquid or air to pass through

porpoise /ˈpɔːpəs/ n [C] sea animal like a small dolphin

porridge /'pɒrɪdʒ/ n [U] soft food made by heating crushed oats in water or milk

port /pɔːt/ n **1** [C] town or city with a harbour **2** [C,U] place where ships load and unload goods or shelter from storms **3** [U] strong sweet dark red wine made in Portugal **4** [U] left side of a ship or aircraft when it is facing forward

portable /'pɔːtəbl/ adj that is easy to carry or move

portal /'pɔːtl/ n [C] website used as a point of entry to the Internet, where information will be useful to a person interested in particular kinds of things: a business ~

porter /'pɔːtə(r)/ n [C] **1** person whose job is to carry luggage, etc at a railway station **2** person whose job is to be on duty at the entrance of a hotel, etc

portfolio /pɔːt'fəʊliəʊ/ n [C] (pl ~s) **1** flat case for carrying documents, drawings **2** (business) set of shares owned by a person or an organization **3** position and duties of a government minister

porthole /'pɔːthəʊl/ n [C] round window in the side of a ship or aircraft

portion /'pɔːʃn/ n [C] **1** part or share of sth **2** amount of food for one person ● **portion** v [PV] **portion sth out** divide sth into shares

portly /'pɔːtli/ adj (-ier, -iest) (esp of an older man) rather fat

portrait /'pɔːtreɪt; -trət/ n [C] **1** painting, drawing or photograph of a person **2** detailed description of sb/sth ● **portrait** adj (computing) (of a document) printed so that the top of the page is one of the shorter sides

portray /pɔː'treɪ/ v [T] **1** make sb/sth appear in a picture; describe sb/sth in a piece of writing **2** describe or show sb/sth in a particular way **3** act a particular role in a film or play ▸ **portrayal** n [C,U]

pose /pəʊz/ v **1** [T] create a threat, problem, etc that has to be dealt with **2** [T] (fml) ask a question **3** [I] ~ **(for)** sit or stand in a particular position, to be photographed, drawn, etc **4** [I] ~ **as** pretend to be sb ● **pose** n [C] **1** position in which sb stands, sits, etc, esp when being photographed, drawn, etc **2** (disapprov) way of behaving that is intended to impress people and is not sincere ▸ **poser** n [C] **1** (infml) difficult question **2** (disapprov) person who behaves in a way that is intended to impress people

posh /pɒʃ/ adj (infml) elegant and expensive

position /pə'zɪʃn/ n **1** [C,U] place where sb/sth is **2** [U] place where sb/sth is meant to be; the correct place: Is everybody in ~? **3** [C,U] way in which sb is sitting or standing or in which sth is arranged: lie in a comfortable ~ **4** [C, usu sing] situation or condition that sb is in: I am not in a ~ to help you. **5** [C] opinion or attitude **6** [C,U] person or an organization's level of importance in relation to others **7** [C] (fml) job [IDM] **in position** in the right or proper place ● **position** v [T] put sb/sth in a particular position

positive /'pɒzətɪv/ adj **1** thinking about what is good in a situation: a ~ attitude **2** useful; good **3** (of a person) certain and confident: I'm ~ he's here. **4** (grammar) complete; real: a ~ pleasure **5** clear and definite: ~ proof **6** (maths) (of a number) greater than zero **7** (tech) of the kind of electric charge carried by protons ▸ **positively** adv definitely; really

possess /pə'zes/ v [T] **1** (fml) have or own sth **2** (usu passive) (lit) (of a feeling, etc) control sb's mind: ~ed by jealousy ▸ **possessor** n [C] (fml) owner

possession /pə'zeʃn/ n **1** (fml) state of having or owning sth **2** [C, usu pl] thing that you own or have with you at one time

possessive /pə'zesɪv/ adj **1** unwilling to share what you own with others **2** (gram) of or showing possession: 'Yours' is a ~ pronoun. ▸ **possessively** adv ▸ **possessiveness** n [U]

possibility /ˌpɒsə'bɪləti/ n (pl -ies) **1** [U] state of being possible **2** [C] something that may happen

possible /'pɒsəbl/ adj **1** that can be done; that can exist **2** reasonable; acceptable ● **possible** n [C] person or thing that might be chosen for sth ▸ **possibly** adv **1** perhaps **2** reasonably: I'll come as soon as I ~ can.

post¹ /pəʊst/ n **1** [U] official system used for sending and delivering letters, parcels, etc **2** [C,U] (one collection or delivery of) letters, parcels, etc **3** [C] job **4** [C] place where sb, eg a soldier, is on duty **5** [C] upright piece of wood, metal, etc supporting or marking sth **6** (the post) [sing] place where a race finishes ■ **postbox** n [C] (GB) public box in the street that you put letters in when you send them ■ **postcard** n [C] card for sending messages by post without an envelope ■ **postcode** n [C] (GB) group of letters and numbers used as part of an address, to make delivery easier ■ ˌpost-ˈhaste adv (old) very quickly ■ **postman** ǀ **postwoman** n [C] person whose job is to collect and deliver letters, etc ∎ **postmark** *n* [C] official mark on a letter, etc, giving the place and date of posting ∎ **post office box** = PO BOX (PO)

0– **post²** /pəʊst/ *v* [T] **1** send a letter, etc to sb by post **2** (*usu passive*) send sb to a place for a period of time as part of their job **3** put a soldier, etc in a particular place to guard a building or an area **4** put a notice, etc in a public place so that people can see it **5** announce sth publicly or officially: *The aircraft and its crew were ~ed missing.* ∎ **'Post-it**™ *(also* **Post-it note)** *n* [C] small piece of coloured sticky paper that you use for writing a note on

postage /'pəʊstɪdʒ/ *n* [U] amount charged for the sending of a letter, etc by post ∎ **postage stamp** *n* [C] *(fml)* = STAMP(1)

postal /'pəʊstl/ *adj* of the post; by post: *~ services* ∎ **postal order** *n* [C] written form for money, to be cashed at a post office

post-date /ˌpəʊst 'deɪt/ *v* [T] write a date on a cheque that is later than the actual date so that the cheque cannot be cashed until then

poster /'pəʊstə(r)/ *n* [C] large printed notice or picture

posterior /pɒ'stɪəriə(r)/ *adj* (*tech*) situated behind or at the back of sth

posterity /pɒ'sterəti/ *n* [U] *(fml)* future generations

postgraduate /ˌpəʊst'ɡrædʒuət/ *n* [C] person already holding a first degree and who is doing advanced study or research

posthumous /'pɒstjʊməs/ *adj* happening after a person has died ▸ **posthumously** *adv*

post-mortem /ˌpəʊst 'mɔːtəm/ *n* [C] **1** medical examination of a body to find the cause of death **2** review of an event after it has happened

0– **'post office** *n* [C] building where postal business takes place: *Where's the main post office?*

postpone /pə'spəʊn/ *v* [T] arrange for sth to happen at a later time than originally planned: *The match was ~d because of the rain.* ▸ **postponement** *n* [C, U]

postscript /'pəʊstskrɪpt/ *n* [C] *(abbr* **PS)** extra message written at the end of a letter

posture /'pɒstʃə(r)/ *n* **1** [U] position in which you hold your body when standing, sitting, etc **2** [C] attitude of mind

posy /'pəʊzi/ *n* [C] (*pl* **-ies**) small bunch of flowers

0– **pot¹** /pɒt/ *n* **1** [C] round container, esp one used for cooking things in: *~s and pans* **2** [C] container of various kinds, made for a particular purpose: *a coffee/plant~* **3** [C] amount contained in a pot

4 [U] *(infml)* = MARIJUANA [IDM] **go to pot** *(infml)* be spoilt or ruined **pots of money** *(GB, infml)* very large amount of money **take pot luck** accept whatever is available, without any choice ∎ **pot-'bellied** *adj* having a fat stomach ∎ **'pothole** *n* [C] **1** large hole in a road made by rain and traffic **2** deep hole worn in rock by water ∎ **'potholing** *n* [U] = CAVING ∎ **'potshot** *n* [C] *(infml)* carelessly aimed shot

pot² /pɒt/ *v* **(-tt-)** [T] put a plant into a flowerpot filled with soil ▸ **potted** *adj* **1** planted in a pot **2** (*of a book*, etc) in a short simple form: *a ~ted history* **3** (*of cooked meat or fish*) preserved in a small container

potassium /pə'tæsiəm/ *n* [U] (*symb* K) soft silver-white metal

0– **potato** /pə'teɪtəʊ/ *n* [C, U] (*pl* **-es**) round vegetable, with a brown or red skin, that grows underground

potent /'pəʊtnt/ *adj* powerful: *~ arguments/drugs* ▸ **potency** /-tnsi/ *n* [U] ▸ **potently** *adv*

potential /pə'tenʃl/ *adj* that can develop into sth or be developed in the future ● **potential** *n* [U] **1** possibility of sth happening or being developed or used **2** qualities that exist and can be developed ▸ **potentiality** /pəˌtenʃi'æləti/ *n* [C] (*pl* **-ies**) (*fml*) power or quality that can be developed ▸ **potentially** /-ʃəli/ *adv*

potion /'pəʊʃn/ *n* [C] *(lit)* drink of medicine, poison, or magical liquid

potter /'pɒtə(r)/ *v* [I] move around in an unhurried relaxed way, doing small unimportant tasks: *I spent the day ~ing around the house.* ● **potter** *n* [C] person who makes clay pots by hand ▸ **pottery** *n* (*pl* **-ies**) **1** [U] (pots, dishes, etc made of) baked clay **2** [C] place where clay pots and dishes are made

potty /'pɒti/ *adj* **(-ier, -iest)** *(GB, infml)* crazy ● **potty** *n* [C] (*pl* **-ies**) *(infml)* bowl that young children use as a toilet

pouch /paʊtʃ/ *n* [C] **1** small usu leather bag carried in a pocket or on a belt **2** pocket of skin on the stomach of some female animals, eg kangaroos

poultry /'pəʊltri/ *n* **1** [pl] chickens, ducks, etc **2** [U] meat from chickens, ducks, etc

pounce /paʊns/ *v* [I] *~ (on)* make a sudden forward attack on sb/sth: *The lion crouched ready to ~.* [PV] **pounce on/upon sth** quickly notice sth that sb has said or done, esp in order to criticize it

0– **pound¹** /paʊnd/ *n* **1** (*symb* £) unit of money in Britain; 100 pence **2** unit of money of several other countries **3** (*abbr* **lb**) measure of weight; 16 ounces (0.454 kilogram) **4** place where lost dogs are kept until claimed by their owners ■ **pound sign** *n* [C] **1** symbol (£) that represents a pound in British money **2** (*US*) = HASH(3)

pound² /paʊnd/ *v* **1** [I,T] hit sth/sb hard many times **2** [I] (of sb's heart) beat quickly and loudly **3** [T] hit sth many times to break it into pieces: *The seeds were ~ed to a powder.*

0━ **pour** /pɔː(r)/ *v* **1** [I,T] (cause a liquid to) flow in a continuous stream: *~ the sauce over the pasta.* **2** [I] (of rain) fall heavily **3** [I] come or go somewhere continuously in large numbers: *In summer tourists ~ into London.* **IDM** **pour cold water on sth** → COLD¹ **[PV]** **pour sth out** express your feelings fully, esp after keeping them hidden: *~ out your troubles*

pout /paʊt/ *v* [I] push your lips forward, esp to show you are annoyed ▶ **pout** *n* [C]

poverty /ˈpɒvəti/ *n* [U] state of being poor ■ **poverty-stricken** *adj* extremely poor

0━ **powder** /ˈpaʊdə(r)/ *n* [U,C] dry mass of fine particles ● *v* [T] put powder on sth: *She ~ed her face and put on lipstick.* ▶ **powdered** *adj* in the form of a powder ■ **powder room** *n* [C] polite word for a women's toilet in a hotel, etc ▶ **powdery** *adj* of or like powder

0━ **power** /ˈpaʊə(r)/ *n* **1** [U] ability to control people or things **2** [U] political control of a country: *seize/lose ~* **3** [U] (in people) ability or opportunity to do sth **4** [U] (also **powers**) [pl] particular ability of the body or mind: *the ~ of speech* **5** (**powers**) [pl] all the abilities of the body or mind **6** [U,C, usu pl] right or authority to do sth **7** [C] country, etc with great influence in world affairs: *a world ~* **8** [U] energy or force that can be used to do work: *nuclear ~* ● **power** *v* [T] supply a machine or vehicle with the energy that makes it work: *~ed by electricity* ■ **power station** *n* [C] building where electricity is produced ■ **power steering** (*GB also* **power-assisted steering**) *n* [U] (in a vehicle) system that uses power from the engine to help the driver change direction

0━ **powerful** /ˈpaʊəfl/ *adj* having great power, influence or strength ▶ **powerfully** *adv*

powerless /ˈpaʊələs/ *adj* without power to control sth; unable to do sth: *~ to act* ▶ **powerlessness** *n* [U]

pp *abbr* **1** pages **2** (*esp GB*) used in front of a person's name when sb signs a business letter on his/her behalf: *pp Laura Bunt*

PR /ˌpiː ˈɑː(r)/ *abbr* public relations

practicable /ˈpræktɪkəbl/ *adj* (*fml*) able to be done; likely to succeed ▶ **practicability** /ˌ-ˈbɪləti/ *n* [U]

0━ **practical** /ˈpræktɪkl/ *adj* **1** concerned with real situations rather than ideas or theories **2** sensible, useful or suitable: *clothing for wearing in bad weather* **3** (of a person) sensible and realistic **4** (of a person) good at making or repairing things ▶ **practicality** /ˌpræktɪˈkæləti/ *n* [C,U] (*pl* **-ies**) ■ **practical joke** *n* [C] trick played on sb ▶ **practically** /-kli/ *adv* **1** almost: *~ no time left* **2** in a realistic or sensible way

0━ **practice** /ˈpræktɪs/ *n* **1** [U] action rather than ideas: *put a plan into ~* **2** [U,C] usual way of doing sth; procedure or custom: *standard ~* **3** [U,C] (time spent) doing an activity regularly or training regularly to improve your skill: *football ~* **4** [U,C] (place) of work or the business of some professional people, eg doctors and lawyers **IDM** **in practice** in reality **be/get out of practice** be or get less good at sth because you have not spent time doing it recently

0━ **practise** (*US* **-ice**) /ˈpræktɪs/ *v* **1** [I,T] do sth repeatedly or regularly to improve your skill: *~ your English* **2** [T] do sth regularly as part of your normal behaviour: *a practising Catholic* **3** [I,T] ~ **(as)** work as a doctor, lawyer, etc **IDM** **practise what you preach** do what you advise others to do ▶ **practised** *adj* experienced; skilled

practitioner /prækˈtɪʃənə(r)/ *n* [C] **1** (*tech*) person who works in a profession, esp medicine **2** (*fml*) person who regularly does an activity, esp one requiring skill

pragmatic /prægˈmætɪk/ *adj* solving problems in a sensible and practical way

prairie /ˈpreəri/ *n* [C,U] large flat area of grass-covered land in North America

0━ **praise** /preɪz/ *v* [T] **1** express your approval or admiration for sb/sth **2** worship God ● **praise** *n* [U] expression of praise ■ **praiseworthy** *adj* deserving praise

pram /præm/ *n* [C] small vehicle on four wheels for a baby to go out in, pushed by hand

prance /prɑːns/ *v* [I] **1** move quickly with exaggerated steps **2** (of a horse) move with high steps

prank /præŋk/ *n* [C] trick that is played on sb as a joke

prattle /ˈprætl/ *v* [I] talk a lot about unimportant things ▶ **prattle** *n* [U]

prawn /prɔːn/ *n* [C] edible shellfish that turns pink when cooked

pray /preɪ/ v [I] **1** speak to God, to give thanks to or to ask for help **2** hope very much that sth will happen: *Let's just ~ for good weather.*

0—**prayer** /preə(r)/ n **1** [C] words which you say to God **2** [C] fixed form of words that you can say when you speak to God **3** [U] act or habit of praying

preach /priːtʃ/ v **1** [I,T] give a religious talk in a church service **2** [T] try to persuade people to accept a particular religion, way of life, etc **3** [I] give sb unwanted advice on morals, behaviour, etc ▸ **preacher** n [C] Christian who preaches at a church service or religious meeting

preamble /priˈæmbl; ˈpriːæmbl/ n [C,U] introduction, esp to a formal document

precarious /prɪˈkeəriəs/ adj not safe or certain; dangerous ▸ **precariously** adv

precaution /prɪˈkɔːʃn/ n [C] action taken in advance to avoid danger or trouble: *take ~s against illness* ▸ **precautionary** adj

precede /prɪˈsiːd/ v [T] come or go before sth/sb in time, place or order: *She~d me in the job.* ▸ **preceding** adj existing or coming before

precedence /ˈpresɪdəns/ n [U] right to come before sb/sth in importance: *take ~ over all others*

precedent /ˈpresɪdənt/ n [C,U] earlier decision or action that is taken as a rule for the future: *set a ~*

precinct /ˈpriːsɪŋkt/ n **1** [C] (GB) commercial area of a town where cars cannot go: *a shopping ~* **2** [C] (US) division of a city, county, etc **3** [usu pl] area around a place or a building, often enclosed by a wall

precious /ˈpreʃəs/ adj **1** of great value **2** (disapprov) (of people and their behaviour) formal, exaggerated and unnatural ● **precious** adv (infml) very: *~ little time*

precipice /ˈpresəpɪs/ n [C] very steep cliff

precipitate /prɪˈsɪpɪteɪt/ v [T] **1** (fml) make sth, esp sth bad, happen sooner than it should: *Illness ~d her death.* **2** ~ into force sb/sth into a particular state ● **precipitate** n [C,U] (chem) solid substance that has been separated from a liquid in a chemical process ● **precipitate** /prɪˈsɪpɪtət/ adj (fml) (of an action or a decision) too hurried ▸ **precipitation** /prɪˌsɪpɪˈteɪʃn/ n **1** [U] fall of rain, snow, etc **2** [U,C] (chem) chemical process in which solid matter is separated from a liquid

precipitous /prɪˈsɪpɪtəs/ adj (fml) dangerously high or steep

precis /ˈpreɪsiː/ n [C] (pl precis /-siːz/) short version of a speech or piece of

---

writing that gives the main points or ideas

0—**precise** /prɪˈsaɪs/ adj **1** clear and accurate **2** exact **3** showing care about small details ▸ **precisely** adv **1** exactly **2** (spoken) used to emphasize that you agree with a statement

precision /prɪˈsɪʒn/ n [U] exactness and accuracy

preclude /prɪˈkluːd/ v [T] (fml) ~ (from) prevent sth from happening or sb from doing sth

precocious /prɪˈkəʊʃəs/ adj (of a child) having developed particular abilities at a younger age than usual ▸ **precociously** adv ▸ **precociousness** n [U]

preconceived /ˌpriːkənˈsiːvd/ adj (of an opinion) formed in advance, before gaining enough knowledge ▸ **preconception** /-ˈsepʃn/ n [C] preconceived idea

precursor /priːˈkɜːsə(r)/ n [C] (fml) ~ (of/to) something that comes before and leads to sth more important

predatory /ˈpredətri/ adj **1** (tech) (of animals) living by killing and eating other animals **2** (written) (of people) using weaker people for their own advantage ▸ **predator** /ˈpredətə(r)/ n [C] predatory animal or person

predecessor /ˈpriːdɪsesə(r)/ n [C] person who did a job before sb else

predestined /ˌpriːˈdestɪnd/ adj already decided by God or by fate

predicament /prɪˈdɪkəmənt/ n [C] difficult or unpleasant situation

predicate /ˈpredɪkət/ n [C] (gram) part of a statement that says sth about the subject, eg 'is short' in 'Life is short.'

predicative /prɪˈdɪkətɪv/ adj (gram) (of an adjective) coming after a verb

0—**predict** /prɪˈdɪkt/ v [T] say that sth will happen in the future ▸ **predictable** adj that can be predicted ▸ **prediction** /-ˈdɪkʃn/ n [C,U] (act of making a) statement saying what you think will happen

predispose /ˌpriːdɪˈspəʊz/ v [T] (fml) influence sb so they are likely to think or behave in a particular way ▸ **predisposition** /-dɪspəˈzɪʃn/ n [C,U]

predominant /prɪˈdɒmɪnənt/ adj **1** most obvious or noticeable **2** having more power or influence than others ▸ **predominance** /-nəns/ n [sing, U] ▸ **predominantly** adv mostly; mainly

predominate /prɪˈdɒmɪneɪt/ v [I] **1** be greater in amount or number than sth/sb else **2** have the most influence or importance

pre-eminent /priˈemɪnənt/ adj (fml) more important, more

---

successful or of a higher standard than others ▶ **pre-eminence** /-nəns/ n [U] ● **pre-eminently** adv to a very great degree; especially

pre-empt /ˌpriˈempt/ v [T] prevent sth from happening by taking action to stop it ▶ **pre-emption** n [U] (business) opportunity given to one person or group to buy goods, shares, etc ● **pre-emptive** adj done to stop sb taking action: a ~ive attack/strike

preen /priːn/ v **1** ~ **yourself** spend a lot of time making yourself look attractive and then admiring your appearance **2** [I,T] (of a bird) clean and smooth its feathers with its beak

prefabricated /ˌpriːˈfæbrɪkeɪtɪd/ adj (esp of a building) made in sections that can be put together later

preface /ˈprefəs/ n [C] introduction to a book ● **preface** v [T] ~ (**with**) begin by saying or doing sth

prefect /ˈpriːfekt/ n [C] **1** (in some British schools) older pupil who has authority over younger pupils **2** (in France) chief administrative officer of an area

0ᵐ prefer /prɪˈfɜː(r)/ v (-rr-) [T] choose one thing rather than sth else because you like it better: I ~ tea to coffee. **IDM prefer charges against sb** ⇒ CHARGE² **1** uses ▶ **preferable** /ˈprefrəbl/ adj more attractive or suitable ▶ **preferably** adv

0ᵐ preference /ˈprefrəns/ n **1** [U, sing] ~ (**for**) liking for sb/sth more than sth else **2** [C] thing that is liked better or best **IDM give (a) preference to sb/sth** treat sb/sth in a way that gives them an advantage over others: P~ will be given to graduates.

preferential /ˌprefəˈrenʃl/ adj giving an advantage to a particular person or group: get ~ treatment

prefix /ˈpriːfɪks/ n [C] (gram) letter or group of letters, eg pre- or un-, placed in front of a word to change its meaning ● **prefix** v [T] add letters or numbers to the beginning of a word or number

0ᵐ pregnant /ˈpregnənt/ adj **1** (of a woman or female animal) having a baby or young animal in the womb **2** full of meaning or feeling ▶ **pregnancy** /-nənsi/ n [U,C, pl **-ies**]

prehistoric /ˌpriːhɪˈstɒrɪk/ adj of the time before recorded history ▶ **prehistory** /ˌpriːˈhɪstri/ n [U]

prejudge /ˌpriːˈdʒʌdʒ/ v [T] (fml) make a judgement about sth before knowing all the facts

prejudice /ˈpredʒudɪs/ n [U,C] unfair dislike of sth/sb **IDM without prejudice (to sth)** (law) without affecting any other legal matter

● **prejudice** v [T] **1** influence sb so that they have an unfair opinion of sb/sth **2** (fml) have a harmful effect on sth ▶ **prejudicial** /ˌpredʒuˈdɪʃl/ adj

prelate /ˈprelət/ n [C] (fml) priest of high rank

preliminary /prɪˈlɪmɪnəri/ adj coming first: a ~ study/report ● **preliminary** n [C] (pl **-ies**) action or event done in preparation for sth

prelude /ˈpreljuːd/ n [C] **1** short, esp introductory, piece of music **2** (written) action, event, etc that acts as an introduction to another

premarital /ˌpriːˈmærɪtl/ adj before marriage: ~ sex

premature /ˈpremətʃə(r)/ adj happening before the normal or expected time ▶ **prematurely** adv

premeditated /ˌpriːˈmedɪteɪtɪd/ adj (of a crime or bad action) planned in advance: ~ murder

premier /ˈpremiə(r)/ adj most important, famous or successful ● **premier** n [C] used esp in newspapers, etc to mean 'prime minister' ▶ **premiership** n [sing]

premiere /ˈpremieə(r)/ n [C] first public performance of a play or film

0ᵐ premise /ˈpremɪs/ n [C] (fml) statement on which reasoning is based

0ᵐ premises /ˈpremɪsɪz/ n [pl] building and land near to it that a business owns or uses: The company is looking for larger ~.

premium /ˈpriːmiəm/ n [C] **1** money paid for an insurance policy **2** extra payment added to the basic rate ■ **Premium Bond** n [C] (GB) government savings certificate that gives a chance of a cash prize

premonition /ˌpriːməˈnɪʃn; ˌprem-/ n [C] feeling that sth unpleasant is going to happen

preoccupation /priˌɒkjuˈpeɪʃn/ n **1** [U] state of thinking about sth continuously **2** [C] something that a person thinks about all the time

preoccupy /priˈɒkjupaɪ/ v (pt, pp **-ied**) [T] take all the attention of sb

0ᵐ preparation /ˌprepəˈreɪʃn/ n **1** [U] ~ (**for**) act of getting ready for sth or making sth ready: work done without ~ **2** [C, usu pl] things you do to get ready for sth or to make sth ready **3** [C] mixture that has been prepared for use as medicine, food, etc

preparatory /prɪˈpærətri/ adj (fml) done in order to prepare for sth ■ **pre·paratory school** (also **prep school**) n [C] **1** (in Britain) private school for children aged between 7 and 13 **2** (in the US) (usu private) school that prepares students for college

0ᵐ prepare /prɪˈpeə(r)/ v [I,T] get or make sth/sb ready to be used to do sth ▸ **prepared** adj **1** ~ (for) ready and able to deal with sth **2** willing to do sth: How much are you ~d to pay?

preposition /ˌprepəˈzɪʃn/ n [C] (gram) word, eg in, from or to, used before a noun or pronoun to show place, position, time or method ▸ **prepositional** /-ˈʃənl/ adj

preposterous /prɪˈpɒstərəs/ adj completely unreasonable; ridiculous ▸ **preposterously** adv

prerogative /prɪˈrɒɡətɪv/ n [C] (fml) right or privilege of a particular person or group

Presbyterian /ˌprezbɪˈtɪəriən/ n [C], adj (member of a) Church governed by officials of equal rank

prescribe /prɪˈskraɪb/ v [T] **1** (of a doctor) tell sb to take medicine or to have treatment: She ~d antibiotics. **2** state with authority what should be done

prescription /prɪˈskrɪpʃn/ n [C] doctor's written instruction for a medicine **2** [C] medicine that your doctor ordered for you **3** [U] act of prescribing medicine

prescriptive /prɪˈskrɪptɪv/ adj (fml) telling people what should be done

0— **presence** /ˈprezns/ n [U] **1** fact of being present in a place **2** (approv) person's appearance and manner

0— **present¹** /ˈpreznt/ adj **1** existing or happening now: the ~ government **2** being in a particular place: Were you ~ at the meeting? ● **present** n **1** [C] thing that you give to sb as a gift **2** (usu the present) [sing] the time now: I'm busy, he's out ~ (= now). **3** (the present) (also the present 'tense) [usu sing] (gram) verb form that expresses an action happening now or at the time of speaking ■ the present 'perfect n [sing] (gram) verb form which expresses an action done in a time period up to the present, formed in English with have/has and a past participle

0— **present²** /prɪˈzent/ v [T] **1** ~ (with, to) give sth to sb, esp formally: ~ her with a book ◇ ~ it to her **2** show or offer sth for people to consider: ~ a report **3** show or describe sth/sb from a particular point of view or in a certain way **4** ~ with cause sth to happen or be experienced: Your request shouldn't ~ us with problems. **5** (of an opportunity, etc) suddenly happen **6** introduce the different sections of a radio or television programme **7** produce a show, play, etc for the public **8** ~ (to) (fml) introduce sb to sb, esp of higher rank **9** ~ yourself officially appear somewhere ▸ **presenter** n [C] person who introduces the different sections of a radio or television programme

presentable /prɪˈzentəbl/ adj fit to

347

appear or be shown in public ▸ **presentably** adv

0— **presentation** /ˌpreznˈteɪʃn/ n **1** [U] act of showing or giving sth to sb **2** [U] way in which sth is presented; appearance **3** [C] meeting at which sth is presented

presently /ˈprezntli/ adv **1** (esp US) now **2** (written) soon: I'll see you ~.

preservative /prɪˈzɜːvətɪv/ n [C,U] substance used to prevent food and wood from decaying ▸ **preservative** adj

0— **preserve** /prɪˈzɜːv/ v [T] **1** keep sth in an unchanged condition **2** prevent food, etc from decaying, esp by treating it in some way **3** keep sb/sth alive, or safe from harm or danger ● **preserve** n [C, usu pl, U] preserved fruit; jam ▸ **preservation** /ˌprezəˈveɪʃn/ n [U]

preside /prɪˈzaɪd/ v [I] ~ (over/at) be in charge of a formal meeting

presidency /ˈprezɪdənsi/ n (pl -ies) [usu sing] **1** job of being president of a country or organization **2** period of time that sb is president

0— **president** /ˈprezɪdənt/ n [C] **1** (also President) leader of a republic, esp the US **2** person in charge of some organizations, clubs, etc ▸ **presidential** /ˌprezɪˈdenʃl/ adj

0— **press¹** /pres/ v **1** [T] push sth closely and firmly against sth **2** [I,T] push or squeeze part of a device, etc to make it work: ~ a button/key/ switch **3** [I] (of a crowd) move in the direction that is mentioned by pushing: The crowd ~ed forward. **4** [T] try repeatedly to persuade or force sb to do sth **5** [T] make sth flat and smooth by using a hot iron **6** [T] squeeze the juice out of fruit or vegetables by using force or weight [IDM] press charges against sb → CHARGE² [PV] press ahead/on (with sth) continue doing sth in a determined way; hurry forward press for sth keep asking for sth ▸ **pressed** adj ~ (for) have barely enough of sth, esp time or money ▸ **pressing** adj urgent: ~ing business

0— **press²** /pres/ n **1** (the press, the Press) [sing, with sing or pl verb] (writers for) newspapers and magazines **2** [sing, U] type or amount of reports that newspapers write about sb/sth: The airline has had a bad ~. **3** [C] machine for printing books, newspapers, etc; process of printing them: Prices are correct at the time of going to ~. **4** [C] business that publishes and prints books: Oxford University P~ **5** [C] machine for pressing sth: a trouser ~ **6** [C, usu sing] act of pushing sth with your hand or with a tool

press

A B C D E F G H I J K L M N O **P** Q R S T U V W X Y Z

■ ˌpress conference n [C] meeting at which a politician, etc answers reporters' questions

0━ pressure /ˈpreʃə(r)/ n 1 [U] force or weight with which sth presses against sth else: *the ~ of her hand on his head* 2 [U, C] (amount of) force produced by a gas or liquid in an enclosed space: *air ~* 3 [U] force or strong persuasion 4 [U] worry caused by the need to achieve or behave in a certain way: *The ~ of work is making her ill.* ■ ˈpressure cooker n [C] airtight pot in which food is cooked quickly by steam ■ ˈpressure group n [C] organized group of people who try to persuade the government, etc to act in a certain way

pressurize (also -ise) /ˈpreʃəraɪz/ v [T] 1 ~ (into) use forceful influence to persuade sb to do sth 2 keep a cabin in an aircraft, etc at a constant air pressure

prestige /preˈstiːʒ/ n [U] respect or admiration caused by sb's success, status, etc ► prestigious /-ˈstɪdʒəs/ adj respected and admired as very important

0━ presumably /prɪˈzjuːməbli/ adv used to say that you think sth is probably true

presume /prɪˈzjuːm/ v 1 [I] suppose that sth is true 2 [I] (fml) behave in a way that shows a lack of respect: *I wouldn't ~ to advise you.*

presumption /prɪˈzʌmpʃn/ n 1 [C] something thought to be true or probable 2 [U] (fml) disrespectful behaviour

presumptuous /prɪˈzʌmptʃuəs/ adj too confident, in a way that shows a lack of respect

presuppose /ˌpriːsəˈpəʊz/ v [T] (fml) 1 accept sth as true and act on that basis 2 depend on sth in order to exist or be true ► presupposition /-ˌsʌpəˈzɪʃn/ n [C, U] (fml)

pretence (US -tense) /prɪˈtens/ n [C, U] act of pretending

0━ pretend /prɪˈtend/ v [I, T] behave in a way that is intended to make people believe that sth is true when in reality it is not

pretension /prɪˈtenʃn/ n [C, usu pl, U] act of trying to appear more important, intelligent, etc than you really are

pretentious /prɪˈtenʃəs/ adj (disapprov) trying to appear more important, intelligent, etc than you really are ► pretentiously adv ► pretentiousness n [U]

pretext /ˈpriːtekst/ n [C] reason that is not true

0━ pretty /ˈprɪti/ adv fairly; very: *I'm ~ sure he'll come back.* [IDM] pretty much/well (spoken) almost; almost

completely ● pretty adj (-ier, -iest) pleasing and attractive: *a ~ girl* ► prettily adv ► prettiness n [U]

prevail /prɪˈveɪl/ v [I] (fml) 1 exist or happen generally 2 win [PV] prevail on/upon sb to do sth (fml) persuade sb to do sth ► prevailing adj 1 (written) most common 2 (of winds) most frequent

prevalent /ˈprevələnt/ adj existing generally; common ► prevalence /-əns/ n [U]

0━ prevent /prɪˈvent/ v [T] stop sb from doing sth; stop sth from happening ► prevention /-ˈvenʃn/ n [U] ► preventive (also preventative /-ˈventətɪv/) adj intended to prevent sth from happening: *~ive medicine*

preview /ˈpriːvjuː/ n [C] showing of a film, play, etc in private before it is shown to the public ● preview v [T] see a film, play, etc before the public and write an account of it for a newspaper, etc

0━ previous /ˈpriːviəs/ adj happening or existing before sth else: *the ~ day* ► previously adv

prey /preɪ/ n [U] animal, bird, etc killed by another for food ● prey v [IDM] prey on sb's mind worry sb greatly prey on/upon sb/sth hunt and catch an animal, etc as prey

0━ price /praɪs/ n 1 [C] amount of money that you have to pay for sth 2 [sing] what must be done or experienced to obtain sth: *a small ~ to pay for freedom* ● price v [T] fix the price of sth ► priceless adj 1 extremely valuable 2 (infml) very funny

prick /prɪk/ v 1 [T] make a very small hole in sth with a sharp point 2 [I, T] (cause sb to) feel a sharp pain in the skin [IDM] prick (up) your ears (of an animal) raise its ears 2 (of a person) listen carefully ● prick n [C] 1 (Δ, sl) penis 2 (Δ, sl) offensive word for an unpleasant man 3 act of pricking sth 4 pain caused by a sharp point

prickle /ˈprɪkl/ n [C] 1 small sharp point growing on a plant or on the skin of an animal 2 slight stinging feeling on the skin ● prickle v [I, T] give sb an unpleasant feeling on their skin ► prickly adj (-ier, -iest) 1 covered with prickles 2 (infml) (of a person) easily annoyed

0━ pride /praɪd/ n 1 [U] feeling of satisfaction that you get from doing sth well 2 [U, sing] person or thing that gives you a feeling of satisfaction or pleasure: *Their daughter was their ~ and joy.* 3 [U] self-respect 4 [U] (disapprov) too high an opinion of yourself 5 [C] group of lions ● pride v [PV] pride yourself on (doing) sth be proud of sth

priest /priːst/ n [C] clergyman of the Christian Church ► the

priesthood n [sing] job or position of being a priest

prig /prɪg/ n [C] (disapprov) very moral person who disapproves of others' behaviour ▸ **priggish** adj

prim /prɪm/ adj (~mer, ~mest) easily shocked by anything rude: ~ and proper

0━ **primary** /'praɪməri/ adj **1** main; most important; basic **2** developing or happening first ▸ **primarily** /praɪ'merəli; 'praɪmərəli/ adv mainly ● **primary** n [C] (pl -ies) (in the US) election in which voters choose candidates for a future election ■ **primary 'colour** (US **primary 'color**) n [C] red, yellow or blue ■ **primary school** n [C] (in Britain) school for children aged between 5 and 11

primate /'praɪmeɪt/ n [C] **1** any animal that belongs to the group of mammals that includes humans, apes and monkeys **2** archbishop

prime /praɪm/ adj **1** main; most important; basic **2** of the best quality ● **prime** n [sing] time in your life when you are strongest or most successful: in the ~ of life ● **prime** v [T] **1** supply sb with information in advance **2** cover wood with primer

0━ **prime minister** (also **Prime 'Minister**) n [C] chief minister in a government

primer /'praɪmə(r)/ n [C] special paint put on wood, metal, etc before the main layer

primeval (also primaeval) /praɪ'miːvl/ adj very ancient

primitive /'prɪmətɪv/ adj **1** belonging to a simple society with no industry, etc: ~ tribes **2** of an early stage of the development of humans or animals: ~ man **3** simple and old-fashioned ▸ **primitively** adv

primrose /'prɪmrəʊz/ n [C] wild plant with pale yellow flowers in spring

0━ **prince** /prɪns/ n [C] **1** male member of a royal family, esp the son of a king or queen **2** male royal ruler of a small country ▸ **princely** adj **1** generous **2** of or for a prince

0━ **princess** /ˌprɪn'ses/ n [C] **1** female member of a royal family, esp the daughter of a king or queen **2** wife of a prince

principal /'prɪnsəpl/ adj most important; main ● **principal** n [C] **1** head of a college or school **2** [usu sing] money lent to sb, on which interest is paid ▸ **principally** /-pli/ adv mainly

principality /ˌprɪnsɪ'pæləti/ n [C] (pl -ies) country ruled by a prince

0━ **principle** /'prɪnsəpl/ n **1** [C, usu pl, U] moral rule or strong belief that influences your actions: It's against my ~s. ◇ I wouldn't wear fur on ~. **2** [C] basic general truth: the ~ of

justice [IDM] **in principle** concerning the basic idea, but perhaps not the details

0━ **print¹** /prɪnt/ v **1** [T] produce letters, etc on paper using a machine that puts ink on the surface **2** [T] produce books, etc by printing them in large quantities **3** [T] produce a photograph from photographic film **4** [I,T] write without joining the letters together [PV] **print sth off/out** produce a document or information from a computer in printed form ▸ **printer** n [C] **1** machine for printing text on paper, esp one attached to a computer **2** person or company that prints books, etc ■ **printout** n [C, U] printed paper produced from a computer

0━ **print²** /prɪnt/ n **1** [U] letters, words, etc in printed form **2** [C, usu pl] mark left on a surface: finger~s **3** [C] picture made by printing from an ink-covered surface **4** [C] photograph printed from a negative [IDM] **in/out of print** (of a book) available/no longer available

0━ **prior** /'praɪə(r)/ adj earlier in time, order or importance: a ~ engagement ■ **prior to** prep (fml) before sth

0━ **priority** /praɪ'ɒrəti/ n (pl -ies) **1** [C] something that you think is more important than other things **2** [U] right of being more important

prise (esp US prize) /praɪz/ v [T] use force to separate sth from sth else

prism /'prɪzəm/ n [C] transparent block of glass that separates light into the colours of the rainbow

0━ **prison** /'prɪzn/ n [C, U] building in which criminals are kept as a punishment ▸ **prisoner** n [C] person kept in prison ■ **prisoner of 'war** n [C] soldier caught by the enemy in war

0━ **privacy** /'prɪvəsi/ n [U] state of being alone and undisturbed

0━ **private** /'praɪvət/ adj **1** of or for the use of one person or group, not the public **2** that you do not want other people to know about; secret **3** not organized or managed by the government; independent: a ~ school **4** not connected with your work; personal: your ~ life **5** where you are not likely to be disturbed; quiet ● **private** n [C] soldier of the lowest rank in the army [IDM] **in private** with no one else present ▸ **privately** adv

privatize (also -ise) /'praɪvətaɪz/ v [T] transfer a company from state to private ownership ▸ **privatization** (also -isation) /ˌpraɪvətaɪ'zeɪʃn/ n [U]

privet /'prɪvɪt/ n [U] evergreen bush often used for garden hedges

privilege /'prɪvəlɪdʒ/ n 1 [C, U] special right or advantage that a particular person or group has 2 [sing] opportunity that gives you great pleasure: a ~ to hear him sing

privileged /'prɪvəlɪdʒd/ adj having special rights and advantages: Only a ~ few were invited.

0–₩ **prize** /praɪz/ n [C] award given for winning a competition, doing good work, etc ● **prize** adj good enough to win a prize: ~ cattle ● **prize** v [T] 1 value sth highly 2 (US) = PRISE

pro /prəʊ/ n [C] (pl ~s) (infml) person who works as a professional, esp in a sport [IDM] **the pros and cons** advantages and disadvantages of sth

pro- /prəʊ; prə-/ prefix in favour of; supporting: pro-democracy

probability /,prɒbə'bɪləti/ n (pl -ies) 1 [U, C] how likely sth is to happen: There is little ~ that you will win. 2 [C] thing that is likely to happen [IDM] **in all probability** (written) it is very likely that

0–₩ **probable** /'prɒbəbl/ adj likely to happen or be true ▸ **probably** adv

probation /prə'beɪʃn/ n [U] (law) 1 system that allows a person who has committed a crime not to go to prison if they behave well and if they see an official (a probation officer) regularly over a period of time: He was put on ~. 2 time of training when you start a new job to see if you are suitable

probe /prəʊb/ v [I, T] 1 ask questions in order to find out secret information 2 examine sth, esp with a long thin instrument ● **probe** n [C] 1 ~ (into) careful investigation of sth 2 spacecraft used for obtaining information 3 long thin metal tool used by doctors for examining the body

0–₩ **problem** /'prɒbləm/ n [C] thing that is difficult to deal with or understand ▸ **problematic** /,prɒblə'mætɪk/ adj full of problems

0–₩ **procedure** /prə'siːdʒə(r)/ n [C, U] usual or proper way of doing sth ▸ **procedural** adj

0–₩ **proceed** /prə'siːd/ v [I] 1 ~ (with/ to) continue; go on 2 (fml) move or go in the direction that is stated

proceedings /prə'siːdɪŋz/ n [pl] (fml) 1 legal action against sb: divorce ~ 2 written report of a meeting, etc

proceeds /'prəʊsiːdz/ n [pl] money obtained from sth; profits

0–₩ **process** /'prəʊses/ n [C] 1 series of things that are done in order to achieve sth: We're in the ~ of selling our house. 2 method of doing or

making sth, esp one used in industry [IDM] **in the process of doing sth** actually still doing sth ● **process** v [T] 1 treat raw material, food, etc in order to change it, preserve it, etc: ~ed food 2 deal officially with a document, request, etc: ~ an application 3 perform a series of operations on data in a computer ▸ **processor** n [C] 1 machine or person that processes things 2 (computing) part of a computer that controls all the other parts of a system

procession /prə'seʃn/ n [C] line of people, vehicles, etc moving along, esp as part of a ceremony

proclaim /prə'kleɪm/ v [T] (fml) publicly and officially tell people about sth important ▸ **proclamation** /,prɒklə'meɪʃn/ n [C, U] (act of making an) official public statement about sth important

procure /prə'kjʊə(r)/ v [T] (fml) obtain sth, esp with difficulty

prod /prɒd/ v (-dd-) 1 [I, T] push sb/ sth with your finger or a pointed object 2 [T] try to make sb do sth, esp when they are unwilling ▸ **prod** n [C]

prodigal /'prɒdɪgl/ adj (fml, disapprov) spending money wastefully

prodigious /prə'dɪdʒəs/ adj (fml) very large or powerful and causing surprise or admiration ▸ **prodigiously** adv

prodigy /'prɒdədʒi/ n (pl -ies) young person who is unusually intelligent or skilful for their age

0–₩ **produce** /prə'djuːs/ v [T] 1 make things to be sold; manufacture 2 grow or make sth as part of a natural process 3 cause a particular result or effect 4 show sth or make sth appear from somewhere 5 be in charge of a play, film, etc for the public to see ● **produce** /'prɒdjuːs/ n [U] things that have been made or grown, esp by farming

0–₩ **producer** /prə'djuːsə(r)/ n [C] 1 person, company or country that grows or makes food, goods or materials 2 person who is in charge of making a play, film, etc

0–₩ **product** /'prɒdʌkt/ n [C] 1 thing that is grown or produced, usu for sale 2 result of a process 3 (maths) quantity obtained by multiplying one number by another

0–₩ **production** /prə'dʌkʃn/ n 1 [U] process of growing or making food, goods or materials 2 [U] quantity of goods produced 3 [C, U] (act of preparing a) play, film, etc for the public

0–₩ **productive** /prə'dʌktɪv/ adj 1 making goods or growing crops, esp in large quantities 2 doing or achieving a lot: a ~ meeting ▸ **productively** adv

productivity /ˌprɒdʌkˈtɪvəti/ n [U] rate of producing goods: P~ has fallen sharply.

profane /prəˈfeɪn/ v [T] (fml) claim showing disrespect for God or holy things: ~ language 2 (tech) not connected with religion; secular ▸ **profanely** adv ▸ **profanity** /prəˈfænəti/ n [C,U] (pl **-ies**) (instance of) profane behaviour or language

0–₩ **profess** /prəˈfes/ v [T] (fml) 1 claim sth, often falsely: I don't ~ to be an expert. 2 state openly that you have a particular belief, etc 3 belong to a particular religion ▸ **professed** adj (fml) (falsely) claimed 2 self-declared

0–₩ **profession** /prəˈfeʃn/ n 1 type of job that needs special knowledge, eg medicine or law 2 statement about what you believe, feel or think about sth

0–₩ **professional** /prəˈfeʃənl/ adj 1 of a profession (1) 2 showing that sb is well trained and highly skilled 3 doing sth as a paid job rather than as a hobby: a ~ golfer ● **professional** n [C] professional person ▸ **professionalism** n [U] skill or qualities of a professional ▸ **professionally** /-ʃənəli/ adv

0–₩ **professor** /prəˈfesə(r)/ n [C] university teacher of the highest rank ▸ **professorial** /ˌprɒfəˈsɔːriəl/ adj ▸ **professorship** n [C] position of a professor

proffer /ˈprɒfə(r)/ v [T] (fml) offer sth to sb

proficient /prəˈfɪʃnt/ adj (written) able to do sth well because of training and practice ▸ **proficiency** /-nsi/ n [U] ▸ **proficiently** adv

profile /ˈprəʊfaɪl/ n [C] 1 side view of the human face 2 description of sb/ sth that gives useful information [IDM] **a high/low profile** a way of behaving that attracts/does not attract attention

0–₩ **profit** /ˈprɒfɪt/ n [C,U] money that you make in business, etc or by selling things 2 [U] (fml) advantage that you get from doing sth ■ **profit margin** n [C] difference between the cost of buying or producing sth and the price that it is sold for ● **profit** v [i] ~ **by/from** gain an advantage or benefit from ▸ **profitable** adj 1 that makes or is likely to make money 2 that gives sb a useful result: a ~ discussion ▸ **profitably** /-əbli/ adv

profound /prəˈfaʊnd/ adj 1 deep; very great: a ~ effect 2 showing or needing great knowledge or thought ▸ **profoundly** adv deeply

profuse /prəˈfjuːs/ adj (fml) produced in large amounts

▸ **profusely** adv ▸ **profusion** /-ˈfjuːʒn/ n [sing, with sing or pl verb, U] (fml) very large quantity of sth: a ~ of flowers ◇ flowers growing in ~

0–₩ **program** /ˈprəʊɡræm/ n [C] 1 (computing) set of instructions for a computer 2 (US) = PROGRAMME ● **program** v (**-mm-** US also **-m-**) [T] 1 (computing) give a set of instructions to a computer to make it perform a particular task 2 (US) = PROGRAMME ▸ **programmer** n [C] person whose job is writing programs for a computer

0–₩ **programme** /ˈprəʊɡræm/ n [C] 1 plan of what is to be done: a ~ of modernization 2 television or radio broadcast 3 list of items in eg a concert or course of study ● **programme** v [T] 1 plan for sth to happen 2 give a machine instructions to do a particular task: ~ the VCR

0–₩ **progress** /ˈprəʊɡres/ n [U] 1 process of improving or developing or nearing the achievement of sth 2 forward movement [IDM] **in progress** (fml) happening at this time ● **progress** /prəˈɡres/ v [i] make progress ▸ **progression** /prəˈɡreʃn/ n 1 [U] process of progressing 2 [C] number of things that come in a series

progressive /prəˈɡresɪv/ adj 1 favouring new, modern ideas: ~ policies 2 happening or developing steadily ● **progressive** n [C] person in favour of new, modern ideas ▸ **progressively** adv

prohibit /prəˈhɪbɪt/ v [T] (fml) 1 stop sth from being done or used, esp by law 2 make sth impossible to do ▸ **prohibition** /ˌprəʊɪˈbɪʃn/ n 1 [U] act of prohibiting sth 2 [C] law or rule that forbids sth ▸ **prohibitive** /prəˈhɪbətɪv/ adj 1 (of prices) so high that people cannot afford to buy or do it 2 preventing people from doing sth ▸ **prohibitively** adv

0–₩ **project¹** /ˈprɒdʒekt/ n [C] planned piece of work designed to find information about sth or to produce sth new

0–₩ **project²** /prəˈdʒekt/ v 1 [T] plan sth for a time in the future 2 [T] estimate sth, based on known facts: ~ the population growth 3 [T] ~ **on(to)** cause light, a film, etc to appear on a screen or surface 4 [i] stick out beyond a surface 5 [i] present sb/sth/yourself to others in a way that gives a good impression

projectile /prəˈdʒektaɪl/ n [C] (fml) object fired from a gun or thrown as a weapon

projection /prəˈdʒekʃn/ n 1 [C] estimate that is based on known facts **2** [U] act of projecting an image of sth onto a surface **3** [C] something that sticks out from a surface

projector /prəˈdʒektə(r)/ n [C] apparatus for projecting pictures onto a screen

the proletariat /ˌprəʊləˈteəriət/ n [sing, with sing or pl verb] (tech) the class of ordinary working people

proliferate /prəˈlɪfəreɪt/ v [I] (written) increase rapidly in number or amount ▸ **proliferation** /prəˌlɪfəˈreɪʃn/ n [U]

prolific /prəˈlɪfɪk/ adj (of a writer, artist, etc) producing many works

prologue (US also **-log**) /ˈprəʊlɒg/ n [C] introductory speech, etc at the beginning of a play, book or film

prolong /prəˈlɒŋ/ v [T] make sth last longer ▸ **prolonged** adj continuing for a long time

promenade /ˌprɒməˈnɑːd/ n [C] paved area for walking next to the beach at a seaside town

prominent /ˈprɒmɪnənt/ adj **1** important or well known **2** noticeable **3** sticking out from sth ▸ **prominence** n [U, sing] state of being important, well known or noticeable ▸ **prominently** adv

promiscuous /prəˈmɪskjuəs/ adj (disapprov) having many sexual partners ▸ **promiscuity** /ˌprɒmɪsˈkjuːəti/ n [U] ▸ **promiscuously** adv

0—¬ **promise** /ˈprɒmɪs/ n **1** [C] statement telling sb that you will definitely do or not do sth **2** [U] sign that sb/sth will be successful: His work shows great ~. ● **promise** v **1** [I,T] tell sb that you definitely do or not do sth **2** [T] make sth seem likely to happen: It ~s to be a hot day. ▸ **promising** adj likely to succeed

promontory /ˈprɒməntri/ n [C] (pl **-ies**) long narrow area of high land that goes out into the sea

0—¬ **promote** /prəˈməʊt/ v [T] **1** help sth to happen or develop **2** advertise a product or service **3** move sb to a higher rank or more senior job ▸ **promoter** n [C] person who organizes or supports sth

0—¬ **promotion** /prəˈməʊʃn/ n [C, U] **1** (instance of) promoting sb/sth **2** advertising or other activity to increase the sales of sth

0—¬ **prompt¹** /prɒmpt/ adj done or acting without delay: a ~ reply ▸ **promptly** adv ▸ **promptness** n [U]

0—¬ **prompt²** /prɒmpt/ v **1** [T] cause sb to decide to do sth; cause sth to happen **2** [I, T] remind an actor of the words if they forget during a performance ● **prompt** n [C] **1** word(s) said to an actor to remind them what to say next **2** (computing) sign on a screen that

shows that the computer has finished doing sth and is ready for more instructions ▸ **prompter** n [C] person who prompts actors

prone /prəʊn/ adj **1** ~ **to** likely to suffer from sth or do sth bad: ~ to infection ◊ accident-~ **2** (fml) lying flat, face downwards

prong /prɒŋ/ n [C] thin pointed part of a fork

pronoun /ˈprəʊnaʊn/ n [C] (gram) word, eg hers or it used instead of a noun

0—¬ **pronounce** /prəˈnaʊns/ v [T] **1** make the sound of a word or letter **2** state sth officially ▸ **pronounced** adj very noticeable ▸ **pronouncement** n [C] formal official statement

0—¬ **pronunciation** /prəˌnʌnsiˈeɪʃn/ n [U, C] way in which a language or a particular word or sound is spoken

0—¬ **proof** /pruːf/ n **1** [U, C] information, documents, etc that show that sth is true **2** [U] process of testing whether sth is true **3** [C, usu pl] copy of printed material which is produced so that mistakes can be corrected **4** [U] standard of strength of alcoholic drink

-proof /pruːf/ adj (in compounds) that can resist sth or protect against the thing mentioned: bullet-~ glass

prop /prɒp/ n [C] **1** piece of wood, metal, etc used to support sth **2** person or thing that helps or supports sb/sth **3** [usu pl] small object used by actors during a performance ● **prop** v (**-pp-**) [T] ~ **(up)** support or keep sth in position

propaganda /ˌprɒpəˈgændə/ n [U] (disapprov) information spread in order to gain support for a political leader, party, etc

propagate /ˈprɒpəgeɪt/ v **1** [T] (fml) spread an idea, a belief, etc among many people: ~ ideas **2** [I,T] (tech) produce new plants from a parent plant ▸ **propagation** /-ˈgeɪʃn/ n [U]

propel /prəˈpel/ v (**-ll-**) [T] move, drive or push sb/sth forward or in a particular direction ▸ **propeller** n [C] blades that turn, to move a ship, helicopter, etc

propensity /prəˈpensəti/ n [C] (pl **-ies**) ~ **(for/to)** (fml) natural tendency to do sth

0—¬ **proper** /ˈprɒpə(r)/ adj **1** (esp GB) right, appropriate or correct **2** (GB, spoken) real; satisfactory: We've not had a ~ holiday in years. **3** socially and morally acceptable **4** according to the exact meaning of the word ▸ **properly** adv correctly ■ '**proper noun** (also '**proper name**) n [C] (gram) name of a particular person, place, etc, written with a capital letter

0─ **property** /ˈprɒpəti/ n (pl -ies)
1 [U] thing(s) owned by sb; possession(s) **2** [C,U] area of land and buildings **3** [C, usu pl] (fml) quality or characteristic that sth has: *the chemical properties of the metal*

prophecy /ˈprɒfəsi/ n (pl -ies) **1** [C] statement that sth will happen in the future **2** [U] power of saying what will happen in the future

prophesy /ˈprɒfəsai/ v (pt, pp -ied) [I,T] say what will happen in the future (done in the past using religious or magic powers)

prophet /ˈprɒfɪt/ n [C] **1** person sent by God to teach people and give them messages **2** person who claims to know what will happen in the future ▶ **prophetic** /prəˈfetɪk/ adj

propitious /prəˈpɪʃəs/ adj (fml) favourable

0─ **proportion** /prəˈpɔːʃn/ n **1** [C, with sing or pl verb] part or share of a whole: *Water covers a large ~ of the earth's surface.* **2** [U] relationship of one thing to another in quantity, size, etc: *The room is very long in ~ to (= relative to) its width.* **3** [U, C] the correct relationship in size, etc between one thing and another **4** (proportions) [pl] measurements or size of sth: *a room of generous ~s* ▶ **proportional** adj of an appropriate size, etc in comparison with sth

0─ **proposal** /prəˈpəʊzl/ n [C] **1** formal suggestion or plan **2** offer of marriage

0─ **propose** /prəˈpəʊz/ v **1** [T] (fml) suggest a plan, idea, etc **2** [T] intend to do sth **3** [I,T] ~ (to) ask sb to marry you

proposition /ˌprɒpəˈzɪʃn/ n [C] **1** idea or plan that is suggested, esp in business **2** thing that you intend to do; task to be dealt with **3** (fml) statement that expresses an opinion ● **proposition** v [T] say to sb in a direct way that you would like to have sex with them

proprietary /prəˈpraɪətri/ adj made by a particular company and sold under a trade name

proprietor /prəˈpraɪətə(r)/ n [C] (fml) owner of a business, hotel, etc

propriety /prəˈpraɪəti/ n [U] (fml) correct social and moral behaviour

propulsion /prəˈpʌlʃn/ n [U] (tech) force that drives sth forward

pro rata /ˌprəʊ ˈrɑːtə/ adv, adj (fml) calculated according to how much of sth has been used, the amount of work done, etc

prosaic /prəˈzeɪɪk/ adj (written) uninteresting; dull

proscribe /prəˈskraɪb/ v [T] (fml) forbid sth by law

prose /prəʊz/ n [U] writing that is not poetry

prosecute /ˈprɒsɪkjuːt/ v [I,T] officially charge sb with a crime in a court of law ▶ **prosecution** /ˌprɒsɪˈkjuːʃn/ n **1** [U,C] process of trying to prove in a court of law that sb is guilty of a crime; process of being charged with a crime **2** (the prosecution) [sing, with sing or pl verb] lawyer(s) that prosecute sb in a court of law ▶ **prosecutor** n [C]

0─ **prospect¹** /ˈprɒspekt/ n **1** [U, sing] ~ (of) possibility that sth will happen **2** [sing] idea of what might or will happen in the future **3** (prospects) [pl] chances of success

prospect² /prəˈspekt/ v [I] ~ (for) search an area for oil, gold, etc ▶ **prospector** n [C]

prospective /prəˈspektɪv/ adj wanting or likely to be or do sth

prospectus /prəˈspektəs/ n [C] **1** printed leaflet advertising a school, college, etc **2** (business) document giving information about a company's shares before they are offered for sale

prosper /ˈprɒspə(r)/ v [I] succeed, esp financially ▶ **prosperity** /prɒˈsperəti/ n [U] success or wealth ▶ **prosperous** /ˈprɒspərəs/ adj successful; rich

prostitute /ˈprɒstɪtjuːt/ n [C] person who has sex for money ● **prostitute** v [T] ~ **sth/yourself** use your skills or abilities to earn money doing sth that others feel is unworthy of you ▶ **prostitution** /ˌprɒstɪˈtjuːʃn/ n [U]

prostrate /ˈprɒstreɪt/ adj lying on the ground, face downwards ● **prostrate** /prɒˈstreɪt/ v ~ **yourself** lie on the ground, face downwards

protagonist /prəˈtæɡənɪst/ n [C] (fml) **1** main person in a play or real event **2** active supporter of a movement, idea, etc

0─ **protect** /prəˈtekt/ v [T] keep sb/ sth safe from harm, injury, etc ▶ **protection** /prəˈtekʃn/ n **1** [U] act of protecting sb/sth; state of being protected **2** [C] thing that protects sb/sth against sth ▶ **protective** adj **1** providing or intended to provide protection: ~ *clothing* **2** ~ **(of/ towards)** wishing to protect sb/sth ▶ **protector** n [C] person or thing that protects

protectorate /prəˈtektərət/ n [C] country that is controlled and protected by a more powerful country

protégé /ˈprɒteʒeɪ/ n [C] person helped and guided by sb important and influential

protein /ˈprəʊtiːn/ n [C,U] natural substance found in meat, eggs, fish, etc which is essential to good health

0— **protest¹** /ˈprəʊtest/ n [C,U] statement or action that shows strong disapproval or disagreement

0— **protest²** /prəˈtest/ v [I,U] **1** ~ **(about/against/at)** show your strong disapproval or disagreement of sb/sth **2** [T] say firmly that sth is true, esp against opposition: He ~ed his innocence. ▶ **protester** n [C] person who makes a public protest

Protestant /ˈprɒtɪstənt/ n [C], adj (member) of any of the Christian groups that separated from the Roman Catholic Church in the 16th century

protocol /ˈprəʊtəkɒl/ n **1** [U] system of fixed rules and formal behaviour used at official meetings **2** [C] (computing) set of rules that control the way data is sent between computers

proton /ˈprəʊtɒn/ n [C] (physics) tiny particle of matter inside an atom, with a positive electric charge

prototype /ˈprəʊtətaɪp/ n [C] first design of sth, eg of an aircraft, from which others are developed

protracted /prəˈtræktɪd/ adj lasting for a long time

protractor /prəˈtræktə(r)/ n [C] instrument for measuring and drawing angles

protrude /prəˈtruːd/ v [I,T] (cause sth to) stick out ▶ **protrusion** /-ˈtruːʒn/ n [C,U]

protuberance /prəˈtjuːbərəns/ n [C] (fml) round part that sticks out of a surface

0— **proud** /praʊd/ adj **1** having a feeling of satisfaction from doing sth well or owning sth **2** (disapprov) having too high an opinion of yourself **3** having self-respect ▶ **proudly** adv

0— **prove** /pruːv/ v (pp ~d US ~n /ˈpruːvn/) **1** [T] use evidence to show sth to be true **2** linking verb be seen or found to be sth: The opposition ~d too strong for him.

proverb /ˈprɒvɜːb/ n [C] well-known phrase or sentence that states the truth or gives advice, eg Waste not, want not. ▶ **proverbial** /prəˈvɜːbiəl/ adj **1** of or expressed in a proverb **2** well known

0— **provide** /prəˈvaɪd/ v [T] ~ **(for)** give sth to sb or make it available for them to use [PV] **provide for sb** supply sb with the things they need to live, eg food and clothing **provide for sth** (fml) make preparations to deal with sth that might happen

0— **provided** /prəˈvaɪdɪd/ (also **providing**) conj ~ **(that)** if; on condition that

providence /ˈprɒvɪdəns/ n [U] the care and kindness of God or fate

▶ **providential** /ˌprɒvɪˈdenʃl/ adj (fml) fortunate

province /ˈprɒvɪns/ n **1** [C] main administrative division of a country **2** (**the provinces**) [pl] (GB) all the parts of a country outside the capital city **3** [sing] (fml) person's particular area of knowledge or responsibility ▶ **provincial** adj **1** of a province (1) or the provinces (2) **2** (disapprov) unwilling to consider new ideas or things ▶ **provincial** n [C] (disapprov) person from the provinces (2)

provision /prəˈvɪʒn/ n **1** [U] act of providing sb with what they want or need **2** [U] ~ **(for)** preparation for future needs **3** (**provisions**) [pl] food supplies **4** [C] conditions in a legal document

provisional /prəˈvɪʒənl/ adj for the present time only and likely to be changed in the future ▶ **provisionally** /-nəli/ adv

provocation /ˌprɒvəˈkeɪʃn/ n **1** [U] act of doing or saying sth deliberately in order to make sb angry **2** [C] something said or done in order to provoke sb

provocative /prəˈvɒkətɪv/ adj **1** intended to cause anger, argument, etc **2** intended to cause sexual desire ▶ **provocatively** adv

provoke /prəˈvəʊk/ v [T] **1** cause a particular feeling or reaction **2** deliberately do sth to annoy sb

prow /praʊ/ n [C] (lit) pointed front part of a ship

prowess /ˈpraʊəs/ n [U] (fml) great skill at doing sth

prowl /praʊl/ v [I] ~ **(about/around)** move about an area quietly, looking for food, sth to steal, etc ▶ **prowl** n [IDM] (be/go) on the prowl (of an animal or a person) moving quietly, hunting or looking for sth

proximity /prɒkˈsɪməti/ n [U] (fml) nearness

proxy /ˈprɒksi/ n (pl **-ies**) **1** [U] authority to act for another person, esp to vote **2** [C] person given this authority

prude /pruːd/ n [C] (disapprov) person easily shocked by sexual matters ▶ **prudish** adj

prudent /ˈpruːdnt/ adj careful and sensible ▶ **prudence** /-dns/ n [U] ▶ **prudently** adv

prune /pruːn/ n [C] dried plum ● **prune** v [T] **1** cut off some of the branches of a tree or bush to encourage further growth **2** cut out unnecessary parts from sth

pry /praɪ/ v (pt, pp **pried** /praɪd/) [I] ~ **(into)** try to find out about sb's private life

PS /ˌpiː ˈes/ abbr postscript; something written at the end of a letter to add sth you have forgotten to say

psalm /sɑːm/ n [C] religious song or poem, esp one of those in the Bible

pseudonym /'sjuːdənɪm/ n [C] name that sb, esp a writer, uses, instead of their real name

psyche /'saɪki/ n [C] (fml) the mind; your deepest feelings

psychedelic /ˌsaɪkə'delɪk/ adj **1** (of drugs) causing sb to see sth that isn't there **2** having very bright colours and strange patterns

psychiatry /saɪ'kaɪətri/ n [U] study and treatment of mental illness
▶ **psychiatric** /ˌsaɪki'ætrɪk/ adj
▶ **psychiatrist** /saɪ'kaɪətrɪst/ n [C] doctor trained in psychiatry

psychic /'saɪkɪk/ adj **1** (also **psychical** /'saɪkɪkl/) connected with or having strange powers of the mind that are not able to be explained by natural laws **2** connected with the mind rather than the body

psychoanalysis /ˌsaɪkəʊə'næləsɪs/ n [U] method of treating some mental illnesses by looking at and discussing the effects of events in the patient's life as possible causes
▶ **psychoanalyse** /ˌsaɪkəʊ'ænəlaɪz/ v [T] treat sb using psychoanalysis
▶ **psychoanalyst** /-'ænəlɪst/ n [C] person who treats patients using psychoanalysis

psychology /saɪ'kɒlədʒi/ n [U] scientific study of the mind and how it influences behaviour
▶ **psychological** /ˌsaɪkə'lɒdʒɪkl/ adj
▶ **psychologist** /saɪ'kɒlədʒɪst/ n [C] student of or expert in psychology

psychopath /'saɪkəpæθ/ n [C] person suffering from a severe mental illness that causes them to behave violently ▶ **psychopathic** /-'pæθɪk/ adj

pt abbr **1** part **2** pint **3** point **4** (Pt.) (esp on a map) port

PTO /ˌpiː tiː 'əʊ/ abbr (GB) please turn over; something written at the bottom of a page to show there is more on the other side

0̶ **pub** /pʌb/ n [C] (GB) building where alcoholic drinks are sold and drunk

puberty /'pjuːbəti/ n [U] stage at which a person becomes physically able to have children

pubic /'pjuːbɪk/ adj of or near the sexual organs

0̶ **public** /'pʌblɪk/ adj **1** of or for people in general **2** of or provided by the government: *money* ◇ *a ~ library* **3** known to many people; not secret **[IDM] in the public eye** often seen on television and mentioned in newspapers, etc ● **public** n [sing, with sing or pl verb] **the** (the public) ordinary people in society in general **2** group of people who share an interest or are involved in the same activity: *the reading ~* **[IDM] in public** when other people, esp strangers, are present ■ **public 'bar** n [C] (GB) bar in a pub with simple and less comfortable furniture than the other bars ■ **public 'company** (ˌpublic ˌlimited company) (US **public corpo'ration**) (abbr **plc, PLC**) n [C] business company that sells shares in itself to the public ■ **public con'venience** n [C] (GB) toilet which the public may use ■ **public 'house** n [C] (fml) = PUB ■ **publicly** adv ■ **public re'lations** n [U] (abbr **PR**) business of obtaining good public opinion of an organization **2** [pl] relationship between an organization and the public ■ **public 'school** n [C] (in Britain) private secondary school for fee-paying pupils

0̶ **publication** /ˌpʌblɪ'keɪʃn/ n **1** [U] act of publishing sth **2** [C] book, magazine, etc

0̶ **publicity** /pʌb'lɪsəti/ n [U] **1** attention that is given to sb/sth by newspapers, television, etc **2** information that attracts public attention to sth; advertising

publicize (also **-ise**) /'pʌblɪsaɪz/ v [T] make sth known to the public; advertise sth

0̶ **publish** /'pʌblɪʃ/ v [T] **1** print and offer a book, etc for sale to the public **2** (fml) make sth known to the public ▶ **publisher** n [C] person or company that publishes books, etc

pucker /'pʌkə(r)/ v [I,T] (cause sth to) form small folds or lines

pudding /'pʊdɪŋ/ n [C, U] (GB) **1** sweet dish eaten at the end of a meal **2** sweet or savoury food made with flour and baked, boiled or steamed

puddle /'pʌdl/ n [C] small pool of water, esp rain

puff /pʌf/ v **1** [I,T] smoke a pipe, cigarette, etc **2** [I,T] (cause smoke, steam, etc) to blow out in clouds **3** [I] (infml) breathe loudly and quickly **[PV] puff (sth) out/up** (cause sth to) swell ▶ **puffed** adj (GB, infml) breathing with difficulty ● **puff** /pʌf/ n [C] **1** act of breathing in smoke from a cigarette, etc **2** small amount of air, smoke, etc that is blown from somewhere ■ **puff 'pastry** n [U] light pastry that forms many layers when baked ▶ **puffy** adj (**-ier, -iest**) (of eyes, faces, etc) looking swollen

puffin /'pʌfɪn/ n [C] N Atlantic seabird with a large brightly coloured beak

0̶ **pull¹** /pʊl/ v **1** [I,T] hold sth firmly and use force in order to move it towards yourself or in a particular direction: *~ the door shut* ◇ *You push and I'll ~.* **2** [T] remove sth from a place by pulling: *~ (out) a tooth* **3** [T] damage a muscle, etc by using too much force [IDM] **pull faces/a face** (at sb) → FACE **pull a fast one** (on sb) (sl) trick sb **pull your finger out** → FINGER **pull sb's leg** (infml) play a joke on sb by making them believe sth untrue **pull your socks up** (GB, infml) try to improve your work or behaviour **pull sth to pieces** criticize sth strongly **pull your weight** do your fair share of the work **pull away (from sth)** (of a vehicle) start moving **pull sth down** destroy a building completely **pull in (to sth) 1** (of a train) enter a station **2** (GB) (of a vehicle) move to the side of the road and stop **pull sth off** (infml) succeed in doing sth difficult **pull out** (of a vehicle) move away from the side of the road and start moving **pull (sb/sth) out (of sth)** (cause sb/sth to) withdraw from sth: ~ *out of a race* **pull over** (of a vehicle) move to the side of the road and stop **pull (sb) through** (help sb to) get better after a serious illness, operation, etc **pull together** act, work, etc together with other people in an organized way and without fighting **pull yourself together** take control of your feelings and behave calmly **pull up** (of a vehicle) stop **pull sb up** (GB, infml) criticize sb for sth they have done wrong ■ **pull-down** 'menu *n* [C] (computing) list of possible choices that appears on a computer screen when you select its title

○➡ **pull²** /pʊl/ *n* **1** [C] act of pulling sth **2** [sing] force or attraction: *the ~ of the river current* **3** [U] (infml) power and influence over other people **4** [C, usu sing] difficult walk up a steep hill

pullet /'pʊlɪt/ *n* [C] young hen

pulley /'pʊli/ *n* [C] device with a wheel and rope, used for lifting things

pullover /'pʊləʊvə(r)/ *n* [C] (esp GB) knitted piece of clothing for the upper body, pulled on over the head

pulp /pʌlp/ *n* [U] **1** soft wet substance that is made by crushing sth, esp wood fibre used for making paper **2** soft part inside some fruit and vegetables ● **pulp** *v* [T] crush or beat sth so that it becomes soft and wet

pulpit /'pʊlpɪt/ *n* [C] raised enclosed platform in a church, from which a priest speaks

pulsate /pʌl'seɪt/ *v* [I] move or shake with a strong regular action ▸ **pulsation** /-'seɪʃn/ *n* [C, U]

pulse /pʌls/ *n* **1** [C, usu sing] regular beating of the arteries as the blood is pumped through them **2** [sing] regular beat in music ● **pulse** *v* [I] move, beat or flow with strong regular movements or sounds

pulverize (also -ise) /'pʌlvəraɪz/ *v* [T]

1 (fml) crush sth to a fine powder **2** (infml) defeat or destroy sb/sth completely

puma /'pju:mə/ *n* [C] large American wild animal of the cat family

pump /pʌmp/ *n* [C] **1** machine for forcing liquid, gas or air into, out of or through sth **2** (GB) light soft shoe worn for dancing or exercise ● **pump** *v* **1** [T] force air, gas or liquid to flow in a particular direction: *The heart ~s blood around the body.* **2** [I] work like a pump; beat **3** [I, T] (cause sth to) move quickly up and down or in and out **4** [T] (infml) try to get information from sb by asking them a lot of questions

pumpkin /'pʌmpkɪn/ *n* [C, U] large round vegetable with thick orange skin

pun /pʌn/ *n* [C] humorous use of words that sound the same or have two meanings, eg 'The soldier laid down his *arms*' ● **pun** *v* (-**nn**-) [I] make a pun

○➡ **punch** /pʌntʃ/ *v* [T] **1** hit sb/sth hard with your fist **2** make a hole in sth with a punch (3) or some other sharp object ● **punch** *n* **1** [C] hard hit made with the fist **2** [U] power to interest people **3** [C] tool or machine for cutting holes in paper, etc: *a hole* ~ **4** [U] drink made of wine or spirits mixed with sugar, lemon, spice etc ■ **'punch-up** *n* [C] (GB, infml) physical fight

punctual /'pʌŋktʃuəl/ *adj* happening or doing sth at the arranged or correct time; not late ▸ **punctuality** /-tʃu'æləti/ *n* [U] ▸ **punctually** *adv*

punctuate /'pʌŋktʃueɪt/ *v* [T] **1** ~ (**with/by**) (usu passive) interrupt sth at intervals **2** [I, T] divide writing into sentences and phrases by using full stops, question marks, etc ▸ **punctuation** /ˌpʌŋktʃu'eɪʃn/ *n* [U] (practice of putting) marks such as full stops and commas in a piece of writing

puncture /'pʌŋktʃə(r)/ *n* [C] small hole in a tyre made by a sharp point ● **puncture** *v* [I, T] get or make a hole in sth

pundit /'pʌndɪt/ *n* [C] person who knows a lot about a subject and often talks about it in public; expert: *political ~s*

pungent /'pʌndʒənt/ *adj* having a strong taste or smell

○➡ **punish** /'pʌnɪʃ/ *v* [T] make sb suffer because they have broken the law or done sth wrong ▸ **punishing** *adj* long and difficult and making you work so hard you become tired ▸ **punishment** *n* **1** [U, C] act or way of punishing sb **2** [U] rough treatment

punitive /'pju:nətɪv/ *adj* (fml) intended as punishment; harsh or severe

punk /pʌŋk/ n [U] (also **punk rock**) loud and aggressive rock music popular in the late 1970s and early 1980s **2** [C] (also **punk rocker**) person who likes punk rock and wears leather clothes, metal chains and has brightly coloured hair **3** [C] (US, infml, disapprov) rude or violent young man or boy

punnet /'pʌnɪt/ n [C] small square basket used as a container for fruit

punt /pʌnt/ n [C] long shallow flat-bottomed boat moved along by a long pole ● **punt** v [I] travel in a punt, esp for pleasure

punter /'pʌntə(r)/ n [C] (GB, infml) **1** customer **2** person who bets money on horse races

puny /'pju:ni/ adj (-ier, -iest) (disapprov) small and weak

pup /pʌp/ n [C] **1** = PUPPY young of various animals, eg seals

o─ **pupil** /'pju:pl/ n [C] **1** person being taught, esp a child in a school **2** small round black area at the centre of the eye

puppet /'pʌpɪt/ n [C] **1** doll that can be made to move, eg by strings attached to parts of its body or by putting your hand inside it **2** (disapprov) person or group whose actions are controlled by another

puppy /'pʌpi/ n [C] (pl **-ies**) young dog

o─ **purchase** /'pɜːtʃəs/ v [T] (fml) buy sth ● **purchase** n [U] act or process of buying sth **2** [C] something bought ▶ **purchaser** n [C] (fml) person who buys sth

o─ **pure** /pjʊə(r)/ adj (-r, -st) **1** not mixed with any other substance; with nothing added **2** not containing harmful substances; clean **3** complete; total: *They met by ~ chance.* **4** without evil thoughts or actions; morally good **5** (of colour, sound or light) very clear; perfect **6** concerned with theory only; not practical: *~ science* ▶ **purely** adv only; completely

purée /'pjʊəreɪ/ n [U, C] smooth thick liquid made by crushing cooked vegetables, fruit, etc in a little water

purgatory /'pɜːɡətri/ n [U] **1** (in Roman Catholic teaching) place after death in which the soul has to be purified by suffering **2** (spoken, hum) any place or state of suffering

purge /pɜːdʒ/ v [T] **1** ~ (of/from) remove unwanted people from a political party, etc: *~ a party of extremists ◇ ~ extremists from the party* **2** ~ (of/from) (written) make yourself/sb/sth pure by getting rid of bad thoughts ● **purge** n [C] act of purging (1)

purify /'pjʊərɪfaɪ/ v (pt, pp **-ied**) [T] make sth/sb pure ▶ **purification** /ˌpjʊərɪfɪ'keɪʃn/ n [U]

purist /'pjʊərɪst/ n [C] person who has strong opinions about what is correct in language, art, etc

puritan /'pjʊərɪtən/ n, adj [C] **1** (disapprov) (of a) person who is very strict in morals **2** (Puritan) (of a) member of a Protestant group in the 16th and 17th centuries who wanted simpler forms of church ceremony ▶ **puritanical** /ˌpjʊərɪ'tænɪkl/ adj (disapprov)

purity /'pjʊərəti/ n [U] state of being pure

purl /pɜːl/ n [U] stitch used in knitting ▶ **purl** v [I,T]

o─ **purple** /'pɜːpl/ adj having the colour of red and blue mixed together

o─ **purpose** /'pɜːpəs/ n **1** [C] reason for which sth is done or made **2** [U] ability to form plans and carry them out **IDM** **on purpose** deliberately ▶ **purposeful** adj showing purpose (2)

purr /pɜː(r)/ [I] (of a cat) make a low vibrating sound expressing pleasure ▶ **purr** n [sing]

o─ **purse** /pɜːs/ n [C] **1** (esp GB) small bag for carrying money, cards, etc, used esp by women **2** (US) = HANDBAG (HAND¹) **3** (sport) sum of money given as a prize in a boxing match ● **purse** v [T] (~ your lips) form your lips into a tight round shape, eg to show disapproval

purser /'pɜːsə(r)/ n [C] officer on a ship responsible for taking care of the passengers, and for the ship's accounts

o─ **pursue** /pə'sjuː/ v [T] (fml) **1** do sth to try to achieve sth over a period of time: *~ a goal/an objective* **2** continue to discuss or be involved in sth: *~ your legal action* **3** follow or chase sb/sth in order to catch them ▶ **pursuer** n [C] (written)

pursuit /pə'sjuːt/ n [fml] **1** [U] act of pursuing sth/sb **2** [C, usu pl] hobby; leisure activity

purvey /pə'veɪ/ v [T] (fml) supply sth, esp food ▶ **purveyor** n [C]

pus /pʌs/ n [U] thick yellowish liquid formed in an infected wound

o─ **push¹** /pʊʃ/ v **1** [I,T] use force on sth in order to move it forward, away or to a different position: *~ a bike up the hill ◇ ~ your way through the crowd* **2** [T] try to persuade sb to do sth that they may not want to do **3** [T] (infml) sell illegal drugs **IDM** **be pushed for sth** (infml) not have enough of sth **PV** **push sb about/ around** (infml) give orders to sb in a rude or unpleasant way **push (sb) for sth** repeatedly ask for sth or try to make sth happen: *They're ~ing for a ban on GM foods.* **push off** (GB, spoken) go away ■ **push-button** adj operated by pressing buttons with your fingers ■ **pushchair** n [C] small folding seat on wheels for a small child ► **pushed** adj 1 ~ to having difficulty doing sth: *be hard ~ed to finish on time* 2 ~ **(for)** not having enough of sth: *be ~ed for time* ► **pusher** n [C] (*infml*) person who sells illegal drugs

0━ **push²** /pʊʃ/ n [C, usu sing] 1 act of pushing sth/sb 2 great effort or attack [**IDM**] **give sb/get the push** (GB, *infml*) dismiss sb/be dismissed from your job

pussy /'pʊsi/ n [C] (pl **-ies**) (also **pussycat**) child's word for a cat

0━ **put** /pʊt/ v (pt, pp **put** pres pt **~ting**) [T] 1 move sth/sb into a particular place or position: *P~ the book on the table. ◊ Her family ~ her in a nursing home.* 2 write or make a mark on sth: *P~ your name here.* 3 bring sth/sb into the state or condition mentioned: *~ yourself at risk.* 4 express sth in a particular way: *She ~ it very politely.* [**IDM**] **put your cards on the table** → CARD **put the clock back** → CLOCK **put it to sb that...** suggest sth to sb to see if they can argue against it **put your oar in** → OAR **put sth right** → RIGHT¹ **put sb/sth to rights** → RIGHT³ [**PV**] **put sth about** (GB, *infml*) cause rumours, etc to pass from one person to another **put yourself/sth across/over (to sb)** communicate your ideas, feelings, etc well to sb **put sth aside** 1 ignore or forget sth, usu a feeling or difference of opinion: *~ aside your differences* 2 save money for a particular purpose **put sth at sth** calculate sb/sth to be a particular age, amount, etc: *I ~ the possible cost at £500.* **put sth away** return sth to its usual place: *~ the cup away in the cupboard* **put sth back** 1 return sth to its usual place: *~ the book back on the shelf* 2 move sth to a later time or date: *~ the meeting back by one hour* 3 move the hands of a clock to show the correct earlier time **put sth by** = PUT STH ASIDE(2) **put sb/sth down** (*infml*) make sb look or seem stupid, esp in front of other people **put sth down** 1 stop holding sth and place it on a table, etc 2 write sth 3 pay part of the cost of sth: *~ down a 5% deposit* 4 stop sth by force: *~ down a rebellion* 5 kill a sick animal **put sth down to sth** consider that sth is caused by sth: *I ~ his failure down to laziness.* **put sth forward** 1 move sth to an earlier time or date 2 move the hands of a clock to show the correct later time 3 suggest sth for discussion: *~ forward a new idea* **put sth in** 1 install equipment or furniture: *~ central heating in*

2 spend a lot of time or make a lot of effort doing sth: *~ in ten hours' work* **put yourself/sb/sth in for sth** enter yourself/sb/sth for a competition **put sb off** 1 cancel a meeting, etc you have made with sb 2 make sb dislike sth/sb or not trust them/it 3 distract sb from sth: *Don't ~ me off when I'm trying to concentrate.* **put sb off sth/sb** make sb lose enthusiasm for or interest in sth/sb **put sth on** 1 dress yourself in sth: *~ a coat on* 2 apply sth to your skin, face, etc 3 switch on a piece of equipment: *~ on the television ◊ ~ on some music* 4 become heavier or fatter: *~ on a stone (in weight)* 5 provide sth specially: *~ on extra trains* 6 produce or present a play, show, etc: *~ on a play* **put sb out** 1 cause inconvenience to sb: *I hope my visit won't ~ you out.* 2 (be put out) be upset or offended **put sth out** 1 take sth outside your house and leave it, eg for sb to collect 2 stop sth from burning or shining: *~ out the lights* 3 publish or broadcast sth: *~ out a warning* **put yourself/sth over (to sb)** = PUT YOURSELF/STH ACROSS(TO SB) **put sb/sth through (to sb)** connect sb by telephone **put sth to sb** 1 offer a suggestion to sb so that they can accept or reject it 2 ask sb a question **put sth up** 1 raise sth: *~ your hand up* 2 build sth or place sth somewhere: *~ a tent up* 3 increase sth: *~ up the rent* 4 provide or lend money **put sb up (at...)** (*esp GB*) stay somewhere for the night **put sb up to sth** (*infml*) encourage sb to do sth wrong **put up with sb/sth** accept sb/sth annoying, unpleasant, etc without complaining: *~ up with bad behaviour* ■ **'put-down** n [C] remark intended to make sb look or feel stupid

putrefy /'pju:trɪfaɪ/ v (pt, pp **-ied**) [I] (*fml*) decay and smell very bad ► **putrefaction** /ˌpju:trɪˈfækʃn/ n [U]

putrid /'pju:trɪd/ adj rotten and bad-smelling

putt /pʌt/ v [I, t] (in golf) hit the ball gently along the ground

putter /'pʌtə(r)/ v [I] (US) = POTTER

putty /'pʌti/ n [U] soft paste used for fixing glass in window frames

puzzle /'pʌzl/ n [C] 1 game, toy that you have to think about carefully in order to answer it or do it: *a crossword* 2 something difficult to understand or explain ● **puzzle** v [T] make sb feel confused when they do not understand sth: *What ~s me is why he didn't return my call.* [**PV**] **puzzle sth out** find the answer to sth by thinking hard **puzzle over/about sth** think hard about sth in order to understand it

PVC /ˌpiː viː ˈsiː/ n [U] strong plastic material

pygmy (also **pigmy**) /ˈpɪgmi/ n [C] (pl **-ies**) **1** (**Pigmy**) member of a race of very short people living in parts of Africa and SE Asia **2** (disapprov) very small person or animal

pyjamas /pəˈdʒɑːməz/ n [pl] loose jacket and trousers worn in bed

pylon /ˈpaɪlən/ n [C] tall steel structure for carrying electric cables

pyramid /ˈpɪrəmɪd/ n [C] **1** structure with a square base and sloping sides meeting at a point, esp one built in ancient Egypt **2** pile of objects in the shape of a pyramid

pyre /ˈpaɪə(r)/ n [C] high pile of wood for burning a dead body on

python /ˈpaɪθən/ n [C] large tropical snake that kills animals by twisting its body tightly round them

Q q

Q, q /kjuː/ n [C, U] (pl **Q's, q's** /kjuːz/) the seventeenth letter of the English alphabet

quack /kwæk/ n [C] **1** sound that a duck makes **2** (infml, disapprov) person who dishonestly claims to have medical knowledge ● **quack** v [I] make the sound of a duck

quad /kwɒd/ n [C] **1** short for QUADRANGLE **2** short for QUADRUPLET

quad bike /ˈkwɒd baɪk/ n [C] motorcycle with four large tyres, used for riding over rough ground ▸ **'quad biking** n [U] activity or sport of riding a quad bike

quadrangle /ˈkwɒdræŋgl/ n [C] open square area with buildings round it, esp in a school or college

quadruped /ˈkwɒdruped/ n [C] (tech) any creature with four feet

quadruple /kwɒˈdruːpl/ v [I,T] become or make sth four times bigger ● **quadruple** /ˈkwɒdrʊpl/ adj, det **1** consisting of four parts, people or groups **2** being four times as much or as many

quadruplet /ˈkwɒdruplət; kwɒˈdruːplət/ n [C] one of four babies born to the same mother at one time

quagmire /ˈkwæɡmaɪə(r), GB also ˈkwɒɡ-/ n [C] **1** area of soft wet ground **2** difficult or dangerous situation

quail /kweɪl/ n [C, U] (meat of a) small brown bird, whose meat and eggs are used for food ● **quail** v [I] (lit) feel or show that you feel very afraid

quaint /kweɪnt/ adj attractive in an

unusual or old-fashioned way
▸ **quaintly** adv

quake /kweɪk/ v [I] shake; tremble
0⃰ **qualification** /ˌkwɒlɪfɪˈkeɪʃn/ n **1** [C, usu pl] exam that you have passed or course of study that you have completed successfully **2** skill or type of experience needed for a particular job **3** [C,U] information added to a statement that modifies or limits it: accept an offer with ~s **4** [U] fact of passing an exam, etc

0⃰ **qualify** /ˈkwɒlɪfaɪ/ v (pt, pp **-ied**) **1** [I,T] have or give sb the qualities, training, etc that are necessary or suitable for sth: She'll ~ as a doctor next year. **2** [T] add sth to a previous statement to make it less general or extreme ▸ **qualified** adj **1** have the necessary qualifications **2** limited in some way: qualified approval

qualitative /ˈkwɒlɪtətɪv/ adj concerned with how good sth is, rather than how much of it there is

0⃰ **quality** /ˈkwɒləti/ n (pl **-ies**) **1** [U,C] (high) standard; how good or bad sth is **2** [C] typical part of sb's/sth's character

qualm /kwɑːm/ n [C] feeling of doubt about whether what you are doing is right

quandary /ˈkwɒndəri/ n [C] (pl **-ies**) state of not being able to decide what to do

quantitative /ˈkwɒntɪtətɪv/ adj concerned with the amount or number of sth rather than how good it is

0⃰ **quantity** /ˈkwɒntəti/ n [C,U] (pl **-ies**) (esp large) amount or number of sth

quarantine /ˈkwɒrəntiːn/ n [U] period when a person or animal is separated from others to prevent the spread of a disease ● **quarantine** v [T] put an animal or person in quarantine

quarrel /ˈkwɒrəl/ n **1** [C] angry argument **2** [U] reason to disagree with sb/sth ● **quarrel** v (-ll- US -l-) [I] ~ (**with**) have an angry argument or disagreement ▸ **quarrelsome** /-səm/ adj (of a person) liking to argue with others

quarry /ˈkwɒri/ n (pl **-ies**) **1** [C] place where stone, slate, etc is dug out of the ground **2** [sing] animal or person that is being hunted or followed ● **quarry** v (pt, pp **-ied**) [T] dig stone, etc from a quarry

quart /kwɔːt/ n [C] measure for liquids, equal to 2 pints (1.14 litres) in the UK and 0.94 of a litre in the US

0⃰ **quarter** /ˈkwɔːtə(r)/ n **1** [C] one of four equal parts of sth; ¼ **2** [C] 15 minutes: a~ to four ◇ (US) a~ of four ◇ a~ past six ◇ (US) a~ after three **3** [C] period of three months **4** [C] part of

a town or city: *the historic* ~ **5** [C] person or group from which help or information may come **6** [C] coin of the US and Canada worth 25 cents **7** (quarters) [pl] accommodation, esp for soldiers: *married* ~*s*
● **quarter** *v* [T] **1** divide sth into four parts **2** (*fml*) provide sb with a place to eat and sleep ■ **quarter-'final** *n* [C] one of four matches in a competition, whose winners play in the semi-finals ■ **'quartermaster** *n* [C] army officer in charge of stores and accommodation

quarterly /'kwɔːtəli/ *adj, adv* (happening or produced) every three months: *I pay my bills* ~.
● **quarterly** *n* [C] (*pl* **-ies**) magazine, etc published four times a year

quartet /kwɔː'tet/ *n* [C] (music for) four players or singers

quartz /kwɔːts/ *n* [U] hard mineral used in making very accurate clocks

quash /kwɒʃ/ *v* [T] **1** (*law*) officially say that a legal decision is no longer valid or correct: ~ *an appeal* **2** (*written*) stop sth from continuing

quaver /'kweɪvə(r)/ *v* [I,T] (of sb's voice) shake because the person is afraid ● **quaver** *n* [C, usu sing] shaking sound in sb's voice

quay /kiː/ *n* [C] platform in a harbour where boats come to load, etc

queasy /'kwiːzi/ *adj* (-ier, -iest) feeling sick; wanting to vomit

0➟ **queen** /kwiːn/ *n* [C] **1** female ruler of an independent state that has a royal family **2** wife of a king **3** woman thought to be the best in a particular group or area **4** (in chess) the most powerful piece **5** playing card with a picture of a queen on it **6** egg-producing female of bees, ants, etc ■ **queen 'mother** *n* [C] mother of a ruling king or queen

queer /kwɪə(r)/ *adj* **1** (*old-fash*) strange or unusual **2** (△, *sl*) homosexual ● **queer** *n* [C] (△, *sl*) homosexual

quell /kwel/ *v* [T] put an end to sth

quench /kwentʃ/ *v* [T] **1** satisfy your thirst by drinking **2** (*written*) put out a fire

query /'kwɪəri/ *n* [C] (*pl* **-ies**) question ● **query** *v* (pt, pp **-ied**) [T] **1** express doubt about whether sth is correct or not **2** (*written*) ask a question

quest /kwest/ *n* [C] (*fml*) long search

0➟ **question¹** /'kwestʃən/ *n* [C] **1** sentence, phrase, etc that asks for information **2** [C] matter that needs to be discussed or dealt with **3** [U] doubt: *His honesty is beyond* ~. **IDM** **in question 1** that is being discussed **2** in doubt; uncertain **out of the question** impossible ■ **'question**

mark *n* [C] mark (?) written at the end of a question

0➟ **question²** /'kwestʃən/ *v* [T] **1** ask sb questions about sth, esp officially **2** express your doubts about sth ▶ **questionable** *adj* that can be doubted

questionnaire /ˌkwestʃə'neə(r)/ *n* [C] ~ **(on/about)** list of questions to be answered to get information

queue /kjuː/ *n* [C] line of people, cars, etc waiting for sth or to do sth
● **queue** *v* [I] wait in a queue

quibble /'kwɪbl/ *v* [I] argue about small unimportant details
● **quibble** *n* [C] argument about a small matter

quiche /kiːʃ/ *n* [C,U] open pie with a filling of eggs, cheese, etc

0➟ **quick** /kwɪk/ *adj* **1** done with speed; taking or lasting a short time **2** moving or doing sth fast: *a* ~ *learner/worker* **IDM** **be quick on the uptake** → UPTAKE **have a quick temper** become angry easily **quick off the mark** → MARK¹ ● **quick** *adv* quickly; fast ● **quick** *n* (the quick) [sing] soft sensitive flesh below the fingernails ▶ **quickly** *adv*
▶ **quickness** *n* [U] ■ **quick-'witted** *adj* able to think quickly; clever

quicken /'kwɪkən/ *v* [I,T] (*written*) become or make sth quicker

quicksand /'kwɪksænd/ *n* [U,C] loose wet deep sand that you sink into if you walk on it

quid /kwɪd/ *n* [C] (*pl* **quid**) (GB, *infml*) one pound in money

0➟ **quiet** /'kwaɪət/ *adj* **1** making little noise **2** without many people or much noise or activity: *a* ~ *life* **3** (of a person) not talking very much ● **quiet** *n* [U] state of being calm without much noise **IDM** **on the quiet** secretly ▶ **quieten** /-tn/ *v* [I,T] (GB) ~ **(down)** become or make sb/sth calmer or less noisy ▶ **quietly** *adv* ▶ **quietness** *n* [U]

quill /kwɪl/ *n* [C] **1** large feather **2** (*also* **quill 'pen**) pen made from a quill feather **3** one of the long sharp spines on a porcupine

quilt /kwɪlt/ *n* [C] **1** decorative padded cover for a bed: *a patchwork* ~ **2** (GB) = DUVET ▶ **quilted** *adj* having two layers of cloth filled with soft material

quin /kwɪn/ *n* (US **quint** /kwɪnt/) *n* [C] = QUINTUPLET

quinine /kwɪ'niːn/ *n* [U] drug from the bark of a S American tree, used in the past to treat malaria

quintet /kwɪn'tet/ *n* [C] (music for) five players or singers

quintuplet /'kwɪntjuplət; kwɪn'tjuːplət/ *n* [C] one of five babies born to the same mother at one time

quip /kwɪp/ *n* [C] quick and clever

remark ● **quip** *v* (**-pp-**) [I] make a quip

quirk /kwɜːk/ *n* [C] **1** strange aspect of sb's personality **2** strange thing that happens, esp accidentally

0━ **quit** /kwɪt/ *v* (**-tt-** pt, pp **quit** *OR* also **~ted**) [I,T] **1** (*infml*) leave your job, school, etc **2** (*infml, esp US*) stop doing sth

0━ **quite** /kwaɪt/ *adv* **1** to some degree; fairly: ~ **hot 2** to the greatest possible degree; completely: ~ *delicious* **3** (*also fml* **quite so**) (*GB*) used to show you agree with sb [IDM] **quite a/the sth** used to show that a person or thing is unusual in some way: *There's a ~ strange story about how they met.*

quiver /ˈkwɪvə(r)/ *v* [I] shake slightly ● **quiver** *n* [C] **1** slight movement in part of your body **2** case for carrying arrows

quiz /kwɪz/ *n* [C] (pl **~zes**) game in which people are asked questions to test their knowledge ● **quiz** *v* (**-zz-**) [T] ask sb a lot of questions in order to get information

quizzical /ˈkwɪzɪkl/ *adj* (of an expression) showing that you are surprised or amused ▶ **quizzically** /-kli/ *adv*

quoit /kɔɪt/ *n* **1** [C] ring thrown onto a small post in the game of quoits **2** (**quoits**) [U] game in which rings are thrown onto a small post

quota /ˈkwəʊtə/ *n* [C] limited number or share that is officially allowed

quotation /kwəʊˈteɪʃn/ *n* **1** [C] group of words taken from a play, speech, etc **2** [U] act of repeating this **3** [C] statement of how much money a piece of work will cost ■ **quo'tation marks** *n* [pl] punctuation marks (' ' *or* " ") used at the beginning and end of a quotation (1)

0━ **quote** /kwəʊt/ *v* [I,T] repeat the exact words that another person has said or written **2** [T] mention an example of sth to support a statement **3** [T] tell a customer how much you will charge for a job or service ● **quote** *n* (*infml*) **1** [C] = QUOTATION(1) **2** [C] = QUOTATION(3) **3** (**quotes**) [pl] = QUOTATION MARKS (QUOTATION)

quotient /ˈkwəʊʃnt/ *n* [C] (*maths*) number obtained by dividing one number by another

Rr

R, r /ɑː(r)/ *n* [C,U] (pl **R's, r's** /ɑːz/) the eighteenth letter of the English alphabet

R & B /ˌɑːr ən ˈbiː/ *abbr* = RHYTHM AND BLUES

rabbi /ˈræbaɪ/ *n* [C] Jewish spiritual leader; teacher of Jewish law

rabbit /ˈræbɪt/ *n* [C] small animal with long ears that lives in a hole in the ground ● **rabbit** *v* [PV] **rabbit on (about sb/sth)** (*GB, infml*) talk continuously about unimportant or uninteresting things

rabble /ˈræbl/ *n* [C] large noisy crowd of people ■ **rabble-rouser** *n* [C] person who makes speeches to crowds of people intending to make them angry or excited

rabid /ˈræbɪd/ *adj* **1** (*disapprov*) having violent or extreme feelings or opinions **2** suffering from rabies

rabies /ˈreɪbiːz/ *n* [U] disease of dogs and other animals causing madness and death

0━ **race¹** /reɪs/ *n* **1** [C] competition of speed, eg in running **2** [sing] situation in which a number of people, groups, etc are competing, esp for political power: *the arms ~* **3** (**the races**) [pl] series of horse races that happen at one place **4** [C,U] one of the main groups that humans can be divided into according to their physical differences, eg colour of skin **5** [C] group of people with the same history, language, etc **6** [C] breed or type of animal or plant ■ **race re'lations** *n* [pl] relationships between people of different races in the same community

0━ **race²** /reɪs/ *v* **1** [I,T] ~ (**against**) compete against sb/sth in a race or races **2** [T] make an animal or a vehicle compete in a race **3** [I,T] (cause sb/sth) to move very fast ■ **racecourse** [C] track where horses race ■ **racehorse** *n* [C] horse that is trained to run in races ■ **racetrack** [C] **1** track for races between runners, cars, bicycles, etc **2** (*US*) = RACECOURSE

racial /ˈreɪʃl/ *adj* **1** happening or existing between people of different races: ~ *discrimination* **2** of race¹(4) ▶ **racially** *adv*

racism /ˈreɪsɪzəm/ *n* [U] (*disapprov*) unfair treatment of other races; belief that some races of people are better than others ▶ **racist** *adj, n* [C]

rack /ræk/ *n* [C] **1** framework, usu of metal or wooden bars, for holding things or hanging things on **2** shelf over the seats in a train, aeroplane, etc for light luggage: *a luggage ~* [IDM] **go to rack and ruin** get into a bad condition ● **rack** *v* (*often passive*) cause sb to suffer great pain [IDM] **rack your brains** try very hard to think of sth

racket /ˈrækɪt/ *n* **1** [C, sing] (*infml*) loud noise **2** [C] (*infml*) dishonest way of getting money **3** (*also* **racquet**) [C] piece of sports

A B C D E F G H I J K L M N O P Q **R** S T U V W X Y Z

equipment used for hitting the ball in tennis, squash, etc **4** (rackets) (also racquets) [U] game played with a ball in a court with four walls
▶ **racketeer** /ˌrækəˈtɪə(r)/ n [C] person involved in a racket (2)

racy /ˈreɪsi/ adj (-ier, -iest) lively, amusing and perhaps about sex
▶ **racily** adv ▶ **raciness** n [U]

radar /ˈreɪdɑː(r)/ n [U] equipment or system for showing the position of solid objects on a screen by using radio waves

radiant /ˈreɪdiənt/ adj **1** showing great happiness, love or health: ~ beauty **2** sending out rays of light or heat ▶ **radiance** /-əns/ n [U]
▶ **radiantly** adv

radiate /ˈreɪdieɪt/ v [I,T] **1** (of a person) send out a particular quality or emotion: She ~s confidence. **2** send out rays of light or heat

radiation /ˌreɪdiˈeɪʃn/ n **1** [U,C] powerful and dangerous rays sent out from a radioactive substance **2** [U] heat, energy, etc, sent out in the form of rays

radiator /ˈreɪdieɪtə(r)/ n [C] **1** apparatus, esp a set of pipes, used for heating a room **2** device for cooling the engine of a vehicle

radical /ˈrædɪkl/ adj **1** basic; thorough and complete **2** new, different and likely to give a great effect **3** favouring thorough political or social change ● **radical** n [C] person with radical (3) opinions
▶ **radically** /-kli/ adv

radii plural of RADIUS

0━ **radio** /ˈreɪdiəʊ/ n (pl ~s) **1** [U,sing] (activity of broadcasting) programmes for people to listen to **2** [C] piece of equipment for listening to radio broadcasts **3** [U] process of sending and receiving messages through the air using electromagnetic waves ● **radio** v [I,T] send a message to sb by radio

radioactive /ˌreɪdiəʊˈæktɪv/ adj sending out energy in the form of rays that can be harmful
▶ **radioactivity** /-ˈtɪvəti/ n [U]

radiography /ˌreɪdiˈɒɡrəfi/ n [U] process or job of taking X-ray photographs ▶ **radiographer** /-fə(r)/ n [C] person working in a hospital whose job is to take X-ray photographs

radiology /ˌreɪdiˈɒlədʒi/ n [U] study and use of different types of radiation in medicine ▶ **radiologist** n [C]

radish /ˈrædɪʃ/ n [C] small crisp red or white root vegetable with a strong taste, eaten raw in salads

radium /ˈreɪdiəm/ n [U] (symb Ra) radioactive chemical element used in the treatment of some diseases

radius /ˈreɪdiəs/ n [C] (pl radii /-diaɪ/) **1** (length of a) straight line from the centre of a circle to the side **2** circular area measured from a central point: within a two-mile ~ of the factory

raffia /ˈræfiə/ n [U] soft fibre from the leaves of a type of palm tree, used for making mats, etc

raffle /ˈræfl/ n [C] way of getting money (esp for charity) by selling numbered tickets that may win prizes ● **raffle** v [T] offer sth as a prize in a raffle

raft /rɑːft/ n [C] **1** flat floating structure of logs fastened together, used as a boat **2** small inflatable boat ▶ **rafting** n [U] sport or activity of travelling down a river on a raft: We went white-water ~ing in Vermont.

rafter /ˈrɑːftə(r)/ n [C] large sloping piece of wood that supports a roof

rag /ræg/ n **1** [C,U] piece of old torn cloth **2** [C] (infml, disapprov) newspaper **3** [U,C] (GB) amusing public event held by students to collect money for charity [IDM] in rags wearing very old torn clothes

rage /reɪdʒ/ n [U,C] feeling of violent anger that is difficult to control [IDM] be all the rage (infml) be very popular and fashionable ● **rage** v [I] **1** show that you are very angry about sth or with sb, esp by shouting **2** (eg of storms) continue in a violent way

ragged /ˈrægɪd/ adj **1** (of clothes) old and torn **2** (of people) wearing old or torn clothes **3** rough; uneven
▶ **raggedly** adv

ragtime /ˈrægtaɪm/ n [U] popular 1920s jazz music

raid /reɪd/ n [C] **1** short surprise attack on an enemy position **2** surprise visit by the police looking for criminals or illegal goods **3** attack on a building, etc in order to commit a crime: a bank ~ ● **raid** v [T] make a raid on sth/sb ▶ **raider** n [C] person who makes a raid (3) on a place

0━ **rail** /reɪl/ n **1** [C] wooden or metal bar put round sth as a barrier or for support **2** [C] bar fixed to the wall for hanging things on: a towel ~ **3** [C, usu pl] steel bar on which trains run **4** [U] railways as a means of transport: travel by ~ ● **rail** v [PV] **rail sth in/off** surround/separate sth with rails ▶ **railing** n [C, usu pl] fence made of upright metal bars
■ **railroad** /-rəʊd/ n [C] (US) = RAILWAY
■ **railway** n [C] **1** track on which trains run **2** system of such tracks, roads from which trains run

0━ **rain** /reɪn/ n [U,sing] water that falls in drops from the clouds ● **rain** v **1** [I] (used with it) fall as rain: It ~ed all day. **2** [I,T] ~ (down/on) (cause sth to) fall on sb/sth in large quantities [PV] **be rained off** (*US* **be rained out**) (of an event) be cancelled or have to stop because of rain ■ **rainbow** /'reɪnbəʊ/ *n* [C] curve of many colours seen in the sky when the sun shines through rain ■ **raincoat** *n* [C] light waterproof coat ■ **rainfall** *n* [U] amount of rain that falls in a certain area during a particular time ■ **rainforest** *n* [C] thick forest in tropical areas with heavy rainfall

rainy /'reɪni/ *adj* (-ier, -iest) having or bringing a lot of rain [IDM] **save, keep, etc sth for a rainy day** save sth, esp money, for a time when you will really need it

0-w **raise** /reɪz/ *v* [T] **1** lift or move sth to a higher level **2** increase the amount or level of sth: ~ *sb's hopes* (= make sb more hopeful) ◇ ~ *your voice* (= speak louder) **3** bring or collect money or people together: ~ *money for charity* ◇ ~ *an army* **4** bring sth up for attention or discussion: ~ *a new point* **5** cause or produce sth; make sth appear: ~ *doubts* **6** (*esp US*) look after a child or young animal until it is able to take care of itself **7** breed farm animals; grow crops [IDM] **raise hell** protest angrily about sth ■ **raise the roof** (cause sb to) make a lot of noise in a building, eg by cheering ■ **raise** *n* [C] (*US* = RISE^3(3))

raisin /'reɪzn/ *n* [C] dried sweet grape

rake /reɪk/ *n* [C] garden tool with a long handle and a row of metal points at the end ● **rake** *v* [I,T] pull a rake over a surface in order to level it or to remove sth: *She ~d the leaves into a pile.* [PV] **rake sth in** (*infml*) earn a lot of money: *She's really raking it in!* **rake sth up** (*infml, disapprov*) remind people of sth unpleasant that happened in the past ■ **rake-off** *n* [C] (*infml*) (usu dishonest) share of profits

rally /'ræli/ *n* [C] (pl -ies) **1** large public meeting, esp one held to support a particular idea or political party **2** (*GB*) race for motor vehicles on public roads **3** long series of hits of the ball in tennis, etc ● **rally** *v* (pt, pp -ied) **1** [I,T] (cause people to) come together to help or support sb/sth **2** [I] become healthier, stronger, etc after a period of illness, weakness, etc [PV] **rally round/around (sb)** (of a group of people) work together to help sb in a time of need

RAM /ræm/ *n* [U] random-access memory; computer memory in which data can be changed and which can be looked at in any order

ram /ræm/ *n* [C] **1** male sheep **2** = BATTERING RAM (BATTER) ● **ram** (-mm-) *v* [T] **1** (of a vehicle) drive into or hit another vehicle with force, esp

deliberately **2** push sth somewhere with force

ramble /'ræmbl/ *n* [C] long walk for pleasure ● **ramble** *v* [I] **1** walk for pleasure, esp in the countryside **2** talk about sth/sb in a confused way, esp for a long time **3** (of a plant) grow wildly ▶ **rambler** *n* [C] ▶ **rambling** *adj* **1** (esp of buildings) extending in many directions irregularly **2** (of speech or writing) long and confused

ramification /ˌræmɪfɪ'keɪʃn/ *n* [C, usu pl] one of the large number of complicated and unexpected results of an action or decision

ramp /ræmp/ *n* [C] **1** slope that joins two parts of a road, building, etc when one is higher than the other **2** (*US*) = SLIP ROAD (SLIP^1)

rampage /ræm'peɪdʒ/ *v* [I] move through a place wildly, usu causing damage ● **rampage** *n* [usu sing] sudden period of wild or violent behaviour, often causing damage: *Football fans went on the ~ in the city.*

rampant /'ræmpənt/ *adj* **1** (of sth bad) spreading uncontrollably **2** (of plants) growing very fast

rampart /'ræmpɑːt/ *n* [C] wide bank of earth built to defend a fort, etc

ramshackle /'ræmˌʃækl/ *adj* (of a house or vehicle) almost collapsing

ran *pt of* RUN^1

ranch /rɑːntʃ/ *n* [C] large farm, esp in the US, where cattle are bred ▶ **rancher** *n* [C] person who owns or manages a ranch

rancid /'rænsɪd/ *adj* (of fatty foods) tasting or smelling bad because no longer fresh

rancour (*US* -cor) /'ræŋkə(r)/ *n* [U] (*fml*) feelings of hatred because you think sb has done sth unfair to you ▶ **rancorous** /-kərəs/ *adj*

random /'rændəm/ *adj* done, chosen, etc without a definite plan or pattern ● **random** *n* [IDM] **at random** without thinking or deciding in advance what is going to happen ■ **random access** *n* [U] (*computing*) ability in a computer to go straight to data items without having to read through items stored previously ■ **random-access memory** *n* [U] (*computing*) = RAM ▶ **randomly** *adv*

randy /'rændi/ *adj* (-ier, -iest) (*infml, GB*) sexually excited

rang *pt of* RING^1

0-w **range^1** /reɪndʒ/ *n* **1** [C, usu sing] group or set of similar things; variety: *sell a wide ~ of books* **2** [C, usu sing] limits between which sth varies **3** [C,U] distance over which sth can be seen or heard **4** [C,U] distance over which a gun or other weapon can hit things: *shot him at close ~*

range

5 [C] line or group of mountains or hills **6** [C] area of land where people can practise shooting

range² /reɪndʒ/ v **1** [I] vary between limits: *Prices ~ from £70 to £100.* **2** [T] (*fml*) arrange people or things in a particular position or order [PV] **range over sth** include a variety of different subjects

ranger /ˈreɪndʒə(r)/ n [C] person whose job is to take care of a forest or large park

0‑w **rank¹** /ræŋk/ n **1** [U, C] position sb has in an organization or in society **2** [C, U] position sb has in the army, navy, etc **3** (**the ranks**) [pl] ordinary soldiers, not officers **4** [C] line or row of people or things: *a taxi ~* ● **rank** v [I, T] be or put sb/sth in a certain position or class: *among the world's best* ■ **the rank and file** n [sing, with sing or pl verb] ordinary members of an organization, not its leaders

rank² /ræŋk/ adj **1** smelling bad **2** (of sth bad) complete **3** (of plants) growing too thickly

rankle /ˈræŋkl/ v [I] cause lasting bitterness or anger

ransack /ˈrænsæk/ v [T] search a place thoroughly leaving it very untidy

ransom /ˈrænsəm/ n [C] money paid to set a prisoner free ● **ransom** v [T] get the freedom of sb by paying a ransom

rant /rænt/ v [I] speak or complain about sth loudly and angrily

rap /ræp/ n **1** [C] quick sharp hit or knock **2** [U] type of modern music with a fast rhythm and words which are spoken fast [IDM] **take the rap (for sb/sth)** (*infml*) be punished, esp for sth you have not done ● **rap** v (**-pp-**) [I, T] hit sth lightly and quickly

rape /reɪp/ v [T] force sb to have sex when they do not want to, by threatening them or using violence ● **rape** n [C, U] **1** crime of forcing sb to have sex with you, esp using violence **2** (*lit*) act of spoiling or destroying an area ▶ **rapist** n [C]

0‑w **rapid** /ˈræpɪd/ adj done or happening very quickly ▶ **rapidity** /rəˈpɪdəti/ n [U] ▶ **rapidly** adv ▶ **rapids** n [pl] part of a river where the water flows very fast, usu over rocks

rappel /ræˈpel/ (*US*) v = ABSEIL

rapport /ræˈpɔː(r)/ n [sing, U] friendly relationship and understanding

rapt /ræpt/ adj (*written*) so deep in thought that you are not aware of other things

rapture /ˈræptʃə(r)/ n [U] (*fml*) great happiness [IDM] **be in, go into, etc raptures (about/over sb/sth)** feel

great pleasure or enthusiasm for sb/sth ▶ **rapturous** adj: *rapturous applause*

0‑w **rare** /reə(r)/ adj (**~r, ~st**) **1** not common **2** (of meat) lightly cooked ▶ **rarely** adv not often ▶ **rareness** n [U]

rarefied /ˈreərɪfaɪd/ adj **1** understood by only a small group of people who share a particular area of knowledge **2** (of air) containing less oxygen than usual

raring /ˈreərɪŋ/ adj ~ **to** (*infml*) very keen to do sth

rarity /ˈreərəti/ n (pl **-ies**) **1** [C] unusual, and therefore interesting, person or thing **2** [U] quality of being rare

rascal /ˈrɑːskl/ n **1** naughty child **2** (*old-fash*) dishonest man

rash /ræʃ/ n **1** [C] area of red spots on a person's skin, caused by illness or a reaction to sth **2** [sing] series of unpleasant things that happen over a short period of time: *a ~ of strikes* ● **rash** adj acting or done without careful thought ▶ **rashly** adv ▶ **rashness** n [U]

rasher /ˈræʃə(r)/ n [C] thin slice of bacon

rasp /rɑːsp/ n **1** [sing] unpleasant harsh sound **2** [C] metal tool used for making rough surfaces smooth ● **rasp** v [I, T] say sth in an unpleasant harsh voice ▶ **rasping** adj

raspberry /ˈrɑːzbəri/ n (pl **-ies**) **1** small dark red berry that grows on bushes **2** (*infml*) rude noise made by sticking out the tongue and blowing

rat /ræt/ n [C] **1** animal like, but larger than, a mouse **2** (*infml*) unpleasant or disloyal person [IDM] **the rat race** (*disapprov*) endless competition for success ● **rat** v (**-tt-**) [PV] **rat on sb** (*infml*) tell sb in authority about sth wrong that sb else has done ▶ **ratty** adj (**-ier, -iest**) (*GB, infml*) irritable

0‑w **rate¹** /reɪt/ n **1** measure of the speed at which sth happens: *a ~ of 3 miles per hour* **2** measure of the number of times sth happens or exists in a period of time: *the birth/divorce ~* **3** fixed price that is charged or paid for sth: *postage ~s* **4** (**rates**) [pl] (in Britain) local tax paid by businesses for land and buildings that they use [IDM] **at any rate** (*spoken*) whatever happens at **this/that rate** (*spoken*) if this/that continues ■ **ratepayer** n [C] (formerly in Britain) person who has to pay rates

0‑w **rate²** /reɪt/ v [T] **1** consider sb/sth in the way that is mentioned: *He is generally ~d as one of the best players.* **2** place sb/sth in a position on a scale in relation to other similar people or things **3** deserve to be treated in a

0̶→ **rather** /ˈrɑːðə(r)/ *adv* **1** fairly; to some degree: *They were ~ surprised.* **2** used to correct sth you have said or to clarify sth: *late night, or ~ early this morning* **[IDM]** **would rather ... (than)** would prefer to: *I'd ~ walk than go by bus.*

ratify /ˈrætɪfaɪ/ *v* (pt, pp **-ied**) [T] make an agreement officially valid by voting for or signing it ▶ **ratification** /ˌrætɪfɪˈkeɪʃn/ *n* [U]

rating /ˈreɪtɪŋ/ *n* **1** [C,U] grade or position of quality **2** [pl] figures showing the popularity of television programmes **3** [C] (*GB*) sailor in the navy who is not an officer

ratio /ˈreɪʃiəʊ/ *n* [C] (*pl* **~s**) relationship between two amounts: *The ~ of men to women was 3 to 1.*

ration /ˈræʃn/ *n* **1** [C] fixed amount of food, fuel, etc allowed to one person, eg during a war **2** (**rations**) [pl] fixed amount of food given regularly to soldiers ● **ration** *v* [T] limit the amount of sth that sb is allowed to have

rational /ˈræʃnəl/ *adj* **1** based on reason rather than emotions **2** (of a person) able to think clearly ▶ **rationally** /-ʃnəli/ *adv*

rationale /ˌræʃəˈnɑːl/ *n* [C] (*fml*) reasons which explain a decision, course of action, belief, etc

rationalize (*also* **-ise**) /ˈræʃnəlaɪz/ *v* **1** [I,T] think and offer reasons for sth that seems unreasonable **2** [T] make changes to a system, business, etc to make it more efficient, esp by spending less money ▶ **rationalization** (*also* **-isation**) /ˌræʃnəlaɪˈzeɪʃn/ *n* [C,U]

rattle /ˈrætl/ *v* [I,T] (cause sth to) make a series of short loud sounds **2** [T] (*infml*) make sb nervous **[PV]** **rattle sth off** repeat sth from memory without having to think too hard ● **rattle** *n* [C] **1** rattling sound **2** baby's toy that produces a rattling sound ■ **rattlesnake** *n* [C] poisonous American snake that makes a rattling noise with its tail

ratty → RAT

raucous /ˈrɔːkəs/ *adj* sounding loud and harsh ▶ **raucously** *adv*

ravage /ˈrævɪdʒ/ *v* [T] badly damage sth ▶ **ravages** (**the ravages of sth**) *n* [pl] the destruction caused by sth

rave /reɪv/ *v* [I] **1** ~ **about** (*infml*) talk with great enthusiasm about sth **2** shout loudly or angrily at sb ■ **rave review** *n* [C] newspaper or magazine article that praises a new film, book, etc. ▶ **raving** *adv, adj* completely (mad)

raven /ˈreɪvn/ *n* [C] large black bird like a crow ● **raven** *adj* (*lit*) (of hair) shiny and black

ravenous /ˈrævənəs/ *adj* very hungry ▶ **ravenously** *adv*

ravine /rəˈviːn/ *n* [C] deep narrow steep-sided valley

ravish /ˈrævɪʃ/ *v* [T] (*lit*) **1** (of a man) force a woman to have sex *(esp passive)* **2** give sb great pleasure *(esp passive)* ▶ **ravishing** *adj* very beautiful

0̶→ **raw** /rɔː/ *adj* **1** not cooked **2** in the natural state: *~ materials* **3** (of people) not experienced **4** (of skin) sore and painful **5** (of the weather) very cold

ray /reɪ/ *n* [C] **1** narrow line of light, heat, etc **2** ~ **(of)** small amount of sth good: *a ~ of hope*

rayon /ˈreɪɒn/ *n* [U] smooth fabric used for making clothes

raze /reɪz/ *v* [T] (*usu passive*) destroy a building, town, etc completely

razor /ˈreɪzə(r)/ *n* [C] instrument used for shaving: *a cut-throat/ disposable ~*

Rd *abbr* (in written addresses) Road

re /riː/ *prep* (*written*) used at the beginning of an email, letter, etc to introduce the subject that it is about

0̶→ **re-** /riː/ *prefix* again: *refill*

0̶→ **reach** /riːtʃ/ *v* **1** [T] arrive at a place; achieve an aim: *~ London* ◇ ~ *an agreement* **2** [I,T] stretch out your hand or arm to touch or take sth: *He ~ed for his gun.* ◇ *Can you ~ the book on the top shelf?* **3** [I,T] go as far as sth: *Their land ~es (down to) the river.* **4** [T] communicate with sb, esp by telephone ● **reach** *n* **1** [sing, U] distance that can be reached: *Medicines should be kept out of ~ of children.* **2** [C, usu pl] part of a river

0̶→ **react** /riˈækt/ *v* [I] **1** ~ **(to)** behave differently as a result of sth **2** ~ **(with)** (*chem*) have an effect on another substance **[PV]** **react against sb/sth** behave in a certain way in opposition to sth

0̶→ **reaction** /riˈækʃn/ *n* **1** [C,U] what you do, say or think as a result of sth that has happened **2** [U] opposition to political or social change **3** [C] (*chem*) change caused in a substance by the effect of another ▶ **reactionary** /-ʃənri/ *n* [C], *adj* (*pl* **-ies**) (person) opposed to political or social change

reactor /riˈæktə(r)/ *n* [C] = NUCLEAR REACTOR (NUCLEAR)

0̶→ **read** /riːd/ *v* (pt, pp **read** /red/) **1** [I,T] look at and understand sth written or printed: *Can you ~ music?* **2** [I,T] go through written words, etc in silence or aloud to others: *~ a book* **3** [T] understand sth: *~ sb's thoughts* **4** [I] (of a piece of writing) have sth written on it; give a particular impression when read: *The sign ~s 'No Entry'.* ◇ *Her reports always ~ well.* **5** [T] (of measuring instruments) show a certain weight, pressure, etc **6** [T] study a subject at university **7** [T] (of a computer or the user) take information from a disk [IDM] **read between the lines** find a meaning that is not openly stated ▸ **readable** adj that is easy or pleasant to read ■ **read-only memory** n [U] (computing) = ROM ■ **read-out** n [C] (computing) display of information on a computer screen

0━ **reader** /ˈriːdə(r)/ n [C] **1** person who reads **2** book that gives students practice in reading **3** (usu Reader) (in Britain) senior university teacher ▸ **readership** n [sing] number or type of people who read a particular newspaper, etc

0━ **reading** /ˈriːdɪŋ/ n **1** act of reading sth **2** [U] books, articles, etc that are intended to be read: *light* (= not serious) ~ **3** [C] way in which sth is understood: *My ~ of the situation is...* **4** [C] amount, etc shown on a measuring instrument **5** [C] (GB) (in Parliament) one of three stages of debate before a bill (2) becomes law

0━ **ready** /ˈredi/ adj (-ier, -iest) **1** ~ **for/to** prepared and able for action or use: ~ *for action* ◇ ~ *to act* **2** easily available: *a* ~ *source of income* **3** willing **4** ~ **to** likely to do sth: *She looked* ~ *to collapse.* **5** quick and clever: *a* ~ *answer* ▸ **readily** adv **1** quickly and easily **2** without hesitation ▸ **readiness** n [U]
● **ready** adv already done: ~*-cooked meals* ● **ready** n [IDM] **at the ready** available to be used immediately ■ **ready-'made** adj ready to use or wear immediately

0━ **real** /rɪəl/ adj **1** existing as a fact **2** true or actual **3** genuine and not false or artificial ● **real** adv (US, infml) very ■ **real estate** n [U] (esp US) **1** property in the form of land and buildings **2** business of selling houses or land ■ **real estate agent** n = ESTATE AGENT (ESTATE)

realism /ˈrɪəlɪzəm/ n [U] **1** acceptance of the facts of a situation **2** (in art and literature) showing of things as they are in real life ▸ **realist** n [C]

0━ **realistic** /ˌrɪəˈlɪstɪk/ adj accepting a situation in a sensible way: *a* ~ *assessment*

0━ **reality** /riˈæləti/ n (pl -ies) **1** [U] true situation and the problems that actually exist in life **2** [C] something actually seen or experienced: *the realities of war* [IDM] **in reality** in actual fact ■ re,ality TV n [U] television shows based on real people (not actors) in real situations, presented as entertainment

0━ **realize** (also -ise) /ˈrɪəlaɪz, GB also ˈrɪəl-/ v [T] **1** understand or

become aware of sth **2** make sth, eg plans or fears, happen **3** (fml) be sold for a particular amount of money ▸ **realization** (also -isation) /ˌriːəlaɪˈzeɪʃn; ˌrɪəl-/ n [U]

0━ **really** /ˈriːəli; ˈriːəli/ adv **1** in reality; truly **2** used to emphasize an adjective or adverb: *I'm* ~ *sorry.* **3** (spoken) used to show interest, surprise, etc at what sb is saying

realm /relm/ n [C] **1** area of interest or knowledge **2** (fml) kingdom

Realtor™ /ˈrɪəltə(r)/ n (US) = ESTATE AGENT (ESTATE)

reap /riːp/ v [T] **1** obtain sth good, esp as a result of hard work **2** [I, T] cut and collect a crop, esp corn

rear[1] /rɪə(r)/ n (usu the rear) [sing] back part of sth [IDM] **bring up the rear** be or come last ● **rear** adj at or near the back of sth ■ the **ˈrearguard** n [C] soldiers protecting the back part of an army

0━ **rear**[2] /rɪə(r)/ v [T] **1** look after young children or animals until they are fully grown **2** breed or keep animals, eg on a farm **3** ~ **(up)** (of a horse) raise itself on its back legs

0━ **reason**[1] /ˈriːzn/ n **1** [C] cause or an explanation for sth that has happened or that sb has done **2** [U] fact that makes it right or fair to do sth **3** [U] power of the mind to think logically, etc: *lose your* ~ (= go mad) **4** [U] what is possible, practical or right: *He needs a job and is willing to do anything within* ~.

reason[2] /ˈriːzn/ v [T] form a judgement about sth after careful thought **2** [I] use your power to think and understand [PV] **reason with sb** talk to sb in order to persuade them to be more sensible ▸ **reasoning** n [U] opinions and ideas based on logical thinking

0━ **reasonable** /ˈriːznəbl/ adj **1** fair; sensible **2** not too expensive ▸ **reasonably** adv **1** quite **2** in a reasonable way

reassure /ˌriːəˈʃɔː(r)/ v [T] remove sb's worries ▸ **reassurance** n [U, C]

rebate /ˈriːbeɪt/ n [C] part of tax, rent, etc paid back

rebel /ˈrebl/ n [C] **1** person who fights against the government **2** person who opposes authority ● **rebel** /rɪˈbel/ v (-ll-) **1** ~ **(against)** fight against or refuse to obey an authority, eg a government ▸ **rebellion** /rɪˈbeljən/ n [C, U] (act of) rebelling ▸ **rebellious** adj

0━ **reboot** /ˌriːˈbuːt/ v [I, T] (computing) (cause a computer to) switch off and then start again immediately

rebound /rɪˈbaʊnd/ v [I] **1** bounce back after hitting sth **2** ~ **(on)** (fml) have unpleasant effects on the doer **3** (business) (of prices, shares, etc) rise again after falling ● **rebound** /ˈriːbaʊnd/ n [IDM] **on the rebound**

while you are sad and confused, esp after a relationship has ended

rebuff /rɪˈbʌf/ n [C] (fml) unkind refusal or answer ▸ **rebuff** v [T]

rebuke /rɪˈbjuːk/ v [T] (fml) speak severely to sb for doing sth wrong ▸ **rebuke** n [C, U]

0▪ **recall** /rɪˈkɔːl/ v [T] **1** (fml) remember sth; remind sb of sth **2** order sb/sth to return or be returned ● **recall** also /ˈriːkɔːl/ n **1** [U] ability to remember sth **2** [sing] official order for sb/sth to return or be given back

recap /ˈriːkæp/ v (-pp-) [I, T] short for RECAPITULATE

recapitulate /ˌriːkəˈpɪtʃuleɪt/ v [I, T] (fml) repeat the main points of what has been said, decided, etc ▸ **recapitulation** /ˌriːkəˌpɪtʃuˈleɪʃn/ n [C, U]

recede /rɪˈsiːd/ v [I] **1** move gradually away or back **2** slope backwards

0▪ **receipt** /rɪˈsiːt/ n **1** [C] piece of paper showing that goods or services have been paid for **2** [U] (fml) act of receiving sth **3** (receipts) [pl] money received by a business, bank or government

receivable /rɪˈsiːvəbl/ adj (business) (of bills, accounts, etc) for which money has not yet been received

0▪ **receive** /rɪˈsiːv/ v [T] **1** get or accept sth sent or given **2** experience or be given a particular type of treatment or injury: I~d a warm welcome from the crowd. **3** accept sb as a member or visitor **4** change broadcast signals into sounds or pictures ▸ **receiver** n [C] **1** part of a telephone that is held to the ear **2** piece of radio or television equipment that changes broadcast signals into sounds or pictures **3** (law) official chosen to take charge of a company that is bankrupt **4** person who buys or accepts stolen goods

0▪ **recent** /ˈriːsnt/ adj that happened, began, etc a short time ago ▸ **recently** adv not long ago

receptacle /rɪˈseptækl/ n [C] (fml) container

0▪ **reception** /rɪˈsepʃn/ n **1** [U] part of a hotel, office building, etc where visitors are received **2** [C] formal social occasion: a wedding ~ **3** [sing] type of welcome that is given to sb: be given a warm ~ **4** [U] quality of radio or television signals received ▸ **receptionist** /-ʃənɪst/ n [C] person whose job is to deal with visitors to a hotel, office building, etc

receptive /rɪˈseptɪv/ adj willing to consider new ideas

recess /rɪˈses/ n **1** [C, U] period of time when work is stopped **2** [C] area of a room where part of a wall is

set back **3** [C, usu pl] secret or hidden part of a place

recession /rɪˈseʃn/ n **1** [C, U] difficult time for the economy of a country: The economy is in deep ~. **2** [U] (fml) backward movement of sth

recipe /ˈresəpi/ n [C] **1** set of instructions for preparing a food dish **2** way of achieving sth: a ~ for disaster

recipient /rɪˈsɪpiənt/ n [C] (fml) person who receives sth

reciprocal /rɪˈsɪprəkl/ adj given and received in return: ~ trade agreements ▸ **reciprocally** /-kli/ adv

reciprocate /rɪˈsɪprəkeɪt/ v [I, T] (fml) behave or feel towards sb in the same way as they behave or feel towards you

recital /rɪˈsaɪtl/ n [C] performance of music or poetry by one person or a small group

recite /rɪˈsaɪt/ v [T] **1** say a poem, etc aloud from memory **2** say aloud a list or series of things ▸ **recitation** /ˌresɪˈteɪʃn/ n [C, U]

reckless /ˈrekləs/ adj not caring about danger or the effects of sth ▸ **recklessly** adv ▸ **recklessness** n [U]

0▪ **reckon** /ˈrekən/ v [T] **1** (infml) think sth: I ~ we ought to go now. **2** calculate an amount, a number, etc [PV] **reckon on sth** rely on sth happening **reckon with sb/sth 1** consider or treat sb/sth as important: a force to be ~ed with (= that cannot be ignored) **2** consider sth as a possible problem: I didn't ~ with getting caught in so much traffic. ▸ **reckoning** n [U, C] **1** calculation **2** time when sb's actions will be judged and they may be punished: the day of ~ing

reclaim /rɪˈkleɪm/ v [T] **1** ask for sth to be given back **2** make land suitable for use ▸ **reclamation** /ˌrekləˈmeɪʃn/ n [U]

recline /rɪˈklaɪn/ v [I] (fml) lie back or down

recluse /rɪˈkluːs/ n [C] person who lives alone and avoids other people

0▪ **recognize** (also -ise) /ˈrekəgnaɪz/ v [T] **1** know again sb/ sth that you have seen, heard, etc before **2** admit that sth exists or is true: They ~d the need to take the problem seriously. **3** accept and approve of sb/sth officially: refuse to ~ a new government **4** give sb official thanks for sth they have done ▸ **recognition** /ˌrekəgˈnɪʃn/ n [U] ▸ **recognizable** adj

recoil /rɪˈkɔɪl/ v [I] **1** (written) move back suddenly in fear, dislike, etc **2** (of a gun) move back quickly when fired ▸ **recoil** /ˈriːkɔɪl/ n [U, sing]

recollect /ˌrekəˈlekt/ v [I, T] remember sth ▸ **recollection** /ˌrekəˈlekʃn/ n **1** [U] ability to remember sth; act of remembering **2** [C] thing that you remember from the past

0–ᴥ **recommend** /ˌrekəˈmend/ v [T] **1** praise sb/sth as suitable for a job/ purpose: Can you ~ a good hotel? **2** advise sb; advise sb to do sth: I ~ leaving/you leave early. ▸ **recommendation** /ˌrekəmenˈdeɪʃn/ n [C, U]

recompense /ˈrekəmpens/ v [T] (fml) reward sb for work; repay sb for losses or harm ● **recompense** n [sing, U] (fml) reward or repayment

reconcile /ˈrekənsaɪl/ v [T] **1** find a way of dealing with two or more ideas, etc that seem to be opposed to each other **2** make people become friends again after an argument **3** ~ **sb/yourself (to)** make sb/yourself accept an unpleasant situation ▸ **reconciliation** /ˌrekənsɪliˈeɪʃn/ n [U, C]

reconnaissance /rɪˈkɒnɪsns/ n [C, U] act of getting information about an area for military purposes

reconnoitre (US -ter) /ˌrekəˈnɔɪtə(r)/ v [I, T] get information about an area for military purposes, by using soldiers, planes, etc

0–ᴥ **record**[1] /ˈrekɔːd/ n **1** [C] written account of facts, events, etc **2** [C] round flat piece of plastic on which sound has been recorded **3** [C] the best result or level ever achieved: a new world ~ in the 100 metres ◇ ~ profits **4** [sing] known facts about sb's character or past [IDM] **off the record** unofficial and not for publication **on record** officially noted ■ **record player** n [C] machine for producing sound from records[1](2)

0–ᴥ **record**[2] /rɪˈkɔːd/ v **1** [T] keep a permanent account of facts or events by writing them down, filming them, etc **2** [I, T] make a copy of music, a film, etc by storing it on tape or a disc to listen to or watch again **3** [T] (of a measuring instrument) show a particular measurement or amount

recorder /rɪˈkɔːdə(r)/ n [C] **1** machine for recording sounds or pictures or both **2** musical instrument played by blowing into one end **3** (GB) judge in certain law courts in Britain and the US

0–ᴥ **recording** /rɪˈkɔːdɪŋ/ n [C] sounds or pictures recorded on a tape or disc

recount[1] /rɪˈkaʊnt/ v [T] (fml) tell sb about sth, esp sth you have experienced

recount[2] /ˌriːˈkaʊnt/ v [T] count sth again, esp votes ▸ **recount** /ˈriːkaʊnt/ n [C]

recoup /rɪˈkuːp/ v [T] get back money that you have spent or lost

recourse /rɪˈkɔːs/ n [U] source of having to, or being able to, use sth that can provide help in a difficult situation: The government, when necessary, has ~ to the armed forces.

0–ᴥ **recover** /rɪˈkʌvə(r)/ v **1** [I] ~ **(from)** get well again after an illness, etc **2** [T] get back sth lost or stolen **3** [T] get control of yourself, your senses, etc again: to ~ consciousness ▸ **recovery** n [U, C, usu sing]

recreation /ˌrekriˈeɪʃn/ n [C, U] (form of) play or amusement or way of spending your free time

recrimination /rɪˌkrɪmɪˈneɪʃn/ n [C, usu pl, U] (act of) accusing and blaming each other

recruit /rɪˈkruːt/ n [C] **1** new member of the armed forces or the police **2** person who joins an organization, company, etc ● **recruit** v [I, T] find sb to join a company, the armed forces, etc ▸ **recruitment** n [U]

rectangle /ˈrektæŋɡl/ n [C] flat four-sided shape with four angles of 90° ▸ **rectangular** /rekˈtæŋɡjələ(r)/ adj

rectify /ˈrektɪfaɪ/ v (pt, pp -ied) [T] put sth right: ~ an error

rector /ˈrektə(r)/ n [C] Anglican priest in charge of a parish ▸ **rectory** /ˈrektəri/ n [C] (pl -ies) rector's house

rectum /ˈrektəm/ n [C] (anat) lower end of the large intestine

recuperate /rɪˈkuːpəreɪt/ v [I] ~ **(from)** (fml) become strong again after an illness, etc ▸ **recuperation** /rɪˌkuːpəˈreɪʃn/ n [U]

recur /rɪˈkɜː(r)/ v (-rr-) [I] happen again ▸ **recurrence** /rɪˈkʌrəns/ n [C, U] repetition ▸ **recurrent** /rɪˈkʌrənt/ adj

recycle /ˌriːˈsaɪkl/ v [T] treat sth already used so that it can be used again

0–ᴥ **red** /red/ adj (~der, ~dest) **1** of the colour of blood **2** (of the face) bright red or pink, because of embarrassment or anger **3** (of hair) reddish-brown **4** (infml, pol) having very left-wing political opinions ■ **red herring** n unimportant fact, event, etc that takes people's attention away from the main point ■ **red tape** n [U] unnecessary official rules that cause delay ● **red** n **1** [C, U] the colour of blood: dressed in ~ **2** [C, U] **red wine 3** [C] (infml, pol) person with very left-wing political opinions [IDM] **be in the red** (infml) owe money to the bank ■ **redhead** n [C] person who has red hair ■ **red-hot** adj so hot that it glows red

redden /'redn/ v [I, T] become or make sth red

redeem /rɪ'diːm/ v [T] **1** make sb/sth seem less bad: *a film with no ~ing features* **2** buy sth back by payment ▸ **redemption** /rɪ'dempʃn/ n [U]

redouble /ˌriː'dʌbl/ v [T] increase or strengthen sth: *~ your efforts*

redress /rɪ'dres/ v [T] (fml) correct sth that is wrong or unfair [IDM] **redress the balance** make a situation equal or fair again ● **redress** n [U] (fml) payment, etc to compensate for sth wrong that has happened to sb

0-∞ **reduce** /rɪ'djuːs/ v [T] make sth less or smaller in size, price, etc [PV] **reduce sb/sth (from sth) to (doing) sth** force sb/sth into a certain state or condition: *He was ~d to tears.* ▸ **reduction** /rɪ'dʌkʃn/ n [C, U] (instance of) reducing sth: *~s in price* **2** [C] small copy of a picture, map, etc

redundant /rɪ'dʌndənt/ adj **1** (of a person) dismissed from a job because no longer needed **2** not needed or useful ▸ **redundancy** /-dənsi/ n [C, U] (pl -**ies**)

reed /riːd/ n [C] **1** tall plant like grass that grows near water **2** (in some wind instruments) piece of cane or metal that vibrates to produce sound

reef /riːf/ n [C] line of rocks, sand, etc just below or above the surface of the sea

reek /riːk/ n [sing] strong unpleasant smell ● **reek** v [I] ~ **(of)** smell unpleasantly of sth

reel /riːl/ n [C] **1** cylinder on which thread, wire, film, etc is wound **2** length of thread, film, etc on one reel **3** (music for a) fast Scottish, Irish or American dance ● **reel** v [I] **1** move unsteadily, eg because you are drunk **2** feel very shocked or upset about sth [PV] **reel sth in/out** wind sth on/off a reel: *I slowly ~ed the fish in.* **reel sth off** say sth quickly without having to think about it

refectory /rɪ'fektri/ n [C] (pl -**ies**) large dining room, eg in a college

0-∞ **refer** /rɪ'fɜː(r)/ v (-**rr**-) [PV] **refer to sb/sth (as sth)** mention or speak about sb/sth **refer to sb/sth 1** describe or be connected to sb/sth **2** look at sth or ask a person for information: *You may ~ to your notes if you want.* **refer sb/sth to sb/sth** send sb/sth to sb/sth for help, advice or a decision: *My GP ~red me to a specialist.*

referee /ˌrefə'riː/ n [C] **1** (sport) official who controls the game in some sports **2** (GB) person who agrees to write a reference (3) for you

0-∞ **reference** /'refrəns/ n **1** [C, U] (act of) referring to sb/sth **2** [C]

number, word or symbol telling you where information may be found **3** [C] letter giving information about sb's character and abilities, esp for a new employer [IDM] **in/with reference to** (written) used to say what you are writing or talking about ■ **'reference book** n [C] book, eg a dictionary or an encyclopedia, looked at for finding information

referendum /ˌrefə'rendəm/ (pl -**dums** or -**da**) n [C, U] direct vote by all the people on a political question

refine /rɪ'faɪn/ v [T] **1** make a substance pure **2** improve sth by making small changes to it ▸ **refined** adj **1** (of a substance) made pure: *~d sugar* **2** (of a person) well educated and polite ▸ **refinement** n **1** [C] small change or addition to sth that improves it **2** [U] process of refining sth **3** [U] quality of being well educated and polite ▸ **refinery** n [C] (pl -**ies**) factory where oil, sugar, etc is refined

reflate /ˌriː'fleɪt/ v [I, T] increase the amount of money in an economy ▸ **reflation** /ˌriː'fleɪʃn/ n [U]

0-∞ **reflect** /rɪ'flekt/ v **1** [T] throw back an image, heat, sound, etc from a surface **2** [T] show the nature of sth or sb's attitude: *The book faithfully ~s his ideas.* **3** [I] ~ **(on)** think deeply about sth [PV] **reflect well, badly, etc on sb/sth** make sb/sth appear to be good, bad, etc to other people ▸ **reflector** n [C] surface that reflects light

reflection /rɪ'flekʃn/ n **1** [C] reflected image, eg in a mirror **2** [U] reflecting of light, heat, etc **3** [C, U] deep thought: *on ~* (= after thinking very carefully)

reflex /'riːfleks/ [C] (also 'reflex action) sudden unintended movement, eg sneezing, made in response to sth

reflexive /rɪ'fleksɪv/ n [C], adj (gram) (word) showing that the action of the verb is performed on the subject: *a ~ verb ◊ In 'I cut myself', 'myself' is a ~ pronoun.*

reflexology /ˌriːfleks'ɒlədʒi/ n [U] treatment in which sb's feet are rubbed in a particular way in order to heal other parts of their body or to make them feel relaxed ▸ **reflexologist** n [C]

re-form /ˌriː'fɔːm/ v [I, T] (cause sth to) form again

0-∞ **reform** /rɪ'fɔːm/ v [I, T] **1** improve a system, organization, etc by making changes to it **2** (cause sb to) behave better than before ● **reform** n [U, C] change or improvement made to a social system, organization, etc ▸ **reformer** n [C] person who works to achieve social and political change

reformation /ˌrefəˈmeɪʃn/ n **1** [U] (fml) act of improving or changing sb/sth **2** (the Reformation) [sing] 16th century religious movement that led to the forming of the Protestant Churches

refract /rɪˈfrækt/ v [T] (physics) make a ray of light bend where it enters water, glass, etc ► **refraction** /-kʃn/ n [U]

refrain /rɪˈfreɪn/ v [I] ~ **(from)** (fml) not do sth ● **refrain** n [C] lines of a song that are repeated

refresh /rɪˈfreʃ/ v [T] make sb feel less tired or hot **IDM** **refresh your/sb's memory** remind yourself/sb of sth by referring to notes, etc ■ re'**fresher course** n [C] course providing training on new ideas and developments in your job ► **refreshing** adj **1** pleasantly new or different **2** making you feel less tired or hot ► **refreshment** n **1** (refreshments) [pl] food and drink **2** [U] (fml) fact of making sb feel stronger

refrigerate /rɪˈfrɪdʒəreɪt/ v [T] make food, etc cold in order to keep it fresh or preserve it ► **refrigeration** /rɪˌfrɪdʒəˈreɪʃn/ n [U]

0🔑 **refrigerator** /rɪˈfrɪdʒəreɪtə(r)/ n [C] (fml) = FRIDGE: *This dessert can be served straight from the ~.*

refuel /ˌriːˈfjuːəl/ v (-ll- US -l-) [I,T] fill sth or be filled with fuel: *The plane landed to ~.*

refuge /ˈrefjuːdʒ/ n [C, U] (place giving) protection from danger, trouble, etc

refugee /ˌrefjuˈdʒiː/ n [C] person forced to leave their country, esp because of political or religious beliefs

refund /ˈriːfʌnd/ n [C] repayment ● **refund** /rɪˈfʌnd/ v [T] pay back money to sb

0🔑 **refusal** /rɪˈfjuːzl/ n [C, U] (instance of) refusing to do, give or accept sth

0🔑 **refuse**[1] /rɪˈfjuːz/ v [I,T] not give, accept or do sth: ~ *to help*

refuse[2] /ˈrefjuːs/ n [U] waste; rubbish

regain /rɪˈgeɪn/ v [T] get sth back; recover sth: ~ *your strength*

regal /ˈriːgl/ adj typical of a king or queen

regalia /rɪˈgeɪliə/ n [U] special clothes worn or objects carried at official ceremonies

0🔑 **regard**[1] /rɪˈɡɑːd/ v [T] ~ **as** think about sb/sth in a particular way: *She is ~ed as the best teacher in the school.* **IDM** **as regards sb/sth** (fml) concerning sb/sth ► **regarding** prep concerning sb/sth; about sb/sth

0🔑 **regard**[2] /rɪˈɡɑːd/ n **1** [U] attention to or concern for sb/sth: *with no ~ for safety* **2** [U] (fml) respect for sb: *have a high ~ for sb* **3** (regards) [pl] kind wishes **IDM** **in/ with regard to sb/sth** concerning sb/sth; about sb/sth ► **regardless of** prep paying no attention to sth

regatta /rɪˈɡætə/ n [C] meeting for boat races

regency /ˈriːdʒənsi/ n (pl -ies) **1** [C] (period of) government by a regent (= person who rules a country in place of the king or queen) **2** (Regency) [sing] period 1811-20 in Britain

regenerate /rɪˈdʒenəreɪt/ v [I,T] give new strength or life to sb/sth ► **regeneration** /rɪˌdʒenəˈreɪʃn/ n [U]

regent /ˈriːdʒənt/ n [C] person who rules instead of a king or queen who is too young, ill, etc

reggae /ˈreɡeɪ/ n [U] West Indian popular music and dance

regime /reɪˈʒiːm/ n [C] (system of) government

regiment /ˈredʒɪmənt/ n [C] large group of soldiers commanded by a colonel ► **regimental** /ˌredʒɪˈmentl/ adj ► **regimented** adj (disapprov) involving strict discipline and/or organization

0🔑 **region** /ˈriːdʒən/ n **1** [C] large area of land **2** [C] division of a country **IDM** **in the region of** about; approximately ► **regional** adj

0🔑 **register** /ˈredʒɪstə(r)/ n **1** [C] (book containing an) official list of names, etc **2** [C] range of the voice or a musical instrument **3** [C,U] (ling) level of language (formal or informal) used in a piece of writing or speech ● **register** v **1** [I,T] record your/sb's/sth's name on an official list **2** (fml) [T] make your opinion known officially or publicly **3** [I,T] (of measuring instruments) show an amount **4** [I,T] (fml) show or express a feeling **5** [T] send sth by post, paying extra to protect it against loss

registrar /ˌredʒɪˈstrɑː(r)/ n [C] keeper of official records

registration /ˌredʒɪˈstreɪʃn/ n [U,C] act of making an official record of sb/sth ■ regi'stration number (also **registration**) (GB) n [C] numbers and letters on a vehicle used to identify it

registry office /ˈredʒɪstri ɒfɪs/ n [C] place where civil marriages take place and where births, marriages and deaths are officially recorded

regret /rɪˈɡret/ v (-tt-) [T] be sorry or sad about sth: *Later, I ~ted my decision to leave.* ► **regrettable** adj that is or should be regretted ► **regrettably** adv

0━ **regret**[2] /rɪ'gret/ n [U,C] feeling of sadness at the loss of sth or because of sth you have done ▶ **regretful** adj sad; sorry

regroup /,ri:'gru:p/ v [I,T] arrange the way people or soldiers work together in a new way: They ~ed their forces and renewed the attack.

0━ **regular** /'regjələ(r)/ adj
1 happening, coming, etc repeatedly at times or places that are the same distance apart ~ breathing **2** usual or normal **3** evenly shaped: a face with ~ features **4** (gram) (esp of verbs, nouns) changing their form in the same way as other verbs, nouns **5** belonging to the permanent armed forces: a ~ soldier ● **regular** n [C] **1** customer who often goes to a shop, restaurant, etc: He's one of our ~s. **2** professional soldier ▶ **regularity** /,regjʊ'lærəti/ n [U] ▶ **regularly** adv at regular times or intervals

regulate /'regjuleɪt/ v [T] control sth by means of rules ▶ **regulation** /,regjʊ'leɪʃn/ n
1 [C, usu pl] official rule or order **2** [U] controlling sth by means of rules ● **regulation** adj as required by rules: in ~ uniform

rehabilitate /,ri:ə'bɪlɪteɪt/ v [T] help sb who has been imprisoned or ill live a normal life again ▶ **rehabilitation** /,ri:ə,bɪlɪ'teɪʃn/ n [U]

rehearse /rɪ'hɜːs/ v [I,T] practise a play, music, etc for public performance ▶ **rehearsal** n [C,U]

reign /reɪn/ n [C] (period of) rule of a king or queen ● **reign** v [I] **1** be king or queen (lit) of a feeling, an idea or atmosphere) be the most obvious feature: Silence ~ed.

reimburse /,ri:ɪm'bɜːs/ v [T] (fml) pay back money to sb that they have spent or lost ▶ **reimbursement** n [U]

rein /reɪn/ n [C, usu pl] long narrow strap for controlling a horse

reincarnate /,ri:ɪn'kɑːneɪt/ v [T] (usu passive) bring sb back in another body after death ▶ **reincarnation** /,ri:ɪnkɑː'neɪʃn/ n [U,C]

reindeer /'reɪndɪə(r)/ n [C] (pl **reindeer**) large deer with antlers, living in cold northern regions

reinforce /,ri:ɪn'fɔːs/ v [T] make sth stronger ▶ **reinforcement** n
1 (reinforcements) [pl] extra soldiers or police officers sent to a place when needed **2** [U, sing] act of making sth stronger

reinstate /,ri:ɪn'steɪt/ v [T] give back a job or position that had been taken away from sb ▶ **reinstatement** n [U]

reiterate /ri'ɪtəreɪt/ v [T] (fml) repeat sth several times ▶ **reiteration** /ri,ɪtə'reɪʃn/ n [sing]

0━ **reject** /rɪ'dʒekt/ v [T] **1** refuse to accept sth/sb **2** send sth back or throw sth away as not good enough ● **reject** /'ri:dʒekt/ n [C] person or thing that has been rejected ▶ **rejection** /rɪ'dʒekʃn/ n [U,C]

rejoice /rɪ'dʒɔɪs/ v [I] (fml) express great happiness about sth ▶ **rejoicing** n [U] happiness; joy

rejuvenate /rɪ'dʒuːvəneɪt/ v [T] make sb/sth look or feel younger and more lively ▶ **rejuvenation** /rɪ,dʒuːvə'neɪʃn/ n [U]

relapse /rɪ'læps/ v [I] go back into a previous or worse state after making an improvement ▶ **relapse** also /'ri:læps/ n [C]

0━ **relate** /rɪ'leɪt/ v [T] **1** ~ (to) show or make a connection between two people or things **2** ~ (to) give a spoken or written report of sth; tell a story [PV] **relate to sth/sb** be connected with sth/sb **2** be able to understand and sympathize with sb/sth ▶ **related** adj of the same family or group; connected

0━ **relation** /rɪ'leɪʃn/ n **1** (relations) [pl] way in which two people, countries, etc behave towards or deal with each other **2** [U,C] way in which two or more things are connected: The fee bears no ~ to the amount of work involved. **3** [C] member of your family ▶ **relationship** n **1** [C] way in which two people, countries, etc behave towards or deal with each other **2** [C] loving and/or sexual friendship between two people **3** [C,U] connection between two or more things

0━ **relative** /'relətɪv/ adj
1 considered in relation to sth else **2** ~ to (fml) with reference to sth **3** (gram) referring to an earlier noun, sentence, or part of a sentence: a ~ clause/pronoun ● **relative** n [C] member of your family ▶ **relatively** adv to a fairly large degree; quite: ~ cheap food ■ **relative clause** n [C] (gram) clause joined to the rest of a sentence by a relative pronoun or adverb ■ **relative 'pronoun** n [C] (gram) pronoun that joins a clause to the rest of a sentence eg who in the woman who came

0━ **relax** /rɪ'læks/ v **1** [I] rest while you are doing sth enjoyable, esp after work **2** [T] become or make sb calmer and less worried **3** [T] allow rules, etc to become less strict ▶ **relaxation** /,ri:læk'seɪʃn/ n **1** [U] ways of resting and enjoying yourself **2** [C] something pleasant you do in order to rest, esp after work ▶ **relaxed** adj calm and not worried

relay /ˈriːleɪ/ n [C] 1 (also ˈrelay race) race in which each member of a team runs, swims, etc one section of the race 2 fresh set of people or animals that replace others that are tired or have finished a period of work 3 electrical device that receives radio and television signals and sends them on again ● relay /ˈriːleɪ; also reˈleɪ/ v [T] receive and send on a message or broadcast

0━ **release** /rɪˈliːs/ v [T] 1 set sb/sth free 2 allow news, etc to be made known; make sth available 3 move sth from a fixed position: ~ the brake ● release n 1 [U, sing] act of releasing sb/sth 2 [C] thing that is made available to the public, esp a new CD or film

relegate /ˈrelɪgeɪt/ v [T] give sb a lower or less important position, rank, etc than before ▸ relegation /ˌrelɪˈgeɪʃn/ n [U]

relent /rɪˈlent/ v [I] become less strict or harsh ▸ relentless adj constant; harsh

0━ **relevant** /ˈreləvənt/ adj connected with what is being discussed ▸ relevance /-əns/ n [U] ▸ relevantly adv

reliable /rɪˈlaɪəbl/ adj that can be trusted to do sth well ▸ reliability /rɪˌlaɪəˈbɪləti/ n [U] ▸ reliably adv

reliant /rɪˈlaɪənt/ adj ~ on dependent on sth ▸ reliance /rɪˈlaɪəns/ n [U] dependence

0━ **relief** /rɪˈliːf/ n 1 [U, sing] lessening or ending of suffering, worry, etc: pain~ 2 [U] food, money, medicine, etc given to people in need 3 [C] person that replaces another when they have finished working for the day 4 [U, C] (way of) carving, etc in which the design stands out from a flat surface ● reˈlief map n [C] map showing the height of hills, etc by shading or colour

relieve /rɪˈliːv/ v [T] 1 reduce or remove an unpleasant feeling or pain 2 make sth less boring, by introducing sth different 3 replace sb who is on duty [PV] relieve sb of sth (fml) take a responsibility or job away from sb: He was ~d of his duties. ▸ relieved adj no longer anxious

0━ **religion** /rɪˈlɪdʒən/ n 1 [U] belief in and worship of God or gods 2 [C] particular system of faith and worship based on such belief

religious /rɪˈlɪdʒəs/ adj 1 of religion 2 (of a person) believing in

and practising a religion ▸ religiously adv regularly

relinquish /rɪˈlɪŋkwɪʃ/ v [T] (fml) stop having sth, esp unwillingly: ~ control

relish /ˈrelɪʃ/ v [T] get pleasure from sth: I don't ~ the idea of getting up so early. ● relish n 1 [U] (written) great enjoyment 2 [U, C] sauce, etc added to food to give it more flavour

reluctant /rɪˈlʌktənt/ adj unwilling ▸ reluctance /-əns/ n [U] ▸ reluctantly adv

0━ **rely** /rɪˈlaɪ/ v (pt, pp -ied) [I] ~ on need or depend on sth/sb; trust sb/ sth

0━ **remain** /rɪˈmeɪn/ v (fml) 1 linking verb continue to be sth: ~ silent 2 [I] still be present after other people/ things have gone or been dealt with: Not much ~ed of the house after the fire. ◇ She ~ed in the house after her friends had left. 3 [I] still need to be done or dealt with: There are only a couple of jobs ~ing now. ▸ remainder n [sing, with sing or pl verb] (written) people, things or time that is left ▸ remains n [pl] 1 ~ (of) parts that are left after others have been eaten, removed, etc 2 (fml) dead body

remand /rɪˈmɑːnd/ v [T] send an accused person away from a law court to wait for their trial at a later date ● remand n [U] (GB) process of keeping sb in prison while they are waiting for trial: He is currently being held on ~.

0━ **remark** /rɪˈmɑːk/ v [I, T] say or write a comment about sb/sth: They all ~ed on his youth. ● remark n [C] something said or written which expresses an opinion, thought, etc ▸ remarkable adj unusual or surprising ▸ remarkably adv

remedial /rɪˈmiːdiəl/ adj aimed at solving a problem, esp by correcting sth that has been done wrong

remedy /ˈremədi/ n [C, U] (pl -ies) 1 way of putting sth right 2 cure ● remedy v (pt, pp -ied) [T] correct or improve sth

0━ **remember** /rɪˈmembə(r)/ v 1 [I, T] have or keep an image in your memory; bring back to your mind a fact, etc that you knew 2 [T] give money, a present, etc to sb: She always ~s my birthday. [PV] remember me to sb used to ask sb to give your greetings to sb else ▸ remembrance /-brəns/ n (fml) 1 [U] act of remembering a past event or a person who is dead 2 [C] (fml) object that causes you to remember sb/sth

0━ **remind** /rɪˈmaɪnd/ v [T] help sb to remember sth important that they must do: R~ me to buy some more milk, will you? [PV] remind sb of sb/sth cause sb to think about sb/sth similar: You ~ me of your father when you do that. ▸ reminder n [C]

something, eg a letter, that causes a person to remember sth

reminisce /ˌremɪˈnɪs/ v [I] ~ **(about)** talk about a happy time in your past ▶ **reminiscence** n [C, pl] remembered experiences ▶ **reminiscent** adj ~ **of** reminding you of sb/sth

remission /rɪˈmɪʃn/ n [U, C] **1** period during which a serious illness improves for a time: *The patient is in* ~. **2** (GB) shortening of the time sb spends in prison, because of good behaviour **3** (fml) act of reducing or cancelling the amount of money sb has to pay

remit /riˈmɪt; ˈriːmɪt/ n [usu sing] (GB) area of activity over which a person or group has authority, control or influence ● **remit** /rɪˈmɪt/ v (-tt-) [T] (fml) **1** send money to a person or place **2** cancel or free sb from a debt or punishment ▶ **remittance** n [C] sum of money remitted

remnant /ˈremnənt/ n [C] small part of sth that is left

remonstrate /ˈremənstreɪt/ v [I] ~ **(with)** (fml) protest or complain about sth/sth

remorse /rɪˈmɔːs/ n [U] ~ **(for)** feeling of being extremely sorry for sth wrong that you have done ▶ **remorseful** adj ● **remorseless** adj (written) **1** unpleasant and not stopping **2** cruel and without pity

0── **remote** /rɪˈməʊt/ adj (-r, -st) **1** ~ **(from)** far away from places where people live **2** far away in time **3** (of a computer, etc) that you can connect to from far away, using an electronic link **4** ~ **(from)** very different from sth **5** (of a person) unfriendly; not interested in others **6** very small: *a* ~ *possibility* ● re,mote con'trol n [C] ability to control an apparatus from a distance using radio or electrical signals **2** [C] device that allows you to operate a television, etc from a distance ▶ **remotely** adv to a very small degree ▶ **remoteness** n [U]

0── **remove** /rɪˈmuːv/ v [T] **1** take sth/sb away or off **2** get rid of sth: ~ *stains/doubts* **3** dismiss sb from a job [IDM] be far, further, furthest **removed from sth** be very different from sth ▶ **removal** n **1** [U] act of removing sth/sb **2** [U, C] (GB) act of moving furniture, etc to a different home ▶ **remover** n [U, C]: *a stain* ~*er*

remunerate /rɪˈmjuːnəreɪt/ v [T] (fml) pay sb for work done ▶ **remuneration** /rɪˌmjuːnəˈreɪʃn/ n [C, U] ▶ **remunerative** /-ərətɪv/ adj profitable

renaissance /rɪˈneɪsns/ n [sing] **1** (the Renaissance) renewed interest in art and literature in Europe in the 14th-16th centuries **2** any similar renewed interest in sth

renal /ˈriːnl/ adj (anat) of the kidneys

render /ˈrendə(r)/ v [T] (fml) **1** cause sb/sth to be in a particular state or condition: *The shock* ~*ed him speechless.* **2** give sb sth: *a reward for services* ~*ed* **3** perform sth **4** translate sth ▶ **rendering** n [C] performance

rendezvous /ˈrɒndɪvuː; -deɪ-/ n [C] (pl **rendezvous** /-vuːz/) **1** (place chosen for) a meeting **2** place where people often meet ● **rendezvous** v [I] meet at an arranged time and place

rendition /renˈdɪʃn/ n [C] (fml) **1** performance of sth, esp a song or piece of music **2** (law) the act of handing over a prisoner or person suspected of a crime for questioning by another country, state, etc.

renegade /ˈrenɪɡeɪd/ n [C] (fml, disapprov) person who leaves one political or religious group to join another

renew /rɪˈnjuː/ v [T] **1** begin sth again: ~ *a friendship* **2** make sth valid for a further period of time: ~ *a passport* **3** emphasize sth by stating or saying it again **4** replace sth old or damaged with sth new of the same kind ▶ **renewable** adj (of energy and natural resources) that is replaced naturally and can be used without the risk of finishing it all: ~*able sources of energy such as wind and solar power* ▶ **renewal** n [C, U]

renounce /rɪˈnaʊns/ v [T] (fml) **1** formally give up a title, position, etc **2** state publicly that you will no longer have anything to do with sb/ sth: ~ *your faith*

renovate /ˈrenəveɪt/ v [T] repair and paint an old building, etc so that it is in good condition again ▶ **renovation** /ˌrenəˈveɪʃn/ n [U, C]

renown /rɪˈnaʊn/ n [U] (fml) fame ▶ **renowned** adj famous

0── **rent** /rent/ n **1** [U, C] money paid regularly for the use of a house, etc **2** [C] torn place in a piece of material or clothing ● **rent** v [I, T] pay money for the use of a house, etc **2** [T] ~ **(out)** allow sth to be used in return for payment of rent ▶ **rental** n [C] amount of rent paid

renunciation /rɪˌnʌnsiˈeɪʃn/ n [C] (fml) act of renouncing sth

reorganize (also -ise) /riˈɔːɡənaɪz/ v [I, T] change the way in which sth is organized ▶ **reorganization** (also **-isation**) /riˌɔːɡənaɪˈzeɪʃn/ n [U, C]

Rep. abbr (US) Republican

rep /rep/ n (infml) **1** [C] = REPRESENTATIVE(2) **2** [U] = REPERTORY

0── **repair** /rɪˈpeə(r)/ v **1** mend sth broken, damaged or torn ● **repair** n [C, U] act of repairing sth: *The* building was in need of ~. **[IDM] in good, bad, etc repair** in a good, bad, etc condition

reparation /ˌrepəˈreɪʃn/ n [C] (fml) money given or sth done to compensate for loss or damage

repatriate /ˌriːˈpætrieɪt/ v [T] **1** send or bring sb back to their own country **2** (business) send money or profits back to your own country ▸ **repatriation** /ˌriːˌpætriˈeɪʃn/ n [U]

repay /rɪˈpeɪ/ v (pt, pp **repaid** /rɪˈpeɪd/) [T] **1** pay back money borrowed **2** give sth to sb or do sth in return for sth they have done for you ▸ **repayment** n [C, U]

repeal /rɪˈpiːl/ v [T] end a law officially ▸ **repeal** n [U]

0—**repeat** /rɪˈpiːt/ v **1** ~ **sth/yourself** say or write sth again or more than once **2** [T] do or produce sth again or more than once ● **repeat** n [C] sth that is repeated ▸ **repeated** adj done again and again ▸ **repeatedly** adv

repel /rɪˈpel/ v (-ll-) [T] **1** drive, push or keep sb/sth away **2** make sb feel horror and disgust ▸ **repellent** adj causing great dislike ▸ **repellent** n [U,C] substance that repels insects

repent /rɪˈpent/ v [I,T] ~ **(of)** (fml) feel and show you are sorry about sth wrong you have done ▸ **repentance** n [U] ▸ **repentant** adj

repercussion /ˌriːpəˈkʌʃn/ n [C, usu pl] indirect and usu bad result of an action or event

repertoire /ˈrepətwɑː(r)/ n [C] all the plays, songs, etc that an actor or musician can perform

repertory /ˈrepətri/ n [U] performance of several plays for a short time using the same actors: a ~ company

repetition /ˌrepəˈtɪʃn/ n [C,U] (act of) repeating sth ▸ **repetitive** /rɪˈpetətɪv/ adj saying or doing the same thing many times, so that it becomes boring

rephrase /ˌriːˈfreɪz/ v [T] say sth again, using different words

0—**replace** /rɪˈpleɪs/ v [T] **1** be used instead of sth/sb else; do sth instead of sb/sth else **2** put a new thing in the place of an old, broken, etc one **3** put sth back in its place ▸ **replacement** n **1** [U] act of replacing one thing with another **2** [C] person or thing that replaces another

replay /ˌriːˈpleɪ/ v [T] **1** (GB, sport) play a sports match again because the previous game was a draw **2** play part of a film, tape, etc again ● **replay** /ˈriːpleɪ/ n [C] replayed sports match, part of a tape, etc

replenish /rɪˈplenɪʃ/ v [T] (fml) make sth full again

replica /ˈreplɪkə/ n [C] exact copy

0—**reply** /rɪˈplaɪ/ v (pt, pp **-ied**) [I,T] give sth as an answer to sb/sth ● **reply** n [C] (pl **-ies**) act of replying to sb/sth

0—**report**[1] /rɪˈpɔːt/ v **1** [I,T] give an account of sth heard, seen, done, etc, esp for a newspaper **2** [T] ~ **(to)** tell sb in authority about a crime, an accident, etc or about sth bad that has happened **3** [I] ~ **to/for** tell sb that you have arrived, eg for work or for a meeting with sb ■ re·ported **speech** n [U] = INDIRECT SPEECH (INDIRECT) ▸ **reporter** n [C] person who reports news for a newspaper or on radio or television

0—**report**[2] /rɪˈpɔːt/ n [C] **1** written or spoken account of sth heard, seen, done, etc **2** (GB) written statement about a pupil's work and behaviour **3** story or piece of information that may or may not be true **4** (written) sound of a gun being fired

repose /rɪˈpəʊz/ v [i] (lit) lie or rest in a particular place ● **repose** n [U] (lit) state of rest

reprehensible /ˌreprɪˈhensəbl/ adj (fml) morally wrong; deserving criticism

0—**represent** /ˌreprɪˈzent/ v **1** act or speak officially on behalf of sb: ~ the Queen **2** linking verb be sth: This figure ~s an increase of 10%. **3** show sb/sth, esp in a picture **4** be a sign or example of sth **5** describe sb/sth in a particular way ▸ **representation** /ˌreprɪzenˈteɪʃn/ n [U,C]

0—**representative** /ˌreprɪˈzentətɪv/ n [C] **1** person chosen to speak or act for sb else or on behalf of a group of people **2** (also infml **rep**) person who works for a company and travels around selling its products
▸ **representative** adj **1** typical of a particular group of people **2** of a system of government in which a small number of people make decisions for a larger group

repress /rɪˈpres/ v [T] **1** try not to have or show an emotion, etc **2** use political force to control a group of people and restrict their freedom ▸ **repression** /rɪˈpreʃn/ n [U] ▸ **repressive** adj harsh or cruel

reprieve /rɪˈpriːv/ v [T] **1** delay or cancel punishment, esp execution ● **reprieve** n [C] **1** order for the delay or cancelling of punishment, esp execution **2** delay before sth bad happens

reprimand /ˈreprɪmɑːnd/ v [T] (fml) express strong official disapproval of sb or their actions ▸ **reprimand** n [C]

reprisal /rɪˈpraɪzl/ n [C,U] (written) violent act towards sb because of sth bad they have done towards you

reproach /rɪˈprəʊtʃ/ v [T] ~ **(for)**

blame or criticize sb for a wrong action ● **reproach** n **1** [U] blame or criticism for sth: *The captain's behaviour is above/beyond ~* (= cannot be criticized). **2** [C] word or remark expressing blame or criticism

0━ **reproduce** /ˌriːprəˈdjuːs/ v **1** [T] make a copy of a picture, piece of text, etc **2** [I,T] produce babies or young ▶ **reproduction** /-ˈdʌkʃn/ n [C,U] ▶ **reproductive** /-ˈdʌktɪv/ adj of or for reproduction of young

reproof /rɪˈpruːf/ n [C,U] (fml) (remark expressing) blame or disapproval

reprove /rɪˈpruːv/ v [T] (fml) tell sb that you do not approve of sth they have done

reptile /ˈreptaɪl/ n [C] cold-blooded egg-laying animal, eg a lizard or snake ▶ **reptilian** /repˈtɪliən/ adj

republic /rɪˈpʌblɪk/ n [C] country governed by a president and politicians elected by the people and where there is no king or queen ▶ **republican** adj of or supporting the principles of a republic ▶ **republican** n [C] **1** person favouring republican government **2** (**Republican**) (US) member of the Republican party

repudiate /rɪˈpjuːdieɪt/ v [T] (fml) refuse to accept sth ▶ **repudiation** /rɪˌpjuːdiˈeɪʃn/ n [U]

repugnant /rɪˈpʌgnənt/ adj (fml) causing a feeling of strong dislike or disgust ▶ **repugnance** /-nəns/ n [U]

repulse /rɪˈpʌls/ v [T] (fml) **1** make sb feel disgust or strong dislike **2** drive back an enemy **3** refuse to accept sb's help, etc ▶ **repulsion** /rɪˈpʌlʃn/ n [U] **1** strong feeling of dislike or disgust **2** (physics) tendency of objects to push each other away ▶ **repulsive** adj very unpleasant

reputable /ˈrepjətəbl/ adj having a good reputation

0━ **reputation** /ˌrepjuˈteɪʃn/ n [C,U] opinion people have of sb/sth, based on what has happened in the past

repute /rɪˈpjuːt/ n [U] (fml) opinion people have of sb/sth (fml) reputed adj generally thought to be sth, although this is not certain: *He is ~d to be the best heart surgeon in the country.* ▶ **reputedly** adv

0━ **request** /rɪˈkwest/ n **1** [C,U] act of politely asking for sth: *make a ~ for more money* **2** [C] thing that you formally ask for ● **request** v [T] (fml) ask for sth politely

0━ **require** /rɪˈkwaɪə(r)/ v [T] (fml) **1** need sth; depend on sth: *My car ~s some attention.* **2** (usu passive) make sb do sth, esp because it is necessary according to a law or set of rules: *You are ~d to pay the fine.* ▶ **requirement** n [C] something needed

requisite /ˈrekwɪzɪt/ n [C], adj (fml) (something) necessary for a particular purpose

0━ **rescue** /ˈreskjuː/ v [T] save sb/sth away from a dangerous or harmful situation ● **rescue** n [C,U] (instance of) saving sb/sth from danger

0━ **research** /rɪˈsɜːtʃ/ n [U,C] ~ (into/ on) detailed study of a subject to discover new facts about it ● **research** /rɪˈsɜːtʃ/ v [I,T] study sth carefully to find out new facts about it ▶ **researcher** n [C]

resemble /rɪˈzembl/ v [T] look like or be similar to another person or thing ▶ **resemblance** n [C,U] fact of being or looking like sb/sth

resent /rɪˈzent/ v [T] feel bitter and angry about sth: *~ his success* ▶ **resentful** adj; ▶ **resentment** n [U,C]

0━ **reservation** /ˌrezəˈveɪʃn/ n **1** [C] arrangement to keep sth for sb, eg a seat in a train, a room in a hotel, etc **2** [C] feeling of doubt about a plan or idea: *I have a few ~s about the plan.* **3** (also **reserve**) [C] area of land in the US that is kept separate for Native Americans to live in

0━ **reserve** /rɪˈzɜːv/ v [T] **1** ask for a seat, table, room, etc to be available for you or sb else at a future time: *~ a table for three at eight o'clock* **2** keep sth for sb/sth, so that it cannot be used by any other person ● **reserve** n **1** [C] supply of sth kept for use when needed **2** [C] piece of land kept for a particular purpose: *a nature ~* **3** [U] quality sb has when they do not talk easily about their feelings, etc **4** [C] extra player in a team who plays if another player cannot **5** (**the reserve**) [sing] (also **the reserves** [pl]) extra military force kept back for use when needed [IDM] **in reserve** available for use if needed ▶ **reserved** adj slow to show your feelings or opinions; shy

reservoir /ˈrezəvwɑː(r)/ n [C] artificial lake where water is stored

reside /rɪˈzaɪd/ v [I] (fml) live in a particular place [PV] **reside in sb/sth** be in sb/sth; be caused by sth

residence /ˈrezɪdəns/ n (fml) **1** [C] (esp large or impressive) house **2** [U] state of living in a particular place: *The Queen is in ~.*

0━ **resident** /ˈrezɪdənt/ n [C], adj (person) living in a place ▶ **residential** /ˌrezɪˈdenʃl/ adj **1** (of an area of a town) having houses, not offices or factories **2** (of a job, course, etc) offering accommodation

residue /ˈrezɪdjuː/ n [C] (tech) small amount of sth that remains after most has been taken or used ▶ **residual** /rɪˈzɪdjuəl/ adj remaining at the end of a process

resign /rɪˈzaɪn/ v [I,T] give up your job, position, etc [PV] **resign yourself to** sth accept sth unpleasant without complaining ▶ **resigned** adj accepting sth unpleasant without complaining

resignation /ˌrezɪɡˈneɪʃn/ n 1 [C, U] (act or formal written statement of) resigning from your job 2 [U] state of being resigned to an unpleasant situation

resilient /rɪˈzɪliənt/ adj able to recover quickly after sth unpleasant, eg shock, injury, etc 2 (of a substance) able to return quickly to its original shape after being bent, etc ▶ **resilience** /-əns/ n [U]

resin /ˈrezɪn/ n [C,U] 1 sticky substance that is produced by some trees 2 similar man-made plastic substance

0🔑 **resist** /rɪˈzɪst/ v [T] 1 refuse to accept sth and try to stop it from happening: ~ change 2 fight back when attacked; use force to stop sth from happening 3 not be damaged or harmed by sth ▶ **resistance** n 1 [U, sing] (action of) resisting sth 2 [U, sing] opposing force: wind ~ance 3 (the Resistance) [sing, with sing or pl verb] secret organization that opposes the enemy in a country controlled by the enemy ▶ **resistant** adj not affected by sth; able to resist sth

resistor /rɪˈzɪstə(r)/ n [C] device that reduces the power in an electric circuit

resolute /ˈrezəluːt/ adj (fml) determined; firm ▶ **resolutely** adv

resolution /ˌrezəˈluːʃn/ n 1 [C] formal decision at a meeting 2 [U] act of solving or settling a problem or dispute 3 [U] quality of being resolute 4 [C] firm decision to do or not do sth: I made a New Year's ~ to lose weight. 5 [U, sing] power of a computer screen, printer, etc to give a clear image: high~ graphics

0🔑 **resolve** /rɪˈzɒlv/ v [T] (fml) 1 find a satisfactory solution to a problem, etc 2 make a firm decision to do sth ● **resolve** n [C, U] (fml) strong determination

resonant /ˈrezənənt/ adj (fml) (of sound) deep, clear and lasting a long time ▶ **resonance** /-nəns/ n [U]

0🔑 **resort** /rɪˈzɔːt/ v [PV] **resort to** sth make use of sth as a means of achieving sth, when nothing else is available: We had to ~ to using untrained staff. ● **resort** n [C] popular holiday centre: a seaside ~

resound /rɪˈzaʊnd/ v [I] 1 (of a sound, voice, etc) fill a place with sound 2 ~ (with) (of a place) be filled with sound ▶ **resounding** adj 1 very

great: a ~ing success 2 loud and clear: ~ing cheers

0🔑 **resource** /rɪˈsɔːs; -ˈzɔːs/ n [C, usu pl] 1 supply of raw materials, etc that a country can use to produce wealth 2 thing that can be used for help when needed ▶ **resourceful** adj (approv) good at finding ways of solving difficulties ▶ **resourcefully** adv

0🔑 **respect** /rɪˈspekt/ n 1 [U, sing] ~ (for) admiration for sb/sth 2 [U, sing] ~ (for) consideration for sb/sth: show ~ for her wishes 3 [C] particular aspect or detail of sth: In some ~s, I agree with you. [IDM] **pay your respects (to sb)** → PAY¹ **with respect to** sth (fml) concerning sth ● **respect** v [T] admire sb/sth; treat sb/sth with consideration

respectable /rɪˈspektəbl/ adj 1 socially acceptable 2 fairly good: a ~ income ▶ **respectability** /rɪˌspektəˈbɪləti/ n [U] ▶ **respectably** adv

respectful /rɪˈspektfl/ adj showing respect ▶ **respectfully** adv

respective /rɪˈspektɪv/ adj of, for or belonging to each one separately ▶ **respectively** adv in the order mentioned

respiration /ˌrespəˈreɪʃn/ n [U] (fml) act of breathing ▶ **respiratory** /rəˈspɪrətri; ˈrespərətri/ adj connected with breathing

respite /ˈrespaɪt/ n [U, sing] short rest from sth difficult or unpleasant

resplendent /rɪˈsplendənt/ adj (fml) very bright; splendid

0🔑 **respond** /rɪˈspɒnd/ v [I] ~ (to) 1 answer sb/sth 2 act in answer to sb/sth 3 react favourably to sth: ~ to treatment

0🔑 **response** /rɪˈspɒns/ n [C, U] 1 answer 2 action done in answer to sth

0🔑 **responsibility** /rɪˌspɒnsəˈbɪləti/ n (pl -ies) 1 [U, C] duty to deal with or take care of sb/sth 2 [U] blame for sth bad that has happened

0🔑 **responsible** /rɪˈspɒnsəbl/ adj 1 ~ (for) having to look after sb/sth or do sth as a duty: ~ for cleaning the car 2 ~ (for) being the cause of sth bad: Who's ~ for this mess? 3 ~ (to) having to report to sb in authority and explain your actions to them 4 trustworthy 5 (of a job) having important duties ▶ **responsibly** adv

responsive /rɪˈspɒnsɪv/ adj reacting quickly and positively to sth

0🔑 **rest¹** /rest/ n 1 (the rest (of sth)) [sing] the remaining part of sth 2 (the rest (of sth)) [pl] the others 3 [C, U] period of relaxing or sleeping 4 [C] object used to support sth: an arm~ 5 [C, U] (music) (sign showing) a pause between notes [IDM] **at rest 1** (tech) not moving 2 dead and therefore free from worry ▶ **restful** *adj* relaxing and peaceful ▶ **restless** *adj* unable to stay still or be happy where you are ▶ **restlessly** *adv*

🔑 **rest²** /rest/ *v* **1** [I,T] relax, sleep or do nothing; not use a part of your body for some time **2** [I,T] ~ **on/against** lean sth on sth [IDM] **rest assured (that...)** (*fml*) used to emphasize that what you are saying will definitely happen **rest on your laurels** (*disapprov*) be so satisfied with your success that you do nothing more [PV] **rest on/upon sb/sth 1** depend on sth **2** look at sb/sth **rest with sb (to do sth)** (*fml*) be the responsibility of sb

🔑 **restaurant** /'restrɒnt/ *n* [C] place where meals can be bought and eaten

restitution /ˌrestɪ'tju:ʃn/ *n* [U] (*fml*) giving back sth stolen, etc to its owner or paying money for damage

restive /'restɪv/ *adj* (*fml*) unable to be still; unwilling to be controlled

restoration /ˌrestə'reɪʃn/ *n* **1** [U,C] act of restoring sth **2** (the Restoration) [sing] period just after 1660 in Britain

restorative /rɪ'stɔ:rətɪv/ *adj* bringing back health and strength

🔑 **restore** /rɪ'stɔ:(r)/ *v* [T] **1** bring back a situation or feeling that existed before **2** bring sb/sth back to a former state or position **3** repair an old building, picture, etc so that it looks as good as it did originally **4** (*fml*) give sth that was lost or stolen back to sb ▶ **restorer** *n* [C] person who restores old buildings, etc

restrain /rɪ'streɪn/ *v* [T] stop sb/sth from doing sth, esp by using physical force ▶ **restrained** *adj* controlled; calm ▶ **restraint** /rɪ'streɪnt/ *n* **1** [C] rule, fact, etc that limits or controls what people can do **2** [U] act of controlling or limiting sth **3** [U] quality of behaving calmly and with control

🔑 **restrict** /rɪ'strɪkt/ *v* [T] limit sth; stop sb/sth from moving freely ▶ **restriction** /rɪ'strɪkʃn/ *n* [C, U] ▶ **restrictive** *adj*

🔑 **result** /rɪ'zʌlt/ *n* **1** [C, U] something that happens because of an action or event **2** [C] final score in a game; marks in an examination **3** [C] answer to a mathematical calculation ● **result** *v* [I] ~ **(from)** happen because of sth else that happened first [PV] **result in sth** make sth happen ▶ **resultant** *adj* (*fml*) caused by the thing just mentioned

resume /rɪ'zju:m/ *v* **1** [I,T] begin sth again after stopping **2** (~ your seat/place/position) [T] go back to the seat or place that you had before

résumé /'rezjumeɪ/ *n* [C] **1** summary **2** (*US*) = CURRICULUM VITAE

resumption /rɪ'zʌmpʃn/ *n* [U, sing] (*fml*) act of beginning sth again after stopping

resurrect /ˌrezə'rekt/ *v* [T] bring sth back into use ▶ **resurrection** /ˌrezə'rekʃn/ *n* **1** (the Resurrection) [sing] (in Christianity) coming back to life of Jesus after his death; time when all dead people will become alive again **2** [U, sing] new beginning for sth which is old or has disappeared

resuscitate /rɪ'sʌsɪteɪt/ *v* [T] (*fml*) bring sb back to consciousness ▶ **resuscitation** /rɪˌsʌsɪ'teɪʃn/ *n* [U]

retail /'ri:teɪl/ *n* [U] selling of goods to the public, usu through shops ▶ **retail** *adv* ● **retail** *v* **1** [T] sell goods to the public **2** [I] ~ **at/for** (*business*) be sold at a particular price ▶ **retailer** *n* [C] person or business that sells goods to the public

🔑 **retain** /rɪ'teɪn/ *v* [T] (*fml*) **1** keep sth; continue to hold or contain sth **2** obtain the services of a lawyer by payment ▶ **retainer** *n* [C] **1** fee paid to sb to make sure they will be available to do work when they are needed **2** (*GB*) reduced rent paid to reserve a flat, etc when you are not there **3** (*old-fash*) servant

retaliate /rɪ'tælieɪt/ *v* [I] repay an injury, insult, etc with a similar one ▶ **retaliation** /rɪˌtæli'eɪʃn/ *n* [U]

retard /rɪ'tɑ:d/ *v* [T] (*fml*) make the development of sth slower

retch /retʃ/ *v* [I] try to vomit but without bringing up anything

retention /rɪ'tenʃn/ *n* [U] (*fml*) action of retaining sth

retentive /rɪ'tentɪv/ *adj* (of the memory) able to remember things well

reticent /'retɪsnt/ *adj* saying little; not saying all that is known ▶ **reticence** /-sns/ *n* [U]

retina /'retɪnə/ *n* [C] (pl ~s or -ae /-ni:/) part of the eye at the back of the eyeball, sensitive to light

retinue /'retɪnju:/ *n* [C, with sing or pl verb] group of people travelling with an important person

🔑 **retire** /rɪ'taɪə(r)/ *v* **1** [I] ~ **(from)** stop doing your job, esp because you have reached a particular age or you are ill **2** [T] tell sb they must stop doing their job **3** [I] (*fml*) leave a place, esp to go somewhere quiet **4** [I] (*lit*) go to bed ▶ **retired** *adj* having retired from work ▶ **retirement** *n* [U] ▶ **retiring** *adj* preferring not to spend time with other people

retort /rɪ'tɔ:t/ *v* [T] reply to a comment quickly or angrily ● **retort** *n* [C, U] quick or angry reply

retrace /rɪˈtreɪs/ v [T] go back along the route you have taken: *She began to ~ her steps towards the house.*

retract /rɪˈtrækt/ v [I,T] **1** take back a statement, offer, etc **2** draw sth in or back: *A cat can ~ its claws.* ▸ **retractable** adj ▸ **retraction** n [C, U]

retread /ˈriːtred/ n [C] tyre made by putting a new rubber surface on an old tyre

retreat /rɪˈtriːt/ v (esp of an army) go back ● **retreat** n [C, U] **1** act of retreating **2** (place for) a period of quiet and rest

retribution /ˌretrɪˈbjuːʃn/ n [U] (fml) severe punishment for sth seriously wrong that sb has done

retrieve /rɪˈtriːv/ v [T] **1** (fml) bring or get sth back **2** (computing) find and get back data that has been stored in a computer's memory **3** make a bad situation better ▸ **retrieval** n [U] act of retrieving sth ◇ **retriever** n [C] dog trained to find and bring back shot birds, etc

retrograde /ˈretrəɡreɪd/ adj (fml, disapprov) going back to an earlier worse condition

retrogressive /ˌretrəˈɡresɪv/ adj (fml, disapprov) returning to old-fashioned ideas or methods instead of making progress

retrospect /ˈretrəspekt/ n [IDM] **in retrospect** looking back on a past event ▸ **retrospective** adj **1** looking back on the past **2** (of a new law or decision) intended to take effect from a particular date in the past

retrovirus /ˈretrəʊvaɪrəs/ n [C] type of virus that causes serious illness

0‑ᴡ **return¹** /rɪˈtɜːn/ v **1** [I] come or go back: *~ home* **2** [T] give, send or put sth back: *~ damaged goods to the shop* ◇ *He didn't ~ my call.* **3** go back to an activity you were doing earlier or a previous state **4** [T] give a decision about sth in a court of law: *The jury ~ed a verdict of guilty.* **5** [T] (GB) elect sb to a political position **6** [T] (business) give a particular amount of money as a profit or loss: *to ~ a high rate of interest*

0‑ᴡ **return²** /rɪˈtɜːn/ n **1** [sing] act of returning to a place **2** [U, sing] action of giving, putting or sending sth/sb back **3** [U, C] amount of profit that you get from sth **4** [C] official report or statement: *fill in a tax ~* **5** [C] (also **re‚turn ˈticket**) (GB) ticket for a journey to a place and back again [IDM] **in return (for sth)** in exchange for or as a payment for sth

reunion /riːˈjuːniən/ n **1** [C] meeting of former friends, colleagues, etc who have not seen one another for a long time **2** [C, U] coming together again after a separation

Rev. (GB also **Revd**) abbr Reverend

rev /rev/ v (-vv-) [I, T] ~ **(up)** increase the speed of an engine: *~ the car (up)*

0‑ᴡ **reveal** /rɪˈviːl/ v [T] **1** make sth known to sb: *~ a secret* **2** allow sth to be seen

revel /ˈrevl/ v (-ll- US -l-) [PV] **revel in sth** enjoy sth very much

revelation /ˌrevəˈleɪʃn/ n **1** [U] making known of sth secret **2** [C] something (esp surprising) that is revealed

revenge /rɪˈvendʒ/ n [U] punishment or injury done to sb because they have made you suffer ● **revenge** v [PV] **revenge yourself on sb** punish or hurt sb because they have made you suffer

revenue /ˈrevənjuː/ n [U, C] income, esp as received by the government

reverberate /rɪˈvɜːbəreɪt/ v [I] (of sound) echo again and again ▸ **reverberation** /rɪˌvɜːbəˈreɪʃn/ n **1** [C, U] loud noise that echoes **2** (**reverberations**) [pl] (usu unpleasant) effects of sth that happens that spread among a large number of people

revere /rɪˈvɪə(r)/ v [T] (fml) have great respect for sb/sth

reverence /ˈrevərəns/ n [U] great respect

reverend /ˈrevərənd/ n [C] (abbr **Rev.**) (title of a) member of the clergy

reverent /ˈrevərənt/ adj feeling or showing great respect for sb/sth ▸ **reverently** adv

reversal /rɪˈvɜːsl/ n [C, U] complete change of sth so that it is the opposite of what it was

0‑ᴡ **reverse** /rɪˈvɜːs/ v **1** [T] make sth the opposite of what it was: *~ a decision* **2** [T] turn sth the other way round **3** [I,T] (cause a vehicle to) move backwards [IDM] **reverse (the) charges** (GB) make a telephone call that will be paid for by the person receiving the call ● **reverse** n **1** (**the reverse**) [sing] the opposite **2** [C] the back of a coin, etc **3** (also re‚verse ˈgear) [U] mechanism used to cause a vehicle move backwards: *put the car into ~ (gear)* ● **reverse** adj opposite in position or order

revert /rɪˈvɜːt/ v [I] ~ **to** go back to a former state, owner or kind of behaviour

0‑ᴡ **review** /rɪˈvjuː/ v **1** [T] consider or examine sth again: *~ the past/a decision* **2** [I,T] write a report of a book, film, etc, giving your opinion of it **3** [T] officially inspect a group of soldiers, etc ● **review** n **1** [U, C] examination of sth, with the intention of changing it if necessary **2** [C] article in a newspaper, etc that gives an opinion of a new book, film, etc **3** [C] inspection of military forces ▶ reviewer n [C] person who writes reviews (2)

0̄ **revise** /rɪˈvaɪz/ v 1 [T] change your opinions or plans, eg because of sth you have learned 2 [T] examine sth again and correct or improve it 3 [I,T] ~ (for) (GB) go over work already done to prepare for an examination ▶ **revision** /rɪˈvɪʒn/ n 1 [C,U] (act of) revising sth 2 [C] corrected version

revitalize (also -ise) /ˌriːˈvaɪtəlaɪz/ v [T] put new life or strength into sth

revive /rɪˈvaɪv/ v 1 [I] become, or make sb/sth become, conscious or healthy and strong again 2 [T] bring sth into use again: ~ old customs ▶ **revival** n [C,U]

revoke /rɪˈvəʊk/ v [T] (fml) officially cancel sth so that it is no longer valid

revolt /rɪˈvəʊlt/ v 1 [I] ~ (against) take violent action against people in power 2 [T] cause sb to feel horror or disgust ▶ **revolt** n [C] protest against those in authority ▶ **revolting** adj extremely unpleasant

0̄ **revolution** /ˌrevəˈluːʃn/ n 1 [C,U] complete change in the system of government, esp by force 2 [C] complete change in conditions or ways of doing things: the computer ~ 3 [C,U] one complete circular movement around a point ▶ **revolutionary** adj 1 of a political revolution 2 involving a great or complete change: a ~ary idea ▶ **revolutionary** n [C] (pl -ies) person who begins or supports a revolution, esp a political one ▶ **revolutionize** (also -ise) /-ʃənaɪz/ v [T] completely change the way sth is done

revolve /rɪˈvɒlv/ v [I] ~ (around) go round sth in a circle [PV] **revolve around/round sb/sth** have sb/sth as the main interest or subject: The story ~s around the old man.

revolver /rɪˈvɒlvə(r)/ n [C] small gun with a revolving container for bullets

revue /rɪˈvjuː/ n [C] show in a theatre, with dances, songs and jokes

revulsion /rɪˈvʌlʃn/ n [U, sing] feeling of disgust or horror

0̄ **reward** /rɪˈwɔːd/ n [C,U] something given in return for work or services or for bringing back stolen property ● **reward** v [T] give sth to sb because they have done sth good, worked hard, etc ▶ **rewarding** adj (of an activity, etc) worth doing; satisfying

rewind /ˌriːˈwaɪnd/ v (pt, pp **rewound** /-ˈwaʊnd/) [i,t] cause a tape, film, etc to go back to the beginning

rhapsody /ˈræpsədi/ n [C] (pl -ies) 1 piece of music in irregular form 2 (written) expression of great delight

rhetoric /ˈretərɪk/ n [U] 1 (disapprov) speech or writing intended to influence people, but that is insincere 2 (fml) art of using words impressively in speech and writing ▶ **rhetorical** /rɪˈtɒrɪkl/ adj 1 (of a question) asked only for effect, not to get an answer 2 intended to influence people, but not completely honest

rheumatism /ˈruːmətɪzəm/ n [U] disease causing pain and stiffness in the muscles and joints ▶ **rheumatic** /ruˈmætɪk/ adj, n [C]

rhino /ˈraɪnəʊ/ n [C] (pl ~s) (infml) = RHINOCEROS

rhinoceros /raɪˈnɒsərəs/ n [C] large heavy thick-skinned animal with one or two horns on its nose

rhododendron /ˌrəʊdəˈdendrən/ n [C] bush with large red, purple, pink or white flowers

rhubarb /ˈruːbɑːb/ n [U] (garden plant) with thick reddish stems that are cooked and eaten like fruit

rhyme /raɪm/ v [I] (of words or lines of a poem) end with the same sound: 'Fall' ~s with 'wall'. ● **rhyme** n 1 [U] (use of) rhyming words at the end of lines in poetry 2 [C] word that rhymes with another word 3 [C] short rhyming poem

0̄ **rhythm** /ˈrɪðəm/ n 1 [C,U] regular pattern of beats or movements 2 [C] regular pattern of changes or events: the ~ of the tides ▶ **rhythmic(al)** /ˈrɪðmɪk(l)/ adj ▶ **rhythm and blues** n [U] (abbr **R&B**) type of music that is a mixture of blues and jazz and has a strong rhythm

rib /rɪb/ n 1 [C] one of the curved bones that go from the backbone to the chest 2 [U,C] way of knitting that produces raised lines ▶ **ribbed** adj (of fabric) having raised lines

ribbon /ˈrɪbən/ n [C,U] narrow strip of material to tie things or for decoration

0̄ **rice** /raɪs/ n [U] white or brown grain that is cooked and eaten

0̄ **rich** /rɪtʃ/ adj 1 having a lot of money or property 2 ~ in containing or providing a large supply of sth: soil ~ in minerals 3 (of food) containing a lot of fat, oil, eggs, etc 4 (of colours, sounds, smells and tastes) strong or deep; very beautiful or pleasing 5 (lit) expensive and beautiful: ~ fabrics ▶ **rich** n [pl] 1 (the rich) rich people 2 (riches) wealth ▶ **richly** adv ▶ **richness** n [U]

rickety /ˈrɪkəti/ adj likely to break or collapse

rickshaw /ˈrɪkʃɔː/ n [C] small light vehicle with two wheels that is pulled by sb walking

A B C D E F G H I J K L M N O P Q **R** S T U V W X Y Z

ricochet /ˈrɪkəʃeɪ/ v (pt, pp **-t-** or **-tt-**) [I] (of a moving object) hit a surface and bounce away when it is at an angle ▶ **ricochet** n [C, U]

0━ **rid** /rɪd/ v (**-dd-** pt, pp **rid**) [IDM] **get rid of sb/sth** make yourself free of sb/sth that you do not want; throw sth away [PV] **rid sb/sth of sb/sth** (written) remove sth/sb that is causing a problem from a place, group, etc

riddance /ˈrɪdns/ n [U] [IDM] **good riddance (to sb/sth)** unkind way of saying that you are pleased sb/sth has gone: He's gone and good ~ to him!

ridden pp of RIDE[1]

riddle /ˈrɪdl/ n [C] **1** difficult or amusing question **2** mysterious event or situation that you cannot explain ● **riddle** v [T] ~ **with** (usu passive) make a lot of holes in sb/sth: a body ~d with bullets

0━ **ride[1]** /raɪd/ v (pt **rode** /rəʊd/ pp **ridden** /ˈrɪdn/) **1** [I, T] sit on a horse, bicycle, etc and control it as it moves **2** [I] travel in a vehicle, esp as a passenger **3** [I, T] float on water or air: surfers riding the waves [PV] **ride up** (of clothing) gradually move upwards, out of position ▶ **rider** n [C] **1** person who rides a horse, bicycle, etc **2** additional remark following a statement

ride[2] /raɪd/ n [C] **1** short journey on a horse or bicycle or in a car, etc [IDM] **take sb for a ride** (infml) cheat or trick sb

ridge /rɪdʒ/ n [C] **1** long narrow piece of high land **2** raised line where two sloping surfaces meet

ridicule /ˈrɪdɪkjuːl/ n [U] unkind comments that make fun of sb ● **ridicule** v [T] make sb/sth look silly

0━ **ridiculous** /rɪˈdɪkjələs/ adj very silly or unreasonable: He looks ~ in that hat. ▶ **ridiculously** adv

rife /raɪf/ adj (sth bad) widespread; common

rifle[1] /ˈraɪfl/ n [C] gun with a long barrel, fired from the shoulder ● **rifle** v [T] ~ **(through)** search quickly through sth in order to find or steal sth

rift /rɪft/ n [C] **1** serious disagreement between people **2** large crack in the ground, rocks or cloud

rig /rɪg/ v (**-gg-**) [T] **1** arrange or influence sth dishonestly for your own advantage: ~ an election **2** fit a ship with masts, sails, etc **3** fit equipment somewhere, sometimes secretly: The lights had been ~ged (up) but not yet tested. [PV] **rig sth up** make or build sth quickly using whatever materials are available ● **rig** n [C] **1** large piece of equipment for taking oil or gas out of the land or sea: an oil~ **2** way that a ship's masts, sails, etc are arranged ▶ **rigging** n [U] ropes, etc that support a ship's masts and sails

0━ **right[1]** /raɪt/ adj **1** morally good or acceptable: I hope we're doing the ~ thing. **2** true or correct: the ~ answer **3** most suitable: the ~ person for the job **4** in a normal or satisfactory condition: That milk doesn't smell ~. **5** of, on or towards the side of the body that is towards the east when a person faces north: my ~ hand [IDM] **(not) in your right mind** (not) mentally normal **on the right track** ▶ TRACK **put/set sth right** correct sth or deal with a problem ■ **right angle** n [C] angle of 90° ▶ **right-angled** adj ▶ **rightly** adv for a good reason; correctly ▶ **rightness** n [U]

0━ **right[2]** /raɪt/ adv **1** exactly; directly: Put it ~ in the middle. **2** all the way; completely: Go ~ to the end of the road. **3** (infml) immediately: I'll be ~ with you (= I am coming very soon). **4** correctly **5** on or to the right side: turn ~ [IDM] **right away/off** immediately; without delay **right now** at this moment; immediately

0━ **right[3]** /raɪt/ n **1** [U, C] what is morally correct or good: He knew he was in the ~ (= had justice on his side). **2** [C, U] moral or legal claim to get sth or to behave in a particular way: You have no ~ to be here. ◇ animal ~s campaigners ◇ By ~s (= if justice were done) half the money should be mine. **3** (rights) [pl] the authority to perform, publish, film, etc a particular work: He sold the ~s for $2 million. **4** (the/sb's right) [sing] right side or direction **5** (the right, the Right) [sing, with sing or pl verb] political groups that most strongly support the capitalist system [IDM] **in your own right** because of your personal qualifications or efforts **put/set sb/sth to rights** correct sth/sth; put things in order ■ **right-hand** adj on the right side of sth ■ **right-handed** adj (of a person) using the right hand for writing, using tools, etc ■ **right-hand 'man** n [sing] main helper and supporter ■ **right of 'way** n [C] (legal permission to use a path that goes across private land) **2** [U] (in road traffic) the right to go first ■ **the right 'wing** n [sing, with sing or pl verb] part of a political party whose members are least in favour of radical change ▶ **right-wing** adj

right[4] /raɪt/ v [T] return sb/sth/ yourself to the normal, upright position: The ship ~ed herself. [IDM] **right a wrong** do sth to correct an unfair situation or sth bad that you have done

righteous /ˈraɪtʃəs/ adj (fml) morally

right and good ▶ **righteously** adv
▶ **righteousness** n [U]

rightful /ˈraɪtfl/ adj (fml) that is correct, right or legal: the ~ owner ▶ **rightfully** adv

rigid /ˈrɪdʒɪd/ adj **1** strict; unwilling or difficult to change **2** stiff and difficult to bend ▶ **rigidity** /rɪˈdʒɪdəti/ n [U] ▶ **rigidly** adv

rigorous /ˈrɪɡərəs/ adj **1** careful and detailed **2** strict; severe ▶ **rigorously** adv

rigour (US -or) /ˈrɪɡə(r)/ n **1** [U] fact of paying careful attention to detail **2** [U] (fml) strictness; severity **3** (the rigours of sth) [pl] the difficulties and unpleasant conditions of sth

rim /rɪm/ n [C] edge of sth circular: the ~ of a cup ● **rim** v (-mm-) [T] (fml) form an edge round sth

rind /raɪnd/ n [U,C] hard outer covering of certain fruits, cheese or bacon

0▬ **ring**[1] /rɪŋ/ v (pt **rang** /ræŋ/ pp **rung** /rʌŋ/) **1** [I,T] ~ (up) telephone sb/sth: I'll ~ you (up) later. **2** [I,T] (cause a bell) to produce a sound: ~ the doorbell ◊ R ~ for the nurse if you need her. **3** [I] ~ (with) (lit) be full of a sound [IDM] **ring a bell** (infml) remind one of sth ● **ring true/hollow/false** give the impression of being sincere/true or not sincere/true [PV] **ring off** (GB) end a telephone conversation ● **ring out** be heard loudly and clearly ● **ring** n **1** [C] sound of a bell **2** [sing] particular quality that words, sounds, etc have: a ~ of truth [IDM] **give sb a ring** (GB, infml) make a telephone call to sb

0▬ **ring**[2] /rɪŋ/ n [C] **1** circular metal band worn on a finger **2** circular band of any kind of material: a key ~ **3** circle: The children stood in a ~. **4** group of people working together, esp illegally: a spy ~ **5** enclosed area in which animals or people perform or compete, with seats around it for an audience: a circus ~ ● **ring** v (pt, pp ~ed) [T] **1** surround sb/sth **2** draw a circle around sth ▪ **ringleader** n [C] (esp lit) person who leads others in doing sth wrong ▪ **ring road** n [C] road built around a town

ringlet /ˈrɪŋlət/ n [C, usu pl] long hanging curl of hair

rink /rɪŋk/ n [C] specially prepared area of ice for skating: ice/skating ~

rinse /rɪns/ v [T] wash sth in clean water: R~ the pasta with boiling water. ● **rinse** n **1** [C] act of rinsing sth **2** [C,U] liquid for colouring the hair

riot /ˈraɪət/ n **1** [C] noisy violent behaviour by a crowd **2** [sing] ~ of collection of a lot of different types of the same thing: a ~ of colour [IDM] **run riot** → RUN[1] ● **riot** v [I] behave in a violent way in a public place,

often as a protest ▶ **rioter** n [C] ▶ **riotous** adj disorderly; wild

rip /rɪp/ v (-pp-) [I,T] tear sth or become torn, often suddenly or violently [PV] **rip sb off** (infml) cheat sb, by charging them too much money, etc ● **rip** n [C] long tear in fabric, paper, etc ▪ **ripcord** n [C] string that you pull to open a parachute ▪ **rip-off** n [C] (infml) something that is not worth what you pay for it

ripe /raɪp/ adj (~r, ~st) **1** (fully grown) and ready to be eaten: ~ apples/ cheese **2 ~ for** ready or suitable for sth to happen ▶ **ripeness** n [U]

ripen /ˈraɪpən/ v [I,T] become or make sth ripe

ripple /ˈrɪpl/ n [C] **1** very small wave or movement on the surface of water **2** short sound of quiet laughter, etc ● **ripple** v [I,T] (cause sth to) move in ripples

0▬ **rise**[1] /raɪz/ v (pt **rose** /rəʊz/ pt ~n /ˈrɪzn/) [I] **1** come or go upwards **2** (written) get up from a lying, sitting or kneeling position: He always rose (= got out of bed) early. **3** (of the sun, moon, etc) appear above the horizon **4** increase in amount or number: Prices have continued to ~. **5** become more successful, important, powerful, etc **6** get stronger: The wind is rising. **7** (fml) rebel against sth **8** slope upwards: rising ground **9** (of a river) start [PV] **rise to sth 1** show that you are able to deal with an unexpected situation, problem, etc: He was determined to ~ to the challenge. **2** react when sb is deliberately trying to make you angry ▶ **rising** n [C] armed rebellion

0▬ **rise**[2] /raɪz/ n [C] **1** increase in a number, amount or level **2** (C) (GB) increase in wages **3** [sing] upward movement or progress: his ~ to power **4** [C] small hill [IDM] **give rise to sth** (fml) cause sth to happen or exist

0▬ **risk** /rɪsk/ n **1** [C] possibility of danger or of sth bad happening in the future **2** [C] ~ (to) person or thing that is likely to cause problems or danger in the future [IDM] **at risk (from/of sth)** in danger of sth unpleasant happening **do sth at your own risk** do sth dangerous and agree to take responsibility for anything bad that happens **run the risk (of doing sth)** take a risk do sth even though you know that sth bad could happen to you ● **risk** v [T] **1** put sth in danger **2** take the chance of sth bad happening to you: ~ getting wet [IDM] **risk your neck** → NECK ▶ **risky** adj (-ier, -iest) dangerous

risotto /rɪˈzɒtəʊ/ n [C,U] (pl ~s) Italian dish of rice cooked with vegetables, etc

rissole /ˈrɪsəʊl/ n [C] small flat mass of minced meat, etc that is fried

rite /raɪt/ n [C] traditional, esp religious, ceremony [IDM] **rite of passage** ceremony or event that marks an important stage in sb's life

ritual /ˈrɪtʃuəl/ n [C,U] **1** series of actions regularly followed, esp as part of a religious ceremony **2** something done regularly and always in the same way ● **ritual** adj of or done as a ritual

0–**rival** /ˈraɪvl/ n [C] person, company or thing that competes with another in sport, business, etc ● **rival** v (-ll- US also -l-) [T] be as good, impressive, etc as sb/sth else ▸ **rivalry** n [C,U] (pl -ies) competition between two people, companies, etc

0–**river** /ˈrɪvə(r)/ n [C] large natural stream of water flowing to the sea

rivet /ˈrɪvɪt/ n [C] metal pin used to fasten pieces of metal, leather, etc together ● **rivet** v [T] **1** hold sb's attention completely **2** fasten sth with rivets ▸ **riveting** adj (approv) so interesting that it holds your attention completely

0–**road** /rəʊd/ n [C] **1** hard surface built for vehicles to travel on **2** the way to achieving sth: be on the ~ to success ■ **roadblock** n [C] barrier placed across the road by the police or army ■ **road hog** n [C] (infml) careless driver ■ **road map** n [C] **1** map that shows the roads of an area **2** set of instructions or suggestions about how to do sth or find out about sth ■ **roadworks** n [pl] (GB) (area where road repairs being done to the road ■ **roadworthy** adj (of a vehicle) fit to be driven on roads

roam /rəʊm/ v [I] walk or travel about with no clear purpose

roar /rɔː(r)/ n [C] deep loud sound (like that) made by a lion ● **roar** v **1** [I] make a deep loud sound **2** [I,T] shout sth very loudly **3** [I] laugh very loudly ▸ **roaring** adj (infml) **1** noisy **2** (of a fire) burning with a lot of flames and heat [IDM] **do a roaring trade (in sth)** (infml) sell sth or sth very quickly **roaring drunk** extremely drunk and noisy

roast /rəʊst/ v [I,T] cook food, esp meat, in an oven or over a fire; be cooked in this way ● **roast** adj cooked in an oven or over a fire: ~ potatoes ● **roast** n [C] **1** large piece of roasted meat: the Sunday ~ **2** (US) party held in sb's garden at which food is cooked over an open fire

0–**rob** /rɒb/ v (-bb-) [T] steal money or property from a person or place ▸ **robber** n [C] person who robs sb/ sth ▸ **robbery** n [C,U] (pl -ies) crime of stealing money or goods from a bank, shop, etc, esp using violence

robe /rəʊb/ n [C] long loose garment

robin /ˈrɒbɪn/ n [C] small brown bird with a red breast

robot /ˈrəʊbɒt/ n [C] machine that can do certain human tasks automatically

robust /rəʊˈbʌst/ adj strong; healthy ▸ **robustly** adv ▸ **robustness** n [U]

0–**rock¹** /rɒk/ n **1** [U,C] hard solid material that forms part of the earth's surface **2** [C] mass of rock standing above the earth's surface or in the sea **3** [C] large stone **4** [U] (also rock music) type of loud modern music with a strong beat, played on electric guitars, etc **5** [U] (GB) hard stick-shaped sweet [IDM] **on the rocks 1** (of a relationship or a business) likely to fail soon **2** (of a drink) served with ice but no water ■ **rock and roll** (also **rock'n' roll**) n [U] type of music popular in the 1950s ■ **rock-bottom** n [U] lowest point ▸ **rockery** n [C] (pl -ies) part of a garden with small rocks and plants

rock² /rɒk/ v [I,T] **1** move gently backwards and forwards or from side to side **2** [T] (written) shock sb/ sth very much [IDM] **rock the boat** (infml) spoil a calm situation ▸ **rocker** n [C] **1** one of the two curved pieces of wood on the bottom of a rocking chair **2** = ROCKING CHAIR [IDM] **be off your rocker** (spoken) be crazy ■ **rocking chair** n [C] chair fitted with rockers that make it move backwards and forwards

rocket /ˈrɒkɪt/ n **1** [C] tube-shaped device filled with fast-burning fuel that is used to launch a missile or spacecraft **2** [C] firework that shoots high into the air **3** [U] (GB) plant with long green leaves that have a strong flavour and are eaten raw in salads ● **rocket** v [I] increase quickly and suddenly; move very fast: Prices are ~ing.

rocky /ˈrɒki/ adj (-ier, -iest) adj **1** of rock; full of rocks **2** difficult and not certain to continue: a ~ marriage

rod /rɒd/ n [C] long thin straight piece of wood, metal, etc: a fishing ~

rode pt of RIDE¹

rodent /ˈrəʊdnt/ n [C] small animal, eg a rat, with strong, sharp front teeth

rodeo /ˈrəʊdiəʊ/ n [C] (pl ~s) (esp in the US) contest of skill in catching cattle with a rope, riding wild horses, etc

roe /rəʊ/ n **1** [U] mass of fish eggs, eaten as food **2** [C] = ROE DEER

■ **'roe deer** *n* [C] (pl **roe deer**) small European and Asian deer

rogue /rəʊg/ *n* [C] (*hum*) person who behaves badly but in a harmless way ▶ **roguish** *adj* (of a person) pleasant and amusing but looking as if they might do sth wrong

0─ **role** /rəʊl/ *n* [C] 1 function or importance of sb/sth 2 actor's part in a play ■ **'role model** *n* [C] person that you admire and try to copy ■ **'role-play** *n* [C] learning activity in which you behave as sb else would behave in certain situations ▶ **role-play** *v* [I,T]

0─ **roll**[1] /rəʊl/ *v* 1 [I,T] (make a round object) move along by turning over and over 2 [I,T] (cause sth to) turn over and over while remaining in the same place: *a dog ~ing in the mud* 3 [I,T] (cause sth to) move smoothly (on wheels or as if on wheels): *The clouds ~ed away.* ◊ *The car began to ~ back down the hill.* 4 [I,T] ~ (**up**) make sth/yourself into the shape of a ball or tube: *~ up a carpet* ◊ *The hedgehog ~ed up into a ball.* 5 [T] make sth flat, by pushing sth heavy over it: *~ pastry* 6 [I] make a long continuous sound: *The thunder ~ed in the distance.* [IDM] **be rolling in money/it** (*infml*) have a lot of money [PV] **roll in** (*infml*) arrive in large quantities **roll up** (*infml*) arrive

0─ **roll**[2] /rəʊl/ *n* [C] 1 something made into a tube: *a ~ of film* 2 (*also* **bread 'roll**) small rounded piece of bread for one person 3 rolling movement 4 official list of names: *the electoral ~* 5 long deep sound: *the ~ of drums*

roller /ˈrəʊlə(r)/ *n* [C] tube-shaped object for pressing sth, smoothing sth, etc ■ **Rollerblade**™ (*US* **Roller Blade**™) *n* [C] boot with a line of small wheels attached to the bottom ▶ **Rollerblade** *v* [I] ■ **'roller skate** *n* [C] boot with two pairs of small wheels attached to the bottom ▶ **roller skate** *v* [I] move over a hard surface wearing roller skates

rolling /ˈrəʊlɪŋ/ *adj* rising and falling gently: *~ hills/waves* ■ **'rolling pin** *n* [C] wooden or glass tube-shaped kitchen utensil for flattening pastry

ROM /rɒm/ *n* [U] (*computing*) read-only memory; computer memory that contains data that cannot be changed or removed

Roman /ˈrəʊmən/ *n* [C] , *adj* (citizen) of Rome, esp ancient Rome ■ **Roman 'Catholic** *n* [C], *adj* (member) of the Christian Church that has the Pope as its leader ■ **Roman Ca'tholicism** *n* [U] ■ **Roman 'numeral** *n* [C] letter, eg V, L or M, or group of letters, used to represent a number

romance /rəʊˈmæns/ *n* 1 [C] love affair 2 [U] love or the feeling of

---

being in love 3 [U] feeling of excitement and adventure 4 [C] story of love, adventure, etc

0─ **romantic** /rəʊˈmæntɪk/ *adj* 1 of or having feelings of love 2 of or suggesting love, adventure and excitement: *a ~ journey* 3 not practical; very imaginative and emotional ● **romantic** *n* [C] imaginative person whose hopes and ideas may not be realistic ▶ **romantically** /-kli/ *adv* ■ **romanticism** /rəʊˈmæntɪsɪzəm/ *n* [U] romantic feelings, attitudes, etc ■ **romanticize** (*also* **-ise**) /rəʊˈmæntɪsaɪz/ *v* [I,T] make sth seem more attractive or interesting than it really is

romp /rɒmp/ *v* [I] play happily and noisily ▶ **romp** *n* [C]

0─ **roof** /ruːf/ *n* [C] 1 top covering of a building, car, etc 2 upper part: *the ~ of the mouth* ▶ **roof** *v* [T] cover sth with a roof ▶ **roofing** *n* [U] material for making roofs ■ **'roof rack** *n* [C] metal frame fixed on top of a car, used for carrying large objects

rook /rʊk/ *n* 1 large black bird like a crow 2 = CASTLE(2) ▶ **rookery** *n* [C] (pl **-ies**) group of trees where rooks nest

0─ **room** /ruːm; rʊm/ *n* 1 [C] part of a building with its own walls, ceiling and door 2 [U] empty space that can be used for a particular purpose: *Is there ~ for me in the car?* 3 [U] possibility of sth happening; opportunity to do sth: *~ for improvement* ▶ **roomy** *adj* (**-ier, -iest**) having plenty of space

roost /ruːst/ *n* [C] place where birds sleep ● **roost** *v* [I] (of a bird) rest or go to sleep somewhere

rooster /ˈruːstə(r)/ *n* [C] (*esp US*) = COCK(1)

0─ **root**[1] /ruːt/ *n* 1 [C] part of a plant that is in the soil and takes in water and food from the soil 2 [C] base of a hair, tooth, etc 3 [C, usu sing] main cause or origin of sth: *Is money the ~ of all evil?* 4 (**roots**) [pl] feelings or connections you have with the place in which you grew up 5 [C] (*ling*) form of a word on which other forms are based [IDM] **take root** become established

root[2] /ruːt/ *v* 1 [I,T] (cause a plant to) grow roots 2 [I] search for sth by turning things over [PV] **root sth/sb out** find the person or thing that is causing a problem and remove or get rid of them ▶ **rooted** *adj* 1 ~ **in** developing from or being strongly influenced by sth: *His problems are deeply ~ed in his childhood experiences.* 2 firmly fixed in one place [IDM] **rooted to the spot** so

---

frightened or shocked that you cannot move

0—ᗒ **rope** /rəʊp/ *n* [C,U] (piece of) very thick strong string [IDM] **show sb/ know/learn the ropes** (*infml*) show sb/know/learn how a particular job should be done ● **rope** *v* [T] tie sb/ sth with a rope [PV] **rope sb in** | **rope sb into sth** persuade sb to join in an activity or to help to do sth **rope sth off** separate one area from another with ropes ● **ropey** (*also* **ropy**) *adj* (**-ier, -iest**) (*GB, infml*) poor in quality, health, etc.

rosary /ˈrəʊzəri/ *n* (*pl* **-ies**) [C] string of beads used by some Roman Catholics for counting prayers **2** (**the Rosary**) [sing] set of prayers said while counting the rosary beads

rosé /ˈrəʊzeɪ/ *n* [U] pink wine

rose[1] *pt of* RISE

rose[2] /rəʊz/ *n* **1** [C] (bush with thorns producing a) flower with a sweet smell **2** [U] pink colour

rosette /rəʊˈzet/ *n* [C] circular decoration made of ribbon, worn by supporters of a political party, etc

roster /ˈrɒstə(r)/ *n* [C] list of people's names and their duties

rostrum /ˈrɒstrəm/ *n* [C] (*pl* **-s** *or* **-tra** /-trə/) raised platform for a public speaker

rosy /ˈrəʊzi/ *adj* (**-ier, -iest**) **1** pink and pleasant in appearance: ~ *cheeks* **2** likely to be good or successful: *a ~ future*

rot /rɒt/ *v* (**-tt-**) [I,T] (cause sth to) decay naturally and gradually ● **rot** *n* [U] process of decaying: (*the rot*) used to describe the fact that a situation is getting worse

rota /ˈrəʊtə/ *n* [C] (*GB*) list of jobs to be done and the people who will do them in turn

rotary /ˈrəʊtəri/ *adj* moving round a central point

rotate /rəʊˈteɪt/ *v* [I,T] **1** (cause sth to) move or turn around a central point **2** (cause sb/sth to) regularly change around: *We ~ the night shift.* ▶ **rotation** /-ˈteɪʃn/ *n* [C,U] action of rotating: *the rotation of the Earth* **2** [C] one complete turn

rotor /ˈrəʊtə(r)/ *n* [C] rotating part of a machine, esp on a helicopter

rotten /ˈrɒtn/ *adj* **1** decayed **2** (*infml*) very bad; terrible

0—ᗒ **rough**[1] /rʌf/ *adj* **1** (of a surface) not level or smooth **2** not exact; not in detail: *a ~ guess/sketch* **3** not gentle or careful; violent **4** (of the sea) having large waves ● **rough** *n* **1** (**the rough**) [sing] part of a golf course where the grass is long **2** [C] (*tech*) first version of a drawing or design, done without much detail [IDM] **in rough** (*esp GB*) not complete; unfinished

▶ **rough-and-ready** *adj* not made but good enough for a particular situation ▶ **roughly** *adv* **1** approximately: *It will cost ~ly £100.* **2** using force ▶ **roughness** *n* [U]

rough[2] /rʌf/ *v* [IDM] **rough it** (*infml*) live without the normal comforts [PV] **rough sb up** (*infml*) hurt sb by hitting them ● **rough** *adv* using force or violence [IDM] **live/sleep rough** live or sleep outdoors, usu because you have no home

roughen /ˈrʌfn/ *v* [I,T] become or make sth rough

roulette /ruːˈlet/ *n* [U] gambling game played with a small ball on a revolving wheel

0—ᗒ **round**[1] /raʊnd/ *adj* **1** shaped like a circle or a ball; curved **2** (of a number) expressed to the nearest 10, 100, etc: *a ~ number* ▶ **roundly** *adv* forcefully ▶ **roundness** *n* [U] (*written*) ● **round trip** *n* [C,U] journey to a place and back again ■ **round-shouldered** *adj* with shoulders that are bent forward

0—ᗒ **round**[2] /raʊnd/ *adv* **1** moving in a circle; on all sides of sth: *spin~* ◇ *The hands of a clock go ~.* ◇ *A crowd gathered ~.* **2** in a circle or curve to face the opposite way: *Turn your chair ~.* **3** at various places in an area: *People stood ~ waiting for something to happen.* **4** to the other side of sth: *We walked ~ to the back of the house.* **5** from one place, person, etc to another: *Pass these papers ~.* **6** (*infml*) to or at sb's house: *I'll be ~ in an hour.*

0—ᗒ **round**[3] /raʊnd/ *n* [C] **1** set of events forming part of a process: *the next ~ of talks* **2** stage in a sports competition **3** stage in a boxing or wrestling game **4** complete game of golf **5** regular route taken by sb delivering or collecting sth: *a postman's ~* **6** number of drinks bought by one person for all the others in a group **7** (*GB*) whole slice of bread; sandwich made from two whole slices of bread **8** bullet

0—ᗒ **round**[4] /raʊnd/ *prep* in a circle: *The earth moves ~ the sun.* **2** on, to or from the other side of sth: *walk ~ the corner* **3** surrounding sth: *a wall ~ the house* **4** in or to many parts of sth: *climb ~ the shop* [IDM] **round here** near where you are now or where you live

round[5] /raʊnd/ *v* [T] **1** go round a corner, bend, etc **2** make sth into a round shape [PV] **round sth off (with sth)** complete sth satisfactorily **round sb/sth up 1** find and bring people, animals or things together: *~ up cattle* **2** increase sth to the nearest whole number

roundabout /ˈraʊndəbaʊt/ *n* [C] (*GB*) **1** road junction where vehicles must go round a circle **2** = MERRY-

adj indirect: a ~ route

rounders /'raʊndəz/ n [U] (GB) team game played with a bat and a ball

rouse /raʊz/ v [T] 1 (fml) wake sb up 2 cause sb to be more active, interested, etc: a rousing speech

rout /raʊt/ v [T] defeat sb easily and completely ● rout n [sing] complete defeat

0—¬ route /ruːt/ n [C] way from one place to another ● route v [T] send sb/sth by a particular route

0—¬ routine /ruːˈtiːn/ n [C,U] regular way of doing things ● routine adj 1 regular or normal 2 (disapprov) ordinary and boring

0—¬ row¹ /rəʊ/ n [C] 1 line of people or things: She sat at a ~ at the back of the room. 2 journey in a rowing boat: We went for a ~ on the lake. [IDM] in a row happening one after another without interruption: This is her third win in a ~. ● row v [I,T] move a boat through the water using oars ▪ rowing boat (US rowboat) n [C] small open boat that you row with oars

0—¬ row² /raʊ/ n [C] 1 serious disagreement; noisy argument 2 [sing] loud unpleasant noise ● row v [I] (GB) have a noisy argument

rowdy /'raʊdi/ adj (-ier, -iest) (of people) noisy and rough ▶ rowdy n [C] (pl -ies) (old-fash, disapprov) rowdy person

0—¬ royal /'rɔɪəl/ adj of or belonging to a king or queen ▶ royal n [C, usu pl] (infml) member of a royal family ▪ royal blue adj deep bright blue ▶ royalist /'rɔɪəlɪst/ n [C] person who supports rule by a king or queen ▶ royally adv (old-fash) splendidly

royalty /'rɔɪəlti/ n (pl -ies) 1 [U] royal person or people 2 [C] payment to an author, etc for every copy of a book, etc that is sold

RSI /,ɑːr es 'aɪ/ n [U] repetitive strain injury; pain and swelling, esp in the arms and hands, caused by performing the same movement many times in a job or an activity

RSVP /,ɑːr es viː 'piː/ abbr (on an invitation) please reply

0—¬ rub /rʌb/ v (-bb-) 1 [I,T] move your hand, a cloth, etc backwards and forwards over a surface 2 [I] (of a surface) move backwards and forwards many times against sth, esp causing pain: My shoes are ~bing. 3 [I] spread a liquid or other substance over a surface while pressing firmly: She ~bed the lotion into her skin. [IDM] rub sb up the wrong way (infml) annoy sb [PV] rub sb/yourself/sth down rub sb or a person, horse, etc hard with sth to make it dry and clean rub sth down make sth smooth by rubbing it with

a special material rub it/sth in (infml) remind sb of sth unpleasant rub (sth) off (sth) remove sth or be removed by rubbing: R~ the dirt off your trousers. rub sth out remove pencil marks, etc by using a rubber ● rub n [C, usu sing] act of rubbing a surface

0—¬ rubber /'rʌbə(r)/ n 1 [U] strong elastic substance used for making tyres, etc 2 [C] (GB) piece of rubber for removing pencil marks from paper, etc 3 [C] (in some card games or sports) competition consisting of a series of games between the same players ▪ rubber band n [C] thin circular strip of rubber, used for keeping papers, etc together

0—¬ rubbish /'rʌbɪʃ/ n [U] 1 (esp GB) things that you throw away 2 nonsense ▶ rubbishy adj (GB, infml) of very poor quality

rubble /'rʌbl/ n [U] bits of broken stone, rocks or bricks

ruby /'ruːbi/ n [C] (pl -ies) dark red precious stone

rucksack /'rʌksæk/ n [C] large bag carried on the back by walkers and climbers

rudder /'rʌdə(r)/ n [C] flat hinged piece at the back of a boat or aircraft, used for steering

ruddy /'rʌdi/ adj (-ier, -iest) 1 (of sb's face) looking red and healthy 2 (lit) red in colour ▶ ruddy adj, adv (GB, infml) mild swear word used to show annoyance: You're a ~ fool!

0—¬ rude /ruːd/ adj (~r, ~st) 1 not polite 2 connected with sex or the body in a way people find offensive 3 (written) sudden and unexpected: a ~ reminder ▶ rudely adv ▶ rudeness n [U]

rudiments /'ruːdɪmənts/ n [pl] (fml) most basic facts of a subject ▶ rudimentary /,ruːdɪ'mentri/ adj (fml) 1 simple; basic 2 undeveloped

ruffle /'rʌfl/ v [T] 1 disturb the smooth surface of sth: He ~d her hair affectionately. 2 upset or annoy sb

rug /rʌg/ n [C] 1 thick piece of material, like a small carpet, for covering part of a floor 2 small blanket

rugby /'rʌgbi/ n [U] kind of football played with an oval ball that may be kicked or carried

rugged /'rʌgɪd/ adj 1 (of the landscape) uneven; rocky 2 (of a man's face) having strong, attractive features

rugger /'rʌgə(r)/ n [U] (infml, esp GB) = RUGBY

0—¬ ruin /'ruːɪn/ v [T] 1 destroy or spoil sth 2 cause sb/sth to lose all their money ● ruin n 1 [U] destruction 2 [U] fact of having no money, of having lost your job, etc: Drink led to his ~. 3 [C, usu pl] parts of a building that remain after it has been destroyed: *the ~s of an old castle* [IDM] **in ruins** destroyed or severely damaged: *The scandal left his reputation in ~s.* ▸ **ruined** adj partly destroyed ▸ **ruinous** adj causing ruin

0━ **rule** /ruːl/ n 1 [C] statement of what may, must or must not be done 2 [C] habit; usual way sth happens: *I go to bed early, as a ~.* 3 [U] government: *under foreign ~* [IDM] **a rule of thumb** rough practical way of doing or measuring sth ● **rule** v 1 [I,T] have authority over a country, group of people, etc 2 [I,T] give an official decision about sth: *The judge ~d in his favour.* 3 [T] draw a line with a ruler [IDM] **rule the roost** (*infml*) be the most powerful member of a group [PV] **rule sb/sth out 1** state that sth is not possible or that sb/sth is not suitable ▸ **ruler** n [C] **1** person who rules or governs **2** straight piece of wood, plastic, etc used for drawing straight lines or for measuring ▸ **ruling** n [C] official decision

rum /rʌm/ n [U] alcoholic drink made from sugar cane

rumble /ˈrʌmbl/ v [T], n [U,C] (make a) deep heavy continuous sound

rummage /ˈrʌmɪdʒ/ v [I] turn things over carelessly while looking for sth

0━ **rumour** (*US* -or) /ˈruːmə(r)/ n [C,U] piece(s) of information spread by being talked about but not certainly true ▸ **rumoured** (*US* -ored) adj reported as a rumour

rump /rʌmp/ n 1 [C] area of flesh at the top of the back legs of a four-legged animal 2 (*rump* ˈsteak) [C,U] piece(s) of good quality beef cut from the rump of a cow

rumple /ˈrʌmpl/ v [T] make sth creased or untidy

rumpus /ˈrʌmpəs/ n [usu sing] (*infml*) noisy quarrel or disturbance

0━ **run¹** /rʌn/ v (-nn- pt ran /ræn/ pp run) 1 [I] move using your legs, going faster than when you walk 2 [T] cover a certain distance by running 3 [I] practise running as a sport: *I go ~ning every morning.* 4 [I,T] take part in a race: *to ~ the marathon* 5 [T] control or manage a business, etc: *~ a hotel* 6 [I,T] (cause sth) to operate or function: *I can't afford to ~ a car any more.* ◇ *The heater ~s on electricity.* 7 [I] (of buses, etc) travel on a particular route 8 [T] (*infml*) drive sb to a place in a car: *I'll ~ you home.* 9 [I] move sth quickly, in a particular direction: *The car ran off the road into a ditch.* 10 [T] move sth in a particular direction: *~ a comb through your hair* 11 [I,T] (cause sth to) lead or stretch from one place to

another: *The road ~s parallel to the river.* 12 [I] continue for a time without stopping: *The play ran for six months.* 13 [T] bring sth into a country illegally and secretly: *~ drugs* 14 [I,T] (cause liquid to) flow: *a river that ~s into the sea* ◇ *I'll ~ you a bath.* 15 [T] (of colour) spread 16 (usu used with adj) become different in a particular (esp bad) way: *Supplies are ~ning low.* ◇ *We're ~ning short of milk.* 17 [T] publish an item or a story in a newspaper, etc 18 [I] ~ **for** (esp *US*) be a candidate in an election for a political position: *~ for president* [IDM] **run amok** suddenly become angry or excited and start behaving violently **run its course** → COURSE **run in the family** → FAMILY **run for it** run in order to escape from sb/sth **run high** (of feelings) be strong and angry or excited **run riot/wild** behave in a very free and uncontrolled way **run the risk (of doing sth)** → RISK **run to seed** → SEED [PV] **run across sb/sth** meet sb or find sth by chance **run after sb/sth 1** chase sb/sth **2** (*infml*) try to have a romantic relationship with sb **run along** (*old-fash*) go away **run away (from sb/sth)** leave a place suddenly; escape from sb/sth **run away with you** control what you completely **run away/off with sb** leave your home, husband, wife etc to have a relationship with sb else **run (sth) down 1** (cause sth to) lose power or stop working **2** (cause sth to) stop functioning gradually or become smaller in size: *The company is being ~ down.* **run sb/sth down 1** hit and injure sb/sth with a vehicle **2** criticize sb/sth in an unkind way **run into sb** meet sb by chance **run into sth** experience difficulties unexpectedly **run sth off** copy sth on a machine **run out** become no longer valid **run out (of sth)** use up or finish a supply of sth **run sb/sth over** (of a vehicle or its driver) knock down and drive over sb/sth **run through sth 1** (*written*) pass quickly through sth **2** discuss, read or examine sth quickly **3** perform, act or practise sth **run to sth 1** be of a particular size or amount **2** (of money) be enough for sth: *Our funds won't ~ to a trip abroad this year.* **run sth up 1** allow a bill, debt, etc to reach a large total: *~ up big debts* **2** make a piece of clothing quickly **3** raise sth, esp a flag **run up against sth** experience a difficulty

■ **ˈrunaway** adj 1 (of a person) having left without telling anyone 2 out of control ▸ **runaway** n [C] child who has left home without telling anyone ■ **ˌrun-ˈdown** adj 1 (of a building, etc) in bad condition 2 (of a person) tired, esp from working too hard ■ **ˈrun-up** n

**[sing] period of time leading up to an event

0¬ **run**² /rʌn/ *n* **1** [C] act of running on foot **2** [C] journey in a car, train, etc **3** [C] period of sth good or bad happening: *a ~ of bad luck* **4** [C] series of performances of a play or film **5** [sing] sudden great demand for sth **6** [sing] enclosed space for domestic animals **7** [C] point scored in cricket or baseball [IDM] **on the run** trying to escape ■ **run-of-the-mill** *adj* ordinary, with no interesting features

rung¹ *pp of* RING¹

rung² /rʌŋ/ *n* [C] step on a ladder

0¬ **runner** /'rʌnə(r)/ *n* [C] **1** person or animal that runs, esp in a race **2** smuggler: *a gun ~* **3** thin strip on which sth slides or moves: *the ~s of a sledge* ■ **runner bean** *n* [C] climbing plant with a long flat green bean container, eaten as a vegetable ■ **runner-up** (*pl* **runners-up**) *n* [C] person who finishes second in a race

0¬ **running** /'rʌnɪŋ/ *n* [U] **1** action or sport of running **2** activity of managing or operating sth [IDM] **make the running** (*GB, infml*) set the pace or standard ● **running** *adj* **1** in succession: *win the championship three years ~* **2** (of water) flowing; supplied to a building **3** continuous: *a ~ battle*

runny /'rʌni/ *adj* (-**ier**, -**iest**) (*infml*) **1** (of the eyes or nose) producing liquid **2** more liquid than usual

runway /'rʌnweɪ/ *n* [C] surface along which aircraft take off and land

rupture /'rʌptʃə(r)/ *n* [C] **1** (*med*) breaking or bursting of sth inside the body; hernia: *the ~ of a blood vessel* **2** (*fml*) ending of friendly relations between people, countries, etc ● **rupture** *v* [I,T] (*med*) (cause sth to) burst or break apart inside the body **2** [T] (*written*) end good relations with sb

0¬ **rural** /'rʊərəl/ *adj* in or of the countryside

ruse /ruːz/ *n* [C] trick

0¬ **rush** /rʌʃ/ *v* [I,T] move or do sth with great speed, often too fast **2** [I,T] do sth of force sb to do sth too quickly **3** [T] try to attack or capture sb/sth suddenly [IDM] **be rushed off your feet** be extremely busy ● **rush** *n* **1** [sing] sudden movement forward made by a lot of people or things **2** [sing, U] situation in which you are in a hurry and need to do things quickly: *I can't stop—I'm in a ~.* **3** [sing, U] (period of) great activity: *the Christmas ~* **4** [sing] sudden demand for goods, tickets, etc **5** [C, usu pl] tall plant like grass that grows near water ■ **rush hour** *n* [C] busy period when many people are travelling to and from work

---

sack

rusk /rʌsk/ *n* [C] hard crisp biscuit for babies to eat

rust /rʌst/ *n* [U] reddish-brown substance formed on metal by the action of water and air ● **rust** *v* [I,T] (cause sth to) become covered in rust ► **rusty** *adj* (-**ier**, -**iest**) **1** covered with rust **2** (*infml*) showing lack of recent practice: *My tennis is a bit ~ these days.*

rustle /'rʌsl/ *v* **1** [I,T] (cause sth dry and light to) make a sound like paper, leaves, etc moving or rubbing together **2** [T] steal farm animals [PV] **rustle sth up (for sb)** (*infml*) make or find sth quickly for sb: *~ up a meal* ● **rustle** *n* [sing] light dry sound

rut /rʌt/ *n* **1** [C] deep track made by a wheel in soft ground **2** fixed and boring way of life: *be in a ~* ► **rutted** *adj* (of a road or path) having deep tracks made by wheels

ruthless /'ruːθləs/ *adj* (*disapprov*) without pity; cruel ► **ruthlessly** *adv*

rye /raɪ/ *n* [U] (grain of a) cereal plant used for making flour and whisky

Ss

S *abbr* south(ern): *S Yorkshire*

S, s /es/ *n* [C, U] (*pl* **S's, s's** /'esɪz/) the nineteenth letter of the English alphabet

sabbath /'sæbəθ/ (the **Sabbath**) *n* [sing] the day of rest, Sunday for Christians, Saturday for Jews

sabotage /'sæbətɑːʒ/ *n* [U] deliberate damaging of an enemy's or rival's equipment, plans, etc ● **sabotage** *v* [T] secretly damage or spoil a machine, a car, sb's plans, etc ► **saboteur** /,sæbə'tɜː(r)/ *n* [C] person who commits sabotage

sabre (*US* **saber**) /'seɪbə(r)/ *n* [C] heavy sword with a curved blade

saccharin /'sækərɪn/ *n* [U] very sweet substance used in place of sugar

sachet /'sæʃeɪ/ *n* [C] small paper or plastic packet for holding sugar, shampoo, etc

0¬ **sack**¹ /sæk/ *n* [C] (contents of a) large bag of strong material for carrying coal, potatoes, etc [IDM] **get the sack | give sb the sack** be dismissed/dismiss sb from a job ■ **sackcloth** (*also* **sacking**) *n* [U] rough material for making sacks ► **sackful** *n* [C] amount held by a sack

0¬ **sack²** /sæk/ *v* [T] **1** (*infml, esp GB*) dismiss sb from a job **2** (of an army, esp in the past) steal or destroy property in a captured city, etc

---

sacrament /'sækrəmənt/ n [C] Christian ceremony, eg baptism or confirmation ▸ **sacramental** /ˌsækrə'mentl/ adj

sacred /'seɪkrɪd/ adj **1** connected with religion or with God: a ~ shrine **2** very important and treated with great respect

sacrifice /'sækrɪfaɪs/ n **1** [U] fact of giving up sth valuable to you for a good purpose **2** [C] valuable thing that you give up for a good purpose: make~s **3** [C,U] ~ (to) act of offering sth valuable to a god ● **sacrifice** v ~ **(to)** **1** [T] give up sth that is valuable to you for a good purpose: ~ a career to have a family **2** [I,T] kill an animal or a person in order to please a god ▸ **sacrificial** /ˌsækrɪ'fɪʃl/ adj

sacrilege /'sækrɪlɪdʒ/ n [U,sing] disrespectful treatment of a holy thing or place ▸ **sacrilegious** /ˌsækrə'lɪdʒəs/ adj

0—**sad** /sæd/ adj (~der, ~dest) **1** unhappy or causing sorrow: a ~ person/song ■ **sadden** v [T] (fml) (often passive) make sb sad: ~dened by his death ■ **sadly** adv **1** unhappily: S~ly, we have no more money. **2** in a sad way: smile ~ly ▸ **sadness** n [U,sing]

saddle /'sædl/ n [C] **1** leather seat for a rider on a horse, bicycle, etc **IDM** in the saddle in a position of authority and control **2** riding a horse ● **saddle** v [T] put a saddle on a horse **[PV] saddle sb with sth** give sb an unpleasant task, etc: I was ~d with cleaning the car. ■ **saddlebag** n [C] bag attached to a saddle

sadism /'seɪdɪzəm/ n [U] (getting sexual pleasure from) cruelty to other people ▸ **sadist** n [C] person who gets pleasure from hurting others ▸ **sadistic** /sə'dɪstɪk/ adj

sae /ˌes eɪ 'iː/ abbr stamped addressed envelope, usu sent to sb when you want a reply

safari /sə'fɑːri/ n [C,U] journey to hunt or watch wild animals, esp in Africa: on ~ in Kenya

0—**safe¹** /seɪf/ adj (~r, ~st) **1** ~ (from) protected from danger and harm: ~ from attack **2** not likely to lead to physical harm or danger: a ~ speed **3** not hurt, damaged, lost, etc: They turned up ~ and sound. **4** (of a place, etc) giving protection from danger, harm, etc **5** careful: a ~ driver **IDM** (as) safe as houses very safe **play (it) safe** be careful; avoid risks **safe and sound** unharmed ■ **safe 'keeping** n [U] fact of sth being in a safe place: Put it in your pocket for ~ keeping. **2** fact of sb/sth being taken care of by a trusted person ▸ **safely** adv ▸ **safeness** n [U]

safe² /seɪf/ n [C] very strong box with a lock, for keeping valuable objects in

safeguard /'seɪfgɑːd/ n [C] ~ (against) something that prevents harm, damage, etc ● **safeguard** v [T] ~ (against) protect sth from loss, harm or damage; keep sth safe

0—**safety** /'seɪfti/ n [U] state of being safe; freedom from danger ■ **safety belt** n [C] = SEAT BELT (SEAT) ■ **safety pin** n [C] pin with a point bent backwards towards the head, that is covered when closed so it cannot hurt you ■ **safety valve** n [C] **1** device which lets gas, liquid, etc escape if the pressure gets too high **2** harmless way of letting out anger, etc

sag /sæg/ v (-gg-) [I] **1** sink or curve down under weight or pressure **2** hang unevenly

saga /'sɑːgə/ n [C] **1** long story full of adventures about people who lived a long time ago **2** long story about events over a period of many years

sage /seɪdʒ/ n **1** [U] herb used for flavouring food **2** [C] (fml) very wise person ● **sage** adj (lit) wise

said pt, pp of SAY

0—**sail¹** /seɪl/ n [C,U] strong cloth used for catching the wind and moving a boat along **2** [sing] trip on a boat: go for a ~ **3** [C] arm of a windmill **IDM** set sail (from/for...) begin a trip by sea

0—**sail²** /seɪl/ v **1** [I] travel on water in a ship, yacht, etc **2** [I,T] control a boat or ship: Can you ~ (a yacht)? **3** [I] begin a journey on water **4** [T] move quickly and smoothly in a particular direction **[PV] sail through (sth)** pass an exam, etc easily ▸ **sailing** n [U] sport of travelling in a boat with sails: go ~ing ■ **sailing boat** n [C] (US 'sailboat) (also 'sailing ship) n [C] boat or ship that uses sails ▸ **sailor** n [C] member of a ship's crew; person who sails a boat

0—**saint** /seɪnt/ n; or before names snt/ n [C] (abbr St) person recognized as holy by the Christian Church because of the way they have lived or died ▸ **saintly** adj (-ier, -iest) of or like a saint; very holy and good

sake /seɪk/ n **IDM** for God's, goodness', heaven's, etc sake used before or after an order or request to express anger, etc: For goodness' ~ hurry up! **for the sake of sb/sth | for sb's/sth's sake** in order to help sb/sth or because you like sb/sth: Please do it for my ~.

0—**salad** /'sæləd/ n [C,U] **1** mixture of raw vegetables, eg lettuce, cucumber and tomato **2** food served with salad: a cheese ~ ■ **salad dressing** n [U,C] sauce of oil, vinegar, etc put on salads

salami /səˈlɑːmi/ n [C] large spicy sausage served cold in slices

0-w **salary** /ˈsæləri/ n [C] (pl **-ies**) (usu monthly) payment for a job
▶ **salaried** adj receiving a salary

0-w **sale** /seɪl/ n [U,C] act of selling sth or being sold **2** [C] period when goods are sold at a lower price than usual: *buy a dress in the ~* s **[IDM] for sale** available to be bought: *They've put their house up for ~.* **on sale 1** (of goods in shops, etc) available to be bought **2** (*esp US*) being offered at a reduced price ■ **salesman** | **salesperson** | **saleswoman** n [C] person who sells goods ■ **salesmanship** n [U] skill in persuading people to buy things

saline /ˈseɪlaɪn/ adj containing salt

saliva /səˈlaɪvə/ n [U] liquid produced in your mouth to help you to swallow food

sallow /ˈsæləʊ/ adj (of sb's skin or face) having an unhealthy yellow colour

salmon /ˈsæmən/ n (pl **salmon**) [C,U] large fish with silver skin and pink flesh that is used for food ■ **salmon 'pink** adj orange-pink in colour, like the flesh of a salmon

salmonella /ˌsælməˈnelə/ n [U] type of bacteria that causes food poisoning

salon /ˈsælɒn/ n [C] shop that gives customers hair or beauty treatment

saloon /səˈluːn/ n [C] **1** (*also* sa'loon car) (*GB*) car with four doors and a boot which is separated from the rest of the interior **2** (*also* sa'loon bar) (*GB*) = LOUNGE BAR (LOUNGE) **3** bar where alcoholic drinks were sold in the western US in the past **4** large comfortable room on a ship, used by the passengers to sit in

0-w **salt** /sɔːlt/ n **1** [U] white substance obtained from mines and sea water, used to flavour food **2** [C] chemical compound of a metal and an acid **[IDM] the salt of the earth** good and honest person **take sth with a pinch of salt** → PINCH ● **salt** v [T] put salt in or on food ■ **salt cellar** (*US* 'salt shaker) n [C] small container for salt ▶ **salty** adj (**-ier, -iest**)

salute /səˈluːt/ n [C] action of raising your right hand to the side of your head as a sign of respect, esp in the armed forces ● **salute** v [I,T] give sb a salute **2** [T] (*fml*) express admiration for sb/sth

salvage /ˈsælvɪdʒ/ n [U] **1** act of saving things that have been or might be lost or damaged, esp in an accident **2** things that are saved from a disaster or an accident ● **salvage** v [T] save sth from loss, wreckage, etc

salvation /sælˈveɪʃn/ n [U] **1** (in Christianity) state of being saved

---

389

sand

from evil **2** way of protecting sb from danger, disaster, etc

0-w **same** /seɪm/ adj **1** exactly the one(s) referred to; not different: *We've lived in the ~ house for ten years.* **2** exactly like the one(s) mentioned: *The ~ thing happened to me last week.* ■ **wallpaper ~s** ● **same** pron (the same) **1** the same thing(s): *I would do the ~.* **2** having the same number, colour, size, etc: *I'd like the ~ as yours.* **[IDM] all the same** in spite of this: *She's quite old, but very lively all the ~.* **be all the same to sb** → ALL **same here** (*spoken*) used to say that sth is also true of you: *'I'm hungry.' 'S~ here.'* ● **same** adv (usu the same) in the same way: *Babies all look the ~ to me.* ■ **sameness** n [U] being the same; lack of variety

samosa /səˈməʊsə/ n [C] spicy Indian food consisting of a triangle of pastry filled with meat or vegetables

0-w **sample** /ˈsɑːmpl/ n [C] one of a number of people or things, or part of a whole, taken for showing what the rest is like: *wallpaper ~s* ● **sample** v [T] test a small amount of sth to see what it is like: *~ our new wine*

sanatorium /ˌsænəˈtɔːriəm/ n (pl **~s** or **-ria** /-riə/) place like a hospital for treating people who are or have been ill

sanctimonious /ˌsæŋktɪˈməʊniəs/ adj (*disapprov*) showing that you feel morally better than others ▶ **sanctimoniously** adv

sanction /ˈsæŋkʃn/ n **1** [C, usu pl] official order that limits trade, etc with a country in order to make it obey a law: *economic ~s* **2** [U] (*fml*) official permission or approval for sth ● **sanction** v [T] give permission for sth to happen

sanctity /ˈsæŋktəti/ n [U] holiness

sanctuary /ˈsæŋktʃuəri/ n (pl **-ies**) **1** [C] area where wild birds or animals are protected and encouraged to breed **2** [C,U] (place offering) safety and protection from arrest, attack, etc: *be offered ~* **3** [C] holy building or part of it that is considered the most holy

0-w **sand** /sænd/ n **1** [U] substance consisting of fine grains of rock, found on beaches, in deserts, etc **2** [U,C, usu pl] large area of sand on a beach ● **sand** v [T] ~ **(down)** smooth sth by rubbing it with sandpaper: *~ (down) the wood* ■ **sandbag** n [C] bag filled with sand, used for stopping bullets, water, etc ■ **sandcastle** n [C] pile of sand made to look like a castle, usu by a child on a beach ■ **'sand dune** = DUNE ■ **'sandpaper** n [U] strong paper with sand glued to it, used for rubbing surfaces smooth

■ 'sandstone n [U] type of stone formed from sand, used in building

▶ sandy adj (-ier, -iest) 1 covered with or containing sand 2 (of hair) yellowish-red

sandal /'sændl/ n [C] type of open shoe attached to the foot by straps

sandwich /'sænwɪdʒ/ n [C] two slices of bread with meat, salad, etc between them: a cheese ~

● sandwich v [T] put sb/sth between two other people or things

sane /seɪn/ adj (~r, ~st) 1 having a healthy mind 2 sensible and reasonable: a ~ policy ▶ sanely adv

sang pt of SING

sanitary /'sænɪtri/ adj 1 free from dirt that might cause disease: poor ~ conditions 2 clean; not likely to cause health problems ■ 'sanitary towel (US 'sanitary napkin) n [C] pad of cotton wool, used by a woman during her period (3)

sanitation /ˌsænɪ'teɪʃn/ n [U] systems that keep places clean, esp by removing human waste

sanity /'sænəti/ n [U] the quality of having a normal healthy mind

sank pt of SINK

sap /sæp/ v (-pp-) [T] make sb/sth weaker; destroy sth gradually ● sap n [U] liquid in a plant or tree that carries food to all its parts ▶ sapling n [C] young tree

sapphire /'sæfaɪə(r)/ n [C] bright blue precious stone ● sapphire adj bright blue in colour

sarcasm /'sɑːkæzəm/ n [U] (use of) ironic remarks, intended to hurt sb's feelings ▶ sarcastic /sɑː'kæstɪk/ adj ▶ sarcastically /-kli/ adv

sardine /ˌsɑː'diːn/ n [C] small young sea fish that is either eaten fresh or preserved in tins [IDM] (packed, crammed, etc) like sardines (infml) pressed tightly together

sari /'sɑːri/ n [C] dress worn esp by Indian women made of a long piece of cloth wrapped round the body

sarong /sə'rɒŋ/ n [C] long piece of fabric wrapped round the waist, worn in Indonesia and Malaysia

sash /sæʃ/ n [C] 1 long piece of cloth worn round the waist or over the shoulder 2 either of a pair of windows that slide up and down inside the main frame ■ sash 'window n [C] window with two frames that slide up and down

sat pt, pp of SIT

Satan /'seɪtn/ n the Devil ▶ satanic (also Satanic) /sə'tænɪk/ adj

satchel /'sætʃəl/ n [C] bag with a long strap for carrying school books

satellite /'sætəlaɪt/ n [C]

1 electronic device that is sent into space and moves around the earth or another planet. It is used for communicating by radio, television, etc and for providing information: ~ television/TV 2 natural object that moves around a larger natural object in space 3 town, country or organization that depends on another larger or more powerful one: ~ states ■ satellite dish n [C] piece of equipment that receives signals from a satellite

satin /'sætɪn/ n [U] silk material that is shiny on one side

satire /'sætaɪə(r)/ n 1 [U] way of criticizing a person, idea or institution, using humour to show their faults: political ~ 2 [C] piece of writing that uses this type of criticism ▶ satirical /sə'tɪrɪkl/ adj ▶ satirize (also -ise) /'sætəraɪz/ v [T] make fun of sb/sth using satire

O─π **satisfaction** /ˌsætɪs'fækʃn/ n 1 [U] feeling of being contented: get ~ from your work 2 [C] something that makes sb contented 3 [U] (fml) acceptable way of dealing with a complaint, etc

satisfactory /ˌsætɪs'fæktəri/ adj good enough for a particular purpose; acceptable: ~ progress ▶ satisfactorily /-tərəli/ adv

O─π **satisfy** /'sætɪsfaɪ/ v (pt, pp -ied) [T] 1 give sb what they want or need; make sb pleased 2 provide what is wanted, needed or asked for: ~ sb's hunger/curiosity 3 give sb proof that sth is true ▶ satisfied adj contented

satnav /'sætnæv/ n [U, C] satellite navigation; device in a vehicle that gives directions while you are driving

O─π **Saturday** /'sætədeɪ; -di/ n [U, C] the seventh day of the week, next after Friday (See examples of use at Monday.)

saturate /'sætʃəreɪt/ v [T] 1 make sth completely wet 2 (usu passive) fill sth/sb completely so that it is impossible to add any more ▶ saturated adj 1 completely wet 2 (chem) (of butter, oils, etc) containing fats that are not easily processed by the body when eaten ▶ saturation /ˌsætʃə'reɪʃn/ n [U]

O─π **sauce** /sɔːs/ n [C, U] thick liquid that is served with food to give it flavour ▶ saucy adj (-ier, -iest) rude ▶ saucily adv

saucepan /'sɔːspən/ n [C] deep metal cooking pot with a lid and a handle

saucer /'sɔːsə(r)/ n [C] small shallow dish on which a cup stands

sauna /'sɔːnə; also 'saʊnə/ n [C] (period of sitting in a) very hot room filled with steam

saunter /'sɔːntə(r)/ v [I] walk in a slow relaxed way ▶ saunter n [sing]

scan

sausage /'sɒsɪdʒ/ *n* [C,U] mixture of chopped meat, flavouring, etc inside a tube of thin skin

savage /'sævɪdʒ/ *adj* **1** fierce and violent: a ~ *animal* **2** involving very strong criticism: a ~ *attack on the education system* ● **savage** *v* [T] **1** (of an animal) attack so violently: *~d by a dog* **2** (*written*) criticize sb/sth severely ▶ **savagely** *adv* ▶ **savagery** *n* [U] cruel and violent behaviour

0̶∞ **save** /seɪv/ *v* **1** [T] ~ (**from**) keep sb/sth safe from harm, loss, etc: ~ *sb's life* **2** [I,T] ~ (**up; for**) keep sth, esp money for future use: ~ (*up*) *for a new car* ∘ *S~ some cake for me!* **3** [T] make sth unnecessary: *That will ~ you a lot of trouble.* **4** [T] (in football, etc) stop the ball going into the net [IDM] **save (sb's) face** (help sb to) avoid embarrassment **save your neck** → NECK ● **save** *n* [C] (in football, etc) act of stopping a goal being scored ● **saving** *n* **1** [C] amount saved: a *saving of £5* **2** (**savings**) [pl] money saved ■ **savings account** *n* [C] bank account in which interest is paid on money saved

saviour (*US* -**or**) /'seɪvɪə(r)/ *n* [C] **1** person who saves sb/sth from danger **2** (**the Saviour**) Jesus Christ

savour (*US* -**or**) /'seɪvə(r)/ *v* [T] **1** enjoy the full taste of sth: ~ *the wine* **2** enjoy a feeling or an experience thoroughly: ~ *your freedom* ● **savour** *n* [usu sing] (*lit*) taste or smell

savoury (*US* -**ory**) /'seɪvəri/ *adj* having a taste that is salty not sweet ● **savoury** *n* [usu sing] (pl -**ies**) savoury dish

saw¹ *pt of* SEE¹

saw² /sɔː/ *n* [C] tool which has a long blade with sharp teeth, for cutting wood, metal, etc ● **saw** *v* (pt -**ed** pp -**n** /sɔːn/ *US also* -**ed**) [I,t] use a saw to cut sth [PV] **saw sth up** cut sth into pieces with a saw ■ **sawdust** *n* [U] tiny pieces of wood that fall from wood as it is sawn ■ **sawmill** *n* [C] factory where wood is cut into boards

saxophone /'sæksəfəʊn/ *n* [C] curved metal musical instrument, often used for jazz

0̶∞ **say** /seɪ/ *v* (pt, pp **said** /sed/) [T] **1** speak or tell sth to sb, using words **2** give an opinion on sth **3** suggest or give sth as an example or a possibility: *You could learn the basics in, let's ~, two months.* **4** make sth clear by words, gestures, etc: *His angry glance said it all.* **5** (of sth written or that can be seen) give particular information: *The book doesn't ~ where he was born.* [IDM] **go without saying** be very obvious that sth is to say in other words **you can say that again** (*spoken*) I agree with you completely ● **say** *n* [sing, U] right to

influence sth by giving your opinion before a decision is made: *have no ~ in what happens* [IDM] **have your say** express your opinion ▶ **saying** *n* [C] well-known phrase or statement

scab /skæb/ *n* **1** dry crust that forms over a wound **2** (*infml*, *disapprov*) worker who refuses to join a strike

scaffold /'skæfəʊld/ *n* [C] **1** platform on which criminals are executed **2** framework of poles and boards round a building for workers to stand on ▶ **scaffolding** *n* [U] framework of poles and boards round a building for workers to stand on

scald /skɔːld/ *v* [T] burn yourself with hot liquid or steam ● **scald** *n* [C] injury to the skin from hot liquid or steam ▶ **scalding** *adj* very hot

0̶∞ **scale¹** /skeɪl/ *n* **1** [sing, U] relative size, extent, etc of sth: *riots on a large ~* **2** [C] range or levels or numbers used for measuring sth: a *salary ~* **3** [C] regular series of marks on an instrument used for measuring **4** (**scales**) (*US also* **scale**) [pl] instrument for weighing people or things: *bathroom ~s* **5** [C] relation between the actual size of sth and its size on a map, diagram, etc that represents it **6** [C] (*music*) series of notes arranged in order of pitch **7** [C] one of the thin pieces of hard material that cover fish, snakes, etc **8** [U] (*GB*) chalky substance left inside kettles, water pipes, etc ▶ **scaly** *adj* (-**ier**, -**iest**)

scale² /skeɪl/ *v* **1** [T] (*written*) climb to the top of sth high **2** [T] remove the scales from a fish [PV] **scale sth up/down** increase/decrease the size or number of sth

scallop /'skɒləp/ *n* [C] shellfish with two fan-shaped shells

scalp /skælp/ *n* [C] skin and hair on top of the head ● **scalp** *v* [T] cut the scalp off sb

scalpel /'skælpəl/ *n* [C] small light knife used by surgeons

scamper /'skæmpə(r)/ *v* [I] run quickly like a child or small animal

scampi /'skæmpi/ *n* [U, with sing or pl verb] (*GB*) large prawns

scan /skæn/ *v* (-**nn**-) **1** [T] examine sth closely: ~ *the horizon* **2** [T] look at a document, etc quickly but not thoroughly: ~ *the newspapers* **3** [T] get an image of an object, part of sb's body, etc on a computer by passing X-rays, etc over it in a special machine **4** [I] (of poetry) have a regular rhythm [PV] **scan sth into sth** | **scan sth in** (*computing*) pass an electronic beam over sth in order to put it into the computer's memory ● **scan** *n* [C] medical test in which a

scandal

machine produces a picture of the inside of the body: *do/have a brain ~* ▶ **scanner** *n* [C] **1** device for examining or recording sth using beams of light sound or X-rays **2** machine which uses X-rays, etc to produce a picture of the inside of the body

scandal /'skændl/ *n* **1** [C,U] action or behaviour that offends or shocks people **2** [U] talk which damages a person's reputation ▶ **scandalize** (*also* -**ise**) /-dəlaɪz/ *v* [T] do sth that people find very shocking ▶ **scandalous** *adj* shocking and unacceptable

scant /skænt/ *adj* (*fml*) hardly any; not enough ▶ **scantily** *adv* **scanty** *adj* (-**ier, -iest**) very small in size or amount

scapegoat /'skeɪpɡəʊt/ *n* [C] person blamed for the wrong acts of another

scar /skɑ:(r)/ *n* [C] **1** mark left on the skin by a wound that has healed **2** permanent mental suffering after a bad experience ● **scar** *v* (-**rr-**) [T] leave a scar on sb

scarce /skeəs/ *adj* (~**r, ~st**) less than is needed; hard to find ▶ **scarcely** *adv* almost not; barely: ~ *enough food* ▶ **scarcity** *n* [C,U] (*pl* -**ies**) lack of sth

scare /skeə(r)/ *v* **1** [T] frighten sb **2** [I] become frightened: *He ~s easily.* ● **scare** *n* [C] feeling or state of fear: *a bomb/health ~* ▶ **scarecrow** *n* [C] figure dressed in old clothes, to scare birds away from crops ▶ **scary** /'skeəri/ *adj* (-**ier, -iest**) (*infml*) frightening

scarf /skɑ:f/ *n* [C] (*pl* **scarves** /skɑ:vz/ *or* ~**s**) piece of material worn round the neck or over the head

scarlet /'skɑ:lət/ *adj* bright red in colour ■ **scarlet 'fever** *n* [C] serious infectious disease that causes red marks on the skin

scathing /'skeɪðɪŋ/ *adj* criticizing sb/ sth very severely ▶ **scathingly** *adv*

scatter /'skætə(r)/ *v* **1** [T] throw or drop things in different directions: ~ *seed* **2** [I] (cause people or animals to) move quickly in various directions ▶ **scatterbrain** *n* [C] (*infml*) person who cannot concentrate for long or forgets things quickly ▶ **scatterbrained** *adj* ▶ **scattered** *adj* spread over a wide area

scavenge /'skævɪndʒ/ *v* [I,T] **1** search through rubbish for things that can be used or eaten **2** (of animals or birds) eat dead animals that have been killed by a car, etc ▶ **scavenger** *n* [C] animal, bird or person that scavenges

scenario /sə'nɑ:riəʊ/ *n* [C] (*pl* ~**s**) **1** imagined series of future events: *a*

nightmare ~ **2** written outline of a play, film, etc

scene /si:n/ *n* [C] **1** place where sth happens: *the ~ of the crime* **2** incident in real life: *~s of horror during the fire* **3** place represented on the stage in a theatre, etc **4** division of play or opera **5** (*the* scene) particular area of activity or way of life: *the fashion ~* **6** view that you see **7** [*usu sing*] loud embarrassing argument: *make a ~* [IDM] **behind the scenes 1** behind the stage of a theatre **2** in secret **on the scene** present ▶ **scenery** *n* [U] **1** natural features of an area, eg mountains **2** painted background used in a theatre stage ▶ **scenic** /'si:nɪk/ *adj* having beautiful natural scenery

scent /sent/ *n* **1** [U,C] pleasant smell **2** [U,C, *usu sing*] smell left behind by a person or animal and that other animals can follow **3** [U] (*esp GB*) perfume [IDM] **on the scent (of sth)** close to discovering sth ● **scent** *v* [T] **1** find sth by using the sense of smell **2** (*written*) suspect the presence of sth: ~ *danger* **3** give sth a particular, pleasant smell: *~ed paper*

sceptic (*US* **sk-**) /'skeptɪk/ *n* [C] person who usu doubts that a statement, claim, etc is true ▶ **sceptical** *adj* ▶ **scepticism** /'skeptɪsɪzəm/ *n* [U,sing] attitude of doubting that claims or statements are true

sceptre (*US* -**er**) /'septə(r)/ *n* [C] decorated rod carried by a king or queen as a symbol of power

schedule /'ʃedjul, *US* 'skedʒuːl/ *n* **1** [C,U] plan that lists all the work that you have to do and when you must do each thing: *production ~s ◇ on/behind ~* (= on time/not on time) **2** [C] (*US*) = TIMETABLE (TIME¹) ● **schedule** *v* [T] arrange for sth to happen at a particular time

scheme /ski:m/ *n* [C] **1** plan or system for doing or organizing sth: *a ~ for raising money* **2** ordered arrangement: *a colour ~* **3** secret or dishonest plan ● **scheme** *v* [T] make secret plans to do sth ▶ **schemer** *n* [C] (*disapprov*) person who plans secretly to do sth for their own advantage

schizophrenia /,skɪtsə'fri:niə/ *n* [U] illness in which the mind becomes separated from actions ▶ **schizophrenic** /-'frenɪk/ *adj, n* [C] (person) with schizophrenia

scholar /'skɒlə(r)/ *n* [C] **1** person who knows a lot about an academic subject **2** student who has been given a scholarship to attend school or university ▶ **scholarly** *adj* ▶ **scholarship** *n* **1** [C] payment given to sb by an organization to help pay for their education **2** [U] serious study of an academic subject

scowl

0—∞ **school** /skuːl/ n [C] place where children go to be educated or where people go to learn a particular skill: *All children should go to* (= attend) ~. ◇ *primary/secondary* ~ ◇ *a driving/riding* ~ **2** [U] process of learning in a school; time during your life when you go to a school: *Is she old enough for* ~? **3** [U] time during the day when children are working in a school: *S~ starts at 9 am.* **4 (the school)** [sing] all the children and staff in a school **5** [C,U] (*US, infml*) (time spent at) a college or university **6** [C] department of a university: *medical* ~ **7** [C] group of artists, writers, etc: *the Dutch* ~ *of painting* **8** [C] large number of fish swimming together ■ **school** v [T] (*fml*) ~ **(in)** train sb/yourself/an animal to do sth ■ **schooling** n [U] education ■ **school-leaver** n [C] (*GB*) person who has just left school ■ **schoolmaster** (fem **schoolmistress**) n [C] teacher in a school, esp a private school

schooner /ˈskuːnə(r)/ n [C] **1** sailing ship with two or more masts **2** tall glass for sherry or beer

0—∞ **science** /ˈsaɪəns/ n **1** [U] knowledge about the structure and behaviour of the natural and physical world, based on facts that you can prove, as by experiments **2** [U,C] particular branch of knowledge, eg physics ■ **science fiction** n [U] fiction dealing with future scientific discoveries, imaginary worlds, etc ► **scientific** /ˌsaɪənˈtɪfɪk/ adj ► **scientifically** /-kli/ adv ► **scientist** /ˈsaɪəntɪst/ n [C] expert in one or more of the sciences

scintillating /ˈsɪntɪleɪtɪŋ/ adj very clever, amusing and interesting

0—∞ **scissors** /ˈsɪzəz/ n [pl] instrument with two blades, used for cutting paper, cloth, etc: *a pair of* ~

scoff /skɒf/ v [I] ~ **(at)** talk about sb/sth in a way that shows you think they are stupid or ridiculous

scold /skəʊld/ v [I,T] (*fml*) speak angrily to sb, esp a child

scone /skɒn/ n [C] small cake made with fat and flour and eaten with butter

scoop /skuːp/ n [C] **1** tool like a large spoon, used for picking up flour, grain, etc or for serving ice cream **2** piece of exciting news obtained by one newspaper, etc before its rivals ● **scoop** v [T] **1** ~ **(up)** move or lift sth with a scoop or sth like a scoop **2** ~ **(up)** move or lift sb/sth with a quick continuous movement

scooter /ˈskuːtə(r)/ n [C] **1** (*also* **motor scooter**) light motorcycle with a small engine and a cover to protect the rider's legs **2** child's vehicle with two wheels, moved by pushing one foot against the ground

scope /skəʊp/ n [U] **1** opportunity to achieve sth: ~ *for improvement* **2** range of things that a subject, an organization, etc deals with [pl]

scorch /skɔːtʃ/ v **1** [T] burn the surface of sth by making it too hot **2** [I,T] (cause sth to) become dry and brown, esp from the heat of the sun or from chemicals: ~*ed grass* ■ **scorch mark** n [C] brown mark made on a surface by burning

0—∞ **score**[1] /skɔː(r)/ n **1** [C] (record of) points, goals, etc in a game **2** [C] copy of written music **3** [C] set or group of twenty **4** (scores) [pl] (*infml*) very many **5** [C] cut in a surface, made with a sharp tool [IDM] **on that/this score** as far as that/this is concerned **settle an old score** have your revenge

0—∞ **score**[2] /skɔː(r)/ v **1** [I,T] win points, goals, etc in a game **2** [I,T] keep a record of the points, goals, etc won in a game **3** [I,T] gain marks in a test or an exam; succeed **4** [T] write music: ~*d for the piano* **5** [T] make a cut or mark on a surface ► **scorer** n **1** (in sports) player who scores points, goals, etc **2** person who keeps a record of the points, etc scored

scorn /skɔːn/ n [U] strong feeling that sb/sth is stupid or not good enough ● **scorn** v [T] **1** feel or show that you do not respect sb/sth **2** refuse sth proudly: ~ *sb's advice* ► **scornful** adj ► **scornfully** adv

scorpion /ˈskɔːpiən/ n [C] small animal with claws and a poisonous sting in its tail

Scotch /skɒtʃ/ n [C,U] (type or glass of) Scottish whisky ■ **Scotch tape**™ (*US*) = SELLOTAPE™

scot-free /ˌskɒt ˈfriː/ adv (*infml*) unpunished: *escape* ~

scoundrel /ˈskaʊndrəl/ n [C] (*old-fash*) person without moral principles

scour /ˈskaʊə(r)/ v [T] **1** search a place thoroughly: ~ *the area for the thief* **2** clean a surface by rubbing it hard with rough material ► **scourer** (*also* **scouring pad**) n [C] small ball of wire or stiff plastic used for cleaning pans

scourge /skɜːdʒ/ n [C] (*written*) cause of great suffering: *the* ~ *of war*

scout /skaʊt/ n **1 (the Scouts)** [pl] organization originally for boys, that trains young people in practical skills **2** [C] member of the Scouts **3** person, aircraft, etc sent ahead to get information about the enemy ● **scout** v [I] ~ **(around/for)** search an area in order to find sth

scowl /skaʊl/ n [C] angry look or expression ● **scowl** v [I] ~ **(at)** look at sb/sth angrily

scrabble /'skræbl/ v [I] ~ (around/about/for) try to do sth in a hurry, often by moving your hands or feet about quickly: *She ~d around in her bag for her glasses.*

scraggy /'skrægi/ adj (-ier, -iest) (disapprov) thin and not looking healthy

scram /skræm/ v (-mm-) [I] (old-fash, sl) go away quickly

scramble /'skræmbl/ v **1** [I] move quickly, often with difficulty, using your hands to help you **2** [I] ~ (for) push, fight or compete with others for sth: ~ *for the best seats* **3** [T] beat and cook eggs **4** [T] mix up a telephone or radio message so that only people with special equipment can understand it ● **scramble** n **1** [sing] difficult walk or climb over rough ground **2** [sing] ~ (for) rough struggle: *a ~ for seats* **3** [C] motorbike race over rough ground

scrap /skræp/ n **1** [C] small piece of sth, esp paper, food, etc: *a ~ of paper* ◇ (fig) *~s of news* **2** [U] unwanted things: ~ *metal* **3** [C] (infml) short fight or quarrel ● **scrap** v (-pp-) **1** [T] cancel or get rid of sth useless **2** [I] (infml) fight with sb ■ **scrapbook** n [C] book of blank pages on which newspaper articles, etc are pasted ■ **'scrap heap** n [C] pile of unwanted things, esp metal [IDM] **on the scrap heap** (infml) no longer wanted or useful ● **scrappy** adj (-ier, -iest) not well organized

scrape /skreɪp/ v **1** [T] remove sth from a surface by moving sth sharp like a knife across it: *She ~d the mud off her boots.* **2** [T] rub sth accidentally so that it gets damaged or hurt: ~ *your arm on the wall* [I,T] (cause sth to) make an unpleasant sound by rubbing against sth: *Don't ~ your chairs on the floor.* **4** [T] make a hole in the ground [IDM] **scrape the (bottom of the) barrel** (disapprov) have to use whatever people or things you can get because nothing better is available [PV] **scrape sth together/up** obtain or collect sth together, but with difficulty ● **scrape** n **1** [sing] action or sound of one thing scraping against another **2** [C] injury or mark made by scraping sth against sth rough **3** [C] (old-fash) difficult situation

0~ **scratch¹** /skrætʃ/ v **1** [I,T] rub your skin with your nails, to stop it itching **2** [I,T] cut or damage your skin or the surface of sth with sth sharp **3** [T] remove sth by rubbing it with sth sharp: *They ~ed lines in the dirt to mark out a pitch.* [IDM] **scratch the surface (of sth)** deal with, understand, or find out only a small part of a subject or problem

0~ **scratch²** /skrætʃ/ n **1** [C] mark, cut or sound made by scratching **2** [sing] act of scratching a part of your body when it itches [IDM] **from scratch** at the beginning up to **scratch** good enough ▶ **scratchy** adj **1** making the skin itch **2** (of a record) sounding bad because of scratches

scrawl /skrɔːl/ v [I,T] write sth quickly or carelessly ● **scrawl** n [C,sing] (piece of) untidy handwriting

0~ **scream** /skriːm/ v **1** [I] give a long sharp cry of fear, pain, anger, etc **2** [T] shout sth in a loud, high voice because of fear, pain, etc ● **scream** n [C] loud sharp cry made by sb who is frightened, excited, etc

screech /skriːtʃ/ v **1** [I,T] make a loud high unpleasant sound; say sth using this sound **2** [I] (of a vehicle) make a loud high unpleasant noise as it moves ● **screech** n [C] loud high screeching cry or sound: *a ~ of brakes*

0~ **screen** /skriːn/ n **1** [C] flat surface on a television, computer, etc on which you see pictures or information **2** [C] large flat surface that films or pictures are shown on **3** [sing,U] films or television in general **4** [C] upright piece of furniture that can be moved to divide a room or to keep one area separate **5** [C] something that hides or protects sth/sb: *a ~ of trees around the house* **6** [C] (esp US) frame with wire netting fastened on a window or a door ● **screen** v [T] **1** hide or protect sb/sth with a screen **2** examine sb/sth for defects, diseases, etc **3** show a film etc on a screen ■ **'screenplay** n [C] script for a film

0~ **screw** /skruː/ n **1** [C] metal pin with a spiral groove cut round its length, used to fasten things together **2** [C] act of turning a screw **3** [sing] (⚠, sl) act of having sex **4** [C] propeller of a ship [IDM] **have a screw loose** be slightly strange in your behaviour ● **screw** v **1** fasten one thing to another with a screw **2** [I] twist sth round in order to fasten it in place: ~ *the lid on* **3** [I] be attached by screwing: *The lid simply ~s on.* **4** [I,T] (⚠, sl) have sex with sb [PV] **screw (sth) up** (sl) do sth badly or spoil sth by doing sth ■ **screw your eyes/face up** tighten the muscles of your eyes/face because of bright light, pain, etc ■ **screwdriver** n [C] tool for turning a screw ● **screwed-'up** adj (infml) upset and confused

scribble /'skrɪbl/ v **1** write sth quickly and carelessly: ~ *(a note) on an envelope* **2** draw meaningless marks on paper, etc ● **scribble** n **1** [U,sing] careless and untidy writing **2** [C] something scribbled

scribe /skraɪb/ n [C] person who

made copies in writing before printing was developed

scrip /skrɪp/ n [C] (business) extra share in a business, given out instead of a dividend

script /skrɪpt/ n **1** [C] written text of a play, speech, film, etc **2** [U] handwriting **3** [U, C] system of writing ● **script** v [T] write the script for a film, etc ■ **scriptwriter** n [C] person who writes scripts for radio, films, etc

scripture /ˈskrɪptʃə(r)/ n **1** (Scripture) (also the Scriptures) [pl] the Bible **2** (scriptures) [pl] holy books of a particular religion ▶ **scriptural** adj

scroll /skrəʊl/ n [C] **1** long roll of paper for writing on **2** design like a scroll, cut in stone ● **scroll** v [I,T] (computing) move text on a computer screen up or down so that you can read different parts of it: ~ down the page ■ **scroll bar** n [C] (computing) strip at the edge of a computer screen that you use to scroll through a file with, using a mouse

scrounge /skraʊndʒ/ v [I,T] (infml, disapprov) get sth from sb by asking them for it rather than by paying for it: ~ (£10) off a friend ▶ **scrounger** n [C]

scrub /skrʌb/ v (-bb-) **1** [I,T] clean sth by rubbing it hard, usu with a brush and soap and water **2** [T] (infml) cancel sth ● **scrub** n **1** [sing] act of scrubbing sth **2** [U] (land covered with) low trees and bushes ■ **scrubbing brush** (US **scrub brush**) n [C] stiff brush for scrubbing floors, etc

scruff /skrʌf/ n [C] (esp GB, infml) a dirty or untidy person [IDM] **by the scruff of the/sb's neck** roughly holding the back of an animal's or a person's neck ▶ **scruffy** adj (-ier, -iest) (infml) dirty and untidy

scruple /ˈskruːpl/ n [C, U] feeling that prevents you from doing sth that you think may be morally wrong: have no ~s about doing sth

scrupulous /ˈskruːpjələs/ adj **1** paying great attention to small details **2** very honest ▶ **scrupulously** adv

scrutinize (also -ise) /ˈskruːtənaɪz/ v [T] (written) look at or examine sb/ sth carefully

scrutiny /ˈskruːtəni/ n (pl -ies) [C, U] (fml) careful and thorough examination

scuba-diving /ˈskuːbə daɪvɪŋ/ n [U] sport or activity of swimming underwater using special breathing equipment. This consists of a container of air which you carry on your back and a tube through which you breathe the air.

scuff /skʌf/ v **1** [T] mark a smooth surface when you rub it against sth rough: ~ your shoes **2** [I,T] drag your feet along the ground when walking

scuffle /ˈskʌfl/ v [I] ~ (with) (of two or more people) fight or struggle with each other ▶ **scuffle** n [C]

sculpt /skʌlpt/ v = SCULPTURE

sculptor /ˈskʌlptə(r)/ (fem sculptress) n [C] person who makes sculptures

sculpture /ˈskʌlptʃə(r)/ n **1** [C, U] work of art that is a solid figure or object made by carving or shaping wood, stone, etc **2** [U] art of making sculptures ● **sculpture** (also **sculpt** /skʌlpt/) v [I,T] make a sculpture

scum /skʌm/ n **1** [U] layer of bubbles or dirt that forms on the surface of a liquid **2** [pl] (infml) insulting word for people that you strongly disapprove of

scurry /ˈskʌri/ v (pt, pp -ied) [I] run with short quick steps: Ants scurried around the crumbs of food. ▶ **scurry** n [sing]

scythe /saɪð/ n [U] tool with a long handle and a curved blade, used for cutting grass, etc ● **scythe** v [I,T] cut grass, corn, etc with a scythe

0̶₋ sea /siː/ n **1** (the sea) [U] (esp GB) salt water that covers most of the earth's surface: to travel by ~ **2** [C] (in proper names) particular area of the sea, sometimes surrounded by land **3** [C] (also **seas** [pl]) movement of the waves of the sea: a rough/calm ~ **4** [sing] ~ **of** large amount of sth covering a large area: a ~ of corn [IDM] **at sea 1** on a ship, etc on the sea **2** confused and not knowing what to do **by sea** in a ship **go to sea** become a sailor **put (out) to sea** leave a port on a ship, boat, etc ■ **seaboard** n [C] part of a country that is along its coast ■ **seafaring** /ˈsiː-feərɪŋ/ adj, n [U] (of) work or travel on the sea ■ **seafood** n [U] fish, shellfish, etc from the sea used as food ■ **seafront** n [sing] part of a town facing the sea ■ **seagoing** adj (of ships) built for crossing the sea ■ **seagull** n [C] = GULL ■ **sea horse** n [C] small fish with a head like a horse ■ **sea legs** n [pl] ability to travel on a ship without being seasick ■ **sea level** n [U] level of the sea used as a basis for measuring the height of land: 50 metres above ~ level ■ **sea lion** n [C] large seal ■ **seaman** n [C] sailor ■ **seamanship** n [U] skill in sailing a boat or ship ■ **seashore** n [usu sing] land close along the edge of the sea ■ **seasick** adj feeling sick from the motion of a ship ■ **seaside** n [sing] (esp GB) place by the sea, esp a holiday resort ▶ **seaward** adj, adv towards the sea ■ **seaweed** n [U] plant growing in the sea, esp on rocks at its edge ■ **seaworthy** adj (of a ship) in a suitable condition to sail

0━ **seal** /siːl/ n **1** [C] sea animal that eats fish and lives around coasts **2** [C] official design or mark, stamped on a document to show that it is genuine **3** [sing] thing that makes sth definite: *The project has been given the PM's ~ of approval* (= official approval). **4** [C] substance that prevents gas, liquid, etc escaping through a crack **5** [C] piece of wax, etc that is placed across a letter or box and which has to be broken before the letter or box can be opened [IDM] **seal of approval** formal approval ■ **sealskin** n [U] skin of a seal, used for clothing ● **seal** v [T] **1** close an envelope by sticking the edges of the opening together **2** close a container tightly or fill a crack, etc **3** (*written*) make sth definite, so that it cannot be changed: *~ a bargain* ◇ *~ sb's fate* [PV] **seal sth off** (of the police, army) prevent people from entering an area: *Police ~ed off the building.*

seam /siːm/ n [C] **1** line where two edges of cloth, etc are joined together **2** layer of coal, etc in a mine

seance /ˈseɪɒns/ n [C] meeting where people try to talk to the spirits of the dead

0━ **search** /sɜːtʃ/ v [I,T] look carefully for sb/sth; examine a particular place when looking for sb/sth: *~ (her pockets) for money* **2** [T] examine sb's clothes, etc in order to find sth they may be hiding: *The youths were arrested and ~ed.* ● **search** n **1** [C] attempt to find sth: *She went out in ~ of* (= looking for) *a drink.* **2** (*computing*) act of looking for information in a computer database or network: *do a ~ on the Internet* [IDM] **in search of** searching for ▶ **searching** (of a book, a question, etc) trying to find out the truth about sth ■ **searchlight** n [C] powerful light that can be turned in any direction ■ **search party** n [C] group of people formed to search for sb/sth ■ **search warrant** n [C] official document allowing a building, etc to be searched by police, etc

0━ **season** /ˈsiːzn/ n [C] **1** any of the four main periods of the year: spring, summer, autumn and winter **2** period when something typically happens: *the rainy ~* ■ **in/out of season** (of fruit, etc) available/not available ● **season** v [T] ~ **(with)** flavour food with salt, pepper, etc ▶ **seasonable** /-əbl/ adj usual or suitable for the time of year ▶ **seasonal** adj happening or

needed during a particular season: *~ trade* ▶ **seasonally** adv ▶ **seasoned** adj **1** (of a person) having a lot of experience of sth **2** (of food) flavoured with salt, pepper, etc **3** (of wood) made suitable for use by being left outside ▶ **seasoning** n [C,U] herb, spice, etc used to season food ■ **season ticket** n [C] ticket that can be used many times within a stated period of time

0━ **seat** /siːt/ n [C] **1** place where you can sit, eg a chair: *Please take a ~* (= sit down). **2** the part of a chair, etc on which you actually sit **3** place where you pay to sit in a train, theatre, etc: *There are no ~s left for the concert.* **4** official position as a member of a council, parliament, etc **5** (*fml*) ~ **of** place where an activity goes on: *the ~ of government* **6** the part of the body which a person sits ● **seat** v [T] **1** (*fml*) give sb a place to sit: *Please be ~ed.* (= sit down) **2** have enough seats for a particular number of people: *The cinema ~s 200.* ■ **seat belt** n [C] strap fastened across a passenger in a car or aircraft ▶ **seating** n [U] seats

secateurs /ˌsekəˈtɜːz/ n [pl] strong scissors used in the garden for cutting small branches, etc

secede /sɪˈsiːd/ v [I] (*fml*) ~ **(from)** (of a state, country, etc) officially leave an organization and become independent ▶ **secession** /sɪˈseʃn/ n [C,U] fact of an area or group becoming independent

secluded /sɪˈkluːdɪd/ adj not visited by many people; isolated ▶ **seclusion** /sɪˈkluːʒn/ n [U] being secluded; privacy

0━ **second** /ˈsekənd/ det, ordinal number **1** next after the first in a series; 2nd: *the ~ person to come* ◇ *He was the ~ to arrive.* **2** next in order of importance, size, etc: *As a dancer, he is ~ to none* (= nobody is a better dancer than he is). **3** another; additional: *a ~ home* [IDM] **second to none** as good as the best: *As a writer, she's ~ to none.* ● **second** adv after one other person or thing in order of importance: *come ~ in a race* ■ **second 'best** n [U] adj next after the best ■ **second-class** adj, adv of or by a class not as good as the best ■ **second-'hand** adj, adv **1** not new; previously owned by somebody else **2** (of news, etc) obtained from a source other than the original ▶ **secondly** adv used to introduce the second of a list of points you want to make ■ **second 'nature** n [U] habit that has become instinctive ■ **second-'rate** adj not of the best quality ■ **second 'thoughts** n [pl] different decision reached after further thought

0━ **second²** /ˈsekənd/ n [C] **1** sixtieth part of a minute **2** (*also infml* **sec**)

very short time: Wait a ~! **3** [C] (*symb* ') (used for measuring angles) sixtieth part of a minute '1'(3) **4** (seconds) [pl] (*spoken*) second helping of food **5** [C,usu pl] item sold at a lower price than usual because it is imperfect **6** [C] (*GB*) level of university degree at British universities ■ ˌsecond 'hand *n* [C] hand on a watch or clock recording seconds

0━▼ **second³** /ˈsekənd/ *v* [T] (in a meeting) officially state that you support a proposal ▶ **seconder** *n* [C] person who seconds a proposal at a meeting

0━▼ **second⁴** /sɪˈkɒnd/ *v* [T] (*esp GB*) **~ (from; to)** send an employee to another department, office, etc, to do a different job for a short period of time ▶ **secondment** *n* [U,C]

secondary /ˈsekəndri/ *adj* **1** less important than sth else: *of ~ interest* **2** developing from something else: *a ~ infection* **3** connected with teaching children of 11 - 18 years

secrecy /ˈsiːkrəsi/ *n* [U] keeping secrets; state of being secret

0━▼ **secret** /ˈsiːkrət/ *adj* **1** (to be) kept from the knowledge or view of others: *~ information* **2** not declared or admitted: *a ~ admirer* **3** (of places) quiet and unknown; secluded ● **secret** *n* **1** [C] something that is known about by only a few people **2** (usu the secret) [sing] best way or the only way to achieve sth: *the ~ of her success* **3** [usu pl] thing that is not fully understood: *the ~s of the universe* [IDM] **in secret** without other people knowing about it ■ ˌsecret 'agent *n* [C] member of a secret service; spy ▶ **secretly** *adv* ■ ˌsecret 'service *n* [usu sing] government department concerned with spying

secretariat /ˌsekrəˈteəriət; -iæt/ *n* [C] administrative department of a large political or international organization

0━▼ **secretary** /ˈsekrətri/ *n* [C] **1** employee who types letters, makes arrangements, etc **2** official of a society, club, etc in charge of writing letters, keeping records, etc ▶ **secretarial** /ˌsekrəˈteəriəl/ *adj* ■ ˌSecretary of 'State *n* [C] **1** (*GB*) head of an important government department **2** (*US*) head of the department that deals with foreign affairs

secrete /sɪˈkriːt/ *v* [T] **1** (of the body) produce a liquid, eg saliva **2** (*fml*) hide sth: *~ money in a drawer* ▶ **secretion** /sɪˈkriːʃn/ *n* (*tech*) **1** [U] process of secreting liquids **2** [C] liquid produced in the body

secretive /ˈsiːkrətɪv/ *adj* liking to hide your thoughts, feelings, etc from other people ▶ **secretively** *adv*

sect /sekt/ *n* [C] small group of

397

people sharing the same religious beliefs ▶ **sectarian** /sekˈteəriən/ *adj* of a sect

0━▼ **section** /ˈsekʃn/ *n* [C] **1** any of the parts into which something is divided **2** department in an organization, institution, etc **3** drawing or diagram of something seen as if cut through from top to bottom ▶ **sectional** *adj* **1** of one particular group within a community or an organization **2** made of separate sections

0━▼ **sector** /ˈsektə(r)/ *n* [C] **1** part of an area of activity, esp of a country's economy: *the private/public ~* **2** division of an area, esp for control of military operations

secular /ˈsekjələ(r)/ *adj* not religious or spiritual: *~ education*

0━▼ **secure** /sɪˈkjʊə(r)/ *adj* **1** free from worry, doubt, etc **2** likely to continue or be successful for a long time: *a ~ job* **3** ~ (against/from) safe **4** unlikely to move, fall down, etc: *a ~ foothold* ● **secure** *v* [T] **1** (*fml*) obtain or achieve sth: *~ a job* **2** close sth tightly: *~ all the doors* **3** ~ (against) protect sth so that it is safe ▶ **securely** *adv*

0━▼ **security** /sɪˈkjʊərəti/ *n* (pl **-ies**) **1** [U] measures to protect a country, building or person against attack, danger, etc: *tight ~ at the airport* **2** [U] protection against sth bad that might happen in the future **3** [U,C] valuable item, eg a house, used as a guarantee that a loan will be repaid **4** (securities) [pl] documents showing ownership of property

sedan /sɪˈdæn/ *n* (*US*) = SALOON(1)

sedate /sɪˈdeɪt/ *adj* calm and dignified ▶ **sedately** *adv*

sedation /sɪˈdeɪʃn/ *n* [U] treatment using sedatives

sedative /ˈsedətɪv/ *n* [C], *adj* (drug) used to calm the nerves or make sb sleep

sedentary /ˈsedntri/ *adj* **1** (of work) done sitting down **2** (of people) spending much of their time seated

sediment /ˈsedɪmənt/ *n* [U] solid material that settles at the bottom of a liquid ▶ **sedimentary** /ˌsedɪˈmentri/ *adj*

seduce /sɪˈdjuːs/ *v* [T] **1** persuade sb to have sex with you **2** persuade sb to do sth they would not usu agree to do ▶ **seduction** /sɪˈdʌkʃn/ *n* [C,U] ▶ **seductive** /sɪˈdʌktɪv/ *adj* very attractive

0━▼ **see** /siː/ *v* (pt **saw** /sɔː/ pp **seen** /siːn/) **1** [T] (often with *can, could*) become aware of sb/sth by using the eyes: *He couldn't ~ her in the crowd.* **2** [I] (often with *can, could*) have or use the power of sight: *It was dark so I couldn't ~ much.* **3** [T] watch a film,

see

TV programme, etc: *Did you ~ the film on TV last night?* **4** [T] (used in orders) look at sth to find information: *S~ page 4.* **5** [T] meet sb by chance: *Guess who I saw last night?* **6** [T] visit sb; consult sb: *Come and ~ us again soon.* ◇ *You should ~ a doctor about that cough.* **7** [T] understand sth: *He didn't ~ the joke.* **8** [T] find sth out by looking, asking or waiting: *I'll go and ~ if she's there.* **9** [I] find sth out or decide sth by thinking or considering: *'Can I go to the party?' 'We'll ~ (= I'll decide later).'* **10** [T] make sure of sth: *~ that the windows are shut* **11** [T] go with sb to help or protect them: *I'll ~ you home.* [IDM] **(not) see eye to eye with sb** (not) agree with sb **see for yourself** check sth yourself in order to be convinced **see how the land lies** → LAND¹ **seeing is believing** (spoken) I need to actually see something to believe it exists or happens **seeing things** (infml) think you can see sth that is not really there **see red** (infml) become very angry **see sense** (infml) become reasonable **see the light 1** finally understand and accept sth **2** begin to believe in a religion **you see** (spoken) used when you are explaining sth to sb [PV] **see about sth** deal with sth **see sb about sth** take advice **see sth in sb/sth** find sb/sth interesting or attractive **see sb off** go to a station, etc to say goodbye to sb who is leaving **see through sb/sth** realize the truth about sb/sth so that you are not deceived **see sth through** continue sth until it is finished **see to sb/sth** deal with sb/sth

see² /siː/ *n* [C] (*fml*) district or office of a bishop

0━ **seed** /siːd/ *n* **1** [C, U] small hard part of a plant from which a new plant can grow **2** [C] (*US* = PIP **3** [C, usu *pl*] origin of a development, etc: *the ~s of doubt* **4** [C] (esp in tennis) one of the best players in a competition, given a position in a list [IDM] **go/run to seed 1** (of a plant) stop flowering as seed is produced **2** (of a person) begin to look untidy, old, etc ● **seed** *v* **1** [I] (of a plant) produce seed **2** [T] plant seeds in an area of ground **3** [T] (esp in tennis) make sb a seed in a competition ▶ **seedless** *adj* (of fruit) having no seeds ▶ **seedling** *n* [C] young plant grown from a seed

seedy /siːdi/ *adj* (**-ier, -iest**) (*disapprov*) dirty and unpleasant, possibly connected with immoral activities ▶ **seediness** *n* [U]

0━ **seek** /siːk/ *v* (pt, pp **sought** /sɔːt/) (*fml*) **1** [I, T] look for sth/ sth **2** [T] to obtain or achieve sth: *~ to end the conflict* **3** [T] ask sb for sth: *~ advice*

▶ **seeker** *n* [C] (used in compounds) person trying to find or get the thing mentioned: *job/asylum-~s*

0━ **seem** /siːm/ *v* [I] give the appearance of being or doing sth: *This book ~s interesting.* ▶ **seeming** *adj* (*fml*) appearing to be sth that may not be true: *a ~ing contradiction* ▶ **seemingly** *adv*

seen *pp* of SEE¹

seep /siːp/ *v* [I] (of liquids) come slowly through sth: *water ~ing through the cracks* ▶ **seepage** /-ɪdʒ/ *n* [U] process of seeping through sth

see-saw /ˈsiː sɔː/ *n* **1** [C] long plank supported in the middle, with a person sitting at each end, rising and falling in turn **2** [sing] situation in which things keep changing from one state to another and back again ● **see-saw** *v* [I] change repeatedly from one state, emotion, etc to another and back again

seethe /siːð/ *v* [I] **1** be angry about sth but try not to show it: *~ing (with rage) at his behaviour* **2** (*written*) (of a place) be full of a lot of people or animals moving around

segment /ˈseɡmənt/ *n* [C] **1** part of something, esp of a circle, marked off or cut off **2** section of an orange, lemon, etc

segregate /ˈseɡrɪɡeɪt/ *v* [T] put people of a different race, etc apart from the rest of the community ▶ **segregation** /ˌseɡrɪˈɡeɪʃn/ *n* [U]

seismic /ˈsaɪzmɪk/ *adj* of earthquakes

seize /siːz/ *v* [T] **1** take hold of sb/sth suddenly and with force **2** be quick to make use of a chance, an opportunity, etc: *~d the chance to get revenge* [PV] **seize up 1** (of machinery) become stuck and stop working **2** (of part of the body) become painful and difficult to move

seizure /ˈsiːʒə(r)/ *n* **1** [C, U] (act of) using force to take sth from sb **2** [C] (*old-fash*) sudden attack of illness

0━ **seldom** /ˈseldəm/ *adv* not often; rarely

0━ **select** /sɪˈlekt/ *v* [T] choose sb/sth carefully from a group of people or things ● **select** *adj* **1** carefully chosen as the best of a larger group **2** (of a society, club, etc) used by people with a lot of money or a high social position ▶ **selection** /-kʃn/ *n* **1** [U] process of choosing sth/sth **2** [C] group of selected things; number of things from which to select ▶ **selective** *adj* **1** affecting only a small number of people or things from a larger group **2** tending to choose carefully

0━ **self** /self/ *n* (pl **selves** /selvz/) *n* [C, U] your own nature; your personality

self- /self/ *prefix* of, to or by yourself or itself ■ self-as'sured *adj* confident ■ self-'catering *adj* (of holiday accommodation) with no meals provided, so you must cook for yourself ■ self-'centred *adj* thinking too much about yourself and not about the needs of others ■ self-'confident *adj* confident in your own ability ▶ self-'confidence *n* [U] ■ self-'conscious *adj* nervous or embarrassed because you are aware of being watched by others ▶ self-'consciousness *n* [U] ■ self-con'tained *adj* 1 not needing or depending on others 2 (GB) (of a flat) having its own kitchen, bathroom and entrance ■ self-con'trol *n* [U] ability to remain calm and not show your emotions ■ self-de'fence (US -defense) *n* [U] something you do to protect yourself when you are being attacked, criticized, etc ■ self-em'ployed *adj* working for yourself and not employed by a company, etc ■ self-es'teem *n* [U] feeling of being happy with your own character and abilities ■ self-'evident *adj* obvious; without need for proof ■ self-'harm *n* [U] injuring yourself deliberately ■ self-'help *n* [U] relying on your own efforts and abilities to achieve things, without the help of others ■ self-im'portant *adj* (*disapprov*) having too high an opinion of yourself ▶ self-im'portance *n* [U] ■ self-in'dulgent *adj* (*disapprov*) allowing yourself to have or do things that you like, esp when you do this too often ▶ self-in'dulgence *n* [U] ■ self-'interest *n* [U] (*disapprov*) fact of sb only considering their own interests and of not caring about things that would help others ■ self-'pity *n* [U] (*disapprov*) feeling of pity for yourself ■ self-re'liant *adj* not depending on others ▶ self-re'liance *n* [U] ■ self-re'spect *n* [U] feeling of pride in yourself that what you say, do, etc is right and good ■ self-'righteous *adj* (*disapprov*) convinced that what you say and do is always morally right, and that other people are wrong ■ self-'sacrifice *n* [U] (*approv*) giving up things you want or need in order to help others ■ 'selfsame *adj* (*written*) identical ■ self-'satisfied *adj* (*disapprov*) too pleased with yourself and your achievements ■ self-'service *n* [U] system in which buyers collect goods themselves and pay at a special desk ■ self-suf'ficient *adj* able to produce everything you need ■ self-'willed *adj* (*disapprov*) determined to do what you want without caring about others

selfish /'selfɪʃ/ *adj* (*disapprov*)

thinking mainly of yourself and your own needs, not of others ▶ 'selfishly *adv* ■ selfishness *n* [U]

0━ **sell** /sel/ *v* (pt, pp **sold** /səʊld/) 1 [I,T] give sth to sb in exchange for money 2 [T] offer sth for people to buy: *Do you ~ stamps?* 3 [I] be bought in the way or numbers mentioned; be offered at the price mentioned: *Does this book ~ well?* 4 [T] make people want to buy sth: *Scandals ~ newspapers.* 5 [T] persuade sb to accept sth as good, useful, true, etc: *~ sb an idea* 6 [T] *~ yourself* present yourself, your ideas, etc in a way which is attractive to others 7 [T] *~ yourself* (*disapprov*) accept money, etc for doing something bad [IDM] sell sb/yourself short not value sb/yourself highly enough ● sell your soul (to the devil) do sth dishonourable for money [PV] sell sth off sell things cheaply because you want to get rid of them ● sell out 1 sell all of sth, eg tickets 2 be disloyal to sb/sth ● sell (sth) up sell your house, business, etc, usu when retiring

Sellotape™ /'seləteɪp/ *n* [U] (GB) thin, clear, sticky plastic tape used for joining, mending, etc things

selves *plural of* SELF

semantics /sɪ'mæntɪks/ *n* [U] (*ling*) study of the meanings of words

semaphore /'seməfɔː(r)/ *n* [U] system of sending signals by holding two flags in various positions ● semaphore *v* [I,T] send a message by semaphore

semblance /'semblans/ *n* [sing,U] *~ of* (*written*) appearance: *create a/ some ~ of order*

semen /'siːmen/ *n* [U] whitish liquid containing sperm, produced by the sex organs of men and male animals

semi- /'semi/ *prefix* half; partly: *~-literate* ■ 'semicircle *n* [C] (*geom*) half a circle ■ 'semicolon *n* [C] the punctuation mark (;) ■ semicon'ductor *n* [C] solid substance that conducts electricity in certain conditions ■ semi-de'tached *adj* (GB) (of a house) joined to another on one side by a shared wall ■ semi-'final *n* [C] either of two matches before the final ■ semi-'skimmed *adj* (GB) (of milk) that has had half the fat removed

seminar /'semɪnɑː(r)/ *n* [C] small group of students meeting for study

0━ **senate** /'senət/ *n* (usu the Senate) 1 [sing] upper house of the law-making assembly in the US, France, etc 2 [C,usu sing, U] governing council of some universities ■ senator (often Senator) *n* [C] member of a senate

send

O─ **send** /send/ v (pt, pp **sent** /sent/) [T] **1** cause sb/sth to be taken to a place, esp by post, radio, etc: ~ a *letter/an email* **2** tell sb to do something by sending them a message: *My parents* ~ *their love.* **3** tell sb to go somewhere or to do sth: *the kids to bed* **4** cause sth/sb to move quickly: *The punch sent him flying.* **5** make sb react in a particular way: ~ *sb to sleep* [PV] **send away (to sb) (for sth)** = SEND OFF (FOR STH) **send sb away** tell sb to leave **send for sb/sth** ask or order that sb should come, or sth be brought to you: ~ *for a doctor* **send off (for sth)** write and ask for sth to be sent to you by post **send sth out 1** send sth to a lot of different people or places: ~ *out wedding invitations* **2** produce sth, eg light, a signal, etc: *The sun* ~ *s out light.* **send sb/sth up** (GB, infml) copy sb/sth in a way that makes them/it seem funny ● **'send-off** n [C] (infml) occasion when people gather to say goodbye to sb

senile /'si:naɪl/ adj weak in body or mind as a result of old age ▶ **senility** /sə'nɪləti/ n [U]

O─ **senior** /'si:niə(r)/ adj **1** ~ (to) higher in rank or status than others **2** (Senior) used after the name of a man who has the same name as his son, to avoid confusion ● **senior** n **1** [sing] person who is older than sb else: *He is three years her* ~. **2** [C, usu pl] older school pupil ● **senior 'citizen** n [C] older person, esp sb who has retired from work ▶ **seniority** /ˌsi:ni'ɒrəti/ n [U] fact of being older or of higher rank than others

O─ **sensation** /sen'seɪʃn/ n [C,U] **1** feeling; the ability to feel **2** [C,U] (cause of) great excitement, surprise, etc ▶ **sensational** adj **1** causing great excitement or interest **2** (infml) wonderful; very good

O─ **sense** /sens/ n **1** [C] one of the five powers (sight, hearing, smell, taste and touch) by which a person is conscious of things **2** [C] feeling about sth important: *a* ~ *of dread* **3** [sing] understanding of the nature or value of sth: *a* ~ *of humour* **4** [U] good practical judgement: *There's no* ~ *in doing that.* **5** (senses) [pl] normal state of mind; ability to think clearly: *take leave of your* ~*s* (= go mad) **6** [C] meaning of a word; way of understanding sth [IDM] **make sense 1** have a meaning that can be understood **2** be a sensible thing to do **3** be easy to understand or explain **make sense of sth** understand sth difficult ● **sense** v [T] become aware of sth even though you cannot see it, hear it, etc: ~ *danger*

senseless /'sensləs/ adj **1** (disapprov) foolish **2** unconscious ▶ **senselessly** adv ▶ **senselessness** n [U]

sensibility /ˌsensə'bɪləti/ n **1** [U,C] ability to experience and understand deep feelings, esp in the arts **2** (sensibilities) [pl] person's feelings

O─ **sensible** /'sensəbl/ adj **1** having or showing good sense (4); practical: *a* ~ *person/idea* **2** (lit) aware of sth ▶ **sensibly** adv

O─ **sensitive** /'sensətɪv/ adj **1** ~ (to) aware of and able to understand other people's feelings: *a* ~ *friend* **2** easily offended or upset: ~ *about his baldness* **3** requiring great care: *a politically* ~ *issue* **4** ~ (to) reacting quickly or more than usual to sth: ~ *skin* ◇ ~ *to light* **5** (of instruments) able to measure very small changes ▶ **sensitivity** /ˌsensə'tɪvəti/ n [U] quality or degree of being sensitive

sensitize (also **-ise**) /'sensətaɪz/ v [T] ~ (to) make sb/sth more aware of sth, esp a problem or sth bad

sensual /'senʃuəl/ adj **1** enjoying physical, esp sexual, pleasures **2** suggesting an interest in physical, esp sexual, pleasure ▶ **sensuality** /-'æləti/ n [U] enjoyment of sensual pleasures

sensuous /'senʃuəs/ adj giving pleasure to the senses ▶ **sensuously** adv ▶ **sensuousness** n [U]

sent pt, pp of SEND

O─ **sentence** /'sentəns/ n **1** [C] (gram) group of words that express a statement, question, etc **2** [C,U] punishment given by a court of law: *a jail/prison* ~ ● **sentence** v [T] state that sb is to have a certain punishment: ~ *sb to death*

sentiment /'sentɪmənt/ n **1** [C,U] (fml) attitude or opinion, esp one based on emotions **2** [U] (disapprov) feelings of pity, romantic love, etc, which may be too strong

sentimental /ˌsentɪ'mentl/ adj **1** of the emotions, rather than reason **2** (disapprov) producing too much emotion ▶ **sentimentality** /-'tæləti/ n [U] (disapprov) the quality of being too sentimental ▶ **sentimentally** adv

sentry /'sentri/ n [C] (pl **-ies**) soldier whose job is to guard sb

O─ **separate¹** /'seprət/ adj **1** ~ (from) forming a unit by itself; not joined to sth else: ~ *rooms* **2** different: *on three* ~ *occasions* ▶ **separately** adv

O─ **separate²** /'sepəreɪt/ v [I,t] (cause people or things to) move apart; divide into different parts or groups **2** [I] stop living together as a couple with your husband, wife or partner ▶ **separation** /ˌsepə'reɪʃn/ n **1** [U, sing] act of separating sb/sth;

state of being separated **2** [C] period of living apart from sb **3** [C] legal agreement by a married couple to live apart

0━ **September** /sep'temba(r)/ n [U, C] ninth month of the year (See examples of use at *April*.)

septic /'septɪk/ adj infected with harmful bacteria: a ~ *wound*

sepulchre (*US* **sepulcher**) /'seplkə(r)/ n [C] (*old-fash*) tomb, esp one cut in rock

sequel /'si:kwəl/ n ~ **(to)** **1** [C] book, film, etc continuing the story of an earlier one **2** [usu sing] thing that happens after or as a result of an earlier event

sequence /'si:kwəns/ n [C, U] set of events, actions, etc which have a particular order

sequin /'si:kwɪn/ n [C] small shiny disc sewn onto clothing as decoration

serene /sə'ri:n/ adj calm and peaceful ▸ **serenely** adv ▸ **serenity** /sə'renəti/ n [U]

sergeant /'sɑ:dʒənt/ n [C] **1** member of one of the middle ranks in the army and the air force, below an officer **2** (in Britain) police officer below an inspector in rank **3** (in the US) police officer just below a lieutenant or captain

serial /'sɪəriəl/ n [C] story, etc broadcast or published in parts ● **serial** adj of or forming a series ▸ **serialize** (*also* -**ise**) /-aɪz/ v [T] produce a story, etc in parts for the television, a magazine, etc ■ **serial number** n [C] number put on a product, eg a camera or television, to identify it

0━ **series** /'sɪəri:z/ n [C] (pl **series**) group of related things, events, etc, occurring one after the other

0━ **serious** /'sɪəriəs/ adj **1** bad or dangerous: a ~ *illness* **2** needing careful thought; important **3** not silly; thoughtful: a ~ *face* **4** ~ **(about)** sincere about sth: *Are you ~ about this plan?* ▸ **seriously** adv ▸ **seriousness** n [U]

sermon /'sɜ:mən/ n [C] speech on religious or moral matters, esp one given in a church

serotonin /ˌserə'təunɪn/ n [U] chemical in the brain that affects how a person feels

serpent /'sɜ:pənt/ n [C] (*lit*) snake

serrated /sə'reɪtɪd/ adj having a series of sharp points on the edge like a saw

serum /'sɪərəm/ n (pl **sera** /-rə/ or ~**s**) [C, U] (*med*) (injection of) liquid which fights disease or poison: *snakebite ~*

0━ **servant** /'sɜ:vənt/ n [C] person who works in sb's house and cooks, cleans, etc for them

0━ **serve** /sɜ:v/ v **1** [I, T] give food or drink to sb at a meal **2** [I, T] attend to customers in a shop **3** [T] be useful to sb in achieving sth **4** [T] provide an area or group of people with sth needed: *This bus ~s our area.* **5** [I] ~ **(as)** be suitable for a particular purpose: *This room ~s as a study.* **6** [I, T] work or perform duties for sb/ sth: ~ *on a committee* **7** [T] spend a period of time in prison: ~ *a life sentence* **8** [T] (*law*) deliver an official document to sb, esp one ordering them to appear in court **9** [I, T] (in tennis, etc) start playing by throwing the ball in the air and hitting it **[IDM] it serves sb right (for doing sth)** (of bad luck, etc) be deserved by sb ▸ **serve** n [C] (in tennis, etc) action of serving the ball to your opponent ▸ **server** n [C] **1** (*computing*) computer or program that manages information or devices shared by several computers connected in a network **2** (*sport*) person who is serving, eg in tennis ▸ **serving** n [C] amount of food for one person

0━ **service** /'sɜ:vɪs/ n **1** [C] system or business that meets public needs: a *bus* ~ **2** (*also* **Service**) [C] organization or a company that provides sth for the public or does sth for the government **3** [U] serving of customers in hotels, restaurants and shops **4** [U] work that sb does for an organization, etc: *ten years'* ~ *in the army* **5** [U] work done by a vehicle: *This car has given good* ~ (= has been reliable). **6** [C, U] maintenance or repair of a vehicle to keep it operating well **7** [C, usu pl] particular skills or help that a person is able to offer **8** [C, usu pl, U] (work done by people) in the army, the navy and the air force **9** [C] religious ceremony **10** (**services**) [sing, with sing or pl verb] (*GB*) place beside a motorway where you can stop for petrol, food, etc **11** [C] (in tennis, etc) act or way of serving the ball **12** [C] complete matching set of plates, dishes, etc **[IDM] at sb's service** ready to help sb **be of service (to sb)** (*fml*) be useful or helpful ● **service** v [T] maintain and repair a car, machine, etc to keep it operating well ▸ **serviceable** adj suitable to be used ■ **service charge** n [C] additional charge on a bill for service in a restaurant, etc ■ **serviceman | servicewoman** n [C] person serving in the armed forces ■ **service station** n [C] = PETROL STATION

serviette /ˌsɜ:vi'et/ n [C] piece of cloth or paper used at meals for protecting your clothes and wiping your hands and lips

0–☞ **session** /'seʃn/ n [C] **1** period spent in one activity: *a recording* ~ **2** meeting or series of meetings of a parliament, law court, etc **3** (in Scotland) school or university year

0–☞ **set**[1] /set/ n **1** [C] group of similar things of the same kind that belong together **2** [C, with sing or pl verb] group of people who spend a similar amount of time together and have similar interests **3** [C] television or radio receiver **4** [C] scenery for a play, film, etc **5** [C] division of a match in tennis, volleyball, etc **6** [C] act of styling hair

0–☞ **set**[2] /set/ v (pt, pp **set**, -tt-) **1** [T] put sb/sth in a particular place or position: ~ *a tray down on the table* **2** [T] cause sb/sth to be in a particular state; start sth happening: ~ *a prisoner free* ◇ ~ *sb thinking* **3** [T] (usu passive) place the action of a play, film or novel in a particular place, time, etc: *The film is* ~ *in London in the 1960s.* **4** [T] prepare sth so that it is ready for use or in position: ~ *the alarm clock for 7 o'clock* **5** [T] arrange plates, knives, forks, etc on a table ready for a meal **6** [T] put a precious stone into a piece of jewellery **7** [T] arrange or fix sth: ~ *a date for the wedding* **8** [T] fix sth so that others copy it or try to achieve it: ~ *a new fashion/record* ◇ ~ *a good example* **9** [T] give sb a piece of work, a task, etc: ~ *an examination* **10** [I] become firm or hard: *The cement has* ~. **11** [T] put a broken bone into the right position to mend **12** [T] ~ **(to)** write music to go with words **13** [I] (of the sun or moon) go down [IDM] **set an example** offer a good standard for others to follow **set eyes on sb/sth** see sb/sth **set foot in/on sth** enter or visit a place **set light/fire to sth** | **set sth on fire** cause sth to start burning **set your heart on sth** | **have your heart set on sth** want sth very much **set your mind to sth** → MIND[1] **set sth right** → RIGHT[1] **set sb/sth to rights** → RIGHT[1] **set sail (from/for...)** begin a journey by sea **set the scene (for sth)** create a situation in which sth can happen or develop **set sb's teeth on edge** (of a sound or taste) make sb feel physically uncomfortable [PV] **set about sth** attack sb and start hitting them **set sb about sth** start doing sth suddenly **set sth back sth** (infml) cost sb a particular amount of money **set sth/sb back** delay the progress of sth/sb by a particular time **set sth back (from sth)** place sth, esp a building, at a distance from sth **set off** begin a journey, etc **set sth off** **1** cause a bomb, etc to explode **2** start a process or series of events **3** make sth look attractive: *This*

colour ~*s off her eyes.* **set on/upon sb** attack sb **set out 1** begin a journey, etc **2** begin a job, task, etc with a particular goal **set sth out 1** arrange or display things **2** present ideas, facts, etc in an orderly way: ~ *out your ideas in an essay* **set to** begin doing sth **set sth up 1** build sth or put sth somewhere: *The police* ~ *up roadblocks.* **2** arrange for sth to happen **3** create sth or start it: ~ *up a business* **set (yourself) up (as sb)** start running a business ■ **'setback** n [C] something that delays progress or development ■ **'set-up** n [C] (infml) **1** way of organizing sth; system **2** situation in which sb makes it seem that you have done sth wrong

set[3] /set/ adj **1** in a particular position **2** planned; fixed and unlikely to change: *We always follow a* ~ *pattern.* ◇ *have* ~ *ideas about sth* ◇ *As people get older, they get more* ~ *in their ways.* **3** (of a restaurant meal) having a fixed price and limited choice of dishes: *a* ~ *menu/lunch* **4** (infml) ready or likely to do sth: ~ *to go* [IDM] **set in your ways** unwilling to change your habits **be set on (doing) sth** be determined to do sth: *She's* ~ *on winning.* ■ **set book** n [C] (GB) book that students must study for an exam

set square /'set skweə(r)/ n [C] triangular instrument used for drawing lines at certain angles

settee /se'tiː/ n [C] (GB) = SOFA

setter /'setə(r)/ n [C] breed of long-haired dog

setting /'setɪŋ/ n **1** [C] surroundings: *a rural* ~ **2** [C] place and time at which the action of film, play or book takes place **3** [C] height, speed, etc at which a machine, etc is or can be set

0–☞ **settle** /'setl/ v **1** [T] put an end to an argument or disagreement: ~ *an argument* **2** [T] decide or arrange sth finally **3** [I,T] make a place your permanent home **4** [I,T] make sb/yourself comfortable: ~*d (back) in the chair* **5** [I,T] (cause sb/sth to) become calm: ~ *sb's nerves* **6** [I] ~ **(on/over)** fall from above and come to rest on sth: *The bird* ~*d on a branch.* **7** [I,T] (cause sth to) sink slowly down: *dust settling on the floor* ◇ *The rain* ~*d the dust.* **8** [I,T] ~ **(up)** pay a debt [PV] **settle down 1** get into a comfortable position, either sitting or lying **2** start to have a quieter way of life, living in one place **settle (down) to sth** begin to give your attention to sth **settle for sth** accept sth that is not quite what you want **settle in** move into a new house, job, etc and start to feel comfortable there **settle on sth** decide to have sth ► **settled** adj not likely to change or move: ~*d weather* ► **settler** n [C] person who goes to live in a new country or region

settlement /'setlmənt/ n **1** [C,U] (action of reaching an) official agreement that ends an argument **2** [C] (law) (document stating the) conditions on which money or property is given to sb: a divorce ~ **3** [U,C] process of people settling in a place; place where they settle

0━ **seven** /'sevn/ number 7 ▸ **seventh** /'sevnθ/ ordinal number, n [C] 7th; the fraction ⅐; one of seven equal parts of sth

0━ **seventeen** /ˌsevn'ti:n/ number 17 ▸ **seventeenth** /ˌsevn'ti:nθ/ ordinal number 17th

0━ **seventy** /'sevnti/ **1** number 70 **2** (the seventies) n [pl] numbers, years or temperatures from 70 to 79 ▸ **seventieth** /'sevntiəθ/ ordinal number 70th

sever /'sevə(r)/ v **1** [T] cut a part of sth from the rest: ~ a limb from the body **2** [T] end sth: ~ relations with sb

0━ **several** /'sevrəl/ det, pron more than two but not very many

0━ **severe** /sɪ'vɪə(r)/ adj **1** very bad, difficult, intense, etc: a ~ storm **2** stern; strict: ~ discipline ▸ **severely** adv ▸ **severity** /sɪ'verəti/ n [U]

0━ **sew** /səʊ/ v (pt ~ed pp ~n /səʊn/) [I,T] make stitches with a needle and thread; fasten cloth, etc with stitches [PV] **sew sth up 1** join or mend sth by sewing **2** (infml) arrange sth satisfactorily: They have the election ~n up = that is settled.

sewage /'su:ɪdʒ/ n [U] used water and human waste carried away from houses and factories by sewers

sewer /'su:ə(r)/ n [C] underground pipe that carries sewage away from houses and factories

sewn pt of SEW

0━ **sex** /seks/ n **1** [U,C] state of being male or female **2** [C] group of all male or all female people: a member of the opposite ~ **3** [U] (sexual activity leading to and including) sexual intercourse ● **sexy** adj (-ier, -iest) sexually attractive ▸ **sexily** adv ▸ **sexiness** n [U]

sexism /'seksɪzəm/ n [U] unfair treatment of people (esp women) because of their sex ▸ **sexist** adj, n [C]

sextant /'sekstənt/ n [C] instrument for measuring the altitude of the sun, etc

sexton /'sekstən/ n [C] person who takes care of a church, churchyard, etc

0━ **sexual** /'sekʃuəl/ adj of sex or the sexes ■ **sexual** '**harassment** n [U] comments about sex, physical contact, etc in the workplace, that a person finds annoying and offensive ■ **sexual** '**intercourse** n [U] physical union of two people

often leading to the production of children ▸ **sexuality** /ˌsekʃu'æləti/ n [U] feelings and activities connected with a person's sexual desires ▸ **sexually** adv

shabby /'ʃæbi/ adj (-ier, -iest) **1** in poor condition; poorly dressed **2** (of behaviour) unfair; mean ▸ **shabbily** adv

shack /ʃæk/ n [C] small, crudely built shed or house

shackle /'ʃækl/ n [C, usu pl] **1** one of a pair of metal rings linked by a chain, for fastening a prisoner's wrists or ankles **2** ~ (of) (fml) anything that prevents freedom of action ● **shackle** v [T] **1** put shackles on sb **2** prevent sb from acting freely

0━ **shade** /ʃeɪd/ n **1** [U] area that is dark and cool because the sun's light does not get to it: sit in the ~ **2** [C] thing that reduces light: a lamp~ **3** [C] ~ (of) (depth of) colour: four ~s of blue **4** [C, usu pl] different kind or level of opinion, feeling, etc: ~s of meaning **5** (a shade) [sing] (written) a little; slightly: a ~ warmer **6** (shades) [pl] (infml) = SUNGLASSES ● **shade** v [T] **1** prevent direct light from reaching sth: ~ your eyes **2** cover a light to reduce brightness **3** darken parts of a drawing, etc [PV] **shade into sth** change gradually into sth else: green shading into blue

0━ **shadow** /'ʃædəʊ/ n **1** [C,U] dark shape that sb/sth's form makes on a surface when they are between the light and the surface: The ship's sail cast a ~ on the water. **2** [U] (also shadows [pl]) darkness in a place or on sth **3** [sing] a very small amount of sth: not a ~ of doubt **4** [sing] strong (usu bad) influence of sb/sth **5** (shadows) [pl] dark areas under sb's eyes, because they are tired, etc ● **shadow** v [T] follow sb and watch sb closely and often secretly ▸ **shadowy** adj **1** dark and full of shadows **2** not clear; mysterious

shady /'ʃeɪdi/ adj (-ier, -iest) **1** giving shade from sunlight; situated in the shade **2** (infml) not entirely honest: a ~ character

shaft /ʃɑ:ft/ n [C] **1** long, narrow, usu vertical passage in a building or underground, eg for entering a mine: a lift ~ **2** long narrow part of an arrow, hammer, golf club, etc **3** metal bar joining parts of a machine or engine together **4** either of two poles between which a horse is fastened to a cart, etc **5** (lit) narrow beam of light, etc

shaggy /'ʃægi/ adj (-ier, -iest) **1** (of hair, fur, etc) long and untidy **2** having long untidy hair, fur, etc

0━ **shake¹** /ʃeɪk/ v (pt shook /ʃʊk/ pp ~n /'ʃeɪkən/) **1** [I,T] (cause sb/sth

shake

to) move quickly from side to side or up and down **2** [I] ~ **(with)** make short quick movements that you cannot control, eg because you are afraid **3** [I] (of sb's voice) sound unsteady, usu because you are afraid, etc **4** [T] shock or upset sb very much: *We were ~n by his death.* [IDM] **shake hands (with sb)** | **shake sb's hand** take sb's hand and move it up and down as a greeting **shake your head** move your head from side to side to indicate 'no' or to show doubt, etc [PV] **shake sb/sth off** free yourself of sb/sth **shake sth up** make important changes in an organization, etc to make it more efficient ■ **shake-up** n [C] major reorganization of a company, etc
► **shakily** /-ɪli/ *adv* ► **shaky** *adj* (-ier, -iest) **1** (of a person) shaking and weak because of illness, etc **2** not firm or safe; not certain

0━ **shake** /ʃeɪk/ *n* [C, usu sing] act of shaking sb/sth

shale /ʃeɪl/ *n* [U] soft stone that splits easily

0━ **shall** /ʃəl; strong form ʃæl/ *modal v* (neg **shall not** short form **shan't** /ʃɑːnt/ *pt* **should** /ʃʊd; neg **should not** short form **shouldn't** /ˈʃʊdnt/) **1** (*old-fash*) used with *I* and *we* to talk about the future: *I shan't be gone long.* **2** used in questions with *I* and *we* for making offers or suggestions or asking for advice: *S~ I open the window?* ◇ *What ~ we do tonight?*

shallot /ʃəˈlɒt/ *n* [C] kind of small onion

0━ **shallow** /ˈʃæləʊ/ *adj* **1** not deep: *a ~ river* **2** (*disapprov*) not serious: *a ~ thinker* ► **shallowness** n [U]
► **shallows** n [pl] shallow place in a river, etc

sham /ʃæm/ *n* (*disapprov*) **1** [sing] situation, feeling, system, etc that is not as good or true as it seems to be **2** [C] person who pretends to be sth they are not **3** [U] pretence ● **sham** *adj* not genuine but intended to seem real: *a ~ marriage* ● **sham** *v* (-mm-) [I,T] pretend sth: *~ illness*

shamble /ˈʃæmbl/ *v* [I] walk without lifting your feet properly

shambles /ˈʃæmblz/ *n* [sing] (*infml*) (a shambles) situation or scene of disorder or confusion

0━ **shame** /ʃeɪm/ *n* **1** [U] feelings of guilt, sadness, etc that you have when you know you have done sth wrong: *feel ~ at having told a lie* **2** [U] (*fml*) ability to feel shame as sth you have done: *He has no ~.* **3** (a shame) [sing] used to say that sth is a cause for feeling sad or disappointed: *It's/ What a ~ you can't come.* **4** [U] loss of respect caused when you do sth wrong: *bring ~ on your family* [IDM]

put sb/sth to shame be much better than sb/sth ● **shame** *v* [T] **1** (*written*) make sb feel ashamed **2** (*fml*) make sb feel they have lost honour or respect [PV] **shame sb into doing sth** cause sb to do sth by making them feel ashamed not to do it
► **shamefaced** /ˌʃeɪmˈfeɪst/ *adj* looking ashamed ► **shameful** *adj* that should make you feel ashamed ► **shamefully** /-fəli/ *adv*
► **shameless** *adj* (*disapprov*) not feeling ashamed of sth you have done

shampoo /ʃæmˈpuː/ *n* **1** [C,U] liquid soap used for washing the hair; a similar liquid used for cleaning carpets, etc **2** [U] act of washing your hair using shampoo
● **shampoo** *v* [T] wash hair or carpets with shampoo

shamrock /ˈʃæmrɒk/ *n* [C, U] small plant with three leaves on each stem, the national emblem of Ireland

shandy /ˈʃændi/ *n* [C,U] drink of beer mixed with lemonade

shan't shall not → SHALL

shanty town /ˈʃænti taʊn/ *n* [C] town or part of a town where poor people live in very bad conditions

0━ **shape** /ʃeɪp/ *n* **1** [C,U] outer form or outline of sth: *a round ~* **2** [U] physical condition of sb/sth: *She's in good ~.* [IDM] **get/knock/lick sth into shape** make sth more acceptable, organized or successful **take shape** develop and become more complete ● **shape** *v* [T] **1** make sth into a particular shape: *S~ the dough into a ball.* **2** have an influence on the way that sb/sth develops [PV] **shape up** develop satisfactorily: *Our plans are shaping up well.*
► **shapeless** *adj* having no definite shape ► **shapely** *adj* (-ier, -iest) (esp of a woman's body) having an attractive curved shape

0━ **share** /ʃeə(r)/ *n* **1** [C, usu sing] part of something divided between two or more people **2** [sing] ~ (of) part that sb has in an activity that involves several people: *your ~ of the blame* **3** [C] ~ (in) one of the equal parts into which the capital of a company is divided and which people buy as a way of investing money ● **share** *v* **1** [I,T] ~ **(with)** have or use sth at the same time as sb else: *~ a house with sb* **2** [T] ~ **(out)** divide sth between two or more people **3** [I,T] have the same feelings, experiences, etc as sb else: *a view that is widely ~d*
► **shareholder** n [C] owner of shares in a company ► **share-out** n [usu sing] act of dividing sth between two or more people

shark /ʃɑːk/ *n* [C] **1** large and sometimes dangerous fish **2** (*infml*,

---

A B C D E F G H I J K L M N O P Q R **S** T U V W X Y Z

disapprov) person who is dishonest in business

shelve

0━ **sharp** /ʃɑːp/ *adj* **1** having a fine cutting edge or point: *a ~ knife* **2** sudden: *a ~ rise/fall* **3** well defined; clear: *a ~ outline* **4** (of people or their mind, eyes, etc) quick to notice things **5** critical or harsh: *~ words* **6** (of sounds) loud and high **7** causing a cutting or piercing feeling: *a ~ wind/pain* **8** (of bends, etc) changing direction suddenly **9** (of tastes) strong and slightly bitter **10** (of clothes or the way sb dresses) fashionable and new **11** (*music*) half a tone higher than the note before it **12** (*music*) above the correct pitch ● **sharp** *n* [C] (*music*) (*symb* ♯) note played half a tone higher than the note named ● **sharp** *adv* **1** exactly: *at seven o'clock* ~ **2** suddenly: *turn ~ left* **3** (*music*) above the correct pitch ▸ **sharpen** *v* [I,T] (cause sth to) become sharp ▸ **sharpener** *n* [C] tool or machine that makes things sharp ▸ **sharply** *adv* ▸ **sharpness** *n* [U]

shatter /'ʃætə(r)/ *v* **1** [I,T] (cause sth to) suddenly break into small pieces **2** [I,T] (cause sb's feelings, hopes or beliefs to) be completely destroyed: *All my illusions were ~ed.* ▸ **shattered** *adj* **1** shocked and upset **2** (*GB, infml*) very tired

0━ **shave** /ʃeɪv/ *v* **1** [I,T] cut hair off the face, etc with a razor **2** [T] cut a small amount off a price, etc [PV] **shave sth off sth** remove a thin layer from a surface ● **shave** *n* [C] act of shaving the face ▸ **shaven** /'ʃeɪvn/ *adj* with all the hair shaved off ▸ **shaver** *n* [C] electric razor ▸ **shavings** *n* [pl] thin pieces of wood which have been shaved off

shawl /ʃɔːl/ *n* [C] large piece of material worn over a woman's shoulders or head or wrapped round a baby

0━ **she** /ʃiː/ *pron* (used as the subject of a *v*) female person or animal mentioned earlier: *My sister says ~ is going.*

sheaf /ʃiːf/ *n* [C] (*pl* **sheaves** /ʃiːvz/) **1** corn, etc tied into a bundle after it has been cut **2** bundle of papers, etc tied together

shear /ʃɪə(r)/ *v* (*pt* ~**ed** *pp* **shorn** /ʃɔːn/ *or* ~**ed**) [T] cut the wool off a sheep ▸ **shears** *n* [pl] garden tool like a large pair of scissors: *a pair of* ~

sheath /ʃiːθ/ *n* [C] (*pl* ~**s** /ʃiːðz/) cover for the blade of a knife, etc

sheathe /ʃiːð/ *v* [T] (*lit*) put sth into a sheath

sheaves *plural of* SHEAF

she'd /ʃiːd/ *short for* SHE HAD; SHE WOULD

shed /ʃed/ *n* [C] small building, usu made of wood, used for storing

things, etc ● **shed** *v* (*pt, pp* **shed** *pres pt* **-dd-**) [T] **1** get rid of sth no longer wanted **2** let sth fall; drop sth: *The lorry ~ its load.* **3** send light over sth **4** (*lit*) allow liquid to pour out: ~ *tears* (= cry) ▸ '**shedload** *n* [C] ~ **(of sth)** (*GB, infml*) large amount of sth, esp money: *The project cost a ~load of money.*

0━ **sheep** /ʃiːp/ *n* [C] (*pl* **sheep**) grass-eating animal kept for food and for its wool ■ '**sheepdog** *n* [C] dog trained to look after sheep ■ '**sheepskin** *n* [U,C] the skin of a sheep with the wool still on it ▸ **sheepish** *adj* looking or feeling embarrassed because you have done sth silly

0━ **sheer** /ʃɪə(r)/ *adj* **1** used to emphasize the size, degree or amount of sth **2** complete: ~ *nonsense* **3** very steep: *a ~ drop* **4** (of cloth, etc) very thin and light ● **sheer** *adv* straight up or down

0━ **sheet** /ʃiːt/ *n* **1** piece of thin fabric used on a bed to lie on or under **2** flat thin piece of a material: *a ~ of glass/paper* **3** wide flat area of water, ice, etc ■ '**sheet music** *n* [U] music printed on single sheets

sheikh (*also* **shaikh**) /ʃeɪk; ʃiːk/ *n* [C] Arab prince or ruler

0━ **shelf** /ʃelf/ *n* [C] (*pl* **shelves** /ʃelvz/) **1** flat piece of wood, etc attached to a wall, etc for things to stand on **2** (*geol*) piece of rock like a shelf on a cliff face or underwater

she'll /ʃiːl/ *short for* SHE WILL

0━ **shell** /ʃel/ *n* [C] **1** hard outer covering of eggs, nuts and some animals, eg snails **2** metal case filled with explosives, to be fired from a large gun **3** walls or outer structure of sth, eg an empty or ruined building [IDM] **come out of your shell** become less shy, quiet, etc ● **shell** *v* **1** [I,T] fire shells at sth **2** [T] remove the shell from nuts, peas, etc [PV] **shell (sth) out (for sth)** (*infml*) pay a lot of money for sth ▸ '**shellfish** *n* [C] (*pl* **shellfish**) creature with a shell that lives in water, esp one of the types that can be eaten, eg a crab

0━ **shelter** /'ʃeltə(r)/ *n* **1** [U] fact of having a place to live or stay **2** [U] protection from rain, danger or attack **3** [C] building, etc that gives people shelter ● **shelter** *v* **1** [T] give sb/sth a place where they are protected from the weather or danger **2** [I] find a place that gives you shelter: ~ *from the rain under a tree*

shelve /ʃelv/ *v* **1** [T] delay dealing with a problem, project, etc **2** [T] put books, etc on a shelf **3** [I] (of land) slope downwards

A B C D E F G H I J K L M N O P Q R **S** T U V W X Y Z

shelves plural of SHELF

shepherd /ˈʃepəd/ (fem **shepherdess** /ˌʃepəˈdes/ old-fash) n [C] person who takes care of sheep
● **shepherd** v [T] guide sb or a group of people somewhere ■ **shepherd's 'pie** n [C, U] (GB) dish of finely chopped meat with mashed potato on top

sheriff /ˈʃerɪf/ n [C] (US) chief law officer in a county

sherry /ˈʃeri/ n [U] strong yellow or brown wine, originally from southern Spain

shied pt, pp of SHY²

0─ **shield** /ʃiːld/ n [C] **1** piece of metal, etc carried by soldiers in the past to protect the body when fighting **2** person or thing used to protect sb/ sth, esp by forming a barrier **3** drawing or model of a shield showing a coat of arms ● **shield** v [T] protect sb/sth from danger, harm or sth unpleasant

0─ **shift** /ʃɪft/ n **1** [C] ● **(in)** change in position or direction **2** [C] (period worked by a) group of workers which starts work as another group finishes: *be on the day/night ~* **3** [U] mechanism on a computer keyboard that allows capital letters, etc to be typed: *a ~ key* ● **shift** v **1** [I,T] (cause sth to) change position or direction **2** [T] (infml) remove sth: *~ a stain*

shifty /ˈʃɪfti/ adj (**-ier, -iest**) not to be trusted ▶ **shiftiness** n [U]

shimmer /ˈʃɪmə(r)/ v [I] shine with a soft light

shin /ʃɪn/ n [C] front part of the leg below the knee ● **shin** v (**-nn-**) (US **shinny**) [PV] **shin up/down sth** climb up or down sth quickly

0─ **shine** /ʃaɪn/ v (pt, pp **shone** /ʃɒn/ or, in sense 3 **~d**) **1** [I] give out or reflect light **2** [T] shine the light from a lamp, etc in a particular direction **3** [T] (infml) polish sth: *~ shoes* **4** [I] very good at sth ● **shine** n [sing] brightness that sth has when light is reflected on it ▶ **shiny** adj (**-ier, -iest**) smooth and bright

shingle /ˈʃɪŋɡl/ n [U] area of small stones on a beach ▶ **shingly** /ˈʃɪŋɡli/ adj

0─ **ship¹** /ʃɪp/ n [C] large boat that carries people or goods by sea ■ **'shipmate** n [C] sailor belonging to the same crew ■ **'shipshape** adj clean and tidy ■ **'shipwreck** n [U,C] loss or destruction of a ship at sea because of a storm, etc ■ **'shipwreck** v [T] (be shipwrecked) be left somewhere after your ship has been lost or destroyed ■ **'shipyard** n [C] place where ships are built

ship² /ʃɪp/ v (**-pp-**) [T] transport or

send sb/sth, esp by ship ▶ **shipment** n **1** [U] process of sending goods from one place to another **2** [C] load of goods shipped ▶ **shipper** n [C] person or company that arranges for goods to be shipped ▶ **shipping** n [U] all the ships of a country, port, etc

shirk /ʃɜːk/ v [I,T] try to avoid work, duty, etc, esp through laziness ▶ **shirker** n [C]

0─ **shirt** /ʃɜːt/ n [C] piece of clothing worn esp by men, for the upper part of the body, with sleeves and buttons

shirty /ˈʃɜːti/ adj (**-ier, -iest**) (GB, infml) annoyed; angry

shit /ʃɪt/ n (⚠, sl) **1** [U] solid waste matter passed from the bowels **2** [sing] act of emptying the bowels **3** [C] (disapprov) unpleasant person ● **shit** v (**-tt-** pt, pp **shat** /ʃæt/ or **shitted**) (⚠, sl) pass solid waste matter from the bowels ● **shit** exclam (⚠, sl) swear word used to show that you are angry ▶ **shitty** adj (**-ier, -iest**) (⚠, sl) unpleasant; very bad

shiver /ˈʃɪvə(r)/ v [I] ● **(with)** shake slightly, esp with cold or fear ● **shiver** n [C] act of shivering ▶ **shivery** adj

shoal /ʃəʊl/ n [C] great number of fish swimming together

0─ **shock** /ʃɒk/ n **1** [U,C] (medical condition or unpleasant feeling caused by) a sudden surprise, fear, worry, etc **2** [C] violent shaking movement, caused by an earthquake, explosion, etc **3** [C] effect caused by an electric current passing through the body ● **shock** v [T] **1** surprise and upset sb **2** offend and disgust sb ▶ **shocking** adj **1** that offends or upsets people: *~ing behaviour* **2** (infml) very bad

shod pt, pp of SHOE

shoddy /ˈʃɒdi/ adj (**-ier, -iest**) of poor quality: *~ work*

0─ **shoe** /ʃuː/ n [C] outer covering of leather, etc for the foot, which does not reach above the ankle [IDM] **be in sb's shoes** | **put yourself in sb's shoes** be in, or imagine yourself in, another person's situation ● **shoe** v (pt, pp **shod** /ʃɒd/) fit a horse with horseshoes ■ **'shoelace** n [C] material like string for fastening a shoe ■ **'shoestring** n [C] [IDM] **on a shoestring** (infml) with a very small amount of money

shone pt, pp of SHINE

shoo /ʃuː/ exclam used to tell an animal or a child to go away ● **shoo** v [T] make animals, etc go away by saying 'shoo'

shook pt of SHAKE¹

0─ **shoot** /ʃuːt/ v (pt, pp **shot** /ʃɒt/) **1** [T] aim and fire with (sth from) a gun or other weapon **2** [T] kill or wound a person or an animal in this way **3** [I,T] (cause sb/sth to) move suddenly or quickly: *Pain shot up his arm.* ◇ *He shot out his hand.* **4** [I,T] make a film or photograph of sth **5** [I] (in football, etc) try to score a goal [IDM] **shoot your mouth off (about sth)** (*infml*) talk indiscreetly about sth ▪ **shooting star** *n* [C] small meteor

shoot² /ʃuːt/ *n* [C] **1** young growth on a plant **2** occasion when sb takes professional photographs: *a fashion ~* **3** group of people shooting animals or birds for sport

0──**shop** /ʃɒp/ *n* [C] **1** (*esp GB*) (part of a) building where goods are sold **2** place where things are repaired or made, esp part of a factory [IDM] **talk shop** talk about your work ▪ **shop** *v* (*-pp-*) **1** go to the shops to buy things: *~ for presents* **2** [T] (*GB, infml*) give information about sb, esp to the police [PV] **shop around (for sth)** search carefully for goods giving the best value ▪ **shop assistant** *n* [C] person serving in a shop ▪ **shop floor** *n* [sing] area in a factory where goods are made ▪ **shopkeeper** *n* [C] owner of a (small) shop ▪ **shoplifter** *n* [C] person who steals things from shops ▶ **shoplifting** *n* [U] ▶ **shopper** *n* [C] person who buys goods from shops ▶ **shopping** *n* **1** act of shopping: *go ~ping* **2** goods bought from shops ▪ **shopping mall** (*esp US*) large group of shops built together under one roof and closed to traffic ▪ **shop steward** *n* [C] official of a branch of a trade union elected by the workers

0──**shore** /ʃɔː(r)/ *n* [C] land along the edge of the sea or a lake ▪ **shore** *v* [PV] **shore sth up** support part of a building, etc with large pieces of wood or metal

shorn *pp of* SHEAR

0──**short¹** /ʃɔːt/ *adj* **1** measuring or covering a small length or distance: *He had ~ hair.* **2** (of a person) small in height **3** lasting or taking a small amount of time: *the ~est day of the year* **4 ~ (of)** not having enough of sth; lacking sth: *~ of money* **5 ~ on** (*infml*) lacking in a certain quality: *~ on tact* **6 ~ (of)** less than the number, amount or distance mentioned: *five miles ~ of our destination* **7 ~ (with)** (of a person) rude to sb: *I was a little ~ with her.* [IDM] **for short** as an abbreviation in short briefly in the short term → TERM **little/nothing short of sth** almost sth ▪ **shortbread** *n* [U] crumbly biscuit made with a lot of butter ▪ **short-change** *v* [T] cheat sb, esp by giving them too little change ▪ **short circuit** *n* [C] electrical fault causing current to flow the wrong way ▪ **short-circuit**

v [I,T] (cause sth to) have a short circuit ▪ **shortcoming** *n* [C] (usu pl) fault in sb's character, a plan, system, etc ▪ **short cut** (*also* **short cut**) **1** route taken to shorten a journey, etc **2** way of doing sth more quickly, efficiently, etc ▪ **shortfall** *n* [C] amount of sth that is less than is needed ▪ **shorthand** *n* [U] system of writing quickly using special symbols ▪ **short-handed** *adj* not having enough workers, helpers, etc ▪ **shortlist** *n* [usu sing] list of candidates, eg for a job, selected from a larger group, from which the final choice is to be made ▶ **shortlist** *v* [T] ▪ **short-lived** *adj* lasting only for a short time ▪ **shortness** *n* [U] ▪ **short sight** *n* [U] inability to see distant objects clearly ▪ **short-sighted** *adj* **1** unable to see distant objects clearly **2** not thinking about the possible future effects of sth ▪ **short-tempered** *adj* easily annoyed ▪ **short-term** *adj* of or for a short period of time ▪ **short wave** *n* [U] (*abbr* **SW**) radio wave with a wavelength of less than 100 metres

short² /ʃɔːt/ *adv* before the agreed or natural time: *a career tragically cut ~ by illness* [IDM] **go short (of)** not have enough of sth **short of (doing) sth** without (doing); unless sth happens: *do anything ~ of murder*

short³ /ʃɔːt/ *n* [C] **1** small strong alcoholic drink **2** short films **3 =** SHORT CIRCUIT (SHORT¹)

shortage /ˈʃɔːtɪdʒ/ *n* [C, U] lack of sth; state of not having enough of sth

shorten /ˈʃɔːtn/ *v* [I,T] (cause sth to) become shorter: *~ a dress*

0──**shortly** /ˈʃɔːtli/ *adv* **1** soon: *We'll leave ~.* **2** in an angry impatient way: *speak ~ to sb*

0──**shot¹** /ʃɒt/ *n* [C] **1 ~ (at)** act of firing a gun, etc; sound of this **2** person who shoots a gun well, badly, etc: *a good/bad ~* **3** remark, etc aimed against sb/sth that you are arguing with or competing with **4** (*infml*) attempt; try: *have a ~ at solving the problem* **5** throw, kick, stroke, etc of the ball in certain sports: *a ~ at goal* **6** photograph; scene in a film **7** (*infml*) small injection of a drug, etc: *a ~ of morphine* [IDM] **like a shot** very quickly **a shot in the arm** something that gives fresh energy to sb/sth **a shot in the dark** answer, etc that is risked in the hope that it may be right **not by a long shot** → LONG¹ ▪ **shotgun** *n* [C] long gun used esp for shooting birds and animals ▪ **the shot-put** *n* [sing] (*also* **shot-putting**) contest in which athletes throw a heavy metal ball as far as possible

should

0⟶ **should¹** /ʃəd; strong form ʃʊd/ **modal v** (neg **should not** short form **shouldn't** /ˈʃʊdnt/) **1** used to show what is right, appropriate, etc, esp when criticizing sb: *You ~ have been more careful.* **2** used to give or ask for advice: *S ~ I apologize to him?* **3** used to say you expect sth is true or will happen: *We ~ arrive before dark.* **4** used to say that sth expected has not happened: *He ~ be here by now.* **5** (GB, fml) used after *I* or *we* instead of *would* to say what you would do if sth else happened first **6** (fml) used to refer to a possible event or situation: *If she ~ come back, please tell me.* **7** used in a *that* clause after certain *adjs*: *I'm anxious that we ~ allow plenty of time.* **8** (GB) used to make polite requests: *I ~ like to make a phone call, please.* **9** used with question words to express lack of interest, disbelief, etc: *How ~ I know?*

should² *pt of* SHALL

0⟶ **shoulder** /ˈʃəʊldə(r)/ *n* [C] **1** either of the two parts of the body between the top of each arm and the neck **2** part of a piece of clothing which covers the shoulder **3** part of sth, eg a bottle or mountain, shaped like a shoulder **[IDM]** **shoulder to shoulder (with sb)** **1** side by side **2** working, fighting, etc together ● **shoulder v** [T] **1** accept the responsibility for sth: *~ the responsibility/blame for sth* **2** push sb/sth out of your way with your shoulder: *~ sb aside* **3** carry sth on the shoulder ■ **'shoulder blade** *n* [C] either of the flat bones of the upper back

shouldn't *short for* SHOULD NOT

0⟶ **shout** /ʃaʊt/ *n* [C] loud cry of anger, fear, etc ● **shout v** [I,T] say sth in a loud voice; speak angrily to sb: *Don't ~ at me!* ◊ *~ (out)* orders **[PV]** **shout sb down** shout in order to prevent sb being heard ■ **shouting** *n* [U] shouts

0⟶ **shove** /ʃʌv/ *v* [I,T] push sb/sth roughly **[PV]** **shove up** (GB, spoken) move in order to make a space for sb to sit down: *S~ up so I can sit down.* ● **shove** *n* [usu sing] strong push

shovel /ˈʃʌvl/ *n* [C] tool like a spade, used for moving earth, stones, coal, etc ● **shovel v** (-ll-, US -l-) [T] **1** lift or move sth with a shovel

0⟶ **show¹** /ʃəʊ/ *v* (pt **-ed**; pp **-n** /ʃəʊn/) **1** [T] make sth clear; prove sth: *The figures ~ that her claims are false.* **2** [T] let sb see sth: *~ your ticket at the gate* **3** [T] help sb to do sth by letting them watch you do it. *She ~ed me how to do it.* **4** [T] point to sth: *S~ me which one you want.* **5** [T] lead or guide sb to a place: *S~ her in.* **6** [T] make it clear that you have a particular quality:

She ~ed great courage. **7** [T] behave in a particular way towards sb: *He ~ed me great kindness.* **8** [I,T] be visible; allow sth to be seen: *Black doesn't ~ the dirt.* **[IDM]** **it goes to show** used to say that sth proves sth **show your face** appear among friends or in public **show your hand/cards** reveal your intentions **[PV]** **show off** (infml, disapprov) try to impress people with your wealth, ability, etc **show up** (infml) arrive: *All the guests ~ed up.* **show (sth) up** (cause sth to) become visible: *The lines ~ed up in the light.* ► **showing** *n* **1** [C] act of showing a film **2** [usu sing] performance: *the company's poor ~ing* ■ **show-off** *n* [C] (infml, disapprov) person who tries to impress people with his/her wealth, ability, etc

0⟶ **show²** /ʃəʊ/ *n* **1** [C] theatre performance, esp one containing singing and dancing **2** [C] programme on television or the radio **3** [C,U] collection of things for public display: *a fashion ~* ◊ *The latest computers will be on ~ at the exhibition.* **4** [C] action or behaviour that shows how you feel: *a ~ of emotion* **5** [U, sing] insincere act: *Her grief is all ~.* ◊ *She does it for ~.* **6** [U] colourful or pleasing sight: *all the ~ of the circus* **7** [C, usu sing] (infml) effort: *put up a good ~* **[IDM]** **a show of hands** raising of hands to vote for or against sth ■ **show business** *n* [U] business of entertaining the public ■ **'showdown** *n* [C] argument, fight, etc that will settle a disagreement ■ **'showjumping** *n* [U] sport of riding a horse and jumping over fences as quickly as possible ■ **'showroom** *n* [C] large shop where goods, esp cars or electrical goods, are put on display ► **showy** *adj* (**-ier, -iest**) intended to attract attention

0⟶ **shower** /ˈʃaʊə(r)/ *n* [C] **1** (room or part of a room containing a) device that sprays water from above for people to wash under **2** act of washing yourself with a shower: *(esp GB) have a ~* ◊ *(esp US) take a ~* **3** short period of rain **4** fall of a large number of things: *a ~ of stones* ● **shower v** **1** [I] wash yourself under a shower **2** [I,T] *~ (with, down, on)* (cause sth to) fall onto sb/sth, esp in a lot of small pieces **3** [T] *~ (with, on)* give a lot of sth to sb: *~ sb with presents* ► **showery** *adj* (of the weather) with frequent showers of rain

shown *pp of* SHOW¹

shrank *pt of* SHRINK

shrapnel /ˈʃræpnəl/ *n* [U] pieces of metal from an exploding bomb

shred /ʃred/ *n* [C] **1** [usu pl] small thin piece torn or cut from sth **2** [usu sing] *~ of* very small amount of sth: *not one ~ of proof* ● **shred v** (-dd-) [T]

cut or tear sth into small pieces
● **'shredder** n [C] machine that tears paper into pieces so that nobody can read what was printed on it

shrewd /ʃruːd/ adj having or showing sound judgement and common sense: a ~ guess ▶ **shrewdly** adv

shriek /ʃriːk/ v **1** [I] give a loud high shout, eg because you are excited **2** [T] say sth in a loud high voice ● **shriek** n [C] loud high shout: a ~ of pain/delight

shrill /ʃrɪl/ adj (of sounds or voices) unpleasantly high and loud ▶ **shrillness** n [U]

shrimp /ʃrɪmp/ n [C] **1** small shellfish, pink when boiled **2** (US) = PRAWN

shrine /ʃraɪn/ n [C] **1** place where people come to worship because it is connected with a holy person or an event **2** any place associated with a deeply respected person, activity, etc

shrink /ʃrɪŋk/ v (pt shrank /ʃræŋk/ or shrunk /ʃrʌŋk/ pp shrunk) **1** [I,T] (cause sth to) become smaller: My shorts shrank in the wash. **2** [I] move back or away from sth out of fear or disgust **[PV] shrink from sth** be unwilling to do sth ▶ **shrinkage** /-ɪdʒ/ n [U] process or amount of shrinking ● **shrunken** /ˈʃrʌŋkən/ adj that has become smaller (and less attractive)

shrivel /ˈʃrɪvl/ v (-ll-, US -l-) [I,T] ~ (up) (cause sth to) become dry and wrinkled from heat, cold or old age

shroud /ʃraʊd/ n [C] **1** cloth wrapped round a dead body **2** thing that covers and hides sth: a ~ of mist ● **shroud** v [T] (usu passive) cover or hide sth: be ~ed in mystery

shrub /ʃrʌb/ n [C] plant with a woody stem, lower than a tree ▶ **shrubbery** n [C,U] (pl -ies) area planted with shrubs

shrug /ʃrʌɡ/ v (-gg-) [I,T] lift your shoulders slightly to express doubt, etc **[PV] shrug sth off** treat sth as unimportant ▶ **shrug** n [usu sing]

shrunk pt, pp of SHRINK

shrunken → SHRINK

shudder /ˈʃʌdə(r)/ v [I] shake with fear, disgust, etc ● **shudder** n [usu sing] strong shaking movement

shuffle /ˈʃʌfl/ v **1** [I] walk without lifting your feet properly **2** [I] move from one foot to another because of embarrassment, etc **3** [T] mix up playing cards to change their order **4** [T] move things into a different position or order ● **shuffle** n [usu sing] **1** slow shuffling walk **2** act of mixing playing cards before a game

shun /ʃʌn/ v (-nn-) (written) avoid sb/sth

shunt /ʃʌnt/ v **1** [I,T] move trains, etc from one track to another **2** [T]

(disapprov) move sb/sth to a different place

shush /ʃʊʃ/ exclam used to tell sb to be quiet

0━ **shut** /ʃʌt/ v (-tt- pt, pp shut) [I,T] **1** (cause sth to) become closed: ~ a book ◇ The window won't ~. **2** (GB) (cause a shop, etc to) stop being open for business: What time does the baker's ~? **[IDM] shut your eyes to sth** deliberately ignore sth **shut up shop** close a business; stop trading, etc **[PV] shut (sth) down** (cause a factory, etc to) stop working **shut sth off** stop the supply of gas, water, etc **shut sb/sth off from sth** separate sb/sth from sth **shut sb up** close a room, house, etc **shut (sb) up** (infml) (cause sb to) stop talking ● **'shutdown** n [C] act of closing a factory, business or switching off a large machine

shutter /ˈʃʌtə(r)/ n [C] **1** wooden or metal cover for a window **2** part of a camera that opens to let light pass through the lens ▶ **shuttered** adj with shutters closed

shuttle /ˈʃʌtl/ n [C] **1** aircraft, bus, etc that travels regularly between two places **2** device for carrying thread in a sewing machine, etc ● **shuttle** v [I] travel between two places frequently **1** [T] carry people between two places, making regular journeys backwards and forwards ■ **'shuttlecock** n [C] cork with feathers in it, used in badminton

0━ **shy** [1] /ʃaɪ/ adj **1** (of people) nervous or embarrassed about meeting others **2** (of animals) easily frightened ▶ **shyly** adv ▶ **shyness** n [U]

shy [2] /ʃaɪ/ v (pt, pp shied /ʃaɪd/) [I] (esp of a horse) turn away suddenly in fear **[PV] shy away (from sth)** avoid doing sth because you are frightened

Siamese twin /ˌsaɪəmiːz 'twɪn/ n [C] one of two people born with their bodies joined together

sibilant /ˈsɪbɪlənt/ adj (lit) making an 's' or a 'sh' sound

sibling /ˈsɪblɪŋ/ n [C] (fml) brother or sister

0━ **sick** /sɪk/ adj **1** ill: care for ~ people in hospital **2** likely to vomit: feel ~ **3** ~ of (infml) bored with or annoyed about sth that has been happening for a long time: I'm ~ and tired of his lies. **4** (infml) (esp of humour) cruel or offensive: ~ jokes **[IDM] be worried sick | be sick with worry** be very worried ● **sick** n **1** [U] (GB) vomit **2** (the sick) [pl] people who are ill ■ **sick leave** n [U] permission to be absent from work, etc because of illness

A B C D E F G H I J K L M N O P Q R **S** T U V W X Y Z

sicken /'sɪkən/ v 1 [T] make sb feel disgusted: *Violence ~s him.* 2 [I] ~ (for) begin to be ill ▸ **sickening** *adj* disgusting

sickle /'sɪkl/ n [C] short tool with a curved blade for cutting grass

sickly /'sɪkli/ *adj* (-ier, -iest) 1 often ill 2 looking ill: *a ~ complexion* 3 making you feel sick: *a ~ sweet smell*

sickness /'sɪknəs/ n 1 [C,U] (type of) illness or disease 2 [U] feeling that you are going to vomit; the fact of vomiting

0—w **side**[1] /saɪd/ n [C] 1 either of the two halves of a surface, an object or an area: *the left-hand ~ of the road* 2 any flat surface that is not the top, bottom, front or back 3 part of sth near the edge and away from the middle: *parked on the ~ of the road* 4 left or right part of a body: *a pain in your ~* 5 either surface of a piece of paper, etc 6 either of two opposing groups of people in games, war, etc 7 one of the opinions held by sb in an argument, a business arrangement, etc 8 aspect of sth: *study all ~s of a question* [IDM] **get on the right/wrong side of sb** please/displease sb **on/from all sides** in/from all directions **on the big, small, etc side** slightly too big, small, etc **on/to one side** 1 out of your way 2 to be dealt with later **side by side** close together **take sides** support sb in a dispute ■ **sideboard** n [C] cupboard with drawers for holding plates, etc ■ **sideburns** (GB also 'sideboards') n [pl] hair that grows down the sides of a man's face in front of the ears ■ **side effect** n [C] indirect, usu bad effect of a drug ■ **sidelight** n [C] either of a pair of two small lights at the front of a car ■ **sideline** n 1 job that is not your main occupation 2 (sidelines) [pl] lines forming the edge of a sports field ■ **sidelong** *adj* to or from the side: *a ~ glance* ■ **side road** n [C] minor road ■ **sidestep** v (-pp-) 1 [T] avoid answering a question 2 [I,T] avoid a blow, etc by stepping to one side ■ **sidetrack** v [T] turn sb's attention away from more important matters ■ **sidewalk** n (US) = PAVEMENT ■ **sideways** *adv* to, towards or from the side

side[2] /saɪd/ v [PV] **side with sb (against sb/sth)** support one person or group in an argument against sb else

siding /'saɪdɪŋ/ n [C] short railway track off the main lines

siege /siːdʒ/ n [C,U] (act of) surrounding a city, etc with armed forces to capture it [IDM] **lay siege to sth** begin a siege of a town, building, etc

sieve /sɪv/ n [C] frame with wire netting through which flour, etc is passed to separate coarse grains from fine grains ● **sieve** v [T] put sth through a sieve

sift /sɪft/ v 1 [T] put flour or some other fine substance through a sieve 2 [T] examine sth very carefully: ~ *(through) the evidence*

sigh /saɪ/ v 1 [I] take a deep breath, expressing sadness, tiredness, relief, etc 2 [T] say sth with a sigh ● **sigh** n [C] act or sound of sighing

0—w **sight**[1] /saɪt/ n 1 [U] ability to see 2 [U] act of seeing sth/sb: *I faint at the ~ of blood.* ◇ *The soldiers have orders to shoot on ~* (= as soon as they see sb). 3 [U] range within which sb/sth can be seen: *They're in ~* (= will happen soon). ◇ *Keep out of ~.* 4 [C] thing seen or worth seeing 5 (sights) [pl] famous buildings, etc of a place: *the ~s of London* 6 [C] device that helps you aim a gun, etc 7 (a sight) [sing] (*infml*) person or thing that looks ridiculous, dirty, etc [IDM] **at/on sight** as soon as sb/sth is seen **in sight** 1 able to be seen 2 near: *The end of the war is in ~.* **a sight for sore eyes** (*spoken*) something very pleasing to see ● **sight** v [T] (*written*) suddenly see sth, esp sth you have been looking for ▸ **sighted** *adj* able to see; not blind ▸ **sighting** n [C] instance of sb/sth being seen ■ **sightseeing** n [U] activity of visiting interesting buildings, etc as a tourist

0—w **sign**[1] /saɪn/ n [C] 1 thing that shows that sb/sth exists or is present: *Headaches may be a ~ of stress.* 2 notice, board, etc that gives a warning, directions, advertises a business, etc: *A road ~* 3 movement of the hand, head, etc to tell sb sth 4 mark or symbol used to represent sth [IDM] **a sign of the times** event, etc typical of its period ● **sign** v [I,T] 1 write your name on a document, letter, etc 2 use sign language to communicate with sb [PV] **sign sth away** give away property, etc by signing a document **sign off** 1 end a letter 2 end a broadcast **sign on** (GB) 1 officially register as unemployed **sign (sb) on/up** (cause sb to) sign an agreement to work for sb ■ **sign language** n [U,C] system of communicating with people who cannot hear, using the hands ■ **signpost** n [C] sign at the side of a road giving information about the direction of places

0—w **signal** /'sɪɡnəl/ n [C] 1 movement or sound that gives sb information, instructions, a warning, etc: *A red light is a danger~.* 2 event, action, etc that shows that sth exists or is likely to happen: *Chest pains can be a warning ~ of heart problems.* 3 device which gives information to train drivers **4** message sent or received by radio waves ● signal v (-ll-, US -l-) **1** [I,T] make a movement or sound to give sb a message, an order, etc **2** [T] be a sign that sth exists or is likely to happen ■ signal box n [C] building beside a railway, from which rail signals are operated

signatory /'sɪgnətri/ n [C] (pl -ies) person, country, etc that has signed an agreement

O─w signature /'sɪgnətʃə(r)/ n [C] person's name as they usu write it, eg at the end of a letter ■ signature tune n [C] short tune that introduces a broadcast or performer

significance /sɪg'nɪfɪkəns/ n [U] meaning; importance

O─w significant /sɪg'nɪfɪkənt/ adj **1** having a special meaning; important **2** full of meaning: a ~ look ▶ significantly adv

signify /'sɪgnɪfaɪ/ v (pt, pp -ied) **1** [T] be a sign of sth; mean sth **2** [T] make your intentions, views, etc known **3** [I] (fml) be of importance; matter

Sikh /siːk/ n [C] person whose religion is Sikhism ● Sikh adj of the Sikhs ▶ Sikhism /'siːkɪzəm/ n [U] religion that developed in Punjab in the late 15th century and is based on a belief that there is only one God

O─w silence /'saɪləns/ n [U,C] **1** complete lack of noise or sound **2** period of not speaking or answering questions: They finished their meal in total ~. ● silence v [T] make sb/sth silent ▶ silencer n [C] device for reducing the noise that a vehicle or gun makes

O─w silent /'saɪlənt/ adj **1** (of a person) saying little or nothing **2** making little or no sound; where there is little or no sound **3** (of a letter in a word) written but not pronounced ▶ silently adv

silhouette /ˌsɪlu'et/ n [C] dark outline of sb/sth against a lighter background ● silhouette v [T] (usu passive) make sth appear as a silhouette: trees ~d against the sky

silicon /'sɪlɪkən/ n [U] (symb Si) chemical element found in rocks and sand, used in making glass and transistors ■ silicon 'chip n [C] very small piece of silicon used to carry a complicated electronic circuit

O─w silk /sɪlk/ n [U] (material made from) fine, soft thread produced by silkworms ▶ silken adj soft, smooth and shiny like silk ■ silkworm n [C] caterpillar (= creature like a worm) that produces silk thread ▶ silky adj (-ier, -iest) soft, shiny and smooth like silk

sill /sɪl/ n [C] flat shelf at the base of a window

O─w silly /'sɪli/ adj (-ier, -iest) showing a lack of thought or good sense; foolish ▶ silliness n [U]

silt /sɪlt/ n [U] sand, mud, etc left behind by moving water ● silt v(PV) silt (sth) up (cause sth to) become blocked with silt

O─w silver /'sɪlvə(r)/ n [U] **1** (symb Ag) shiny white precious metal **2** articles, coins, etc of silver **3** the colour of silver ● silver adj made of or looking like silver ■ silver 'jubilee n [C] 25th anniversary of an important event ■ silver 'medal n [C] medal given to the person who wins the second place in a competition ■ silver-'plated adj (of spoons, dishes, etc) covered with a thin layer of silver ■ silversmith n [C] person who makes or sells silver articles ■ silver 'wedding n [C] 25th anniversary of a wedding ▶ silvery adj like silver

O─w similar /'sɪmələ(r)/ adj ~ (to) like sb/sth but not exactly the same ▶ similarly adv

similarity /ˌsɪmə'lærəti/ n (pl -ies) **1** [U,sing] state of being like sb/sth but not exactly the same **2** [C] similar feature, characteristic, etc

simile /'sɪməli/ n [C,U] (tech) word or phrase that compares sth to sth else, eg as white as snow

simmer /'sɪmə(r)/ v [I,T] (cause sth to) boil gently **2** [I] ~ with be almost unable to control an emotion: ~ing with anger [PV] simmer down become calm after being angry

O─w simple /'sɪmpl/ adj **1** easily understood; not difficult: a ~ problem **2** plain: ~ food **3** consisting of only a few parts; not complicated in structure: ~ forms of life **4** (of a person) ordinary; not special: a ~ country girl **5** (of a person) not very intelligent; not mentally normal **6** (gram) used to describe the present or past tense of a verb that is formed without an auxiliary verb, eg I love him. ▶ simply adv **1** used to emphasize how easy or basic sth is: Simply add hot water and stir. **2** absolutely **3** in a way that is natural and plain

simplicity /sɪm'plɪsəti/ n [U] quality of being easy to understand or use [IDM] be simplicity itself be very simple

simplify /'sɪmplɪfaɪ/ v (pt, pp -ied) [T] make sth easier to do or understand ▶ simplification /-fɪ'keɪʃn/ n [C,U]

O─w simulate /'sɪmjuleɪt/ v **1** pretend to have a particular feeling: ~ interest **2** create particular conditions that exist in real life for training or study purposes ▶ simulation n [C,U]

simultaneous /ˌsɪmlˈteɪniəs/ *adj* happening or done at the same time ▸ **simultaneously** *adv*

sin /sɪn/ *n* **1** [C] offence against God's laws **2** [U] act of breaking a religious or moral law ● **sin** *v* (**-nn-**) [I] commit a sin; do wrong ▸ **sinful** /-fl/ *adj* morally wrong or wicked ▸ **sinfulness** *n* [U] ▸ **sinner** *n* [C] person who has committed a sin

⊶ **since** /sɪns/ *prep* (with perfect tenses) from a stated time in the past until a later past time, or until now: *I haven't seen him ~ Tuesday.* ● **since** *conj* **1** from the time when: *It's twenty years ~ I've seen her.* **2** because; as: *S~ I have no money, I can't buy it.* ● **since** *adv* (with perfect tenses) from a stated time in the past onwards: *I met her last summer and haven't seen her ~.*

⊶ **sincere** /sɪnˈsɪə(r)/ *adj* **1** (of feelings, etc) genuine: *~ friendship* **2** (of people) not deceiving others; honest ▸ **sincerely** *adv* ▸ **sincerity** /sɪnˈserəti/ *n* [U]

sinew /ˈsɪnjuː/ *n* [C, U] strong band of tissue that joins a muscle to a bone ▸ **sinewy** *adj* muscular; tough

⊶ **sing** /sɪŋ/ *v* (*pt* **sang** /sæŋ/ *pp* **sung** /sʌŋ/) **1** [I, T] make musical sounds with your voice in the form of a song or tune **2** [I] make a high ringing sound ● **singer** *n* [C] ▸ **singing** *n* [U]

singe /sɪndʒ/ *v* [I, T] (cause the surface of sth to) be blackened by burning ▸ **singe** *n* [C] slight burn on cloth, etc

⊶ **single** /ˈsɪŋɡl/ *adj* **1** only one: *a ~ apple* **2** (of a person) not married **3** for the use of one person: *a ~ bed* **4** (GB) (of a ticket) for a journey to a place but not back again [IDM] (**in**) **single file** (in) one line, one behind the other ● **single** *n* **1** [C] (GB) ticket allowing travel to a place but not back again **2** [C] tape, CD, etc with only one song on each side **3** (**singles**) [U] (esp in tennis) game with one person on each side ● **single** *v* [PV] **single sb/sth out** (**for sth/as sb/sth**) choose sb/sth from a group for special attention ■ **single-handed** *adj, adv* (done) by one person without help ■ **single-minded** *adj* giving all your attention, energy, etc to one aim ■ **single 'parent** *n* [C] parent caring for a child on their own ▸ **singly** /ˈsɪŋɡli/ *adv* one at a time

sing-song /ˈsɪŋsɒŋ/ *n* **1** [C] informal occasion at which people sing songs together **2** [sing] way of speaking with a rising and falling rhythm

singular /ˈsɪŋɡjələ(r)/ *adj* **1** (*gram*) referring to one person: *a ~ verb* **2** (*fml*) very great or obvious **3** (*lit*) unusual; strange ● **singular** *n* [C]

(*gram*) form of a noun or verb that refers to one person or thing ▸ **singularly** *adv* (*fml*) very; in an unusual way

sinister /ˈsɪnɪstə(r)/ *adj* suggesting evil or danger ● **place**

⊶ **sink** /sɪŋk/ *v* (*pt* **sank** /sæŋk/ *pp* **sunk** /sʌŋk/) **1** [I] go down below the surface or towards the bottom of a liquid or sth soft **2** [T] damage a boat or ship so that it goes below the surface of the sea, etc **3** [I] move slowly downwards: *She sank to the ground.* ◊ *The building is ~ing.* **4** [I] decrease in value, strength, etc **5** [T] make a deep hole in the ground: *~ a well* [PV] **sink in/into sth 1** (of liquids) go down into another substance **sink sth into sth** invest a lot of money in sth ● **sink** *n* [C] large open container in a kitchen with taps, used for washing the dishes in

sinuous /ˈsɪnjuəs/ *adj* curving; twisting

sinus /ˈsaɪnəs/ *n* [C] hollow space in the bones of the head behind the nose

sip /sɪp/ *v* (**-pp-**) [I, T] drink sth, taking a very small amount each time ● **sip** *n* [C] very small amount of a drink that you take into your mouth

siphon (*also* **syphon**) /ˈsaɪfn/ *n* [C] tube used for moving liquid from one container to another, using pressure from the atmosphere ● **siphon** *v* [T] **1** move a liquid from one container to another using a siphon **2** (*infml*) remove money from one place to another, esp illegally

⊶ **sir** /sɜː(r)/ *n* [C] **1** (*fml*) used as a polite way of addressing a man: *Can I help you, ~?* **2** (**Dear Sir/Sirs**) used at the beginning of a formal business letter **3** (**Sir**) used before the name of a knight or baronet

sire /ˈsaɪə(r)/ *n* [C] (*tech*) male parent of an animal, esp a horse ● **sire** *v* [T] be the male parent of an animal, esp a horse

siren /ˈsaɪrən/ *n* [C] device for producing a loud noise as a signal or warning: *an ambulance ~*

sirloin /ˈsɜːlɔɪn/ (*also* **sirloin steak**) *n* [C, U] good quality beef that is cut from a cow's back

⊶ **sister** /ˈsɪstə(r)/ *n* [C] **1** girl or woman who has the same mother and father as another person **2** (**Sister**) (GB) senior hospital nurse **3** (**Sister**) female member of a religious group, esp a nun ● **sister** ▸ fellow woman ▸ **sisterhood** *n* **1** [U] close relationship between women with shared ideas and aims **2** [C, with sing or pl verb] group of women living together in a religious community ▸ **sisterly** *adj* of or like a sister

A B C D E F G H I J K L M N O P Q R **S** T U V W X Y Z

sit /sɪt/ v (-tt- pt, pp **sat** /sæt/) **1** [I] rest your weight on your bottom with your back upright **2** [T] put sb in a sitting position: *She sat the child on the chair.* **3** [I] (of objects) be in a particular place: *The box sat unopened on a shelf.* **4** [I] have an official position as sth or as a member of sth: *She ~s on several committees.* **5** [I] (of a parliament, law court, etc) meet in order to do official business **6** [I] (*GB*) do an exam [IDM] **sit on the fence** avoid becoming involved in deciding or influencing sth **sit tight 1** stay where you are **2** refuse to take action, etc [PV] **sit about/around** spend time doing nothing very useful **sit back** relax and do nothing: *~ back and watch television* **sit for sb/sth** be a model for an artist or a photographer **sit in** occupy a building, etc as a protest **sit in on sth** attend a class, discussion, etc as an observer **sit on sth** (*infml*) have received a letter, report, etc from sb and then not replied or taken any action concerning it **sit up 1** not go to bed until later than usual **2** (cause sb to) take a sitting position ▪ **'sit-in** n [C] act of occupying a building, etc as a protest

sitcom /'sɪtkɒm/ n [C,U] regular programme on television that shows the same characters in different amusing situations

O—**site** /saɪt/ n [C] **1** place where a building, etc is or will be situated **2** place where sth happened or that is used for sth: *a caravan ~* **3** (*computing*) place on the Internet where a company, an organization, etc puts information ● **site** v [T] build or position sth in a particular place

sitting /'sɪtɪŋ/ n [C] **1** time during which a parliament or law court meets **2** time when a meal is served in a hotel, etc to a group of people at the same time **3** act of posing for a portrait or photograph [IDM] **sitting duck** person or thing that is easy to attack ▪ **'sitting room** n [C] (*GB*) room in a house where people sit together, watch TV, etc

situate /'sɪtʃueɪt/ v [T] (*fml*) build sth in a particular position ▶ **situated** *adj* **1** in a particular place or position: *The hotel is beautifully ~d in a quiet spot near the river.* **2** (*fml*) (of a person, an organization, etc) in the stated circumstances

O—**situation** /ˌsɪtʃu'eɪʃn/ n [C] **1** all the circumstances and things happening at a certain time and in a certain place **2** (*written*) position of a town, building, etc **3** (*old-fash*) job ▪ **situation 'comedy** = SITCOM

O—**six** /sɪks/ *number* 6 [IDM] **at sixes and sevens** (*infml*) in confusion

▶ **sixth** /sɪksθ/ *ordinal number, n* [C] 6th; the fraction ⅙; each of six equal parts of sth

O—**sixteen** /ˌsɪks'tiːn/ *number* 16
▶ **sixteenth** /ˌsɪks'tiːnθ/ *ordinal number*

O—**sixty** /'sɪksti/ **1** *number* 60 **2** (**the sixties**) n [pl] numbers, years or temperatures from 60 to 69
▶ **sixtieth** /'sɪkstiəθ/ *ordinal number*

O—**size** /saɪz/ n [U,C] how large a person or thing is **2** [C] standard measurement of clothes, shoes, etc: *~ five shoes* ● **size** v [T] mark the size of sth [PV] **size sb/sth up** (*infml*) form a judgement of sb/sth ▶ **sizeable** /-əbl/ *adj* fairly large

sizzle /'sɪzl/ v [I], n (make the) hissing sound of sth cooking in fat

skate /skeɪt/ n [C] **1** boot with a steel blade attached to the bottom of it for moving over ice = ICE SKATE (ICE[1]) **2** = ROLLER SKATE (ROLLER (ICE[1]) [IDM] **get/put your skates on** (*infml*) hurry up ● **skate** v [I] move on skates [IDM] **be skating on thin ice** be taking a risk [PV] **skate over/round sth** avoid talking about sth directly ▶ **skater** n [C] ▪ **'skateboard** n [C] short, narrow board with small wheels at each end, for standing and riding on for fun ● **skater** n [C]

skeleton /'skelɪtn/ n [C] **1** structure of bones that supports the body **2** main structure that supports a building, etc **3** basic outline of a plan, etc **4** smallest number of people needed to provide a service, etc: *a ~ staff* [IDM] **a skeleton in the cupboard** secret which you are ashamed of ▪ **'skeleton key** n [C] key that opens several different locks

skeptic, skeptical, skepticism (*US*) = SCEPTIC, SCEPTICAL, SCEPTICISM

sketch /sketʃ/ n [C] **1** simple drawing that is done quickly and without detail **2** short funny scene on television, in the theatre, etc **3** short description of sth ● **sketch** v [I,T] **1** make a quick drawing of sb/sth **2** give a general description of sth ▶ **sketchy** *adj* (*-ier, -iest*) not done thoroughly; lacking detail

skewer /'skjuːə(r)/ n [C] pointed wood or metal pin for holding meat, vegetables, etc together during cooking ● **skewer** v [T] push a skewer into sth

O—**ski** /skiː/ n [C] long narrow strip of wood, etc attached to special boots for moving over snow ● **ski** v (pt, pp **skied** *pres pt* **~ing**) [I] move over snow on skis, esp as a sport: *go ~ing* ▶ **skier** n [C]

skid /skɪd/ n [C] uncontrollable sideways sliding movement of a vehicle on ice ● **skid** v (-dd-) [I] (usu of a vehicle) move sideways or forwards in an uncontrollable way

skies plural of SKY

0⃞ **skilful** (US **skillful**) /ˈskɪlfl/ adj good at sth, esp sth that requires special ability: a ~ player ▸ **skilfully** adv

0⃞ **skill** /skɪl/ n [C, U] ability to do sth well ▸ **skilled** adj ~ (in/at) **1** having enough ability, experience, etc to be able to do sth well **2** (of a job) needing special abilities or training: ~ed work

skim /skɪm/ v (-mm-) **1** [T] remove fat, cream, etc from the surface of a liquid **2** [I, T] move lightly over a surface, barely touching it **3** [I, T] ~ **(through)** read sth quickly

0⃞ **skin** /skɪn/ n **1** [C, U] layer of tissue that covers the body **2** [C, U] skin of a dead animal, used for making leather, etc **3** [C, U] outer layer of some fruit and vegetables **4** [C, U] thin layer that forms on the surface of some liquids, eg boiled milk [IDM] **by the skin of your teeth** by a narrow margin **get under sb's skin** (infml) annoy sb **it's no skin off my, your, his, etc nose** (infml) it does not matter to me, you, him, etc **make your skin crawl** make you feel afraid or disgusted **(nothing but/all/only) skin and bone** (infml) extremely thin ● **skin** v [T] (-nn-) take the skin off an animal, a fruit or a vegetable ■ **skin-deep** adj (of a feeling, etc) not deep or lasting ■ **skinflint** n [C] (disapprov) person who does not like spending money ■ **skinhead** n [C] young person with very short hair, esp one who is violent ■ **skin-tight** adj (of clothing) fitting very closely to the body ■ **skinny** adj (-ier, -iest) (disapprov) very thin

skint /skɪnt/ adj (GB, infml) having no money

skip /skɪp/ v (-pp-) **1** [I] move forwards lightly and quickly making a little jump with each step **2** [I] jump over a rope swung under your feet as you jump **3** [T] not do sth that you usu do or should do: to ~ lunch/a class **4** [T] leave out sth that would normally be the next thing you would do, read, etc: ~ part of the book **5** [I] move from one place to another quickly **6** [I, T] leave a place quickly or secretly: ~ the country ● **skip** n [C] **1** skipping movement **2** large metal container for rubbish, etc

skipper /ˈskɪpə(r)/ n [C] captain of a small ship or a sports team ● **skipper** v [I, T] be the captain of a ship or team

0⃞ **skirt** /skɜːt/ n [C] **1** piece of women's clothing that hangs from the waist ● **skirt** v [T] be or go

round the edge of sth: a wood ~ing the field **2** avoid talking about a subject, esp because it is embarrassing ■ **skirting board** n [C, U] narrow piece of wood fixed along the bottom of the walls in a house

skittle /ˈskɪtl/ n **1** [C] wooden or plastic object used in the game of skittles (skittles) [U] game in which players try to knock over as many skittles as possible by rolling a ball at them

skulk /skʌlk/ v [I] hide or move around, trying not to be seen

skull /skʌl/ n [C] bone structure that forms the head

skunk /skʌŋk/ n [C] small N American animal that sends out a strong smell when attacked

0⃞ **sky** /skaɪ/ n [C, U] (pl **skies** /skaɪz/) the space above the earth, where we see clouds, the sun, moon and stars ■ **skydiving** n [U] sport in which you jump from a plane and fall for as long as you safely can before opening your parachute ■ **sky-high** adj very high; too high ■ **skylark** n [C] small bird that sings as it flies high in the sky ■ **skylight** n [C] window in a sloping roof ■ **skyline** n [C, usu sing] outline of buildings, hills, etc against the sky ■ **skyscraper** n [C] very tall building

slab /slæb/ n [C] thick flat piece of stone, etc

slack /slæk/ adj **1** not stretched tight: a ~ rope **2** (of business) not having many customers or sales; not busy: Trade is ~. **3** (disapprov) giving little care, attention or energy to a task ● **slack** v [I] work less hard than you should do or than you usu do [PV] **slack off (on sth)** do sth more slowly or with less energy than before ● **slack** (the slack) n [U] part of a rope that is hanging loosely [IDM] **take up the slack 1** improve the way money or people are used in an organization **2** tighten a rope ▸ **slacker** n [C] (infml, disapprov) person who is lazy and avoids work ▸ **slackness** n [U]

slacken /ˈslækən/ v [I, T] **1** ~ **(off/up)** (cause sth to) gradually become slower, less active, etc **2** (cause sth to) become less tight

slag /slæg/ n **1** [U] waste matter remaining when metal has been removed from rock **2** [C] (GB, sl) offensive word for a woman, used to suggest that she has a lot of sexual partners ● **slag** v (-gg-) [PV] **slag sb off** (GB, sl) say cruel or critical things about sb ■ **slag heap** n [C] large pile of slag (1) from a mine

slam /slæm/ v (-mm-) **1** [I, T] (cause sth to) shut with great force **2** [T] throw or knock sth somewhere with great force: ~ a book against the wall **3** [T] (infml) criticize sb/sth very strongly ● **slam** n [C] noise of sth being slammed

slander /'slɑːndə(r)/ n [U, C] (offence of) saying sth false about sb that damages their reputation ● **slander** v [T] say sth false about sb
▸ **slanderous** adj

slang /slæŋ/ n [U] very informal words and expressions used in spoken conversation, esp by a particular group of people

slant /slɑːnt/ v **1** [I,T] (cause sth to) slope in a certain direction **2** [T] often (disapprov) present information from a particular point of view, esp unfairly ● **slant** n [C] **1** sloping position **2** point of view

slap /slæp/ v (**-pp-**) [T] **1** hit sb/sth with the palm of the hand **2** put sth on a surface carelessly, esp because you are angry: ~ paint onto the wall ● **slap** n [C] action of hitting sb/sth with the palm of the hand [IDM] **a slap in the face** action seemingly intended as a deliberate insult to sb ● **slap** adv (also **slap 'bang**) (infml) straight: The car ran ~ into the wall.

slapdash /'slæpdæʃ/ adj done or doing things too carelessly and quickly

slapstick /'slæpstɪk/ n [U] comedy in which people fall over, knock each other down, etc

slap-up /'slæp ʌp/ adj (GB, infml) (of a meal) large and very good

slash /slæʃ/ v **1** [T] make a long cut with a sharp object, esp in a violent way **2** reduce sth by a large amount: ~ prices ● **slash** n [C] **1** sharp movement made with a knife, etc in order to cut sb/sth **2** long narrow wound or cut **3** symbol (/) used to show alternatives, as in 'lunch and/ or dinner'

slat /slæt/ n [C] thin, narrow piece of wood, metal, etc

slate /sleɪt/ n **1** [U] dark grey stone that splits easily into thin, flat layers **2** [C] small thin piece of slate used for covering roofs ● **slate** v [T] criticize sb/sth severely, esp in a newspaper

slaughter /'slɔːtə(r)/ n [U] **1** killing of animals for their meat **2** cruel killing of many people at once ● **slaughter** v [T] **1** kill an animal, usu for its meat **2** kill a large number of people or animals violently **3** (infml) defeat sb/ sth completely in a game, competition, etc ▪ **'slaughterhouse** n [C] place where animals are killed for food

slave /sleɪv/ n [C] **1** person who is legally owned by and forced to work for another **2** ~ (**of/to**) person controlled by a habit, etc: a ~ to drink ● **slave** v [I] work very hard: ~ away in the kitchen ● **slavery** n [U] **1** state of being a slave **2** system of using slaves

slaver /'slævə(r)/ v [I] (usu of an

animal) let saliva run out of the mouth, esp because of hunger or excitement

slavish /'sleɪvɪʃ/ adj (disapprov) lacking originality or independence: a ~ copy ▸ **slavishly** adv

slay /sleɪ/ v (pt **slew** /sluː/ pp **slain** /sleɪn/) [T] (lit or US) kill sb/sth violently

sledge /sledʒ/ (also **sled** /sled/) n [C] vehicle for travelling over snow, with long strips of wood or metal instead of wheels

sledgehammer /'sledʒhæmə(r)/ n [C] heavy hammer with a long handle

sleek /sliːk/ adj **1** smooth and shiny: ~ hair **2** often (disapprov) looking well dressed and rich

0—**sleep¹** /sliːp/ v (pt, pp **slept** /slept/) **1** [I] rest with your eyes closed and your mind and body not active **2** [T] have enough beds for a particular number of people: a flat that ~s six [IDM] **sleep like a log/baby** (infml) sleep well **sleep tight** (spoken) used to wish sb a good night's sleep [PV] **sleep around** (infml, disapprov) have sex with a lot of people **sleep in** stay in bed after the time you usu get up in the morning **sleep sth off** recover from drunkenness, etc by sleeping **sleep on sth** leave a problem, etc to the next day **sleep through sth** not be woken by a noise **sleep together|sleep with sb** (infml) have sex with sb ▸ **sleeper** n [C] **1** person who sleeps (bed in a) sleeping car **2** beam of wood supporting the rails of a railway track ▪ **'sleeping bag** n [C] thick warm bag for sleeping in, eg when camping ▪ **'sleeping car** n [C] railway carriage fitted with beds ▪ **'sleeping pill** (also **'sleeping tablet**) n [C] pill containing a drug that helps sb to sleep ▸ **sleepy** adj (**-ier, -iest**) **1** needing or ready for sleep **2** (of places, etc) without much activity: a ~ little town ▸ **sleepily** adv

0—**sleep²** /sliːp/ n **1** [U] condition when the body is at rest with the eyes closed, mostly at night: It's late – go to ~. **2** [sing] period of sleep [IDM] **go to sleep** begin to sleep **put sb to sleep** (infml) make sb unconscious before an operation by using an anaesthetic **put sth to sleep** kill a sick or injured animal by giving it drugs so that it dies without pain ▸ **sleepless** adj without sleep

sleet /sliːt/ n [U] falling snow mixed with rain ● **sleet** v (used with it) fall as sleet: It's ~ing outside.

sleeve /sliːv/ n **1** [C] part of a piece of clothing that covers the arm **2** stiff envelope for a record [IDM]

have/keep sth up your sleeve keep a plan, idea, etc secret until you need it

sleigh /sleɪ/ n [C] sledge (= vehicle that slides over snow), esp one pulled by horses

sleight /slaɪt/ n [IDM] **sleight of hand** skilful movements of your hand that others cannot see

slender /'slendə(r)/ adj 1 (approv) (of people) slim 2 thin or narrow 3 small in amount or size: to win by a ~ margin ▸ **slenderness** n

slept pt, pp of SLEEP[1]

slice /slaɪs/ n [C] 1 thin flat piece cut off sth, esp bread or meat 2 (infml) part or share of sth: a ~ of the credit 3 utensil with a wide blade for cutting or lifting sth, eg cooked fish [IDM] **a slice of life** film, play or book that gives a realistic view of ordinary life ● **slice** v 1 [T] ~ (**up**) cut sth into pieces 2 [I] cut sth easily (as if) with a sharp blade: a knife slicing through butter

slick /slɪk/ adj 1 done (too) smoothly and efficiently 2 (disapprov) (of people) speaking easily and smoothly but in a way that seems insincere 3 smooth and slippery

slide[1] /slaɪd/ v (pt, pp **slid** /slɪd/) 1 [I,T] (cause sth to) move smoothly over a smooth or wet surface 2 [I,T] (cause sth to) move quickly and quietly so as not to be noticed 3 [I] move gradually into a worse situation [IDM] **let sth slide** neglect sth: He began to let things ~. ■ **slide rule** n [C] instrument like a ruler with a part that slides, used for calculating numbers

slide[2] /slaɪd/ n 1 [C, sing] change to a lower or worse situation 2 [C] structure with a steep slope for children to play on 3 [C] picture on photographic film projected onto a screen 4 [C] glass plate onto which sth is examined under a microscope ■ **slideshow** (also **slide-show**) n [C] (computing) display of images on a computer

slight[1] /slaɪt/ adj 1 not serious or important: a ~ headache 2 small and thin in size [IDM] **not in the slightest** not at all ▸ **slightly** adv 1 a little: feel ~ly better 2 slenderly: a ~ly built boy ▸ **slightness** n [U]

slight[2] /slaɪt/ v [T] treat sb rudely and without respect; insult sb ● **slight** n [C] critical or offensive remark ▸ **slightingly** adv

slim /slɪm/ adj (**-mer**, **-mest**) 1 (approv) not fat or thick; slender 2 small: a ~ chance of success ● **slim** v (**-mm-**) [I] eat less, etc to reduce your weight ▸ **slimmer** n [C] person who is slimming ▸ **slimness** n

slime /slaɪm/ n [U] any unpleasant

thick liquid substance ▸ **slimy** adj (**-ier**, **-iest**) 1 like or covered with slime 2 (infml, disapprov) polite, friendly, etc in a way that is not sincere or honest

sling /slɪŋ/ n [C] band of material looped round an object, eg a broken arm, to support or lift it ● **sling** v (pt, pp **slung** /slʌŋ/) [T] (infml) throw sth/sb carelessly or with force

slink /slɪŋk/ v (pt, pp **slunk** /slʌŋk/) [I] move as if you do not want to be seen or are ashamed

slip[1] /slɪp/ v (**-pp-**) 1 [I] slide accidentally and (almost) fall: He ~ped (over) in the mud. 2 [I] slide out of position or out of your hand: The plate ~ped from my hand. 3 [I,T] (cause sth to) move quietly and quickly, without being seen: He ~ped the coin into his pocket. 4 [I] fall to a lower level; become worse 5 [I,T] put clothes on or take them off easily and quickly: ~ on a coat [IDM] **let slip sth** accidentally reveal secret information **let slip (through your fingers)** miss or fail to use an opportunity **slip your mind** (of sb's name, etc) be forgotten [PV] **slip up** (infml) make a careless mistake ■ **slip road** n [C] (GB) road for joining or leaving a motorway ■ **slipstream** n [sing] stream of air behind a fast-moving vehicle ■ **slip-up** n [C] (infml) careless mistake

slip[2] /slɪp/ n [C] 1 small mistake: make a few ~s 2 small piece of paper: pay- ◇ betting ~ 3 act of slipping 4 piece of women's underwear, worn under a dress or a skirt [IDM] **give sb the slip** (infml) escape from sb

slipper /'slɪpə(r)/ n [C] loose soft shoe worn in the house

slippery /'slɪpəri/ adj (**-ier**, **-iest**) 1 (also infml **slippy**) difficult to hold, stand or move on, because it is smooth, wet or polished 2 (infml) (of people) that you cannot trust 3 (infml) (of problems, etc) difficult to deal with [IDM] **the/a slippery slope** course of action that can easily lead to serious problems or disaster

slipshod /'slɪpʃɒd/ adj done or doing things without care

slit /slɪt/ n [C] long narrow cut, tear or opening ● **slit** v (**-tt-** pt, pp **slit**) [T] make a slit in sth

slither /'slɪðə(r)/ v [I] move somewhere smoothly, often close to the ground

sliver /'slɪvə(r)/ n [C] long thin piece of sth: a ~ of glass

slob /slɒb/ n [C] (infml, disapprov) dirty, untidy, lazy person

slog /slɒg/ v (**-gg-**) [I] (infml) 1 work hard and steadily at sth boring or difficult: ~ (away) at sth 2 walk somewhere with difficulty: ~ up the hill ● **slog** n [U, C, usu sing] period of hard work or effort

slogan /ˈsləʊɡən/ n [C] easily remembered phrase used in advertising

slop /slɒp/ v (-pp-) **1** [I] (of a liquid) move around in a container, often so that some liquid spills over the edge **2** [T] cause sth to spill: *Don't ~ the water all over the floor!* [PV] **slop about/around** (of liquids) move around esp in a container ● **slop** n [U] (*also* **slops** [pl]) **1** waste food, sometimes fed to animals **2** dirty waste water

0━ **slope** /sləʊp/ n **1** [C] area of rising or falling ground **2** [C, usu pl] area of land that is part of a mountain or hill: *ski ~s* **3** [sing, U] amount by which sth slopes ● **slope** v [I] be at an angle; have a slope [PV] **slope off** (GB, infml) go somewhere quietly, esp to avoid sth/sb

sloppy /ˈslɒpi/ adj (-ier, -iest) **1** that shows a lack of care, thought or effort: *~ work* **2** (of clothes) loose and shapeless **3** (infml) romantic in a silly way: *a ~ love story* **4** containing too much liquid
▶ **sloppily** adv ▶ **sloppiness** n [U]

slosh /slɒʃ/ v **1** [I, T] (cause liquid to) move about noisily or spill over the edge of sth: *~ water all over the floor* **2** [I] walk noisily in water or mud
▶ **sloshed** adj (sl) drunk

slot /slɒt/ n [C] **1** long narrow opening: *put a coin in the ~* **2** position, time or opportunity for sb/sth in a plan, schedule, etc: *~s for advertisements on television* ● **slot** v (-tt-) [T] make a slot for sth; place sth in a slot [PV] **slot sth/sb in** manage to find a position, time or opportunity for sb/sth

sloth /sləʊθ/ n **1** [C] S American animal that lives in trees and moves very slowly **2** [U] (fml) laziness
▶ **slothful** adj

slouch /slaʊtʃ/ v [I] stand, sit or move in a lazy way ● **slouch** n [sing] slouching posture, walk, etc [IDM] **be no slouch** (infml) be very good at sth

slovenly /ˈslʌvnli/ adj untidy; dirty
▶ **slovenliness** n [U]

0━ **slow¹** /sləʊ/ adj **1** taking a long time; not fast: *a ~ vehicle* **2** not acting immediately **3** not quick to learn: *a ~ child* **4** not very busy; containing little action: *Sales are ~ this month.* **5** (of a watch or clock) showing a time earlier than the correct time [IDM] **slow off the mark** → MARK¹ ● **be slow on the uptake** → UPTAKE ● **slow** adv at a slow speed: *~-moving traffic* [IDM] **go slow (on sth)** show less enthusiasm for achieving sth ■ **slowcoach** (US **slowpoke**) n [C] (infml) person who moves, works, etc too slowly
▶ **slowly** adv ▶ **slowness** n [U]

slow² /sləʊ/ v [I, T] **~ (down/up)** (cause sth/sb to) go at a slower speed or be less active ■ **slowdown** n [C] **1** reduction of speed or activity **2** (US) = GO-SLOW (GO¹)

sludge /slʌdʒ/ n [U] (anything resembling) thick soft wet mud

slug /slʌɡ/ n [C] **1** small soft creature like a snail but without a shell **2** (infml) small amount of a strong alcoholic drink **3** (infml, esp US) bullet ● **slug** v (-gg-) [T] (infml) hit sb/sth hard

sluggish /ˈslʌɡɪʃ/ adj moving, reacting or working more slowly than normal ▶ **sluggishly** adv

sluice /sluːs/ n [C] (*also* **sluice gate**) sliding gate for controlling the flow of water in a canal, etc ● **sluice** v [T] wash sth with a stream of water

slum /slʌm/ n [C] very poor area of a city where the houses are dirty and in bad condition ● **slum** v (-mm-) [T] (infml) spend time in places that are much worse than you are used to [IDM] **slum it** accept conditions that are worse than those you are used to ▶ **slummy** adj

slumber /ˈslʌmbə(r)/ v [I] (lit) sleep ● **slumber** n [U, C, usu pl] (lit) sleep

slump /slʌmp/ v [I] **1** fall in price, value, number, etc suddenly and steeply **2** sit or fall down heavily ● **slump** n [C] sudden fall in prices, trade, etc

slung pt, pp of SLING

slur /slɜː(r)/ v (-rr-) [T] **1** pronounce words in a way that is not clear, usu because you are drunk or tired **2** damage sb's reputation by making false statements about them ● **slur** n [C] damaging remark: *a ~ on her name*

slush /slʌʃ/ n [U] **1** melting, dirty snow **2** (infml, disapprov) silly sentimental stories, films, etc ■ **slush fund** n [C] (disapprov) money kept for illegal purposes, esp in politics ▶ **slushy** adj (-ier, -iest)

slut /slʌt/ n [C] (disapprov, offens) **1** woman who has many sexual partners **2** lazy or untidy woman ▶ **sluttish** adj

sly /slaɪ/ adj (disapprov) acting or done in a secret and dishonest way ● **sly** n [IDM] **on the sly** secretly ▶ **slyly** adv ▶ **slyness** n [U]

smack /smæk/ n **1** [C] (sound of a) sharp hit given with your open hand **2** [C] (infml) loud kiss **3** [U] (infml) the drug heroin ● **smack** adv suddenly and forcefully: *run ~ into a wall* ● **smack** v **1** [T] hit sb with your open hand **2** [I, T] (cause sth to) hit sth with a lot of force and a loud noise [IDM] **smack your lips** → LIP [PV] **smack of sth** seem to contain or involve an unpleasant quality

small

O─ **small** /smɔːl/ adj **1** not large in size, number, degree, amount, etc: *a ~ house* **2** young: *~ children* **3** unimportant; slight: *a ~ problem* **4** not doing business on a large scale: *~ businesses* **IDM** **look/feel small** look/feel stupid, weak, ashamed, etc **the small hours** period of time very early in the morning, soon after midnight **small wonder (that...)** → WONDER ● **small n** [sing] (the ~ of the/sb's back) the lower part of the back where it curves in ▪ **small arms** n [pl] light weapons carried in the hand ▪ **small fortune** n [usu sing] a lot of money ▪ **smallholding** n [C] (GB) small piece of land used for farming ▪ **small-minded** adj (disapprov) mean and selfish ▶ **smallness** n [U] ▪ **smallpox** n [U] serious infectious disease that leaves permanent scars on the skin ▪ **small talk** n [U] polite conversation about everyday social matters

O─ **smart¹** /smɑːt/ adj **1** clean and neat; well dressed: *a ~ appearance/ person* **2** (esp US) intelligent: *a ~ answer* **3** connected with fashionable people: *a ~ restaurant* **4** quick or hard: *We set off at a ~ pace.* ● **smarten** /ˈsmɑːtn/ v [PV] **smarten (yourself/sb/sth) up** make yourself/sb/sth look neater and more attractive ▶ **smartly** adv ▪ **smartness** n [U]

smart² /smɑːt/ v [I] feel a sharp stinging pain: *The smoke made my eyes ~.*

O─ **smash** /smæʃ/ v [I, T] (cause sb to) break violently into small pieces: *~ a cup on the floor* **2** [I, T] (cause sb to) move with great force against sth solid: *They ~ed into the wall.* **3** [T] hit sth/sb very hard **4** [T] defeat or destroy sth/sb ● **smash** n [sing] **1** sound or act of breaking sth noisily into pieces **2** (GB) [C] accident in which one vehicle hits another: *a car ~* **3** [C] (in tennis) hard, downward stroke (also **smash 'hit**) [C] play, song, etc that is suddenly very successful ▪ **smashing** adj (old-fash, GB, infml) very good ▪ **smash-up** n [C] car crash

smattering /ˈsmætərɪŋ/ n [sing] *~ of* small amount of sth, esp knowledge of a language: *a ~ of French*

smear /smɪə(r)/ v [T] **1** cover a surface with an oily or soft substance: *His face was ~ed with blood.* **2** damage sb's reputation by saying untrue things about them ● **smear** n [C] **1** oily or dirty mark **2** untrue remark about sb that is intended to damage their reputation, esp in politics: *a ~ campaign* **3** small amount of a substance taken from the body, to be tested for disease

O─ **smell¹** /smel/ v (pt, pp **smelt** /smelt/ or **smelled**) **1** [I] *~ (of)* have a particular smell: *~ good/of soap* **2** [T] (often with can, could) notice or recognize a particular smell: *Can you ~ gas?* **3** [T] put your nose near sth to test its smell: *~ the flowers* **4** [I] have a bad smell: *Your feet ~.* **5** [I] have the sense of smell: *Can birds ~?* **IDM** **smell a rat** (infml) suspect that sth is wrong

O─ **smell²** /smel/ n **1** [C, U] quality of sth that people and animals sense through their noses **2** [sing] unpleasant smell: *What a ~!* **3** [U] ability to sense things with the nose **4** [C] act of smelling sth: *Have a ~ of this.* ▶ **smelly** adj (**-ier, -iest**) (infml) having an unpleasant smell

O─ **smile** /smaɪl/ n [C] expression of the face with the corners of the mouth turned up, showing amusement, happiness, etc ● **smile** v [I] make a smile appear on your face ▶ **smilingly** adv

smirk /smɜːk/ v [I], n [C] (give a) silly self-satisfied smile

smithereens /ˌsmɪðəˈriːnz/ n [pl] [IDM] **smash, blow, etc sth to smithereens** destroy sth completely by breaking it into pieces

smitten /ˈsmɪtn/ adj *~(with/by)* **1** suddenly feeling that you are in love with sb: *I'm rather ~ with her.* **2** severely affected by a feeling, disease, etc

smock /smɒk/ n [C] loose comfortable piece of clothing like a long shirt

smog /smɒg/ n [U, C] mixture of fog and smoke

O─ **smoke¹** /sməʊk/ n **1** [U] usu white, grey or black vapour produced by sth burning **2** [C] act of smoking a cigarette, etc **IDM** **go up in smoke 1** be completely burned **2** result in failure ▪ **'smokescreen** n [C] **1** something you do or say in order to hide your real intentions **2** cloud of smoke used to hide soldiers, ships, etc during a battle ▶ **smoky** adj (**-ier, -iest**)

O─ **smoke²** /sməʊk/ v [I, T] breathe smoke from a cigarette, etc; use cigarettes, etc as a habit **1** [I] produce smoke **3** [T] preserve meat or fish with smoke [PV] **smoke sb/sth out** fill a place with smoke to force sb/sth out ▶ **smoker** n [C] person who smokes tobacco regularly ▶ **smoking** n [U] activity of smoking cigarettes, etc

O─ **smooth** /smuːð/ adj **1** (of a surface) completely flat and even, without any lumps, holes, etc: *~ skin* **2** (of a liquid) free from lumps **3** happening or continuing without any problems **4** (of movement)

even and regular: *a ~ ride*
5 (*disapprov*) (of a person, esp a man) polite and pleasant, but seeming insincere **6** (of sounds or tastes) pleasant and not bitter or harsh ● **smooth** *v* [T] make sth smooth **(PV)** **smooth sth over** make problems, etc seem less important ▶ **smoothly** *adv* ▶ **smoothness** *n* [U]

smother /ˈsmʌðə(r)/ *v* [T] **1** kill sb by covering their face so that they cannot breathe **2** ~ **(with/in)** cover sth/sb thickly or with (too much of sth: *a cake ~ed in cream* ◇ *She ~ed him with kisses.* **3** prevent sth from developing or being expressed: ~ *a yawn* **4** put out a fire by covering it with sth

smoulder (*US* **smol-**) /ˈsmoʊldə(r)/ *v* [i] burn slowly without flame: *~ing ashes* ◇ (*fig*) *Hate ~ed within her.*

smudge /smʌdʒ/ *n* [C] dirty mark ● **smudge** *v* **1** [T] touch or rub sth, esp wet ink or paint, so that it is no longer clear **2** [i] (of wet ink, etc) become blurred: *Her lipstick had ~d.*

smug /smʌɡ/ *adj* (**-gg-**, **-gest**) (*disapprov*) too pleased with yourself ▶ **smugly** *adv* ▶ **smugness** *n* [U]

smuggle /ˈsmʌɡl/ *v* [T] take goods, people, etc illegally or secretly into or out of a place or country: *drugs into the country* ◇ ~ *a letter into prison* ▶ **smuggler** *n* [C] ▶ **smuggling** *n* [U]

smut /smʌt/ *n* **1** [U] (*infml*) vulgar stories, pictures, etc about sex **2** [C] (black mark made by a) bit of dirt, soot, etc ▶ **smutty** *adj* (**-ier**, **-iest**)

snack /snæk/ *n* [C] small quick meal, usu eaten instead of or between main meals

snag /snæɡ/ *n* [C] **1** hidden or unexpected difficulty **2** sharp or rough piece of an object that sticks out ● **snag** *v* (**-gg-**) [T] (cause sth to) catch or tear on sth rough or sharp

snail /sneɪl/ *n* [C] small soft animal that moves very slowly and has a shell on its back

0⟋ **snake** /sneɪk/ *n* [C] reptile with a very long thin body and no legs **(IDM)** **a snake (in the grass)** (*disapprov*) person who pretends to be a friend but who cannot be trusted ● **snake** *v* [i] follow a twisting path

snap /snæp/ *v* (**-pp-**) **1** [I,T] (cause sth to) break suddenly with a sharp noise **2** [I,T] (cause sth to) open or close with a sudden sharp noise: *His eyes ~ped open.* **3** [I,T] ~ **(at)** say sth in an impatient, usu angry, voice **4** [i] ~ **(at)** (of a dog, etc) try to bite sb/sth: *The dog ~ped at her ankles.* **5** [I,T] (*infml*) take a photograph **6** [i] suddenly be unable to control your feelings any longer: *My patience finally ~ped.* **(IDM)** **snap your fingers** make a clicking noise with your

---

sniff

---

fingers to attract attention, etc **snap out of it/sth** (*infml*) get out of a bad, unhappy, etc mood **(PV)** **snap at sth** try to catch with the teeth: (*fig*) ~ *at the chance to go on holiday* **snap sth up** buy sth quickly and eagerly ● **snap** *n* **1** [C] sudden sharp noise, esp made by sth breaking **2** [C] (*also* 'snapshot) photograph, usu one taken quickly **3** [C] sudden short period of cold weather ● **snap** *adj* done quickly, without careful thought: *a ~ decision* ● **snappy** *adj* (**-ier**, **-iest**) **1** (of a remark, title, etc) clever, amusing and short **2** (*infml*) attractive and fashionable **3** speaking to people bad-temperedly

snare /sneə(r)/ *n* [C] **1** trap for catching small animals and birds **2** situation which traps sb ● **snare** *v* [T] catch sth, esp an animal, in a snare

snarl /snɑːl/ *v* [i] (of dogs, etc) show the teeth and growl **2** [I,T] speak or say sth in an angry voice **(PV)** **snarl (sth) up** (*infml*) (cause sth to) become confused or tangled ■ 'snarl-up *n* [C] (*GB*, *infml*) situation in which traffic is unable to move ● **snarl** *n* [C] act or sound of snarling

snatch /snætʃ/ *v* [I,T] (try to) take sb/sth suddenly or steal sth: ~ *the child from her father* **2** [T] take or get sth quickly, usu because there is not much time: ~ *some sleep* ● **snatch** *n* [C] **1** short part of a conversation or some music that you hear: *~es of conversation* **2** act of moving your hand quickly to take or steal sth: *a bag ~*

sneak /sniːk/ *v* **1** [i] go somewhere quietly and secretly: ~ *past sb* **2** [T] do sth or take sb/sth somewhere secretly: ~ *money from the box* **3** [i] (*old-fash*) tell an adult that another child has done sth wrong ● **sneak** *n* [C] (*old-fash*) person who sneaks(3) ▶ **sneaker** *n* [C] (*US*) = TRAINER(1) (TRAIN²) ▶ **sneaking** *adj* secret: *a ~ing respect for sb* ◇ *a ~ing suspicion* ▶ **sneaky** *adj* (**-ier**, **-iest**) (*infml*) done or acting in a secret and sometimes dishonest way

sneer /snɪə(r)/ *v* [i] ~ **(at)** show that you have no respect for sb/sth by your expression or words ● **sneer** *n* [C] sneering look, smile, etc

sneeze /sniːz/ *v* [i] have air come noisily and uncontrollably out through your nose and mouth, eg because you have a cold **(IDM)** **not to be sneezed at** (*infml*) good enough to be accepted ● **sneeze** *n* [C] act of sneezing or the noise you make when sneezing

sniff /snɪf/ *v* **1** [i] draw air in through the nose, producing a sound **2** [I,T] ~ **(at)** breathe air in through the

---

nose in order to smell sth: ~ *(at) the roses* [IDM] **not to be sniffed at** good enough to be accepted [PV] **sniff sb/ sth out** discover or find sb/sth by looking ● **sniff** n [C] act or sound of sniffing

snigger /'snɪgə(r)/ n [C] quiet unpleasant laugh ● **snigger** v [I] ~ **(at)** laugh in a quiet unpleasant way

snip /snɪp/ v (**-pp-**) [I,T] cut sth with scissors using short quick strokes ● **snip** n **1** [C] act or sound of cutting sth with scissors **2** (a snip) [sing] (*GB, infml*) thing that is cheap and good value: *It's a ~ at only £10.*

snipe /snaɪp/ v **1** shoot at sb from a hiding place **2** criticize sb unpleasantly ▸ **sniper** n [C] person who shoots at sb from a hidden position

snippet /'snɪpɪt/ n [C] small item of news, information, etc: ~*s of gossip*

snivel /'snɪvl/ v (**-ll- *US* -l-**) [I] cry or complain in a miserable way

snob /snɒb/ n [C] (*disapprov*) person who respects social position or wealth too much ▸ **snobbery** n [U] behaviour of a snob ▸ **snobbish** *adj*

snog /snɒg/ v (**-gg-**) [I,T] (*GB, infml*) (of two people) kiss each other, esp for a long time

snooker /'snuːkə(r)/ n [U] game played with 15 red balls and 7 of other colours on a long table ● **snooker** v [T] place sb in a difficult position

snoop /snuːp/ v [I] ~ **(around/round)** find out private things about sb, esp by looking secretly around a place

snooze /snuːz/ v [I], n [C] (*infml*) (have a) short sleep, esp during the day

snore /snɔː(r)/ v [I] breathe noisily while sleeping ● **snore** n [C] sound of snoring

snorkel /'snɔːkl/ n [C] tube that allows a swimmer to breathe air while under water ● **snorkel** v (**-ll-** *US* -l-) [I] swim with a snorkel

snort /snɔːt/ v **1** [I] force air out loudly through the nose, esp to show that you are angry or amused **2** [T] (*sl*) take drugs by breathing them in through the nose ● **snort** n [C] act or sound of snorting

snout /snaʊt/ n [C] nose of an animal, esp a pig

0–π **snow¹** /snəʊ/ n [U] frozen water falling from the sky in soft, white flakes, or a mass of this on the ground, etc ■ **snowball** n [C] ball of snow for throwing in play ■ **snowball** v [I] grow quickly in size, importance, etc ■ **snowboarding** n [U] sport of moving over snow on a long wide board called a snowboard ■ **snowdrift** n [C] deep pile of snow that has been blown together by the

wind ■ **snowdrop** n [C] type of small white spring flower ■ **snowman** n [C] figure of a man made from snow ■ **snowplough** (*US* -**plow**) n [C] vehicle or machine for pushing snow off roads, etc ■ **snowstorm** n [C] heavy fall of snow, esp with a strong wind

0–π **snow²** /snəʊ/ v [I] (used with *it*) fall as snow: *It ~ed all day.* [PV] **be snowed in/up** be unable to leave a place because of heavy snow **be snowed under (with sth)** have more things, esp work, than you feel able to deal with: *He is ~ed under with work.* ▸ **snowy** *adj* (**-ier, -iest**)

snub /snʌb/ v (**-bb-**) insult sb, esp by ignoring them when you meet ● **snub** n [C] deliberately rude action or comment ● **snub** *adj* (of a nose) short, flat and turned up at the end ▸ **snub-nosed** *adj*

snuff /snʌf/ n [U] powdered tobacco that is sniffed into the nose ● **snuff** v [T] ~ **(out)** put out a candle by pinching the flame with your fingers or by covering it with sth [IDM] **snuff it** (*GB, hum, sl*) die [PV] **snuff sth out** (*written*) put an end to sth

snug /snʌg/ *adj* **1** warm and comfortable **2** tight-fitting: *a ~ jacket* ▸ **snugly** *adv*

snuggle /'snʌgl/ v [I] ~ **(up/down)** lie or get close to sb for warmth or affection

0–π **so¹** /səʊ/ *adv* **1** to such a great degree: *not so big as I thought* **2** very: *I'm so glad to see you.* **3** used to refer back to sth already mentioned: *'Is he coming?' 'I hope so.'* **4** also: *You are young and so am I.* **5** (*spoken*) used to agree that sth is true: *'It's Friday today, not Thursday.' 'So it is.'* **6** (*spoken*) used to show sb how to do sth or how sth happened: *Stand with your arms out, so.* [IDM] **and so on (and so forth)** used at the end of a list to show that it continues in the same way **so as to do sth** with the intention of doing sth: *He drove fast so as not to be late.* **so much for sth** nothing further needs to be said or done about sth **so much so that** to such an extent that ■ **'so-and-so** n [C] (*infml*) **1** some person or other **2** annoying and unpleasant person: *That so-and-so lied to me.* ■ **so-called** *adj* used to show that you do not think the word being used is appropriate: *Her so-called friends refused to help her.*

0–π **so²** /səʊ/ *conj* **1** used to show the reason for sth: *He was hurt so I helped him.* **2** used to show the result of sth: *Nothing more was heard from her so people thought she was dead.* **3** ~ **(that)...** used to show the purpose of sth: *I gave you a map so (that) you wouldn't get lost.* **4** used to introduce the next part of a story: *So she went and told the police.* [IDM] **so**

A B C D E F G H I J K L M N O P Q R **S** T U V W X Y Z

what? (*spoken*) and what does it matter?: *'She lied to me.' 'So what?'*

soak /səʊk/ v **1** [T] put sth in liquid for a time so that it becomes completely wet: ~ *the beans overnight* **2** [I] become completely wet by being put in liquid for a time: *I'm going to ~ in a hot bath.* **3** [T] make sb/sth completely wet: *The rain ~ed the spectators.* [PV] **soak sth up** take in or absorb liquid: *Paper ~s up water.* ● **soak in** [C] act of soaking sth/sb ▶ **soaked, soaking** adj completely wet

0─ **soap** /səʊp/ n **1** [U,C] substance used with water for washing your body **2** [C] (*infml*) = SOAP OPERA ● **soap** v [T] rub yourself/sb/sth with soap ■ **soap opera** [C,U] story about the lives and problems of a group of people which is broadcast several times a week on the radio or TV ▶ **soapy** adj

soar /sɔː(r)/ v [I] **1** rise very quickly: *~ing prices* **2** (of birds, etc) fly or go high up in the air

sob /sɒb/ v (**-bb-**) [I] cry noisily, taking sudden sharp breaths [PV] **sob your heart out** cry noisily for a long time ● **sob** n [C] act or sound of sobbing ■ **sob story** [C] (*disapprov*) story that sb tells you just to make you feel sorry for them

sober /ˈsəʊbə(r)/ adj **1** not drunk **2** serious and responsible: *a ~ person* ● **sober** v [I,T] (*cause sb to*) behave or think in a more serious and sensible way [PV] **sober up** (*cause sb to*) become no longer drunk ▶ **soberly** adv

soccer /ˈsɒkə(r)/ n [U] = FOOTBALL(1)

sociable /ˈsəʊʃəbl/ adj friendly; liking company ▶ **sociably** adv

0─ **social** /ˈsəʊʃl/ adj **1** of society and the way it is organized: *~ reforms* **2** of your position in society: *~ class* **3** of activities in which people meet each other for pleasure: *a busy ~ life* **4** (of animals, etc) living in groups **5** = SOCIAL ■ **social science** [C,U] subjects concerning people within society, eg sociology, economics ■ **social security** n [U] government payments to help the unemployed, disabled, etc ■ **social worker** n [C] person employed to provide help and advice on health, housing, social security, etc ▶ **socially** adv

socialism /ˈsəʊʃəlɪzəm/ n [U] political and economic theory that land, industries, etc should be owned by the state ▶ **socialist** adj, n [C]

0─ **socialize** (*also* -ise) /ˈsəʊʃəlaɪz/ v [I] mix socially with others

0─ **society** /səˈsaɪəti/ n (pl **-ies**) **1** [U] people in general, living together in communities **2** [C,U] particular

community of people **3** [C] organization of people with a common interest: *a drama ~* **4** [U] the group of people in a country who are rich, fashionable and powerful: *a ~ wedding* **5** [U] (*fml*) state of being with other people

sociology /ˌsəʊsiˈɒlədʒi/ n [U] study of the nature and growth of society and social behaviour ▶ **sociologist** n [C] expert in sociology ▶ **sociological** /-ˈlɒdʒɪkl/ adj

0─ **sock** /sɒk/ n [C] **1** piece of clothing worn over the foot and ankle, esp inside a shoe **2** (*infml*) hard blow, esp with the fist ● **sock** v [T] (*infml*) hit sb hard

socket /ˈsɒkɪt/ n [C] **1** device in a wall that you put a plug into in order to connect electrical equipment to the power supply **2** curved hollow space in which sth fits or turns

sod /sɒd/ n [C] (GB, ⚠, *sl*) **1** used to refer to a person you are annoyed with **2** thing that causes problems

soda /ˈsəʊdə/ n **1** [U,C] = SODA WATER **2** (*US*) [U,C] sweet fizzy drink made with soda water flavoured with fruit **3** [U] chemical substance used for making soap, glass, etc ■ **soda water** [U,C] (*glass of*) water containing a gas to make it bubble

sodden /ˈsɒdn/ adj very wet

sodium /ˈsəʊdiəm/ n [U] (*symb* Na) soft silver-white metal found naturally only in compounds, eg salt

sofa /ˈsəʊfə/ n [C] long comfortable seat with raised ends and back for two or more people

0─ **soft** /sɒft/ adj **1** not hard or stiff: *a ~ pillow* **2** (of surfaces) smooth and pleasant to touch: *~ skin* **3** (of light or colours) not too bright or strong **4** (of sounds) not loud **5** (of outlines) not having sharp angles or hard edges **6** ~ **(on)** (too) kind and gentle: *Don't be too ~ on the class.* **7** (*disapprov*) too easy: *a ~ job* **8** (*infml*, *disapprov*) weak and lacking in courage **9** (*infml*, *disapprov*) stupid or crazy [IDM] have a soft spot for sb/sth (*infml*) like sb/sth ■ **soft-boiled** adj (of eggs) boiled for a short time so that the yellow part (yolk) stays soft ■ **soft drink** [C] cold drink that does not contain alcohol ■ **soft drug** n [C] illegal drug (eg cannabis) not likely to cause addiction ■ **soft-hearted** adj kind, sympathetic and emotional ▶ **softly** adv ▶ **softness** n [U] ■ **soft-pedal** v (**-ll-** *US* **-l-**) [I,T] (*infml*) treat sth as less important than it really is ■ **soft-soap** v [T] (*infml*) persuade sb to do sth by saying nice things to them ■ **software** n [U] programs, etc used to operate a computer

soften /ˈsɒfn/ v **1** [I,T] (cause sth) to become softer **2** [T] make sth easier to accept: *try to ~ the shock* [PV] **soften sb up** (*infml*) try to persuade sb to do sth for you by being very nice first

soggy /ˈsɒɡi/ adj (**-ier, -iest**) very wet or heavy with water ▸ **sogginess** n [U]

0— **soil** /sɔɪl/ n [C,U] upper layer of earth in which plants grow ● **soil** n [I,T] (*fml*) (cause sth to) become dirty

sojourn /ˈsɒdʒən/ n [C] (*lit*) temporary stay in a place

solace /ˈsɒləs/ n [C,U] (*fml*) (thing that gives) comfort or relief from sadness, etc

solar /ˈsəʊlə(r)/ adj of the sun: ~ *power* ■ the '**solar system** n [sing] the sun and its planets

sold pt, pp of SELL

solder /ˈsəʊldə(r)/ n [U] type of metal which melts easily, used for joining together harder metals, etc ● **solder** v [T] join pieces of metal with solder ● **soldering iron** n [C] tool that is heated and used for joining metals together

0— **soldier** /ˈsəʊldʒə(r)/ n [C] member of an army ● **soldier** v [PV] **soldier on** continue without that you are doing in spite of difficulties

sole /səʊl/ adj **1** only; single: *the ~ owner* **2** not shared: *have ~ responsibility* ▸ **solely** adv only; not involving sb/sth else ● **sole** n **1** [C] bottom surface of the foot or a shoe **2** [U,C] (pl **sole**) flat sea fish used for food ● **sole** v [T] repair a shoe by replacing the sole

solemn /ˈsɒləm/ adj **1** not happy or smiling **2** done in a serious, formal way: *a ~ promise* ▸ **solemnly** adv ▸ **solemnness** n [U]

solemnity /səˈlemnəti/ n (pl **-ies**) (*fml*) **1** [U] quality of being solemn **2** (**solemnities**) [pl] (*fml*) formal things people do at a serious event

solicit /səˈlɪsɪt/ v **1** [I,T] ~ (**for**) (*fml*) ask for sth, eg support, money, etc **2** [I,T] (of a prostitute) offer sex to sb for money

solicitor /səˈlɪsɪtə(r)/ n [C] (*GB*) lawyer who prepares legal documents, advises clients, etc

0— **solid** /ˈsɒlɪd/ adj **1** not in the form of a liquid or gas: *Water becomes ~ when it freezes.* **2** having no holes or spaces inside **3** strong and well made **4** that you can rely on: ~ *arguments* **5** of the same substance throughout: ~ *gold* **6** (*infml*) without a pause; continuous: *sleep ten hours ~* **7** (*geom*) (of a shape) having length, width and height; not flat **8** in complete agreement: *The workers were ~ on this issue.* ● **solid** n [C] **1** substance or object that is

solid, not a liquid or gas **2** (*geom*) shape with length, width and height ▸ **solidly** adv ▸ **solidity** /səˈlɪdəti/ n [U]

solidarity /ˌsɒlɪˈdærəti/ n [U] ~ (**with**) support by one person or group for another because they share feelings, opinions, aims, etc

solidify /səˈlɪdɪfaɪ/ v (pt, pp **-ied**) [I,T] (cause sth to) become solid or firm

solitaire /ˌsɒlɪˈteə(r)/ n **1** [U] (*US*) = PATIENCE(3) **2** [C] (piece of jewellery with a) single jewel: *a ~ ring*

solitary /ˈsɒlətri/ adj **1** done alone, without other people **2** remote **3** only one; single: *a ~ visitor*

solitude /ˈsɒlɪtjuːd/ n [U] state of being alone

solo /ˈsəʊləʊ/ n [C] (pl **~s**) piece of music, dance, etc (to be) performed by one person: *a clarinet ~* ● **solo** adj, adv **1** done by one person alone, without any help: *a ~ flight* **2** of or performed as a musical solo: *music for ~ flute* ▸ **soloist** n [C] person who performs alone

solstice /ˈsɒlstɪs/ n [C] time at which the sun is furthest north or south of the equator

soluble /ˈsɒljəbl/ adj **1** that can be dissolved in liquid **2** (*fml*) (of a problem) that can be solved ▸ **solubility** /-ˈbɪləti/ n [U]

0— **solution** /səˈluːʃn/ n **1** [C] ~ (**to**) way of dealing with a problem or difficult situation **2** [C] ~ (**to**) answer to a puzzle **3** [C,U] liquid in which sth is dissolved **4** [U] process of dissolving a solid or gas in a liquid

0— **solve** /sɒlv/ v [T] find the answer to a problem, etc ▸ **solvable** adj

solvent /ˈsɒlvənt/ adj having enough money to pay your debts ● **solvent** n [U,C] liquid able to dissolve another substance ▸ **solvency** /-ənsi/ n [U] (*written*) state of not being in debt

sombre (*US* **somber**) /ˈsɒmbə(r)/ adj **1** dark coloured or dull: ~ *colours* **2** serious and sad: *a ~ mood* ▸ **sombrely** adv ▸ **sombreness** n [U]

0— **some**[1] /sʌm; weak form səm/ det **1** an unspecified number or amount of: *Have ~ milk.* ◇ ~ *children* **2** unknown or not named: *She's living at ~ place in Surrey.* **3** approximately: ~ *twenty years ago* **4** large amount of sth: *for ~ time*

0— **some**[2] /sʌm/ pron **1** an unspecified number or amount: *S~ of these books are quite useful.* **2** part of an amount or number: *S~ of the guests didn't stay for long, but most did.* ◇ *S~ people have very bad manners.*

0— **somebody** /ˈsʌmbədi/ (also **someone** /ˈsʌmwʌn/) pron **1** an unknown or unnamed person: *There's ~ at the door.* **2** an important person: *She really thinks she's ~.*

somehow /'sʌmhaʊ/ adv **1** in some way; by some means: *We'll get there ~.* **2** for some reason: *S~ I just don't think she'll ever come back.*

someone = SOMEBODY

somersault /'sʌməsɔːlt/ n [C] movement in which sb turns over completely, with their head over their head ● **somersault** v [I] turn over completely in the air

something /'sʌmθɪŋ/ pron **1** an unknown or unnamed thing: *I want ~ to eat.* **2** (infml) a significant thing: *I'm sure she knows ~ about this.* **3** (infml) used to show that a description or an amount, etc is not exact: *a new company aimed at thirty-~s* (= people between 30 and 40 years old) [IDM] **or something** (infml) or another thing similar to the one mentioned: *The car hit a tree or ~.* **something like a sb/sth** rather similar to sb/sth: *It looks ~ like a melon.* **2** approximately sb/sth

sometime /'sʌmtaɪm/ adv at an unspecified point in time: *~ in May*

sometimes /'sʌmtaɪmz/ adv occasionally: *I ~ receive letters from him.*

somewhat /'sʌmwɒt/ adv quite; rather: *I was ~ surprised.*

somewhere /'sʌmweə(r)/ (US **someplace**) adv in, at or to an unknown or unnamed place: *It's ~ near here.* [IDM] **get somewhere** → GET

son /sʌn/ n [C] **1** [C] male child of a parent **2** used as a form of address by an older man to a younger man or boy: *What's your name, ~?* ■ **'son-in-law** (pl **'sons-in-law**) husband of your daughter

sonata /sə'nɑːtə/ n [C] music for one or two instruments, usu with three or four parts

song /sɒŋ/ n **1** [C] short piece of music with words that you sing **2** [U] songs in general; music for singing [IDM] **for a song** (infml) at a very low price **a song and dance (about sth)** unnecessary fuss

sonic /'sɒnɪk/ adj (tech) relating to sound or the speed of sound

sonnet /'sɒnɪt/ n [C] poem containing 14 lines with 10 syllables each

soon /suːn/ adv **1** a short time from now; a short time after sth has happened: *We will ~ be home.* **2** early; quickly: *How ~ can you be ready?* [IDM] **as soon as** at the moment that: *He left as ~ as he heard the news.* ◇ *Please send it as ~ as possible.* **no sooner...than...** (written) used to say that sth happens immediately after sth else: *No ~er had she arrived than she had to leave again.* **the sooner the better** as quickly as possible **I, etc would sooner do sth (than do sth else)** prefer

to do sth (than do sth else): *I would ~er die than marry you.*

soot /sʊt/ n [U] black powder produced when wood, coal, etc is burnt ▶ **sooty** adj (-ier, -iest) covered with or black with soot

soothe /suːð/ v [T] **1** make sb who is upset, etc feel calmer **2** make a painful part of your body feel more comfortable ▶ **soothing** adj

sop /sɒp/ n [C] something offered to please sb who is angry, disappointed, etc

sophisticated /sə'fɪstɪkeɪtɪd/ adj **1** having or showing experience of the world and culture **2** (of a machine, system, etc) complicated and refined: *weapons* ▶ **sophistication** /sə,fɪstɪ'keɪʃn/ n [U]

soppy /'sɒpi/ adj (-ier, -iest) (infml) silly and sentimental

soprano /sə'prɑːnəʊ/ n [C] (pl **-s**) adj (music for, or singer with the) highest singing voice of women

sorcerer /'sɔːsərə(r)/ (fem **sorceress** /-əs/) n [C] (in stories) person with magic powers, helped by evil spirits ▶ **sorcery** n [U] magic that uses evil spirits

sordid /'sɔːdɪd/ adj **1** immoral or dishonest **2** very dirty and unpleasant ▶ **sordidly** adv ▶ **sordidness** n

sore /sɔː(r)/ adj **1** (of a part of the body) painful, and often red, esp because of infection **2** (esp US, infml) upset and angry: *feel ~* [IDM] **a sore point** subject that makes you feel angry or upset when it is mentioned **stand/stick out like a sore thumb** be very noticeable in an unpleasant way ● **sore** n [C] painful infected area on the skin ▶ **sorely** adv greatly: *~ly needed* ▶ **soreness** n [U]

sorrow /'sɒrəʊ/ n [C,U] feeling of great sadness because sth very bad has happened ● **sorrow** v [I] (lit) **~ (at/over)** feel or express great sadness ▶ **sorrowful** adj

sorry /'sɒri/ adj (-ier, -iest) **1** feeling sad and sympathetic: *I'm ~ to hear that your father's ill.* **2** feeling sad and ashamed about sth that has been done: *She was ~ for her past crimes.* **3** feeling disappointment and regret: *I was genuinely ~ to leave.* **4** poor and causing pity: *in a ~ state* [IDM] **be/feel sorry for sb** feel pity or sympathy for sb **I'm sorry** (spoken) **1** used when you are apologizing for sth **2** used for disagreeing with sb **3** used for introducing bad news: *I'm ~ to tell you that you've failed.* ● **sorry** exclam **1** used for apologizing for sth: *S~ I'm late.*

2 (*GB*) used for asking sb to repeat sth that you have not heard

0━ **sort¹** /sɔːt/ n [C] group of people or things that are alike in some way [IDM] **out of sorts** feeling ill or upset **sort of** (*infml*) to some extent: ~ *of pleased that it happened*

0━ **sort²** /sɔːt/ v [T] ~ (**out**) arrange things in groups in a particular order: ~ (*out*) *the good and bad apples* [PV] **sort sth out** (*infml*) **1** put sth in good order **2** deal with a problem ▶ **sorted** *exclam* (*spoken*) used to say sth has been done successfully: '*Did you book the hotel?*' '*Yes, ~!*'

SOS /ˌes əʊ 'es/ n [sing] urgent message for help sent by radio, etc

so-so /ˌsəʊ 'səʊ; *adj, adv* (*infml*) average; neither very well nor very badly: '*How are you feeling?*' '*So-so.*'

soufflé /ˈsuːfleɪ/ n [C,U] dish of eggs, milk, cheese etc beaten together and baked until it rises

0━ **soul** /səʊl/ n **1** [C] spiritual part of a person, believed to exist after death **2** [C,U] emotional and intellectual energy: *put ~ into your work* **3** [sing] perfect example of a good quality: *She's the ~ of discretion.* **4** [U] person: *not a ~ to be seen* **5** [U] = SOUL MUSIC ■ '**soul-destroying** *adj* (of work) very dull and boring ▶ **soulful** *adj* showing deep feeling ▶ **soulfully** *adv* ▶ **soulless** *adj* (of a person) feeling no emotion ■ **soul music** n [U] type of music that expresses feelings of African American musicians ■ '**soul-searching** n [U] careful examination of your thoughts and feelings

0━ **sound¹** /saʊnd/ n **1** [U] something you can hear: *the ~ of drums* **2** [sing] idea or impression that you get of sb/sth from what sb says or what you read: *I don't like the ~ of him.* ■ '**sound barrier** n [C] point at which an aircraft's speed equals that of sound ■ '**sound effect** n [usu pl] sound other than speech or music used in a film, play, etc ■ '**soundproof** *adj* made so that sound cannot pass through it or into it ■ '**soundproof** v [T] make a room, etc soundproof ■ '**soundtrack** n [C] music, etc used in a film

0━ **sound²** /saʊnd/ v **1** [I] give a certain impression: *His story ~s genuine.* **2** [I,T] (cause sth to) produce a sound **3** [T] give a signal by making a sound: ~ *the alarm* **4** [T] (*tech*) pronounce sth: *Don't ~ the 'b' in 'dumb'.* **5** [I,T] (*tech*) measure the depth of the sea or a lake with a weighted line [PV] **sound off** (**about sth**) (*infml*) express your opinions loudly or aggressively **sound sb out**

(**about/on sth**) try to find what sb thinks about sth

sound³ /saʊnd/ *adj* **1** sensible; that can be relied on: *a man of ~ judgement* **2** good and thorough: *She has a ~ grasp of the issues.* **3** in good condition; not hurt or ~. **4** deep: *be a ~ sleeper* ● **sound** *adv* deeply: ~ *asleep* ▶ **soundly** *adv* deeply or well ▶ **soundness** n [U]

soup /suːp/ n [U] liquid food made by cooking meat, vegetables, etc together in water [IDM] **in the soup** (*infml*) in difficulties

sour /ˈsaʊə(r)/ *adj* **1** having a sharp bitter taste **2** not fresh: ~ *milk* **3** not cheerful; bad-tempered [IDM] **go/turn sour** stop being pleasant or satisfactory ● **sour** v [I,T] (cause sth to) become sour ▶ **sourly** *adv* ▶ **sourness** n [U]

0━ **source** /sɔːs/ n [C] place, person or thing that you get sth from or where sth starts: *renewable energy ~s* ◇ *the ~ of a river* ● **source** v [T] (*business*) ~ (**from**) get sth from a particular source

0━ **south** /saʊθ/ n [U, sing] (*abbr* **S**) **1** (*the south*) point of the compass, to the right of a person facing the sunrise **2** (*the south, the South*) southern part of a country, region or the world ● **south** *adv* (*abbr* **S**) **1** in or towards the south **2** (of winds) from the south ● **south** *adv* towards the south ■ **south-'east** n [sing] *adj, adv* (*abbr* **SE**) (direction or region) halfway between south and east ▶ ˌsouth-'eastern *adj* ▶ **southerly** /ˈsʌðəli/ *adj, adv* **1** in or towards the south **2** (of winds) from the south ▶ **southern** (*also* **Southern**) /ˈsʌðən/ *adj* of or in the south part of the world or a region ▶ **southerner** n [C] person born or living in the southern part of a country ▶ **southward** /ˈsaʊθwəd/ *adv* towards the south ▶ **southward(s)** *adv* ■ ˌsouth-'west n [sing] *adj, adv* (*abbr* **SW**) (direction or region) halfway between south and west ▶ ˌsouth-'western *adj*

souvenir /ˌsuːvəˈnɪə(r)/ n [C] thing kept as a reminder of a person, a place or an event

sovereign /ˈsɒvrɪn/ n [C] (*fml*) king or queen ● **sovereign** *adj* **1** (of a country or state) free to govern itself; independent **2** having complete power ▶ **sovereignty** /ˈsɒvrənti/ n [U] complete power to govern a country

sow¹ /saʊ/ n [C] adult female pig

sow² /saʊ/ v (pt ~**ed** pp ~**n** /saʊn/ or ~**ed**) **1** [I,T] plant or spread seeds in or on the ground **2** [T] introduce or spread feelings, etc: ~ *discontent*

soya bean /ˌsɔɪə biːn/ n [C] type of bean grown as food and for its oil

spa /spɑː/ n [C] (place with a) spring of mineral water

0→ **space** /speɪs/ n **1** [U] amount of an area or a place that is empty and available for use: *There's not enough ~ here.* **2** [C] area or place that is empty: *a parking ~* **3** [U] large area of land that has no buildings on it **4** (*also* **outer** **space**) [U] the universe outside the earth's atmosphere **5** [C, usu sing] period of time: *within the ~ of a day* **6** [U] whole area in which all things exist and move [IDM] **look/stare/gaze into space** look straight ahead of you without looking at a particular thing, usu because you are thinking about sth ● **space** v [T] ~ (**out**) arrange things so that they have regular spaces between them ■ '**space-age** *adj* (*infml*) very modern ■ '**spacecraft** /'spaceship** n [C] vehicle for travelling in space ■ '**space shuttle** n [C] spacecraft designed to be used, eg for travelling between the earth and a space station ■ '**space station** n [C] large structure that is sent into space and remains there as a base for people working in space

spacial *adj* is SPATIAL

spacious /'speɪʃəs/ *adj* having a lot of space ▶ **spaciousness** n [U]

spade /speɪd/ n [C] **1** long-handled tool with a flat blade and sharp edge for digging **2** playing card with black figures shaped like leaves ■ '**spadework** n [U] hard work done as preparation for sth else

spaghetti /spə'geti/ n [U] long thin pieces of pasta that look like string

spam /spæm/ n [U] (*infml*) advertising material sent by email to people who have not asked for it ▶ **spamming** n [U] practice of sending mail, esp advertisements, through the Internet to a large number of people

span /spæn/ n [C] **1** time that sth lasts or is able to continue: *the ~ of a person's life* **2** range or variety of sth **3** distance or part between the supports of a bridge or an arch ● **span** v (**-nn-**) [T] **1** last all through a period of time; cover sth: *a life ~ning fifty years* **2** stretch right across sth

spaniel /'spænjəl/ n [C] breed of dog with long ears that hang down

spank /spæŋk/ v [T] hit sb, esp a child, several times on their bottom as a punishment ▶ **spank** n [C]

spanner /'spænə(r)/ (*US* **wrench**) n [C] tool for holding and turning nuts onto bolts, etc

spar /spɑː(r)/ v (**-rr-**) [I] ~ (**with**) **1** practise boxing **2** argue, usu in a friendly way

0→ **spare¹** /speə(r)/ *adj* **1** additional to what is needed: *two ~ chairs* **2** kept in case you need to replace the one you usually use; extra: *a ~*

---

spawn
key/tyre **3** (of time) free from work **4** (*written*) (of people) thin ● **spare** (*also* **spare part**) n [usu pl] new part for a car, machine, etc used to replace an old or broken part ■ **spare 'tyre** (*US* ~ **tire**) n [C] extra wheel for a car

spare² /speə(r)/ v [T] **1** be able to give money, time, etc for a purpose: *Can you ~ a few minutes?* ◊ *You should ~ a thought for* (= think about) *those who clean up after you.* **2** ~ **sb/ yourself (from)** save sb/yourself from having to go through an unpleasant experience **3** (*lit*) allow sb/sth to escape harm, damage or death: *~ a prisoner's life* **4** do sth well without limiting the time, money or effort involved: *No expense was ~d* (= a lot of money was spent). [IDM] **spare a thought for** consider (sb/sth) when making a decision ▶ **sparing** *adj* careful to give or use only a little of sth ▶ **sparingly** *adv*

spark /spɑːk/ n [C] **1** tiny flash of light produced by sth burning or an electric current being broken **2** [usu sing] small amount of a quality or feeling: *not a ~ of decency in him* ● **spark** v **1** [T] ~ (**off**) cause sth to start or develop, esp suddenly **2** [I] produce sparks ■ '**spark plug** (*also* '**sparking plug**) n [C] device for lighting the fuel in an engine

sparkle /'spɑːkl/ v [I] shine brightly with flashes of light. (*fig*) *Her conversation ~d.* ● **sparkle** n [C, U] act of sparkling: (*fig*) *a performance lacking in ~* ▶ **sparkling** /'spɑːklɪŋ/ *adj*

sparrow /'spærəʊ/ n [C] common small brown and grey bird

sparse /spɑːs/ *adj* not crowded or thick: *a ~ population* ▶ **sparsely** *adv* ▶ **sparseness** n [U]

spasm /'spæzəm/ n **1** [C, U] sudden uncontrollable tightening of a muscle **2** [C] sudden strong feeling or reaction ▶ **spasmodic** /-'mɒdɪk/ *adj* **1** done or happening at irregular intervals **2** (*tech*) caused or affected by spasms ▶ **spasmodically** *adv*

spat *pt, pp of* SPIT

spate /speɪt/ n [sing] large number of usu unpleasant things coming all at once: *a ~ of robberies*

spatial /'speɪʃl/ *adj* (*fml or tech*) of or concerning space ▶ **spatially** *adv*

spatter /'spætə(r)/ v **1** [I,T] cover sb/ sth with drops of liquid, dirt, etc **2** [I] fall on a surface in drops ● **spatter** n [sing] shower of drops of liquid

spatula /'spætʃələ/ n [C] tool with a flat flexible blade used for mixing and spreading things

spawn /spɔːn/ n [U] eggs of fish and frogs ● **spawn** v **1** [I,T] (of fish or frogs) lay eggs **2** [T] cause sth to develop or be produced

O┄ **speak** /spiːk/ v (pt **spoke** /spəʊk/ pp **spoken** /'spəʊkən/) **1** [I] make sb talk about sth; use your voice to say sth: *I was ~ing to her about my plans. ◇ Please ~ more slowly.* **2** [T] be able to use a language: *~ French* **3** [I] make a speech to an audience **4** [T] say or state sth: *~ the truth* [IDM] **be on speaking terms (with sb)** be willing to be friendly towards sb, esp after an argument **speak your mind** express your opinion openly [PV] **speak for sb** state the views or wishes of a person or group **speak out (against sth)** state your opinions publicly, esp in opposition to sth **speak up 1** speak more loudly **2** say what you think, esp to support or defend sb/sth ▸ **speaker** *n* [C] **1** person who makes a speech **2** person who speaks a particular language: *a French ~* **3** part of a radio or piece of musical or computing equipment that the sound comes out of

spear /spɪə(r)/ *n* [C] weapon with a metal point on a long shaft ● **spear** *v* [T] push or throw a spear through sth/sb ▸ **spearhead** *n* [C] person or group that begins an activity or leads an attack ▸ **spearhead** *v* [T] begin an activity or lead an attack

spearmint /'spɪəmɪnt/ *n* [U] kind of mint used esp in making sweets

O┄ **special** /'speʃl/ *adj* **1** of a particular kind; not common **2** of or for a certain person or purpose **3** exceptional in amount, degree, etc: *~ treatment* ● **special** *n* [C] **1** thing that is not usu available that is provided on one occasion: *a television ~ about the elections* **2** (*US, infml*) reduced price in a shop ▸ **specialist** *n* [C] person who is an expert in a particular subject, profession, etc ▸ **specially** *adv* particularly

speciality /ˌspeʃi'æləti/ (*esp US* **specialty**) *n* [C] (*pl* -**ies**) **1** type of food or product that a restaurant or place is famous for **2** sb's special interest, skill, subject, etc

specialize (*also* -**ise**) /'speʃəlaɪz/ *v* [I] ~ **(in)** become an expert in a particular area of work, study or business: *~ in modern history* ▸ **specialization** (*also* -**isation**) /ˌspeʃəlaɪ'zeɪʃn/ *n* [U]

species /'spiːʃiːz/ *n* [C] (*pl* **species**) group into which animals, plants, etc that are able to breed with each other are divided

O┄ **specific** /spə'sɪfɪk/ *adj* **1** detailed and precise: *~ instructions* **2** relating to one particular thing, etc: *for a ~ purpose* ▸ **specifically** /-kli/ *adv*

specification /ˌspesɪfɪ'keɪʃn/ *n* [C,U] detailed description of how sth is, or should be, designed or made

specify /'spesɪfaɪ/ *v* (pt, pp -**ied**) [T] state details, materials, etc clearly and precisely

specimen /'spesɪmən/ *n* [C] **1** small amount of sth that shows what the rest is like: *a ~ of her work* **2** small quantity of blood, etc taken from sb to be tested for disease

speck /spek/ *n* [C] small spot; tiny piece of dirt, etc

speckle /'spekl/ *n* [usu pl] small spot, esp one of many, on feathers, etc ▸ **speckled** *adj*

spectacle /'spektəkl/ *n* **1** (**spectacles**) [pl] (*fml*) = GLASSES **2** [C,U] impressive and exciting performance or event **3** [C] impressive sight or view

spectacular /spek'tækjələ(r)/ *adj* very impressive ▸ **spectacularly** *adv*

spectator /spek'teɪtə(r)/ *n* [C] person watching a show or sports event

spectrum /'spektrəm/ *n* [usu sing] (*pl* -**tra** /-trə/) **1** image of a band of colours as seen in a rainbow **2** (*written*) wide range of related qualities, ideas, etc: *a ~ of opinions*

speculate /'spekjuleɪt/ *v* **1** [I,T] form opinions without having complete knowledge **2** [I] buy and sell goods, shares, etc, hoping to make a profit but risking loss ▸ **speculation** /-'leɪʃn/ *n* [C,U] ▸ **speculative** *adj*

sped *pt, pp of* SPEED

O┄ **speech** /spiːtʃ/ *n* **1** [C] formal talk given to an audience: *make a ~* **2** [U] power, act or way of speaking ▸ **speechless** *adj* unable to speak, eg because of deep feeling

O┄ **speed** /spiːd/ *n* **1** [C,U] rate at which sb/sth moves: *a ~ of 10 kilometres an hour ◇ travelling at full ~* **2** [U] quickness of movement: *move with great ~* ● **speed** *v* (pt, pp) (**sped** /sped/ *or* ~**ed**) **1** [I] (*written*) go quickly **2** drive faster than the speed allowed by law: *The police caught him ~ing.* [PV] **speed (sth) up** (cause sth) to go faster: *~ up production* ■ **speedboat** *n* [C] boat with a motor that can travel very fast ■ **speed camera** *n* [C] (*GB*) machine which takes pictures of vehicles that are being driven too fast. These pictures are then used as evidence so that the drivers can be punished. ■ **speed dating** *n* [U] event at which single people meet and talk to each other for a short time, in the hope of finding partners ■ **speed hump** (*esp GB*) (*US* **speed bump**) *n* [C] raised area across a road to make traffic go slower ■ **speed limit** *n* [C] highest speed at which you can legally drive on a particular road ■ **speedometer** /spiː'dɒmɪtə(r)/ *n* [C] instrument showing the speed of a vehicle, etc ■ **speedway** n [C,U] (track used for) racing motorbikes ▸ **speedy** adj (-ier, -iest) quick

0— **spell**¹ /spel/ n [C] **1** short period of time during which sth lasts: a ~ of warm weather **2** period spent doing a certain activity: a ~ at the wheel (= driving) **3** (condition produced by) words supposed to have magic power: (fig) under the ~ of a fascinating man ■ **spellbound** adj with the attention held (as if) by a magic spell

0— **spell**² /spel/ v (pt, pp **spelt** /spelt/ or **-ed**) **1** [I,T] say or write the letters of a word in the correct order **2** [T] (of letters) form words when in a particular order: C-A-T spells cat. **3** [T] have sth, usu sth bad, as a result: The crop failure spelt disaster for farmers. [PV] **spell sth out** make sth easy to understand ■ **spellcheck** (also **spellchecker**) n [C] computer program that checks your writing to see if your spelling is correct ▸ **spellcheck** v [T] ■ **spelling** n **1** [U] act of forming words correctly from individual letters; ability to do this **2** [C] way in which a word is spelt

spelunking /spɪˈlʌŋkɪŋ/ n [U] (US) = CAVING

0— **spend** /spend/ v (pt, pp **spent** /spent/) **1** [I,T] ~ (on) pay out money for goods, services, etc **2** [T] use time for a purpose; pass time: ~ a week in hospital **3** [T] use energy, effort, etc until it has all been used: ~ your energy cleaning the house [IDM] **spend a penny** (old-fash, GB, infml) go to the toilet ■ **spendthrift** n [C] (disapprov) person who wastes money ▸ **spent** adj used up

sperm /spɜːm/ n [C] male sex cell which fertilizes a female egg

spew /spjuː/ v [I,T] (cause sth to) come out in a stream **2** ~ (sth) (up) to vomit

sphere /sfɪə(r)/ n [C] **1** completely round solid shape **2** range of interests, activities, influence, etc ▸ **spherical** /ˈsferɪkl/ adj round

0— **spice** /spaɪs/ n [C,U] one of various types of powder or seed that come from plants and are used in cooking **2** [U] extra interest or excitement: add ~ to a story ● **spice** v [T] add spice to sth ▸ **spicy** adj (-ier, -iest) **1** containing spice **2** exciting and slightly shocking

spick /spɪk/ adj [IDM] **spick and span** clean and tidy

0— **spider** /ˈspaɪdə(r)/ n [C] small creature with eight legs, esp one that spins a web to trap insects ▸ **spidery** adj long and thin, like the legs of a spider: ~y handwriting

spied pt, pp of SPY

spike /spaɪk/ n [C] **1** thin object with a sharp point **2** (usu pl) metal point

attached to the sole of a running shoe, etc **3** long pointed group of flowers that grow together on a single stem ● **spike** v [T] **1** push a sharp piece of metal, wood, etc into sb/sth **2** add alcohol, poison or a drug to sb's drink or food without them knowing ▸ **spiky** adj (-ier, -iest)

spill /spɪl/ v (pt, pp **spilt** /spɪlt/ or **-ed**) [I,t] (cause liquid or powder to) run over the side of the container [IDM] **spill the beans** (infml) reveal a secret

0— **spin** /spɪn/ v (-nn- pt pp **spun** /spʌn/ or **span** /spæn/) **1** [I,T] (cause sth to) turn round and round quickly **2** [I,T] make thread from wool, cotton, etc by twisting it **3** [T] (of a spider or silkworm) produce thread from its body to make a web or cocoon: Spiders ~ webs. **4** [T] compose a story [PV] **spin sth out** make sth last as long as possible ● **spin** n [C,U] **1** very fast turning movement **2** [sing, U] (infml) way of presenting information, esp in a way that makes you or your ideas seem good **3** [C] short ride in a car for pleasure [IDM] **in a (flat) spin** very confused, worried or excited ■ **spin doctor** n [C] (infml) person whose job is to present information to the public about a politician, etc in the most positive way possible ■ **spin dryer** (also ~ **drier**) n [C] (GB) machine that spins clothes to dry them ■ **spin-off** n [C] product, etc resulting indirectly from another activity

spinach /ˈspɪnɪdʒ/ n [U] plant with large green leaves, cooked and eaten as a vegetable

spinal /ˈspaɪnl/ adj (anat) of the spine (1)

spindle /ˈspɪndl/ n [C] **1** thin rod for winding thread by hand in spinning **2** bar on which part of a machine turns ▸ **spindly** /ˈspɪndli/ adj (-ier, -iest) long and thin

spine /spaɪn/ n [C] **1** row of small bones that are connected together down the middle of the back **2** sharp point on some animals and plants, eg the cactus **3** part of the cover of a book where the pages are joined together ■ **spine-chilling** adj very frightening ▸ **spineless** adj (disapprov) cowardly ▸ **spiny** adj (-ier, -iest) (of animals or plants) having sharp points

spinster /ˈspɪnstə(r)/ n [C] (old-fash often disapprov) unmarried woman

spiral /ˈspaɪrəl/ n [C] **1** curve winding round a central point: A snail's shell is a ~. **2** continuous harmful increase or decrease in sth ● **spiral** adj moving in a continuous curve winding round a central point:

A B C D E F G H I J K L M N O P Q R **S** T U V W X Y Z

spire *a ~ staircase* • **spiral** v (-ll- *US* -l-) [I]
1 move in a spiral **2** increase rapidly

spire /ˈspaɪə(r)/ n [C] pointed tower, esp of a church

0─ **spirit** /ˈspɪrɪt/ n **1** [U,C] person's thoughts and feelings or soul **2** (spirits) [pl] state of mind: *in high ~s* (= cheerful) **3** [C] person: *What a generous ~!* **4** [U] courage or energy: *act with ~* **5** [sing] mental attitude; state of mind: *It depends on the ~ in which it was done.* **6** [U] real meaning or purpose of sth **7** [C] soul without a body; ghost **8** [C, usu pl] strong alcoholic drink, eg whisky [IDM] **in spirit** in your thoughts • **spirit** v [T] take sth away quickly or mysteriously • **spirited** *adj* lively, brave, etc **2** having the mood stated: *high-/low-~ed*

0─ **spiritual** /ˈspɪrɪtʃuəl/ *adj* **1** connected with the human spirit rather than the body **2** religious • **spiritual** n [C] religious song as originally sung by black slaves in the US ▸ **spiritually** *adv*

spit /spɪt/ n **1** [U] saliva **2** [C] narrow point of land jutting out into the sea, etc **3** [C] metal spike which holds meat, etc for roasting • **spit** v (-tt- pt, pp **spat** /spæt/) **1** [T] force liquid, food, etc from the mouth **2** [I] force saliva out of your mouth, often as a sign of lack of respect **3** [T] say sth angrily: *He was ~ting abuse at the judge.* **4** [I] (used with *it*) rain lightly [IDM] **be the spitting image of sb** → IMAGE

0─ **spite** /spaɪt/ n [U] feeling of wanting to hurt or upset sb: *do sth out of ~* [IDM] **in spite of sth** without being prevented by the conditions mentioned: *They went out in ~ of the rain.* • **spite** v [T] deliberately annoy or upset sb • **spiteful** *adj* unkind

splash /splæʃ/ v **1** [I] (of liquid) fall noisily onto a surface **2** [T] make sb/ sth wet by throwing liquid: *~ water on the floor* **3** [I] move through water making drops fly everywhere: *People were ~ing around in the pool.* [PV] **splash sth across/over sth** put a photograph, news story, etc in a place where it will be easily noticed **splash out (on sth)** (*infml*) spend a lot of money on sth • **splash** n [C] sound or act of, or mark made by, splashing

spleen /spliːn/ n [C] organ that controls the quality of the blood in the body

splendid /ˈsplendɪd/ *adj* **1** very impressive: *a ~ view* **2** (*old-fash*) excellent ▸ **splendidly** *adv*

splendour (*US* -dor) /ˈsplendə(r)/ n [U] grand and impressive beauty

splice /splaɪs/ v [T] join two pieces of a rope, film, tape, etc together

splint /splɪnt/ n [C] piece of wood or metal tied to a broken arm or leg to keep it still and in position

splinter /ˈsplɪntə(r)/ n [C] sharp piece of wood, glass, etc broken from a larger piece • **splinter** v [I,T] (cause sb) to break into splinters • **splinter group** n [C] (esp in politics) group that has separated from a larger one

0─ **split** /splɪt/ v (-tt- pt, pp **split**) **1** [I,T] (cause a group of people to) divide into separate or opposing parts: *Arguments ~ the group.* **2** [T] divide sth into parts and share it with others: *~ the profits* **3** [I,T] (cause sth) to tear along a straight line: *The box ~ open).* **4** [T] cut sth's skin and make it bleed **5** [I] **~ (from/with)** leave sb and stop having a relationship with them: *He ~ with his wife in June.* [IDM] **split hairs** pay too much attention to small differences **split your sides (laughing/with laughter)** laugh very much [PV] **split up (with sb)** stop having a relationship with sb • **split** n **1** [C] separation or division **2** [C] crack or tear made by splitting **3** (the splits) [pl] act of sitting with the legs stretched in opposite directions: *a gymnast doing the ~s* • **split perso'nality** n [C] mental disorder in which one person seems to have two distinct personalities ■ **split 'second** n [C] very short moment

splutter /ˈsplʌtə(r)/ v **1** [I,T] speak quickly and with difficulty, because you are angry or embarrassed **2** [I] make a series of short explosive sounds: *The fire ~ed.* • **splutter** n [C] short explosive sound

0─ **spoil** /spɔɪl/ v (pt, pp or ~ed) **1** [T] ruin the value or pleasure of sth: *Rain ~ed our holiday.* **2** [T] harm the character of a child by lack of discipline **3** spoil sb/yourself [T] make sb/yourself happy by doing sth special **4** [I] (of food, etc) become bad • the spoils n [pl] (*fml*) stolen goods, profit, etc • **'spoilsport** n [C] person who ruins others' enjoyment

spoke[1] /spəʊk/ n [C] rod connecting the centre of a wheel to the edge

spoke[2] pt of SPEAK

0─ **spoken** pp of SPEAK

0─ **spokesman** /ˈspəʊksmən/ (pl **-men**) (*also* **spokesperson** (pl **-people**) (fem **spokeswoman** (pl **-women**) n [C] person speaking as the representative of a group, etc

sponge /spʌndʒ/ n **1** [C, U] (piece of) a) soft light substance that is full of holes and can hold water easily **2** [C] simple sea animal with a body full of holes from which natural sponge is obtained **3** [C,U] (*GB*) = SPONGE CAKE • **sponge** v **1** [T] wipe sb/ yourself/sth with a sponge **2** [T] remove sth using a wet cloth or

sponge 3 [I,T] (*infml, disapprov*) get money, food, etc from people without offering anything in return: ~ *money off/from your friends*
■ **'sponge cake** n [C,U] (*GB*) soft light cake ▶ **spongy** adj (**-ier, -iest**)

sponsor /'spɒnsə(r)/ n [C] **1** person, company, etc that pays for an event **2** person or company that supports sb by paying for their training or education ● **sponsor** v [T] **1** pay for an event, programme, etc as a way of advertising **2** pay sb money if they do sth for charity ▶ **sponsorship** n [U]

spontaneous /spɒn'teɪniəs/ adj done, happening, etc naturally and not planned: *a ~ offer of help* ▶ **spontaneity** /ˌspɒntə'neɪəti/ n [U] ▶ **spontaneously** adv

spoof /spuːf/ n [C] (*infml*) humorous copy of a film, TV programme, etc

spooky /'spuːki/ adj (**-ier, -iest**) (*infml*) frightening

spool /spuːl/ n [C] reel for thread, film, tape, etc

0~ **spoon** /spuːn/ n [C] utensil with a shallow bowl on a handle, used for putting food, eg soup, into the mouth ● **spoon** v [T] lift and move food with a spoon ■ **'spoon-feed** v [T] (*disapprov*) teach people sth in a way that does not make them think for themselves

sporadic /spə'rædɪk/ adj occurring only occasionally ▶ **sporadically** /-kli/ adv

spore /spɔː(r)/ n [C] (*biol*) small cell like a seed produced by some plants, eg mushrooms

0~ **sport** /spɔːt/ n **1** [U] activity done for pleasure or exercise, usu according to rules **2** [C] particular form of sport: *water ~* s [IDM] **be a (good) sport** (*infml*) be generous, cheerful and pleasant ● **sport** v [T] have or wear sth proudly: *a new beard* ▶ **sporting** adj **1** of sport **2** fair and generous in your treatment of others [IDM] **a sporting chance** a reasonable chance of success ■ **'sports car** n [C] low fast car, often with a roof that can be folded back ■ **'sportsman** (pl **-men**) **'sportswoman** (pl **-women**) n [C] person who takes part in sport ■ **'sportsmanship** n [U] quality of being fair and generous, esp in sport ■ **sport u'tility vehicle** n [C] (*abbr* **SUV**) (*esp US*) type of large car, made originally for travelling over rough ground ▶ **sporty** adj (**-ier, -iest**) good at or liking sport

0~ **spot** /spɒt/ n [C] **1** small esp round mark of a different colour from the surface it is on **2** small dirty mark on sth **3** small red and infected mark on the skin **4** place: *a secluded ~* **5** (*infml*) ~ of small amount: *a ~ of tea* [IDM] **in a (tight) spot** (*infml*) in a difficult situation **on the spot**

---

spread

1 immediately: *an on-the-~ parking fine* **2** actual place where sth is happening ● **spot** v (**-tt-**) [T] see or notice sth/sb [IDM] **be spotted with sth** be covered with small round marks of sth ▶ **spotted** adj marked with spots ▶ **spotless** adj completely clean ▶ **spotty** adj (**-ier, -iest**) (of a person) having a lot of spots on the skin

spotlight /'spɒtlaɪt/ n [C] (lamp used for sending a) strong light directed at a particular place ● **spotlight** v [T] (pt, pp **spotlit** /-lɪt/ or, in sense 2 **-ed**) **1** shine a spotlight on sb/sth: *a spotlit stage* **2** direct attention at a problem, situation, etc

spouse /spaʊs/ n [C] (*fml* or *law*) husband or wife

spout /spaʊt/ n [C] pipe through which liquid pours: *a ~ on a teapot* [IDM] **be/go up the spout** (*GB, sl*) go wrong; be spoilt ● **spout** v **1** [I,T] (cause liquid) to come out of sth with great force **2** [T] (*infml, disapprov*) speak a lot about sth; repeat sth in a boring or annoying way

sprain /spreɪn/ v [T] injure a joint in your body by suddenly twisting it: *~ an ankle* ▶ **sprain** n [C]

sprang pt of SPRING²

sprawl /sprɔːl/ v [I] **1** sit or lie with your arms and legs spread out in a relaxed or awkward way **2** spread untidily over a large area ▶ **sprawl** n [C, usu sing, U] large area covered with buildings that spreads into the countryside in an ugly way: *urban ~*

0~ **spray** /spreɪ/ n **1** [U,C] liquid sent through the air in tiny drops **2** [U,C] substance that is forced out of a container, eg an aerosol, in the form of tiny drops: *hair~* **3** [C] device or container that turns liquid into tiny drops **4** [C] small branch of a tree or plant, esp for decoration ● **spray** v [I,T] cover sb/sth with very small drops of liquid

0~ **spread** /spred/ v (pt, pp **spread**) **1** [T] extend the surface of sth by unfolding it: *The bird ~ its wings.* **2** [T] put a substance on a surface: *~ butter on bread* **3** [I,T] (cause sth to) become more widely known, felt, etc: *~ disease* **4** [T] extend over an area or period of time ● **spread** n **1** [U] growth or increase of sth: *the rapid ~ of the disease* **2** [U,C] soft food that you put on bread **3** [usu sing] extent or width of sth **4** [C] (*infml*) a lot of food on a table ■ **spread'eagled** adj in a position with your arms and legs spread out ■ **'spreadsheet** n [C] computer program for displaying and changing rows of figures

---

A B C D E F G H I J K L M N O P Q R **S** T U V W X Y Z

sprightly /ˈspraɪtli/ adj (-ier, -iest) lively and active ▸ **sprightliness** n [U]

0— **spring¹** /sprɪŋ/ n 1 [U, C] season of the year between winter and summer, when plants begin to grow 2 [C] length of coiled wire which returns to its shape after being pulled or pressed: *bed*-~s 3 [U] ability of a spring to return to its original position 4 [C] place where water comes naturally to the surface from under the ground 5 [C] quick sudden jump ● **spring-clean** v [T] clean a house, etc thoroughly, including the parts you do not usu clean ▸ **spring clean** n [sing] ▸ **springy** adj (-ier, -iest) returning quickly to the original shape when pushed, pulled, etc

spring² /sprɪŋ/ v (pt **sprang** /spræŋ/ pp **sprung** /sprʌŋ/) 1 [I] jump or move suddenly: ~ (up) from your *chair* ~ **(on)** do sth, ask sth or say sth that sb is not expecting: *She sprang the news on me.* 2 [T] [IDM] **spring a leak** (of a boat, etc) begin to leak [PV] **spring from sth** have sth as a source or an origin **spring up** appear or develop quickly

sprinkle /ˈsprɪŋkl/ v [T] throw small pieces of sth or drops of liquid on sth ▸ **sprinkler** /-klə(r)/ n [C] device for sprinkling water in drops on grass, plants, etc

sprint /sprɪnt/ v [I, T] run at full speed ● **sprint** n [C] fast run ▸ **sprinter** n [C]

sprout /spraʊt/ v [I, T] produce leaves, etc or begin to grow: (fig) *houses* ~*ing (up) on the edge of town* ● **sprout** n [C] 1 = BRUSSELS SPROUT 2 new part of a plant

sprung pp of SPRING²

spun pp of SPIN

spur /spɜː(r)/ n [C] 1 sharp pointed object worn on the heel of a rider's boot, used to make the horse go faster 2 thing that encourages sb to try or work harder [IDM] **on the spur of the moment** without planning in advance ● **spur** v (-rr-) [T] ~ **(on)** encourage sb to do sth or try harder to achieve sth

spurn /spɜːn/ v [T] reject or refuse sb, an offer, etc

spurt /spɜːt/ v 1 [I, T] (cause liquids, etc to) come out in a sudden burst 2 [I] make a sudden effort in a race, contest, etc ● **spurt** n [C] 1 sudden burst of liquid, etc 2 sudden burst of energy, speed, etc 3 sudden rush of liquid, etc

sputter /ˈspʌtə(r)/ v [I] make a series of spitting sounds

spy /spaɪ/ n [C] (pl **-ies**) person who tries to get secret information about another country, organization, or person ● **spy** v (pt, pp **-ied**) 1 [I, T] ~ **(on)** collect secret information about sb/sth 2 [T] (*lit* or *fml*) suddenly see or notice sb/sth

squabble /ˈskwɒbl/ v [I], n [C] (have a) quarrel, usu about sth unimportant

squad /skwɒd/ n [C, with sing or pl verb] small group of people working as a team: *a football* ~

squadron /ˈskwɒdrən/ n [C, with sing or pl verb] group of military aircraft or ships

squalid /ˈskwɒlɪd/ adj (disapprov) 1 dirty and unpleasant 2 morally bad ▸ **squalidly** adv

squall /skwɔːl/ n [C] 1 sudden violent wind 2 loud cry, esp from a baby ● **squall** v [I] cry noisily

squalor /ˈskwɒlə(r)/ n [U] dirty and unpleasant conditions

squander /ˈskwɒndə(r)/ v [T] ~ **(on)** waste time, money, etc in a stupid or careless way

0— **square¹** /skweə(r)/ adj 1 having four straight equal sides and four angles of 90° 2 forming an angle of 90°: ~ *corners* 3 equal to a square with sides of a stated length: *six metres* ~ *a* [infml] having paid all the money owed to sb: *Here's the £10 I owe you—now we're* ~. 5 (*sport*) (of two teams) having the same number of points 6 honest; fair: ~ *dealings* [IDM] **a square meal** a satisfying meal **a square peg in a round hole** (*GB, infml*) person who does not feel happy or comfortable in a particular situation ● **square** adv directly; not at an angle ▸ **squarely** adv 1 directly; not at an angle or to one side: *I looked her* ~*ly in the eye.* 2 directly or exactly; without any uncertainty ▸ **squareness** n [U] ▸ **square root** n [C] (*maths*) number which when multiplied by itself gives a particular number: *The* ~ *root of 4 is 2.*

0— **square²** /skweə(r)/ n [C] 1 shape or area with four equal sides and four angles of 90° 2 four-sided open area in a town 3 result when a number is multiplied by itself [IDM] **back to square one** a return to the situation you were in at the beginning of a project, task, etc

square³ /skweə(r)/ v 1 [T] ~ **(off)** make sth have straight edges and corners 2 [T] multiply a number by itself 3 [T] make sth straight or level 4 [T] (*infml*) bribe sb [PV] **square sth off** mark off in squares **square (sth) with sth** make two ideas, facts or situations agree or be consistent with each other: ~ *the theory with the facts* **square up (with sb)** pay money that you owe

squash /skwɒʃ/ v 1 [T] press sth so that it becomes soft, damaged or flat 2 [I, T] push sb/sth or yourself into a space that is too small: ~ *ten people into a car* **3** [T] stop sth from continuing; destroy sth because it is a problem for you ● **squash** *n* **1** [U] game for two players, played with rackets and a rubber ball in a walled court **2** [C,U] (*GB*) drink made from fruit juice **3** [C,U] (*pl* **squash** *or* **~es**) type of vegetable that grows on the ground, eg a pumpkin or marrow **4** [sing] (*infml*) crowd of people squashed together

squat /skwɒt/ *v* (**-tt-**) [I] **1** sit with your legs bent under your body **2** occupy empty buildings, land, etc without permission ● **squat** *adj* short and wide or fat ● **squat** *n* [C] building occupied by squatters ▸ **squatter** *n* [C] person who lives in a building, etc without permission and without paying rent

squawk /skwɔːk/ *v* [I] **1** (of birds) make a loud harsh sound **2** speak in a loud sharp voice because you are angry, surprised, etc ▸ **squawk** *n* [C]

squeak /skwiːk/ *v* [I,T], *n* [C] (make a) short high sound that is not very loud ▸ **squeaky** *adj* (**-ier, -iest**)

squeal /skwiːl/ *n* [C] long high cry or sound ● **squeal** *v* [I] **1** make a long high sound **2** (*infml, disapprov*) give information, esp to the police about sth illegal sb has done

squeamish /ˈskwiːmɪʃ/ *adj* **1** easily made sick by unpleasant sights or situations, esp the sight of blood **2** easily shocked, offended, etc ▸ **squeamishly** *adv* ▸ **squeamishness** *n* [U]

0̶ⁿ **squeeze** /skwiːz/ *v* **1** [T] press sth firmly, esp with your fingers: ~ *a sponge* **2** [T] ~ (**from/out of**) get liquid out of sth by pressing or twisting it hard **3** [I,T] force sb/sth/ yourself into or through a small space: ~ *into the back seat* [PV] **squeeze sth out of/from sb** get sth by putting pressure on sb, using threats, etc ● **squeeze** *n* **1** [C, usu sing] act of pressing sth **2** [sing] condition of being squeezed **3** [C, usu sing] (difficulty caused by a) reduction in the amount of money, jobs, etc available

squelch /skweltʃ/ *v* [I] make a sucking sound as when feet are lifted from mud ● **squelch** *n* [C] squelching sound

squid /skwɪd/ *n* [C,U] sea creature with ten long arms around its body

squint /skwɪnt/ *v* [I] **1** look at sth with your eyes partly shut **2** (*GB*) (of an eye) look in a different direction from the other eye ● **squint** *n* [C, usu sing] disorder of the eye muscles which causes each eye to look in a different direction

squirm /skwɜːm/ *v* [I] **1** move by twisting the body about **2** feel embarrassment or shame ▸ **squirm** *n* [C] squirming movement

squirrel /ˈskwɪrəl/ *n* [C] small bushytailed animal with red or grey fur

squirt /skwɜːt/ *v* **1** [I,T] force liquid, gas, etc out in a thin fast stream through a narrow opening; be forced out in this way **2** [T] hit sb/sth with a stream of water, gas, etc ● **squirt** *n* [C] thin fast stream of a liquid

St *abbr* **1** (used in addresses) Street **2** Saint

stab /stæb/ *v* (**-bb-**) [I,T] **1** push a pointed weapon into sb, killing or injuring them **2** make a short, forceful movement with a finger, etc [IDM] **stab sb in the back** betray sb ● **stab** *n* [C] **1** act of stabbing sb/sth **2** sudden sharp pain **3** attempt to do sth: *have a ~ at sth* ▸ **stabbing** *adj* (of pain) very sharp and sudden

0̶ⁿ **stable**¹ /ˈsteɪbl/ *adj* **1** firmly fixed; not likely to move, change or fail **2** (of a person) calm and reasonable; balanced ▸ **stability** /stəˈbɪləti/ *n* [U] ▸ **stabilize** (*also* **-ise**) /ˈsteɪbəlaɪz/ *v* [I,T] (cause sth to) become firm, steady and unlikely to change ▸ **stabilizer** (*also* **-iser**) *n* [C] device that keeps sth steady

0̶ⁿ **stable**² /ˈsteɪbl/ *n* [C] building in which horses are kept ● **stable** *v* [T] put or keep a horse in a stable

stack /stæk/ *n* [C] **1** (usu neat) pile: *a ~ of books* **2** pile of hay, straw, etc stored in the open **3** tall chimney or group of chimneys **4** (**stacks**) [pl] (*infml*) ~ (**of**) large number of sth ● **stack** *v* [T] **1** arrange things in a pile **2** fill sth with piles of things

stadium /ˈsteɪdiəm/ *n* (*pl* **~s** *or* **-dia** /-diə/) *n* [C] large sports ground, with seats for spectators

0̶ⁿ **staff** /stɑːf/ *n* **1** [C, usu sing] all the workers employed in an organization considered as a group **2** (*US*) people who work at a school or university, but who do not teach students **3** [C, with sing or pl verb] group of senior army officers **4** [C] strong stick used as a support when walking ● **staff** *v* [T] (provide people to) work in an institution, company, etc

stag /stæg/ *n* [C] male deer

0̶ⁿ **stage** /steɪdʒ/ *n* **1** [C] period or step in development, growth, etc: *at an early ~ in her life* **2** [C] separate part that a process, etc is divided into **3** [C] raised platform on which actors perform plays **4** (often **the stage**) [sing] acting as a profession: *go on the ~* (= be an actor) **5** [sing] place where important things happen, esp in politics [IDM] **be/go on the stage** be/become an actor ● **stage** *v* [T] produce a performance of a play, etc ■ **stagecoach** *n* [C] vehicle pulled by horses, which was

used in the past to carry passengers
■ **stage 'manager** n [C] person in charge of a theatre stage

stagger /'stægə(r)/ v **1** [I] walk unsteadily **2** [T] shock or surprise sb very much **3** [T] arrange events, etc so that they do not happen together ▸ **stagger** n [C]

stagnant /'stægnənt/ adj **1** (of air or water) not moving and therefore smelling bad **2** not developing, growing or changing

stagnate /stæg'neɪt/ v [I] **1** stop developing or making progress **2** be or become stagnant ▸ **stagnation** /-ʃn/ n [U]

staid /steɪd/ adj (of appearance, behaviour, etc) dull, quiet and serious ▸ **staidly** adv ▸ **staidness** n [U]

stain /steɪn/ v **1** [T] leave marks that are difficult to remove on sth **2** [I] become marked **3** [T] colour wood, fabric, etc ● **stain** n **1** [C] dirty mark that is difficult to remove **2** [U] liquid used for colouring wood, etc **3** [C] thing that harms sb's reputation, etc ■ **stained glass** n [U] pieces of coloured glass, often used to make patterns in windows ▸ **stainless 'steel** n [U] type of steel that does not rust

0-▪ **stair** /steə(r)/ n **1** (stairs) [pl] set of steps built between two floors inside a building: *a flight of ~s* **2** [C] one of a series of steps: *sitting on the bottom ~* ■ **staircase** | **stairway** n [C] set of stairs inside a building

stake /steɪk/ n **1** [C] strong pointed wooden or metal post pushed into the ground to support sth, etc **2** [C] money that sb invests in a company: *I have a ~ in the company's success.* **3** [C, usu pl] sum of money risked or gambled [IDM] **at stake** that can be won or lost, depending on the success of a particular action ● **stake** v **1** [T] risk money or sth important on the result of sth **2** support sth with a stake [IDM] **stake (out) a/your claim (to/for/on sth)** say or show publicly that you think sth should be yours (*infml*) [PV] **stake sth out** watch a place secretly, esp for signs of illegal activity

stale /steɪl/ adj **1** (of food, etc) not fresh **2** no longer interesting because too well known **3** no longer able to do sth well because you have been doing the same thing for too long ▸ **staleness** n [U]

stalemate /'steɪlmeɪt/ n [C,U] **1** position in chess in which no further move can be made **2** stage in an argument, etc in which no further discussion seems possible

stalk /stɔːk/ n [C] thin stem that supports a flower, leaf or fruit and

joins it to another part of the plant ● **stalk** v **1** [I,T] move slowly and quietly towards an animal or a person, in order to kill, catch or harm it or them: *He ~ed his victim as she was walking home.* **2** [T] illegally follow and watch sb over a long period of time **3** [I] walk in an angry or proud way ▸ **stalker** n [C] **1** person who follows and watches another person over a long period of time **2** person who follows an animal in order to kill it

stall /stɔːl/ n [C] **1** compartment for one animal in a stable **2** table or small open shop, etc from which things are sold in the street **3** (the stalls) [pl] seats in a theatre nearest the stage ● **stall** v **1** [I,T] (cause a vehicle or an engine to) stop suddenly because of lack of power or speed **2** [I] delay doing sth so that you have more time **3** [T] make sb wait so that you have more time to do sth

stallion /'stæliən/ n [C] male horse, esp one used for breeding

stamina /'stæmɪnə/ n [U] energy and strength to work hard, run long distances, etc

stammer /'stæmə(r)/ v [I,T] speak with difficulty, repeating sounds or words before saying things correctly ● **stammer** n [sing] tendency to stammering speech

0-▪ **stamp¹** /stæmp/ n [C] **1** (*also fml* **'postage stamp**) small piece of printed paper stuck on envelopes, parcels, etc to show that postage has been paid: *a ~ album* **2** tool for printing the date or a mark on a surface **3** words, design, etc made by stamping sth on a surface **4** small piece of paper stuck on a document to show that an amount of money has been paid **5** act of stamping with the foot ■ **stamp album** n [C] book for keeping postage stamps collected as a hobby

0-▪ **stamp²** /stæmp/ v **1** [I,T] put your foot down with force on the ground, etc **2** [T] ~ **A on B**; ~ **B with A** print a design, the date, etc onto sth using a special tool **3** [T] make a feeling show clearly on sb's face, in their actions etc: *The crime had revenge ~ed all over it.* **4** [T] stick a stamp on a letter or parcel [PV] **stamp sth out** get rid of sth bad, unpleasant or dangerous, esp by using force

stampede /stæm'piːd/ n [C] sudden rush of people or animals, eg through fear ● **stampede** v [I,T] (cause animals or people to) move in a stampede

stance /stæns/ n [C] **1** way of standing, esp when striking the ball in golf, cricket, etc **2** attitude, opinion: *her ~ on nuclear arms*

0-▪ **stand¹** /stænd/ n **1** [usu sing] attitude or opinion **2** [C] strong effort to defend yourself or your opinion: *make a ~ against job losses* **3** [C] table or upright structure where things are sold or displayed **4** [C] piece of furniture for holding a particular type of thing: *a music ~* **5** [C] building where people stand or sit to watch sports contests, etc **6** [usu sing] = WITNESS BOX (WITNESS)

0→ **stand²** /stænd/ v (pt, pp **stood** /stʊd/) **1** [I] be on your feet; be upright **2** [I] get up onto your feet from another position **3** [T] put sth/ sb in an upright position: *~ the ladder against the wall* **4** [I] be in a certain place, condition or situation: *the house ~s on the corner* **5** [I] be a particular height: *She ~s five foot six.* **6** [I] ~ **at** be at a particular level, amount, height, etc **7** [I] (of an offer, decision, etc) be still valid: *My decision ~s.* **8** [T] (used esp with can't, couldn't) strongly dislike sb/ sth: *I can't ~ her brother.* **9** [T] be able to survive or tolerate sth without being harmed or damaged: *His heart won't ~ the strain.* **10** [T] buy a drink or meal for sb: *~ sb a meal* **11** [I] ~ (**for/as**) be a candidate in an election: *~ for parliament* [IDM] **it stands to reason** (*infml*) it must be obvious to any sensible person who thinks about it **stand a chance (of doing sth)** have the possibility of succeeding or achieving sth **stand fast/firm** refuse to move back; refuse to change your opinions **stand your ground** → GROUND¹ **stand on your own (two) feet** be independent **stand out like a sore thumb** → SORE [PV] **stand by 1** be present while sth bad happens without doing anything **2** be ready for action **stand by sb** help or support sb, esp in a difficult situation **stand by sth** still believe sth you said, decided or agreed earlier **stand down** resign from a job, etc; withdraw **stand for sth 1** be an abbreviation or symbol for sth: *PO ~s for Post Office.* **2** (not stand for sth) not tolerate sth: *She won't ~ for disobedience.* **stand in (for sb)** take the place of sb **stand out (as sth)** be much better or more important than sb/sth **stand out (from/against sth)** be easily seen; be noticeable **stand sb up** (*infml*) deliberately not meet sb you have arranged to meet **stand up for sb/sth** support or defend sb/sth **stand up to sb** resist sb **stand up to sth** remain in good condition in spite of hard use, etc ■ **standby** n [C] person or thing to be used as a substitute, esp in case of emergency [IDM] **on standby** ready to do sth immediately if needed or asked ■ **stand-in** n [C] person who does sb's job for them for a short time ■ **stand-offish** /ˌstænd ˈɒfɪʃ/ *adj* (*infml*) (of people) unfriendly

433

starry

■ **standpoint** n [usu sing] point of view

0→ **standard** /ˈstændəd/ n [C] **1** thing used as a measure **2** (normal or expected) level of quality: *the ~ of her school work* **3** special flag ● **standard** *adj* of the normal or usual kind: *~ sizes of paper* ▸ **standardize** (*also* **-ise**) v [T] make sth conform to a fixed standard of size, shape, quality, etc ■ **standard lamp** n [C] tall lamp with a base on the floor ■ **standard of 'living** n [C] level of comfort, wealth, etc enjoyed by a particular group of people

standing /ˈstændɪŋ/ n [U] **1** position or reputation of sb within a group of people or an organization **2** period of time sth has existed: *debts of long ~* ▸ **standing** *adj* permanent and established: *a ~ joke*

stank *pt* of STINK

stanza /ˈstænzə/ n [C] group of lines in a poem

staple /ˈsteɪpl/ n [C] **1** small piece of bent wire for holding sheets of paper together **2** main article or product ● **staple** v [T] fasten or secure sth with a staple (1) ● **staple** *adj* forming the main part of sth: *Their ~ diet is rice.* ▸ **stapler** n [C] device for putting staples into paper, etc

0→ **star** /stɑː(r)/ n [C] **1** large ball of burning gas seen as a point of light in the sky at night **2** figure with five or more points resembling a star, often used to show quality **3** famous singer, actor, etc **4** planet or force believed to influence a person's life: *born under a lucky ~* ● **star** v (**-rr-**) **1** [I] be the main actor in a film, etc **2** [T] (of a film, etc) have sb as the main actor ▸ **stardom** n [U] status of being a star (3) ■ **starfish** n [C] sea animal shaped like a star ▸ **starry** *adj*

starboard /ˈstɑːbəd/ n [U] right side of a ship or an aircraft when it is facing forward

starch /stɑːtʃ/ n [U] **1** white, tasteless food substance found in potatoes, rice, etc **2** starch in powdered form or as a spray, used for making clothes, etc stiff ● **starch** v [T] make clothes, sheets, etc stiff using starch ▸ **starchy** *adj* (**-ier, -iest**)

0→ **stare** /steə(r)/ v [I] ~ (**at**) look at sb/sth for a long time ● **stare** n [C] staring, often unfriendly, look

stark /stɑːk/ *adj* **1** looking severe, without colour or decoration **2** unpleasant and impossible to avoid: *the ~ reality of life in prison* **3** clearly very different to sth: *in ~ contrast* ● **stark** *adv* completely: *~ naked*

starling /ˈstɑːlɪŋ/ n [C] common small bird with dark shiny feathers

starry → STAR

A B C D E F G H I J K L M N O P Q R **S** T U V W X Y Z

0━ **start¹** /stɑːt/ n **1** [C, usu sing] point at which sth begins; act of beginning sth **2** (the start) [sing] place where a race begins **3** [C] amount of time or distance that sb has as an advantage over others in a race **4** [C, usu sing] sudden movement of the body because of surprise, fear, etc

0━ **start²** /stɑːt/ v **1** [I,T] begin doing sth **2** [I,T] (cause sth to) start happening: When does the class ~? ◇ ~ a fire **3** [I,T] (cause a machine or vehicle to) begin running: The car won't ~. **4** [I,T] ~ (up) (cause sth to) begin to exist: ~ a business **5** [I] ~ (out) begin a journey [IDM] **start the ball rolling → BALL** [PV] **start off** begin to move **start sb off (on sth)** cause sb to begin doing sth **start out** begin to do sth, esp in business or work ▶ **starter** n [C] **1** (esp GB) first course of a meal **2** person, horse, car, etc that starts a race **3** device to start an engine [IDM] **for starters** (spoken) first of all

startle /ˈstɑːtl/ v [T] shock or surprise sb

starve /stɑːv/ v [I,T] (cause sb to) suffer or die from hunger [IDM] **be starving (for sth)** | **be starved** (infml) feel very hungry [PV] **starve sb/sth of sth** not give sth that is needed: Her children were ~d of love. ▶ **starvation** /-ˈveɪʃn/ n [U]

0━ **state¹** /steɪt/ n **1** [C] condition of a person or thing: a poor ~ of health **2** (also State) [C] country **3** (also State) [C] organized political community forming part of a larger country: Ohio is a ~ in America. **4** (also the State) [U, sing] government of a country **5** [U] very formal ceremony: buried in ~ ▶ **state** (also State) adj **1** of the state (4) **2** connected with the leader of a country attending an official ceremony of a particular state (3), esp in the US: ~ police ▶ **stately** adj (-ier, -iest) impressive in size, appearance or manner ■ **stately ˈhome** n [C] (GB) large, impressive house of historical interest

0━ **state²** /steɪt/ v [T] formally write or say sth, esp clearly and firmly ▶ **statement** n [C] **1** formal account of events, views, etc **2** financial report: a bank ~ment

statesman /ˈsteɪtsmən/ n [C] (pl -men) wise, experienced and respected political leader ▶ **ˈstatesmanship** n [U] skill in managing state affairs

static /ˈstætɪk/ adj not moving ● **static** n [U] **1** atmospheric disturbance affecting radio broadcasts **2** (also ˌstatic elecˈtricity) electricity which collects on the surface of objects

0━ **station** /ˈsteɪʃn/ n [C] **1** place where trains stop so that people can get on and off **2** building, etc where a service is organized: a bus ~ **3** radio or TV company ● **station** v [T] send sb, esp from one of the armed forces, to work in a certain place ■ **ˈstation wagon** n [C] (US) = ESTATE CAR (ESTATE)

stationary /ˈsteɪʃənri/ adj not moving: ~ traffic

stationer /ˈsteɪʃənə(r)/ n [C] person who owns or manages a shop selling paper, envelopes, etc for writing ▶ **stationery** /-ʃənri/ n [U] materials for writing and for using in an office

statistics /stəˈtɪstɪks/ n **1** [pl] information shown as numbers **2** [U] the science of collecting and explaining statistics ▶ **statistical** /-kl/ adj ▶ **statistically** /-kli/ adv ▶ **statistician** /ˌstætɪˈstɪʃn/ n [C] expert in statistics

0━ **statue** /ˈstætʃuː/ n [C] figure of a person, an animal, etc in wood, stone, bronze, etc ▶ **statuette** /ˌstætʃuˈet/ n [C] small statue

stature /ˈstætʃə(r)/ n [U] (written) **1** importance gained from achievement or ability **2** (person's) size or height

0━ **status** /ˈsteɪtəs/ n [U] person's legal, social or professional position ■ **ˈstatus symbol** n [C] item showing sb's importance, wealth, etc

status quo /ˌsteɪtəs ˈkwəʊ/ n [sing] the situation as it is now

statute /ˈstætʃuːt/ n [C] law passed by a parliament, council, etc ▶ **statutory** /-tri/ adj fixed or required by law

staunch /stɔːntʃ/ adj (of a supporter, etc) loyal ▶ **staunchly** adv

stave /steɪv/ v (pt, pp –d or **stove** /stəʊv/) [PV] **stave sth in** break or damage sth by making part of it fall inwards **stave sth off** (pt, pp –d) delay danger, etc

0━ **stay** /steɪ/ v [I] **1** be or remain in the same place or condition: ~ at home ◇ ~ sober **2** live in a place temporarily as a guest or visitor: ~ at a hotel [IDM] **stay put** (infml) remain where you are or where sb/sth is [PV] **stay away (from sb/sth)** not go near sb or sth **stay in** not go out **stay on** continue studying, working, etc. somewhere for longer than expected **stay out** continue to be outdoors or away from your home at night **stay over** sleep at sb's house for one night **stay up** not go to bed ● **stay** n [C] **1** period of staying; visit: a long ~ in hospital **2** rope or wire supporting a ship's mast, a pole, etc [IDM] **a stay of execution** (law) delay in carrying out the order of a court ■ **ˌstaying ˈpower** n [U] = STAMINA

steadfast /ˈstedfɑːst/ adj firm and unchanging ▸ **steadfastly** adv

0━ **steady** /ˈstedi/ adj (-ier, -iest) **1** even and regular: a ~ speed **2** not changing and not interrupted; not supported **3** firmly fixed or supported; not moving: hold the ladder ~ **4** (of a person) reliable: a ~ worker ● **steady** adv steadily ● **steady** v (-ied) (cause sb/sth/yourself to) stop moving, shaking or falling ▸ **steadily** adv in a regular way

steak /steɪk/ n [C, U] (thick slice of) meat or fish

0━ **steal** /stiːl/ v (pt **stole** /stəʊl/ pp **stolen** /ˈstəʊlən/) **1** [I, T] ~ (from) take sb's property without permission **2** [I] move secretly and quietly **3** [T] obtain sth suddenly or secretly: ~ a kiss [IDM] **steal the show** attract the most attention

stealth /stelθ/ n [U] fact of doing sth in a quiet or secret way ▸ **stealthy** adj (-ier, -iest)

0━ **steam** /stiːm/ n [U] **1** hot gas that water changes into when it boils **2** power produced from steam under pressure, used to operate engines, etc: a ~ train/engine [IDM] **run out of steam** (infml) lose energy and enthusiasm and stop doing sth ● **steam** v **1** [I] send out steam **2** [I] move, work, etc by steam power **3** [T] place food over boiling water so that it cooks in the steam [PV] **steam (sth) up** (cause sth to) become covered with steam ■ **steam engine** n [C] engine driven by steam ▸ **steamer** n [C] **1** boat or ship driven by steam **2** vessel in which food is steamed ■ **steamroller** n [C] slow heavy vehicle used for flattening new roads ▸ **steamy** adj

0━ **steel** /stiːl/ n [U] hard metal made from iron and carbon, used for knives, machinery, etc ● **steel** v ~ yourself (for/against sth) prepare yourself to deal with sth unpleasant: She ~ed herself for disappointment.

0━ **steep**[1] /stiːp/ adj **1** (of a slope) rising or falling sharply **2** (infml) (of a price or demand) too much; unreasonable ▸ **steeply** adv ▸ **steepness** n [U]

steep[2] /stiːp/ v [IDM] **be steeped in sth** (written) have a particular quality: a city ~ed in history [PV] **steep sth in sth** leave sth in a liquid for a long time in order to flavour it **steep yourself in sth** (written) spend a lot of time thinking or learning about sth

steeple /ˈstiːpl/ n [C] tall pointed tower of the roof of a church ■ **steeplechase** n [C] race for horses or athletes with obstacles such as fences and water to jump over ■ **steeplejack** n [C] person who repairs steeples, tall chimneys, etc

0━ **steer** /stɪə(r)/ v [I, T] direct the course of a boat, car, etc [IDM] **steer**

clear (of sb/sth) → CLEAR[1] ■ **steering wheel** n [C] wheel used for controlling the direction that a vehicle goes in

stem /stem/ n [C] **1** main long thin part of a plant above the ground **2** long thin part like a stem, eg on a wine glass ● **stem** v [T] (-mm-) stop sth that is flowing from spreading or increasing [PV] **stem from sth** be the result of sth

stench /stentʃ/ n [C] strong, very unpleasant smell

stencil /ˈstensl/ n [C] **1** thin sheet of metal, etc with letters or designs cut in it **2** letters, etc made by putting ink, etc through holes on a stencil ● **stencil** v (-ll- US -l-) [I, T] produce letters, etc with a stencil

0━ **step**[1] /step/ n [C] **1** act of lifting your foot and putting it down in order to walk; sound this makes **2** way that sb walks: I heard her ~ on the stair. **3** distance covered when you take a step **4** one of a series of actions done to achieve sth or that form part of a process: take ~s to help her ◇ I'll explain it to you ~ by ~. **5** flat place for the foot when going from one level to another: A flight of ~s led up to the door. **6** (steps) [pl] = STEPLADDER [IDM] **in/out of step (with sb/sth)** **1** putting/not putting your feet down at the same time as others **2** agreeing/not agreeing with others' ideas **mind/watch your step 1** walk carefully **2** behave carefully **step by step** gradually ■ **stepladder** n [C] folding ladder with steps

0━ **step**[2] /step/ v (-pp-) [I] **1** lift your foot and move it in a particular direction or put it on or in sth **2** move a short distance [IDM] **step on it** (spoken) go faster or hurry **step out of line** behave badly or break the rules [PV] **step aside/down** resign from a position or job, esp so sb else can have it **step in** help sb in a dispute or difficult situation **step sth up** increase sth ■ **stepping stone** n [C] **1** one of a line of flat stones used to cross a stream, etc **2** stage towards achieving sth

step- /step-/ prefix related as a result of one parent marrying again: ~mother

stereo /ˈsteriəʊ/ n **1** [C] machine that plays CDs, cassettes, the radio, etc that has two separate speakers **2** [U] system for playing recorded music, in which the sound is directed through two channels: broadcast in ~ ▸ **stereo** adj: ~ sound

stereotype /ˈsteriətaɪp/ n [C] fixed idea of what sb/sth is like

sterile

sterile /ˈsteraɪl/ adj **1** not able to produce children or young **2** clean and free from bacteria **3** having no result: *an ~ argument* **4** (of land) not able to produce crops ► **sterility** /stəˈrɪləti/ *n* [U] ► **sterilize** (*also* **-ise**) /ˈsterəlaɪz/ *v* [T] **1** kill the bacteria in sth **2** make a person or animal unable to have babies or young

sterling /ˈstɜːlɪŋ/ *n* [U] money system of Britain ■ **sterling** *adj* (*fml*) of excellent quality

stern /stɜːn/ *adj* severe, strict or serious ► **sternly** *adv* ■ **stern** *n* [C] back end of a ship

steroid /ˈsterɔɪd; ˈstɪər-/ *n* [C] powerful chemical product in the body or taken as a drug

stethoscope /ˈsteθəskəʊp/ *n* [C] instrument for listening to the beating of the heart, etc

stew /stjuː/ *v* [T] cook sth slowly in liquid in a closed dish ■ **stew** *n* [C, U] dish of stewed meat, etc [IDM] **get (yourself/sb)/be in a stew (about/over sth)** (*infml*) become/feel very nervous or upset about sth

steward /ˈstjuːəd/ *n* [C] **1** (*fem* **stewardess** /ˌstjuːəˈdes/) person who takes care of passengers on a ship, an aircraft or a train **2** person who helps to organize a large public event, eg a race

0➔ **stick**[1] /stɪk/ *n* [C] small thin piece of wood that has fallen from a tree **2** [C] = WALKING STICK (WALK[1]) **3** [C] long thin piece of sth: *a ~ of chalk* **4** [U] (*GB, infml*) criticism or harsh words: *The referee got a lot of ~ for his decision.* [IDM] **give sb stick** (*infml*) punish or criticize sb

0➔ **stick**[2] /stɪk/ *v* (*pt, pp* **stuck** /stʌk/) **1** [I,T] (cause sth, usu a sharp object) to be pushed into sth: *~ the knife into the cheese* **2** [I,T] (cause sth to) be fixed to sth else, esp with glue **3** [T] (*infml*) put sth somewhere, esp quickly or carelessly: *S~ it in the bag.* **4** [I] become fixed in one position and impossible to move: *The key stuck in the lock.* **5** [T] (*GB, infml*) tolerate sb/sth unpleasant: *I can't ~ this job any longer.* [IDM] **stick your neck out** (*infml*) take risks **stick your nose into sth** → NOSE[1] **stick your oar in** → OAR **stick out like a sore thumb** → SORE **stick to your guns** (*infml*) refuse to change your mind about sth **stuck in a groove** → GROOVE [PV] **stick around** (*infml*) not go away **stick at sth** keep on with sth **stick by sb** continue to support sb **stick (sth) out** continue to be further out than sth else or come through a hole: *~ your tongue out* **stick it/sth out** continue to the very end **stick to sth** continue doing or using sth and not want to change it **stick up** point upwards or be above a surface **stick up for sb/yourself/sth** defend or support sb/

yourself/sth ■ **sticker** *n* [C] sticky label ■ **sticking plaster** *n* [C, U] = PLASTER(3) ■ **stick-in-the-mud** *n* [C] (*infml, disapprov*) person who refuses to try anything new ► **sticky** *adj* (**-ier, -iest**) **1** like or covered with glue **2** (*infml*) difficult: *a ~ situation*

0➔ **stiff** /stɪf/ *adj* **1** not easily bent, folded, etc: *~ cardboard* **2** hard to stir, move, etc: *a ~ paste* **3** more difficult or severe than usual: *a ~ climb* ◇ *~ breeze* **4** (of a person) not friendly or relaxed [IDM] **(keep) a stiff upper lip** keep calm and hide your feelings in spite of pain or difficulty ● **stiff** *adv* (*infml*) very much: *bored ~* ► **stiffly** *adv* ► **stiffness** *n* [U]

stiffen /ˈstɪfn/ *v* [I,T] become or make sth difficult to bend, move, etc

stifle /ˈstaɪfl/ *v* **1** [T] prevent sth from happening: *~ a yawn* **2** [I,T] (cause sb to) have difficulty breathing

stigma /ˈstɪɡmə/ *n* [U,C, usu sing] mark of shame

stile /staɪl/ *n* [C] step used to climb over a fence, etc

stiletto /stɪˈletəʊ/ *n* [C] (*pl* **~s** *or* **~es**) woman's shoe with a very high narrow heel; heel on such a shoe

0➔ **still**[1] /stɪl/ *adv* **1** up to now or the time mentioned and not finishing: *She is ~ busy.* **2** in spite of what has just been said: *It's raining. S~, we must go shopping.* **3** even: *Tom is tall, but Mary is ~ taller.*

0➔ **still**[2] /stɪl/ *adj* **1** not moving; calm and quiet: *Keep ~ while I brush your hair.* **2** (*GB*) (of a drink) not containing bubbles of gas ● **still** *v* [I,T] (*lit*) become or make sth calm or quiet ● **still** *n* [C] **1** photograph of a scene from a film **2** equipment for making strong alcoholic drinks ■ **stillborn** *adj* **1** born dead **2** not successful; not developing

stilt /stɪlt/ *n* [C] one of two poles with a support for the foot, used for walking raised above the ground

stilted /ˈstɪltɪd/ *adj* (of speech, behaviour, etc) stiff and unnatural

stimulant /ˈstɪmjələnt/ *n* [C] drink, drug, etc that increases bodily or mental activity

stimulate /ˈstɪmjuleɪt/ *v* [T] **1** make sth develop; encourage sth: *~ discussion* **2** make sb interested and excited about sth ► **stimulating** *adj* ► **stimulation** /ˌstɪmjuˈleɪʃn/ *n* [U]

stimulus /ˈstɪmjələs/ *n* [C] (*pl* **-li** /-laɪ/) something that stimulates sb/sth: *a ~ to hard work*

0➔ **sting** /stɪŋ/ *v* (*pt, pp* **stung** /stʌŋ/) **1** [I,T] (of an insect or a plant) touch your skin or make a small hole in it so that you feel a sharp pain **2** [I,T] (cause sb to) feel a sharp pain: *The smoke made my eyes ~.* **3** [T] make sb feel angry or upset ● **sting** *n* [C] **1** sharp, often poisonous organ of some insects, eg bees **2** wound

made when an insect stings you
3 any sharp pain

stingy /ˈstɪndʒi/ *adj* (**-ier, -iest**) (*infml*) unwilling to spend or give money, etc ▸ **stingily** /-əli/ *adv* ▸ **stinginess** *n* [U]

stink /stɪŋk/ *v* (*pt* **stank** /stæŋk/ or **stunk** /stʌŋk/; *pp* **stunk**) [I] **1** have a strong unpleasant smell **2** seem very bad or dishonest [**PV**] **stink sth out** fill a place with a bad smell ● **stink** *n* (*infml*) **1** [C] very unpleasant smell **2** [*sing*] lot of trouble and anger about sth: *kick up a* ~ (= complain a lot and cause trouble)

stint /stɪnt/ *v* [I,T] ~ **on** give sb only a small amount of sth ● **stint** *n* [C] fixed amount of work, etc

stipulate /ˈstɪpjuleɪt/ *v* [T] state sth as a necessary condition ▸ **stipulation** /-ˈleɪʃn/ *n* [U]

0—**stir** /stɜː(r)/ *v* (**-rr-**) **1** [T] mix a liquid by moving a spoon, etc round and round in it **2** [I,T] (cause sb/sth to) move **3** [T] excite sb or make them feel sth strongly: *a book that* ~s *the imagination* **4** [I,T] (*GB, infml*) try to cause trouble [**PV**] **stir sb up** encourage sb to do sth ● **stir** *n* [*sing*] excitement or shock ▸ **stirring** *adj* exciting ● **stir-fry** *v* [T] cook thin strips of vegetables or meat quickly in very hot oil: *~-fried chicken* ▸ **stir-fry** *n* [C]: *Let's have a ~-fry tonight.*

stirrup /ˈstɪrəp/ *n* [C] one of two metal rings attached to a horse's saddle which support the rider's feet

stitch /stɪtʃ/ *n* **1** [C] single passing of a needle and thread through cloth, etc to join or decorate sth or through skin to close a wound **2** [C] one turn of the wool round the needle in knitting **3** [C,U] style of sewing or knitting that you use to get the pattern you want **4** [C, usu *sing*] pain in the side caused by running [**IDM**] **not have a stitch on | not be wearing a stitch** be naked in stitches (*infml*) laughing a lot ● **stitch** *v* [T] sew sth

stoat /stəʊt/ *n* [C] small brown furry animal, larger than a rat

0—**stock** /stɒk/ *n* **1** [C,U] supply of goods available for sale in a shop **2** [C,U] ~ (**of**) supply of sth available for use **3** [C, usu *pl*, U] share in a company, bought as a way of investing money **4** [U] = LIVESTOCK **5** [U] liquid in which bones, etc have been cooked, used for soup, etc [**IDM**] **in/out of stock** available/not available to buy **take stock (of sth)** review a situation ● **stock** *adj* not interesting because it has been used too often: *a ~ phrase* ■ **stockbroker** *n* [C] person who buys and sells stocks (3) and shares for other people ■ **stock exchange** *n* [C] place where stocks (3) are bought and sold ■ **stock**

437

stone

market *n* [C] business of buying and selling shares in companies and the place where this is done ■ **stockpile** *v* [T] buy large quantities of sth and keep it for use in the future ▸ **stockpile** *n* [C] ■ **stock-'still** *adv* without moving at all ■ **stocktaking** *n* [U] process of making a list of all the goods in a shop or business

stock² /stɒk/ *v* [T] **1** (of a shop) keep a supply of a particular type of goods to sell **2** fill sth with food, books, etc [**PV**] **stock up (on/with sth)** buy a lot of sth to use later

stockade /stɒˈkeɪd/ *n* [C] tall strong fence, built for defence

stocking /ˈstɒkɪŋ/ *n* either of a pair of thin coverings for a woman's feet and legs

stocky /ˈstɒki/ *adj* (**-ier, -iest**) (of a person) short, with a strong, solid body ▸ **stockily** *adv*

stodge /stɒdʒ/ *n* [U] (*sl*) heavy solid food ▸ **stodgy** *adj* (**-ier, -iest**) **1** heavy and solid **2** dull

stoic /ˈstəʊɪk/ *n* [C] person who suffers without complaint ▸ **stoical** *adj* ▸ **stoically** /-kli/ *adv* ▸ **stoicism** /ˈstəʊɪsɪzəm/ *n* [U] patient suffering, etc

stoke /stəʊk/ *v* [I,T] ~ (**up; with**) add fuel to a fire, etc ▸ **stoker** *n* [C] person whose job is to add fuel to a fire, etc, esp on a ship or steam train

stole¹ /stəʊl/ *n* [C] wide band of fabric, etc worn around the shoulders

stole² *pt* of STEAL

stolen *pp* of STEAL

0—**stomach** /ˈstʌmək/ *n* **1** [C] organ in the body where food is digested **2** [C] front part of the body below the chest [**IDM**] **have no stomach for sth 1** not want to eat sth **2** not have the desire or courage to do sth: *have no ~ for a fight* ● **stomach** *v* [T] approve of and be able to enjoy sth

0—**stone** /stəʊn/ *n* **1** [U] solid mineral substance found in the ground, used for building **2** [C] piece of rock **3** [C] jewel **4** [C] hard seed of some fruits, eg the cherry **5** [C] (*pl* **stone**) unit of weight, 14 pounds (6.35 kilograms) **6** [C] piece of hard material that can form in a body organ: *kidney ~s* [**IDM**] **a stone's throw** a short distance away ● **stone** *v* [T] **1** throw stones at sb/sth **2** take the stone out of fruit ■ the 'Stone Age *n* [*sing*] early period in human history when tools, etc were made of stone ▸ **stoned** *adj* (*sl*) under the influence of drugs or alcohol ■ **stone 'deaf** *adj* completely unable to hear

stony /'stəʊni/ adj (-ier, -iest)
1 having a lot of stones **2** hard and unsympathetic ▸ **stonily** /-ɪli/ adv

stood pt, pp of STAND

stool /stuːl/ n [C] small seat without a back

stoop /stuːp/ v [I] bend your body forwards and downwards [PV] **stoop to sth** lower your standards to do sth wrong ● **stoop** n [sing] stooping position

0━ **stop**[1] /stɒp/ n [C] **1** act of stopping or stopping sth: The car came to a ~. **2** place at which buses, etc stop regularly **3** (GB) = FULL STOP (FULL) [IDM] **put a stop to sth** stop sth from happening: It's time to put a ~ to the violence.

0━ **stop**[2] /stɒp/ v (-pp-) **1** [I,T] (cause sb/sth to) no longer move or function: We decided to ~ for the night. ◇ The engine ~ped. ◇ He was ~ped by the police. **2** [I,T] (make sb/sth) no longer continue to do sth: (spoken) ~ it! You're hurting me. ◇ The phone never ~s ringing. **3** [I,T] (cause sth to) end or finish **4** [T] prevent sb from doing sth or sth from happening: ~ her (from) leaving **5** [I] (GB, infml) stay somewhere for a short time **6** [T] prevent money from being paid: ~ a cheque [PV] **stop off (at/in...)** make a short visit somewhere during a trip **stop over (at/in...)** stay somewhere for a short time during a journey ■ **stopcock** n [C] tap that controls the flow of liquid or gas through a pipe ■ **stopgap** n [C] temporary substitute ■ **stopover** n [C] short stay somewhere between two parts of a journey ▸ **stoppage** /-prɪdʒ/ n [C] period when work is stopped ■ **stopper** n [C] object that fits into the top of a bottle to close it ■ **stop press** n [U] late news added to a newspaper

storage /'stɔːrɪdʒ/ n [U] **1** (space used for) keeping sth in a place until it is needed **2** (computing) process of keeping information, etc on a computer; way in which it is kept

0━ **store** /stɔː(r)/ n [C] **1** large shop selling many different types of goods **2** (US) any shop, large or small **3** quantity of sth kept for use as needed **4** place where goods are kept [IDM] **in store (for sb)** waiting to happen to sb: What's in ~ for us today? **set/put (great, etc) store by sth** consider sth to be important ● **store** v [T] **1** ~ (away/up) put sth somewhere and keep it for future use **2** keep information or facts in a computer or your brain

storey /'stɔːri/ n [C] floor or level of a building

stork /stɔːk/ n [C] large, long-legged wading bird

0━ **storm** /stɔːm/ n [C] **1** period of very strong winds, rain, etc **2** violent show of feeling: a ~ of protest [IDM] **take sth/sb by storm 1** be extremely successful **2** capture a building by sudden violent attack ● **storm** v **1** [T] suddenly attack a place **2** [I] speak, move, etc angrily ▸ **stormy** adj (-ier, -iest)

0━ **story** /'stɔːri/ n (pl -ies) **1** description of past or imaginary events **2** news report **3** (infml) lie **4** (US) = STOREY

stout /staʊt/ adj **1** (of a person) rather fat **2** strong and thick **3** (fml) determined and brave ● **stout** n [U,C] strong dark beer ▸ **stoutly** adv

0━ **stove** /stəʊv/ n [C] closed apparatus burning wood, coal, etc used for cooking, etc

stow /stəʊ/ v [T] ~ (away) put sth in a safe place ■ **stowaway** n [C] person who hides on a ship or an aircraft to avoid paying

straddle /'strædl/ v [T] sit or stand with one of your legs on either side of sb/sth

0━ **straight**[1] /streɪt/ adv **1** not in a curve or at an angle; in a straight line: walk ~ **2** by a direct route; immediately: Come ~ home. **3** in or into a level or upright position: Sit up ~. **4** honestly, directly: Tell her ~ what you think. [IDM] **go straight** (infml) stop being a criminal and live an honest life ■ **straightaway** adv immediately

0━ **straight**[2] /streɪt/ adj **1** not bent or curved: a ~ line **2** level, upright or parallel to sth **3** clean and neat **4** honest and direct **5** (US) (of alcoholic drinks) not mixed with water or anything else **6** (infml) = HETEROSEXUAL [IDM] **keep a straight face** stop yourself from smiling or laughing ● **straight** n [C] straight part of a racetrack or road ▸ **straightness** n [U]

straighten /'streɪtn/ v [I,T] make sth or become level, tidy, etc

straightforward /ˌstreɪt'fɔːwəd/ adj **1** easy to understand or do **2** honest ▸ **straightforwardly** adv

0━ **strain**[1] /streɪn/ n **1** [U,C] pressure on sb/sth because they have too much to do or deal with; the problems and anxiety that this produces: a marriage under great ~ **2** [U,C] pressure put on sth when a physical force stretches or pushes it: put ~ on a rope **3** [C,U] injury caused by stretching a muscle too much **4** [C] type of a virus, an insect, etc

strain[2] /streɪn/ v **1** [T] injure a muscle, etc by stretching it too much **2** [I,T] make the greatest possible effort to do sth: I ~ed my ears (= listened very hard) to hear what he was saying. **3** [T] force or push sth beyond a normal or acceptable limit **4** [T] pass food, etc through a sieve, cloth, etc to separate the solid part from the liquid ▶ **strained** *adj* forced and unnatural ▶ **strainer** *n* [C] kitchen utensil with a lot of small holes in it for straining tea, etc

strait /streɪt/ *n* [C] **1** (*also* **straits** [pl]) narrow stretch of water connecting two seas (**straits** [pl] difficulty, esp because of lack of money: *The firm is in dire ~s.*

straitjacket /ˈstreɪtdʒækɪt/ *n* [C] jacket with long sleeves tied round a violent person to prevent movement

strait-laced (*also* **straight-laced**) /ˌstreɪt ˈleɪst/ *adj* (*disapprov*) morally strict or serious

strand /strænd/ *n* [C] **1** single piece of thread, wire, hair, etc **2** one of the different parts of an idea, plan, story, etc

stranded /ˈstrændɪd/ *adj* in a helpless position, unable to move, etc

o── strange /streɪndʒ/ *adj* **1** not familiar, unknown **2** unusual; odd: *What ~ ideas you have!* ▶ **strangely** *adv* **strangeness** *n* [U] ▶ **stranger** *n* [C] **1** person you do not know **2** person in a place they have not been in before

strangle /ˈstræŋgl/ *v* [T] kill sb by squeezing their throat ■ **stranglehold** *n* [sing] strong hold on sb/sth: *They have a ~hold on the economy.* ▶ **strangler** *n* [C]

strap /stræp/ *n* [C] strip of leather, plastic, etc used for fastening or support ● **strap** *v* (**-pp-**) [T] fasten, carry or hold sth in place with a strap ▶ **strapping** *adj* (of people) big and strong

strata *plural* of STRATUM

strategic /strəˈtiːdʒɪk/ *adj* **1** done as part of a plan meant to achieve a purpose or gain an advantage **2** connected with getting an advantage in a war ▶ **strategically** /-kli/ *adv*

o── strategy /ˈstrætədʒi/ *n* [C] **1** plan intended to achieve a particular purpose **2** [U] (skill in) planning sth, esp the movement of armies in war ▶ **strategist** *n* [C] person skilled in strategy

stratosphere /ˈstrætəsfɪə(r)/ *n* [sing] layer of the atmosphere between about 10 and 50 km above the earth

stratum /ˈstrɑːtəm/ *n* [C] (pl **-ta** /-tə/) **1** (*geol*) horizontal layer of rock, etc in the earth **2** (*written*) class in a society

straw /strɔː/ *n* **1** [U] dry, cut stems of wheat, barley, etc **2** [C] single stem or piece of straw **3** [C] thin tube of

plastic, etc that you suck a drink through [IDM] **the last/final straw** last in a series of bad events that finally makes a situation intolerable

strawberry /ˈstrɔːbəri/ *n* [C] (pl **-ies**) (plant with) small juicy red fruit with tiny seeds on its surface

stray /streɪ/ *v* [I] move away from the right path, etc ● **stray** *adj* **1** (of animals) lost from home: *a ~ dog* **2** separated from other things or people of the same kind ● **stray** *n* [C] animal or person that has got lost or separated from others

streak /striːk/ *n* [C] **1** long thin line that is a different colour from the rest **2** bad quality in sb's character: *a ~ of cruelty* **3** brief period: *a ~ of good luck* ● **streak** *v* **1** [T] mark sth with streaks **2** [I] move very fast ▶ **streaky** *adj* (**-ier, -iest**) marked with streaks

o── stream /striːm/ *n* [C] **1** small narrow river **2** steady flow of people, liquid, things, etc: *a ~ of abuse* **3** (*esp GB*) group of pupils with the same level of ability [IDM] **with/against the stream** with/ against the majority ● **stream** *v* [I] **1** flow as a stream **2** move freely, esp in the wind or water: *with her long hair ~ing* ▶ **streamer** *n* [C] long narrow ribbon of paper ■ **streamline** *v* [T] **1** give sth a smooth even shape so that it moves easily through air and water **2** make a system, etc more efficient, esp in a way that saves money ▶ **streamlined** *adj*

o── street /striːt/ *n* [C] road with houses and buildings on one or both sides [IDM] **streets ahead (of sb/sth)** (*infml*) much better or more advanced than sb/sth else (**right) up your street** (*infml*) in your area of interest, etc ■ **streetcar** *n* [C] (*US*) = TRAM

o── strength /streŋθ/ *n* **1** [U] quality or degree of being strong **2** [C] way in which sb/sth is strong, effective, etc: *Her intelligence is one of her ~s.* **3** [U] number of people available: *The army is below ~.* [IDM] **on the strength of sth** because sb has been influenced by sth: *buy it on the ~ of his advice* ▶ **strengthen** *v* [I, T] become or make sth stronger

strenuous /ˈstrenjuəs/ *adj* needing great effort ▶ **strenuously** *adv* ▶ **strenuousness** *n* [U]

o── stress /stres/ *n* **1** [C,U] pressure or worry caused by the problems in sb's life **2** [U,C] pressure put on sth that can damage it or make it lose shape **3** [U] emphasis: *She lays great ~ on punctuality.* **4** [U,C] (*ling*) extra force used when speaking a particular word or syllable ● **stress** *v* [T] **1** emphasize a fact, an idea, etc

2 (ling) give extra force to a word or syllable when saying it

0— **stretch** /stretʃ/ v **1** [I,T] make sth wider, longer or looser by pulling it **2** [I] (be able to) be stretched **3** [I,T] put your arms or legs out straight and tighten your muscles **4** [I] extend over an area: *fields ~ing for miles* **5** [T] make use of all sb's skills, intelligence, etc [IDM] **stretch your legs** (infml) go for a short walk after sitting for some time [PV] **stretch (yourself) out** lie at full length

● **stretch** n **1** [C] area of land or water **2** [C] continuous period of time: *ten hours at a ~* **3** [C,U] act of stretching a part of your body **4** [U] ability to stretch, eg of a rope ▶ **stretchy** adj (-ier, -iest) that can be made longer or wider without breaking or tearing

stretcher /ˈstretʃə(r)/ n [C] frame covered with canvas for carrying sb who is sick or injured

0— **stricken** /ˈstrɪkən/ adj ~ (by/with) affected or overcome by sth bad: ~ *with terror*

0— **strict** /strɪkt/ adj **1** that must be obeyed exactly: *a ~ diet* **2** demanding that rules, esp rules of behaviour, should be obeyed: *a ~ teacher* **3** exactly defined: *the ~ sense of a word* ▶ **strictly** adv ▶ **strictness** n [U]

stride /straɪd/ v (pt **strode** /strəʊd/) (not used in the perfect tenses) [I] walk with long steps: *We strode across the snowy fields.* ● **stride** n [C] long step: *He crossed the room in two ~s.* [IDM] **take sth in your stride** accept and deal with sth difficult without letting it worry you too much

strident /ˈstraɪdnt/ adj (esp of a voice) loud and insistent: ~ *protests*

strife /straɪf/ n [U] (fml or lit) state of conflict

0— **strike**[1] /straɪk/ v (pt, pp **struck** /strʌk/) **1** [T] hit sb/sth hard **2** [T] attack sb/sth, esp suddenly **3** [T] (of a thought or an idea) come into sb's mind suddenly: *An awful thought has just struck me.* **4** [T] give sb a certain impression: *She ~s me as a clever girl.* **5** [T] put sb suddenly into a particular state: *struck dumb* **6** [I] (of workers) refuse to work as a protest **7** [T] produce a flame by rubbing sth against a surface: ~ *a match* **8** [I,T] show the time by making a ringing noise, etc: *The clock struck (four).* **9** [T] discover gold, etc by digging or drilling [IDM] **strike a bargain/deal** make an agreement with sb in which both sides have an advantage **strike camp** remove tents, etc **strike a chord (with sb)** say or do sth that makes people feel sympathy or enthusiasm **strike it rich** become

suddenly rich [PV] **strike sb/sth off (sth)** remove sb/sth's name from sth, eg a list **strike out 1** start being independent **2** (US, infml) fail or be unsuccessful **strike up (with sb)** begin a friendship, conversation, etc

0— **strike**[2] /straɪk/ n **1** act of stopping work for a period of time as a protest: *Firefighters are threatening to come out on ~.* **2** military attack **3** sudden discovery of sth valuable, esp oil

0— **striking** /ˈstraɪkɪŋ/ adj attracting attention, beautiful

0— **string**[1] /strɪŋ/ n **1** [C,U] (length of) fine cord for tying things, etc **2** [C] series of things threaded on a string: *a ~ of beads* **3** [C] series of things or people coming one after another: *a ~ of accidents* **4** (computing) [C] series of characters (= letters, numbers, etc) **5** [C] stretched piece of wire on a musical instrument **6** (the strings) [pl] the players of these instruments in an orchestra [IDM] **(with) no strings (attached)** with no special conditions or restrictions ▶ **stringy** adj (-ier, -iest) (disapprov) like string

string[2] /strɪŋ/ v (pt, pp **strung** /strʌŋ/) [T] **1** tie or hang sth in place, esp as a decoration **2** put a series of small objects on string, etc **3** put a string or strings on a violin, tennis racket, etc [PV] **string along (with sb)** go somewhere with sb for a while **string sb along** (infml) allow sb to believe sth that is not true **string sth out** make sth last longer than expected or necessary ■ **strung 'up** adj (GB, infml) (of a person) tense and nervous

stringent /ˈstrɪndʒənt/ adj (of rules, etc) very strict ▶ **stringently** adv

0— **strip** /strɪp/ v (-pp-) **1** [I,T] take off clothes, coverings, parts, etc **2** [T] ~ **(down)** separate a machine, etc into parts to be cleaned or repaired **3** [T] ~ **of** take sth from sb as a punishment: ~ *sb of his liberty* ● **strip** n long narrow piece of material, land, etc ■ **strip cartoon** = COMIC STRIP (COMIC) ■ **stripper** n [C] person who performs a striptease ■ **striptease** n [C,U] entertainment in which a person takes their clothes off in front of an audience

0— **stripe** /straɪp/ n [C] **1** long narrow band on a surface that is different in colour, material, etc **2** (often a V-shaped) badge worn on a uniform, showing rank ▶ **striped** (also **stripy, stripey**) adj having stripes

strive /straɪv/ v (pt **strove** /strəʊv/ pp **striven** /ˈstrɪvn/) [I] (fml) try very hard to achieve sth: ~ *to succeed*

strode pt of STRIDE

0— **stroke**[1] /strəʊk/ n [C] **1** act of hitting a ball, eg in tennis, cricket

2 single movement of the arm when hitting sb/sth **3** any of a series of repeated movements in swimming or rowing **4** [usu sing] act of moving your hand gently over a surface **5** mark made by moving a pen or brush across a surface **6** ~ (of) single successful action or event **7** sound made by a bell **8** sudden serious illness when a blood vessel in the brain bursts [IDM] **at a (single) stroke** | **at one stroke** at a single stroke with a single immediate action

0-w **stroke²** /strəʊk/ v [T] move your hand gently over a surface, sb's hair, etc

0-w **stroll** /strəʊl/ n [C] slow relaxed walk ● **stroll** v [I] walk somewhere in a slow relaxed way ▶ **stroller** n [C] **1** person enjoying a relaxed way **2** (US) = PUSHCHAIR (PUSH¹)

0-w **strong** /strɒŋ/ adj (~er /-ŋgə(r)/ ~est /-ŋgɪst/) **1** having great power **2** having a powerful effect on the mind or body: a ~ drug **3** able to resist attack or influence: a ~ will **4** not easily hurt, broken, changed, etc **5** having the stated number: an army 2000 ~ **6** having a lot of flavour: ~ cheese **7** (of a drink) containing a lot of a substance: ~ coffee [IDM] **be strong on sth 1** be good at sth **2** have a lot of sth **going strong** (infml) continuing to be healthy, active or successful ■ **stronghold** n [C] **1** place where a cause has strong support **2** castle ▶ **strongly** adv

strove pt of STRIVE

struck pt, pp of STRIKE¹

0-w **structural** /ˈstrʌktʃərəl/ adj of the way sth is built or organized ▶ **structurally** adv

0-w **structure** /ˈstrʌktʃə(r)/ n **1** [C, U] way in which the parts of sth are put together, etc **2** [C] thing built of parts, esp a building ● **structure** v [T] arrange or organize sth

0-w **struggle** /ˈstrʌɡl/ v [I] **1** try hard to do sth or move somewhere when it is difficult: ~ to earn a living **2** fight against sb/sth **3** fight sb or try to get away from them: How did she manage to ~ free? ● **struggle** n **1** [C] hard fight **2** [sing] something that is difficult for you to do or achieve

strung pt, pp of STRING²

strut /strʌt/ v (-tt-) [I] walk in a proud, angry, etc way ● **strut** n [C] piece of wood or metal to strengthen a framework

stub /stʌb/ n [C] **1** short remaining end of a pencil, cigarette, etc **2** piece of a cheque left in the book ● **stub** v (-bb-) [T] **1** accidentally hit your toe against sth [PV] **stub sth out**

---

put out a cigarette, etc by pressing it against sth hard

stubble /ˈstʌbl/ n [U] **1** lower stems of corn, etc, left in the ground after harvest **2** short growth of beard ▶ **stubbly** /-bli/ adj

stubborn /ˈstʌbən/ adj **1** having a strong will; too determined **2** difficult to move, remove, cure, etc: a ~ cough ▶ **stubbornly** adv ▶ **stubbornness** n [U]

stubby /ˈstʌbi/ adj (-ier, -iest) short and thick

stuck¹ pt, pp of STICK²

stuck² /stʌk/ adj **1** unable to move or continue **2** ~ **with** (infml) unable to get rid of sb/sth that you do not want: ~ with sb all day [IDM] **get stuck in (to sth)** (infml) begin to do sth enthusiastically

stud /stʌd/ n **1** [C] small piece of jewellery pushed through a hole in your ear, nose, etc **2** [C] small round piece of metal attached to sth, esp for decoration **3** [C, usu pl] one of several metal or plastic objects on the sole of a football boot, etc **4** [C, U] animal, esp a horse, kept for breeding; place where such animals are kept **5** [C] (infml) man regarded as a good sexual partner ▶ **studded** adj decorated with small raised pieces of metal

0-w **student** /ˈstjuːdnt/ n [C] **1** (GB) person who is studying at a college or university **2** (US) person studying at secondary school **3** any person interested in a particular subject

0-w **studio** /ˈstjuːdiəʊ/ n (pl ~s) **1** workroom of a painter, photographer, etc **2** room(s) where films, or radio or television programmes are made

studious /ˈstjuːdiəs/ adj spending a lot of time studying or reading ▶ **studiously** adv

0-w **study¹** /ˈstʌdi/ n (pl -ies) **1** [U] (also studies [pl]) process of learning sth **2** [C] piece of research that examines a subject in detail: a ~ of the country's economy **3** [C] room used for reading, writing, etc **4** [C] drawing or painting of sth, esp one done for practice **5** [C] piece of music played as an exercise

0-w **study²** /ˈstʌdi/ v (pt, pp -ied) **1** [I,T] give time and attention to learning sth **2** [T] watch or look at sb/sth carefully to find out sth

0-w **stuff¹** /stʌf/ n [U] (infml) **1** used to refer to a substance, material, group of objects, etc when you do not know the name: What's this sticky ~ on the carpet? ◇ Where's all my ~ (= possessions)? **2** used to refer generally to things people do, say, think, etc: I've got loads of ~ to do

---

A B C D E F G H I J K L M N O P Q R **S** T U V W X Y Z

today. [IDM] **do your stuff** (*infml*) show what you can do

stuff² /stʌf/ v [T] **1** fill sth tightly with sth **2** fill a vegetable, chicken, etc with another type of food **3** (*infml*) fill yourself/sb with food **4** fill the body of a dead animal with material to give it the original shape [IDM] **get stuffed** (*GB, spoken*) used to tell sb rudely to go away or that you do not want sth ▸ **stuffing** n [U] **1** mixture of food used to stuff (2) a chicken, etc **2** soft material used to fill cushions, soft toys, etc

stuffy /'stʌfi/ *adj* (**-ier, -iest**) **1** (of a room) not having enough fresh air **2** (*infml*) (of people) formal and dull ▸ **stuffiness** n [U]

stumble /'stʌmbl/ v [I] **1** hit your foot against sth and almost fall **2** make a mistake or stop as you speak [PV] **stumble across/on/upon sth/sb** discover sth/sb unexpectedly ▸ **stumble** n [C] act of stumbling ■ **stumbling block** n [C] something that prevents progress

stump /stʌmp/ n [C] **1** part of a tree left in the ground after the rest has been cut down, etc **2** anything left after the main part has been cut or broken off **3** (in cricket) one of the three upright pieces of wood at which the ball is aimed ■ **stump** v **1** [T] (*infml*) ask sb a question that is too difficult for them to answer **2** [I] walk in a noisy heavy way ▸ **stumpy** *adj* (**-ier, -iest**) short and thick

stun /stʌn/ v (**-nn-**) [T] **1** make sb unconscious by hitting them on the head **2** shock sb so much that they cannot think or speak **3** impress sb very much ▸ **stunning** *adj* very attractive

stung *pt, pp* of STING

stunk *pp* of STINK

stunt /stʌnt/ n [C] **1** dangerous thing done as entertainment, esp as part of a film **2** thing done to attract attention ■ **stunt** v [T] stop or slow the growth or development of sb/sth ■ **stuntman** | **stuntwoman** n [C] person employed to do dangerous scenes in place of an actor in a film, etc

stupendous /stjuː'pendəs/ *adj* amazingly large, good, etc ▸ **stupendously** *adv*

0️⃣ **stupid** /'stjuːpɪd/ *adj* showing a lack of intelligence or good sense ▸ **stupidity** /-'pɪdəti/ n [C,U] ▸ **stupidly** *adv*

stupor /'stjuːpə(r)/ n [C,U] condition of being almost unconscious from shock, drink, etc

sturdy /'stɜːdi/ *adj* (**-ier, -iest**) strong and solid ▸ **sturdily** /-ɪli/ *adv*

stutter /'stʌtə(r)/ v [I,T], n = STAMMER

sty /staɪ/ n [C] **1** (pl **sties**) = PIGSTY (PIG) **2** (*also* **stye**) (pl **sties** or **styes**) inflamed swelling of the eyelid

0️⃣ **style** /staɪl/ n **1** [C,U] particular way in which sth is done **2** [C] design of sth, esp clothes **3** [U] quality of being fashionable and elegant **4** [C,U] features of a book, painting, building, etc that make it typical of an author, period, etc: *a fine example of Gothic* ~ [IDM] **be more sb's style** be what sb prefers or what suits sb: *Big cars are more my* ~. ● **style** v [T] design, make or shape sth in a particular way ▸ **stylish** *adj* (*approv*) fashionable ▸ **stylist** n [C] person who styles people's hair ▸ **stylistic** /-'lɪstɪk/ *adj* of the style an artist uses in a particular piece of art, writing or music ▸ **stylized** (*-ised*) *adj* drawn, written, etc in a way that is not natural or realistic

stylus /'staɪləs/ n [C] **1** needle used for reproducing sound from records **2** (*computing*) pointing device shaped like a pen for use with palmtops, etc

suave /swɑːv/ *adj* confident, elegant and polite, sometimes in a way that seems insincere

sub /sʌb/ n [C] (*infml*) **1** short for SUBMARINE **2** substitute, esp in cricket or football

subconscious /ˌsʌb'kɒnʃəs/ *adj* of feelings that influence your behaviour, even though you are not aware of them ▸ **subconscious** n [sing] (the/your subconscious) part of your mind containing feelings you are not aware of ▸ **subconsciously** *adv*

subcontinent /ˌsʌb'kɒntɪnənt/ n [C] large land mass forming part of a continent

subdivide /ˌsʌbdɪ'vaɪd/ v [I,T] divide sth again into smaller parts ▸ **subdivision** /-dɪ'vɪʒn; 'sʌbdɪvɪʒn/ n [C,U]

subdue /səb'djuː/ v [T] **1** bring sb/sth under control, esp by using force **2** calm or control your feelings

0️⃣ **subject¹** /'sʌbdʒɪkt/ n [C] **1** thing or person being discussed, described or dealt with: *the* ~ *of the book* **2** area of knowledge studied in a school, etc **3** (*gram*) noun or phrase which comes before a verb and which performs the action of that verb or is described by it, eg *the book in The book is green.* **4** person who has the right to belong to a country

subject² /səb'dʒekt/ v [T] (*fml*) bring a nation or group under your control, esp by using force [PV] **subject sb/sth to sth** (*written*) make sb/sth experience sth unpleasant: ~ *sb to criticism* ▸ **subjection** /-ʃn/ n [sing]

subject³ /'sʌbdʒekt; -dʒɪkt/ *adj* ~ **to 1** likely to be affected by sth, esp sth bad: ~ to frequent colds **2** depending on sth to be completed or agreed: ~ to confirmation **3** under the authority of sth/sb: ~ to the law

subjective /səb'dʒektɪv/ adj **1** influenced by personal feelings **2** (phil) having no existence outside the mind; imaginary ▶ **subjectively** adv ▶ **subjectivity** /-'tɪvəti/ n [U]

sublet /ˌsʌb'let/ v (-tt-, pt, pp **sublet**) [I,T] (of a tenant) rent a house, flat, etc to sb else

sublime /sə'blaɪm/ adj of the greatest and highest kind ▶ **sublimely** adv

submarine /ˌsʌbmə'riːn/ n [C] ship that can travel under water

submerge /səb'mɜːdʒ/ v **1** [I,T] (cause sth to) go under water **2** [T] (written) hide ideas, feelings, etc completely ▶ **submersion** /səb'mɜːʃn/ n [U]

submission /səb'mɪʃn/ n [U] **1** acceptance of sb's power over you **2** [U,C] (act of presenting sb in authority with a) document, proposal, etc for consideration

submissive /səb'mɪsɪv/ adj always willing to obey others ▶ **submissively** adv ▶ **submissiveness** n [U]

submit /səb'mɪt/ v (-tt-) **1** [T] give a document, proposal, etc to sb in authority so they can study or consider it **2** [I] accept the power of sb/sth over you

subordinate /sə'bɔːdɪnət/ adj **1** lower in rank **2** of less importance ● **subordinate** n [C] person who is lower in rank or position than sb else ● **subordinate** /sə'bɔːdɪneɪt/ v [T] ~ (to) treat sb/sth as less important than sb/sth else

subscribe /səb'skraɪb/ v [I] ~ (to) **1** pay money once a year to receive regular copies of a newspaper, etc **2** agree to pay a sum of money regularly to be a member of an organization, charity, etc [PV] **subscribe to sth** (fml) agree with an opinion, theory, etc ▶ **subscriber** n [C] ▶ **subscription** /səb'skrɪpʃn/ n [C,U] money paid to a charity, to receive a magazine regularly, to belong to a club, etc

subsequent /ˈsʌbsɪkwənt/ adj ~ (to) following ▶ **subsequently** adv afterwards

subservient /səb'sɜːviənt/ adj (disapprov) too willing to obey others ▶ **subservience** /-əns/ n [U] ▶ **subserviently** adv

subside /səb'saɪd/ v [I] **1** (of water, etc) return to the normal level **2** (of land or a building) sink lower **3** become less strong, active, loud, etc ▶ **subsidence** /-ns; 'sʌbsɪdns/ n [C,U] (instance of) subsiding (2)

subsidiary /səb'sɪdiəri/ adj connected with sth but less important than it: a ~ role ● **subsidiary** n [C] (pl -ies) company controlled by another larger company

subsidy /'sʌbsədi/ n [C] (pl -ies) money granted, esp by a government, to help an industry, a theatre, etc ▶ **subsidize** (also -ise) /'sʌbsɪdaɪz/ v [T] give a subsidy to sb or an organization to help pay for sth

subsist /səb'sɪst/ v [I] manage to stay alive, esp with little food and money ▶ **subsistence** n [U] state of having just enough money to stay alive

0-- **substance** /'sʌbstəns/ n **1** [C,A] type of solid, liquid or gas that has particular qualities **2** [U] (written) quality of being based on facts or the truth: a speech with little ~ **3** [U] most important or main part of sth

0-- **substantial** /səb'stænʃl/ adj **1** large: a ~ amount **2** solidly built ▶ **substantially** adv **1** very much **2** mainly

substantiate /səb'stænʃieɪt/ v [T] prove a claim, etc by giving facts

0-- **substitute** /'sʌbstɪtjuːt/ n [C] person or thing taking the place of another ● **substitute** v [I,T] ~ (for) serve or use sb/sth instead of sb/sth else ▶ **substitution** /ˌsʌbstɪ'tjuːʃn/ n [U,C]

subsume /səb'sjuːm/ v [T] (fml) include sth in a group and not consider it separately

subterfuge /'sʌbtəfjuːdʒ/ n [U,C] (fml) secret, usu dishonest, way of behaving or doing sth

subterranean /ˌsʌbtə'reɪniən/ adj (fml) under the ground

subtitle /'sʌbtaɪtl/ n [C] **1** (usu pl) words printed on a film, translating the dialogue, giving the dialogue for deaf viewers, etc **2** secondary title of a book, etc

subtle /'sʌtl/ adj **1** not very noticeable or obvious: a ~ difference **2** clever: a ~ plan **3** good at noticing and understanding things ▶ **subtlety** n [U,C] (pl -ies) ▶ **subtly** /'sʌtli/ adv

subtract /səb'trækt/ v [T] ~ (from) take a number or amount away from another number or amount ▶ **subtraction** /-ʃn/ n [U,C]

suburb /'sʌbɜːb/ n [C] residential area of a town away from the centre ▶ **suburban** /sə'bɜːbən/ adj ▶ **suburbia** /sə'bɜːbiə/ n [U] (life lived by people in) suburbs

subvert /səb'vɜːt/ v [T] (fml) try to destroy the authority of a political, religious, etc system ▶ **subversion** /-ʃn/ n [U] ▶ **subversive** adj trying to subvert sth

A B C D E F G H I J K L M N O P Q R **S** T U V W X Y Z

subway

subway /'sʌbweɪ/ *n* [C] **1** pedestrian tunnel beneath a road, etc **2** (US) underground railway system in a city

○━ **succeed** /sək'siːd/ *v* **1** [I] ~ **(in)** achieve what you are trying to achieve or do well in your job, etc: ~ *in winning the race* **2** [T] come next after sb/sth and take their/its place or position: ~ *sb as president* **3** [I] ~ **(to)** gain the right to sth when sb dies

○━ **success** /sək'ses/ *n* **1** [U] achievement of your aims, fame, wealth, etc **2** [C] person or thing that succeeds ▸ **successful** *adj* ▸ **successfully** *adv*

succession /sək'seʃn/ *n* **1** [C, usu sing] series of people or things that follow each other in time or order: *They had three children in quick* ~. **2** [U] regular pattern of one thing happening after another [IDM] **in succession** one after the other ▸ **successive** *adj* coming one after the other ▸ **successor** *n* [C] person or thing that follows another

succinct /sək'sɪŋkt/ *adj* expressed briefly and clearly ▸ **succinctly** *adv* ▸ **succinctness** *n* [U]

succulent /'sʌkjələnt/ *adj* **1** (of fruit and meat) juicy and delicious **2** (of plants) thick and fleshy

succumb /sə'kʌm/ *v* [I] ~ **(to)** (*fml*) stop resisting temptation, illness, etc

○━ **such** /sʌtʃ/ *det, pron* **1** of the type already mentioned: ~ *countries as France* ◇ *He said he didn't have time or made some* ~ *excuse.* **2** of the type that you are just going to mention: *There is no* ~ *thing as a free lunch.* **3** used to emphasize the degree of sth: *Don't be in* ~ *a hurry.* [IDM] **as such** as the word is usu understood ■ **such-and-such** *pron, det* used for referring to sth without saying exactly what it is ■ **suchlike** *pron, det* (things) of the same kind

○━ **suck** /sʌk/ *v* [I,T] **1** take liquid, air, etc into your mouth using the lips **2** [T] hold a sweet, etc in the mouth and lick it with your tongue **3** [T] (of a pump, etc) take liquid, air, etc out of sth **4** [T] pull sb/sth with great force in one direction: *The current* ~*ed her under the water.* ● **suck up** *n* [usu sing] act of sucking ▸ **sucker** *n* [C] **1** (*infml*) person that is easily tricked or persuaded to do sth **2** ~ **for** (*infml*) person who likes sth very much: *a* ~*er for old films* **3** organ on the body of some animals that enables them to stick to a surface **4** rubber disc that sticks to a surface when you press against it

suckle /'sʌkl/ *v* [T] feed a baby or young animal with milk from the breast

suction /'sʌkʃn/ *n* [U] process of causing a vacuum, esp so that two surfaces stick together

○━ **sudden** /'sʌdn/ *adj* happening unexpectedly and quickly ▸ **suddenly** *adv* ▸ **suddenness** *n* [U]

sudoku /su'dəʊku:/ *n* [U,C] number game with 81 squares in which you have to write the numbers 1 to 9 in a particular pattern: *Alison is addicted to* ~.

suds /sʌdz/ *n* [pl] mass of bubbles that forms on soapy water

sue /su:; sju:/ *v* [I,T] make a legal claim against sb in a court of law

suede /sweɪd/ *n* [U] soft leather with one rough side

suet /'su:ɪt; 'sju:ɪt/ *n* [U] hard animal fat used in cooking

○━ **suffer** /'sʌfə(r)/ *v* **1** [I] ~ **(from)** be badly affected by a disease, pain, sadness, etc **2** [T] experience sth unpleasant, eg injury, defeat or loss **3** [I] become worse: *Her work* ~*ed when she was ill.* [IDM] **not suffer fools gladly** have little patience with people you think are stupid ▸ **suffering** *n* [U] (also **sufferings**) [pl] physical or mental pain

suffice /sə'faɪs/ *v* [I] (*fml*) be enough for sb/sth

○━ **sufficient** /sə'fɪʃnt/ *adj* enough ▸ **sufficiency** /-nsi/ *n* [sing] (*fml*) sufficient quantity ▸ **sufficiently** *adv*

suffix /'sʌfɪks/ *n* [C] (*gram*) letter or group of letters added to the end of a word to change its meaning

suffocate /'sʌfəkeɪt/ *v* **1** [I,T] (cause sb to) die from not being able to breathe air **2** (be suffocating) [I] be very hot with very little fresh air: *Open a window. It's suffocating in here!* ▸ **suffocation** /ˌsʌfə'keɪʃn/ *n* [U]

○━ **sugar** /'ʃʊɡə(r)/ *n* [U] sweet substance obtained from various plants ● **sugar** *v* [T] add sugar to sth ■ **sugar cane** *n* [U] tall tropical grass from which sugar is made ▸ **sugary** *adj* **1** containing sugar; sweet **2** (*disapprov*) too sentimental

○━ **suggest** /sə'dʒest/ *v* [T] **1** put forward an idea or plan for consideration **2** put an idea into sb's mind ▸ **suggestion** /-tʃən/ *n* **1** [C] idea, plan, etc that you mention for sb to think about **2** [U,C, usu sing] reason to think that sth, esp sth bad, is true ▸ **suggestive** *adj* making sb think about sth, esp about sex ▸ **suggestively** *adv*

suicide /'su:ɪsaɪd; 'sju:-/ *n* [C,U] act of killing yourself deliberately: *commit* ~ **2** [C] action likely to ruin your career, position in society, etc **3** [C] (*fml*) person who commits suicide ▸ **suicidal** /-'saɪdl/ *adj*

1 wanting to kill yourself **2** likely to lead to death or disaster

0~ **suit**[1] /suːt/ *n* [C] **1** jacket and trousers (or skirt) of the same material **2** set of clothing worn for a particular activity **3** any of four sets of playing cards (spades, hearts, diamonds, clubs) ▸ **suitcase** *n* [C] case for carrying clothes, etc when travelling

0~ **suit**[2] /suːt/ *v* **1** [I,T] be convenient or useful for sb/sth **2** [T] (esp of clothes, colours, etc) make you look attractive: *Blue ~s you.* [IDM] **suit yourself** (*infml*) do as you want ▸ **suitable** /ˈsuːtəbl; -ɪə-/ *adj* right or appropriate for a purpose ▸ **suitably** *adv* ▸ **suitability** /-ˈbɪləti-/ *n* [U] ▸ **suited** *adj* right or appropriate for sb/sth

suite /swiːt/ *n* [C] **1** set of matching pieces of furniture **2** set of rooms, eg in a hotel **3** piece of music in three or more parts

sulk /sʌlk/ *v* [I] (*disapprov*) refuse to speak because you are annoyed with sb ▸ **sulky** *adj* (*-ier, -iest*)

sullen /ˈsʌlən/ *adj* (*disapprov*) silent and bad-tempered ▸ **sullenly** *adv* ▸ **sullenness** *n* [U]

sulphur (*US sulfur*) /ˈsʌlfə(r)/ *n* [U] (*symb* S) yellow element that burns with a bright flame ■ **sulphuric acid** (*US sulfuric ~*) /sʌlˈfjʊərɪk ˈæsɪd/ *n* [U] (*chem*) (*symb* H₂SO₄) strong colourless acid

sultan /ˈsʌltən/ *n* [C] ruler of certain Muslim countries

sultana /sʌlˈtɑːnə/ *n* [C] small dried grape without seeds, used in cakes, etc

sultry /ˈsʌltri/ *adj* (*-ier, -iest*) **1** (of the weather) hot and uncomfortable **2** (*written*) (of a woman) sexually attractive

0~ **sum** /sʌm/ *n* [C] **1** amount of money **2** total obtained by adding together numbers or amounts **3** simple problem that involves calculating numbers ● **sum** *v* (*-mm-*) [PV] **sum (sth) up** give a summary of sth **sum sb/sth up** form or express an opinion of sb/sth

0~ **summary** /ˈsʌməri/ *n* [C] (*pl* -**ies**) short statement giving only the main points of sth ● **summary** *adj* **1** (*fml*) giving the main points only; brief **2** done without delay: *a ~ execution* ▸ **summarize** (*also* -ise) /-raɪz/ *v* [T] give a summary of sth

0~ **summer** /ˈsʌmə(r)/ *n* [C,U] warmest season of the year ▸ **summery** *adj* like or suitable for summer

summit /ˈsʌmɪt/ *n* [C] **1** highest point of sth, esp a mountain **2** meeting of two or more heads of government

summon /ˈsʌmən/ *v* [T] **1** (*fml*) order sb to appear in a court of law **2** (*fml*)

order sb to come to you **3** ~ (**up**) make an effort to find a quality within yourself: *~ (up) all your courage*

summons /ˈsʌmənz/ *n* [C] (*pl* -**es** /-zɪz/) order to appear in a court of law ● **summons** *v* [T] order sb to appear in a court of law

0~ **sun** /sʌn/ *n* **1** (*the sun, the Sun*) [sing] star round which the earth moves and which gives it heat and light **2** (*usu the sun*) [sing, U] light and heat from the sun **3** [C] any star around which planets move [IDM] **under the sun** used to emphasize that you are talking about a large number of things ● **sun** *v* (*-nn-*) [T] ~ **yourself** lie in the sun ■ **sunbathe** *v* [I] sit or lie in the sun ■ **sunbeam** *n* [C] ray of sunlight ■ **sunburn** *n* [U] painful red skin caused by too much time spent in the sun ■ **sunburnt** *adj* suffering from sunburn ■ **sunglasses** *n* [pl] glasses with dark lenses to protect the eyes from the sun ■ **sunlight** *n* [U] light from the sun ■ **sunny** *adj* (*-ier, -iest*) **1** bright with sunlight **2** cheerful ■ **sunrise** *n* [U] dawn ■ **sunshade** *n* [C] object like an umbrella to keep off the sun ■ **sunshine** *n* [U] light and heat of the sun ■ **sunstroke** *n* [U] illness caused by spending too much time in the sun ■ **suntan** *n* [C] browning of the skin caused by exposure to sunlight

0~ **Sunday** /ˈsʌndeɪ; -di/ *n* [C,U] the first day of the week, next after Saturday (See examples of use at *Monday*.)

sundry /ˈsʌndri/ *adj* (*fml*) various ▸ **sundries** *n* [pl] (*written*) various small items

sung *pp* of SING

sunk *pp* of SINK

sunken /ˈsʌŋkən/ *adj* **1** that has fallen to the bottom of the sea **2** (of eyes or cheeks) hollow **3** lower than the surrounding area

0~ **super** /ˈsuːpə(r); ˈsjuː-/ *adj* (*infml*) excellent

superb /suːˈpɜːb; sjuː-/ *adj* excellent ▸ **superbly** *adv*

supercomputer /ˈsuːpəkəmpjuːtə(r); ˈsjuː-/ *n* [C] powerful computer with a large amount of memory and a very fast central processing unit

superficial /ˌsuːpəˈfɪʃl; ˌsjuː-/ *adj* **1** of or on the surface only **2** not thorough or deep: *a ~ knowledge* ▸ **superficiality** /ˌsuːpəˌfɪʃiˈæləti/ *n* [U] ▸ **superficially** *adv*

superfluous /suːˈpɜːfluəs; sjuː-/ *adj* more than you need or want ▸ **superfluously** *adv*

superhighway /ˈsuːpəhaɪweɪ; ˈsjuː-/ *n* [C] way of quickly sending information such as video, sound and pictures through a computer network, esp the Internet: *the information ~*

superhuman /ˌsuːpəˈhjuːmən; ˌsjuː-/ *adj* having much greater power, knowledge, etc than is normal

superimpose /ˌsuːpərɪmˈpəʊz; ˌsjuː-/ v [T] **~ (on)** put one image on top of another

superintend /ˌsuːpərɪnˈtend; ˌsjuː-/ v [I,T] (*fml*) be in charge of sth and make sure everything is working, being done, etc as it should be ▸ **superintendent** n [C] **1** person who superintends sth/sb **2** senior police officer

0⃞ **superior** /suːˈpɪəriə(r); sjuː-/ *adj* **1** higher in rank, importance, quality, etc **2** (*disapprov*) showing that you think you are better than others ● **superior** n [C] person of higher rank, status or position ▸ **superiority** /suːˌpɪəriˈɒrəti/ n [U]

superlative /suːˈpɜːlətɪv; sjuː-/ *adj* **1** excellent **2** (*gram*) of adjectives or adverbs, expressing the highest degree, eg *best, worst, most* ● **superlative** n [C] superlative form of an adjective or adverb

0⃞ **supermarket** /ˈsuːpəmɑːkɪt; ˈsjuː-/ n [C] large shop selling food, household goods, etc

supernatural /ˌsuːpəˈnætʃrəl; ˌsjuː-/ *adj* seeming magical, etc, because it cannot be explained by the laws of nature

superpower /ˈsuːpəpaʊə(r); ˈsjuː-/ n [C] one of the most powerful nations in the world

supersede /ˌsuːpəˈsiːd/ v [T] take the place of sth/sb

supersonic /ˌsuːpəˈsɒnɪk; ˌsjuː-/ *adj* faster than the speed of sound

superstar /ˈsuːpəstɑː(r)/ n [C] very famous performer

superstition /ˌsuːpəˈstɪʃn; ˌsjuː-/ n [U,C] (idea, practice, etc based on) the belief that particular events bring good or bad luck ▸ **superstitious** *adj*

supervise /ˈsuːpəvaɪz; ˈsjuː-/ v [I,T] be in charge of sb/sth and make sure everything is done correctly ▸ **supervision** /ˌsuːpəˈvɪʒn/ n [U] ▸ **supervisor** n [C] person who supervises sb/sth

supper /ˈsʌpə(r)/ n [C,U] last meal of the day

supple /ˈsʌpl/ *adj* easily bent; not stiff ▸ **suppleness** n [U]

supplement /ˈsʌplɪmənt/ n [C] **1** thing added to sth else **2** additional section of a book, newspaper, etc ● **supplement** /ˈsʌplɪment/ v [T] **~ (with)** add sth to sth in order to improve or complete

it ▸ **supplementary** /-ˈmentri/ (*US* **supplemental** /-ˈmentl/) *adj* additional

0⃞ **supply** /səˈplaɪ/ v (pt, pp **-ied**) [T] provide sb/sth with sth that they need or want, esp in large quantities: *~ gas to a house* ◇ *~ sb with food* ● **supply** n (pl **-ies**) **1** [C] amount of sth that is provided or available to use **2** [pl] things such as food, medicines, fuel, etc needed by a group of people, eg an army: *food supplies* **3** [U] act of supplying sth ▸ **supplier** n [C] person or company that supplies goods, etc

0⃞ **support** /səˈpɔːt/ v [T] **1** help or encourage sb by showing that you agree with them, by giving money, etc: *~ a political party* **2** provide sb with what is necessary to live, esp money: *~ a family* **3** hold sth/sb in position; prevent sth/sb from falling **4** help to show that sth is true **5** (*GB*) like a particular sports team, watch their games, etc ● **support** n [U] **1** encouragement and help you give to sb/sth **2** [U] sympathy and help that you give to sb in a difficult situation **3** [C] thing that supports sth ▸ **supporter** n [C] ▸ **supportive** *adj* giving encouragement, help, etc

0⃞ **suppose** /səˈpəʊz/ v [T] **1** think or believe that sth is true or possible: *There's no reason to ~ she's lying.* **2** pretend sth is true; imagine what would happen if sth were true: *Let us ~, for example, that you have lost your passport.* [IDM] **be supposed to do/be** be expected or required to do/ be sth according to a rule, an arrangement, etc: *I'm ~d to make coffee for the visitors.* **not be supposed to do sth** not be allowed to do sth ▸ **supposedly** /-ɪdli/ *adv* according to what is generally thought or believed ▸ **supposing** *conj* used to ask sb to imagine that sth is true

supposition /ˌsʌpəˈzɪʃn/ n [C] idea that you think is true but cannot prove **2** [U] act of believing or claiming sth to be true

suppress /səˈpres/ v [T] **1** put an end to sth, often by force: *~ a revolt* **2** prevent sth from being known: *~ the truth* ▸ **suppression** /-ʃn/ n [U]

supreme /suːˈpriːm; sjuː-/ *adj* **1** highest in rank or position **2** greatest in degree ▸ **supremacy** /suːˈpreməsi; sjuː-/ n [U] ▸ **supremely** *adv*

surcharge /ˈsɜːtʃɑːdʒ/ n [C] payment additional to the usual charge

0⃞ **sure** /ʃɔː(r)/ *adj* **1** confident that you know sth or that you are right: *Are you ~ you don't mind?* **2 ~ of** certain that you will receive sth or that sth will happen **3 ~ to** certain to do sth or to happen: *He's ~ to be late.* **4** reliable: *a ~ cure for colds* [IDM] **be**

sure to do sth used to tell sb to do sth

make sure (of sth/that...) 1 do sth in order to make certain that sth else happens **2** check that sth is true or has been done ● **sure** *adv* (*infml, esp US*) **1** used to say 'yes' to sb **2** used to emphasize what you are saying: *It ~ is cold!* [IDM] **sure enough** as was expected: *I said he would be late and ~ enough, he was.* ▸ **surely** *adv* **1** used for expressing hope, certainty, etc: *S~ly not!* **2** (*fml*) certainly

surety /'ʃʊərəti; 'ʃɔːr-/ *n* (*pl* -ies) [C, u] (*law*) **1** money given as a promise that you will pay a debt, appear in court, etc **2** person responsible for the conduct or debt(s) of another

surf /sɜːf/ *n* [U] large waves in the sea, and the white foam that they produce as they fall on the shore ● **surf** *v* [I, T] **1** take part in the sport of riding on waves on a surfboard **2** [T] ~ **the net/Internet** use the Internet ■ **surfboard** /'sɜːfbɔːd/ *n* [C] long narrow board used for surfing ▸ **surfing** *n* [U] **1** sport of riding on top of the waves using a board **2** activity of looking at different things on the Internet

0‑w **surface** /'sɜːfɪs/ *n* **1** [C] outside or top layer of sth **2** [C, usu sing] layer of an area of water **3** [sing] outward appearance of sb/sth ● **surface** *v* **1** [I] come up to the surface of water **2** [I] suddenly appear or become obvious **3** [I] (*infml*) wake up or get up **4** [T] put a surface on a path, road, etc ■ **surface mail** [U] letters, etc sent by land or sea, not by air

surfeit /'sɜːfɪt/ *n* [usu sing] ~ **(of)** (*fml*) too much of sth

surge /sɜːdʒ/ *v* [I] **1** move forward or upward like waves **2** fill sb with a strong feeling ● **surge** *n* [C] **1** sudden increase **2** sudden forward or upward movement

surgeon /'sɜːdʒən/ *n* [C] doctor who performs surgical operations

surgery /'sɜːdʒəri/ *n* (*pl* -ies) **1** [U] medical treatment of injuries and diseases by cutting open the body **2** [C] place where a doctor, dentist, etc sees their patients

surgical /'sɜːdʒɪkl/ *adj* of, by or for surgery ▸ **surgically** /-kli/ *adv*

surly /'sɜːli/ *adj* (-ier, -iest) bad-tempered and rude ▸ **surliness** *n* [U]

surmount /sə'maʊnt/ *v* [T] (*fml*) **1** deal successfully with a difficulty, etc *a church ~ed by a tower*

0‑w **surname** /'sɜːneɪm/ *n* [C] name shared by all the members of a family

surpass /sə'pɑːs/ *v* [T] (*fml*) do or be better than sb/sth

surplus /'sɜːpləs/ *n* [C] amount of money, etc beyond what is needed

0‑w **surprise** /sə'praɪz/ *n* [U, C] (*usu* pleasant feeling caused by) sth sudden or unexpected [IDM] **take sb by surprise** surprise sb by happening unexpectedly ● **surprise** *v* [T] **1** cause sb to feel surprised **2** attack, discover, etc sb suddenly and unexpectedly: ~ *a burglar* ▸ **surprised** *adj* feeling or showing surprise ▸ **surprising** *adj* ▸ **surprisingly** *adv*

surrender /sə'rendə(r)/ *v* [I, T] **1** ~ **(yourself) (to)** stop fighting against an enemy, etc and allow yourself to be caught, etc **2** [T] give up sth/sb when you are forced to [PV] **surrender (yourself) to sth** (*fml*) allow a feeling, habit, etc to control your actions ▸ **surrender** *n* [U, sing] act of surrendering

0‑w **surround** /sə'raʊnd/ *v* [T] **1** be or move all around sb/sth ● **surround** *n* [C] (*usu* decorative) edge or border ▸ **surrounding** *adj* that is near or around sth ▸ **surroundings** *n* [pl] everything around sb/sth

surveillance /sɜː'veɪləns/ *n* [U] close watch kept on sb suspected of doing wrong, etc: *under ~*

0‑w **survey** /sə'veɪ/ *v* [T] **1** look at or study the whole of sth **2** measure and make a map of an area of land, etc **3** (*GB*) examine a building to make sure it is in good condition ● **survey** /'sɜːveɪ/ *n* [C] **1** investigation of the opinions, behaviour, etc of a group of people **2** act of examining and measuring an area of land to make a map of it **3** (*GB*) examination of the condition of a building **4** general view or study of sth ▸ **surveyor** /sə'veɪə(r)/ *n* [C] person whose job is to examine buildings and record the details of areas of land

survival /sə'vaɪvl/ *n* **1** [U] state of continuing to live or exist, despite danger **2** [C] thing that has survived from an earlier time

0‑w **survive** /sə'vaɪv/ *v* [I, T] continue to live or exist (longer than sth): ~ *an accident ◇ She ~d her husband.* ▸ **survivor** *n* [C] person who continues to live, despite almost being killed

susceptible /sə'septəbl/ *adj* **1** ~ **to** likely to be affected by sb/sth: ~ *to cold* **2** easily influenced ▸ **susceptibility** /sə,septə'bɪləti/ *n* [U]

0‑w **suspect** /sə'spekt/ *v* [T] **1** think that sth is possible: *We ~ that he's dead.* **2** feel doubt about sb/sth: ~ *the truth of his statement* **3** ~ **(of)** feel that sb is guilty of sth: ~ *sb of lying* ● **suspect** /'sʌspekt/ *n* [C] person

suspected of doing wrong, etc
● **suspect** /'sʌspekt/ *adj* not to be relied on or trusted

suspend /sə'spend/ *v* [T] **1 ~ (from)** hang sth from sth else: ~ *a lamp from the ceiling* **2** delay sth: ~ *judgement* **3 ~ (from)** officially prevent sb from doing their job, going to school, etc for a time: *They ~ed the two boys from school.*

suspenders /sə'spendəz/ *n* [pl] **1** (*GB*) short elastic straps for holding up stockings or socks **2** (*US*) = BRACES (BRACE(3))

suspense /sə'spens/ *n* [U] uncertainty or worry about what may happen

suspension /sə'spenʃn/ *n* [U, C] **1** act of suspending sb from their job, etc or of delaying sth **2** springs, etc that support a car so the driver cannot feel bumps in the road
■ **su'spension bridge** *n* [C] bridge hanging on steel cables attached to towers

0━ **suspicion** /sə'spɪʃn/ *n* **1** [U,C] feeling that sth is wrong, sb has done wrong, etc: *arrested on a ~ of murder* **2** [C] feeling that sth is true, though you have no proof **3** [sing] small amount of sth: *a ~ of sadness* ▶ **suspicious** *adj* having or causing suspicion ▶ **suspiciously** *adv*

sustain /sə'steɪn/ *v* [T] **1** keep sb/sth alive or in existence **2** (*fml*) suffer: *an injury* **3** (*fml*) support a weight

sustenance /'sʌstənəns/ *n* [U] (*fml*) (nourishing quality of) food or drink

SUV /,es juː 'viː/ *n* [C] (*esp US*) = SPORT UTILITY VEHICLE (SPORT)

SW *abbr* = SHORT WAVE (SHORT¹)

swab /swɒb/ *n* [C] piece of cotton wool, etc used for cleaning wounds, taking a sample for testing, etc ● **swab** *v* (**-bb-**) [T] clean a wound, etc with a swab

swagger /'swægə(r)/ *v* [I] (*disapprov*) walk or behave in a proud and confident way
● **swagger** *n* [sing] (*disapprov*) way of walking that seems too confident

0━ **swallow** /'swɒləʊ/ *v* **1** [I,T] cause food, etc to go down your throat **2** [I] **~ (up)** use up sth completely: *earnings ~ed up by bills* **3** [T] accept that sth is true; believe sth: *I'm not ~ing that story!* **4** [T] hide your feelings **5** [T] accept an insult, etc without complaining ● **swallow** *n* [C] **1** small bird with a forked tail **2** act of swallowing or amount swallowed

swam *pt of* SWIM

swamp /swɒmp/ *n* [C,U] (area of) soft wet land ● **swamp** *v* [T] **1** make sb have more of sth than they can deal with: ~*ed with requests* **2** fill or cover

sth with water ▶ **swampy** *adj* (**-ier, -iest**) having swamps

swan /swɒn/ *n* [C] large white water bird with a long thin neck ● **swan** *v* (**-nn-**) [I] (*GB, infml, disapprov*) go around enjoying yourself in a way that annoys others or makes them jealous ● **swansong** *n* [sing] last performance or last work of a musician, poet, etc

swanky /'swæŋki/ *adj* (**-ier, -iest**) (*infml, disapprov*) fashionable and expensive

swap (*also* **swop**) /swɒp/ *v* (**-pp-**) [I,T] **~ (with)** give sth to sb in exchange for sth else: ~ *seats with sb* ● **swap** *n* [C] act of swapping or sth swapped

swarm /swɔːm/ *n* [C] large group of insects, esp bees ● **swarm** *v* [I] move in large numbers [PV] **swarm with sb/sth** be full of people or things: *beaches ~ing with people*

swat /swɒt/ *v* (**-tt-**) [T] hit sth, esp an insect, with a flat object

sway /sweɪ/ *v* **1** [I,T] (cause sth to) move from side to side **2** [T] persuade sb to believe sth or do sth ● **sway** *n* **1** [U] movement from side to side **2** (*lit*) power or influence over sth

0━ **swear** /sweə(r)/ *v* (*pt* **swore** /swɔː(r)/ *pp* **sworn** /swɔːn/) **1** [I] **~ (at)** use offensive or rude words, usu because you are angry **2** [T] make a serious promise to do sth: *She made him ~ not to tell anyone.* **3** [I,T] say or promise sth solemnly, esp in a court of law [PV] **swear by sth** be certain that sth is good or useful **swear sb in** make sb promise to do a job correctly, be loyal to a country, etc ■ **'swear word** *n* [C] rude or offensive word

0━ **sweat** /swet/ *n* **1** [U] liquid which comes through the skin when you are hot, nervous etc **2** [usu sing] state of being covered with sweat **3** [U] hard work or effort ● **sweat** *v* [I] **1** produce sweat **2** (*infml*) be worried or nervous [IDM] **sweat blood** (*infml*) work very hard
■ **'sweatshirt** *n* [C] long-sleeved cotton sweater ▶ **sweaty** *adj* (**-ier, -iest**) (causing sb to be) hot and covered with sweat

0━ **sweater** /'swetə(r)/ *n* [C] knitted woollen or cotton piece of clothing for the upper body

swede /swiːd/ *n* [C,U] large round yellow root vegetable

0━ **sweep¹** /swiːp/ *v* (*pt, pp* **swept** /swept/) **1** [T] clear dust, dirt, etc using a brush, broom, etc **2** [T] carry or move sb/sth quickly: *The sea swept him along.* **3** [I,T] (of weather, fire, etc) pass quickly over an area: *A huge wave swept (over) the deck.* **4** [I] move in a proud way: *She swept from the room.* **5** [I] (of a place, etc) form a long smooth curve: *The coast ~s northwards.* [IDM] **sweep sb off their** feet make sb suddenly fall in love with you **sweep sth under the carpet** hide sth embarrassing or scandalous ▸ **sweeper** n [C] person or thing that sweeps ▸ **sweeping** adj **1** having a wide effect: ~ing changes **2** too general: a ~ing statement

sweep² /swiːp/ n **1** [C] act of cleaning a room, etc with a broom **2** [C] smooth curving movement **3** [U] range of an area, piece of writing, etc: the broad ~ of a novel **4** [C] movement over an area, eg to search for sth **5** [C] = CHIMNEY SWEEP (CHIMNEY)

O─ **sweet** /swiːt/ adj **1** tasting like sugar **2** smelling pleasant: Don't the roses smell ~! **3** pleasant or attractive: a ~ face **4** fresh and pure: the ~ smell of the countryside **5** lovable: a ~ little boy **IDM** have a **sweet tooth** (infml) like food that contains a lot of sugar ● **sweet** n [C] **1** small piece of sth sweet, eg boiled sugar, chocolate, etc **2** dish of sweet food ■ **sweetcorn** n [U] type of maize with sweet yellow seeds ■ **sweeten** v [I,T] become or make sth sweet ■ **sweetener** n [C] substance used to make food taste sweeter ■ **sweetheart** n [sing] used to address sb in a way that shows affection ● **sweetly** adv ● **sweetness** n [U] ■ **sweet-talk** v [T] ~ (into) try to persuade sb to do sth by saying nice things to them

O─ **swell** /swel/ v (pt **swelled** /sweld/ pp **swollen** /ˈswəʊlən/ or **swelled**) [I,T] **1** (cause sth to) become greater in size, thickness, quantity, etc: a swollen ankle **2** (cause sth to) curve outwards ● **swell** n [U,sing] slow rise and fall of the sea's surface ▸ **swelling** n [C] swollen place on the body

swelter /ˈsweltə(r)/ v [I] be uncomfortably hot

swept pt, pp of SWEEP¹

swerve /swɜːv/ v [I] change direction suddenly: The car ~d to avoid her. ▸ **swerve** n [C]

swift /swɪft/ adj quick, prompt: a ~ reply ▸ **swiftly** adv ▸ **swiftness** n [U] ● **swift** n [C] small bird similar to a swallow

swig /swɪɡ/ v (**-gg-**) [T] (infml) drink sth in large amounts

swill /swɪl/ v [T] **1** clean sth by pouring large amounts of water in, on or through it **2** (infml) drink sth in large amounts: ~ tea ● **swill** n [U] waste food that is given to pigs to eat

O─ **swim** /swɪm/ v (pt **swam** /swæm/ pp **swum** /swʌm/ **-mm-**) **1** [I,T] (of a person) move through water using the arms and legs: to ~ the Channel **2** [I] spend time swimming for pleasure: I go ~ming twice a week. **3** [I] (of a fish, etc) move through or

across water **4** [I] ~ (in/with) be covered with liquid **5** [I] seem to be moving around: His head swam. ● **swim** n [sing] period of time during which you swim: go for a ~ **IDM in the swim (of things)** (infml) involved in things that are happening ▸ **swimmer** n [C] person who swims ■ **swimming costume** | **swimsuit** n [C] piece of clothing worn by women and girls for swimming ■ **swimming pool** n [C] area of water that has been created for people to swim in ■ **swimming trunks** n [pl] shorts worn by boys and men for swimming

swindle /ˈswɪndl/ v [T] get money, etc from sb by cheating ● **swindle** n [usu sing] situation in which sb uses illegal methods to get money from sb/sth ▸ **swindler** n [C] person who gets money, etc by swindling

O─ **swing** /swɪŋ/ v (pt, pp **swung** /swʌŋ/) [I,T] **1** (cause sth to) move backwards and forwards while hanging from a fixed point: ~ your arms **2** (cause sth to) turn or change direction quickly: ~ round the corner **3** (cause sb/sth to) change from one opinion, mood, etc to another: a speech that ~s the voters **IDM swing into action** start doing sth quickly ● **swing** n **1** [C] swinging movement or rhythm **2** [C] change from one opinion or situation to another **3** [C] seat hanging from a bar, etc for swinging on **4** [U] type of jazz with a smooth rhythm, played esp in the 1930s **IDM go with a swing** be lively and enjoyable **swings and roundabouts** (GB, infml) situation in which there are gains and losses

swingeing /ˈswɪndʒɪŋ/ adj (GB, written) large in amount, etc; severe

swipe /swaɪp/ v **1** [I,T] hit sb/sth with your hand, etc by swinging your arm **2** [T] (infml) steal sth **3** [T] pass a credit card, etc through a special machine that is able to read the information stored on it ● **swipe** n [C] swinging blow ■ **swipe card** n [C] plastic card with information recorded on it which can only be read by an electronic device: Access to the building is by ~ card only.

swirl /swɜːl/ v [I,T] (cause air, water, etc to) move or flow with twists and turns ● **swirl** n [C] swirling movement or pattern

swish /swɪʃ/ v [I,T] (cause sth to) move through the air with a hissing sound ● **swish** n [sing] movement or sound made by sth moving quickly ● **swish** adj (infml) fashionable or expensive

O─ **switch** /swɪtʃ/ n [C] **1** device for making and breaking an electrical circuit: a light ~ **2** change from one thing to another: a ~ from gas to

swivel

electricity ● **switch** v **1** [I,T] (cause sth to) change from one thing to another: ~ *to using gas* **2** [T] exchange one thing for another: ~ *the dates of the exams* [PV] **switch sth off/on** turn a light, machine, etc off/on by pressing a button or switch ■ **'switchboard** n [C] central part of a telephone system used by a company, etc where calls are answered and put through to the appropriate person, etc

swivel /'swɪvl/ v (-ll- US -l-) [I,T] (cause sth to) turn (as if) on a central point: ~ *(round) in your chair*

0— **swollen** pp of SWELL

swoop /swu:p/ v [I] (of a bird or plane) fly downwards suddenly, esp in order to attack sth/sth: (fig) *Police ~ed (on the house) at dawn.* ● **swoop** n [C] **1** swooping movement **2** sudden attack

swop = SWAP

sword /sɔ:d/ n [C] weapon with a long steel blade fixed in a handle ■ **'swordfish** n [C] large sea fish with a long thin pointed upper jaw

swore pt of SWEAR

sworn[1] pp of SWEAR

sworn[2] /swɔ:n/ adj **1** made after you have promised to tell the truth: *a ~ statement* **2** (~ enemies) people, countries, etc that hate each other

swum pp of SWIM

swung pt, pp of SWING

syllable /'sɪləbl/ n [C] unit into which a word can be divided, usu containing a vowel: *'Table' has two ~s.* ▶ **syllabic** /sɪ'læbɪk/ adj

syllabus /'sɪləbəs/ n [C] list of subjects, etc in a course of study

syllogism /'sɪlədʒɪzəm/ n [C] logical argument in which a conclusion is drawn from two statements

0— **symbol** /'sɪmbl/ n [C] sign, mark, object, etc that represents sth: *The Dove is a ~ of peace.* ▶ **symbolic** /sɪm'bɒlɪk/ adj of or used as a symbol ▶ **symbolically** adv ▶ **symbolism** /'sɪmbəlɪzəm/ n [U] (use of) symbols ▶ **symbolize** (also -ise) /'sɪmbəlaɪz/ v be a symbol of sth

symmetry /'sɪmətri/ n [U] **1** exact match in size and shape of the two halves of sth **2** quality of being very similar or equal ▶ **symmetric** /sɪ'metrɪk/ (also **symmetrical** /-ɪkl/) adj

0— **sympathetic** /ˌsɪmpə'θetɪk/ adj **1** kind to sb who is hurt or sad; showing understanding and care: *~ looks* **2** showing that you approve of sb/sth or that you share their views **3** (of a person) easy to like: *a ~ character in a novel* ▶ **sympathetically** /-kli/ adv

sympathize (also -ise) /'sɪmpəθaɪz/ v

[I] ~ **(with)** **1** feel sorry for sb; show that you understand their problems **2** support sb/sth ▶ **sympathizer** (also -iser) n [C] person who supports a cause, party, etc

0— **sympathy** /'sɪmpəθi/ n (pl -ies) [U,C, usu pl] **1** (capacity for) sharing or understanding the feelings of others **2** act of showing support for or approval of an idea, cause, etc

symphony /'sɪmfəni/ n [C] (pl -ies) long musical composition, usu in three or four parts, for an orchestra

symptom /'sɪmptəm/ n [C] **1** change in the body that is a sign of illness **2** sign, usu of sth bad: *~s of discontent* ▶ **symptomatic** /-'mætɪk/ adj being a sign of an illness or problem

synagogue /'sɪnəgɒg/ n [C] building used by Jews for religious worship and teaching

synchronize (also -ise) /'sɪŋkrənaɪz/ v [I,T] (cause sth to) happen at the same time or move at the same speed as sth else: ~ *watches*

syndicate /'sɪndɪkət/ n [C] group of people or companies that join together for business ● **syndicate** /'sɪndɪkeɪt/ v [T] (usu passive) sell an article, a photograph, etc to several different newspapers, etc

syndrome /'sɪndrəʊm/ n [C] (med) set of symptoms which are a sign of an illness, etc

synonym /'sɪnənɪm/ n [C] word with the same meaning as another ▶ **synonymous** /sɪ'nɒnɪməs/ adj

synopsis /sɪ'nɒpsɪs/ n [C] (pl -opses /-siːz/) summary or outline of a book, play, etc

syntax /'sɪntæks/ n [U] (ling) (rules for) making sentences out of words and phrases ▶ **syntactic** /sɪn'tæktɪk/ adj of syntax

synthesis /'sɪnθəsɪs/ n [U,C] (pl -theses /-siːz/) combining of separate parts to make a single whole ▶ **synthetic** /sɪn'θetɪk/ adj artificial, not natural: ~ *fabric* ▶ **synthesize** (also -ise) /'sɪnθəsaɪz/ v [T] make sth by combining separate things ▶ **synthetically** /sɪn'θetɪkli/ adv

syphilis /'sɪfɪlɪs/ n [U] serious venereal disease

syphon = SIPHON

syringe /sɪ'rɪndʒ/ n [C] device with a needle for injecting liquids into the body, etc ● **syringe** v [T] clean sth with a syringe

syrup /'sɪrəp/ n [U] thick sweet liquid

0— **system** /'sɪstəm/ n [C] **1** organized set of ideas, etc: *a ~ of government* **2** [C] group of parts that are connected or work together **3** [sing] human or animal body, when considered as the organs and processes that make it function ▶ **systematic** /-'mætɪk/ adj based on

A B C D E F G H I J K L M N O P Q R **S** T U V W X Y Z

order, following a fixed plan
▸ **systematically** /-kli/ *adv*

Tt

T, t /tiː/ *n* [C,U] (pl **T's, t's** /tiːz/) the twentieth letter of the English alphabet ■ **T-shirt** *n* [C] informal shirt with short sleeves and no buttons

ta /taː/ *exclam* (*GB, sl*) thank you

tab /tæb/ *n* [C] small piece of cloth, paper, etc that sticks out from the edge of sth, used to give information about it, or to hold it, pull it, etc ■ **tab key** *n* [C] button on a keyboard that you use to move to a certain fixed position in a line of a document that you are typing

tabby /'tæbi/ *n* [C] (pl **-ies**) (*also* **tabby cat**) cat with grey or brown fur and dark stripes

0▸ table /'teɪbl/ *n* [C] 1 piece of furniture with a flat top on legs 2 list of facts or figures arranged in columns or rows ● **table** *v* [T] present sth formally for discussion ■ **tablecloth** *n* [C] cloth for covering a table, esp during meals ■ **tablespoon** *n* [C] large spoon for serving food ■ **tablespoonful** *n* [C] amount contained in a tablespoon ■ **table tennis** *n* [U] indoor game in which a small light ball is hit over a low net on a table

0▸ tablet /'tæblət/ *n* [C] 1 small hard piece of medicine 2 small bar of soap 3 flat piece of stone, etc with words cut into it

tabloid /'tæbloɪd/ *n* [C] newspaper with small pages, short news articles and many pictures of famous people

taboo /tə'buː/ *n* [C] (pl **~s**) something that is forbidden because of a strong religious or social custom ▸ **taboo** *adj*: *in the days when sex was a ~ subject* ■ **ta'boo words** *n* [pl] words that many people consider offensive or shocking

tabulate /'tæbjuleɪt/ *v* [T] arrange facts, figures, etc in a table (2) ▸ **tabulation** /-'leɪʃn/ *n* [U]

tacit /'tæsɪt/ *adj* understood without being said: *~ agreement* ▸ **tacitly** *adv*

tack /tæk/ *n* 1 [U,sing] course of action: *change* ~ 2 [C] small nail with a flat head 3 [C] long loose stitch ● **tack** *v* [T] sew sth together with loose stitches

0▸ tackle /'tækl/ *v* 1 [T] deal with a problem, piece of work, etc 2 [T] speak to sb frankly about sth 3 [I,T] (in football, etc) try to take the ball away from sb 4 [T] deal with sb violent or threatening, eg a thief ● **tackle** *n* 1 [C] act of tackling sb in football, etc 2 [U] equipment

needed for a certain sport, esp fishing

tacky /'tæki/ *adj* (**-ier, -iest**) (*infml*) cheap and bad taste: *~ jewellery*

tact /tækt/ *n* [U] skill of not offending people by saying or doing the right thing ▸ **tactful** *adj* having or showing tact ▸ **tactfully** *adv* ▸ **tactless** *adj* ▸ **tactlessly** *adv*

tactic /'tæktɪk/ *n* 1 [C, usu pl] method used to achieve sth 2 (**tactics**) [pl] art of arranging and moving armies in a battle ▸ **tactical** *adj* of tactics: *a ~al move* ▸ **tactician** /tæk'tɪʃn/ *n* [C] expert in tactics

tadpole /'tædpəʊl/ *n* [C] small creature that grows into a frog or toad

tag /tæg/ *n* 1 [C] small piece of paper, fabric, etc attached to sth to show its cost, owner, etc 2 [U] (*GB*) game in which one child chases and tries to touch another ● **tag** *v* (**-gg-**) [T] fasten a tag to sth [PV] **tag along (behind/with sb)** go somewhere with sb, esp uninvited

0▸ tail /teɪl/ *n* 1 [C] long movable part at the end of the body of an animal, bird, etc 2 [C] part of sth that sticks out at the back like a tail: *the ~ of an aircraft* 3 (**tails**) [U] side of a coin without a person's head on it 4 [C] (*infml*) person employed to follow sb ● **tail** *v* [T] follow sb closely to watch what they do [PV] **tail away/off** become gradually less or quieter ■ **tailback** *n* [C] long line of traffic reaching back along a road ▸ **tailless** *adj* ■ **tail light** *n* [C] red light at the back of a car, bus, etc ■ **tailpipe** *n* [C] (*esp US*) = EXHAUST(2) ■ **tailwind** *n* [C] wind blowing from behind a moving vehicle, etc

tailor /'teɪlə(r)/ *n* [C] maker of men's clothes, eg coats and jackets ● **tailor** *v* [T] 1 make or adapt sth for a particular purpose, person, etc 2 cut out and sew sth: *a well-~ed suit* ■ **tailor-made** *adj* 1 perfectly suitable: *a ~-made course of study* 2 (of clothes) made by a tailor for a particular person

taint /teɪnt/ *v* [T] spoil sth by adding a bad quality ● **taint** *n* [sing] trace of a bad quality

0▸ take¹ /teɪk/ *v* (pt **took** /tʊk/ pp **~n** /'teɪkən/) 1 [T] carry sth/sb or cause sb to go from one place to another: *T~ an umbrella with you.* ◇ *She took a friend home.* 2 [T] get hold of or reach sb/sth: *~ her hand* ◇ *She took him in her arms.* 3 [T] remove and use sth, esp without permission or by mistake; steal sth: *Who has ~n my bicycle?* 4 [T] get sth from a certain source: *This line is ~n from a poem by Keats.* 5 [T] capture a place or person; get control of sth: *He was ~n prisoner.* **6** [T] (*fml*) buy a newspaper or magazine regularly: *He ~s The Times.* **7** [T] eat or drink, etc sth: *Do you ~ sugar in your tea?* **8** [T] find out and record sth; write sth down: ~ *notes* ◇ ~ *the names of the volunteers* **9** [T] photograph sb/sth **10** [T] test or measure sth: ~ *sb's pulse/ temperature* **11** [T] accept or receive sth: ~ *advice* ◇ ~ *the blame* ◇ *Will you ~ £450 for the car?* **12** [T] be able to bear sth: *He can't ~ being criticized.* **13** [T] react to sth/sb in the way stated: *I wish you'd ~ me seriously.* **14** [T] consider sth/sb to be sb/sth: *What do you ~ me for?* **15** [T] have a particular feeling, opinion, etc: ~ *pleasure in being cruel* **16** [T] used with nouns to show that a specific action is being performed: ~ *a bath/ walk/holiday* **17** [T] need or require a particular amount of time: *The work took four hours.* **18** [T] wear a particular size in clothes or shoes: *What size shoes do you ~?* **19** [T] have enough space for sth/sb; be able to hold a certain quantity: *The car ~s five people.* **20** [T] do an exam or a test: ~ *a driving test* **21** [T] be the teacher in a class: *She ~s us for French.* **22** [T] study a subject at school, college, etc **23** [T] use a means of transport, a road, etc: ~ *a bus into town* ◇ ~ (= turn into) *the first road on the left* **24** [T] be successful; work: *The smallpox injection did not ~.* [IDM] **take heart** → HEART **take it on/upon yourself to do sth** decide to do sth without asking permission or advice **take it/a lot out of sb** make sb very tired **take its course** → COURSE [PV] **take sb aback** shock and surprise sb **take after sb** be like your mother or father in appearance or character **take sth apart** separate the parts of a machine, etc **take sth away 1** subtract one amount from another: ~ *5 from 10, and that leaves 5.* **2** buy a meal at a restaurant and take it somewhere else to eat **3** cause sth to disappear: *a pill to ~ the pain away* **take sb/ sth back** remove sb/sth from a place **take sb/ sth back 1** admit that sth you have said is wrong **2** agree to receive sb/ sth back: *This shop only ~s goods back if you have your receipt.* **take sb back (to...)** cause sb to remember sth **take sth down 1** remove a structure by separating it into pieces **2** make a written record of sth **take sb in** deceive sb: *Don't be ~n in by him.* **take sth in 1** absorb sth into the body, eg by breathing **2** make a piece of clothing narrower or tighter **3** include or cover sth: *The trip took in several cities.* **4** take notice of sth

with your eyes **5** understand and remember sth: *I couldn't ~ in everything she said.* **take off 1** (of an aircraft) leave the ground **2** (of a project, etc) become successful quickly **take sth off** (*infml*) imitate sb **take sth off (sth)** **1** remove clothes, etc: ~ *off your coat* **2** take time as a break from work: ~ *a week off to go on holiday* **3** stop a public service, TV programme, etc **4** deduct an amount from the total: ~ *50p off (the price)* **take sth on** begin to have a quality, appearance, etc **take sb on 1** accept sb as an opponent **2** employ sb **take sb/sth on** (of a vehicle, aircraft, etc) allow passengers, fuel, cargo, etc to be loaded **take sb out** go to a restaurant, etc with sb you have invited: ~ *her out to dinner* **take sth out 1** remove or extract a part of the body: ~ *out a tooth* **2** obtain an official document for payment: ~ *out a licence* **take it out of sb** (*infml*) exhaust: *That run really took it out of me.* **take it/sth out on sb** (*infml*) show your anger, etc by being unkind to sb, although it is not their fault **take over (from sb)** begin to have control of sb else's duties, responsibilities, etc **take sth over** gain control of a business, company, etc, esp by buying shares **take to sth 1** go away to a place, esp to escape from danger: ~ *to the woods to avoid capture* **2** begin to do sth as a habit; develop an ability for sth: *I took to cycling ten miles a day.* **take to sb/sth** begin to like sb/sth **take sth up 1** shorten a piece of clothing **2** learn or start to do sth, esp for pleasure: ~ *up cycling/chess* **3** continue sth unfinished **4** occupy time or space: *This table ~s up half the room.* **5** accept an offer **take up with sb** (*infml*) begin to be friendly with sb, esp sb with a bad reputation **take sth up with sb** speak or write to sb about sth **take sth upon oneself** assume (responsibility) for sth **be taken with sb/sth** find sb/sth interesting or attractive ■ **takeaway** (US *'takeout*) *n* [C] **1** restaurant from which food is taken to be eaten somewhere else **2** meal bought at this type of restaurant: *have a ~away* ■ **'take-off** *n* [C] **1** start of a flight, when an aircraft leaves the ground **2** imitation of sb ■ **'takeover** *n* [C] act of taking over a business, etc

take² /teɪk/ *n* [C] period of filming without stopping

taker /'teɪkə(r)/ *n* [C] person who accepts an offer

takings /'teɪkɪŋz/ *n* [pl] amount of money that a shop, theatre, etc receives

talcum powder /'tælkəm paʊdə(r)/

(*also* talc) n [U] perfumed powder for the skin

tale /teɪl/ n [C] **1** story: ~s of adventure **2** report or account of sth **3** lie: Don't tell ~s.

talent /ˈtælənt/ n [C, U] natural ability to do sth well: have a ~ for music ▸ **talented** *adj* having talent; skilled

0— **talk**¹ /tɔːk/ v **1** [I] say things; speak to give information: He was ~ing to a friend. **2** [I, T] discuss sth: This is serious. We need to ~. We ~ed politics all evening. **3** [I] say words in a language: Can the baby ~ yet? **4** [I] gossip **5** [I] give information to sb, esp unwillingly: Has the prisoner ~ed yet? [PV] **talk down to** speak to sb as if they were less important or intelligent than you **talk sb into/out of sth** persuade sb to do/not to do sth **talk sth over (with sb)** discuss sth thoroughly ▸ **talkative** /ˈtɔːkətɪv/ *adj* liking to talk a lot ▸ **talker** n [C] ■ **talking point** n [C] subject for discussion ■ **talking-to** n [sing] (*infml*) serious talk with sb who has done sth wrong

0— **talk²** /tɔːk/ n **1** [C, U] conversation or discussion **2** (**talks**) [pl] formal discussions between governments, etc: peace ~s **3** [C] speech or lecture on a particular subject **4** [U] (*infml*) words that are spoken but without facts, etc to support them: Don't pay any attention to him. He's all ~.

0— **tall** /tɔːl/ *adj* **1** of more than average height **2** of the height that is mentioned: Tim is six feet ~. [IDM] **be a tall order** (*infml*) be very difficult to do **a tall story** story that is difficult to believe

tally /ˈtæli/ n [C] (pl -**ies**) record of money spent, points scored in a game, etc ● tally v (pt, pp -**ied**) [I] ~ (**with**) be the same as or match another person's account, another set of figures, etc

talon /ˈtælən/ n [C] curved claw of a bird, eg an eagle

tambourine /ˌtæmbəˈriːn/ n [C] small shallow drum with metal discs round the edge, shaken or hit with the hand

tame /teɪm/ *adj* (~r, ~st) **1** (of animals) trained to live with people; not wild or fierce: a ~ monkey **2** (*infml*) not interesting or exciting: The film has a rather ~ ending. **3** (*infml*) (of a person) easily controlled ● tame v [T] make sth tame or easy to control: ~ a lion ▸ **tamely** *adv* ▸ **tameness** n [U] ▸ **tamer** n [C] person who tames animals: a lion ~r

tamper /ˈtæmpə(r)/ v [I] ~ **with** interfere with or change sth without authority

tampon /ˈtæmpɒn/ n [C] piece of cotton material that a woman puts

453

inside her vagina to absorb blood during her period (3)

tan /tæn/ n **1** [C] brown colour of the skin from sunlight **2** [U] yellowish brown colour ● tan v (**-nn-**) **1** [T] make animal skins into leather **2** [I, T] (cause skin to) go brown from sunlight [IDM] **tan sb's hide** (*infml*) beat sb hard

tandem /ˈtændəm/ n [C] bicycle for two riders [IDM] **in tandem (with sb/sth)** working closely together with sb/sth

tandoori /tænˈdʊəri/ n [C, U] (dish of meat, etc in this) style of Indian cooking using a clay oven

tang /tæŋ/ n [C, usu sing] strong sharp taste or smell

tangent /ˈtændʒənt/ n [C] **1** straight line that touches a curve but does not cross it [IDM] **fly/go off at a tangent** change suddenly from one line of thought, action, etc to another

tangerine /ˌtændʒəˈriːn/ n [C] kind of small sweet orange

tangible /ˈtændʒəbl/ *adj* **1** that can clearly be seen to exist: ~ proof **2** that you can touch and feel ▸ **tangibly** *adv*

tangle /ˈtæŋɡl/ n [C] confused mass of string, hair, etc **2** [sing] confused state: in a ~ ● tangle v [I, T] (cause sth to) become twisted into a confused mass: ~d hair [PV] **tangle with sb/sth** become involved in a fight or argument with sb

tango /ˈtæŋɡəʊ/ n [C] (pl -**s**) (music for a) South American dance

0— **tank** /tæŋk/ n [C] **1** large container for liquid or gas **2** armoured fighting vehicle with guns

tankard /ˈtæŋkəd/ n [C] large metal mug for beer

tanker /ˈtæŋkə(r)/ n [C] ship, lorry, etc that carries large quantities of liquid or gas

tantalize (*also* -**ise**) /ˈtæntəlaɪz/ v [T] tease sb by offering sth that they want and then not allowing them to have it

tantamount /ˈtæntəmaʊnt/ *adj* ~ **to** having the same effect as sth

tantrum /ˈtæntrəm/ n [C] outburst of bad temper, esp by a child

0— **tap** /tæp/ n [C] **1** device for controlling the flow of liquid or gas from a pipe or container **2** light hit with your hand or fingers [IDM] **on tap** available to be used at any time ● tap v (**-pp-**) **1** [I, T] hit sb/sth quickly and lightly: ~ sb on the back **2** make use of a source of energy, knowledge, etc that already exists: ~ a country's resources **3** [T] fit a device to a telephone so that sb's calls can be listened to secretly **4** [T] draw

tap

A B C D E F G H I J K L M N O P Q R S **T** U V W X Y Z

liquid from sth ■ **'tap dance** n [U,C] style of dancing in which you make tapping steps on the floor with special shoes

0—**tape** /teɪp/ n **1** [U] long narrow strip of magnetic material used for recording sounds, pictures, etc **2** [C] cassette that contains sounds (and pictures) that have been recorded: *a blank ~* **3** [C,U] (piece of a) narrow strip of material: *sticky ~* **4** [C] piece of tape stretched across the place where a race will finish ■ **tape** v [T] **1** record sound, etc on magnetic tape **2** fasten sth by sticking or tying it with tape [IDM] **have (got) sb/sth taped** (GB, *infml*) understand sb/sth fully ■ **'tape measure** n [C] strip of cloth or thin metal, marked for measuring things ■ **'tape recorder** n [C] apparatus for recording and playing sound on magnetic tape

taper /ˈteɪpə(r)/ v [I,T] (cause sth to) become gradually narrower [PV] **taper off** gradually become less in number ■ **taper** n [C] long thin candle

tapestry /ˈtæpəstri/ n [C,U] (pl -ies) (piece of) heavy cloth with a picture or pattern woven into it, used for covering walls

tar /tɑː(r)/ n [U] thick black sticky substance, hard when cold, used for making roads, preserving wood, etc ● **tar** v (-rr-) [T] cover sth with tar [IDM] **be tarred with the same brush (as sb)** be thought to have the same fault, etc as sb else

tarantula /təˈræntʃələ/ n [C] large hairy poisonous spider

0—**target** /ˈtɑːɡɪt/ n **1** [C,U] result that you try to achieve: *achieve a sales ~* **2** [C] object or person aimed at when attacking **3** [C] object that people practise shooting at ● **target** v [T] aim sth at sb/sth

tariff /ˈtærɪf/ n [C] **1** tax on goods coming into a country **2** list of prices for rooms, meals, etc in a hotel

Tarmac™ /ˈtɑːmæk/ n [U] **1** mixture of tar and broken stones for making road surfaces **2** (the tarmac) area covered with Tarmac, esp at an airport

tarnish /ˈtɑːnɪʃ/ v [I,T] (esp of metal surfaces) (cause sth to) lose brightness: *Brass ~es easily.* **2** lessen the quality of sb's reputation

tarpaulin /tɑːˈpɔːlɪn/ n [C,U] (sheet of) heavy waterproof cloth

tart /tɑːt/ n [C] **1** open pie containing jam or fruit **2** (GB, *infml*, *disapprov*) sexually immoral girl or woman ● **tart** v [PV] **tart yourself up** (GB, *infml*) make yourself more attractive by putting on nice clothes, etc **tart sth up** (GB, *infml*) decorate or improve the appearance of sth

● **tart** adj **1** having an unpleasant sour taste **2** (of remarks, etc) quick and unkind: *a ~ reply* ▸ **tartly** adv ▸ **tartness** n [U]

tartan /ˈtɑːtn/ n [U,C] (woollen cloth with a) pattern of coloured stripes crossing each other, esp of a Scottish clan

tartar /ˈtɑːtə(r)/ n [U] hard substance that forms on the teeth

0—**task** /tɑːsk/ n [C] piece of (esp hard or unpleasant) work that has to be done [IDM] **take sb to task (for/over sth)** criticize sb strongly for sth they have done ■ **'task force** n [C] group of people organized for a special (esp military) purpose ■ **'taskmaster** n [C] person who gives others work to do, often work that is difficult

tassel /ˈtæsl/ n [C] bunch of threads tied at one end, hanging as decoration from sth

0—**taste**¹ /teɪst/ n **1** [C,U] quality that different foods and drinks have that allows you to recognize them when you put them in your mouth: *a sweet/sour ~* **2** [U] sense that allows you to recognize a food or drink in your mouth **3** [C,usu sing] small quantity of food or drink **4** [C] person's ability to choose things that others recognize as being of good quality or appropriate: *Your choice of colours shows good ~.* **5** [C,U] personal liking [IDM] **be in good/bad, etc taste** be suitable/ offensive, etc **a taste of your own medicine** → MEDICINE ▸ **tasteful** adj showing good taste (4) ▸ **tastefully** adv ▸ **tasteless** adj **1** (of food) having no flavour **2** showing bad taste (4) ▸ **tastelessly** adv ▸ **tasty** adj (-ier, -iest) having a pleasant flavour

0—**taste**² /teɪst/ v **1** linking verb ~ **(of)** have a particular flavour: *~ bitter/sweet* **2** [T] be able to recognize flavours in food and drink **3** [T] test the flavour of sth: *She ~d the soup.* **4** [T] have a short experience of sth: *~ freedom*

tatters /ˈtætəz/ n [pl] [IDM] **in tatters 1** torn in many places **2** ruined ▸ **tattered** adj old and torn; in bad condition

tattoo /təˈtuː/ n [C] (pl ~s) **1** picture or design marked permanently on sb's skin by making holes with a needle and filling them with coloured ink **2** outdoor show by members of the armed forces, with music, marching, etc ● **tattoo** v [T] mark sb's skin with a tattoo

taught pt, pp of TEACH

taunt /tɔːnt/ v [T] say unkind or insulting words to sb in order to upset them ● **taunt** n [C] taunting remark

taut /tɔːt/ adj tightly stretched ▸ **tautly** adv ▸ **tautness** n [U]

tautology /tɔːˈtɒlədʒi/ n [C, U] (pl **-ies**) (of language) unnecessary repeating of the same idea in different words ▸ **tautological** /-ˈlɒdʒɪkl/ adj

tavern /ˈtævən/ n [C] (lit) pub; inn

tawny /ˈtɔːni/ adj brownish-yellow

0━ **tax** /tæks/ n [C, U] money that has to be paid to a government for public services ● **tax** v [T] **1** put a tax on sb/sth **2** require sb to pay a tax **3** need a lot of physical or mental effort: ~ *sb's patience* ▸ **taxable** adj (of money) that you have to pay tax on: ~ *income* ▸ **taxation** /-ˈseɪʃn/ n [U] (system of) raising money by taxes ■ **tax-free** adj on which tax need not be paid ■ **taxpayer** n [C] person who pays taxes, esp income tax

0━ **taxi** /ˈtæksi/ n [C] (also **taxicab**) car with a driver which may be hired ● **taxi** v [I] (of an aircraft) move along the ground before or after flying ■ **taxi rank** n [C] place where taxis wait to be hired

0━ **tea** /tiː/ n **1** [U] dried leaves of a bush grown in China, India, etc **2** [U, C] hot drink made by pouring boiling water onto tea leaves **3** [U, C] hot drink made by pouring boiling water onto the leaves of other plants: *mint* ~ **4** [U, C] light early evening meal ■ **tea bag** n [C] small paper bag containing tea leaves ■ **tea caddy** /-kædi/ n [C] (pl **-dies**) n [C] small tin in which tea is kept ■ **tea chest** n [C] (GB) large light wooden box in which tea is packed ■ **tea cosy** n [C] (pl **-ies**) cover to keep a teapot warm ■ **teacup** n [C] cup from which tea is drunk ■ **teapot** n [C] container in which tea is made and served ■ **tea set** (also **tea service**) n [C] set of cups, plates, etc for serving tea ■ **teaspoon** n [C] small spoon for stirring tea ■ **teaspoonful** n [C] amount contained in a teaspoon ■ **tea strainer** n [C] device for pouring tea through to stop tea leaves going into the cup ■ **teatime** n [U] (GB) time at which tea is served ■ **tea towel** (also **tea cloth**) n [C] cloth used for drying washed dishes and cutlery

0━ **teach** /tiːtʃ/ v (pt, pp **taught** /tɔːt/) [I, T] give lessons to sb; give sb knowledge, skill, etc: *He taught me art.* ◇ ~ *a child (how) to swim* ▸ **teacher** n [C] person who teaches, esp in a school ▸ **teaching** n **1** [C, usu sing, U] work of a teacher: *earn a living by* ~*ing* **2** [C, usu sing, pl, U] ideas of a particular person or group: *the* ~*ings of Lenin*

teak /tiːk/ n [U] strong hard wood of a tall Asian tree

0━ **team** /tiːm/ n [C, with sing or pl verb] **1** group of people playing on the same side in a game: *a football* ~ **2** group of people working together: *a* ~ *of surgeons* ● **team** v [I] ~ **up (with)** work together with another person or group ■ **team spirit** n [U] (approv) desire and willingness of people to work together as a team ■ **teamwork** n [U] organized cooperation

0━ **tear**[1] /teə(r)/ v (pt **tore** /tɔː(r)/ pp **torn** /tɔːn/) **1** [T] damage sth by pulling it apart or into pieces or by cutting it on sth sharp: ~ *a sheet of paper* **2** [I] become torn: *This cloth* ~*s easily.* **3** [T] remove sth from sth else by pulling it forcefully: ~ *a page out of a book* **4** [I] move somewhere very quickly: *We tore home.* **5** [T] badly affect or damage sth: *a country torn by civil war* [IDM] **be torn between A and B** be unable to choose between two things or people [PV] **tear sth down** pull or knock down a building, wall, etc **tear sth up** pull a piece of paper into small bits ■ **tear** n [C] hole made in sth by tearing ■ **tearaway** n [C] (infml) young person who is difficult to control

0━ **tear**[2] /tɪə(r)/ n [C, usu pl] drop of liquid that comes from your eye when you cry [IDM] **in tears** crying: *She left the room in* ~*s.* ■ **teardrop** n [C] single tear ▸ **tearful** adj crying or likely to cry ▸ **tearfully** adv ■ **tear gas** n [U] gas that stings the eyes, used by the army, etc ■ **tear jerker** n [C] (infml) story, film, etc likely to make people cry

tease /tiːz/ v [I, T] laugh at sb and make fun of them playfully or unkindly ● **tease** n [C] person who likes teasing people ▸ **teaser** n [C] (infml) difficult problem or question

teat /tiːt/ n [C] **1** rubber end on a baby's feeding bottle **2** animal's nipple

tech /tek/ n [C] (infml) short for TECHNICAL COLLEGE (TECHNICAL)

0━ **technical** /ˈteknɪkl/ adj **1** concerned with the practical use of machinery, methods, etc in science or industry **2** concerned with the skills needed for a particular job, sport, etc **3** of a particular subject: *the* ~ *terms of physics* **4** in a strict legal sense ■ **technical college** n [C] college that teaches practical subjects ▸ **technicality** /-ˈkæləti/ n [C] (pl **-ies**) technical point or small detail, esp one that seems unfair ▸ **technically** /-kli/ adv

technician /tekˈnɪʃn/ n [C] person with a practical, mechanical or industrial skill

0━ **technique** /tekˈniːk/ n [C] way of doing sth, esp one that needs special skills **2** [U,sing] skill with which sb is able to do sth practical

technocrat /'teknəkræt/ n [C] expert in science, engineering, etc who has a lot of power in politics and/or industry

o━ **technology** /tek'nɒlədʒi/ n [U] study and use of science for practical tasks in industry, business, etc ▶ **technological** /-'lɒdʒɪkl/ adj ▶ **technologist** n [C] expert in technology

teddy bear /'tedi beə(r)/ n [C] soft furry toy bear

tedious /'ti:diəs/ adj long and boring: a ~ lecture ◇ ~ work ▶ **tediously** adv

tee /ti:/ n [C] **1** (in golf) flat area from which a player starts at each hole **2** piece of wood, plastic, etc on which you put a golf ball before you hit it ● **tee** v [PV] **tee off** hit a golf ball from a tee **tee (sth) up** prepare to hit a golf ball by placing it on a tee

teem /ti:m/ v [I] (used with it) (of rain) fall very heavily [PV] **teem with sth** be full of animals, people, etc moving around

teenage /'ti:neɪdʒ/ adj (for people who are) between 13 and 19 years old: ~ fashions ▶ **teenager** n [C] person who is between 13 and 19 years old

teens /ti:nz/ n [pl] years of a person's life when they are between 13 and 19 years old: Both girls are in their ~s.

teeter /'ti:tə(r)/ v [I] stand or move unsteadily

teeth plural of TOOTH

teethe /ti:ð/ v [I] (of a baby) grow its first teeth ● **teething troubles** n [pl] problems that occur when first using a new system

teetotal /,ti:'təʊtl/ adj never drinking alcohol ▶ **teetotaller** n [C]

telecommunications /,telikə,mju:nɪ'keɪʃnz/ n [pl] technology of sending signals, images and messages over long distances by radio, television, satellite, etc

telegram /'telɪɡræm/ n [C] message sent by telegraph and then phoned

telegraph /'telɪɡrɑːf/ n [U] method of sending messages over long distances, using wires that carry electrical signals ● **telegraph** v [I,T] send a message by telegraph ▶ **telegraphic** /-'ɡræfɪk/ adj

telemarketing /'telimɑːkɪtɪŋ/ n [U] = TELESALES

telepathy /tə'lepəθi/ n [U] direct communication of thoughts from one person to another without using speech, writing, etc ▶ **telepathic** /,telɪ'pæθɪk/ adj

o━ **telephone** /'telɪfəʊn/ n [C,U] (machine used in a) system for talking to sb over long distances using wires or radio ● **telephone** v [I,T] (fml, esp GB) speak to sb by telephone ● **telephone booth** n [C] = PHONE BOOTH (PHONE) ■ **telephone box** n [C] = PHONE BOX (PHONE) ● **telephone directory** n [C] book that lists the names, addresses and telephone numbers of people in a particular area ■ **telephone exchange** n [C] place where telephone calls are connected ■ **telephone number** n [C] number of a particular telephone, that you use when you make a call to it

telephonist /tə'lefənɪst/ n [C] person whose job is to make telephone connections in an office or at a telephone exchange

telephoto lens /,telɪfəʊtəʊ 'lenz/ n [C] special lens that produces a large clear picture of a distant object being photographed

telesales /'teliseɪlz/ n [U] method of selling things and taking orders for sales by telephone

telescope /'telɪskəʊp/ n [C] long tube-shaped instrument with lenses, for making distant objects appear nearer and larger ● **telescope** v [I,T] become or make sth shorter by sliding sections inside one another ▶ **telescopic** /-'skɒpɪk/ adj

teletext /'telitekst/ n [U] computerized service providing information on television screens

o━ **television** /'telɪvɪʒn/ n (abbr TV) **1** [C] (also **television set**) piece of electrical equipment with a screen on which you can watch moving pictures and sounds **2** [U] programmes broadcast on television **3** [U] system, process or business of broadcasting television programmes ▶ **televise** /'telɪvaɪz/ v [T] broadcast sth on television

telex /'teleks/ n **1** [U] system of sending typed messages round the world by telephone lines **2** [C] message sent by telex ● **telex** v [I,T] send a message by telex

o━ **tell** /tel/ v (pt, pp told /təʊld/) **1** [T] make sth known to sb in words: I told her my name. **2** [T] give information about sth **3** [I] (infml) reveal a secret: You promised not to~. **4** [T] order or advise sb to do sth: I told them to go. **5** [I,T] know, see or judge sth correctly: I think he's happy - it's hard to ~. **6** [I] ~ (on) have an effect on sb/sth, esp a bad one: All this hard work is ~ing on him. [IDM] **all told** with all the people or things counted **I told you (so)** (infml) I warned you that this would happen **tell tales (about sth/on sb)** tell sb about sth that another person has done wrong **tell the time** read the time from a clock, etc [**PV**] **tell A and B apart** be able to see the difference between A and B **tell sb off (for (doing) sth)** (infml) speak angrily to sb for doing sth wrong **tell on sb** (infml) inform against sb: *John told on his sister.* ▶ **teller** *n* **1** person who receives and pays out money in a bank **2** person who counts votes, esp in a parliament ▶ **telling** *adj* effective: *a ~ing argument*

telltale /ˈtelteɪl/ *n* [C] (disapprov) child who tells an adult what another child has done wrong ● **telltale** *adj* showing that sth exists or has happened: *a ~ blush*

telly /ˈteli/ *n* [C, U] (pl **-ies**) (infml) short for TELEVISION

temerity /təˈmerəti/ *n* [U] (fml) extremely confident and rude behaviour: *He had the ~ to call me a liar.*

temp /temp/ *n* [C] (infml) person, esp a secretary, employed for a short time

temper /ˈtempə(r)/ *n* **1** [C, usu sing, U] fact of becoming angry very easily: *He's got a quick ~.* **2** [C, usu sing] short period of feeling very angry: *fly into a ~* **3** [C] state of the mind: *be in a foul ~* [**IDM**] **keep/lose your temper (with sb)** manage/fail to control your anger ● **temper** *v* [T] make sth less extreme: *justice ~ed with mercy* ● **-tempered** (used to form compound adjectives) having a certain temper: *a bad~ed man*

temperament /ˈtemprəmənt/ *n* [U, C] person's character shown in the way they behave or react to sb/ sth ▶ **temperamental** /ˌ-ˈmentl/ *adj* **1** having a tendency to become angry, etc easily: *Children are often ~al.* **2** connected with sb's personality ▶ **temperamentally** /ˌ-ˈtəli/ *adv*

temperate /ˈtempərət/ *adj* **1** (tech) (of climate) free from extremes of heat and cold **2** (fml) behaving in a calm controlled way

0— **temperature** /ˈtemprətʃə(r)/ *n* [C, U] **1** measurement in degrees of how hot or cold sth is **2** measurement of how hot sb's body is: *Does he have a ~ (= is it higher than normal because of illness)?*

tempest /ˈtempɪst/ *n* [C] (fml) violent storm ▶ **tempestuous** /temˈpestʃuəs/ *adj* stormy, violent: (fig) *a ~uous love affair*

temple /ˈtempl/ *n* [C] **1** building used in the worship of a god or gods, esp in the Hindu and Buddhist religions **2** flat part on each side of the forehead

tempo /ˈtempəʊ/ *n* [C] (pl **~s** or, in sense 1 **tempi** /ˈtempiː/) **1** (tech) speed or rhythm of a piece of music

2 speed of any movement or activity: *the ~ of city life*

temporal /ˈtempərəl/ *adj* (fml) **1** of the real physical world, not spiritual matters **2** of or limited by time

0— **temporary** /ˈtemprəri/ *adj* lasting for only a short time ▶ **temporarily** /ˈtemprərəli; ˌtempəˈrerəli/ *adv*

tempt /tempt/ *v* [T] **1** attract sb or make sb want to do or have sth **2** (try to) persuade sb to do sth, esp sth wrong or unwise: *Nothing would ~ me to live here.* ▶ **temptation** /tempˈteɪʃn/ *n* **1** [C, U] desire to do or have sth that you know is bad or wrong **2** [C] thing that tempts you ▶ **tempting** *adj* attractive: *a ~ing offer*

0— **ten** /ten/ *number* 10 ▶ **tenth** ordinal number **1** [C] 10th; the fraction ¹⁄₁₀; each of ten equal parts of sth

tenable /ˈtenəbl/ *adj* **1** (of an opinion) that can be reasonably defended **2** (of a job or position) that can be held for the stated time

tenacious /təˈneɪʃəs/ *adj* very determined to get or keep sth ▶ **tenacity** /təˈnæsəti/ *n* [U]

tenant /ˈtenənt/ *n* [C] person who pays rent for the use of a building, land, etc ▶ **tenancy** /-ənsi/ *n* (pl **-ies**) **1** [C] period of time that you rent a house, land, etc for **2** [C, U] right to live or work in a house, etc that you rent

0— **tend** /tend/ *v* **1** [I] **~ to** be likely to do sth: *He ~s to make too many mistakes.* **2** [T] care for sb/sth: *shepherds ~ing their sheep*

tendency /ˈtendənsi/ *n* [C] (pl **-ies**) **1** way a person or thing is likely to behave or act: *a ~ to talk too much* **2** new custom that is starting to develop: *an increasing ~ for parents to help at school*

tender /ˈtendə(r)/ *adj* **1** gentle, kind and loving **2** (of food) easy to bite through or cut **3** (of part of the body) painful to touch **4** easily hurt or damaged ▶ **tenderly** *adv* ▶ **tenderness** *n* [U] ● **tender** *v* **1** [I] **~ (for)** make a formal offer to do work at a stated price: *~ for the construction of the new motorway* **2** [T] (fml) offer or give sth to sb: *He ~ed his resignation.* ● **tender** *n* [C] formal offer to do work at a stated price

tendon /ˈtendən/ *n* [C] strong band of tissue that joins a muscle to a bone

tenement /ˈtenəmənt/ *n* [C] large building, esp in a poor part of a city, divided into flats

tenet /ˈtenɪt/ *n* [C] (fml) principle; belief

tenner /'tenə(r)/ n [C] (GB, infml) £10 (note)

tennis /'tenɪs/ n [U] game for two or four players who hit a ball across a net with a racket ■ **'tennis court** n [C] marked area on which tennis is played

tenor /'tenə(r)/ n **1** [C] (man with a) singing voice with a range just below the lowest woman's voice **2** [sing] musical part written for a tenor voice **3** [sing] (fml) (the tenor of sth) general meaning of sth
● **tenor** adj (of a musical instrument) with a range of notes similar to those of a tenor voice: a ~ saxophone

tenpin bowling /ˌtenpɪn 'bəʊlɪŋ/ n [U] game in which a ball is rolled towards ten bottle-shaped pins, in order to knock them down

tense /tens/ adj (~r, ~st) **1** nervous and worried **2** stretched tightly
● **tense** v [I,T] make your muscles tight and stiff, esp because you are not relaxed: He ~d his muscles.
▶ **tensely** adv ● **tense** n [C] (gram) verb form that shows the time of the action or state: the present/past/future~

0━ **tension** /'tenʃn/ n **1** [U,C, usu pl] situation in which people do not trust each other or feel unfriendly towards each other: political ~(s) **2** [U] mental, emotional or nervous strain **3** [U] state or degree of being stretched: the ~ of the rope

0━ **tent** /tent/ n [C] shelter made of nylon, etc that is supported by poles and ropes and is used esp for camping

tentacle /'tentəkl/ n [C] long thin part of certain creatures (eg an octopus) used for feeling, holding, etc

tentative /'tentətɪv/ adj made or done to test sth; not definite: make a ~ offer ▶ **tentatively** adv

tenterhooks /'tentəhʊks/ n [pl] [IDM] **(be) on tenterhooks** (be) in a state of anxious waiting

tenth → TEN

tenuous /'tenjuəs/ adj so weak or uncertain that it hardly exists

tepid /'tepɪd/ adj slightly warm

0━ **term** /tɜːm/ n **1** [C] word or phrase used as the name of sth: technical ~s **2** [C,U] (esp GB) division of the school or university year: summer/spring ~ **3** [C] fixed period of time: the president's ~ of office [IDM] **in the long/short/medium term** used to describe what will happen a long, short, etc time in the future ● **term** v [T] (fml) use a particular name or word to describe sth/sb

terminal /'tɜːmɪnl/ n [C] **1** building(s) for passengers or goods, esp at an airport or port **2** (computing) piece of equipment that joins the user to a central computer system **3** (tech) point at which connections can be made in an electric circuit ● **terminal** adj of an illness that will cause death and cannot be cured ▶ **terminally** /-nəli/ adv

terminate /'tɜːmɪneɪt/ v [I,T] come or bring sth to an end ▶ **termination** /ˌtɜːmɪ'neɪʃn/ n [U,C] (fml) ending of sth: the termination of a contract

terminology /ˌtɜːmɪ'nɒlədʒi/ n [U,C] (pl -ies) special words and expressions used in a particular subject

terminus /'tɜːmɪnəs/ n [C] (pl -ni /-naɪ/ or ~es) last station or stop at the end of a railway line or bus route

termite /'tɜːmaɪt/ n [C] insect that eats wood

terms /tɜːmz/ n [pl] **1** conditions of an agreement or a contract **2** conditions of sale or payment **3** way of expression: I'll explain this in general ~ first. [IDM] **be on good, friendly, bad, etc terms (with sb)** have a good, friendly, bad etc relationship with sb **come to terms with sth** learn to accept sth unpleasant or difficult **in terms of sth** concerning sth

terrace /'terəs/ n [C] (GB) long row of houses joined together in one block **2** [C] flat area outside a house, restaurant, etc **3** (terraces) [pl] (GB) wide steps where spectators can stand at a football ground, etc **4** [C] one of a series of flat areas of ground that are cut into a hillside like steps ● **terraced** adj formed into terraces: ~d houses ◇ a ~d hillside

terrain /tə'reɪn/ n [C,U] (written) area of land: hilly ~

terrestrial /tə'restriəl/ adj **1** (tech) of or living on the land **2** of the planet Earth **3** (of television and broadcasting systems) operating on earth rather than from a satellite

0━ **terrible** /'terəbl/ adj **1** causing great fear, harm or unhappiness: a ~ war/accident **2** unhappy or ill **3** (infml) very bad: What ~ food! ▶ **terribly** adv (infml) extremely: terribly busy

terrier /'teriə(r)/ n [C] kind of small lively dog

terrific /tə'rɪfɪk/ adj **1** (infml) excellent; wonderful **2** very large; very great: a ~ amount of work ▶ **terrifically** /-kli/ adv extremely

terrify /'terɪfaɪ/ v (pt, pp -ied) [T] make sb feel very frightened: I'm terrified of dogs.

territorial /ˌterə'tɔːriəl/ adj of land or territory

territory /'terətri/ n [C,U] (pl -ies) **1** area of land under the control of a ruler, country, etc: Spanish ~ **2** area of land claimed and defended by one person or animal **3** area for which sb is responsible

terror /'terə(r)/ n **1** [U] feeling of extreme fear **2** [C] person, thing or situation that makes you very afraid ▶ **terrorism** /-rɪzəm/ n [U] use of violence for political purposes ▶ **terrorist** adj, n [C] ▶ **terrorize** (also -ise) v [T] use threats or violence to make people do as they are told

terse /tɜːs/ adj using few, often unfriendly, words ▶ **tersely** adv ▶ **terseness** n [U]

0– **test** /test/ n [C] **1** examination of a person's knowledge or ability: an intelligence ~ ◊ a driving ~ **2** medical examination to discover what is wrong with you, etc: a blood ~ **3** experiment to discover whether sth works, etc: a nuclear ~ ■ **test** v [T] check how well sth works or examine sb's health or mental abilities ■ **'test match** n [C] international cricket or rugby match ■ **test tube** n [C] small glass tube, closed at one end, used in chemical experiments

testament /'testəmənt/ n (fml) **1** [C, usu sing, U] ~ (to) thing that clearly shows or proves sth **2** [C] (Testament) either of the two main divisions of the Bible: the New T~ **3** [C] = WILL²(4)

testicle /'testɪkl/ n [C] either of the two glands of the male sex organ that produce sperm

testify /'testɪfaɪ/ v (pt, pp -ied) [I, T] make a statement that sth happened or that sth is true, esp in a law court

testimonial /ˌtestɪ'məʊniəl/ n **1** formal written statement, often by a former employer, about sb's character, abilities, etc **2** thing given to sb to show honour or thanks

testimony /'testɪməni/ n [U, C] (pl -ies) formal statement of truth, esp in a law court

tetanus /'tetənəs/ n [U] serious disease, caused by infection of a cut, causing muscles to become stiff

tête-à-tête /ˌteɪt ɑː 'teɪt/ n [C] private conversation between two people

tether /'teðə(r)/ n [C] rope or chain used to tie an animal to sth ● **tether** v [T] tie an animal to sth so that it cannot move very far

0– **text** /tekst/ n **1** [U] main printed part of a book or magazine **2** [U] any form of written material: a computer that can process ~ **3** [C] (infml) = TEXT MESSAGE **4** [C] written form of a speech, play, article, etc **5** [C] book, play, etc that is studied **6** [C] short passage of the Bible, etc as the subject of a sermon ● **text** v [T] send sb a written message using a mobile phone: I'll ~ you when I get

in. ■ **'textbook** n [C] book that teaches a particular subject, used in schools, etc ■ **'text message** (also infml text) n [C] written message sent from one mobile phone to another ▶ **'text-messaging** n [U] ▶ **textual** /'tekstʃuəl/ adj (written) of or in a text

textile /'tekstaɪl/ n [C, usu pl] any type of fabric made by weaving

texture /'tekstʃə(r)/ n [C, U] way a surface or fabric feels or looks, eg how rough or smooth it is

0– **than** /ðən; strong form ðæn/ conj, prep **1** used for introducing the second part of a comparison: Sylvia is taller ~ me. **2** used after more or less and before expressions of time, distance, etc: It cost more ~ £100. ◊ It's less ~ a mile to the station.

0– **thank** /θæŋk/ v [T] tell sb that you are grateful for sth ▶ **thankful** adj grateful ▶ **thankfully** adv ▶ **thankless** adj unpleasant or difficult to do and unlikely to bring any thanks: a ~less task ▶ **thanks** n [pl] exclam (words or actions) used to show that you are grateful for sth **[IDM] thanks to sb/sth** because of sb/sth ■ **thanks'giving** n **1** [U,C] (Thanks'giving (Day)) public holiday in the US and Canada **2** [U] (fml) expression of thanks to God

0– **'thank you** used to show that you are grateful for sth or to accept an offer: Thank you for your letter. **[IDM] no, thank you** used for refusing an offer politely

0– **that** /ðæt/ det, pron (pl **those** /ðəʊz/) **1** used to refer to a person or thing that is not near the speaker: Look at ~ man over there. **2** used to refer to sb/sth that has already been mentioned or is known about: Have you forgotten about ~ money I lent you last week? **3** (fml) used for referring to people or things of a particular type: Those present were in favour of change. **4** used to introduce a part of a sentence which refers to the person, thing or time you have been talking about: Where's the letter ~ came yesterday? ◊ The pen (~) you gave me is a nice one. **[IDM] that is (to say)** used to say what sth means or to give more information ● **that** adv to that degree; so: The film wasn't ~ bad. ● **that** conj used after some verbs, adjectives and nouns to introduce a new part of the sentence: She said (~) the story was true.

thatch /θætʃ/ n [C, U] roof covering of dried straw, reeds, etc ● **thatch** v [T] cover a roof, etc with a thatch

thaw /θɔː/ v **1** [I, T] (cause ice and snow to) melt **2** [T] (cause frozen food, etc to) become liquid or soft again: Leave the meat to ~. **3** [I]

There's the soup to heat, ~ there's the bread to butter.

thence /ðens/ *adv* (old-fash or fml) from that place

theology /θiˈɒlədʒi/ *n* [U] study of religion and God ▶ **theological** /ˌθiːəˈlɒdʒɪkl/ *adj*

theorem /ˈθɪərəm/ *n* [C] mathematical statement that can be proved by reasoning

0‒**theory** /ˈθɪəri/ *n* (pl **-ies**) **1** [C, U] formal set of ideas intended to explain why sth happens or exists: *Darwin's ~ of evolution* **2** [U] principles on which a particular subject is based ▶ **theoretical** /ˌθɪəˈretɪkl/ *adj*

therapeutic /ˌθerəˈpjuːtɪk/ *adj* designed to help treat an illness

therapy /ˈθerəpi/ *n* [C, U] treatment of a physical problem or an illness ▶ **therapist** *n* [C]

0‒**there** /ðeə(r)/ *adv* **1** (there is, are, was, were, etc) used to show that sth exists or happens: *T~'s a pub round the corner.* **2** in, at or to that place or position: *We'll soon be ~.* ◇ *I took one look at the car and offered to buy it ~* — *and then/then and ~* (= immediately). ◇ *Hello, is Bob ~ please?* (= used when calling sb on the phone) **3** at that point (in a story, etc): *Don't stop ~!* **4** used for calling attention to sth: *T~'s the bell for lunch.* ● **there** *exclam* used to express satisfaction that you were right about sth or to show that sth annoys you: *T~! You've woken the baby!* [IDM] **there, there!** used to persuade a small child to stop crying

thereabouts /ˌðeərəˈbaʊts/ *adv* near that place, number, year, etc

thereafter /ˌðeərˈɑːftə(r)/ *adv* (fml) after that

thereby /ˌðeəˈbaɪ/ *adv* (fml) by that means; in that way

0‒**therefore** /ˈðeəfɔː(r)/ *adv* for that reason

thereupon /ˌðeərəˈpɒn/ *adv* (fml) immediately; because of that

thermal /ˈθɜːml/ *adj* **1** (*tech*) of or caused by heat **2** (of clothes) designed to keep you warm in cold weather

thermometer /θəˈmɒmɪtə(r)/ *n* [C] instrument for measuring temperature

Thermos™ (*also* **Thermos flask**) /ˈθɜːməs flɑːsk/ *n* [C] type of vacuum flask

thermostat /ˈθɜːməstæt/ *n* [C] device that automatically keeps a building, engine, etc at an even temperature

thesaurus /θɪˈsɔːrəs/ *n* [C] (pl **-es** or **-ri** /-raɪ/) book of words grouped together according to their meanings

these *plural of* THIS

---

become friendlier and less formal ● **thaw** *n* [C, usu sing] (warm weather causing) thawing

0‒**the** /ðə; *strong form* ðiː/ *definite article* **1** used for referring to a particular thing: *T~ sky was blue.* ◇ *Please close ~ window.* **2** all the people, things, etc of the same kind: *T~ dog is a popular pet.* **3** used for referring to a group or nationality: *~ rich* ◇ *~ French* **4** used before certain geographical names: *~ Mediterranean* ◇ *~ Atlantic (Ocean)* **5** used with musical instruments: *play ~ piano* **6** (used with a unit of measurement) every: *paid by ~ hour* **7** used with a superlative: *~ best day of your life* [IDM] **the more, less, etc..., the more, less, etc...** used to show that two things change to the same degree: *T~ more I read, ~ less I understand.*

0‒**theatre** (*US theater*) /ˈθɪətə(r)/ *n* **1** [C] building in which plays are performed **2** (**the theatre**) [sing] work of acting in, producing, etc plays **3** [C] hall or room for lectures **4** [C, U] (*GB*) = OPERATING THEATRE (OPERATE) ■ **theatregoer** *n* [C] person who frequently sees plays at the theatre ▶ **theatrical** /θiˈætrɪkl/ *adj* **1** of the theatre **2** (of behaviour) exaggerated in order to attract attention

theft /θeft/ *n* [U, C] (crime of) stealing sth from a person or place

0‒**their** /ðeə(r)/ *det* of or belonging to them: *They have lost ~ dog.* ▶ **theirs** /ðeəz/ *pron* of or belonging to them: *That dog is ~s, not ours.*

0‒**them** /ðəm; *strong form* ðem/ *pron* **1** (used as the object of a v or prep) people, animals or things mentioned earlier: *Give ~ to me.* ◇ *Did you eat all of ~?* **2** used instead of *him* or *her*: *If anyone comes, ask ~ to wait.*

0‒**theme** /θiːm/ *n* [C] **1** subject of a talk, book, etc **2** repeated tune in a piece of music ■ **theme park** *n* [C] large park which has machines for people to ride on which are based on a single idea ■ **theme music/song/tune** *n* [C] music played at the beginning and end of a film, TV programme, etc

0‒**themselves** /ðəmˈselvz/ *pron* **1** used as a reflexive when the people or animals doing an action are also affected by it: *They hurt ~.* **2** used for emphasis: *They ~ have often made that mistake.* [IDM] **(all) by themselves 1** alone **2** without help

0‒**then** /ðen/ *adv* **1** at that time: *I was still unmarried ~.* **2** next; after that: *We stayed in Rome and ~ in Naples.* **3** used to show the logical result of sth: *If you miss that train ~ you'll have to get a taxi.* **4** also:

---

thesis /ˈθiːsɪs/ n [C] (pl **theses** /ˈθiːsiːz/) **1** long piece of writing on a subject, done as part of a university degree **2** statement or theory supported by arguments

0⎯ **they** /ðeɪ/ pron (used as the subject of a v) **1** people, animals or things mentioned earlier **2** used instead of *he* or *she* to refer to a person whose sex is not known: *If anyone comes later, ~'ll have to wait.* **3** people in general: *T~ say we're going to have a hot summer.*

they'd /ðeɪd/ short for THEY HAD, THEY WOULD

they'll /ðeɪl/ short for THEY WILL

they're /ðeə(r)/ short for THEY ARE

they've /ðeɪv/ short for THEY HAVE

0⎯ **thick** /θɪk/ adj **1** having a large distance between opposite sides or surfaces: *a ~ slice of bread* ◇ *a wall 2 feet* ~ **2** growing closely together in large numbers: *~ hair* ◇ *a ~ forest* **3** (of a liquid) not flowing very easily **4** difficult to see through; difficult to breathe in: *a ~ fog* **5** (*GB, infml*) stupid: *slow to learn or understand things* ● **thick** adj thickly: *spread the butter too ~* [IDM] **thick and fast** quickly and in large quantities ● **thick** n [U] [IDM] **in the thick of sth** involved in the busiest part of sth **through thick and thin** even when there are problems or difficulties ▶ **thicken** v [I,T] become or make sth thick: *~en the soup* ▶ **thickly** adv ▶ **thickness** n **1** [U] state of being thick **2** [C] distance between opposite sides or surfaces or sides: *4 centimetres in ~ness* **3** [C] layer of sth ■ **thick-set** adj (esp of a man) having a strong heavy body ■ **thick-skinned** adj not sensitive to criticism, etc

thicket /ˈθɪkɪt/ n [C] mass of trees or bushes growing closely together

0⎯ **thief** /θiːf/ n [C] (pl **thieves** /θiːvz/) person who steals sth from another person or place ▶ **thieving** /ˈθiːvɪŋ/ n [U] (*infml*) act of stealing things

thigh /θaɪ/ n [C] part of the human leg between the knee and the hip

thimble /ˈθɪmbl/ n [C] small cap of metal or plastic worn over the end of the finger to protect it while sewing

0⎯ **thin** /θɪn/ adj (~ner, ~nest) **1** having a small distance between opposite sides or surfaces **2** (of a person or part of the body) not fat **3** not growing closely together or in large amounts: *~ hair* **4** containing more liquid than is normal or expected: *~ soup* **5** easy to see through: *a ~ mist* **6** weak; feeble: *a ~ excuse* ● **thin** n [IDM] **the thin end of the wedge** event or action that is the beginning of sth more serious or unpleasant ● **thin** adv thinly: *cut the bread too ~* ● **thin** v (-nn-) [I,T] become or make sth thin ▶ **thinly** adv ▶ **thinness** n [U]

0⎯ **thing** /θɪŋ/ n **1** [C] any unnamed object: *What is that ~ on the table?* **2** (things) [pl] personal possessions, clothes, etc: *Bring your swimming ~s.* **3** (a thing) [sing] used with negatives to mean 'anything': *I haven't got a ~ to wear.* **4** [C] fact, event, situation or action; what sb says or thinks: *A terrible ~ happened last night.* ◇ *There's another ~ I want to ask you.* **5** (things) [pl] general situation as it affects sb: *Hi Mike. How are ~s?* **6** [C, usu sing] what is needed or socially acceptable: *do/ say the right/wrong ~* **7** [C] (with an adjective) (*spoken*) used to talk to or about a person or animal, to show how you feel about them: *She's a sweet little ~.* [IDM] **for one thing** used for introducing a reason **have a thing about sb/sth** (*infml*) have a strong like or dislike of sb/sth in a way that seems strange **the thing is** (*spoken*) used to introduce an important fact, reason or explanation

0⎯ **think** /θɪŋk/ v (pt, pp **thought** /θɔːt/) **1** [T] have a particular idea or opinion about sth/sb; believe sth: *Do you ~ it's going to rain?* **2** [I] use your mind to form opinions, make decisions, etc **3** [I,T] imagine sth: *I can't ~ why he came.* **4** [T] expect sth: *The job took longer than we thought.* **5** [I,T] have sth as a plan or intention: *I ~ I'll go for a swim.* [IDM] **think aloud** say what your thoughts are as you have them **think better of it/of doing sth** decide not to do sth after thinking further about it **think nothing of (doing) sth** consider an activity to be normal or easy **think the world, highly, a lot, not much, poorly, little, etc of sb/sth** have a very good, bad, etc opinion of sb/ sth: *I don't ~ much of her idea.* [PV] **think about/of sb/sth 1** consider sb/ sth when you are doing or planning sth **2** consider doing sth **think of sth/sb 1** have an image or idea of sth/sb in your mind: *When I said that I wasn't ~ing of anyone in particular.* **2** create an idea in your imagination: *Can you ~ of a way to raise money?* **3** (used esp with *can*) remember sth: *I can't ~ of her name.* **4** imagine sth: *Just ~ of the expense!* **5** consider sth/ sb in a particular way: *I ~ of this place as my home.* **think sth out/through** consider sth carefully and thoroughly **think sth over** consider sth carefully before reaching a decision **think sth up** invent or devise a plan, etc ● **think** n [sing] [IDM] **have a think (about sth)** (*infml*) think carefully about sth ▶ **thinker** n [C] person who thinks seriously about things in a particular way: *a quick ~*

0→ **thinking** /ˈθɪŋkɪŋ/ n [U] process of thinking; opinions about sth ● **thinking** adj intelligent

0→ **third** /θɜːd/ ordinal number, n [C] 3rd; the fraction ⅓; each of three equal parts of sth ■ **third deˈgree** n [sing] IDM **give sb the third degree** (infml) question sb for a long time; use threats or violence to get information from sb ► **thirdly** adv ■ **third ˈparty** n [C] (fml or law) person other than the two main people involved ■ **third-party inˈsurance** n [U] insurance that covers you if you injure sb or damage their property ■ the **third ˈperson** n [sing] (gram) set of pronouns and verb forms used by a speaker to refer to other people or things: 'They are' is the ~ person plural of the verb 'to be'. ■ **thirdˈrate** adj of very poor quality ■ the **Third World** n [sing] way of referring to the developing countries of the world in Africa, Asia and Latin America

thirst /θɜːst/ n 1 [U, sing] feeling of needing or wanting a drink 2 [sing] ~ (for) strong desire for sth: a ~ for knowledge ● **thirst** v [PV] **thirst for sth** (lit) be very eager for sth: ~ for revenge

0→ **thirsty** /ˈθɜːsti/ adj (-ier, -iest) feeling or causing thirst: We were hungry and ~. ► **thirstily** /-ɪli/ adv

0→ **thirteen** /ˌθɜːˈtiːn/ number 13 ► **thirteenth** /-ˈtiːnθ/ ordinal number

0→ **thirty** /ˈθɜːti/ number 1 30 2 (the thirties) n [pl] numbers, years or temperatures from 30 to 39 ► **thirtieth** /ˈθɜːtiəθ/ ordinal number

0→ **this** /ðɪs/ det, pron (pl **these** /ðiːz/) 1 (being) the person or thing nearby, named or understood: Is ~ your bag? 2 used for introducing sb or for showing sth to sb: Jo, ~ is Pete. 3 (infml) used when you are telling a story or telling sb about sth: Then ~ man came in. ● **this** adv to this degree; so: It was about ~ high.

thistle /ˈθɪsl/ n [C] wild plant with prickly leaves and esp purple flowers

thong /θɒŋ/ n [C] 1 narrow strip of leather used to fasten sth 2 piece of underwear for men or women that has only a very narrow strip of fabric at the back

thorn /θɔːn/ n 1 [C] sharp pointed part on the stem of some plants, eg roses 2 [C,U] tree or bush that has thorns IDM **a thorn in sb's flesh/side** person or thing that constantly annoys sb ► **thorny** adj (-ier, -iest) 1 causing difficulty or disagreement: a ~y problem 2 having thorns

0→ **thorough** /ˈθʌrə/ adj 1 done completely and carefully 2 (of a person) doing work carefully, with attention to detail ■ **ˌthoroughˈgoing** adj (written) very thorough; complete: a ~going revision ► **thoroughly** adv ► **thoroughness** n [U]

thoroughbred /ˈθʌrəbred/ n [C], adj (animal, esp a horse) of pure breed

thoroughfare /ˈθʌrəfeə(r)/ n [C] (fml) public road or street

those plural of THAT

0→ **though** /ðəʊ/ conj 1 in spite of the fact that: They bought the car, even ~ they couldn't really afford it. 2 and yet; but: It's possible, ~ unlikely. ● **though** adv however

thought[1] pt, pp of THINK

0→ **thought**[2] /θɔːt/ n 1 [C] something that you think of or remember 2 [U] power or process of thinking 3 [C] feeling of care or worry 4 [U,C] intention or hope of doing sth 5 [U] particular way of thinking: modern scientific ~ IDM **have second thoughts** change your opinion after thinking about sth again **on second thoughts** used to say that you have changed your opinion ► **thoughtful** adj 1 quiet, because you are thinking 2 (approv) showing that you think about other people ► **thoughtfully** adv ► **thoughtless** adj not caring for other people; selfish ► **thoughtlessly** adv

0→ **thousand** /ˈθaʊznd/ number 1 1000 2 (a thousand or thousands (of)) (infml) large number: There were ~s of people there. ► **thousandth** /ˈθaʊznθ/ ordinal number

thrash /θræʃ/ v 1 [T] beat a person or an animal with a stick, whip, etc 2 [I,T] (cause sth to) move about violently: He ~ed about in the water. 3 [T] defeat sb very easily in a game [PV] **thrash sth out** discuss a problem thoroughly in order to decide sth ► **thrashing** n [C] 1 beating 2 defeat

0→ **thread** /θred/ n 1 [C,U] (length of) cotton, silk, wool, etc used in sewing 2 [C] line of thought connecting parts of a story 3 [C] raised spiral line round a screw or bolt ● **thread** v [T] 1 put a thread through a narrow opening or tube: ~ a needle 2 join objects, eg beads, together by passing sth long and thin through them 3 pass film, tape, etc into position on a machine [IDM] **thread your way through sth** move carefully through sth ■ **threadbare** adj (of cloth) worn

0→ **threat** /θret/ n 1 [C,U] statement of an intention to punish or harm sb 2 [U,C, usu sing] possibility of trouble, danger or disaster 3 [C] person or thing likely to cause trouble or danger: He is a ~ to society.

0→ **threaten** /ˈθretn/ v 1 [T] make a threat or threats against sb; use sth

A B C D E F G H I J K L M N O P Q R S **T** U V W X Y Z

as a threat: They ~ed to kill all the passengers. **2** [I,T] seem likely to happen or cause sth unpleasant: Danger ~ed. **3** [T] be a danger to sth ▸ **threatening** adj ▸ **threateningly** adv

0━ **three** /θriː/ number **3** ▸ **three-dimensional** adj having length, breadth and depth

thresh /θreʃ/ v [T] separate grains of corn, etc from the rest of the plant, using a machine or by beating

threshold /ˈθreʃhəʊld/ n [C] (fml) **1** floor at the bottom of a doorway, considered as the entrance to a building or room **2** point of beginning sth: on the ~ of a new career

threw pt of THROW

thrift /θrɪft/ n [U] (approv) careful use of money ▸ **thrifty** adj (-ier, -iest)

thrill /θrɪl/ n [C] **1** strong feeling of excitement or pleasure **2** sudden strong feeling that produces a physical effect ● **thrill** v [T] excite or please sb very much ▸ **thriller** n [C] book, play or film with an exciting story, esp about crime or spying

thrive /θraɪv/ v [I] grow well and strong; prosper: a thriving business

0━ **throat** /θrəʊt/ n [C] **1** tube in the neck that takes food and air into the body **2** front part of the neck

throb /θrɒb/ v (-bb-) [I] (of the heart, pulse, etc) beat, esp more quickly and strongly than usual ▸ **throb** n [C]

throes /θrəʊz/ n [pl] **IDM** in the **throes of (doing) sth** in the middle of a difficult activity

thrombosis /θrɒmˈbəʊsɪs/ (pl -ses /-siːz/) n [C,U] serious medical condition caused by a thick mass of blood forming in a blood vessel or the heart

throne /θrəʊn/ n **1** [C] special chair used by a king or queen in official ceremonies **2** (the throne) [sing] position of being king or queen

throng /θrɒŋ/ n [C] (fml) large crowd of people ● **throng** v [I,T] go somewhere or be present somewhere in large numbers

throttle /ˈθrɒtl/ v [T] attack or kill sb by squeezing their throat to stop them breathing ● **throttle** n [C] device controlling the flow of fuel into an engine

0━ **through** /θruː/ prep **1** from one end or side of sth/sb to the other: The train went ~ the tunnel. ◇ The bullet went straight ~ him. **2** from the beginning to the end of an activity, situation or period of time: He won't live ~ the night. **3** past a barrier, stage or test: He drove ~ a red light. ◇ smuggle drugs ~ customs **4** (US) (also infml thru) until, and including: Monday ~ Thursday **5** by means of; because of: The accident happened ~

463 / **throw**

lack of care. ● **through** adv **1** from one end or side of sth to the other: Put the coffee in the filter and let the water run ~. **2** from the beginning to the end of sth **3** past a barrier, state or test: Our team is ~ to the semi-finals. **4** connected by telephone: I tried to ring you but I couldn't get ~. **IDM** **through and through** completely ● **through** adj **1** allowing a direct journey: a ~ train **2** ~ (with) (esp US) used to show you have finished using sth or have ended a relationship with sb

0━ **throughout** /θruːˈaʊt/ prep, adv **1** in or into every part of sth: They're sold ~ the world. **2** during the whole period of time of sth: I watched the film and cried ~.

0━ **throw** /θrəʊ/ v (pt threw /θruː/ pp ~n /θrəʊn/) **1** [I,T] send sth through the air with some force, by moving the arm **2** [T] put sth in a particular place quickly and carelessly **3** [T] move sth suddenly and forcefully: I threw open the windows. **4** [T] move (a part of) your body suddenly and forcefully: ~ up your hands in horror **5** [T] make sb fall to the ground **6** [T] cause sb/sth to be in a certain state: Hundreds were ~n out of work. **7** [T] direct sth at sb/sth: She threw me an angry look. ◇ The trees threw long shadows on the grass. **8** [T] (infml) confuse, upset or surprise sb: The interruptions threw him. **9** [T] (tech) make a clay pot, etc on a potter's wheel **10** [T] move a switch, etc to operate sth **11** [T] (throw a party) give a party **IDM** **throw cold water on sth** → COLD¹ **throw a fit** → FIT³ **throw sb in at the deep end** (infml) ask sb to do sth new and difficult for which they are unprepared **throw in the towel** admit defeat **throw light on sth** → LIGHT¹ **throw your weight about/around** (infml) use your position of power aggressively in order to achieve what you want **[PV] throw sth away|throw sth out 1** get rid of sth unwanted **2** fail to make use of sth; waste sth **throw sth in** include sth with what you are selling, without increasing the price **throw yourself/sth into sth** become involved in an activity with enthusiasm **throw sb/sth off** manage to get rid of sth/sb that is annoying, etc **throw oneself on sb/sth** (fml) depend completely on sb/sth for help, etc: ~ oneself on the mercy of others **throw sb out (of...)** force a troublemaker to leave a place **throw sth out 1** reject a plan, idea, etc **2** = THROW STH AWAY **throw sth together** make or prepare sth quickly **throw (sth) up** vomit **throw sth up 1** make people notice sth

thru

2 leave your job ● **throw** n [C] **1** act of throwing sth, esp a ball or dice **2** distance over which sth is thrown **3** loose cover for a sofa, etc
■ **thrower** n [C]

thru (US) = THROUGH

thrush /θrʌʃ/ n [C] bird with a brown back and brown spots on its chest

thrust /θrʌst/ v (pt, pp **thrust**) [I,T] push sth/sb suddenly and forcefully in a particular direction ● **thrust** n **1** (the thrust) [sing] main point of an argument, etc **2** [C] sudden strong movement that pushes sth/sb forward **3** [U] (tech) force produced by an engine to push a plane, etc forward

thud /θʌd/ n [C] dull sound of a heavy object hitting sth softer ● **thud** v (-**dd-**) [I] strike or fall with a thud

thug /θʌg/ n [C] violent and dangerous person

0─ thumb /θʌm/ n [C] short thick finger set apart from the other four [IDM] **thumbs up/down** used to show that sth has been accepted/rejected **under sb's thumb** (of a person) completely controlled by sb
● **thumb** v [T] ask for a free ride from passing motorists by signalling with your thumb: to ~ a lift [PV] **thumb through sth** turn the pages of a book quickly to get a general idea of it
■ **thumbnail** n [C] nail at the tip of the thumb ■ **thumbnail 'sketch** n [C] very short description of sth
■ **'thumbtack** n [C] (US) = DRAWING PIN (DRAWING)

thump /θʌmp/ v [I,T] hit sb/sth hard, esp with your fist **2** [I] beat strongly: His heart ~ed with fear.
● **thump** n [C] (noise of a) heavy blow

thunder /'θʌndə(r)/ n [U] **1** loud noise that follows a flash of lightning **2** loud noise like thunder: the ~ of guns ● **thunder** v **1** [I] (used with it) sound with thunder: It's been ~ing all night. **2** [I] move somewhere very fast, often with a loud noise **3** [T] say sth in a loud angry voice
■ **'thunderbolt** n [C] (written) flash of lightning that comes at the same time as the noise of thunder and that hits sth ■ **'thunderclap** n [C] loud crash of thunder ■ **thunderous** adj very loud: ~ous applause
■ **'thunderstorm** n [C] storm of lightning, thunder and heavy rain

0─ Thursday /'θɜːzdeɪ; -di/ n [U,C] the fifth day of the week, next after Wednesday (See examples of use at Monday.)

0─ thus /ðʌs/ adv (fml) **1** in this way; like this **2** as a result of this

thwart /θwɔːt/ v [T] (fml) prevent sth or their plans from succeeding

thyme /taɪm/ n [U] kind of herb used in cooking

thyroid /'θaɪrɔɪd/ (also 'thyroid gland) n [C] gland in the neck that affects the body's growth

tiara /ti'ɑːrə/ n [C] piece of jewellery like a small crown, worn by a woman

tic /tɪk/ n [C] sudden unconscious moving of the muscles, esp in the face

tick /tɪk/ n [C] **1** (GB) mark ✓ showing that sth is correct or has been dealt with **2** small bloodsucking insect **3** (also 'ticking) light repeated sound of a clock or watch **4** (GB, infml) moment: I'll be with you in a ~. ● **tick** v **1** [I] (of a clock, etc) make short light repeated sounds **2** [T] (off) put a mark (✓) next to an item on a list, an answer, etc [IDM] **what makes sb tick** what makes sb behave in the way they do [PV] **tick sb off** (infml) speak angrily to sb because they have done sth wrong **tick over** keep working or operating steadily

0─ ticket /'tɪkɪt/ n [C] **1** printed piece of card or paper that gives you the right to travel on a bus, enter a cinema, etc **2** label attached to sth in a shop, etc giving the price or size of sth **3** official notice of an offence against traffic laws: a parking ~

tickle /'tɪkl/ v **1** [T] touch part of sb's body lightly, esp so as to make them laugh **2** [I,T] have or cause an itching feeling in a part of the body: My throat ~s. **3** [T] amuse and interest sb ● **tickle** n [usu sing] act or feeling of tickling ■ **ticklish** adj **1** (of a person) sensitive to being tickled **2** (infml) (of a problem) needing to be dealt with carefully

tidal /'taɪdl/ adj of or caused by tides ■ **'tidal wave** n [C] very large ocean wave

tide /taɪd/ n [C,U] regular rise and fall in the level of the sea **2** [C] flow of water that happens as the sea rises and falls: Beware of strong ~s. **3** [C, usu sing] direction in which opinions, events, etc seem to be moving ● **tide** v [PV] **tide sb over (sth)** help sb through a difficult period by providing what they need ■ **'tidemark** n [C] highest point reached by a tide on a beach

tidings /'taɪdɪŋz/ n [pl] (old-fash) news

0─ tidy /'taɪdi/ adj (-ier, -iest) **1** neat; orderly: a ~ room/girl **2** (infml) (of an amount of money) fairly large: a ~ sum of money ▶ **tidily** adv ■ **tidiness** n [U] ● **tidy** v (pt, pp -ied) [I,T] make sth look neat by putting things where they belong: ~ (up) the room

tie[1] /taɪ/ v (pres pt **tying** /'taɪɪŋ/) **1** [T] fasten sth to sth or hold things together using string, rope, etc: A label was ~d to the handle. ◇ ~ (up) a *parcel* **2** [T] make a knot in a piece of string, ribbon, etc: ~ *your shoelaces* **3** [I] be closed or fastened with a knot, etc: *Does this dress* ~ *in front?* **4** [T] connect or link sb/sth closely with sb/sth else **5** [T] ~ **(to)** restrict sb and make them unable to do everything they want: *be* ~*d by a contract/promise* **6** [I, T] (of two teams, etc) have the same number of points: *The two teams* ~*d.* [PV] **tie sb down (to (doing) sth)** limit sb's freedom **tie in (with sth)** match or agree with sth **tie sb up 1** tie sb's arms or legs with rope so that they cannot move or escape **2** (*infml*) (*usu passive*) cause sb to be busy: *I'm a bit* ~*d up now; can you call back later?* **tie sth up** invest money so that it is not easily available for use

0—m **tie²** /taɪ/ *n* [C] **1** long narrow strip of material worn round the neck, esp by men, with a knot at the front **2** piece of string or wire, used for fastening or tying sth **3** strong connection between people and organizations: *family* ~*s* **4** thing that limits sb's freedom of action **5** equal score in a game, etc ▪ **tiebreaker** *n* [C] way of deciding the winner when competitors have the same score

tier /tɪə(r)/ *n* [C] row or layer of sth that has several rows or layers placed one above the other

tiff /tɪf/ *n* [C] slight argument

tiger /ˈtaɪɡə(r)/ *n* [C] large fierce animal of the cat family, yellowish with black stripes ▪ **tigress** /ˈtaɪɡrəs/ *n* [C] female tiger

0—m **tight** /taɪt/ *adj* **1** held or fixed in position firmly; difficult to move or undo: *a* ~ *knot* **2** (of clothes) fitting closely: *These shoes are too* ~. **3** very strict and firm: *Security is* ~ *at the airport.* **4** with people or things packed closely together **5** difficult to manage because there is not enough of sth, esp money or time: *a* ~ *schedule* **6** (*GB, infml, disapprov*) unwilling to spend money; not generous **7** (*-tight*) made so that sth cannot get in or out: *air-* ◇ *water-* [IDM] **a tight spot/corner** very difficult or dangerous situation ▪ **tight** *adv* tightly: *The bags are packed* ~. ▪ **tighten** /taɪt/ *v* [I, T] (cause sth to) become tighter: ~ *(up) the screws* ▪ **tight-fisted** *adj* (*infml*) unwilling to spend money ▪ **tightly** *adv* ▪ **tightness** *n* [U] ▪ **tightrope** *n* [C] rope stretched high up on which acrobats perform ▪ **tights** *n* [pl] piece of clothing made of very thin fabric that fits closely over a woman's hips, legs and feet

tile /taɪl/ *n* [C] thin usu square piece of baked clay or other material for covering roofs, walls and floors [IDM] **have a night on the tiles** (*GB, infml*) stay out late enjoying yourself ▪ **tile** *v* [T] **1** cover a surface with tiles: *a* ~*d*

bathroom **2** (*computing*) arrange several windows on a computer screen

0—m **till¹** *conj, prep* = UNTIL

till² /tɪl/ *n* [C] drawer or box for money in a shop, bank, etc ▪ **till** *v* [T] prepare and use land for growing crops

tiller /ˈtɪlə(r)/ *n* [C] handle used for turning the rudder of a boat

tilt /tɪlt/ *v* [I, T] (cause sth to) move into a position with one side or end higher than the other ▪ **tilt** *n* [C] sloping position [IDM] **(at) full tilt** as fast as possible

timber /ˈtɪmbə(r)/ *n* **1** [U] trees grown to be used in building, etc **2** [U] wood prepared for use in building, etc **3** [C, usu pl] wooden beam used in building a house or ship ▪ **timbered** *adj* built of wooden beams

0—m **time¹** /taɪm/ *n* **1** [U] what is measured in minutes, hours, days, etc: *As* ~ *went by we saw less and less of each other.* **2** [U] the time shown on a clock in minutes and hours: *What* ~ *is it?* **3** [U, C] time when sth happens or when sth should happen: *It's* ~ *for lunch.* ◇ *What* ~ *do you finish work?* **4** [U] an amount of time; the amount of time available to work, rest, etc: *He never takes any* ~ *off* (= time spent not working). ◇ *What a waste of* ~! **5** (*a time*) [*sing*] period of time during which you do sth or sth happens: *I lived in Egypt for a* ~. ◇ *Her parents died a long* ~ *ago.* **6** [U, pl] period of time; age: *in prehistoric* ~*s* **7** [C] occasion: *He failed the exam three* ~*s.* **8** [C, U] how long sb takes to run a race or complete an event: *The winner's* ~ *was 11.6 seconds.* **9** [U] (*music*) speed of a piece of music: *dance in* ~ *to the music* [IDM] **ahead of your time** having advanced or new ideas that other people use or copy later **all the time**, **the whole time** during the whole period **at a time** separately at all times always **at one time** at a period of time in the past **at times** sometimes **behind the times** old-fashioned in your ideas, methods, etc **do time** (*infml*) spend time in prison **for the time being** for a short period of time but not permanently **from time to time** occasionally **have no time for sb/sth** dislike sb/sth **have the time of your life** (*infml*) enjoy yourself very much **in time** after a period of time when a situation has changed **it's about/high time** (*spoken*) used to say that you think sb should do sth soon: *It's high* ~ *you went to bed.* **on time** not late or early; punctual(ly) **take your time** use as much time as you need without hurrying **time after time | time and** (time) again often; on many or all occasions ■ 'time bomb n [C] bomb set to explode at a certain time ■ 'time limit n [C] period of time during which sth must be done ▶ times 1 prep (infml) multiplied by sth: 5 ~s 2 is 10. 2 n [pl] used in comparisons to show how much more, better, etc sth is than sth else: three ~s as long as sth ■ 'timescale n [C] period of time it takes for sth to happen or be completed ■ 'timeshare (also 'timesharing) n [U] arrangement in which a holiday home is owned by several people who use it for a short time each year ■ 'time signal n [C] signal broadcast on the radio that gives the exact time of day ■ 'time switch n [C] switch that can be set to operate automatically at a certain time ■ 'timetable n [C] 1 list showing the times at which trains, buses, etc depart or arrive 2 list showing the times at which the various subjects are taught at school

time² /taɪm/ v [T] 1 choose the time or moment for sth: She ~d her arrival for shortly after 3. 2 measure the time taken for sth to happen or for sb to do sth ▶ timer n [C] device used to measure the time that sth takes; device that starts or stops a machine working at a particular time ▶ timing n [U] (skill in) choosing the best moment to do sth

timely /'taɪmli/ adj (-ier, -iest) occurring at just the right time

timid /'tɪmɪd/ adj shy and not brave or self-confident ▶ timidity /tɪ'mɪdəti/ n [U] ▶ timidly adv

O─ tin /tɪn/ n 1 [U] (symb Sn) soft silver-white metal 2 (also 'tin can) [C] (GB) metal container for food: a ~ of beans ▶ tinned adj (of food) preserved in a can: ~ned peaches ■ 'tinfoil n [U] very thin sheets of metal, used for wrapping food in ▶ tinny adj (-ier, -iest) (disapprov) (of a sound) light, high and unpleasant ■ 'tin-opener n [C] (GB) tool for opening tins of food

tinge /tɪndʒ/ v [T] ~ (with) 1 add a small amount of colour to sth 2 add a small amount of a particular emotion or quality to sth: admiration ~d with envy ● tinge n [C, usu sing] small amount of a colour, feeling or quality: a ~ of sadness in her voice

tingle /'tɪŋɡl/ v [I] 1 (of a part of your body) feel as if a lot of small sharp points are pushing into it 2 ~ with feel an emotion strongly: ~ with excitement ● tingle n [C, usu sing] tingling feeling

tinker /'tɪŋkə(r)/ v [I] ~ (with) make small changes to sth to repair it, esp in a way that may not be helpful

tinkle /'tɪŋkl/ v [I] make a series of

light high ringing sounds ● tinkle n [usu sing] tinkling sound

tinsel /'tɪnsl/ n [U] strip or thread of shiny material used as a Christmas decoration

tint /tɪnt/ n [C] (esp pale) shade of colour ● tint v [T] add a small amount of colour to sth

O─ tiny /'taɪni/ adj (-ier, -iest) extremely small

O─ tip /tɪp/ n [C] 1 thin pointed end of sth: the ~s of your fingers 2 small part put on or over the end of sth: a stick with a rubber ~ 3 small piece of advice about sth practical 4 small amount of extra money given to sb who has done a service: leave the waiter a ~ 5 (GB) place where you can take rubbish and leave it 6 (GB, infml, disapprov) untidy place [IDM] on the tip of your tongue just about to be remembered or spoken the tip of the iceberg small sign of a much larger problem ● tip v (-pp-) 1 [I,T] (cause sth to) move so that one end or side is higher than the other 2 [T] (esp GB) make sth come out of a container or its position by holding or lifting it at an angle 3 (GB) [I,T] leave rubbish somewhere outdoors in order to get rid of it 4 [I,T] give a tip (4) to sb: ~ the waiter 5 [T] say in advance that sb/sth will be successful 6 [T] cover the end or edge of sth with a colour, substance, etc: ~ped cigarettes [PV] tip sb off (about sth) (infml) warn sb that sth, esp sth illegal is about to happen ■ 'tip-off n [C] secret warning ■ 'tip-top adj (infml) excellent

tipple /'tɪpl/ n [C] (infml) alcoholic drink

tipsy /'tɪpsi/ adj (-ier, -iest) (infml) slightly drunk

tiptoe /'tɪptəʊ/ n [IDM] on tiptoe/ tiptoes standing or walking on the front part of your foot, with your heels off the ground: stand on ~ to see over sb's head ● tiptoe v [I] walk quietly: She ~d out.

O─ tire¹ /'taɪə(r)/ v [I,T] (cause sb to) become tired: The long walk ~d them (out). ▶ tired adj 1 feeling that you need rest or sleep 2 ~ of bored with sb/sth: I'm ~d of watching television. ▶ tiredness n [U] ▶ tireless adj (approv) putting a lot of hard work and energy into sth over a long time ▶ tiresome adj annoying or boring

O─ tire² (US) = TYRE

tissue /'tɪʃuː/ n 1 [U] (also tissues [pl]) mass of cells that form the different parts of humans, animals and plants: nerve ~ 2 [C] piece of soft paper used as a handkerchief 3 [U] (also 'tissue paper) very thin soft paper, used esp for wrapping things

O─ tit /tɪt/ n [C] 1 (⚠, sl) woman's breast 2 small bird of various kinds [IDM] tit

for tat situation in which you do sth bad to sb because they have done the same to you

titbit /ˈtɪtbɪt/ n [C] **1** small tasty piece of food **2** small piece of gossip, etc

titillate /ˈtɪtɪleɪt/ v [T] excite sb, esp sexually

☞ **title** /ˈtaɪtl/ n **1** [C] name of a book, play, picture, etc **2** [C] word, eg Lord, Mrs or Professor, used for showing sb's rank, profession, marital status, etc **3** [C] position of being the winner of a competition, esp a sports competition **4** [U, C] (law) right to own sth ▸ **titled** adj having a title such as Lord, Lady, etc ■ **title deed** n [C] legal document proving that sb is the owner of a house, etc ■ **title role** n [C] part in a play, etc that is used as the title

titter /ˈtɪtə(r)/ v [I] give a nervous or silly little laugh ▸ **titter** n [C]

TNT /ˌtiː en ˈtiː/ n [U] powerful explosive

☞ **to¹** /tə; before consonants /tə/; before vowels /tu/; strong form /tuː/ prep **1** in the direction of sth: walk to the shops **2** situated in the direction mentioned from sth: Place the cursor to the left of the first word. **3** as far as sth: Her hair fell to her waist. **4** reaching a particular state: rise to power **5** used to show the end or limit of a range or period of time: from May to July **6** before the start of sth: It's ten (= minutes) to three. **7** used to show the person or thing that receives sth: I gave it to Peter. **8** used to show a relationship between one person or thing and another: She's married to Mark. ◇ the key to the door **9** used to show a comparison or ratio: I prefer tea to coffee. ◇ We won by 6 goals to 3.

☞ **to²** before consonants /tə/; before vowels /tu/; strong form /tuː/ (used before the simple form of a v to form the infinitive) **1** used to show purpose or intention: I went out to buy food. **2** used to show the result of sth: It was too hot to go out. **3** used to show the cause of sth: I'm sorry to hear that. **4** used to show an action that you want or are advised to do: I'd love to go to Paris. **5** used instead of the whole infinitive: 'Will you come?' 'I hope to.'

to³ /tuː/ adv (of a door) in or into a closed position: Push the door to. [IDM] **to and fro** backwards and forwards

toad /təʊd/ n [C] animal like a frog

toadstool /ˈtəʊdstuːl/ n [C] kind of fungus, esp one that is poisonous

toast /təʊst/ n **1** [U] slices of bread that have been made brown by heating them on both sides **2** [C] act of a group of people wishing sb happiness, success, etc by drinking a glass of sth, esp alcohol, at the same time: propose a ~ to sb ● **toast** v **1** [T] wish happiness, success, etc to sb by drinking wine, etc: ~ the bride and bridegroom **2** [I, T] (cause sth, esp bread, to) turn brown by heating it in a toaster, etc **3** [T] warm a part of your body by placing it near a fire ▸ **toaster** n [C] electrical machine for toasting bread

tobacco /təˈbækəʊ/ n [U] (plant having) leaves that are dried and used for smoking in cigarettes, pipes, etc ▸ **tobacconist** /-kənɪst/ n [C] shop or person that sells tobacco, cigarettes, etc

toboggan /təˈbɒɡən/ n [C] long narrow sledge (= vehicle that slides over snow) used for sliding down slopes ● **toboggan** v [I] travel down a slope on snow using a toboggan

☞ **today** /təˈdeɪ/ adv, n [U] **1** (on) this day **2** (at) this present time: the young people of ~

toddle /ˈtɒdl/ v [I] (esp of a young child) walk with short unsteady steps ▸ **toddler** n [C] small child that has just learned to walk

to-do /təˈduː/ n [C, usu sing] (pl ~s) (infml) unnecessary excitement or anger about sth

☞ **toe** /təʊ/ n [C] **1** one of the five small parts that stick out from the foot **2** part of a sock, shoe, etc that covers the toes [IDM] **keep sb on their toes** make sure that sb is ready for action by doing things that they are not expecting ● **toe** v [IDM] **toe the line** obey orders ■ **toenail** n [C] hard layer covering the end of a toe

toffee /ˈtɒfi/ n [C, U] (piece of) hard sticky sweet made by heating sugar, butter, etc

☞ **together** /təˈɡeðə(r)/ adv **1** with each other: They went for a walk ~. **2** so that two or more things touch or are joined with each other: Tie the ends ~. **3** in or into agreement ~ at the same time: They both spoke ~. [IDM] **together with** including; in addition to ● **together** adj (infml, approv) (of a person) well organized and confident ▸ **togetherness** n [U] feeling of friendliness or love

toggle /ˈtɒɡl/ n [I, T] (computing) press a key or set of keys on a computer keyboard in order to move from one program to another, etc

toil /tɔɪl/ v [I] (fml) ~ (away) work hard and/or for a long time ● **toil** n [U] (fml) hard, unpleasant and tiring work

☞ **toilet** /ˈtɔɪlət/ n [C] (room containing a) bowl used for receiving and taking away waste matter from the body ■ **toilet paper** n [U] paper used for cleaning your bottom after you have used the toilet ▸ **toiletries** n [pl] things, eg soap and toothpaste, that you use for cleaning your teeth, etc ■ **'toilet roll** n [C] roll of toilet paper

token /'təʊkən/ n [C] **1** round flat piece of metal used instead of a coin to operate some machines, etc **2** (GB) piece of paper that you pay for and that sb can exchange for goods in a shop: *a book* ~ **3** symbol or sign: *a* ~ *of my affection* ● **token** *adj* small; not serious: *a* ~ *gesture*

told *pt, pp of* TELL

tolerate /'tɒləreɪt/ v [T] **1** allow sb to do sth that you disagree with or dislike: *I won't* ~ *such behaviour.* **2** accept sb/sth unpleasant without protesting: ~ *heat/noise* ▶ **tolerable** /-rəbl/ *adj* fairly good; that can be tolerated ▶ **tolerably** *adv* fairly ▶ **tolerance** /-rəns/ *n* [U] willingness or ability to tolerate sb/sth: *religious/ racial tolerance* ▶ **tolerant** /-rənt/ *adj* able to accept what other people say or do even if you do not agree with it ▶ **toleration** /ˌtɒləˈreɪʃn/ *n* [U] action or practice of tolerating sb/sth

toll /təʊl/ *n* **1** [C] money that you pay to use a particular road or bridge **2** [C] amount of damage or the number of deaths caused by a war, disaster, etc: *the death* ~ *has now reached 7000* **3** [sing] sound of a bell ringing with slow regular strokes ● **toll** *v* [I,T] (of a bell) ring slowly and repeatedly, esp as a sign that sb has died

0━ **tomato** /təˈmɑːtəʊ/ *n* [C] (pl ~**es**) (plant with a) soft red fruit eaten raw or cooked as a vegetable

tomb /tuːm/ *n* [C] place, esp with a stone monument, where a dead body is buried ■ **'tombstone** *n* [C] stone monument over a tomb

tomboy /'tɒmbɔɪ/ *n* [C] young girl who enjoys games and activities traditionally associated with boys

tomcat /'tɒmkæt/ *n* [C] male cat

0━ **tomorrow** /təˈmɒrəʊ/ *adv, n* [U] **1** (on) the day after today **2** (in) the near future

0━ **ton** /tʌn/ *n* [C] unit for measuring weight, 2240 pounds in Britain, 2000 pounds in the USA **2** (tons) [pl] (*infml*) a lot: ~*s of money*

0━ **tone**[1] /təʊn/ *n* **1** [C] quality of sb's voice, esp expressing a particular emotion: *speaking in hushed* ~*s* **2** [sing] general quality or character of sth, eg a style of writing: *the serious* ~ *of the article* **3** [C] quality of a sound, esp that of a musical instrument **4** [C] shade of a colour **5** [C] signal on a telephone line: *the dialling* ~ **6** [C] (*music*) one of the five longer differences in pitch between one note and the next ▶ **tone-'deaf** *adj* unable to hear the differences between musical notes

tone[2] /təʊn/ *v* **1** [T] ~ (**up**) make your muscles, skin, etc firmer and stronger: *Exercise* ~*s up the body.* **2** [I] ~ (**in; with**) match the colour of sth [PV] **tone sth down** cause sth to become less forceful or intense

tongs /tɒŋz/ *n* [pl] tool with two parts joined at one end, used for picking up and holding things

0━ **tongue** /tʌŋ/ *n* **1** [C] soft part in the mouth that moves around, used for talking, tasting, licking, etc **2** [U,C] tongue of some animals, cooked and eaten **3** [C] (*fml*) language **4** [sing] particular way of speaking: *He has a sharp* ~. **5** [C] long narrow piece of leather under the laces on a shoe [IDM] **with your tongue in your cheek | with tongue in cheek** saying sth that you do not intend to be taken seriously; joking ■ **tongue-tied** *adj* unable to speak because of shyness or nervousness ■ **tongue-twister** *n* [C] word or phrase that is difficult to say

tonic /'tɒnɪk/ *n* **1** (*also* **tonic water**) [U,C] clear fizzy drink, often mixed with a strong alcoholic drink, eg gin **2** [C,U] medicine that gives strength or energy **3** [C,U] liquid that you put on your hair or skin to make it healthier

0━ **tonight** /təˈnaɪt/ *adv, n* [U] (during the) evening or night of today

tonnage /'tʌnɪdʒ/ *n* [U,C] amount of cargo a ship can carry

0━ **tonne** /tʌn/ *n* [C] metric unit of weight; 1000 kilograms

tonsil /'tɒnsl/ *n* [C] either of the two small organs at the back of the throat ▶ **tonsillitis** /ˌtɒnsəˈlaɪtɪs/ *n* [U] painful swelling of the tonsils

0━ **too** /tuː/ *adv* **1** to a higher degree than is allowed or desirable: *You're driving* ~ *fast!* **2** in addition; also: *She plays the guitar and sings* ~.

took *pt of* TAKE[1]

0━ **tool** /tuːl/ *n* [C] instrument that you hold in your hand and use for working on sth

0━ **toot** /tuːt/ *n* [C] short high sound from a car horn or whistle ● **toot** *v* [I,T] (cause sth to) make a short high sound

0━ **tooth** /tuːθ/ *n* (pl **teeth** /tiːθ/) **1** [C] any of the hard white objects in the mouth, used for biting and chewing food **2** [C] narrow pointed part that sticks out of an object, eg on a comb or saw [IDM] **get your teeth into sth** (*infml*) put a lot of effort or enthusiasm into sth that is difficult enough to keep you interested **in the teeth of sth** in spite of problems, etc ■ **'toothache** *n* [U,C, usu sing] pain in a tooth or ~teeth ■ **'toothbrush** *n* [C] brush for cleaning your teeth ▶ **toothed** /tuːθt/ *adj* having teeth ▶ **toothless** *adj* ■ **'toothpaste** *n* [U] substance that you put on a brush and use to clean your teeth ● **'toothpick** *n* [C] short pointed piece of wood, etc, used for removing food from between your teeth

0—■ **top**¹ /tɒp/ *n* **1** [C] highest part or point of sth: *at the ~ of the hill* **2** [C] upper flat surface of sth: *the ~ of the table* **3** [sing] highest or most important rank or position **4** [C] thing that you put on the end of sth to close it: *a pen/bottle ~* **5** [C] piece of clothing worn on the upper part of the body **6** [C] toy that spins on its pointed end [**IDM**] **at the top of your voice** as loudly as you can ● **from top to bottom** very thoroughly ● **get on top of sb** (*infml*) be too much for sb to manage or deal with ● **on top of sth** **1** in addition to sth **2** in control of a situation ● **on top of the world** very happy or proud ● **over the top** ‖ **OTT** (*esp GB, infml*) unacceptably extreme or exaggerated: *His performance in the film is a bit over the ~.* ● **top** *adj* highest in position, rank or degree: *a room on the ~ floor* ◇ *at ~ speed* ■ **top 'brass** *n* [sing, with sing or pl verb] (*infml*) people in the most important positions in a company, etc ■ **top 'dog** *n* [usu sing] (*infml*) person, group, etc that is better than all the others, esp in a competition ■ **top 'hat** *n* [C] man's tall formal black or grey hat ■ **top-'heavy** *adj* too heavy at the top ■ **topless** *adj, adv* (of a woman) with the breasts bare ■ **topmost** *adj* (*written*) highest ■ **top 'secret** *adj* needing to be kept completely secret ■ **topsoil** /ˈtɒpsɔɪl/ *n* [U] layer of soil nearest the surface

0—■ **top²** /tɒp/ *v* (**-pp-**) [T] **1** be higher than an amount: *Exports have ~pped £100m.* **2** be in the highest position on a list **3** put sth on top of sth else: *a cake ~ped with icing* **4** ~ **yourself** (*infml*) kill yourself deliberately [**PV**] **top sth up** fill up a partly empty container: *~ up sb's drink*

topic /ˈtɒpɪk/ *n* [C] subject for discussion or study ● **topical** *adj* of present interest: *~al issues*

topple /ˈtɒpl/ *v* [I,T] **1** (cause sth to) become unsteady and fall: (*fig*) *The crisis ~d the government.*

torch /tɔːtʃ/ *n* [C] **1** (*GB*) small electric light held in the hand **2** piece of wood soaked in oil, etc for carrying as a light ● **torchlight** /ˈtɔːtʃlaɪt/ *n* [U] light of torch or torches

tore *pt* of TEAR¹

torment /ˈtɔːment/ *n* [U,C] (person or thing that causes) extreme suffering ● **torment** /tɔːˈment/ *v* [T] **1** (*written*) make sb suffer very much **2** annoy sb in a cruel way ● **tormentor** *n* [C]

torn *pp* of TEAR¹

tornado /tɔːˈneɪdəʊ/ *n* [C] (pl **~es**)

---

total

violent destructive storm with circular winds

torpedo /tɔːˈpiːdəʊ/ *n* [C] (pl **~es**) long narrow bomb that travels underwater and is used for destroying ships ● **torpedo** *v* [T] attack and destroy sth (as if) with a torpedo

torrent /ˈtɒrənt/ *n* [C] **1** large amount of water moving very quickly **2** large amount of sth that comes suddenly and violently: *a ~ of abuse* ▶ **torrential** /təˈrenʃl/ *adj* (of rain) falling in large amounts

torso /ˈtɔːsəʊ/ *n* [C] (pl **~s**) main part of the human body, not including the head, arms or legs

tortilla /tɔːˈtiːə/ *n* [C] **1** thin Mexican pancake, usu eaten hot and filled with meat, cheese, etc **2** Spanish dish made with eggs and potatoes fried together

tortoise /ˈtɔːtəs/ *n* [C] slow-moving animal with a hard shell ■ **tortoiseshell** *n* [U] hard yellow and brown shell of some turtles, used for making ornaments

tortuous /ˈtɔːtʃuəs/ *adj* **1** full of bends **2** not direct; complicated

torture /ˈtɔːtʃə(r)/ *v* [T] cause extreme pain to sb, as a punishment or to force them to say sth ● **torture** *n* **1** [U] act of torturing sb **2** [C,U] (*infml*) (thing that causes) mental or physical suffering ▶ **torturer** *n* [C]

Tory /ˈtɔːri/ *n* [C] (pl **-ies**) (member) of the Conservative Party

toss /tɒs/ *v* **1** [T] throw sth lightly or carelessly **2** [T] move your head suddenly upwards, esp to show annoyance **3** [I,T] (cause sb/sth to) move restlessly from side to side: *I kept ~ing and turning all night.* **4** [T] shake or turn food in order to cover it with oil, butter, etc: *~ a salad* **5** [I,T] decide sth by throwing a coin and guessing which side will be on top when it falls: *Let's ~ to see who goes first.* ● **toss** *n* [C] act of tossing sth: *with a ~ of her head* ■ **toss-up** *n* [sing] even chance

tot /tɒt/ *n* [C] **1** (*infml*) very small child **2** (*esp GB*) small amount of alcoholic drink ● **tot** *v* (**-tt-**) [**PV**] **tot sth up** (*infml*) add up numbers to make a total

0—■ **total** /ˈtəʊtl/ *n* [C] complete number or amount: *The repairs come to over £500 in ~.* [**IDM**] **in total** altogether ● **total** *adj* complete: *the ~ profit* ● **total** *v* (**-ll-** *US also* **-l-**) [T] **1** reach a particular total: *The number of visitors ~led 15 000.* **2** ~ (**up**) add up the numbers of sth/sb and get a total ▶ **totality** /təʊˈtæləti/ *n* [C,U] (*fml*) whole amount; state of being complete or

---

A B C D E F G H I J K L M N O P Q R S **T** U V W X Y Z

whole ▶ **totally** adv completely: ~ly blind

totalitarian /təʊˌtæləˈteəriən/ adj (disapprov) (of a system of government) in which there is only one political party that has complete power and control over the people

totter /ˈtɒtə(r)/ v [I] **1** walk or move unsteadily **2** be weak and seem likely to fall

0—**touch**[1] /tʌtʃ/ v [I,T] put your hands or fingers onto sb/sth: *The dish is hot—don't—(it)!* **2** [I,T] (of two or more things, surfaces, etc) be or come so close together that there is no space between: *The two wires ~ed.* **3** [T] eat, drink or use sth: *He hasn't ~ed any food for two days.* **4** [T] cause sb to feel sympathetic or upset: *We were greatly ~ed by your thoughtfulness.* **5** [T] be as good as sb in skill, quality, etc: *No one can ~ him as an actor.* **[PV] touch wood** touch sth made of wood to avoid bad luck **[PV] touch down** (of an aircraft) land **touch sth off** make sth begin, esp a violent situation **touch on/upon sth** mention sth briefly **touch sth up** improve sth by changing or adding to it slightly ■ **touchdown** n [C,U] moment when a plane or spacecraft lands ▶ **touched** adj feeling happy and grateful ▶ **touching** adj causing feelings of pity or sympathy ■ **touch screen** n [C] (computing) display device which allows you to use a computer by touching areas on the screen

0—**touch**[2] /tʌtʃ/ n **1** [U] sense that enables you to be aware of things when you put your hands on them **2** [C,usu sing] act of putting your hands or fingers on sb/sth **3** [sing] way sth feels when you touch it: *The material has a velvety ~.* **4** [C] small detail: *put the finishing ~es to the project* **5** [sing] way of doing sth: *Her work has that professional ~.* **6** [C,usu sing] ~ **of** very small amount: *a ~ of frost in the air* **7** [U] (in football/rugby) part of the pitch outside the sidelines: *The ball is in ~.* **[IDM] be, get, keep, etc in touch (with sb)** communicate with sb ■ **touch-and-'go** adj uncertain; risky

touchy /ˈtʌtʃi/ adj (-ier, -iest) easily offended

0—**tough** /tʌf/ adj **1** having or causing difficulties: *a ~ problem* **2** very firm; severe: *~ laws to deal with terrorism* **3** strong enough to deal with difficult situations **4** (of meat) difficult to cut and chew **5** not easily cut or broken **[IDM] tough luck** (infml) used to show sympathy for sth unfortunate that has happened to sb ▶ **toughen** /ˈtʌfn/ v [I,T] become or make sth/sb stronger ▶ **toughness** n [U]

toupee /ˈtuːpeɪ/ n [C] small wig worn on a bald part of a man's head

0—**tour** /tʊə(r)/ n [C] **1** journey made for pleasure during which several places are visited: *a round-the-world ~* **2** act of walking around a town, building, etc in order to visit it: *I went on a guided ~* (= by sb who knows the place) *of the palace.* **3** official series of visits to different places by a sports team, famous person, etc ● **tour** v [I,T] travel around a place, eg to perform, advertise sth, etc ▶ **tourism** /ˈtʊərɪzəm/ n [U] business of providing hotels, special trips, etc for tourists ▶ **tourist** n [C] person who visits places for pleasure

tournament /ˈtɔːnəmənt/ n [C] series of games or contests: *a chess ~*

tourniquet /ˈtʊənɪkeɪ/ n [C] bandage twisted tightly round an injured arm or leg to stop it bleeding

tout /taʊt/ v **1** [I,T] try to get people to buy your goods or services, esp in an annoyingly direct way **2** [T] (GB) sell tickets for sports matches, etc at very high prices ● **tout** n [C] person who buys tickets for sports events, etc and then sells them at a higher price

tow /təʊ/ v [T] pull a car or boat behind another vehicle, using a rope, chain, etc ● **tow** n [C] act of towing a vehicle **[IDM] in tow** (infml) following closely behind on tow being towed ▶ **towpath** n [C] path along the bank of a canal or river

0—**towards** /təˈwɔːdz/ (also **toward** /təˈwɔːd/) prep **1** in the direction of sb/sth: *walk ~ the door* **2** getting closer to achieving sth: *steps ~ unity* **3** close(r) to a point in time: *~ the end of the 19th century* **4** in relation to sb/sth: *friendly ~ tourists* **5** with the aim of obtaining sth: *The money will go ~ a new car.*

0—**towel** /ˈtaʊəl/ n [C] piece of fabric or paper for drying things, esp your body ▶ **towelling** (-l- US) n [U] thick soft cloth used for making towels

0—**tower** /ˈtaʊə(r)/ n [C] tall narrow (part of a) building, esp of a church or castle **[IDM] a tower of strength** person who can be relied on to give a lot of help or support ● **tower** v **[PV] tower over/above sb/sth** be much higher or taller than sb/sth ■ **tower block** n [C] (GB) very tall block of flats or offices ▶ **towering** adj very tall; very great

0—**town** /taʊn/ n **1** [C] place with many buildings and houses, larger than a village **2** [sing] all the people who live in a particular town **3** [U] main business or shopping area of a town: *I gave her a lift into ~.* **4** [U] particular town where sb works or lives or one which has just been referred to: *I'll be in ~ again next week.* **5** [sing,U] life in towns as opposed to life in the country [IDM] **go to town (on sth)** (infml) do sth with great energy and enthusiasm **(out) on the town** (infml) visiting restaurants, clubs, etc for entertainment, esp at night ■ **town 'clerk** n [C] official in charge of town or city records ■ **town 'council** n [C] group of officials who govern a town ■ **town 'hall** n [C] buildings with the offices of the town's local government ■ **township** n [C] (in South Africa in the past) a town where black citizens live

toxic /'tɒksɪk/ adj (fml) containing poison; poisonous

O━ toy /tɔɪ/ n [C] thing for children to play with ● **toy** v [PV] **toy with sth 1** consider an idea or plan, but not seriously **2** play with sth and move it around carelessly: ~ with a pencil

O━ trace /treɪs/ v [T] **1** discover or find sb/sth after looking for them/it carefully: I cannot ~ the letter. **2** find the origin or cause of sth **3** describe a process or the development of sth **4** follow the shape or outline of sth; draw a line or lines on sth **5** copy sth by drawing on transparent paper placed over it ● **trace** n [C,U] **1** mark, sign, etc showing that sb/sth was present in a place: ~s of an ancient civilization ◇ disappear without ~ **2** (C) very small amount of sth: ~s of poison in his blood ▸ **tracing** n [C] copy of a drawing, map, etc made by tracing (5) ■ **tracing paper** n [U] transparent paper used for making tracings

trachea /trə'kiːə/ n [C] (pl ~s or, in scientific use, ~e /-kiːiː/) (anat) tube that carries air to the lungs

O━ track /træk/ n [C] **1** rough path or road **2** [C, usu pl] series of marks left by a moving vehicle, a person or an animal **3** [C,U] rails that a train moves along **4** [C] course or circuit for racing **5** [C] piece of music or song on a record, CD or tape [IDM] **(be) hot on sb's/sth's tracks** → HOT **keep/lose track of sb/sth** have/not have information about what is happening or where sb/sth is **make tracks** (spoken) leave a place **on the right/wrong track** thinking in the right/wrong way **stop/halt sb in their tracks | stop/halt/freeze in your tracks** (infml) suddenly make sb stop by frightening or surprising them; suddenly stop because sth has frightened or surprised you: The horse stopped dead in its ~s. ● **track** v [T] follow sb/sth by following the marks, signs, etc they have left behind [PV] **track sb/sth down** find sb/sth after searching in different places ▸ **tracker** n [C] ■ **track record** n [C] past achievements of a person or organization ■ **tracksuit** n [C] loose warm suit worn by athletes, etc during training

tract /trækt/ n [C] **1** (tech) system of connected organs or tubes in the body: the respiratory ~ **2** large area of land **3** short article on a religious, political or moral subject

traction engine /'trækʃn endʒɪn/ n [C] large vehicle, driven by steam, used in the past for pulling heavy loads

tractor /'træktə(r)/ n [C] motor vehicle used for pulling farm machinery

O━ trade¹ /treɪd/ n **1** [U] business of buying, selling or exchanging goods or services **2** [C] particular type or area of business: She's in the book ~. **3** [U,C] job, esp one needing training and skill with the hands: He's a carpenter by ~. ■ **trademark** (abbr **TM**) n [C] name or symbol used on a product by a manufacturer ■ **trade name** n [C] = BRAND NAME (BRAND) ■ **tradesman** n [C] person, eg a shopkeeper, who sells goods ■ **trade union** n [C] organization of workers, formed to protect their interests and get better working conditions ■ **trade 'unionist** n [C] member of a trade union

O━ trade² /treɪd/ v **1** [I,T] ~ (in) buy and sell things **2** [T] ~ (for) exchange sth for sth else: to ~ secrets [PV] **trade sth in (for sth)** give sth used in part payment for sth new **trade on sth** take unfair advantage of sth ▸ **trader** n [C]

O━ tradition /trə'dɪʃn/ n [C,U] (set of) customs, beliefs or practices passed from one generation to the next ▸ **traditional** /-ʃənl/ adj ▸ **traditionally** adv

O━ traffic /'træfɪk/ n [U] **1** vehicles on a road at a particular time **2** movement of ships or aircraft along a route **3** movement of people or goods from one place to another: commuter ~ **4** ~ (in) illegal trade in sth ● **traffic** v (-ck-) [PV] **traffic in sth** buy and sell sth illegally ▸ **trafficker** n [C] ■ **traffic island** n [C] raised area for pedestrians in the middle of a busy road ■ **traffic jam** n [C] long line of vehicles on a road that cannot move or can only move very slowly ■ **traffic light** n [C, usu pl] set of coloured lights that control the flow of traffic at a road junction ■ **traffic warden** n [C] person whose job is to check that people do not park their cars in the wrong place

tragedy /'trædʒədi/ n (pl -ies) [C,U] **1** very sad event or situation, esp one involving death **2** serious play with a sad ending; plays of this type

tragic /'trædʒɪk/ adj **1** making you feel very sad, usu because sb has died: a ~ accident **2** connected with tragedy (2) ▸ **tragically** /-kli/ adv

trail

trail /treɪl/ n [C] **1** line, sign, series of marks, etc left by sb/sth showing where they have been **2** path through the countryside **[IDM] (be) hot on sb's trail** → HOT ● **trail** v **1** [I,T] (cause sth to) be pulled along behind sb/sth, usu along the ground **2** [I] walk slowly because you are tired or bored, esp behind sb else **3** [I] ~ **(by/in)** lose in a game, etc **4** [T] follow sb/sth by looking for signs they have left behind **5** [I] (of plants) grow along the ground or hang down loosely ▸ **trailer** n [C] **1** truck or container with wheels, that is pulled along by another vehicle **2** (US) vehicle without an engine, that can be pulled by a car or truck or used as a home when it is parked **3** series of short pieces from a new film, shown to advertise it

0-w **train**[1] /treɪn/ n [C] **1** line of carriages or trucks joined together and pulled along by a railway engine **2** number of people or animals moving in a line **3** series of connected things: a ~ of thought **4** part of a long dress that spreads out on the ground behind the wearer

0-w **train**[2] /treɪn/ v [I,T] **1** receive or give sb teaching, practice or exercise: a football team **2** [T] make a plant grow in a certain direction: ~ roses up a wall **[PV]** **train sth at/on sb/ sth** (written) aim a gun, camera, etc at sb/sth ▸ **trainee** /ˌtreɪˈniː/ n [C] person being taught how to do a particular job ▸ **trainer** n [C] **1** [usu pl] shoe worn for sports or as a piece of informal clothing **2** person who trains people or animals ▸ **training** n [U] preparation; practice

traipse /treɪps/ v [I] (infml) walk in a tired way

trait /treɪt/ n [C] particular quality in your personality

traitor /ˈtreɪtə(r)/ n [C] person who betrays their country, friends, etc

tram /træm/ n [C] passenger vehicle powered by electricity that runs on rails set in the road

tramp /træmp/ v [I,T] walk with heavy or noisy steps, esp for a long time ● **tramp** n [sing] **1** person with no house or job who travels from place to place **2** [sing] (the tramp of sb/ sth) sound of sb's heavy footsteps

trample /ˈtræmpl/ v **1** [I,T] ~ **(on/ over)** step heavily on sb/sth so that you crush or harm them/it with your feet **2** [I] ~ **(on/over)** treat sb's rights or feelings and treat them as if they were unimportant

trampoline /ˈtræmpəliːn/ n [C] strong cloth held by springs in a frame, on which gymnasts jump up and down

trance /trɑːns/ n [C] sleep-like condition of the mind

tranquil /ˈtræŋkwɪl/ adj (fml) calm; quiet ▸ **tranquillity** (US also -l-) /-ˈkwɪləti/ n [U] calm quiet state ▸ **tranquillize** (also -ise) (US also -l-) v [T] make a person or animal calm, esp by giving them a drug ▸ **tranquillizer** (also -iser) (US also -l-) n [C] drug used to reduce anxiety ▸ **tranquilly** adv

transact /trænˈzækt/ v [T] (fml) do business with a person or an organization ▸ **transaction** /-ˈzækʃn/ n **1** [C] piece of business done between people **2** [U] (fml) ~ **of** process of doing sth

transatlantic /ˌtrænzətˈlæntɪk/ adj of travelling or communications across the Atlantic Ocean

transcend /trænˈsend/ v [T] (fml) be or go beyond the usual limits of sth: ~ human knowledge

transcontinental /ˌtrænzˌkɒntɪˈnentl/ adj crossing a continent

transcribe /trænˈskraɪb/ v [T] **1** record thoughts, speech or data in written form **2** (tech) show the sounds of speech using a phonetic alphabet: ~d in phonetic symbols **3** arrange a piece of music so that it can be played by a different instrument, etc ▸ **transcript** /ˈtrænskrɪpt/ n [C] written or printed copy of words that have been spoken ▸ **transcription** /-ˈskrɪpʃn/ n [U, C]

0-w **transfer**[1] /trænsˈfɜː(r)/ v (-rr-) **1** [I,T] move from one place, job, etc to another: He was ~red to the sales department. **2** [T] give the possession of sth to sb else ▸ **transferable** adj that can be transferred (2): This ticket is not ~able. ▸ **transference** /ˈtrænsfərəns/ n [U]

0-w **transfer**[2] /ˈtrænsfɜː(r)/ n **1** [U,C] (instance of) moving sb/sth from one place, job, etc to another **2** [C] design that can be transferred from one surface and stuck onto another

transfix /trænsˈfɪks/ v [T] (fml) (usu passive) make sb unable to move, think or speak because of fear, astonishment, etc

0-w **transform** /trænsˈfɔːm/ v [T] completely change the appearance or character of sth ▸ **transformation** /-məˈmeɪʃn/ n [C, U] ▸ **transformer** n [C] apparatus that changes the voltage of an electric current

transfusion /trænsˈfjuːʒn/ n [C, U] act or process of putting one person's blood into sb else's body

transgress /trænzˈgres/ v [I,T] (fml) go beyond the limit of what is morally or legally acceptable ▸ **transgression** /-ˈgreʃn/ n [C, U]

transient /ˈtrænziənt/ *adj* lasting for only a short time

transistor /trænˈzɪstə(r); -ˈsɪst-/ *n* [C] **1** small electronic device used in computers, radios, etc for controlling the electric current **2** (*also* **transistor** (**radio**)) small radio with transistors ▸ **transistorized** /-təraɪzd/ *adj* having transistors

transit /ˈtrænzɪt; -sɪt/ *n* [U] process of travelling or being moved from one place to another: *goods damaged in ~*

transition /trænˈzɪʃn; -ˈsɪʃn/ *n* [U,C] (instance of) changing from one state or condition to another ▸ **transitional** /-ʃənl/ *adj*

transitive /ˈtrænsətɪv/ *adj* (*gram*) (of a verb) used with a direct object, eg *washed* in 'He washed the cups.'

transitory /ˈtrænsətri/ *adj* lasting for only a short time

0— **translate** /trænsˈleɪt/ *v* [I,T] **1** put sth written or spoken into a different language: ~ (*the book*) *from French into Russian* **2** ~ (**into**) (cause sth to) be changed into a different form: ~ *words into action* ▸ **translation** /-ˈleɪʃn/ *n* [C,U] ▸ **translator** *n* [C]

translucent /trænsˈluːsnt/ *adj* allowing light to pass through, but not transparent

transmission /trænsˈmɪʃn/ *n* (*fml*) **1** [U] act of passing sth from one trapdoor, place or thing to another: *the ~ of the disease* **2** [C] television or radio broadcast **3** [U,C] parts of a vehicle that pass power to the wheels

transmit /trænsˈmɪt/ *v* (**-tt-**) [T] **1** send an electronic signal, radio or television broadcast, etc **2** pass sth from one person to another: *sexually ~ted diseases* ▸ **transmitter** *n* [C] device that transmits radio or television signals

transnational /ˌtrænzˈnæʃnəl/ *adj* (*business*) operating in or between many different countries, without being based in any particular one

0— **transparent** /trænsˈpærənt/ *adj* **1** (of glass, plastic, etc) allowing you to see through it: *Glass is ~.* **2** easily understood; obvious ▸ **transparency** /-rənsi/ *n* (pl **-ies**) **1** [C] small piece of photographic film in a frame **2** [U] quality of being transparent ▸ **transparently** *adv*

transplant /trænsˈplɑːnt; trænz-/ *v* [T] **1** take an organ, skin, etc from one person, animal, part of the body, etc and put it into or onto another **2** move a growing plant and plant it somewhere else **3** (*fml*) move sb/sth to a different place or environment ▸ **transplant** /ˈtrænsplɑːnt; ˈtrænz-/ *n* **1** [C,U] medical operation in which a damaged organ, etc is replaced with

another: *have a heart ~* **2** organ, etc that is used in a transplant operation

0— **transport** /trænˈspɔːt/ *v* [T] move goods or people from one place to another ● **transport** /ˈtrænspɔːt; *esp US* transportation /ˌtrænspɔːˈteɪʃn/ *n* [U] **1** (system for) carrying people or goods from one place to another **2** vehicle or method of travel ▸ **transporter** *n* [C] large vehicle used for carrying cars

transpose /trænˈspəʊz/ *v* [T] **1** (*fml*) change the order of two or more things **2** (*fml*) move sth to a different place or change sth into a different form **3** (*music*) write or play a piece of music in a different key[1](5) ▸ **transposition** /ˌtrænspəˈzɪʃn/ *n* [C,U]

transverse /ˈtrænzvɜːs/ *adj* (*tech*) situated across sth ▸ **transversely** *adv*

transvestite /trænzˈvestaɪt/ *n* [C] person who enjoys wearing the clothes of the opposite sex

0— **trap** /træp/ *n* [C] **1** device for catching animals **2** plan for catching or deceiving sb **3** light two-wheeled carriage **4** (*sl*) mouth ● **trap** *v* (**-pp-**) [T] **1** keep sb in a dangerous place, etc that they want to get out of but cannot **2** catch an animal in a trap **3** trick or deceive sb ■ **trapdoor** *n* [C] small door in a floor or ceiling ▸ **trapper** *n* [C] person who catches animals

trapeze /trəˈpiːz/ *n* [C] bar hung from two ropes, used by acrobats for swinging on

trash /træʃ/ *n* [U] **1** (*US*) = RUBBISH **2** (*infml*) material, writing, etc of very low quality ■ **trash can** *n* [C] (*US*) = DUSTBIN (DUST) ▸ **trashy** *adj* (**-ier, -iest**) (*infml*) of very low quality

trauma /ˈtrɔːmə/ *n* **1** [C,U] emotional shock producing a lasting harmful effect **2** [C,U] (*infml*) very upsetting, unpleasant experience ▸ **traumatic** /trɔːˈmætɪk/ *adj*

0— **travel** /ˈtrævl/ *v* (**-ll-** *US* **-l-**) **1** [I,T] go from one place to another, esp over a long distance: ~ *abroad/across Africa/around the world* **2** [I] move or go at a particular speed or in a particular direction: *Light ~s faster than sound.* ● **travel** *n* **1** [U] act or activity of travelling: *space ~* **2** (**travels**) [pl] time spent travelling, esp for pleasure ■ **travel agent** *n* [C] person whose job is to make arrangements for people wanting to travel ▸ **travelled** (*US* **-l-**) *adj* (of a person) having travelled the amount mentioned: *a well-~ writer* ▸ **traveller** (*US* **-l-**) *n* **1** person who is travelling or who often travels **2** (*GB*) person who does not live in one place, but who travels around, esp as part of a group ■ **traveller's cheque** n [C] cheque that can be exchanged abroad for the money of the country you are in

traverse /trə'vɜːs/ v [T] (fml) cross an area of land or water

travesty /'trævəsti/ n [C] (pl **-ies**) very bad imitation or representation of sth: a ~ of justice

trawl /trɔːl/ v [I,T] fish with a large wide net dragged along the bottom of the sea ▶ **trawler** n [C] fishing boat used for trawling

tray /treɪ/ n [C] flat piece of wood, plastic, etc, used for carrying things, esp food

treacherous /'tretʃərəs/ adj **1** disloyal or deceitful **2** dangerous: ~ tides ▶ **treacherously** adv ▶ **treachery** /-tʃəri/ n [U,C] (pl **-ies**)

treacle /'triːkl/ n [U] thick sticky liquid made from sugar ▶ **treacly** adj

tread /tred/ v (pt **trod** /trɒd/ pp **trodden** /'trɒdn/) **1** [I] put your foot down while stepping or walking **2** [T] press or crush sth with your feet **3** [I,T] walk somewhere [IDM] **tread on sb's toes** (infml) offend sb **tread water** keep yourself upright in water by moving your legs up and down ● **tread** n **1** [sing] way sb walks or the sound sb makes when they walk **2** [C] raised pattern on a tyre of a vehicle **3** [C] upper surface of a step or stair

treason /'triːzn/ n [U] crime of betraying your country, eg by helping its enemies ▶ **treasonable** /-zənəbl/ adj: a ~able offence

treasure /'treʒə(r)/ n **1** [U] collection of gold and silver, jewels, etc **2** [C] highly valued object or person ● **treasure** v [T] have or keep sth that is extremely valuable to you ▶ **treasurer** n [C] person in charge of the money, accounts, etc of an organization ■ **treasure trove** /trəʊv/ n [U] treasure found hidden and claimed by no one

treasury /'treʒəri/ n (the Treasury) [sing, with sing or pl verb] government department that controls public money

0-w treat /triːt/ v [T] **1** behave in a particular way towards sb/sth: They ~ their children badly. **2** consider or deal with sth in a particular way: ~ it as a joke **3** give medical care to a person, an injury, etc: ~ a patient **4** use a chemical substance to clean, protect, preserve, etc sth: ~ crops with insecticide **5** pay for sth that sb/you will enjoy and that they/you do not usu have or do ● **treat** n [C] sth very pleasant or enjoyable, esp sth that you give sb or do for them

treatise /'triːtɪs, -tɪz/ n [C] long formal written work on one subject

0-w treatment /'triːtmənt/ n [U,C] way of treating a person or thing: medical ~

treaty /'triːti/ n [C] (pl **-ies**) formal agreement between countries: a peace ~

treble /'trebl/ det three times as much or as many: He earns ~ my salary. ● **treble** n **1** [U] high tones or part in music or a sound system **2** [C] (boy who sings with a) child's high voice ● **treble** v [I,T] become or make sth three times as much or as many ● **treble** adj high in tone: a ~ recorder

0-w tree /triː/ n [C] tall plant with a wooden trunk and branches ▶ **treeless** adj without trees

trek /trek/ v (**-kk-**) [I] n [C] (make a) long hard journey, esp on foot

trellis /'trelɪs/ n [C] light wooden framework used for supporting climbing plants

tremble /'trembl/ v [I] **1** shake uncontrollably from fear or cold **2** shake slightly: The leaves ~d in the breeze. **3** be very anxious ● **tremble** n [C, usu sing] feeling, movement or sound of trembling: a ~ in her voice

tremendous /trə'mendəs/ adj **1** very great: a ~ explosion **2** extremely good ▶ **tremendously** adv

tremor /'tremə(r)/ n [C] **1** small earthquake: earth ~s **2** slight shaking movement in a part of your body

trench /trentʃ/ n [C] long narrow channel dug in the ground, eg for drainage or to protect soldiers

0-w trend /trend/ n [C] general change or development: the ~ towards smaller families ■ **trendsetter** n [C] person who starts a new fashion or makes it popular ▶ **trendy** adj (**-ier, -iest**) (infml) very fashionable

trespass /'trespas/ v [I] ~ (**on**) go on sb's private land without their permission ▶ **trespass** n [U,C] ▶ **trespasser** n [C]

trestle /'tresl/ n [C] wooden or metal structure with legs, used for supporting a flat surface ■ **trestle table** n [C] table supported on trestles

0-w trial /'traɪəl/ n [C,U] **1** examination in a law court before a judge (and jury) to decide if sb is guilty or innocent: He's on ~ for murder. **2** [C,U] (act of) testing how good sth is **3** [C] cause of worry or difficulty [IDM] **on trial 1** being tried in a law court **2** being tested and examined **trial and error** process of solving a problem by trying various methods until you find one that is successful ■ **trial run** n [C] test of how well sth new works

0→ **triangle** /'traɪæŋgl/ n [C] flat shape with three straight sides and three angles ▶ **triangular** /-'æŋgjələ(r)/ adj

tribe /traɪb/ n [C] group of people of the same race, customs, language, etc living in a particular area, often under the rule of a chief ▶ **tribal** adj ■ **tribesman** /ˈtraɪbzmən/ **tribeswoman** n [C] member of a tribe

tribunal /traɪˈbjuːnl/ n [C] type of court with the authority to settle certain kinds of problems

tributary /ˈtrɪbjətri/ n [C] (pl -ies) river or stream that flows into a larger river or a lake

tribute /ˈtrɪbjuːt/ n [C,U] act, statement or gift intended to show your respect or admiration for sb: *pay ~ to her courage*

0→ **trick** /trɪk/ n [C] 1 something done to deceive sb or to annoy them as a joke: *play a ~ on sb* 2 clever or skilful action intended to entertain people: *conjuring ~s* 3 way of doing sth that works well 4 cards played or won in one round of a game [IDM] **do the trick** (infml) succeed in doing what is needed or wanted ● **trick** v [T] deceive sb: *He was ~ed into giving away all his money.* ▶ **trickery** n [U] (written) deception; cheating ▶ **tricky** adj (-ier, -iest) 1 difficult to do or deal with: *a ~y situation* 2 (of a person) deceitful

trickle /ˈtrɪkl/ v [I] flow in a thin stream: *Tears ~d down her cheek.* ● **trickle** n [C] slow or thin flow of sth: *a ~ of blood*

tricycle /ˈtraɪsɪkl/ n [C] vehicle like a bicycle, but with one wheel at the front and two behind

tried pt, pp of TRY¹

trifle /ˈtraɪfl/ n 1 (a trifle) [sing] (fml) small amount 2 [C] thing of little value or importance 3 [C,U] sweet dish made of cream, cake, jelly, etc [IDM] **a trifle** (fml) slightly: *They felt a ~ sad.* ● **trifle** v [I] [PV] **trifle with sb/ sth** (fml) treat sb/sth without genuine respect ▶ **trifling** adj unimportant

trigger /ˈtrɪgə(r)/ n [C] part of a gun that you press in order to fire it ● **trigger** v [T] ~ (**off**) make sth happen suddenly

trill /trɪl/ n [C] 1 repeated short high sound made, esp by a bird's voice or a bird 2 (music) quick repeated playing of two different notes ● **trill** v [I,T] sound or sing with a trill

trilogy /ˈtrɪlədʒi/ n [C] (pl -ies) group of three related books, plays, etc

trim /trɪm/ v (-**mm**-) [T] 1 make sth neater, smaller, better, etc by cutting parts from it 2 decorate sth, esp around its edges ● **trim** n [C,U, usu sing] act of cutting a small amount

off sth, esp hair [IDM] **in** (**good, etc**) **trim** (infml) in good condition or order ● **trim** adj (~**mer, ~mest**) (approv) 1 (of a person) looking slim and attractive 2 neat and tidy ▶ **trimming** n (trimmings) [pl] extra things that it is traditional to have with a meal, etc: *roast beef with all the ~mings* (= vegetables, sauce, etc) 2 [U,C, usu pl] material used to decorate sth, eg along its edges

trimester /traɪˈmestə(r)/ n [C] (US) = TERM(2)

trinity /ˈtrɪnəti/ n [sing] (**the Trinity**) (in Christianity) union of Father, Son and Holy Spirit as one God

trinket /ˈtrɪŋkɪt/ n [C] small piece of jewellery, etc of little value

trio /ˈtriːəʊ/ n [C] (pl ~**s**) 1 group of three people or things 2 (music for) a group of three players or singers

0→ **trip** /trɪp/ n [C] 1 (usu short) journey to a place and back again, esp for pleasure 2 (sl) experience caused by taking a drug causing hallucinations 3 act of falling down ● **trip** v (-**pp**-) 1 [I] ~ (**over/up**) catch your foot on sth and fall all over 2 [T] ~ (**up**) catch sb's foot and make them fall or almost fall 3 [I] (lit) move with quick light steps [PV] **trip** (**sb**) **up** (deliberately cause sb) to make a mistake ▶ **tripper** n [C] person visiting a place for a short time for pleasure

tripartite /traɪˈpɑːtaɪt/ adj (fml) having three parts or groups

tripe /traɪp/ n [U] 1 lining of a cow's or pig's stomach, used as food 2 (infml) nonsense

triple /ˈtrɪpl/ adj having three parts or involving three people or groups ● **triple** v [I,T] become or make sth three times as much or as many

triplet /ˈtrɪplət/ n [C] one of three children born to the same mother at one time

triplicate /ˈtrɪplɪkət/ n [IDM] **in triplicate** 1 done three times 2 (of documents) copied twice, so that there are three copies in total

tripod /ˈtraɪpɒd/ n [C] support with three legs, eg for a camera

trite /traɪt/ adj uninteresting and not original

triumph /ˈtraɪʌmf/ n 1 [C] great achievement or success 2 [U] feeling of joy and satisfaction that you get from a great success or victory ● **triumph** v [I] ~ (**over**) defeat sb/ sth; be successful ▶ **triumphal** /-ˈʌmfl/ adj done to celebrate a great success or victory ▶ **triumphant** /-ˈʌmfənt/ adj showing great joy and satisfaction because you have triumphed ▶ **triumphantly** adv

trivia /ˈtrɪviə/ n [U] unimportant matters, details or information

trivial /ˈtrɪvɪəl/ *adj* not important or serious; not worth considering ▶ **triviality** /ˌtrɪviˈæləti/ *n* [C,U] (pl **-ies**) ▶ **trivialize** (*also* **-ise**) *v* [T] make sth seem less important, etc than it really is

trod *pt* of TREAD

trodden *pp* of TREAD

trolley /ˈtrɒli/ *n* [C] **1** small vehicle with wheels that is pushed by hand and used for carrying things: *a supermarket ~* **2** small table on wheels for serving food **3** (*US*) = TRAM

trombone /trɒmˈbəʊn/ *n* [C] brass musical instrument with a sliding tube ▶ **trombonist** /-ɪst/ *n* [C] person who plays the trombone

troop /truːp/ *n* **1** (troops) [pl] soldiers, esp in a large group **2** [C] group of people or animals ● **troop** *v* [I] walk somewhere together as a group ▶ **trooper** *n* [C] soldier of low rank in the part of an army that uses tanks or horses

trophy /ˈtrəʊfi/ *n* [C] (pl **-ies**) **1** prize given for winning a competition **2** something kept as a reminder of a victory or success

tropic /ˈtrɒpɪk/ *n* **1** [C, usu sing] one of the two imaginary lines drawn around the world 23°26′ north (the Tropic of Cancer) or south (the Tropic of Capricorn) of the equator **2** (the tropics) [pl] area between the two tropics, which is the hottest part of the world

0→ tropical /ˈtrɒpɪkl/ *adj* of the tropics: *~ fish/islands*

trot /trɒt/ *v* (**-tt-**) [I] **1** (of a horse or its rider) move fairly quickly, at a speed faster than a walk but slower than a gallop **2** run with short steps [PV] **trot sth out** (*infml, disapprov*) give the same facts, explanations, etc that have often been used before: *~ out the same old excuses* ● **trot** *n* [sing] trotting phase [IDM] **on the trot** (*infml*) one after the other

0→ trouble /ˈtrʌbl/ *n* **1** [C,U] (situation causing a) problem, worry or difficulty: *You shouldn't have any~ finding the house.* **2** [U] illness; pain: *heart ~* **3** [U] something that is wrong with a machine, vehicle, etc: *engine ~* **4** [U] situation that is difficult or dangerous; situation in which you might be criticized or punished: *A yachtsman got into ~ off the coast and had to be rescued.* ◇ *He's always in ~ with the police.* **5** [C,U] angry or violent situation: *the ~s in Northern Ireland* **6** [U] extra work or effort: *I don't want to put you to any ~.* [IDM] **get into trouble** **1** have serious difficulties **2** do sth deserving punishment **get sb into trouble** (*infml*) make (an unmarried

woman) pregnant **take the trouble to do sth** do sth even though it involves effort ● **trouble** *v* **1** [T] make sb worried or upset **2** [T] (*fml*) (used in polite requests) disturb sb because you want to ask them sth: *I'm sorry to ~ you, but could you tell me the way to the station?* **3** [I] (*fml*) make an effort; bother ▶ **troubled** *adj* worried ■ **troublemaker** *n* [C] person who causes trouble ▶ **troublesome** *adj* causing trouble, pain, etc over a long time

trough /trɒf/ *n* [C] **1** long narrow container for animals to feed or drink from **2** low area between two waves **3** area of low air pressure

troupe /truːp/ *n* [C, with sing or pl verb] group of actors, dancers, etc

0→ trousers /ˈtraʊzəz/ *n* [pl] (*esp GB*) piece of clothing that covers the body from the waist down and is divided into two to cover each leg separately: *a pair of ~*

trout /traʊt/ *n* [C,U] (pl **trout**) common freshwater fish that is used for food

trowel /ˈtraʊəl/ *n* [C] **1** small garden tool with a curved blade **2** small tool with a flat blade, used for spreading cement, etc

truant /ˈtruːənt/ *n* [C] child who stays away from school without permission: *play (= be a) ~* ▶ **truancy** /-ənsi/ *n* [U]

truce /truːs/ *n* [C] agreement between enemies to stop fighting for a period of time

0→ truck /trʌk/ *n* [C] **1** (*esp US*) = LORRY **2** (*GB*) open railway vehicle for carrying goods or animals **3** vehicle that is open at the back, esp for carrying goods, etc: *a farm ~* [IDM] **have/want no truck with sb/sth** refuse to deal with sb; refuse to consider sth

trudge /trʌdʒ/ *v* [I,T] walk slowly or with difficulty ● **trudge** *n* [C, usu sing] long tiring walk

0→ true /truː/ *adj* (**~r**, **~st**) **1** connected with facts rather than things that have been invented or guessed: *Is it ~ she's leaving?* **2** real: *my ~ feelings for you* **3** faithful; loyal: *a ~ friend* **4** being an accurate version or copy of sth: *a ~ copy* [IDM] **come true** (of a hope, dream, etc.) become reality **true to form** behaving as you would expect sb to behave, esp when this is annoying ● **true** *n* [IDM] **out of true** not straight or in the correct position

0→ truly /ˈtruːli/ *adv* sincerely: *feel ~ grateful* **2** really: *a ~ brave action*

trump /trʌmp/ *n* [C] (*also* **'trump card**) (in some card games) card of a suit that is chosen to have a higher value in a game [IDM] **come up/turn up trumps** (*infml*) be unexpectedly helpful or generous ● **trump** *v* [T] (in some games) play a trump card that beats sb else's card [PV] **trump sth up** (usu passive) invent a false accusation: *~ed-up charges* • **trump card** *n* [C] **1** = TRUMP **2** something that gives you an advantage over others

trumpet /ˈtrʌmpɪt/ *n* [C] brass musical instrument with a long curved tube that you blow into • **trumpet** *v* **1** [I,T] declare sth loudly **2** [I] (of an elephant) make a loud noise ▸ **trumpeter** *n* [C] trumpet player

truncate /trʌŋˈkeɪt/ *v* [T] shorten sth by cutting off the top or end

truncheon /ˈtrʌntʃən/ *n* [C] (*esp GB*) short thick stick carried as a weapon by a police officer

trundle /ˈtrʌndl/ *v* [I,T] (cause sth to) roll or move somewhere slowly and noisily

trunk /trʌŋk/ *n* **1** [C] thick main stem of a tree **2** [C] (*US*) = BOOT(2) **3** [C] long nose of an elephant **4** (**trunks**) [pl] shorts worn by men or boys for swimming **5** [C] large strong box for storing or transporting clothes, etc **6** [C, usu sing] human body apart from the head, arms and legs • **trunk road** *n* [C] (*GB*) important main road

truss /trʌs/ *v* [T] **1** tie up sb's arms and legs so that they cannot move **2** tie the legs and wings of a chicken, etc before cooking it • **truss** *n* [C] **1** padded belt worn by sb suffering from a hernia **2** framework supporting a roof, bridge, etc

⚬▬ **trust¹** /trʌst/ *n* **1** [U] ~ **(in)** belief that sb/sth is good, sincere, etc and will not try to harm or deceive you **2** [C,U] (*law*) (arrangement for the) holding and managing of money or property for others: *money kept in a ~* **3** [C] (*money*) organization, etc that invests money that is given or lent to it and uses the profits to help a charity [IDM] **take sth on trust** believe sth without proof ▸ **trusting** *adj* ready to trust others ▸ **trustingly** *adv* ▸ **trustworthy** *adj* reliable ▸ **trusty** *adj* (-**ier**, -**iest**) (*old-fash or hum*) that you have had for a long time and have always been able to rely on

⚬▬ **trust²** /trʌst/ *v* [T] **1** have confidence in, believe that sb is good, sincere, etc: *You can ~ me.* **2** believe that sth is true or correct or can be relied on: *He ~ed her judgement.* **3** (*fml*) hope and expect that sth is true: *I ~ you are well.*

trustee /trʌˈstiː/ *n* [C] person or organization that has control of money, etc that has been put into a trust for sb

⚬▬ **truth** /truːθ/ *n* (pl ~**s** /truːðz/) **1** [sing] true facts about sth, rather than things that have been invented or guessed: *tell the ~* **2** [U] quality or state of being based on fact: *There's*

not a grain of ~ in what he says. **3** [C] fact that is generally accepted as true: *scientific* ~**s** ▸ **truthful** *adj* **1** (of a person) saying only what is true **2** (of a statement) giving only the true facts about sth ▸ **truthfully** *adv* ▸ **truthfulness** *n* [U]

⚬▬ **try¹** /traɪ/ *v* (pt, pp **tried**) **1** make an attempt to do or get sth: *He tried to escape.* **2** [T] use, do or test sth to see if it is satisfactory, enjoyable, etc: *Have you tried this new soap?* **3** [T] ~ **(for)** examine and decide a case in a law court: *He was tried for murder.* [IDM] **tried and tested/trusted** (*US*) **tried and true** that you have used or relied on successfully in the past **try your hand (at sth)** attempt to do sth **try it on (with sb)** (*GB, infml*) behave badly towards sb or try to get sth from them, even though this will make them angry **try sb's patience** make sb feel impatient [PV] **try sth on** put on a piece of clothing to see if it fits and how it looks **try sb/sth out (on sb)** test or use sb/sth to see how good or effective they are ▸ **trying** *adj* annoying or difficult to deal with

try² /traɪ/ *n* [C] (pl -**ies**) **1** [usu sing] attempt **2** (in rugby) points scored by a player touching the ball down behind the opponents' goal

tsar /zɑː(r)/ *n* [C] title of the emperor of Russia in the past ▸ **tsarina** /zɑːˈriːnə/ *n* [C] title of the empress of Russia in the past

tsetse fly /ˈtsetsi flaɪ/ *n* [C] African fly that bites humans and animals and can cause a serious disease called 'sleeping sickness'

T-shirt → **T, t**

tsunami /tsuːˈnɑːmi/ *n* [C] very large wave in the sea, often caused by an earthquake, which destroys things when it reaches the land

tub /tʌb/ *n* [C] **1** open container, used for washing clothes in, etc **2** small plastic or paper container with a lid, used for food, etc: *a ~ of margarine* **3** (*esp US*) = BATH(1)

tuba /ˈtjuːbə/ *n* [C] brass musical instrument that you play by blowing and that produces low notes

tubby /ˈtʌbi/ *adj* (-**ier**, -**iest**) (*infml*) (of a person) short and fat

⚬▬ **tube** /tjuːb/ *n* **1** [C] long hollow pipe of rubber, plastic, etc, esp for carrying liquids **2** [C] soft metal or plastic container for pastes, paints, etc **3** [C] hollow tube-shaped organ in the body **4** (**the tube**) [sing] (*GB*) (in London) underground railway system ▸ **tubing** *n* [U] metal, plastic, etc in the shape of a tube ▸ **tubular** /ˈtjuːbjələ(r)/ *adj* made of or shaped like tubes

tuber /'tju:bə(r)/ *n* [C] short thick rounded part of an underground stem on some plants, eg potatoes

tuberculosis /tju:ˌbɜːkjʊ'ləʊsɪs/ *n* [U] (*abbr* **TB**) serious infectious disease that affects the lungs

TUC /ˌtiː juː 'siː/ *abbr* Trades Union Congress; organization to which many British trade unions belong

tuck /tʌk/ *v* [T] **1** push the loose ends of sth into sth else so that it is tidy: *He ~ed his shirt into his trousers.* **2** put sth in a tidy, comfortable or hidden position [PV] **tuck in**| **tuck into sth** (*infml*) eat food eagerly **tuck sb in/up** make sb feel comfortable in bed by pulling the covers up around them ● **tuck** *n* [C] **1** fold sewn into a piece of clothing **2** medical operation in which skin and/or fat is removed, to make sb look thinner or younger

○▬ **Tuesday** /'tjuːzdeɪ, -di/ *n* [C,U] the third day of the week, next after Monday (See examples of use at *Monday*.)

tuft /tʌft/ *n* [C] bunch of hair, grass, etc

tug /tʌg/ *v* (**-gg-**) [I,T] ~ **(at)** pull sth hard, often several times ● **tug** *n* [C] **1** (*also* **tugboat**) small powerful boat that pulls ships into harbours **2** sudden hard pull

tuition /tju'ɪʃn/ *n* [U] (*fml*) (fee for) teaching sth: *have private ~*

tulip /'tjuːlɪp/ *n* [C] large brightly coloured spring flower, shaped like a cup, on a tall stem

tumble /'tʌmbl/ *v* **1** [I,T] (cause sb to) fall downwards **2** [I] ~ **(down)** fall suddenly and dramatically **3** [I] move or fall somewhere in a relaxed, uncontrolled way [PV] **tumble to sth/ sb** (*infml*) suddenly understand sth ● **tumble** *n* [C, usu sing] fall ■ **tumbledown** *adj* falling to pieces ■ **tumble 'dryer** | **tumble-'drier** *n* [C] machine for drying washed clothes

tumbler /'tʌmblə(r)/ *n* [C] straight-sided drinking glass

tummy /'tʌmi/ *n* [C] (*pl* **-ies**) (*infml*) stomach

tumour (*US* **-or**) /'tjuːmə(r)/ *n* [C] mass of diseased cells growing in the body

tumult /'tjuːmʌlt/ *n* [U,C, usu sing] (*fml*) **1** noisy confusion involving a large number of people **2** confused state ▶ **tumultuous** /tjuː'mʌltʃuəs/ *adj* (*fml*) very loud; involving strong feelings, esp of approval: *~uous applause*

tuna /'tjuːnə/ *n* [C,U] (*pl* **tuna** or **~s**) large sea fish eaten as food

○▬ **tune** /tjuːn/ *n* [C] series of musical notes that are sung or played in a particular order [IDM] **be in/out of tune (with sb/sth)** be/not be in

agreement with sb/sth **in/out of tune** be/not be singing or playing the correct musical notes to sound pleasant **to the tune of sth** (*infml*) used to emphasize how much money sth cost: *I was fined to the ~ of £1000.* ● **tune** *v* [T] **1** adjust a musical instrument to the correct pitch **2** adjust an engine so that it runs smoothly **3** ~ **(in)** adjust the controls on a radio or television so that you can receive a particular programme or channel [PV] **tune in (to sth)** listen to or watch a radio or television programme ▶ **tuneful** *adj* having a pleasant tune ▶ **tunefully** *adv* ▶ **tuner** *n* [C] person who tunes musical instruments, esp pianos ■ **'tuning fork** *n* [C] small steel fork that produces a certain musical note when you hit it

tunic /'tjuːnɪk/ *n* [C] **1** loose piece of clothing covering the body down to the knees, as worn in ancient Greece **2** (*GB*) tightly fitting jacket worn as part of a uniform by police officers, soldiers, etc

○▬ **tunnel** /'tʌnl/ *n* [C] underground passage, eg for a road or railway ● **tunnel** *v* (**-ll-** *US* **-l-**) [I,T] dig a tunnel under or through the ground

turban /'tɜːbən/ *n* [C] head covering worn by a Muslim or Sikh man, consisting of a long cloth wound round the head

turbine /'tɜːbaɪn/ *n* [C] engine driven by a wheel that is turned by a current of water, steam, air or gas

turbulent /'tɜːbjələnt/ *adj* confused; violent or uneven: *~ passions/seas* ▶ **turbulence** /-ləns/ *n* [U]

tureen /tjʊ'riːn, tə'-/ *n* [C] large deep dish from which soup or vegetables are served

turf /tɜːf/ *n* (*pl* **~s** or **turves**) **1** [C,U] (cut piece of) short grass and the surface layer of soil held together by its roots **2** (the **turf**) [sing] sport of horse racing ● **turf** *v* [T] cover an area of ground with turf [PV] **turf sb out (of sth)**| **turf sb off sth** (*GB*, *infml*) force sb to leave a place, an organization, etc

turkey /'tɜːki/ *n* [C] large bird, used for food **2** [U] meat from a turkey

turmoil /'tɜːmɔɪl/ *n* [U,sing] state of confusion or disorder

○▬ **turn¹** /tɜːn/ *v* **1** [I,T] (cause sth to) move around a central point: *The Earth ~s around the sun.* ◇ *~ a key in a lock* **2** [I,T] move (a part of) your body so as to face or start moving in a different direction: *She ~ed to look at me.* ◇ *Don't ~ your back on me!* **3** [I,T] (cause sth/sb to) change the direction it/they are facing or moving in: *She ~ed the jumper inside out.* **4** [I] (of a road or river) curve in a particular direction **5** [T] aim or point sth in a particular direction: *She ~ed her attention back to me.*

6 (usu used with an adj) (cause sth to) change into a particular state or condition: *The milk has ~ed sour.* ◇ *She's just ~ed 50.* **7** [I, T] ~ (from) sth **into** (cause sth to) pass from one state to another: *Caterpillars ~ into butterflies.* [IDM] **be well, badly, etc turned out** be well, badly, etc dressed **not turn a hair** show no emotion when sth shocking, surprising, etc happens **turn your back on sb/sth** reject sb/sth that you have previously been connected with **turn a blind eye (to sth)** pretend not to notice sth bad that is happening **turn the clock back** → CLOCK **turn a deaf ear to sb/sth** ignore or refuse to listen to sb/sth **turn your hand to sth** begin to learn a practical skill **turn your nose up at sth** (*infml*) refuse sth, esp because you do not think it is good enough for you **turn over a new leaf** change the way of life to become a better, more responsible person **turn the tables (on sb)** gain an advantage over sb who had an advantage over you **turn tail** turn and run away **turn up trumps** → TRUMP [PV] **turn (sb) against sb** (cause sb to) become unfriendly or opposed to sb **turn sb away (from sth)** refuse to allow sb to enter a place **turn (sb/sth) back** return the way you have come; make sb/sth do this **turn sb/sth down** refuse sb, their offer, etc **turn sth down** adjust a cooker, radio, etc to reduce the heat, sound, etc it produces **turn sb in** (*infml*) take sb to the police to be arrested **turn sth off** stop the flow or operation of sth: *~ off the tap* **turn sb off** (*infml*) cause sb to be bored or not sexually excited **turn sth on** start the flow or operation of sth: *~ on the radio* **turn out 1** be present at an event **2** happen in the way that is mentioned: *Everything ~ed out well.* **turn sb out (of/from sth)** force sb to leave a place **turn sth out 1** switch a light or fire off **2** empty sth, esp to clean it: *~ out the cupboards* **3** produce sth: *The factory ~s out 500 cars a week.* **turn sth over 1** make sth change position so that the other side is facing upwards or outwards **2** think carefully about sth **3** do business worth the amount that is mentioned **turn sth/sb over to sb** give control of sth/sb to sb: *The thief was ~ed over to the police.* **turn to sb/sth** go to sb/sth for help, advice, etc **turn sth/sb up 1** adjust a cooker, radio, etc to

---

479

tussle

increase the heat, sound, etc ■ **'turn-off** *n* [C] road that leads away from a main road ■ **'turnout** *n* [C, usu sing, U] number of people who attend an event ■ **'turnover** *n* [sing] amount of business done by a company: *Their annual ~over is £10 million.* ■ **'turn-up** *n* [C] **1** [usu pl] folded-up end of a trouser leg **2** (*infml*) surprising and unexpected event: *He offered to help? That's a ~-up for the books!*

0— **turn²** /tɜːn/ *n* [C] **1** act of turning sb/sth around **2** change of direction in a vehicle, on a road, etc **3** time when sb in a group of people should or is allowed to do sth: *It's your ~ to choose.* **4** unusual or unexpected change in what is happening: *Business has taken a ~ for the worse.* **5** short performance or piece of entertainment **6** (*old-fash*) feeling of illness [IDM] **at every turn** everywhere or every time you try to do sth **done to a turn** (*GB*) (of food) cooked just long enough **in turn 1** one after the other **2** as a result of sth in a series of events **speak/talk out of turn** say sth that you should not because it is the wrong time or it offends **take turns (in sth/to do sth)** | **take it in turns** do sth one after the other: *The children took it in ~s to play on the swing.*

turning /ˈtɜːnɪŋ/ *n* [C] road that leads off another ■ **'turning point** *n* [C] time at which an important change happens

turnip /ˈtɜːnɪp/ *n* [C, U] round white, or white and purple, root vegetable

turnpike /ˈtɜːnpaɪk/ *n* [C] (*US*) road which drivers have to pay to use

turnstile /ˈtɜːnstaɪl/ *n* [C] entrance gate that turns in a circle when pushed and allows one person through at a time

turntable /ˈtɜːnteɪbl/ *n* [C] flat circular surface that turns round, on which a record is placed in a record player

turpentine /ˈtɜːpəntaɪn/ *n* [U] strong-smelling colourless liquid used for cleaning off or thinning paint

turquoise /ˈtɜːkwɔɪz/ *adj* greenish-blue in colour ● **turquoise** *n* [C, U] type of greenish-blue precious stone

turret /ˈtʌrət/ *n* [C] **1** small tower on top of a building **2** small metal tower on a ship, plane or tank that can turn round and from which guns are fired

turtle /ˈtɜːtl/ *n* [C] large reptile with a hard round shell, that lives in the sea

tusk /tʌsk/ *n* [C] either of a pair of very long pointed teeth of an elephant and some other animals

tussle /ˈtʌsl/ *v* [I], *n* [C] (have a) rough fight or argument

---

A B C D E F G H I J K L M N O P Q R S **T** U V W X Y Z

tut /tʌt/ (also tut-'tut) exclam used for showing disapproval, annoyance, etc

tutor /'tju:tə(r)/ n [C] **1** private teacher, esp of one pupil **2** (GB) university teacher who guides the studies of a student ● **tutor** v [I,T] teach sb or work as a tutor ▸ **tutorial** /tju:'tɔːriəl/ n [C] teaching period for a small group of students ▸ **tutorial** adj connected with the work of a tutor

tuxedo /tʌk'si:dəʊ/ n [C] (pl ~s) (US) = DINNER JACKET (DINNER)

0-w **TV** /ˌti: 'vi:/ n [C, u] television

twang /twæŋ/ n [C] **1** used to describe a way of speaking, esp one in which the sounds are produced through the nose **2** sound made when a tight string is pulled and released ● **twang** v [I,T] (cause sth to) make a twang (2)

tweak /twi:k/ v [T] **1** pull or twist sth: ~ a child's nose **2** make slight changes to a machine, system, etc to improve it ▸ **tweak** n [sing]

tweed /twi:d/ n **1** [U] thick woven woollen fabric that has small spots of different coloured thread in it **2** (tweeds) [pl] clothes made of tweed

tweet /twi:t/ n [C] short high sound made by a small bird

tweezers /'twi:zəz/ n [pl] small tool with two long thin parts joined at one end, used for pulling out or picking up very small things

0-w **twelve** /twelv/ number 12 ▸ **twelfth** /twelfθ/ ordinal number

0-w **twenty** /'twenti/ number **1** 20 **2** (the twenties) [pl] numbers, years or temperatures from 20 to 29 ▸ **twentieth** /'twentiəθ/ ordinal number

0-w **twice** /twaɪs/ adv two times: I've read this book ~. ◇ Your room is ~ as big as mine.

twiddle /'twɪdl/ v [I,T] twist or turn sth with your fingers, often because you are nervous or bored

twig /twɪg/ n [C] small thin piece of a branch of a bush or tree ● **twig** v (-gg-) [I,T] (GB, infml) suddenly realize or understand sth

twilight /'twaɪlaɪt/ n [U] (time of) faint light just after sunset

twill /twɪl/ n [U] strong woven fabric with diagonal lines

0-w **twin** /twɪn/ n [C] either of two children born to the same mother at one time ● **twin** adj similar, one of a matching pair: ~ beds (= two single beds)

twine /twaɪn/ n [U] strong string ● **twine** v [I,T] (cause sth to) twist or wind around sth

twinge /twɪndʒ/ n [C] **1** sudden sharp pain **2** ~ (of) sudden short feeling of an unpleasant emotion: a ~ of guilt

twinkle /'twɪŋkl/ v [I] **1** shine with an unsteady light: stars twinkling in the sky **2** (of sb's eyes) look bright with happiness or amusement ▸ **twinkle** n [sing]: a ~ in her eyes

twirl /twɜːl/ v [I,T] (cause sb/sth to) move or spin round and round **2** [T] curl or twist sth with your fingers ● **twirl** n [C] action of a person spinning around

0-w **twist** /twɪst/ v **1** [I,T] (cause sth to) bend or turn into a particular shape: The car was a pile of ~ed metal. **2** [I,T] turn your body, or a part of your body, around: She ~ed (her head) round. **3** [T] turn sth around in a circle with your hand: I nervously ~ed the ring on my finger. **4** [I] (of a road or river) have many bends **5** [T] injure part of your body, esp your ankle, wrist or knee, by bending it awkwardly **6** [T] wind sth around or through an object: The phone cable has got ~ed (= wound round itself). **7** [T] deliberately change the meaning of what sb has said: ~ the facts [IDM] twist sb's arm (infml) persuade or force sb to do sth **twist sb round your little finger** (infml) get sb to do anything you want ● **twist** n [C] **1** action of turning sth with your hand or turning a part of your body **2** unexpected change or development in a story or situation: by a strange ~ of fate **3** thing that has been twisted into a particular shape: mineral water with a ~ of lemon

twit /twɪt/ n [C] (GB, infml) silly or annoying person

twitch /twɪtʃ/ n [C] small sudden uncontrollable movement of the muscles ● **twitch** v **1** [I] (cause a part of the body to) make a sudden quick movement **2** [I,T] give sth a short sharp pull; be pulled in this way

twitter /'twɪtə(r)/ v [I] **1** (of a bird) make short high sounds **2** talk quickly in an excited or nervous way ▸ **twitter** n [sing]

0-w **two** /tu:/ number 2 [IDM] **put two and two together** guess the truth from what you see, hear, etc ■ ˌtwo-'faced adj (infml, disapprov) deceitful or insincere ▸ **twofold** adj, adv **1** having two parts **2** twice as many or as much ■ ˌtwo-way adj allowing movement or communication in two directions

tycoon /taɪˈkuːn/ n [C] (infml) person who is successful in business or industry and has become rich and powerful

tying → TIE[1]

0-w **type** /taɪp/ n **1** [C] (one of a) group of things or people with certain features in common; kind or sort: many different ~s of computers

2 [U] letters that are printed or typed: *italic* ~ ■ **type** *v* [I,T] write sth using a word processor or typewriter ■ **typecast** /ˈtaɪpkɑːst/ *v* (pt, pp **typecast**) [T] (usu passive) constantly give an actor the same kind of part to play ■ **typescript** *n* [C,U] typed copy of sth ■ **typewriter** *n* [C] machine that prints letters on paper by means of keys that are pressed with the fingers ■ **typing** *n* [U] activity or job of using a typewriter or word processor to write sth ■ **typist** *n* [C] person whose job is to type letters, etc in an office

typhoid /ˈtaɪfɔɪd/ *n* [U] serious infectious disease that causes fever and sometimes death

typhoon /taɪˈfuːn/ *n* [C] very violent tropical storm

typhus /ˈtaɪfəs/ *n* [U] serious infectious disease causing fever and purple spots on the body

0‒┐ **typical** /ˈtɪpɪkl/ *adj* having the usual qualities of a particular thing or person: *a* ~ *case* ▸ **typically** /-kli/ *adv*

typify /ˈtɪpɪfaɪ/ *v* (pt, pp **-ied**) [T] be a typical feature or example of sth

typist → TYPE

tyrannical /tɪˈrænɪkl/ *adj* of or like a tyrant

tyrannize (*also* **-ise**) /ˈtɪrənaɪz/ *v* [I,T] ~ **(over)** (*written*) use your power to treat sb cruelly and unfairly

tyranny /ˈtɪrəni/ *n* [U] unfair or cruel use of power or authority

tyrant /ˈtaɪrənt/ *n* [C] person who has complete power in a country and uses it in a cruel and unfair way

0‒┐ **tyre** /ˈtaɪə(r)/ *n* [C] thick rubber ring that fits around the edge of a wheel of a bicycle, car, etc

Uu

U, u /juː/ *n* [C,U] (pl **U's, u's** /juːz/) the twenty-first letter of the English alphabet ■ **U-turn** *n* [C] **1** turn of 180° that a vehicle makes so that it can move forward in the opposite direction **2** (*infml*) complete change in policy or behaviour

ubiquitous /juːˈbɪkwɪtəs/ *adj* (*fml*) seeming to be present everywhere; very common

udder /ˈʌdə(r)/ *n* [C] part of a cow, goat, etc that produces milk

UFO /ˌjuː ef ˈəʊ; ˈjuːfəʊ/ *n* [C] (pl **~s**) Unidentified Flying Object, esp a spacecraft believed to have come from another planet

ugh /ɜː; ʊx/ *exclam* used for expressing disgust: *Ugh! What a horrible smell!*

0‒┐ **ugly** /ˈʌgli/ *adj* (**-ier, -iest**) **1** unpleasant to look at

2 threatening, likely to be violent ▸ **ugliness** *n* [U]

UK /ˌjuː ˈkeɪ/ *abbr* the United Kingdom

ulcer /ˈʌlsə(r)/ *n* [C] open sore area on the skin or inside the body ■ **ulcerate** /ˈʌlsəreɪt/ (*med*) *v* [I,T] (cause sth to) become covered with ulcers ▸ **ulcerous** *adj*

ulterior /ʌlˈtɪəriə(r)/ *adj* (of a reason for doing sth) hidden: *an* ~ *motive*

0‒┐ **ultimate** /ˈʌltɪmət/ *adj* last, final or most extreme ▸ **ultimately** *adv* in the end

ultimatum /ˌʌltɪˈmeɪtəm/ *n* [C] (pl **~s** or **-ta** /-tə/) final statement of conditions to be agreed to without discussion: *issue an* ~

ultrasound /ˈʌltrəsaʊnd/ *n* **1** [U] sound that is higher than human beings can hear **2** [U,C] medical process that produces an image of what is inside your body: *have an* ~ *scan*

ultraviolet /ˌʌltrəˈvaɪələt/ *adj* (*physics*) of or using electromagnetic waves that are just shorter than those of violet light in the spectrum and that cannot be seen: ~ *rays* (= that cause the skin to go darker)

umbilical cord /ʌmˌbɪlɪkl ˈkɔːd/ *n* [C] tube that joins an unborn baby to its mother

0‒┐ **umbrella** /ʌmˈbrelə/ *n* [C] **1** folding frame covered with cloth, used as a protection from rain **2** thing that contains or includes many different parts or elements

umpire /ˈʌmpaɪə(r)/ *n* [C] (in tennis, baseball, etc) person who sees that rules are obeyed ■ **umpire** *v* [I,T] act as an umpire in a game

umpteen /ˌʌmpˈtiːn/ *det* (*infml*) very many: *read* ~ *books on the subject* ▸ **umpteenth** /ˈtiːnθ/ *det*: *for the* ~*th time*

UN /ˌjuː ˈen/ *abbr* the United Nations

0‒┐ **unable** /ʌnˈeɪbl/ *adj* ~ **to** not having the skill, strength, knowledge, etc to do sth

unaccountable /ˌʌnəˈkaʊntəbl/ *adj* (*fml*) that cannot be explained ▸ **unaccountably** *adv*

unaccustomed /ˌʌnəˈkʌstəmd/ *adj* (*fml*) **1** ~ **to** not in the habit of doing sth; not used to sth: ~ *to speaking in public* **2** unusual

unanimous /juˈnænɪməs/ *adj* in or showing complete agreement: *a* ~ *decision* ▸ **unanimity** /ˌjuːnəˈnɪməti/ *n* [U] (*written*)

unanswerable /ʌnˈɑːnsərəbl/ *adj* that cannot be questioned or disagreed with

unarmed /ˌʌnˈɑːmd/ *adj* without weapons

A B C D E F G H I J K L M N O P Q R S T **U** V W X Y Z

unassuming /ˌʌnəˈsjuːmɪŋ/ adj not attracting attention to yourself; modest

unattached /ˌʌnəˈtætʃt/ adj 1 not married or involved in a romantic relationship 2 not connected with a particular group or organization

unattended /ˌʌnəˈtendɪd/ adj not looked after; alone: ~ luggage

unavoidable /ˌʌnəˈvɔɪdəbl/ adj impossible to avoid or prevent

unaware /ˌʌnəˈweə(r)/ adj ~ (of) not knowing or realizing that sth exists or is happening ▶ **unawares** /-ˈweəz/ adv when not expected: catch/take sb ~s (= surprise sb)

unbalanced /ˌʌnˈbælənst/ adj slightly crazy; mentally ill

unbearable /ʌnˈbeərəbl/ adj that cannot be tolerated or endured ▶ **unbearably** adv

unbeatable /ʌnˈbiːtəbl/ adj that cannot be beaten: ~ value for money

unbelievable /ˌʌnbɪˈliːvəbl/ adj that cannot be believed; astonishing ▶ **unbelievably** adv

unborn /ˌʌnˈbɔːn/ adj not yet born

unbroken /ʌnˈbrəʊkən/ adj not interrupted or disturbed: ~ sleep

unbutton /ʌnˈbʌtn/ v [T] undo the buttons on a piece of clothing

uncalled for /ʌnˈkɔːld fɔː(r)/ adj (of behaviour or remarks) not fair or appropriate

uncanny /ʌnˈkæni/ adj (-ier, -iest) strange and difficult to explain

unceremonious /ˌʌnˌserəˈməʊniəs/ adj (written) done roughly and rudely ▶ **unceremoniously** adv

0— **uncertain** /ʌnˈsɜːtn/ adj 1 not sure; doubtful: be ~ about what to do 2 likely to change; not reliable: ~ weather ▶ **uncertainly** adv ▶ **uncertainty** n [C, U] (pl -ies)

uncharitable /ʌnˈtʃærɪtəbl/ adj unkind or unfair

unchecked /ʌnˈtʃekt/ adj not controlled or stopped

uncivilized (also -ised) /ʌnˈsɪvəlaɪzd/ adj (of behaviour, etc) rude

0— **uncle** /ˈʌŋkl/ n [C] brother of your father or mother; husband of your aunt

0— **uncomfortable** /ʌnˈkʌmftəbl/ adj 1 (of clothes, furniture, etc) not letting you feel physically comfortable 2 embarrassed; not relaxed ▶ **uncomfortably** adv

uncommon /ʌnˈkɒmən/ adj not existing in large numbers or in many places ▶ **uncommonly** adv (fml) extremely; unusually

uncompromising /ʌnˈkɒmprəmaɪzɪŋ/ adj unwilling to change your opinions, decisions, etc

unconcerned /ˌʌnkənˈsɜːnd/ adj not interested or worried

unconditional /ˌʌnkənˈdɪʃənl/ adj without conditions or limits: ~ love

0— **unconscious** /ʌnˈkɒnʃəs/ adj 1 in a state like sleep because of injury or illness: She was knocked ~. 2 (of feelings, thoughts, etc) happening without you realizing or being aware; not deliberate: ~ impulses 3 not aware of sb/sth ▶ **unconsciously** adv

uncool /ʌnˈkuːl/ adj (infml) not considered acceptable by fashionable young people

uncountable /ʌnˈkaʊntəbl/ adj (gram) (of nouns) that cannot be made plural or used with a or an, eg water, bread and information

uncouth /ʌnˈkuːθ/ adj (of a person or their behaviour) rude or socially unacceptable

uncover /ʌnˈkʌvə(r)/ v [T] 1 remove sth that is covering sth 2 discover sth secret or hidden

undaunted /ʌnˈdɔːntɪd/ adj (written) not discouraged or afraid

undecided /ˌʌndɪˈsaɪdɪd/ adj not having decided sth; not certain

undeniable /ˌʌndɪˈnaɪəbl/ adj true or certain; that cannot be denied ▶ **undeniably** adv

0— **under** /ˈʌndə(r)/ prep 1 below sth: Have you looked ~ the bed? 2 covered by sth: Most of the iceberg is ~ the water. 3 less than; younger than: ~ £50 4 used to say who or what controls, governs or manages sb/sth: She has a staff of 19 working ~ her. 5 according to an agreement, a law or system: ~ the terms of the contract 6 experiencing a particular process; affected by sth: a hotel ~ construction ◊ You'll be ~ anaesthetic so you won't feel anything. 7 using a particular name: She wrote ~ the name of George Eliot. ● **under** adv in or to a lower place, esp under water

under- prefix 1 (in nouns and adjectives) below: an ~current 2 (in adjectives and verbs) not enough: ~ripe

underarm /ˈʌndərɑːm/ adj 1 connected with a person's armpit: ~ deodorant 2 (sport) (of the way a ball is thrown) with the hand kept below the level of the shoulder ▶ **underarm** adv

undercarriage /ˈʌndəkærɪdʒ/ n [C] the part of an aircraft, including its wheels, that supports it when it is landing and taking off

undercharge /ˌʌndəˈtʃɑːdʒ/ v [I,T] charge too little for sth, usu by accident

underclothes /ˈʌndəkləʊðz/ n [pl] (fml) = UNDERWEAR

undercover /ˌʌndəˈkʌvə(r)/ adj, adv working or done secretly, esp as a spy

undercurrent /ˈʌndəkʌrənt/ n [C] hidden thought or feeling: *an ~ of bitterness*

undercut /ˌʌndəˈkʌt/ v (-tt- pt, pp ~cut) [T] sell goods or services at a lower price than your competitors

underdeveloped /ˌʌndədɪˈveləpt/ adj (of a country) having few industries and a low standard of living

underdog /ˈʌndədɒg/ n [C] person, etc thought to be in a weaker position, and so unlikely to win a competition

underdone /ˌʌndəˈdʌn/ adj (esp of meat) not completely cooked

underestimate /ˌʌndərˈestɪmeɪt/ v [T] **1** think or guess that the amount, cost or size of sth is smaller than it really is **2** not realize how good, strong, determined, etc sb really is: ~ *the enemy's strength*

underfed /ˌʌndəˈfed/ adj having had too little food to eat

underfoot /ˌʌndəˈfʊt/ adv under your feet: *The grass was wet* ~.

undergo /ˌʌndəˈgəʊ/ v (pt -went /-ˈwent/ pp -gone /-ˈgɒn/) [T] experience sth, esp a change or sth unpleasant

undergraduate /ˌʌndəˈgrædʒuət/ n [C] university or college student studying for their first degree

0— underground /ˈʌndəgraʊnd/ adj **1** under the surface of the ground **2** operating secretly and often illegally, esp against a government ● **underground** /-graʊnd/ n [sing] **1** (the Underground) (GB) underground railway system in a city **2** (the underground) [with sing or pl verb] secret political organization ● **underground** /ˌʌndəˈgraʊnd/ adv **1** under the surface of the ground **2** in or into a secret place in order to hide from the police, etc: *He went* ~ *to avoid arrest.*

undergrowth /ˈʌndəgrəʊθ/ n [U] bushes and plants growing thickly under trees

underhand /ˌʌndəˈhænd/ adj done secretly and dishonestly

underlie /ˌʌndəˈlaɪ/ v (pt -lay /-ˈleɪ/ pp -lain /-ˈleɪn/ pres pt lying) [T] (fml) be the basis or cause of sth

underline /ˌʌndəˈlaɪn/ v [T] **1** draw a line under a word, letter, etc **2** emphasize that sth is important

undermanned /ˌʌndəˈmænd/ adj not having enough workers to be able to function well

undermine /ˌʌndəˈmaɪn/ v [T] **1** gradually weaken sth, esp sb's confidence or authority: *Repeated failure ~d his confidence.* **2** make sth weaker at the base, eg by digging under it

0— underneath /ˌʌndəˈniːθ/ prep, adv under or below sth else

underpants /ˈʌndəpænts/ n [pl]

1 (GB) piece of men's underwear worn under their trousers **2** (US) piece of underwear worn by men or women under trousers, a skirt, etc

underpass /ˈʌndəpɑːs/ n [C] road or path that goes under a railway, another road, etc

underprivileged /ˌʌndəˈprɪvəlɪdʒd/ adj not having the standard of living, rights, etc enjoyed by others in society

underrate /ˌʌndəˈreɪt/ v [T] not recognize how good, important, etc sb/sth really is

underscore /ˌʌndəˈskɔː(r)/ v (esp US) = UNDERLINE

underside /ˈʌndəsaɪd/ n [C] side or surface that is underneath

the undersigned /ˌʌndəˈsaɪnd/ n [C] (pl **the undersigned**) (fml) the person who has signed that particular document: *We, the ~ agree to…*

0— understand /ˌʌndəˈstænd/ v (pt, pp **-stood** /-ˈstʊd/) **1** [I,T] know or realize the meaning of words, a language, what sb says, etc: *She can* ~ *French perfectly.* **2** [T] know or realize how or why sth happens, works, etc: *I don't* ~ *why she was fired.* **3** [I,T] know sb's character well: *No one ~s me.* **4** [I,T] (fml) have been told: *I* ~ *that you wish to leave.* [IDM] **make yourself understood** make your meaning clear ▶ **understandable** adj seeming normal and natural; that can be understood ▶ **understandably** adv ▶ **understanding** n **1** [U, sing] knowledge **2** [C, usu sing] informal agreement **3** [U] sympathy ▶ **understanding** adj sympathetic and willing to forgive others

understate /ˌʌndəˈsteɪt/ v [T] state that sth is smaller, less important or less serious than it really is: ~ *the extent of the problem* ▶ **understatement** /ˈʌndəsteɪtmənt/ n [C, U]

understudy /ˈʌndəstʌdi/ n [C] (pl **-ies**) actor who learns the part of another actor in a play so that they can play that part if necessary

undertake /ˌʌndəˈteɪk/ v (pt **-took** /-ˈtʊk/ pp **-n** /-ˈteɪkən/) [T] (fml) **1** make yourself responsible for sth and start doing it **2** [I] ~ **to agree or promise to do sth** ▶ **undertaking** n [C] **1** important and/or difficult task or project **2** (fml) promise or agreement to do sth

undertaker /ˈʌndəteɪkə(r)/ n [C] person whose job is to arrange funerals

undertone /ˈʌndətəʊn/ n [C] ~ **(of)** hidden meaning or feeling [IDM] **in an undertone** in a quiet voice

undervalue /ˌʌndəˈvæljuː/ v [T] not recognize how good, valuable or important sb/sth really is

underwater /ˌʌndəˈwɔːtə(r)/ adj, adv found, used or happening below the surface of water

underwear /ˈʌndəweə(r)/ n [U] clothing worn next to the skin and under other clothes

underworld /ˈʌndəwɜːld/ n [sing] **1** people and activities involved in crime in a particular place **2** (the underworld) (in mythology) home of the dead

underwrite /ˌʌndəˈraɪt/ v (pt -wrote /-ˈrəʊt/ pp -written /-ˈrɪtn/) [T] (tech) accept financial responsibility for sth so that you will pay money in case of loss or damage ▶ **underwriter** n [C] person or organization that underwrites insurance policies, esp for ships

undesirable /ˌʌndɪˈzaɪərəbl/ adj not wanted or approved of; likely to cause trouble ● **undesirable** n [C, usu pl] person who is not wanted in a particular place

undeveloped /ˌʌndɪˈveləpt/ adj (of a place, land, etc) not yet used for agriculture, industry, building, etc

undies /ˈʌndiz/ n [pl] (infml) = UNDERWEAR

undo /ʌnˈduː/ v (pt -did /-ˈdɪd/ pp -done /-ˈdʌn/) [T] **1** open sth that is fastened, wrapped or tied: ~ a button/zip **2** destroy the effect of sth: He undid all my good work. ▶ **undoing** n [sing] cause of sb's failure

undoubted /ʌnˈdaʊtɪd/ adj certain; accepted as true ▶ **undoubtedly** adv

undress /ʌnˈdres/ v [I,T] take off your clothes; remove sb else's clothes ▶ **undressed** adj not wearing any clothes

undue /ˌʌnˈdjuː/ adj (fml) too much: with ~ haste ▶ **unduly** adv

undulate /ˈʌndjuleɪt/ v [I] move up and down gently like a wave: The road ~s through the hills.

undying /ʌnˈdaɪɪŋ/ adj (fml) that will last for ever: ~ love

unearth /ʌnˈɜːθ/ v [T] **1** find sth in the ground by digging **2** discover sth by chance or after searching for it: ~ the truth

unearthly /ʌnˈɜːθli/ adj unnatural and therefore frightening [IDM] **at an unearthly hour** (infml) very early, esp when this is annoying

uneasy /ʌnˈiːzi/ adj (-ier, -iest) worried or anxious ▶ **uneasily** adv ▶ **uneasiness** n [U]

uneconomic /ˌʌnˌiːkəˈnɒmɪk; ˌʌnˌek-/ adj not producing profit

unemployed /ˌʌnɪmˈplɔɪd/ adj not having a job ▶ **the unemployed**

n [pl] unemployed people ▶ **unemployment** /-ˈplɔɪmənt/ n [U]

unequal /ʌnˈiːkwəl/ adj **1** in which people are treated differently or have different advantages in a way that seems unfair **2** (~ to) different in size, amount, etc **3 ~ to** (fml) not capable of doing sth ▶ **unequally** adv

unequivocal /ˌʌnɪˈkwɪvəkl/ adj (fml) having a completely clear meaning ▶ **unequivocally** adv

uneven /ʌnˈiːvn/ adj **1** not level or smooth **2** varying in quality

unexpected /ˌʌnɪkˈspektɪd/ adj causing surprise because it is not expected ▶ **unexpectedly** adv

unfailing /ʌnˈfeɪlɪŋ/ adj (approv) that you can rely on to always be there and always be the same

unfair /ʌnˈfeə(r)/ adj ~ (on/to) not right or just: ~ remarks/ competition ▶ **unfairly** adv

unfaithful /ʌnˈfeɪθfl/ adj ~ (to) having sex with sb who is not your husband, wife or usual partner

unfamiliar /ˌʌnfəˈmɪliə(r)/ adj **1** ~ (to) that you do not know or recognize **2** ~ **with** not having any knowledge or experience of sth: I'm ~ with this type of computer.

unfasten /ʌnˈfɑːsn/ v [T] undo sth that is fastened

unfinished /ʌnˈfɪnɪʃt/ adj not complete: We have some ~ business.

unfit /ʌnˈfɪt/ adj **1** not of an acceptable standard; not suitable: ~ for human consumption **2** not capable of doing sth, eg because of illness **3** (of a person) not in good physical condition because you have not taken exercise

unfold /ʌnˈfəʊld/ v [I,T] **1** (cause sth folded to) become open or flat **2** (cause sth to) gradually be made known: as the story ~ed

unforeseen /ˌʌnfɔːˈsiːn/ adj unexpected

unforgettable /ˌʌnfəˈɡetəbl/ adj that cannot be easily forgotten

unfortunate /ʌnˈfɔːtʃənət/ adj **1** unlucky **2** that makes you feel sorry: an ~ remark ▶ **unfortunately** adv

unfounded /ʌnˈfaʊndɪd/ adj not based on facts

unfriendly /ʌnˈfrendli/ adj (-ier, -iest) not kind or pleasant to sb

unfurl /ʌnˈfɜːl/ v [I,T] (cause sth that is curled or rolled tightly to) open: The leaves slowly ~ed.

unfurnished /ʌnˈfɜːnɪʃt/ adj (of a rented room, etc) without furniture

ungainly /ʌnˈɡeɪnli/ adj moving in a way that is not graceful

ungodly /ʌnˈɡɒdli/ adj (old-fash) not showing respect for God; wicked [IDM] **at an ungodly hour** very early or very late and therefore annoying

ungrateful /ʌnˈɡreɪtfl/ adv not expressing thanks for sth that sb has done for you

unguarded /ʌnˈɡɑːdɪd/ adv careless, esp in speech

0= **unhappy** /ʌnˈhæpi/ adj (-ier, -iest) not happy; sad ▶ **unhappily** adv ▶ **unhappiness** n [U]

unhealthy /ʌnˈhelθi/ adj (-ier, -iest) **1** not having or showing good health **2** harmful to your health

unheard-of /ʌnˈhɜːd ɒv/ adj that has never been known or done; very unusual

unicorn /ˈjuːnɪkɔːn/ n [C] (in stories) white horse with a long straight horn on its forehead

unidentified /ˌʌnaɪˈdentɪfaɪd/ adj not recognized or known; not identified

0= **uniform** /ˈjuːnɪfɔːm/ n [C, U] special set of clothes worn by all members of an organization or group, eg the army or schoolchildren ● **uniform** adj not varying; regular ▶ **uniformed** adj: ~ed police officers ▶ **uniformity** /-ˈfɔːməti/ n [U, sing]

unify /ˈjuːnɪfaɪ/ v (pt, pp -ied) [T] join people, things, parts of a country, etc together to form a single unit ▶ **unification** /ˌjuːnɪfɪˈkeɪʃn/ n [U]

unilateral /ˌjuːnɪˈlætrəl/ adj done by one member of a group or organization without the agreement of the other members: a ~ decision

0= **union** /ˈjuːniən/ n **1** [C] = TRADE UNION (TRADE[1]) **2** [C] club or association **3** [C] group of countries or states **4** [U, sing] (fml) act of joining or state of being joined together: a summit to discuss economic and monetary ~ ■ the **Union Jack** n [sing] national flag of the United Kingdom

0= **unique** /juˈniːk/ adj **1** being the only one of its kind **2** very special or unusual: a ~ singing voice **3** ~ (to) belonging to or connected with one particular person, place or thing: The koala is ~ to Australia. ▶ **uniquely** adv

unisex /ˈjuːnɪseks/ adj designed to be used by both men and women

unison /ˈjuːnɪsn/ n [IDM] **in unison (with sb/sth) 1** done or said at the same time **2** (of people or organizations) working together and in agreement with each other

0= **unit** /ˈjuːnɪt/ n [C] **1** single thing, person or group **2** (business) single item of the type of product that a company sells: What's the ~ cost? **3** group of people with a specific job or function: the university research ~ **4** small machine that has a special function or is part of a larger machine: the central processing ~ of a computer **5** standard of

measurement: The metre is a ~ of length.

0= **unite** /juˈnaɪt/ v [I, T] (cause people or things to) join together or become one with others ■ the **United Kingdom** n [sing] (abbr **(the) UK**) England, Scotland, Wales and Northern Ireland ■ the **United Nations** n [sing, with sing or pl verb] (abbr **(the) UN**) association of many countries which works for peace, better conditions, etc

unity /ˈjuːnəti/ n [U, sing] state of being in agreement and working together

universal /ˌjuːnɪˈvɜːsl/ adj done by or involving all the people in the world or in a particular group ▶ **universally** adv

0= **universe** /ˈjuːnɪvɜːs/ n (the universe) [sing] everything that exists in space, including all the stars and planets

0= **university** /ˌjuːnɪˈvɜːsəti/ n [C, U] (pl -ies) institution for advanced teaching and research

unkempt /ˌʌnˈkempt/ adj not kept tidy: ~ hair

0= **unkind** /ˌʌnˈkaɪnd/ adj unpleasant or unfriendly; slightly cruel

0= **unknown** /ˌʌnˈnəʊn/ adj not known or identified

unleaded /ˌʌnˈledɪd/ adj (of petrol) not containing lead and therefore less harmful to the environment

unleash /ʌnˈliːʃ/ v [T] (fml) ~ **(on)** suddenly release a powerful force

0= **unless** /ənˈles/ conj if ...not: You will fail ~ you work harder.

0= **unlike** /ˌʌnˈlaɪk/ adj, prep different from a particular person or thing

0= **unlikely** /ʌnˈlaɪkli/ adj **1** not likely to happen; not probable: He's ~ to get better. **2** not the person, thing or place that you would normally expect: an ~ candidate for the job

0= **unload** /ˌʌnˈləʊd/ v **1** [I, T] remove things from a vehicle or ship; empty the contents of sth **2** [T] ~ **(on/onto)** (fml) pass the responsibility for sb/ sth to sb else

unlock /ˌʌnˈlɒk/ v [T] open a door, etc using a key

0= **unlucky** /ʌnˈlʌki/ adj having or bringing bad luck

unmanned /ˌʌnˈmænd/ adj (of a machine, vehicle or place) not having or needing a person to control or operate it

unmask /ˌʌnˈmɑːsk/ v [T] show the true character of sb

0= **unmentionable** /ʌnˈmenʃənəbl/ adj too shocking or embarrassing to be spoken about

unmistakable /ˌʌnmɪˈsteɪkəbl/ adj that cannot be mistaken for sb/sth else ► **unmistakably** adv

unmitigated /ʌnˈmɪtɪgeɪtɪd/ adj (fml) completely bad: an ~ disaster

unmoved /ʌnˈmuːvd/ adj not feeling any pity or sympathy: He was ~ by her tears.

unnatural /ʌnˈnætʃrəl/ adj 1 not natural or normal: an ~ silence 2 not expected or acceptable: ~ behaviour

0̅ʉ unnecessary /ʌnˈnesəsəri/ adj not needed; more than is needed ► **unnecessarily** adv

unnerve /ʌnˈnɜːv/ v [T] cause sb to lose confidence or courage

unnoticed /ʌnˈnəʊtɪst/ adj not seen or noticed

unobtrusive /ˌʌnəbˈtruːsɪv/ adj (fml) not attracting unnecessary attention

unofficial /ˌʌnəˈfɪʃl/ adj without the approval or permission of sb in authority

unpalatable /ʌnˈpælətəbl/ adj 1 (of facts, ideas, etc) unpleasant and not easy to accept: his ~ views 2 not pleasant to taste

0̅ʉ unpleasant /ʌnˈpleznt/ adj 1 not pleasant 2 not kind, friendly or polite ► **unpleasantness** n [U]

unprecedented /ʌnˈpresɪdentɪd/ adj never having happened or been done before

unpredictable /ˌʌnprɪˈdɪktəbl/ adj that cannot be predicted: I never know how she will react, she's so ~.

unprintable /ʌnˈprɪntəbl/ adj (of words, etc) too offensive or shocking to be printed

unqualified /ʌnˈkwɒlɪfaɪd/ adj 1 not qualified for a job: ~ to teach 2 not limited; complete: an ~ disaster

unquestionable /ʌnˈkwestʃənəbl/ adj that cannot be doubted; certain ► **unquestionably** adv

unravel /ʌnˈrævl/ v (-ll- US -l-) 1 [I,T] (cause sth woven or knotted to) separate into threads 2 [T] explain sth that is difficult to understand or mysterious: ~ a mystery

unreal /ʌnˈrɪəl/ adj 1 so strange that it is more like a dream than reality 2 not related to reality: ~ expectations ► **unreality** /ˌʌnriˈæləti/ n [U]

0̅ʉ unreasonable /ʌnˈriːznəbl/ adj not reasonable or fair

unreliable /ˌʌnrɪˈlaɪəbl/ adj that cannot be trusted or depended on

unremitting /ˌʌnrɪˈmɪtɪŋ/ adj never relaxing or stopping

unrest /ʌnˈrest/ n [U] political situation in which people are angry and likely to fight or protest

unrivalled (US -l-) /ʌnˈraɪvld/ adj better or greater than any other

unroll /ʌnˈrəʊl/ v [I,T] (cause sth to) open from a rolled state and become flat

unruffled /ʌnˈrʌfld/ adj (of a person) calm

unruly /ʌnˈruːli/ adj not easy to control

unsavoury (US -vory) /ʌnˈseɪvəri/ adj unpleasant or offensive; not considered morally acceptable: Her friends are all ~ characters.

unscathed /ʌnˈskeɪðd/ adj not harmed

unscrupulous /ʌnˈskruːpjələs/ adj without moral principles; not honest or fair

unseat /ʌnˈsiːt/ v [T] 1 remove sb from a position of power 2 cause sb to fall off a horse, etc

unseemly /ʌnˈsiːmli/ adj (old-fash) (of behaviour, etc) not polite or suitable

unsettle /ʌnˈsetl/ v [T] make sb feel upset or worried, esp because a situation has changed: Changing schools might ~ the kids.

unsightly /ʌnˈsaɪtli/ adj not pleasant to look at

unsound /ʌnˈsaʊnd/ adj 1 not acceptable; not holding acceptable views: politically ~ 2 (of a building, etc) in poor condition; weak **IDM of unsound mind** (law) mentally ill

unspeakable /ʌnˈspiːkəbl/ adj that cannot be described in words, usu because it is so bad

unstuck /ʌnˈstʌk/ adj **IDM come unstuck 1** become separated from sth it was stuck to **2** (infml) (of a person, plan, etc) fail completely, with bad results

unswerving /ʌnˈswɜːvɪŋ/ adj (fml) strong and not changing: ~ loyalty

unthinkable /ʌnˈθɪŋkəbl/ adj impossible to imagine or accept

0̅ʉ untidy /ʌnˈtaɪdi/ adj (-ier, -iest) not neat or ordered

untie /ʌnˈtaɪ/ v (pt, pp ~d pres pt untying) [T] undo a knot in sth; undo sth that is tied

0̅ʉ until /ənˈtɪl/ (also **till** /tɪl/) prep, conj up to the point in time or the event mentioned: Wait ~ the rain stops.

untold /ʌnˈtəʊld/ adj (fml) too great to be measured

untoward /ˌʌntəˈwɔːd/ adj (fml) unexpected or unfortunate

unused¹ /ˌʌnˈjuːzd/ adj never having been used; not being used at the moment

unused² /ʌnˈjuːst/ adj ~ **to** not having much experience of sth; not used to sth: She was ~ to talking about herself.

0̅ʉ unusual /ʌnˈjuːʒuəl/ adj different from what is usual or normal;

interesting because it is different
▶ **unusually** adv

unveil /ˌʌnˈveɪl/ v [T] **1** remove a covering from a painting, statue, etc so that it can be seen for the first time **2** introduce a new plan, product, etc to the public for the first time

unwarranted /ʌnˈwɒrəntɪd/ adj (fml) not deserved or justified

unwieldy /ʌnˈwiːldi/ adj difficult to move or control, because it is large or heavy

unwind /ʌnˈwaɪnd/ v (pt, pp **-wound** /-ˈwaʊnd/) **1** [I,T] undo sth that has been wrapped into a ball or around sth **2** [i] (infml) relax

unwitting /ʌnˈwɪtɪŋ/ adj (written) not aware of what you are doing or the situation you are involved in
▶ **unwittingly** adv

unwrap /ʌnˈræp/ v (**-pp-**) [T] take off the paper, etc that covers or protects sth

0— **up** /ʌp/ adv **1** towards or in a higher position: He jumped up from his chair. **2** to or at a higher level: She turned the volume up. ◦ Prices are going up. **3** to the place where sb/ sth is: A car drove up and he got in. **4** to or at an important place: go up to London **5** to a place in the north of a country: He's moved up north. **6** into pieces or parts: tear the paper up **7** completely: The stream has dried up. **8** out of bed: Is Pete up yet? **9** (spoken) used to say that sth is happening: What's up? **[IDM] be up to sb** be sb's duty or responsibility; be for sb to decide **up against sth** (infml) facing difficulties or problems **up and down 1** moving upwards and downwards: The boat bobbed up and down in the water. **2** backwards and forwards: walk up and down **3** sometimes good and sometimes bad **up for sth 1** on offer for sth; being considered for sth **2** willing to take part in an activity: We're going clubbing. Are you up for it? **up to sth 1** as far as a particular number, level, etc: My car takes up to four people. **2** until sth: up to now **3** as high or as such sth **3** capable of sth: She's not up to the job. ● **up** prep **1** to or in a higher position: climb up the stairs **2** along or further along a road, etc: There's another telephone box up the road. ● **up** adj **1** directed or moving upwards: the up escalator **2** (infml) cheerful **3** (of a computer system) working ● **up** v (**-pp-**) **1** [i] (infml) (up and...) suddenly move or do sth unexpected: He just upped and left without telling anyone. **2** [T] increase the price or amount of sth: The buyers upped their offer. ■ **up-and-coming** adj (infml) likely to be successful and popular in the future

■ **ups and downs** n [pl] mixture of good and bad experiences

upbringing /ˈʌpbrɪŋɪŋ/ n [sing, U] way in which a child is cared for and taught how to behave while it is growing up

update /ˌʌpˈdeɪt/ v [T] **1** make sth more modern **2** give sb the most recent information about sth ● **update** n [C]: a news ~

upheaval /ʌpˈhiːvl/ n [C, U] big change that causes a lot of confusion, worry and problems

uphill /ʌpˈhɪl/ adv towards the top of a hill or slope ● **uphill** adj **1** sloping upwards **2** difficult to win; requiring a lot of effort: an ~ battle/task

uphold /ʌpˈhəʊld/ v (pt, pp **-held** /-ˈheld/) [T] **1** support sth: ~ the law **2** confirm a legal decision

upholster /ʌpˈhəʊlstə(r)/ v [T] cover a chair, etc with soft material (padding) and fabric ● **upholsterer** n [C] ▶ **upholstery** n [U] materials used in upholstering

upkeep /ˈʌpkiːp/ n [U] cost or process of keeping sth in good condition: the ~ of a house

upland /ˈʌplənd/ n [C, usu pl] area of high land situated away from the coast

upload /ˌʌpˈləʊd/ v [T] (computing) move data to a larger computer system from a smaller one ● **upload** /ˈʌpləʊd/ n [U] (computing) act or process of uploading

upmarket /ˌʌpˈmɑːkɪt/ adj (infml) designed for or used by people who belong to a high social class: an ~ restaurant

0— **upon** /əˈpɒn/ prep (fml) = ON²

0— **upper** /ˈʌpə(r)/ adj at or near the top of sth; situated above sth else: the ~ lip **[IDM] gain, get, have, etc the upper hand** get an advantage over sb so that you are in control ● **upper** n [C] top part of a shoe attached to the sole ■ the **upper class** n [C] social group considered to have the highest social status and more money and/or power than others ▶ **upper class** adj ■ **uppermost** adj (written) **1** higher or nearer the top than other things **2** more important than other things: These thoughts were ~most in his mind at the time. ● **uppermost** adv (written) in the highest position; facing upward

upright /ˈʌpraɪt/ adj **1** (of a person) not lying down, and with the back straight **2** placed in a vertical position **3** (of a person) moral and honest ● **upright** n [C] piece of wood, metal or plastic that is placed vertically in order to support sth

uprising /ˈʌpraɪzɪŋ/ n [C] fighting by ordinary people against those in power

uproar /ˈʌprɔː(r)/ n [U,sing] (outburst of) noise and excitement or anger ▸ **uproarious** /ʌpˈrɔːriəs/ adj (written) very noisy

uproot /ˌʌpˈruːt/ v [T] **1** pull a tree, etc out of the ground **2** ~ yourself/sb (cause sb to) leave a place where you/they have lived for a long time

○ᴀ **upset** /ˌʌpˈset/ v (-tt- pt, pp **upset**) [T] **1** make sb feel worried, unhappy or annoyed: be ~ by the bad news **2** cause sth to go wrong: ~ all our plans **3** make sb feel sick after they have eaten or drunk sth: Milk ~s her stomach. **4** cause sth to fall over by hitting it accidentally: ~ a glass of water ● **upset** adj unhappy or disappointed because of sth unpleasant that has happened ● **upset** /ˈʌpset/ n **1** [C] situation in which there are unexpected problems or difficulties **2** [C] illness in the stomach causing sickness and diarrhoea: a stomach ~ **3** [U,C] feelings of unhappiness and disappointment

upshot /ˈʌpʃɒt/ n (the upshot) [sing] ~ (of) final result of a series of events

○ᴀ **upside down** /ˌʌpsaɪd ˈdaʊn/ adv, adj in a position with the top where the bottom usu is: The canoe floated ~ in the river. [IDM] **turn sth upside down 1** make a place untidy when looking for sth **2** cause large changes and confusion in a person's life: His death turned her world ~.

upstage /ˌʌpˈsteɪdʒ/ v [T] attract attention away from sb else and onto yourself

○ᴀ **upstairs** /ˌʌpˈsteəz/ adv, adj to or on a higher floor

upstanding /ˌʌpˈstændɪŋ/ adj (fml) behaving in a moral and honest way

upstart /ˈʌpstɑːt/ n [C] (disapprov) person who has just started a new job but who behaves as if they are more important than other people

upstream /ˌʌpˈstriːm/ adv along a river, in the opposite direction from the way the water flows

uptake /ˈʌpteɪk/ n [IDM] **be quick/slow on the uptake** be quick/slow to understand sth

uptight /ˌʌpˈtaɪt/ adj (infml) anxious and/or angry about sth

up to date /ˌʌp tə ˈdeɪt/ adj **1** modern; fashionable: This technology is bang up to date. **2** having all the most recent information: up-to-date records

○ᴀ **upward** /ˈʌpwəd/ adj pointing towards or facing a higher place ▸ **upwards** (esp US **upward**) adv **1** towards a higher place or position **2** towards a higher amount or price

uranium /juˈreɪniəm/ n [U] radioactive metal used in producing nuclear energy

○ᴀ **urban** /ˈɜːbən/ adj of a town or city ▸ **urbanized** (also -ised) adj (of an area, country, etc) having a lot of towns, streets, factories, etc, rather than countryside

○ᴀ **urge** /ɜːdʒ/ v [T] **1** try hard to persuade sb to do sth: They ~d her to come back soon. **2** recommend sth strongly: ~ caution **3** (written) use force to make a person or an animal move more quickly ● **urge** n [C] strong desire to do sth: a sudden ~ to run away

○ᴀ **urgent** /ˈɜːdʒənt/ adj needing to be dealt with immediately ▸ **urgency** /-dʒənsi/ n [U] ▸ **urgently** adv

urine /ˈjʊərɪn/ n [U] liquid waste that is passed from the body ▸ **urinate** v [I] pass urine from the body

URL /ˌjuː ɑː(r) ˈel/ abbr (computing) uniform/universal resource locator; the address of a World Wide Web page

urn /ɜːn/ n [C] **1** container for holding the ashes of a dead person **2** large metal container for serving tea or coffee

US /ˌjuː ˈes/ abbr United States (of America): a US citizen

○ᴀ **us** /əs; strong form ʌs/ pron (used as the object of a v or prep) me and another or others; me and you

USA /ˌjuː es ˈeɪ/ abbr United States of America: visit the ~

usage /ˈjuːsɪdʒ/ n **1** [U,C] way in which words are used in a language: a guide to modern English ~ **2** [U] fact of sth being used; how much sth is used: Car ~ is expected to increase.

USB /ˌjuː es ˈbiː/ abbr universal serial bus; system for connecting other pieces of equipment to a computer ■ **USB ˈflash drive** (also ˌUSB ˈflash disk, USˈB drive/stick) n [C] (abbr **UFD**) (computing) small device that is used for storing and moving data onto a computer

○ᴀ **use¹** /juːz/ v (pt, pp **~d** /juːzd/) [T] **1** do sth with a machine, a method, an object, etc for a particular purpose: Can I ~ your phone? **2** take a particular amount of a liquid, substance, etc in order to achieve or make sth: This type of heater ~s a lot of electricity. **3** (disapprov) take advantage of sb unfairly; exploit sb [PV] **use sth up** finish sth completely ▸ **usable** adj ▸ **user** n [C] person or thing that uses sth ■ **ˌuser-ˈfriendly** adj easy for people to use or understand

○ᴀ **use²** /juːs/ n **1** [U,sing] act of using sth; state of being used: The 12th-century chapel is still in ~ today. **2** [C,U] purpose for which sth is used; way in which sth is or can be used: a tool with many ~s **3** [U] right or opportunity to use sth, eg sth that belongs to sb else: You can have the

~ of my car. **4** [U] ability to use your mind or body: *He lost the ~ of his legs.* **[IDM] be of use (to sb)** (fml) be useful **come into/go out of use** start/stop being used in time **it's no use (doing sth)** | **What's the use (of doing sth)?** used to say that there is no point in doing sth because it will not be successful: *It's no ~ I can't persuade her.* **make use of sth/sb** use sth/sb, esp in order to gain an advantage ▶ **useful** /'ju:sfl/ *adj* that can help you to do or achieve what you want ▶ **usefully** *adv* ▶ **usefulness** *n* [U] **useless** *adj* **1** not useful **2** (*infml*) not very good at sth: *I'm ~less at maths.* ▶ **uselessly** *adv*

0-m **used¹** /ju:st/ *adj* **~ to** familiar with sth; in the habit of doing sth: *You will soon be/get ~ to the weather.*

0-m **used²** /ju:zd/ *adj* that has belonged to or been used by sb before: *~ cars*

0-m **used to** /'ju:st tə; before vowels and finally 'ju:st tu/ *modal v* used to say that sth happened frequently or continuously during a period in the past: *I ~ play football when I was a boy.*

usher /'ʌʃə(r)/ *n* [C] person who shows people where to sit in a church, public hall, etc ● **usher** *v* [T] take or show sb where they should go **[PV] usher sth in** (fml) be the beginning of sth new or make sth new begin ▶ **usherette** /,ʌʃə'ret/ *n* [C] (*GB*) woman whose job is to lead people to their seats in a theatre or cinema

0-m **usual** /'ju:ʒuəl/ *adj* existing, done, happening, etc most often: *We'll meet at the ~ place.* ▶ **usually** *adv* in the way that is usual or most normal; most often: *I ~ly walk to work.*

usurp /ju:'zɜ:p/ *v* [T] (fml) take sb's position and/or power without having the right to do this ▶ **usurper** *n* [C]

utensil /ju:'tensl/ *n* [C] tool that is used in the house: *kitchen ~s*

uterus /'ju:tərəs/ *n* [C] (anat) = WOMB

utility /ju:'tɪləti/ *n* (pl **-ies**) **1** [C] public service such as an electricity, water or gas supply **2** [U] (fml) quality of being useful **3** [C] (*computing*) piece of computer software that performs a particular task ■ **utility room** *n* [C] room in a private house which contains equipment such as a washing machine, freezer, etc

utilize (also **-ise**) /'ju:təlaɪz/ *v* [T] (fml) use sth, esp for a practical purpose ▶ **utilization** (also **-isation**) /-'zeɪʃn/ *n* [U]

utmost /'ʌtməʊst/ *adj* greatest; most extreme: *of the ~ importance*

● **utmost** *n* [sing] the greatest amount possible: *I will do my ~* (= try as hard as possible) *to persuade her.*

utter /'ʌtə(r)/ *adj* complete; total: *~ darkness* ● **utter** *v* [T] (fml) make a sound with your voice; say sth: *to ~ a groan* ▶ **utterance** /-rəns/ *n* [U,C] (fml) spoken word or words ▶ **utterly** *adv* completely

U-turn → U, u

V v

V, v /vi:/ *n* [C,U] (pl **V's, v's** /vi:z/) **1** the twenty-second letter of the English alphabet **2** Roman numeral for 5 **3** volt(s)

v *abbr* **1** (also **vs**) (in sport or a legal case) versus (= against) **2** (infml, written) very

vacancy /'veɪkənsi/ *n* [C] (pl **-ies**) **1** job that is available for sb to do **2** room that is available in a hotel, etc

vacant /'veɪkənt/ *adj* **1** not filled or occupied; empty **2** showing no sign that the person is thinking of anything: *a ~ expression*

vacate /və'keɪt/ *v* [T] (fml) leave a building, seat, etc empty; make sth available for sb else

0-m **vacation** /və'keɪʃn/ *n* **1** [C] period when universities are closed **2** [U,C] (*US*) = HOLIDAY

vaccinate /'væksɪneɪt/ *v* [T] **~ (against)** protect sb against a disease by injecting them with a vaccine ▶ **vaccination** /-'neɪʃn/ *n* [C,U]

vaccine /'væksi:n/ *n* [C, U] substance that is put into the blood and that protects the body from a disease

vacuum /'vækjuəm/ *n* [C] (pl **~s**) **1** space that is completely empty of all matter or gases **2** [usu sing] situation in which sb/sth is missing or lacking: *a ~ in his life since his wife died* **3** [usu sing] act of cleaning sth with a vacuum cleaner ● **vacuum** *v* [I,T] clean sth with a vacuum cleaner ■ **vacuum cleaner** *n* [C] electrical machine that sucks up dirt and dust from floors ■ **vacuum flask** *n* [C] container with a vacuum between its two walls, used for keeping liquids hot or cold

vagabond /'vægəbɒnd/ *n* [C] (old-fash) person who has no home or job and who travels around

vagina /və'dʒaɪnə/ *n* [C] (anat) passage from the outer female sex organs to the womb

vagrant /'veɪgrənt/ *n* [C] (fml or law) person who has no home or job, esp one who begs ▶ **vagrancy** /-rənsi/ *n* [U]

vague /veɪg/ adj (~r, ~st) **1** not clear in a person's mind **2** not having or giving enough information about sth ▶ **vaguely** adv **vagueness** n [U]

vain /veɪn/ adj **1** unsuccessful: a ~ attempt **2** (disapprov) too proud of your own abilities, appearances, etc [IDM] **in vain** unsuccessfully ▶ **vainly** adv

vale /veɪl/ n [C] (in poetry or place names) valley

valentine /'væləntaɪn/ n [C] **1** (also **'valentine card**) card sent to sb you love on St Valentine's Day (14th February) **2** person that you send a valentine to

valet /'væleɪ; 'vælɪt/ n [C] **1** man's personal male servant **2** (GB) hotel employee whose job is to clean the clothes of hotel guests **3** (esp US) person who parks your car for you at a hotel or restaurant

valiant /'væliənt/ adj very brave ▶ **valiantly** adv

0‑w **valid** /'vælɪd/ adj **1** that is legally and officially acceptable: The ticket is ~ until 1st May. **2** based on what is logical or true **3** (computing) that is accepted by the system: a ~ password ▶ **validate** v [T] (fml) make sth valid ▶ **validity** /və'lɪdəti/ n [U]

0‑w **valley** /'væli/ n [C] low land between hills or mountains, often with a river

valour (US -or) /'vælə(r)/ n [U] (lit) great courage, esp in war

0‑w **valuable** /'væljuəbl/ adj worth a lot of money **2** very useful: ~ advice ▶ **valuables** n [pl] valuable things, esp jewellery

valuation /,vælju'eɪʃn/ n **1** professional judgement about how much money sth is worth **2** [C] estimated value that has been decided on

0‑w **value** /'væljuː/ n **1** [U,C] amount of money sth is worth **2** [U] worth of sth compared with its price: This large packet is good ~ at 99p. **3** [U] quality of being useful or important: the ~ of regular exercise ◇ [pl] principles: high moral ~s ● **value** v [T] **1** think that sb/sth is important: I really ~ her as a friend. **2** decide that sth is worth a particular amount of money ■ **value 'added tax** n [U] = VAT ▶ **valueless** adj (fml) without value or worth ▶ **valuer** n [C] person whose job is to estimate how much property, land, etc is worth

valve /vælv/ n [C] **1** device for controlling the flow of a liquid or gas in one direction only **2** structure in the heart that lets blood flow in one direction only

vampire /'væmpaɪə(r)/ n [C] (in stories) dead person who sucks the blood of living people

0‑w **van** /væn/ n [C] covered vehicle with no side windows, used for carrying goods

vandal /'vændl/ n [C] person who commits acts of vandalism ▶ **vandalism** /-dəlɪzəm/ n [U] crime of deliberately damaging public property, etc ▶ **vandalize** (also -ise) /-dəlaɪz/ v [T] deliberately damage or destroy public property, etc

vanguard /'vænɡɑːd/ n (the vanguard) [sing] **1** leaders of a movement in society, eg in politics, art, industry, etc **2** front part of an advancing army

vanilla /və'nɪlə/ n [U] flavouring that comes from a plant and is used in sweet foods, eg ice cream

vanish /'vænɪʃ/ v [I] **1** disappear suddenly **2** stop existing: Her hopes of finding a new job have ~ed.

vanity /'vænəti/ n [U] **1** (disapprov) too high an opinion of yourself: She had no personal ~ (= about her appearance). **2** (lit) quality of being unimportant

vanquish /'væŋkwɪʃ/ v [T] (lit) defeat sb completely

vaporize (also -ise) /'veɪpəraɪz/ v [I,T] (cause sth to) turn into gas

vapour (US -or) /'veɪpə(r)/ n [C,U] mass of very small drops of liquid in the air, eg steam: water ~

0‑w **variable** /'veəriəbl/ adj often changing; likely to change ● **variable** n [C] situation, number or quantity that can vary or be varied ▶ **variably** adv

variant /'veəriənt/ adj, n [C] (being a) different form of sth: ~ spellings

0‑w **variation** /,veəri'eɪʃn/ n **1** [C,U] change, esp in the amount or level of sth: ~(s) in temperature **2** [C] (music) repetition of a simple tune in a different form

varicose vein /,værɪkəʊs 'veɪn/ n [C] swollen painful vein, esp in the leg

0‑w **varied** /'veərid/ adj **1** of many different types **2** not staying the same, but changing often: a ~ life

0‑w **variety** /və'raɪəti/ n (pl -ies) **1** [sing] ~ (of) several different sorts of the same thing: a wide ~ of interests **2** [U] quality of not being the same: a life full of ~ **3** [C] type: rare varieties of birds **4** [U] entertainment with singing, dancing, comedy, etc: a ~ act

0‑w **various** /'veəriəs/ adj **1** several different: This dress comes in ~ colours. ◇ She took the job for ~ reasons. **2** (fml) having many different features ▶ **variously** adv

varnish /'vɑːnɪʃ/ n [U,C] (liquid used for giving a) hard shiny surface on wood, etc ● **varnish** v [T] put varnish on the surface of sth

0‑w **vary** /'veəri/ v (pt, pp -ied) **1** [I] be different in size, amount, etc: Car prices ~ greatly. **2** [I, T] (cause sth to) change or be different according to the situation: ~ *your route*

vase /vɑːz/ *n* [C] container made of glass, etc, used esp for holding cut flowers

0—¬ vast /vɑːst/ *adj* extremely large: *a ~ desert* ▸ **vastly** *adv*: *~ly improved* ▸ **vastness** *n* [U]

VAT /ˌviː eɪ ˈtiː; væt/ *abbr* value added tax; tax added to the price of goods or services

vat /væt/ *n* [C] large container for holding liquids, esp in industrial processes

vault /vɔːlt/ *n* [C] **1** room with thick walls, esp in a bank, where valuable things are kept safe **2** room under a church or cemetery, used for burying people **3** arched roof **4** jump made by vaulting ● **vault** *v* [I, T] ~ (**over**) jump over sth using your hands or a pole to push you: ~ (*over*) *a wall* ▸ **vaulter** *n* [C] person who vaults: *a pole~er*

VCR /ˌviː siː ˈɑːr/ *abbr* = VIDEO CASSETTE RECORDER (VIDEO)

VD /ˌviː ˈdiː/ *abbr* = VENEREAL DISEASE

VDU /ˌviː diː ˈjuː/ *n* [C] visual display unit; machine with a screen like a television that displays information from a computer

veal /viːl/ *n* [U] meat from a calf (= a young cow)

veer /vɪə(r)/ *v* [I] change direction

0—¬ vegetable /ˈvedʒtəbl/ *n* [C] plant, eg potato, bean or onion, eaten as food: *root ~s, such as carrots* ◊ *a ~ garden/patch*

vegetarian /ˌvedʒəˈteəriən/ *n* [C] person who does not eat meat or fish ▸ **vegetarian** *adj*: *a ~ restaurant*

vegetate /ˈvedʒəteɪt/ *v* [I] (of a person) spend time doing very little and feeling bored

vegetation /ˌvedʒəˈteɪʃn/ *n* [U] (written) plants in general

veggie /ˈvedʒi/ *n* [C], *adj* (GB, infml) = VEGETARIAN

vehement /ˈviːəmənt/ *adj* (written) showing very strong feelings, esp anger ▸ **vehemence** /-məns/ *n* [U] ▸ **vehemently** *adv*

0—¬ vehicle /ˈviːəkl/ *n* [C] **1** something such as a car, bus or lorry that carries people or goods from place to place **2** ~ (**for**) way of expressing sth: *Art may be a ~ for propaganda.*

veil /veɪl/ *n* [C] **1** covering for a woman's face **2** [sing] (written) something that hides sth else: *a ~ of mist* ● **veil** *v* [T] **1** cover your face with a veil **2** (lit) cover with sth else that hides it partly or completely

vein /veɪn/ *n* **1** [C] any of the tubes that carry blood from all parts of the body to the heart **2** [C] thin line in a leaf or an insect's wing **3** [C] layer of metal or mineral in rock: *a ~ of gold*

4 [sing] particular style or manner: *in a comic ~*

velocity /vəˈlɒsəti/ *n* [U, C] (pl -ies) (fml or physics) speed

velvet /ˈvelvɪt/ *n* [U] cloth made of cotton, silk, etc with a thick soft surface on one side ▸ **velvety** *adj* soft like velvet

vendetta /venˈdetə/ *n* [C] long bitter quarrel between families who try to harm or kill each other

vending machine /ˈvendɪŋ məʃiːn/ *n* [C] machine from which you can buy cigarettes, drinks, etc by putting coins into it

vendor /ˈvendə(r)/ *n* [C] **1** person who sells food, sweets, newspapers, etc, usu outside on the street **2** (law) person who is selling a house or other property

veneer /vəˈnɪə(r)/ *n* **1** [C, U] thin layer of wood or plastic glued to the surface of cheaper wood **2** [sing] ~ (**of**) false outer appearance: *a ~ of politeness* ● **veneer** *v* [T] cover the surface of sth with a veneer of wood, etc

venerable /ˈvenərəbl/ *adj* (fml) deserving respect because of age, importance, etc

venerate /ˈvenəreɪt/ *v* [T] (fml) feel and show great respect for sb/sth ▸ **veneration** /-ˈreɪʃn/ *n* [U]

venereal disease /vəˌnɪəriəl dɪˈziːz/ *n* [C, U] (abbr **VD**) any disease caught by having sex with an infected person

vengeance /ˈvendʒəns/ *n* [U] (fml) act of punishing or harming sb in return for what they have done to you [**IDM**] **with a vengeance** (infml) to a greater degree than is expected or usual

vengeful /ˈvendʒfl/ *adj* (fml) showing a desire for revenge

venison /ˈvenɪsn; -zn/ *n* [U] meat from a deer

venom /ˈvenəm/ *n* [U] **1** poison of certain snakes, spiders, etc **2** (written) strong bitterness or hate ▸ **venomous** *adj*: *a~ous snake/ glance*

vent /vent/ *n* [C] hole for air, gas, liquid to pass through [**IDM**] **give (full) vent to sth** (fml) express a feeling, esp anger, strongly: *give~ to your feelings* ● **vent** *v* [T] (written) ~ (**on**) express feeling, esp anger, strongly: *He ~ed his anger on his brother.*

ventilate /ˈventɪleɪt/ *v* [T] allow fresh air to enter and move around a room, building, etc ▸ **ventilation** /-ˈleɪʃn/ *n* [U] ▸ **ventilator** *n* [C] **1** device or opening for letting fresh air come into a room **2** piece of equipment that helps sb to breathe

A B C D E F G H I J K L M N O P Q R S T U **V** W X Y Z

by pumping air in and out of their lungs

ventriloquist /ven'trɪləkwɪst/ n [C] person who can make their voice appear to come from another person

0━ **venture** /'ventʃə(r)/ n [C] business project or activity, esp one that involves taking risks: *The project is a joint ~.* ● **venture** v **1** [I] go somewhere even though you know it might be dangerous or unpleasant **2** [T] (*fml*) say or do sth carefully, esp because it might offend sb **3** [T] risk losing sth valuable or important if you are not successful at sth ■ **'venture capital** n [U] (*business*) money lent to sb to buy buildings, equipment, etc when they start a business

venue /'venjuː/ n [C] place where people meet for an organized event, eg a concert

veranda (*also* **verandah**) /vəˈrændə/ n [C] (*esp GB*) platform with an open front and a roof, built along one side of a house

verb /vɜːb/ n [C] (*gram*) word or phrase that expresses an action (eg *eat*), an event (eg *happen*) or a state (eg *exist*)

verbal /'vɜːbl/ adj **1** relating to words: *Applicants must have good ~ skills.* **2** spoken, not written: *a ~ agreement* **3** (*gram*) relating to verbs: *a ~ noun* ▶ **verbally** /-bəli/ adv in spoken words ■ **verbal 'noun** n [C] noun derived from a verb, eg *swimming* in: *Swimming is a good form of exercise.*

verbose /vɜːˈbəʊs/ adj (*fml*, *disapprov*) using more words than are needed ▶ **verbosity** /vɜːˈbɒsəti/ n [U]

verdict /'vɜːdɪkt/ n [C] **1** decision reached by a jury in a law court: *return a ~ of guilty/not guilty* **2** ~ (**on**) opinion or decision formed after you have tested or considered sth

verge /vɜːdʒ/ n [C] piece of grass at the edge of a path or road [IDM] **on/ to the verge of (doing) sth** very near to the moment when sb does sth or sth happens: *He was on the ~ of tears.* ● **verge** v [PV] **verge on/to sth** be very close to an extreme state or condition

verify /'verɪfaɪ/ v (pt, pp -**ied**) [T] make sure that sth is true ▶ **verifiable** adj ▶ **verification** /ˌverɪfɪˈkeɪʃn/ n [U]

veritable /'verɪtəbl/ adj (*fml* or *hum*) rightly named; real: *a ~ liar*

vermin /'vɜːmɪn/ n [pl] **1** small animals or insects that are harmful to crops, birds and other animals **2** (*disapprov*) people who are harmful to society

vernacular /vəˈnækjələ(r)/ adj, n [sing] (in or of the) language spoken in a particular area or by a particular group

versatile /'vɜːsətaɪl/ adj having many different skills or uses ▶ **versatility** /ˌvɜːsəˈtɪləti/ n [U]

verse /vɜːs/ n **1** [U] writing arranged in lines, each having a regular pattern **2** [C] set in a poem or song **3** [C] short numbered division of a chapter in the Bible

versed /vɜːst/ adj ~ **in** (*fml*) knowledgeable about or skilled in sth: *He had become well ~ in employment law.*

0━ **version** /'vɜːʃn/ n [C] **1** copy of sth that is slightly different from the original: *the film ~ of the play* **2** description of an event, etc from the point of view of one person: *There were three ~s of what happened.*

versus /'vɜːsəs/ prep (abbr **v**, **vs**) against: *England ~ Brazil*

vertebra /'vɜːtɪbrə/ n [C] (pl **-brae** /-briː/) any of the small bones that are connected together to form the backbone ▶ **vertebrate** /'vɜːtɪbrət/ n [C], adj (*tech*) (animal) having a backbone

0━ **vertical** /'vɜːtɪkl/ adj (of a line, pole, etc) going straight up or down from a level surface or from top to bottom in a picture, etc: *the ~ axis of the graph* ● **vertical** n [C] vertical line or position ▶ **vertically** /-kli/ adv

vertigo /'vɜːtɪɡəʊ/ n [U] feeling of dizziness and fear, caused by looking down from a high place

0━ **very** /'veri/ adv **1** to a great degree; extremely: *~ little/quickly* **2** used to emphasize a superlative or before *own*: *the ~ best quality* ◇ *his ~ own car* (= belonging to him and nobody else) [IDM] **very likely** → LIKELY ● **very** adj **1** actual: *This is the ~ book I want!* **2** extreme: *at the ~ end* **3** used to emphasize a noun: *The ~ thought of it upsets me.*

vessel /'vesl/ n [C] **1** (*fml*) large ship or boat **2** (*old-fash* or *tech*) container used for holding liquids, eg a cup

vest /vest/ n [C] **1** (*GB*) piece of underwear worn under a shirt, etc next to the skin **2** special piece of clothing that covers the upper body: *a bulletproof ~* **3** (*US*) = WAISTCOAT(WAIST) ● **vest** v [PV] **vest in sb/sth** (*law*) (of power, property, etc) belong to sb/sth legally **vest sth in sb/sth** | **vest sb with sth** (*fml*) **1** give sb the legal right or power to do sth: *the authority ~ed in her* **2** make sb the legal owner of land or property ■ **vested 'interest** n [C] ~ (**in**) personal reason for wanting sth to happen, esp because you benefit from it

vestige /ˈvestɪdʒ/ n [C] (fml) **1** small remaining part of sth **2** used in negative sentences to say that not even a small amount of sth exists: *not a ~ of truth in the report*

vet /vet/ n [C] doctor skilled in the treatment of sick animals ● vet v (-tt-) [T] find out about sb's past life and career in order to decide if they are suitable for a particular job

veteran /ˈvetərən/ n [C] person with long experience, eg as a soldier ■ **veteran 'car** n [C] car made before 1916, esp before 1905

veterinarian /ˌvetərɪˈneərɪən/ n (US) = VET

veterinary /ˈvetnrɪ; ˈvetərənərɪ/ adj connected with caring for the health of animals ■ **veterinary surgeon** n [C] (GB, fml) = VET

veto /ˈviːtəʊ/ n (pl ~es) **1** [C, U] official right to refuse to allow sth to be done, esp a law being passed **2** [C] ~ (on) occasion when sb refuses to allow sth to be done ● veto v [T] stop sth from happening or being done by using your official authority: ~ a proposal

vex /veks/ v (old-fash or fml) annoy or worry sb ▶ **vexation** /vekˈseɪʃn/ n [C, U] ▶ **vexed** adj (of a problem) very difficult and causing a lot of discussion

0━ **via** /ˈvaɪə/ prep **1** through a place **2** by means of a particular person, system, etc: *I heard about the sale ~ Tim.*

viable /ˈvaɪəbl/ adj (esp of a plan or business) capable of succeeding ▶ **viability** /-ˈbɪlətɪ/ n [U]

viaduct /ˈvaɪədʌkt/ n [C] long high bridge carrying a road or railway across a valley

vibrate /vaɪˈbreɪt/ v [I, T] (cause sth to) move from side to side very quickly and with small movements: *The house ~s whenever a heavy lorry passes.* ▶ **vibration** /-ˈbreɪʃn/ n [C, U]

vicar /ˈvɪkə(r)/ n [C] Anglican priest in charge of a church and the area around it (parish) ▶ **vicarage** /ˈvɪkərɪdʒ/ n [C] vicar's home

vice /vaɪs/ n **1** [U] criminal activities that involve sex or drugs: *plain-clothes detectives from the ~ squad* **2** [C, U] evil or immoral behaviour or quality in sb's character: (hum) *Cigarettes are my only ~.* **3** [C] tool with two metal jaws that hold sth firmly

vice- /vaɪs/ prefix next in rank to sb and able to represent them or act for them: ~*president*

vice versa /ˌvaɪs ˈvɜːsə/ adv the other way round: *We gossip about them and ~* (= they gossip about us.)

vicinity /vəˈsɪnətɪ/ n (the vicinity) [sing] area around a particular place

vicious /ˈvɪʃəs/ adj acting or done with evil intentions; cruel and violent ■ **vicious 'circle** n [sing] situation in which one problem causes another problem, which then makes the first problem worse ▶ **viciously** adv

0━ **victim** /ˈvɪktɪm/ n [C] person who has been attacked, injured or killed as the result of a crime, disease, accident, etc: ~*s of the flood* ▶ **victimize** (also -ise) v [T] make sb suffer unfairly ▶ **victimization** (also -isation) /ˌvɪktɪmaɪˈzeɪʃn/ n [U]

victor /ˈvɪktə(r)/ n [C] (lit) winner

0━ **victory** /ˈvɪktərɪ/ n [C, U] (pl -ies) success in a game, an election, a war, etc ▶ **victorious** /vɪkˈtɔːrɪəs/ adj having won a victory

0━ **video** /ˈvɪdɪəʊ/ n (pl ~s) **1** [U, C] (box containing a) type of magnetic tape used for recording moving pictures and sound **2** [C] copy of a film, programme, etc that is recorded on videotape **3** [C] (GB) = VIDEO CASSETTE RECORDER ● **video** v [T] record a television programme using a video recorder; film sb/sth using a video camera ■ **video camera** n [C] special camera for making video films ■ **video cas'sette recorder** n (abbr **VCR**) (also **'video recorder**) n [C] machine for recording and playing films and TV programmes on video ■ **'videoconferencing** n [U] system enabling people in different parts of the world to have a meeting by watching and listening to each other using video screens ■ **'videotape** n [U, C] = VIDEO(1)

vie /vaɪ/ v (pres pt **vying** /ˈvaɪɪŋ/) [I] ~ **with** compete with sb

0━ **view¹** /vjuː/ n **1** [C] personal opinion about sth; attitude towards sth: *In my ~, nurses deserve better pay.* **2** [U, sing] used when you are talking about whether you can see sth or whether sth can be seen in a particular situation: *The lake soon came into ~.* **3** [C] what can be seen from a place: *a wonderful ~ from the top of the mountain* [IDM] **in full view (of sb/sth)** completely visible; directly in front of sb/sth **in view of sth** considering sth: *In ~ of the weather, the event will be held indoors.* **on view** being shown in public **with a view to (doing) sth** (fml) with the intention of doing sth ■ **'viewdata** n [U] information system in which computer data is sent along telephone lines and shown on a television screen ■ **'viewfinder** n [C] part of a camera that you look through to see the area that you are photographing ■ **'viewpoint** n [C] way of thinking about a subject

0━ **view²** /vjuː/ v [T] **1** think about sb/sth in a particular way: ~ *the*

vigil /'vɪdʒɪl/ n [C,U] period of time when people stay awake, esp at night, to watch a sick person, say prayers, etc: *His mother kept a round-the-clock ~ at his bedside.*

vigilant /'vɪdʒɪlənt/ *adj* (*fml*) very careful to notice any signs of danger or trouble ▶ **vigilance** /-əns/ *n* [U] ▶ **vigilantly** *adv*

vigilante /ˌvɪdʒɪ'læntɪ/ *n* [C] member of a group who try to prevent crime or punish criminals in their community, esp because they think the police are not doing their job

vigour (*US* -or) /'vɪɡə(r)/ *n* [U] energy, force or enthusiasm ▶ **vigorous** *adj* strong or energetic ▶ **vigorously** *adv*

vile /vaɪl/ *adj* (~r, ~st) (*infml*) very unpleasant: *~ weather* **1** (*fml*) wicked; completely unacceptable ▶ **vilely** /'vaɪllɪ/ *adv*

villa /'vɪlə/ *n* [C] (*GB*) house for holiday makers, eg in the countryside: *rent a ~ in Tuscany*

0-w **village** /'vɪlɪdʒ/ *n* [C] very small town situated in a country area ▶ **villager** *n* [C] person who lives in a village

villain /'vɪlən/ *n* [C] **1** main bad character in a story, play, etc **2** (*GB*, *infml*) criminal **IDM the villain of the piece** (*hum*) person or thing to be blamed for a problem, damage, etc

vindicate /'vɪndɪkeɪt/ *v* [T] (*fml*) **1** prove that sth is true or that you were right to do sth **2** prove that sth is not guilty of sth ▶ **vindication** /-'keɪʃn/ *n* [C,U]

vindictive /vɪn'dɪktɪv/ *adj* wanting to harm or upset sb who has harmed you ▶ **vindictively** *adv* ▶ **vindictiveness** *n* [U]

vine /vaɪn/ *n* [C] climbing plant, esp one that produces grapes as its fruit ▶ **vineyard** /'vɪnjəd/ *n* [C] area of land planted with vines for making wine

vinegar /'vɪnɪɡə(r)/ *n* [U] bitter liquid made from malt, wine, etc, used to add flavour to food or to preserve it ▶ **vinegary** *adj*

vintage /'vɪntɪdʒ/ *n* [C] year in which a particular wine was made ● **vintage** *adj* **1** old and of very high quality **2** (*GB*) (of a vehicle) made between 1917 and 1930

vinyl /'vaɪnl/ *n* [U,C] kind of strong flexible plastic

viola /vi'əʊlə/ *n* [C] stringed musical instrument slightly larger than a violin

violate /'vaɪəleɪt/ *v* [T] **1** (*fml*) go against or refuse to obey a law, an agreement, etc **2** (*fml*) disturb or not respect sb's peace, privacy, etc **3** damage or destroy a holy place ▶ **violation** /-'leɪʃn/ *n* [U,C]

0-w **violent** /'vaɪələnt/ *adj* **1** involving or caused by physical force: *a ~ attack* **2** showing or caused by very strong emotion: *a ~ argument* **3** very strong and sudden: *a ~ thunderstorm* ▶ **violence** /-ləns/ *n* [U] **1** violent behaviour **2** physical or emotional force or energy ▶ **violently** *adv*

violet /'vaɪələt/ *n* **1** [C] small plant with sweet-smelling purple or white flowers **2** [U] bluish-purple colour

violin /ˌvaɪə'lɪn/ *n* [C] stringed musical instrument held under the chin and played with a bow ▶ **violinist** *n* [C] violin player

VIP /ˌviː aɪ 'piː/ *n* [C] Very Important Person; famous or important person who is treated in a special way

viper /'vaɪpə(r)/ *n* [C] poisonous snake

viral → VIRUS

virgin /'vɜːdʒɪn/ *n* [C] person who has never had sex ● **virgin** *adj* **1** pure or natural and not changed, touched or spoiled: *~ snow* **2** with no sexual experience ▶ **virginity** /və'dʒɪnətɪ/ *n* [U] state of being a virgin

virile /'vɪraɪl/ *adj* having the strength and (esp sexual) energy considered typical of men ▶ **virility** /və'rɪlətɪ/ *n* [U]

virtual /'vɜːtʃuəl/ *adj* **1** almost or very nearly the thing described: *The deputy manager is the ~ head of the business.* **2** made to appear to exist by the use of computer software: *~ memory/space* ● **virtual re'ality** *n* [U] images created by a computer that appear to surround the person looking at them and seem almost real

0-w **virtually** /'vɜːtʃuəlɪ/ *adv* **1** in every important respect; almost or very nearly: *V~ all the students passed the exam.* **2** by the use of computer software that makes sth appear to exist

virtue /'vɜːtʃuː/ *n* **1** [U] (*fml*) behaviour or attitudes that show high moral standards **2** [C] particular good quality or habit: *Patience is a ~.* **3** [C,U] attractive or useful quality: *The great ~ of the plan is its cheapness.* **IDM by/in virtue of sth** (*fml*) by means of or because of sth ▶ **virtuous** *adj* morally good

0-w **virus** /'vaɪrəs/ *n* [C] **1** tiny living thing that causes infectious disease **2** (*fml*) disease caused by a virus **3** instructions hidden within a computer program that are designed to cause faults or destroy data ▶ **viral** /'vaɪrəl/ *adj* like or caused by a virus: *a viral infection*

visa /'viːzə/ *n* [C] official mark put on

a passport allowing the owner to visit or leave a country

viscount /'vaɪkaʊnt/ n [C] (in Britain) nobleman of a rank below an earl and above a baron ▶ **viscountess** n [C] **1** woman who has the rank of a viscount **2** wife of a viscount

vise (US) = VICE(3)

0➔ **visible** /'vɪzəbl/ adj that can be seen ▶ **visibility** /-'bɪləti/ n [U] condition of the light or weather for seeing things clearly over a distance ▶ **visibly** adv clearly

0➔ **vision** /'vɪʒn/ n **1** [U] ability to see; area that you can see from a particular position **2** [C] idea or picture in your imagination: ~s of great wealth **3** [U] wisdom in planning the future: problems caused by lack of ~

visionary /'vɪʒənri/ adj (approv) original and showing vision (3) **2** relating to dreams or strange experiences ▶ **visionary** n [C] (pl -ies) person who has the ability to think about or plan the future in an intelligent, imaginative way

0➔ **visit** /'vɪzɪt/ v [I, T] go to see a person or place for a period of time: ~ a friend/Rome **2** [T] make an official visit to sb, eg to carry out checks or give advice [PV] visit with sb (US) spend time with sb, esp talking socially ● **visit** n [C] act or time of visiting sb/sth: pay a ~ to a friend ▶ **visitor** n [C] person who visits a person or place

visor /'vaɪzə(r)/ n [C] movable part of a helmet, covering the face

vista /'vɪstə/ n [C] (fml) **1** (lit) beautiful view **2** (written) range of things that might happen in the future: The job will open up new ~s for her.

visual /'vɪʒuəl/ adj of or connected with seeing or sight ■ **visual 'aid** n [usu pl] picture, video, etc used in teaching to help people understand sth ■ **visual dis'play unit** n [C] (computing) = VDU ▶ **visualize** (also -ise) v [T] form a mental picture of sb/sth ▶ **visually** adv

0➔ **vital** /'vaɪtl/ adj **1** necessary or very important: a ~ part of the machine **2** connected with or necessary for staying alive **3** (written) (of a person) full of energy and enthusiasm ▶ **vitality** /vaɪ'tæləti/ n [U] energy and enthusiasm ▶ **vitally** /'vaɪtəli/ adv extremely; in an essential way ■ **vital sta'tistics** n [pl] **1** figures that show the numbers of births and deaths in a country (esp GB, infml) **2** measurements of a woman's chest, waist and hips

vitamin /'vɪtəmɪn/ n [C] natural substance found in food that is an essential part of what humans and

animals eat to help them stay healthy

vitriolic /ˌvɪtri'ɒlɪk/ adj (fml) (of language or comments) very angry and bitter

vivacious /vɪ'veɪʃəs/ adj (approv) having a lively and attractive personality ▶ **vivaciously** adv ▶ **vivacity** /vɪ'væsəti/ n [U]

vivid /'vɪvɪd/ adj **1** (of memories, a description, etc) producing very clear pictures in your mind: a ~ description **2** (of light, colours, etc) very bright ▶ **vividly** adv

vivisection /ˌvɪvɪ'sekʃn/ n [U] experiments on living animals for scientific research

vixen /'vɪksn/ n [C] female fox

0➔ **vocabulary** /və'kæbjələri/ (pl -ies) n **1** [C, U] all the words that a person knows or uses: the ~ of a three-year-old **2** [C] all the words in a language **3** [C, U] list of words with their meanings, esp in a book for learning a foreign language

vocal /'vəʊkl/ adj **1** connected with the voice **2** expressing your opinions freely and loudly ● **vocal** n [C, usu pl] part of a piece of music that is sung, rather than played on an instrument: backing ~s ■ **vocal 'cords** n [pl] thin strips of muscle in the throat that move to produce the voice ▶ **vocalist** /-kəlɪst/ n [C] singer ▶ **vocally** /-kəli/ adv

vocation /vəʊ'keɪʃn/ n [C, U] **1** (fml) type of work or way of life that you believe is esp suitable for you: She believes that she has found her true ~ in life. **2** belief that a particular type of work or way of life is esp suitable for you ▶ **vocational** /-ʃənl/ adj connected with the skills, knowledge, etc that you need to do a particular job: ~al training

vociferous /və'sɪfərəs/ adj (fml) expressing your opinions in a loud and confident way: a ~ group of demonstrators ▶ **vociferously** adv

vodka /'vɒdkə/ n [U] strong Russian alcoholic drink

vogue /vəʊɡ/ n [C, U] fashion for sth: a new ~ for low-heeled shoes

0➔ **voice** /vɔɪs/ n **1** [C, U] sounds produced through the mouth by a person speaking or singing: recognize sb's ~ ◇ He's lost his ~ (= he cannot speak). **2** [U, sing] (right to express) your opinion: They should be allowed a ~ in deciding their future. ● **voice** v [T] tell people your feelings or opinions about sth

void /vɔɪd/ n [C] (fml) [usu sing] large empty space ● **void** adj **1** ~ (of) (fml) completely lacking sth (law) (of a contract, etc) not valid or legal ● **void** v [T] (law) state officially that sth is no longer valid

volatile /ˈvɒlətaɪl/ *adj* likely to change (in mood or behaviour) suddenly and unexpectedly

vol-au-vent /ˈvɒl əʊ vɒ̃/ *n* [C] small light pastry case filled with meat, fish, etc in a cream sauce

volcano /vɒlˈkeɪnəʊ/ *n* (pl **~es** or **~s**) mountain with an opening (crater) through which hot melted rock, gas, etc are forced out
▶ **volcanic** /-ˈkænɪk/ *adj*

volition /vəˈlɪʃn/ *n* [U] (*fml*) power to choose sth freely or to make your own decisions: *He left of his own ~ (= because he wanted to).*

volley /ˈvɒli/ *n* [C] **1** (in tennis, football, etc) hit or kick of the ball before it touches the ground **2** many bullets, stones, etc that are fired or thrown at the same time ● **volley** *v* [I,T] (in some sports) hit or kick the ball before it touches the ground: *He ~ed the ball into the back of the net.* ■ **volleyball** *n* [U] game in which a ball is thrown over a net

volt /vəʊlt/ *n* [C] (*abbr* **V**) unit for measuring the force of an electric current ▶ **voltage** *n* [C] electrical force measured in volts

voluble /ˈvɒljʊbl/ *adj* (*fml*) talking a lot ▶ **volubly** *adv*

0~ **volume** /ˈvɒljuːm/ *n* **1** [U,C] amount of space occupied by a substance **2** [U] amount of sth: *The ~ of exports fell last month.* **3** [U] amount of sound produced by a radio, television, etc: *the ~ control on the TV* **4** [C] (*fml*) book, esp one of a series

voluminous /vəˈluːmɪnəs/ *adj* (*fml*) **1** (of clothing) very large; using a lot of material: *a ~ skirt* **2** (of writing) very long and detailed

voluntary /ˈvɒləntri/ *adj* **1** done willingly, without being forced to: *Attendance is ~.* **2** (of work) done without payment: *a ~ organization* ▶ **voluntarily** /-trəli/ *adv*

volunteer /ˌvɒlənˈtɪə(r)/ *n* [C] **1** person who offers to do sth without being forced or paid **2** person who chooses to join the armed forces without being forced to join ● **volunteer** *v* [I,T] offer to do sth without being forced or paid to do it **2** [T] suggest sth or tell sb sth without being asked **3** [I] ~ **for** join the armed forces voluntarily

voluptuous /vəˈlʌptʃuəs/ *adj* (*written*) **1** (of a woman) having a full and sexually desirable figure **2** (*lit*) giving you physical pleasure ▶ **voluptuously** *adv*

vomit /ˈvɒmɪt/ *v* [I,T] bring food from the stomach back out through the mouth ● **vomit** *n* [U] food from the stomach that has been vomited

0~ **vote** /vəʊt/ *n* **1** [C] formal choice that you make in an election or at a meeting in order to choose sb or decide sth **2** [C] ~ **(on)** occasion when a group of people vote on sth: *have/take a ~ on an issue* **3** (the vote) [sing] total number of votes in an election: *She obtained 40% of the ~.* **4** (the vote) [sing] right to vote in political elections ● **vote** *v* [I,T] formally express an opinion, support for sb, etc by marking a paper or raising your hand: *~ for/against sb* ◇ ~ *on the suggestion* **2** [T] suggest sth or support a suggestion that sb has made ▶ **voter** *n* [C]

vouch /vaʊtʃ/ *v* [PV] **vouch for sb** say that sb will behave well and that you will be responsible for their actions **vouch for sth** say that you believe that sth is true or good because you have evidence for it

voucher /ˈvaʊtʃə(r)/ *n* [C] piece of paper that can be exchanged for certain goods or services

vow /vaʊ/ *n* [C] formal and serious promise, esp a religious one, to do sth ● **vow** *v* [I,T] make a formal promise to do sth or a formal statement that sth is true

vowel /ˈvaʊəl/ *n* [C] **1** speech sound in which the mouth is open and the tongue is not touching the top of the mouth, the teeth, etc **2** letter that represents a vowel sound, eg *a, e, i, o* and *u*

voyage /ˈvɔɪdʒ/ *n* [C] (*written*) long journey, esp by sea or in space ● **voyage** *v* [I] (*lit*) travel, esp in a ship ▶ **voyager** *n* [C]

vs *abbr* (*esp US*) = VERSUS

vulgar /ˈvʌlɡə(r)/ *adj* **1** showing a lack of good taste; not polite, elegant or well behaved **2** rude and likely to offend ▶ **vulgarity** /vʌlˈɡærəti/ *n* [U]

vulnerable /ˈvʌlnərəbl/ *adj* weak and easily hurt physically or emotionally ▶ **vulnerability** /ˌvʌlnərəˈbɪləti/ *n* [U]

vulture /ˈvʌltʃə(r)/ *n* [C] **1** large bird that eats the flesh of dead animals **2** person who hopes to gain from the troubles or suffering of others

vying *pres part* VIE

W w

W *abbr* **1** west(ern): *W Yorkshire* **2** watt(s)

W, w /ˈdʌbljuː/ *n* [C,U] (pl **W's, w's** /ˈdʌbljuːz/) the twenty-third letter of the English alphabet

wacky /ˈwæki/ *adj* (**-ier, -iest**) (*infml*) funny or amusing in a slightly crazy way

wad /wɒd/ *n* [C] **1** thick pile of papers, banknotes, etc folded or rolled together **2** mass of soft material: *a ~ of cotton wool*

waddle /ˈwɒdl/ v [I] walk with short steps, swinging from side to side, like a duck ▸ **waddle** n [sing]

wade /weɪd/ v [I] walk with an effort through sth, esp water or mud [PV] **wade in|wade into sth** (*infml*) enter a fight, argument or argument in a forceful or insensitive way **wade through sth** deal with or read sth that is boring and takes a lot of time ■ **'wading bird** (*also* **'wader**) n [C] long-legged bird that feeds in shallow water

wafer /ˈweɪfə(r)/ n [C] **1** thin crisp light biscuit, eaten with ice cream **2** very thin round piece of special bread given by a priest during Communion

waffle /ˈwɒfl/ v **1** [C] small crisp pancake with a pattern of raised squares **2** [U] (*GB, infml*) language that uses a lot of words but does not say anything important or interesting ● **waffle** v [I] (*GB, infml, disapprov*) talk or write using a lot of words but without saying anything important or interesting

waft /wɒft/ v [I,T] (cause sth to) move gently through the air: *The scent ~ed into the room.* ▸ **waft** n [C]

wag /wæɡ/ v (**-gg-**) [I,T] (cause sth to) move from side to side: *The dog ~ged its tail.* ▸ **wag** n [C]

0─┳ **wage** /weɪdʒ/ n [C] (*also* **wages** [pl]) regular amount of money that you earn, usu every week, for work or services: *fight for higher ~s* ◇ *a ~ increase* ● **wage** v [T] ~ (**against/on**) begin and continue a war, campaign, etc: *~ a war on poverty*

wager /ˈweɪdʒə(r)/ n [C], v [I,T] (*old-fash or fml*) = BET

waggle /ˈwæɡl/ v [I,T] (cause sth to) move with short movements from side to side or up and down

wagon /ˈwæɡən/ n [C] **1** railway truck for carrying goods (*GB also* **waggon**) **2** vehicle with four wheels, pulled by horses and used for carrying heavy loads

wail /weɪl/ v [I] **1** make a long loud high cry, esp because you are sad or in pain: *a ~ing child* **2** (of things) make a long high sound: *~ing sirens* ● **wail** n [C] long loud high cry

0─┳ **waist** /weɪst/ n [C] **1** area around the middle of the body between the ribs and the hips **2** part of a piece of clothing that covers the waist ■ **'waistcoat** n [C] (*GB*) short piece of clothing with buttons down the front but no sleeves, often worn under a man's jacket ■ **'waistline** n [C] measurement of the body around the waist

0─┳ **wait** /weɪt/ v **1** [I] ~ (**for**) stay where you are or delay doing sth until sb/sth comes or sth happens: *We had to ~ an hour for the train.* ◇ *I'm ~ing to see the manager.* **2** [T] ~ (**for**) hope or watch for sth to happen, esp for a long time: *He is ~ing for his opportunity.* **3** [T] be left to be dealt with at a later time: *The matter isn't urgent; it can ~.* [IDM] **I, they, etc can't wait/can hardly wait** used when you are emphasizing that sb is very excited about sth or keen to do it: *I can't ~ to tell her the news!* **wait and see** used to tell sb to be patient and wait to find out about sth later **wait on sb hand and foot** (*disapprov*) do everything that sb wants ■ **wait on sb** act as a servant to sb, esp by serving food to them **wait up (for sb)** wait for sb to come home before you go to bed ● **wait** n [C, usu sing] act or time of waiting: *We had a long ~ for the bus.* ▸ **waiter** (*fem* **waitress** /ˈweɪtrəs/) n [C] person whose job is to serve customers at their tables in a restaurant, etc ■ **'waiting list** n [C] list of people who are waiting for sth that is not yet available ■ **'waiting room** n [C] room where people can sit while they are waiting, eg for a train or to see a doctor

waive /weɪv/ v [T] choose not to insist on a rule or right in a particular situation: *~ a fee*

0─┳ **wake¹** /weɪk/ v (*pt* **woke** /wəʊk/ *pp* **woken** /ˈwəʊkən/) [I,T] ~ (**up**) (cause sb to) stop sleeping: *What time did you ~ up?* [IDM] **your waking hours** time when you are awake [PV] **wake up to sth** become aware of sth; realize sth

wake² /weɪk/ n [C] **1** occasion before a funeral when people gather to remember the dead person **2** track left on the surface of water by a moving ship [IDM] **in the wake of sb/sth** coming after or following sb/sth

waken /ˈweɪkən/ v [I,T] (*written*) (cause sb to) wake from sleep

0─┳ **walk¹** /wɔːk/ v **1** [I] move or go somewhere by putting one foot in front of the other on the ground, but without running **2** [T] go somewhere with sb on foot, esp to make sure they get there safely: *I'll ~ you home.* **3** [T] take an animal for a walk [PV] **walk away/off with sth** (*infml*) **1** win sth easily **2** steal sth **walk into sth** (*infml*) **1** become caught in an unpleasant situation, esp because you are careless: *~ into a trap* **2** get a job very easily **walk out** (*infml*) (of workers) go on strike **walk out (of sth)** leave a meeting, etc, esp in order to show your disapproval **walk out on sb** (*infml*) suddenly leave sb that you are having a relationship with: *How could he ~ out on her and the kids like that?* **walk (all) over sb** (*infml*) treat sb badly

■ **walkabout** n [C] (GB) occasion when an important person walks among ordinary people to meet and talk to them ▶ **walker** n [C] person who walks ■ **walking stick** n [C] stick that you carry and use as a support when walking

■ **Walkman™** n [C] (pl ~s) small cassette or CD player with headphones that you carry with you and use while you are moving around ■ **walk-on** adj (of a part in a play) small and with no words to say ■ **walkout** n [C] sudden strike by workers ■ **walkover** n [C] easy victory

0─■ **walk²** /wɔːk/ n [C] journey on foot, usu for pleasure or exercise: My house is a five-minute ~ from the shops. **2** [C] path or route for walking **3** [sing] way of walking: a slow ~ [IDM] **a walk of life** a person's job or position in society

walkie-talkie /ˌwɔːki ˈtɔːki/ n [C] (infml) small radio that you can carry with you and use to send or receive messages

0─■ **wall** /wɔːl/ n [C] **1** long upright solid structure of stone, brick, etc that surrounds, divides or protects sth **2** any of the upright sides of a room or building **3** something that forms a barrier or prevents progress: Investigators were confronted by a ~ of silence. **4** outer layer of sth hollow, eg an organ of the body: the abdominal ~ [IDM] **go to the wall** (infml) (of a company or organization) fail because of lack of money **up the wall** (infml) crazy or angry: Dad will go up the ~ if I'm late. ● **wall** v [T] surround an area, town, etc with a wall or walls: a ~ed garden [PV] **wall sth/sb in** surround sth/sb with a wall or barrier **wall sth off** separate one place or area from another with a wall **wall sth up** block sth with a wall or bricks

■ **wallflower** n [C] garden plant with sweet-smelling flowers ■ **wallpaper** n [U] **1** paper, usu with a coloured design, for covering the walls of a room **2** background pattern or picture on your computer screen ■ **wallpaper** v [T] cover the walls of a room with wallpaper ■ **wall-to-'wall** adj covering the floor of a room completely

0─■ **wallet** /ˈwɒlɪt/ n [C] small flat case, esp for carrying paper money and credit cards

wallop /ˈwɒləp/ v [T] (infml) hit sb/sth very hard ▶ **wallop** n [sing]

wallow /ˈwɒləʊ/ v [I] ~ (in) **1** (of animals or people) roll about in mud, water, etc **2** take pleasure in sth: ~ in luxury/self-pity

Wall Street /ˈwɔːl striːt/ n [U] US financial centre and stock exchange in New York City

wally /ˈwɒli/ n [C] (pl **-ies**) (GB, infml) stupid person

walnut /ˈwɔːlnʌt/ n **1** [C] (tree producing a) large nut with a hard round shell in two halves **2** [U] brown wood of the walnut tree, used for making furniture

walrus /ˈwɔːlrəs/ n [C] large sea animal with thick fur and two long outer teeth (tusks)

waltz /wɔːls/ n [C] (music for a) graceful ballroom dance ● **waltz** v [I] **1** dance a waltz **2** (infml) walk or go somewhere in a very confident way: I don't like him ~ing into the house as if he owns it.

WAN /wæn/ n [C] (pl ~s) (computing) wide area network; system in which computers in different places are connected, usu over a large area

wan /wɒn/ adj (written) looking pale and weak

wand /wɒnd/ n [C] long thin stick used by a magician

0─■ **wander** /ˈwɒndə(r)/ v [I, T] walk around a place with no special purpose: ~ round the streets ◇ ~ away from the subject **2** [I] (of sb's thoughts) move away from the subject: You ~ to the point. ▶ **wanderer** n [C] ▶ **wanderings** n [pl] (written) journeys from place to place

wane /weɪn/ v [I] **1** gradually become weaker or less important **2** (of the moon) appear slightly smaller each day after being round and full ● **wane** n [sing] [IDM] **on the wane** (fml) becoming smaller, less important or less common

wangle /ˈwæŋɡl/ v [T] ~ (from/out of) (infml) get sth that you want by persuading sb or by a clever plan: ~ an extra week's holiday

0─■ **want¹** /wɒnt/ v **1** [I, T] have a desire or wish for sth: They ~ a new car. ◇ I ~ to go home. **2** [I, T] (infml) need sth: The grass ~s cutting. **3** [I] ~ **to** (infml) used to give advice to sb, meaning should: You ~ to be more careful. **4** [T] feel sexual desire for sb **5** [T] (fml) lack sth [PV] **want sb for sth** (esp in negative sentences) (fml) lack sth that you really need: They ~ for nothing (= they have everything they need). ▶ **wanted** adj being searched for by the police in connection with a crime: America's most ~ed man ▶ **wanting** adj ~ (in) (fml) **1** not having enough of sth **2** not good enough: The new system was tried and found ~ing.

want² /wɒnt/ n **1** [C, usu pl] sth that you need or want **2** [U, sing] ~ of (fml) lack of sth: die for ~ of water

WAP /wæp/ abbr wireless application protocol; technology that links devices such as mobile phones to the Internet: a ~ phone

war /wɔ:(r)/ n [C,U] **1** (instance or period of) armed fighting between countries: *the First World W~* ◇ *an at ~* **2** struggle or competition: *a trade ~* ◇ *the ~ on drugs* [IDM] **have been in the wars** (*spoken*) have been injured in a fight or an accident ■ **'warfare** n [U] activity of fighting a war: *chemical ~* ■ **'war game** n [C] practice battle used as a training exercise ■ **'warhead** n [C] explosive front end of a missile ■ **'warlike** *adj* (*fml*) **1** aggressive and wanting to fight **2** connected with fighting wars ■ **'warpath** n [IDM] **(be/go) on the warpath** (*infml*) (be) angry and wanting to fight or punish sb ▶ **'warring** *adj* involved in a war: *~ring tribes* ■ **'warship** n [C] ship used in war ■ **'wartime** n [U] period of war

warble /'wɔ:bl/ v [I,T] (esp of a bird) sing with rapidly changing notes ▶ **warbler** n [C] bird that warbles

ward /wɔ:d/ n [C] **1** separate room in a hospital for people with the same type of medical condition **2** (in Britain) division of a local government area **3** (*law*) person, usu a child, under the protection of a guardian ▶ **ward** v [PV] **ward sb/sth off** protect or defend yourself from danger, illness, attack, etc

warden /'wɔ:dn/ n [C] person responsible for taking care of a particular place and for making sure rules are obeyed: *the ~ of a youth hostel*

warder /'wɔ:də(r)/ n [C] (fem **wardress** /'wɔ:drəs/) (*GB*) guard in a prison

wardrobe /'wɔ:drəʊb/ n [C] **1** tall cupboard for hanging clothes in **2** [usu sing] the clothes that a person has **3** [usu sing] department in a TV or theatre company that takes care of the clothes the actors wear

ware /weə(r)/ n **1** [U] (in compounds) manufactured goods of the type mentioned: *silver~* **2** (**wares**) [pl] (*old-fash*) things that sb is selling ■ **'warehouse** n [C] large building for storing goods

warm /wɔ:m/ *adj* **1** fairly hot; between cool and hot: *~ water* **2** (of clothes, buildings, etc) keeping you warm or staying warm in cold weather: *a ~ jumper* **3** friendly and enthusiastic: *a ~ welcome* **4** (of colours) creating a comfortable feeling or atmosphere ■ **warm** v [T] (cause sth/sb) to become warm/er [PV] **warm to/towards sb/sth 1** begin to like sb/sth **2** become more interested in sth ■ **warm up** prepare for physical exercise or a performance by doing gentle exercises or practice ■ **warm (sb/sth) up** (cause sb/sth) to become more lively or enthusiastic ■ **warm-'blooded** *adj* (of animals) having a

constant blood temperature ■ **warm-'hearted** *adj* (of a person) kind ▶ **warmly** *adv* ▶ **warmth** n [U] state or quality of being warm

warn /wɔ:n/ v [T] tell sb in advance about a possible danger or difficulty: *I ~ed her that it would cost a lot.* ◇ *They were ~ed not to climb the mountain in bad weather.* ▶ **warning** n **1** [C,U] statement, event, etc telling sb that sth bad may happen in the future: *He didn't listen to my ~ing.* **2** [C] statement telling sb that they will be punished if they continue to behave in a certain way ▶ **warning** *adj*: *~ing signs of trouble ahead*

warp /wɔ:p/ v [I,T] (cause sth to) become bent or twisted: *Some wood ~s in hot weather.* **2** [T] influence sb so that they behave in an unacceptable or shocking way: *a ~ed mind*

warrant /'wɒrənt/ n [C] legal document giving sb authority to do sth: *a ~ for his arrest* ■ **warrant** v [T] (*fml*) make sth necessary or appropriate in a particular situation ▶ **warranty** n [C,U] (pl -**ies**) written agreement in which a company promises to repair or replace a product if there is a problem

warren /'wɒrən/ n [C] (*also* **rabbit warren**) **1** system of holes and underground tunnels where wild rabbits live **2** (*disapprov*) building or part of a city with many narrow passages or streets

warrior /'wɒriə(r)/ n [C] (*fml*) (esp in the past) soldier; fighter

wart /wɔ:t/ n [C] small hard lump on the skin

wary /'weəri/ *adj* (-**ier**, -**iest**) looking out for possible danger or difficulty ▶ **warily** *adv*

was /wəz; strong form wɒz/ *third pers sing pres tense* BE

wash[1] /wɒʃ/ v **1** [T] make sth/sb clean using water and usu soap: *~ your hands/clothes* **2** ~ (**yourself**) [I,T] make yourself clean using water and usu soap: *I had to ~ and dress in a hurry.* **3** [I] (of clothes, fabrics, etc) be able to be washed without damage: *Does this sweater ~ well?* **4** [I,T] (of water) flow or carry sth in a particular direction: *Pieces of the wreckage were ~ed ashore.* [IDM] **wash your hands of sb/sth** refuse to be involved with or responsible for sb/sth **sth won't/doesn't wash (with sb)** used to say that sb's explanation, excuse, etc is not valid or acceptable: *That excuse just won't ~ with me.* [PV] **wash sb/sth away** (of water) remove or carry sb/sth away to another place ■ **wash sth down (with sth) 1** clean sth large or a

wash

surface with a lot of water **2** drink sth while or after eating food: *We had bread and cheese ~ed down with beer.* **wash sth out 1** wash the inside of sth to remove dirt, etc **2** remove a substance from sth by washing **3** (of rain) make a game, an event, etc end early or prevent it from starting **wash (sth) up** wash plates, glasses, etc after a meal ▸ **washable** *adj* that can be washed without being damaged ■ **washbasin** *n* [C] bowl with taps that is fixed to a wall in a bathroom, used for washing your hands and face in ■ **washed out** *adj* **1** (of fabric or colours) no longer brightly coloured **2** (of a person) pale and tired ■ **washing-up** *n* [U] (GB) (act of washing the) dirty plates, glasses, pans, etc left after a meal ■ **washing-up liquid** *n* [U] (GB) liquid soap for washing dishes, pans, etc ■ **washout** *n* [C] (*infml*) complete failure ■ **washroom** *n* [C] (US, old-fash) toilet

wash² /wɒʃ/ *n* **1** [C, usu sing] act of cleaning sth by using water and usu soap: *give the car a good ~* **2** (the wash) [sing] (sound made by the) movement of water caused by a passing boat

washer /'wɒʃə(r)/ *n* [C] **1** small flat ring of metal, plastic, etc for making a screw or joint tight **2** (*infml*) = WASHING MACHINE (WASHING)

0–┳ **washing** /'wɒʃɪŋ/ *n* [U] **1** act of washing sth: *I do the ~* (= wash the clothes) *in our house.* **2** clothes, sheets, etc that are waiting to be washed or that have been washed: *hang the ~ out on the line* ■ **washing machine** *n* [C] electric machine for washing clothes ■ **washing powder** *n* [U] soap in the form of powder for washing clothes

wasn't /'wɒznt/ = BE

wasp /wɒsp/ *n* [C] flying insect with black and yellow stripes and a sting in its tail

wastage /'weɪstɪdʒ/ *n* [U, sing] fact of losing or destroying sth, esp because it has been used carelessly **2** [U] amount of sth that is wasted **3** [U] reduction in numbers of employees or students: *natural ~*

0–┳ **waste¹** /weɪst/ *v* [T] **1** use more of sth than is necessary or useful **2** not make good or full use of sb/ sth: *~ an opportunity* [PV] **waste away** (of a person) become thin and weak

0–┳ **waste²** /weɪst/ *n* [U, sing] **~ (of)** act of using sth in a careless or unnecessary way: *a ~ of time/money* ◊ *I hate to see good food go to ~* (= thrown away). **2** [U] materials that are no longer needed and are thrown away: *industrial ~* **3** (wastes) [pl] large area of land where there are few people, animals or plants:

the frozen ~s of Siberia ● **waste** *adj* **1** (of land) not suitable for building or growing things and therefore not used: *~ ground* **2** no longer useful and to be thrown away: *~ paper* ▸ **wasteful** *adj* causing waste: *~ful processes* ▸ **wastefully** *adv* ■ **waste-paper basket** *n* [C] container for waste paper

0–┳ **watch¹** /wɒtʃ/ *v* **1** [I, T] look at sb/ sth carefully for a period of time **2** [T] take care of sb/sth for a short time: *Can you ~ my bags for me while I go to the loo?* **3** [T] (*infml*) be careful about sth: *~ your mouth on the low ceiling* [IDM] **watch your step** → STEP¹ [PV] **watch out** (spoken) used to warn sb about sth dangerous **watch over sb/ sth** (*fml*) take care of sb/sth; protect and guard sb/sth ▸ **watcher** *n* [C] person who watches and studies sb/ sth regularly

0–┳ **watch²** /wɒtʃ/ *n* **1** [C] small clock worn on the wrist **2** [sing, U] act of watching sb/sth carefully in case of danger or problems: *keep / a)s close ~ on her* **3** [C, U] fixed period of time, usu while others are asleep, during which sb watches for any danger so that they can warn others; the person who does this: *I'm on first ~.* [IDM] **be on the watch (for sb/sth)** be looking carefully for sb/sth, esp in order to avoid danger: *Be on the ~ for thieves.* ■ **watchdog** *n* [C] person or group of people whose job is to protect people's rights ▸ **watchful** *adj* paying attention to what is happening in case of danger, accidents, etc ■ **watchman** /'wɒtʃmən/ *n* [C] (pl **-men** /-mən/) person whose job is to guard a building, esp at night ■ **watchword** *n* [C] word or phrase that expresses sb's beliefs or attitudes

0–┳ **water¹** /'wɔːtə(r)/ *n* **1** [U] clear colourless liquid that falls as rain, is found in rivers, etc and is used for drinking **2** [U] area of water, esp a lake, river, etc: *He fell into the ~.* **3** (waters) [pl] the water in a particular lake, river, sea or ocean **4** [U] surface of a mass of water: *She dived under the ~.* **5** (waters) [pl] area of sea or ocean belonging to a particular country: *in British ~s* ■ **water cannon** *n* [C] machine that produces a powerful jet of water, used for breaking up crowds ■ **water closet** *n* [C] (*abbr* **WC**) (old-fash) toilet ■ **watercolour** (US -color) *n* **1** (watercolours) [pl] paints that you mix with water, not oil, and use for painting pictures **2** [C] picture painted with these paints ■ **watercress** *n* [U] plant that grows in running water, with leaves used as food ■ **waterfall** *n* [C] place where a stream or river falls from a high place ■ **waterfront** *n* [C, usu sing] part of a town or area that is next to water, eg in a harbour ■ **waterhole** (*also* **watering hole**) *n* [C] pool in a hot country, where animals go to drink ■ **waterlogged** /-lɒɡd/ *adj* **1** (of soil, a field, etc) extremely wet **2** (of a boat) full of water ■ **watermark** *n* [C] design in some kinds of paper that can be seen when the paper is held up to the light ■ **watermelon** /-melən/ *n* [C, U] large round dark green fruit with red flesh and black seeds ■ **watermill** *n* [C] mill next to a river in which the machinery for grinding grain into flour is driven by the power of the water turning a wheel ■ **waterproof** *n* [C], *adj* (coat) that does not let water through ▸ **waterproof** *v* [T] make sth waterproof ■ **watershed** *n* [C] **1** event or period of time that marks an important change **2** line of high land separating river systems ■ **waterside** *n* [sing] edge of a river, lake, etc ■ **waterski** *v* [i] ski on water while being pulled along by a boat ▸ **waterskiing** *n* [U] ■ **water table** *n* [C] level below which the ground is filled with water ■ **watertight** *adj* **1** that does not allow water to get in or out **2** (of an excuse, plan, argument, etc) containing no mistakes, faults or weaknesses ■ **waterway** *n* [C] river, canal, etc along which boats can travel ■ **waterworks** *n* [C, with sing or pl verb] building with pumping machinery, etc for supplying water to an area [IDM] **turn on the waterworks** (*infml, disapprov*) start crying

water² /ˈwɔːtə(r)/ *v* **1** [T] pour water on plants, etc: ~ *the lawn* **2** [I] (of the eyes) become full of tears **3** [I] (of the mouth) produce saliva **4** [T] give water to an animal to drink [PV] **water sth down 1** make a liquid weaker by adding water **2** change a speech, piece of writing, etc to make it less offensive ■ **watering can** *n* [C] container with a long spout, used for watering plants

watery /ˈwɔːtəri/ *adj* **1** containing too much water **2** (of colours) pale; weak

watt /wɒt/ *n* [C] unit of electrical power

0━ wave /weɪv/ *v* **1** [I,T] move your hand or arm from side to side in the air to attract attention, as a greeting, etc **2** [I,T] show where sth is, show sb where to go, etc by moving your hand in a particular direction: *The guard ~d us on.* **3** [T] hold sth in your hand and move it from side to side: ~ *a flag* **4** [i] move freely and gently, while one end or side is held in position: *branches ~ing in the wind* [PV] **wave sth aside/away** not accept sth because you do not think it is important ● **wave** *n* [C] **1** raised line

of water that moves across the surface of the sea, etc **2** sudden increase in a particular feeling or activity: *a ~of panic* **3** movement of your arm or hand from side to side: *with a ~ of his hand* **4** form in which heat, sound, light, etc is carried: *radio ~s* **5** (of hair) slight curl ■ **wavelength** *n* [C] **1** distance between two similar points on a wave of energy, eg light or sound **2** size of a radio wave used by a particular radio station, etc ▸ **wavy** *adj* (**-ier, -iest**) having curves; not straight: *a wavy line ◇ wavy hair*

waver /ˈweɪvə(r)/ *v* [i] **1** be or become weak or unsteady **2** hesitate about making a decision **3** move unsteadily

wax /wæks/ *n* [U] soft easily-melted sticky or oily substance used for making candles, polish, etc ● **wax** *v* **1** [T] polish or cover sth with wax **2** [T] remove hair from a part of the body using wax **3** [i] (of the moon) seem to get gradually bigger until its full form is visible **4** [i] (~ lyrical, eloquent, etc) (*written*) become lyrical, eloquent, etc when speaking or writing

0━ way¹ /weɪ/ *n* **1** [C] method, style or manner of doing sth: *the best ~ to help people ◇ the rude ~ in which she spoke to us* **2** (ways) [pl] habits: *She is not going to change her ~s.* **3** [C, usu sing] route or road that you take in order to reach a place: *ask sb the ~ to the airport* **4** [C, usu sing] route along which sb/sth is moving or that sb/sth would take if there was nothing stopping them/it: *Get out of my ~! I'm in a hurry.* **5** [C] road, path, etc **6** [C, usu sing] (in a) particular direction: *He went the other ~.* **7** [sing] distance or period of time between two points: *It's a long ~ to London.* **8** [C] particular aspect of sth: *In some ~s, I agree with you.* **9** [sing] particular condition or state: *The economy's in a bad ~.* [IDM] **by the way** (*spoken*) used to introduce a new subject when talking **by way of sth** (*fml*) as a form of sth: *say something by ~ of introduction* **get/ have your (own) way** get or do what you want, esp when sb has tried to stop you **give way** break or fall down **give way (to sb/sth) 1** stop resisting sb/sth; agree to do sth that you do not want to do: *give ~ to their demands* **2** (*GB*) allow sb/sth to be or go first: *Give ~ to traffic coming from the right.* **3** be replaced by **go out of your way (to do sth)** make a special effort to do sth **go your own way** do what you want in the/sb's way stopping sb from moving or doing sth **make way (for sb/sth)** allow sb/sth to pass **(there is) no way**

(*infml*) used to say that there is no possibility that you will do sth or that sth will happen **on your/the/its way**
1 going or coming **on your way**
1 no longer blocking sb/sth or causing inconvenience: *I moved my legs out of the ~ to let her get past.* **2** finished **3** far from a town or city **4** unusual **under way** having started and making progress **way of life** typical beliefs, habits and behaviour of a person or group

way² /weɪ/ *adv* (used with a preposition or an adverb) very far; by a large amount: *She timed the race ~ ahead of the others.* ■ **way-out** *adj* (*infml*) unusual or strange

waylay /weɪˈleɪ/ *v* (*pt, pp* **-laid** /-ˈleɪd/) [T] stop sb from going somewhere, eg in order to talk to them or attack them

wayward /ˈweɪwəd/ *adj* (*written*) difficult to control: *a ~ child*

WC /ˌdʌbljuː ˈsiː/ *abbr* (GB) (on signs and doors in public places) water closet; toilet

0— **we** /wiː/ *pron* (used as the subject of a v) I and another person or other people: *We are all going to visit him.*

0— **weak** /wiːk/ *adj* **1** not physically strong: *still ~ after his illness* **2** easily bent, broken or defeated: *a ~ joint/ team* **3** easy to influence; not having much power: *a ~ leader* **4** not good at sth: *~ at mathematics* **5** not convincing: *a ~ argument* **6** not easily seen or heard: *~ sound/light* **7** containing a lot of water: *~ tea*
▶ **weaken** *v* [I,T] become or make sb/ sth weak ■ **weak-¦kneed** *adj* (*infml*) lacking courage or strength ▶ **weakling** *n* [C] (*disapprov*) weak person ▶ **weakly** *adv* ▶ **weakness** *n* **1** [U] lack of strength, power or determination **2** [C] fault or defect: *We all have our little ~nesses.* **3** [C, usu sing] difficulty in resisting sth/sb that you like very much: *a ~ for cream cakes*

0— **wealth** /welθ/ *n* **1** [U] large amount of money, property, etc that a person or country owns **2** [U] state of being rich **3** [sing] *~ of* large amount of sth: *a ~ of information* ▶ **wealthy** *adj* (**-ier, -iest**) rich

wean /wiːn/ *v* [T] gradually stop feeding a baby with its mother's milk and start giving it solid food [PV] **wean sb off/from sth** cause sb to stop doing sth gradually

0— **weapon** /ˈwepən/ *n* [C] something, eg a gun, bomb or sword, used in fighting ▶ **weaponry** *n* [U] weapons

0— **wear¹** /weə(r)/ *v* (*pt* **wore** /wɔː(r)/ *pp* **worn** /wɔːn/) **1** [T] have sth on your body as a piece of clothing, an ornament, etc: *a ~ dress* **2** [T] have your hair in a particular style; have a beard or moustache **3** [T] have a particular expression on your face: *a ~ smile* **4** [T] (cause sth to) become thinner, smoother or weaker through continuous use or rubbing: *The carpets are starting to ~.* **5** [I] stay in good condition after being used for a long time: *These shoes have worn well.* **6** [T] (*infml*) accept or allow sth [PV] **wear (sth) away** (cause sth to) become thinner, smoother, etc by continuously using or rubbing it **wear (sth) down** (cause sth to) become gradually smaller, smoother, etc **wear sb/sth down** gradually make sb/sth weaker or less determined **wear off** gradually disappear or stop **wear on** (written) (of time) pass, esp slowly **wear (sth) out** (cause sth to) become useless because of constant wear or use **wear yourself/sb out** make yourself/ sb feel very tired

wear² /weə(r)/ *n* [U] **1** (in compounds) clothes for a particular purpose or occasion: *mens~* **2** fact of wearing sth: *clothes for everyday ~* **3** amount or type of use that sth has over time: *There's a lot of ~ in these shoes yet.* **4** damage or loss of quality from use: *The carpet is showing signs of ~.* [IDM] **wear and tear** damage to objects, furniture, etc caused by normal use

weary /ˈwɪəri/ *adj* (**-ier, -iest**) very tired ▶ **wearily** *adv* ▶ **weariness** *n* [U] ● **weary** *v* (*pt, pp* **-ied**) [I,T] *~ (of)* become or make sb feel tired

weasel /ˈwiːzl/ *n* [C] small wild animal with reddish-brown fur

0— **weather¹** /ˈweðə(r)/ *n* [U] condition of sun, wind, temperature, etc at a particular place and time [IDM] **under the weather** (*infml*) slightly ill
■ **weather-beaten** *adj* (of a person or their skin) rough and damaged because the person spends a lot of time outside ■ **weather forecast** *n* [C] description on the TV, etc of what the weather will be like tomorrow, etc ■ **weatherman** (pl **-men** /-men/) (fem **weathergirl**) *n* (*infml*) person on the TV or radio who tells people what the weather will be like ■ **weatherproof** *adj* that keeps out rain, wind, etc ■ **weathervane** *n* [C] metal object on the roof of a building that turns round to show the direction of the wind

weather² /ˈweðə(r)/ *v* [I,T] (cause sth to) change shape or colour because of the effect of the sun, rain, etc **2** [T] come safely through a difficult experience: *~ a storm/crisis*

weave /wiːv/ *v* (*pt* **wove** /wəʊv/ *or* in sense 4 ~d *pp* **woven** /ˈwəʊvn/ *or* in sense 4 ~d) **1** [I,T] make fabric, a carpet, a basket, etc by crossing threads or strips across, over and under each other **2** [T] make sth by twisting flowers, pieces of wood, etc together: ~ *flowers into a garland* **3** [T] compose a story **4** [I,T] move along by twisting and turning to avoid obstructions: ~ *through the traffic* ● **weave** *n* [C] way in which threads are arranged in a piece of woven fabric ► **weaver** *n* [C] person whose job is weaving fabric

0⟶ **web** /web/ *n* **1** [C] net of fine threads made by a spider **2** (the Web) [sing] = WORLD WIDE WEB (WORLD) **3** [C] complicated pattern of closely-connected things **4** [C] skin that joins the toes of ducks, frogs, etc ● **webbed** *adj* (of a bird or animal) having pieces of skin between the toes ■ **webcam** (also **ˈWebcam**) *n* [C] (*computing*) video camera connected to a computer that is connected to the Internet, so that its images can be seen by Internet users ■ **webcast** *n* [C] (*computing*) live video broadcast of an event sent out on the Internet ■ **ˈwebmaster** *n* [C] (*computing*) person responsible for particular pages of information on the World Wide Web ■ **ˈwebsite** *n* [C] (*computing*) place connected to the Internet, where a company, organization, etc puts information that can be found on the World Wide Web

we'd /wiːd/ = WE HAD, WE WOULD

wed /wed/ *v* (*pt, pp* **-ded** *or* **wed**) [I,T] (*old-fash*) marry

0⟶ **wedding** /ˈwedɪŋ/ *n* [C] marriage ceremony ■ **ˈwedding ring** *n* [C] ring worn to show that you are married

wedge /wedʒ/ *n* [C] **1** piece of wood, metal, etc with one thick end and one thin pointed end, used for splitting sth or to keep two things separate **2** something shaped like a wedge: *a ~ of cake* ● **wedge** *v* [T] put or squeeze sth into a narrow space to fix it in place: ~ *the door open*

wedlock /ˈwedlɒk/ *n* [U] (*old-fash or law*) state of being married

0⟶ **Wednesday** /ˈwenzdeɪ; -di/ *n* [C,U] the fourth day of the week, next after Tuesday (See examples of use at *Monday*.)

wee /wiː/ *adj* (*infml*) very little ● **wee** *n* [sing] act of passing liquid waste (urine) from the body: *do/have a ~* **2** [U] urine ► **wee** *v* [I]

weed /wiːd/ *n* [C] **1** wild plant growing where it is not wanted, eg in a garden **2** (*GB, infml*) thin weak person ● **weed** *v* [I,T] remove weeds from the ground [PV] **weed sth/sb out** get rid of sth/sb: ~ *out the lazy students* ► **weedy** *adj* (*-ier, -iest*) **1** (*GB, infml*) having a thin weak body **2** full of weeds

0⟶ **week** /wiːk/ *n* [C] **1** period of seven days, esp from Monday to Sunday **2** period spent at work in a week: *a 35-hour ~* [IDM] **week after week** [week in, week out] every week ■ **ˈweekday** *n* [C] any day except Saturday and Sunday ■ **ˈweekˈend** *n* [C] Saturday and Sunday ► **weekly** *adj, adv* happening or appearing every week or once a week ► **weekly** *n* [C] (*pl* **-ies**) newspaper or magazine that is published once a week

weep /wiːp/ *v* (*pt, pp* **wept** /wept/) [I,T] (*fml*) cry ● **weeping** *adj* (of some trees) with branches that hang downwards

0⟶ **weigh** /weɪ/ *v* **1** *linking verb* have a certain weight: ~ *10 kilograms* **2** [T] measure how heavy sb/sth is: *She ~ed herself on the scales.* **3** [T] ~ **(up)** consider sth carefully before deciding sth: ~ *up the pros and cons* **4** [T] have an influence on sb's opinion or the result of sth: *His past record ~s heavily against him.* [IDM] **weigh anchor** lift an anchor out of the water before sailing away [PV] **weigh sb/sth down** make sb/sth heavier so they are not able to move easily **2** make sb feel worried or depressed **weigh in (with sth)** (*infml*) join in a discussion, argument, etc by saying sth important **weigh on sb** make sb anxious or worried **weigh sth out** measure an amount of sth by weight

0⟶ **weight** /weɪt/ *n* **1** [U,C] how heavy sth is, which can be measured in kilograms, etc: *I've put on (= gained) ~.* ◊ *She wants to lose ~ (= become less heavy or fat).* **2** [U] fact of being heavy **3** [C] heavy object **4** [sing] great responsibility or worry: *The news was certainly a ~ off my mind (= I did not have to worry about it any more).* **5** [U] importance, influence or strength: *opinions that carry ~* **6** [C,U] unit or system of units by which weight is measured **7** [C] piece of metal known to weigh a particular amount: *a 100-gram ~* [IDM] **over/under weight** weighing too much/ too little **put on/lose weight** (of a person) become heavier/lighter ● **weight** *v* [T] ~ **(down)** attach a weight to sth to keep it in position or to make it heavier ► **weighted** *adj* ~ **towards/against/in favour of** arranged in such a way that one person or thing has an advantage/a disadvantage ► **weightless** *adj* having no weight ► **weightlessness** *n* [U] sport of lifting heavy weights ► **weightlifter** *n* [C] ► **weighty** *adj* (*-ier, -iest*) (*fml*) **1** important and serious **2** heavy

weir /wɪə(r)/ n [C] wall across a river to control its flow

weird /wɪəd/ adj **1** (infml) unusual or different; not normal **2** (written) strange; unnatural: ~ shrieks
▸ **weirdly** adv ▸ **weirdness** n [U]

○━ **welcome** /ˈwelkəm/ v [T] **1** greet sb in a friendly way when they arrive somewhere **2** be pleased to receive or accept sth: The decision has been ~d by everyone. ● **welcome** exclam used as a greeting to a person who is arriving: W~ home! ● **welcome** n [C,U] greeting or reception ● **welcome** adj **1** received with or giving pleasure: a ~ change **2** ~ to used to say that you are very happy for sb to do sth if they want to: You're ~ to use my car. [IDM] **you're welcome** (esp US) used as a polite reply when sb thanks you for sth

weld /weld/ v [T] join pieces of metal together by heating their edges and pressing them together ● **weld** n [C] joint made by welding ● **welder** n [C] person whose job is welding metal

welfare /ˈwelfeə(r)/ n [U] health, comfort and happiness ■ **welfare state** (the ˌWelfare ˈState) n [usu sing] system of social services for people who are ill, unemployed, old, etc, paid for by the government

we'll /wiːl/ = WE SHALL, WE WILL

○━ **well**[1] /wel/ exclam used to express hesitation, surprise, acceptance, etc: W~,... I don't know about that. ◇ W~, ~, so you've come at last! ◇ Oh, very ~ then, if you insist. ● **well** adj (better /ˈbetə(r)/ best /best/) **1** in good health: feel/get ~ **2** in a satisfactory state or condition: All is not ~ at home. **3** advisable; a good idea: It would be ~ to start early.

○━ **well**[2] /wel/ adv (better /ˈbetə(r)/ best /best/) **1** in a good, right or satisfactory way: The children behaved ~. **2** thoroughly and completely: Shake the mixture ~. **3** to a great extent or degree: drive at ~ over the speed limit **4** (can/could well) easily: She can ~ afford it. **5** (can/could/may/might well) probably: You may ~ be right. **6** (can/could/may/might well) with good reason: I can't very ~ leave him now. [IDM] **as well (as sb/sth)** in addition to sb/sth; too **be well out of sth** (infml) be lucky that you are not involved in sth **do well** be successful **do well to do sth** be sensible or wise to do sth **leave/let alone** not interfere with sth satisfactory **may/might (just) as well do sth** do sth because it seems best in the situation you are in, although you may not really want to do it **very well** (used for showing agreement, often with some unwillingness) **well and truly**

(infml) completely **well done** used to express admiration for what sb has done **well in (with sb)** (infml) be good friends with sb, esp sb important **well off** (infml) **1** having a lot of money **2** in a good situation ■ **well adˈvised** adj acting in the most sensible way ● **well-being** n [U] state of being comfortable, healthy or happy ■ **well ˈbred** adj having or showing good manners ■ **well conˈnected** adj (fml) (of a person) having important or rich friends or relatives ■ **well ˈdone** adj (of food, esp meat) cooked thoroughly ■ **well ˈearned** adj much deserved ■ **well ˈheeled** adj (infml) rich ■ **well inˈformed** adj having or showing wide knowledge ■ **well inˈtentioned** adj intending to be helpful, but not always succeeding ■ **well ˈmeaning** adj = WELL INTENTIONED ■ **well-nigh** /ˌwel ˈnaɪ/ adv (fml) almost ■ **well ˈread** adj having read many books; knowledgeable ■ **well ˈspoken** adj having a way of speaking that is considered correct or elegant ■ **well ˈtimed** adj done or happening at the right time or at an appropriate time ■ **well-to-ˈdo** adj rich ■ **well-ˈwisher** n [C] person who wishes another success, happiness, etc

well[3] /wel/ n [C] **1** deep hole in the ground from which people obtain water **2** = OIL WELL (OIL) **3** narrow space in a building for a staircase or lift ● **well** v [I] ~ (up) (of a liquid) rise to the surface of sth and start to flow: Tears ~ed up in his eyes.

wellington /ˈwelɪŋtən/ (also ˌwellington ˈboot) (also /infml/ welly) n [C] waterproof rubber boot that reaches to the knee

○━ **well ˈknown** adj known about by a lot of people; famous: His books are well known.

welter /ˈweltə(r)/ n [sing] (fml) large and confusing amount of sth

wend /wend/ v (old-fash or lit) move slowly somewhere: He ~ed his way home.

went pt of GO[1]

wept pt, pp of WEEP

we're /wɪə(r)/ short for WE ARE (BE)

were /wə(r)/; strong form wɜː(r)/ pt of BE

weren't /wɜːnt/ = WERE NOT (BE)

werewolf /ˈweəwʊlf/ n [C] (pl -wolves /-wʊlvz/) (in stories) person who sometimes turns into a wolf, esp when the moon is full

○━ **west** /west/ n [U, sing] (abbr W) **1** (the west) direction that you look towards to see the sun set; one of the four points of the compass **2** (the West) Europe and N America, contrasted with eastern countries **3** (the West) (US) western side of the

US ● **west** *adj* (*abbr* **W**) **1** in or towards the west **2** (of winds) blowing from the west ● **west** *adv* towards the west ▶ **'westbound** *adj* travelling towards the west: ~*bound traffic* ◇ **westerly** *adj* **1** in or towards the west **2** (of winds) blowing from the west ▶ **westward** *adv, adj* towards the west

0─► **western** /'westən/ *adj* (*abbr* **W**) (*also* **Western**) of the west part of the world or a particular country ● **western** *n* [C] film or book about life in the western US in the 19th century, usu involving cowboys ▶ **westerner** *n* [C] person who comes from or lives in the western part of the world, esp western Europe or N America ● **westernize** (*also* -**ise**) *v* [T] bring ideas or ways of life that are typical of western Europe and N America to other countries

0─► **wet** /wet/ *adj* (~**ter**, ~**test**) **1** covered or soaked with liquid, esp water: ~ *grass/hair* ◇ *My shirt was ~ through* (= completely wet). **2** (of weather, etc) with rain: *a* ~ *climate* **3** (of paint, cement, etc) not dry or solid **4** (GB, *infml, disapprov*) (of a person) lacking a strong character ■ **wet 'blanket** *n* [C] (*infml, disapprov*) person who prevents others from enjoying themselves ● **wet** *n* [C] (*infml*) wet weather; rain **2** (GB, *infml, disapprov*) person who lacks a strong character: *Don't be such a ~!* ● **wet** *v* (-**tt**- *pt, pp* **wet** *or* ~**ted**) [T] make sth wet ■ **'wetsuit** *n* [C] rubber clothing worn by underwater swimmers to keep warm

we've /wiːv/ *short for* WE HAVE

whack /wæk/ *v* [T] (*infml*) hit sb/sth very hard ● **whack** *n* [C,usu sing] (*infml*) (sound made by the act of hitting sb/sth very hard **2** (GB) share of sth; amount of sth [IDM] **out of whack** (*esp US, infml*) (of a system or machine) not working as it should because its parts are not working together correctly ▶ **whacked** *adj* (GB, *infml*) very tired ● **whacking** *n* [C] (*old-fash, infml*) beating ▶ **whacking** (*also* **whacking great**) *adj* (GB, *infml*) used to emphasize how big or how much sth is ▶ **whacky** = WACKY

whale /weɪl/ *n* [C] very large sea animal hunted for its oil and meat [IDM] **have a whale of a time** (*infml*) enjoy yourself very much ▶ **whaler** *n* [C] **1** ship used for hunting whales **2** person who hunts whales ▶ **whaling** *n* [U] activity or business of hunting and killing whales

wharf /wɔːf/ *n* [C] (pl ~**s** *or* **wharves** /wɔːvz/) flat structure built beside the sea or a river where boats can be tied up and goods unloaded

0─► **what** /wɒt/ *pron, det* **1** used in questions to ask for particular information about sb/sth: *W~ time is it?* ◇ *W~ are you reading?* **2** the thing(s) that: *Tell me ~ happened next.* **3** used to say that you think that sth is esp good, bad, etc: *W~ a good idea!* [IDM] **what about...?** → ABOUT **what for?** for what purpose or reason?: *W~ is this tool used for?* ◇ *W~ did you do that for?* **what if...?** what would happen if...? **what is more** used to add a point that is even more important **what's what** (*spoken*) what things are useful, important, etc **what with sth** used to list the various reasons for sth

0─► **whatever** /wɒt'evə(r)/ *det, pron* **1** any or every; anything or everything: *You can eat ~ you like.* **2** used when you are saying that it does not matter what sb does or wants, because the result will be the same: *Keep calm, ~ happens.* **3** used in questions to show surprise or confusion: *W~ do you mean?* ● **whatever** (*also* **whatsoever**) *adv* (used for emphasis) not at all; not of any kind: *no doubt ~*

wheat /wiːt/ *n* [U] (plant producing) grain from which flour is made

wheedle /'wiːdl/ *v* [I,T] (*disapprov*) persuade sb to give you sth or do sth by saying nice things that you do not mean: *She ~d the money out of her brother.*

0─► **wheel** /wiːl/ *n* **1** [C] one of the circular objects under a car, bicycle, etc that turns when it moves **2** [C,usu sing] the circular object used to steer a car, etc or ship: *A car swept past with Jon at the ~.* ● **wheel** *v* **1** [T] push or pull sth that has wheels **2** [I] move or turn in a circle [IDM] **wheel and deal** do a lot of complicated deals in business or politics, often dishonestly ■ **'wheelbarrow** *n* [C] small open container with one wheel and two handles, that you use outside to carry things ■ **'wheelchair** *n* [C] chair with wheels for sb who is unable to walk ▶ **-wheeled** (forming compound adjectives) having the number of wheels mentioned: *a three-~ed vehicle*

wheeze /wiːz/ *v* [I] breathe noisily and with difficulty ● **wheeze** *n* [C] high whistling noise that your chest makes when you cannot breathe easily ▶ **wheezy** *adj* (-**ier**, -**iest**)

whelk /welk/ *n* [C] small shellfish that can be eaten

0─► **when** /wen/ *adv* **1** (used in questions) at what time; on what occasion: *W~ did you come?* **2** used after an expression of time to mean at or on which: *Sunday is the day ~ few people work.* ◇ *Her last visit to the town was in May, ~ she saw the new hospital.* ● **when** pron *when/which time: 'I've got a new job.' 'Since ~?'* ● **when** conj **1** at or during the time that: *It was raining ~ we arrived.* **2** after: *Call me ~ you've finished.* **3** considering that; although: *Why buy a new car ~ your present one runs well?*

O━ **whence** /wens/ adv (old-fash) from where

O━ **whenever** /wen'evə(r)/ conj **1** at any time that; on any occasion that: *Ask for help ~ you need it.* **2** every time that: *I go ~ I can.* ● **whenever** adv (used in questions to show surprise) when

O━ **where** /weə(r)/ adv **1** (used in questions) in or to what place or situation: *W~ does he live?* **2** (used after words or phrases that refer to a place or situation) at, in or to which place: *one of the few countries ~ people drive on the left* ● **where** conj (in) the place or situation in which: *Put it ~ we can all see it.*

■ '**whereabouts** adv used to ask the general area where sb/sth is: *W~abouts did you find it?* ● '**whereabouts** n [U, with sing or pl verb] place where sb/sth is: *Her ~abouts is/are unknown.* ■ ,**where'as** conj used to compare or contrast two facts: *He gets to work late every day ~ she is always early.* ■ ,**where'by** adv (fml) by which; because of which ■ ,**whereu'pon** conj (written) and then; as a result of this

O━ **wherever** /weər'evə(r)/ conj **1** in any place: *I'll find him, ~ he is.* **2** in all places; everywhere: *Crowds of people queue to see her ~ she goes.* ● **wherever** adv (used in questions for showing surprise) where

wherewithal /'weəwɪðɔːl/ n (the wherewithal) [sing] the money, things or skill needed for a purpose: *Does he have the ~ to buy a car?*

whet /wet/ v (**-tt-**) increase your desire for or interest in sth: *The book will ~ your appetite for more of her work.*

O━ **whether** /'weðə(r)/ conj used to express a doubt or a choice between two possibilities: *I don't know ~ to accept or refuse.*

O━ **which** /wɪtʃ/ **1** pron, det used in questions to ask sb to be exact about one or more people or things from a limited number: *W~ way shall we go up the hill or along the road?* **2** used to be exact about the thing(s) that you mean: *Houses ~ overlook the sea cost more.* **3** used to give more information about sth: *His best film, ~ won several awards, was about Gandhi.*

whichever /wɪtʃ'evə(r)/ det, pron **1** used to say what feature or quality is important in deciding sth: *Choose ~ brand you prefer.* **2** used to say that it does not matter which, as the result will be the same: *W~ way you travel, it is expensive.*

whiff /wɪf/ n [C] **1** slight smell **2** slight sign or feeling of sth

O━ **while** /waɪl/ conj **1** during the time that sth is happening: *Her parents died ~ she was still at school.* **2** at the same time as sth else is happening **3** used to contrast two things: *She likes tea, ~ I prefer coffee.* **4** although: *W~ I want to help, I don't think I can.* ● **while** n [sing] period of time: *for a long ~* ● **while** v [PV] **while sth away** spend time in a pleasant, lazy way

whilst /waɪlst/ conj (fml) = WHILE

whim /wɪm/ n [C, U] sudden wish to do or have sth, esp when it is unnecessary

whimper /'wɪmpə(r)/ v [I] make low weak crying noises ● **whimper** n [C]

whimsical /'wɪmzɪkl/ adj unusual and not serious, in a way that is either amusing or annoying

whine /waɪn/ n [C] long high unpleasant sound or cry ● **whine** v [I] **1** complain in an annoying, crying voice: *a child that never stops whining* **2** make a long high unpleasant sound: *The dog was whining* to come in.

whinny /'wɪni/ n [C] (pl **-ies**) quiet sound made by a horse of a horse ▶ **whinny** v (pt, pp **-ied**) [I]

whip /wɪp/ n [C] **1** piece of leather or rope fastened to a handle, used for hitting people or animals [C] **2** (member of a political party who gives an) order to members to attend and vote in a debate ● **whip** v (**-pp-**) **1** [T] hit a person or an animal hard with a whip **2** [I,T] (cause sth to) move quickly and suddenly: *A branch ~ped across the car window.* **3** [T] remove or pull sth quickly and suddenly: *He ~ped out a knife.* **4** [T] stir cream, etc very quickly until it becomes stiff [PV] **whip sb/sth up** try to make people excited or feel strongly about sth **2** quickly make a meal or sth to eat ▶ **whipping** n [C,usu sing] act of hitting sb with a whip, as a punishment ■ '**whip-round** n [C] (GB, infml) money given by a group of people in order to buy sth for sb

whirl /wɜːl/ v **1** [I,T] (cause sb/sth to) move around quickly in a circle **2** [I] spin; feel confused: *Her mind was ~ing.* ● **whirl** n [sing] **1** movement of sth spinning around: (fig) *Her mind was in a ~* (= a state of confusion). **2** number of events or activities happening one after another [**IDM**] **give sth a whirl** (*infml*) try sth to see if you like it or can do it ■ **whirlpool** *n* [C] strong circular current of water ■ **whirlwind** *n* [C] **1** tall column of quickly circulating air **2** situation in which a lot of things happen very quickly ▸ **whirlwind** *adj* happening very fast: *a ~wind romance*

whirr (*esp US* **whir**) /wɜː(r)/ *n* [C, usu sing] continuous low sound of a machine working or a bird's wings moving quickly ● **whirr** (*esp US* **whir**) *v* [I] make a continuous low sound like the parts of a machine moving

whisk /wɪsk/ *v* [T] **1** beat eggs, cream, etc into a stiff light mass **2** take sb/sth somewhere very quickly and suddenly: *They ~ed him off to prison.* ● **whisk** *n* [C] kitchen utensil for beating eggs, etc

whisker /ˈwɪskə(r)/ *n* **1** [C] long stiff hair near the mouth of a cat, etc **2** (**whiskers**) [pl] hair on the side of a man's face

whisky (*US* **whiskey**) /ˈwɪski/ *n* [U, C] (*pl* **-ies**) strong alcoholic drink made from grain

0**¬ whisper** /ˈwɪspə(r)/ *v* **1** [I, T] speak very quietly to sb so that others cannot hear what you are saying **2** [I] (*written*) (of leaves, the wind, etc) make a soft quiet sound ● **whisper** *n* [C] **1** low quiet voice or the sound it makes **2** (*also* **whispering**) (*written*) soft quiet sound

whist /wɪst/ *n* [U] card game for two pairs of players

0**¬ whistle** /ˈwɪsl/ *n* **1** instrument that produces a clear high sound, esp as a signal **2** sound you make by forcing your breath out when your lips are closed **3** high loud sound produced by air or steam being forced through a small opening ● **whistle** *v* [I, T] make a high sound or a musical tune by forcing your breath out when your lips are closed **2** [I] (of a kettle or other machine) make a high sound **3** [I] move quickly with a whistling sound: *The bullets ~d past us.*

0**¬ white** /waɪt/ *adj* (**~r, ~st**) **1** having the colour of fresh snow or milk **2** of a pale-skinned race of people **3** (of the skin) pale because of illness or emotion **4** (*GB*) (of tea or coffee) with milk added ● **white** *n* **1** [U] colour of fresh snow or milk **2** [C, usu pl] member of a race of people who have pale skin **3** [C, U] part of an egg that surrounds the yellow part (yolk) **4** [C, usu pl] white part of the eye ■ **whiteboard** *n* [C] large board with a smooth white surface that teachers, etc. write on with special pens: *an interactive ~board* (= that is linked to a computer) ■ **white-'collar** *adj* of

office workers, not manual workers ■ **white 'elephant** *n* (usu sing) something expensive but useless ■ **the 'White House** *n* [sing] (official home of the) President of the USA ■ **white 'lie** *n* [C] small harmless lie ▸ **white** *v* [I, T] become or make sth white or whiter ▸ **whiteness** *n* [U, sing] ■ **White 'Paper** *n* [C] (*GB*) official report explaining government plans before a new law is introduced ■ **whitewash** *n* **1** [U] mixture of lime or chalk and water, used for painting walls white **2** [U, sing] (*disapprov*) attempt to hide unpleasant facts about sb/sth ● **whitewash** *v* [T] **1** cover a wall, etc with whitewash **2** (*disapprov*) try to hide unpleasant facts about sb/sth ■ **white 'water** *n* [U] part of a river that looks white because the water is moving very fast over rocks: *~-water rafting*

whittle /ˈwɪtl/ *v* [I, T] shape a piece of wood by cutting small pieces from it [**PV**] **whittle sth away** make sth gradually decrease in value or amount: *The value of our savings is being slowly ~d down by inflation.* **whittle sth down** reduce the size or number of sth

whizz (*esp US* **whiz**) /wɪz/ *v* [I] (*infml*) **1** move very quickly, making a high continuous sound: *A bullet ~ed past me.* **2** do sth very quickly ■ **whizz-kid** (*esp US* **whiz-kid**) /ˈwɪz kɪd/ *n* [C] (*infml*) person who is very good and successful at sth, esp at a young age

whizzy /ˈwɪzi/ *adj* (*infml*) having features that make use of advanced technology: *a ~ new mobile phone*

0**¬ who** /huː/ *pron* **1** used in questions to ask about the name, identity or function of sb: *W~ is the woman in the black hat?* ◇ *W~ are you phoning?* **2** used to show which person or people you mean: *The people ~ called yesterday want to buy the house.* **3** used to give more information about sb: *My husband, ~ has been ill, hopes to see you soon.*

0**¬ whoever** /huːˈevə(r)/ *pron* **1** the person or people who: *W~ says that is a liar.* ◇ *You must speak to ~ is the head of the department.* **2** used to say that it does not matter who, since the result will be the same: *W~ rings, I don't want to speak to them.* **3** (used in questions for showing surprise) who: *W~ heard of such a thing!*

0**¬ whole** /həʊl/ *adj* **1** full; complete: *He told us the ~ story.* **2** not broken or damaged: *She swallowed the sweet ~.* [**IDM**] **go the whole hog** (*infml*) do sth thoroughly ● **whole** *n* **1** [C] thing that is complete in itself: *Four quarters make a ~.* **2** (**the whole**)

[sing] ~ **of** all that there is of sth: *the* ~ *of her life* [IDM] **on the whole** considering everything; in general ■ **whole'hearted** *adj* (*approv*) complete and enthusiastic ▶ **whole'heartedly** *adv* ■ **wholemeal** *adj* containing whole grains of wheat, etc, including the husk: ~*meal flour/bread* ■ **whole 'number** *n* [C] (*maths*) number that consists of one or more units, with no fractions ▶ **wholly** *adv* completely: *I'm not wholly convinced.*

wholesale /'həʊlseɪl/ *adj, adv* **1** of goods that are bought and sold in large quantities, esp so they can be sold again to make a profit **2** (esp of sth bad) happening or done to a very large number of people or things: *the ~ slaughter of animals* ▶ **wholesaler** *n* [C] trader who sells goods wholesale

wholesome /'həʊlsəm/ *adj* **1** good for your health **2** morally good

0**━ whom** /huːm/ *pron* (*fml*) used instead of 'who' as the object of a verb or preposition: *W~ did she invite?* ◇ *The person to ~ this letter is addressed died two years ago.*

whoop /wuːp/ *n* [C] loud cry of happiness or excitement ● **whoop** *v* [I] shout loudly because you are happy or excited: ~*ing with joy*

whooping cough /'huːpɪŋ kɒf/ *n* [U] infectious disease, esp of children, that makes them cough and have difficulty breathing

whore /hɔː(r)/ *n* [C] (*old-fash*) female prostitute

0**━ whose** /huːz/ *det, pron* **1** used in questions to ask who sth belongs to: *W~ (house) is that?* **2** used to say which person or thing you mean: *He's a man ~ opinion I respect.* **3** used to give more information about a person or thing: *Isobel, ~ brother he was, had heard the story before.*

0**━ why** /waɪ/ *adv* **1** used in questions to ask the reason for or purpose of sth: *W~ are you late?* **2** used to give or talk about a reason: *That's ~ she left so early.* [IDM] **why not?** used to make or agree to a suggestion: *W~ not write to him?*

wick /wɪk/ *n* [C] burning piece of string, etc in a candle or oil lamp [IDM] **get on sb's wick** (*GB, infml*) annoy sb

wicked /'wɪkɪd/ *adj* **1** morally bad **2** (*infml*) slightly bad but in a way that is amusing or attractive: *a ~ grin* **3** dangerous, harmful or powerful **4** (*sl*) very good: *Their new song's ~.* ▶ **wickedly** *adv* ▶ **wickedness** *n* [U]

wicker /'wɪkə(r)/ *n* [U] thin sticks of wood woven together to make

baskets, etc ■ **'wickerwork** *n* [U] baskets, furniture, etc made of wicker

wicket /'wɪkɪt/ *n* [C] **1** (in cricket) set of three sticks (stumps) at which the ball is bowled **2** area of grass between the two wickets

0**━ wide** /waɪd/ *adj* (~**r**, ~**st**) **1** measuring a lot from one side to the other: *a ~ river* **2** measuring a particular distance from one side to the other: *12 metres ~* **3** including many different things: *a ~ range of interests* **4** far from what is aimed at: *His shot was ~ (of the target).* [IDM] **give sb/sth a wide berth** not go too near sb/sth; avoid sb/sth **wide of the mark** not accurate ● **wide** *adv* as far or fully as possible: *He was ~ awake.* ◇ *The door was ~ open.* ■ **wide-'eyed** *adj* **1** with your eyes fully open because of fear, surprise, etc **2** inexperienced; naïve ▶ **widely** *adv* **1** by a lot of people; in or to many places: *It is ~ly known that...* ◇ *He has travelled ~ in Asia.* **2** to a large degree; a lot: *Prices vary ~ly from shop to shop.* ▶ **widen** *v* [I,T] become or make sth wider ■ **widespread** *adj* existing or happening over a large area

widow /'wɪdəʊ/ *n* [C] woman whose husband has died ● **widow** *v* [T] (*usu passive*) cause to become a widow or widower ▶ **widower** *n* [C] man whose wife has died

0**━ width** /wɪdθ; wɪtθ/ *n* [U, C] measurement from one side of sth to the other; how wide sth is

wield /wiːld/ *v* [T] **1** have and use power, authority, etc **2** hold sth, ready to use it as a weapon or tool: *~ an axe*

0**━ wife** /waɪf/ *n* [C] (pl **wives** /waɪvz/) woman that a man is married to

wig /wɪg/ *n* [C] piece of artificial hair that is worn on the head

wiggle /'wɪgl/ *v* [I,T] (cause sth to) move from side to side or up and down in short quick movements: *~ your toes* ▶ **wiggle** *n* [C]

wigwam /'wɪgwæm/ *n* [C] type of tent used by Native Americans in the past

wiki /'wɪki/ *n* [C] (*computing*) type of website that allows visitors to add, remove and change information

0**━ wild** /waɪld/ *adj* **1** living or growing in natural conditions; not kept in a house or on a farm: ~ *animals/plants* **2** (of land) in its natural state; not changed by people **3** lacking discipline or control: *The boy is ~ and completely out of control.* **4** full of very strong feeling: ~ *applause/cheers* **5** not carefully planned; not sensible or accurate: *a ~ guess* **6** ~ **about** (*infml*) very enthusiastic about sb/sth

7 affected by storms and strong winds: ~ *weather* [IDM] **run wild** → RUN¹ ● **wild** *n* **1** (**the wild**) [sing] natural environment that is not controlled by people **2** [pl] area of a country far from towns and cities ■ **wild card** *n* [C] **1** (in card games) card that has no value of its own and takes the value of any card the player chooses **2** (*computing*) symbol that has no meaning of its own and can represent any letter ■ **wildcat 'strike** *n* [C] sudden unofficial strike by workers ■ **wild 'goose chase** *n* [C] (*infml*) search for sth that is impossible for you to find and so wastes your time ■ **wildlife** *n* [U] wild animals, birds, etc ▶ **wildly** *adv* **1** in a way that is not controlled **2** extremely: *The story had been ~ly exaggerated.* ▶ **wildness** *n* [U]

wilderness /ˈwɪldənəs/ *n* [C, usu sing] large uncultivated area of land [IDM] **in the wilderness** no longer in an important position, esp in politics

wiles /waɪlz/ *n* [pl] clever tricks intended to deceive sb

wilful (*US also* **willful**) /ˈwɪlfl/ *adj* (*disapprov*) **1** (of sth bad) done deliberately **2** determined to do what you want; not caring about what others want ▶ **wilfully** *adv*

0━ **will¹** /wɪl/ *modal v* (short form **'ll** /l/ neg **will not** short form **won't** /wəʊnt/ pt **would** /wəd/ strong form /wʊd/ short form **'d** /d/ neg **would not** short form **wouldn't** /ˈwʊdnt/) **1** used for talking about or predicting the future: *You'll be in time if you hurry.* ◇ *How long ~ you be staying in Paris?* **2** used for showing that sb is willing to do sth: *They won't lend us any more money.* **3** used for asking sb to do sth: *W~ you come this way please?* **4** used for ordering sb to do sth: *W~ you be quiet!* **5** used for stating what you think is probably true: *That ~ be the postman at the door.* **6** used for stating what is generally true: *If it's made of wood, then it ~ float.* **7** used for describing habits: *She would sit there, hour after hour, doing nothing.* ◇ *He '~ smoke between courses at dinner* (= it annoys you).

0━ **will²** /wɪl/ *n* **1** [C,U] ability to control your thoughts and actions to achieve what you want to do: *He has an iron ~/a ~ of iron.* **2** [U,C] strong determination to do sth that you want to do: *the ~ to live* [sing] what sb wants to happen in a particular situation: (*fml*) *It is God's ~.* **4** [C] legal document saying what is to happen to sb's property and money after they die: *to make a ~* [IDM] **at will** whenever or wherever you like ■ **willpower** *n* [U] determination to do sth; strength of mind

---

will³ /wɪl/ *v* [T] **1** use the power of your mind to do sth or to make sth happen: *She ~ed her eyes to stay open.* **2** (*fml*) formally give your property or possessions to sb after you die, by means of a will

0━ **willing** /ˈwɪlɪŋ/ *adj* **1** ~ (**to**) not objecting to doing sth; having no reason for not doing sth: *I'm perfectly ~ to discuss the problem.* **2** ready or pleased to help; done enthusiastically: ~ *helpers* ▶ **willingly** *adv* ▶ **willingness** *n* [U]

willow /ˈwɪləʊ/ *n* [C] tree with thin flexible branches

wilt /wɪlt/ *v* **1** (of plants) bend, lose their freshness and begin to die **2** (*infml*) become weak or tired or less confident

wily /ˈwaɪli/ *adj* (**-ier, -iest**) clever at getting what you want, esp by deceiving people

wimp /wɪmp/ *n* [C] (*infml, disapprov*) person who is not strong, brave or confident

0━ **win** /wɪn/ *v* (**-nn-** pt, pp won /wʌn/) *v* **1** [I,T] be the most successful in a game, competition, etc **2** [T] get sth as a result of a competition, race, election, etc **3** [T] achieve or get sth that you want, esp by your own efforts: *try to ~ support for your proposals* [IDM] **win (sth) hands down** (*infml*) win sth easily [PV] **win sb around/over/round (to sth)** get sb's support by persuading them that you are right ● **win** *n* [C] success; victory ▶ **winner** *n* [C] ▶ **winning** *adj* **1** that wins or has won sth **2** attractive; pleasing: *a ~ning smile* ▶ **winnings** *n* [pl] money won in a competition, etc

wince /wɪns/ *v* [I] show pain, distress, etc by a sudden slight movement of the face ● **wince** *n* [C, usu sing]

winch /wɪntʃ/ *n* [C] machine for lifting or pulling heavy weights using a rope or chain ● **winch** *v* [T] move by using a winch

0━ **wind¹** /wɪnd/ *n* **1** (also **the wind**) [C,U] air that moves quickly as a result of natural forces: *gale-force ~s* **2** [U] gas that forms in the stomach and causes discomfort **3** [U] breath that you need when you do exercises: *I need time to get my ~ back after running so far.* [IDM] **get wind of sth** (*infml*) hear about sth secret or private **put the wind up sb** (*GB, infml*) make sb frightened ● **wind** *v* [T] make sb unable to breathe for a short time ■ **windfall** *n* [C] **1** amount of money that sb/sth wins or receives unexpectedly **2** fruit, esp an apple, blown off a tree by the wind ■ **wind instrument** *n* [C] musical instrument (eg an oboe) that you blow into to produce

---

A B C D E F G H I J K L M N O P Q R S T U V **W** X Y Z

sounds ■ **windmill** n [C] **1** building with machinery for grinding grain into flour that is driven by the power of the wind turning long arms (sails) **2** tall thin structure with parts that turn round, used to change wind power into electricity ■ **windpipe** n [C] passage for air from the throat to the lungs ■ **windscreen** (US **windshield**) n [C] window across the front of a motor vehicle ■ **windscreen wiper** (US **windshield wiper**) n [C] blade with a rubber edge that moves across a windscreen to make it clear of rain ■ **windsurfing** n [U] sport of sailing on water standing on a long narrow board with a sail ▶ **windsurfer** n [C] ■ **windswept** adj **1** (of a place) not protected against strong winds **2** looking as though you have been in a strong wind: ~swept hair ▶ **windy** adj (-ier, -iest) with a lot of wind: a ~y day

0━ **wind²** /waɪnd/ v (pt, pp **wound** /waʊnd/) **1** [I,T] (of a road, river, etc) have many bends and twists: The river ~s (its way) through the countryside. **2** [T] wrap or twist sth around itself or sth else **3** [T] ~ **(up)** make a clock, etc work by turning a key, handle, etc to tighten the spring **4** [I,T] ~ **forward/back** operate a tape, film, etc so that it moves nearer to its ending or starting position: He wound the tape back to the beginning. [PV] **wind sth back, down, forward, etc** cause sth to move backwards, down, etc, eg by turning a handle: ~ a window down **wind down 1** (infml) (of a person) rest or relax after a period of activity **2** (of a piece of machinery) go slowly and then stop **wind sth down 1** bring a business, an activity, etc to an end gradually over a period of time **2** make sth move downwards by turning a handle, etc: ~ the window down **wind up** (infml) (of a person) find yourself in a particular place or situation: We eventually wound up in a little cottage by the sea. **wind (sth) up** bring a speech, meeting, etc to an end **wind sb up** (infml) deliberately say or do sth to annoy sb **wind sth up 1** stop running a company, business, etc and close it completely **2** make sth, eg a car window, move upwards by turning a handle, etc

0━ **window** /ˈwɪndəʊ/ n [C] **1** opening (usu filled with glass) in a wall, vehicle, etc to let in light and air **2** glass at the front of a shop and the area behind it where the goods are displayed **3** area within a frame on a computer screen, in which a particular program is operating or in which information of a particular type is shown ■ **window box** n [C] long narrow box outside a window, in which flowers are grown ■ **window dressing** n [U] act of arranging goods attractively in a shop window ■ **windowpane** n [C] piece of glass in a window ■ **window-shopping** n [U] looking at goods in shop windows, usu without intending to buy ■ **windowsill** n [C] narrow shelf below a window, either inside or outside

0━ **wine** /waɪn/ n [U,C] alcoholic drink made from grapes or other fruit ● **wine** v [IDM] **wine and dine (sb)** entertain sb or be entertained by going to restaurants, enjoying good food and drink, etc

0━ **wing** /wɪŋ/ n **1** [C] one of the parts of the body of a bird or insect that it uses for flying **2** [C] one of the long flat surfaces that stick out from the sides of a plane and support it in flying **3** [C] part of a large building that sticks out from the main part: add a new ~ to a hospital **4** [C] (GB) part of a car above the wheel **5** [C] one section of an organization that has a certain function or whose members share the same opinions: the left/right ~ **6** [C] (in football, hockey, etc) far left or right side of the sports field **7** (the wings) [pl] sides of the stage in a theatre that are hidden from the audience [IDM] **take sb under your wing** take care of and help sb less experienced than you are ● **wing** v [I,T] (lit) fly somewhere [IDM] **wing it** (infml) do sth without planning or preparing it first ▶ **winged** adj having wings ▶ **winger** n [C] (in football, hockey, etc) attacking player who plays towards the side of the pitch ■ **wingspan** n [C] distance between the end of one wing and the end of the other when the wings are fully stretched

wink /wɪŋk/ v [I] **1** ~ **(at)** close one eye and open it again quickly **2** (written) shine with an unsteady light; flash on and off ● **wink** n [C] act of winking, esp as a signal to sb [IDM] **have forty winks** (infml) sleep for a short time, esp during the day **not get/have a wink of sleep** | **not sleep a wink** not be able to sleep

winkle /ˈwɪŋkl/ n [C] small shellfish, like a snail, that can be eaten

winner, winning → WIN

0━ **winter** /ˈwɪntə(r)/ n [U,C] coldest season of the year ● **winter** v [I] (fml) spend the winter somewhere ■ **winter sports** n [pl] sports that people do on snow or ice ▶ **wintry** /-tri/ adj

wipe /waɪp/ v [T] rub a surface with a cloth, your hand, etc, or rub sth against a surface, in order to remove dirt or liquid from it: ~ the dishes with a cloth ◇~ your feet on the mat ◇ Use that cloth to ~ up the mess. **[PV] wipe sb/sth out** destroy or remove sth completely: *War ~d out whole villages.* **wipe sth up** remove dirt or liquid from sth with a cloth: *~ up the milk you spilt* ◇ ~ *up* (= dry) *the cups* ● **wipe** *n* [C] **1** act of cleaning sth with a cloth **2** special piece of thin cloth or soft paper that you use to clean away dirt and bacteria

0-▪ **wire** /ˈwaɪə(r)/ *n* **1** [C,U] (piece of) metal in the form of a thin thread **2** [C] (*infml, esp US*) = TELEGRAM telegram ● **wire** *v* [T] **1** connect a building, piece of equipment, etc to an electricity supply, using wires **2** connect sth/sb to a piece of equipment, esp using a tape recorder or computer system **3** (*US*) send sb a message by telegram ▸ **wiring** *n* [U] system of wires that supply electricity to a building, etc ▸ **wiry** *adj* **1** (of a person) thin but strong **2** strong and rough, like wire

wireless /ˈwaɪələs/ *adj* lacking or not needing wires ● **wireless** *n* [C] (*old-fash*) radio

0-▪ **wisdom** /ˈwɪzdəm/ *n* [U] **1** ability to make sensible decisions and give good advice because of the experience and knowledge that you have **2** ~ **of** how sensible sth is ▪ **wisdom tooth** *n* [C] any of the four large back teeth that do not grow until you are an adult

0-▪ **wise** /waɪz/ *adj* (~**r**, ~**st**) having or showing experience, knowledge and common sense **[IDM] be none the wiser | not be any the wiser** knowing no more than before ▸ **wisely** *adv*

0-▪ **wish** /wɪʃ/ *v* **1** [T] want sth to happen or be true even though it is unlikely or impossible: *I ~ I was/were taller.* ◇ *She ~ed she hadn't eaten so much.* **2** [T] ~ **to** (*fml*) want to do sth; want sth to happen: *I ~ to speak to the manager.* **3** [I] ~ **(for)** think very hard that you want sth, esp sth that can only be achieved by good luck or magic: *He has everything he could possibly ~ for.* **4** [T] say that you hope sb will be happy, lucky, etc: *~ sb good luck/a happy birthday* ● **wish** *n* **1** [C] desire or longing for sth: *I have no ~ to interfere, but...* **2** [C] thing that you want to have or to happen **3** (**wishes**) [pl] used esp in a letter or card to say that you hope sb will be happy, successful, etc: *Dad sends his best ~es.* ▸ **wishful** *adj* ▪ **wishful thinking** *n* [U] belief that sth will come true simply because you wish it

wishy-washy /ˈwɪʃi wɒʃi/ *adj* (*infml, disapprov*) weak or feeble; not firm or clear

wisp /wɪsp/ *n* [C] **1** small thin piece of hair, grass, etc **2** long thin line of smoke or cloud ▸ **wispy** *adj*: *~y hair*

wistful /ˈwɪstfl/ *adj* thinking sadly

about sth that you would like to have, esp sth in the past that you can no longer have ▸ **wistfully** /-fəli/ *adv*

wit /wɪt/ *n* **1** [C,U, *sing*] (person who has the) ability to say or write things that are both clever and amusing **2** (**wits**) [pl] your ability to think quickly and clearly and to make good decisions **[IDM] be at your wits' end** be so worried by a problem that you do not know what to do next **be frightened/scared/terrified out of your wits** be very frightened **have/keep your wits about you** be alert and ready to act ▸ **witticism** /ˈwɪtɪsɪzəm/ *n* [C] clever and amusing remark ▸ **witty** *adj* (**-ier, -iest**) able to say or write clever, amusing things ▸ **wittily** *adv*

witch /wɪtʃ/ *n* [C] woman believed to have evil magic powers ▪ **witchcraft** /-krɑːft/ *n* [U] use of magic powers, esp evil ones ▪ **witch doctor** *n* [C] person believed to have special magic powers to heal people ▪ **witch-hunt** *n* [C] attempt to find and punish people with ideas that are thought to be unacceptable or dangerous to society

0-▪ **with** /wɪð/ *prep* **1** in the company or presence of sb/sth: *live ~ your parents* ◇ *leave a child ~ a babysitter* **2** having or carrying sth: *a coat ~ two pockets* ◇ *a girl ~ blue eyes* **3** using sth: *cut it ~ a knife* **4** used to say what fills, covers, etc sth: *Fill the bottle ~ water.* **5** in opposition to sb/sth; against sb/sth: *argue ~ Rosie* **6** concerning; in the case of: *be patient ~ them* **7** used to show the way in which sb does sth: *He behaved ~ great dignity.* **8** because of; as a result of: *tremble ~ fear* **9** because of sth and as it happens: *Skill comes ~ experience.* **10** in the same direction as sth: *sail ~ the wind* **11** in spite of sth: *W~ all her faults, I still love her.* **[IDM] be with me/you** (*infml*) be able to understand what sb is talking about: *I'm afraid I'm not quite ~ you.* **be with sb (on sth)** support sb and agree with what they say: *We're all ~ you on this one.* **be with it** (*infml*) **1** fashionable **2** understanding what is happening around you

0-▪ **withdraw** /wɪðˈdrɔː; wɪθ'd-/ *v* (*pt* **-drew** /-ˈdruː/ *pp* **~n** /-ˈdrɔːn/) **1** [I,T] (cause sth/sb to) move back or away from a place or situation: *~ troops from the battle* **2** [T] stop giving or offering sth to sb: *The drug was ~n from sale.* **3** [I,T] (cause sb/sth to) stop taking part in sth or being a member of an organization: *calls for Britain to ~ from the EU* **4** [T] take money out of a bank account ▸ **withdrawal** /-ˈdrɔːəl/ *n* [C,U] (act

wither

of) withdrawing ■ with'drawal symptoms n [pl] unpleasant effects experienced by a person who has stopped taking a drug they are addicted to ▶ with'drawn adj (of a person) unusually quiet and shy

wither /'wɪðə(r)/ v 1 [I,T] (cause a plant to) dry up and die 2 [I] become less or weaker, esp before disappearing completely: All our hopes just ~ed away. ▶ withering adj making sb feel silly or ashamed: a ~ing look

withhold /wɪð'həʊld; wɪθ'h-/ v (pt, pp -held /-held/) [T] (fml) ~ (from) refuse to give sth to sb: ~ permission

0─ within /wɪ'ðɪn/ prep not further than sth; inside: ~ an hour ◇ ~ the city walls ◇ ● within adv (fml) inside

0─ without /wɪ'ðaʊt/ prep 1 not having, experiencing or showing sth: You can't buy things ~ money. 2 not in the company of sb: Don't go ~ me. 3 used with the -ing form to mean 'not': He left ~ saying goodbye.

withstand /wɪð'stænd; wɪθ's-/ v (pt, pp -stood /-stʊd/) [T] (fml) be strong enough not to be hurt or damaged by extreme conditions, the use of force, etc: ~ an attack

0─ witness /'wɪtnəs/ n [C] 1 person who sees an event take place and is able to describe it 2 person who gives evidence in a law court 3 person who signs a document to confirm that another person's signature is real 4 (fml) sign or proof ● witness v [T] 1 see sth happen because you are there when it happens: ~ an accident 2 be present when an official document is signed ■ 'witness box (US 'witness stand) n [C] place in a court of law where people stand to give evidence

witticism, witty ⇒ WIT

wives plural of WIFE

wizard /'wɪzəd/ n [C] 1 man believed to have magic powers 2 person who is very good at sth: a financial ~

wizened /'wɪznd/ adj (written) looking smaller and having wrinkles because of old age

wobble /'wɒbl/ v [I,T] (cause sth to) move from side to side unsteadily ▶ wobbly adj (infml) unsteady: a wobbly chair

woe /wəʊ/ n 1 (old-fash or hum) 1 (woes) [pl] troubles and problems that sb has 2 [U] great unhappiness ▶ woeful adj 1 very bad or serious 2 (lit) very sad

wok /wɒk/ n [C] large bowl-shaped Chinese cooking pan

woke pt of WAKE¹

woken pp of WAKE¹

wolf /wʊlf/ n [C] (pl wolves /wʊlvz/) fierce wild animal of the dog family

● wolf v [T] ~ (down) (infml) eat sth quickly and greedily

0─ woman /'wʊmən/ n (pl women /'wɪmɪn/) 1 [C] adult female human being 2 [U] women in general 3 [C] woman who comes from the place mentioned, does the job mentioned, etc: a business~ ▶ womanhood n [U] (fml) state or qualities of being a woman ▶ womanizer (also -iser) n [C] (disapprov) man who has sexual relationships with many different women ■ 'womankind n [U] (old-fash, fml) women in general ▶ womanly adj (approv) (of a woman) behaving, dressing, etc in the way that is expected of a woman ■ Women's Libe'ration (also infml Women's Lib) n [U] movement that aimed to achieve the same social and economic rights for women as men

womb /wuːm/ n [C] organ in a woman's body in which a baby develops before it is born

won pt, pp of WIN

0─ wonder /'wʌndə(r)/ v 1 [I,T] feel curious about sth; ask yourself questions: I ~ who she is. 2 [I] used to make polite requests: I ~ if you can help me. 3 [I] ~ (at) (fml) be very surprised by sth: She ~ed at her own stupidity. ● wonder n 1 [U] feeling of surprise and admiration 2 [C] thing or quality in sth that fills you with surprise and admiration: the ~s of modern medicine ◇ a ~ drug [IDM] do/work wonders have a very good effect or result it's a wonder (that)... (spoken) it is surprising or strange: It's a ~ that they weren't all killed. (it's) no/little/ small wonder (that)... it is not surprising ▶ wonderful adj very good, pleasant or enjoyable ▶ wonderfully adv

wonky /'wɒŋki/ adj (GB, infml) unsteady; not straight

won't /wəʊnt/ short for WILL NOT (WILL¹)

woo /wuː/ v [T] 1 try to get the support of sb: ~ voters 2 (old-fash) (of a man) try to persuade a woman to marry him

0─ wood /wʊd/ n 1 [U,C] hard material that the trunk and branches of a tree are made of 2 [C] (also woods [pl]) area of trees, smaller than a forest [IDM] not out of the wood(s) (infml) not yet free from difficulties or problems ▶ wooded adj covered with trees ▶ wooden adj 1 made of wood 2 not showing enough natural expression, emotion or movement ■ 'woodland n [U] land covered with trees ■ 'woodpecker n [C] bird with a long sharp beak that makes holes in tree trunks to find insects ■ 'woodwind n [sing, with sing or pl verb] (players of) wind instruments, eg the flute

and the clarinet ■ **'woodwork** n [U]
1 parts of a building made of wood
2 activity or skill of making things
from wood ▶ **'woodworm** n [U, C]
(damage caused by) a small worm
that eats wood ▶ **woody** adj **(-ier, -iest) 1** of or like wood **2** covered
with trees: a ~y hillside

woof /wʊf/ exclam (infml) word used
to describe the sound made by a
dog

○━ **wool** /wʊl/ n [U] **1** soft hair of
sheep and some other animals
2 thread or cloth made from
animal's wool, used for knitting
▶ **woollen** (US -l-) adj made of wool
▶ **woollens** (US -l-) n [pl] clothes
made of wool ▶ **woolly** (US also -l-)
adj (-ier, -iest) **1** made of or looking
like wool **2** (of people or their ideas)
confused; not clear ▶ **woolly** n
(pl -ies) (infml) woollen sweater

○━ **word** /wɜːd/ n **1** [C] written or
spoken unit of language **2** [C] thing
that you say; remark or statement:
Have a ~ with Mick and see what he
thinks. ◊ Don't say a ~ about it.
3 [sing] promise that you will do sth
or that sth is true: I give you my ~ that
I will come back. ◊ You'll just have to
take my ~ for it (= believe me).
4 [sing] piece of information or
news: If ~ gets out about the affair,
he'll have to resign. [IDM] **by word of
mouth** because people tell each
other and not because they read
about it **have/exchange words (with
sb) (about sth)** argue or quarrel with
sb **in a word** (spoken) used for giving
a very short, usu negative, answer or
comment **in other words** used to
introduce an explanation of sth
(not) in so/as many words (not)
using the exact words sb said, but
suggested indirectly **say/give the
word** give an order; make a request:
Just say the ~, and I'll go. **take sb's
word for it** believe that sb is telling
the truth **too funny, silly, etc for
words** (infml) extremely funny, silly,
etc **word for word** exactly the
same words ▶ **word** v [T] express sth
in words ▶ **wording** n [U, C, usu sing]
words used in a piece of writing or
speech ■ **word-perfect** adj able to
say sth from memory without
making any mistakes ■ **'word
processing** n [U] use of a computer
to create, store and print a piece of
text, usu typed in from a keyboard
■ **'word processor** n [C] computer
that runs a word processing
program and is usu used for writing
letters, reports, etc ▶ **wordy** adj
(-ier, -iest) using too many words,
esp formal ones

wore pt of WEAR[1]

○━ **work[1]** /wɜːk/ v [I, T] do sth that
requires mental or physical effort,
esp as part of a job: I've been ~ing
hard all day. ◊ Doctors often ~ long

hours. **2** [I] have a job: She ~s for an
engineering company. **3** [I] ~ **(for)**
make efforts to achieve sth: a
politician who ~s for peace **4** [T]
manage or operate sth to gain
benefit from it: ~ the land (= grow
crops on it, etc) **5** [I] function;
operate: The lift is not ~ing. **6** [T]
make a machine, device, etc
operate: Do you know how to ~ the
coffee machine? **7** [I] have the
desired result; be successful: Will
your plan ~? **8** [T] make a material
into a particular shape or form by
pressing, stretching it, etc: ~ clay/
dough **9** [I, T] move or pass to a
particular place or state, usu
gradually: He ~ed his way to the top
of his profession. [IDM] **work loose
→** LOOSE **work to rule** follow the
rules of your job strictly in order to
cause delay, as a form of protest
against your employer, etc **work
wonders →** WONDER [PV] **work sth
off** get rid of sth by using physical
effort: He ~ed off his anger by digging
the garden. **work out 1** train the
body by physical exercise **2** develop
in a successful way: Things ~ed out
well for us. **work out (at sth)** be equal
to a particular amount: The total ~s
out at £180. **work sb out** (infml)
understand sb's character **work sth
out 1** calculate sth: ~ out the new
price **2** find the answer to sth; solve
sth: ~ out a problem **3** plan or think
of sth: ~ out a new scheme **work sb/
yourself up (into sth)** make sb/
yourself reach a state of great
excitement, anger, etc **work sth up**
develop or improve sth with some
effort: I can't ~ up any enthusiasm for
his idea. **work up to sth** develop or
move gradually towards sth
▶ **worker** n [C] person who works
■ **'workout** n [C] period of physical
exercise ■ **,work-to-'rule** n [C] act or
working strictly according to the
rules to cause delay, etc, as a protest

○━ **work[2]** /wɜːk/ n **1** [U] the job that
a person does esp in order to earn
money: He's been looking for ~ for a
year. ◊ to be in/out of ~ (= have/not
have a job) **2** [U] the duties you have
and the activities you do as part of
your job: Police ~ is mainly routine.
3 [U] tasks that need to be done: I've
plenty of ~ for you to do. **4** [U] place
where you do your job: I go to ~ at 8
o'clock. **5** [U] use of physical strength
or mental power in order to do or
make sth: Do you like hard ~? **6** [U]
thing produced as a result of work:
an artist whose ~ I admire **7** [C] piece
of writing, art, music etc: the ~s of
Shakespeare **8** (works) [pl] activities
involving building or repair: road~s
9 (works) [C, with sing or pl verb]
place where industrial processes are

carried out: *a gas~s* **10** (the works) [pl] moving parts of a machine, etc [IDM] **at work 1** having an effect on sth **2 ~ (on)** busy doing sth **get (down)/set to work** begin **have your work cut out** have sth difficult to do, esp in the available time **in work/out of work** having/not having a job ■ **'workbench** *n* [C] long heavy table used for working with tools, etc ■ **'workbook** *n* [C] book with questions to be answered, usu in the spaces provided ■ **'workforce** *n* [C, with sing or pl verb] total number of workers in a factory, industry, etc ■ **'workload** *n* [C] amount of work to be done by sb ■ **'workman** *n* [C] man whose job involves work with his hands ■ **'workmanlike** *adj* done well; skilful ■ **'work of 'art** *n* [C] excellent painting, sculpture, etc ■ **'workshop** *n* [C] **1** room or building where things are made or repaired **2** period of group discussion and practical work ■ **'work-shy** *adj* (GB, *disapprov*) not wanting to work; lazy ■ **'workstation** *n* [C] desk and computer at which a person works ■ **'worktop** *n* [C] flat surface in a kitchen, on which food is prepared

workable /'wɜːkəbl/ *adj* (of a system, an idea, etc) that can be used successfully: *a ~ plan*

workaholic /ˌwɜːkə'hɒlɪk/ *n* [C] (*infml*) person who finds it difficult to stop working

0~ **working** /'wɜːkɪŋ/ *adj* **1** having a paid job: *the ~ population* **2** of or for work: *~ hours/clothes* **3** good enough, esp as a basis for further improvement: *a ~ knowledge of Russian* [IDM] **in running/working order** (esp of machines) working well ● **working** *n* [C, usu pl] **1** way a machine, organization, etc operates **2** parts of a mine or quarry where coal, metal, etc has been dug from the ground ■ **working 'capital** *n* [U] (*business*) money that is needed to run a business rather than to buy buildings, equipment, etc at the beginning ■ **working 'class** *n* [C] social class whose members do not have much money, etc and are usu employed to do manual work ■ **working-class** *adj* ■ **'working party** *n* [C] group of people that study and report on a subject

0~ **world** /wɜːld/ *n* **1** (the world) [sing] the earth, its countries and people **2** [C, usu sing] particular part of this: *the French-speaking ~* **3** [C] planet: *There may be other~s out there.* **4** [C] people or things of a certain kind or activity: *the insect ~* ◇ *the ~ of sport* **5** [sing] person's environment, experiences, friends, etc: *Parents are the most important people in a child's ~.* **6** [sing] our society; all the people in the world: *I don't want the whole~ to know about it.* **7** [sing] state of human existence: *this ~ and the next* (= life on earth and after death) [IDM] **do sb/sth the world of good** make sb feel much better; improve sth **how, why, etc in the world** (*infml*) used for emphasis and to show surprise or annoyance: *How in the ~ did you manage to do it?* **out of this world** (*infml*) absolutely wonderful **a/the world of difference** (*infml*) used to emphasize how much difference there is between two things ■ **world-'class** *adj* as good as the best in the world ■ **world-'famous** *adj* known throughout the world ▶ **worldly** *adj* (*written*) **1** of material, not spiritual, things **2** having a lot of experience of life ▶ **worldliness** *n* [U] ■ **world 'power** *n* [C] country with great influence on international politics ■ **world 'war** *n* [C] war involving many important countries ■ **'worldwide** *adj, adv* happening all over the world ■ **the ˌWorld Wide ˈWeb** (*also* the Web) (*abbr* WWW) *n* [sing] international multimedia system of sound, pictures and video for finding information on the Internet

worm /wɜːm/ *n* [C] **1** small long thin creature with no bones or legs: *birds looking for ~s* **2** young form of an insect **3** (*infml, disapprov*) weak worthless person ● **worm** *v* [I,t] use a twisting and turning movement, esp to move through a narrow place: *He ~ed his way through the narrow tunnel.* [PV] **worm your way/ yourself into sth** (*disapprov*) make sb like you or trust you, in order to gain some personal advantage

worn[1] *pp* of WEAR[1]

worn[2] /wɔːn/ *adj* damaged by use or wear ■ **worn 'out** *adj* **1** (of a thing) badly damaged and no longer usable **2** (of a person) extremely tired

0~ **worry** /'wʌri/ *v* (pt, pp **-ied**) **1** [I,t] **~ (about)** (cause sb/yourself to) be anxious about sb/sth: *Don't ~ about me. I'll be fine.* ◇ *What worries me is how I'm going to get home.* **2** [T] annoy or disturb sb **3** [T] (of a dog) attack animals by chasing and/or biting them ▶ **worried** *adj* anxious; troubled ● **worry** *n* (pl **-ies**) **1** [U] state of worrying about sth **2** [C] something that worries you ▶ **worrying** *adj* that makes you worry

0~ **worse** /wɜːs/ *adj comparative of* BAD **1** of poorer quality or lower standard; less good: *Her work is bad,*

but his is ~. **2** more serious or severe: *an even ~ tragedy* **3** more ill or unhappy: *She got ~ in the night.*
● **worse** *adv* comparative of BADLY **1** less well: *She cooks badly, but I cook ~.* **2** more seriously or severely: *It's raining ~ than ever.* [IDM] **be worse off** be poorer, unhappier, etc than before or than sb else ● **worse** *n* [U] more problems or bad news [IDM] **be none the worse (for sth)** not be harmed by sth **the worse for wear** (infml) worn, damaged or tired ▶ **worsen** *v* [I,T] (cause sth to) become worse than it was before

0— **worship** /ˈwɜːʃɪp/ *n* [U] **1** practice of showing respect for God or a god by saying prayers, etc **2** strong feeling of love and respect for sb/sth ● **worship** *v* (-pp- *US* -p-) **1** [I,T] show respect for God or a god, by going to church, praying, etc **2** [T] love and admire sb very much ▶ **worshipper** /ˈwɜːʃɪpə(r)/ *n* [C]

0— **worst** /wɜːst/ *adj* superlative of BAD of the poorest quality or lowest standard; worse than any other person or thing of a similar kind: *the ~ storm for years* ● **worst** *adv* superlative of BADLY most badly or seriously ● **worst** *n* (the worst) [sing] the worst part, state, event, etc [IDM] **at (the) worst** used for saying what is the worst thing that can happen **if the worst comes to the worst** if the situation becomes too difficult or dangerous

0— **worth** /wɜːθ/ *adj* **1** having a value in money, etc: *a car ~ £55000* **2** used to recommend the action mentioned because you think it may be useful, enjoyable, etc: *The book is ~ reading.* **3** important, good or enjoyable enough to make sb feel satisfied, esp when effort is involved: *The job is hard work but it's ~ it.* [IDM] **for all sb/it is worth** (infml) making every effort **worth your while** interesting or useful for sb to do ● **worth** *n* [U] **1** amount of sth that a certain sum of money will buy: *a pound's ~ of apples* **2** financial, practical or moral value of sb/sth ▶ **worthless** *adj* **1** having no value **2** (of a person) having no good qualities ■ **worth'while** *adj* useful or interesting, and worth the time, money or effort spent

worthy /ˈwɜːði/ *adj* (-ier, -iest) **1** ~ (of) deserving sth: *~ of blame* **2** deserving respect

0— **would** /wəd/; strong form wʊd/ *modal v* (short form **'d** /d/) neg **would not** short form **wouldn't** /ˈwʊdnt/) **1** used as the past form of *will* when reporting what sb has said or thought: *He said he ~ be here at nine o'clock.* **2** used for describing the result of sth imagined: *She'd look better with short hair.* **3** used for making polite requests: *W~ you open*

a window, please? **4** used in offers or invitations: *W~ you like a sandwich?* **5** used to say what you like, love, hate, etc: *I'd love a cup of coffee.* **6** used to give advice: *I ~n't drink any more, if I were you.* ■ **would-be** *adj* used to describe sb who is hoping to become the type of person mentioned: *~-be parents*

0— **wound**[1] /wuːnd/ *n* [C] injury to the body, esp one made with a weapon: *a bullet ~* ● **wound** *v* [T] **1** injure part of the body **2** hurt sb's feelings

0— **wound**[2] /waʊnd/ *pt, pp* of WIND[2]

wove *pt* of WEAVE

woven *pp* of WEAVE

wow /waʊ/ *exclam* (infml) used to express great surprise or admiration

wrangle /ˈræŋɡl/ *v* [I], *n* [C] (take part in) an angry argument that lasts for a long time

0— **wrap** /ræp/ *v* (-pp-) **1** [T] cover sth completely in material; fold sth round sth/sb: *~ (up) a parcel ◇ W~ the bandage round your leg.* **2** [I,T] (computing) cause text to be carried over to a new line automatically as you reach the end of the previous line; to be carried over in this way: *The text ~s around if it is too long to fit the screen.* [IDM] **be wrapped up in sb/ sth** (infml) be so deeply involved with sb/sth that you do not pay enough attention to others [PV] **wrap (sb/yourself) up** wear warm clothes **wrap sth up** (infml) complete a task, agreement, etc ● **wrap** *n* **1** [C] piece of fabric that a woman wears around her shoulders **2** [U] paper, plastic, etc. that is used for wrapping things in: *We stock a wide range of cards and gift ~.* **3** [sing] used when making a film to say that filming has finished: *Cut! That's a ~.* **4** [C] type of sandwich made with a cold thin pancake (tortilla) rolled around meat or vegetables ▶ **wrapper** *n* [C] piece of paper wrapped round sth, eg a sweet or newspaper ▶ **wrapping** *n* [C, U] something used for covering or packing sth [IDM] **under wraps** (infml) being kept secret until some time in the future

wrath /rɒθ/ *n* [U] (old-fash or fml) extreme anger

wreak /riːk/ *v* [T] (fml) do great damage or harm to sb/sth

wreath /riːθ/ *n* [C] (pl ~s /riːðz/) circle of flowers and leaves, esp one placed on a grave as sign of respect for sb who has died

wreathe /riːð/ *v* [T] (written) (usu passive) ~ (in/with) cover or surround sth: *hills ~d in mist*

wreck /rek/ *n* [C] **1** ship that has sunk or been very badly damaged **2** car, plane, etc that has been very badly damaged in an accident **3** [usu sing] (*infml*) person who is in a bad physical or mental condition ● **wreck** *v* [T] **1** damage or destroy sth **2** spoil sth completely: *The weather~ed all our plans.* ▶ **wreckage** *n* [U] remains of a vehicle, etc that has been badly damaged or destroyed

wren /ren/ *n* [C] very small brown bird

wrench /rentʃ/ *v* [T] **1** twist or pull sth/sb/yourself violently: ~ *the door open* **2** twist or injure a part of your body ● **wrench** *n* **1** [C] (*esp US*) metal tool for holding or turning things **2** [sing] sad and painful separation **3** [C, usu sing] sudden and violent twist or pull

wrestle /ˈresl/ *v* [I] **1** ~ (**with**) fight sb by holding them and trying to throw them to the ground **2** ~ **with** struggle to deal with a problem ▶ **wrestler** *n* [C] person who wrestles as a sport

wretch /retʃ/ *n* [C] unfortunate or unpleasant person

wretched /ˈretʃɪd/ *adj* **1** feeling ill or unhappy: *His toothache made him feel~.* **2** extremely bad or unpleasant **3** extremely annoying ▶ **wretchedly** *adv* ▶ **wretchedness** *n* [U]

wriggle /ˈrɪgl/ *v* [I,T] move with quick short twists and turns: *Stop wriggling and sit still!* [PV] **wriggle out of (doing) sth** (*infml*) avoid doing sth unpleasant ▶ **wriggle** *n* [C]

wring /rɪŋ/ *v* (*pt, pp* **wrung** /rʌŋ/) [T] **1** ~ (**out**) twist and squeeze sth wet to get the water out of it **2** twist a bird's neck in order to kill it [IDM] **wring your hands** squeeze and twist your hands because you are sad, anxious, etc [PV] **wring sth from/out of sb** obtain sth from sb with difficulty ▶ **wringer** *n* [C] machine for wringing clothes that are wet ■ **wringing** 'wet *adj* very wet

wrinkle /ˈrɪŋkl/ *n* [C, usu pl] small fold or line in the skin, esp caused by age ● **wrinkle** *v* [I,T] (cause sth to) form wrinkles ▶ **wrinkly** *adj*

0–ᵐ **wrist** /rɪst/ *n* [C] joint between the hand and the arm ■ **wristwatch** *n* [C] watch that you wear on your wrist

writ /rɪt/ *n* [C] legal document ordering sb to do or not to do sth

0–ᵐ **write** /raɪt/ *v* (*pt* **wrote** /rəʊt/ *pp* **written** /ˈrɪtn/) [T] **1** mark letters or numbers on a surface, esp with a pen or pencil **2** [I,T] produce sth in written form so that people can read, perform or use it, etc: ~ *a report/novel* **3** [I,T] put information, greetings, etc in a letter and then

send it to sb: *She promised to ~ to me every week.* **4** [T] put information in the appropriate places on a cheque or form **5** [I,T] (*computing*) record data in the memory of a computer [IDM] **be written all over sb's face** (of a feeling) be very obvious from the expression on sb's face [PV] **write sth down** write sth on paper to remember or record it **write off/ away (to sb/sth) (for sth)** write a letter to an organization, etc to order sth, ask for information, etc **write sb/sth off 1** ~ **(as)** decide that sb/sth is a failure and not worth paying attention to **2** (*business*) cancel a debt **3** (*GB*) damage sth, esp a vehicle, so badly that it is not worth repairing **write sth out** write sth in full **write sth up** make a full written record of sth ■ **'write-off** *n* [C] **1** (*GB*) vehicle so badly damaged that it is not worth repairing **2** (*business*) act of cancelling a debt and accepting that it will never be paid ■ **'write-up** *n* [C] article giving sb's opinion of a new book, play, etc in a newspaper

0–ᵐ **writer** /ˈraɪtə(r)/ *n* [C] **1** person whose job is writing books, stories, etc **2** person who has written a particular thing: *the ~ of the article*

writhe /raɪð/ *v* [I] twist or move your body about, esp because you are in pain

0–ᵐ **writing** /ˈraɪtɪŋ/ *n* **1** [U] activity of writing **2** [U] books, articles, etc in general **3** (**writings**) [pl] written works of an author **4** [U] person's handwriting ■ **'writing paper** *n* [U] (usu good quality) paper for writing letters on

0–ᵐ **written** *pp* of WRITE

0–ᵐ **wrong** /rɒŋ/ *adj* **1** not true or correct; mistaken: *a ~ answer* ◊ *prove that sb is ~* **2** causing problems or difficulties; not as it should be: *What's ~ with your foot?* **3** not suitable, right or what you need: *catch the ~ train* **4** not morally right or honest: *It is ~ to steal.* ● **wrong** *adv* in a way that produces a result that is not correct or that you do not want: *You've spelt my name ~.* [IDM] **go wrong 1** make a mistake **2** (of a machine) stop working correctly **3** experience problems or difficulties ● **wrong** *n* **1** [U] behaviour that is not honest or morally acceptable: *know the difference between right and ~* **2** [C] (*fml*) dishonest or illegal act [IDM] **in the wrong** responsible for an accident, mistake, etc **on the wrong track** → TRACK ● **wrong** *v* [T] (usu passive) (*fml*) treat sb badly or unfairly ■ **'wrongdoer** *n* [C] person who does sth dishonest or illegal ■ **'wrongdoing** *n* [U] ▶ **wrongful** *adj* (*law*) not fair, morally right or legal: *She sued her employer for ~ful*

dismissal. ▶ **wrongfully** *adv*
▶ **wrongly** *adv*

wrote *pt of* WRITE

wrought iron /ˌrɔːt ˈaɪən/ *n* [U] form of iron used to make decorative fences, gates, etc

wrung *pt, pp of* WRING

wry /raɪ/ *adj* **1** showing that you are both amused and disappointed or annoyed: *a ~ face* **2** amusing in an ironic way: *a ~ smile* ▶ **wryly** *adv*

WWW /ˌdʌblju: dʌblju: ˈdʌblju:/ *abbr* = THE WORLD WIDE WEB (WORLD)

WYSIWYG /ˈwɪzɪwɪg/ *abbr* (*computing*) what you see is what you get; what you see on the computer screen is exactly the same as will be printed

Xx

X, x /eks/ *n* [C,U] (pl **X's, x's** /ˈeksɪz/) **1** the twenty-fourth letter of the English alphabet **2** Roman numeral for 10 **3** (*maths*) unknown quantity **4** used to represent a kiss at the end of a letter, etc

xenophobia /ˌzenəˈfəʊbiə/ *n* [U] (*disapprov*) great dislike or fear of foreigners

Xerox™ /ˈzɪərɒks/ *n* [C] **1** process for producing copies of letters, documents, etc using a special machine **2** copy made using Xerox ▶ **xerox** *v* [T] make a copy of a letter, document, etc by using Xerox

Xmas /ˈkrɪsməs; ˈeksməs/ *n* [C,U] (*infml, written*) used as a short way of writing 'Christmas'

X-ray /ˈeks reɪ/ *n* [C] **1** [usu pl] type of radiation that can pass through objects and make it possible to see inside them **2** photograph made by X-rays: *a chest* ~ ● **X-ray** *v* [T] photograph and examine bones and organs inside the body, using X-rays

xylophone /ˈzaɪləfəʊn/ *n* [C] musical instrument with a row of wooden bars that are hit with small wooden hammers

Yy

Y, y /waɪ/ *n* [C,U] (pl **Y's, y's** /waɪz/) the twenty-fifth letter of the English alphabet ■ **Y-fronts**™ *n* [pl] (*GB*) men's underpants with an opening in the front sewn in the form of an inverted Y

yacht /jɒt/ *n* [C] large sailing boat, often with an engine and a place to sleep on board, used for pleasure trips and racing ▶ **yachting** *n* [U]

sport or activity of sailing or racing yachts

yam /jæm/ *n* [C, U] large root of a tropical plant that is cooked as a vegetable

Yank /jæŋk/ *n* [C] (*GB, infml* often *disapprov*) person from the US

yank /jæŋk/ *v* [I,T] pull sb/sth hard, quickly and suddenly

yap /jæp/ *v* (**-pp-**) [I] **1** (of small dogs) make short sharp barks **2** (*infml*) talk in a silly, noisy and usu irritating way

0--- yard /jɑːd/ *n* [C] **1** (*GB*) area outside a building, usu with a hard surface and a surrounding wall **2** (*US*) = GARDEN(1) **3** (usu in compounds) area of land used for a special purpose or business: *a boat* ~ **4** (*abbr* **yd**) unit for measuring length equal to 3 feet (0.9144 of a metre) ■ **yardstick** *n* [C] standard used for judging how good or successful sth is

yarn /jɑːn/ *n* **1** [U] thread that has been spun for knitting, weaving, etc **2** [C] (*infml*) long story

yashmak /ˈjæʃmæk/ *n* [C] piece of cloth covering most of the face, worn by some Muslim women

0--- yawn /jɔːn/ *v* [I] **1** open your mouth wide and breathe in deeply, usu because you are tired or bored **2** (of a large hole or empty space) be very wide and often frightening: *a ~ing gap* ● **yawn** *n* [C] act of yawning

yd *abbr* (pl **~s**) = YARD(4)

0--- yeah /jeə/ *exclam* (*infml*) yes

0--- year /jɪə(r); also jɜ:(r)/ *n* [C] **1** period of 365 days (or 366) from 1 January to 31 December: *The museum is open all (the) ~ round* (= during the whole year). **2** period of 12 months, measured from any particular time **3** period of 12 months connected with a particular activity: *the financial/school* ~ **4** (*esp GB*) (at a school, etc) level that you stay in for one year: *She was in my ~ at school.* **5** [usu pl] age; time of life: *He was 14 ~s old when it happened.* [IDM] **year in, year out | year after year** every year for many years ▶ **yearly** *adj, adv* (happening) every year or once a year

yearn /jɜːn/ *v* [I] ~ **for/to** (*lit*) want sth very much: *He ~ed for his home.* ▶ **yearning** *n* [C,U] (*written*) strong and emotional desire

yeast /jiːst/ *n* [C,U] fungus used in making beer and wine, or to make bread rise

yell /jel/ *v* [I,T] shout loudly ● **yell** *n* [C] loud shout

0--- yellow /ˈjeləʊ/ *adj* **1** of the colour of lemons or butter **2** (*infml, disapprov*) easily frightened ● **yellow** *n* [U,c] the colour of

lemons or butter ● **yellow** *v* [I,T] (cause sth to) become yellow: *The papers had ~ed with age.*
▸ **yellowish** *adj* slightly yellow
■ **Yellow 'Pages**™ (*US also* **yellow 'pages**) *n* [sing with *sing* or *pl* verb] telephone directory listing companies, etc by the service they provide

yelp /jelp/ *n* [C] (make a) short sharp cry, esp of pain

yen /jen/ *n* [C] 1 (*pl* **yen**) unit of money in Japan 2 [usu sing] strong desire: *I've always had a ~ to travel.*

0─ **yes** /jes/ *exclam* used when accepting, agreeing, etc: *Y~, I'll come with you.* ● **yes** *n* [C] answer that shows you agree with an idea, a statement, etc

0─ **yesterday** /'jestədeɪ, -di/ *adv, n* [U] 1 (on) the day before today 2 (in) the recent past

0─ **yet** /jet/ *adv* 1 used in negative sentences and questions to talk about sth that has not happened but that you expect to happen: *They haven't come ~.* ◇ *I have not met him (= I have not met him yet).* 2 at some future time: *She may surprise us all ~.* 3 used to emphasize an increase in number, amount or the number of times sth happens: *~ another government report* 4 still: *I have ~ to meet him.* (= I have still not met him.) ● **yet** *conj* in spite of what has just been said: *a clever ~ simple idea*

yew /ju:/ *n* [C,U] 1 (*also* **yew tree**) small tree with dark green leaves and red berries 2 wood of the yew

Y-fronts → Y, y

yield /ji:ld/ *v* 1 [T] produce or provide sth, eg a profit, result or crop: *The tax increase would ~ £10 million a year.* 2 [I] **~ (to)** stop resisting sth/sb; agree to do sth that you do not want to do: *~ to temptation* 3 [T] (*fml*) allow sb to win, have or take control of sth that has been yours up until now ● **yield** *n* [C,U] total amount of crops, profits, etc produced: *a ~ of three tonnes of wheat per hectare*
▸ **yielding** *adj* 1 (of a substance) soft and easy to bend 2 (of a person) willing to do what others want

yippee /jɪ'pi:/ *exclam* (*infml*) used to express pleasure or excitement

yob /jɒb/ *n* [C] (*GB, infml*) rude, noisy and aggressive young man
▸ **yobbish** *adj*: *~ behaviour*

yodel /'jəʊdl/ *v* (**-ll-** *US* **-l-**) sing or call in the traditional Swiss way, with frequent changes from the normal voice to high notes

yoga /'jəʊgə/ *n* [U] 1 Hindu philosophy that teaches you how to control your body and mind 2 system of exercises for your body and for controlling your breathing

yoghurt /'jɒgət/ *n* [U,C] thick white liquid food made by adding bacteria to milk and often flavoured with fruit

yoke /jəʊk/ *n* 1 [C] piece of wood placed across the necks of two oxen so that they can pull heavy loads 2 [sing] (*fml*) harsh treatment or control: *freed from the ~ of slavery*

yokel /'jəʊkl/ *n* [C] (*hum* or *disapprov*) person from the countryside

yolk /jəʊk/ *n* [C,U] yellow part of an egg

yonder /'jɒndə(r)/ *adj, adv* (*old-fash*) (that is) over there

0─ **you** /ju:/ *pron* (used as the subject of a v or as the object of a v or prep) 1 person or people being spoken to or written to 2 used for referring to people in general: *It's easier to fly with the wind behind ~.*

you'd /ju:d/ *short for* YOU HAD, YOU WOULD

you'll /ju:l/ *short for* YOU WILL

0─ **young** /jʌŋ/ *adj* (**~er** /-ŋgə(r)/ **~est** /-ŋgɪst/) having lived or existed for a short time: *a ~ woman/nation* ● **young** *n* [pl] 1 young animals or birds; offspring 2 (**the young**) young people as a group ▸ **youngish** *adj* fairly young ▸ **youngster** /-stə(r)/ *n* [C] (*infml*) young person or child

0─ **your** /jɔ:(r)/ *adj* belonging to you: *How old are ~ children?* ▸ **yours** /jɔ:z/ *pron* 1 of or belonging to you: *Is that book ~?* 2 (*usu* Yours) used at the end of a letter before signing your name: *Y~s faithfully/sincerely/truly*

you're /jʊə(r), jɔ:(r)/ = YOU ARE (BE)

0─ **yourself** /jɔ:'self/ *pron* (*pl* **-selves** /-'selvz/) 1 used as a reflexive when the person or people doing sth are also the person or people affected by it: *Have you hurt ~?* 2 used for emphasis: *You told me so ~.* [IDM] (all) **by yourself/yourselves** 1 alone 2 without help

0─ **youth** /ju:θ/ *n* (*pl* **~s** /ju:ðz/) 1 [U] time or state of being young: *in my ~* 2 [C] young man 3 (*also* **the youth**) [pl] young people considered as a group ▸ **youthful** *adj* young; seeming young: *a ~ful appearance* ■ **youth hostel** *n* [C] building that provides cheap and simple accommodation to young people who are travelling

you've /ju:v/ *short for* YOU HAVE

yuck /jʌk/ *exclam* (*infml*) used to express disgust

yum /jʌm/ (*also* **yum-'yum**) *exclam* (*infml*) used to show that you think sth tastes or smells very nice
▸ **yummy** *adj* (*infml*) very good to eat

yuppie /'jʌpi/ n [C] (infml often disapprov) young professional person, esp one who is ambitious and earns a lot of money

Zz

Z, z /zed/ n [C, U] (pl **Z's, z's** /zedz/) the twenty-sixth letter of the English alphabet

zany /'zeɪni/ adj (-ier, -iest) (infml) strange or unusual in an amusing way

zeal /ziːl/ n [U, C] (written) energy and enthusiasm ▶ **zealous** /'zeləs/ adj (written) full of zeal

zealot /'zelət/ n [C] often (disapprov) person who is very enthusiastic about sth, esp religion or politics

zebra /'zebrə; 'ziːbrə/ n [C] African wild animal like a horse with black and white stripes on its body
■ **zebra 'crossing** n [C] (GB) area on the road marked with black and white stripes where people may cross

zenith /'zenɪθ/ n [C] (fml) highest point of sth

0━ **zero** /'zɪərəʊ/ number **1** 0; nought **2** temperature, pressure, etc that is equal to zero on a scale: *The temperature was ten degrees below* (= -10°C). **3** lowest possible amount or level; nothing at all ● **zero v** [PV] **zero in on sb/sth 1** fix all your attention on the person or thing mentioned **2** aim a gun, etc at the person or thing mentioned ■ **'zero hour** n [U] time when an important event, an attack, etc is to start

zest /zest/ n **1** [sing, U] enjoyment and enthusiasm **2** [U, sing] quality of being interesting and enjoyable **3** [U] outer skin of an orange or lemon

zigzag /'zɪgzæg/ n [C] line that turns right and left at sharp angles ● **zigzag v** (-gg-) [I] move forward with sudden sharp turns first to the left and then to the right: *The path ~s up the cliff.*

zinc /zɪŋk/ n [U] (symb Zn) bluish-white metal

zip (also **'zip fastener**) /zɪp/ n [C] device for fastening clothes, bags, etc, consisting of two rows of metal or plastic teeth that you can pull together to close sth or pull apart to open it ● **zip v** (-pp-) [T] **1** open or close sth with a zip **2** (computing) make computer files, etc smaller so that they use less space on a disk, etc ■ **'Zip code** n [C] (US) = POSTCODE (POST¹) ▶ **zipper** n [C] (esp US) = ZIP

zither /'zɪðə(r)/ n [C] flat musical instrument with many strings

zodiac /'zəʊdiæk/ n (the zodiac) [sing] imaginary band in the sky

containing the positions of the sun, moon and planets, divided into twelve equal parts: *the signs of the zodiac*

zombie /'zɒmbi/ n [C] (infml) person who seems only partly alive, without any feeling or interest in what is happening

0━ **zone** /zəʊn/ n [C] area or region with particular features or uses: *a time* ◇ *a nuclear-free* ~

zoo /zuː/ n [C] (pl **-s**) park where living animals are kept for people to look at ■ **'zookeeper** n [C] person who works in a zoo taking care of the animals

zoology /zəʊ'ɒlədʒi; zu'ɒl-/ n [U] scientific study of animals and their behaviour ▶ **zoological** /,zəʊə'lɒdʒɪkl; ,zuːə'l-/ adj ▶ **zoologist** n [C] student of or expert in zoology

zoom /zuːm/ v [I] **1** move or go somewhere very fast **2** (of prices, etc) increase suddenly and sharply [PV] **zoom in/out** (of a camera) show the object that is being photographed from closer/further away, using a zoom lens ■ **'zoom lens** n [C] camera lens that can make the object being photographed appear bigger or smaller

zucchini /zu'kiːni/ n [C] (pl **zucchini** or **~s**) (US) = COURGETTE

Common irregular verbs

Where two forms are given, consult the entry to see if there is a difference in meaning.

Infinitive	Past Tense	Past Participle	Infinitive	Past Tense	Past Participle
arise	arose	arisen	forecast	forecast/~ed	forecast/~ed
awake	awoke	awoken			
be	was/were	been	foresee	foresaw	foreseen
bear	bore	borne	foretell	foretold	foretold
beat	beat	beaten	forget	forgot	forgotten
become	became	become	forgive	forgave	forgiven
befall	befell	befallen	forgo	forwent	forgone
begin	began	begun	forsake	forsook	forsaken
bend	bent	bent	freeze	froze	frozen
beset	beset	beset	get	got	got/gotten
bet	bet	bet	give	gave	given
bid	bid/bade	bid/bidden	go	went	gone
bite	bit	bitten	grind	ground	ground
bleed	bled	bled	grow	grew	grown
blow	blew	blown	hang	hung/~ed	hung/~ed
break	broke	broken	have	had	had
breed	bred	bred	hear	heard	heard
bring	brought	brought	hide	hid	hidden
broadcast	broadcast	broadcast	hit	hit	hit
build	built	built	hold	held	held
burn	burnt/~ed	burnt/~ed	hurt	hurt	hurt
burst	burst	burst	keep	kept	kept
buy	bought	bought	kneel	knelt	knelt
cast	cast	cast	knit	~ted/knit	~ted/knit
catch	caught	caught	know	knew	known
choose	chose	chosen	lay[1]	laid	laid
cling	clung	clung	lead[1]	led	led
come	came	come	lean	~ed/leant	~ed/leant
cost	cost/~ed	cost/~ed	leap	leapt/~ed	leapt/~ed
creep	crept	crept	learn	learnt/~ed	learnt/~ed
cut	cut	cut	leave	left	left
deal	dealt	dealt	lend	lent	lent
dig	dug	dug	let	let	let
do[1]	did	done	lie[2]	lay	lain
draw	drew	drawn	light	lit/~ed	lit/~ed
dream	dreamt/~ed	dreamt/~ed	lose	lost	lost
drink	drank	drunk	make	made	made
drive	drove	driven	mean	meant	meant
dwell	dwelt	dwelt	meet	met	met
eat	ate	eaten	mislay	mislaid	mislaid
fall	fell	fallen	mislead	misled	misled
feed	fed	fed	misspell	misspelt/~ed	misspelt/~ed
feel	felt	felt			
fight	fought	fought	mistake	mistook	mistaken
find	found	found	mow	mowed	mown
flee	fled	fled	outdo	outdid	outdone
fling	flung	flung	outgrow	outgrew	outgrown
fly	flew	flown	outshine	outshone	outshone
forbid	forbade	forbidden	overcome	overcame	overcome

Infinitive	Past Tense	Past Participle	Infinitive	Past Tense	Past Participle
overdo	overdid	overdone	sow	sowed	sown/~ed
overhang	overhung	overhung	speak	spoke	spoken
overhear	overheard	overheard	speed	sped/~ed	sped/~ed
override	overrode	overridden	spend	spent	spent
overrun	overran	overrun	spell	spelt/~ed	spelt/~ed
oversee	oversaw	overseen	spill	spilt/~ed	spilt/~ed
overshoot	overshot	overshot	spin	spun	spun
oversleep	overslept	overslept	spit	spat	spat
overtake	overtook	overtaken	spread	spread	spread
overthrow	overthrew	overthrown	spring	sprang	sprung
partake	partook	partaken	stand	stood	stood
pay	paid	paid	stink	stank/	stunk
podcast	podcast	podcast	stride	strode	—
put	put	put	strike	struck	struck
quit	quit	quit	string	strung	strung
read	read	read	strive	strove	striven
repay	repaid	repaid	swear	swore	sworn
rewind	rewound	rewound	sweep	swept	swept
rid	rid	rid	swell	swelled	swollen/~ed
ride	rode	ridden	swim	swam	swum
ring¹	rang	rung	swing	swung	swung
rise	rose	risen	take	took	taken
run	ran	run	teach	taught	taught
saw	sawed	sawn	tear	tore	torn
say	said	said	tell	told	told
see	saw	seen	think	thought	thought
seek	sought	sought	throw	threw	thrown
sell	sold	sold	tread	trod	trodden
send	sent	sent	typecast	typecast	typecast
set	set	set	undercut	-cut	-cut
sew	~ed	sewn	undergo	-went	-gone
shake	shook	shaken	underlie	-lay	-lain
shear	sheared	shorn/~ed	understand	-stood	-stood
shed	shed	shed	undertake	-took	-taken
shine	shone	shone	underwrite	-wrote	-written
shit	shat/~ted	shat/~ted	undo	undid	undone
shoe	shod	shod	unwind	unwound	unwound
shoot	shot	shot	upset	upset	upset
show	showed	shown	wake	woke	woken
shrink	shrank	shrunk	waylay	waylaid	waylaid
shut	shut	shut	wear	wore	worn
sing	sang	sung	weave	wove	woven
sink	sank	sunk	wed	~ded/wed	~ded/wed
sit	sat	sat	weep	wept	wept
slay	slew	slain	win	won	won
sleep	slept	slept	wind	wound	wound
slide	slid	slid	withdraw	withdrew	withdrawn
sling	slung	slung	withhold	withheld	withheld
slink	slunk	slunk	withstand	withstood	withstood
slit	slit	slit	wring	wrung	wrung
smell	smelt/~led	smelt/~led	write	wrote	written

Geographical names

Afghanistan /æfˈɡænɪstæn/   Afghan /ˈæfɡæn/

Africa /ˈæfrɪkə/   African /ˈæfrɪkən/

Albania /ælˈbeɪniə/   Albanian /ælˈbeɪniən/

Algeria /ælˈdʒɪəriə/   Algerian /ælˈdʒɪəriən/

Angola /æŋˈɡəʊlə/   Angolan /æŋˈɡəʊlən/

Antarctica /ænˈtɑːktɪkə/   Antarctic /ænˈtɑːktɪk/

(the) Arctic /ˈɑːktɪk/   Arctic /ˈɑːktɪk/

Argentina /ˌɑːdʒənˈtiːnə/   Argentinian /ˌɑːdʒənˈtɪniən/

Armenia /ɑːˈmiːniə/   Armenian /ɑːˈmiːniən/

Asia /ˈeɪʃə, ˈeɪʒə/   Asian /ˈeɪʃn, ˈeɪʒn/

Australia /ɒˈstreɪliə/   Australian /ɒˈstreɪliən/

Austria /ˈɒstriə/   Austrian /ˈɒstriən/

Azerbaijan /ˌæzəbaɪˈdʒɑːn/   Azerbaijani /ˌæzəbaɪˈdʒɑːni/

(the) Bahamas /bəˈhɑːməz/   Bahamian /bəˈheɪmiən/

Bahrain /bɑːˈreɪn/   Bahraini /bɑːˈreɪni/

Bangladesh /ˌbæŋɡləˈdeʃ/   Bangladeshi /ˌbæŋɡləˈdeʃi/

Barbados /bɑːˈbeɪdɒs/   Barbadian /bɑːˈbeɪdiən/

Belarus /ˌbeləˈruːs/   Belarusian /ˌbeləˈruːsiən/

Belgium /ˈbeldʒəm/   Belgian /ˈbeldʒən/

Benin /beˈniːn/   Beninese /ˌbenɪˈniːz/

Bhutan /buːˈtɑːn/   Bhutanese /ˌbuːtəˈniːz/

Bolivia /bəˈlɪviə/   Bolivian /bəˈlɪviən/

Bosnia and Herzegovina /ˌbɒzniə ən ˌhɜːtsəɡəˈviːnə/   Bosnian and Herzegovinian /ˈbɒzniən ən ˌhɜːtsəɡəˈvɪniən/

Botswana /bɒtˈswɑːnə/   Botswanan /bɒtˈswɑːnən/

Brazil /brəˈzɪl/   Brazilian /brəˈzɪliən/

Brunei /bruːˈnaɪ/   Bruneian /bruːˈnaɪən/

Bulgaria /bʌlˈɡeəriə/   Bulgarian /bʌlˈɡeəriən/

Burkina Faso /bɜːˌkiːnə ˈfæsəʊ/   Burkinan /bɜːˈkiːnən/

Burma /ˈbɜːmə/ (now officially Myanmar)   Burmese /bɜːˈmiːz/

Burundi /bʊˈrʊndi/   Burundian /bʊˈrʊndiən/

Cambodia /kæmˈbəʊdiə/   Cambodian /kæmˈbəʊdiən/

Cameroon /ˌkæməˈruːn/   Cameroonian /ˌkæməˈruːniən/

Canada /ˈkænədə/   Canadian /kəˈneɪdiən/

(the) Central African Republic /ˌsentrəl ˌæfrɪkən rɪˈpʌblɪk/   Central African /ˌsentrəl ˈæfrɪkən/

Chad /tʃæd/   Chadian /ˈtʃædiən/

Chile /ˈtʃɪli/   Chilean /ˈtʃɪliən/

China /ˈtʃaɪnə/   Chinese /ˌtʃaɪˈniːz/

Colombia /kəˈlɒmbiə/   Colombian /kəˈlɒmbiən/

Congo /ˈkɒŋɡəʊ/   Congolese /ˌkɒŋɡəˈliːz/

Costa Rica /ˌkɒstəˈriːkə/   Costa Rican /ˌkɒstəˈriːkən/

Côte d'Ivoire /ˌkəʊt diːˈvwɑː/   Ivorian /aɪˈvɔːriən/

Croatia /krəʊˈeɪʃə/   Croatian /krəʊˈeɪʃn/

Cuba /ˈkjuːbə/   Cuban /ˈkjuːbən/

Cyprus /ˈsaɪprəs/   Cypriot /ˈsɪpriət/

(the) Czech Republic /ˌtʃek rɪˈpʌblɪk/   Czech /tʃek/

(the) Democratic Republic of the Congo /deməˌkrætɪk rɪˌpʌblɪk əv ðə ˈkɒŋɡəʊ/   Congolese /ˌkɒŋɡəˈliːz/

Denmark /ˈdenmɑːk/   Danish /ˈdeɪnɪʃ/

East Timor /ˌiːst ˈtiːmɔː(r)/   East Timorese /ˌiːst tɪməˈriːz/

Ecuador /ˈekwədɔː(r)/   Ecuadorian, -ean /ˌekwəˈdɔːriən/

Egypt /ˈiːdʒɪpt/   Egyptian /iˈdʒɪpʃn/

El Salvador /el ˈsælvədɔː(r)/   Salvadorean /ˌsælvəˈdɔːriən/

England /ˈɪŋɡlənd/   English /ˈɪŋɡlɪʃ/

Equatorial Guinea /ˌekwətɔːriəl ˈɡɪni/   Equatorial Guinean /ˌekwətɔːriəl ˈɡɪniən/

Eritrea /ˌerɪˈtreɪə/   Eritrean /ˌerɪˈtreɪən/

Estonia /eˈstəʊniə/   Estonian /eˈstəʊniən/

Ethiopia /ˌiːθiˈəʊpiə/   Ethiopian /ˌiːθiˈəʊpiən/

Europe /ˈjʊərəp/   European /ˌjʊərəˈpiːən/

Fiji /ˈfiːdʒiː/	Fijian /fɪˈdʒiːən/
Finland /ˈfɪnlənd/	Finnish /ˈfɪnɪʃ/
France /frɑːns/	French /frentʃ/
(the) FYROM /ˌfɔːmə juːˈɡəʊslɑːv rɪˈpʌblɪk əv ˌmæsəˈdəʊniə/	Macedonian /ˌmæsəˈdəʊniən/
Gabon /ˈɡæˈbɒn/	Gabonese /ˌɡæbəˈniːz/
(the) Gambia /ˈɡæmbiə/	Gambian /ˈɡæmbiən/
Georgia /ˈdʒɔːdʒə/	Georgian /ˈdʒɔːdʒən/
Germany /ˈdʒɜːməni/	German /ˈdʒɜːmən/
Ghana /ˈɡɑːnə/	Ghanaian /ɡɑːˈneɪən/
Great Britain /ˌɡreɪt ˈbrɪtn/	British /ˈbrɪtɪʃ/
Greece /ɡriːs/	Greek /ɡriːk/
Grenada /ɡrəˈneɪdə/	Grenadian /ɡrəˈneɪdiən/
Guatemala /ˌɡwɑːtəˈmɑːlə/	Guatemalan /ˌɡwɑːtəˈmɑːlən/
Guinea /ˈɡɪni/	Guinean /ˈɡɪniən/
Guyana /ɡaɪˈænə/	Guyanese /ˌɡaɪəˈniːz/
Haiti /ˈheɪti/	Haitian /ˈheɪʃn/
Holland /ˈhɒlənd/	Dutch /dʌtʃ/
Honduras /hɒnˈdjʊərəs/	Honduran /hɒnˈdjʊərən/
Hungary /ˈhʌŋɡəri/	Hungarian /hʌŋˈɡeəriən/
Iceland /ˈaɪslənd/	Icelandic /aɪsˈlændɪk/
India /ˈɪndiə/	Indian /ˈɪndiən/
Indonesia /ˌɪndəˈniːʒə/	Indonesian /ˌɪndəˈniːʒn/
Iran /ɪˈrɑːn/	Iranian /ɪˈreɪniən/
Iraq /ɪˈrɑːk/	Iraqi /ɪˈrɑːki/
Ireland /ˈaɪələnd/	Irish /ˈaɪrɪʃ/
Israel /ˈɪzreɪl/	Israeli /ɪzˈreɪli/
Italy /ˈɪtəli/	Italian /ɪˈtæliən/
Jamaica /dʒəˈmeɪkə/	Jamaican /dʒəˈmeɪkən/
Japan /dʒəˈpæn/	Japanese /ˌdʒæpəˈniːz/
Jordan /ˈdʒɔːdn/	Jordanian /dʒɔːˈdemiən/
Kazakhstan /ˌkæzækˈstæn/	Kazakh /kæˈzæk/
Kenya /ˈkenjə/	Kenyan /ˈkenjən/
Korea, North /ˌnɔːθ kəˈrɪə/	North Korean /ˌnɔːθ kəˈrɪən/
Korea, South /ˌsaʊθ kəˈrɪə/	South Korean /ˌsaʊθ kəˈrɪən/
Kuwait /kʊˈweɪt/	Kuwaiti /kʊˈweɪti/
Kyrgyzstan /ˌkɜːɡɪˈstæn/	Kyrgyz /kɜːɡɪz/
Laos /laʊs/	Laotian /ˈlaʊʃn/
Latvia /ˈlætviə/	Latvian /ˈlætviən/
Lebanon /ˈlebənən/	Lebanese /ˌlebəˈniːz/
Lesotho /ləˈsuːtuː/	Sotho /ˈsuːtuː/
Liberia /laɪˈbɪəriə/	Liberian /laɪˈbɪəriən/
Libya /ˈlɪbiə/	Libyan /ˈlɪbiən/
Lithuania /ˌlɪθjuˈeɪniə/	Lithuanian /ˌlɪθjuˈeɪniən/
Luxembourg /ˈlʌksəmbɜːɡ/	Luxembourg /ˈlʌksəmbɜːɡ/
Madagascar /ˌmædəˈɡæskə(r)/	Madagascan /ˌmædəˈɡæskən/
Malawi /məˈlɑːwi/	Malawian /məˈlɑːwiən/
Malaysia /məˈleɪʒə/	Malaysian /məˈleɪʒn/
(the) Maldives /ˈmɔːldiːvz/	Maldivian /mɔːlˈdɪviən/
Mali /ˈmɑːli/	Malian /ˈmɑːliən/
Malta /ˈmɔːltə/	Maltese /mɔːlˈtiːz/
Mexico /ˈmeksɪkəʊ/	Mexican /ˈmeksɪkən/
Micronesia /ˌmaɪkrəˈniːziə/	Micronesian /ˌmaɪkrəˈniːziən/
Moldova /mɒlˈdəʊvə/	Moldovan /mɒlˈdəʊvən/
Mongolia /mɒŋˈɡəʊliə/	Mongolian /mɒŋˈɡəʊliən/
Montenegro /ˌmɒntɪˈniːɡrəʊ/	Montenegrin /ˌmɒntɪˈniːɡrɪn/
Morocco /məˈrɒkəʊ/	Moroccan /məˈrɒkən/
Mozambique /ˌməʊzæmˈbiːk/	Mozambican /ˌməʊzæmˈbiːkən/
Myanmar /miˌænˈmɑː(r)/	⊃ Burma
Namibia /nəˈmɪbiə/	Namibian /nəˈmɪbiən/
Nepal /nɪˈpɔːl/	Nepalese /ˌnepəˈliːz/
(the) Netherlands /ˈneðələndz/	Dutch /dʌtʃ/
New Zealand /ˌnjuː ˈziːlənd/	New Zealand /ˌnjuː ˈziːlənd/

Nicaragua /ˌnɪkəˈrægjuə/	Nicaraguan /ˌnɪkəˈrægjuən/
Niger /niːˈʒeə(r)/	Nigerien /niːˈʒeəriən/
Nigeria /naɪˈdʒɪəriə/	Nigerian /naɪˈdʒɪəriən/
Northern Ireland /ˌnɔːðən ˈaɪələnd/	Northern Irish /ˌnɔːðən ˈaɪrɪʃ/
Norway /ˈnɔːweɪ/	Norwegian /nɔːˈwiːdʒən/
Oman /əʊˈmɑːn/	Omani /əʊˈmɑːni/
Pakistan /ˌpɑːkɪˈstɑːn/	Pakistani /ˌpɑːkɪˈstɑːni/
Panama /ˈpænəmɑː/	Panamanian /ˌpænəˈmeɪniən/
Papua New Guinea /ˌpæpjuə ˌnjuː ˈgmi/	Papua New Guinean /ˌpæpjuə ˌnjuː ˈgɪniən/
Paraguay /ˈpærəgwaɪ/	Paraguayan /ˌpærəˈgwaɪən/
Peru /pəˈruː/	Peruvian /pəˈruːviən/
(the) Philippines /ˈfɪlɪpiːnz/	Philippine /ˈfɪlɪpiːn/
Poland /ˈpəʊlənd/	Polish /ˈpəʊlɪʃ/
Portugal /ˈpɔːtʃʊɡl/	Portuguese /ˌpɔːtʃʊˈgiːz/
Qatar /ˈkæˈtɑː(r)/	Qatari /kæˈtɑːri/
Romania /ruˈmeɪniə/	Romanian /ruˈmeɪniən/
Russia /ˈrʌʃə/	Russian /ˈrʌʃn/
Rwanda /ruˈændə/	Rwandan /ruˈændən/
Saudi Arabia /ˌsaʊdi əˈreɪbiə/	Saudi /ˈsaʊdi/
Scandinavia /ˌskændɪˈneɪviə/	Scandinavian /ˌskændɪˈneɪviən/
Scotland /ˈskɒtlənd/	Scottish /ˈskɒtɪʃ/
Senegal /ˌsenɪˈgɔːl/	Senegalese /ˌsenɪgəˈliːz/
Serbia /ˈsɜːbiə/	Serbian /ˈsɜːbiən/
(the) Seychelles /seɪˈʃelz/	Seychellois /ˌseɪʃelˈwɑː/
Sierra Leone /siˌerə liˈəʊn/	Sierra Leonean /siˌerə liˈəʊniən/
Singapore /ˌsɪŋəˈpɔː(r)/	Singaporean /ˌsɪŋəˈpɔːriən/
Slovakia /sləʊˈvækiə/	Slovak /ˈsləʊvæk/
Slovenia /sləʊˈviːniə/	Slovene /ˈsləʊviːn/
Somalia /səˈmɑːliə/	Somali /səˈmɑːli/
South Africa /ˌsaʊθ ˈæfrɪkə/	South African /ˌsaʊθ ˈæfrɪkən/
South Sudan /ˌsaʊθ suˈdɑːn/	South Sudanese /ˌsaʊθ ˌsuːdəˈniːz/
Spain /speɪn/	Spanish /ˈspænɪʃ/
Sri Lanka /sri ˈlæŋkə/	Sri Lankan /sri ˈlæŋkən/
Sudan /suˈdɑːn/	Sudanese /ˌsuːdəˈniːz/
Suriname /ˈsʊərɪnɑːm/	Surinamese /ˌsʊərɪnəˈmiːz/
Swaziland /ˈswɑːzilænd/	Swazi /ˈswɑːzi/
Sweden /ˈswiːdn/	Swedish /ˈswiːdɪʃ/
Switzerland /ˈswɪtsələnd/	Swiss /swɪs/
Syria /ˈsɪriə/	Syrian /ˈsɪriən/
Tajikistan /tæˌdʒiːkɪˈstæn/	Tajik /tæˈdʒiːk/
Tanzania /ˌtænzəˈniːə/	Tanzanian /ˌtænzəˈniːən/
Thailand /ˈtaɪlænd/	Thai /taɪ/
Trinidad and Tobago /ˌtrɪnɪdæd ən təˈbeɪɡəʊ/	Trinidadian /ˌtrɪnɪˈdædiən/, Tobagonian /ˌtəʊbəˈgəʊniən/
Tunisia /tjuˈnɪziə/	Tunisian /tjuˈnɪziən/
Turkey /ˈtɜːki/	Turkish /ˈtɜːkɪʃ/
Turkmenistan /tɜːkˌmenɪˈstɑːn/	Turkmen /ˈtɜːkmen/
Uganda /juːˈgændə/	Ugandan /juːˈgændən/
Ukraine /juːˈkreɪn/	Ukrainian /juːˈkreɪniən/
(the) United Arab Emirates /juːˌnaɪtɪd ˌærəb ˈemɪrəts/	Emirati /emɪˈrɑːti/
(the) United Kingdom /juːˌnaɪtɪd ˈkɪŋdəm/	British /ˈbrɪtɪʃ/
(the) United States of America /juːˌnaɪtɪd ˌsteɪts əv əˈmerɪkə/	American /əˈmerɪkən/
Uruguay /ˈjʊərəgwaɪ/	Uruguayan /ˌjʊərəˈgwaɪən/
Uzbekistan /ʊzˌbekɪˈstæn/	Uzbek /ˈʊzbek/
Venezuela /ˌvenəˈzweɪlə/	Venezuelan /ˌvenəˈzweɪlən/
Vietnam /ˌvjetˈnæm/	Vietnamese /ˌvjetnəˈmiːz/
Wales /weɪlz/	Welsh /welʃ/
(the) West Indies /ˌwest ˈɪndiz/	West Indian /ˌwest ˈɪndiən/
Yemen /ˈjemən/	Yemeni /ˈjeməni/
Zambia /ˈzæmbiə/	Zambian /ˈzæmbiən/
Zimbabwe /zɪmˈbɑːbwi/	Zimbabwean /zɪmˈbɑːbwiən/